The New York Times

SUPERSIZED BOOK OF SUNDAY CROSSWORDS

The New York Times

SUPERSIZED BOOK OF SUNDAY CROSSWORDS
500 Puzzles

Edited by Will Shortz and Eugene T. Maleska

ST. MARTIN'S GRIFFIN ✠ NEW YORK

ACROSS

1. "The Cape Cod Lighter" writer
6. Speak abusively to
11. Swear words
15. Hunt assemblage
19. Like a shoe
20. Add ___ of salt
21. Cicatrix
22. Classic New Yorker cartoonist
23. The God, literally
24. Undeliverable piece of mail
25. Toaster, e.g.
27. Crystal-lined stone
28. Ample shoe width
29. Precious one
31. Progeny
32. With 39- and 54-Across, the beginning of the story
36. Javits Center designer
37. Dark grayish green
38. Dolt
39. See 32-Across
50. Takes too much, briefly
51. Chinese truth
52. Lloyd Webber musical role
53. Code word for "K"
54. See 32-Across
63. Take care of
64. Start for bees or breeze
65. Noted Expos name
66. Put away
67. Dental mold
70. S.A.T. subj.
72. Flash
74. Insult, slangily
77. Bangkok teacher, on Broadway
78. Anonymous one
80. Literature Nobelist Pirandello
83. With 94- and 106-Across, the end of the story
90. Panache
91. "I told you so!"
92. Harris of "thirty-something"
93. Fluffy scarf
94. See 83-Across
103. Newton of the N.F.L.
104. "O Henry, ___ thine eyes!": Shak.
105. Put ___ show
106. See 83-Across
117. Tidal flood
118. Island near Quemoy
119. Louis who said "L'etat c'est moi"
120. North of Virginia
121. Heating conduit
123. Early pamphleteer
125. Rope with a loop
126. Say "z" imperfectly
127. Ready for service
128. Church V.I.P.
129. Flower with a showy head
130. Pot builder?
131. 1985 Cher film
132. Baby Moses was hidden among them
133. Author Hite

DOWN

1. Midwest tribe
2. Used an awl
3. Grant
4. Make suitable again
5. Holds fast
6. Best-selling 1993 pop album
7. "Bye"
8. Simonized
9. "Do ___ say . . ."
10. Mark Twain novel whose plot is encapsulated in this puzzle
11. Hollywood statue
12. Barbados cherry
13. Count, as votes
14. It ended in 1806: Abbr.
15. Problematic construction site
16. Clear
17. Boredom
18. Shopper, often
26. Silvers sarge
30. Like some humor
33. Radio code sound
34. ___ piece (consistent)
35. Doce meses, en Espana
39. Dangerous group
40. Popular ice cream brand
41. Suffix meaning "to become"
42. Stock page heading
43. W.C. co-star
44. Foldable items
45. "It's O.K. with me"
46. Old studio
47. Carnival girl, in the movies
48. Actor McCowen
49. Shot
55. Males
56. ___ of roses
57. Very much
58. Part of a bray
59. Card
60. Whole
61. W.W. I soldier
62. Increase
68. Wind dir.
69. Mai ___
71. Sentimentality
73. Stockbroker's offering
74. A couple of bucks?
75. Not occupied
76. Valuables
79. Lucci's elusive prize
81. Mongolian desert
82. Smooth
84. Literary olio
85. Calendar abbr.
86. Overhead figures?
87. Flandre flavoring
88. Pavement caution
89. ID of a sort
95. Like some court proceedings
96. Scotch refusal
97. Marathoner's need
98. Shoots over
99. ___ canto
100. Persuade by trickery
101. Some sweaters
102. Somewhat high
106. Electronics pioneer Nikola
107. Toss one's ___ the ring
108. Get rid of
109. Kool-Aid flavor
110. Hearty dinner entree
111. Zinc ___
112. Penalized
113. Diamond middleman?
114. Winged
115. Potassium compound
116. "The Wreck of the Mary ___"
122. Spitz-type dog
124. Bath beverage

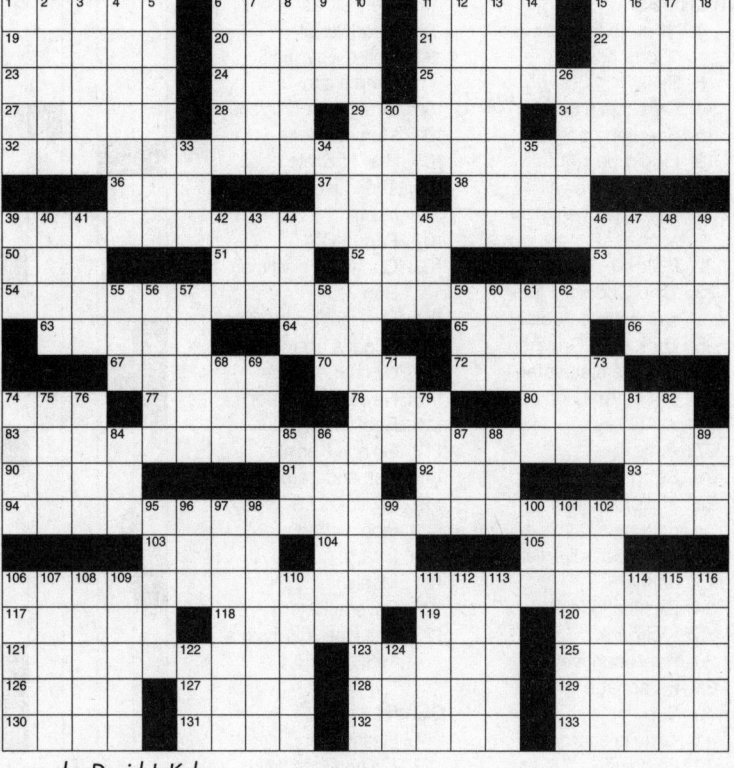

by David J. Kahn

ACROSS

1. "It" in the old slogan "Gotta have it"
6. Stinky
11. Crescent's tip
15. Sceptors' go-withs
19. Liquid part of fat
20. Poem's farewell
21. "God ha' mercy on such ___"
22. Pullover
23. "The Goodbye Girl" star suffers audibly
25. Look from Groucho
26. Foreign statesman whose real first name is Aubrey
27. Annex
28. Beggar's cry
29. Philippine lady ricochets
32. Aproned advertising animal
34. Destinations
35. Kickback
36. Reproductive cell
38. Parsonage
40. Sup
41. Tequila source
42. Foldaway
43. Novelist-critic dances
49. Form of a thank-you
50. Theater acronym
52. Bottom line
53. "To a Steam Roller" poet
54. 1942 Oscar winner reacts to a bad pun
58. Troubadour
61. Locker room supply
62. Set upon
63. Twosome
65. Member of the order Isoptera
67. "The Munsters" actress sang
70. Popular Polynesian port
73. E.T.O. battle town
74. Shining
78. Big name in Hawaii
79. Shows curiosity
81. Two-time Tony winner did a no-no
84. Its symbol is a crescent and star
86. Mausoleum opening?
88. Steak order
89. Old dagger
90. "Casino" co-star does firming exercises
94. Shaver
95. Pantheon figures
96. Manner, as of writing
97. Headwork?
99. Noted Egyptian temple site
100. One of the Clintons
103. Memo order
104. Port of Crete
105. 1964 Oscar winner roams
107. Part of B.A.
108. Canadian politician Bob
111. Like most cupcakes
112. Super's apartment number, maybe
113. Newswoman stops
116. Rooster locale
117. Coin in Kerman
118. Kett and James
119. Six-time U.S. Open tennis champ
120. Pizazz
121. Moolah
122. Several Peters
123. She was a lady in a 1932 tune

DOWN

1. Fleshy fruit
2. Airline since 1948
3. Ambassador takes a husband
4. Sonny's sibling
5. Slapdash
6. Wife abroad
7. Genesis name
8. Tellico Dam overseer: Abbr.
9. Sea between Italy and Greece
10. Send away
11. Salesman's duties
12. Like some books
13. Administer an oath to
14. Rate
15. "Lulu," e.g.
16. Perfect slave
17. Mame's onus
18. King's desires
24. What George couldn't tell
30. Cousins of cassowaries: Var.
31. Perpendicular to the keel
33. They protect banks
36. Police target
37. Hub of old Athens
38. One-track
39. Win
40. Former New York Senator
42. Parking places

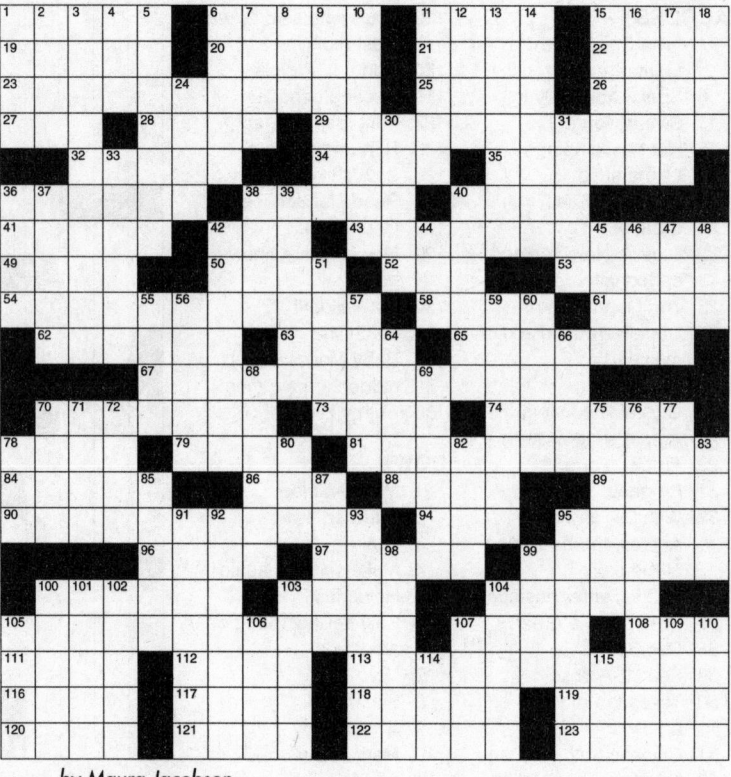

by Maura Jacobson

44. Pinch hitter
45. Reply to the Little Red Hen
46. Annapolis mascot
47. Shield border
48. Not long to wait
51. Pennies, perhaps
55. 50's TV's "The Martha ___ Show"
56. ___ hoot
57. Nazarenes and others
59. Forwarded
60. Hardly the creme de la creme
64. Of the cheekbone
66. Year in Ivan the Terrible's reign
68. Marine organisms
69. Jimmy's successor
70. Swanky
71. ___ breve
72. Liqueur flavor
75. Nail down
76. Columnist reacted angrily
77. "If a body ___ body . . ."
78. Bad-mouth
80. End of Madama Butterfly's name
82. Sturdy wagon
83. Escritoire
85. Flick
87. 1980 Carly Simon hit
91. Make business connections
92. Shakespeare's Fairy Queen
93. Hollywood hopeful
95. Wailer
98. Tournament news
99. Lady of a stuttering song
100. Almost princely
101. Jean Renoir film heroine
102. Ream
103. Allan-___ (Sherwood Forest figure)
104. Salad ingredient
105. Baloney
106. Patricia of "A Face in the Crowd"
107. Controversial apple spray
109. Longfellow's bell town
110. Isabella d'___ (famed beauty)
114. Times Sq., e.g., on the IRT
115. Film "Contessa"

ACROSS

1. Perfume
6. Tie
12. Individually, in a way
20. Truman biographer Miller
21. Sub feature
22. Ups and downs
23. TURKEY
25. SWEET POTATOES
26. Town near Oakland
27. Closeout
28. Home in the woods
29. Words of acquiescence
30. Rose fancier
33. Kind of chair
38. SQUASH
45. Some Dadaist works
49. "Voila!"
50. Conduct
51. Composer Khachaturian
52. Funny ones
54. "That ___ lie!"
55. Gathering places
56. Henry ___
57. Regulars
59. Suffix with Rock
61. Skill tested with Zener cards
62. Resounds
63. BRUSSELS SPROUTS
66. The Way
68. Lobster part
69. Pen noise
70. Big name in sportswear
75. Kind of jet
76. STUFFING
79. Stings
83. One who looks at books
85. "Flash Gordon" originator ___ Raymond
86. Rival of Athens
87. Separated
88. Equips with better materiel
90. Sound-stage cry
92. Theater drop
93. Scope
94. Soul
95. What wine shouldn't be
97. Earth tones
98. GRAVY
102. Stage direction
103. Hoof sound
104. Kind of ground
109. Bali Ha'i, in "South Pacific"
113. Iranian money
116. "My Left Foot" Oscar-winner Fricker
117. CHESTNUTS
121. APPLE PIE
123. Band attraction
124. San ___
125. Harden
126. Dinner ender
127. Atlas features
128. Father-and-daughter Hollywood duo

DOWN

1. Perth ___, N.J.
2. Opposite of eau
3. Dumas's ___ Mousquetaires
4. King and others
5. More rubicund
6. Civil War inits.
7. They may be caught at the shore
8. Italian sports car, informally
9. Bordered by a ridge
10. Protozoan
11. Pointer
12. "Sweet Swan of ___!": Jonson
13. Valenciennes, e.g.
14. Eastern V.I.P.'s
15. Business combine
16. Uris hero ___ Ben Canaan
17. ___ Tin Tin
18. Hot spot, in lunch counter lingo
19. Tee predecessor
24. Attended
31. "Where's Daddy?" playwright
32. Elicits
34. Sisal or yucca
35. "West Side Story" song
36. Send
37. Rigs
39. X, to Xenophon
40. "One Flew Over the Cuckoo's Nest" author
41. Goddess with a lyre
42. Some pens
43. Screenwriter, often
44. Bandleader Baxter
45. Curacao neighbor
46. Up
47. Young fowl
48. Rocket section
53. Hamlet's "___ and arrows"
55. Greek brandies
58. Mideast capital
60. March need
62. Sea anemones, e.g.
64. Dawning
65. Salute
67. Beggar's quest
71. Do a legislator's job
72. Missionary Junipero ___
73. Kind of sleeve
74. Red-coated cheeses
76. Airstrip
77. Style of furnishing
78. Part of a metropolitan region
79. Satisfy
80. Actor Redgrave
81. About
82. Gettysburg general
84. Hosiery purchase
88. "A Yank in the ___" (1941 movie)
89. Knightwear
91. W.B.A. result
95. Office machines
96. "___ dabba doo!"
99. Baltimore's ___ Park
100. Saxon's foe
101. Deflected
105. Marie Antoinette, e.g.
106. Bring on
107. Beautify
108. Spare locales
110. It's a put-on
111. Kipling's "___ we forget!"
112. Direction in Durango
114. Auto racer Luyendyk
115. Reason for a brushoff?
117. Gametes
118. Cambodia's ___ Nol
119. Seventh-century date
120. N.T. book
121. Bon ___
122. Nasdaq listings: Abbr.

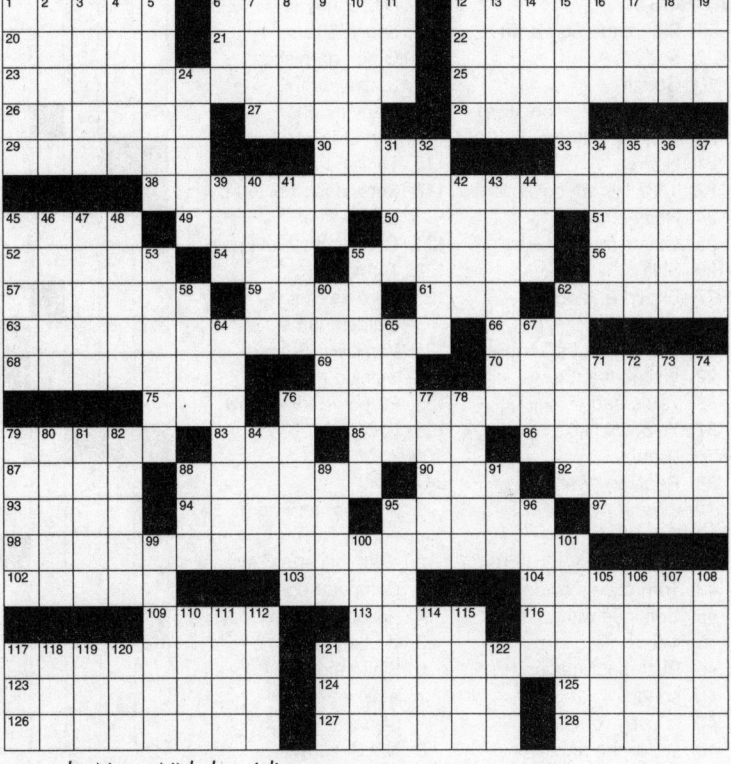

by Nancy Nicholson Joline

ACROSS

1. Site of the Sun Bowl
7. Busy
13. Couch
19. ___ acid (preservative)
20. Biblical tempter
21. Honors
22. 1837 literary collection
24. Hairy-chested
25. Gloaming, to poets
26. Shift
27. Expert at ledger-demain?
28. "Paradise Lost" figure
29. Visited the future
36. Tad's dad
37. Yevtushenko's "Babi ___"
38. Reply to "Who's there?"
39. Repute
40. Like Falstaff
43. Turn state's evidence
45. Continue without the words
46. Rush-hour traffic speed
47. "Cosby" co-star
49. ___ in the right direction
51. She loved Theseus
53. Kind
54. Silent signals
56. Bridge or wrestling feat
59. Bran source
60. Tinker with, in a way
62. Reprimands
66. Covering
70. Winsor McCay's "Little" one
71. Game-winning cry
72. Auto's comfort quality
73. Pioneering 1982 film
74. 100
76. Pronto
77. Fine-grained wood
79. Out of here
80. Do some punching
82. Beginning Latin word
83. Caboose
87. Grimm creature
90. Noted X-1 pilot
92. Romantic painter Vedder
93. "Up" positions
96. Religious ideal
97. Greenpeace concern
98. Recognition
99. Bowwow
101. Zeniths, e.g.
103. ___-mo
104. Hit song lyric of 1929 and 1968
109. Green garnishes
110. Sugary suffix
111. Many moons
112. Part of i.p.s.
115. Trinket: Var.
117. Show once hosted by Bud Collyer
121. Gentleman thief Lupin
122. Torments
123. Barbara Bush's maiden name
124. Van Dyke Emmy-winning role
125. Prepared for a blow
126. Excoriate

DOWN

1. 90 (degrees) from norte
2. "Bad Influence" star
3. Computer command
4. Epitome of simplicity
5. "Buttery" legume
6. Staff range
7. Alaska Senator Stevens
8. N.Y.C. subway
9. Difference in days between the lunar and solar year
10. Site of the ancient Pythian Games
11. Find after a long search
12. Scores: Abbr.
13. Maul
14. "Dombey and Son" woman
15. War film starring Martin Balsam
16. Where singer Billy Ocean was born
17. Migratory fish
18. Storm heading: Abbr.
20. With subterfuge
23. Cuprite, e.g.
28. Like some college honors
30. Leaping before looking
31. Headset, to hams
32. "Phooey!"
33. The Buckeyes
34. Cut down
35. First name in mysteries
40. Point in the right direction
41. More obvious
42. Sealskin wearer
44. Convincing evidence
46. Org. once headed by Allen Dulles
48. Multiplication symbol
49. Kind of price
50. Repetition for rhetorical effect
52. Anti-Communist soldier
55. Dinner and a movie, perhaps
57. A.B.A. members: Abbr.
58. ___-tung
61. Bandanna-clad product "spokesman"
63. Prefix with plasm
64. Scorpion attack
65. Transude
67. Aspect
68. "My Cup Runneth Over" singer
69. Gun sound
74. Its slogan was once "Find out how good we really are"
75. Part of a count
78. French shield
81. Clear-eyed
83. Southpaw's strength
84. Betting game ending
85. Like a warm-up exercise, comparatively speaking
86. Heritage
88. Words to live by
89. Shake a leg
91. Straddling
94. Classic Japanese theater
95. Miser
99. Shorty
100. "The African Queen" director
102. Rotisserie league concern
103. Rests
105. Sultan Qabus bin Said, e.g.
106. Coming-of-age period
107. Thumbs-down response
108. Jet
113. Do aquatints
114. First president of South Korea
115. Gender ___
116. Obsolescent preposition
117. Use a shuttle
118. One of a pack?
119. Set the pace
120. F. D. R. agcy.

by Ray Hamel

5

ACROSS

1. Capital of Germany?
6. Person in a hammock
12. TV's Maverick
16. Toward the rudder
21. 1993 N.B.A. Rookie of the Year
22. Certain Alaskan
23. It can go round the world
24. In a distinguished way
25. Move
27. Modern Maturity grp.
28. [Not that one again!]
29. Heavy marble
30. Joyce and Synge, e.g.
32. Fresh air, slangily
33. Cabinet dept.
34. Start for girl
35. Other, in Oaxaca
37. Price discount factors
42. Avoid guile
48. Prepare for more shots
49. Disobeyed a zoo sign?
50. Symphony in E flat major
51. Chef d'etat, once
52. High mark
53. Stroke
56. Dashboard letters
57. Street fight?
59. Academy freshman
60. On one's toes
61. Jimmies
64. Unhappy one
65. Sound of laughter
66. Part of Q.E.D.
67. They are round and pound
68. Emulates Delilah
69. French 101 verb
70. Humerus neighbor
71. Soup ingredient
72. Sanctified
73. Genealogical abbr.
74. Words at a shootout
77. "It's ___ cry from . . ."
81. Boardwalk buy
83. Prefix with polar
84. River known to the ancients as Obringa
85. "My Friend" of 50's TV
86. Pulled out
89. Certain Alaskan
90. Try to get the lead, maybe
91. Certain Dodge
92. Put
93. Chandelier pendant
94. Prepared with bread crumbs, in cookery
95. "Happy Birthday" writers
96. Mariner's danger
97. Theological inst.
98. 1896 decision ___ v. Ferguson
100. Prohibition
101. Keogh relative
102. TV series with Sgt. O'Rourke
105. Source of cork
106. Scientific discovery of 1868
107. 1939 film with a Best Actor performance
111. Like some stockings
113. Hardly humble
114. ___-memoire
115. Farthest: Abbr.
116. Agree
119. Pirates' domain
123. Works
128. Like a bunch
129. ___ Bear
130. Business book, with "The"
133. Mark Twain prop
134. Extremely sharp
135. Home on the range
136. The "voice" in Bloch's "Voice in the Wilderness"
137. S-shaped
138. Prefix with -gon
139. The prince in "The Prince and the Pauper"
140. Grant's successor

DOWN

1. Pacifier
2. Duty
3. Beaver material
4. "Peter Rabbit," for one
5. Stick together
6. Quit
7. Dimethyl sulfate and others
8. Cousin of calypso
9. Kon-___ (Heyerdahl raft)
10. Bright green hummingbirds
11. Garcia Lorca's "Dona ___ la soltera"
12. Just barely
13. Globe-trot
14. Fictional Jane
15. Bang-up
16. Sweater material
17. Russian wolfhound
18. Peek follower
19. Spanish custard
20. Sharon's co-star in 80's TV
26. Checks on clothing
31. Red-eye cause
36. Song syllable
37. Up a tree
38. Abounding
39. Attentive
40. Be extra sure
41. Leisure
42. Look-see
43. Weighty reading?
44. Nurses
45. ___ Hall (Robert Southey's home)
46. Dearest
47. Seat groupings
49. Man ___
53. Made watertight
54. Hardly melodious
55. Private road feature
57. Hooch hounds
58. Occasion for bows and whistles?
62. Make further corrections
63. Black
64. Tiny
66. Not original
67. Military hat adornments
68. Banana oil
72. Mental acuity
75. Singaraja is its capital
76. Tablecloths and napkins, maybe
78. Giveaway
79. In the mood
80. Return payments?
82. Horace volume
86. Young fellow
87. The gold of the conquistadors
88. Important West Indies crop
89. Kind of plate
93. It can curl your hair
94. Stew ingredients
95. It's on the agenda
97. Tablet
99. Like dachshunds
102. Message starter
103. Song words before "We stand on guard for thee!"
104. Letters from Greece
106. Break out, in a way
108. "Slavonic Dances" composer
109. Napoleon locale
110. Conceive
111. Abide
112. Happy as a clam
116. Black Hawk and tribesmen
117. Deuce follower
118. Form of discipline
120. Jog, e.g.
121. Stupendous
122. Cold weather meal
124. Georgia ___
125. Concert sites
126. Bank (on)
127. Lockmaker
131. W.W. II org.
132. Spanish article

by Manny Nosowsky

ACROSS

1. They emerge in the spring
8. 1997 Peter Fonda title role
12. Haunted house décor
16. Mil. award
19. Reprimander's reading
20. Settled, as a quarrel
22. Explorer of the Canadian Arctic
23. Parent's ploy
25. Sue Grafton's "___ for Alibi"
26. Kind of fire
27. Chemist Remsen, discoverer of saccharin
28. Soupçon
29. Displays displeasure
31. Old-fashioned cold remedy
32. Racer's path
33. W.W. II gen.
34. Ear-piercing pooch
35. Irritate
41. Shepherds' woolen plaids
42. Rhone's capital
43. Chromatin component
44. Overcome utterly
46. God-___
49. Royal irritant of lore
50. Motor-driven
52. Raised-eyebrow remarks
55. 1940 John Wayne drama
60. William ___, the Father of Photography
62. Cause for a shootout
63. Red-blooded
64. "___ soit qui mal y pense"
66. Word in four French department names
67. "Momo" author Michael
69. Stand in an atelier
70. Neoprene gasket
72. It's served in shreds
73. More than desires
75. Stuff
76. Ad-lib
78. Dockworker's org.
79. "Sex for Dummies" author
81. Typewriter feature
84. Fed. stipend
85. Mimics 113-Across
87. Appetite
88. "The best ___ to come!"
89. Tre ___ (piano player's direction)
91. More, in Madrid
92. Stephen King's home
95. Creation of Burr Tillstrom
97. Completely mistaken
103. In heaven
105. Sloth, for one
106. Refuse visitors
107. Part of some E-mail addresses
109. "Master of the World" director William
110. Disney's "___ and the Detectives"
112. Hydrocarbon suffix
113. Cloven-hoofed animals
115. Content of some pits
116. Exert oneself to the utmost
120. ___-Manguean (Indian language group)
121. Hypnotized
122. Mideast entity
123. Cyst
124. Cold war force
125. Grand duke's father
126. Like a golf ball

DOWN

1. Receive
2. Disney's Michael
3. Dr. in an H. G. Wells novel
4. Checklist part
5. With 36-Down, like some service uniforms
6. Broomball surface
7. Tried hard
8. College in East Orange, N.J.
9. Ballad
10. Impress clearly
11. Spiny anteater
12. Certain boxer, informally
13. Shogun's capital
14. Classic gangster nickname
15. Surveillance equipment
16. Climbing the corporate ladder
17. Breezed
18. Abbr. preceding multiple surnames
21. 1953 movie that shares the name of a Texas town
24. Participates in a vigil, maybe
30. Hydrophane or isopyre
32. "Look here!"
36. See 5-Down
37. Steve of Aerosmith
38. One with pin tales?
39. Picnic pest
40. Part of the Net, for short
45. Indignant, with "up"
46. Sits in on
47. They cant
48. British P.M. during the American Revolution
49. Spanish specie
50. Average American, they say
51. Holding
53. Where Puff frolicked
54. Eisenhower appointee to the Supreme Court
56. Nemesis
57. "___ le roi!" (Bastille cry)
58. "Eight Men Out" star
59. Like peacocks, among all birds
61. Start of many French titles
65. "Splendor in the Grass" screenwriter
68. Part of some E-mail addresses
71. Card player's cry
74. Hutch
77. One of the Power Rangers
80. Cached
82. No-hitter king
83. Certain plaintiff, at law
86. Colonial leader?
90. Actress Lena
91. Little sucker
92. "___ Mrs. Jones" (#1 hit of 1972)
93. Let down, perhaps
94. Contingencies
95. Bow (to)
96. Eastern Christian
98. Familiar with
99. Indonesian island
100. Chief river of British Columbia
101. Not of the cloth
102. Philanthropize
104. Spotted ___
108. Russian politician Alexander
111. "Breezy" star, 1973
113. Thick of things
114. Dr. Johnny Fever's station
117. Adderley of hard bop
118. Victrola mfr.
119. Last words of Little Jack Horner

by Frank Longo

ACROSS

1. Playwright Norman
7. 1943 Bogart film
13. Where suits are put on
20. Colorless ketone
21. Canadiens and Canucks
22. Milieu
23. He should have written "What Makes Sammy Run"
25. TV role for Penny
26. Kind of chance
27. Suffix with human
29. Toot
30. Fork-tailed flier
31. He should have written "Fear of Flying"
35. Handle, as insurance claims
38. Like some heads
39. Explorer Vasco da ___
40. ___ Lobos
43. Sprang
44. Magnate
45. Sight at post offices
47. Robbins and Russert
48. Coach
49. "Yikes!"
51. ___ vie
52. What candles may signify
53. He should have written "Green Eggs and Ham"
56. Social reformer Jacob
57. O.R. workers
58. Erskine Caldwell title character
59. Seaman's description
60. Start
62. Blade attachments
64. Tommy Dorsey's "___ Always You"
65. Seeress
66. Wasted
68. Rancher's enemy
70. Stuffy
72. Frequent direction givers: Abbr.
75. Challenge, metaphorically
76. He should have written "Postcards From the Edge"
79. Certain fighter
80. Many a Gary Cooper pic
82. Canadiens or Canucks
83. Crash locale in "Alive"
84. V-chips block it
85. Strong objections
87. Oodles
88. 72-Across recommendation
89. José or Juan
90. Kind of collar
91. Where Jimmy Carter taught after his Presidency
92. Nosebleed seats
93. She should have written "On the Beach"
95. Lorelei Lee's creator
96. Communicate
99. U.S.N.A. grad
100. Piece of dust
104. Gang of Four members
106. He should have written "Arrowsmith"
110. Cabalist
111. Temporarily away
112. More virtuous than thou
113. Common cleanser
114. Eats one's heart out
115. Barbecue offerings

DOWN

1. They report to lt. cols.
2. Reynolds film "Rent-___"
3. Civil War major general Jesse
4. Business undertakings
5. Most popular
6. "Java" man
7. Blab
8. B.T.U. producers
9. Chop down
10. Friend of mon frère
11. Fix some origami
12. Marxlike
13. Disney Store purchase
14. Bart Starr's alma mater
15. Libation
16. Touch up
17. Social misfit
18. Sister of King Arthur
19. Suffix with pun
24. Cape ___
28. Grunt : Vietnam :: ___ : W.W. II
31. Foreknowledge
32. Muscateer?
33. When dark comes o'er the land
34. He was lost in books
35. Hitching post
36. Condescend
37. He should have written "Hotel"
38. 1928 hit with the lyric "I'm in heaven when I see you smile"
40. He should have written "Love Story"
41. Song of the past
42. View à la Shakespeare
44. They have their own lines
46. Telephone user
48. Moon of Neptune
49. Fades
50. Square dance partner
53. TV's Peter
54. "Paradise Lost" character
55. Pops, e.g.
61. Over in Germany
63. Coastline feature
64. Mosque V.I.P.
65. Pumps have them
66. Goes to market
67. Miss's accessory
68. Be prophetic
69. John's "Pulp Fiction" partner
70. Hoax
71. Plain-speaking radio talk show host
73. ___-ground missile
74. Ford predecessor
77. Sea ___
78. Little Richard's hometown
81. Mentions
84. It gets a licking
86. On the schedule
87. Wee, to Burns
88. Tree trauma
91. Sect member during the time of Christ
92. Ark contents
93. Ways of walking
94. Benefit from
95. Not in the profession
96. Baby sitter's banes
97. ___ fide (in bad faith)
98. Combine
100. Parker and Waterman
101. Minty Mexican plant
102. Soup vegetable
103. Slips
105. Title for Mrs. Perón
107. Panama City's home: Abbr.
108. Pro
109. Didn't hold

by Randolph Ross

COUNTDOWN

by Charles Deber

ACROSS

1. God "the most merciful"
6. Bird of myth
9. Slanted: Abbr.
13. Blacksmith's tools
18. Prefix with grain
19. Show presenter, for short
20. Pioneering Russian spacecraft series
21. Lawn game
22. Sight off the coast of Salerno
24. Bugs
25. Be creative
26. Spanish weeks
27. Expo '70 host
29. Saw red
30. Last-minute ticket acquirer, maybe
31. "Well done!"
32. Broadly
34. Certain annuity plan
36. 1998, e.g., in fancy language
41. Piglike animals
44. Cleveland team, for short
46. Minneapolis-to-Fargo hwy.
47. Man, in old Rome
48. Rock's Burdon and Carmen
49. Transmit via computer
50. Seventh-century date
51. Some porcelain
53. Worker ___
54. Math ratio
55. Orchestra member
58. Gulf of ___ (arm of the Baltic)
59. No longer in enemy hands
62. Heather lands
63. Footnote word
65. A new look at an 18th-century English writer
69. Fabric with nubby yarn
72. First name in stand-up
73. Big name in computer games
77. Like a wayward G.I.
78. Nautical passageway
80. Bustles
82. Mouths
83. "From Here to Eternity" wife
85. Oil driller's setup
86. On again
88. Sing like Bing
90. Non-P.C. suffix
91. Express
93. Institution since 1701
94. Close and Ford
95. Nurses and police officers, e.g.
98. Neighbors of Ethiopians
100. Enemies of the Iroquois
101. Consider, with "over"
103. Kind of set
107. Place to go with a flashlight
110. He coached 347 N.F.L. wins
111. Menu section
112. Like our numbers
113. Apocalypse
114. 1773 Tea Party, e.g.
116. Survey respondent
117. Let go of
118. Back muscle, for short
119. TV actress Taylor
120. Jacket choice
121. Sushi supplies
122. Poetic preposition
123. Seconds: Abbr.

DOWN

1. Collect
2. "12 Angry Men" director
3. Pack animal
4. Monopoly avenue next to the B.&O. Railroad
5. Sellers of record players
6. Brownish
7. Sugar ending
8. Feature of classical architecture
9. Kind of artery
10. Bomb
11. "Crazy Love" singer
12. Song syllables
13. Vases of a "La Bohème" character
14. ___ radical
15. Fast shuffle, so to speak
16. Sandwich base
17. Very beginning
21. Item that's often stubbed
23. Composer Saint-___
28. Not a good person with secrets
32. Democrats fight it
33. "___ long . . ."
35. Representation
37. Writer Welty
38. Roundish
39. Forehead feature
40. Source of an omen, maybe
41. Zoom
42. Drury Lane composer of the 1700's
43. The Panthers of the Big East Conference
45. Success for a returning space shuttle
49. "Do you ___?"
52. Target of many a wound
54. 1991–92 U.S. Open champ
56. Not streamlined
57. Parts of 69-Down
60. Catlike
61. ___-Tiki
62. Tiny model
64. Casey of County General Hospital
66. Pilgrimage sites
67. Lean
68. Berlin's "___ Lost in His Arms"
69. See 57-Down
70. Soaked
71. Sculpture subjects
74. In a minute
75. Maker of a brand name?
76. Lacking
79. Early wheels
80. O.K.
81. Per ___
84. Insouciant
87. Chart holder
88. The 1990's, politically speaking
89. Vintner's cache
92. William or Henry
94. Sparkle
96. Weak
97. Train
99. Carol starter
102. Mountains, so to speak
104. "Difficult years"
105. Position
106. Met singer Simon
107. Kirk, e.g.: Abbr.
108. Straight, after "in"
109. Low tract
110. Recovering from a charley horse
113. Onetime Presidential inits.
115. Dory feature

ACROSS

1. Like gazpacho
5. "Pronto!"
9. Put
13. Kindergarten lesson
17. Actress Cheri of "S.N.L."
19. Clouted
20. Cubemaker Rubik
21. College appointment
22. Food for thought?
24. Fair
25. Ares' mother
26. Comparable to a pancake
27. Pain killer?
30. Bakery product
31. Kind of jet
32. Sprang
33. Plea for a TV cop?
40. Clio hopefuls
42. Lead for a Lab
43. Ryan known as "The Ryan Express"
44. Short cut
45. Blacken
48. Tanked (up)
51. Where they tell off-color prayers before meals?
55. Elect
56. Ribs
58. Half of the "Rich Girl" duo, in 70's pop
59. Snake, for one
60. Salted away
62. Famed reproach
63. Springs
64. Julia Child using miso, e.g.?
70. Actress Swenson and others
73. "___ be in England"
74. About which
78. Short wave?
79. Semidiameters
81. Donahue of "Get a Life"
84. Year in Vigilius's papacy
85. Wit in need of washing?
88. Junta, say
90. Faulkner title start
91. They precede kisses
92. "Ivan IV" composer
94. Son of Judah
95. Army refusal
97. Do well as a temptress?
101. One of the King Sisters
103. Lunks
105. Eloise's ilk
106. What one used to do in Kremlin heat?
111. Bribe, informally
114. "Oliver!" choreographer White
115. Picnic pest, in this puzzle?
116. Balding lion's lament?
119. Windows picture
120. Neolith, e.g.
121. Whopper creators
122. Overall stuff
123. Permits
124. "My treat"
125. Kind of child
126. Make over

DOWN

1. Part of an ear
2. ___ cosa (something else)
3. Gamboling places
4. "Up on the Roof" singers, with "the"
5. Bowling alley inits.
6. Remote post?
7. Suffix with symptom
8. See 104-Down
9. Tenant
10. Reason to ask "What's cookin'?"
11. Piece of The Rock
12. Start with step or stop
13. Stick
14. Result of a video viewer's spill?
15. Worries
16. Catch
18. Do parquetry
19. Bank robber Willie
23. Singer Almond or actor Singer
28. Hard wood
29. Extinguishes
33. Things like Audi's rings
34. Customize
35. Spain's ___ Brava
36. Swarms
37. Popular fashion magazine
38. Holstein abode
39. Sum of the parts
41. Stops running
44. Waited (for) until long after dark
46. Bit
47. Merlot, Médoc, etc.
49. Belief system
50. Judge
52. Ancient Germanic invader
53. Pro ___
54. Idaho, slangily
57. Town that's home to Ohio Northern University
61. Honored Hindu
62. Mil. arena abroad
63. Cubic meter
65. Difficult situation
66. Kind of stitch
67. Suffix meaning inflamed
68. Botanical beard
69. Restaurateur Toots
70. Itself, in a Latin phrase
71. New Jersey hoopsters
72. Bad photo of a shoelace problem?
75. Minneapolis suburb
76. "___ River"
77. Ogre
79. Commercial prefix meaning "convenient to use"
80. Worship
81. Release
82. One of Judy Garland's girls
83. Rapper in "Tank Girl"
86. Japanese-American
87. It goes around the middle
89. Light and filmy
93. Chicken choices
96. Large amounts
97. Popular car, again
98. Tempe sch.
99. TV actor Katz
100. Flip
101. Bubbling
102. Thrusting weapon
104. With 8-Down, Asian capital
107. Peace-keeping grp.
108. Town on the Vire
109. Hebrew letter
110. Touchable
112. Compos mentis
113. Lady in Arthurian legend
117. Assay
118. Funnyman Philips

by Cathy Millhauser

by Rich Norris

ACROSS

1. Political V.I.P.
5. Where roads meet: Abbr.
9. They're full of beans
13. "My Dinner With Andre" playwright
18. "Love is a Hurtin' Thing" singer
20. Tinny-sounding instrument
21. "He fain would write ___": Browning
23. Jazzman Chick
24. Frequented, as a restaurant
25. Tickle
26. Magna ___
27. Troublemakers, at times
28. Beginning of a quote
32. Speech bobbles
33. Sound barrier breaker, for short
34. Newt
35. Poetic preposition
36. Off-burned item
37. Nutritional amt.
38. Quote, part 2
45. Mars: Prefix
47. Closing document
48. Do a vet's job
49. That, in Toledo
50. Sudden
52. Hacienda room
54. Some default consequences
58. A fl. oz. contains six
61. Flourless cakes
63. Maryland athlete, for short
65. Pig ___
67. King of old comics
69. Quote, part 3
74. After-dinner offering
75. Two-syllable foot, in poetry
76. Something to pass
77. Old college building feature
80. "Major" animal
82. Quote, part 4
83. ___ avis
85. Guido's high note
86. Capital on the Missouri
88. Hit
92. Sch. subject
93. Quote, part 5
100. Robt. ___
101. Undersides
102. "Cheerio!"
103. Four-time Oscar-winning composer
105. "Puppy Love" singer
107. Don Pasquale and others
109. Schmoozes
111. Strainer
112. Tree decoration
114. Get ___ (access)
117. Snack bar drink
119. Shot up
120. Quote, part 6
128. Thurman of "Henry & June"
129. Strange
130. The New Yorker illustrator Irvin
131. Put in stitches
132. "___ Haw"
135. VCR button: Abbr.
136. End of the quote, and its author
142. 1964 role for Audrey
144. Hood of "Our Gang" comedies
145. Threepeater's threepeat
146. Like the sea lion
147. Pass on
148. Kind of mentality
149. Get around
150. Nostalgic, in a way
151. Cha cha cha, e.g.
152. 1963 Newman co-star
153. Artist Magritte
154. Rhône's capital

DOWN

1. Unwanted children?
2. Swearing
3. Kind of deal
4. Thick piece
5. Drop abruptly
6. The 45th of 50
7. Political journal since 1865, with "The"
8. Battlement openings
9. Agreement
10. Colorful fish
11. Conductor Antal ___
12. Disagreements
13. Least adequate
14. Doll
15. Main conduit
16. Flake
17. City ESE of Miami
19. Pricey
20. Family room pieces
22. Long-tailed parrot
29. "The Lineup" grp.
30. Golf club part
31. Onetime Davis Cup coach
39. Blood line
40. "Cool!"
41. Lazybones
42. Way-off
43. Pupil protector
44. Register key
45. Hrs. in Halifax
46. Frat letters
51. Trouble
53. Old flatboats
55. Reach on the road, perhaps
56. Unmentioned
57. Convene
59. Investigation
60. The Trojans, for short
62. Record holders?
64. Vatican period
66. Game declaration by Ivana?
68. Stew ingredient
70. Took place
71. Sounds
72. Breaks up
73. Bar orders
77. ___ dixit
78. Quartet member
79. Mideast land
81. Sanctuaries
84. French friend
87. Smell like
89. Applications
90. Medicinal shrub
91. Like some parties
94. Driver's lic. stat
95. Actor Keach
96. Prohibited
97. Fake
98. Untrustworthy, to 60's–70's collegians
99. Split
104. Unfamiliar
106. Urban passages
108. Publicity
110. Washed with lots of water
113. Coach Karolyi
115. Poi, essentially
116. Like a brigadier general
118. "Zip-___-Doo-Dah"
120. Doctors
121. Cheese ___
122. Glib
123. Finishes a book?
124. Hold
125. Access
126. Certain case, in Latin grammar
127. Pet provider
133. Diciembre follower
134. "The Return of the Native" heath
137. Gymnast Korbut
138. Dumbarton denizen
139. Shelley's alma mater
140. Ballet movement
141. Critic Pauline
143. Kill with a click

ACROSS

1. Son of Zeus
5. Caucus selection
13. On-line feature
18. Apple seeds' site
19. Poisonous shrub
20. Spheres
22. Make jerky
23. Hypochondriac?
26. Run out
28. Van Morrison's "___ the Mystic"
29. Oscar winner Kedrova
30. Go right
31. None too brainy
32. Former mile record-holder
33. Magical symbol
36. Christmas leapers, in song
38. Bolt down
39. Pub order
41. Overcast
42. Classroom accessory
43. Like denim
45. Showed fright, in a way
47. Soccer team
48. "Vissi d'arte," e.g.
49. Like the Trojan horse
51. Food stat.
52. D.C. setting
53. Quick-starting worker?
56. American naturalist John
57. Bernie's partner in songwriting
58. Checks
59. Cudgel
60. Jet follower
63. Sibyl
64. North Dakota city
65. Upside-down sleeper
66. Stay near the shore
67. TV adjustment: Abbr.
68. Ottoman, e.g.
69. Late puppeteer Lewis
70. Hyperion, for one
71. x and y
72. Grade-C movies?
74. It may be lent or bent
77. Addr. book entry
78. Dramatists' devices
79. Bartlett's abbr.
80. Water cannon target
82. Colorings
83. Take offense
86. Certain suit
87. Secluded
88. Drop off
90. Clansman's wear
91. Meager
92. Commuter's home, perhaps
94. On
95. Slog
97. Interminable time
98. Eastern royal
100. Some bends
102. Less original
103. Ancient Greek puzzle?
108. ___ libre (poetry style)
109. Deceive
110. Pacific Rim capital
111. Year, on monuments
112. Florists' units
113. Sticky-toed critter
114. "Nana" actress

DOWN

1. Consented
2. Roll of coins
3. Wild-eyed orator?
4. Percolates
5. Fuller construction
6. High priest at Shiloh
7. Multitudinous
8. Took in
9. No-see-um
10. "Later!"
11. Common base
12. Prior to
13. The Three Bears, e.g.
14. Grad student's grilling
15. Queen Elizabeth's daggers?
16. Prefix with sex
17. Everglades evergreen
21. Source of growth
24. Story of a siege
25. Take umbrage at
27. Like Monica Seles, by birth
32. Prompt
34. Block house?
35. Waxed
37. ___ Miss
40. Oil of ___
44. Warmth
45. Not legitimate evidence
46. Bygone request
47. Woodrow's second First Lady
49. Carrion feeders
50. Stew ingredient
51. Snuffy Smith, for one
53. Coordinate
54. It may be on a roll
55. Worthless talk
56. Tiki carvers
59. Hold responsible
60. Unfulfilled potential?
61. First of all
62. Co-star of Mia in "Another Woman"
64. Coke, sometimes
65. Shucks
66. They often brown-bag it
68. Matchmaking industry?
69. Huff
70. Like the little finger
72. Long-time Moore co-star
73. Links rental
74. Takes back the lead?
75. Reduce engine heat, in a way
76. Courts
78. Hokkaido people
81. ___-mile (freight unit)
82. Like locoweed
83. Cavern sight
84. One of the Andrews Sisters
85. 1964–65 Wimbledon winner Roy
87. ___ Tomb
88. Raring to go
89. Watering hole
93. European capital
96. They go with the flow
99. Jot
101. Brain area
102. Bunch
104. Singer, of a sort
105. Take steps
106. 16-year-old's want
107. 401(k) alternative

by John Wolting

12   WARNING: CONGESTION!

by Nelson Hardy

ACROSS

1. Crowning
8. Lawrence Welk favorites
14. Slope sight
18. Kind of case
19. Not set
21. Dynamic beginning
22. "You don't have to cook all night"?
24. The Vamp
25. Angle shape
26. Computerphile
27. Celebrity
29. Guard
32. Nonplussed
34. Corker
35. Cobb and others
36. Get hoary
37. Bender
39. Target
41. Nicotine source
43. Idle question to a bakery chef?
48. Polish
50. Pun-prone poet
51. Jog
52. Bridge section
54. Send all over the place
56. Hurricane or tornado
60. Press one's suit
61. "Our Gang" member
62. ___ strip
65. Jester Jay
66. Lots
68. W.W. II field
69. Decision for newlyweds?
74. Tiny taste
75. Highway ___
77. Fashion designer Schiaparelli
78. Some snares
80. Places for studs
81. Designate
84. Dune
86. Actor Baskin of "Air Force One"
87. Party
89. ___-pointe (ballet position)
90. Branches
94. Develop
96. Jed Clampett, in Beverly Hills?
100. Strict
102. Commercial prefix with vision
103. Be short of
104. It might show its face in Vegas
105. Female gametes
107. Stalk in a swamp
109. Lace part
112. Cleave
114. Zealot
117. Starch tree
118. Singer's syllable
119. Over the bounding main
120. Restrict windfall profits?
126. Break
127. Exhibits fear
128. Dregs
129. The Charleses' canine
130. Expunges
131. Forthcoming

DOWN

1. It's game
2. Plains dweller
3. School org.
4. "Politically Incorrect" host
5. Spotted cats
6. Mild-flavored onion
7. A Turner
8. Whence the phrase "pass the buck"
9. Binge, in a way
10. Neighbor of Syr.
11. Strikeout symbols, in baseball
12. "Forever Your Girl" singer
13. Excellent, in British lingo
14. Checks
15. What maligned celebrities would like to do?
16. Collection
17. Laughs loudly
19. Cattle feed
20. Narrow margin
23. Spitz stroke
28. Gordon or Ginsburg
29. Stooge
30. Turkish leader
31. Some parties
33. 1984–88 Olympic skating champ
38. "___ be in England . . ."
40. Plaint at a door
42. French film award
44. Spicy cuisine
45. It's not up to par
46. Expiate
47. Pooh pal
49. Oft-toasted Melba
53. Kunta Kinte's slave name
55. Aristophanes play, with "The"
57. Chops up, in a way
58. Feodor, e.g.
59. Drugstore dispensations
61. Crave, with "over"
62. Haggard of C & W
63. "The Stunt Man" star
64. Loving phrase for a British policeman?
67. Years of Caesar's reign
70. Memory unit
71. Swordsman
72. Good ___
73. Game played for the Thomas Cup
76. Swains
79. King Harald's predecessor
82. Ex-wife of Mickey and Frank
83. Old Spanish viceroyalty
85. "The ___ Report" (1976 best seller)
87. Ticket stub, e.g.
88. Kind of moth
91. Harass
92. Eshkol's successor
93. Popeye's ___ Pea
95. Perkins who wrote "Blue Suede Shoes"
97. Washington's Birthday event
98. Infidel
99. Deal with
101. Professor's goal
105. "Butterfield 8" author
106. Wedgwood products
108. Inhibit
110. Passages
111. Hindrances to settlements
113. Equestrian's attire
115. Facts and figures
116. Start of a 1961 nonsense song
121. Small ammo
122. Prefix with angle or athlete
123. "Star Trek: D.S.9" character
124. 1980's TV drama "___ House"
125. Born

by Brendan Emmett Quigley

ACROSS

1. Cough medicine ingredient
7. Time changes?
12. Finishes
18. Rachmaninoff song, with "The"
19. Earth threatener
21. Attitudinize
22. Duck and dodge
24. Not according to Hoyle
25. He played Bob in "La Bamba"
26. Patois
27. Mexican restaurant entree
29. Part of NATO: Abbr.
30. Coagulation protein
32. Forgets one's lines, e.g.
34. Hunted
35. Marathoner's complaint
38. Book end?
39. Danielle Steel's "Message From ___"
40. Note in the B major scale
42. E'en if
43. Warhol subject
46. Diner offering
49. Receivers of children's "telephones"
51. Last word of the year, often
52. Beamed
54. Wahoos of the A.C.C.
55. Logging-on requirement
56. Baseball V.I.P.'s
57. Mexican beans?
58. "Abdul Abulbul ___" (1927 tune)
59. Cry of pain
60. Hard up
62. Fryolator fill
64. Place for padding or paddling
65. Like clothes at the laundromat
68. Exert pressure (on)
69. Béjart of ballet
71. Some are cheap
72. First name in 60's rock
73. Co-___ (appropriates)
74. "Demian" author
77. Fulfilled
78. 1924 gold medal swimmer
81. Cager Longley
82. Without
83. "Meet the Press" host Russert
84. Like punkies, vis-à-vis fleas
85. Kind of cuisine
87. Excalibur, e.g.
90. Minnesota twins?
91. Actresses Eleniak and Alexander
93. Maritime inits.
94. Dutch piano center
95. Bone: Prefix
96. Part of WATS
98. Charging need
100. Soprano Swarthout
102. Celtic Neptune
103. Night: Prefix
104. Bounce
106. Kind of radio
109. Unoccupied
111. Animal of American folklore
115. Went wide of
116. Drain blocker
117. Very detailed
118. Lipton competitor
119. "See ya"
120. Spliced, so to speak

DOWN

1. They, in Calais
2. Scafell ___ (highest point in England)
3. "The Whiffenpoof Song" singers
4. Wine order
5. When Macbeth slays Duncan
6. Chicago hrs.
7. Professor ___
8. Vouchsafe
9. "Make ___!" (captain's order)
10. Legal precedent
11. Trifle
12. Controversial premiere of 1879, with "A"
13. 1952 Winter Olympics site
14. When Nancy is hot
15. Tchaikovsky dancers
16. Hot
17. Nice girl?
20. Defaulter's worry
21. A lot
23. Women's groups
28. Giraffes' cousins
31. One with light locks
33. WellCare, for one
34. Start to mature
35. One of the Near Islands
36. XXX, in a way
37. General Mills cereal
39. Twaddle
41. Gig gear
43. Asian capital of 2.6 million
44. Best Supporting Actress of 1992
45. Diminutive suffix
47. Lake of Geneva resort
48. Cutting
50. Old yellers
53. Lincoln in-law
56. Econ. concern
57. Some royal tombs
58. "2001" extras
61. W.W. II gen.
63. Skipped
64. Shot
65. Gone out with
66. Agenda listing
67. Exaggerator's suffix
69. Lawn wrecker
70. "Crystal Silence" jazzman
72. Booed
75. Venn diagram representation
76. Georgia was one: Abbr.
79. Time to give up
80. Highlands tongue
82. Year in Sylvester II's papacy
83. Gustatory sensor
84. So far
86. "We Do Our Part" org.
88. Non's opposite
89. Goes back on one's word
92. Curvilinear
95. Royal fern
96. Poe's middle name
97. "Somewhere in Time" star
99. Rights
100. Beginning, in slang
101. Clinton was one
103. Uncovered
105. Luke Skywalker, e.g.
107. Family troubles
108. Flyspeck
110. Canine command
112. ___ mort (melancholy)
113. 325i or Z3
114. Crossed (out)

ACROSS

1. Launch of July 1962
8. The "E" in E. L. Doctorow
13. Rattles, for 1-Across
20. Trapped
21. 1930's–40's director Zoltan ___
22. Secondary result
23. Hardly used
24. Writer who said "Satire is what closes Saturday night"
26. Pulitzer-winning biographer Leon
27. Sundial letters
29. Junglelike
30. Ere
31. "I wish you a meretricious and a happy New Year" penner
37. Mom-and-pop grp.
40. Kind of condor
41. Dealer's nemesis
42. Smart
46. Patches again
48. One of the Allies of W.W. II
51. 0 degrees
53. Anxious
54. Where the smart set sat [answer to be entered in the appropriate manner]
57. Green, maybe
58. 1966 movie that won Best Original Score
60. Novel by 47-Down
61. Universités
62. Island in French Polynesia
63. Gov. Landon
65. "___ on $45 a Day"
67. A reduced state
68. Park toy
71. Made for a mortise
73. Binary ___
76. Thoroughly confine
78. Plaza abbr.
79. Handlebar feature
82. Bun, for one
84. Japanese portal
86. Prairielike
89. Sanford of "The Jeffersons"
90. See 54-Across
92. French flier
93. Center or end
95. Snick-or-___
96. Taras Bulba, notably
97. Munich's river
98. Matador's opponent
101. Like some diets
103. Word before "loves me" and "loves me not"
104. "From Bed to Worse" writer
108. Floor
112. Eastern pooh-bah
113. Games grp.
114. ___-American
118. She said "You can lead a horticulture, but you can't make her think"
123. More eccentric
125. Certain sweaters
126. Zaps, in a way
127. Treater's words
128. Nocturnal noisemaker
129. Upriver spawner
130. Reversion

DOWN

1. Scrabble draw
2. Site of Vance Air Force Base
3. Camp locale
4. Rock layer
5. Lot
6. With 87-Down, Wit's End resident called "Old Vitriol and Violets"
7. Goes back to the start
8. Hosp. test
9. Mr. X
10. In the majority?
11. Leaking
12. Loose overcoat
13. Name as a price
14. Grant giver, for short
15. Waters
16. Back talk
17. San ___
18. Brand of daminozide
19. Neck band?
25. Collection of legends
28. Whom "I Like"
32. Summoned, as a butler
33. Island southeast of Borneo
34. Schools for engrs.
35. "What ___ the odds?"
36. "Papillon" star
37. "No ___!" (slangy O.K.)
38. Drift
39. "'Tis ___ bagatelle!"
42. Editor who "looked like a dishonest Abe Lincoln"
43. Handy
44. Buntlines, e.g.
45. Pigtail
47. She replied to Noël Coward's "You look almost like a man!" with "And so do you"
49. Nursery rhyme residence
50. Confute
52. Dean Smith's sch.
54. See 54-Across
55. Buenos ___
56. See 54-Across
59. Leisure
64. One facing life, maybe
66. Smut
69. Loner
70. East wind, in Greek myth
72. Chanel fragrance
73. Hot dog garnish
74. Haven
75. Casualty of 1997
77. Subatomic particle
80. Abstractions
81. Gorgeous Georgian?
83. J.F.K. or F.D.R.
85. Sherlock's lady friend
87. See 6-Down
88. 52-Down rival
91. It's a gas
94. Bean
96. ___ Mounds (Illinois historical site)
99. Collect
100. They may be vital
102. Chem. or biol.
104. So out it's in
105. Guitar sound
106. Winner of a noted 1978 Supreme Court case
107. Comedian Smirnoff
108. Wife of Esau
109. Glandular fever, for short
110. Medea rode on it
111. Kind of suit
115. Done, in Verdun
116. Sleep phenomena
117. Utah city
119. Turn left
120. Fashion inits.
121. Snake ___
122. Alphabetic sequence
124. Actress Massen of "Tokyo Rose"

by Christopher Hurt

ACROSS

1. Court conference
8. Cakes of a sort
13. Gotham City do-gooder
19. It began around 1100 B.C. in Europe
20. Fires
21. In a New York minute
22. 1960's foursome
23. Monumental foursome
25. 1996 Tony winner
26. Tight
27. You wouldn't want to be caught in one
28. Bean ___
29. Singer in a field
32. ___ Varner, Faulkner woman
33. German electricity-producing city
35. Baseball stats
36. Photographer Goldin
37. Silent
39. Tin Pan Alley org.
44. Noncash deposit
45. Literary foursome
48. ___-ran
49. Semiannual occurrence
51. Components of some campaigns
52. Country club figure
53. Pitch
54. Ransom ___ Olds
55. Fields of activity
57. Certain turn-on
58. "O For a Thousand Tongues" composer
59. Changes a file listing, e.g.
61. Not staccato
65. French F.B.I.
67. Con: Var.
68. Critical foursome
71. White wine aperitif
72. Native-born Israelis
75. Fenway Park locale
76. Their words are divine
80. Get via roving eyes
81. Outwits
83. Tex-Mex snacks
85. "Eldorado" rock group
86. Bickerer in the "Iliad"
87. ___ de Triomphe
88. "We ___ the World"
90. Rocky Mountain pass
92. Bankrolls
93. Court foursome
96. Dedicated
97. Symbols of obstinacy
99. A "Doctor Zhivago" setting
100. One of Ophelia's flowers
101. Tennis legend Lacoste
102. Super Bowl XXXII outcome
104. Some Pablo Neruda works
106. Enters cyberspace
108. Duchamp contemporary
111. "The Crying Game" star
112. Home of Ephesus
114. Corn ___
115. TV foursome
118. Annual foursome
122. What une plume writes on
123. Scroogelike
124. Rustled
125. Devotes
126. Brahman, e.g.
127. Spanish saint and namesakes

by Nancy Nicholson Joline

DOWN

1. Rival, perhaps
2. Dander
3. Edmond O'Brien film noir, 1950
4. Consigns
5. Bundles
6. Mulder of "The X-Files," for one
7. Word with cure or room
8. Barbecue
9. Overdid the flattery
10. Jolly Roger feature
11. Like Radio City Music Hall
12. Latvia, once: Abbr.
13. Ellington contemporary
14. Greek Minerva
15. Nursery rhyme boy
16. Alphabetical foursome
17. Prefix with phobia
18. Indigence
20. Total
24. Overcoats
29. Inferior
30. Jim Palmer was one
31. Yuletide foursome
32. Like Baby Bear's porridge
34. Noted alpine tunnel
36. Like Miss Congeniality
38. Cries on seeing a cute baby
40. Like "The Bonfire of the Vanities"
41. Lucky foursome
42. It may be fixed
43. Oater group
45. Bills paid in Italy
46. Surgeons' tools
47. Signs of approval
50. Bucs' home
56. Ken-L Ration competitor
60. Lackland, e.g.
62. Rod
63. Does penance
64. The housewife in "Diary of a Mad Housewife"
66. Decree
69. Way out of the public eye
70. "Get outta here!"
72. Either end of Alaska
73. Parts
74. Variety of herring
77. Tramp
78. Weather whipping boy
79. Soaked
82. Awakening
84. Santa ___
88. Penultimate word of Warner Brothers cartoons
89. Like the sound of a gong
91. Big tips
94. Castro's predecessor
95. Kind of spoon
98. Went through channels?
103. Squints (at)
105. Sad music
106. "Gigi" composer
107. "Live"
108. Venomous ones
109. Gather
110. "___ down now!"
113. Miss in a 1934 song
114. Sound before "Yeah, you!"
116. Palindromic diarist
117. U.S. Army medal
119. Words of understanding
120. Org. in the Mapplethorpe brouhaha
121. Newsmaking 60's grp.

ACROSS

1. Kaiser, once
4. "Die Fledermaus" maid
9. Irritate
13. Slow movement
19. Flap
20. Biological group
21. Inner: Prefix
22. Whalesucker
23. Gong worn on the head?
26. Plug for a cask
27. Having the biggest lip?
28. Set-tos
30. In a bit
31. "Oh, I see"
32. Ran riot
33. Beat
35. First note at the Moulin Rouge?
40. Contest for Atalanta
43. Wheelhouse direction
44. Check mates
45. Strauss opera
47. Cambodia's Lon ___
48. Dallas icemen
50. Baja cheer
51. Birling surface
52. Pulitzer Prize category
54. Rug rat
55. Fast Chinese food?
61. Biol. subject
62. Ingle glowers
63. Diamond flaw?
64. What you will
66. Clean
69. Downhill gold medalist of 1994
70. Travelers' gear
71. Rival of Billie Jean
72. Kind of skirt
74. Author Puzo
75. Women, slangily
76. Off-limits craziness?
79. Flight
82. ___ alia
84. Popular card game
85. Start of the fifth century
86. More than see
88. "Rock 'N' Roll Is King" group
89. Prevents
92. Having tears
94. Skim along
95. Crossword grid feature
97. Dog pedigree?
100. "Hernando's Hideaway," e.g.
101. Go formal
102. Auto of long ago
103. It may be thrown into a pot
104. They make connections
106. Nautical hanger-on
111. Lit up
113. Farewell to balloting?
115. Where Mark Twain is buried
116. Director Riefenstahl
117. Backgammon piece
118. Fatima's spouse
119. Optimally
120. Hebrides tongue
121. Bars
122. Vintage

DOWN

1. Notable opening of 10/7/82
2. Fall guy?
3. Alitalia stop
4. Hercule's creator
5. Humbles
6. Chimp in space
7. The hots
8. Olive relative
9. Weasel out
10. Buck features
11. Mount
12. Go (over)
13. ___ Nova (music style)
14. Left
15. Key of Mendelssohn's Symphony No. 3
16. Disco fruit?
17. Press agent?
18. Meal starter
24. U.P.S. inquiry
25. "It's ___ World" ('62 sitcom)
29. Foil on the stage
32. Renaissance fiddle
34. Opposite of heter-
35. Calculate astrologically
36. ___-relievo
37. Straight
38. "Becket" star
39. Cheap magazines
40. Ground meal
41. Partner, redundantly
42. Delights
46. To boot
49. Show disdain for
53. Tangent or secant
56. "Adam's Rib" actress
57. Confine
58. Home of the Black Bears
59. Exhibit vanity
60. Millennium makeup
62. Use a thurible
65. Less upfront
66. Flies in the face of
67. With nothing left over
68. Drummer's affliction?
70. Go "poof!"
72. Tick off
73. Continuous-play tape
74. Member of a corps
77. Best in the regatta
78. Garbage haulers
79. Caron role
80. Speller's phrase
81. Allocate, with "out"
83. Corrects the ledger
87. In good financial shape
90. Brit. money
91. Multiplex multitude
92. Sphagnous
93. Gullywasher
96. Henry James title character
98. The Love Bug, of Disney films
99. Señor on the Sullivan show
101. Utility room item
103. Revolver inventor
105. Suffix with collect
106. 1976 Kiss hit
107. 1966 N.L. batting champ
108. "So long!"
109. Be a couch potato
110. Arthurian lady
111. Where the buoys are
112. Not dis
114. Lombard Street feature

by Richard Silvestri

ACROSS

1. Pill popper's pop
7. It's supposed to come first
13. Rotating bodies
20. On the decline?
21. Old French colony
22. Turned a deaf ear to
23. Head man on ice?
25. Envoys
26. 10th anniversary gift
27. African plains grazer
28. India/Pakistan events
30. Strip off
31. Look of one needing a comeuppance
33. Man to "tell 'em what they won" on many game shows
36. College credits
38. Christie detective
40. Early "S.N.L." star
43. "Out!"
47. Absent-minded barber's request?
51. Light of the moon
52. Lounging
53. Here's one pour vous
54. Woofer output
55. Kind of bar
56. Psis' predecessors
57. Not doing well in a race
60. Peeples of "North Shore," 1987
62. Sandwiches for dessert
63. Comparatively stewed
65. Boat propellers
67. Marabou, for one
69. Make final
70. Chan's silent "You got me"?
73. Stand in
76. They can go to blazes
77. "C'mon, be ___"
78. Saint-___ (Loire's capital)
80. 10, in a way
83. N.L. Central team inits.
85. Ham
87. "There!"
88. University of California site
89. La la starter
91. Prefix with duct
92. Sign-on requirement, often
94. Like a 911 call: Abbr.
95. Remnants in Ohio?
99. Nimble
100. Operatic passage
101. Coffeecake
102. Joltless joe
104. "Jerusalem Delivered" poet
106. Stool, in a manner of speaking
110. Paler than pale
112. Fasten with a pop
115. Kabuki alternative
117. Italian note
118. Cubist before Rubik
120. Gift holders?
124. Why plants turn to the sun
125. Unreadable
126. Kind of center
127. Sling mud
128. What to do
129. Most curious

DOWN

1. Autograph holders
2. Don't leave at the doorstep
3. Kind of geometry
4. Parking place
5. Bons mots
6. Neighbor of Mo.
7. Airline to Stockholm
8. Rhine whine
9. Electrical unit
10. Rags have them
11. Sticking point
12. Ties up the phone
13. Light lager
14. "T" size: Abbr.
15. Worry
16. Flood survivor's pet?
17. Art Deco illustrator
18. Got ready to drive, with "up"
19. Old sit-in org.
24. Aquarium staple
29. Sandwich filler
32. —
34. Vocally
35. Reason to go back to school
37. Forms grp.
39. Pot containers
41. "The light dawns!"
42. Bruce of "Family Plot"
44. Vaudeville dancer's accessory
45. Ray of film
46. Building blocks, e.g.
47. Milk: Prefix
48. Work ___
49. Snow, in Bordeaux
50. Soprano Scotto
55. Welsh dog
58. Old Dodge
59. Purplish-red
61. "___ Grows in Brooklyn"
64. Gimlets and screwdrivers
66. Hit (the brakes)
68. Fast exodus
71. European language of one million
72. Czechs' cousins
73. Bag
74. Opened
75. Worrier's handful
76. Abominable Snowman?
79. Timeless, in olden times
80. Monthly occurrence
81. Dewy
82. "Did you ___?"
84. Off one's rocker
86. Son of Vespasian
90. Part of H.R.H.
93. Guide and protector
95. Dump
96. Trying
97. Never, never, never
98. Little PC pictures
103. Mate's assent
105. Playwright Chekhov
107. Satirical production
108. "Bonanza" deputy and others
109. Sets upon
110. Something to put on?
111. Old English bard
113. Three oceans touch it
114. Hungry feeling
116. "___ be in England"
118. Sch. group
119. Viper's sound
121. Put two and two together
122. Large amount
123. Lassie's mate

by Nancy Salomon

by Henry Hook

ACROSS

1. Meager
5. Pen name
8. Tried to lose?
15. Mediocre
19. Hawaiian winter wind
20. She danced with John in "Pulp Fiction"
21. Woman in Charles's life
22. Relaxation
23. Start of a quip
26. Mysterious character
27. They let you know you're wanted
28. Solar system mockup
29. Vacillated
31. Abundance
32. Tykes
33. The other team in "Damn Yankees"
34. Homer Simpson's exclamation
36. Ike's command: Abbr.
37. Inheritance?
38. Dickens the sketchwriter
41. Suffix with macro-
44. As soon as
46. C's in shop class?
50. Town SE of Bakersfield, Calif.
52. Scepter adornment
54. Family
55. Zulus, e.g.
56. Political practice, perhaps
58. Quip, part 2
62. Forster's "___ With a View"
63. Gull
65. Asia Minor region
66. Quip, part 3
69. Like a banshee
71. Without
72. Gone by
76. Quip, part 4
78. Tolkien tree-man
79. "The Player" director, 1992
80. Article in El Pais
81. Citric cooler
82. Addams Family member
84. E-9: Abbr.
88. Painter Anthony Van ___
91. Spread out
92. Calendar units: Abbr.
93. Unsurprising
95. Japanese honorific
97. Ilex, for one
99. Noted site of foreign study
102. Kind of train
105. Nearly sacrificed son
110. Expurgated, with "up"
111. "Tobacco Road" father Jeeter ___
112. Actress Dolores
113. Plant-growth retardant
114. End of the quip
117. Bean town?
118. More blackened
119. Animation unit
120. Take out of context?
121. Secretary, for one
122. Lev Bronstein's alias
123. Fire
124. Tried to beat the tag

DOWN

1. Captains, informally
2. O.K. for the diet-conscious
3. Architect Jones
4. "Politically Incorrect" host
5. Chums
6. 1965 Yardbirds hit "___ Man"
7. Lakeside sight
8. Build up
9. Enjoyed
10. The Sage of Concord
11. Easter emblem
12. Toymaker, maybe
13. Largo, vis-à-vis presto
14. Adirondack lake
15. Big pistol manufacturer
16. 1985 newsmaking ship Achille ___
17. "Roots" Emmy winner
18. Follows
24. Cézanne's "Boy in ___ Vest"
25. Madness?
30. Colorado resort
32. Horse's halter
33. Cordwood measure
35. Publisher Adolph
38. Tolerate
39. "Oops!"
40. Emil ___, 1948–52 Czech track gold medalist
42. Did some scouting
43. Impart erroneously
45. They're on top of things
47. "The Drew Carey Show" woman
48. Entreaty
49. Partake at 30-Down
50. As yet unscheduled: Abbr.
51. Dense clouds
53. Fetched, to a hillbilly
57. Free-for-all
58. Duck
59. Nevertheless
60. Wedding vow infinitive
61. Bennett song start
63. Vladivostok villa
64. Nouvelle Calédonie, e.g.
67. Thrice daily, in pharm.
68. Preface
69. Jets or Sharks
70. Makeup lessons?: Abbr.
73. Gen. Bradley
74. Flees
75. Modern-day evidence
76. Clear the tables
77. Mix up
79. Writer Quindlen
83. Sans pass
85. Mideast leader beginning 1981
86. "Chacun ___ goût"
87. Marilyn Monroe's birthday
89. "The Screwtape Letters" writer
90. Name in Chinese history
94. Multipurpose conjunction
96. One with a lot of paperwork
98. Ukraine's capital
99. Almost boil
100. Stan's pal
101. Lots and lots
103. Bottom line
104. "All My Children" role
106. Coasters
107. Synthetic fiber
108. Garlicky mayonnaise
109. Intimidated
111. Trent of the Senate
112. Lowland
115. CC
116. Spell

ACROSS

1. Spot on a cliff
5. Pound (down)
9. First baseball player to make $1 million a year
13. Big splash
18. "Thérèse Raquin" novelist
19. Girl in a #1 Everly Brothers hit
20. Part of a meter
21. Ruth's mother-in-law
22. Turning points
23. Critic Judith
24. Genius?
26. Beige shirt with khaki pants?
29. "Bulworth" star
30. "Yo!"
31. Grp. in peace accords
32. Person of high position
33. A new twist?
39. Toshiba competitor
42. "The Last Time I Saw Paris" composer
43. Wagner heroine
44. Twist
48. Solely
49. Job for a seamstress
52. Part of a plane
53. Partner of Brahma and Vishnu
54. Rather soft
56. Like many a castle
58. Not just given
59. Farm sound
60. Calmer
62. Kilmer communicates with the deaf?
64. Headline trumpeting a new wedding veil?
68. Hairdo for the office?
70. "Phantom Lady" actress, 1944
71. Far East carrier, for short
73. Black Sea locale
74. Challenging reply
76. Answers
78. "Seven" or "10," e.g.
79. Qatar's capital
81. Took steps
84. "Here ___ Again" (1987 #1 hit)
85. Writer Harte
86. St. ___ , Switzerland
88. Agape
89. Journal unit
90. Ex-hoopster Dave, after he went to Washington?
93. His name's an anagram of "gaoler"
96. Calendar abbr.
97. Supply boat
102. Split
103. Places where graft is most common?
108. Case for Ace Ventura?
110. Having fine threads
111. The Miners of the N.C.A.A.
112. Kind of bit
113. Cutlass, e.g.
114. Great interest
115. Repeated cry in a children's argument
116. Obdurate
117. Word after who or what
118. Gamepieces
119. Certain constellation star

DOWN

1. Bohemian, e.g.
2. "Good Times" star, in 70's TV
3. Calm
4. Needing a pat on the back, say
5. Gang's domain
6. ___ were
7. Like a golf ball in the rough
8. Czar of 1682–1725
9. European capital
10. Fabrication
11. Home of the Cyclones
12. TV's "The ___ Today"
13. Sportscaster Dick
14. Stone size
15. Hesitant
16. Concord
17. Baby
19. Absolutely clean
25. Hearty entree
27. Goal-oriented activity
28. Rikki-tikki-___
32. Plate ump's call
34. A little work
35. Belief that all natural objects have souls
36. Lord's worker
37. A three or a five, for instance
38. Literary inits.
39. Sound at the door
40. 37-Down, e.g.
41. How "Lili Marlene" is played
44. Laughs hysterically
45. Psalms writer
46. Still
47. Rolls
50. "Take two" was his motto
51. Receipts
53. Disrespect
55. Sits, slangily
57. Sad
58. Tigers foe
60. Concert sites
61. Each
62. Of the belly
63. Ancient greeting
65. ___ dixit
66. Dapper ones
67. Funny one
68. Starting point
69. Lilac, e.g.
72. Tour grp.
74. Shred
75. Owns, once
76. Kind of sale
77. Sauce ingredient
79. Ready to come out of the oven
80. Ending of many Web site names
82. One who stays up late
83. Make some fast food
86. 1993 A.F.C. Rookie of the Year Rick
87. Bite, so to speak
90. Flaubert creation
91. Strengthen
92. Revolt
93. Eskimo-___ (language group)
94. Discharge
95. Ancient Greek physician
98. Leftover
99. Woman of "Today"
100. It happens
101. Aggressive
102. Workers in columns
103. Battery
104. Tips
105. A bell ringer closes it: Abbr.
106. Wallop
107. Wherry equipment
109. Runner Sebastian

by Joe DiPietro

by Fred Piscop

ACROSS

1. Conduct, in a way
6. Innocent
10. Pasta or potato, to an athlete
14. Saint in Italy
19. Showy flower
20. Daminozide, commercially
21. 'Hood
22. Edit, as a soundtrack
23. The exterminator ordered ___
25. The horologist ordered ___
27. Em, for example
28. Song word after "Aba"
30. Cell division process
31. Introduction to physics?
33. Disinfest
36. Blue book filler
37. Razor-billed bird
40. Stampeders
42. Gray wolf
43. Pantry pest
44. The inept furniture mover ordered ___
48. The wild pitcher ordered ___
53. Illegal parker's worry
54. Petitions
56. Liszt's "La Campanella," e.g.
57. Old shoe polish brand
60. Discloses
61. Withdraws, with "out"
63. Beneficiary of nepotism: Abbr.
64. Evening event
66. Rival of Helena
68. Domino, e.g.
69. The real estate agent ordered ___
72. The comedian ordered ___
74. Politico Bayh
75. Cremona craftsman
77. River crosser, perhaps
78. Campaign feature, maybe
79. Hardly a blabbermouth
80. Pump, e.g.
82. 1962 Paul Anka hit
86. "The Last Command" locale
88. Giggled
91. Longer in the tooth
92. The used-car dealer ordered ___
94. The mama's boy ordered ___
97. Initials since 1933
98. Whence the Magi, with "the"
100. Port of Egypt
101. "Hoo" preceder
102. More cluttered
105. Fore-and-after
107. Like some questions
110. Showstoppers?
112. One of TV's Mavericks
114. Vacillate
117. The panhandler ordered ___
120. The munitions expert ordered ___
123. Crow's home
124. Ham's punctuation
125. Bit of fast food
126. Land
127. He was a real dummy
128. Channels
129. Pack
130. Like smokestacks

DOWN

1. Office dupes, for short
2. Result of a crack?
3. Diamond family name
4. Actress Massey
5. Whole bunch
6. Like some coifs
7. Climber's challenge
8. Duster
9. Scratch
10. Sporty car
11. "Exodus" role
12. Nickelodeon cartoon character
13. Toto's creator
14. Masks
15. Balloon or dirigible
16. Milton, for one
17. Saint ___ (Florida county)
18. Having made substantial gains?
24. Flexible
26. Two-stage missile
29. Place for bats?
32. Kill ___ killed
34. "SOS" singers
35. Directly opposed
37. "Hamlet" quintet
38. Unsettling comment from a pilot
39. Apteryx australis
41. Slowest on the uptake
45. Scribes
46. Smoking gun
47. "L'___ c'est moi"
49. Slander
50. "Foreign Affairs" author Alison
51. ___ Rogers St. Johns
52. Took out
55. Oahu-to-Maui dir.
58. Major defense contractor
59. Lively
62. Caterpillar constructions
65. Navigation units
67. Diatribes
68. Raise again . . . and again
69. Pertaining to 73-Down
70. Seed structure
71. Word of politeness
73. Hospital supply
76. Professional suffix
77. Ring fighter
79. Reached the vanishing point
81. Bully
83. Wired
84. Utah state flower
85. Give or take
87. Gesturer
89. Cousin of a canvasback
90. Time of decision
93. Goa garment
95. Tries not to attract attention
96. Car bomb?
99. Gets serious, with "up"
102. Vanquishes
103. Let out
104. Halitosis fighter
106. Younger siblings, traditionally
108. Crows' homes
109. Prefix with -pathy
111. Square-ended vessel
113. The "id" in "id est"
115. Sleekly designed
116. Flaw
118. Hollywood autobiography subtitled "My Story"
119. Bit of Florida
121. Nonpolluting
122. El adjoiner

ACROSS

1. 1997 N.H.L. M.V.P. Dominik
6. Kind of range
11. Not right?
18. Romeo, e.g.
20. Two for the road
21. Ennoble
22. + 43
24. Sticks
25. Like jambalaya
26. Once, once
28. Papas in films
29. "___ speak"
32. − 32
36. What's-his-face
38. Won over
39. "The Black Cat" writer
42. Mentor's charge
43. Blacken, as steak
45. Acropolis figure
47. Tolkien creature
48. − 3
54. Like wedding cakes
55. Rtes.
56. Key rings?
57. Designer Cassini
59. Uniform alternative
60. "Casablanca" role and others
62. Unkind look
63. "Maid of Athens, ___ part": Byron
64. "Wheel of Fortune" request
65. − 41
70. "Foucault's Pendulum" author
71. Progress impeders
73. Toward the caboose
74. Writer Fannie
76. Up
77. Dry fuel
78. Eritrean capital
81. "___ vous plait"
84. Rodeo grounds features
86. − 31
88. Suffix with corpus
89. Its main street is Last Chance Gulch
90. Santa's spot?
91. Deadly virus
93. Wall Street whiz
94. Homers reach them
99. Sponges
101. − 90 or − 94, among others
104. Depilatory brand
105. Less tanned
108. Dirt
109. Item on a list
111. One who studies irises
113. − 100
119. Like a gridiron
120. Omega competitors
121. Like the heavens
122. Calculator figures
123. Glyceride, e.g.
124. Wake the dead?

DOWN

1. That ship
2. It may be pint-sized
3. Saucehound
4. Lacking vigor
5. See 58-Down
6. Indian princess
7. C.D. offering: Abbr.
8. Safe-products org.
9. Paul Bunyan, e.g.
10. Develop
11. Podium speaker
12. U.N. arm
13. Running late
14. Three-time Wimbledon champ
15. Pink, so to speak
16. Solar deity
17. ___-majesté
19. Coral assemblies
20. Graphic head?
23. 60's–70's Italian P.M.
27. Site of many losses
29. Daisy relative
30. Unflawed
31. + 29 or + 44 or + 69, etc.
33. Burning passions
34. Crucifix letters
35. "I earn that ___": "As You Like It"
37. "L'Absinthe" painter
39. − 29
40. Ring combination
41. Lady of a 1932 song
43. Quarter-millennium
44. 1940's Tigers All-Star Newhouser
46. Posting in a French store
49. Ship sunk at Pearl Harbor
50. "Can't do it"
51. Beethoven's birthplace
52. Zeno's home
53. Rustic pipe
58. With 5-Down, a TV gourmet
61. Emissary
62. Elton John, e.g.
64. Pollen container
66. Actress Mary et al.
67. Bring in
68. Stuff
69. Doctor Zhivago
71. Nickname for Alexander
72. Loud
75. Advertising figures
78. Give ___ of one's own medicine
79. Traffic caution
80. Engineer's sch.
82. Words after "Well"
83. Minimal
85. Mordant Mort
87. Book after Neh.
92. Male slave
95. Privileged classes
96. Zeus, to Cronus
97. Pour out freely
98. Squares things
99. Streep's "___ in the Dark"
100. The slightest amount
101. C.S.A. general
102. House & Garden topic
103. Bugs
105. "Passion" star Negri
106. Kind of indigestion
107. Capital of Denmark in the Middle Ages
110. Gonzo
112. Avg.
114. Potted
115. Island guitar
116. "My man!"
117. Go wrong
118. Ham sandwicher

by Jim Page

ACROSS

1. It finds itself in hot water
7. Comics debut of 1941
13. No longer shrink-wrapped
19. Socks pattern
20. It didn't keep Little Boy Blue awake
21. Jinx
22. Breakfaster's favorite drama?
25. Crime mystery writer Paretsky
26. Fluency
27. Discredit
28. Resort souvenir
29. Breakfaster's query?
35. Associate of Zhou
38. Have breakfast, e.g., in Germany
39. Church part
40. Nasty
44. Waters and Mertz
46. Whispered call
47. ACTH or thyroxine
50. Bright-colored blooms
52. E. coli, for one: Abbr.
53. Heads toward
54. Fielding brother
55. Breakfaster's personal credo?
58. "Jaws" sighting
59. Loose, in a manner of speaking
60. The L of L-dopa
61. Dry as a bone
62. Is in peak singing condition?
64. Marked by drinking
66. First name in jeans
68. Williams and Kennedy
70. "The Conqueror Worm" poet
71. One way to run
74. Peel
76. 1997 Peter Fonda title role
78. Isle of Man man
81. Dolt
82. Breakfaster's maids?
85. Just
86. Remove all restrictions on
88. L'eau lands?
89. Mouthed but not spoken
91. "Amadeus" role
92. Cause of a non sequitur
93. Salt of element #53
94. Meg's "Prelude to a Kiss" co-star
95. Wear well
96. Feeding tube?
99. Formerly named
100. How a breakfaster views himself?
106. Cap initials at Busch Stadium
109. Have a loan from
110. Make
111. Part of the eye
115. Waiters' reaction after breakfast was over?

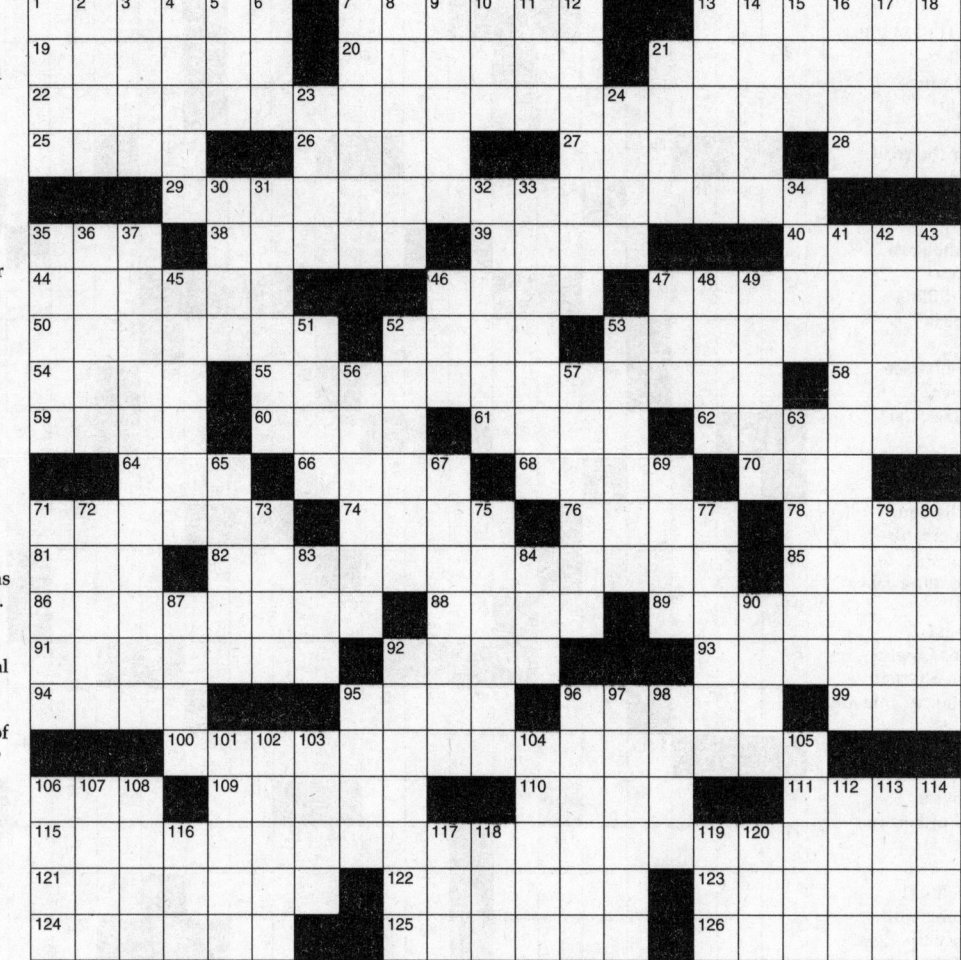

by Manny Nosowsky

121. ___ Forest (W.W. I battle site)
122. "Bewitched" husband
123. One in the can
124. Holiday driver, in a phrase
125. Place beside
126. Sharp-pointed instrument

DOWN

1. ___ Ski Valley, N.M.
2. Author Bombeck
3. Golden-___
4. Legally
5. It may be involved in a draft
6. Pick up
7. Wear off
8. Bran accompanier
9. Like some chairs
10. ___ et ubique (here and everywhere)
11. Female name suffix
12. Swellhead
13. Roasters
14. Second of a historical trio
15. Cedar ___ (lumber source)
16. "Capital!"
17. Plain Jane
18. Astronaut Slayton
21. Actress McClurg
23. "No ___ allowed"
24. Confront
30. Start with pad or port
31. Lash out at
32. Violinist Heifetz
33. Surprise challenger
34. Mashed dish
35. Cross, of a sort
36. Eric Rohmer's "___ of Winter"
37. Breakfaster's sad comment?
41. Breakfaster's U.N. guest?
42. How tuna may be packed
43. Screendom's Laura and Bruce
45. Escape artist
46. Hand, informally
47. "Gotcha!"
48. "Is that all right?"
49. Swab again
51. Illustrator Silverstein
52. Second-rate film
53. Kind of linebacker
56. Opposed
57. Jams
63. Run a charity, e.g.
65. Giggle
67. Black to the max
69. Will be, to Doris Day
71. March music maker
72. Ear part
73. Wrong end?
75. Enlarge
77. Observation
79. Select or elect
80. Paris school
83. It releases a dangerous spray
84. Spirit
87. It may be polished
90. 1956 Allen Ginsberg poem
92. Dodger name of fame
95. Lo-cal
96. Flow stoppage
97. Capital city spelled with an umlaut
98. Registered, with "up"
101. Sondheim song "We're ___ Be All Right"
102. Oscar winner Edmund of "Miracle on 34th Street"
103. Golfer Ballesteros
104. Prefix with transmitter
105. Scrumptious
106. Try
107. Like some traffic
108. Runners
112. Kind of chops
113. Renaissance art patron
114. "I'd hate to break up ___"
116. ___ Kippur
117. Easy mark
118. Dadaist Jean
119. It might halt traffic on the Rhine
120. Many a worker

ACROSS

1. ___ salad
6. Attempts
11. Churchill's "few"
14. Cassius's costume
18. Welcome sight
19. The Sorbonne, e.g.
20. Paella pot
22. Comet competitor
23. Q: ___ A: Later
27. Café additive
28. "Beverly Hills 90210" restaurant owner and others
29. Passionate desire
30. Originate
31. Sister of Terpsichore
33. Happy-lark go-between
34. Open, in a way
35. Q: ___ A: Out
44. It's charged
45. Egg manufacturer
46. Hallow ending
47. ___ Bator
48. Indian Prime Minister, 1991–96
49. The others
51. Sch. supporters
52. River of Tours
53. Aeronautical feat
54. Q: ___ A: O.K.
59. Some computer keys
60. Med. drips
61. Comprise
62. Payments for releases
64. Genetic inits.
65. Took off a ship
68. Just beat
69. Play to the camera
70. Five-time Kentucky Derby winner
71. Q: ___ A: Friends
79. "B.C." creator
80. Teased teen-agers
81. Laugh syllable
82. First name in cosmetics
83. Charlottesville-to-Richmond dir.
84. Romanian ruler known as "the Impaler"
85. Rye filler
86. Craggy peak
88. Part of X-X-X
89. Q: ___ A: I don't have any
95. "Jug handles"
96. Bond rating
97. Descriptive words for Ben Jonson
98. Painter El ___
100. "Makin' Whoopee" songwriter
102. Vault
103. Tierra del Fuego, e.g.
107. Q: ___ A: I don't need one
111. Tuner
112. Crewmate of Scotty
113. Instant
114. Words of wisdom
115. Not rash
116. Vegas action
117. Bury
118. Code name

DOWN

1. Hood
2. A few laughs
3. Actor Morales
4. Tailor, at times
5. Atl. speedster
6. Blood component
7. Colorless ketone
8. Farm females
9. Frazier foe
10. Gets into trouble, maybe
11. Popular fast-food chain, informally
12. Very much
13. Winter woe
14. Exotic vacation spot
15. Spanish eyes
16. Willing
17. Fire
21. Button sources
24. Greatly admiring
25. Poi party
26. Joyce's homeland
32. One who believes "practice makes perfect"
33. Per annum
34. Genesis
35. On the same side as
36. Santa sounds
37. Poetically sufficient?
38. "___ pray"
39. Harbor markers
40. He directed Marlon
41. Good routine
42. Like an angel
43. Bushwhacker, e.g.
50. Tried to hit, in dialect
51. Geneva Convention concern
52. Hot rocks
53. Trails
55. Like some shows
56. Israeli day
57. Dog, Down Under
58. Tour operator, at times
62. Go over old territory?
63. Renée of the silents
64. Area covers
65. Press
66. Staff sgt., e.g.
67. Charlie of the 60's Orioles
69. Confuse
70. Weather prefix
71. "That was close!"
72. Neighborhood
73. Cheers
74. Master's ordeal
75. "If ___ nickel . . ."
76. Put ___ (ask hard questions of)
77. Eye drop
78. "Darn it!"
85. China's Yellow Emperor
86. Arsonist
87. N.C.A.A. World Series site
90. Irk
91. Western city or its radio station
92. Diamond Head locale
93. "Well begun is half done" writer
94. Nut
98. Classic Italian car
99. Tom Clancy hero
100. Actor MacLachlan
101. Month of l'été
102. Busy
104. Capone trademark
105. Totes
106. Suit to ___
107. O.E.D. entries
108. Container
109. Directional suffix
110. Cartesian conclusion

by Randolph Ross

24 KVETCHES

by Cathy Millhauser

ACROSS

1. Heath ___ (flowering perennial)
6. Some are inflatable
11. 1980's Geena Davis sitcom
15. During
19. Verdi's Aïda, e.g.
20. Dazzle
21. Lover of Aphrodite
22. Goya's Maja is one
23. Movie kvetch in the woods?
25. Arbitrary decree
26. Old Pontiacs
27. Catchers in tag
28. "There's Something About ___ (That Reminds Me of You)"
29. Newborn's bed
31. Leg scratchers
34. Madras wear
35. Robert ___
37. Kvetch's game show?
40. Charges
42. Basis of the marine food chain
45. Job ad letters
46. Seles rival
48. Pavarotti possessive
49. What kvetches do at grocery stores?
55. Steeping gadget
57. Prefix with light or night
58. Rock's ___ Heep
59. Prefix with sphere or system
61. Surfeited
62. Spot for a nosh
65. ___ apple
67. Mrs. Flagston of the comics
68. Remember a kvetch in one's will?
72. Maj. Houlihan portrayer in "M*A*S*H"
74. Round trip?
75. Contradicts
79. No-waist dresses
81. Visit
82. More than irked
84. Newcomer, briefly
85. Cloaks
87. Angry kvetching?
91. Annihilation
92. They often don't speak to each other
94. "-speak"
95. Tangent, e.g.
96. By ___ (via)
98. Nickname for a kvetch maven?
104. "The Thief of Bagdad" star, 1940
105. Football's Flash Herber
106. Primitive time
110. Small pipe organ
112. Reject
114. Triangle part
115. Susan Lucci's eluder
117. Procter & Gamble soap
118. Film title kvetch?
121. Kind of club
122. French quarters
123. Heard cases
124. Pronouncement
125. Surround
126. Richard of "Final Analysis"
127. Riding lawnmower maker
128. "The Devil and Daniel Webster" writer

DOWN

1. Comparable to a fiddle
2. A deadly sin
3. Tibiae neighbors
4. Brink
5. Legal matter
6. Rue
7. Transversely
8. Bugs
9. Subdued
10. Big initials at Indy
11. Occasion for a game plan?
12. Stemming
13. Get back, as authority
14. Piedmont province
15. Actress Bassett
16. Kiddie kvetches' game?
17. Oft-broken promise
18. ___ Arc, Ark.
24. Indian percussion rhythm
29. Cousin of "Phooey!"
30. Like some Clement Moore snow
32. Kind of meet
33. Train in a celebrated song
34. ___ Pea (Popeye's kid)
36. Ancient Roman officials
38. Prefix with store
39. Middle English letter
41. Realtor sign add-on
42. "Rigoletto" has three
43. Croquet site
44. Yago Sant' ___ (wine brand)
47. N.R.C. predecessor
50. Low note provider
51. Curtain call call
52. Drying frames
53. Overhaul
54. Fink
56. Human apes
60. Some fraternity members
63. Actor Montgomery
64. A lot of tea
65. Lawyer: Abbr.
66. '54 defense pact
69. "___ your pardon?"
70. Bleacher feature
71. Feudal estate
72. Journalist Alexander et al.
73. Zephyr's kvetching?
76. Premed subj.
77. Elusive creature
78. Arty Big Apple area
79. Small merganser
80. What an "F" may indicate
82. ___ jure (by law)
83. Site of a wreck
86. Begin wedding plans
88. "Able was ___ . . ."
89. Birdhouse dweller
90. Undone?
93. Peace Corps director Sargent
97. Minded
99. Sheathe
100. Daughter of Ingrid Bergman
101. Illegal lender
102. Big step
103. Conclusion of many firm names
107. Detective Pinkerton
108. Followers
109. Wading bird
111. Cassini with designs on Jackie
112. Withered
113. ___-dieu (kneeling bench)
115. Prod
116. Year in Leo IX's papacy
118. Bouquet sender's abbr.
119. Brew milieu
120. Strummer's instrument

ACROSS

1. Like some Swift writing
7. Gallery event
14. "My Cup Runneth Over" singer, 1967
20. Zane Grey classic
21. Blows the joint
22. Egghead
23. Fence builder's job?
25. Storied raider
26. Writer Ferber
27. Minds, with "to"
28. Green hole
29. Chinese dynasty when Jesus lived
30. Roots may need this
31. El ___
32. Bygone music genre
35. Giving the once-over
37. Architect's job?
42. Winner's look
44. Least bit of concern
45. Pre-Columbian Peruvian
46. Strip
47. Singer profiled in "Sweet Dreams"
48. Unit of 97-Across
49. Push to the limit
50. Ends of letters, briefly
51. Steeple musician's job?
57. "What Kind of Fool ___"
58. Authority, metaphorically
59. Like an empty ship at sea
60. Judge's cry
64. Ball park licensee
67. Fliers with narrow waists
69. Cinch
70. Singed parts, usually
71. Kind of drum
73. Chaney, the Man of a Thousand Faces
75. "Fancy that!"
76. Sculptor's job?
82. ___-Magnon
84. Shoe color
85. Drive
86. Puts to flight
87. Runners' location
88. Rock projection
90. It's fit to be tried
91. Leaves
92. Politician's job?
96. 1970 hit "Hitchin' ___"
97. Poet's concern
98. It's not free of charge
99. Natl. Popcorn Poppin' Month
102. Time div.
103. Main ingredient in a Monte Carlo
105. Like some pitches
109. Tudor queen
110. Bear
112. Feather packer's job?
115. Sen. Gaylord ___, who originated Earth Day
116. Make more precipitous
117. ___ Park, N.Y.
118. They're driven in droves
119. Some TV spots
120. One with a light workload?

DOWN

1. Barbara Stanwyck film "Woman ___"
2. Word before "go"
3. Just like ewe?
4. Mercury org.
5. Chemical suffix
6. Stealthy
7. Fortas and Lincoln
8. Cessation
9. Poet laureate of 1692
10. Maintain, as attention
11. Warmly welcomes, perhaps
12. "Fairy tale"
13. Alien force, briefly
14. Isaac's eldest
15. Decked out
16. Gardner of "The Snows of Kilimanjaro"
17. Automatons
18. Magnifies
19. Manager of five straight World Series champions
24. Screen
28. Like some lenses
31. Best-selling author Carr
33. Reagan prog.
34. Middle: Prefix
36. Chatterboxes
37. Like some vases
38. "Grab ___!"
39. Clinker
40. Photo process
41. Hack
42. Covered with goo
43. Potential space colony activity
47. Want
48. Andy Capp's wife
52. Make muffs
53. VCR button
54. Kind of I.R.A.
55. Hosp. hot spots
56. Bamboozle
61. Bench locale
62. Builds
63. Offends olfactorily
65. Put in plaintext
66. City in Kyrgyzstan
67. Servicewoman, acronymically
68. "Speak!" response
69. Exterior lineman
71. "Puh-lease!"
72. Generic
73. Access the Web
74. Rousing cheer
77. Longing
78. Long in politics
79. Bombeck of "At Wit's End"
80. Oscilloscope inventor Karl
81. Forsaken
82. Mozart solo feature
83. Arouse again
87. Pollen bearers
89. Snagged
90. Disrespects
91. Ballyhoo
93. Guerrilla's campaign
94. Lipton rival
95. Lowdown
99. Spring locales
100. Belief
101. One catching his opponent's ear?
104. Longs
106. Blockhead
107. Classical decorative object
108. Landers and others
109. Start of something big
111. Purpose
112. Clock std.
113. Time for les vacances
114. Something to chew on

by Harvey Estes and Nancy Salomon

ACROSS

1. Be unwarrantably bold
8. Occultism
14. Modus operandi
20. One seen at trackside
22. Moonstruck
23. Lizard with a serrated crest
24. Start of an imaginary soliloquy
27. Inoffensive
28. Accepted
29. Kind of ticket
30. Enzyme suffix
31. Part 2 of the soliloquy
41. Walker's aid
42. Uris novel "___ 18"
43. Buddhist who has attained Nirvana
44. Sitter's charge
47. Halfwit
48. Tierra-Fuego bridge
49. Spirited meeting?
52. Part 3 of the soliloquy
61. Ref's call
62. Part of many Arab names
63. Favorite
64. International money
65. Part 4 of the soliloquy
72. Prefix with nucleotide
73. French cleric
74. Controversial teachings
75. Promising words
76. Part of a G.I.'s address
79. 50's baseball nickname
81. Samantha's daughter on TV
85. 1976 album "Olé ___"
86. Declinations
87. 1939 Humphrey Bogart role
88. Rattling trains
89. Catch, as flies
90. Type
92. Part 5 of the soliloquy
103. To me, to Mimi
104. Psychoanalyst Fromm
105. Introduction to marketing?
106. Picnic spoiler
107. Part 6 of the soliloquy
114. Popular van Gogh painting
115. She's a deer
116. Kind of tin
117. Brillo rival
118. Entanglement
120. Holds
122. Pickle place
123. Part 7 of the soliloquy
133. Took place
134. Airport feature
135. Nasser's org.
136. Genoan V.I.P., once
137. End of the soliloquy
147. Put on ice
148. Arbitrates
149. Bawl out
150. One of the Munsters
151. It has its ups and downs
152. African menaces

by David J. Kahn and Hillary B. Kahn

DOWN

1. Smarten up
2. Ham's need
3. Dangerous bacteria
4. Lets fly
5. Actor Tognazzi
6. Zinger
7. Elusive one
8. Word with wheel or engine
9. At all
10. Dog-scolding word
11. "What's in ___?"
12. Put aboard
13. Land around the Brahmaputra Valley
14. Station in space
15. Something to stroke
16. King of song
17. "Very funny!"
18. Quick round of tennis
19. Stunt man, e.g.
21. ___ la Plata
22. Obfuscate
25. "The Birth of a Nation" grp.
26. Journalist Nellie
32. One ___ (ball game)
33. "I'm a Stranger Here Myself" poet
34. Put on the throne
35. Insect nests
36. Narrow valley
37. Reach on foot
38. "The ___ Love"
39. Killer whale
40. Classical music features
44. Noted Yugoslav patriot
45. Mixed dish
46. Fill-in
49. 1979 exile
50. Naturalness
51. Churchill contemporary
53. Checkup
54. Second degree?
55. Go ___ for
56. When repeated, an old-fashioned cry
57. Spinner
58. "Here's ___ your eye!"
59. Southwest land
60. Dummies
66. Grated on
67. Fatuous
68. Abate
69. Theological belief
70. Long Island community
71. Reef, maybe
76. Oilman Kashoggi
77. Blurb, e.g.
78. Part of a yoke
80. Flashlight carriers
82. Definitive word
83. Cacao exporter
84. Veep before Ford
91. First name in opera
93. More smooth
94. Artist with collectible lithos
95. Equivocator's forte
96. Some I.B.M. products
97. Tail
98. A year in the life of St. Anselm
99. Barked
100. Muzzles
101. Popular snack cracker
102. Explosives
108. Parched
109. Oberhausen one
110. "___ lay me down . . ."
111. Target of a bang-up job?
112. Actress Taylor
113. Sinn ___
118. Bandage
119. Legit
121. Gulf war weapons
122. Father-and-daughter actors
123. Swagger
124. Depot abbr.
125. Narc activities
126. Person with a mike
127. 1982 Michener epic
128. "Bali ___"
129. Word on a ticket
130. Teams up with
131. Type size
132. Reminders
138. "Nightmare" street
139. Kitty in "The Killers," 1946
140. Hamilton is on it
141. Flower on a French shield
142. Author LeShan
143. Just-hired
144. Rod
145. Common possessive
146. It has a bite and hops

ACROSS

1. "Say You, Say Me" singer, 1985
7. Gets rid of
13. Goalie's area
19. 1804 symphony
20. Chiang Kai-shek's capital
21. Lizard
22. Salesman's sprees?
24. Puts forward
25. In addition
26. Gridiron specialist
27. Prepare mushrooms
29. Full deck, to Caesar?
30. Scottish landowner
32. B.&O. stop
33. Seat option
34. Saltimbocca base
35. Tilde wearers
36. Fall wear?
40. Wallop
41. $C_{14}H_9C_{15}$
42. Best Actress of 1987
43. Minimum
44. Took five
45. Little bit
46. Potato chip brand
47. Roper undertaking
48. Peter Pan's loss
52. "Red Red Wine" and "Gitarzan"?
55. Long haul
59. Flush
60. Aurifies
61. Prime time for Nick
62. Hot issue?
63. Like the Kara Kum
64. Groundwork
65. Boy-meets-girl event
66. Construction piece
67. Called up
68. Send out
69. Something to read
70. Insinuating
71. Take off
72. Akin to barrel-chested?
74. "I'll Take ___" (Bob Hope film)
75. Not walk straight
77. Suffered a sell-off
78. Little white thing
79. Rock group?
82. Be a cast member of
84. Tops
85. Cookbook abbr.
88. Actor Burton
89. Obnoxious Presidential advisers?
91. Take a loss on, so to speak
92. Child's appliance
93. Dungeons & Dragons sort
94. Attorney's deg.
95. Judge Kenneth
97. To be, in Barcelona
98. Kafka hero Gregor
99. Captivate
102. Florentine flower
103. Confuse
105. The Bible?
108. Holiday quenchers
109. One by one?
110. Jazz star
111. Annette, in "Beach Blanket Bingo"
112. Hereditary ruler
113. Like some college programs

by Rich Silvestri

DOWN

1. Made merry
2. Greatest source of 1840's immigration
3. Be composed (of)
4. It's quarry
5. Water cooler
6. Clanton foe
7. Loud speaker
8. Magdalene College student
9. Subject of a Car and Driver rating
10. Takeoff artist
11. Part of w.p.m.
12. Pantywaists
13. Societal division
14. Con
15. Poetic preposition
16. Close
17. Fill to the brim
18. Put fodder away
21. ___ Ste. Marie
23. Without a cent
28. Helper, in brief
31. No, for one
33. "Halt!" to a salt
34. Queue at the bank?
37. Plug in the mouth
38. Veldt sights
39. Spanish royalty
40. Bud
44. Conundrum
46. Bebe Neuwirth TV role
47. Man of Principle
48. Winter wear
49. Every 60 minutes
50. Dior creation
51. L.A. team vehicle?
52. Short stay
53. One way to stand
54. Put the kibosh on
56. Overzealous
57. Duck
58. An original Mouseketeer
60. Anwar's predecessor
64. Cut at an angle
65. Saudi city
69. Kind of acid
70. Candy, in Canterbury
73. Ethyl acetate, e.g.
74. Fourier series function
76. It's always in verse
78. Tower site
79. Made annotations
80. Whodunit motive, perhaps
81. Garden-variety
82. Prepares for a shoot
83. Given the go-ahead
84. Minor malady
85. Dainty restaurant
86. Without exception
87. Flattered
89. Improvises chords
90. Strident sounds
93. Distance between rails
96. Put off
98. Blackthorn fruit
99. Balanced
100. Gulf of Finland feeder
101. Dudley Do-Right's org.
104. Three min. in the ring
106. TV Tarzan
107. Musician's pride

ACROSS

1. Discussed thoroughly, with "out"
7. Florentine family name
13. Flattened at the poles
19. Diffuse
20. Medium-sweet sherry
22. Introduction
23. Song from "Holiday Inn"
25. Meteorological menace
26. Holiday in Hue
27. Skyrocket
28. Bamako is its capital
30. Univ. awards
31. Modest bathing suit
34. Lustrous hue
38. Notre Dame name
39. Feature of some modems
40. 99-Down, Down Under
41. Oft-scripted Baroness Orczy novel
50. Smash letters
52. Limerick language
53. One of the Reiners
54. Gospel music award
55. Moonshine
58. Cautious stock inv.
60. Spring bloomer
63. Op. ___
64. Botanist's workplace
66. 74-Down's opposite
68. Constriction worker?
70. 6-pointers
71. Theme of this puzzle
75. Small shot
76. Landed a haymaker
77. Sked guesses
78. Quits working
80. Name of 13 popes
81. "Iceland" star
83. Cager Kukoc
85. React to a bad joke, perhaps
86. Gore's grp.
88. Infielder Joey ___
90. Warehouse supply: Abbr.
92. Shoe box marking
93. Peaked
100. "Hot Diggity" singer
101. Aurora's counterpart
102. Crack team?: Abbr.
103. Boiled holiday treat
108. Loaf locale
113. Get wind of
114. Mountain lake
115. Slapstick ammo
116. Suffix with duct
117. Theseus' land
120. Counterirritant concoction
125. First Olympic Hall of Fame gymnast
126. Under political attack, maybe
127. Plan
128. Stalk
129. Cartoon cat
130. Oater groups

by Brendan Emmett Quigley

DOWN

1. Popular book genre
2. Wheyfaced
3. Whack
4. In great demand
5. Journal addendum?
6. Cut
7. Code name
8. Medicine Nobelist Metchnikoff
9. Afro and bob
10. "Just Another Girl on the ___" (1993 drama)
11. Cause for pause
12. Soul singer Hayes
13. Stadium cheer
14. ___ Paese cheese
15. Fred Mertz, notably
16. Exiter's exclamation
17. Hint
18. Nephew of Cain
21. Where Dick Button won gold
24. Epitaph starter
29. S.D.I. concern
32. "Phooey!"
33. Fury
34. Bud, to Lou
35. Business biggie
36. Ford Sterling played one
37. Exiter's exclamation
39. Chilean president, 1964–70
41. Delicious
42. Holy war
43. Starwort, e.g.
44. Most difficult to believe
45. Buttinsky
46. Feeling lousy
47. Chopin works
48. Exhibits, basically
49. Answer to "Shall we?"
50. "Put a lid on it!"
51. Kind of float
56. Revolutionary name
57. Pawn
59. Speaker's spot
61. Putting up with
62. Dictionary abbr.
65. "Here comes trouble!"
67. Inc. relative
69. Have ___ (overreact)
72. Open-mouthed quintet
73. "À votre ___!"
74. Chabrier's "Le Roi malgré ___"
75. Palace or prison, e.g.: Abbr.
79. "I told you so!"
82. D.S.M. recipient
84. "Singing journalist" Phil
87. Guards, collectively
89. Yemeni port
91. Slalom maneuver
94. Henri or Pierre, e.g.
95. Roadie's load
96. Shutout
97. Dress (up)
98. Shepherd's locale
99. Stripling
103. Nursery rhyme boy
104. Starbucks serving
105. Stops up
106. Solicits, with "up"
107. Map of the Aleutians, usually
108. Fussbudget
109. House mem.
110. What anglers want that campers don't
111. "Mr. Belvedere" actress Graff
112. School clique, maybe
113. Kind of seal
115. Ready for surgery
118. Whisper sweet nothings
119. Cape ___
121. Chi preceder
122. Humerus locale
123. Year abroad
124. Most letters in D.C.

ACROSS

1. Men in the hood?
5. Head lock
10. "Damn Yankees" vamp
14. School subj.
18. "La Bohème," updated
19. Back-country
20. Dostoyevsky novel, with "The"
22. Digging, so to speak
23. Sgt. Snorkel's dog
24. Labor organizer's cry
25. Full shopping cart?
27. Coffee filter?
30. Small-time
31. "The Benefactor" novelist
32. Whirlpool whereabouts
33. Captain Kirk's log entry
35. Commemorative pillar
38. They, to Thibaudet
40. Mayflower Compact signer
41. Journalist's question
44. Drama in three acts?
47. Be reasonable
51. Wifey's mate
53. Little or Short
54. Is near bankruptcy
56. Poltergeist manifestation
57. Area east of the Bosporus
58. Mountain goat's perch
59. Matriculate
61. "Superman II" villainess
62. Pat Nixon's real first name
64. Like party punch
66. Farm alarms
68. Kind of division
70. Not sharply defined, as a computer image
72. Drag queen's collection
73. Food fish
77. Like some undercover cops
79. Loafer, e.g.
83. Seat of Allen County, Kansas
84. Port on the English Channel
86. Like a Windsor tie
88. The Blue Devils
89. John known as "The Father of Television"
91. Body that includes SHAPE
92. Mystical saying
93. He caught Larsen's perfect game
94. Plumed headgear
95. Apply cosmetics to wild animals?
98. Stirrup site
99. Wharton's farmer
102. Brownie
103. N.B.A. Rookie of the Year, 1993
105. Goofing, with "up"
108. Org. founded by Samuel Gompers
110. Nagana carrier
114. Talmud Torah teacher
115. Bromo salesman?
119. December 25?
121. Go gaga over
122. One in a receiving line?
123. Bogarde of "Darling"
124. Pick up on
125. Comparatively congenial
126. Shore soarer
127. Nordstrom competitor
128. A little night music
129. Brats
130. Kind of organ

by Fran and Lou Sabin

DOWN

1. The second plague, in Exodus
2. From an earlier era
3. Composer Bruckner
4. Strong porters
5. Weary walker
6. They're always made at home
7. The Phantom of the Opera
8. Renders replete
9. Less lively
10. Luce publication
11. Olfactory input
12. "Turandot" slave
13. Of an arterial trunk
14. Plastered at a picnic?
15. Mint bar
16. Cubic meter
17. Divided
21. Car in a Beach Boys tune
26. Like much of Chile
28. Spruce
29. Feeler
34. Jazz pianist Billy
36. Unbelievable one
37. Knock for a loop: Var.
39. Bad-mouth
41. Journalist's question
42. "Not another word!"
43. Tony's cousin
45. 8 ½" × 14"
46. Land alternative
48. Like some consequences
49. Pre-1991 atlas abbr.
50. Subjects of Mendelian experiments
52. Robinson and Thomas?
55. Vulgarian
58. Switch-hit?
59. Out of this world
60. Like some interpretations
63. Bushy hair
65. Ranch hand
67. Baseball's Maglie
69. Mouth widener
71. Clinch
73. They're all in the family
74. Ancient mariner
75. Others, to Ovid
76. Tars
78. Down Under dog
80. Unalloyed
81. Creole vegetable
82. Close in on
85. Student-focused org.
87. One who makes an admission?
90. Bread
92. Brutes
93. Brute
96. Tel Aviv carrier
97. Trades
100. 1936 Olympics hero
101. Car-racing class
104. Libertine
105. Olive brown
106. Bob Cratchit, e.g.
107. Understanding
109. Showed the way, in a way
111. "So ___!"
112. Hanging net
113. Flubbed a fly
114. Fashionable dressers
116. Head set
117. Central points
118. Attend Andover, e.g.
120. Watson-Crick model

by Rich Norris

ACROSS

1. Lemony, say
7. "Time Cycle" composer Lukas ___
11. One of a secretive trio
19. Utica's county
20. "Yeah, sure"
21. School part
22. Eastern European hill?
24. West African fliers?
25. Subjects for special fx artists
26. Alley prowler
27. Afford without a problem
29. Smudge
30. Driver's invitation
33. Most hectic
35. Coeur d'___
36. Oriental Miss Universe?
39. Pretentious
41. "Domani" singer
42. Boxers' beefs
43. Fax cover-page word
44. "Married to the ___" (1988 film)
47. Six-time N.L. home run champ
48. Bumped into
49. Break out
50. Increase in strength, with "up"
51. Suspected
55. Restored photo, perhaps
59. Means
61. Resting place
63. Central European sensors?
65. Southeast Asian go-getter?
67. Eastern European vestments?
68. Hint
69. Five-time Emmy-winning actress
70. Similarity symbol, in math
71. Lure with music
75. On the quiet side?
76. "To what do I ___ . . ."
78. Hip friend
80. Yet, poetically
81. Contribute
82. Turmoil
83. Shade of brown
86. Fastened, in a way
89. Hung. neighbor
90. Mideast exam administrators?
92. Western law enforcement group
95. Gorilla
97. City on the Allegheny
98. London's ___ of Court
99. Glorify
100. Hackneyed
101. Bygone pol. cause
104. Far Eastern nourishment?
108. South central Asian gems?
112. Deviations
113. Promising words
114. Move stealthily
115. Office supply items
116. Succeeding
117. "Potemkin" setting

DOWN

1. Furnace fuel
2. Letter of approval?: Abbr.
3. Souvenir shop items
4. Mo. or Miss.
5. First name in exiles
6. Saloon
7. Shoot
8. Oriental tie
9. Epicurean
10. Increases
11. Spikes
12. Patriots' grp.
13. Nice view
14. School grp.
15. Hard on the feet
16. Papal vestment
17. Squelch
18. Kind of test
21. 1990 Best New Artist Grammy winner
23. Attached houses?: Abbr.
28. Isles
31. Spanish seer?
32. Tecs
33. Sugar source
34. Royal residence of early Ireland
35. It can help if you're short
36. Throw away
37. "I can't ___ thing"
38. Tournament helper
40. The Twelve Tables' contents
43. Hardly hide
44. Bucks
45. ___ probandi
46. Buzzer
48. Noted Charlton Heston role
50. Student, at times
52. Color on the Irish flag
53. Hullabaloo
54. Kewpie doll features
55. Period of time
56. Messed up
57. Out
58. "___ to Pieces" (1965 hit)
60. Style of expression
62. Self-conscious laugh
64. Keep an ___ the ground
65. Stale
66. Islands dish
67. Combine
69. Farm call
72. Witnesses
73. Lecherous look
74. Parts to tie
77. Dating
78. [Sans warning!]
79. Blame
82. Word of lawyerly advice
83. Suffix with motor
84. Rain gear material
85. Campaign
86. Maintains
87. Whiz
88. Penn, e.g.: Abbr.
89. Take on
90. Attendance preventers
91. Go around in circles
92. Galileo, for one
93. Bridge call, for short
94. Condescending type
96. Handheld instruments
100. Bounce
102. Old Oldses
103. Fishing, perhaps
105. Spot for a computer
106. St. Augustine's locale: Abbr.
107. Suffix with fact
109. Swing in a ring
110. Thrice daily, in prescriptions
111. Expose, poetically

ACROSS

1. Slow-witted
4. Gum site
8. Norms: Abbr.
12. O. Henry specialty
17. When to call, in some want ads
19. "The Alienist" author Carr
21. Kind of cut
22. Blazing stars
23. Carom
24. "Like me"
25. "A waking dream," according to Aristotle
26. Supports a scheme
27. Very old I.R.S. employee?
31. They're good for the biceps
32. "___ Mio"
33. Delighted condition?
36. On the lam
37. Some western New York legislation?
41. Hallow ending
42. Class
44. Blueprint item
45. Blockage
46. Orch. section
47. Office mail
50. Big inits. in cellular technology
53. Madison and Monroe
57. Cry of economic liberation?
65. Part of Latin I conjugation
66. Just make, with "out"
68. Steamed
69. Anthology
70. Hobbyist purchases
71. I.R.S. target in Calif.?
74. Colosseum cover-up
75. Guarantee
77. Something to lend
78. Clockmaker Terry
79. Follow
80. Assessment of a comedian?
83. Tom and Diane
85. Subj. for immigrants
86. "The Time Machine" race
88. Actress Scala
89. Company recruits, for short
93. Mammilla
97. Let out
99. Sot sound
102. Stones' request of their accountant?
107. "The House of Blue Leaves" playwright
109. Tommy of "Finian's Rainbow"
110. English dramatist George
111. Bulldog, e.g.
113. April 15 greeting?
117. Language from which "mako" comes
119. Side in a debate
120. Jaleel White role on "Family Matters"
121. Cold coating

by Randolph Ross

122. Quite dissimilar
123. "___ happens . . ."
124. Brouhaha
125. Intimate
126. "Saturday Night Live" announcer
127. Jiffs
128. Fast fleet
129. H.M.O. personnel

DOWN

1. Disaster
2. Fictional friend of Isaac of York
3. One may be honorable
4. Diving duck
5. Slips past
6. De-bused, e.g.
7. Mother of Castor and Pollux
8. Trains
9. Slattern
10. Exhaust
11. Popeye's ___ Pea
12. Place for a male trio
13. Emotionless
14. In general
15. Styron's Turner
16. Proposal response
18. D.C. team, for short
20. ___ chocolates
28. Searches
29. Davis was its Pres.
30. "Friends" co-star
34. ___-Coat (floor wax brand)
35. Not necessarily exact: Abbr.
38. Einstein's birthplace
39. Poetic measures
40. Crowning point
43. Like a tundra
46. Plays matchmaker
48. Funny brothers
49. Rust
51. Bearing
52. Follower: Suffix
53. Nicholson film "The Two ___"
54. ___ acid
55. Disputed island in the East China Sea
56. Music with jazzlike riffs
58. Like some arrangements
59. Embarrassed
60. Just beat
61. One of the Jacksons
62. Desert home
63. Rocker Bob
64. Cafeteria supply
67. Handy abbr.
72. Get ___ for effort
73. Loop runners
76. Manhattan ingredient
81. ___ Loma, Calif.
82. Delete
84. Extemporize
87. Tchaikovsky's Symphony No. 5 ___ minor
89. Bygone sports cars
90. Accepted the bait
91. David Brinkley's autobiography
92. Practiced yellow journalism
94. Sweep
95. Germfree
96. Something awful
98. Let in advance
99. Twice as perilous
100. Lou Gehrig or Cal Ripken
101. They're swung in church
103. Winter 1997–98 newsmaker
104. Writer Josephine
105. Nevada town
106. "___ pray"
108. 180, so to speak
112. Strikes out
114. Lukas of "Witness"
115. Rainbows
116. Jaguar models
117. It works according to scale
118. King intro

ACROSS

1. Outputs from El Chichón
6. Bellyached
12. The Scourge of God
18. Cassandra, e.g.
20. Additions at school?
22. Neptune satellite
23. Conductor Georg got high praise from his peers?
26. Like a solar event
27. Panache
28. Come-ons
29. Hides
30. Go-carts
33. Curtain material
35. Chunk
37. Half of a Vegas duo
38. D.C. figures: Abbr.
39. Wiped out
43. "Blueberry Hill" singer is the only portly person in the family?
50. Analogous (to)
51. "Bravo!"
52. King's title, for short
53. Baseball's Caminiti
54. Burden
55. Bonaparte aide
56. Numerical prefix
58. Change for the better
60. Overthrew
64. O.T. book read at Purim
66. Antiquated
69. Japanese violinist is bored by her Calif. performance?
75. Church assembly
76. Small field
77. Computer language
78. Virile
81. ___ ghost
83. "7 Faces of Dr. ___" (1964 movie)
85. Salon stuff
86. Clay, now
87. Some radios, for short
90. Thin skin
93. Stadium level
94. Rap Queen loves her supporters?
98. Lender's protection
99. Fan sounds
100. Amalgamate
101. ___-Cat
102. Three-time N.F.L. M.V.P. Brett
104. Show biz's Peggy and Mama
107. Twilight, old-style
111. Composed
114. "The Wild Duck" playwright
116. Given to burrowing, maybe
118. Pianist Ruth's audience knows exactly when to clap?
122. Armpit, anatomically
123. One surrounded by raised hands
124. Tampa neighbor
125. Sotheby's visitor
126. William Jennings ___ "Cross of Gold" speech
127. Mosquito type

DOWN

1. Shakes off
2. Hard as ___
3. Singer with a falsetto
4. Playing a part from
5. Is tricked by
6. Venetian boat song
7. Chemical ending
8. Ultimate
9. Reduced in number
10. Board members
11. Big name in paperbacks
12. Take-out counter?
13. Chirrup
14. Most well-kept
15. Pour ___
16. "St. Elmo's Fire" actor
17. Raggedy ___ (dolls)
19. Newt
21. Drivel
24. Component of "fully loaded"
25. Redresser
31. "Beat the Clock" TV host
32. Glanced at
34. Ferry terminus, maybe
36. Salaam
38. Marginal notation
40. Get off on
41. Composed
42. Make (one's way)
43. Fact or factoid
44. Safari sight
45. Kind of review
46. Mail or fax
47. Injury around a horse's hoof
48. News head
49. Hindu incarnation
57. Birds-feather link
59. Best-selling computer game
61. Nibble
62. Stand in the sun, say
63. German one
65. Wriggly creature
67. Develop
68. Traffic caution
70. Freudian concerns
71. Jaguars and such
72. "Live free ___" (New Hampshire motto)
73. Snowfall
74. Lulus
78. Retailer's place
79. Game ending?
80. Give as an example
82. Group of poems
84. Service sites
88. Sportscaster Albert
89. "Funny Girl" co-star
91. Weather stats
92. Maximum limits?
93. English novelist Anthony
95. Where home is
96. Adar's predecessor
97. Food eaten
103. Confuse
104. French equivalent of the Oscar
105. Impatient
106. Prince, e.g.
108. Made smooth, in a way
109. "Go fly ___!"
110. Old Persians
111. Hunk
112. Shout in bad weather?
113. Saharan
115. Kind of appeal
117. Some football linemen: Abbr.
119. Scull
120. "Give ___ rest!"
121. Blokes

by David J. Kahn

ACROSS

1. Rikki-Tikki-___
5. 1990's group Salt-N-___
9. Headpiece?
13. Off
18. February 1991 headline
20. Jordanian tongue
22. Like un ami to une amie
23. ___ Foundation (leading philanthropic organization)
24. Mrs. Yeltsin
25. Join for a ride
26. 60's-70's German chancellor
27. Charleson of "Chariots of Fire"
29. Highway caution
31. Ushered (in)
32. Southern Mexican
36. Kind of plan
37. Suffix with room
38. Much-discussed 1991 film
40. Outlet type
43. Composer Bartók
44. Bar sounds
45. Rein
47. "Theogony" poet
51. Angle, in a way
55. Low tie
56. NASA connector
57. Happening
58. Cruise catcher
59. Settles
60. Hot shots
64. Govt. investigation grp.
65. Former TV host John
66. High riser
67. Milton's "Lycidas," for one
69. "Oh, sure!"
73. Dweller in Shiloh
75. Friendly questioning, in court
77. Religious leader ___ Muhammad
78. Treat
81. Clink
82. What that is, in a 1953 song
83. Skirts
84. Ancient land west of the Rhine
87. Author ___ Le Guin
88. Converted palace
89. Dance move
90. Axes
92. Communism battler, with "the"
93. Not a job for a claustrophobe
97. Inits. on a Soyuz rocket
101. 1964 Streisand song
103. "She-Goat" artist
104. Home of Wheeler Air Force Base
105. Certain hammers
109. Ratio symbols
110. Decreaser?
112. Name after a name
113. Go's mate
115. Buzzers
118. Polo man?
119. Reagan adviser
120. Add up
121. Relevant
122. Fictional pirate
123. Squeezed (out)
124. Epitome of thinness

DOWN

1. Sound quality
2. Ham saver
3. Undeveloped
4. 90–110, normally
5. Finish
6. Afr. nation
7. Little, in Lyon
8. Pope of 772
9. Role for Mia
10. Openings
11. 1994 Peace Nobelist
12. "Spartacus" actress
13. It calls for a blessing
14. What some theaters won't do
15. Visored cap
16. A Walton
17. Flight
19. Like some numbers: Abbr.
21. Terrorist of renown
28. Do something
30. Line carrier
33. Netcom competitor
34. 1797–8 to-do
35. Soft drink brand
39. Greetings
41. Information source
42. Site of Jesus' first miracle
43. Slows (down)
45. It's unpleasant to be in
46. Figurative powerhouse
47. Big name in book publishing
48. Jolliet's 1669 discovery
49. Expires
50. To begin with
52. "Casablanca" actor
53. As a team
54. N.B.A. stats
55. Endorse
57. Rock blaster
61. Kind of raise
62. 1985 Nelligan title role
63. Some jewelry
66. Letter opener
68. Airfone corporation
70. Jewel
71. Nobleman
72. Certain Brooklyn-Manhattan train
74. Treasure-trove
76. "Make ___ good one"
77. They perform a balancing act
78. Bud
79. Acknowledge
80. "___ lost me"
84. Property receivers
85. Draw
86. Escape, in a way
87. Off-balance
89. Speaking block
91. His "E" was the same as J. R.'s
93. Deal (with)
94. Ardent cry
95. Fi lead
96. Message on a dirty car
97. Picnic staple
98. Harrier, for one
99. V.I.P.
100. Puckered
102. Downs spot
105. 1993 Sugar Bowl winner, for short
106. "When I Was ___"
107. Way to get to N.Y.C.
108. Supporter of botany
111. Calls
114. Operation
116. Sturdy one
117. Small music-maker

by Robert H. Wolfe

by Emily Cox and Henry Rathvon

ACROSS

1. Purloin a sirloin?
7. Not for sure
13. Hangers around the house
19. Necessitate
20. ___ de Balzac
21. Something too easily broken
22. Overdo the diet
23. Director Martin Scorsese's anagrammatic claim
25. Where a pupil sits
26. Recess for a joint
28. Emmy-winning Daly
29. Rotten egg
30. Jockey Eddie Arcaro's anagrammatic motto
32. Hors d'oeuvre cheese
33. Cartoon skunk Le Pew
34. Masthead figs.
35. Queen's servants
36. King of comedy
37. Hole-making bug
38. Fine subjects
39. Ulysses S. Grant's anagrammatic advice regarding hangovers
43. Protectors from splats
46. Cried "Yee-haw!"
47. Poetic preposition
48. A point in Mexico
49. Song-and-dance shows
50. Spree
51. Sternward
54. Artist Piet Mondrian's anagrammatic epigram
57. Capitalist?
59. Congress-thwarting move
60. Author ___ Mae Brown
61. Jackknife, e.g.
62. Farm prefix
63. Toothless
65. Kevin Costner's anagrammatic lament about his videos
69. What Leary tripped on
70. Wheel track
71. Sunshine in Québec
72. Babe Ruth, on the Yankees
73. Intent
74. Without rocks
75. Sneaker bottoms
76. Carmen Miranda's anagrammatic ballroom tip
80. What an ostiary guards
81. Oxlike antelope
82. Footless critter
83. Stuff in a muffin
84. Slugger's stat
87. Greet with old-fashioned etiquette
88. Bath's county
89. Len Deighton's anagrammatic avowal on writing
93. Beatles' "___ Loser"
94. MacGraw's namesakes
95. Any spider
96. Glaciated mountain peak
97. Poet Denise Levertov's anagrammatic urging
100. Tasselly hem
102. Blow up
103. Let
104. Melt down, as fat
105. "Sophie's Choice" author
106. Helmet plumes
107. Lots and lots

DOWN

1. Have a hearth
2. Virgin
3. Domestic flights
4. Ankles
5. Ullmann of moviedom
6. Classic work of Euclid
7. Trilled calls
8. Plantain lily
9. Bit of clowning
10. Whence the word "troll"
11. Canadian prairie tribe
12. Aye-aye
13. Many a lecturer
14. Setting for "Don Pasquale"
15. Org. with a much-quoted journal
16. Lobster part
17. Coop flier
18. Rustic sow-and-sows?
21. Like a Nosy Parker
24. Maroon
27. Mudder fodder
31. Shade
32. B. B.'s bag
33. Prepare to be shot
36. Quaker in the woods
37. Carrier in a canal
38. Auteur's order
39. Bara the "vamp"
40. Gad about
41. "It's ___ move"
42. Get a rise out of?
43. Whine pathetically
44. Urban transports
45. Emulated Demosthenes
46. Composed
50. Rock's Bon ___
51. Silky goat
52. Like fast marches
53. Tots' wheels, for short
55. Psychic shock
56. Oven ___
57. School door sign
58. Brit's accented reply
61. Rational faith in God
64. Put to the proof
65. Without letup
66. "Pure ___" (1994 jazz album)
67. Drive out of one's lane
68. Buff, so to speak
71. Grafting bud
73. Teen-y problem
74. Tariff
75. Alternately
76. Mocks
77. Foodstuff
78. How some country stars sing
79. Product of erosion
80. Trio abroad
83. Runs colorfully
84. Name in a Beach Boys title
85. In old show biz, he was no dummy
86. Forward line players, in soccer
88. Set straight
89. Singer Cara
90. Cupid's stock
91. Start
92. Like whose eyes, in a Ben Jonson verse?
94. Of planes and flying
95. Say it's so
98. Alternate: Abbr.
99. Mythical monster
101. Abbr. on a boombox

by Frank Longo

ACROSS

1. Overhaul
7. Inge dog
12. Oysters Rockefeller ingredient
19. Cry of success
21. Gretzky was one
22. Dragon's land, in song
23. Soprano Gluck kidnapped by a fundamentalist group?
25. Raging
26. River to the Ohio
27. Actor Baldwin trapped in a heavenly phenomenon?
29. Telescope-maker ___ Clark
32. Green around the gills
34. "Mickey" singer Basil
35. Flees to a J.P.
36. Supermodel Evangelista stuck in a dead end?
39. Party giver's abbr.
41. Overcurious
42. Poster material
43. VCR adjuncts
45. "___-Kid" (1995 comedy)
48. Sign, slangily
49. Where Jekyll became Hyde
52. Actress Garr discovered at a statue site?
58. Reporter under Perry White
61. Aspen asset
62. A abroad
63. Davy Jones's domain
64. Cowboy, at times
66. Remnant
68. Queequeg's captain
69. Actor Williams found in a 17th-century poem?
75. Near-miss exclamation
76. Casa chamber
77. "Mr. Clemens and Mark Twain" author Justin
78. Spitchcock
79. Like new recruits
82. A&W alternative
84. Like a flu sufferer, often
88. Singer Cochran unearthed in the food pyramid?
91. Gift for a haole
92. Aladdin's monkey
93. Consumer Reports employee
94. Years on end
96. Race with gates
99. "The Statue" actress Virna
102. Claim on an orange juice carton
105. Witticist Bombeck caught in a newspaper feature?
108. Strapped
111. Hebrides island
113. Letters on some 747's
114. Peace
115. Artist Warhol accosted by the British police?
118. Hersey hamlet
120. Bach work
121. Statesman Doria seen in an idealistic vision?
126. Pricey homes
127. Bolshevism founder
128. Bradshaw was one
129. Calorie-crammed course
130. High-fives
131. Clinkers

DOWN

1. Periphery
2. First name in screwball comedy
3. Different sp.
4. Inflexible
5. Dillon of "A Christmas Story"
6. Arizona Indian
7. ___ Canals
8. "Java" trumpeter
9. "The Mill on the Floss" writer
10. Tip sheet buyer
11. Indo-Europeans
12. Part of a brake
13. Puerto Rican port
14. Totally
15. Avis alternative
16. City known in ancient times as Beroea
17. Discontinues
18. Reason for excommunication
20. Sri Lankan language
24. TV angel Munroe
28. "Les Misérables," e.g.
29. Simmering
30. Treeless tract
31. Singer Carr
33. Tennis do-over
37. Blazing
38. Actor Montand
40. Major fish exporter
44. "The Dunwich Horror" star
46. "Ladders to Fire" novelist
47. Philosopher Lao-___
50. Added stipulations
51. Contacts, modern-style
53. Holding a grudge
54. Fine-tune
55. "Hard Road to Glory" author
56. Uncluttered
57. Apply, as ointment
59. CNN anchor Bernard
60. 100 qintars
65. Check the figures
67. Distort
68. Word on monuments
69. 1966 Beatles concert site
70. Alternative to high water
71. ___ Mountains, part of the Tien Shan range
72. Ill-fated German admiral
73. Getting on in years
74. Actress Grey
75. It's catching
79. Retrovirus component
80. Masquerade
81. Display dolor
83. Lay up
85. Film actor Albert
86. Torpedo vessel
87. Short and stout
89. Brief operatic solos
90. Stonehenge worshiper
95. Lepidopterist's accessory
97. Hellespont victim
98. Gunsmith
99. Spoke like Sylvester
100. Lest
101. Mister Ed productions
103. Charles and others
104. Fabergé egg glaze
106. "Never Wave at ___" (Rosalind Russell flick)
107. Drumroll-accompanying exclamations
109. Top-drawer
110. One playing the field
112. Where the action is
116. Democratic donkey designer
117. Plumbing problem
119. Cost of cards
122. Powers that be
123. "Hold On Tight" group
124. ___ Lingus
125. Title choice

ACROSS

1. Backside
5. Chaff
10. Fluff up
15. Alum, for one
19. First name in daredeviltry
20. Fixed the pilot
21. Mix, in a way
22. Mixed bag
23. Part of a girl's magazine dealing with makeup?
25. Attempt to irritate?
27. Kind of sauce: Var.
28. Treasure State capital
30. Straight
31. Sing in a full, happy voice
33. Await judgment
34. Fowl place
35. Tops in quality
38. On the horizon
40. Goldbrick
44. Maker of the game Pong
45. Cinematographer Nykvist
46. Got up
48. 1969 Peace Prize grp.
49. "___ Bell" (Stephen Foster song)
50. Go parasailing
51. Has a bug
52. E.T.S. offering
53. Connecticut Bulldog
54. Sleeves of a sports jacket?
58. Milk, in combinations
59. Dorm companion
61. Former West African capital
62. Infer
63. Epitome of hardness
64. Garfield's middle name
65. Grow past the hour
66. Shampooing aftermath
68. Utter impulsively
69. Kitchen cloths
72. Beautiful Berry
73. Little one bypasses the altar?
75. Script ending
76. Audio effect
77. Appealing
78. Sale caveat
79. Winter Palace resident
80. Afore
81. Kitchen gadgets
83. Slide in sleet
84. Swell top
85. Religious knights
87. Eucharistic plate
89. Help for a mountaineer
90. "Phooey!"
91. Jam session feature
92. Used stickum
94. Put forward
97. Emulate Isamu Noguchi
99. Side by side
103. Grange lacrosse team?
105. Philly champion?
107. Member of the Winnebago nation
108. Like "The X-Files"
109. Stowe character
110. Court defense
111. Bryn ___ College
112. 52-Across and the like
113. Electrical setup
114. Cap'n Hawks of "Show Boat"

DOWN

1. Cause for Chapter 11
2. Eye layer
3. Bugaboo
4. In a flap?
5. Timber problem
6. Force back
7. Pay stretcher
8. Something to heave
9. Increase the slope of
10. Random bits
11. Veldt sight
12. ___ breve
13. Helios, to the Romans
14. Mask features
15. Tone down
16. Succulent plant
17. Penn Station initials
18. "Hold the Line" rock group
24. Ankles
26. Rank
29. Gambling spot
32. Washing
34. Directs a hoedown
35. Phony
36. Author Calvino
37. Country's border?
39. At this point
40. Hurts badly
41. Army dog?
42. Overjoy
43. Chopper part
45. Out of ___ (grouchy)
47. Pool shot
50. Protection against tampering
52. Devonshire dad
54. "Get ready for the camera!"
55. Collector's book
56. Sojourn
57. Small type
58. Backing for plasterwork
60. One of the Thomases
62. Krypton and xenon
64. Tattered Tom's creator
65. Fat or wax
66. Night cover
67. Button material
68. Bunches of bits
69. Plying with pills
70. Understand
71. Mattress brand
73. Sounds of contentment
74. Winnebago, e.g.
77. Vestibule item
79. Sideboard
81. Bow on the screen
82. Married people
83. Cork
84. 1920 Colette novel
86. Go for
88. The lot
89. Tube, over here
91. Theater backdrop
93. Caruso portrayer
94. Bit of physics
95. ___ precedent
96. Cold powder
97. Antitoxins
98. Prefix with com
100. Before long
101. Fax
102. Yarborough component, perhaps
104. O.A.S. member: Abbr.
106. Nada

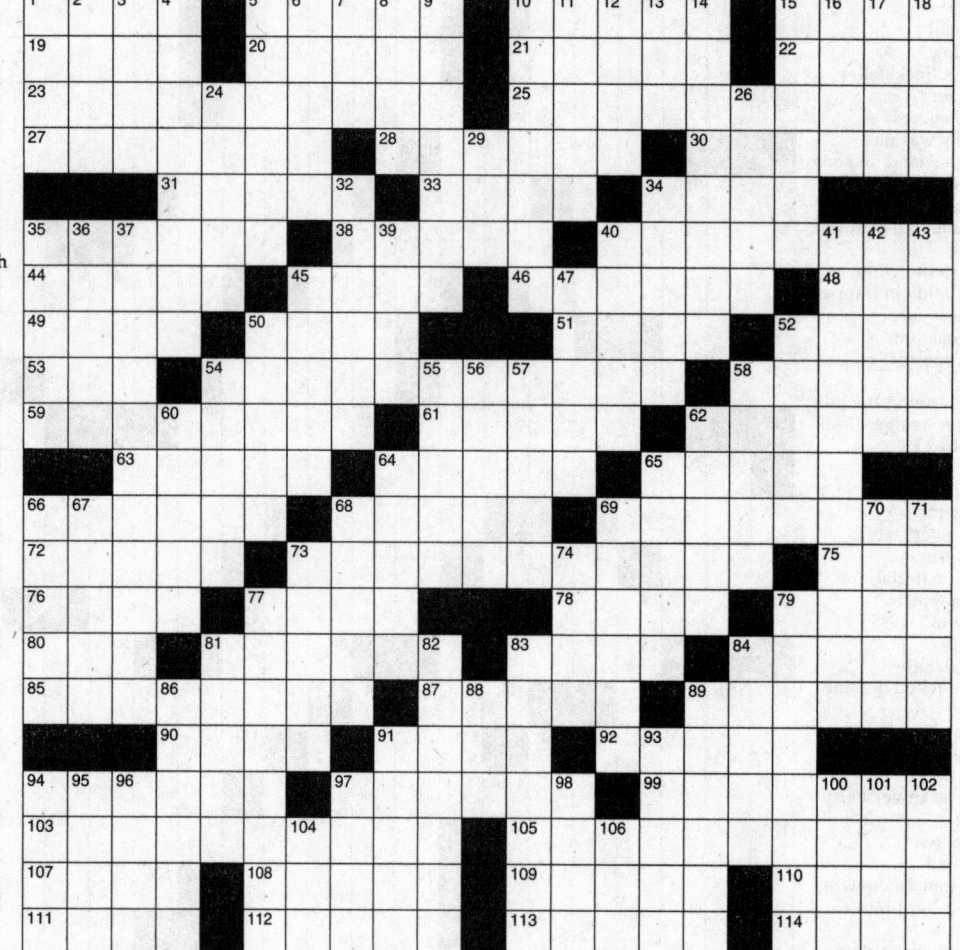

by Richard Silvestri

ACROSS

1. Displaces
6. Atomic
12. Lowly ones
17. Portuguese city
19. Batting a thousand
21. Mercury : Sable :: Ford : ___
23. Poet's outlook on life?
25. Fighting force
26. Good earth
27. Grab
28. Poet's favorite 1972 hit?
30. Objective
32. Many people sit around it
34. With 68-Down, "Fame" actress
35. Shakespearean couplet description?
41. Did derbies
42. Derbies
43. Roar of the crowd
44. Ebon
47. What one gets reading poetry?
52. Pen
55. Iranian city
56. General assemblies
57. Meal starter
59. Don't waste
60. Sans nuts, e.g.
62. "Taras Bulba" author
65. Tamper-resistant
66. Result of poetic license?
70. Crows
71. Stand for Steen
72. "Eleni" director Peter
73. Too hot for tots
74. "Brain Trust" Prez
75. Bats
77. Hi-fi buys
80. Substance in soaps
82. What a disaffected Japanese poet might become?
87. Outdated poet suffix
88. Tel. listing abbr.
90. Kyrgyzstan's ___ Mountains
91. Certain vertebrae
92. Opinion of Keats poetry?
98. Some "Aïda" singers
101. Labor activist Chavez
102. Forum wear
103. Talk about Tennyson poems?
105. Hose hue
107. "Hard Lines" poet
111. Correction section
112. Conclusion of many a poet?
116. Emmy-winning Rob
117. Arabs, Hebrews, etc.
118. Hitches
119. She's married . . . with niños
120. Contend, colloquially
121. Designer Simpson

by Cathy Millhauser

DOWN

1. More than simmer
2. Machinating
3. Provincial capital in the Dominican Republic
4. Vow taker
5. Jeff's "77 Sunset Strip" partner
6. Kinetic art form
7. "The Gondoliers" nurse
8. Pew locale
9. Suffix akin to -ity
10. Crag
11. Fictional Dinsmore and Venner
12. Lance
13. Pesky insect
14. Unconfirmed reports
15. Body build
16. Khartoum's country
18. Merlin of football and TV
20. Roof type
22. All there
24. Old-timer, of sorts
29. Xylophone striker
31. Senator of 1967 censure
32. High: Prefix
33. Flatten, in Britain
35. Babylon's land
36. Perfume billed as "The forbidden fragrance"
37. Swindle
38. Next
39. Wild things
40. Poetic contraction
44. 10,000,000 ergs
45. Krupp works site
46. Ticked (off)
48. Reaches over
49. Friend of Coleridge
50. Hankered
51. It's got ewe covered
53. Crinkly cloth
54. Springs
58. "___ can eat!"
60. Sacred poem
61. It's played with matches
63. Need to reimburse
64. "The Fisher King" director
65. Bacchus attendant
66. Filmdom's Robert and Alan
67. People
68. See 34-Across
69. Horse height measure
70. Open wide
74. Chevy Chase title role
76. Sooner migrant
77. Bats
78. Manx "Thanks!"
79. Abide
81. Cabbage collector, for short
83. "Ford ___ better idea" (old slogan)
84. Winged
85. "Odyssey" peak
86. Protected, in a way
89. Tailor's tool
92. St. John, e.g.
93. Joust contestant
94. Job preceder
95. Pointless
96. Venetian official, once
97. Give off
98. Stand at wakes
99. Relevant, to lawyers
100. Neighbor of Turkey
104. Give a hoot
105. Derby doings
106. Noble, in Nuremberg
108. Church projection
109. King of a Handel oratorio
110. Promotional overkill
113. Peruvian Sumac
114. Lead head?
115. Actress Long

INDIAN CORN

ACROSS

1. Instrument superseded by the viol
8. W.W. I Allied plane
10. Switch's partner
14. Unappetizing fare
18. Dangerous strain
19. "I understand!"
20. Put ___ question
21. Bagpipe part
22. Primitive Indian?
24. Former White House nickname
25. Rebelled
26. Not happy with
27. Words before "about"
29. Indian comic strip character?
31. Take a powder
33. Country name
35. "Carousel" choreographer
36. Where the Knicks play: Abbr.
39. PC menu selection
40. Simmons rival
42. Ending with iron or tin
43. Stopover for young Indians?
46. Hydroplane part
48. Brewery fixture
51. Anderson of sitcoms
52. C in a C scale, e.g.
54. What the Indian said after taking out a car loan?
57. Some computer program sequences
59. Bound collection
61. "The Capeman" composer
62. Kind of bank
63. Tot's cry
64. It bollixes up the machinery
66. Neighed
68. Indian's interpretation of Robert Browning?
73. In condensed format
76. "Well done!" in Italy
77. Vintner's prefix
80. One of L.B.J.'s beagles
81. Make a new connection with
83. Rest stop lineup
86. Jordan dropped it in 1949
88. Sound effects in an Indian haunted house?
91. Metronome settings
93. Dietary, in ads
94. It's sometimes "junk"
95. ___ one's heels
97. Indian weatherman's forecast?
99. Echo
102. Advantage
104. Current: Prefix
105. Trainer's workplace, perhaps
106. Paint remover component
109. Give off intense light

110. "___ Thief" (1950 movie)
112. Indian's "Well, sorr-r-ry!"?
114. Detriment
116. Citroën model name
120. He caught his adversary's ear
121. Often underreported income
123. What the Indian said after his son's road test?
125. Does a warm-up (for)
126. "Biscuit" introduced in 1912
127. Jazz singer Jones
128. "The Family Circus" cartoonist
129. "Tom Thumb" star Tamblyn
130. Downright blue
131. It may be common
132. Bridge seats

DOWN

1. RCA products: Abbr.
2. River through Aragón
3. Yahoo

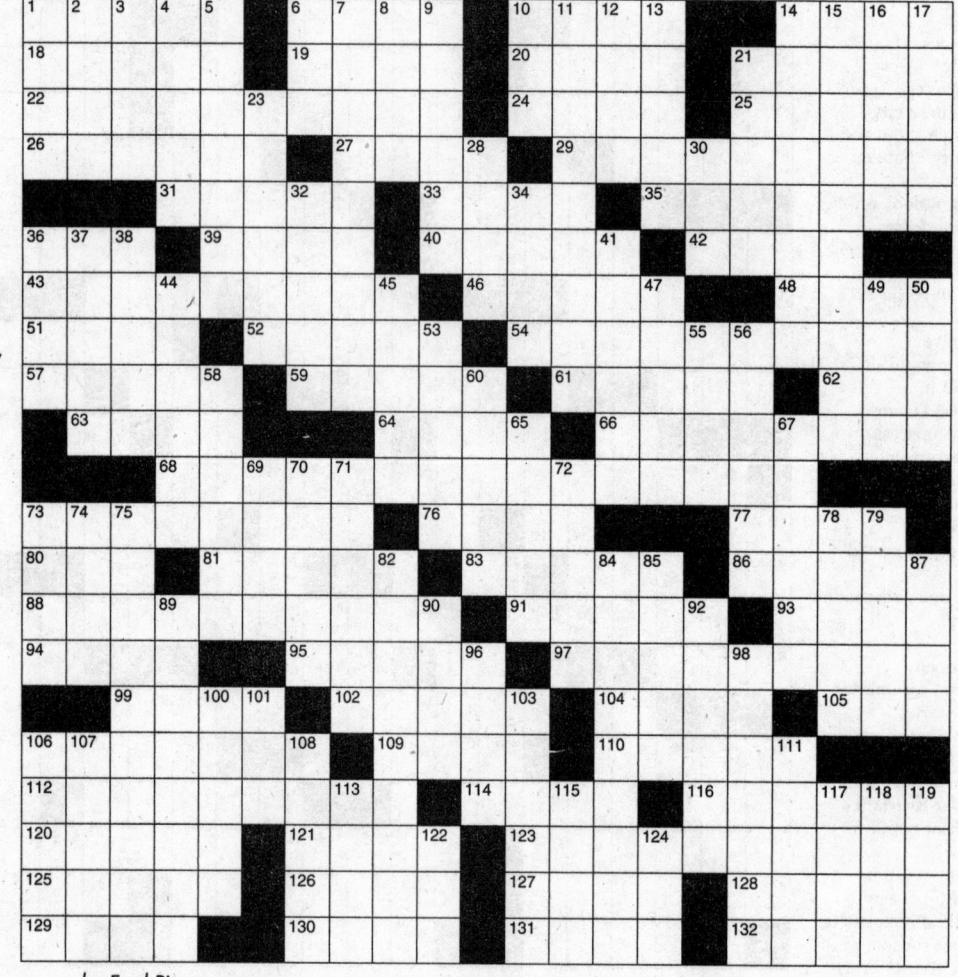

by Fred Piscop

4. Cary of "The Princess Bride"
5. Former W.B.C. lightweight champion
6. Flag
7. Mekong River capital
8. "...and shall bring forth ___": Matt.
9. Drive participants
10. Action at Christie's
11. Lorelei Lee's creator
12. Restlessness
13. Puffed, as a reefer
14. Bronco's locale
15. Store come-on
16. Hoopster/actor
17. p., as in Plymouth
21. College major
23. Like a body in Newton's first law
28. Lagoon perimeter
30. Patch up
32. Some choristers
34. "Road" film destination
36. Weigh, with "over"
37. Urban playing site
38. Salami choice
41. Turning about the vertical

44. "Fantasia" dancers
45. Loyal subject
47. Language of India
49. Roy Rogers, né Leonard ___
50. Initiated, with "off"
53. West Indies native
55. Florida city, informally
56. Disentangle
58. Husband of Ops, in myth
60. They often accompany ejections
65. Precept
67. Channel swimmer Gertrude
69. It's found in sticks
70. Kind of kitchen
71. South American stamp word
72. Temple of Zeus site
73. One who takes orders
74. Sleek, in car lingo
75. Some wimple wearers
78. Babes in the woods
79. Bunk position
82. Black and white cartoon character
84. Like a jam

85. He notched 363 victories
87. Big name in games
89. Bibliophilic data
90. Long story
92. Martian feature
96. "Oh, go on!"
98. Cornmeal slab
100. High times?
101. Hartebeest kin
103. Female fowl
106. New York "Place" name
107. South American rodent
108. Hail
111. Lost
113. Goo
115. ___-tiller
117. "Stupid ___ stupid does"
118. Garment slit
119. Cool drinks
122. "Old" country
124. Author Fleming

ACROSS

1. Heart monitor sound
4. Small lizards, old-style
8. "Be that as ___ . . ."
13. Befuddled
18. Genesis brother
20. Grandson of Methuselah
21. Horde
22. Does some exercises
23. Retaliatory tactics
26. PC fixers
27. One of a comical pair
28. Undercover types
29. Ground
31. Rap sheet letters
32. Engineer
34. Lunch order
35. Put away
37. Hot times abroad
38. Words of support
39. Clinton and Bush, e.g.
40. Jerk
42. D.C. toiler
43. ___-Foy, city near Quebec
44. Strains in the winter?
45. Having more leeway
46. Iran or Iraq vis-à-vis OPEC
52. Store stock: Abbr.
53. Myopic Mr.
56. Mail-order specification
57. Minneapolis suburb
59. Hue and cry
61. Columbian vessel
64. Certain pass
67. Took for oneself
69. Old airline name
71. Ball participant
73. Attached, in a way
75. Gulf of Aden country
77. It has a lot to offer
78. Cape town
79. Subject of Form 1040, line 15a
81. Quake
82. Novel ending
85. Shoot-'em-up
90. Draw up, as cloth
92. Reveals, poetically
93. First mistake
94. W.W. II agcy.
97. "On the Rebound" pianist Floyd
99. Ward of "My Fellow Americans"
100. Lug
102. Cut, old-style
103. Single-celled organism
104. Kind of phenomena
105. It's read regularly
107. "As Time Goes By" singer in "Casablanca"
108. Cartoonist Wilson
110. Elvis's middle name
111. City SSE of Gainesville
112. Pang
114. Inventor's goal
117. Outré
118. Ohio natives
119. Annina in "Der Rosenkavalier"
120. Ratio of AB to BC, say
121. All in ___ work
122. Aquarium denizen
123. Boardroom bigwigs
124. Some E.R. cases

DOWN

1. Flatters
2. Cut off
3. "If elected I will not serve" candidate of 1968
4. Copenhagen-to-Riga dir.
5. Popular retirement destination
6. Glazed fabric
7. Polishes
8. Roadblock requests
9. More than loyal
10. Aesop's foible?
11. Heads off
12. Recently: Abbr.
13. Decree
14. Movie projection?
15. Revulsed
16. Elevates
17. Blockhead
19. Parts of a curriculum
24. Hole opener
25. Anticipatory question
30. Chop
33. Pro ___
36. Pound sound
39. Common street name
41. Dominion ended by Francis II: Abbr.
43. Shutterbug
44. Delirium
46. Storage of a kind
47. Hint
48. Basso Pinza
49. ___ canto
50. Ijsselmeer Dam site
51. Actress Tushingham and others
53. Year in the papacy of Innocent III
54. Like a bump on ___
55. Plymouth poky
58. Calls home, as a tree
60. Made a new hole
62. Menlo Park monogram
63. Hosts
65. A6 manufacturer
66. "Fantasy Island" props
68. Destructive 1964 Florida hurricane
70. "The Silent Clowns" author
72. Type of 46-Down
74. ___ grata
76. "Coming Home" subject, briefly
80. Slowed musical passage
82. "Go back!" on a PC
83. Clobbered
84. Rum-based liqueur
86. Argues vehemently
87. Cause for a magnifying glass
88. Social
89. Contender
91. Graycoat
94. Where Algonquin Park is
95. Approach the end of an ocean trip
96. Brightly colored attire
98. Piano piece
99. Field
100. Takeoff locale
101. "Becket" actor, 1964
102. Factions
105. "This means ___!"
106. "The Simpsons" tavern owner
109. Assist illegally
112. American competitor
113. Marinaro and McMahon
115. That, in Toledo
116. Kind of pad

by Rich Norris

ACROSS

1. Some calisthenics
7. Hardly stars
14. Promote
20. Avid
21. Japanese art of flower arranging
22. Take away
23. Gave in church
24. Indexed early man?
26. Ancient porch
27. "___ of troubles": Hamlet
29. Secret devices
30. It may lead to a strike
31. Twisted person
33. Some campers
34. Wall Street worker
36. Reply to "Is it Mr. or Professor Chomsky?"
40. Together
41. Hill climber
42. Like fabric by the yard
43. How some people seem to know
45. Old despot
48. Hugs
50. Staten Island Ferry litter?
55. Enterprise log signature
56. Toast for the holidays
58. Long time
59. Its cap. is Charleston
60. Showed, with "out"
63. Kind of test
64. They battle the Indians
66. Reply to "How many Senators are there, child?"
70. Big name in computers
73. Friction easer
74. Wire
77. One of the Whitneys
78. From ___ Z
79. Oxford university since 1844
82. Part
84. Molly Pitcher, for example?
87. Sang
89. Indochine locale
90. East, in Essen
91. Electronic snoop
94. Words with word or way
95. Low voice
98. What the overheated passengers called the airline?
100. Nightclub charge
103. Line up well
105. Static
106. Brews
107. Site for Seurats
109. Chairs for prayers?
110. Answer, in brief
114. Question about a flashlight that lacks batteries?
117. Precisely
119. Sharp as a tack
120. "I like that!"
121. Family split?
122. Like the other evil
123. Some kids' bedtime reading
124. Nike rival

DOWN

1. NCO club members
2. Vacate
3. "For ___ us a child . . ."
4. Shocked
5. Common article
6. Some recyclables
7. "Great shot!"
8. Tex. neighbor
9. School org.
10. F.B.I. sting of the late 70's
11. Wall builder
12. Author Bagnold and others
13. Sometimes cracked container
14. City whose name is Spanish for "ash tree"
15. Library ref.
16. Least of all
17. TV debut of 1/14/52
18. "Luann" cartoonist Greg ___
19. Held another session
25. Portfolio contents, for short
28. "The ___ the limit!"
32. Goes to bat
33. Some pointers
35. Wave catchers
36. Moolah
37. In the dark
38. "Wheel of Fortune" songstress, 1952
39. Has
40. Abbr. in car ads
43. Sizing up
44. Like some deities
46. ". . . ___ forgive our debtors"
47. Go crazy
49. "Bottoms up!"
51. Walked awkwardly
52. Bloomsbury group member
53. "The Grapes of Wrath" family
54. More, in Monterrey
56. Continued
57. Sum (up)
61. 80's TV adventure
62. Full chorus, in music
65. The first one opened in Detroit in 1962
67. Occupies quarters
68. Israeli city on the Gulf of Aqaba
69. Some radios
70. Bunny boss, briefly
71. Director Kazan
72. Pate toppers
75. Was admitted to
76. "Maria ___" (1933 song)
80. 1984 skiing gold medalist
81. "If ___ be so bold . . ."
83. Cracker cheese
85. China rose, e.g.
86. Infantile remark
87. Make an impression
88. Dadaist collection
92. Modern mall features
93. Feel in one's bones
96. Fort ___ (where Billy the Kid was gunned down)
97. Dirty stuff
98. Mishandle
99. Bubble
100. Taj ___
101. Admission of defeat
102. Tiny amphibians
103. "___ coffee?"
104. Babe and Baby
108. Like workhorses
109. Jokes (around)
111. Pin, in a way
112. Clinton denial
113. Look-see
115. Got into a jam?
116. Seine contents
118. Full of: Suffix

by Manny Nosowsky

ACROSS

1. Rum-soaked cake
5. Tall, slender hound
11. Practical joke
15. Bleached
19. 12th-century poet
20. Neckwear accessory
21. Uzbek sea
22. Fashion house ___-Picone
23. "At 9 A.M. breakfast will be supplied by ___"
25. Prohibit
27. Mastic, for one
28. "At 11 A.M. ___ will speak"
30. Comics sound
31. Unusually smart
34. First name in TV talk
35. Like R. L. Stine stories
36. "At 1 P.M. ___ will sing . . ."
39. Govt. property org.
40. River near Chantilly
41. O'Donnell and Perez
42. ". . . a tune from one of their ___"
48. Modern office staples
49. Jackson and Leigh
50. Handle a joystick
51. In post-career mode: Abbr.
52. Dance invitation response
53. Axis Powers, once
54. Jamaican sect member
56. "At 3 P.M. President Clinton will ___ . . ."
61. First name among sopranos
62. The less-used end
63. Nonexistent
64. Key of Mendelssohn's Symphony No. 3
66. Kind of alcohol
67. ". . . on the subject of ___"
74. Initiated, legally
76. Europe/Asia dividers
77. Actress Suzanne
78. Ambient music pioneer
79. Mount Vernon, e.g.
81. Wristbone-related
82. Abbr. on a Mayberry envelope
85. "At 5 P.M. the Philatelic Society will discuss some ___"
87. Knot-tying place
88. Actress Ward
89. Hosts
90. "And at 7 P.M. there'll be a showing of the 60's film ___ . . ."
92. Snail trail
95. Slick, so to speak
98. Some pops: Abbr.
99. Wage news
100. ". . . starring ___ . . ."
103. Goes limp
104. Call to action
105. ". . . unless ___"
110. Grouper grabbers

by Merl Reagle

111. Numerous
112. Dario Fo forte
113. Infamous Roman
114. Cobbler's need
115. Places for coats
116. Lively intelligence
117. Jersey Standard's other name

DOWN

1. Conk
2. Without form
3. Without foundation
4. Gallery event
5. British gun
6. It can be fresh or hot
7. Singer Peggy
8. Put ___ fight
9. Brick baker
10. Dr. Scholl products
11. I love: Fr.
12. Ball partner
13. City on the Ganges
14. Basic: Abbr.
15. Human-powered taxi
16. Province of Spain
17. Tongue-lasher?
18. Access
24. Ticket
26. Slangy tag-team member
29. TV dog
30. Boarding place
31. Sorry individual
32. Barcelona buck
33. Colorful spiral seashell
37. Mary of Peter, Paul and Mary
38. My, to Mimi
39. Lead pumper
42. [see other side]
43. Collins juice
44. Quite a while
45. Bearish
46. Underground systems
47. Fire escape route
49. Jupiter
50. "___, the heavens were opened": Matt. 3:16
52. Glove fabric
53. Film changes
55. Sheriff Lobo portrayer
56. Wound with sound
57. He's a weasel
58. Flatten
59. Talus area
60. Loss-prevention device
65. Blackbird
68. 1984 Peace Nobelist
69. "Dies ___"
70. Familiars, often
71. Writer Singer and inventor Singer
72. Apathy
73. Drives forward
75. Prepare to land
80. Subj. of 60's protest
81. He helped topple Batista
82. Slaps a new head on
83. Dentists' kids, probably
84. Have the guts
86. Prodigious
87. Shift
88. Like some triangles
90. Dam agcy.
91. Hockey's Lindros
92. Hollywood dive?
93. Ostracized one
94. Ready to spit
95. Caterpillar hairs
96. Via
97. Case workers: Abbr.
101. Summer getaway, perhaps
102. School orgs.
103. Big letters in public broadcasting
106. Race car sponsor
107. Columbus, for one: Abbr.
108. Christina's dad
109. Prelude to a hickey

ACROSS

1. Where the 1986 World Series was won
5. Lot
9. Automotive pioneer
13. Prepare to go home, in a way
19. Onetime America's Cup champ
21. Kind of service
22. List ender
23. Coffee addict's meal?
25. Special correspondent
26. "Soap" spinoff
27. Humpty Dumpty short?
29. Like ghost stories
33. Saying nothing
35. Nets
36. Awakened
37. Computer program input
41. Ticket place: Abbr.
42. Sch. subject
45. Plowing woe
46. Hydrocarbon derived from petroleum
47. 1962 NASA success
49. An otherwise well-behaved liar?
53. One-on-one sport
55. Chanel fragrance
56. "___ precaution . . ."
57. "Voices Carry" vocalist Mann
58. 90's actor Epps
59. Luke's "90210" role
60. Panay seaport with a repetitive name
62. Landscaper's tool
64. Cupronickel, e.g.
65. Method for mixing cards, Illinois-style?
70. Divided into sections
72. Highflier's home?
73. Oceanus and brothers
75. Some construction beams
76. Part of a wagon train
77. Profit
79. Jump causer
81. Old "Tonight Show" theme writer
82. Grade
83. Tot's plaything?
86. Fumes
88. Gathering places
90. Sale item label
91. Wife, with "the"
92. Crew need
93. No-goodnik
95. Nobel or Celsius, e.g.
96. ___ Ababa
98. Had
99. Sells
101. What to serve stew in?
105. Hard
108. Natural gas component
109. Ice cream as still life?
115. Passes
116. Perfectly healthy, to the Army
117. Person who cracks a whip
118. Can't stand
119. Kind of home or room
120. Russian river
121. Tax

DOWN

1. Gal of song
2. 1970's Chinese premier
3. Erhard's discipline
4. Part of a toll-free long-distance number
5. Less exposed
6. Identical
7. Haughtiness
8. Woodworking groove
9. Control
10. Blockers, e.g.
11. Vestige
12. Twilled fabric
13. Verbal dueling
14. God, with "the"
15. Cords
16. Purina alternative
17. "Later!"
18. Brickmaker's furnace
20. Jewish teacher
24. Sentence completer
28. Swiveling part
29. Family head
30. Some Bach compositions
31. Ranch infestation?
32. Underway to over there
34. Consumer
38. French clergyman
39. Bassoon, basically
40. Was overrun
42. Yeast, fruit and nuts?
43. Tree with pods
44. "The Gift of the Magi" feature
48. Monster in the Strait of Messina
50. Scottish landowners
51. Thread: Prefix
52. "___ cloud nine!"
54. One of Henry VIII's six
58. Flirt with, maybe
59. Less sane
61. "Wozzeck" and "Jenufa"
62. St. Patrick's home
63. ___ gratia
66. Land on the Rubicon
67. Guys
68. Smallpox symptom
69. Let go
70. Suffix with endo- or proto-
71. Li'l one
74. Gold coins of ancient Rome
76. Central vein of a leaf
77. One of a ballroom couple
78. Sport ___ (trucklike vehicles)
80. O. Henry Award-winning author Tillie ___
82. Whiplash preventer
83. Flawlessly
84. English poet Dowson
85. Cuss (out)
87. Marmots and such
89. Savers by profession
94. Had too much of
95. "What ___ thou?"
96. Swiftly
97. Deep, unnatural sleep
100. Jean Renoir film heroine
101. Basis
102. ___ Reader (eclectic magazine)
103. Great, in slang
104. Dwindle
106. Rossini subject
107. Singer Adams
110. Basketball Hall-of-Famer Holman
111. Down
112. Somewhat exotic meat
113. Abbr. after a general's name, maybe
114. Aim

by Dave Tuller

ACROSS

1. Theater worker
8. Hank Aaron or Jesse Owens, e.g.
16. "Wild Thing" group, with "the"
22. Day in Hollywood
23. Breakdown
24. Capital of Zimbabwe
25. Part 1 of a prophecy by Martin Luther King Jr.
28. Marshal Dillon portrayer
29. Cone-shaped heaters
30. Grocery area
31. More than suggestive
32. Track pick, informally
33. Sharp
34. Jalopy
36. Fr. holy woman
37. Prophecy, part 2
48. Holmes girl
49. Soup holder
50. What Moses did
51. Prophecy, part 3
58. Bob Hope's "___ Russia $1,200"
59. 1/6 fl. oz.
60. Extinct New Zealanders
61. Brown of renown
62. Sludge
64. Swindle
67. Seesaw quorum
69. Prepare to surf, perhaps
71. Category
72. Joint protection
73. Unpopular slice
75. Wreck
77. "___ here" (store sign)
78. Time to act
79. Prophecy, part 4
83. Big name in games
85. Mer makeup
87. Riveter of song
89. Some wait for this
90. Cooperative interaction
93. Hundred smackers
95. Halfhearted
98. Charisse of "Silk Stockings"
100. Laszlo player in "Casablanca"
101. Kin's partner
102. Child's play
103. Grape brandy
105. Kind of trip
107. Pretense
108. Prophecy, part 5
114. Salad topper
115. Where suits are pressed
116. Laundry woe
117. Prophecy, part 6
126. Split
127. Memorable 1995 hurricane
128. Buffoon
129. Half and half
130. Famous redhead
132. Make sense
135. Poker challenge
138. Shade
141. End of the prophecy
145. Whip
146. Bête noire
147. Correction, of sorts
148. "Grand" hotels

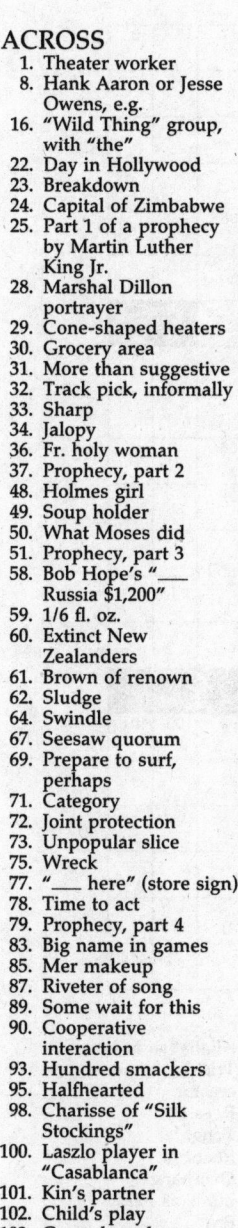

by Ed Early and Bob Klahn

149. Well-worn
150. Biased

DOWN

1. Yielding
2. Enthusiastic
3. Moon shade
4. Make way?
5. Architect ___ van der Rohe
6. Literary olios
7. "___ Kelly" (Jagger film)
8. Vinegar radical
9. Item of interest
10. Mrs. Alfred Hitchcock
11. Short orders
12. "Wonderful!"
13. Film rating org.
14. Spot of wine?
15. Missouri town near the George Washington Carver National Monument
16. "Lyin' Eyes" singers
17. "Awesome!"
18. Like some votes
19. Most festive
20. Wall Street analysts' concern
21. Letter getter
26. Cameo carvings
27. Red or Card, for short
33. Geared down, perhaps
35. Crusty ones
38. Had a heart but used a club?
39. Some trains
40. Brit. award
41. 8 ½" × 11" size: Abbr.
42. It's often served at home
43. Two-toned treat
44. Savage
45. Plaster of paris
46. Fotomat abbr.
47. "Love thy neighbor" is one
51. Speedily
52. Admitted
53. Make up one's mind
54. Detached
55. Hole in the wall?
56. Unrivaled
57. The first Mrs. Copperfield
58. "E-w-w-w!"
63. Code breaker
65. Here and there?
66. 11-Down extra
68. Very early
70. Old car with a 389 engine
71. Senator who made the rounds
74. "i" lid
76. "For ___ sow..."
79. Model Cheryl
80. Cool, once
81. Violinist Paganini
82. Operative
84. Tennyson's "___ and Enid"
85. Theologian who opposed Martin Luther
86. "Oh, right!"
88. Wishing spot
90. Excluding
91. Tomorrow's woman
92. Giant gains: Abbr.
94. Mary Tyler Moore catch phrase on "The Dick Van Dyke Show"
96. Elaborate Japanese porcelain
97. Lifeboat support
99. Snuggery
102. Clairvoyants
104. Soothsay
106. Unified whole
109. Venus's home
110. Shavetails: Abbr.
111. Berlin-to-Cologne dir.
112. Problem of the middle ages?
113. "___ geht's?"
117. Something to catch or save
118. Unrefined
119. "Peer Gynt" dancer
120. Fake fanfare
121. Dracula's mother-in-law?
122. Mutually fee-free
123. O.B.E., for one
124. Performance extension
125. Thatched
131. Powwow
133. Wrist attachment
134. Swamp thing
135. "___ hollers..."
136. Rubber Duck, for one
137. Baïonnette, e.g.
138. Prowling Wolfe
139. River to the Caspian
140. "Now I see!"
142. It goes to extremes
143. Polo Grounds legend
144. "___ Ramsey" (70's western)

ACROSS

1. Signals at sea
8. "War and Peace" heroine
15. Indian dwelling
20. Like Miss Congeniality
21. Christie and others
22. Madonna role
23. Tar?
25. Connoisseur
26. Reception site, maybe
27. Catty comments
28. Even
29. Red ___
30. Tolkien creatures
31. Sprint competitor
32. Crazy, in Cannes
33. Distance between pillars
36. Yorkshire river
37. 60's org.
38. Heyum?
41. Some are "great"
42. Common setting for a joke
43. Mme., in Madrid
44. Check out
46. Not separately
50. Last choice on some lists
53. Come-___
56. Destined
57. Commitment
59. Encouraging words
61. Sleuth Lupin
62. Kind of mail
63. Minnie?
66. Phone trio
67. A.A.A. recommendations
68. Eliot's Grizabella, e.g.
69. Popular White House souvenir
70. It precedes "com"
71. Part of a comparison
72. "Exodus" role
73. Furner?
76. They move in a charged atmosphere
77. Request of an equestrian
79. Corn ___
80. Multipurpose truck, for short
81. "Home Alone" actor
82. Meg, among the "little women"
83. Stranger
85. Teach, with "up"
87. Strong
90. Prog. Cons. rival, in Canada
92. Med. drama sites
93. Guns
95. Purty?
99. L-1011 alternative
102. Athos, to Porthos
103. Salon offering
104. Cable inits.
105. Less than diddly
106. Bank posting
107. Broadcasting feed
109. "Aladdin" prince and namesakes
111. Whip
112. Two-dimensional extent
113. Mexican waters
114. Hail?
117. Critical
118. Becomes understood
119. "Your Show of Shows" name
120. Person with a net, perhaps
121. Begins to like
122. Waterloos

by Nancy Joline and Peg Conner

DOWN

1. Dissipates
2. Threaten
3. Fairy tale characters
4. All's partner
5. 16th President, familiarly
6. Inklings
7. ___ Lake, N.Y.
8. Nopes
9. ___-old
10. It's only skin-deep
11. Museum room, maybe
12. "Leaving Las Vegas" actress
13. Participatory
14. "Don't ___!"
15. Hercules
16. Elliptical
17. Dah?
18. Pied-___
19. Port on the Loire
24. Dweebs
32. Kind of house
34. Movie ratings
35. It paves the way
38. Spar
39. Show disapproval
40. Caterer's need
41. "Hamlet" has five
42. Deposits
45. Drogheda's locale
46. Welcoming or parting gesture
47. Like some corners
48. Mayun?
49. Poland Spring competitor
51. Hit a four-bagger
52. Nicholas Gage book
54. Intensify
55. Restrains
58. Available
60. Mubarak's predecessor
64. Turn topsy-turvy
65. Dog treats
68. Procession
71. La Scala features
73. It may be feathered
74. Was bossy?
75. Antique shop item
78. Perfect ones
81. Actor's goal
84. London greeting
86. Occasion calling for grace
88. Easter starter
89. Onetime U.N. effort site
91. Cause for hitting the forehead
93. Sack
94. Baryshnikov, e.g.
96. Actor Alan of "Hope & Gloria"
97. Haunt
98. Like some cousins
99. Allahabad attire
100. Tristram Shandy's creator
101. Rags
103. Toughie
106. Roam
108. Overhang
110. Limp, as hair
111. Pro ___
114. Attention-getter
115. It may be thrown
116. Napoléon, for one

ACROSS

1. River name meaning "where the goods are brought in"
8. "Shane" man
12. He's well-sooted for the job
19. Womb-related
20. Mine, in Amiens
21. Most volatile emotionally
22. "Hey, babe, wanna sit with me on the plane?"
24. Transport to ecstasy
25. Game for two of four
26. "While we're in the air, write an essay on aviation"
28. "Don't waste your breath!"
31. Still
32. Some M.I.T. grads
33. Spree
36. Nods, perhaps
37. "I'm an unattractive woman who'll gab the whole trip"
43. Revolt
45. Burden
48. Deanna of "Star Trek: T.N.G."
49. "Mulholland Falls" actor
50. One of the clan
51. Bad-mouth
53. "___ out!" (ump's cry)
55. Manor near Twelve Oaks
56. "Follow orders in this plane area or else!"
62. Court huddle
64. Twice 79-Down
65. Sen. Cochran
66. Roman called "The Elder"
68. Trackers, e.g.
69. "Prepare to do a spoof on airports"
73. Accused's retort
74. Middling
75. Cross letters
76. Sine ___ non
79. Pilot's wear
82. "Executives, today's lesson is on jet financing"
86. Years of Nero's reign
87. Found groovy
89. Bush, for one
90. Bits
91. Bank deals
93. A Bear
96. Prefix with biology
98. Housekeeping
99. "First I'll read, then watch the movie, then . . ."
101. Fen-___ (diet drug combo)
103. Through working: Abbr.
104. Astonish
105. Spanish article
107. Lions and tigers and bears, e.g.
109. "What's that knitter doing during air turbulence?"
114. Rhyme scheme
118. Conspicuousness
119. "My suitcase is better than yours"
122. Pollen, e.g.
123. Lake near Jacobs Field
124. Put into motion
125. North Pole family
126. Pick-me-up
127. Bums steers?

DOWN

1. Darts' places
2. Siouan speaker
3. Jets, e.g.
4. Gold braid
5. Among, in poetry
6. "Wheel of Fortune" buy
7. Used a thurible
8. Wash against
9. Part of a Latin trio
10. "Indeed!"
11. Examine closely
12. Assemblage
13. Psychoanalyst Karen
14. Joy of wild animals?
15. Split
16. Chow ___
17. Secy.
18. Last in line, usually
21. "Don't blame ___ voted for . . ."
23. Zeit or polter follower
27. One telephone button
29. They're missing from a roll
30. Contest
33. American finch
34. Beeish
35. Diving bird
38. Lichtenstein, for one
39. ___ condolence
40. Spills the beans
41. Gillette brand
42. Landing ___
44. It's "here" in Le Havre
46. Pitches
47. Greek letters
52. Basic sugar
54. Hardships
57. Discontinued, with "out"
58. "Wild!" to a dude
59. Ice cream brand
60. Teller
61. Airport monitor abbr.
63. Lacking
67. Tom Joad, e.g.
69. Harassing
70. Watch chain
71. 1997 Rose Bowl winner: Abbr.
72. 50% of Bonn
73. Porch with a view
76. Doha's land
77. Treatment
78. Plus
79. See 64-Across
80. Hydroxyl-carbon compound
81. Small English coins
83. ___ d'Orléans
84. Veto
85. First name in horror
88. Lass
92. Trees, e.g.
94. N.F.L. sacker Bryce ___
95. Poe's "___ Lee"
97. Aria area
98. Mayo, for one
100. Pang
102. Jet's home
106. Computer game pioneer
107. Sire
108. French toast
109. Convention site
110. Stewpot
111. Place
112. Not spec.
113. Pre-weekend cry
115. Canaanite deity
116. Fishing luck
117. Home of the Cyclones
118. Small pouch
120. Old French coin
121. Change for a dol.

by Mark Danna

ACROSS

1. Heist gain
5. East German secret police
10. "Star Wars" princess
14. Attack moves
20. S
23. Alpo competition
24. P
25. Threatening finale
26. Clinton has two
27. Buys or leases
28. Miller hero
30. Downed
31. Shakespeare, e.g.
32. Here on the authority of
35. Ripken, Jr. and Sr.
36. "And I Love ___"
37. Had the know-how
39. Mo. parts
40. Hot
42. Knots
43. "Cabaret" director
45. Tract
46. 1968 track and field gold medalist
48. Former Swedish P.M. Palme
49. J
55. Water around the ljsselmeer
56. Wrap
58. Medium-range U.S. missiles
59. Some feasts
60. Dolphin leader
62. She's put out to pasture
63. Horror film staple
66. Vocal style
69. Sat at home
70. First "M" of M&M's
73. Heroine of Tennessee Williams's "Summer and Smoke"
74. N
79. Basso Pinza
80. Existentialist concern
81. From Tabriz
82. Wayne genre
83. Whitish
84. Printed
86. Popular museum exhibits
88. Anatomical cavities
91. Irk
92. Big dictionary section
93. Break
96. L
101. Pinball paths
102. Hill and Bryant
103. Horseshoer's need
104. Hostilities
107. Greek architectural feature
108. Circus
110. Wheat part
112. Old-time actresses Markey and Bennett
113. Oscar-winning Gibson
114. Moravian, e.g.
116. Some clouds
118. Bit of fancy footwork
119. Live
120. Correo ___ (airmail)
122. Make eights, maybe
124. Kind of hotel
127. Unlearned

by Matt Gaffney

129. M
133. Made out
134. G
135. Positions
136. The best
137. Call it quits
138. Complete

DOWN

1. "Dog Day Afternoon" character
2. Blame
3. Switch settings
4. "The Crucifixion" painter
5. Tariff co-sponsor of 1930
6. Common powder
7. When the sun goes down
8. Near misses, maybe
9. "Wie geht es ___?" (German greeting)
10. Flight
11. Two or more periods
12. "___ be all right"
13. Partner-to-be
14. Toast
15. Alerts
16. "Bravo!"
17. Choctaw for "red people"
18. Attached, in a way
19. Derisive
20. Not just any
21. Remnants
22. Ski run
29. "Buddy"
31. Bit of a drag
33. Thin nails
34. Yesteryear
37. King ___ Trio (popular 40's combo)
38. ___ d'amore
39. Baby
41. Actress Harper
42. Bettors bet on them
43. Dickens alias
44. Traveled horizontally
46. Cold one
47. Heroine of 1847
50. Alley mewers
51. Lover of Pyramus
52. The duck in "Peter and the Wolf"
53. Armor-plated warship
54. Black Sea port, new-style
56. Kind of path or pay
57. ___ about (approximately)
60. Karate school
61. Blows away
63. Run for it
64. First name in bridge
65. Pinup features
66. Over
67. Shah ___ Pahlavi
68. Game-ending pronouncement
70. Have it in mind
71. When shadows almost disappear
72. Grand slam foursome
73. Lawyers: Abbr.
75. Touch, say
76. Largest Greek island, to locals
77. Rawls and Reed
78. 1968 Chemistry Nobelist Onsager
84. Santa ___
85. Egyptian menaces
87. Seemingly forever
88. Greek cheese
89. Reaches
90. On-line periodical, for short
91. Subject of a 1982 best seller
93. Mapmaker's aid
94. Crackerjacks
95. They follow signatures
96. Underground network
97. Forum locale
98. R-rating reason
99. Followers
100. Late evening
101. End in ___
105. What to do "in St. Louis"
106. An Acura
108. Ingot
109. Geometrical solid
110. Major command
111. Minerva's domain
114. Full
115. English university town
117. Took steps
118. Quick holiday
121. Very
123. New Zealander
124. London's ___ Square
125. Runner Rosie
126. On the other side of the street: Abbr.
128. Alias
130. Unproven facility
131. Hung. neighbor
132. Alphabet trio

by Frances Hansen

ACROSS

1. 1962 Tommy Roe hit
7. "I'd rather not hear about it!"
14. Go with the flow
19. "Casablanca" producer
20. Meteorological effects
21. "Beggars can't be choosers" et al.
22. Start of a verse
25. Ring thing
26. Toothpaste-approving grp.
27. "I Know" singer Farris
28. Christian ___
29. "Olympia" painter
31. Every, in prescriptions
32. Tot's transport
36. They may have soft shells
37. Filippo Lippi's title
38. Finger, so to speak
42. Muezzin's call to prayer
43. Unnerve
44. Plum pudding ingredient
45. From Umbria: Abbr.
46. Verse, part 2
52. Dolly, for one
53. Lust after
54. Sailplanes
55. Stag
56. O.K.
58. Attribute
60. Mug
61. Designer in J.F.K.'s White House
63. Take under one's wing
65. Thin
68. Nice touch
70. "Caught" star Maria Conchita ___
73. ___-garde
74. Netanyahu's predecessor
75. Starbuck's captain
76. Its capital is Altdorf
78. Verse, part 3
83. Galley feature
84. "How now! ___?": Hamlet
85. Caesar's wings
86. Malodorous
87. Christian Science founder
88. RR stop
89. Jelly Roll Morton biographer Alan
91. Locale of Ptolemy's lighthouse
93. Good name for a chef?
94. Hardly a sissy
95. West of Hollywood
96. Patch up
99. Princess Yasmin ___ Khan
100. Obvious clue
105. End of the verse
109. Person in a booth
110. ___ Trail (Everglades highway)
111. Testify under oath
112. Nervous, with "up"
113. Clytemnestra's killer
114. Sprung up

DOWN

1. Draft
2. Harness part
3. K-6: Abbr.
4. St. Pierre and Miquelon
5. Refuse
6. Classify
7. All there
8. Plunk
9. One of Knute's successors
10. Cheese made of 52-Across's milk
11. Cuts into
12. French Revolution leader
13. Toledo-to-Akron dir.
14. Extra
15. Not-so-mild oath
16. Stravinsky ballet
17. A Dumas
18. Lao-___
21. Lively, to Liszt
23. Dona ___ (Las Cruces' county)
24. The Magi, notably
29. Hampton Court feature
30. They're nonreturnable
32. Kind of warden
33. Boston Symphony conductor
34. Christmas tree hangings
35. Even one
36. Napoleon relative
37. W.W. II tyrant
38. Certain rating
39. Friend of Aramis
40. See 72-Down
41. Bugs bugs him
43. Desktop publisher's supply
44. Social climber's concern
47. Affirm under oath
48. Ragwort variety
49. Strange "gift"
50. They may be modified
51. Richard Leakey's birthplace
57. Set back?
58. Making no progress
59. Sticks in the mud
60. Stalin's persecuted peasant
62. Bygone delivery person
64. Source of the Truckee River
65. It may be toxic
66. Work around
67. Broken
69. Shakespearean verb ending
71. Babydoll
72. With 40-Down, Down East university town
74. Discompose
75. Bon Ami alternative
77. Rubs the wrong way
79. More odious
80. Crimson Tide, for short
81. Panache
82. Blue Eagle inits.
89. Mesquite or mimosa, e.g.
90. Muscateers?
91. Shanxi shrine
92. Marilu of "Taxi"
93. Socked away
94. Helga's husband
95. Thou squared
96. First South Korean president
97. Hard to hold
98. Mayberry's Goober
100. Biol., geol., etc.
101. Name of two ancient Egyptian kings
102. Cries of surprise
103. Kind of wave
104. The Untouchables, e.g.
105. "Naughty!"
106. W.W. II arena
107. Make an antimacassar
108. Cockney residence

HEY, IT'S A LIVING

ACROSS

1. Calculating machine inventor, 1642
7. Reach
14. Protest
20. Delphi temple god
21. Invented word
22. Fingerprint features
23. Supper
24. Job for a restaurant server?
26. Pesticide
28. Had dinner at home
29. Three-way joint
30. Professional org.
33. Milne marsupial
34. Yugoslav novelist ___ Andric
35. Mildew cause
39. Job for a statistician?
43. Hurting the most
44. Alan and Adam
45. Blintzes, e.g.
49. Dustup
50. Player for coach Marv Levy
51. Embargoes
52. Job for a plastic surgeon?
57. Skid row look
60. Tomato-impact noises
61. ___ man
62. 70's All-Star ___ Otis
63. Most like a wallflower
64. Worry
66. Job for a mathematician?
72. Plays the siren
73. Quark/antiquark particles
74. Rudolf's refusal
75. Man-mouse link
76. Food on a tray
77. What squeaky wheels get
82. Job far a relay racer?
85. Like Mongolia
86. Photography woe
87. Scull
88. Summoned
90. Jack
92. Styx ferryman
95. Job for a critic?
97. London institution
99. Rhine feeder
100. Second-century date
101. Thumbs up
102. Airport info: Abbr.
103. 1978 disaster film, with "The"
105. Ripoffs
108. Job for a debutante?
113. Panama party
117. Screenfuls
118. Caught by surprise, with "on"
119. Athlete's assignment
120. Lohengrin and others
121. Toast opening
122. Tempt

by Nancy Salomon

DOWN

1. Course number
2. Goon
3. Bread, maybe
4. Sound of shutters in the wind
5. Minor-party candidate
6. Avon products
7. Parrot
8. Word ending in "o" in Esperanto
9. Compass pt.
10. Solve
11. Check words
12. Chill
13. Not strong
14. Have a title
15. Scholarly type
16. One to remember, for short
17. Spiels
18. Like the best ruse
19. "Women Who Run With the Wolves" author
25. Collections
27. Landscaper's need
30. Iraqis, e.g.
31. Singing Osmond
32. Shackle site
34. Woes of the world
36. Dew times
37. Push
38. Speaker's name
40. It's west of Dublin
41. Benedictines
42. They're not free of charge
46. Frees
47. Like carpet
48. Outburst
51. Ring holder
53. Synchronized
54. Lone Star State sch.
55. Christmas stocking item
56. Lady of a 1918 hit
58. Big name in morning radio
59. "___ won't be afraid" (1961 pop lyric)
60. Classic Alan Ladd western
63. Dish out messily
64. Ruckus
65. Place for bouquets
66. Delete, with "out"
67. Money in the making
68. Mrs. Katzenjammer, e.g.
69. Wards (off)
70. Manner of speech
71. Stage of a race
76. Bank
77. 1982 Disney film
78. Al from New Orleans
79. Cosmetics brand
80. Urbane
81. Marine fliers
83. Chesterfield or ulster
84. Mata ___
85. Way off
89. Violate, with "on"
90. Cold symptom
91. Bibliophile's concern
92. Some trim
93. Screenwriter Mankiewicz
94. Leaves home?
96. Hotshot
97. Kind of approval
98. Buckle opener
99. Passion
104. It's just for openers
105. Unbending
106. Shot shooter
107. Branch
109. Swellhead's excess
110. Anthem preposition
111. Letters before many state names
112. "___ Girls" (Kelly musical)
114. Tackle moguls
115. Shamus
116. "___ we having fun yet?"

ACROSS

1. Ending with way or sea
6. Commercial fuel
13. Questions closely
19. Placed on a pedestal
21. Nazareth native
22. Expire
23. MASH member
24. Songbird's lament?
26. Extract
27. Without ___ (daringly)
28. Rand Corporation employee
29. Trophy locale
30. Sot
33. Hun king, in myth
35. B.O. sign
36. Match
38. Story of trouble in the Oriole clubhouse?
42. More inclined
44. Pitch in
45. Prefix with -verse
46. Emulate Webster
49. New York neighborhood
50. Slip
51. Not our
53. Approaches
54. You, abroad
55. Having parasites in the hair?
57. Kind of test
59. Farm creature
60. Is faithful
61. 1954 Maxwell Anderson play, with "The"
64. Where on parle français, perhaps
65. Looked
66. ___ paper, used for postage stamps
69. Turk. borders it
70. Hangs back
72. Mad states
73. Big bird
74. "The Open Window" writer
75. Like Jack Haley in "The Wizard of Oz"?
78. Short snort
79. "Phooey!"
82. Like pear tree leaves
83. Pothook shape
84. Go without
85. Auerbach of "The Jack Benny Show"
86. Julio, for one
87. Record label abbr.
88. Shop talk
89. Risk a blowout?
93. Clause connector
94. KLM competitor
97. MacLaine movie "Guarding ___"
98. Summer discomfort
100. L.A.P.D. call
103. It has pull
106. ___ the Hyena ("Li'l Abner" character)
107. Front line
109. Acknowledgment from Gen. Montgomery?
113. Pax ___
114. What's left
115. Horton Foote's "Tender ___"
116. Wet floor
117. Farm device
118. Largest in scope
119. Without any pizazz

DOWN

1. Big, so to speak
2. Designer Simpson
3. Statue of a repairman?
4. Actor Stoltz
5. Elocutionist
6. Part of a footnote abbr.
7. Circular
8. Reply to "Am too!"
9. Not on time for
10. Goldfinger portrayer ___ Frobe
11. Subject of a 1996 Oscar-winning documentary
12. Part of R.S.V.P.
13. Bowl setting
14. Dodge
15. Swenson of "Benson"
16. Towers
17. Like some landings
18. Dictator's assistant
20. Affect
25. Caron role
31. Food group
32. Goldbrick
33. "Tomorrow" show
34. Classic sports car, informally
37. Want ad abbr.
39. Had second thoughts
40. Dr. of rap
41. Some Monte Carlo Rally winners
42. Goes after
43. Showy, scarlet flower
47. Story of adoptive jungle dwellers?
48. Looking up to
50. Duck down
51. Prepared to drive
52. Suffers from
55. Sticky stuff
56. Otto I's realm: Abbr.
58. Total
61. Loser at Fredericksburg
62. Sign of spring
63. Conked out
66. Lap dog
67. Connecticut collegian
68. Back blocker
71. Size
72. Aug. setting
75. The Pyramids, e.g.
76. Actresses Judith and Dana
77. Discovery grp.
80. Rio relative
81. Dispatched
84. Standings stat
87. Moves (oneself)
88. Practiced for a rodeo
90. "Primal Fear" star
91. Show for which Liza Minnelli won a 1978 Tony
92. Presidential nickname
94. Eye sores
95. Emerged
96. Prepare, as mushrooms
99. Letter opener
101. Control ___
102. Bunch name
104. Jeremy's singing partner
105. Site of some Millais works, with "the"
106. G.P.O. items
108. Barbra's 1968 co-star
110. 100th anniversary of the Potemkin mutiny
111. Senate approval
112. Fast way to J.F.K.

by Randolph Ross

ACROSS

1. Tater
5. Start of a palindrome
10. Figurehead site
14. Silent one
19. Mata ___
20. Yankee Conference town
21. Piquant
22. "Yond Cassius has ___ and hungry look": Julius Caesar
23. President's vision?
26. You can get a rise out of it
27. High spots
28. Dances for Desi
29. Mario Cuomo, e.g.
30. Fraternity letters
31. Lasting forever
32. Red ___
33. President's bird?
38. Spoiled child, perhaps
41. Athletic type, supposedly
42. Bones, in anatomy
43. Architectural flute
46. ___-mo
47. Innocent, e.g.
48. Stable locks
50. Place to buy a pie
52. Prankster
53. President's injuries?
58. ___-Unis
59. Parts of a baseball schedule
61. Archenemies, maybe
63. Czar's reply to protesters
64. Broad sash
65. Flaubert's birthplace
66. ___ Khan
68. Shot, e.g.
71. They do the thinking
74. Superiors
79. Bar at night, perhaps
81. President's testament?
83. Annex
84. Banker types
86. London gallery
87. Spring time in Lisbon
88. Boston's Bobby
89. ___ Prayer
91. Leave a mark on
93. Big garden products brand
94. Look into again, as a case
96. President's takeover?
100. Misjudge
101. Fictional weaver
102. Mouths
103. Does high-tech surgery, in a way
105. One of the Brady bunch
106. Baby's pastime
111. Protected bird
112. President's weapon?
114. Rice-
115. ". . . ___ saw Elba"
116. "Let ___ Cake"
117. Bewilder
118. Part of a ship's bow
119. Reddish-brown gem
120. One-sided tilts
121. Victory, to Wagner

DOWN

1. Popular dog name
2. Easter egg hunt sight
3. Constellation animal
4. Plan to take off
5. Angora
6. Sound reveille
7. Gives, old-style
8. Chemical suffix
9. The mornings after
10. Early infant: Var.
11. Some shades
12. Kind of liner
13. "Swiss Family Robinson" author Johann
14. President's fog?
15. Nikita's successor
16. President's beam?
17. El ___
18. Airing
24. Link
25. Noted jazz bandleader
31. Nordrhein-Westfalen city
33. Hardly stimulating
34. Bouquet
35. Surprisingly cold
36. Busy one
37. Etiquette subjects
38. Emerald City V.I.P., with "the"
39. Bluebloods
40. Get hot under the collar?
44. Some rtes.
45. Upswing
48. Ape
49. Pink-slip
51. Old-fashioned heating devices
53. Apprehend
54. Aloof ones
55. Prefix with modulator
56. Stammerer's phrase
57. The 21st, e.g.: Abbr.
60. Dinner for the Cratchits
62. Mercury model
65. Electrical unit
67. Goop
68. Hardwear?
69. Often-recited Christmas poet
70. President's line?
72. Pitcher
73. Unwanted coat?
74. Honor
75. Snippet
76. Alliance until 1977
77. Root of diplomacy
78. Single-master
80. President's article of apparel?
82. Flight path
85. Fed. holiday, often
87. "Happy Days" father, informally
90. Less available
91. Actress Braga
92. Maid
93. Expo '70 site
95. Shows pride in one's appearance
97. Corsage staple
98. Attacks
99. Founds
101. Spanish actress Carmen ___
103. Mother of Judah
104. Where Shah Jahan is entombed
105. U.K. honors
106. French tire
107. Common conjunctions
108. Sons of, to a sabra
109. Seep
110. Standard force
113. "Yo te ___"

by Charles Deber

ACROSS

1. Shakespearean prince
4. In stitches
8. Lacked, briefly
13. Footnoted
18. Moscow's locale: Abbr.
19. Swift Malay boat
20. Grammy-winning Carey
21. One of the 12 tribes of Israel
22. Strip's bête noire
24. Poppy plant derivative
25. Seasonal songs
26. Experienced one
27. Plug
29. She follows an order
30. Math branch: Abbr.
31. They may be just
33. More apt to bore
35. Early alias of 68-Across
38. Snow construction
39. "Finnegans Wake" wife
40. Prime
42. Évian, notably
43. Best Director of 1992
47. Fashion designer Pucci
49. Noble
50. Direction at sea
51. Bra specification
53. Promotes
54. "___ Davis Eyes" (1981 #1 song)
55. News broadcast closer
57. Maynard G. of 60's TV
59. Peeper pleaser
61. Revulsion
63. "Dallas" Miss
65. Counting aid
67. Old geographical inits.
68. Strip's creator, born 11/26/22
72. Door sign
74. Having a gap
76. Depth: Prefix
77. Clean-lined
79. Manhattan neighborhood
82. Loud, resonant sound
84. Great Western Forum player
85. "The Prince and the Pauper" star, 1937
87. ___ profit
89. Pound sound
91. Giving
92. Western wolf
93. Grease pencil, for one
94. Skaters do them
96. Wing
97. Stove or washer: Abbr.
98. Gremlins, Pacers, etc.
101. Fluid ___
102. Strip's cry of disgust
104. "Hooray!"
106. Monorail vehicle
110. Mariner's dir.
111. Checkup sounds
112. Fully anesthetized
114. "... two mints ___!"

DOWN

115. Adam of "Chicago Hope"
117. Short shots
119. Predecessor of the strip
121. Clark's big role
122. French town opposite Brighton
123. First name in exploration
124. The Lion of God
125. Particles
126. Cloyingly charming
127. Young newts
128. Capitol Hill V.I.P.: Abbr.

DOWN

1. Brought on
2. Designer Simpson
3. Alan and Cheryl
4. Song ___
5. Slip up
6. Strip's smallest character
7. Baby caretaker
8. Popular proverb from the strip
9. Greek nickname
10. Steak ___ (flambéed dish)
11. With 80-Down, Frieda's do in the strip
12. Next
13. Treat on a toothpick
14. Sicilia or Capri
15. Strip's apparition
16. Sushi offering
17. E.R. figures
20. Wear black, perhaps
23. Old-fashioned cold remedies
28. Training overseer?: Abbr.
32. Stepped
34. Unracy
35. Start with Cone or Cat
36. Playmobile
37. When to sing 25-Across
41. Petit chanteur
43. Brings in
44. Restrained, after "on"
45. Strip's comforter
46. "Melancholia" engraver
48. Seine sight
49. Govt. antidiscrimination org.
52. ___-mell
54. 1992 Earth Summit host
56. Jelly ingredient
58. Blister
60. R.B.I. producers, often
62. Whale of a captain?
64. Book before Job: Abbr.
66. Sister of Helios
69. Pub fixture
70. Tobacco mouthful
71. Kind of card
73. They're not cool
75. River known for disastrous floods
78. Japanese hand scroll
80. See 11-Down
81. Indy quest
83. Strip's trademark remark
85. Dog hounder
86. "Damn Yankees" vamp
88. Type of tide
90. Fierceness
93. Abbr. on a ticket
95. Schedule listings
97. Airline employees
99. Perfume, as at Mass
100. But, to Brutus
103. Pool
105. "The best ___ to come"
107. Rum mixers
108. Hopping joint?
109. Gum
111. Pierce player on TV
113. Stylish magazine
115. Humerus site
116. Density symbol
118. DHL alternative
120. Plastered

by Christopher Hurt and Derek Tague

ACROSS

1. Hater of green eggs and ham
7. Puzzle solver's exclamation
14. Foil giant
19. Iago's wife
20. "Amadeus" antagonist
21. Clips
22. Keep in touch with the kids I raised?
24. Family life, figuratively
25. Transport for Tarzan
26. Cove
27. Dismissal
28. Big name in action films catches game?
31. Thwart the progress of United We Stand?
34. Boxcar rider, maybe
35. Run-D.M.C., e.g.
36. Seven: Prefix
37. Looks for
40. Auberge
41. TV's "Murder ___"
42. Dome home
47. Constellation north of Taurus
49. Costal fracture?
52. Tidbit
55. Deborah's "The King and I" co-star
56. Uniform decoration
57. Businesses
61. Updates an atlas
63. Spud bud
64. Actress Sorvino
65. Teetotaler's choice
66. Something too tough for talons?
68. "Like ___ not!"
69. Not name
70. Free
71. Beat
72. St. ___ University
73. Investor's concern
75. "___ in apple"
76. Draw forth
78. Country legend tees off?
80. Thick vegetable soup
85. Hilton alternative
86. Ad ___
87. Atlantis docked with it
90. Pressure, in a way
91. Garth Brooks's birthplace
93. Former Davis Cup coach
95. Tasty
96. Sculptor's creation?
101. Overfill airplane areas?
104. Loser
105. "Gotcha"
106. Vacuum tube filler
107. "I Will Survive" singer
108. Psycho with intense desires?
114. Touches up
115. Rival of Oprah
116. Pledge
117. "Bullitt" director Peter
118. Unfriendly quality
119. Book of the Apocrypha

DOWN

1. Like some wine
2. Grp. with a staff in its symbol
3. Pressure unit
4. Algonquian Indian confederation
5. Prepare to shoot
6. Old-fashioned contraction
7. Cousin of -esque
8. Kind of curve
9. Jazzman Mose
10. "Mi ___ Loca" (Pam Tillis hit)
11. Poet's adverb
12. Burn up
13. Shanty material
14. Lots
15. Buzz off
16. Mother Teresa, notably
17. Right at the beginning?
18. "It's worth ___!"
21. The Beatles' "___ Woman"
23. Links rental
27. Pres. initials
28. Crack in the cold, maybe
29. "Frank & Jesse" co-star
30. First name in shipping
31. Glee clubs
32. Kind of artery
33. The U.A.E. belongs to it
38. P.I.'s
39. South, to the south
42. "___ Man Answers" (1962 comedy)
43. "The Taming of the Shrew" servant
44. Bebe's "Cheers" role
45. King of the fairies
46. To astronomers, they're hot and blue
48. Comparatively cantankerous
49. Durable wood
50. Nervous
51. Dial letters
53. Beverage for Beowulf
54. 528i or Z3, e.g.
57. Toast
58. Hardly handsome
59. "Twelfth Night" countess
60. It may be pending
62. Israel's first U.N. representative
63. Squeezed (out)
66. "Phooey!"
67. Tucked away
72. Ballet jump
74. Spiker's barrier
75. Dispatch boat
77. Old radio's ___ Stoopnagle
79. Pandora's boxful
81. Poster material
82. Pastor, sometimes
83. Proceed
84. Loaf pair
87. Man alternative
88. Archipelago components
89. Christogram letter
91. Crying
92. Cinerary vessel
94. On a par, in Paris
96. Not forthright
97. Andes climber
98. To date
99. Department north of Nièvre
100. Elbows
102. Pouring pot
103. "___ Dei"
105. Calling company?
108. ___ de coeur (pained utterance)
109. Sinbad's transport
110. Loser to Norton, 1973
111. It may be natural
112. Sade's "Is ___ Crime"
113. Young and Coleman

by Frank Longo

ACROSS

1. Bygone geographical inits.
4. Area south of the Atlas Mountains
10. Copier
14. Spots
17. Western Athletic Conf. team
19. Five-time Sugar Bowl champs
21. Opera based on two Wedekind plays
22. Popular 20's auto
23. Conservative group
25. Newspaper employee
27. Arouse
28. Parting words
30. Wolfgang Köhler's movement
31. Where the current enters
32. Ran
33. His real name was Ernesto
35. Site of ancient Samos
36. Kind of eng.
37. Boys
38. Tour de France activity
40. Trenton-to-Newark dir.
41. Parts of hoops
42. Hair-dyeing job
44. P.R., so to speak
45. "The Magus" setting
47. St. Lawrence Seaway terminus
48. Sultanate on the South China Sea
52. Apt. divisions
53. Canary relatives
54. ___ hawk (American bird)
55. Host
58. High ground
59. The Fighting Tigers, for short
60. Fa follower
61. ___-di-dah
62. Wreck
64. San ___ (Marin County seat)
67. Literary monogram
68. George's brother
69. Woosnam of the P.G.A.
70. Demonstrated, in a dramatic way
72. Ogees, e.g.
74. Meteorological concern
76. Grave
77. Heat meas.
78. Mogadishu resident
79. Jamie Lee in "Halloween"
80. Home runs, in baseball slang
83. Resentment
84. A one ___ chance
85. Character builder?
86. Nav. rank
88. Place for a target group?

92. Rocky Lane spoke for him
93. Slangy turndown
94. Some museum rooms
95. With 89-Down, a casino cry
96. Nuremberg negative
97. Andy Kaufman role on "Taxi"
99. Family reunion attender
101. In installments
104. More comely
105. As tight as possible?
107. Area for improvement?
109. Payroll service giant, initially
110. Big sports event sponsor
111. Excel
112. Nobelist Wiesel
113. Thou
114. Kind of student
115. Drove
116. Scholarly prof.'s degree

by Rich Norris

DOWN

1. Superficial
2. Adding some color to
3. Kids' game
4. Controversial 70's-80's sitcom
5. "That's ___!"
6. Ushers in
7. LSD and others
8. Set
9. New York stadium name
10. High mountain
11. Rid
12. Gen. Robt. ___
13. "The Deer Hunter" event
14. Fashion label since 1975
15. Handle, as goods
16. "The Volcano Lover" novelist
18. Motley
20. R-V connection
24. English source
26. Prepare for an emergency, in a way
29. Lawn-care products brand

32. Recognition
34. Talk (over)
37. Some contractions
38. Certain tournament
39. RNA sugar
41. Special ed course
42. Part of an address
43. "Romeo Is Bleeding" actress
46. "Maid of Athens, ___ we part": Byron
47. Supermarket section
49. Retreats
50. Jagged
51. British ___
53. Marienbad, for one
54. Covered
55. 1981 Literature Nobelist Canetti
56. Video game adventurer
57. Kind of school
58. Beverage servers
63. More compliant
65. To ___
66. "___ sher!"
71. Nagy of Hungary
73. Ask (for)
75. Proxy votes
76. Serenaded

77. Ring
79. Come-on
80. "Happy Days" type
81. Building manager's schedule
82. Hooey
85. Caused distress
87. Was overrun
88. Not uniform
89. See 95-Across
90. Parlor treat
91. Panhandle site
92. Nixon's "In the Arena," e.g.
96. Suitable spot
97. Ballad
98. Suffix with concession
100. Rabin's predecessor
102. Marksmanship org. founded in 1871
103. Georgia ___
104. Mister Rogers, for one
106. Clarinetist Lewis
108. Early evictee

ACROSS

1. Strikes out
6. Res ___ loquitur
10. Drink mixer
15. Actor ___ Phillips
19. Atlanta institution
20. Biblical kingdom
21. Shade of green
22. Some eagles
23. Burdened
24. Ranch menace
25. Nathan Hale was one
26. "So ___"
27. Ill omen
29. Echolocation device
31. ___ Sutcliffe, early Beatle
32. Kind of vaccine
33. Suffix with 20-Across
34. Kind of pigeon
37. Played
39. Got on
41. N.B.A. center Longley and others
42. Nags they're not
43. First golfer to win all four majors
46. Like a March wind
48. Schoolboy collars
49. Command at sea
50. Flourish
52. Astronaut Bean et al.
53. Oktoberfest sight
54. Leaf collectors?
55. Suffix with free
56. One of a watery quintet
60. Sign
61. Powwow
64. Gay Nineties bon vivant
66. "___ cannot wither her": Shak.
67. Cabins and such
68. Tickles
69. "Wow"
70. Comics girlfriend
72. Quiet craft
73. 60's chess champ
74. This, to Cervantes
75. Space station supply
76. Affair
77. Welles's "The Third Man" role
78. Lets go of
80. Steamboat stops
82. Target
83. F.B.I. storage
84. Creepers
85. Weasels' cousins
87. Lights out
89. Hang
90. Pocahontas's husband
91. Undiminished
92. Yule decorations
94. Skater Midori
95. Wine choice
99. Poetic time of day
100. Dentist's instruction
102. Vegas bookings
105. Originator of cutout dresses
107. ___-um (gnat)
109. "Picnic" playwright
110. Sole supporter?
111. Padre's brothers
112. Preliminary drudgery
113. Live wire, so to speak
114. Like Pegasus
115. Cheers
116. Kind of organ
117. Goals
118. Cub Sandberg and others

DOWN

1. Wallops
2. Union Pacific terminus
3. Runway sight
4. It may be continental
5. In ___ (harmonious)
6. Ineffective
7. Not flat, as hair
8. "The Maltese Falcon" role
9. Ruffle
10. Intimate
11. Needing Dramamine, maybe
12. Some synthetics
13. Eager
14. "Jacta est ___" ("The die is cast")
15. Neighbor of Syr.
16. Electra's brother
17. "Welcome aboard" sloganeer
18. Ear ornaments
28. Where Slyne Head is
30. Sell down the river, in a way
35. Best Picture of 1968
36. Ruminates
38. Ceremonial burner
40. Much-discussed drug
42. Hem and haw
43. Gorge
44. Squares accounts
45. Most foul
46. Best Picture of 1995
47. Splits
48. Precocious 1955 fictional heroine
51. Plunges
52. Decree
57. E. L. Doctorow best seller
58. Think tank member
59. Grommets
61. Way of standing
62. Wears off
63. Sarges' superiors
64. Kimberley features
65. Chem. majors' degrees
68. Still going
71. Tea
72. A Jackson
76. General Motors' birthplace
77. Strictly speaking
79. Composer Bernstein
81. Overwhelms
82. Woof alternative
83. Jai alai locale
84. They're always thin
86. Loads
87. Kind of contract
88. Marilyn's "Bus Stop" role
89. Transfer
90. Fixed
92. Maine Senator
93. Nasty
96. Milieu for Queen Elizabeth 2
97. What a star may stand for
98. ___ Park, Colo.
101. Without restraint
103. A party to
104. Bar on wheels
106. Hook shape
108. Scrape (out)

by Nancy Nicholson Joline

ACROSS

1. Split
7. Skiing type
13. Pressing machines
20. Closer to base?
21. See 60-Across
22. Impute
23. Start of a verse
26. Azerbaijani neighbor
27. Missouri feeder
28. Salt, perhaps
29. Faxed
30. Land in Genesis
32. European fruit tree
34. Leases
36. River inlet
39. Jack in oaters
41. Agt. such as Ness
43. B.C. Judean king
47. Part of A.D.
49. Sounding startled
52. Power problem
55. Old record label
56. Part 2 of the verse
60. With 21-Across, an 1861 literary hero
61. Kind of sax
62. Route
63. "___ It Romantic?"
64. Changes a Life sentence?
65. B. A. Baracus's group
66. Tag
68. Suddenly shrinks
70. Costa del Sol section
73. Launch of 7/10/62
77. Ferber's "Giant" ranch
79. Caravan maker
81. Basso Tajo
82. Yours, in Yonne
85. Mrs. David Copperfield
87. Month after Nisan
88. What optimists have
89. Part 3 of the verse
94. Afore
95. It's often underfoot
96. Stopped lying
97. Art Deco notable
98. Mythical queen of Thebes
100. Dickens girl
102. Medicare-eligible, maybe
104. Draft org.
105. Neighbor of 26-Across
108. Kissers
111. Burden of proof
113. Stand in ceremony?
116. Verdant
118. Head lock
120. Clearing
124. End of the verse
128. Kind of counter
129. Dogear mark
130. Custodians, colloquially
131. Custody
132. Impaired
133. Neverending, once

by Cathy Millhauser

DOWN

1. ___-plié (ballet movement)
2. Actor-songwriter Novello
3. Start of a cheer
4. Kristen on "Ryan's Hope"
5. Mock
6. Goof
7. Lowell and Tan
8. Mahayana monks
9. Ragú rival
10. Book extra
11. Fresh
12. Lassie creator Knight
13. Slalom champ Phil
14. Cinereous
15. Cpl., e.g.
16. ___ Pointe, Mich.
17. In play
18. Bacheller's "___ Holden"
19. Spanish muralist
24. Expression of respect
25. Coward

31. King Harald's predecessor
33. Student body pres., e.g.
35. Lt. Kojak
36. Grower
37. Private
38. Like some of the early English
40. Peter Weiss drama "___/Sade"
42. "The Clan of the Cave Bear" author
44. Rotations, in garages
45. Awaited sign
46. Tabloid talk
48. Handel's "Messiah," e.g.
50. Drag
51. Attar source
53. Related on the father's side
54. Diving bird
57. Actor Davis
58. Wandering
59. Old-fashioned cooker

65. Famed furrier's family
67. Name meaning "My God is he"
69. Burdened
71. Shows wild instability
72. "Battlestar Galactica" commander
74. Some church lighting
75. Advisories
76. Media executive Steven and others
78. Incendiary sinner
80. Actress Scacchi
82. Yemeni capital
83. Geometric solids
84. Muffin topper
86. Equipped
90. One in a heat
91. Like elvers
92. 1931 Dracula portrayer
93. Receptive
99. Miter wearer
101. Snit
103. Waiting place in a park

106. Sergeant York
107. "The Caine Mutiny" captain
109. Father of Paris
110. Brains
112. Incline
113. Gumshoe
114. Avis pair
115. Latin pronoun
117. High: Ger.
119. Variety listing
121. Say it's so
122. "After Dark, My Sweet" actor, 1990
123. Highland tongue
125. Christina's father
126. Singsong syllable
127. Literary inits.

ACROSS

1. Red-faced
8. Metal found in meteors
14. Defiled
20. 1963 Hepburn-Grant film
21. Social instability due to a breakdown in values
22. Mandarin, e.g.
23. Like some Greek odes
24. Standup comedian who wrote "Letters From an Adult Child"
26. Byrnes and Hall
27. Exaction
29. Long, in a way
30. Badminton call
32. "ER" doc
34. John Hancock: Abbr.
35. "___ Mio"
39. Before, once
41. Joins, as long-lost friends
45. Shoe with a puckered seam
47. Construction piece
48. Summarizes concisely
52. "___ y Plata" (Montana's motto)
53. Choose by divine election
54. Is suitable (for)
55. Plastics workers
57. Needle
58. Slow
61. Football positions: Abbr.
63. Stairmaster part
64. Give out
65. "Oh, ___!"
66. Fly-by-night
68. ___ vu
69. U.S. Foreign aid, mostly
71. 70's TV detective
74. Lump together
76. Heads up
77. Some retreats
78. Not miss ___
79. Superlative
80. Appreciates
81. Stares absentmindedly
82. One of the Bobbsey twins of fiction
84. Object of decoration
86. Redline
87. Org. for advocates
88. "Sleeping Gypsy," "The Snake Charmer," etc.
93. "At Random" autobiographer

95. Port with a natural harbor
96. Crabwise
97. 50's political inits.
98. Land
100. School of whales
102. Sci. course
103. Arles water
105. Mine railway
109. Quartet for first graders
111. ". . . or ___ me?"
114. Tree surgeon, maybe
118. Odds and ends
120. Hardened
121. Theater area
122. Unusual house shape
123. Ticks off
124. Clerk
125. Kind of sandwich

DOWN

1. Ne plus ultra
2. Like plowhorses
3. Try to get mystical messages
4. Was mentioned
5. Magazine since 1952
6. Bowdlerize, with "out"
7. Politesse
8. Reports by phone
9. "Double Fantasy" artist
10. Spell
11. Flandre friend
12. Bank rights
13. Late afternoon, usually
14. Kind of list
15. "There ___ losers . . ."
16. Most collectible
17. Hospital V.I.P.'s
18. Something that can get in the way
19. Place for a VCR
25. Useless
28. She was Jennifer on "WKRP"
31. Fictional detective Philip
33. Room in the game Clue
36. Popular feature in poetry
37. Emulated a siren
38. College founded by a king
39. Pleased as punch
40. Switch tags
42. Incomparable ending
43. Montgomery's field: Abbr.
44. Code word for "S"
46. Seaplane inventor Glenn

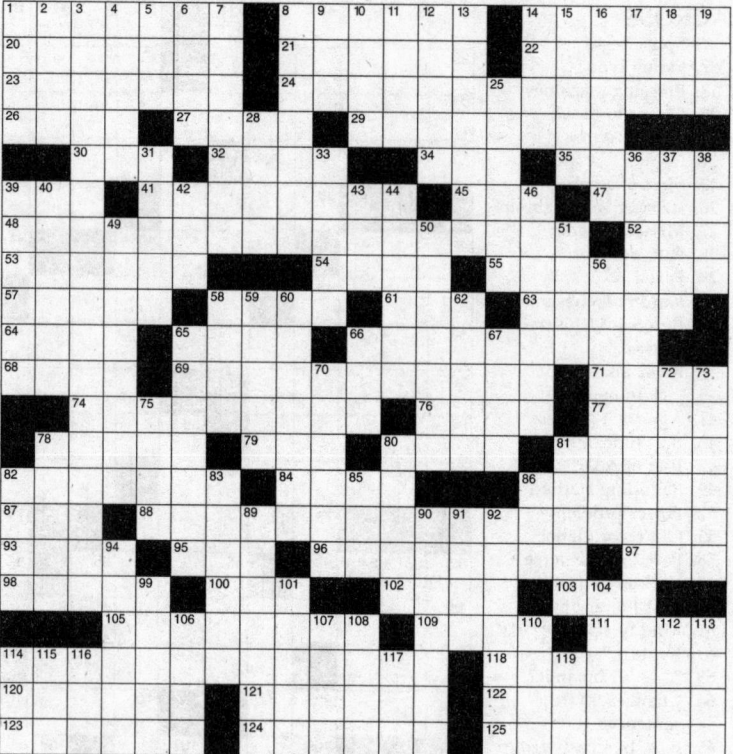

by David J. Kahn

49. Grape yields
50. Early influence on Baryshnikov
51. Car weight without fuel or load
56. Traveled unaccompanied
58. Asphalt
59. "Animal House" frat man
60. Urdu is spoken here
62. Muzzle
65. Old French headdress
66. Peg with a concave top
67. Stars
70. Directs
72. Three-time A.L. M.V.P.
73. Review, as damage
75. Cut
78. Harry's Veep
80. Edam relative
81. River at Liège
82. Veneer
83. Poser
85. Former French toastee?
86. "Midnight Lace" actress, 1960
89. Lions
90. Bill collector?
91. Med lab specimen

92. Admit a mistake, so to speak
94. Old Ford model
99. Intro
101. Daring
104. Set sights on
106. Boosts
107. "Be ___!"
108. Big name in computers
110. Chief, in Italian
112. Sikorsky or Stravinsky
113. Where Dollywood is: Abbr.
114. Familial moniker
115. Tolkien creature
116. "___ hora es?"
117. Part of an itin.
119. A lot of Colo.

ACROSS

1. Puts down
8. Puts up
14. Passover breads
20. Surplus
21. Fish that hitches rides
22. Broadcast, e.g.
23. Order to a longshoreman?
25. Surgical probe?
26. Busy
27. Caesar, for one
28. Civil rights leader Medgar
30. Antique car owner's need, for short
31. Perfect number
32. Order to a C.P.A.?
35. Fatigues
38. The Gipper
41. Robert Blake TV series
43. City on the Saône and Rhone
44. That Geller feller
45. Garden pests
46. Snaps of the fingers
48. Order to an art gallery worker?
52. Kind of sale
53. Spleen
54. Le ___ Noël
55. Telecast over
56. Where to hear "O patria mia"
60. Give thumbs down
61. Some dances
63. Breathing fire
64. Polished
66. "Takin' it ___ Streets" (1976 hit)
68. Order to a quarterback?
72. Over and done with
73. Family once called "the landlords of New York"
75. Hurray for José
76. Old "S.N.L." name
78. Pindar work
79. Gimlet or screwdriver
80. Soap seller
83. Dweeb
84. Anthem contraction
85. Wreck
87. Order to an editor?
91. Like Burns's "schemes o' mice an' men"
94. Thick locks
95. Crew tool
96. Siouan language
97. Makes potable, in a way

99. Grabs in monopolistic fashion
102. Strength: Var.
104. Order to a surgeon?
106. Gun grp.
108. Up to
109. Close to, once
111. Navy NCO
112. Kind of quarter
114. Making redundant
116. Order to a sloppy senator?
120. Park, for one
121. One who minds
122. One out?
123. Troubles
124. Rococo
125. Burr and Hamilton, e.g.

DOWN

1. Goldbrick
2. More level
3. Do piano work
4. Bank offerings, for short
5. Hill's partner
6. It may need stroking
7. Word with high or hunting
8. Like loose soil
9. Call, in a way
10. Hosp. employee
11. Sticks together
12. Three-legged stand
13. Letter encl.
14. Billiard shot
15. Small British island
16. Order to a D.A. with a hung jury?
17. Whole slew of
18. Like early postcards
19. Pepper, e.g.
24. "What's the ___?"
29. Congo neighbor
32. One with a successful day on Wall Street
33. Indian ox
34. Push
36. Baja opposite
37. Snake sound
39. Calendar abbr.
40. Can-opening aid
42. Ticket info, maybe
45. Jewish pledge of faith
47. They're on a sched.
48. Imply
49. Musical composition
50. Adjoining
51. Medium pace
52. Use the spade again
55. Fan sound

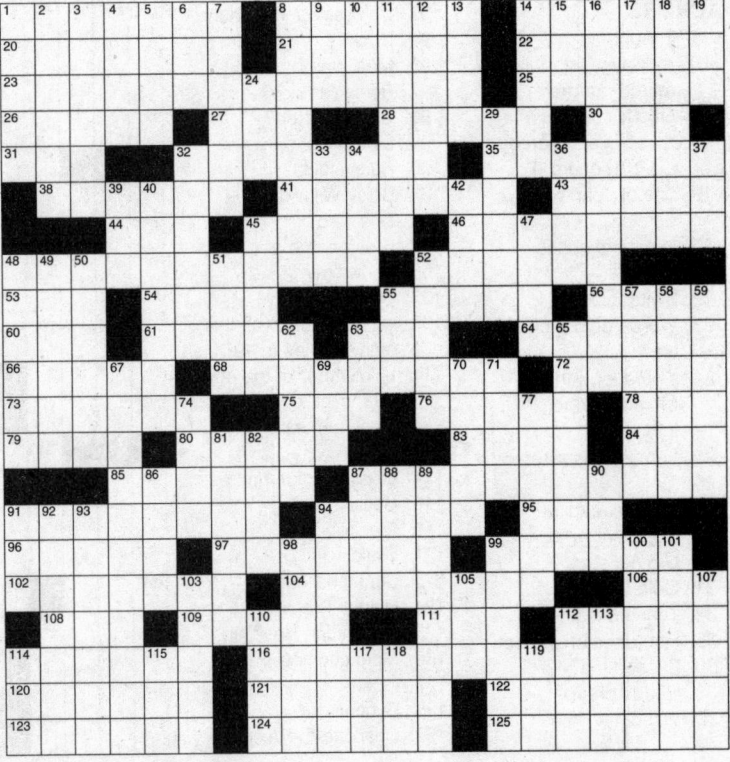

by Nancy Salomon

57. Not alfresco
58. Transferred the title
59. Bean counters
62. "Cheers!"
63. Fannie ___
65. Progress
67. Order to a cue card handler?
69. Tarzan portrayer
70. Quirks
71. Sch. type
74. 1986 Starship hit
77. Recover from a drenching
81. Knight's fair lady
82. Off the mark
86. Flair
87. Fountain treat
88. Not backing
89. Prescription for burnout
90. Common correlatives
91. 40's-50's music
92. Showing a lot of feeling
93. Sendups
94. Actress Stapleton
98. Rock climber
99. Uplifted
100. Open a package, maybe

101. Supermarket employee
103. Pens
105. Vs.
107. Primes the pot
110. Sonar signal
112. Time-honored name?
113. It's east of the Caspian
114. Dynamite
115. It fits under a head
117. Nabokov novel
118. End amount
119. Big Ten inits.

ACROSS

1. Freight
6. ← Player with this retired number
12. Overly smooth
15. ". . . this sceptered ___": "Richard II"
19. Site of Joan of Arc's demise
20. Dutch royal house
21. Goof
22. Switchblade
23. Words before clear or way
24. ← Player with this retired number, informally
25. Famed railsplitter
26. TV
27. Mideast capital
29. Center of Anytown, U.S.A.
31. Golfer Juli
33. Tennis's Nastase
35. Film director ___ Lee
36. Exceed
38. Hearty cheer
39. Without a date
42. "___ at 'em!"
44. Johnson of "Laugh-In"
45. Throat projection
47. Where the Paraná River is: Abbr.
48. First name in horror
49. Prank
50. Honored
51. Shadow companion
53. Dumps
56. "East of Eden" co-star
57. Garlic segment
58. State tree of Missouri
59. Transcript
60. ← Season record for which 3-Down had this number
62. Caviar
63. Gypsy, traditionally
65. ___-European
69. Upper, in Saxony
70. Open tract
72. Champ of 10/30/74
73. New Mexico resort
74. Colleague of Farrar and Maleska
75. Travel aid
78. Hex, of a sort
80. Convention activity
82. Pathetic
84. Waxy bloomer
87. Cousin of a loon
88. Clippers
91. Roosevelt quartet
92. Parrot's word

93. It's missing in manana
94. Duck
95. Meat stamp
97. Romanian coin
98. Copier button
99. Slow-moving
100. Race official
102. Boxer Willard
103. Uris hero
104. Brand name at picnics
106. Know-how
107. London gallery
109. ← Team that won this many games in 1961
111. ← Member of the only A.L. team to win this many games in a season
114. Classic action figures
118. Boast
119. Free (of)
121. Wield
123. Supercharger
124. Height: Prefix
125. Debenture, basically
126. More cunning
127. Open
128. Bygone era
129. Charlotte-to-Raleigh dir.
130. ← Season record for which Rickey Henderson had this number
131. Actress Young and others

DOWN

1. Lit ___ (college course)
2. Top-flight
3. ← Player with this retired number
4. ← Player with this retired number
5. "Peyton Place" actor
6. Decimate, with "down"
7. ___ and Thummin (Judaic objects)
8. Obeisance
9. Kind of skate
10. Curing, in a way
11. Noted Virginia family
12. Shade of green
13. Umpire
14. Movement
15. Practitioners' suffix
16. ← Season record for which Grover Cleveland Alexander had this number
17. One smeared in England
18. Big name in batteries

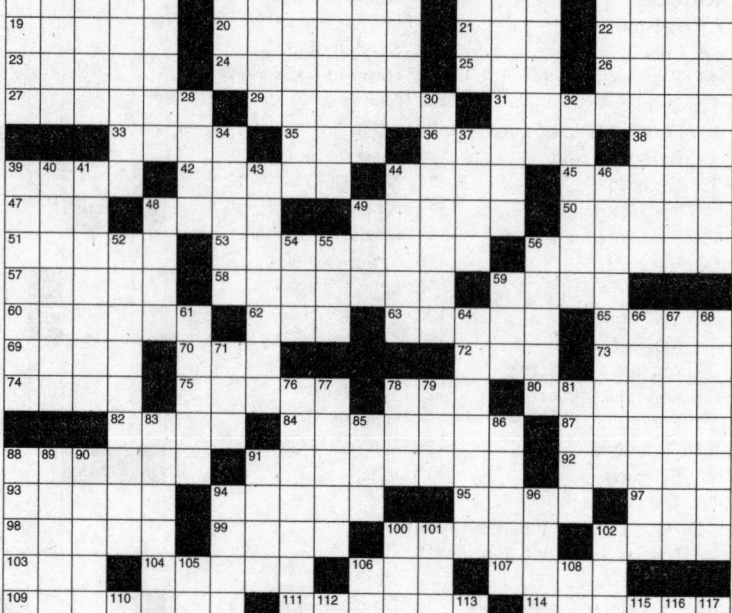

28. Blue ___
30. Sink
32. ← Player with this retired number
34. Sought lampreys
37. Western Athletic Conference team
39. Skating jump
40. Object with three round projections
41. Nickname
43. Like certain elections
44. ← Player with this retired number
46. Clothing
48. Rabbit or Fox preceder
49. Murmur
52. Swampy tract
54. Hubris source
55. Nor. neighbor
56. First TV series to show a baby being born, 1955
59. 60's chess champ
61. Impugns
64. Harshest sentence
66. Enclosed part of a blimp
67. ← Season record for which Earl Webb had this number
68. Bony

71. Printemps follower
76. Region of 101-Down
77. Rundown
78. Vegetable container
79. Plastic ___ Band
81. Turkish title
83. "___ Good Times Really Over" (1982 country hit)
85. Golly
86. Good will, e.g.
88. Meower
89. V.I.P.
90. "Hamlet" locale
91. Custard
94. What an apostrophe may signal
96. Bummer
100. Superlarge drink
101. Where Firenze is
102. Insipid
105. Spooky
106. Let in
108. Emperor after Vespasian
110. Tae ___ do
112. The latest
113. Carol
115. Killer whale
116. "My People" author
117. Absorbs, with "up"
120. Scheduled
122. Many mos.

by Derrick Niederman

ACROSS

1. Old Turkish aristocracy
6. ___ Gailey of "Miracle on 34th Street"
10. "He" and "she" follower
14. Hold off
19. Wasn't upright
20. Actress Anderson
21. Crown
22. Mideast's Gulf of ___
23. Heckles, say
25. Rare book dealer's abbr.
26. 1989 Tom Hanks film, with "The"
27. UXS
29. Examines closely
30. Temper
31. Afr. nation
32. Obeyed a flasher
33. Timely girl's name
34. Deplorable
35. Bleat
36. In ___ (not yet moved)
37. Down
39. "To Evening," e.g.
40. 0X
44. Early American orator Fisher ___
45. Jerusalem artichoke, e.g.
48. Tabloid, maybe
49. Pays what's expected
51. Western tribe
52. Problem for a dentist
54. "___ Baby" ("Hair" song)
56. They lack refinement
58. ___ Town
59. Razor-billed bird
60. Cutty ___
61. Some theater
64. Mil. drop site
65. TH000X
68. Grp. that conducts many tests
69. Runner's jersey
71. Pro side
72. One of 13 Popes
73. French count, maybe
74. Flurries
75. Not solid
76. Old-fashioned lady
77. "___ agnus Dei" (Christian phrase)
78. Former
81. Roll
82. Inevitable
83. Spell
85. IX
90. Copy
91. Bluejacket
92. Before long
93. Player's grp.
94. Barbecue sound
97. Tangs
99. Tie again
102. Stable nibble
103. Shooter
104. Temple architectural features
105. bXw
109. Jousting
110. Morales of "La Bamba"
111. Free of criticism
112. King protectors
113. Regnum
114. Ring foe
115. Noted Civil War biography
116. Pick up
117. Spawning fish
118. Ending with hoop
119. Chicago's ___ Expressway

DOWN

1. Common defenses
2. Equus and others
3. Covered, in a way
4. Over
5. Decoration for a newlywed's car
6. Threw toward
7. Fibrous
8. Inner beginner
9. Dropping, in a manner of speaking
10. Indy occurrence
11. Soft drink name
12. "Who's there?" reply
13. Figure in a murder mystery
14. Lightly touches
15. Accouter
16. 10 X
17. It's on its way out
18. Struggles with, as a varmint
24. Let go
28. Kind of horn
36. Afternoon fare
38. Gray
40. Onetime Chicago V.I.P.
41. Early wheels
42. Eastern verse
43. Suffix with glass
44. A celebrity may have one
45. Big brass
46. More romance
47. ? X
50. Breaks down, in a way
52. Kind of society
53. "Star Wars" name
54. Showed wonderment
55. Warner ___
57. Win over
60. Eye-opening problem
61. Word in a billet-doux
62. Pion's place
63. Saddled
65. What's more
66. Film director Sam
67. S.C. Johnson spray
70. Joint deposit?
73. Kind of ears
75. Announcement makers, for short
76. Tony-winning producer Theodore
79. Some TNT sports coverage
80. Backside
81. Certain illustrations
82. Utensils
83. Church events
84. Shoe style
86. Major news media
87. Sicilian resort
88. Object of a charity search
89. More than "Gosh!"
91. Dangerous pest
94. "___ Nacht" (German Christmas carol)
95. Fine liner fabric
96. Nobel and others
98. Summits
100. Succeed
101. Hoops
106. Cat's-paw, e.g.
107. Rhine feeder
108. Sped

by Robert H. Wolfe

ACROSS

1. In a fog
7. Fattening sites
12. School founded by a brewer
18. Comic Judy
19. Fusilli's shape
20. Delta, for one
21. John Knowles book about the tortoise's winning strategy?
23. Paper launched in 1944
24. Its setting is a setting
25. Color close to aqua
26. Makes sound
28. Slumber party guest
29. Public outcry
32. Frasier's brother
35. Debate position
36. Diamond corners
37. John Kennedy Toole book about a desert union?
41. Luke's sister
42. "Whip It" singers
43. Wrong
44. Parkers plug them
46. Peruvian coin
47. Musical based on "La Bohème"
48. "___ So Fine"
51. Discussion groups
52. Sine, cosine and tangent
55. Recess
57. Duke is part of it, for short
58. Henry James story about a mutiny?
62. Minimal swimwear
65. Tour-planning org.
66. Island ring
67. Islam's largest branch
68. Jane Austen book about Rosa Parks?
74. Moral misdeed
75. Ring combo
76. Patch sort
77. Strasberg subject
80. Was a pioneer
81. Door feature
84. Horror director Craven
85. Kite-flying need
86. Be cyclical
87. Writer Tarbell and others
89. Superwide shoe specification
90. Thomas Hardy book about a taxpayer's deductions for groceries?
96. Prophets
97. City on Guanabara Bay
98. Pianist Peter and family
99. Doughy snack
101. Robust
102. Start of many Latin American place names
104. Dubai native
106. Filing asst.
107. It's not wall-to-wall
109. John Grisham book about fashion show critics?
114. Ordinary
115. Sheathe
116. Frosh topper
117. Sudden contractions
118. TV event of January 1977
119. Baseball card number

DOWN

1. Harts
2. Coin of Córdoba
3. Lacking in substance
4. Trophy
5. Pilot's projection: Abbr.
6. Blowgun ammo
7. Relieved
8. Service award
9. 401(k)'s kin
10. Singly
11. Happy colleague
12. Competes
13. Radius setting
14. Campaign poster inscriptions
15. Gary of "Forrest Gump"
16. Guitarist Segovia
17. Cassette parts
19. Sobersided
20. 1984 Steve Martin/Lily Tomlin film
22. Dido's love
27. Like appreciative fans
30. "Jefferson in Paris" star
31. Use a prie-dieu
33. 1974 foreign-language hit
34. Knowledge, in France
36. Stirs
38. Historic event
39. Upended umlaut
40. Alice's cat
44. Kind of shop or language
45. Prepared for transmission
48. Meddles

49. Vespers time
50. Ross's forte
51. Recon unit
52. Win
53. "Computers for people" company
54. Old five-centesimi coin
56. Heart ward, for short
59. Swindled
60. Sinn ___
61. Behavioral quirk
63. Clear
64. Rubbernecks
69. Time being
70. Field marshal Rommel
71. Actor Baker
72. Precarious
73. Corroded
78. Floorboard sound
79. Soundtrack album, e.g.
82. Scandal reaction
83. Bobby Orr, from 1966 to 1976
85. It has its ups and downs
86. Enjoys a favorite book
88. "Die Fledermaus" composer
90. Shred
91. "All's Well That Ends Well" heroine
92. Cad

93. "Deed I Do" singer
94. Andean beast
95. Morale
96. Pillow covers
100. He introduced the Easter egg roll on the White House lawn
102. Stars
103. Cry of despair
105. Rum cake
108. Fishes-Bull go-between
110. "The Island of the Day Before" author
111. Snitch
112. In addition
113. Quick punch

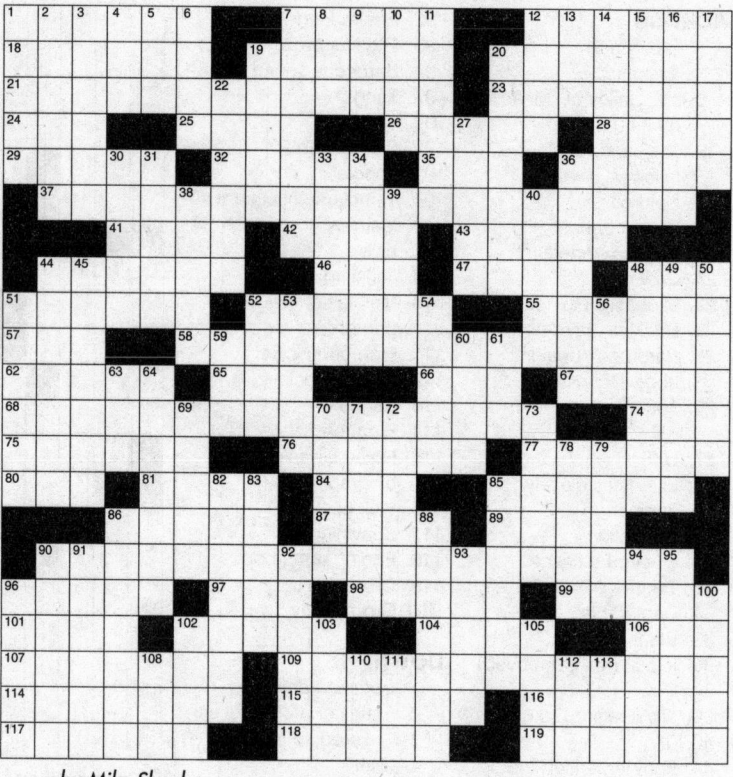

by Mike Shenk

ACROSS

1. March event
7. ___ law (i=v/r)
11. They may appear in the long run
16. "The Phantom of the Opera" star, 1962
19. Appear
20. TV actress Spelling
21. Sound from the bleachers
22. She played Sarah in "The Bible"
23. Hardly Mensa material
25. Kind of session
26. Understanding
27. Hard rock, maybe
28. Suburb north of Seattle
29. Mole, for one
30. Directional suffix
31. Warhol icon Sedgwick
33. Medit. nation
34. Tricked
35. Stem joint
36. "The ___ Adventure" ("Star Wars" spinoff)
37. Group of planes
39. Bitsy beginning
40. Like
41. "Gilligan's Island" actress
43. 1974 hit subtitled "Touch the Wind"
45. Composer Prokofiev
46. "Exodus" role
47. John of York
48. Pizzeria patron
49. Property of housepets?
50. Tackled
51. Hay morsel
52. Reassurer's words
54. Animation
55. Perfect
57. Ending with blind or broad
58. Kilowatt-hour fraction
59. Congratulations, of a sort
60. Decline
62. Bereavements
64. "It Happened One Night" producer
67. Violinist Jean-___ Ponty
68. Dosage amts.
71. Diamond of records
73. Nigerian language
74. Book stores?
76. Cozened
77. First Lady of 1900
80. Magazine that debuted 2/17/33
82. Cheer
83. ___ Darya (Asian river)
84. When repeated twice, a 1964 pop hit
85. Botswanan problem
86. Go-getters
88. Portray
90. Grenoble's river
91. Battle of Coronel admiral, 1914
92. Drunk's woe, with "the"
94. "The Dark at the Top of the Stairs" playwright
95. Better than never?
96. Pancreas, e.g.
97. Time to look ahead
98. First name in spydom
99. "___ only knew"
100. Intersecting street
101. Sammy Davis Jr. had one
103. Drop the ball
105. Small songbird
106. Come about
107. Site of Chief Big Foot's last stand
109. Clockmaker Terry
110. ___ citato
111. Not well-done
112. They're not in the nuclear family
113. Matter for a judge
114. Thrills
115. "My Way" songwriter
116. Sensible to the nth degree

DOWN

1. ___ Fjord (inlet of the Skagerrak)
2. Preview programs for computers
3. Contract
4. Transfix
5. Possible change in Russia
6. Not lethargic
7. Idle
8. Center of a roast
9. Rocky Lane spoke for him
10. Tom Sawyer's half brother
11. One letting go
12. Couch potatoes, often
13. "The Furys" novelist James
14. Wrapped up
15. School reward
16. Lausanne lies on it
17. Is intemperate
18. Quirks, say
24. "These Dreams" singer, 1986
29. Maniacal
32. Guitar-picking pioneer Everly
35. Math calculation
36. North Holland seaport
37. Delicate
38. In a difficult position
40. Tackle
42. Open tract
44. Drip site
45. Ethel Merman and Jack Benny, e.g.
52. "Children of the Albatross" author
53. Conductor ___ Klas
56. Hold
57. Logging-on need
59. Sorority letter
61. Torpedo
62. A.M.A. members
63. Disgusted
64. .6102 cubic inch
65. Frederick Forsyth best seller, with "The"
66. 1975 James Taylor hit
68. Euripidean work
69. Angler's hope
70. Chaldeans
72. The maximum, often
74. ___-majesté
75. Turns away
76. Put to use
78. Duds at work
79. Pot grower?
81. To be, in Bordeaux
87. Cave
89. Inlet
91. Oscar Madison, for one
93. Donald's daughter
96. Bellyache
98. Kind of hound
100. U.S.N. personnel
101. Enter
102. Itchings
104. Unwind
107. Depression-era inits.
108. Resource to be tapped?

by Frank Longo

ACROSS

1. Cry of relief
7. Actress Campbell of "Martin"
12. Greenery
19. Stainless
20. Bony
21. Mammals like camels
22. Minnie's mama
24. Amount of fun
25. James Whitcomb Riley's "___ I Went Mad"
26. Make waves, for short?
27. Request for permission
29. A small one is white
30. Jodie's mom or dad
34. Unmannered
38. Changing places
41. Tops
42. Lawn mower maker
44. Where area code 813 is: Abbr.
45. Pad, so to speak
46. Zip
47. Partridge locales?
49. Side-channel, in Canada
50. Mel's daughters
54. Farm females
55. Tentativeness
57. Synthetic fiber
58. Mawkish
59. Life's strange turns
60. Throws off
61. Not esto or eso
62. Univ. grant source
63. Member of Glenn's family
67. Elemental ending
70. Competitor of Bloomies
72. Part of a candlelight ceremony, maybe
73. Where zebras and giraffes graze
75. They travel on foot
77. Subatomic particle
78. Unruffled
80. Soprano in "Louise"
81. Michael J.'s kids
83. Understand
84. Gym equipment
86. One for Juan
87. Kind of alphabet
88. Hurricane heading: Abbr.
89. 50's–60's teen idol
90. French bench
92. Hoarder
94. Side in a Euro conflict
96. Jasmine's family member
99. Uranians, e.g.
101. Kind of exhaust
102. Provide, as with legal authority
103. Lizard, old-style
106. Hitched
110. Member of Joyce's family
114. Sautéed fish dish
115. Lots of potatoes
116. Designer Pucci
117. Follows a sidewalk preacher
118. First name in cosmetics
119. Holds off

DOWN

1. Tip
2. God with iron gloves
3. Midnight or beyond
4. Hair color
5. Initial instruction
6. Cherished name in Calcutta
7. Kitchen meas.
8. Suffix with Manhattan
9. "Able" one
10. Capital once known as Salisbury
11. Masefield's "___ That Pass By"
12. Testing site
13. Ben-Gurion carrier
14. Liqueur flavor
15. Traveler
16. Close friend, in slang
17. Hoedown date
18. Squiggly shape
20. "What's to become ___?"
23. Dog bowl bits
28. Investor's concern
30. Certain camera shot
31. Union demand
32. Charles's game
33. ". . . ___ a good-night!"
35. Anita, Bonnie, Ruth and June
36. Sore labour's bath, to Shakespeare
37. Flip, in a way
38. Return, as chips
39. Doubleday et al.
40. Donna's sons
43. Penn Sta. traffic
46. Big Apple's 30 Rock occupant
47. Ship commanded by Martin Pinzón

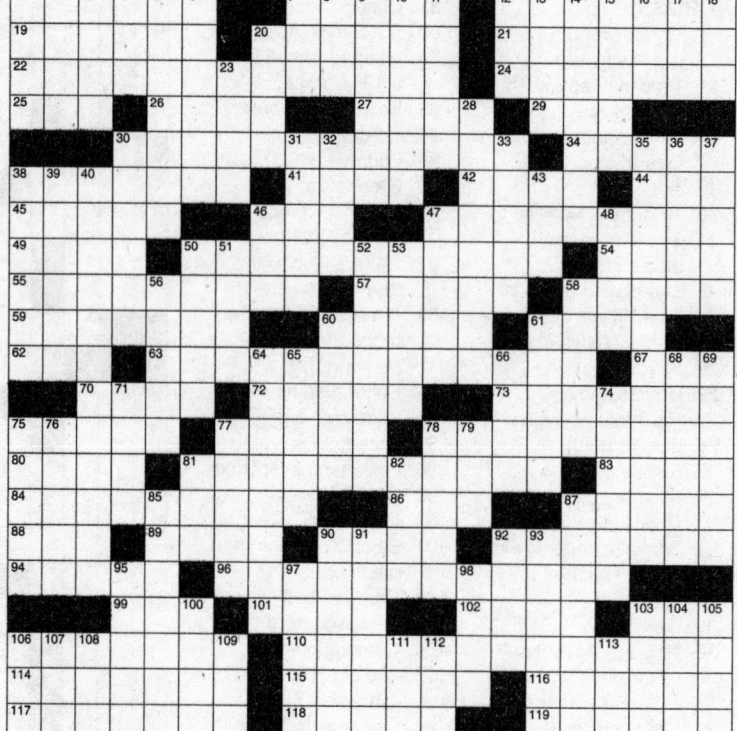

by Randolph Ross

48. Caboose
50. Highlanders
51. ___ many words
52. "Give me an example, smarty"
53. Bar's partner
56. Sounds of time passing
58. Allen or Martin
60. He played Robin and Don Juan
61. Tracks
64. "Braveheart" setting
65. Bridge positions
66. Tropical spot
68. Nervousness
69. Climbing plant with a dye-yielding root
71. Burnoose wearer
74. Straddling
75. Deliveries to a butcher
76. Cut back
77. Silvers role
78. Shell
79. Tic-tac-toe failure
81. Football Hall-of-Famer Ford
82. Candid Allen
85. Fortification
87. Spring part
90. S.A.T.'s
91. Solvent
92. Stress, for one

93. Tousled
95. Old Texaco star
97. Broadway salute to Blake
98. Times to call, in classifieds
100. Elated
103. Vogue rival
104. So-so
105. Terrible time
106. Vandalize
107. Honest name
108. Grammy category
109. Paris's Parc ___ Princes
111. Not just any
112. Ground breaker
113. Tiny carp?

ACROSS

1. Routine responses?
6. Least amiable
12. One who sets up shots
18. Make ___ for
20. Radiators and such
22. Camden Yards player
23. One of the Beverly Hillbillies
24. The World ___
25. Lab vessel
26. View surreptitiously
28. Concubine's room
29. Tart
30. How the celebrity's mom and dad survived?
37. Contemptible one
38. Theme park transport
39. Hit man, so to speak
40. Novelist Nin
42. Name of three English rivers
43. Be against change
47. How the case of commercial espionage is halted?
52. ___ du Diable
53. Cry of delight
54. Bitter, to a Brit
55. Chatter
56. Nonplussed
58. Birchbark
60. Bowling game
63. Commute overseas regularly?
68. Quit
69. Top
70. More monumental
71. Short test for brains?
72. Base figure: Abbr.
73. Annual hoops event, familiarly
74. Taste
77. Evening hours, to Larry King?
87. Ready for a vacation
88. Sundance's girl
89. Pour ___ troubled waters
90. Where the Via del Corso runs
91. Elath resident
94. Small toymakers: Var.
95. President Bush writes part of his autobiography?
101. Andretti, for one
102. 1920's White House nickname
103. Greenish-yellow hue
104. Sit in on
106. "King Rat" novelist
110. Birdie of Broadway's "Bye Bye Birdie"
113. Diving instructions, maybe
114. Barely perceptible
115. Heavy hammer
116. Lay hold of
117. ___ verite
118. Krupp family city

DOWN

1. Muslim pilgrimage: Var.
2. Cousin of a lemur
3. Weekly radio program
4. Heatless
5. It can go in brackets
6. Angry words
7. Animator's sheet
8. Words before and after "what" for Popeye
9. LAX abbr.
10. Counterpart for madame
11. Wall Street figure
12. Stole
13. Hardware
14. Chutists' needs
15. Keen
16. 80's TV divorcee
17. Strapped
19. Arizona native
21. Mayo Clinic test
27. S.A. country
30. Master
31. Not dissonant, musically
32. Beat it!
33. Emulate Tyra Banks
34. Agassi, at times
35. Challenger of Stalin
36. Sign of damage
41. Mollify
43. When repeated, cry at a celebratory party
44. Intimidate, with "out"
45. "To fetch ___ . . ."
46. Combining the ideal characteristics of its variety
48. Nipped, with "out"
49. 1973 World Series stadium
50. Reached in amount
51. "The Time Machine" people
56. Letters on a telephone bill
57. Redressed, with "for"
58. Williams title start
59. "So then what?"
60. Specter
61. Left and right, maybe
62. Midpoint: Abbr.
63. Camp vehicles
64. Strain
65. Big name in golf
66. Light: Prefix
67. Tax-free bond, briefly
74. Banking game
75. "See ya!"
76. English 101 subject
78. Most gamesome
79. Having equal angles
80. Salinger dedicatee
81. Interpret
82. She had a "Tootsie" role
83. List ender
84. Tpkes.
85. "Das Rheingold" locale
86. Telephone connections
91. Leaning to the right
92. Corned beef alternative
93. Important sports org.
95. Exams for advanced study, briefly
96. Noted stationer
97. "Coffee ___?"
98. Churchly: Abbr.
99. Some office equipment
100. Eleve's place
105. Letters after Gov. Jeanne Shaheen's name
107. Sportscaster Scully
108. Compass heading
109. Thrash
111. Sensitive subject, often
112. Stereo site

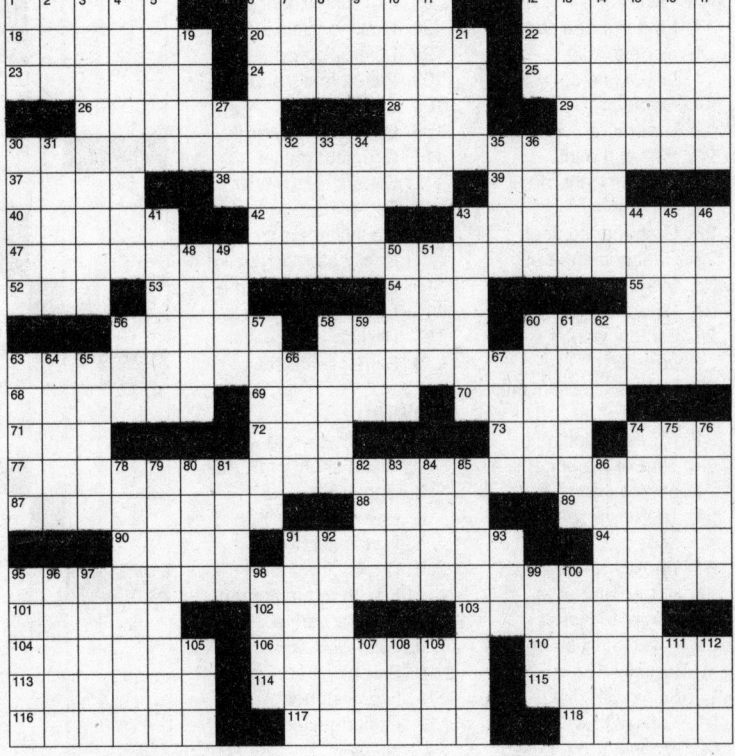

by David J. Kahn

64 CLOTHES CALL

ACROSS

1. Kindergarten stuff
5. Deduce
11. Like some socks
14. Outdoes
19. Loser in an upset
20. Part of the iris bordering the pupil
21. Implant
22. Grammar subject
23. Dancer's apparel?
26. Money substitute
27. Preacher's apparel?
28. Factory worker's apparel?
30. Florida's ___ National Forest
31. "Cheers" setting
33. Start of many criminal case names
34. The universe on day one
37. Unexpected blows
39. Actor Peter et al.
43. Home, to Hans
44. Psychiatrist's apparel?
49. Brutally dismiss
50. Suffix with disk
51. Kansas town
52. Amount to be raised, maybe
53. A regular type
54. Cable network, briefly
55. Miner's apparel?
59. Burns's partner
60. "Ditto"
62. Send
63. Earthy deposits
64. Conners
65. Saki, really
66. Author Marsh
68. Separates, in a way
70. Now
71. Election times
74. ___ as a pig
75. Projectionist's apparel?
77. One of the 13 orig. colonies
78. Rhineland town heavily bombed in W.W. II
79. Apt family name in "The Wizard of Oz"
80. Constellation animal
81. "___ cost to you!"
82. Suffix with special
83. Entomologist's apparel?
87. Silent actress Naldi
88. Highly seasoned stew
90. TV Mr.
91. Joyous hymn
92. Country
95. Govt. intelligence org.
96. Meeting room staple
99. Referee's apparel?
103. Pro athlete's apparel?
107. ___ friends
108. Lawyer's apparel?
111. Compact matter
112. Elevs.
113. Flower part
114. Mountain known locally as Mongibello
115. Kind of skill or home
116. Luggage marking
117. Restful
118. Barrier breakers

DOWN

1. 1956 Peck role
2. Island south of Borneo
3. Plagiarize
4. Free
5. Nero's successor
6. Dizzy
7. Edison contemporary
8. Holler's partner
9. Polar worker
10. Snitch
11. Fed. watchdog
12. Opportunities, so to speak
13. Resided
14. 1956 Marilyn Monroe film
15. Collectible Dutch print
16. Hindu garment
17. Letters of rejoicing
18. Library Card Sign-Up Mo.
24. Gumshoes
25. Sealy competitor
29. Ivy Leaguer
31. Fella
32. "___ Lay Dying"
34. Castle locale
35. Kind of yoga
36. Mechanic's apparel?
37. One of the Marianas
38. Become suddenly aware
40. Engineer's apparel?
41. Shine
42. Penn and others
44. Certain office worker
45. Surf sounds
46. Composer Siegmeister
47. Old dagger
48. Paper size: Abbr.
53. Highlander's pride
55. Treasure site
56. Day after mercredi
57. Skeletal parts
58. Saint ___ College of California
59. Stock up
61. Form of Spanish "to be"
65. Continue
66. Sip
67. Intimate
68. Master
69. 4×4 name
70. E-Z Pass payment
71. One of the Monkees
72. Nosy one
73. Longtime G.M. chief Alfred
75. Evil, to Yves
76. 1884 literary hero, informally
79. Physicist Ohm
81. Lab reports
83. Son's designation, with "the"
84. Hollywood's B. D. and Anna May
85. Certain H.S. teams
86. Good bond rating
89. Yankee
91. Anne McCaffrey's dragon land
93. Don Marquis character
94. Airs
96. Wonderland message
97. "Men in Black" menace
98. River at Lyon
99. Malt liquor yeast
100. South Seas adventure story
101. Delete
102. Onetime athletic org.
103. Lasting effect
104. Belt-tightening
105. 1971 Grammy song "___ No Sunshine"
106. Child welfare grps.
109. It's got your no.
110. Downed

by Michael S. Maurer

ACROSS

1. Mailing supply
7. Leaves of metal
12. Coped
19. A Musketeer
20. Cliched movie ending
21. Better
22. Most ghastly
23. Hose-wielding serf, perhaps?
25. Slangy acumen
26. 1977 film killer
27. "The Clan of the Cave Bear" author
28. Charlotte's web site
29. Developmental period
30. Trumpeter Ziggy
31. Rabin's successor
33. Fact about unladylike habits?
37. Chow
41. Cries akin to "Shucks!"
42. Clingmans Dome locale: Abbr.
43. T or F, e.g.: Abbr.
44. Overhauled
46. Charleston dancer
49. "This means ___!"
51. Expert witness at a trial
52. Samplers
53. Ones peeking at rams and ewes?
56. Winter Palace dweller, once
57. Loser to Braddock, 1935
58. Emollient source
59. Rent
60. Famed Chicago boat?
65. Invitation word
69. "Help!" in France
70. Pilgrim's pronoun
71. Blood: Prefix
75. Long-winded oration of Andrew, e.g.?
78. Heavenly host
81. Bureaucratic stuff
82. John Dos Passos trilogy
83. Pass in some bowls
84. Yak in the pulpit
85. Qt. couple
87. More than chuckle
89. The Nittany Lions: Abbr.
90. Early pulpit
91. Stifling of a happy bird?
96. Hotfoot it
98. Refreshing spot
99. Get nosy
100. Vacation sites
104. Ancient Roman wheel
105. Lt. Kojak
106. Prefix with graph
109. Seedy place?
112. Live, as a game ball
113. Pen
114. Habituates
115. The Green Wave
116. Popular Christmas gift
117. Like Batman
118. Volcano, e.g.

by Cathy Millhauser

DOWN

1. Napkin holders
2. Composer Khachaturian
3. Back talk, to one prophet?
4. Crop up
5. Conversation starter
6. J. F. K. jet set
7. 1995 cop on the spot
8. Like some garages
9. Montreal, for one
10. Guitar designer Fender
11. Buckle up
12. Stephen King title
13. Capacious
14. Member-supported org.
15. Abu Dhabi denizen
16. "Naked Maja" painter
17. By any chance
18. Laura or Bruce of film
20. Hot
24. Political debates, often
30. Washstand toppers
32. Palmists, e.g.
33. Go with the wind
34. Certain fledgling
35. Suffix with hoop
36. Modern Maturity grp.
38. Emulate Mia
39. Thomas Mann's "___ Kroger"
40. Mean grin
44. Event for those who know the ropes
45. Irish offshoot
47. Span. coin: Abbr.
48. Short wave?
49. Coaster rider's cry
50. Makes bubbly
51. Swamp critter
53. ___ law (ancient code)
54. Worked with alfalfa
55. Additionally
57. Hecklers' chorus
61. Nobel-winning Bunche
62. Captain Hook's sidekick
63. Ostrich cousin
64. Sharpen
65. Kvetch
66. Kind of hat or house
67. Web user's need
68. Cornerstone abbr.
72. Afore
73. Irish side dish?
74. Humble
76. Guadalajara lunch
77. "Tom Thumb" star Tamblyn, 1958
78. Kind
79. Ruin
80. Cast aspersions on
85. It's a snap
86. Huge
87. Mended
88. ___ Hound (Canis Major)
91. Low-frequency speaker
92. Tallies
93. Pakistani city
94. Unfold
95. Big hit
97. Hag
100. Bursae
101. Fore-and-after's fore
102. Tops
103. Remote location
106. Rests
107. Silver hair
108. ___ and terminer
110. Weimar "with"
111. Spanish queen until 1931

ACROSS

1. Buzzing
6. Billiard stroke
11. Name in computer software
16. Hinder
21. Oscar Madison's secretary
22. Hero of the first opera written for TV
23. Ain't right?
24. Leaf
25. GREEN
27. GREEN
29. Bank deposit
30. Keep for oneself
31. Concert finale
32. ___ League
33. Kansas city
35. Raiders' chief
38. Subjects of modern mapping
39. Bitty's partner
40. V-chips block it
42. Column couple
44. Trojan War figure
46. GREEN
52. Corsair and Citation, for two
56. ___-a-porter
57. Feature of Roy Lichtenstein's art
58. Genealogist's abbr.
59. Eastern attire
61. Dit's partner
62. Come to
65. Kind of testing
67. Novarro of silents
69. City on the Mohawk
71. Jimmy Dorsey's "___ Mine"
72. Watering holes
74. GREEN
77. GREEN
79. George ___
80. Stretch
81. Colleen
82. Detergent
83. French toast portion?
85. Easily handled, as a ship
87. Lhasa ___
90. Beethoven's "Choral" Symphony
93. Service station offering
94. GREEN
98. GREEN
101. Commencement
102. Voyage preceder
103. 1993 N.B.A. Rookie of the Year
104. "Forget it!"
105. Where firings take place on a daily basis
107. Spicy stew
109. Mineral suffix
110. Gospels follower
112. Commuters' ways
114. Financial aid criterion
116. Dexterity
117. What some fans do
119. GREEN
123. Smoking container
126. Foam at the mouth
127. Petitions
128. Pulitzer dramatist Connelly
131. Ancient city in 2-Down
133. Food item usually picked wild
136. Abases
140. Jerusalem's Mosque of ___
141. Aristocracies
143. Arm
145. Granada greeting
146. GREEN
148. GREEN
150. Reason for 55-Down's rebellion
151. Underground worker
152. Petitions
153. Math measurements
154. Blackthorn fruits
155. Colonel's insignia
156. Digression
157. To wit: Lat.

DOWN

1. Out of place
2. Aleppo's land
3. Coloratura's specialty
4. Provoke
5. Bowl sound
6. County in NW Ireland
7. City once called Philadelphia
8. One born on a kibbutz
9. Most likely to collapse
10. Annex
11. Victoria, e.g.
12. Rubber gasket
13. With 15-Down, some chains
14. Outfoxed
15. See 13-Down
16. Newt
17. Costly sweaters
18. Say suddenly
19. Target
20. 1955 film robot
26. Lewis of children's TV
28. Rankle
34. Go-ahead
36. Takeoff, approx.
37. The Lone Ranger's real identity
41. It may be living or dead
43. She's still with Stiller
45. Ignominy
46. Squarely
47. ___-Detoo
48. Some Balts
49. Lonesome George of early TV
50. Address nos.
51. Shades
53. Woman on TV's "Ab Fab"
54. They're fit to be tied
55. 1786 Springfield insurrectionist
59. Lounge
60. Assumed names
63. Off
64. Vietnamese port
66. Populous place
68. Team V.I.P.: Abbr.
70. Flat sign
73. Discerning
75. Shoptalk
76. Hole enlarger
78. Sicilia, for one
79. Shipmate of Starbuck
84. Panzer
86. ___-tat
87. French 101 verb
88. It's spotted in westerns
89. Driving hazard
91. Sgts., e.g.
92. Service station offering
94. Private
95. Sub
96. Rally
97. Record
99. Winged
100. Film used for recording tapes
101. Dairy aisle buy
106. Bush leaguers
108. Advances
111. Tall player
113. Sting
115. Pat
118. Grow together
119. Babbling
120. Id moderator
121. Pasta go-with
122. "Yuck!"
124. Banned Wilde drama
125. Desdemona's faithful servant
128. Shapes
129. Film director Jon
130. Sly character
132. Celebrate
134. Name in Chinese politics
135. Actor Christopher
137. The world according to Arp
138. Object of frequent sightings
139. "___ Isn't So" (Hall & Oates hit)
142. Desiccated
144. Language that gave us the word "whisky"
147. C.I.A. forerunner
148. Tax pro
149. Calendar abbr.

by Nancy Nicholson Joline

ACROSS

1. Like putty in one's hands, maybe
7. Teen's woe
14. Rum cocktail
20. Rockville ___, L.I.
21. Musical instrument with finger holes
22. Tigers' school
23. Soup ingredient
24. Start of a quip by 67-Across
26. Backgammon impossibility
27. Tab topic
29. Ring thing
30. It has a red coat
31. Quipu maker
33. It might be sung on one's birthday
37. Skins
39. Part 2 of the quip
44. Exploits
45. Hot
46. Say further
47. Place, as a bet
48. Traveller's check
49. Lucky draw
50. Drudge
52. Sharp taste
53. With 56-Down, city near Knoxville
56. See 72-Across
59. Withdraws
61. Part 3 of the quip
65. Trouble
66. Show stoppers
67. Author of the quip
69. Bumbling beast
72. With 56-Across, like some shares
73. Part 4 of the quip
75. Zones
79. Ball girls
80. Downing and others: Abbr.
81. Some W.B.C. outcomes
82. Briny
83. Suffers from
85. Examines, with "over"
86. Prado treasure
87. Charles, e.g.
88. Norwegian king
92. Beet variety
94. Part 5 of the quip
101. 50's TV comedian
102. Concurred
103. Pig
104. ___-humanite (crime against humanity): Fr.
105. Historic grp.
107. Airport line
109. Alert, for short
110. End of the quip
115. Elusive subject, familiarly
117. Deep-frying need
118. Ex-con, maybe
119. Rubber ring
120. Ticket order
121. Jacks or better, in poker
122. Blurs

DOWN

1. Nova follower
2. Spelling
3. What pronouns refer to
4. Local org.
5. Skater Heiden
6. Struck out
7. Shalikashvili's predecessor
8. 90's brew
9. Warp, say
10. It comes before adolescence
11. "___ Darlin' " (1957 hit)
12. Sphinx
13. Copy to a floppy
14. Enthusiastic exclamation
15. They're boring
16. In the same place
17. Deli option
18. Composer Khachaturian
19. A keeper may keep it
25. Ties up
28. Contact, perhaps
32. Hanging clear of the bottom
34. A.M. TV offering
35. Mythical bird
36. "___ questions?"
38. Relief
40. Female octopus
41. "Pillow Talk" actress
42. 1993 Kevin Kline comedy
43. Choice beef cuts
48. Bust, so to speak
49. Bleated
50. Fugitive's trail
51. "Jurassic Park" girl
52. Its slogan was once "The things we do to make you happy"
53. Wrinkle-resistant fabric
54. Govt. agent's employer
55. Opera's ___ Te Kanawa
56. See 53-Across

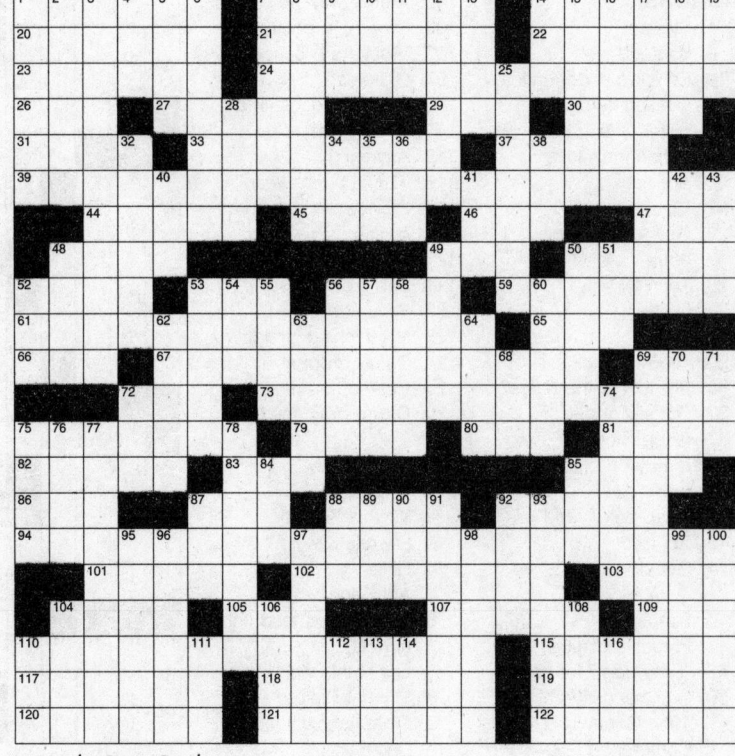

by Peter Gordon

57. Biting
58. Pea stabbers
60. Olympics great Janet
62. He doubted God's ability to bring water out of a rock
63. Wards (off)
64. Film director Buñuel
68. New York ___
69. Popular dessert
70. "The Dukes of Hazzard" spinoff
71. Jour. staff
72. Airline to Karachi
74. Attacks
75. It might have the shakes
76. Tannish
77. TV pal of Mary and Rhoda
78. Ought to have, informally
84. Certain look
85. Accelerator
87. Map abbr.
88. Saturn's wife
89. ___ Fresnos, Tex.
90. Black and tan ingredient
91. Bordeaux business owner
92. Popular cereal
93. Stashes
95. Absentee
96. Where the Tagus flows
97. Cap attachment
98. Conditions of equilibrium
99. More silly
100. ___ Field
104. British emblem
106. ___ Snaps (dog treats)
108. Petticoat junction
110. "Name him!"
111. England's Isle of ___
112. Before, in poetry
113. Sun. follower?
114. Big cheer
116. Compass dir.

ACROSS

1. Steady
6. Sauteed dish
10. Edison's middle name
14. Dessert item
19. Silver Ghost, informally
20. Lohengrin's love
21. Activist
22. Up
23. Title for a cleric's book?
25. Teen fantasy?
27. Do type
28. Gone
29. 1995 Pitt flick
30. Product of the press?
32. Quickly apply
37. Goodfellow ___, Tex.
40. It may be black or green
41. Deep bell sound
42. Mr. Hyde, e.g.
44. Cybernetics pioneer ___ Wiener
46. Firm
48. Pinochle combo
49. "Dirty dog," for one
50. City discussed at the 1954 Geneva Conference
52. Senate support
54. Cows, maybe
55. Opposite of baja
56. Black spot
58. Kind of expression
60. They cross the line
62. ___ one
64. Bank deposit
65. Sewing tool
66. Masseuse's target
67. "Was ___ blame?"
68. Program
70. Ring org.
73. 70-Across weapon
75. Miss America attire
77. Dweller across the strait from Singapore
79. Stadium sight
81. Horrible
84. Prefix with mechanics
85. Thick fog, in slang
86. "___-Man" (1974 spy/sci-fi film)
88. Center of activity
89. Wit
90. Part of a W.W. II exclamation
91. Search for x
93. Bit of business attire
96. Kind of apparel
99. Foreign refusal
100. Shower with flowers
101. Certain model railroads

102. Ardent and then some
103. Cavern, in poetry
105. "Backdraft" concern
107. Old piece
109. Wedding locale in a Crosby film
112. Anorexic?
116. Simple beachwear?
119. Provide, as with some quality
120. For fear that
121. Split, so to speak
122. Pen patter
123. Not thinking straight
124. Douay prophet
125. Heart of the matter
126. Desert drainage basin

DOWN

1. Support ___
2. Virginia Senator
3. Lily relative
4. Hints
5. Artsy one
6. Engage in a food fight at KFC?
7. Out of this world
8. Sight at Dulles
9. "That'll show you!"
10. Deem
11. Screw (up)
12. Hero-worship
13. Like Australia's western plateau
14. Famous Tuesday Club member
15. ___ bark beetle
16. Actress Myrna
17. Repeatedly
18. Ultimate
24. Fin
26. Bounce
30. Do a salon job
31. Hitchhiker from Calcutta?
33. Hammer in manufacturing
34. Tiny Christmas decoration?
35. Was coquettish with
36. Auction actions
37. Cochise player Michael in 50's TV
38. Succeed
39. Unbearably hot holiday?
41. Quite a thrill
43. Capriole
45. Small fastener
47. Foreign refusal
51. Jerks
53. 1953 title role for Rita Hayworth
56. Treat

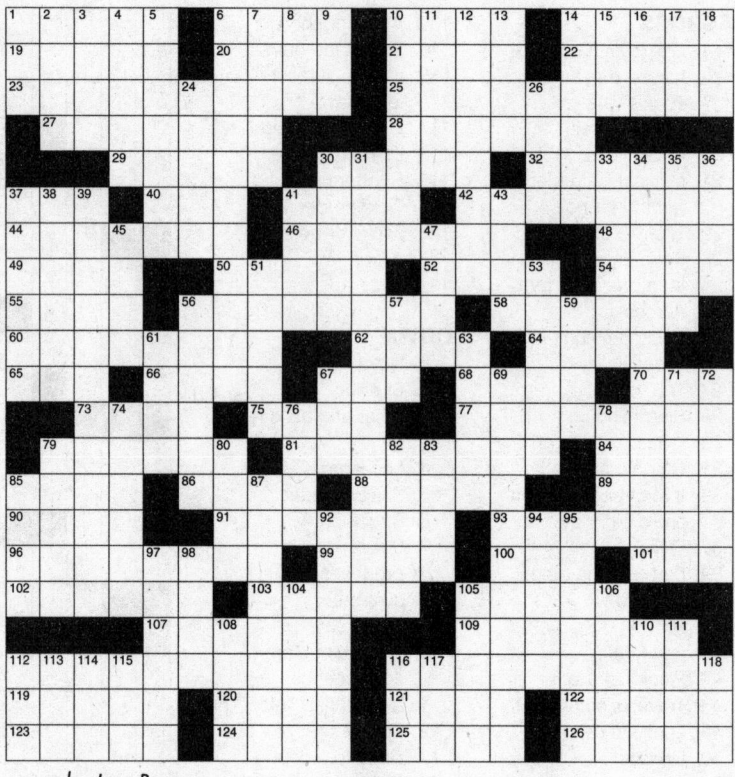

by June Boggs

57. Talk fondly
59. "Field of Dreams" setting
61. What a padlock may fasten
63. Org.
67. Where Mt. Carmel is: Abbr.
69. Kindly spirit?
71. Inner-city area
72. Current terminals
74. Disable
76. With bated breath
78. Small fastener
79. City ESE of Bombay
80. Water ring
82. Chilling
83. Go up and down the dial
85. Budge
87. Whitens
92. It might come out of a summit
94. Rose-red dye
95. Stove workspace
97. Fictional ghost
98. It passes between decks
104. Clangor
105. Be ready for
106. It meant nothing to Caesar
108. Capital of Manche

110. North or South district in Hawaii
111. Black
112. Drops outside
113. Musician Brian
114. Hubbub
115. Procter & Gamble soap
116. Oomph
117. Year in Nero's reign
118. Agcy. overseeing Fed. records

ACROSS

1. Favorite Degas subject
8. Behave
11. ___-Ball
15. It often has its arms out front
18. Gorged oneself
19. Classified
21. "Windsor Forest" poet
22. Dinner offerings
24. Services, in a way
25. "Mr. Basketball" Holman et al.
26. Gray remover, maybe
27. "Suzanne" songwriter
28. Orbital point
29. "The Simpsons" tavern
31. Show of affection
33. Backgammon piece
34. Oater affirmative
36. Engine conduits
37. Hits errantly, in golf
38. Impassioned
41. State to be in
42. Word with ready or shy
44. Reef
45. Hair-raising site?
47. Undercover operation
52. #2 at the 1994 U.S. Open
54. Swing voter: Abbr.
55. Lodge
56. CD-___
57. Ice cream parlor order
59. "La vita nuova" poet
60. Captures, in a way
63. Rachmaninoff's "___-tableaux"
64. Indian stringed instruments
65. Make up
66. Like some muscles
67. Poop
68. Impetuous
69. Listen: Sp.
70. British noble, briefly
72. "___ in my memory lock'd": Ophelia
73. Certain berth
76. Kind of pie
79. Community spirit
81. Majors in acting
82. Ruling groups
83. Farm resident
84. Part of a split personality
86. Orchestral works
88. Considerable irritant
91. Word in many business names
92. "Star Trek" role
93. Soup kitchen offering
97. Taradiddles
100. Puffball relative
101. Release upon
102. Hotfooted it
104. Clock sound
106. Make money
107. Health care group
110. Sews up
111. Reserved
112. Totals
113. Christie contemporary
114. Musical syllables
115. Never, in Nuremberg
116. Least irrigated

DOWN

1. Butler's expletive
2. Col. Hannibal Smith's group
3. Cool
4. Relative of an agate
5. Plumbing piece
6. Chancel entrance display
7. Collar inserts
8. Collar
9. Animator's unit
10. Parcels
11. "___ Is Love" (1962 hit)
12. They provide prayer support
13. Brings in
14. 1997 U.S. Open champ
15. Long-term pollution concern
16. Data transmission path
17. Actress Armstrong and others
20. Tend the hearth
21. Toaster treat
23. Couple or so
28. Word before and after "to"
30. Parasol
32. Quite a while
35. Fund-raising grp.
37. Seemed funny
38. Sit-up benefactors
39. Squeal
40. Travels of Shane, e.g.
41. Locale
42. Mention
43. Breeze through
46. Items in sync?
47. Imaginary
48. Chaplin and others
49. Mil. transports
50. "Are you nervous?" response, a la Don Knotts
51. Diamond execs

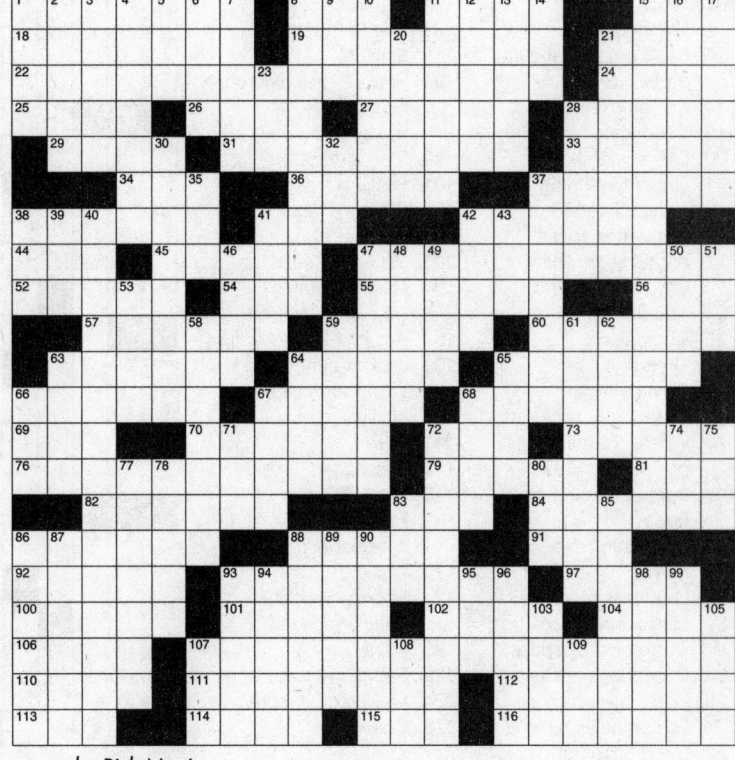

by Rich Norris

53. Gist
58. Hairsplitters
59. Pronouncements
61. Charge with
62. Bribe money, in slang
63. Chacon of the 1962 Mets
64. Still-life subject
65. Hasty
66. Pocket item
67. Holiday purchases
68. Diamond target
71. Company that made Photophones
72. Ford sobriquet
74. Sniggler's quest
75. Fam. reunion attendee
77. Castle features
78. "Paper Moon" actor or actress
80. Breakfast orders, briefly
83. J. F. K. posting
85. Emulated Mme. Defarge
86. Kind of meeting
87. Prize
88. Aquarium acquisitions
89. Track and field events
90. Secure
93. Topps rival
94. Gaucho gear
95. Mil. address
96. Longtime Guy Lombardo record label
98. City on the Oregon Trail
99. Dumbarton denizens
103. New Look designer
105. Measure of speed
107. Presidential monogram
108. Star Wars, initially
109. "___ dreaming?"

ACROSS

1. Cutaneous
7. Rock group that sang "Let's Go"
14. Splendid
19. Conductor Toscanini
20. Like some shoes
21. Grammy-winning single of 1958
22. Groundskeeper's bagful at an Atlantic City newspaper?
24. Armpit
25. Companion
26. Oregon ___
27. Playboy Khan
28. Library ref.
29. Where "Falstaff" premiered, 1893
32. Start of a string of 13 Popes
34. Dish alternative, maybe
36. Loudness measure
37. Musician who co-starred in "Trespass"
38. Descartes conclusion
39. Horse owned by a Boston newspaper?
42. Hired hands at Microsoft
44. Sponsorship
46. Camera since 1924
47. Bank sitters
49. Some picture frames
52. Used rubber
56. Garden, in a way
57. Correspondence to the editor of an Allentown newspaper?
60. Allan-___
61. Obviously sleep-deprived
63. End of a Burns title
64. Prepare to get juice
65. Madonna's "La ___ Bonita"
67. Kind of law
69. Yeshiva product
71. Off, so to speak
72. Drink with 87-Across
74. Concert memento
76. Like a clover leaf
78. Take over, in a way
79. Columbia, S.C., newspaper's security department?
81. Vane dir.
84. Like a mule
86. Mars, to Aries, in astrology
87. Ingredient in a 72-Across
89. Thunderstruck
91. ___ facto
93. Like Chippendale furniture
94. Way into the bathroom at a Macon newspaper?
99. Start to function?
101. Snake oil, purportedly
102. Hungary was a member of it
103. Suffix with sect
104. Named before
106. Do some roadwork
107. Automobile sticker fig.
108. Jack-in-the-box part
109. I.Q. recordholder Marilyn ___ Savant
111. Prize
113. Associated
115. Shell shot at a Harrisburg newspaper?
120. Come
121. Nobel physicist Becquerel
122. Frank
123. Rather awkward
124. Mouthing off more
125. Crackers

DOWN

1. Skip, as a stone on water
2. Muff
3. Hwy.
4. Sweet wine
5. Some insurance fraud
6. ___ Tay, Scotland
7. Part of an old Greek fleet
8. In the know about
9. Subject of a psych. experiment
10. Do
11. Permanent-magnet alloy
12. Seize again
13. 60's campus grp.
14. Popular theater name
15. Bulldog
16. Big goon
17. 50's–60's "What's My Line?" panelist
18. Beginning of a tape
21. Harper, for one
23. "Come Back, Little Sheba" wife
27. Edits
29. Book before Nahum
30. Likeness: Prefix
31. Come-on at a Lakeland newspaper?
33. "Enough!"
35. Handsome, as Henri
36. Carmichael classic
38. Sharon, for one
40. Attorney-to-be's exams
41. In base 8
43. Shipping dept. stamp
45. Pupil's reward
48. Roy Rogers's real surname
50. A great dist.
51. ". . . and last in the American League" team
53. Recruiter at a Wichita newspaper?
54. Inter ___
55. Say it ain't so
58. ___ squares (statistical method)
59. Malcontent
62. They're full of beans
64. A bobby pin may hold it
65. "Look at me, ___ . . ."
66. Start of some Italian church names
68. Tutsi foe
70. ___-a-brac
73. Cutting down
75. Misrepresent
77. Eddie Rickenbacker's 94th ___ Squadron
79. City on Resurrection Bay
80. Great Fire of London diarist
82. Pelvic bones
83. Tempter
85. Acting Day
88. Gets via computer
90. Prefix with 1-Across
92. Name dropper?
94. Gong in an orchestra set
95. Run out
96. Hybrid cats
97. Humidor item
98. Fife player
100. "As You Like It" servant
105. In unison
106. "Jurassic Park" mosquito preserver
108. Roman historian
110. Some B'way shows
112. Bird whose male hatches the eggs
114. Bad-mouth
115. Stage setups, for short
116. "Superman ___"
117. ___ bind
118. Baseball's Dykstra
119. Before, once

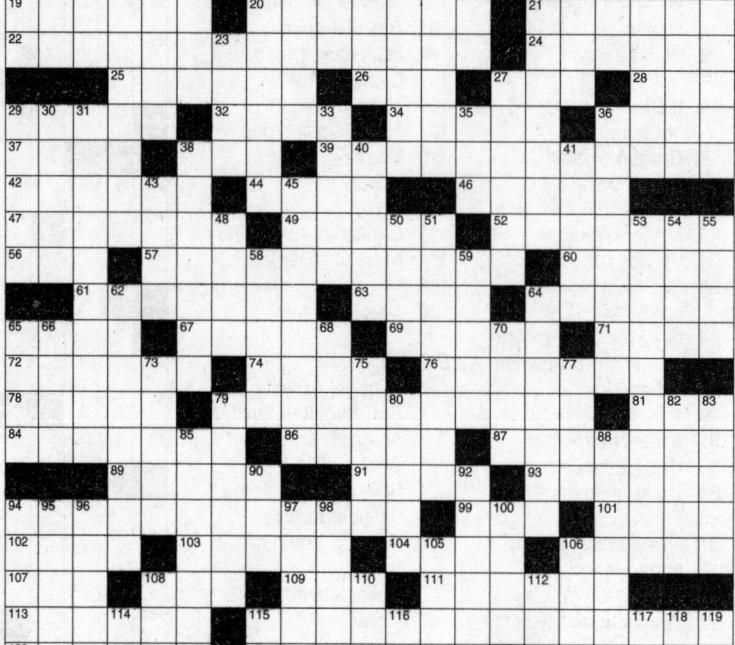

by Fred Piscop

ACROSS

1. It comes in a scoop
5. Small club, say
9. Underlying
14. Essential parts
19. Butcher's cut
20. Luxembourg town where George Patton is buried
21. Daughter of William the Conqueror
22. On ___ (reveling)
23. First name in mystery
24. Grand
25. Tree knots
26. ___ Domingo
27. Seat setting
28. 1997 Stanley Cup finals player
31. Unexplained skill
32. Harried
33. Scraps
34. "Little House on the Prairie" co-star Karen
35. Counts, e.g.
37. 20's–50's papal name
38. Transfer and messenger materials
39. Yoga practitioner
40. Filmmaker Gus Van ___
41. What to call a lady
42. Letter trio
45. F-4's
48. Former Toronto pitching ace
50. Noted name in civil rights
51. Dark times, briefly
52. Good cheer
53. Where Europe was divided
54. Sales worker
55. Country name, 1937–49
57. With 17-Down, a temporary urban home
58. Characters in "Julius Caesar" and "The Merchant of Venice"
60. Stadium sounds
62. Close one
66. Spa: Abbr.
67. Like a prize-winning witch's costume
69. Rightful
70. Financial page inits.
72. ___ kwon do
73. Reams
74. Zip
75. Former Eur. carrier
77. Like very few games
79. Aldrin's craft
80. Strength
83. Lao-___
84. Sugar ___
85. Somewhat
86. Kick
87. Handful, maybe
88. It may be laid on thick
89. Scythe handle
90. Ogle
94. Word with pepper or paper
95. Covering
96. Intl. group since 1948
99. Voltaire, e.g.
102. Color of some hummingbird throats
103. Noted Civil War biography
104. Big name now out
105. Start of a cheer
106. Site of a 70's revolution
107. "___ my case"
108. Violate a treaty, perhaps
109. Land of literature
110. One of the Ringling Brothers
111. They run in the blood
112. Pick up
113. Depilatory brand
114. Throw off

DOWN

1. ___ France
2. Charles and others
3. They have suns and red, white and blue fields
4. Small roll
5. Title site in a Sondheim musical
6. Tippy canoe area
7. Microphone inventor Berliner
8. Place to play b-ball
9. Charter Baseball Hall-of-Famer
10. "___ only"
11. They're bound to work
12. "___ Have to Do is Dream"
13. Pasta dishes
14. Turkish pooh-bahs
15. W.W. II Axis members: Abbr.
16. Prizes for Tommy Tune
17. See 57-Across
18. Outlet
29. Accomplishments
30. A pusher may push it
32. Give more medicine
36. ___'acte
37. Annoyance
38. Recherche
39. Try
40. Basic Halloween costume
41. Breakfast offering
42. Divisions politiques
43. King called "le Bel"
44. Be rewarded at work
45. Ring around the end of a post
46. 1996 biography "Citizen ___"
47. Spelling on TV
48. Med. nation
49. Hounds
56. Conditions
57. Any vessel
58. Coll. course
59. Ahas
61. Edge
63. Horace, for one
64. Sheepdog with fine matted hair
65. Wrong for the situation
68. Yacht's dir.
71. Catch slyly
74. Reply from Boris
75. Dins
76. This and that
78. "Step ___!"
80. Headdress, maybe
81. 1974 hit by Chicago
82. Unaware
84. Bric-a-___
87. ___ Reader's Encyclopedia (classic literary reference)
88. Their home is the Astrodome
89. Rock guitarist ___ Ray Vaughan
90. Shoot
91. "Voila!"
92. "I Love a Parade" composer
93. "Touched by an Angel" co-star
94. Where to see "The Last Supper"
95. Lit
97. Decrease
98. Bishops' group
100. Beat it
101. Broiler
102. Guadalquivir and others

by Robert H. Wolfe

ACROSS

1. Unrehearsed
8. Clear, in a way
13. Two-time U.S. Open champ
18. Showing again
20. Starting again
21. Jump for joy
22. MAC
24. Action star Jean-Claude Van ___
25. Tear down, in England
26. Taro root
27. Mom's specialty
28. Palette color
29. ___ Na Na
31. HARD DRIVE
35. White-tailed bird
36. Site of the Outback Bowl
38. One
39. One-___
41. Baseball's Moises
42. Theater group, for short
43. Lugubrious
46. Asian open sedan chair
49. Wipe the floor with
50. With 87-Down, early commercialists
51. "Happy" first name
53. Place for a cashier, maybe
54. Author Auletta
55. Coups de grace
56. BACKUP
58. Test killer
59. Vermeer contemporary
61. It means "place without water" in Mongolian
62. Wide shoe specification
63. Interviewed
64. CHIP
68. Some cuts
71. Anthem contraction
72. TV Maverick
73. Words on a quarter
76. Fire ___
77. MOUSE
79. Technique
80. A.C.C. team
82. Volcano near Catania
83. Warner on horseback
84. Press into service
85. "Are you ___ out?"
86. Discuss
88. Roman or Greek, e.g.
89. Not a picky specification
90. A year in the life of Attila

91. Tic-Tac rival
93. "The Last Supper," e.g.
96. "Somewhere in Time" actor
97. Har-___ (tennis surface)
99. WEB SITE
103. Legal point
104. Took on
106. Le Figaro article
107. Contender
108. Author Dinesen
110. Limber
111. NETWORK
116. Recruit's response
117. Luncheonette
118. Radiator features
119. Certain Art Deco works
120. Show off
121. Traveled by double-ripper

DOWN

1. Ball
2. Not agin
3. BIT
4. ___ run of bad luck
5. Bristle, botanically
6. Second-generation Japanese
7. Pol. designation for Gov. Jeanne Shaheen
8. Mark
9. Envelope abbr.
10. "The Young Man From Atlanta" playwright
11. Tracks
12. Nabber's cry
13. Noted ice cream maker
14. Conclusion of a term
15. HACKER
16. Bugs's foil
17. Grave
19. Not as accomplished
20. Shakespearean verb with thou
23. Soaking
29. Cheerless
30. Lunar phenomena
32. People of influence
33. Auto with Teletouch transmission
34. Eight is enough for this
37. Fix
40. Surrounded (by)
44. Executor, sometimes
45. Word in some magazine titles
47. ___ arch
48. Square

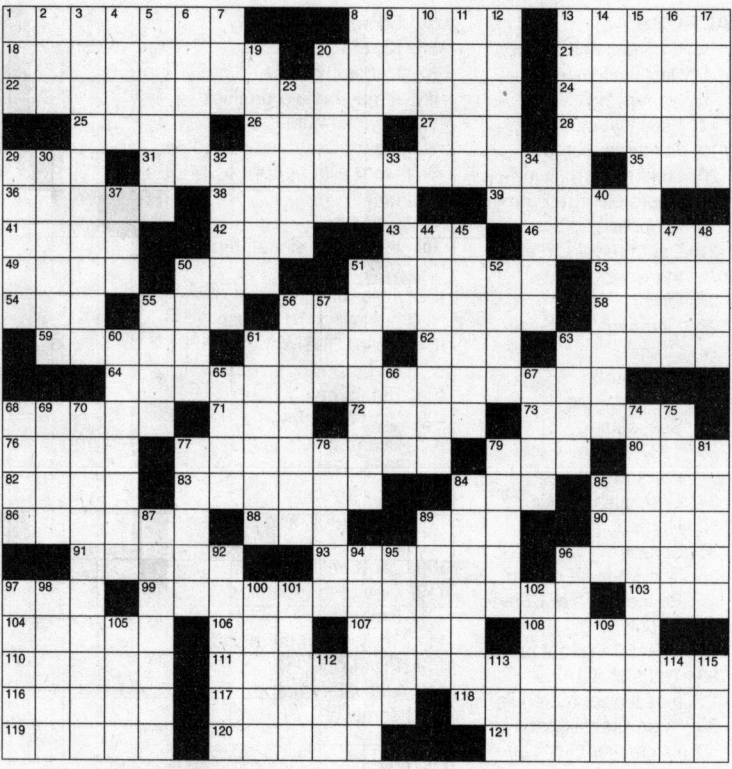

by David J. Kahn

50. Church receptacle
51. FLOPPY DISK
52. "Mermaids" actress
55. Florida vacation spot, with "the"
56. Blackmailer, e.g.
57. 1860's White House name
60. Get ready to fly
61. Shin armor
63. Scads
65. Bind, so to speak
66. Direct ending
67. Menace
68. Film director Nicolas
69. Doing
70. DIGITAL MONITOR
74. PRODIGY
75. Unfold
77. Soup for a cold
78. 40's–50's TV drama sponsor
79. "Do ___ like"
81. Early spring sign
84. Opens
85. Word with bag or cap
87. See 50-Across
89. Best seller "Angela's ___"
92. Speaks impertinently to
94. Fall back
95. Uplift

96. Kind of price
97. Macduff was one
98. Hardship
100. Bad luck, old-style
101. "Cool!"
102. Kind of hemp
105. Mario of the N.B.A.
109. Not much
112. Suffix with bow
113. Up, as a vote
114. Tpke.
115. Either of two books of the Apocrypha: Abbr.

ACROSS

1. Sleeping spots
7. Rats
12. Mark of official approval
18. White-knuckled
20. Pointless
21. Breathing aid
22. 1944 film
25. See 45-Down
26. With 60-Down, bid
27. Blasted a hole in
28. Boots
29. "The Road Runner" background sights
33. "___ mud in your eye!"
35. Pitcher Fernandez
37. Fan letdown
38. "The First Wives' Club" members
40. Latin clarification
42. Make an outstanding design?
45. 1965 film
51. Skirt
52. English churchyard features
53. Dealer in piece goods
54. Literally, "goddess"
55. They're toasted at luncheons
56. Shooting match
58. Domingo y lunes
62. Word of encouragement
63. City of northern Finland
64. Certain drop
65. Singer Jackson
67. 1986 or 1994 film
72. Habituates
73. "James and the Giant Peach" author
74. Dole's Senate successor
75. Intl. air hub
76. Big name in video games
77. Golden ___ (seniors)
79. Ball throwers
80. It played the Platters' platters
81. Hoglike animals
84. Auto with models 900 and 9000
85. Locale of ancient Ur
86. 1951 film
91. Unfair shake
92. Relaxation in 63-Across
93. Exciting experience, in slang
94. En-graved letters?
95. "That feels good!"
97. Was in knots
100. Recesses
103. If A = B and B = C, then A = C, e.g.
106. "Serpico" author Peter
108. Glass-___ Currency Act, 1913
110. Impolite reply
112. 1948 film
118. Helmsman
119. Like some walks
120. Successful person
121. Bootlicker
122. Theroux's "The Happy ___ of Oceania"
123. Bay, county or city of Ireland

DOWN

1. Super Bowl XIV participants
2. Late bedtime
3. Daisy variety
4. Request to a guest
5. Kenyan independence leader ___ Mboya
6. Look for damages
7. Former Chief Justice Harlan ___ Stone
8. Breaks
9. More than nod
10. Contentious political assembly
11. Antivenins
12. British F.B.I.
13. First name in folk
14. Third Chinese dynasty
15. Two-time president of Texas
16. Snob
17. Actress Harper and others
19. Computer game ___ City
21. Isao ___ of the P.G.A.
23. Slangy turndown
24. Coming up
30. Crayola color
31. Canceled
32. Questionnaire datum
34. Author LeShan
36. "Edward Scissorhands" star
39. Strait of Messina menace
41. Iron: Prefix
43. "The Simpsons" bartender
44. With 111-Down, vulture or hawk
45. With 25-Across, voiced an opinion
46. Satanic moniker
47. Southern swarmer

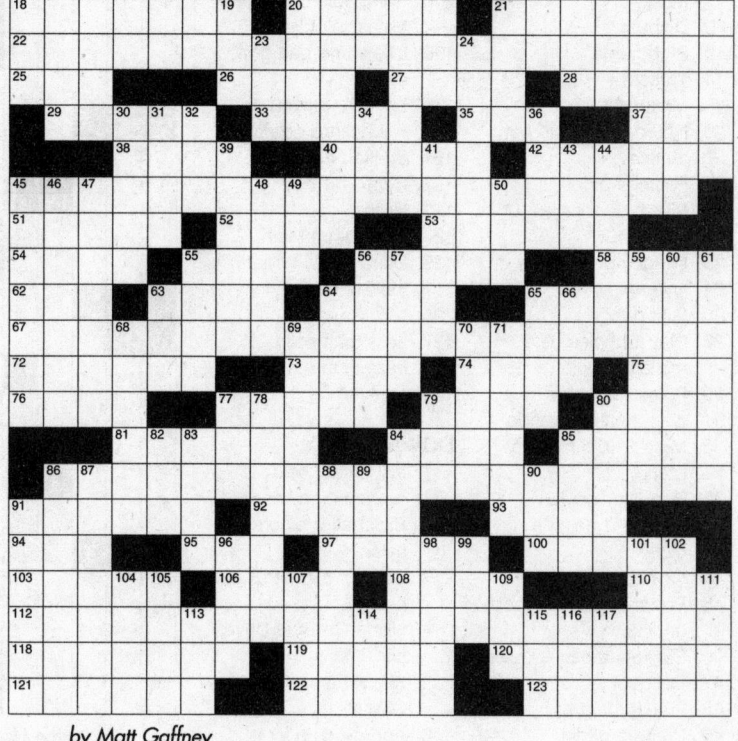

by Matt Gaffney

48. Lull
49. Sympathetic sounds
50. A Turner
55. Pays the price for
56. Namesakes of a son of Adam
57. Swiss theologian Barth
59. Site of a famous flag-raising
60. See 26-Across
61. Real-life sailor on whom Crusoe was based
63. Words of praise
64. Paul I, e.g.
65. Pot contents
66. 18, 19 and 20 of a series
68. Henry Clay, for one
69. West-central Texas city
70. Double fold
71. Challenger of the dragon Smaug
77. Boost
78. "The Pelican Brief" author
79. Case workers, for short
80. Arches
82. 90's film autobiography subtitled "My Story"
83. Bear of literature
84. Fish that sings when mating
85. Bit
86. Embodiment of impractical chivalry
87. They make calls from home
88. Some TV's
89. The Tar Heels: Abbr.
90. Mouths
91. Loud and rude
96. 1944 Bing Crosby hit
98. Cuddly film creatures of 1983
99. Opium ___
101. Jostle
102. Historic rival of Florence
104. City near Provo
105. Vidal's "___ Breckinridge"
107. Prefix with -vert
109. Riot-stopping grps.
111. See 44-Down
113. Mid.
114. Wheaton of "Stand By Me"
115. Seasonal drink
116. Actress Thurman
117. Country singer McDaniel

ACROSS

1. Must
6. Dispute
10. Strip name
14. Thrash
19. Make suit, as a suit
20. Noted Sao Paulo-born athlete
21. Pastoral pipe
22. "God ___ refuge . . .": Psalm 46
23. Wingding
24. Jive men
25. Golf pro?
27. Play 18 holes of miniature golf?
30. Place for a lace
31. It's a matter of pride
32. Mr. ___ (old mystery game)
33. Rodents, jocularly
35. Weekend golfer's club?
41. Golf course?
45. Pizzeria ___ (fast food chain)
46. Sunken treasure locale
47. Bouquet ___
48. French biography
49. Prepare garlic, perhaps
52. Victimizes
54. Stamps
56. Go quietly
57. Dino, to Fred and Wilma
58. Canaanite's deity
60. Bird holder
61. ___ del Corso, Rome
63. 1770 patriot Attucks
66. The stuff of folk tales
67. Divots, for instance?
72. "___ gut" (German praise)
74. Nonets
75. ___ Gabriel
76. Where the action is
78. Recognizes
79. Overseas relative
82. Word before and after "of the"
86. Fails to
88. Preppy, e.g.
91. Robert Devereux's earldom
92. Woodworker's tool
93. Lacking fresh air
95. Approaching
97. Kind of scores
98. Golfer's coverup?
100. Nostalgic for golf?
103. "Slithy" creatures
104. Fine, informally
105. Staff
106. "King Solomon's Mines" plot line
109. Like some bad golf shots?
116. L.P.G.A. player?
120. Haphazard collection
121. Spotted animal
122. Corn
123. Hollow
124. Ivy League team
125. Daughter of William the Conqueror
126. "Er . . . um . . ."
127. Less than solid
128. Laze in the tub
129. Introvert

DOWN

1. Instrument held between the knees
2. Baseball brothers' name
3. Copy of a photo, briefly
4. Like a Car and Driver car
5. Spanish essayist ___ y Gasset
6. Abbreviation for a pound
7. Oviform: egg:: pyriform: ___
8. Quarter of a quartet, maybe
9. Check the boundaries again
10. Teacher, frequently
11. Federal agcy., 1946–75
12. Lexicographer's conclusion
13. Pother
14. Many a Beijing commuter
15. Out
16. Music category
17. Couch potato's passion
18. At one time, at one time
26. ___ pain
28. Rogers and Clark
29. Basic ___
33. Wharton degree
34. Swimmer's stopper
35. Arithmetic homework
36. Condo
37. Have ___ of (not allow)
38. "Ed Wood" star, 1994
39. Not easy to find
40. "Oh, right!"

42. The Land of the Blessed
43. Exactitude
44. New Hampshire college town
47. Grind
50. Popular tourist attractions
51. "Essays of ___"
53. Parting words
55. Ancient money
59. Act like
62. Last word of Shelley's "Adonais"
63. Take it easy
64. Mail abbr.
65. Graduating class: Abbr.
67. Old joke
68. Waiting
69. Storm dir.
70. Whiteheads, e.g.
71. Rest
72. Time's 1977 Man of the Year
73. Slowly destroy
77. Rather and Jennings, e.g.
79. Sri Lankan exports
80. Cross inscription
81. Memo starter
83. Org.

84. Furniture wood
85. Office phone nos.
87. Mrs. Walton of "The Waltons"
89. Wedding
90. Work areas
94. Blvds.
96. Brute
99. Verse
100. By and large
101. Diet
102. Enthusiastic yes
106. Ventura County's ___ Valley
107. Composer Khachaturian
108. Pate base
110. It melts in your mouth
111. One of the Sinatras
112. Sign of impatience
113. Kind of mitt
114. Drop
115. Award of merit
117. First name in dictators
118. Meaning, for short
119. Brownie

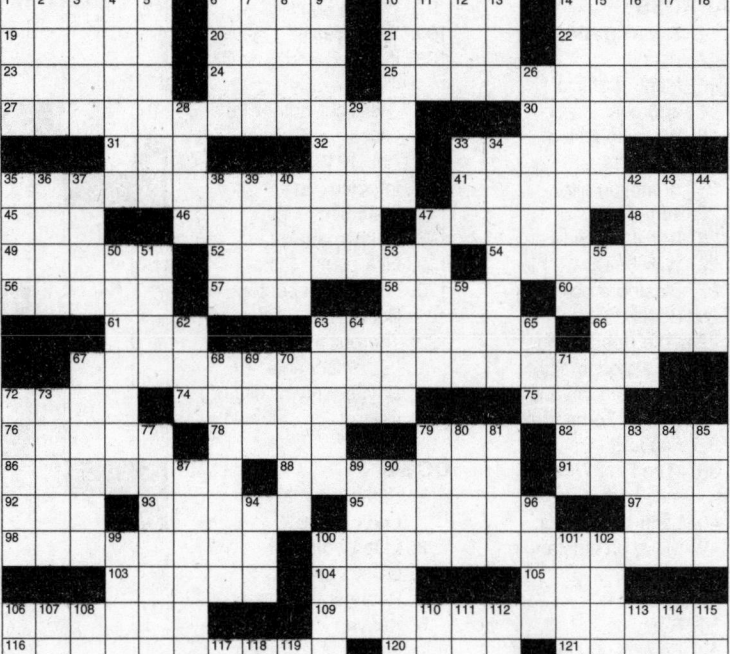

by Karen Hodge

ACROSS

1. Take for a spin?
7. Lincoln's Secretary of State
13. Pop follower
16. Curly conker
19. For him and her
20. Information like 15-Down
21. Aerialist's get up
23. Shoot-out?
25. Ran against
26. Journal conclusion
27. Everglades deposit
28. Bolts down
29. Without words
30. Mr. Hyde, for one
32. Cousin of a bandore
33. Drained
34. Stood by
36. Some of the best Impressionist art?
40. DH stat
43. Scots tongue
44. Riding for a fall
46. Construction piece
47. Go over
48. Jerk
50. Canute's foe
52. Mining waste
53. Year St. Eugene became Pope
54. Second-rate missile?
57. Harangue
58. Teacher's deg.
61. Exmoor exclamation
62. Surrey, e.g.
63. "Stand By Me" director
64. Scholarly
66. Formal accessories
67. Pelts
68. Dieter's temptation
69. Lose one's balance?
70. With the intent
71. Monogram of Macavity's creator
72. Swedish imports
73. When to go shopping?
75. "When You ___ Love" (1912 tune)
76. Olympus Mons's locale
77. "Phooey!"
78. Spot maker
83. Sounds of disapproval
84. Personal quirks
85. "Phooey!"
87. Naturalness
88. Comic Philips
89. Trip fare?
93. Cretaceous
95. Middle of a TV trio
97. Touched the tarmac
98. 1944 Preminger movie

99. Positions of authority
102. Obote's deposer
103. Post
104. 1959 Kingston Trio hit
107. Photography aids
108. Tennis player's bad end?
111. Cheese dish
112. C₄H₈, e.g.
113. Tickled pink
114. Affirmative on board
115. Connections
116. Heavy
117. It's good for what ails you

DOWN

1. Rustic
2. Responsibility
3. Catch of the day, perhaps
4. Digital communication?: Abbr.
5. Crow's home
6. Spreads out
7. Galley mark
8. Vocalized pauses
9. Get smart
10. Use a joystick
11. This person's revolting
12. Fancy fellows?
13. Gobs

14. Do the walls over
15. Officer Dibble's nemesis, in cartoons
16. Setting of a sci-fi slave story?
17. Pitcher Hershiser
18. Where debris gets caught
22. Peg away
24. Down
31. Bit of gossip
32. Senate Agriculture Committee head
34. Basketball Hall-of-Famer Unseld
35. Cycloid section
36. Pacer's burden
37. Four-minute men
38. Die down
39. Old bay, maybe
41. Fishermen, at times
42. Opposite
45. Simple organism
47. Money substitute
49. Two cents worth
51. Promotes
52. Slipped in sleet
53. Not coastal
55. People on line
56. Big piece
57. Sunfish
58. Put on a pedestal
59. Good form

60. "Backdraft" by the Bolshoi?
65. Shankar and others
66. Spread out
67. Exact moment
69. Directly
70. Cremona collectible
74. Fortuneteller's tool
76. Short time?
79. Honey
80. Sled dog
81. Set, as a price
82. Marshal at Waterloo
84. Receptive
86. Checkout device
89. "I, Claudius" star
90. Hot dish
91. Thunderhead's mother, in film
92. Sounded swinish
94. Giant get-together
96. Pluckable
98. Pastoral setting
99. Other, in the barrio
100. Row
101. Mach 1 fliers
102. Uzbekistan's ___ Sea
103. British gun
105. Headed for overtime
106. Capp of the comics
109. Pilot's heading
110. 1971 McCartney album

by Richard Silvestri

ACROSS

1. Stew
7. Like tea
13. These might play into the wrong hands
21. Two-time Wimbledon winner Gibson
22. It goes "pssst!"
24. Positively planning
25. Funnies romantic
27. ___ of habit
28. Penn name
29. Shade of purple
30. State of agitation
32. Award for Samuel Beckett
33. Features on some stationery
34. Peak of NE Greece
36. Former service site
38. Funnies flapper
43. Shadowy places
48. Exceeded
49. Like some vbs.
50. Capital of Togo
51. H.S. subject
52. Baseball's Duren and Sandberg
53. Talk of the town?
56. The Mustangs: Abbr.
57. Mountain transport
58. Word repeated in "Elegy in a Country Churchyard"
59. Funnies flier
62. In ___ (beset by difficulties)
63. Little one
64. Spoilers
65. Singer Billy Ray
66. W.W. II Japanese aircraft
67. "Far out!"
69. New York Met tenor Alfredo
70. Flavors
71. Another funnies flier
78. Tired of everything
81. "All ___" (1967 Temptations hit)
82. University officials
86. Emulate Romeo and Juliet
87. Like some computer encoding systems
88. They give you fits
92. Rock-and-Roll Hall of Fame architect
93. Took steps
94. Funnies victim
96. Strike out
97. Mucho
98. Balmoral, e.g.
99. Untrustworthy types
100. Like some keys
101. Midsummer ___ (June 23)
102. Tree protuberance
104. Part of a drying-out period, maybe
105. Loud voice from the "Iliad"
107. 1960's Maoists
110. Funnies fighter
113. ___ Lingus
114. Professor's prize
116. Ombrometers measure them
117. Carbon compound
120. Check, in a way
122. More or less, informally
123. "Things"
127. Vista
129. Big-eyed funnies character
133. Like a Carreras concert
134. Holes in the head
135. Coveted
136. In peace
137. Feeds a crowd
138. Actress Katharine et al.

DOWN

1. Aphorisms
2. Nobelist Wiesel
3. Pillar of heaven, to Pindar
4. Like a dime
5. Nickname in magazine publishing
6. Ring site
7. Spoiled bunch
8. Work on a tough stain, e.g.
9. 10th-century explorer
10. Got the gold
11. Northern Amer.
12. Cream serving
13. Big-eared funnies character
14. Memo starter
15. Chest protector
16. Raiding grp.
17. Lay to rest
18. "Three men in ___"
19. Actress Petty
20. Old-time dagger
23. Grazing sites
26. "The ___ Sanction" (1970's thriller)
31. Cookbook amt.
33. Johns
34. Dunderheads
35. Doughnutlike
37. French soul
38. Typos
39. Knock down
40. Natural
41. Writer Akins and others
42. Dirty fighter
44. Proper words
45. Like some Christians
46. Science fiction magazine since 1930
47. Way out
53. Corral
54. Penn., e.g.
55. Anatomical prefix
56. Chocolate ___
57. Start of a how-to title
59. Ring sport
60. Even
61. Swimming great Diana
62. People of the Sun
64. Based (in)
68. Pilfers
69. Pasted but good
72. Funnies gumshoe
73. Available
74. Become tiresome
75. Places for drawings?
76. Brag
77. "Show Boat" composer
78. Medicine man
79. Breakfast place
80. Like Seurat paintings
83. Inviting, as inspection
84. Do a double take
85. Club name since 1892
87. Come to mind
88. Cause of jungle fever
89. Lower
90. Ruffle
91. "___ Amigos" (1973 western)
95. "Star Wars" planet
96. Classic Ferrari
100. Where Alice worked
102. Letter before ar
103. Tell tales
105. Barbecue pieces
106. Colorful bird
108. In large supply
109. Date
110. Like some Western law
111. Investigator
112. Plague
115. Collars
117. Heroic poetry
118. Place to be picked up?
119. Lulu
121. Disney's "___ and the Detectives"
122. Writer's Market abbr.
123. Some execs
124. Sponsorship
125. Nautical heading
126. 1917 revolutionaries
128. Kurasawa film
130. Genetic stuff
131. Loony bird
132. One of the "virgins" of "Two Virgins"

by Randolph Ross

ACROSS

1. Where heads are put together
6. Skater Harding and others
12. "___ behold!"
17. Tulle's schools
19. Popeye's son
21. Founding editor of the O.E.D.
22. How jewelers get absolution?
24. Per
25. "Le Comte Ory" composer
26. Cut forage
27. Super Bowl XXIX winners, informally
28. Midwestern jewelry article?
33. Cut forests
36. Ends
37. Mechanical method
38. Character actress Tessie
41. Oscar-winning "Love Story" composer
42. More than big
44. Tamperer hamperer
48. Patron of jewelers?
52. Exudation
54. Fills the cracks
55. "Snow White" dwarf
57. Notorious Bugs
58. Subjects of planning
61. Actress of "Fame" fame
62. Pippi Longstocking creator Lindgren
63. Green
65. Where crazy jewels end up?
68. Powers that be
69. Section of a pas de deux
72. Diamond great
73. "Hansel and Gretel" role
76. Stale
77. Mustachioed detective
79. Run
82. Bend
84. Jewelry disaster?
87. Surprise cries
88. "Picnic" playwright's kin
90. ___ Canals
91. Second-oldest country in the Western Hemisphere
92. Adenauer, a k a Der ___
93. Position
96. Family man
97. Part of a jeweler's education, with "the"?
103. Sal and others
104. Kind of diagram
105. Comeback
110. Banderillero's target
111. Jeweler's ultimatum?
115. Late-night name
116. "The Mighty Ducks" star
117. Bring to a boil?
118. Angora, merino, etc.
119. "Springtime-fresh" smokes
120. Wind-up toys?

DOWN

1. Fourfront?
2. Dos cubed
3. Wing tips' tips
4. Country rocker Joe et al.
5. Triage team member
6. Literary inits.
7. Mine
8. Sparks on the screen
9. Aches
10. Breathing problem
11. Assail
12. Predatory
13. Rocket gasket
14. Spinning
15. Button material
16. Photography supplies
18. ___ depth finder
20. Shoot for, with "to"
21. Possible source of mermaid legends
23. Long
29. Math class, for short
30. Writer Dinesen
31. Diamond and others
32. Jersey girl?
33. "Chicago Hope" setting: Abbr.
34. Biblical barterer
35. Platinum item of jewelry?
39. Tolkien tree creatures
40. Plugging away
42. Wide expanse
43. Acting family of TV and film
44. Smudge
45. Help at the jeweler's?
46. Over
47. Imparts
49. Peachy-keen
50. O.T. book
51. Driving hazard
53. German river
56. Perry Como's "___ Loves Mambo"
59. Gateway Arch-itect, to friends
60. Floodgate
62. Song words before gal or shadow
63. Mariner's need
64. Fictional Italian town
66. Others: Sp.
67. Acad.
70. Hair applications
71. Ugandan with abandon
74. A lot
75. Turkish title
77. Prefix with dactyl
78. Preference
80. Grammy-winning Ford
81. Tennyson heroine
83. Swedish soprano Birgit
85. Land subjugated by 106-Down
86. "The Last Days of Pompeii" heroine
89. Washer setting
92. Honors
93. 100 agorot
94. Writer famous for locked-room mysteries
95. Roman title
97. "The Hobbit" hero Baggins
98. Opening
99. Do maintenance work on
100. Rubbish
101. Anatomical roofs
102. Grit
103. Word in Morris code?
106. Ahab's father
107. Showed disdain
108. Shoe-touting bulldog
109. Tours seasons
112. Figurative brink
113. Pro ___
114. Bar measures: Abbr.

by Cathy Millhauser

ACROSS

1. Like some appliances
5. Cremona name
10. Spite
16. Halloween get-up
19. Inveigh (against)
20. Actor Alain
21. 50's–70's Dodgers manager Walt
22. Slip
23. 1936 film
26. Where Maracana Stadium is
27. "La Navarraise" heroine
28. Wheezy chest sounds
29. Nursery rhyme character who "fell fast asleep"
31. Daiquiri flavor
33. ___ clock (self-winding timepiece)
34. Fiasco
35. Emergency supply
36. Of the upper hipbone
37. Started eating
38. City on the North Platte
40. "It Happened One Night" star
42. Printemps month
45. Prayer word
46. Waiting area for the Robert E. Lee
48. One of a Latin trio
49. Ursula Andress's birthplace
50. Get better, so to speak
52. "Meet John Doe" star
56. P. C. Wren's Beau
57. Rank below abbess
59. Kind of space
60. Name in Keats's "On First Looking Into Chapman's Homer"
61. 3–2, e.g.
62. Some poker payments
63. Faineance
64. Home for Heidi
66. Plow part
67. Abel, for one
70. Put an edge on
71. "You Can't Take it With You" star
73. 1958 Pulitzer author
74. British royal, informally
75. Former Eur. airline
76. Alternative to Corinthian
78. Inexperienced
79. Ref's decision
80. Born May 18, 1897, he directed all the films named in this puzzle
84. Wheedle
86. 60's series set in post-Civil War
88. Appropriate
89. Spread out
90. St. ___, first American links locale
92. Pakistan's chief river
93. Odalisques serve them
95. Contradicts
96. Respected one
97. Barbecue offering
98. One of Princess Yasmin's names
99. 1946 film
105. Private eye
106. Tennis doubles player
107. Utters
108. Like some votes
109. St. Agnes's ___ (January 20)
110. Salad start
111. Ballet ___
112. Like a 103-Down, maybe

DOWN

1. Usher's offering
2. "Wheels"
3. Served the purpose
4. Make a killing
5. Contribute during preparation
6. Famous party giver
7. Marine ___
8. Moreover
9. Physics topic
10. Griffith TV role
11. Fugard's "A Lesson From ___"
12. W.W. II transports: Abbr.
13. Four-time Japanese P.M.
14. Sounds from the lea
15. Make heroic
16. 1951 film
17. Posthumous Plath book
18. Fumble
24. Nail polish
25. Island next to Leyte
30. You can stand this!
31. Oregonian
32. 1944 film
33. Part of a tennis court
34. Except
35. Rascal
36. Their work goes down the tubes
37. Hall-of-___
39. Shopping street in London's West End
41. Shows surprise
43. Puccini's "Vissi d'___"
44. Don Juan's mother
47. Like Asia's reaches
49. Woman's wide lace collar
51. Pianist-actor Wilson
53. "Over There" composer
54. Louise de la Ramee's pen name
55. The Water Rat's friend
56. Sticky stuff
58. Reconsidered
60. Father
62. Typewriter sound
63. Snub, in a way
64. Chin
65. It means "Out of my way!"
66. Game of chance
67. Young hog
68. Dominions
69. Hero of 1898
71. Steinbeck family
72. Early weather satellite
75. Plymouth Colony leader
77. Character actor J. ___ Naish
80. Emancipation
81. Western backdrops
82. Caller on Miss Mullens, in Longfellow
83. Sack
85. Guy in the street
87. TV actress Meyers
90. Moderate
91. Beersheba's locale
92. Grant Wood, notably
93. Knife handles
94. Wrong
96. Title for Kiri Te Kanawa
97. Rap duo ___ Kross
100. Bernadette, e.g.: Abbr.
101. Six-foot runner?
102. George's brother
103. Certain letter
104. Nevada county seat

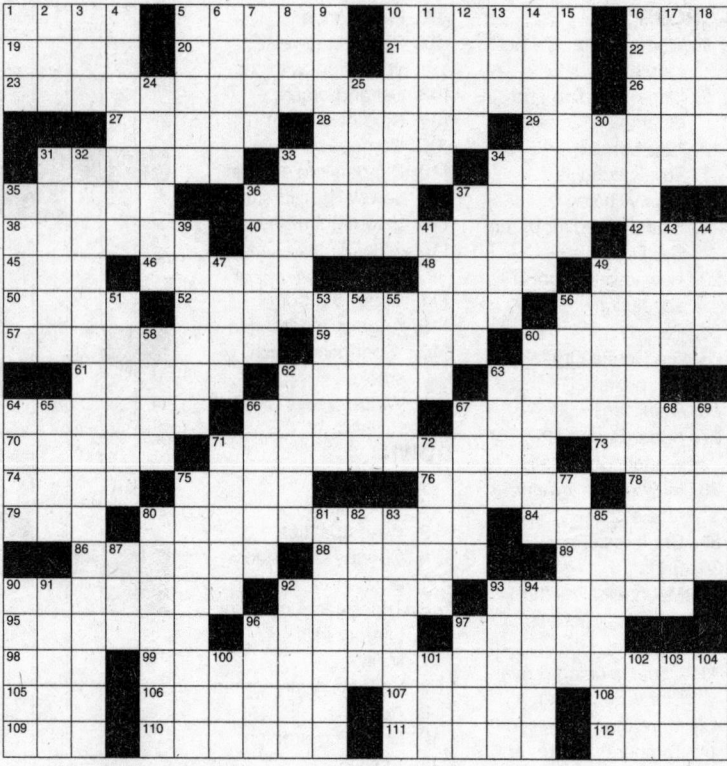

by Frances Hansen

ACROSS

1. Device
7. Crescent features
12. 1986 P.G.A. Championship winner
19. Tell el ___, Nile excavation site
20. Richards of "Jurassic Park"
22. Fair
23. 1980 Oscar winner
25. Makes available
26. Faint
27. Alvarado of "Little Women," 1994
29. Primatologists' subjects
30. More like Mrs. Rumpole of books and TV
33. Some are deciduous
34. London park name
36. Scarlett's mother
37. Three-time Pulitzer-winning playwright
41. Tiny one of fiction
44. Candy counter name
45. "___ go bragh"
46. Mark of uncertainty
48. Tombstone letters
49. Like a streaker
51. ___ Na Na of rock
54. St. Francis ___ (French prelate)
55. Prevarication
59. View from Chamonix
61. Indian prince
62. Perkins's killer role
63. ___ Detoo, "Star Wars" android
65. They blow with the wind
66. Boggy land
67. Form of ID
70. Tolkien forest giant
71. Insults
73. Where Diana Vreeland reigned
74. Milne creature
76. Like some stories
77. Special-care job at the cleaner's
79. Reads the riot act to
84. Accommodates
86. Dallas-to-San Antonio dir.
88. Contest in "Ivanhoe"
89. Bachelor's last words
90. One in an incubator
91. Uffizi attraction
93. Storage area
95. Fairy tale creature
96. Sailor's top
101. Bit of earthenware
102. Tax ___
104. Waterfall
105. Museum guides
107. 1960 #1 hit "___ Angel"
109. First name on "Saturday Night Live"
110. Deficiency
111. Mother-of-pearl source
114. It might make a report for a construction crew
120. Duped
121. More crushed
122. "South Pacific" nurse
123. Pedal parts
124. Yucky
125. Requiring a tie

DOWN

1. Hood's rod
2. Aramis, to Athos
3. Weir
4. Brings in
5. What vines do
6. 1600-foot-deep lake in the Western U.S.
7. "All the Way" lyricist Sammy
8. Neighbor of Arg.
9. Word to a boxer, maybe
10. Paisleys, e.g.
11. Rumbled, in a way
12. Hope-Crosby film destination
13. Prefix with duct or form
14. Gunn of "Treasure Island"
15. Escalator feature
16. Sulked
17. Flu feature
18. Cowboy affirmatives
21. Santa ___, California track
24. Time past
28. Whaler's org.
30. "The game ain't over till it's over" speaker
31. Kind of acid
32. Was quiescent
33. Red ___ (sushi order)
34. "___ Johnny!"
35. Senate sounds
38. Mocking
39. St. Paul's architect
40. Eliot hero
42. Personification of peace, in myth
43. Painted Desert features
47. New York's ___ Lakes
49. Lunch counter order
50. Passing remarks?
52. Mad one of fiction
53. Santo Domingo-born All-Star
56. First U.S. college to award degrees to women
57. Strikes out
58. Hindus' holy river
60. They may be felt on the head
64. Writer Santha Rama ___
65. Dramatist Lope de ___
66. Like Watergate-era Washington
68. Balder and Odin
69. Knicks great Monroe
71. Problem for a lawn mower
72. Classify
75. Sondheim's "___ While I'm Around"
77. Like some stoves
78. Worn
80. Cry of Caesar
81. Arrive at, as a solution
82. It's the law
83. Drawer oddments?
85. Word with park or plan
87. Big circus name
92. Bunk
93. Whistle-blower
94. Valley crosser
97. British mil. decoration
98. Feet containers
99. Maker of the Grand Canyon, in myth
100. Touch up
103. Shoreline feature
106. Upright
107. M. Hulot's creator
108. "My People" author
109. Eye
110. Not solid
112. Lunch time, maybe
113. Chill
115. Spots
116. Crossed
117. They, in Toulon
118. U.S.S.R., today
119. Essential

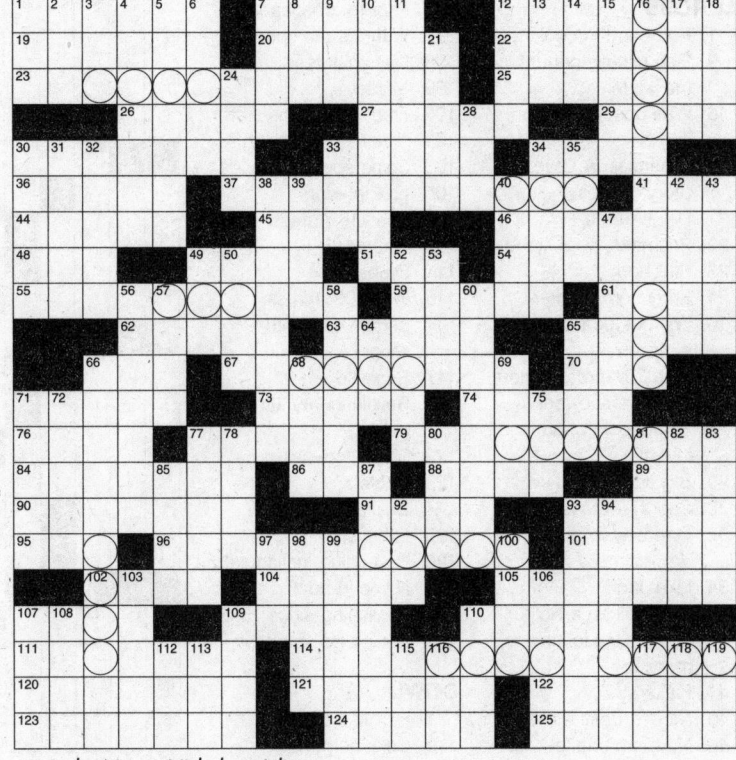

by Nancy Nicholson Joline

ACROSS

1. Pod used in cooking
9. Fish usually caught in the winter
13. Was upset and then some
20. "Enemies, A Love Story" actress
21. De ___ hotel
22. Prismatic, as a stone
23. Stubborn
24. Early comic writer
26. Without means of support?
27. With 30-Across, where to find a snowcap
28. Symphonic poem inventor
29. Big snowfall
30. See 27-Across
32. One way to get things down
34. Like Jack
36. They roll on a Rolls
38. Old White House moniker
41. Flake off
43. Nice 'n Easy maker
46. Northern capital
47. Friend for Rover or Fido
48. Mad as a hornet
49. Lose forward momentum
51. Jack Mercer supplied his voice
53. Kind of personality
55. With 63-Across, pretty good
58. "___ coffee?"
59. African ranger
63. See 55-Across
65. "___ It Kinda Fun" (1945 song)
66. PBS supplier
68. Most blue?
70. Gil Blas's creator
72. Emergency room cases, for short
73. "___ joy keep you" (start of a Sandburg poem)
75. See 81-Across
77. Arrive, but just barely
79. Kick up ___ (complain)
81. With 75-Across, unmentionables
82. Jack
85. Sharp-toothed creatures
87. Vegan morsels
93. Way up a hill
94. Prior to, poetically
95. Warm, so to speak
98. Livestock feed
99. Medley
100. French surname start
101. "I've heard enough!"
103. Some speech sounds
105. Lt.'s inferior
106. See 116-Across
109. Lecherlike
111. Drops
116. With 106-Across, phrase said with a sneer
117. Bonelike
120. Revolutionary turned politico
122. Thrust forward
123. Noble
124. Dusseldorf donkey
125. Exhaust
126. Is of value, colloquially
127. Name in book publishing since 1943
128. Having no spark left

DOWN

1. Hardly a fop
2. Colo. neighbor
3. See 67-Down
4. Saint in Brazil
5. Had to do with
6. Some bands
7. British isles
8. Tampa-to-Jacksonville dir.
9. Wounds with words
10. Wounds
11. Words to live by
12. Democrat's opponent?
13. Astaire and Rogers, e.g.
14. O.K.'d: Abbr.
15. Willy Wonka creator
16. Jai ___
17. Platy propellers
18. Don Juan's mother
19. Feeler
25. Onetime Olympics host
27. North of Virginia
30. Book after Amos: Abbr.
31. Pound sound
32. Call to attention
33. Hello, of sorts
35. Year in Edward the Confessor's reign
37. Fire damage
38. See 39-Down
39. With 38-Down, almost positive
40. Puts forth
42. Judge to be
44. King Harald's father
45. Actionable statements
50. Opening for a dermatologist
52. Linguist Mario
54. Classified information?
56. Mantel piece
57. Cousin of "Omigod!"
60. Parenthesis, essentially
61. Oner
62. Many years
63. NATO capital
64. Oriole's origin
66. Allegedly at fault
67. With 3-Down, features of some ads
69. F.C.C. concerns: Abbr.
71. Comics cry
74. Gray of "Gray's Manual of Botany"
76. Jocular suffix
78. "___ each life . . ."
80. In ___ (harmonious)
83. Puffed up
84. God offended by Daphnis
86. Clothes line
88. Take the grand prize
89. "The Bell Jar" writer
90. Uncomplicated
91. ___ Khan
92. Gets rid of, as stock
96. "Who'll volunteer?"
97. It's added to the bill
102. Colored
104. Parlor piece
107. Some Canadian fliers
108. Actor Conrad of old films
110. "If I ___ betting man . . ."
111. Halls of music
112. Skirt style
113. ___ uproar
114. Knight fight
115. Clockmaker Thomas
117. French department or river
118. Out of action
119. Proof of ownership
121. Shepherd's setting
122. Walker, briefly

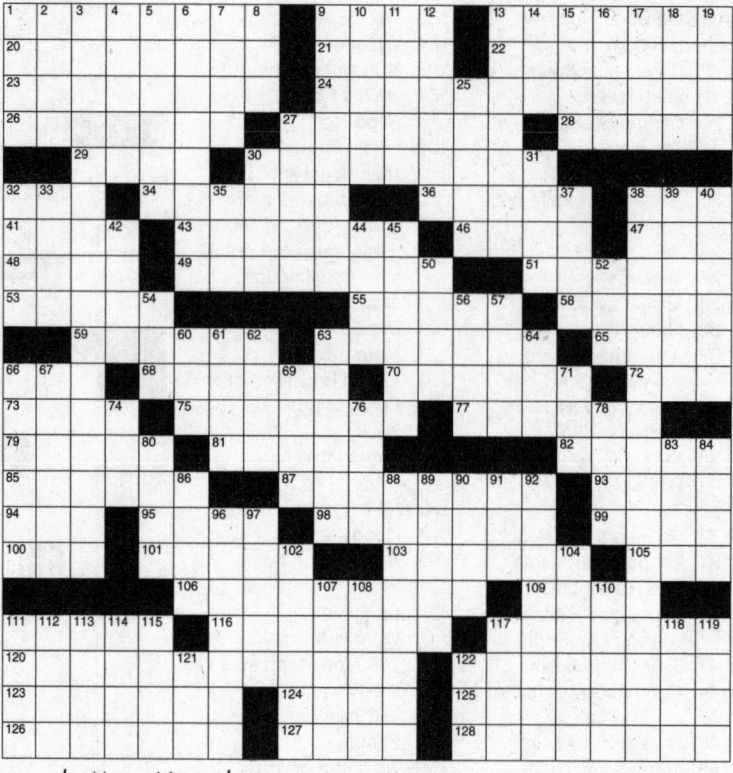

by Manny Nosowsky

ACROSS

1. Campus cafeteria arrangement
9. Soft drink brand
15. Spot, biblically
20. "The Witching Hour" author
21. Dorsal part of the midbrain
22. Merchant Nordstrom
23. Flip through a magazine?
25. "The Canterbury Tales" pilgrim
26. Returnee's "hello!"
27. Dickens boy
28. Mars's opposite
29. Bogies
30. Appearances
31. Powerful Washington lobby
34. "If ___ broke . . ."
35. Near, in Niedersachsen
36. Get a 3 on a 3, e.g.
37. Blackens
39. From the source
40. From the capital of Eritrea
43. Gets mentioned by a magazine?
45. Unvarnished
46. Says a myth that's amiss?
47. Prefix with god
48. Three-time Masters winner
51. Manx or Persian
52. Present
57. One magazine's view?
61. Neighbor of Mauritania
62. When repeated, comment to an apologizer
63. Stiller's comedy partner
64. Left-lane type
67. Movie segment
68. Like an oversized magazine?
70. City of Brittany
72. A.T.M. need
73. Guards
74. Coordinate in the game battleships
76. Back way
79. Spill, as blood
80. Force behind a magazine?
85. Herons' haunts
89. "Deal!"
90. X's on a map
91. U.S.S.R. successor
92. "Die Meistersinger" soprano
93. Bellyached
94. 20 Questions category
96. Prominent U.S. mayor
98. Held off
99. Old Pontiac
101. Shining example?
102. Fades (out)
103. Adler of Sherlock Holmes stories
104. Gracing a magazine's cover?
108. Around
109. "___ serious?"
110. Southeast Asian tongue
111. More fitting
112. Saddam Hussein, e.g.
113. They're useful in making contacts

DOWN

1. Cousin of the xylophone
2. Them
3. Orange County city
4. Inveigled
5. Big balls
6. "You come here often?" e.g.
7. Whiz
8. Counselor at Troy
9. Stands
10. "And I Love ___"
11. Show biz group
12. Dazes
13. Sandwich filler
14. Green card, informally
15. Certain neurotransmitter
16. Finely done
17. Some professors
18. Common alarm clock setting
19. Bridge support
24. Piece of disinformation
31. Larrup
32. Ninja's motion
33. As the crow cries
34. "___ not back in an hour . . ."
36. Foe of the Sioux
38. Red Sea nation
41. Amounts to carry
42. Files
43. Jazz group member
44. 51-Across, for one
46. Switzerland's ___ Leman
48. Poultry plant worker
49. Florida Congressman ___ Hastings

50. Operation locations, for short
51. Get tough
53. Brunch fare
54. Point of depression
55. G, F and C
56. St. Patrick's locale
57. Recent fighter
58. According to
59. Make it
60. Disgruntledness
64. Any car, affectionately
65. Goddess mentioned in "The Raven"
66. Computer key
68. "Peanuts" boy
69. "Lord's Prayer" pronoun
71. Like some sports contracts
72. Vim
75. One First Lady's maiden name
76. Piedmont wine city
77. Collateral, maybe
78. Gets the short end of the stick
80. Where Montego Bay is
81. Braggart's vacation?
82. 1955 Wimbledon and U.S. Open champ
83. Sinners do it
84. Fine porcelain

85. Fraction of an inch
86. Curtis and others
87. News locale of 5/28/53
88. Assents
91. "That's impossible!"
95. Bank worry
96. Resign, as an office
97. ". . . ___ cost to you!"
99. Sheepskin holder
100. Rubber roller
102. Brazilian national hero
105. Under: Prefix
106. Overly
107. Silver filling?

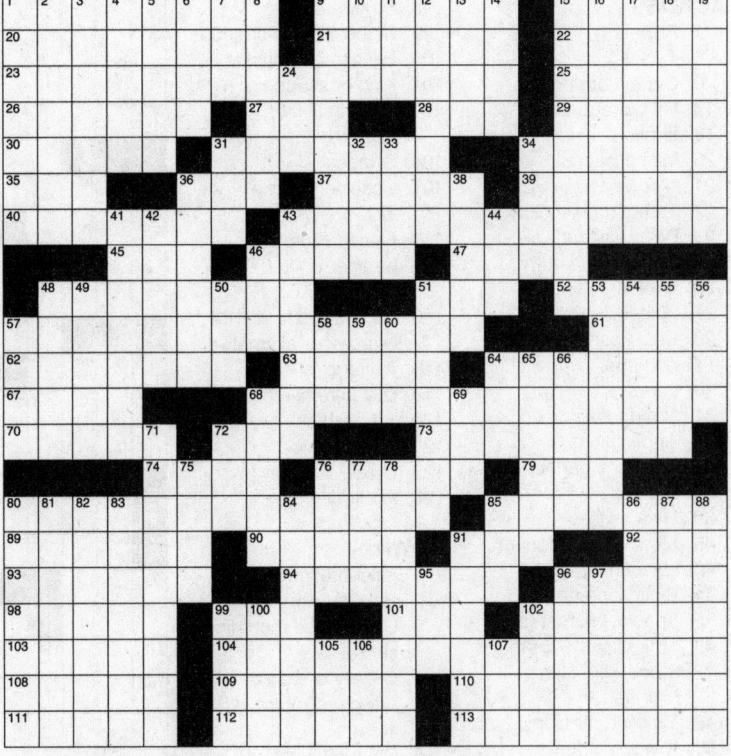

by Matt Gaffney

ACROSS

1. Appears
6. Tackle
9. Certain apartment
13. Fly out of a jungle
19. Implied
20. Like a bairn
21. "Are you ___ out?"
22. Terrigenous rocks
23. Ballet dancer's cookout?
26. Sublet
27. Polaris, in Paris
28. Bottle contents, perhaps
30. Lao-___
31. Not dorsal
34. Applications
35. Feather's partner
36. Rations
39. Litter's littlest
40. Most like sphagnum
43. Hit man
44. Biblical no-no
45. Special-interest grps.
48. "The Day the Earth Stood Still" star Michael
49. Timeline division
50. X years before Hastings
51. Wash. Sq. campus
52. Quiescent
53. Showman's good buys?
56. Certain skirts
58. Finds an easy chair
61. Where basketball and volleyball were first played
62. "Yer darn ___!"
64. Position
65. Envelope abbr.
68. Sir Charles's pet fish?
71. V-neck garment
72. Unruly hair
74. The "A" of A&M Records
75. Its pitch is high
77. Orange ___
78. Provokes
79. Silent screen star's drink makers?
84. Oxford's skyline
86. Mother of Zephyrus
88. "B.C." cartoonist
89. Stadium sound
90. Glycerol-based solvent
91. Congenial song ending
92. Apr. addressee
93. Single out for praise
94. Beat against
96. Wood stack
98. Spiked staffs
99. Camera type, for short
100. Big name in games
101. Kind of shopping
103. Exclamation of surprise
104. Scrapes
107. Codeine, for one
111. Tell
113. French sculptor's weather-front detectors?
116. It's a fault's fault
117. High water alternative
118. Average fellow?
119. Day to remember
120. "___ Fables"
121. Drifting
122. Ogle
123. Acclivity

DOWN

1. Palpebral swelling
2. How the Amazon flows
3. Effect in the recording studio
4. Cheevy of Edwin Arlington Robinson verse
5. Old rural sights
6. Tangoing number
7. Prepare to drag
8. Rubber stamp
9. Played fast and loose with the facts
10. As soon as
11. Boners
12. Braid, to Brigitte
13. Simpson's attorney?
14. Nickname for a big dog
15. Canal site
16. Quotation compiler's singer?
17. Feeling
18. Benzocaine, for one
24. This guy's a doll
25. "How Can We Be Lovers" singer
29. Favorite game of President Clinton
32. Nugatory
33. Tiff
36. Manner
37. Beige hue
38. Pair with a plow
41. Bumbling
42. Bound
44. Pants
46. Noted acting family's nobleman?
47. Fandango accompaniment
50. Thalberg's studio
52. Hokkaido native
54. Phonetic contractions
55. Pens and needles
57. Pronouncements
59. Desktop pub. items
60. Match maker?
63. Fish hawk
64. Warmongers rattle them
65. Cleo's undoing
66. Useful article
67. Hungarian composer's boat songs?
69. Chow
70. Senile ones
73. The "K" of RKO
76. Neighbor of Minn.
78. Transmitter
80. Queen's county
81. Language maven Partridge
82. Interest level
83. "___ a Woman" (Beatles tune)
85. Scottish playwright's haircutters?
87. Silver category
90. Like the gang, in song
91. Stores
93. Lawmaking locale
95. Hercule's creator
97. Behind the line of scrimmage
98. Power bikes
99. Rather, informally
102. Tabby's mate
104. On
105. Maiden loved by Hercules
106. Pueblo pot
108. Dynamic introduction
109. Junket
110. To be, to Brutus
112. "Yo te ___"
114. Tofu base
115. Have markers out

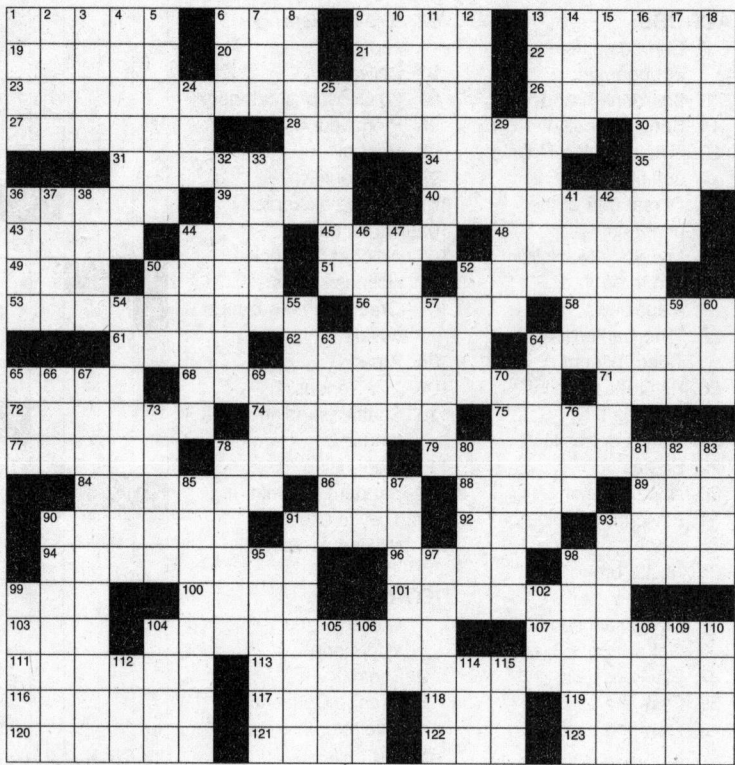

by Charles M. Deber

ACROSS

1. Workplace overseer, for short
5. Placido domicile
9. Diamond, e.g.
13. Beatles hit of 1965
17. Popular newspaper column
19. Alma mater visitor
20. ___ vincit amor
22. Water color
23. JUST LISTED!
26. Hardly Herculean
27. Have a yen (for)
28. Jennifer of "Flashdance"
29. Winkers and blinkers
31. Instrument for a merengue
34. Award for Eric Bogosian
35. Inclined
36. Address
37. OPEN FLOOR PLAN!
42. Miniature sci-fi vehicles
43. French possessive
45. Sea dog
46. Milo of "Barbarella"
47. Comic Philips
48. MANY UPGRADES!
54. Two in a million?
55. Unfortunate price to pay
57. Mideast pooh-bah
58. Blue book filler
59. "___ Tu" (1974 hit)
60. Two caliphs
61. Start to byte
62. Milanese monsieur
64. Stadium stats
65. NICE MOLDING!
69. Flat parts
70. They pay for quarters
72. Pervading tone
73. Bondman
74. 120-pound Australians
75. Actors McKellen and Holm
78. Art Deco designer
79. Lincoln's first Vice President
82. Chinese dynasty
83. COLONIAL CHARM!
86. That: Sp.
87. Terminator
89. Suffix with cash
90. ___-Cat
91. Hold up
92. FULL BASEMENT!
98. Rower, e.g.
100. Some earrings
101. Dagwood's sweetheart before Blondie

102. Sweetheart
103. Shot glass?
106. The "tacho" in tachometer
107. Short story-writer
108. Secular
109. PARKLIKE SETTING!
115. Actor Alan
116. Collar
117. Bath cooler
118. Saint Catherine's birthplace
119. It's out on a lime
120. Skates in water
121. Part of B.P.O.E.
122. Not own

DOWN

1. Mo. when oysters "R" in season
2. Cinema admonition
3. Laugh syllable
4. Fireplace receptacles
5. Clicker
6. Cold porter
7. Water-light phenomenon
8. Protozoan
9. Makes out in a lawsuit
10. Reformer Jessie
11. Genetic carrier, for short
12. Bread for tacos
13. Unfortunate
14. Latin counterpart of "iso-"
15. Bergman's "Casablanca" surname
16. Yields
18. Words of agreement
21. Shakespearean title start
24. Reveals, as a secret
25. Web user's woe
30. Matriculate
31. Sad sort
32. Subject for a wine connoisseur
33. GAS INCLUDED!
35. Glass cookware brand
38. Renowned "regretter"
39. INDOOR POOL!
40. Some fishermen
41. Out
44. Drum major's hat
48. Banging
49. Not orig.
50. Pop musician Lofgren
51. Dog show worker
52. Like the Sahara
53. Brit. record label
56. Diets
59. Huge, old-style

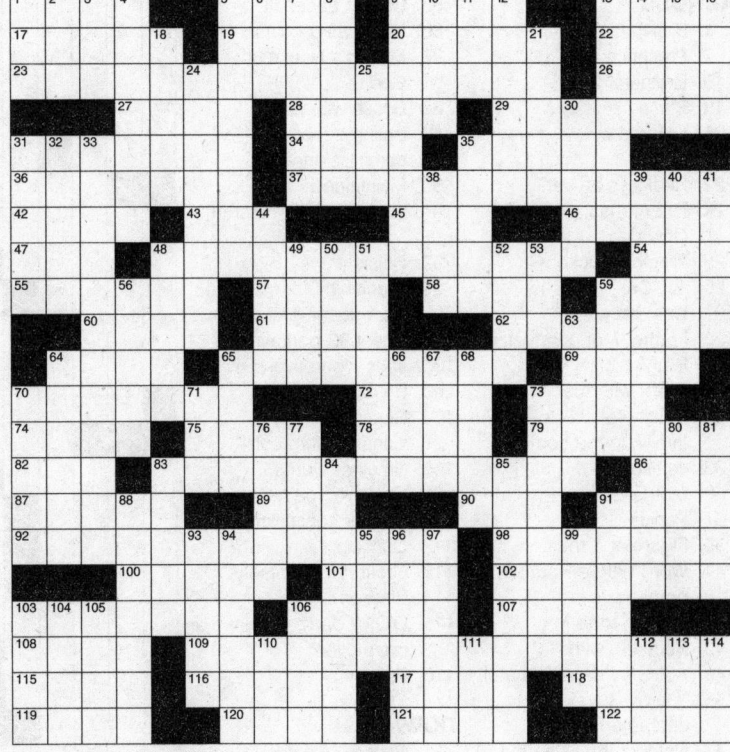

by Cathy Millhauser

63. Gather gradually
64. Oft-grated cheese
65. Hurdle for an atty.-to-be
66. ___ song
67. Campus military org.
68. "Awake and Sing!" playwright
70. Make new A-line lines
71. ___ Tin Tin
73. Oater action
76. Innocents
77. Ragout
80. First-generation Japanese
81. The Hunchback's "our"
83. Oldest known city in Belgium
84. Tramps
85. Hooks up or lays down, e.g.
88. Upright
91. Holy Roman Emperor, 840–55
93. Hindu ascetics
94. Kitchen drawer item
95. Waste allowance of old
96. Crop up
97. Kind of symmetry
99. Writers Henry and Philip

103. Put-down
104. ___ Bowl
105. Use a shuttle
106. Skier Chaffee
110. Domingo, for one
111. Hunky-dory
112. Pipe joint
113. It's accommodating
114. Put an end to something?

ACROSS

1. Brawl
7. Presence
15. Brothers' titles
19. Place
20. Cleared out, in a way
21. Matter
22. Reckless arrival?
24. ___ Arenas, port in 93-Down
25. Tropical cuckoo
26. ___-Cat
27. University V.I.P.
28. Former Met conductor Bruno
29. Prefix with fuel
30. Smallville, U.S.A., family, in the comics
33. Jettison
36. Mother ___
37. Punkie
39. Figure at a roast
41. Word before Rodham, perhaps
42. "___ no idea!"
43. Become, with "to"
45. Actress Peeples et al.
46. "Hardy Boys" character
47. Naldi of the "Ziegfeld Follies"
48. Extols
49. Real estate ad abbr.
50. Zero hour for Will Kane, in a film
51. Convened anew
52. Computer magazine
53. Biblical heirs, with "the"
54. "No food or drink" site, perhaps
56. "I knew it!"
57. Storyteller
58. Grating
59. Exchange figures
62. Philippine island
64. Early 20th-century French art style
66. Diamond status
68. Alley sounds
69. Warren Moon, once
70. A lot of time
72. Norwegian coin
73. Made a lot of noise
75. "A Hard Road to Glory" athlete-author
76. Baker
77. Loquacious
80. Anatomical passage
81. Rumple
82. Colgate rival
83. Hail ___
84. Bulbous flower, for short
85. Blue of baseball
86. Plans, as a course
87. Muslim's House of God
88. Boost, with "up"
89. Acting baseball commissioner Bud
90. Maintained
91. Jack London's "Martin ___"
92. Hoists
94. Glacial ice formation
96. ___ rigueur (literally)
99. Agent 99 portrayer
101. Jobs, figuratively
103. Be a pain
104. Reach capacity, slangily, with "out"
105. "In other words . . ."
106. Decisive spa service?
111. Spica's constellation
112. Consign
113. Groundhog, notably
114. Slacken
115. D'Oyly Carte production
116. Puts in

DOWN

1. Causes of some scratches
2. Cox of "St. Elsewhere"
3. Temporary talent scarcity?
4. Saturn, for one
5. Their motto is "North to the future"
6. "Keystone Kops" producer
7. Alphabetic sequence
8. Sailing pronoun
9. Inst.
10. Name of 11 ancient Egyptian rulers
11. Transfix
12. Actor Vincent of "Alive"
13. Writer Wolitzer
14. "Fables in Slang" author
15. Questionable ancestry?
16. 1961 Bobby Vee hit
17. Come before
18. Eyed
21. One doing a balancing job
23. Trick
28. Stimulate
31. Romantic bit of film making?
32. Brat's look
34. Atheist's E-mail, maybe?
35. She played Thelma in "Thelma & Louise"
38. Marcel Duchamp subject
40. Sky-___ (TV news aid)
43. Austrian composer Berg
44. Tumult
46. Some apartments
49. "___ dear . . ."
50. Polite refusal
51. They exist from hand-to-mouth
53. Beethoven's "___ Solemnis"
54. No longer dirt
55. River at Avignon
57. Humble
58. Schoolbag item
60. Vacuum malfunction result?
61. Least equivocal
63. Prehistoric medical supply?
65. Was shown
67. Revival gear
71. Words of understanding
74. American record-holder Steve Scott, e.g.
75. Quattros and others
76. Kind of testimony
77. Get some coffee, perhaps
78. Don's world
79. Identifying equipment
81. .001 inch
82. Arrives, officially
84. Baltimore suburb ___ Burnie
85. Trace
86. It may involve finger-pointing
89. Ancient Greek coin
93. Where the Bio-Bio flows
95. Margin
97. Bar selection
98. Managers, sometimes
100. Experimental rock pioneer
102. Jazz style
106. ___-Magnon
107. Part of a workout
108. Court figure: Abbr.
109. Rural sight
110. Lt. hopeful

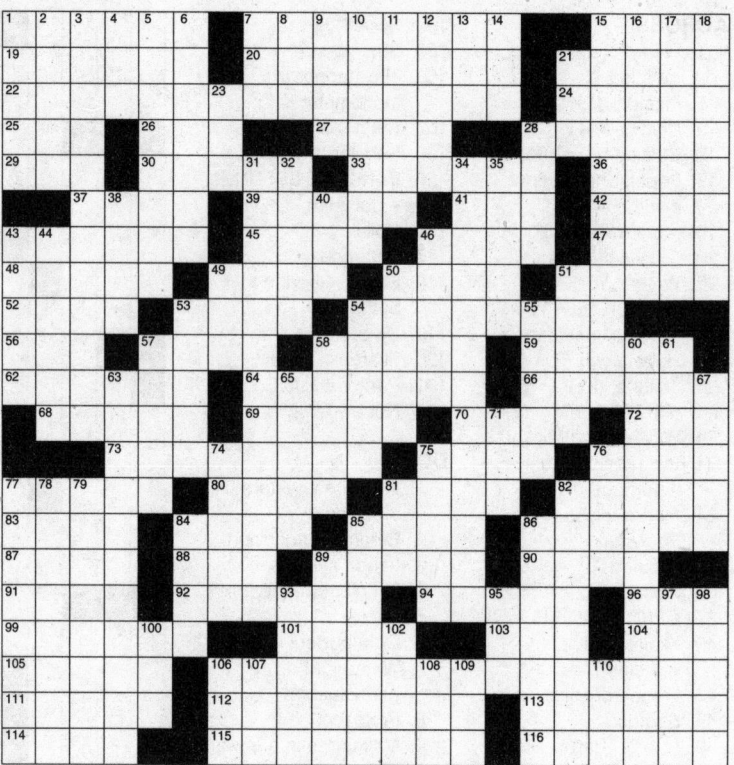

by Rich Norris

ACROSS

1. One may be checkered
5. Night light
9. April honoree
13. Fairy tale figures
17. Baseball's Tommie
18. Devour
20. ___ Fjord
21. Part of a monk's title
22. Beginning of a thought by the 72-Across 102-Across 80-Across
26. Bedtime genie
27. Stamp of approval?: Abbr.
28. Patsies
29. Sushi supplies
30. Scrooge's look
31. Quilters' klatch
32. "Dr. Zhivago" name
34. Type choices
35. Mocking
40. End of the thought
44. ___-de-sac
45. Seat of Garfield County, Okla.
46. Olympics jump
47. Not theirs
48. Canon competitor
49. P.M. hours, to a bard
50. 80-Across's field
54. Practices girth control
55. With grace
58. ___-class (airplane section)
59. Two Tudors
60. Regatta
61. Catch of the day, maybe
62. Somewhat, to Salieri
63. Part of a rainbow
66. Palestrina piece
67. Ale, e.g.
71. Tearjerkers, sometimes
72. Like 80-Across
74. Lacto-___-vegetarian
75. Beer variety
76. Lady Macbeth, for one
77. Crazy quilt
78. Corp. V.I.P.'s
79. "Peer Gynt" character
80. See 22-Across
85. E-mail
87. Bar, at the bar
88. Taxi door info
89. Personals, e.g.
90. Isle on which Apollo was born
91. Protection for some I.R.A.'s
93. Item on a list
97. Each
98. Vexes
102. What 80-Across became in 1996
106. Start of a Dickens title
107. River to the Fulda
108. Certain string ensemble
109. "Eugene Onegin" mezzo-soprano
110. Famous tiger
111. Root beer brand
112. Eliot character
113. Old news agency

DOWN

1. Dog's "dogs"
2. Mideast title
3. Spotted
4. Bid
5. Only U.N. member whose flag is not rectangular
6. Clears
7. Ear: Prefix
8. Mother Teresa, for one
9. Most enamored (of)
10. Pianist Levant
11. 1982 country hit "Same ___ Me"
12. Gobs
13. Peddled
14. ___ vera
15. "Dumb & Dumber" actress
16. Caesar and others
19. Jump (on)
21. Trickery
23. "That is . . ."
24. "___ directed"
25. Chutzpah
30. Not go directly
32. Eye makeup
33. Dress style
34. Godliness
35. Oporto's river
36. Young Fontaine role
37. With increased reserve
38. Cuckoo
39. Bar request
40. Trickle
41. Black, yellow and white
42. Jean-Claude Duvalier, e.g.
43. Big bar order
48. Second-fiddle
51. Prefix with linear
52. Plottage
53. Liking
54. Art style, familiarly
56. Rubbish
57. Yard sale staples
59. Associate
61. Roman sandal
62. Jewish holiday
63. Faith in Turkey
64. Static
65. Historical info
66. Gangster's gals
67. Nodule
68. Verb for thou
69. Call to mind
70. Santa ___, Calif.
72. Sit for a photo
73. Nincompoops
76. Erects, as a contraption
78. Loon
80. Duck walk
81. Sorry sorts
82. "It must have been ___ news day"
83. Visit
84. Bit of NASA equipment
86. With a level head
90. In a fog
91. Overexposed to the sun
92. T. S. Eliot book-essay
93. Premed class: Abbr.
94. Computer programming phrase
95. Israel's Abba
96. He once had stable work on TV
99. Wife in "Come Back, Little Sheba"
100. Brain scans, for short
101. Timetable listings: Abbr.
103. Rhoda's TV mom
104. Head, in slang
105. Liverpool-to-Newcastle dir.

by Elizabeth C. Gorski

ACROSS

1. Haughty refusal
6. Sternward
11. Surveyor's chart
15. Where scissors are made?
18. St. Theresa's birthplace
19. Edit, possibly
21. "An American in Paris" actress
23. ___ Orchestra (popular 30's band)
24. The Beatles' "I'm ___"
25. Case
26. Slangy refusal
27. Pop setting for a Mussorgsky work?
29. Spiral ___
32. Products of gamma rays
33. Thatching palm
34. Horus's father
35. Kind of fence
38. Comes down pretty hard
40. Pop Anthony Burgess novel?
43. Prefix with drama
44. Louis I, to Charlemagne
45. College building
46. "___ beam up" ("Star Trek" order)
48. Big dogs, for short
52. Glides
57. Pop title role in a 1993 film?
62. Epithet of Athena
63. Pitchers, in a way
64. Trifling
65. Disagreeable sorts, in slang
66. Actress Russo
67. Pop dance team, informally?
71. Hero sandwich
73. Joule fragments
74. Containing the 58th element
75. Alaska's first governor
77. Dig
78. 30's crooner Columbo
82. Pop western of 1960?
91. Garden section: Var.
92. Catacomb recess
93. Weed with purplish flowers: Var.
94. Old alms box
95. ___ de pont (bridgehead)
96. Phoenician, e.g.
97. Pop 50's-60's TV star?
105. A season: Abbr.
106. Medieval kingdom in western Europe
107. Morgan le Fay's brother
108. Sheepherders of the Southwest
110. Commences, as an adventure
111. Gaines rival
112. ___ Rogers St. Johns
113. Scale notes
114. Aid for Santa
115. "Oh boy!"
116. ___-tresses (orchid)

DOWN

1. Collar
2. Dissolve
3. Where charges may show up
4. Pop Peace Nobelist?
5. "Norma ___"
6. Kind of summit
7. Hungarian revolutionary Kun
8. M.P.'s prize
9. Fearless one
10. Vibrating effect
11. 1957 Nabokov novel
12. Scourge of serge
13. Amphora handle
14. "Jour de Fete" star
15. Kin of "Sacre bleu!"
16. Swallows
17. Shallow bay on England's east coast
20. Swedish money
22. "Cleopatra" extra
28. Jimmy Carter alma mater: Abbr.
29. Linguist Chomsky
30. Tavern need: Abbr.
31. Solicit
35. Obsession, e.g.
36. Soph. and others
37. Cricket wicket
38. Mideast inn
39. Math amts.
41. 1984–88 Olympic figure-skating gold medalist
42. "No kidding!"
47. Cyst
48. Truman's birthplace
49. Burlesque activity
50. Part of morning calisthenics
51. Holdup
53. Pop product at a barbershop?
54. "It was ___ joke!"
55. Protest in no uncertain terms
56. Ed.'s request
57. 1978 Irving character
58. Graphic beginning
59. Alphabet quartet
60. Tormented
61. Draws
65. Language authority Mario
67. Unclear
68. Fastballer known as "The Express"
69. Bills
70. Waves at, perhaps
72. One of a storied threesome
76. Goose egg
77. Lion's prey
79. Open, in a way
80. How a siren walks
81. He sank with the Scharnhorst
82. Park item
83. Insulin, e.g.
84. Ones providing arms
85. Thin, overseas
86. Picture, commercially
87. Cold pack?
88. Dance
89. Hero robot of the comics
90. Certain intersection
98. Rank below marquis
99. ___ prius (trial court)
100. Grandson of Adam
101. Tiny payment
102. Mississippi feeder
103. Bergman in "Casablanca"
104. Without ___ of hope
108. Old-time Yankee great Chase
109. Eur. airline

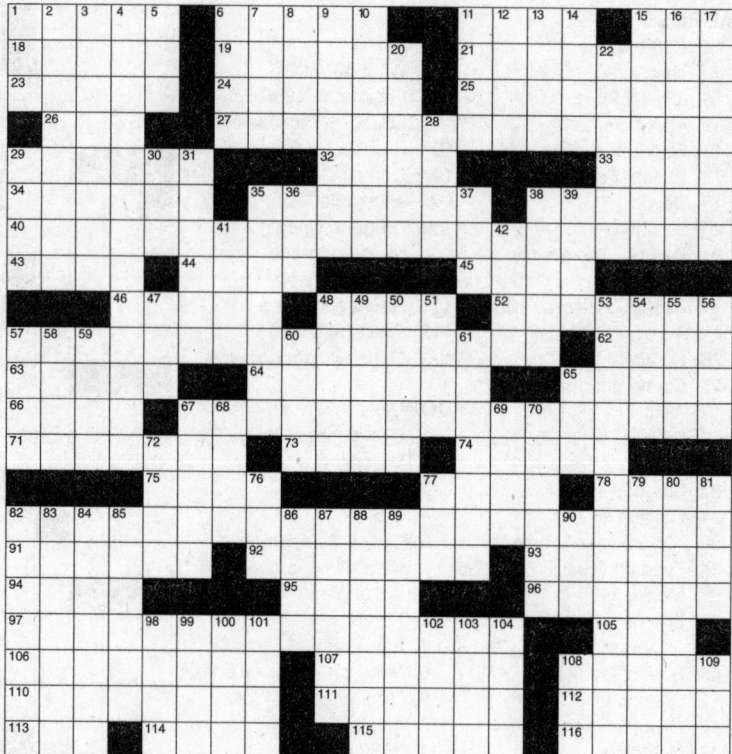

by Bryant White

ACROSS

1. Cruelty
7. Conspicuous success
12. Deliver
16. Metered rental
19. 1979 Vanessa Redgrave title role
20. "You ___ Beautiful"
21. Naturalness
22. Santa ___ winds
23. PLASTIC SURGEON
25. Trisyllabic cadences
27. Landon from Kansas
28. GARDENER
30. Play to ___ (deadlock)
31. Hamlin's "L.A. Law" co-star
32. A pop
33. "Yikes!"
34. Fraternity letters
35. Lively ones
36. Storm type
38. ___ Friday
39. Reddish brown
40. Curator's deg.
42. Really enjoys oneself
45. Female friend of Franco
46. Feel-good times
49. Cassio's adversary
50. Injured, in a way
51. Eye problem
52. Herb used in pickling
55. Order
57. Valueless item
58. Neighbor of Turk.
60. Take-home
61. Slave of Amneris
63. St. Louis pro
65. Old English letter
66. BASKETBALL REFEREE
70. Quite some time
71. Even
72. Royal Ascot time
73. House vote
74. Blue
75. Economic stat.
76. Org. involved in Bosnia
78. Small endocrine
82. Early German
84. Some schools, informally
86. Perceive
87. Baby oil brand
89. Interest
90. Kind of error
92. Crisis points?: Abbr.
93. Actress North
94. Tricked
95. Lime and others
98. Zestful
99. Short dog, for short
100. Joined
102. Force: Lat.
103. Ax
106. Old Norse collection
107. MARRIAGE COUNSELOR
110. ___ Piedras, P.R.
111. Enhearten
113. CATTLE BREEDER
115. Bird with a white tail
116. Expos V.I.P.
117. Copier, for short
118. Anna Pavlova, e.g.
119. 37-Down, in Oberhausen
120. Squeal
121. Fatty ___
122. Longed

by David J. Kahn

DOWN

1. Leaves for a restaurant?
2. Quick
3. Bats
4. Sheraton's parent
5. Boutique
6. "The ___ redden in the sun": Bryant
7. Take home
8. Bomb aftermaths
9. 1969 Paul Revere & the Raiders hit
10. Drenched
11. Rip, but not Van Winkle
12. Harbor sight
13. Certain hose
14. Bavarian river
15. Sparkle
16. FISHING BOAT CAPTAIN
17. 1493 Columbus landing site
18. Most abject
24. Ribald
26. More primitive
29. Kind of computer
35. TOY DESIGNER
36. With 96-Down, movie pioneer
37. N.F.C. ___
38. Dotty
39. Pasty
40. City near Hartford
41. BAIL BONDSMAN
43. Exposer
44. JUDGE
46. Judy Blume best seller
47. CHIROPRACTOR
48. Words with were or know
50. Joins
53. Amazon, e.g.
54. It fits in a lock
56. Florida game fish
59. Stepping places
62. Finis
64. Pipelines
67. Bro. or sist.
68. King, Pope or Emperor
69. Fleischer's Olive ___
77. March ender, maybe
79. Burning
80. Shortage
81. Comet competitor
83. Brings into play
85. Part of a bray
88. "Twelfth Night" countess
89. Overhangs
90. Become emotional
91. Arm-twisted
93. Family room feature
96. See 36-Down
97. Leftovers?
99. Word of mouth
100. ___ nerve
101. Wynonna's mother
103. 1993 Aerosmith hit
104. Seating request
105. Wrote down
107. Slipper without a back
108. West Point inits.
109. Ring results
112. Right to influence
114. Cambodia's ___ Nol

ACROSS

1. Sponge
6. Iconoclastic comedian
10. South Africa's first P.M.
15. Sap
20. Think a lot of
21. Ensemble part
22. Commandment subjects
23. Pineapple island
24. Sailor's cry
26. Forty?
28. Continue to the end
29. Stuffing seasoning
31. Clear
32. 1936 Loretta Young title role
33. Itches
34. Second person in the Bible
36. Approaching
38. First name in society
39. Take the wrong way?
40. 1932 skiing gold medalist Utterstrom
41. Agamemnon's sister-in-law
43. Dog on "Frasier"
46. Heiress, maybe
48. Subject of monthly reading
49. Indy racer Guthrie
52. Monitor
53. Flushing stadium
54. Onetime SAC chief and family
55. Downyflake rival
56. Put on a show
58. Virus type
60. Part of the Winnebago nation
61. Less ruddy
62. Dreary
65. New York nosh
67. Trembling
69. Hydrocarbon suffixes
70. Class division
73. Sandhurst send-offs
75. Earned a citation?
76. Barber of renown
77. Lure of New Orleans
79. Churchill Downs drink
81. "We Do Our Part" org.
84. Parsley's pungent relative
86. Where Mocha is
88. Hardly enthusiastic
89. Largest land carnivore
90. Concerns
93. Pluck
95. Dessert wine
97. Part of "the works"
98. Women's casual slacks
100. G.I.'s suppliers
102. Truth, to Trotsky
103. Senator succeeded by Cleland
104. Liturgy
105. 8-Down sound
108. Beauts
109. Sound of reproach
110. Deposit
112. Guard of myth
114. Kind of footing
115. Plug
116. Blue-green
117. Not yet scheduled
119. Head for the ranch?
121. "___ Playing Our Song" (1979 song)
123. Calyx components
124. Pizarro's capital
128. Home of the Riksdag
129. Stalemate
130. Joss
132. Odysseus, e.g.
134. Antique sale listing
137. Lure of New Orleans
139. Reference marks
140. A la King?
141. Individual share
142. Two-time U.S. Open winner
143. First name in cosmetics
144. Stumped
145. Dallas Cowboy's emblem
146. Assignation

DOWN

1. Like some skits
2. Allan-___
3. Single-named 60's singer
4. Zane and Lady Jane
5. A Saarinen
6. Reassure
7. Former org. of the Pacers and the Spurs
8. Guffaw
9. Mother of 41-Across
10. "Phooey!"
11. It circles Uranus
12. Morrison and others
13. Lunch counter request
14. Start of a Faulkner title
15. TV family name
16. "Dallas" co-star
17. Kind of suit
18. Heavenly gift
19. Site of a famous campanile
22. Boxcars
25. Western copper center
27. Feverish
30. Place to put a tiger?
35. ___ Bridge, St. Louis
37. La Mediterranee, e.g.
39. Parts of pedigrees
42. And the following: Lat.
43. Fine fur
44. Mickey
45. Spoils, with "on"
47. "What's with ___?"
48. CH4
49. Heebie-jeebies
50. The Rome of Hungary
51. Loyalist
52. Westernizer of Russia
54. Became unglued
55. Leaf gatherer
57. Make squiggles
59. Tunnel traveler
61. Founder of New York's Public Theater
63. Claustrophobe's nightmare, for short
64. Tense
66. Cartesian conclusion
68. Gone
71. Monk, maybe
72. Branched
74. Motor oil additives
77. Prized game fish
78. Reason for an R rating
80. Addams portrayer, in film
82. Produced no more
83. Some are restricted
85. It's a scorcher
87. Frostiness
89. Vegetarian's staple
90. Practice
91. ___ probandi
92. Beat it
94. Gave off, as vapor
96. Steelhead, e.g.
99. Fruit pastry
101. Slump
106. Philodendron, e.g.
107. Held on the stage
110. Early arrival
111. Blackmore heroine
112. "Blue River" actress, 1995
113. Collectible, maybe
114. Sauce made with pine nuts
115. Hawk
116. Crow's home
118. Deli necessity
119. Lab specimens
120. Principle
122. Like good computer screens, informally
124. Great Western Forum player
125. With aloof disdain
126. Prides of lions
127. Existential woe
128. Last item
131. Wood sorrels
133. Graft recipient
135. Bing Crosby's record label
136. Org. founded in 1970
138. Interim rulers

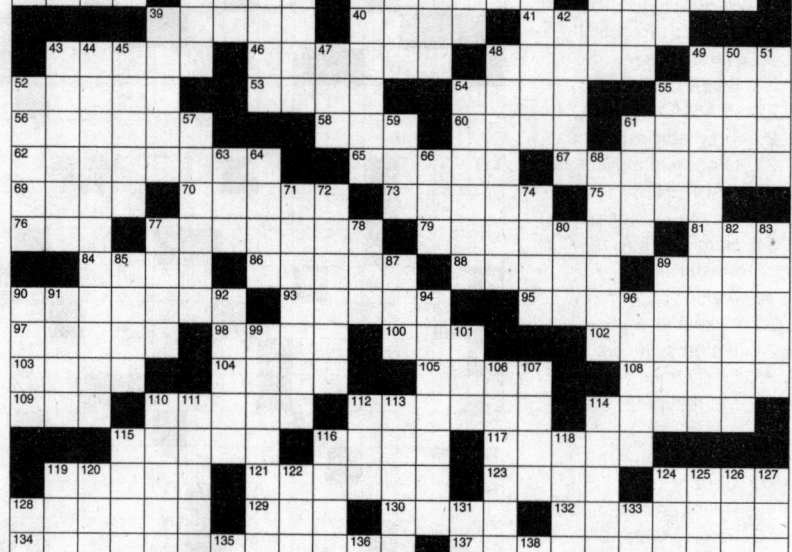

by June Boggs

ACROSS

1. Follow
8. Cases
15. Unmemorized words
20. Begin, e.g.
21. Less stirred
22. Winslow Homer's home
23. Be ecstatic
26. King of the 18th dynasty
27. Parodied, with "up"
28. Poetic contraction
29. Even though
30. Tiny bit
33. Go to bat for
35. Sault ___ Marie
36. Okla. football rival
37. "Women and Love" author
40. Neighbor of Minn.
41. Garish
42. Paris-to-Marseilles dir.
43. Song from the Beatles' "Sgt. Pepper's" album
48. Rocker Joan
49. Principle of philosophy
50. Old Alka-Seltzer mascot
51. Finder's cry
53. Slippery ___
54. Land of the Chosen people
55. "Diary of a Genius" author
57. Bring upon oneself
61. Stout relative
62. With 86-Down, partner of buts
63. Brunch beverage
65. ___ incognita
66. Musical measures
68. Some gold diggers
72. Watch word
73. Not chronic
75. Approached
76. Nice view
78. Fraternity letter
79. Pool contents?
80. "It's ___ . . . World"
81. Bow in the theater
83. Reunion group
84. B flat's equivalent
87. 1985 N.L. Cy Young Award winner
88. Ally of the U.S.
89. Raised
92. Slots
96. King's title: Abbr.
97. Melville foretopman
98. Singer Janis
99. Rockefeller Center muralist
100. Chemical suffix
101. Hosp. areas
102. Sandinista foe
105. Cruise in style
109. Reception helper
111. Performs, for King James
112. Downwind
115. Dauphin's father
116. 1970 Chicago hit
121. Waste maker
122. Partly coincide
123. Show up
124. Vocalist John
125. Hounds
126. American and Swiss

DOWN

1. Strains, in a way
2. Exhaust
3. Where Sir Arthur Evans excavated
4. Hall-of-Famer Hubbard
5. Slimmer swimmer
6. Some Ivy Leaguers
7. Water barrier
8. It's quarried in Vermont
9. Continuous sound
10. Celebrated
11. Galore
12. Like some floors
13. Presumptive person?
14. Full house indicator
15. Sashayed
16. Brush carelessly
17. Poet's prerogative
18. Most pitch-black
19. Optimal option
24. Objective
25. First published work by 39-Down
31. Antonio's role in "Evita"
32. Aguirre portrayer
34. Very alluring
35. Whisky drink
38. Alert
39. The Sage of Concord
41. Charpentier opera or its heroine
43. "Ben-Hur" author
44. Round trip of sorts
45. Spot
46. Humphrey's "High Sierra" co-star
47. Malefactor
48. Jamie Lee's mom
49. It's often in hot water
52. Supplies
55. Treated to supper
56. Surrounded by
58. Fair play
59. Ragamuffins
60. Yard chore
63. "___ Breckinridge"
64. Easily maneuverable military forces
67. Place
69. Raised
70. City with a Latin quarter
71. Composed
74. Drain trap shape, at times
77. Petered out
81. Provincetown catch
82. Tennis shot
85. Like some wages
86. See 62-Across
87. Chap
89. Get some air
90. Urban modernization
91. Chomolungma's more familiar name
93. "Do the Right Thing" extras
94. Way down?
95. Spanish diminutive suffix
97. Hammered
102. Recesses
103. Coarse files
104. Former ring king
106. Riding accessories
107. Representative location
108. Rollers?
110. Division word
111. Midler's "___ Las Vegas"
113. Big cheese
114. Use acid
117. A gift in O. Henry's "The Gift of the Magi"
118. Squeal
119. Good ___ boy
120. Old-style interjection

by Harvey Estes

ACROSS

1. Erect
6. "Casablanca" role
10. Legend, e.g.
15. Winston Churchill's "___ Country"
19. ___ vincit amor
20. Distress
21. Signals are used to switch them
22. Leader of philosophical skepticism
23. What a tipsy actor does?
26. Priests' vestments
27. Sets for med. dramas
28. "Video Companion" author
29. Pool
30. Reine's spouse
32. Year in Claudius's reign
33. Wallace of "E.T."
34. Like 20-Across, often
35. It may drip
36. Brought about
38. What a sweet tooth demands?
41. Words with hole or two
42. Commercial thoroughfare
45. "Gunsmoke" bartender
46. Mme., in Madrid
47. Nuts
48. "On Broadway" co-writer Cynthia
49. Social climber's goal
52. Loose overcoat
55. Like the Archbishop of York
57. Code word
59. Plenty
60. Yup's alternative
61. Aisle?
65. Some are holy
68. Access
70. Work done on the premises?
71. Broadway hit subtitled "A Musical Arabian Night"
72. Italian auto maker Bugatti
73. Had one's foot in the door?
76. Prefix with sphere
77. "thirty-something" actor
78. Social addition
79. Disney World transport
81. Wingdings
83. "Love Affair" star, 1994
86. Der ___ (Adenauer)
87. Striker's cry
89. "The Crying Game" star
91. Student datum
92. Fools
93. 200 milligrams
95. San Diego Zoo attraction?
100. Conquered quickly
102. Fleet fleet?
103. Deep blue
104. Nobelist Hammarskjold
107. Maria, for one
108. List ender
109. Constrain
110. Rush
111. Low note
112. Biting
114. Goings-on at the church fair?
118. "___ la Douce"
119. Had dinner delivered
120. Like one side of a ship
121. Laertes and Ophelia
122. They, in Trieste
123. Nashville ___ (60's pop group)
124. Trade center
125. Ano nuevo time

DOWN

1. Enticed, with "in"
2. Dean Martin topic
3. Taken
4. ___ Roger de Coverley (country dance)
5. Abated
6. Flip
7. Emulated Groucho Marx
8. Miro compatriot
9. Holly Hunter in "The Piano"
10. Recess
11. Plains family
12. Cycle starter
13. Payback
14. Luxury car ___ Martin
15. "Gotcha!"
16. Offerings at a downscale eatery?
17. Encompassing
18. Lives
24. They go to waist
25. Spurts of activity
31. Uganda's Amin
35. "___ was a cunning hunter": Genesis
37. Relaxes
38. Nursery rhyme girl
39. L.I. zone
40. Veridicality
42. Classic Gershwin song
43. Landlord's need
44. Government fashion decree?
49. Summer needs
50. Mai ___
51. Or's go-with
53. Stirring up
54. City WSW of Milano
56. European airline
57. Place for a throne
58. Problem for a suited-up diver?
62. "___, 'tis true I have gone here and there": Shak.
63. Preoccupied
64. Tour organizer, for short
66. Enumerate
67. Wraps
69. Sports car feature
73. Having learned a lesson
74. Japan's largest lake
75. Waiting period, seemingly
80. Tabula ___
82. Curtail
83. Persiflage
84. Easter features
85. ___-Freudian
87. F.D.R.'s Fala, e.g.
88. Blini accompaniments
90. Forbear
92. "The House of the Spirits" author
94. Sei halved
96. Kurds and Turks
97. Ice-T or Eazy-E
98. Sulking
99. Word for the diet-conscious
101. In a box, in a way
104. "Death, Be Not Proud" poet
105. Choler
106. Artist's plaster
110. Large hall
113. ___ kwon do
115. Small section of a dictionary
116. Country ___
117. Golfer Woosnam

by Nancy Nicholson Joline

ACROSS

1. Suffix with land or city
6. Hanged
14. Unhitched?
20. Clio contender
21. Attack
22. Like socks in a drawer
23. Noted guitarist
26. Some learning
27. Kernel
28. The Thames borders it
29. Word of reproach
30. Tiny type size
32. Numbskull
34. Bandleader Paul
38. Roman mine
39. Atom
40. Chiang ___-shek
43. Marcus and George
44. Four-time Indy winner
50. Noted youth grp.
51. ___ Mujeres, Mexico
52. Furtive sort
53. They don't want to fight
55. Should
57. Attached at the base, botanically
63. Druggie
64. Early empire builder
65. Recipe amt.
67. Italian city where Giotto painted
69. "Surprised by Joy" autobiographer
74. Metric weights
75. It may be high in the afternoon
76. Count (on)
77. Introductory material
78. Loss by decay
81. Wasn't sociable
83. Strike location
84. General announcement?
86. Stagger
88. Not the best service
89. "My Little Chickadee" star
96. Medieval weapon
97. Laugh syllable
98. Artillery shell component
99. A substantial amount of Louisiana
100. Goes around
102. Tricked
103. Rolls
107. Vitamin C source
108. Refuse
112. No longer stuck on
114. Understanding words
115. Three-time N.F.L. M.V.P.
121. Understanding
122. Computer offering
123. Not be fast
124. They're out in a game
125. Prepares for a rough ride
126. Cardinal points?

DOWN

1. Buffalo wing?
2. Modern information medium
3. Tiny amount
4. Where gelato was invented
5. Like a member of the U.S.N.
6. Sober-minded
7. Comaneci achievements
8. Kind of comb
9. City area
10. "Frasier" character
11. Lions' prey
12. Indians with a sun dance
13. It may be struck
14. Eponymous Belgian town
15. Actor Holm
16. An end to peace
17. 1994 A.L. home run king
18. Soft
19. Garden tools
24. Homes with domes
25. Cold war threat
31. Elvis Costello's "My ___ True"
33. Grave marker
35. Silver treat
36. First name in 1936 politics
37. Early 80's sitcom
39. "Othello" courtesan
40. Name in 1993 news
41. Bill the Cat pronouncement, in the funnies
42. Alibi ___ (liars, of a sort)
44. Shanghai
45. G.I. entertainment
46. Greek cafe
47. Shrovetide dish
48. Legal grounds for action
49. Poetic preposition
54. Gray and Moran
56. Argot
58. Getting around well
59. "My gal"
60. The best
61. Kind of estimate
62. Got a flat boot?
64. "___ deal!"
66. Some government appropriations
68. The plus column
70. Pin down
71. Kind of oil
72. Ogle
73. "The Courtship of Miles Standish" character
79. Travel (about)
80. Drop acid?
82. Preceded
83. Travels back and forth
85. Abbr. in a help wanted ad
87. Application
89. Lynette ___, first female Harlem Globetrotter
90. Took in, maybe
91. Actor Stephen
92. Congratulations, of a sort
93. Palindromic English river
94. Chants
95. Authorize
96. Beseech
101. ___-Anne-des-Plaines, Quebec
102. Lake Volta's country
103. Ho-hum TV fare
104. Adlai's '56 running mate
105. Like some apartments
106. Most likely winners
109. Butts
110. Rat-___
111. Pokey
113. Start of a classic Latin quote
116. Broodmare
117. Had fare
118. Med. specialty
119. Tiny terror
120. ___ Saud (former Mideast leader)

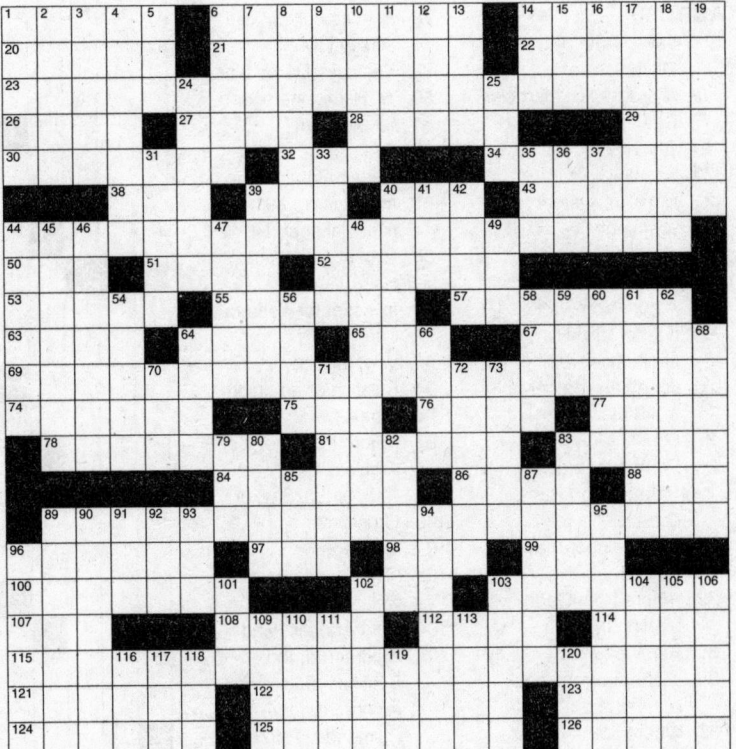

by Matt Gaffney

ACROSS

1. Lake name of two Olympics
7. "Pardon me, Marcello"
12. Bay
19. The dawn
20. Seesaw
21. Nervous system stimulant
23. Amore from Judy Garland, 1948
25. Amore from Jan Garber and His Orchestra, 1926
26. Jonathan's father, in the Bible
27. Sour
28. Romance, e.g.
29. "Too-Ra-Loo-Ra-Loo-___"
30. When dinner may be served
32. Amore from Dean Martin, 1955
35. Reply courtesy, briefly
36. ___ embarrassment (be mortified)
37. Where black is white, for short?
38. Muse for Milton
39. All alternative
40. It turns out Its.
41. Footnote abbr.
43. Griffith and Gibb
44. Rundown
45. It may be picked up in bars
46. Ruth's "Laugh-In" foil
47. "Bye!"
48. Star of 50's TV's "Private Secretary"
51. Amore from Andy Williams, 1965
54. "I do," e.g.
57. Express
58. Like an oxeye window
59. Example of Peke speak?
60. Metro entrance
62. Above, in Berlin
63. Subway passages
65. "Good ___!"
67. Lick ___ promise
68. Music for a baseball team?
70. Ore delivery, maybe
71. Vacation spot
72. Striking likeness
74. "The Spanish Tragedy" dramatist
75. Amore from Anita Baker, 1986
78. Actress called "The Jersey Lily"
79. Kentucky Derby times
80. W. Hemisphere land
81. Strike down
82. Aim
85. Certain South Asian
87. Initials in a 1991 financial scandal
88. Org. at Constitution Hall
91. Investigator's sources
92. Purplish
93. Verb for you
94. Relative of an onion
96. About
97. Amore from the Archies, 1969
99. Rapper ___ Shakur
100. Grunts
101. Simoleons
102. "The Age of Reason" writer
104. Cold Adriatic wind
105. Amore from the Beatles, 1968
107. Amore from the Diamonds, 1957
110. Parent's armful
111. Singer Waters
112. For one
113. The sun and moon
114. Sillies
115. Meals in a hall

DOWN

1. Thrusting fencing maneuver
2. Kook
3. Provokes
4. "Gangsta's Paradise" singer
5. Provoke
6. During office hours
7. Needed smelling salts
8. Encrustation
9. Part of the soft palate
10. Pastor's sch.
11. Major C.P.A. employer
12. Strokes for Solti
13. It's inclined to provide shelter
14. Dark area
15. Ravel's "Ma mere ___" ("Mother Goose")
16. Franklin's 1936 foe
17. Like a beauty queen
18. Contained
22. Where to catch a moray
24. View
28. Gloomy
31. Scully and Mulder's obsession
33. Telepathic
34. Court demand
35. "Away!"
39. Common on-line activities
42. Military wear
43. Precincts
44. ___ Winston Churchill
45. It's just south of Des Plaines
46. Coming
47. ___ noir
48. Spirit
49. Cry of delight
50. That's the way it goes
52. "Bury Me in a Free Land" poet
53. Presque Isle locale
54. French score
55. On in years
56. Pooped
58. Relative of the English horn
61. Code letter after Sierra
64. Uintah Reservation Indians
65. Auctioneer's aid
66. Coin worth about 19 cents
69. Autocrats
71. Sunday reading
73. Charge
76. Fourth of July?
77. Truman's Missouri birthplace
78. Swiss tourist center
79. Lapel item, sometimes
82. Land
83. Kind of tour
84. Garden root
85. Fierce woman
86. Wings
87. Words read with feeling?
88. Some antennas
89. Cupidity
90. Fixes, as furniture
92. 1937 DuPont invention
93. Marbles
95. Classic cause of a fall
97. ___ Tuesday
98. ___ creek
101. 1977 Cy Young winner from the Yankees
103. Dutch treat
106. Letter from St. Paul: Abbr.
107. Standing prerequisite
108. Suffix with Samson
109. Do a Little bit

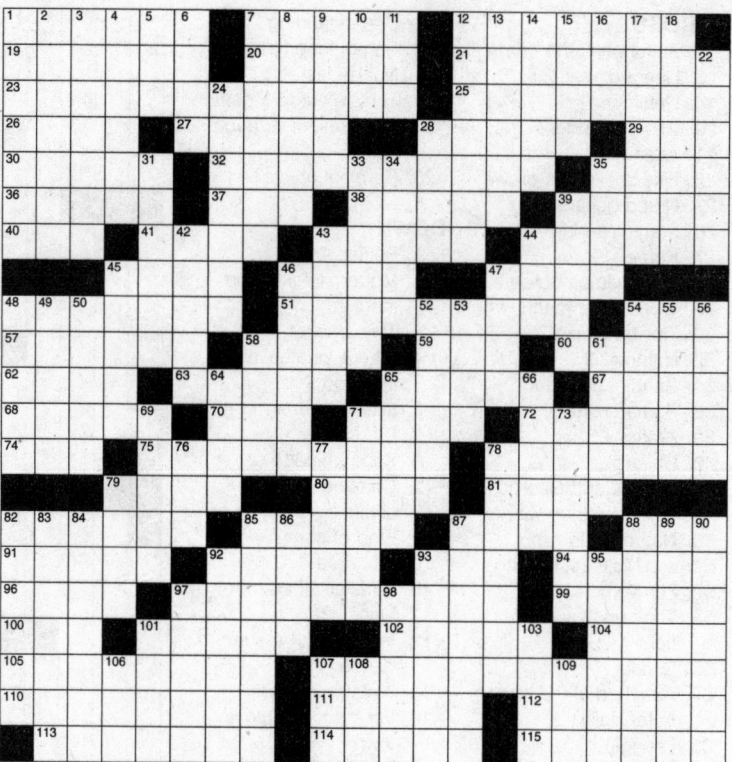

by Dean Niles

ACROSS

1. Spanish poet Federico Garcia ___
6. Jacuzzi user
12. Look everywhere in
17. Indisposed
19. Make it big
20. Popular porters
22. Welty's "One Writer's Beginnings," e.g.
23. Stretched one's neck
24. Mexican state or a product that originated there
25. Whole-grain food
27. Specialist in a duck blind
29. "___ Where My Money Goes" (early 1900's song)
30. Chuck alternative
32. The thing is?
33. G.P. grp.
34. Highest honor
35. Colorful clumps of grass
40. Trimming tool
42. Platitudes
44. Army leader?
45. Province in Italy's Northern League
46. Blue Eagle initials
47. Adult
48. Locate
49. Conviction
52. Kingdom of Minos
53. Lies limply
56. Drink for Drac
57. Nurse
58. Street of mystery
60. Go cold turkey
62. Columbia athlete
63. Fill the hold
64. Flying jib, e.g.
65. Pull strings?
66. Get fresh with
67. More than miffed
69. Toiling
70. Christmas ___
71. Advanced course
73. Whiz
75. "___ a Moon Out Tonight" (1961 hit)
76. "___ Three Lives"
77. Missouri, e.g.
78. East end
79. Jelly ingredient
82. Secretary, at times
83. Crime statistics
87. Western airline name
88. Emma Lazarus
90. Muscle-building unit
92. Put up
93. To be, to Benita
94. Word in a promise
95. Hot issue?
96. Area near the crown
102. One who teases a nobleman
105. Squeaking
106. "Stalag 17" star
108. Inherent character
109. They're dispensed in litres
110. Ancient
111. School of painting
112. Marsh plant
113. Break
114. Cobbler's stock

DOWN

1. Kind of particle
2. "Saw the air too much with your hand," in Shakespeare's words
3. Like Uranus vis-a-vis Jupiter
4. A cock does it
5. Speller's phrase
6. God of wine
7. Unpaid debt
8. Sing-a-long syllable
9. Posterior
10. In any way
11. The scarlet letter
12. Bygone kings
13. Philippine island
14. City WNW of Mascara
15. Overshadow
16. Flower clusters
18. Not be perfect
20. Changes back
21. Guy Lombardo hit of 1937 or Jimmy Dorsey hit of 1957
26. Silo occupant
28. Franklin's flier
31. Grabbed
35. Hung out to dry
36. Bomber initials
37. Bring (out)
38. Single
39. Cod piece?
40. "___ Peach" (Allman Brothers album)
41. Got lucky at poker
43. General Grant's horseshoer
45. Like the flu
47. Hail
48. Alley challenge
49. Beer holders: Abbr.
50. Walt Disney's middle name
51. Unbound
52. Chest material
53. Done in
54. Like some excursions
55. Go furtively
57. Unit of capacitance
59. Distillation product
61. Chuck
63. Closet contents
68. "South Pacific" hero
69. Fends off
70. Make confetti
72. Trojan princess of a Mozart opera
74. Maintain
75. Alas., once
77. Costa, anatomically
79. Get ready to leave
80. Renowned Manhattan eatery
81. Suggest
82. Concern
83. Overflows
84. Captain, e.g.
85. Slander
86. A fistful
88. Home of England's Opera North
89. Off-peak calls?
91. ( ), informally
93. Marker
95. Loose-limbed
97. Prepare for action
98. Toil wearily
99. "___ Lap" (1983 film)
100. Balcony section
101. Engr.'s specialty
103. Bambi's aunt
104. Devil-may-care
107. Bambi's aunt

by Richard Silvestri

ACROSS

1. Alternative to orchestra
5. Indispensables
10. Puts in stitches
14. 1965 jazz album
18. Where Innsbruck is
19. Bubbling
20. One of the Baldwin brothers
21. Thwart
22. City NNE of Tampa
23. Jefferson's portrayer in a 1995 film
24. Java neighbor
25. Kind of collar
26. Mangles
27. Dickens novel transmuted
30. Bargain
32. Hale
33. ___ Fein
34. Effort
35. Boxing titlist with 57 KO's
37. 60's Secretary of the Interior
41. More to the point
45. U.S. ship transmuted
48. Prefix with -gram
49. Music hall
51. Opening word?
52. Believer, informally
53. City on the Rhein
54. Eagerly expectant
56. Bandar ___ Begawan (Brunei's capital)
57. Addition column
58. "L.A. Law" lawyer
59. Native of the Land of the Thunder Dragon
62. Write painstakingly
64. 1955 play transmuted
70. Schoolmarm's hairdos
71. Spread ingredient
72. Ottoman authority
75. Bettors bet on them
78. "___ la guerre"
81. Billionth: Prefix
82. Drink on the drink
83. Fab competitor
84. Atheist Madalyn et al.
86. Rock's opposite, often
89. Fiend
90. 50's TV catch phrase transmuted
93. Deer playmate, in song
95. Consummate
96. Idyllic spots
97. Twosome
98. C minor and others
101. "Xanadu" rock group
102. Water-skier's need
107. Cary Grant movie transmuted
111. German poet Heinrich
112. Astronomer's sighting
113. Lounge
114. Story subtitled "The Yeshiva Boy"
115. Tuckered out
116. Another time
117. Stylish gent, in Britain
118. Knobby
119. Like non-oyster months?
120. Ivy League team
121. Want ad listings: Abbr.
122. "Holy cow!"
123. Storied Phoenician port

DOWN

1. Ecole
2. Clint's "co-star" Clyde, for one
3. Cable channel transmuted
4. Adaptable
5. Decreed
6. W.W. II menace
7. Crack
8. Small, reddish monkey
9. Santa's load
10. Throws a monkey wrench into
11. Airline name drawn from Hosea
12. Joins
13. Some Asimov books
14. Eastern pooh-bah
15. Lounge
16. Produced fiction
17. ___ maison (indoors): Fr.
18. No longer mint
28. Prepares for action
29. Not free
31. Passionate about
35. Masquerade mask
36. Rose bouquet
38. Deuce follower
39. ___-majeste
40. Amphibious vehicles, for short
41. Dutch tourist attraction
42. What's all the screaming about?
43. Holdover
44. Rope used to hang banditos
46. Town in many an oater
47. One of the Karamazov brothers
50. Jazz players are found here
55. Scaler's spike
57. "Well, well, well!"
59. Furnace measure, for short
60. El jefe
61. Open
63. Maj.'s superior
65. Sit-ups strengthen them
66. Cooper of "My Fair Lady"
67. Wine: Prefix
68. Irish lullaby syllables
69. 1996 Coen brothers film
73. Trail mix
74. "The Night of the Hunter" screenwriter
75. Soft drink brand
76. Lifeless
77. Singer Marvin
79. Incidental
80. Considerations pro and con
82. Blues singer transmuted
84. Eyeballed
85. Jim-dandy
87. Exists as an activating force
88. Case for an ophthalmologist
91. Chicago suburb
92. Pain reliever
94. "Lady Lindy"
99. Resort east of Sevastopol
100. Prier
102. Non-bear bear
103. Rowing team
104. Dorothy, for the Tin Man
105. Cordial flavoring
106. Addition column
107. Vanished
108. Where Hansel was headed
109. A penny short of a dime
110. Actor ___ Carroll
112. Drop off for a bit

by Suzie Elliott

ACROSS

1. Mogul capital of India
5. Pundit
10. Dead duck
15. Torme forte
19. Dinner's often on him
20. "Les Miz" setting
21. 1836 battle site
22. Like some traffic
23. Movie about a boy's Presidential aspirations?
25. ___ Drusilla (mother of Tiberius)
26. Trigger puller?
27. Home of the Minotaur
28. Tango maneuver
29. Places for races
30. 95-Down finisher
31. Cause of inflation?
32. Presidential biography by Noel Coward?
36. Italian wine region
37. ___ Hall (historic Princeton site)
39. Bank deposit
40. Great time
41. "That is to say . . ."
42. Stuffed shirt
44. "Dirty Hands" playwright
46. China setting
47. Spruce
50. Gulf
52. Christie's "___ M?"
53. Country guitar player, e.g.
56. At bat stat
57. What the First Lady's critics did over a bottle of bathtub gin?
61. Indianapolis's ___ Dome
62. Cliff hanger?
64. Rembrandt van ___
65. Skittish
66. Dreamscape artist
67. One of the Horae
68. Current choice
70. Exclusive
71. Pickle flavoring
72. Basketball maneuver
73. Shelved for now
75. Hollow
76. Pizazz
77. Gained a lap
78. Mathematical rules governing the Vice President's macarena?
81. Hard-rock connection
82. Turn into something big
84. Memo starter
85. Prominent tower
86. Agonize
87. Rec center
88. At the scene
91. 1984 Peace Nobelist
93. Children's author Eleanor
95. New Deal proj.
96. Narrowly defeats
98. S.A.T. score
102. 60's draft deferment category
103. Vice President's wife at the Starlight Diner?
106. Belfast grp.
107. Baseball Hall-of-Famer Waite ___
108. Basil's "Captain Blood" co-star
109. Catch on
110. Pert
112. Flood avoider
113. Timex rival
114. Head and tail of the victorious First Cat?
116. Avalon, for one
117. Chihuahua bites
118. Bye word
119. Atlantic City attraction
120. "Clueless" lead role
121. "___ Canyon"
122. Skein game?
123. Contemporary of Garbo

DOWN

1. Depth charge
2. Extolment, in hymns
3. Cowboys
4. Be a partner in crime
5. Obsolete geog. abbr.
6. Like unkept yards
7. Stands by for
8. "Aida" setting
9. Returns home?
10. Lively dance in duple time
11. "Sleuth" co-star
12. Old 48-Down kingdom
13. Iago's wife
14. Rake over the coals
15. Arrive in droves
16. Star of a sitcom in which the First Daughter learns syntax?
17. Whitney Houston's record label
18. Get, as a radio broadcast
24. Prohibit
33. One of Nintendo's Mario Brothers
34. African antelope
35. Detroit brew
38. Scout
41. Essex exclamation
43. Kitchen fixture
45. Comings and goings
46. With a twist?
47. Gallivant
48. Basque, e.g.
49. Where the President went without collecting $200?
51. Hitchcock classic
53. Defiant words
54. Overshadow
55. Umbrella alternative
57. Balmoral Castle river
58. Biblical witch's locale (1 Sam. 28)
59. Off one's trolley
60. Humbert Humbert's obsession
63. Publicity
66. Burns and Allen, e.g.
69. Staff leaders
71. Inc. listings
73. "The Three Sisters" sister
74. On the clothesline
78. Moves like a comet
79. Band command
80. Purple shade
83. Into the wind
86. It's a wrap
88. Not neat
89. 60-Down's creator
90. Show piece?
92. Clipped
93. Italian or Mexican, e.g.
94. Rushing sound
95. Terrorist tactic
97. Coin of the realm
99. Actress Jacqueline
100. Sleuth Lupin
101. Attacks violently
103. They're held for questioning
104. Words of resignation
105. Short dogs, for short
111. Grills
114. Wilt
115. Good name for a lawyer?

by Bob Klahn

ACROSS

1. "___ It Be Magic" (Manilow song)
6. Country place for Yeltsin
11. 16-Down, for one
16. Recipe amt.
20. Prefix with -pathy
21. Contemporary author Canin
22. Kind of cross
23. They get what's left
25. More aloof
26. Car in a Beach Boys song
27. Irregular
28. Longhorn rival
29. . . . faith healer, but I . . .
33. Cadiz Mrs.
34. "The heck with you!"
35. Large group
36. Cherish
37. Trig figure: Abbr.
38. Grenoble's river
40. It's good in Paris
42. Benchmarks: Abbr.
43. Exchange
48. Convertiplane, e.g.
49. Shipping hazard
50. . . . publisher of e. e. cummings's works, but I . . .
55. Country singer Tillis
58. Each
59. "Shrovetide Revelers" artist
60. Coeur d'___, Idaho
61. Crockett's last stand
63. Past its prime
64. "Mister ___" (1957 Tony Curtis film)
65. Go through
66. Visit
67. Singer Janis
68. Cha, cha, cha, e.g.
69. Neologism
70. . . . masseur, but I . . .
78. Works into a passion
79. Cowboy gear
80. Smithfield product
81. Combs
82. Collapses
83. Product of Sweden
85. Former chairman of CBS
90. Say "fo'c'sle," e.g.
91. San ___, Calif.
92. Eastern title
93. Violinmaker Amati
94. Address book info: Abbr.

95. . . . mime, but I . . .
99. Wasn't straight
100. Many paintings
101. Releases, in a way
102. Runner Zatopek
106. Cover
107. Word on all U.S. coins
109. Misc. ending
110. Corelli composition
112. Office
113. Dinsmore the prig
115. Cousin of "ugh!"
118. . . . sumo wrestler, but I . . .
124. Free
125. Disinclined
126. Tropical palm
127. Triangular peninsula
128. Minneapolis suburb
129. Big name in the metals industry
130. Do
131. Baylor of basketball fame
132. Overcharge
133. Limitlessly
134. Hell, with "the"
135. It's a wrap

DOWN

1. Prepares to strike, maybe
2. March honor
3. Punic War city
4. National emblem of Wales
5. Quiz whiz Charles Van ___
6. Oust
7. One of Pete Rose's records
8. Does gym-class exercises
9. Like Hannah's heart, in song
10. Connective tissue of prose
11. Warm-up act
12. Made without milk or meat
13. Thermosetting resin
14. Farrier's tool
15. On the safe side?
16. Massenet work
17. Sires
18. Official impression
19. Set an asking figure
24. Has the earmarks of
30. Figure
31. Daggers, in printing

32. Dancer Jeanmaire
38. Autostrada's place
39. Bribes
40. Word with date or trust
41. Slime
43. Moore starter
44. Intent
45. Polo grounds?
46. Field of honor fight
47. Suffix with differ
48. Badge of battle
49. Work on a whaling ship
51. River of Avignon
52. Retina layers
53. Beth Preceder
54. "Mack the Knife" singer
55. Tree also called a custard apple
56. Bygone computer
57. It may be advanced
62. Extended
64. Tops off
65. Galley notations
66. Popular PC shooting game
67. Mid-month, in old Rome

68. Go downhill, in a way
69. Complain
70. Furnace button
71. Truce word
72. Swelter
73. Unit of data transmission
74. Casmerodius albus, commonly
75. Spieled
76. Carpetlike
77. Slip
82. Like Hitler's "diaries"
83. Got wind of, old-style
84. Feels punk
85. Small songbirds
86. It stands for something
87. François Boucher's "Nude Lying on a ___"
88. Fast pace
89. Have the ___ for
91. Year in St. Leo IX's papacy
92. "No returns"
93. Vatican emissary
96. To whom the

Kaaba is dedicated
97. 4-H participant
98. Exhibits more stamina
102. Architectural suffix
103. Diamond elevations
104. Ab ___ (from the beginning)
105. Many a novella watcher
107. Old Jutland resident
108. "Cosby" co-star
109. Puts in
111. Fine-tune
112. Slot
113. Kind of wheel
114. Road race maneuvers
115. Beat it!
116. Profit
117. "Die Lorelei" poet
119. Exuberance
120. Court plea, informally
121. Bullfighter's cloak
122. Disney's Aladdin, e.g.
123. To the ___ (completely)

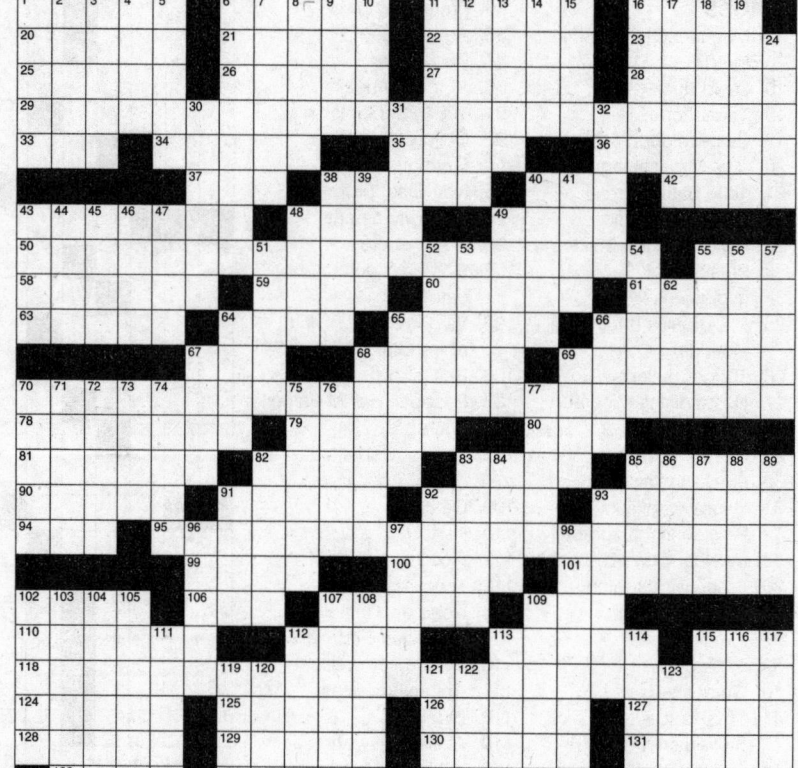

by Mel Rosen

ACROSS

1. Blah
6. Airplane engines
13. Remind again and again of an error
20. Stopped lying
21. Get hot under the collar
22. Very hot under the collar
23. Buck Rogers's female companion
24. It opens with a 75-bar bassoon solo
26. Poor surfer
27. Ref. set
28. Zodiac symbol
29. Like Abner
30. "1,001 Arabian Nights" hero
31. Quills
34. Roman way
35. Fr. religieuse
36. Charged
39. Parade decorations
41. Monumental
42. Esophagus
44. Completes a graveside ceremony
45. Country singer Black
46. Droopy-eared one
48. Follow, as advice
49. Social activities
50. Noted Dixieland clarinetist
52. Unequaled
54. The sun, the moon and the stars
55. Implant
56. Notorious London prison
58. Like some stocks, for short
61. Initials on a rocket
62. Rum cocktail
65. Circles and such
66. Fiesta, e.g.
67. Mystery writer Josephine
68. Italian province or its capital
70. Disney deer
71. Caesar's well
72. Sitcom originally titled "These Friends of Mine"
73. Bouquets
77. Scotland yards?
80. Corps unit
81. Basins
82. Neural transmitters
83. "Happy Days" role
85. Papal capes
86. Engine stats
87. It gives players a cushion
89. Bird calls
92. Meteorological datum
93. Tennis player Ramirez
94. ___ del Fuego
96. Bailey's bailiwick
97. "Walking on Thin Ice" singer
98. Those playing the role of Boris Godunov
100. Athos, to Porthos
101. Writer Rogers St. Johns
103. Like a samaritan's help
107. Tangle
108. Implement
109. Staffing
110. Goddess of peace
111. Crook
112. Understanding
113. Cause for an insurance claim

DOWN

1. Derisive laugh
2. Jim Palmer, notably
3. Preventing an attack, in a way
4. Cadets' inits.
5. Drink for Beowulf
6. Camera setting
7. Not the prayerful sort
8. "You ___ worry . . ."
9. Clash
10. Major record co.
11. Sounds of reproof
12. Display item
13. Ransackers
14. Indy 500 family
15. Some Protestants: Abbr.
16. Sale item abbr.
17. Pilot's nightmare
18. Firing up
19. Overlooks
25. Gene Autry pic
31. His feast day is April 11
32. The unmarried woman in "An Unmarried Woman"
33. Submitted
37. Ditties
38. Arabic letter
40. Makes amends
41. Writer Wiesel
43. Hard to describe
45. Holiday decorations
46. State oratorically
47. Intrinsically
48. Fighting
49. Show senility
51. Idle
52. Capital of Guam
53. One of the Canaries
57. The place
58. 1960 Sinatra movie
59. Roberts of "Charlie's Angels"
60. Salad green
62. Fr. girls
63. Bothers
64. Actually
69. Behind the times
71. It gets into a pickle
72. Seabirds
74. Small African antelope
75. Noted workshop chief
76. Ship, in poetry
77. English writers Derek and Christopher
78. Advocate
79. "The Electric Kool-Aid Acid Test" author
80. 1974 Chicago hit
83. Furniture protector
84. Roulette player's opponent
85. Unrest
87. Steed's movement
88. Position oneself to hear better
90. Pageant element
91. Low tracts
95. Chip feature
98. Engage in logrolling
99. Cartoonist Drake
101. Dry
102. Defy
104. Mauna ___
105. Bank figure: Abbr.
106. "___ moment"

by Wayne Robert Williams

ACROSS

1. Attack severely
7. Sweet, dark wine
14. Saw-billed duck
18. Dutch city on the Rhine
19. Bacchanalian activity
20. Silly
21. Venomous snake
23. Girl, informally
24. "M*A*S*H" regular
25. Noted Riverdale High student
26. Insanity and others
28. Ballerina Spessivtseva
29. Philbrick's "___ Three Lives"
30. Some wts.
32. Silver coins of ancient Greece
33. Pot-au-___ (meat and vegetable dish)
34. ___ were
35. Bossy remark?
36. Spanish arm
37. Rat Pack member
44. Make, as bread
45. Captain of the Half Moon
46. Quarterback's cry
47. Sugar source
49. Victim in a 1932 mystery, with "the"
51. It comes from a fountain
54. Perfect
55. Division of a long poem
56. List shortener
57. Swamp
60. Separates
63. Writers Meyer and Ira
64. One who wails
65. Other: Fr.
66. "The Dark at the Top of the Stairs" writer
67. Planetarium
68. Comic punctuation from a drummer
70. Prepares, in a way
72. Chivvy
73. Help the cause
74. Pitch
75. "Arabian Nights" hero
84. First name in hoteliers
85. Charles, e.g.
86. Offend olfactorily
87. Suffix with portrait
88. Schubert piece
89. Schmear
90. Half-million selling
91. Jack-o'-lantern feature
92. Bargain hunter's joy
94. Axis divisions
96. Tropical tree of the soapberry family
97. Commence
98. Popular cocktail
102. Hold off
103. Blows to smithereens
104. Rouge roulette bet
105. Some beans
106. Solvent compounds
107. Like most gates

DOWN

1. Shortens
2. Worm for bait
3. One of the Leeward Islands
4. Head of Thermopylae?
5. One of L.B.J.'s beagles
6. Mystery author Lathen
7. Chopper
8. "This is ___!" (police cry)
9. 1948 Hitchcock thriller
10. South of Mexico
11. "___ live and breathe!"
12. Cheryl and Diane of Hollywood
13. Nautical direction
14. 17th-century rationalist
15. Hypothetical animal
16. Abbreviations for weekend days
17. Reasons
19. Year St. Augustine was born
20. They undergo mitosis
22. Prayer
27. Ones voting yes
30. Vociferous
31. ___ nova
34. Plot to plant
35. "The Ten Commandments" location
36. Michael Jackson's first #1 hit
38. Where Triton is
39. ___-El (Superman's real name)
40. Doodad
41. United Nations vote
42. Opinions
43. "Relax!"
47. Feldspar, e.g.
48. Uniqueness
49. Horned Frogs' sch.
50. Solo in space
51. Come together
52. Arapaho foe
53. Trattoria offering
54. Vietnamese river or delta
58. Celtic Poseidon
59. Small swimmers
61. Man of courage, to Kipling
62. Hollywood workplace
68. Emerson of tennis
69. Chief Vedic god
70. Wine shipment
71. Biographer Winslow
73. Kind of fingerprint
74. Branch railroad, e.g.
76. Intelligently planned progresses
77. Flipper
78. Suitable for service
79. Blast furnace apparatuses
80. Chariot-driving Greek god
81. Ready to ambush
82. The East, en España
83. Broke a rule of play
88. Migratory songbird
89. Al ___
90. Just touch
91. Pioneer in medicine
92. Macarena and others
93. Jacob's first wife
94. Opposed, in Dogpatch
95. Clockmaker Thomas
99. ___ angelica (organ stop)
100. Singer Sumac
101. Overseas title

by Bryant White

ACROSS

1. Madrid's Paseo del ___
6. Swagger
13. Modern dance giant
19. Reading on the Richter scale
20. Declaimed, as "A Visit From St. Nicholas"
21. Barrio resident
22. Start of a verse
25. Outdid
26. Introduction to conservatism
27. Not the lowest prices
28. Social reformer Dorothea
29. Word with guard or chard
31. Take steps
32. Order to the "Ship of State"
36. Like Atalanta
37. Its point is to make holes
38. Swarthy
42. Yearn
43. Zoom
44. Matty or Moises
45. Chief Theban deity
46. Part 2 of the verse
52. Writer Santha Rama ___
53. Plains Indian
54. Slickers
55. Word from a fencer
56. Seat of an empire?
58. 1980 Oscar winner
60. Theodor ___ (Dr. Seuss)
61. Name that means "heavenly"
63. Wild asses
65. "Passages" writer Gail
68. Most like the Magi
70. Joining forces
74. Thomas of TV
75. Tolkien tree-men
76. It has a Minor part
77. PBS benefactor
78. Part 3 of the verse
84. Cobbler's form
85. Rival of Scipio
86. Hecuba's home
87. Mariposa lily
88. W.W. II landing craft
89. Printers' widths
90. Letter opener?
92. Famous Christian
94. Bee: Prefix
95. On the sordid side
96. From ___ Z
97. Rubble
100. Socks, e.g.
101. D'Oyly Carte offering
106. End of the verse
110. New Jersey's state tree
111. Engine fluid
112. She played Anastasia in "Anastasia"
113. Begets
114. Popular Mouseketeer
115. Chart holder

DOWN

1. Shore (up)
2. Zebras
3. Last of a Latin trio
4. Fish also called mahimahi
5. Source
6. Thin nail
7. Padre, for short
8. It's not returnable
9. Barbarino on "Welcome Back, Kotter"
10. Certify
11. Deejay's disks
12. Harem room
13. Group in robes
14. "Nick of Time" Grammy winner
15. Girl lead-in
16. Sound setup
17. Indigo source
18. Epigram
19. Nashville sch.
23. Put the whammy on
24. Make use of
29. Pole, for example
30. "The stockings ___ hung . . ."
32. Gerald's predecessor
33. Shoot for
34. Ideas, opinions, etc.
35. Sign of summer
36. Liver, in Le Havre
37. Subject of an 1867 sale
38. 67-Down, for one
39. Cherubs
40. 1950 Max Ophuls film "La ___"
41. Prepare to propose
43. Pit
44. Sign of stress?
47. By hook or by crook
48. Po land
49. Muldaur's "___ Woman"
50. They have edible shells
51. Women advisers
57. Cousins of margays

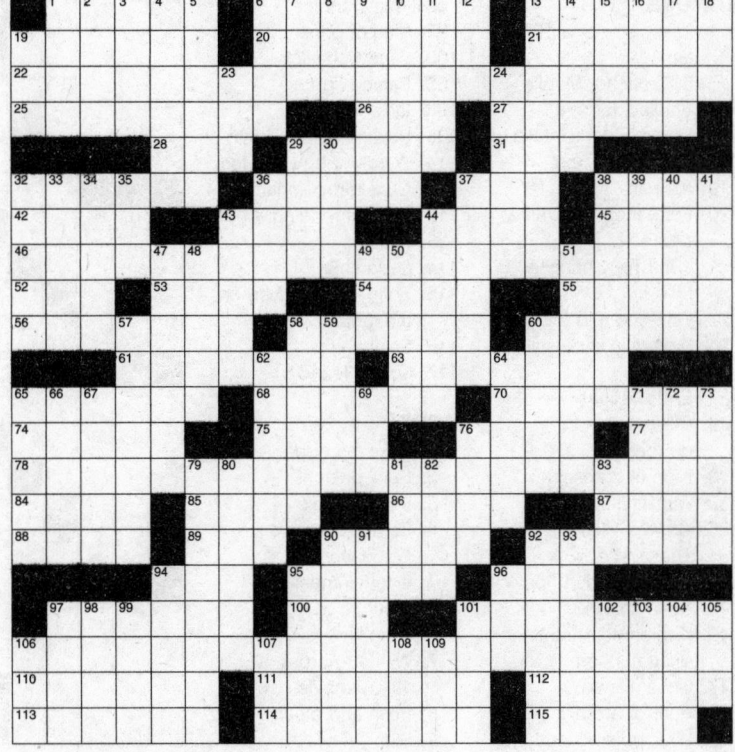

by Frances Hansen

58. Strong ale
59. Genoese creation
60. Bottled spirits?
62. Dieter's bane
64. Not reserved
65. Slight
66. Laugh track sounds
67. Artist Max
69. N.Y.C. zone
71. Enlargement, maybe
72. Mont Blanc covering
73. Burt Reynolds flick
76. Energy source
79. They produce chips off the old block
80. Leave no trace
81. News squib
82. Carhop's burden
83. O.T. book
90. " 'Tis the ___ to be jolly"
91. Be a snitch
92. Glenda Jackson biopic
93. Name in 1993 headlines
94. Indo-European
95. Offshoot
96. Galoot
97. Like still waters, maybe
98. "Das Rheingold" earth goddess
99. Knitted item
101. Bone: Prefix
102. Work units
103. King Hiram's home
104. Drudgery
105. What's more
106. "___ Winterbourne"
107. Elvis's label
108. Welcome giver
109. Sugar lover

ACROSS

1. Title sister of a 1970 film
5. 50's pitcher Maglie
8. Shelley, for one
13. Bodybuilder's intake
18. Hydrangea, e.g.
19. A Khan
20. Further shorten, as a board
21. 1982 Tony nominee Milo
22. One-one and two-two
24. Women's shoe style
26. Bridger
27. Ends of lines
29. Classical earth goddess
30. Kind of cracker
32. Hamilton's prov.
33. Glow
34. Those who work
38. Given life, perhaps
43. See 7-Down
46. Contemporary author-illustrator Jon
47. Unvarnished
48. Roar of a crowd
49. Love personified
50. React angrily
51. Illinois city
52. "De ___ Poetica" (ancient treatise)
53. Arles article
54. Orchestra member
56. Caruso was one
57. Feature of James Monroe's estate
59. Palindrome girl
60. Lourdes is one
61. Coif
63. Trauma sites, for short
64. Suntanning areas
66. Ran for one's wife?
68. November honorees
70. Armada component
73. Teases
74. Quieting down
78. Tee follower
79. Western Hemisphere abbr.
80. ___ team (assault unit)
81. Extreme amount
82. Bug shots?
83. Scale notes
84. List in a hurry?
85. Stonehenge builder
86. All, in stage directions
87. Difference
89. Sound mind, in a phrase
91. Partner for Clark
92. Crosspiece

93. Potato choice
97. Kind of panel
100. Sandwich filler
105. Parade figure
106. Indy 500 gear
108. Beyond control
110. Words with eye or fore
111. Certain repairman
112. Cockpit reading: Abbr.
113. Furious
114. ___ a time
115. Song much played on the radio
116. Shaft
117. To ___ (exactly)

DOWN

1. Bake, as eggs
2. Betel palm
3. Honking time
4. Its slogan was once "Wide world of entertainment"
5. Delhi gown
6. Long time
7. With 43-Across, a 1940's movie cowboy
8. Bean and others
9. Stop
10. Writer Dinesen
11. ___ doute (certainly): Fr.
12. Prefix with light
13. Stuck
14. Dump
15. Pearl player, in a 1996 sitcom
16. Shade of red
17. Red tag locale
18. Alone
23. "For the life ___ . . ."
25. Confined
28. Monopoly equipment
31. Barbary beast
33. Off ___ (occasionally)
35. Extended
36. "___ in Calico" (1946 song)
37. Saint Philip ___ (Renaissance figure)
38. Fashionable shop
39. Bag
40. Holiday bird
41. "Rocket Man" John
42. Tractor man John
43. Kind of land
44. Brothers' name of 40's–50's music
45. Monthly synagogue observance
47. Lyricist Sammy et al.
50. "Pretty stupid, huh?" declarer

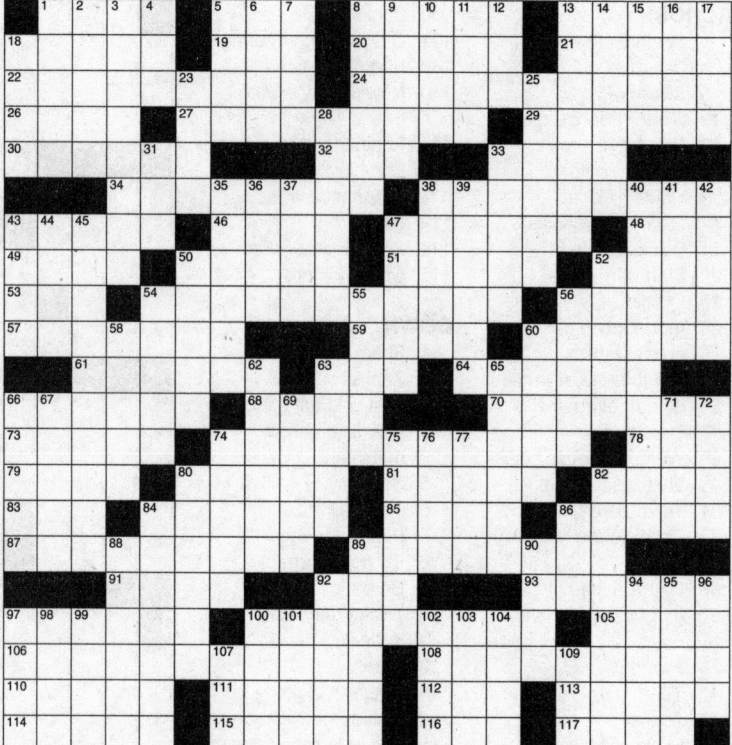

by A. J. Santora

52. Old Houston hockey team
54. Lake Indians
55. Raspy
56. Addams Family member
58. VCR
60. Public relations gambit
62. Small eggs
63. One of filmdom's Coen brothers
65. Certain discriminators
66. Daughter of Mnemosyne
67. Restrict
69. "Women Who Run With the Wolves" author
71. French suffix
72. Spilt ___
74. Toast start
75. They're a pain
76. Looked over
77. Rijksmuseum artist
80. From Odense
82. Standing-room-only show
84. Do needlework
86. ___ hunch
88. Biblical miracle worker
89. Hardly a naif
90. Bullets

92. Extort from
94. Nautical order
95. Bud Grace comic strip
96. Connecticut Senator
97. Prefix with -morph
98. 1982 Disney film
99. More than a peeve
100. In addition
101. Old Dodge
102. Frost
103. Kind of skirt
104. Dist. ___
107. Greek letter
109. Marlins locale: Abbr.

ACROSS

1 Rodeo rope
6 City north of Des Moines
10 Sch. supporters
14 Esau's wife
18 Travel section advertiser
19 ___ wire
20 "Elektra" baritone
21 Army mascot
22 ROB'S
24 BRIDGET'S
26 Neigh. of Scot.,
27 JOHN'S
29 Escapee
30 Anarchist Goldman
33 Gladly, in olden times
34 Night rumblers
35 Asia-Africa link
37 Org. once headed by Lewis Strauss
40 Half of D
41 Conceit
42 Exaggerator's suffix
43 Yucca fiber
44 NANCY'S
48 They're checked at checkpoints
49 Record collections
50 Adam was his father
51 Yellow-breasted bird
55 Pale
56 Cockatoo cousin
57 Approved model: Abbr.
58 Contrary girl
59 Seventh Muslim month
61 Gershwin's "___ It a Pity?"
63 Flustered one
67 Luau staple
69 BRANFORD'S
72 Actress Charlotte
73 Monotonous
75 Organic compound
76 "___ people go"
78 Adolescent
79 Engine starter: Abbr.
81 Stage actor Edmund and others
83 Group with the hit "Waterloo"
86 Silk wrap
87 Vier minus eins
89 Jumping-off point?
90 Pines
91 JEFF'S
94 Innisfree and others
95 Rain protector
98 Be in the red
99 Unit of sound
100 Road curve
101 Liturgical music
102 Removes to a distance
104 And that's not all
106 Fliers' org.
107 Behave arrogantly
108 LAURA'S
112 "To ___ their golden eyes": Shakespeare
115 JAMIE LEE'S
117 CHRISTIE'S
120 German donkey
121 Shake awake
122 Ship to Colchis
123 Renaissance instruments
124 Give a hand
125 Snack
126 Longtime New Yorker editor
127 Worth of the stage

DOWN

1 "The Women" playwright
2 Straight ___ arrow
3 MARIA'S
4 Part of R.S.V.P.
5 Bruins great
6 Sam Shepard's "___ of the Mind"
7 Pert lass
8 "Did you ___!"
9 Typeface line
10 Sign up early
11 Four: Prefix
12 Enzyme suffix
13 Muscles
14 Jeanne's love
15 Firth of Tay port
16 Birch-family trees
17 Lord of San Simeon
20 Study of light
23 Due point: Abbr.
25 Nonplus
28 Changes course, nautically
31 Rubber region
32 ___ van der Rohe
34 Provide space for
35 Hindu god
36 Osiris's wife
37 Cordial
38 Folk singer Andersen
39 Channel port
45 Certain reporters
46 Canio's wife in "Pagliacci"
47 Crowning point
52 SHARI'S
53 Scope
54 City in the Crusades
56 Neighbor of Algeria
57 Caressed
60 O.T. book after Isa.
62 Big-band vocalist Wynn
64 Hypochondriac's preoccupation
65 Gifts for fathers
66 Margaret's father's monogram
67 Sets
68 Militarily fit
70 "I wander'd till ___": Arnold
71 Heavy tool
74 Deep blue
77 Mason or Norman
80 Xjclmzit obwny, e.g.
82 Long time
84 Stayed
85 Office abbr.
87 Decline
88 Some whiskies
89 New Hampshire state flower
90 Personal quirks
92 Raymond Smullyan topic
93 Rounded and notched, as a leaf
95 Softened
96 Words before cannon or wire
97 Pupil's protection
103 Pastoral poem
105 "Zigeunerliebe" composer
106 Durham campus: Abbr.
108 Heat measures, for short
109 Spanish peso
110 Quiche ingredients
111 Greek letters
113 Ball ___
114 European tongue
116 Kanga's child
118 Big name in New Haven
119 Soft coat

by Nancy Scandrett Ross

ACROSS

1 Pronto
4 Letterman's turf
7 Pretty, in ancient Rome
12 Summerhouse
18 Perfume label word
19 Clinton Cabinet member
21 Wanted poster datum
22 Rant about
23 Sch. grp.
24 Headline of January 1896
27 Chair style
29 Excite, in slang
30 Some people take a shine to it
31 "Peter Pan" dog
32 Be of importance, old-style
34 Public relations concern
37 Yawner's feeling
39 Quaff introduced in 1896
42 Cordage grass
46 Pouch
47 "Yippee!"
48 They're helpless
50 Corn byproduct
51 Hardly gregarious
52 Office holder?
55 Neighbor of B.C.
56 The ___ Reader (1990's magazine)
57 Richie's dad, to Fonzie
58 1896 dramatic work
62 Marquand sleuth
64 Cheek-related
66 Longtime Philly conductor
67 Architect I.M.
68 "Not that again!"
70 Wearer of pointy footgear
71 Unisex garb
75 Gunk
76 Washington Monument, e.g.
80 Soap Box Derby site
81 1951 Lanza role
84 Her advice column debuted in 1896
87 Oklahoma city
88 Book after Joel
89 Bed size
91 Dutch treat
92 Jam ingredient?
93 Book course
94 Yellow Sea port
98 Skedaddled

100 "The Birth of a Nation" grp.
101 Product of the rumor mill
103 1896 event, absent since A.D. 394
107 "All ___ Is the Girl" ("Gypsy" song)
109 Shouted
110 Through
111 Patches things up?
114 Antlered beasts
116 Individual
118 Green-skinned pear
121 It was the talk of Chicago, July 1896
126 Stomach muscles
127 Yearbook
128 Bye at the French Open?
129 Nonpayment result
130 Boulogne business abbr.
131 Give the same old story
132 Goalie's stats
133 Aachen article
134 Chess pcs.

DOWN

1 Invigorates, with "up"
2 Appointment
3 First Ford auto, completed in 1896
4 Brittle
5 Put on the line
6 Catch
7 Tropical trees
8 Ivy Leaguer
9 Kind of algebra: Abbr.
10 Colleen
11 Soap title start
12 Tradables introduced in 1896
13 Sports org.
14 Garden bloom
15 Literary pseudonym
16 Kind of companion
17 Choreographer White
20 Start of the "flying down" song
25 Doorframe part
26 Square
28 N.R.C. forerunner
33 He played TV's Mike Hammer
35 Prizm, e.g.
36 Wet wiggler
38 Boom times
39 "Oklahoma!" star

40 "The Bronx Zoo" author
41 Explorer Amundsen
43 Old Sunday paper section
44 Salon application
45 Remedy for dry toast
46 Super Bowl XXI M.V.P.
49 In a bad way
53 Equi-
54 In accordance with
56 Inuit craft
58 Small combos
59 Muslim bigwig
60 Noted name in wine
61 Out of shape
63 Stop worrying
65 Black ___
69 & 72 Snacks introduced in 1896
73 Brownies
74 Lewis Carroll's Boojum
76 Valhalla V.I.P.
77 Beat it
78 Yon maiden

79 Marlowe contemporary
81 A little lower
82 "What ___ mind reader?"
83 Campus mil. grp.
85 Jeanne ___
86 Erstwhile larva
90 Nowhere near
94 Shipping unit
95 Mom's specialty
96 Scottish river
97 Casus ___ (legal situation)
99 Hogan dwellers
102 Something to sneeze at
104 Incubator noise
105 Sluggard
106 Chaps
108 "The Dancing Class" artist
111 Rumble reminder
112 Piscivorous flyer
113 Practice
115 Pop
117 Satellite broadcast
119 Last writes?
120 Versatility list

122 Erie Canal mule
123 Actress Ullmann
124 Inferior mark
125 Number-cruncher

by Henry Hook

ACROSS

1 Rhythmic music in 4/4 time
6 Teutonic cry
9 Drink topped with nutmeg
13 Rotters
17 All points bulletin
18 Words after "You can't fire me!"
20 Shine's companion
21 Early TV backdrop
22 "___ saturated fats"
23 Watch over
24 As well
25 Carriage
26 Marlon Brando title role
29 Jean Stapleton title role
31 Actress Thompson
32 ___ poison
33 Demonstrate
35 Lightens
36 Wynonna's mom
38 Opposite of fortis, in phonetics
39 Cliff-dwelling bird
40 Fred Astaire title role
44 Pounds
48 William Tell's home
49 Remove by dissolving
50 Iniquities
52 Bulldog
53 Travel guide, of a sort
55 Faye Dunaway title role
60 "That is ___ . . ."
61 Robert Burns' "The Bonnie ___ Thing"
62 Poetic dusk
63 Christian and others
64 Lachrymose
68 Sit still for
69 Turkish title
71 Patient's complaint
74 Female goat
75 Jargon suffix
76 Availing
80 Priscilla Lane and others' title roles
84 Black, in a way
86 Common "Wheel of Fortune" purchase
87 With 122-Across, Richard Starkey
88 About one-ninth of an orchestra
90 Friend of Pooh
91 Isengrim's foe in fable
93 Elvis Presley and others' title roles
98 Cries of pain
99 Rhubarb
100 French kind
101 Poetry-reading Muse
104 Wound
105 Chopin's "Étude ___ Major"
106 Saroyan's "My Name Is ___"
110 Jacques Tati title role
112 Lon Chaney Jr. title role
115 Brief upturn
116 Flag down
118 Black tea
119 Ty's folks
120 Old-timer in Wiesbaden
121 Actress Jeffreys
122 See 87-Across
123 Sound from the nest
124 Imitation morocco
125 Cancelled
126 "Metric" prefix
127 Parts of ski runs

DOWN

1 Popeye's buddies
2 Hilo hi
3 Imitated a Persian
4 Highwayman
5 ___ time (never)
6 Etching on copperplate
7 Snippy
8 ". . . never married, and that's ___": Burton
9 ___ Lippo Lippi
10 Amy Lowell poem
11 Point in question
12 Working class member
13 Wish, at times
14 Name on a "Wanted" poster
15 Industrialist John
16 Some camcorders
18 Notorious
19 Tube
27 Wags
28 Symbol of one's troth
30 ___ Draco (James Bond's wife)
34 Japanese-American
37 Nocturnal lemur
39 Actress Corby et al.
40 Conduit
41 "King ___" of old comics
42 Lowers, in a way
43 Bijou
44 Top of a platter
45 Grandpa Walton portrayer
46 Lohengrin's love
47 Perches
51 Prez's stand-in
54 "Marius the Epicurean" author Walter
56 Wise baby?
57 Reagan Attorney General
58 This could raise a red flag
59 Dogie catcher
65 Legendary Robin et al.
66 18 holes, generally
67 Peterman
70 The Merry Macs' "___ Song"
71 Way off
72 Pitcher David
73 The Kingfish, to friends
77 Biblical letters
78 M-G-M symbol
79 Umberto and kin
81 Use as a resource
82 Adds artificiality, with "up"
83 Holy person's title
84 One who says "Amen"
85 Loving one
89 Shaped like a sword
92 Closed
94 Medical suffix
95 Urban hangouts of yore
96 Shakespearean works
97 Manatees
99 Inasmuch (as)
101 Block
102 Jacob Abbott hero
103 Singer Kerr
104 Texas plain
107 Hardly sophisticates
108 "Three Tall Women" playwright
109 Mizzens
111 Earl Derr Biggers hero
113 Authorize
114 Dumas novel
117 One of 13 popes

by Ernie Furtado

ACROSS

1 Lacked a herd mentality
8 ___ St. Vincent Millay
12 Algonquian speakers
20 Speaker's skill
21 Genealogist's work
22 Make a fitting change
23 Movies
25 Big demand
26 Stick with a point
27 Literally, "way of the gods"
28 Kind of blue
29 Jay or em follower
31 Serve brilliantly
32 Serkin's support
38 Queen's home?
42 Get-together: Abbr.
43 Country rocker Steve
44 Whip severely
45 Fly out of Africa?
49 Itsy-bitsy
50 Valuable strings
51 String and Windsor, e.g.
53 Fanfare maker
55 They hang by the neck
56 Part of G.E.: Abbr.
57 Seriously harmed
58 Overindulges, with "on"
59 Physical beginning
60 Band of seven
61 Real card
62 They carry programs
65 Give a hint
67 Crack at an easy target
69 Banking feature in real estate
71 Cough med. dosage, often
72 Ammo provider
74 Shake a leg
76 Use of oilstone
77 Skirt
78 Old TV's "___ Space"
79 "Major" suffix
80 Pre-meal ritual
83 Stuck, in a way
84 Epic achievement
85 Pumping, in a way
86 CBS's Rather
87 Singer Brewer
90 Poly ___ (college course, for short)
91 Crime fighters' tactic
92 Calf's place
93 Kitchen add-on
95 Like most bowl games
98 Jazz style
101 Cleveland player
102 Library volume
103 Buckeye
106 Lullaby start
110 Ravel, e.g.
114 You, now
116 Court psychiatrist
117 "A Death in the Family" author
118 Financially O.K.
119 Lab testers
120 Spoils
121 Eliot's "___ Among the Nightingales"

DOWN

1 Rolls, for stew
2 Stumble
3 Campaign
4 Stick on
5 Cry after "Tag"
6 Bungle
7 Goes blonde?
8 Code of conduct
9 Radio-controlled plane
10 "Eye of ___" (recipe item)
11 Fabulous guy?
12 Having a notched edge
13 Witch's work
14 Author Calvino
15 Indy 500 leaders
16 Frank Norris novel, with "The"
17 Shiloh priest
18 Seek a little love
19 Son to Val and Aleta
24 ___ Na Na
30 Every lily has two
33 "___ a man with seven . . ."
34 Bite-sized pastries
35 Word-of-mouth
36 Like Chaucer's feldes or bokes
37 Minus
38 Give it a go
39 Roofers, at times
40 Cradle site, in rhyme
41 "___ Entertain You"
46 Boxed in
47 Would-be spouse
48 Irish patriot Robert
49 Word after "I thee"
50 Curtain fabric
52 Sucker play
54 Lovebirds' hangout?
55 Mixed-veggie cooker
58 More nuts
60 Football Hall-of-Famer Ken
61 Elbow
62 Sit-in
63 Kind of lens
64 Kind of pie
66 Granolith
68 Initiates an attack
70 Person in a big white hat?
73 Russian fighter
75 Over
77 "I can take ___!"
78 K-O interval
80 Mandrake the Magician's nemesis
81 Regarding
82 Stowe gear
83 Shakespeare's "ancient"
86 Hot spots
88 Word to a dog
89 Novelist France
92 Unlikeliest, as an alibi
94 Metamorphose
96 Lab stain
97 Type of stock certificate
98 He wrote "Carmen"
99 Lava does it
100 Good buddy
104 Quasimodo's creator
105 '87 Costner film role
107 Where one's goose is cooked
108 Artist Magritte
109 Like some salon conversation
110 Hatchback, e.g.
111 Bullfight cry
112 She played Alice in "Alice"
113 Identify, in slang
115 Piglet's mom

by Manny Nosowsky

ACROSS

1. ___ Na Na
4. Capitoline Museum site
8. ___ blank
13. Flying Eagle, 1856–58
17. TV/film director Averback et al.
18. Pre-fax transmission
19. "O Sanctissima," e.g.
20. 1934 Douglas Freeman biography
21. Post ___ (surgical follow-ups)
22. "___ Street Blues"
23. Fireplace
24. Writer Wiesel and others
25. "Independence Day" setting
28. Clique
30. Cheek
31. Remainder of Rennes
33. Foot comforter
34. Loose
35. Go one better
37. Scotland yards?
38. "The Wonder Years" years
39. Charity event
40. Mademoiselle's mother
41. W.W. II hero
42. Stayed at home
43. "Odyssey" peak
46. 229-year-old TV alien
49. Word with care or mare
50. Axioms
52. ___ nothing
54. Twisted entertainment?
59. Early computer
60. Produce foliage
61. Bully
62. Add more lanes to
64. Millay work
65. ___ a minute
66. Seattle player, for short
67. Sunken treasure site
69. One who can't get out
70. Shells
72. Some library vols.
73. Suffix with practical
74. Where Navajo Mountain is
75. ___ du jour
78. Giant's word
81. First of all
84. Type inclined to stress
86. Optimist
88. Buddhist sermons
91. Clad
93. Dishevel
94. Jack-in-the-pulpits, e.g.
95. Part of a Gilbert and Sullivan chorus
96. Travels overseas
98. Puts at risk
100. Starting over
102. Bond
103. Large quantity
105. Mendelssohn's "A Mid-summer Night's Dream"
106. Actress Peeples
107. Film producer De Laurentiis et al.
108. Temple pilasters
109. Harmony parts
110. Sharp-nosed fish
111. Isn't robust
112. "Miracle on 34th Street" actor John
113. Mexican bread
114. Q's tail

DOWN

1. Randy Barnes's Olympic gold-winning event
2. Like A-frames
3. Maintained
4. Lowered, as a mast
5. Five Norwegian kings
6. Singer Etheridge and others
7. Suit, so to speak
8. Seventh-century date
9. Easily beat
10. Special vocabularies
11. Tom and Thomas
12. A as in Absalom
13. Popular pizza brand
14. "Sense and Sensibility" sister
15. Razz
16. Title roles for MacLaine and Kinski
18. Hearty entrées
20. Conductor Fritz
26. Chocolate drink
27. Wandering
29. Coleridge poem
32. Auto indus. regulator
36. Weapon of war
39. Howls
40. Like some pronouns: Abbr.
42. U.S. Pacific atoll
44. Toronto All-Star pitcher Dave
45. 1953 Paramount hit
46. TV host Stewart
47. "Jules and Jim" situation
48. Stew
49. Kitchen gizmo
51. First, Second or Third state
52. Not just in the head
53. Advance
54. Send
55. Consolidate
56. Farm unit
57. Two to eight
58. Cathartic drug
61. French Sudan, today
63. Campbell song
64. Fictional pirate
66. Riffraff
68. Cadet's course, for short
71. Ancient charm
76. It may take some hops
77. Twit
78. Frank
79. Awake before another
80. Griffith and others
81. Nobles, colloquially
82. Pedestal parts
83. League: Abbr.
85. "___ I Kissed You" (Everly Brothers song)
86. Drifters
87. Like some card hands
88. Toast words
89. Muse with a globe
90. Acting idly
91. Parthenon sculpture
92. Concord
93. Portable art
97. Blackouts
99. Quicksand, e.g.
101. "Now!"
104. Capt.'s direction

by Robert H. Wolfe

ACROSS

1 Davos denizens
6 Profess
10 Environs of 1-Across
14 Seasons
19 Appropriate
20 Poet laureate Nahum
21 Butterflies
22 March
23 BBBB
25 EEEE
27 "I was at my girlfriend's," e.g.
28 In flight
30 Straight
31 Turn to twilight
34 One, of a kind
36 Graf ___
37 Ring shouts
38 TTTT
42 Common dog's name
46 "Dear old ___"
47 Clouds
48 Actress Gilbert of "Roseanne"
49 Fur piece
50 Certain postings
52 Captain's heading
53 1969 Medicine Nobelist Salvador ___
55 Scene of vice
56 Comportment
58 Stadium parking lot activity
61 Game item
62 Caribou and elk
63 Let slip
64 Gift
66 Addis ___
67 QQQQ
68 Niacin and others
69 Early round
70 Greets the day
71 Pinch pennies
72 Member of the crew
73 Beef, venison et al.
75 Settled
78 Batter's stat
79 R2D2, for one
80 Bridge builder's deg.
82 Boeing customer
83 Salon offerings
85 ___ about (approximately)
87 It's over from Dover
89 Start of many movements' names
90 Michener genre
91 IIII
93 Medical suffix
94 Ballad subject, maybe
96 Truth ___
97 Catches, in a way
99 Kickback, of a sort
102 Overseas friend
104 Boot
106 OOOO
108 UUUU
113 First name in makeup
114 Maison follower
115 Deco illustrator
116 Midmorning
117 Misses
118 Easter supplies
119 Was attractive
120 Block

DOWN

1 Educ. edifice
2 It may be pitched
3 One of Plato's "Dialogues"
4 Lectures
5 Phraseology
6 "Three men in ___"
7 Bean flavoring
8 Nonspecific abbr.
9 Shifts a portrait
10 Yields
11 Green piece
12 Tontine, e.g.
13 ___ Lanka
14 Steps over a fence
15 Most showy
16 It could be a credit to anyone
17 Shopping aid
18 Scurried
24 All-nighter
26 Pool exercise
29 Kirkconnell, in ballad
31 Numerical prefix
32 "13 Days to Glory" subject
33 CCCC
35 "All ___" (1984 comedy)
36 "First ___ see . . ."
39 "The Country Girl" dramatist
40 Races
41 Goes ballistic
43 PPPP
44 Liquid fats
45 Something to believe in
47 JJJJ
49 YYYY
51 Nonpareil
54 Type of valve
57 Floyd of the Grand Ole Opry
58 Actress Braga
59 Flood point
60 Feverish fits
63 Andiron
65 Walks awkwardly
66 Sheba's locale
67 Thin layer
69 They receive many calls
71 Lance
74 Sentences
76 Children's song refrain
77 Refuse
80 Azerbaijan's capital
81 Hall-of-Fame Pirate
84 Like eagles
86 Abides
87 Was deflected
88 Long Island airport town
91 Skye, e.g.
92 One of the March sisters
93 Carpet fibers
95 Attachés
98 More than serious
99 Opposite of tout
100 To be: Lat.
101 Commend, as for honors
102 Court sort, for short
103 Apportion
105 Prospect
107 Sleep on it
109 Flightboard abbr.
110 Model Aesop character
111 ___ Te Ching
112 Sovereign ruler: Abbr.

by Charles M. Deber

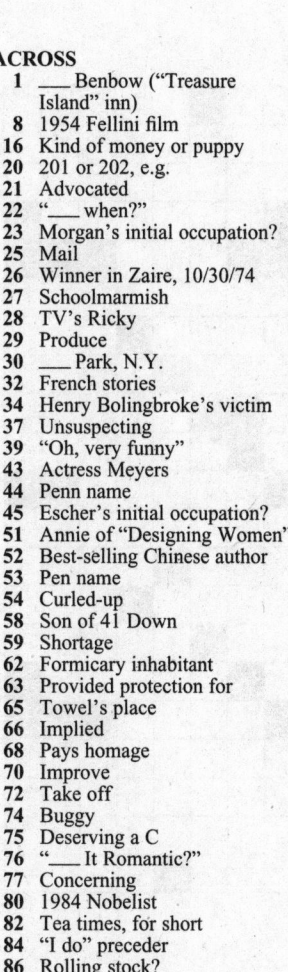

by Randolph Ross

ACROSS

1 ___ Benbow ("Treasure Island" inn)
8 1954 Fellini film
16 Kind of money or puppy
20 201 or 202, e.g.
21 Advocated
22 "___ when?"
23 Morgan's initial occupation?
25 Mail
26 Winner in Zaire, 10/30/74
27 Schoolmarmish
28 TV's Ricky
29 Produce
30 ___ Park, N.Y.
32 French stories
34 Henry Bolingbroke's victim
37 Unsuspecting
39 "Oh, very funny"
43 Actress Meyers
44 Penn name
45 Escher's initial occupation?
51 Annie of "Designing Women"
52 Best-selling Chinese author
53 Pen name
54 Curled-up
58 Son of 41 Down
59 Shortage
62 Formicary inhabitant
63 Provided protection for
65 Towel's place
66 Implied
68 Pays homage
70 Improve
72 Take off
74 Buggy
75 Deserving a C
76 "___ It Romantic?"
77 Concerning
80 1984 Nobelist
82 Tea times, for short
84 "I do" preceder
86 Rolling stock?
87 A sir
90 They're seen after a shower
93 Company once headed by Henry Luce
96 Poetic monogram
97 Loud fellow
98 Clear tables
100 ___ woe
101 They're designed in Hollywood
102 Ovid's "The ___ Love"
103 Literature Nobelist Nelly
105 Bar opening
106 Michener title
107 cummings's initial occupation?
112 Initials for a pound
116 Rock video award
117 Kuwaiti V.I.P.
118 A bit of mischievousness
119 20th-century events
122 Chant
126 Clumsy ships
129 Mother's kin
130 A little night music
134 Cooked up stories
135 Religious ideal
136 Energize
137 Barnum's initial occupation?
143 "Politics of Ecstasy" author
144 Honing device
145 Fetters
146 Heathrow visitors
147 Parrots
148 Topic in tax law

DOWN

1 As ___ (usually)
2 Lawrence's initial occupation?
3 Gym protection
4 Here, in Le Havre
5 Fabulous flyer
6 Having more talent
7 Mrs. Arrowsmith
8 1969 Paul Revere and the Raiders hit
9 Silver-gray
10 Exceeded the limit
11 Binge at the bar
12 Ways of Paris
13 Light ___
14 Winter mo.
15 "Modern Fables" writer
16 Personnel directors
17 Like a morning bed
18 Nova ___
19 Legalistic locator
20 Cracked open
22 Cakemaker Lee
24 Trifling amount
29 Lewis's initial occupation?
31 Hops are dried in them
32 Keat's "The ___ of St. Agnes"
33 Yonder yacht
35 Actors McKellen and Holm
36 Dernier ___
38 "___ You I Love"
40 Parabolic path
41 Heavenly queen
42 Mingling with
45 Empty head
46 Gulf nation
47 Game often played with hexagonal chips
48 ___ pin
49 ___ Manifesto (1854 proclamation)
50 Bears do it
51 Prune
55 Connects with
56 Housman's initial occupation?
57 Tennis calls
59 Salinger's initial occupation?
60 Compass dir.
61 Spellbound
63 Take's mate
64 Brit. award
66 Media initials since 1980
67 "Can you ___?"
69 N N N
71 O.K.
73 Implied
77 G.T.E. rival
78 Month before Adar
79 Forward
81 Press extension
82 Early hrs.
83 Greek salad topping
85 It's inspired
87 Brief résumé
88 To be, in Bogotá
89 Hardy heroine
91 Midwestern tribe
92 South American capital
94 Choice word
95 Prosecutor Jaworski
99 Wooden wedge
101 "Now you ___ . . ."
103 Traumatize
104 Grade school subj.
106 Loaded letters
108 NASA walk, for short
109 Sleeve
110 Where rakes progress
111 ___ pickle
112 Increases
113 Polo participants
114 Haberdasher's offering
115 Lets out
120 Gainsay
121 Etchers' equipment
123 "Deutschland über ___"
124 Mar. tourney
125 Titter
127 Diamond quartet
128 They're plowed
131 Kind of prof.
132 Gyro holder
133 Robert Burns, e.g.
137 Luau serving
138 That guy
139 Request of Vanna
140 Q-U filler
141 Sen. Sessions's state: Abbr.
142 How some stand

ACROSS

1 Bumps one's gums
5 Miles of film
10 Barefaced
14 Model for the writer La Fontaine
19 I.R.S.'s tax portion, seemingly?
21 The buck private stops here
23 Fridge device
24 Marry feisty lady?
25 Gizmos for office files
26 ___ Fernando
27 Friendless
28 Mind
29 Retiring
31 Sandra Bullock film, with "The"
32 Jenny Lind, e.g.
34 Show over-anticipation
35 "Henry IV" role
40 Kind of jacket
41 Street vendor's offering
42 Abductor of Helen
43 Start of a drive
44 Summer abroad
45 Slalom markers
47 George Meredith novel, with "The"
49 Ominous cloud
50 Check
52 Day's end
54 Red River delta city
55 Musical standouts
57 Inclines
58 Speaker's aid
59 Runs in place
60 Lounges
61 Overhaul
62 Manhattan buyer
64 Monte ___
65 Sleeper's problem
68 Word of surrender
69 Tacking on
71 Madonna's record label
72 White sheet
73 Like some teeth
75 Rubes, in old slang
77 Metro vehicle
78 Like words after la: Abbr.
79 Big leaf containers
80 Dry up and shrink
82 Skeptical comment
84 Hie
86 Pack extra
87 Batters
88 Go (for)
89 Nation reunited in 1990
90 ___ of faculty
91 Gives lip service
94 Yugo. neighbor
95 Big barker
99 Condemned inventor?
101 Tentacled creature
103 Unseemly
104 Newton's choreography?
105 Inscribed pillar
106 Pasture, in poetry
107 Something to believe in
108 Beginning to do well?

DOWN

1 Iona College athlete
2 Edison's middle name
3 Let it all out
4 Writer of two biblical epistles
5 Unperturbed
6 Star, e.g.
7 "Darn!"
8 Long ___
9 "And I Love ___"
10 Bawl over
11 Upright
12 Calculator feature: Abbr.
13 "Charlie and the Chocolate Factory" author
14 Relevance
15 Clown Kelly
16 Letter closer
17 "___ word . . ."
18 Educ. org.
20 In hiding
22 Like an evening landscape
26 Where baby dragons come from?
29 Refuse
30 Kind of exchange
32 Spat
33 Roulette profit?
34 Last sip bits
35 Misses the boat
36 ___ Nova (old musical style)
37 No matter how heavy?
38 One in a pen
39 Name of three popes
40 Stack part
41 Darts
42 Canvasses
46 Kickoff
48 Jug size
49 Kitchen utensils
51 Lunar ___
53 1912 Olympic decathlon champ
54 Card collection
56 Nasty, formally
58 Projection
60 Nordland natives
61 Took to jail
62 Bungles
63 Place to beach a boat
64 Hugh le roi
65 One on two wheels
66 They fill perimeters
67 Word purrfect?
70 Quantity purchase
73 What's in it
74 Bon or mon follower
76 Stuck
79 Highest level
81 Turner of tunes
83 Unlicensed anesthesiologist
85 Kind of service
86 Solidified
87 Hit on the head
89 1945 trio's site
90 Eddy of "Rebel-'Rouser"
91 "Critique of Pure Reason" writer
92 "Let ___ Me"
93 Counterfeit
95 "Sexual Healing" singer, 1982
96 Contest winner's cry
97 In years past
98 Will of "The Waltons"
99 Minn. neighbor
100 Compass dir.
101 Former U. of Texas athletic org.
102 Pitch sensitivity

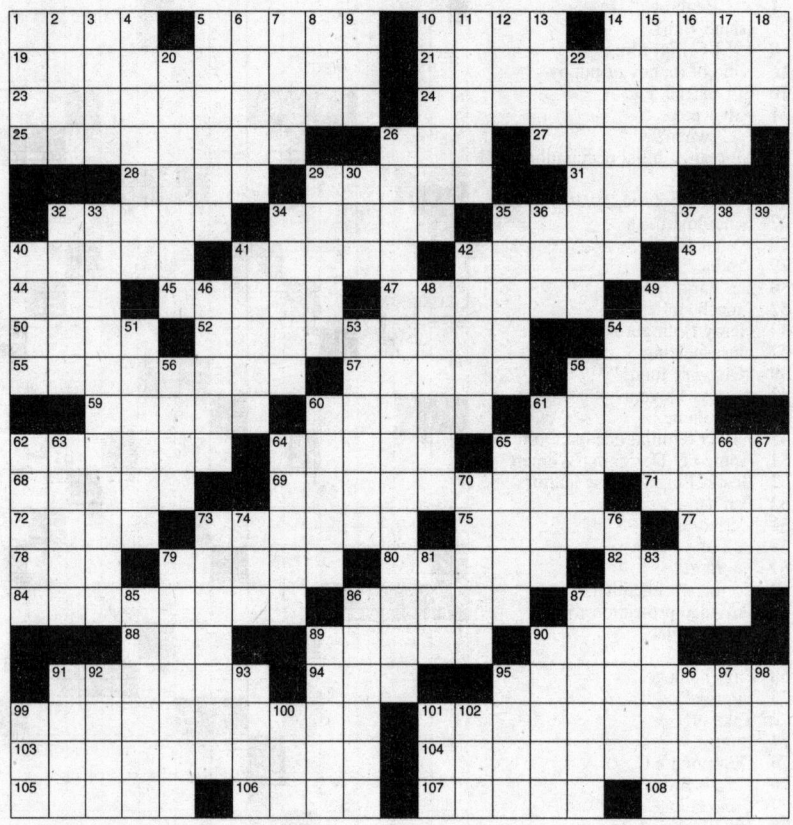

by Harvey Estes

ACROSS

1 Her Majesty: Abbr.
5 Euripides tragedy
10 Southwestern sights
15 Wharton deg.
18 Feet
19 Anemic in the extreme
20 Double duty?
21 Auction conclusion
22 Season's greetings from Athens
25 Jet affliction
26 Oklahoma Indian
27 ___ bodkins
28 Paisley and Fleming
29 Subscribe to
31 Season's greetings from Seoul
34 Controversial coat material
35 "Steppenwolf" author
36 Game show group
37 Mideast carrier
38 Wear well
39 Store money
41 Go out with a bang
42 Actor Mineo
43 Uncle of note
46 Oklahoma city
47 Provide with information
50 Mother of Horus
52 Denton of "Our Miss Brooks"
54 Season's greetings from Rome
57 Start for plop or plunk
59 Some steak orders
60 ___ Rock (Australian tourist site)
61 Major-league
63 Nagy of Hungary
64 Season's greetings from Oslo
68 "Lucky Jim" author
69 Kind of tax
71 Desk-box words
72 Orange container
73 Jerk
74 Season's greetings from Paris
78 Overcharged
79 Half a train toot
81 Rules
82 ___ Friday
83 Simile center
84 Hwys.
85 Gerard and Hodges
86 Lunchtimes
88 Fort ___, Ontario
90 Diving position
91 "Inside the Third Reich" writer
94 First of a Roman trio
98 The other woman
100 Season's greetings from Madrid
102 Marble
103 Babysitter's bane
104 ___ du Diable
105 Sixth-century date
106 Street of film
107 Season's greetings from Dublin
112 J.F.K. info
113 Travel book?
114 Come to the fore
115 ___ homo
116 U.S.C.G. call
117 City on the Aire
118 Lee and Roosevelt
119 Unwelcome growth

DOWN

1 "Mayor" author
2 Have no taste for
3 Nome's domes
4 Eva's half sister?
5 Kangaroo pouches
6 Biblical judge
7 Create wardrobes
8 What's left
9 Without a key
10 "No ___" (menu line)
11 Sorbonne summer
12 Ray
13 Treat, as glass
14 Have car trouble
15 Season's greetings from Oahu
16 MTV bad boy
17 Silver
19 Third degrees
23 Red-and-white containers
24 Adm.'s outfit
30 The Galápagos, e.g.
32 C.I.A. predecessor
33 Tot's timeout
34 Point of view
37 "Tales From Shakespeare" writer
40 Cereal box abbr.
41 E.M.K. is one
42 Teutonic triumph
43 Lines
44 Biblical language
45 Season's greetings from Manchester
47 Signaled
48 Folk history
49 Ready a rifle
51 Descendants of Noah
53 "___ was the sky so deep a hue": Warner
54 Tournament pass
55 Touch upon
56 Diamond girl
58 Grayish green
60 Comrade
62 O'Hara's home
64 Day-___
65 Aware of
66 Accepts an invitation
67 Summer mo.
70 Spanish eyes
72 Acted craftily
75 Nobelist poet Karlfeldt et al.
76 River to the Ubangi
77 Greek consonants
78 ___ Tomé
80 "Golden Boy" playwright
82 Early times
85 1841 ballet
86 Pince-___
87 Lab work: Abbr.
88 Hosts
89 Bridge over the Grand Canal
90 Mescal
91 Suit materials
92 Ambulance supply
93 Choice word
95 Cite, as reasons
96 Spitefulness
97 With revisions
99 Kidney-related
100 60's–70's crime drama, with "The"
101 Wings
108 Sonny
109 Undignified mount
110 "...man ___ mouse?"
111 Chop

by Randolph Ross

ACROSS

1 60's teens
5 Bit of kelp, e.g.
9 Italian wine city
13 Pioneering hypnotist
19 Drop
20 Where the kip is currency
21 Roll up
22 Run out
23 Like many a jailbird?
26 Goad
27 Haughty look
28 Body passage
29 Horned vipers
31 Deutschland song
32 Transporting white envelopes?
37 Cartoonist Browne
40 Witticism
41 Mitigates
42 Erstwhile catalogue
46 Opposed, in oaters
48 Farm alarm
52 Kind of tunnel
53 Dethrone
55 Ill effect of some rock?
59 Long Island Sound city
60 Nightclub
61 Dummy
62 Singer Tennille
63 Dappled
64 Saying
66 Méditerranée, e.g.
68 Hits the hay
70 Chemical endings
71 Gold mine for brew lovers?
74 Author Umberto et al.
76 Imagine
78 CBer's "bear"
79 Porky Pig's girlfriend
82 Stage doings
84 Eighth-century Chinese poet
85 East Lansing sch.
87 Beauty parlor procedures
88 Showy wrap
89 Result of too much filing by the manicurist?
92 Where the bees are
93 A Dionne
95 Some smiths
97 Leeds's river
98 Low-lying areas
99 Expanse

102 Brit. lexicon
104 Classicist's subj.
105 Direction to the special effects guy?
111 Deposit
114 "Good Luck, Miss Wyckoff" writer
115 Appear
116 Wonderland cake message
120 Nitrogen compounds
122 These may have been given to Ishmael?
126 Kind of wheel
127 Cartoonist Peter
128 King's address
129 Rombauer of cookbook fame
130 Drops of water, e.g.
131 It's "east" of Toledo
132 Chuck
133 Australian hoppers

DOWN

1 Liverwort kin
2 Arabian land
3 Joint
4 Beef on the hoof
5 Garment under a chasuble
6 Lambaste
7 Convicted crime boss John
8 Pale
9 Mil. post
10 Latin possessive
11 "The Crucible" happenings
12 "Maybe"
13 Bright group
14 River of Somersetshire
15 Bee participant
16 The south of France
17 Perry's creator
18 Saxophone, e.g.
24 Recipient of a beating
25 Physics unit
30 Canadian chiefs
33 Sewer worker of 50's TV
34 Eponymous British Bobby
35 Swiss river
36 Danish writer Dinesen
37 Smears
38 Light
39 Play an amorous detective?

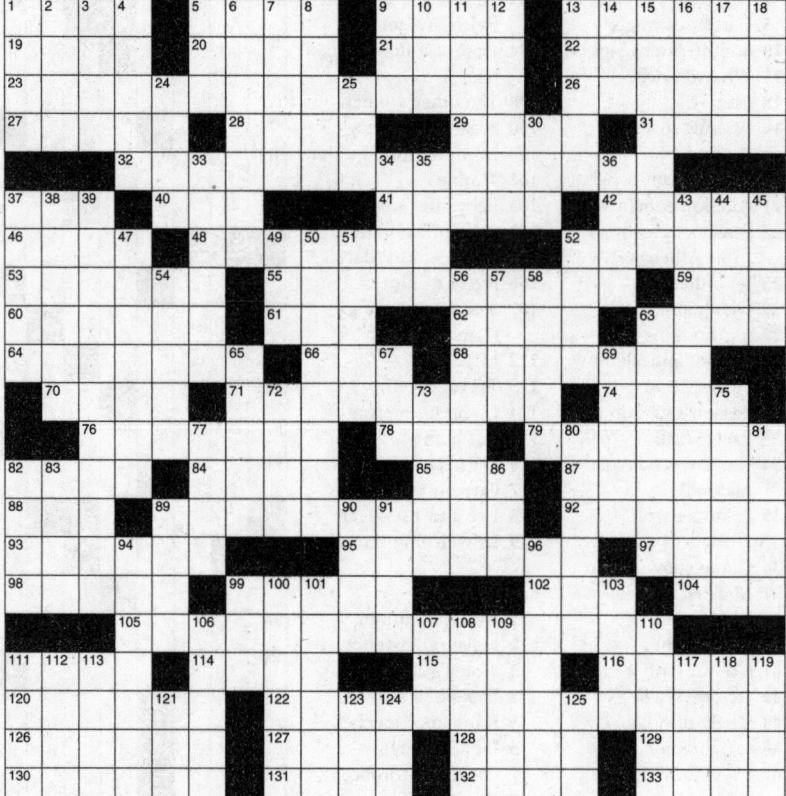

by Cathy Millhauser

43 Where the criminal seaman ended up?
44 Martha of "Hellzapoppin"
45 Inuit conveyance
47 Some fishermen
49 C.I.A., once
50 Indecent
51 Saved for future viewing
52 Third-century date
54 Emerge
56 Secures with seat belts
57 Broke clods
58 Successful
63 Money: Lat.
65 Range
67 Old Fox sitcom
69 Put a new point on
72 Artist's workspace
73 Non-italic
75 Notched range
77 End in ___
80 Slip remover
81 To date
82 Slumbering
83 Robin Cook book
86 Little: Suffix

89 Actress Virna
90 Print indelibly
91 Actress Talbot
94 Map explanations
96 Gadabouts
99 Lacrosse squad
100 Jamaican music
101 Muslim moguls
103 Vier preceder
106 They hold tight
107 "-y" equivalent
108 Part of L.C.M.
109 Sun: Prefix
110 Mr. Arafat
111 Reindeer herder
112 Sheik Abdel Rahman
113 Conn of "Benson"
117 By way of, old-style
118 Office note
119 Those, to Juanita
121 Hackberry, for one
123 Bang maker
124 Me, it's often said
125 Jazzman Montgomery

ACROSS

1 Supermarket section
6 In re
10 Emmy-winning actress Neuwirth
14 Help for the memory-challenged
19 Bulldog
20 From the flock
21 Seldom seen
22 Bypass
23 Teacake
24 Small whirlwind
26 Jerry Rice, e.g., informally
27 Kato's boss
29 Couch
30 Seat of Jackson County, Texas
31 Stock option
32 Aristophanes play that caused a buzz
34 "Baywatch" types
38 Because
39 "Awake, faire Muse," e.g.
40 Lay waste to
41 Nursery rhyme start
49 Excitedly active
51 Former First Lady
52 Revolutionary War hero
53 Cork's place
54 ___ Park, Calif.
55 Produce an effect, as medicine
56 Ones involved in match play
57 Dog's problem
58 African monarchy
60 Caron role
61 Offer
62 Region of Nicaragua
66 Sculptured
70 Brand
71 Bulldozer, e.g.
75 Fanatical
76 Actress Adams et al.
78 1959 Kingston Trio hit
79 Sirens
81 "___ Shoes" (American spiritual)
82 Time's 1977 Man of the Year
83 Inquiry: Abbr.
84 Like some roofs
85 1939 tale of a tarnished Tinseltown, with "The"
88 To be, to Henri
89 Dory's need
90 Becoming slower, musically: Abbr.
91 Place to buy redeye
94 Nickname of Sophocles
99 Them: Fr.
100 Ramses I's successor
101 Early riser?
102 Tale of a butchered Piggy
109 1960–61 A.L. M.V.P.
110 Item sacred to Athena
111 Liberated city of September 1944
112 First name in cosmetics
113 Nil ___ bonum
114 Occupational name endings
115 The "her" of "Leave Her to Heaven"
116 Ancient relic: Var.
117 MTV target
118 Copper
119 Silver, e.g.

DOWN

1 Best-selling CD-ROM game
2 Per
3 Kind of root
4 Glassy sound
5 Hit the roof
6 Pilgrim couple
7 Executive hotel offering
8 Mary Roberts Rinehart volume
9 Paper nautilus and others
10 English goose
11 Sun shade
12 Actress Ekland
13 Member of a conger line?
14 Like some magazine subscriptions
15 Madonna movie role
16 Jargons
17 "___ but dazzling darkness": Vaughan
18 1996 loser to Netanyahu
25 London's ___ Lane
28 Netherlands city
29 Detroit offering
33 See 36-Down
34 Author Stoker
35 Stereotype
36 With 33-Down, polar phenomena
37 Diamond and others
38 Accelerated
41 Gaboriau detective
42 Texas home of the Bears
43 Actress Lenore
44 Day-___
45 Give birth on the farm
46 Predicament
47 Impetus
48 One going in the right direction?
50 Came up quickly
51 Dickensian cries
56 Falafel holders
57 Lithium and others
59 Quite a load
60 Misled, or worse
61 Literary monogram
63 Expected
64 Jazz group, maybe
65 "___ the day!" (Shakespearean phrase)
66 Part of a crossword
67 Music whose name means "color"
68 "___ Like That" (Bernstein/Sondheim song)
69 One of the Corleones
72 Desk item
73 Sister of Clio
74 1930's-ish, e.g.
76 Skier Phil
77 Orange drink
78 New wine
80 Strike one as
82 Attempts
83 Hardly practical
86 Intent
87 Well-made product?
91 Bidding
92 Had a little lamb?
93 Loots
94 Tops
95 Destroy
96 Baker's offering
97 Having greater reserve
98 "Heartbreak House" heroine
99 North Carolina politician Sam
100 Adamantine
103 Seine tributary
104 Unfettered
105 Ice-cream truck song
106 "Winnie-___-Pu"
107 C.S.A.'s Robert ___
108 Computer command
110 N.Y. neighbor

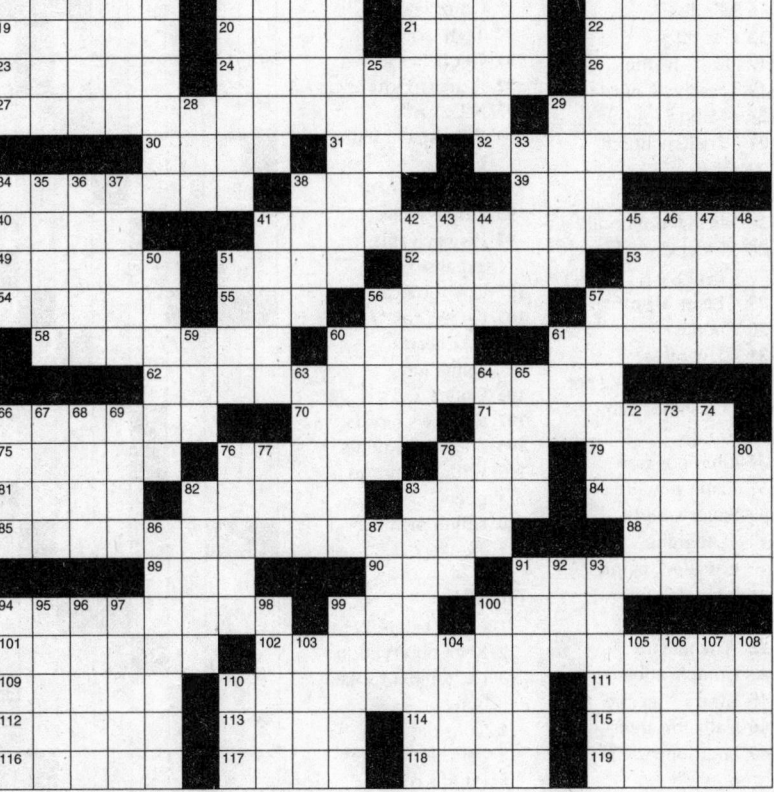

by Jonathan Schmalzbach

ACROSS

1 Ancient storyteller
6 Minded
11 Cut off
17 Bird's wattle
19 Dissolved substance
20 Waiting
21 Parisian church
22 Drifts
23 Frisked
24 Michigan monoliths
26 Model Cheryl
28 Cosmo, e.g.
29 Chemical suffix
30 Zoomed
31 Cleverness
32 Hide-and-seek spot
33 "West Side Story" group
34 Ohio noggins
37 Piano practice
39 Sailor's reply
40 "Laughing Cavalier" painter
41 Nine, in combinations
42 A whole lot
43 Complications
45 Kind of service
46 Calls the shots
49 "___ longa, vita brevis"
50 Colorado bylaw
53 Cheer leader?
54 Declined
57 In the raw
58 Fleeced
59 Palindromic singer
60 Lift: elevator:: bridewell: ___
61 Start of a Shakespeare title
62 Calendar col.
63 Miracles' "Going to a ___"
64 Wright wing?
65 Less up-to-date
67 Lodgings
68 "Radio Days" director
69 Animation frame
70 Alabama residence
72 It's past due
73 Colorful shells
75 Opening notes
76 Made still
80 "___ chance!"
81 Ballerina Shearer
83 Mystique
84 All ___ sudden
85 Señor Cervantes
87 California chap
89 Mr. Pecksniff of "Martin Chuzzlewit"
90 Tech. school
91 Get better
92 Actress Virna ___
93 N.C.A.A. tournament nail-biters
94 Make fun of
95 Hoyle subject
97 Pennsylvania expanse
101 Cochise's cohorts
103 God of the Nile
105 Red heart, sometimes
106 Gofers
107 Eat one's words
108 Stew ingredients
109 Without end, to poets
110 Union member
111 Honkers

DOWN

1 Letter before beth
2 Keen observation
3 Doctored a broken bone
4 Considers
5 Pain, so to speak
6 Pupil's coat
7 Nautical heading
8 Grand slam foursome
9 J.F.K. info
10 Ordain
11 Difficulty
12 Cookbook amts.
13 Put away
14 Illinois college
15 Fold
16 Beats around the bush
18 Starts of auto races
19 Attacks
20 Summer treats
25 Linen fabric
27 Bird-plane link
31 Go off
32 Scourge
33 More than jiggle
35 Blues street
36 Home of Phillips University
37 Country crossings
38 Cut away the center of
40 Like #4 pencils
44 Chinese weight
45 Tidbit
46 Fists
47 Hint
48 Fishing lure
50 Soprano Amelita ___ Curci
51 Guess Who hit of 1970
52 Compact material
54 Pilot's option
55 Plantation worker
56 Montana entranceway
57 Squeals
61 Unkeyed, musically
63 Jollity
65 Walloped
66 Phone feature
67 Kerchief for protecting straightened hair
68 What the fat lady sings?
71 Middle of a wheel, often
72 Become
74 Praise
76 Resembling
77 Directly competitive
78 Not long after, in olden times
79 Morse T
81 Country singer Bandy et al.
82 Figures of speech?
83 In
85 Pool that isn't
86 Sulky
88 "The Graduate" character
89 Military movement
91 Unwelcome greeting
95 Timely question
96 "Take this"
97 Costa ___
98 "Hoc ___ in votis" ("This was among my wishes"): Horace
99 Problem group
100 Jazz pianist Allison
102 Midpoint: Abbr.
104 Salon offering

by Richard Silvestri

ACROSS

1 "Mayday!"
4 M.Sgt.'s inferior
7 D.E.A. worker
11 "#," to a proofreader
16 Tear to shreds
18 Mideast airline
20 Expression of trouble
21 Natalie played her
22 Jean-Jacques Rousseau work
23 City on Norton Sound
24 Part
25 Noble, in a way
26 Ibexes
27 Simon & Garfunkel's first hit, with "The"
30 Torn to shreds
32 Clear
33 Refinery
34 Spotted
35 ___ polloi
36 Marvy
37 Collect
38 Treated unfairly
41 First name in fashion
42 Wiesbaden, for example
45 Answers
48 Escapes alive
53 Up
54 Mess of hair
56 Not working
57 L'chaim, e.g.
58 More plump
60 Building block maker
61 Encase
63 How dogs kiss
64 Resident's suffix
65 Pricey
66 Triple Crown winner War ___
69 Female lobsters
70 Sites of many brawls
74 One-twelfth of a pica
75 "Later"
76 Felix, for one
77 More or less vertical, to a sailor
78 Book before Isaiah
82 With bated breath
84 Physics unit
85 Workers in Detroit make a dash for it
86 Pickled
88 Grand Canyon transportation
90 Sports club
92 Dr Seuss's "___ Ran the Zoo"
93 Out of the wind
97 Orchestrate
100 White House brass?
101 Value judges
103 Military moves carrying a warning
106 Travel guide
107 Oeuf layer
108 Computer symbol
109 Kitchen tubful
110 Bluffer's ploy
111 Stage direction
112 Like praseodymium
113 Hired soldier, in slang
114 Comic Johnson and namesakes
115 Sine qua nons
116 Oscar's cousin
117 "For shame!"
118 Lugubrious

DOWN

1 Italian painter Martini
2 Narcotic
3 Dire Straits' first hit
4 Dog's gift
5 Go all out
6 "Caligula" author
7 Helped get well
8 Give ___ (care)
9 Place-kicker Benirschke
10 Kings and queens
11 Says "cheese"
12 Expert groups
13 Isn't for a lot of people?
14 Medea's aunt
15 Diner
16 "Live" host
17 Nudge
19 Football Hall of Famer Dawson
28 "The Selfish Gene" topic
29 Effigy
31 Ricky Nelson's "Sweeter ___ You"
36 Vitamin bottle abbr.
37 Hand lotion ingredient
39 Until now
40 Clairvoyant's skill
41 City south of Hamar
42 32-card game
43 "Nonsense!"
44 Penny ___
45 Battle of Britain grp.
46 Wing, perhaps
47 Average guy
49 Where Caodaism is practiced
50 Outlines
51 Cheap accommodations
52 Susan Lucci and John Beradino, for two
55 Jazz's Kid ___
59 Link for give and go
60 Deceive
61 Astounded condition
62 She's possessive
65 Fed. loan agcy.
66 Basilica part
67 "Let's Make a Deal" option
68 Chinese dynasty, 1368–1644
69 Nimbus
71 Poet's contraction
72 Bad, in Barcelona
73 Light blue
75 Movie pooch
76 Arnett's net
79 Seat of Cass County
80 Unstoppable, as a plan
81 Unsafe?
83 Character created by Anne Nichols
87 TV series about the Reeds
88 Boohooed
89 Racing brothers
90 "___ Miller"
91 Chop
94 Humbert Humbert's passion
95 Cleared
96 Whistling sounds
97 Poplar tree
98 River from the Alps
99 Paperboy's path
100 Assault
101 Shoelace tip
102 F.D.R.'s mother
104 Ponzi scheme
105 Michelle, par example

by Peter Gordon

114 COLOR ME IRISH!

ACROSS

1 "I'm Still in Love with You" singer
4 Dartmouth's nickname
8 Listing
13 Band with the Grammy-winning album "Dookie"
17 Transportation Secretary Federico
19 Biblical spy
20 Vaughan of jazz
21 Bundle up
22 Gulf north of Somalia
23 Japanese dog breed
24 Walleyed look
25 George Orwell's alma mater
26 Frog's lament, in song
29 Carnival's end
30 Snow White's sister
31 Maiden's lack
32 Its capital is Asmara
34 Not neath
35 Attacked vigorously
38 Some heirs
39 Radio feature
41 ___ marchés (bargains)
42 Man with a bad hair day?
44 Suspect in Clue
47 Like the Owl and the Pussy-Cat's boat
48 Kind of section
49 Superabound
50 "But ___!"
51 Not a dupl.
52 Non-Latino, maybe
53 1965 hit "___ La La"
54 Simpletons
55 Sherlock Holmes movie, with "The"
57 Thumbs-down
59 1995 college football champs
62 Drip
63 Blue
64 Hideaway
65 1973 Charlton Heston sci-fi film
69 Paisley of Northern Ireland
70 Where to watch the birdie?
74 Prehistoric invention
75 Kick out
77 Skip a syllable
79 Kind of crocodile
80 Troubles
81 Attempt
83 "Egad!"
84 Bearded antelopes
85 Unruly hair
86 Neglect to take
88 Amphetamines, in street talk
89 One who works with meters and feet
90 World Cup org.
91 Grad student's bane
93 Strip bark?
94 Army Vietnam group
97 Med. specialty
98 House of sale, to Shakespeare
102 1971 Pan-American Games host city
103 Tom Jones sang this in 1967
108 Qualified
109 Simple people
110 Island with a Great Hall
111 "Blondie" character
112 Precipitate
113 Crete's capital
114 Chopin offering
115 1969 Kingsley Amis novel, with "The"
116 Slave Scott
117 ___ a time
118 Unabridged dictionary, e.g.
119 Needle point?

DOWN

1 "___ of star-crossed lovers" (Romeo and Juliet)
2 Resulted in
3 Inexperience
4 Like bricks
5 Pelvic bones
6 Comes down with
7 Site of Lambeau Field
8 Gives in
9 "Mon Oncle" director
10 Rafsanjani's land
11 Generosity
12 Place to sit before going on
13 Intermediate dojo students
14 Librarian's device
15 Separate
16 Quidnunc
18 Classic juvenile book by L.M. Montgomery
19 Supply with dishes
27 City in Utah County
28 Box-social action
33 Caravansary
35 Cash, in slang
36 Indigo plant
37 "Gadzooks," e.g.
39 Dynamic beginning
40 Kneecap, e.g.
41 Car hood, to a Brit
43 Base
44 Ginnie and Fannie of finance
45 Take a flier
46 Hyson or gunpowder
47 Bam's cousin
48 Kind of terrier
50 St. Patrick's Day activity
53 Señor Ferrari player in "Casablanca"
54 Pluck
56 Winter air
58 Excellent bond rating
60 Slips past
61 1990 Best Actress
65 Used a natatorium
66 One of the three rivers of Three Rivers Stadium
67 Cry of pain
68 The legal profession, in slang
70 Singing voice
71 Best hand in baccarat
72 Flood
73 Graham and Joe, e.g.
76 Drive the getaway car, perhaps
78 Year B.C. in which Crassus died
81 Tex-Mex staple
82 Sanitation engineer
86 Interjection of disgust
87 1924 Michael Arlen novel about London society
89 "Teach"
90 Monthly Meeting member
92 Chang's twin
93 Cropped up
94 Work permit
95 Well-dressed elephant
96 Miss Dunn of "Heartbreak House"
98 Bottom of a platter
99 Mediterranean oaks
100 Woodhouse and Peel of fiction
101 Sierra ___
104 A as in Aachen
105 Wave of water coming aboard a ship
106 Singing part
107 Place ruled by a lord?

by Peter O'Gordon

ACROSS

1 Fortuneteller's aids
7 Fraternal fellow
10 Magnetic flux symbol
13 People with flashlights
19 Farthest point
20 "___ Dance" (Pointer Sisters hit)
22 Sartre play
23 Sot, perhaps
24 Strands
25 Half of a nursery rhyme name
26 Congregates?
29 Overpermissive
30 Family girl
31 Tax
32 Rainbow: prefix
34 Upholstery fabric
39 Poseidon's realm
42 Admitted
45 Introverts
47 Complain, in a way
49 Beat, as grain
50 Collectibles?
53 ___-majesté
55 Devoted
56 Music critic Downes
57 ___ probandi (legal doctrine)
58 Geyser sight
59 Madres' kin
60 Abbr. for Jesse Jackson
61 "Put Your Head on My Shoulder" singer
62 Erupting
64 Storm or Tracker
65 ___ Lanka
66 Novelty?
69 Preteen
72 Liquor-free
74 Iroquois tribe
75 Not give ___
76 Lady in a garden
77 Rakehell
79 Lepidopterans
80 Swell suffix?
81 At another time
82 Arkin of "Catch-22"
83 River near Kassel
84 Halve?
87 Produce additional interest
89 In a sleeping position
91 Engraving instrument
92 Candidate
94 Ethyl acetates
97 Susquehanna River town
98 Hugh Hefner's Muse?
99 Branch
100 It fits in a lock
102 Terminal abbr.
104 A B C's?
113 Make a fresh mix?
115 People who want to lose
116 Open house, perhaps
117 International language system
118 Spellbind
119 Forte
120 They may be glazed over
121 Pepper, for one: Abbr.
122 Archaic exclamations
123 Cover

DOWN

1 Home of ancient Irish kings
2 Copyists
3 Small deer
4 Look up and down
5 Overflow
6 Some Tuzla residents
7 Tangle up
8 Bucolic settings
9 Late rocker Cobain
10 Show
11 Dear
12 Technical sch.
13 Shaded part of a plant
14 Tart
15 Fringe
16 Erupt?
17 Actress Moreno
18 Charon's river
21 Horns
27 Soused
28 Lose no time
33 Reduce taxes, in Britain
34 Overwhelms
35 Swelling wave
36 Human being?
37 Hollywood's Penn
38 Directional suffix
40 Zoo attractions
41 Not be a passive victim
42 It prohibited slavery
43 Agcy. once headed by Edward R. Murrow
44 Some scholars, for short
46 "Silver" star
48 Extreme
51 Soapberry tree
52 Most charming
54 Full of parody
58 Fiji's capital
61 ___ day now
62 Black cuckoos
63 Physique
64 Commerce stat.
67 "Toward Freedom" autobiographer
68 Brewery fixtures
70 Deponent
71 Mean
73 Impressive Impressionist
77 ___ avis
78 Corrida cheers
79 Soldiers
80 "Uh-huh"
81 Author Seton
84 Its atomic number is 83
85 Savings-account abbr.
86 "___ My Party"
88 Expert in Mideast culture
90 10, to a gymnast
93 Vetoes
95 Family dinners
96 Baseball Hall-of-Famer Crawford
99 Handily handling
101 Lulls
102 Like the Negev
103 Start from scratch
105 Time of danger
106 Country crooner McCoy
107 1962 film villain
108 Noted ark-itect
109 Patio component
110 Geometry topic
111 Easter ends it
112 Mr. Pecksniff of "Martin Chuzzlewit"
114 Germanic war god

by Frank A. Longo

ACROSS

1 World-weary
6 Licensing ___
10 Eng. network
13 Biblical incense spice
19 Faulty
20 Christmas present peekers do it
22 Tune
23 Wages
24 Side door, perhaps?
27 The Iliad, e.g.
28 Microscopic life
29 Weapon in action-thrillers
30 Finback whale
32 Room extensions
33 ___-do-well
34 Suspect in a whodunit game?
38 Kind of farm
39 Igor and Dr. Watson: Abbr.
41 Spaghetti-western attire
42 Lyric poem
43 Dynasty after the T'ang
44 Outlet for N.Y. horseplayers
46 Robe adornment
47 Revolution site of 1979
48 Getting ___ years
49 French seasoning
52 Mil. offshoot
55 Common Market inits.
57 A.M.A. members
58 Morning awakener, for some
59 ___ particle
60 "Get ___ of this!"
62 "Elephant Boy" boy
64 Ringbearer in "The Lord of the Rings"
66 Mineral suffix
67 Stinking
69 Joys
72 Zoological duct
75 Sentence subject
77 Flogging, e.g.?
80 Conscious of
81 Numskulls
82 Jocular Johnson
83 Union action?
87 Judah's second son
88 Cooler
89 Trattoria fare
90 Name tag
92 Strip for Spot
93 Ice cream thickeners
95 Coin in 47-Across
97 Honkers
98 Pierce Arrow rival
99 Shrewd
101 ___ amore (with love)
103 "Under a Glass Bell" author
105 Eastern "holies"
106 50-Down, once: Abbr.
107 Westernmost of the Aleutians
108 Give-and-take
110 South Africa's ___ Paul Kruger
112 Fresh
114 Séance sounds
115 Like some coats and paper
117 Loosen rigging
120 Thomas Moore's "The Harp That Once Through ___ Halls!"
124 "___ you sure?"
125 Baseball star?
128 Topic: Sp.
129 Sugar source
131 Bests
132 One who's taken vows
133 Medicinal amts.
134 Disburse
136 Spencer Tracy movie?
140 Faces the wind while stationary, at sea
141 Portuguese writer José Maria ___ de Queiroz
142 Agamemnon's mother
143 Bogart's "High Sierra" role
144 Tailor, in old Rome
145 Napoleonic marshal
146 Nurses
147 Quiet

DOWN

1 Long-toed aquatic bird
2 Soap substitutes, in the Southwest
3 Sad songs
4 Grass used for making paper
5 Brit. medal
6 Cunning, in a way
7 Yeanling's mother
8 Fish-eating bird
9 Despotic jurisdictions
10 Where to get French bread?
11 Premolar
12 Authors
13 Naut. heading
14 On delayed-broadcast
15 Heaps
16 State officers?
17 Shipbuilder's pin
18 Ophthalmologist's implement
20 Flattens
21 Humble toiler
25 Dancers cut it
26 Word with strong or straight
31 Terhune's "___ Dog"
35 Mancinelli opera "___ e Leandro"
36 Playwright David
37 Stimpy's chum
40 Buckle holder
43 Forte
45 Large pill
49 "Maude" or "Frasier" e.g.
50 Where the kroon is spent
51 Beatles character?
53 Shoppers' receptacles
54 Actress Barbara
56 Red chalcedony
57 Children's entertainers
58 Nonsense
61 Summary
63 Turkish ___
64 More kittenlike
65 In medias ___
68 Make roses safe to handle
70 Berber language
71 Water spirits
73 Scorpius's red giant
74 Powerful speaker
76 Cambodia's Lon ___
78 Ancient Mideast nomads
79 Warhol subject
84 Strong cart
85 Cosmonaut's home
86 Red dye
91 Fix a fracture
94 Oxlike antelopes
96 Mothers with pride?
99 Candy cubes
100 Tranquillity
101 Some boaters
102 Sandwich style
104 Vincent Lopez's theme song
108 Traffic warning
109 Like jokers
111 Kind of wheels
113 "Embarkation of Cythera" artist
116 Record holder?
117 Extremist
118 Aurora's doings
119 Soixante minutes
121 Lido, e.g.
122 Hypodermic needle holder
123 Was smart
125 Poetic patchwork
126 Film "7 Faces of Dr. ___"
127 Gene material
130 For fear that
135 Palme ___ (award at Cannes)
137 ___ de coeur
138 Caveman in Moo
139 The Blue Carbuncle, to Holmes

by Bryant White

ACROSS

1 Visiting reporter's interviewees
7 Water vessel
11 Mediterranean port
15 Shelley's "___ to Liberty"
18 It works like a charm
19 Boy of Bogotá
20 Simoleons
21 See 71-Across
22 Rag
23 Novel featuring Napoleon
26 Former trucking indus. overseer
27 Temperately
29 First word of Montana's motto
30 Professional grp.
31 Romanian money
32 Will-wisp connection
33 Lathered
35 Kind of bomber
39 Mythical monster
41 Language akin to Ojibwa
42 Bon ___
45 Montreal skaters, in the sports pages
46 Red-coated cheese
49 How some hogs are raised
52 Theological subj.
53 Baseball stat
54 Rob's wife on "The Dick Van Dyke Show"
55 Littlest
56 Name of four Scottish kings
58 Jam into
60 Bushy clump
63 Booking term
64 Tropical maladies
66 Dinghy's thingies
67 O, e.g.
68 Singer Simone
69 Knitter's need
70 Dress splendidly
71 With 21-Across, symbol of madness
72 "Love Makes the World Go Round" singer Jackson
73 Silver skates boy
74 Slipped
75 XX
76 Hindu mister
77 So-called "Great Precious Conqueror"
79 Place to put your feet up
81 Lewis of Lamb Chop fame
83 Month in Paris
84 Shooter ammo
85 Part of a long-distance company's 800 number
86 Aloud
87 Ted Williams wore it
88 Brooklet
89 Maiden designation?
90 ___-eyed
91 Ecol. police
93 Fouled offensively?
96 Attribute of Athena
99 Buyer's caution
102 "Oh, But ___" (1946 song)
103 Confederate Robert ___
107 Telecommunications giant
108 Old corporate nickname
113 Honorary letter
114 Like Western land, to the pioneers
115 Sent
116 Poet's time of day
117 Kind of chop
118 Print shop order
119 Hardy figure
120 Lobby sign
121 Gaelic
122 Supporters of the 18th Amendment
123 Season ___

DOWN

1 Lips
2 Eclipses and the like?
3 Dairy dish
4 Author Robbe-Grillet et al.
5 "I ___ Song Go . . ."
6 Anna of "Nana"
7 House coats?
8 Be victorious
9 Markey of "Tarzan"
10 Ardent lover
11 Showdown site
12 Canyon thrill-seeker
13 Jai ___
14 Operas by Boito and Mascagni
15 #1 song of 1964
16 Dictated
17 Convert secretly
24 Feat of Klee?
25 Phone trio
28 Baseball's Mr. Tiger
34 Puts one past
36 "The Cosby Show" son and others
37 One addressed as "my lord"
38 It can wait
40 Cockpit figure
42 Actor Assante et al.
43 More grainy
44 1995 Best Picture nominee
47 Yearly payment
48 Flight board abbr.
50 Full of dope
51 Vogue
54 Noted explorer
57 Actor James
59 Bloody, so to speak
61 Make go
62 Cold war period
65 Actress Rowlands
67 Two-handed snack
69 Cut
70 Sides in Avalon Hill games
74 Bring home
75 Tired
77 Terr. until 1889
78 Year in St. Peter's life
80 Blab
82 Cultivated
86 Sexy walk
88 Ransoms
90 Lifts
92 Naples staples
94 Lose
95 Thrash out
97 Meditation words
98 Author ___ Binchy
100 Reserve
101 Archeological bit
104 Admit
105 Overseas student
106 Tribal leader
109 Pun's finish
110 "Deutschland ___ alles"
111 ". . . ___ 'clock scholar"
112 Midwife's action

by Robert H. Wolfe

118 CELEBRITY TYPES

In e-mail messages, faces are sometimes created by combinations of letters, numbers and punctuation marks, as :-(for a frowning face. Tilt your head 90 degrees to the left to view.

by Dean Niles

ACROSS

1 Register Message
7 Slippery ___
10 Clayey deposit
14 Florentine statue
19 Guyana's ___ Indians
20 Kind of flour
21 Jai ___
22 "___, shine; for thy light is come...": Isaiah
23 Vietnam seaport
24 ==}: ‡]]
27 Bone cavities
28 "Indeed!" once
29 Former gold coins of Spain
30 Bye-bye
32 A good deal
34 78-Across's shoe width
35 Short spans
37 8(: o)
41 Battle site of 1944
45 Bud
46 It starts "In the name of Allah..."
47 Dada papa
48 Implanted
49 Basra resident: Var.
51 Evidence left behind
54 Kind of neck
56 Drama kudos
57 Certain solvents
59 [g - }]
62 Mark ___, Oliver of 1968 film
63 Game full of traps
64 Newspaper space
65 ___ Lee cheesecake
67 Tank
68 Hideaway
69 Get-together
71 First name in erotica
73 Garlicky dish
78 *‡(: o) }
80 Square-cut-cigar
81 Jazz style
82 Sign of a smash
83 Singer Bob Marley, e.g.
85 Cotton thread
86 1919 Edith Day musical
87 Teacher's grp.
89 One of the archangels
91 Hog's thigh
92 Brute
93 I8 - #) ‘‘‘‘‘
97 Towel tag
98 Want-ad initials
99 Caboose position
100 Kumiss imbiber
102 Convoke
107 Spoors
110 Author Calvino
113 cI[: -=)I
115 Speculator
116 Begrime, in Britain
117 When les étoiles come out
118 Dweller on the Mekong
119 Freshen
120 Slight
121 Preserve, in a way
122 Cry of pain
123 Criminal evidence

DOWN

1 Nothing, in Nogales
2 Port south of Cartagena
3 *‡ : -)}}}
4 Stars and bars, e.g.
5 Hawaiian island
6 Record from the heart: Abbr.
7 Jacob's twin
8 Western livestock peril
9 Eucalyptus, e.g.
10 Literally, "high-souled"
11 ___ rigueur (to the fullest extent): Fr.
12 Mover's equipment
13 Symbols of purity
14 Pre-Raphaelite Rossetti
15 Bowed, in music
16 Early stringed instrument
17 ___ Royale National Park
18 Studies
25 Call on a yawl
26 Encouraging words from a student
28 Riding whips
31 Comic Philips
33 Theologian Kierkegaard
35 Fast pitch
36 ___ Naval Weapons Station, N.J.
38 Passenger balloon part
39 Hang of it
40 Rises, as water
41 Ferber book
42 Wind around
43 Kind of soup
44 Indulges to the extreme, informally
46 Early TV medium
48 Battery type
50 Kit ___ (candy bar brand)
52 Contemporary
53 Wife of Henry II
55 Literary pseudonym
58 Feature
60 Ontario-Quebec border river
61 High-calorie snack
63 Port in 1943 fighting
66 Crowd sounds
69 Dried out
70 ___ hole (modern worry)
72 "To wrap up..."
74 Christina's father
75 (¶ -)
76 Kind of extremes
77 Tabloid twosomes
78 North Atlantic sighting
79 ___ de Lion
80 Stone memorials
81 Such is a life
84 Chorus sound
88 Old recording disk
90 Prefix meaning "outer"
93 Vast desert
94 Give some slack
95 Beethoven's "___ Quartet"
96 One way to convey information
97 John Wayne film
98 Welsh actor Williams
101 One making rapid strides
102 S&L deposit
103 "Out!"
104 ___ vaccine
105 First name in mysteries
106 S.A. country
108 Bye-bye
109 Be close to
111 Riga denizen
112 Assayers assay them
114 With it
115 Twaddle

ADDLEPATED ADS

ACROSS

1 "Tales from Shakespeare" co-writer
5 Assays
10 First word of "The Raven"
14 Rybinsk Reservoir site
19 Author Wiesel
20 Kind of acid
21 Artificial
22 Wickerwork material
23 Dry cleaner's ad
27 D'Oyly Carte offering
28 Arduous journey
29 Bleeds
30 Netman Ilie
31 Forest opening
32 Mlle., across the Pyrenees
33 Faulkner's "___ Lay Dying"
34 Rafsanjani's country
35 Oklahoma Indian
36 Bunyan's Blue Ox
40 Pest controller's ad
47 Recherché
48 Mirrored
49 Like marcelled hair
50 Like ___ from the blue
51 Greek letters
52 Urban miasma
53 Richard of "Pretty Woman"
54 Hooked grass-cutter
55 Singer with the Four Knights
56 Henley crew-member
57 Clout
58 Figures
59 Grocery-store ad
67 ___ account (absolutely not)
68 Billy Budd's captain
69 Doctrine
70 Burns's "Scots Wha ___"
71 Blocked, as a river
74 Miss Muller, of a Whittier poem
75 Dream stages
76 Physicist Niels
77 The ancient Mariner's cry
78 Estella, to Miss Havisham
79 Amneris's rival
80 C'est ___ (it's his)
81 Charlady's ad

86 "Untouchable" Eliot
87 Make a lap
88 Feather: Prefix
89 Yearling's mom
90 Kett of old funnies
91 Bacheller's "___ Holden"
92 Proem
96 Word provider?
100 Caesar's wife
101 Stripper, notably
102 Pharmacy ad
105 Together
106 Crystal gazer
107 ___ and a day (legal time limit)
108 Noisy-le-Sec seasons
109 Cheap, poorly-made furniture
110 Separate the laundry
111 Inclines
112 Dare, in Dogpatch

DOWN

1 It makes you pucker up
2 Tap in a confirmation service
3 Radio equipment
4 Excises of a sort
5 1982 Dustin Hoffman role
6 Use a solvent
7 Antitoxins
8 Nervous twitch
9 Kiltie's country
10 Repeatedly
11 London stoolie
12 Prompter's hint
13 As an old hand
14 Electric-battery inventor
15 Sonja Henie's home
16 One who's recumbent
17 Lady's partner
18 The humanities
24 It inflates your dough
25 Gladiators' stamping ground
26 Eulogize
31 "Peer Gynt" composer
32 Italian white wine
34 Sense of a sentence
36 Ohio University mascot
37 Running wild
38 Big Ben, for one
39 Tasso's patron
40 Songbirds
41 Cause heartburn

42 Sappho's Muse
43 New Jersey mountain range
44 Midnight
45 Bogart in "High Sierra"
46 Toussaint L'Ouverture's land
52 Dive suddenly, as a whale
53 Shield
54 Emma of "Dynasty"
57 Spurious
58 Bleak
60 Funny papers
61 Toll
62 Pistil part
63 Fischer-Dieskau's musical forte
64 "___ Night" (Christmas carol)
65 A Minor Prophet
66 Spooky
71 Homer's was "rosy-fingered"
72 Late tennis great
73 Baseball's "Say Hey Kid"
74 Devilfish

75 On high
76 Like some lies
78 Role for 101-Down
79 Kind of highway
82 Bar, legally
83 Isaac Stern stroke
84 Passions
85 'Twixt
90 County on the Thames
91 Make an effort
92 Popular pie variety
93 Queen of the Misty Isles
94 First discovered asteroid
95 Dadaist Max
96 Sailor
97 Cuban dough
98 Tang
99 Companion of the Pinta
100 On-line person
101 Perlman of "Cheers"
103 Recent prefix
104 Ship rope

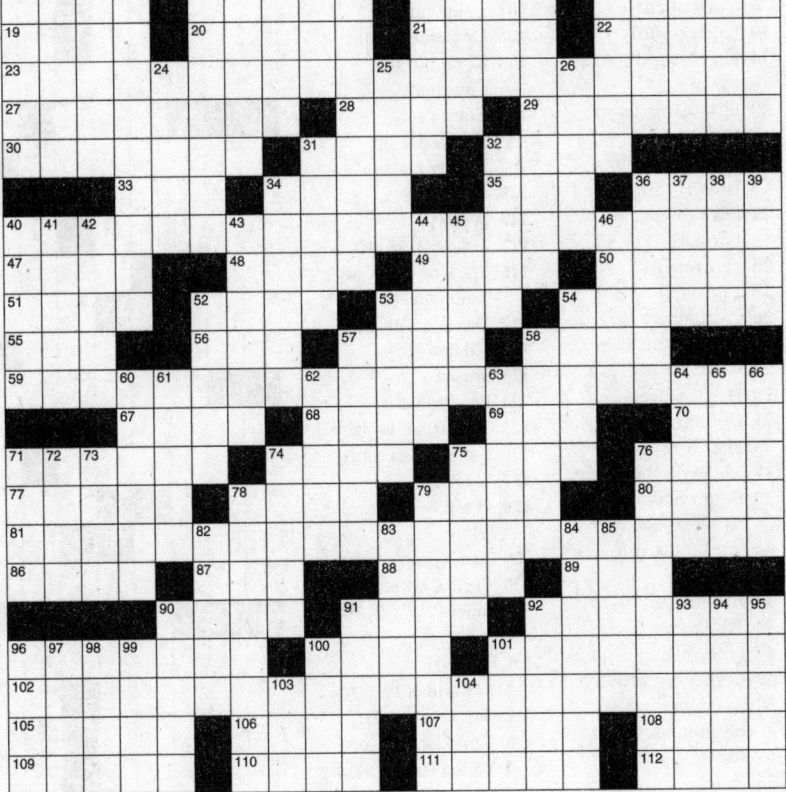

by Frances Hansen

A LOT OF HOGWASH

ACROSS

1 Crack
6 Current choice
10 Latch (onto)
14 Knock hard
19 "Vive ___!"
20 First name in Websters
21 ___ Nui (Easter Island)
22 Film director Forman
23 Hogwash
25 Vim
26 Capital, e.g.
27 Seat on the aisle
28 Early nuclear org.
29 Hogwash
31 Golden time
35 Had down
37 Miles per hour, e.g.
38 Susan Sontag's "___ as Metaphor"
39 "Apologia pro vita ___"
40 Bangers
44 Tumbler
45 Hogwash
49 Centers of activity
50 Academic benchmark
51 Rim supports
53 Ruins
55 Physique, slangily
56 Turkish title
58 Northamptonshire river
59 Pizazz
60 Kind of pie
63 Farm vermin
65 Most thirsty
67 Mosslike growth on marine rock
68 Eastern court members
70 It may have a big head
71 Cylindrical
73 Badge
75 Refugee, for one
78 Scenic balcony
81 Small sea bird
82 It may really smell
83 Hayley Mills role in "The Parent Trap"
85 Wolf: Prefix
86 ___ Lanka
87 Nolan Ryan, notably
89 Beachwear
91 Old Pontiac
92 "Cómo ___ usted?"
94 Hogwash
96 Frothy
98 Hide among pioneers?
101 Chest muscle
102 Opposite of all
104 Gone but not forgotten
105 Composer Khachaturian
107 Hoodwinked
108 Hogwash
112 Seemly
115 Celestial Altar
116 ___ sine qua non (requisite)
117 Dental exam part
118 Hogwash
123 Snowy ___
124 Borderline
125 Mountain denizen
126 Foreign assembly
127 Shelve
128 "Laugh-In" regular Alan
129 Anniversary item
130 Boris Godunov and others

DOWN

1 Franklin's 1936 foe
2 Atl. coast state
3 Feminist measure
4 Banks family nanny
5 Not rising or falling, as a sea
6 "Wheel of Fortune" purchase
7 Musician's ___ mark
8 Common town name ending
9 Physicals
10 Diving bird
11 McKenzie, Brackman TV series
12 Form of silica
13 Herb once thought to be an aphrodisiac
14 Street ___
15 Bridge boo-boo
16 Rick's film love
17 Low digits
18 O.T. book
24 Has a tab
30 ___ Claire, Wis.
31 Fitting work
32 Empty portion of a bottle
33 Hogwash
34 Champion
36 No for an answer
39 Film specification
40 Reds' owner Marge
41 Hogwash
42 Escherich's medical discovery
43 The hit, usually
46 Endorses
47 Go full-bore
48 Medical suffix
52 Thick mush of cornmeal
54 Dry-dock support
57 Have efficacy
59 Hogwash
61 Above, in Berlin
62 Get a lode of this!
64 1953 Pulitzer playwright
66 Answer to "Pourquoi?"
69 Forwarded
72 High-ranking
73 Let up
74 Infirmary call
76 70's Italian P.M.
77 Group values
79 93, e.g.
80 Stayed (with)
84 Took the spoils
88 Popular potted plants
89 Pertaining to the subject
90 Juvenal, for one
93 Amu Darya's outlet
95 Baden-Baden is one
97 Exteriors
99 Sudoriparous
100 Clobbers
103 Toward the mouth
105 "Nor iron bars ___": Lovelace
106 Spanish royalty
108 Scored 100 on
109 Summon
110 Knitting stitch
111 Language in Lahore
113 Coppertone ingredient
114 Take a hike
119 Pink-slip
120 Some trial evidence
121 Roman domestic deity
122 French connections

by Dean Niles

ACROSS

1 Abraham's Oscar role
8 Some Oklahomans
15 Compel compliance of
22 First name in the ring
23 Where drinks are not a treat
24 Trays
25 Random threesome
27 Comedic threesome
28 As originally positioned
29 Polynesian wreath
30 "___ Darlin'" (1959 song)
31 Realize
32 Telecom giant
33 Spanish things
35 Red, white and blue team
37 Caps for chaps
39 Composer ___ Carlo Menotti
40 Bad luck threesome
45 Clint's "In the Line of Fire" co-star
46 Assist
47 60's fashion
48 Year in Trajan's reign
49 El ___
51 Justice chief
52 Dwarfed tree
54 Sports page abbr.
56 Bizarre
60 Reconnaissance groups
62 Shakespearean threesome
67 Bad ___, Germany
68 Absolute worst
70 Verbally
71 Bass attachment
72 Weight
73 Med. printout
74 Chucks
76 Item in a chest
77 "Now it's clear!"
78 Yuletide threesome
82 Literary threesome
84 Galley features
85 Flooring
86 Kind of abrasive
89 G.R.F.'s Veep
90 Rose fancier
91 Grown-up elver
92 Horne and Olin
93 Rabbit's tail
95 Spook group
98 Old TV threesome
101 Kind of room
103 Attempts
104 60's–70's record label
105 Street shaders
108 A Karamazov brother
109 Jumper
113 Kind of bag
115 Dog command
116 Napa Valley sight
117 "Sighted sub, sank ___"
120 Deli threesome
125 Barbra's "A Star Is Born" co-star
126 Attacks
127 Hymn word
128 Dressy wear
129 Hems
130 German article
131 Energy unit
133 Born
135 Olympic swimmer Rowdy
139 Religious threesome
141 Digital threesome

144 Equivocating
145 Radiant
146 Dreamer's opposite
147 Struck out
148 Mañana
149 Concurs

DOWN

1 King of ancient Egypt
2 Cosmetic name
3 Hightails
4 Dashboard item
5 Tina Brown, e.g.
6 Withdraw as a judge
7 Bug
8 Teen trial
9 Range of operation
10 Silvery-gray
11 Finger bone
12 Dugout
13 1929 Wallace Thurman play
14 Jazz trombonist
15 Core
16 Actress Richardson
17 Bomb
18 Ab ___ (from the top)
19 A Jackson
20 Canea resident
21 Early ascetic
26 Hall-of-Fame Dodger manager
31 "Letting Go" novelist
34 Maximally

36 Parties
38 Implied
39 More like TV's Oscar
40 ___ diem
41 Construction member
42 Washroom sign
43 Begley Sr. and Jr.
44 Shuttle-service plane
50 Poker need
52 Bloke
53 Aggregate
55 Board's partner
57 "___ Dreams" (1986 song)
58 Allude
59 ___ Park, Colo.
61 Unpopular org. in the 70's
63 Iowa college
64 Legislative bodies
65 Grind
66 Sweet young things of stage
69 Blanche DuBois' sister
73 Performing groups
75 See 130-Across or 87-Down
76 Violinist Jean ___ Ponty
78 Shaving products
79 National capital whose name means "military post"
80 Heath plant
81 Yesterday, on the Yonne
82 Beethoven's "___ Solemnis"
83 Soho "so long"
86 100 centimos
87 75-Down, Spanish-style

88 Synthetic
92 Bit of psychedelia
94 Holiday scene
95 Kind of center or duty
96 Fatuous
97 Keats' "The Eve of St. ___"
99 Exploit
100 ___ Linda, Calif.
102 Like some real estate parcels
106 Campus letter
107 Nut from a Chinese tree
110 Gain
111 Kind of economy
112 Chant ending
114 Chess finale
117 Oblique
118 Hit it big
119 Book of prayers
121 Two-channel
122 Actress Ryder
123 Musicians' transitions
124 Two-1 creatures
130 Issue
132 Defraud
134 Wired
136 Nürnberg negative
137 Formerly, formerly
138 J.F.K. sights
140 Pilot's heading
141 Report card abbr.
142 1961 Heston role
143 New Deal agcy.

by Nancy Nicholson Joline

ACROSS

1 Declined
6 Sound of sawing wood
11 This isn't it
15 Part of the second qtr.
18 Conger's cousin
19 Caught congers
20 Land of ancient Ephesus
22 Rap's Dr. ___
23 At the office Mr. Ridder ___
26 Fondue, for one
27 Shady bunch
28 Razor brand
29 To be, to Balzac
30 Marx born Leonard
32 "Agnus ___"
33 At the bank Mr. Ridder ___
37 Woe
40 Windward's opposite
41 Dwarfish
42 Kempt
43 Gudrun's victim
45 Tours "Sure!"
47 Procedure: Abbr.
48 In the gym Mr. Ridder ___
55 LXVII x III
58 Court king Arthur
59 Deco artist's pseudonym
60 Bungle
64 Back at work Mr. Ridder ___
69 Wax-and-tint art form
70 Alchemical, astrological, etc.
71 HBO alternative
72 Home of Proteus and Valentine
73 Bobsledding track
74 In the parking lot Mr. Ridder ___
80 Type of twill
81 Rembrandt's "The ___ of Europa"
82 Where leopards get spotted
83 Interjections
84 At the restaurant Mr. Ridder ___
90 Case makers, for short
93 Inlet
94 Turturro of "Angie"
95 Like gentlemen's agreements
98 Inventor Otis
101 Broker's tip, perhaps
103 Lined, as a furnace hearth
106 At the dessert bar Mr. Ridder ___
111 Arctic explorer John
112 Black cats and others
113 Best Picture of '58
114 Locale of Shakespeare's "fiery portal"
115 Stolen item that's often returned
116 Lt. Columbo, e.g.
117 In his bedroom Mr. Ridder ___
122 Writer LeShan
123 Some are gray
124 Astronomer Tycho
125 Brand X
126 Patriotic women's org.
127 Swallow hole?
128 Pioneer in calculus notation
129 Sweet girl of old song

DOWN

1 Fixes firmly
2 Kind of algebra
3 Cliché
4 Grub
5 Give a new hue
6 Rows
7 "Toward Freedom" autobiographer
8 City on the Allegheny
9 Short play?
10 Tokugawa shogunate capital
11 ___ balance (have a decisive effect)
12 Muslim nymph
13 Kitties need them
14 Make equal
15 More than devotees
16 Tingling
17 Calmly lies
21 Primitive: Prefix
24 Applies with cotton balls
25 Ancient Iranian
31 Worked (up)
34 Colombian city
35 Whiffenpoof Society members
36 Commercial award
38 Ernie Bilko creator Hiken
39 Ordinal number ender
43 Seuss's "Horton Hears ___"
44 1969 Oates novel
45 Half of sedecim
46 "Under Hawaiian Skies" accompaniment
49 Toast, in diner slang
50 Figure-eight half
51 Tree good for carving on
52 Supply
53 It's burnt or raw
54 Princess's need
55 Swamp critters, for short
56 Stash
57 Acquire
61 Simon Legree's creator
62 "Alice in Wonderland" cat
63 Initials, maybe
65 Expenditure
66 Topps rival, to baseball card collectors
67 Like some roofs
68 Sra., across the Pyrenees
72 Glass: Sp.
74 Vier preceder
75 ___ avis
76 Unveil, in poetry
77 Alligator logo name
78 Ice cream ___
79 Narrow berth
85 Visually blah
86 F.D.R.'s dog
87 Some are essential
88 Was awarded
89 Mere morsel
90 Downgraded
91 San Francisco Bay city
92 Brandy-Cointreau concoction
96 Acceptable, in some books
97 Reins cats and dogs?
99 Hill V.I.P.: Abbr.
100 "___ luego!"
101 Most discerning
102 Markey who played Tarzan's Jane
103 "Mutt and Jeff" cartoonist Bud
104 Little on the end
105 Movie title rider
107 Share a view
108 Girls of Spain
109 Float decoration
110 Cousin of a potter's wheel
115 Graceful bird
118 Coffee container
119 Brit. award
120 Land on the Rio de la Plata: Abbr.
121 Stroke for Seles

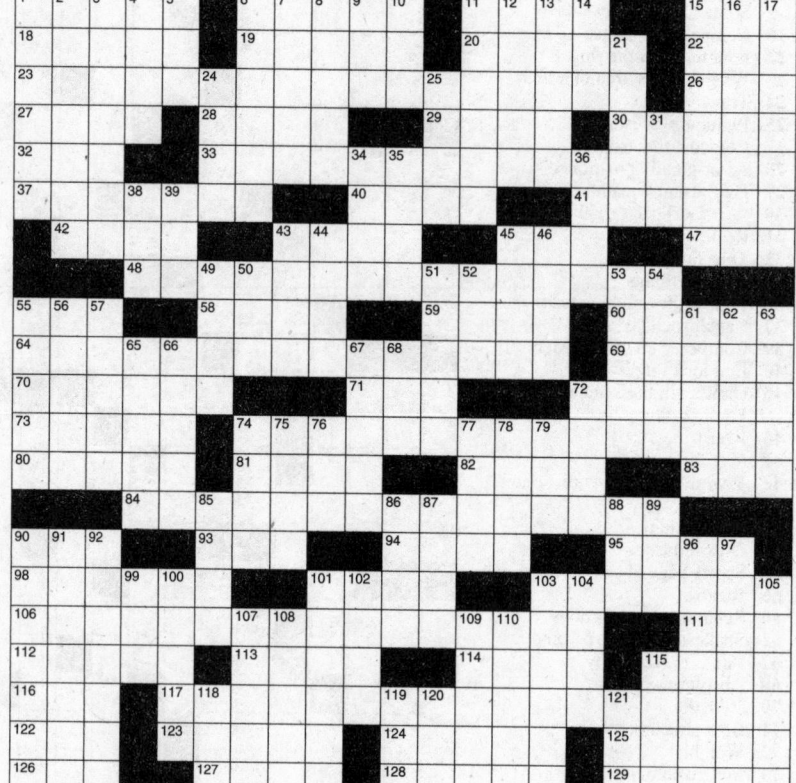

by Cathy Millhauser

ACROSS

1 Public
6 Vending machine items
11 "Here I go . . . !"
19 Province around Peiping
20 News brief
21 Shows how it happened
22 Quickly, in a grove?
24 Forest friend?
25 Punches in
26 Guiding light: Var.
28 Guanacos' kin
31 Demoiselle
32 First tiers
35 Cutup
36 Like the north wind
38 Dunces
40 Track passes
41 Weather map details
43 320 rods
44 World atlas abbr.
45 1960's sports org.
46 "Slow down"
47 Dogcatcher's quarry
48 Wing shape
50 "Cry ___ River"
51 1987 Best Actress
53 Soot mark
56 It stands for something
57 Stray
58 Listen to the trees?
61 Made a basketball foul
63 Girasol
65 Disdainful one
67 Out the window
68 Turns over a new leaf
71 Logger's "yes"?
73 Must, with "to"
76 Highway diversion
77 Clown's props
79 News
80 Writer LeShan
81 Ivy-covered
83 Bibliographical suffix
84 Longtime Steelworkers chief
86 Custom
87 Crimson rival
88 Like some proportions
90 Magazine
93 Pad
94 According to Isaiah, it "shall lie down with the kid"
96 Popular record label

97 1956 perfect game pitcher Don
99 Take in
100 Speak to deaf ears
101 Belafonte forte
102 Trellis climber
105 Like Lindsay Wagner, in 70's TV
107 Timber wolf's little cousin?
110 Evergreen song favorite?
115 Faith
116 English V.I.P.'s
117 Massey of old films
118 Term
119 Folklore figure
120 Astringent fruit

DOWN

1 "What have we here?"
2 Encyc. part
3 Prefix with -taph
4 Makes plain
5 After that
6 One down at the heels?
7 Sports figures?
8 Pop
9 Workshop
10 Ladies of LaMancha
11 Kind of student
12 Collared or jellied dishes
13 North American hawk
14 Like some bandits
15 Slim
16 Protection money paid to the police
17 Get-together: Abbr.
18 Barcelona bruin
20 Milks, in a way
23 Electronic game name
27 Each and every
28 Like some hearts
29 Casual shoe
30 Arboreal consensus?
31 Equine hue
33 Hard-to-find shade giver?
34 Oscar, for one
36 Certifying exams
37 Baby docs
38 Song from "Cymbeline"
39 Music holder
42 Viewed
43 Strong java
47 Like pipe tobacco
49 Hall-of-Famer Slaughter

51 MacGregor, for Rob Roy
52 Sabers' features
53 Pursues
54 George V's wife
55 "Oklahoma!" aunt
59 ___ Gay
60 One way to order whiskey
62 Hopalong Cassidy's portrayer
64 N.F.L.'s ___ Rozelle Award
66 "Ivanhoe" damsel
68 Caper
69 Members of a diaspora
70 Serious
72 Beverage nut
74 Some of Bartlett's quotations
75 Declines
78 Forbes competitor
82 Pets
84 Part of N.C.A.A.: Abbr.
85 Rouge or noir, e.g.
89 On duty
90 Stemming

91 Phrase of agreement
92 Cattle-grazing area
93 Kind of battery
95 Easter festivity
96 Sun Devils' sch.
98 Outs
101 Nap sacks
103 Suffix with phosphor
104 It's stingo, in British lingo
105 Soother
106 "Bonne ___!"
107 Modern office needs
108 Before
109 Woodlawn, e.g.: Abbr.
111 Cable choice
112 ___-hoo
113 Chicago-Detroit dir.
114 1937 song "___ It Rain?"

by Diane C. Baldwin

ACROSS

1 Needled
7 Neighbor of Ala.
10 Where to 'ang one's 'at
13 Its capital is Dispur
18 Tempt
19 Create a new look
21 More platitudinous
23 I-beam projection
24 Lightweight cotton fabric
25 Like an August day
26 CHALTUPID
29 Island in a river
31 Helpful PC key
32 Light rowboat
33 Magazine founded 11/23/36
34 VISSADAGE
39 '60s Tarzan
40 Song syllable
43 Tree trunks
44 Cylindrical buildings
45 Computer storage acronym
47 Jezebel's husband
48 Kind of clock
50 Thimbleful
51 JASOWB
54 Mouth off
55 Relief
57 Multicolored
58 Lively intelligence
59 Second-century date
60 Saintly ring
62 Printings
64 SNILTIR
69 Raconteur
70 Lhasa ___ (terrier)
71 Bearded revolutionary
72 "The Graduate" role
73 Grub
75 Artifice
77 Parade passageway
81 GAINBEAK
83 Barbarian
84 The Joker, on TV
86 Old French coins
87 Like: Suffix
88 Donnybrook
90 The "L" of L. Frank Baum
91 ___ gestae
92 Judge Lance
94 BEDORISING
97 Lulu
98 Dudes
99 Philosophical universal
100 Mudhole
101 SPORETAFF
109 Hospital worker
110 Fan
111 "Flash Gordon," e.g.
114 Seaport on the Loire
115 Tractable
116 Vacuum tube type
117 Temperamental
118 One-handed Norse god
119 Curious
120 Browning work

DOWN

1 British pilots' grp.
2 Unsatisfactorily
3 Metazoan stages
4 It can be a sacrifice
5 So
6 Intensify
7 Gallic characteristic
8 Riga native
9 Oriental pram-pusher
10 Warlike
11 Carnival exhibit
12 First sch.
13 Pardon, once
14 Pompous
15 ___ à manger (dining room): Fr.
16 Kind of clef
17 First name in TV talk
20 Bulova rivals
22 Kind of flour
27 Adherents
28 Fragrant resin
29 Coptic bishops' titles
30 Actress Massey
35 Electricity generators
36 Prefix with bar or bath
37 ___ Cook Jr. of "The Maltese Falcon"
38 Beau Brummell
40 Radon isotope
41 Garden work
42 Does lookout at a heist
46 It's south of Brigham City
47 Ancient Rome's ___ Forum
49 Raphael's "Triumph of ___"
51 God-loving
52 Reply to a bad choice
53 "___ World Turns"
56 Famous beach
57 Sits heavily
59 Siberian salt lake
61 Slacken
63 Medics
64 Factor in sentencing, perhaps
65 Discovery of March 13, 1781
66 Swipes
67 Hydrox alternatives
68 Insects' antenna sockets
69 More novel
74 With embarrassment
76 Intact, as a pharaoh's tomb
77 Univalent chemical group
78 Amnesty
79 Macramé, e.g.
80 Pooh's prize
82 Capital of Deux-Sèvres
83 "Yo!"
85 Flamenco cheer
88 Mike Connors role
89 List ender
92 Connate
93 Wee
95 Judge
96 Uses a crane
97 Keats' "___ Psyche"
101 Nickelodeon cartoon character
102 Term finisher, often
103 Words before time or expense
104 Float
105 Rock's Salt-N-Pepa, e.g.
106 Embraced
107 Claudius' successor
108 Actress Gray
112 American fabulist
113 Give the go-ahead

by Frank A. Longo

ACROSS

1 Urania, e.g.
5 Drug ___
9 Made a suborbital flight
14 "Rob Roy" author
19 ___ errand of mercy
20 Closet
21 Oil source
22 En ___ (roulette bet)
23 504 marbles
25 Bar staple
26 Electrolysis particle
27 Saint of Hollywood
28 Illustrate
29 "Best of . . ." volume
31 With intelligence
32 Capital near the Murrumbidgee River
34 Whereabouts
35 D, for one
36 Leeway
38 Small porch
40 Is partly redundant
44 Like Russia
49 Angela Lansbury role
53 Son of Bani, in the Bible
54 Bellwether's belle?
56 Golden quality
57 Ape
59 False rumor
62 Horse of 50's TV
63 Some fractions
65 Fracases
67 Spectate
68 Proverb giving a clue to this puzzle
73 Stadium cry
74 Surgeon's work
75 Is a forerunner of
76 Incentive of a sort
79 Pulverize the spuds some more
81 Dwellers by the English Channel
82 Forecast
84 Dealer's price
85 Acronym in 70's news
87 Proof word
88 Scheherazade's string of tales?
90 Tyrannical
93 Resell, in a way
95 November honorees
96 One of the Cartwrights
100 French Lick and others
104 Worshiper
107 Freshen
109 Finale of a 151-move chess game
111 Tennis score
112 1,001 log holders
114 Pay
115 Brazilian port
117 1,049 steamships
118 Like krypton
119 Chew the scenery
120 Gaze amorously
121 Kind of pool
122 1,000 boats
123 Groups of pills, e.g.
124 Secretary: Abbr.
125 Cardinal Slaughter

DOWN

1 1,000 poems
2 Pioneering computer of 1951
3 Doc of 30's pulps
4 Pottery surface
5 Cautious
6 Tubular pasta
7 "Zip-___-Doo-Dah"
8 Judge's matter
9 Star of TV's "Addams Family"
10 Squished square
11 Bancroft, Meara and 98 others
12 ___ Lilly & Co.
13 Well-behaved
14 Survey
15 Four and twenty blackbirds (and 76 more)
16 Antelope with spikelike horns
17 Lake catch
18 Itchy, in a way
24 Noted wine family
28 Persecuted priest
30 New Zealand woodcarvers
32 Mulligrubs
33 Hwy.
36 Combines again
37 Boston sports legend
39 Fort's defense
41 Auto-biographies
42 Gore, for example
43 Bundles up
45 Chemical salt
46 Wall Street figure
47 Good hole card
48 Saul's grandfather
49 70's dress
50 Revival cry
51 1,099 regal garments
52 Whiten, as a plant
55 Noted Folies Bergère designer
58 Electrical gauges
60 Like an alias
61 Village
64 Tart
66 Frozen desserts
69 Amenhotep IV's sole deity
70 Word of thanks
71 Tiananmen Square crusher
72 ___ buco
76 Dashboard reading: Abbr.
77 Silkworm
78 Draw forth
80 Optimist
83 Made heavy
86 Big belly
89 Highway caution
91 Cinematographer Nykvist
92 Darling
94 "___ Republic"
97 Vitamin C source
98 Shiny fabric
99 Caterer's food warmer
100 Curtain fabric
101 Full assemblies
102 Pointer
103 Brat's smile
105 ". . . ___ which will live in infamy"
106 Bathroom décor
107 Shoelace tip
108 Curves
110 Bar members, for short
112 A little over a million dollars?
113 Afflictions
116 Latin I word
117 Bird that's an anagram of 116-Down

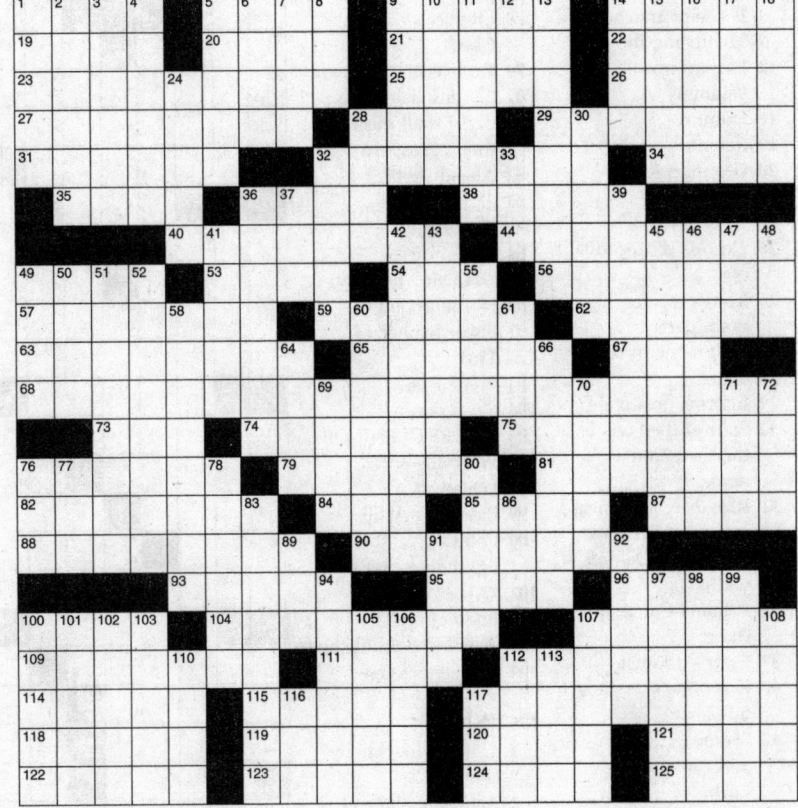

by Ernst Theimer

SO BIG

ACROSS

1 Teleflora rival
4 It's semi-attached
7 That being the case
12 Eastern music
16 Willingly
18 Dummy
19 Remote
20 Groupies follow them
22 OPENLY
25 Express disapproval of
26 Kind of grandparent
27 First name in rock
28 Sauté
29 Informs positively
30 Start of the Sons of the Covenant's name
31 Rice dish with meat
32 Insult, modern-style
33 They come before yodhs
34 Panama Canal, in slang
37 Ewer's adjunct
40 Exert one's influence
42 "Some ___ meat and canna eat": Burns
43 "You Are My Destiny" singer
44 Prefix with dollar
45 "Looking for ___" (Gershwin hit)
46 Actress Carter
47 BARELY
52 Exemplary
53 Suffers humiliation
54 Heckelphones
55 Japanese naval base north of Nagasaki
56 St. ___ fire
57 Falsify, in a way
58 Words on a Wonderland cake
59 More lenient
61 Northerly region of myth
63 Where Empress Zauditu ruled
66 Mailboxes
67 SILENT FILM CAPTION
69 They're worth bonuses, in cards
70 Unwanted look
71 Subject of Ishmael's narration
72 ___ the kill
73 Certain therapy
74 Smooth talkers, perhaps
78 Ellerbee's "___ It Goes"
79 Go over the lines
81 "...my dainty ___! I shall miss thee": Prospero
82 Ahead: Abbr.
83 ___ time (eventually)
84 Arles articles
85 "Bad air," literally
89 Housekeeping
91 Oscar winner of 1961
93 Press agents?
94 ___ a dozen
95 STEERS CLEAR OF
97 Worrying sort
98 Whitebait
99 Baseball's Ashby
100 Point of ___ (British lighthouse site)
101 "Alice" diner
102 Body of art?
103 Detail of pointillism
104 Urgent message

DOWN

1 ___ coin (decide by chance)
2 Actress Yothers et al.
3 They can be bad
4 Conclusions
5 Extra: Abbr.
6 Tight wrapper?
7 Braided breads: Var.
8 Not a democrat
9 Canceled
10 Columbia Pictures co-founder Harry
11 Lizard, old-style
12 Vulgarians
13 Another name for God
14 FLIP OUT
15 Banned plant-growth retardant
17 Revealing comments
18 Vitus Bering and others
21 Farm home
23 Sen. Hatch
24 Movie based on an Isaac Bashevis Singer story
28 Kind of back or bank
30 At the base of
31 Attribute to
33 "Presumed Innocent" author
34 Netanyahu and others
35 Godwin's "The Adventures of ___ Williams"
36 Aloha
37 Unsophisticate
38 "The Cherry Orchard" girl
39 DEFIES DANGER
40 Cigars
41 Latest thing
44 Screwup
46 Certain designated section
48 Apices
49 Finish, finally
50 Have ___ (revel)
51 Copland ballet
52 Suffix in camera names
55 Indian master
58 Actor Hawke of "Alive"
59 Trimmer
60 Stand
61 Faulkner's "___ Thirteen"
62 Daughter of Cronus
63 One of the Barrymores
64 Poet Coolbrith et al.
65 Apropos of
67 Pointed
68 Breaks, in a way
70 Lash, the cowboy
74 Freeloaders
75 Acclaim
76 Auto maker Maserati
77 Tuscany province
78 Wing it
80 Canine cover
82 Fraught
85 No longer speaking to
86 Calhoun and others
87 Speaker's need
88 Remains to be seen?
89 Driver's aid
90 What's wrapped up in the whole ball of wax?
91 Prom night rental
92 Fini
93 Storehouse
95 Astron. clock setting
96 Pile

by Alex K. Justin

by Bryant White

ACROSS

1 Ticks off
7 Gunlock catch
11 Pythias' friend
16 Half of a Samoan port
20 1950's terrorist
21 Cankerous
23 Ran "Ran," e.g.
24 Viscera
25 "Cat's Eye" novelist?
27 Sugar suffix
28 Pupil watcher
30 Showoffs
31 Ale holder
32 One of a dozen
33 Treebeard and others of Middle-earth
34 Kapow!
35 Pope Paul II's successor?
41 1971 Fonda-Sutherland thriller
42 Hanoi holidays
43 Land of Evangeline
49 Straight, to Stradivari
52 Dweller along the Platte
54 Roman rhetorician who wrote "Institutio Oratoria"
55 "I'm c-c-c-cold!"
56 Slaves of the Morlocks, in fiction
57 Normandy department
58 Timeless, in poesy
59 In wild confusion
60 Hook's opposite
62 "Eat at ___"
63 Oscar winner in "The Big Country"
64 Picks out
65 Old German coin: Var.
66 LAX letters
67 Subjects to abusive tricks
69 Many buttons
70 Segar's Olive
71 Fine
73 Cousin of a truffle
74 Acclaimed Philly conductor
75 Kindergartner's trio
78 Courteous guy
79 Navigational aid
80 Slob's home
81 Semisheer fabric
83 Scanty
86 "The Kinsman Saga" author Ben
87 Highlands tongue
88 Chou ___
89 Opinion, forward or backward
90 Townships near Johannesburg
92 June bug
93 Dart
94 Brightest star in Lepus
95 Gumption
97 1920's jazz dance
99 It's good in Mexico
100 Fifth-century B.C. philosopher
101 Prefix with glider
102 Victor in music
104 "Funeral in Berlin" author?
107 "Eugen Onegin" girl
108 Prankish person
112 Like Mahler's Symphony No. 4
113 Penpoint
115 Judicious
118 Gunpowder alternative
123 "Foucault's Pendulum" penman
124 Noted mountaineer?
126 Kittenish
128 Respected member
129 Emphasize
130 Like lightning
131 Littoral fliers
132 Bassoonlike
133 Blackmailed
134 They're loath to come out of their shells

DOWN

1 ___-Hawley Tariff Act of 1930
2 Foot segment
3 Four-time Pulitzer-winning playwright?
4 Spock's org.
5 Corrida luminary
6 Film genre
7 Japanese entertainment
8 Susa was its capital
9 Israel's Bay of ___
10 Mil. unit
11 "Splish Splash" hitmaker of 1958
12 Controversial explosion
13 Gumshoe's hands
14 Genetic lab materials
15 Willem I's land: Abbr.
16 Temporary lodgings: Var.
17 Of a liquid's specific gravity
18 Mercator's field: Abbr.
19 Tout's concern
22 Exceptional
23 Onetime British Prime Minister?
26 Quite a joke
29 Jigger of rum, e.g.
36 Queen of the Adriatic
37 Citer's end word
38 Deteriorated, as relations
39 Slow climbers
40 Ryder rental
41 See 45-Down
44 Jeanne d'Arc, e.g.: Abbr.
45 Classic 1941 film, with 41-Down
46 British secondary school exam
47 They thrive on inflation
48 Actor Holm et al.
50 Sulky contest
51 Items for the disposal
52 Rigatoni sauce
53 Soothe
57 Pilot's decision
61 Best Actor of 1955?
64 Crimson crawler
67 "I am dead, ___, Wretched queen, adieu!"
68 Star-studded altar
69 ___ Mongolia
72 Chemical conclusion
73 Take up new residence at
74 Interpret wrongly
75 1960 World Series hero?
76 Demand
77 Mercury, e.g.
78 Bar supply
79 ___ fat (diet phrase)
80 Verified
82 Lit
83 Poke with a pike
84 Aymara is spoken here
85 Elizabeth I's mother
86 Small concession
87 Circus Maximus V.I.P.
90 Tag info
91 Numbskull
96 Commercial prefix with star
97 "Frasier" and "Maude," e.g.
98 Follower
103 Pick up
105 Ending with beat or peace
106 Kind of plate
108 Puerto Rico's third-largest city
109 Pressed upon
110 Careful
111 Bow, e.g.
114 Singers Bill and Jimmy
115 Ending with centi- or milli-
116 Swan genus
117 Basil, for one
119 Chow
120 Even, to Yvonne
121 Crown
122 Used binoculars
125 Tray material
127 European mil. grp.

ACROSS

1 Yacht heading
4 Parson/author of note
9 Odds and ends
13 Churls
18 Kaye's "___ Big Girl Now"
19 Incensed
20 Carpet surface
21 Cove
22 Opera for singer Cook?
25 Smallest amounts
26 Sealed
27 Cosine's reciprocal
28 Modern transportation
29 Alternative to Midway
30 How Ms. Shore paid for dinner?
33 Chang's twin
34 Cat ___
37 Brooks or Allen
38 Sun or moon
39 Competitor of Pringles
41 Skillful, facetiously
42 Muck
44 Refrain syllable
45 Estevez film "___ Man"
46 Comedian Sherman
47 Soak
49 Osso ___ (veal dish)
52 Didn't bid again
56 Mallorca Mrs.
57 Low
58 One-man Robert Morse play, 1990
59 Graced
60 Presided over
62 Military headgear
64 Provide lodging for
65 Man in a fez
66 Stage shows
67 On ___ boat to China
68 Fettered
69 Façade feature
70 Model airplane, e.g.
71 Battle stat.
72 Flying formation
73 Part of a chemical reaction
74 Slight
76 Talk insincerely
78 Mounted lancer
79 "What's the ___?"
81 LAX posting
82 "Mighty Lak' a Rose" composer Ethelbert
83 Rx writers
86 Clinton Cabinet member
87 Mideast grp.
88 Scrooge's cry
90 Hatfields and McCoys, e.g.
92 Police department abbr.
93 Song for artist Bonheur?
97 Model material
98 People
100 Beginning for 102-Across
102 Results of 100-Across
103 They may be blank
104 Folk song about an old gossip columnist?
108 Hound
109 Singer Braxton
110 Dentist's supply, once
111 Gay Nineties, e.g.
112 Hard rain?
113 Midterm, for one
114 Apportioned
115 Nonacademic degree

DOWN

1 Family member
2 Wreck
3 Aviation legend
4 Lohengrin's request for an update?
5 Auction follower
6 Greek H's
7 Reflected
8 Display item
9 Kind of cord
10 Cultivated land
11 Pipe fitting
12 Minuscule
13 Streaked gray, as an animal's coat
14 Popular science magazine
15 Solo at Popeye's wedding?
16 Hires new staff, in a way
17 Comic actor Arnold
21 Abu Dhabi bigwig
23 Hamlet
24 Roof topper
28 Fairy queen
29 Brit. decoration
31 Miffed
32 Archbishop of Canterbury Thomas ___
35 Ready to go
36 Irritated
40 N.Y.P.D. alert
43 Like Lear
44 Intern
45 Density symbol, in physics
47 Sinkside device
48 Provincetown catch
50 Angler's baskets
51 Waited longer than
52 Vestlike clerical garments
53 Early name in talking machines
54 Fictional aunt's padding material?
55 Woody's boy
56 Running mate of 1972
60 All the tea in China
61 Rubicund
62 What Mrs. Lindberg got at the rooming house?
63 Demon's doing
65 Colleague of 86-Across
66 Hire, as a lawyer
68 Cousin of MI6 in spy stories
69 Give birth, in a way
71 Speedometer info
73 Friend of Fidel
75 Hair arrangement
77 Introduce, with "out"
78 Given free range, as cattle
80 Moisture collector
83 Vanishing delivery people
84 Piece of cake, maybe
85 It sends checks to A.A.R.P. members
86 Avis auto
87 "Hey, you!"
88 Spend time without one's wife, informally
89 Salve ingredient
91 Polite address
92 Flying saucers
94 Seine tributary
95 Precipitates
96 Put an ___ (halt)
99 1990 Indy 500 winner Luyendyk
101 Satirist Mort
104 Initials in telecommunications
105 "Friend or ___?"
106 "___ Haw"
107 Cheery yell

by R. M. Hopkins

ACROSS

1 Some "A-Tisket, A-Tasket" renditions
6 Sleeper's easer
9 Sleeper's woe
16 Wrap up
17 Media exec Roger
19 Turn off
21 Unpaid activity, generally
23 Unobtrusive way in
24 Get ___ of
25 Ho-hum
27 Steal
28 Alphabet string
29 Six-string
30 Subject of Shelley's "Adonais"
31 3-D coordinate
33 Certain cuisine
34 High ways?
35 Contract's contents
36 To ___ mildly
37 X'ed, in a way
38 Hymnal standard
40 Modern Persian
41 Chinese premier, 1949–76
42 Eyes, in poetry
43 "Candid Camera" sound
44 60's Canadian P.M.
47 A lot of "Deck the Halls"
49 Yale Bowl hosts
50 Things sailors bring back
52 Testing org.
53 Like some solutions
54 Ruination
55 One-liner, e.g.
56 Mojavelike
57 Even more tasteless
58 Minn. neighbor
59 Family V.I.P.'s
60 Helen Hunt Jackson romance, 1884
62 CD-___
63 People in Germany
65 Emmy-winning show host, 1955–56
66 Draws forth
67 "Just ___ thought!"
68 Formerly besieged Bosnian town
69 Pronto!
70 Kin
71 Crazies
73 Maximizes effectiveness, as of skills
75 Like some losers
76 Lay off
77 Look-alike, maybe
78 Striking out
82 Word with sign or time
84 Brimless topper
85 Thrills
86 The "S" in R.S.V.P.
87 Autumn bouquet
88 Big shot
89 Roman martyr of A.D. 304
90 Ascetic
91 Lummox
92 Helping hand
93 Of vivid mental imagery
95 Like Cheerios
96 Sweltering
99 Much-decorated W.W. I hero
101 Drain of color
102 The Supremes and others
103 Goddess whom Milton called "heavenly born"
104 Tipsy
105 Name part
106 "Sailor's Song" start

DOWN

1 Literally, coast people
2 Limited end?
3 Wake Island, e.g.
4 Sound of collapse
5 Indian weight
6 American workers
7 Throw for ___
8 Vedic deity
9 Many college grads
10 Bring to light
11 Pranks
12 Page sound
13 Berlin connection
14 1957 Elvis hit
15 Leaf apertures
16 Toiled
17 Skiers' rental, maybe
18 Fit
20 Football Hall-of-Famer Stautner
22 Wagner oeuvres
26 Humdinger
30 Carhop's offering
32 I's predecessor, at times
33 Cartoon superhero
35 Balkan capital
36 Bel ___ cheese
37 Cartoonist Addams
39 Some patients' intake
40 Fire starter
41 Places for bunnies?
43 Dishonest persons' temptation
44 7 on a dial
45 Reckons
46 Nothings
47 50's singer Julius
48 Restaurant roll?
49 "The Hot Zone" virus
51 Early moralist
53 Beat it
56 Gri-gri
59 Stroll
61 Worships
64 Cries at a circus
65 Birchbark
68 "Cinderella" event
72 Castor's slayer
74 Iris fancier?
75 Philosopher implicated in a conspiracy against Nero
77 Nipper or Checkers
78 Disallows
79 One of a related set of atoms
80 OPEC member
81 "Ivan Susanin" composer
82 Gush feeling
83 Dairy deliveries
84 So far
85 ___ Friday
88 Book after Jonah
89 Mountain home
90 "Get Yer ___ Out" (Rolling Stones album)
92 Is bedbound
94 Bruce of "That Championship Season"
95 Other, to Ortega
97 Nanki ___ (Mikado's son)
98 Fronted
100 Kook

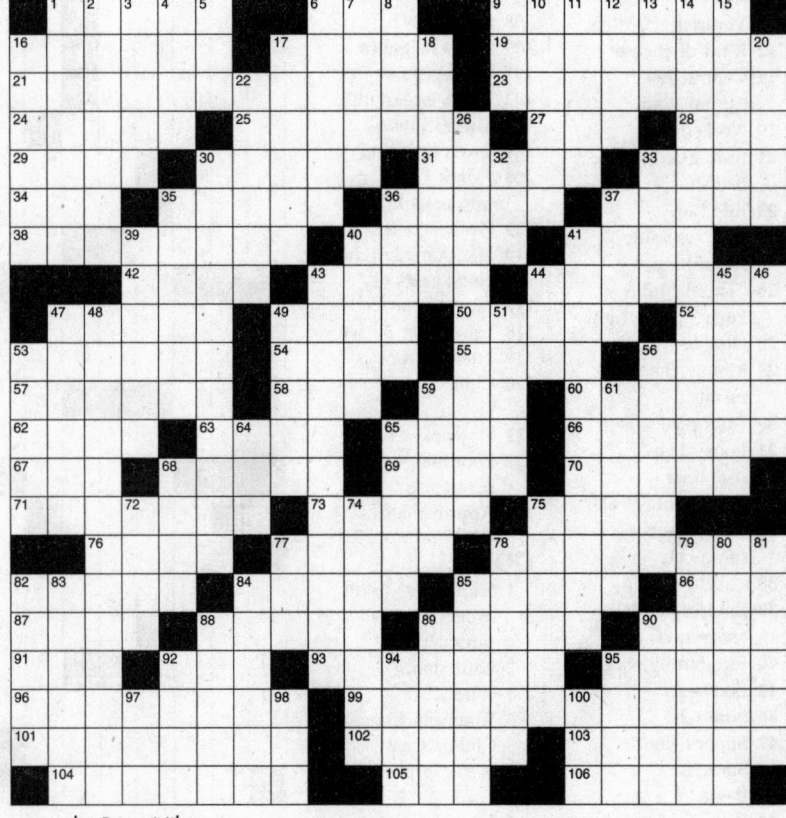

by Dean Niles

ACROSS

1 Ripoffs
6 Ventricles' outlets
12 Kind of cheese
18 Central Asian capital
19 Necked
21 Immigrant, to the British
23 Riled up
24 Dog assessing shoplifting, e.g.?
26 "The Birthday Party" playwright
28 Double-crosser
29 Money-changer's profit
30 Faux pas
31 Look-alikes' container
32 Jean Laffite et al.
35 Triple-decker sandwich
38 ___ du Diable
39 Environmentally concerned
40 Intrafamily chat?
44 Bombast
46 Sun. talk
47 Supervision
48 Stretch
49 Passé
52 Fathers
53 ___ di Como, Italia
54 What laid-off workers need to remember?
60 Do an antique dealer's job
61 Handed down
62 Idol's place
66 Something to believe in
67 Capone's nemesis
68 Audi rival
70 Charlottesville sch.
71 Made a successful stand
75 Used a stethoscope
79 Fox and others, informally
80 Falsely sent legal panel to insane asylum?
82 Variety of cotton
83 Papal tribunals
84 "This ___ stickup!"
85 Alpinist's need
86 Landed
87 Grazing land
90 Ice-T servings?
94 Inexpensive
Sherlock Holmes job?
99 Part of TNT
100 Thai's neighbor
101 Cravings
102 Treaty site of 1925
103 Musical notes
104 Cost of playing
106 "Mark Trail" cartoonist Ed
109 Firing squad order
110 Like some knights
112 Hobo gridlock?
117 Kind of pie
118 Latecomer, perhaps
119 Lustrous fabrics
120 China ___ (showy bloom)
121 Slowpokes
122 Poor man's penthouse
123 Approximates

DOWN

1 Ship officer (with orders for this puzzle?)
2 Latin dance
3 Wild ___
4 American Kennel Club outcast
5 Is in Morpheus' arms
6 Uraeus, in ancient Egypt
7 Run
8 Spinner
9 High-calorie desserts
10 Compilation
11 Bristle
12 Hired escort
13 Cell component
14 U.N.C. athletic grp.
15 High points
16 Mexican revolutionary Zapata
17 "The King of Kings" director
20 Archaeological site
22 Throw off
25 Fitting places
27 Sugarloaf Mountain site
33 Hosp. staffers
34 Get-together
36 Nude
37 Rail at
41 ___ a one
42 H.S.T. or R.M.N.
43 Batting equipment
45 Nailed obliquely
50 Swiss canton
51 Matter of retaliation
52 Vichy et al.
54 Fuss
55 Gaelic
56 Seductress
57 Ball teams
58 Like Yale since 1969
59 Nav. officer
60 Society event
62 Deal
63 Outfit for Pavlova
64 State
65 1980 Kenny Rogers hit
68 First graders' work
69 "___ live and breathe!"
72 Merge
73 Like many furniture sprays
74 Posture
75 Powerful explosive
76 Ring around the collar?
77 Some sports scores
78 Open a bit
80 Future stallion
81 Elevator inventor
82 Basketball center, e.g.
83 King's ___
85 Tiny people
87 Friction match
88 Loosely woven fabric
89 Kind of ball or bill
91 New Year's bowl site
92 Vixen's mate
93 Swoosie Kurtz TV series
94 Road parts
95 Puts on
96 Slip-on
97 Unseparated
98 Oklahoma city
105 Lab item
107 Sot's woe
108 Race, in a way
111 Low hill
113 ___ et amo (expression of mixed feelings)
114 Sound unit
115 ___ standstill
116 Ill. time

by Jacques Liwer

ACROSS

1 Blurred
8 Straighten, as the legs
15 Of a minor domain
20 Cassava dish
21 Little Warsaw, e.g.
22 Missouri tributary
23 Extra effort
25 Hereditary factors
26 Barrels
27 Wizened
28 Prefix with meter or motor
29 Senior
30 Author profiled in "Shadowlands"
32 River of Amiens
34 Botanical suffix
36 Moola
38 Baths
39 Dum-dum
44 Like Coast Guard rescues
46 1953 Ricardo Montalban western
48 Country singer Steve
49 Excuse
51 Welcome uncivilly
52 Shows excitement
54 ___ Fail (ancient crowning stone)
55 Medicinal doses
59 Gorge
60 Ex-superpower
62 Blackthorn
63 Easily imposed upon
65 South American monkey
66 Thin layer
68 Changing pitch
71 Editor's marks
75 Steve Martin song "King ___"
77 Not a neatnik
78 Cigarette substances
80 Invitation notation
81 Another finisher
85 Amplify
88 Osaka O.K.
89 Funnel-shaped flowers
91 Mod ending
92 Piano composition
94 Perform
95 Lacking support
99 Laundry stinker
100 Square element
102 Dance in France
103 Appropriate
104 Playwright Ayckbourn et al.
105 Desert lilies
107 Car style
110 Murder, e.g.
114 TV host John
116 Singer James
118 Columnist Bombeck
119 Cutting out
120 Monopolize
123 Himalayan kingdom
124 Make unnecessary
125 "The Doctor in Spite of Himself" dramatist
126 Tea treat
127 Kind of diving
128 "The End of the World" singer Davis

DOWN

1 Unbelievable bargain
2 "My Dinner with Andre" director Louis
3 1970 Creedence Clearwater Revival hit
4 Most underhanded
5 Sticky stuff
6 Old French coins
7 Gertrude and Ophelia, e.g.
8 Fast-paced
9 Japanese drama
10 One of baseball's Boyers
11 Kimono
12 Unusually narrow, in a way
13 No-show job
14 Blue
15 Fairway description
16 Played for a fool
17 Bamboo stalk
18 Years and years
19 For fear that
24 Refuse
29 Light-colored wood
31 Ice fall
33 Dance in 4/4 time
35 Bargain model: Prefix
37 Takes to the limit
39 Danish change
40 Former Canadian P.M. Wilfrid
41 Highland tongue
42 Dog dogger
43 Experiment
44 Top-notch
45 Relative of 41-Down
47 Aussie flier
50 Drying powder
53 Boob tubes
56 Old French coins
57 Celebrated hostess Mesta
58 Former Pac. pact
61 Prepare tabloid pictures
64 Trunk bulge
67 Petrify
69 Architectural spiral
70 Snatch
72 Leslie Caron film, with "The"
73 Duck
74 Peeping Tom
76 ___ chi (meditative exercise)
79 German city
81 Mimic
82 Film maker Riefenstahl
83 Unaccompanied
84 U.S.-Mex.-Can. concordat
86 Wide receiver Don
87 Inventor Howe
90 Coming
93 Pelee Island location
96 Not down a break, in tennis
97 Herbal quaff
98 One of the deadly sins
101 Shifty
105 Skating gold medalist John et al.
106 Parts of pipes
108 "That's ___"
109 First to spot a comet, usually
110 Strikes out
111 Head honcho
112 Contemporary of Tu Fu
113 Son of Judah
115 Slight person
117 One way to run
120 Atlantic food fish
121 66, e.g.: Abbr.
122 Staffordshire product

by Wayne Robert Williams

132 NOTHING GAINED

ACROSS

1 Summer weather stat.
4 Western treaty grp.
7 Book of 150 songs
13 Hibernated, with "up"
18 Like some canvases
20 Orville Wright or Pete Rose, e.g.
21 Join
22 Victim of calumny
23 Film about an R-rated oracle?
25 Last cameo appearances?
27 Centaur killed by Hercules
28 Longtime Mex. ruling party
29 Like Gen. Schwarzkopf
30 Brought along
32 Sub powerer
35 Flowering shrub
39 Get (from)
43 Kind of statesman
44 Long-running "Popeye" spinoff?
49 Intro
50 "The Burghers of Calais" sculptor
51 Licks
55 Enemy of the Sioux
58 New York's ___ Island
61 Tropical climber
63 Rap's Dr. ___
64 Flowery Greek couple?
68 Watch
70 Shows flexibility
71 Jazz grp.
72 Flunky
73 Spotted
74 Traditional song for a medfly?
80 Tributary of the Tennessee
81 Soul singer Bryson
83 Shredded
84 Neighbor of Aus.
85 Newspaper department
87 Hazing target, once
89 More mysterious
92 1996 thriller that's a must?
99 Area code 208
102 Periodic weather disruption
103 Christian Science practitioner
104 Lifetime domain
107 Bubbly drinks
110 Suffix with bass
111 H.E.W. offshoot
112 Observation
116 Debtor's fasteners?
120 Stick baseball great?
124 Expresses anger toward
125 Shampoo instruction
126 Very
127 Ones who speak
128 "Damn Yankees" part
129 General command
130 Potassium hydroxide
131 Like some jobs

DOWN

1 Hip New York City area
2 Surroundings
3 "___ a man who wasn't there"
4 Song lead-in for "di" or "da"
5 Sharp
6 Take care of
7 Detachable container
8 Blowout
9 Rich person's suffix
10 Subdivision subdivisions
11 Third all-time record home-run hitter
12 Muzzle
13 Paul Newman title role
14 See 46-Down
15 Clear
16 Unending, old-style
17 Atheist
18 Plant groupings
19 Skier's peak
24 Fighting Tigers of the Southeastern Conf.
26 "Perfesser" Casey
31 "Bingo ___ Yale" (Porter song)
33 Accelerate
34 Exploded
36 16 tablespoons
37 Abbr. on a sale item
38 Ornaments
40 Religious believer: Abbr.
41 "___ you so!"
42 ___ for (alluring)
45 "Put ___ on it!"
46 With 14-Down, "Walking on Thin Ice" singer
47 Makeup artist
48 Traveler's house
52 Curtain detail
53 Sort of sorting
54 Merchant
55 Like a sculpture
56 Old Roman politico
57 Curmudgeons
59 Actress Russo
60 Clunky shoe
62 Say so
65 Check one
66 Surmounting
67 Billionth: Prefix
69 Concert ending
72 Listless
74 "Archers of St. George" artist
75 Bigger than big
76 Shell rival
77 Warbling
78 Dickens forger
79 From the Continent
82 Center starter
86 Successor to Schmidt
88 Time without end
90 Capt.'s heading
91 River inlet
93 1985 movie "Izzy and ___"
94 Small change
95 Daughter of Cadmus
96 Puffed out, as apparel
97 Tights
98 Some German Surrealist paintings
99 Ethereal fluids
100 Showy flower
101 Without
105 Play about Capote
106 Part of v.v.
108 No-good
109 Like floodwater
113 Kind of court
114 Zoning measure
115 Mother of Zeus
117 Hoopster Thurmond
118 Standardized test, for short
119 Leader of A.D. 54
121 She-bear, in Sonora
122 Cub house
123 One that's seeded

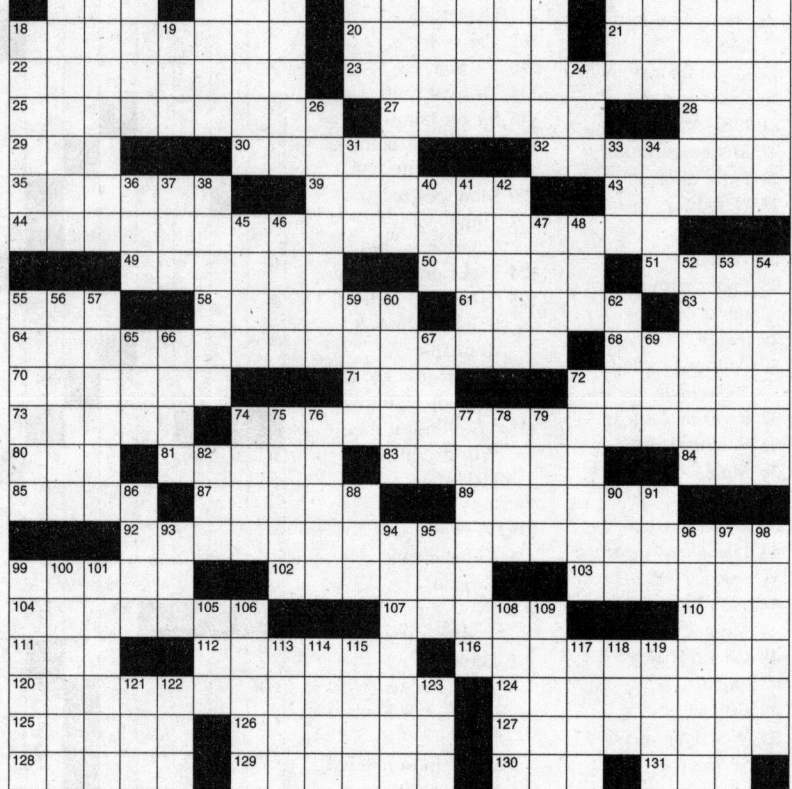

by Dean Niles

ACROSS

1 Prospective
9 Air Force facility
13 Peaches' singing partner
17 Kind of number
21 Writer's voice
22 "To Autumn" and others
23 Colleague of Jimmy and Bjorn
24 Western Indian
25 Kurt Vonnegut novel
28 Lady of Spain
29 Many, many years
30 Eastern prince
31 First name in morning TV
32 Rang
34 "What ___!"
37 Prefix with system
38 Confessed
39 Lodges troops
40 Archaeological site
42 Louisa May Alcott novel
46 Bank deposit?
47 "Three men in ___"
49 A small one is white
50 Denouement
51 Verb tense: Abbr.
52 Discounted
55 Autos since 1989
57 Funny
58 It may have several scènes
60 Anna Quindlen bestseller
63 Put aside, in a way
65 Lang of comics' Smallville
66 ___ Canals
67 Earned status
71 Like a used car
74 Certain joint
75 A.A. Milne title
79 Observant type
80 Miss Piggy's pronoun
81 Per team
82 One way to rest
84 Hardly friendly
85 Kind of political party
87 J.D. Salinger collection
89 Whip
90 Some doubles players
91 Feast of Saint ___ (January event)
92 Part of R.S.V.P.
93 Term of address at court
94 Embellished
96 Chekhov work, with "The"
101 British levy
102 ___ Lingus
104 Scott of "Charles in Charge"
105 Opens for viewing
106 ___-disant (self-styled)
107 Addison's partner
109 Scale meas.
111 Exam for jrs.
112 White-tailed flier
113 T.S. Eliot opus
116 "M*A*S*H" protocol
120 Made sense
122 Debate arguments
123 G.I. address
125 Nape
126 Historic German city
127 Put out
129 Paul Anka's first hit
131 Yeoman's yes
132 Kyrgyzstan's ___ Mountains
133 Aeschylus tragedy

by Randolph Ross

138 It gets a brushoff
139 By means of
140 Melody
141 One for the road?
142 Female sweetheart
143 ___ a one
144 Assists, e.g.
145 Reconnaissance craft

DOWN

1 Defeat an incumbent
2 Picasso's daughter
3 Rubbernecker
4 Tulsa sch.
5 S.I. or TV Guide
6 Spillane's "___ Jury"
7 Words of denial
8 Alexander's home
9 1922 Physics Nobelist
10 Fuss
11 Subject of "Sunday in the Park With George"
12 Cores
13 CD player ancestor
14 Some Ivy Leaguers
15 "6 Rms ___ Vu"
16 Paging
17 Most common, statistically
18 Dickens classic
19 Eventuate
20 Disk jockey's need
26 Do a second lube job
27 Prod
33 Loop loopers

35 "In the Heat of the Night" setting
36 Pear-shaped instrument
38 Radiance
39 Handcuffs
41 Projecting skirt
43 Oscar-winning musical
44 Japanese vegetable
45 Weatherized a house
48 Candle contents
52 Broadway composer Cy
53 Accompanied
54 Agatha Christie mystery
56 Grimm character
58 Mountain ridges
59 When repeated, middling, in Milano
61 Trucks for hire
62 Garden work
64 "Operator" singer
68 Garage sale caveat
69 TV control knob
70 Uncover
72 Smiley's creator
73 Cause of cough
75 Diarists
76 ___ off (sporadically)
77 Score after deuce
78 Art Nouveau jeweler Lalique
79 Seals, as a crate
83 Buffalo's county
86 "___ blue as blue . . ."
88 "¿Cómo ___ usted?"
91 "Doe, ___ . . ."

93 Interference
95 Enjoy thoroughly
97 Sword handles
98 Ring wear
99 Scholarly org.
100 Battle souvenirs
101 The "Her" of "Her voice was ever soft, gentle and low"
103 Must-take coll. course
104 University of Cincinnati team
106 Hurricane protection
107 Loses a liking for
108 Plant of the pea family
110 Bad mark
113 Medicine testing agcy.
114 Bad booze
115 Involuntary actions
117 Boot-shaped land
118 Most happy-go-lucky
119 Discharges
121 Discharges
124 Victorious
127 By any chance
128 Mucho
129 Regular fare
130 A.B.A. member
134 Foerster opera
135 Literary collection
136 Fireplace shell
137 Ranch suffix

ACROSS

1 Dresden's river
5 Went out with the waves
10 Corporate problem
14 Was unyielding
18 Part of an estate
19 "If you could ___ now!"
20 Unacceptable for this puzzle?
22 Robert of the C.S.A.
23 Cardiac fitness assessment
25 Awed, in a way
27 Block components
28 Barnaby Jones portrayer
30 Hatchet handle
31 English Channel feeder
32 Not aye
33 Blood pigment
34 Goaded
38 Discourage
40 Crème ___
44 Actor Frobe of "Goldfinger"
45 "When I Fall in Love" singers
48 TV cartoon pal
49 "Nicholas Nickleby" Tony winner
50 Sigmoid swimmers
51 Passbook amts.
52 Told to go
53 Compass reading
54 Squirrellike mammals
58 Pound parts
59 Like some bikes
62 DARE target group
63 Nonvine wine source
64 Grace verb
65 Some battle participants
66 Pintail ducks
68 Drum or guitar type
70 Coaster cries
71 Uniformity
74 ". . . called for his fiddlers ___"
75 '83 play-based movie
77 Asian holiday
78 Need Ban
79 Fifth word of "America"
80 Crossword worker?
81 Leather attachment
82 C.P.R. giver, perhaps
83 Longest-running network TV show
87 Etta of old comics
88 Wayne's world
90 Pulitzer columnist Goodman
91 Noted name in Mideast talks
92 Often-changed lines
93 Perry's creator
94 Mrs., abroad
96 "___ Foolish Things"
98 Plant, perhaps
99 Retainers
103 First choice
105 Kind of agreement
108 Deprived, once
109 Pesach repast
110 Show some muscle
111 Extra-large shoe width
112 Little red critters
113 Nair competitor
114 Olympic pointers?
115 Bunch

DOWN

1 Mag. wheels
2 "Why don't we?"
3 Oscar: Felix:: Ernie: ___
4 Pulitzer-winning critic Richard
5 Chelmsford's county
6 The Divine Miss M
7 Sex education subject?
8 Miami couple
9 Wane in warring
10 Finishing order
11 Cockney's assistant
12 Existed
13 J.A. Prufrock's creator
14 Greeks' ancestor
15 Abbr. on a mountain sign
16 Majesty's start
17 Flemish composer ___ Prés
21 Devilish designs
24 Parakeet treat
26 Macho ones
29 Shade of red
33 Cannabis plants
34 Snowy ___
35 They come in skeins
36 SSgt. Barry Sadler's group
37 Alf, Mork, etc.
38 Struck out
39 Additionally
40 Pearson and Barrymore
41 Mary Quant was one
42 Accordingly
43 Log
45 Spots for chapeaux
46 Old "Tonight Show" starter
47 Utopias
52 Moon: Prefix
55 Charger, e.g.
56 Charming person?
57 "Don't You Know" singer
58 Hammer's end
60 Stylishly polished
61 That Cosmos guy
65 Coating
66 Pals of Olaf and Lars
67 Poetic ponds
68 Sow, maybe
69 Kind of park
70 Sharpens
71 Krupp Works site
72 Otto's preceder
73 Keeps
75 Those times
76 Withered
79 Jailbirds
81 Manage, with "out"
83 Noted resignee of 1988
84 "Babes in Toyland" composer
85 Vogue competitor
86 Promise recipient
89 Cause for alarms
91 Skunk LePew
93 Roast host
94 Downing Street distance
95 Lunch sandwiches
96 Nonkosher
97 Weight
98 "The Neverending Story" writer
99 Child support?
100 Tayside tios
101 Virginia ___
102 Antique knife
103 Early start?
104 Poet's time
106 Not local: Abbr.
107 Do darts

by Cathy Millhauser

ACROSS

1 Not so fast
8 Deck supervisors
14 Making even
21 By the sea
22 Bulletin board fastener
23 Puff's land, in song
24 Actress Barbara shows affection for E.M.T.'s?
27 Biblical birthright seller
28 Detecting device
29 Dynamite sound
30 Proceeds
31 Barker and Bell
34 Preschool group?
35 C.E.O.'s degree
38 Colorado tributary
40 That: Sp.
41 Naughty but nice women fail to reimburse Doris?
48 Brief freedom?
49 Table scraps
50 "There was ___ woman who . . ."
51 "Une baignade" artist
55 Capri suffix
56 "Just kidding!"
57 Did nothing
59 Cheese choice
62 Rent
63 Dumas heroes exploit losers?
70 Marathoner's ordeal
71 Strenuous
72 Buttercup relatives
73 Imbue
75 Role for Liz in '63
76 Get better in barrels
78 Monthly check sender: Abbr.
79 Kind of fingerprint
80 Rossner title character acts derisively?
86 "Cheers" network
89 Furthermore
90 Tarzan creator's monogram
91 Marvin Lee ___, a.k.a. Meat Loaf
92 Spring perennial
96 "Omnibus" host Cooke
99 Open auto of old
101 Strip at a swim meet
102 Fumbler defaces parts of diamonds?
108 "Cómo ___ usted?"
109 Part of 36-Down
110 Abbr. on some hulls
111 N.T. book before James
112 Juno, for one
113 Note elevators
116 "White Christmas" record label
119 Prompter beginning
120 1970 Jackson 5 hit
121 Dustin persona wheels young Dr. Westheimer?
127 Provider of home runs?
130 Shell, to old poets
131 Son of Odin
132 "What did I tell you!"
133 Third king of Judah
134 Actress Demich of 60's filmdom
136 Compass pt.
138 Varnish ingredients
141 Holm and Hunter
145 Ingénue's elderly beau bespeckles Della's mug?
151 Ezra Pound contemporary
152 More strapped
153 Singer Lynn
154 Books stored horizontally
155 "Gunsmoke" star
156 Sawyer of ABC News

by Cathy Millhauser

DOWN

1 Pine (for)
2 Two-year-olds' chorus
3 Operatic basso Enzo ___
4 Undertake
5 Ordinal adjective
6 Menlo Park monogram
7 TV Tarzan's kin
8 Warm welcomes
9 ___ buco (veal dish)
10 His act was antitrust
11 Pkg. carrier
12 Zilch
13 Impudent nobody
14 "Ease on Down the Road" musical
15 Bandleader Edmundo
16 In the dark
17 Place for hangers-on?
18 TV's Kristen or Graff
19 Dweebs
20 Art base
22 Wine grape
25 Deborah, Graham and Jean
26 Stick-in-the-mud
32 In concurrence
33 A loser to Harry in '48
36 "I'm not supplying," on invitations
37 Madam Polly
39 Article on Mont Blanc
41 Tropical tree-hangers
42 Hip
43 40's singer Ray
44 Aleutian island
45 LuPone of "Evita"
46 Sticks on
47 Best
52 Beef cut
53 Miss Brooks portrayer
54 "The Gondoliers" girl
57 Tackled moguls
58 Oxygen-dependent organism
60 "I ___ Thief" (1935 film)
61 Big name in burlesque
64 Kind of sch.
65 Normandy battle site
66 Surround with trees
67 Soufflé sine qua non
68 Majesty start
69 Discount chain
74 Chatter
75 Arrange systematically
77 Gives weapons, old-style
81 Growl
82 "Verrry interesting" Johnson
83 Mind set?
84 Singer Vikki
85 Enterprise helmsman
86 Theaters near you
87 Cheek makeup
88 Roma is one
93 Two-seated carriage
94 Behind on bills
95 Seder period
97 Plunge in
98 Flight destination in a 1933 title
100 Routine
103 Bare: Prefix
104 Do some salaaming
105 Diamond of Queens
106 Peach ___
107 Heels, e.g.
114 Guiding light
115 Teriyaki ingredient
117 Blubber
118 Rust
119 Steak order
122 Goodies
123 Enrapture, slangily
124 Insurance claim particulars
125 Create smocking
126 Fund ___
127 Service program
128 Pizza part
129 Star of Orion's left foot
135 Simba's "Lion King" love
137 Novelist O'Brien
139 Football's Armstrong
140 Ego
142 Dumas novel
143 "Phooey!"
144 Young oyster
146 ___-eyed
147 Ending akin to -ist
148 Cub house
149 ___ Locks (Great Lakes passage)
150 Necessitate an "Oops!"

ACROSS

1 Caribbean resort
6 Mine, in Marseille
10 Ballerina Spessivtseva
14 Sir abroad
17 Cobbler's supply
18 Copy cats
19 Official language of China
20 Stag goers
21 Spiffy, as clothes
24 Some M.I.T. grads
25 Straight
26 Rio seven
27 Hibernated
28 Grandma
29 Venue for figure skaters
32 Not a happy time
35 Early TV sex symbol
38 "___ tu" (Verdi aria)
39 On both sides of
40 Gave the once-over
41 Pitcher's target
43 Wizened
44 Future corp. exec., maybe
47 One full of grace
52 No gentlemen, they
54 Get the message
55 Judge Lance
56 Racing's Luyendyk
57 "...ready ___!"
58 Hawaiian hardwood
60 Scorecard division
64 Vino center
65 Hit protest song of 1970
68 When Solomon Grundy married
71 "Call Me Irresponsible" songwriter
72 ___-Rooter
73 "The Volcano Lover" novelist
74 Plentiful
76 Pile up
78 By
80 Journal end
81 Conk
84 Radio transmission, briefly
87 Gene Wilder flick
91 Suffix with witch or hatch
92 Julio Iglesias hit
94 Tarlatan skirt
95 Shoulder of a lock bolt
96 Come before
99 ___ Paul's
100 German native
101 Assistant of a sort
104 Detective's discovery
106 Sub in a tub
107 Fathers
109 Hieroglyphic representation
110 Govt. investigators
114 Small pocket
115 Premiere of 10/11/75
119 Palindromic lady
120 Them, with "the"
121 Photographer Arbus
122 Contradict
123 Electrical unit
124 "Make do" amount
125 Tolkien tree giants
126 Be in control

DOWN

1 Alliance: Abbr.
2 Womanizer
3 Forelimb part
4 Storytelling occasions
5 Simile center
6 Polygon perpendiculars
7 Swift
8 First word of Montana's motto
9 Creeds
10 Productions
11 Potential troublemaker
12 Ob-___ (medical specialist)
13 Summer mo.
14 Leading
15 Actress Davis
16 Gold check
18 Turns one's hair gray
19 Ships, in poetry
22 French-Belgian river
23 Island south of Livorno
28 Compass heading
30 Bag carrier
31 "Service ___ smile"
33 Joan of art
34 "___ Billie Joe" (1967 song)
35 H or S, in Morse code
36 Fever
37 ___ club
42 Draining
44 Brainy bunch
45 Stock, in cookery
46 John who played Gomez
48 "Vingt ans après" figure
49 "...I'll tell ___ lies"
50 Rule
51 Retreats
53 Hint
58 Kind of end
59 Barley beard
61 Muckraker Tarbell
62 "...to ___ few"
63 Kind of cab
65 Hold forth
66 Hit out of the park
67 Frommer title
69 French political division
70 Pinch
75 Bandleader Lanin
77 Winter wear
79 Dowdy person
81 Estonian, e.g.
82 Melville work
83 ___ Station
85 48-day period in Judaism
86 Couturières
88 Pull forcibly on
89 Ashcans, in London
90 Padding site
93 Decaying substances
96 Mideast letters
97 Hang around
98 Regarded
100 "Entertainment Tonight" host
101 Pickup person
102 Cole Porter's "___ Paris"
103 Rise up
105 Comics dog
108 De ___ ("Justine" novelist)
111 Miss equivalent
112 60's singer Sands
113 Not e'en once
115 Condiment at Maxim's
116 Actress Sue ___ Langdon
117 Feminine force
118 Recipe measure: Abbr.

by Ernie Furtado

ACROSS

1 One who pitches
6 Dickens's Defarge
12 Like every other book page
18 Break off
19 Kind of insurance program
21 Makeshift abode
22 What egotists want to be
24 "No"
25 Pennsylvania city
26 Not his or hers
27 "___ Dream" ("Lohengrin" soliloquy)
29 Impenetrable
30 Tooth layer
32 Kind of sack
34 "Steppenwolf" author
36 Thinness
38 Yawned
41 Hero follower
44 Worldwide
48 Actors' agents
50 Tibetan mountain people
53 Site of ancient Sheba
54 Blue expanse in France
55 False handle
57 To have, in Le Havre
58 "Buddenbrooks" author
59 Comic's necessity
61 Map Abbr.
62 Fran Drescher TV role
63 These are hardly modern art
65 Bottom of the barrel
67 Hodgepodge
69 Protest grp. of the 60's
70 Kind of camera
72 Windsor, e.g.
74 Diane to Woody, often
77 Newswoman Magnus
78 Alexander or Peter
80 "Liberty" locale
85 Bean, for one
87 Stinker
89 Absolutely pristine
91 Settled, as a deal
92 Idi Amin, e.g.
93 Corrigendum
95 Actor Chaney
96 Brazilian state
97 Fusilli and ziti
99 Confounds
101 Kind of charge
102 Tolkien forest giant
103 Preference
105 Novelist Allende
107 O.K.
110 Hospital workers, for short
111 Recovers
116 Snail's trail
118 Grounds
122 Bluster
123 Peace Nobelist Myrdal
124 One in a pool, perhaps
126 Big Apple landmark, informally
130 1969 Indy winner
131 Places for studs
132 Dairy Queen order
133 Serves with sauce?
134 Nonexperts
135 Wine-drinking occasion

DOWN

1 Heightened
2 Name in lawn equipment
3 Cheech of Cheech and Chong
4 Advantage
5 Classic opening
6 Sports team since 1962
7 Drink made from a packet
8 Racket
9 Not genuine
10 Knightwear?
11 Piccadilly Circus statue
12 Well-worn
13 Mr. of film
14 Folketing assemblers
15 Niblicks
16 Olympic marks
17 Charity
19 Have significance
20 Bambi's aunt
23 Newspaper edition
28 "___ Bop" (1984 hit)
31 Tabriz locale
32 More than clean
33 Novelist Rand
35 Publisher's staff, for short
37 Gossip bit
38 Hair-care article
39 Lover of Apollo
40 Job follower
42 Interpretations
43 St. ___ River (Superior-Huron link)
44 Jock's favorite school time
45 Spring
46 Former Dodge model
47 Part of N.B.
49 Proportion
51 Grimm fellow
52 "The Loco-Motion" singer Little ___
54 Failed intention
56 Fancy headgear
59 Began, with "off"
60 Contiguous
64 Actor Richard
66 Electronic reading
68 Eased gently
71 Ascertains
73 Unaffected
74 Two-door
75 Club newsletter
76 Old Glory
79 Excess
81 Medicine container
82 Sonar blip
83 Curb
84 Merchandising event
86 Horse's bit
88 Pompano event
90 Sub ___
94 Murder ___
96 Campanile feature
98 Véronique, e.g.: Abbr.
100 Zola's "The ___ of Father Mouret"
101 Luau
104 Rainbow, for one
106 Joint Chiefs, e.g.
108 Skips
109 "Beau ___"
110 Of late
112 Shop fixture
113 Ancient yarn
114 Call up
115 Less cracked
116 Spectators' spots
117 Vega's constellation
119 Antiquate
120 ___ Mountains
121 First name on the Supreme Court
122 Kind of plaid
125 Third word of "America"
127 CD-___
128 Actor Vigoda
129 Clod

by Nancy Nicholson Joline

ACROSS

1 Haphazard growth
7 Country on the Gulf of Guinea
12 Went off welfare
19 Summary
20 Popular support group
21 Gourmet
22 "Don't tell me what to say on the air," said ___
24 Change the layout
25 Clear the boards
26 Gets better
27 Simple card game
29 Complainer
30 Flew off the handle
31 Type of belly button
32 Singer Watley et al.
34 Poetic monogram
35 Québec time off
36 Voting group
37 Voting district
38 Foot parts
41 What "nobody doesn't like"
44 Bank holdings
46 "It's ___!"
47 Retailer R.H. ___
48 Davis of "Jungle Fever"
49 Of the lower part of a pistil
52 Report card listing
53 Brief moments
54 Sometimes it must be followed
55 Old Pontiac
56 Unlike the king's English
58 Munich Mister
59 Campus program, for short
60 Mr. Moto reply
61 Mobs
62 Clift of "The McLaughlin Group"
64 Consonant (with)
66 Bit
67 Word with smoke or cow
69 Feeling
70 Expenditure
71 Kind of particle
72 Not work
73 ___-majesté
74 Make tracks
75 They feel for you
77 One who yearns
78 She, in Siena
79 Condition
80 Dark
81 Pub vessel
85 1961 Best Actor for "Judgment at Nuremberg"
87 Collar stiffener
88 Cautious
90 Apiece
91 Additionally
92 "Down by the Salley Gardens" poet
94 "Norma Rae" director Martin
95 Outbuilding
97 Flubs
99 Sticky stuff
100 Obvious pleasure
101 Port St. ___, Fla.
102 Actress Parsons
105 "Republican Congressmen don't like me," said ___
108 Chills, so to speak
109 Contacts, modern-style
110 "Sense and Sensibility" director
111 Salon employee
112 Boy of old song
113 Tough ones

DOWN

1 Parts of orreries
2 How some taxes are levied
3 Parlay a bet
4 Have ___ of nerves
5 Ready for the Information Age
6 Trip starter
7 "I won my 1984 Tony by just a few votes," said ___
8 Stalwart
9 Raggedy ones
10 Cambodia's Lon ___
11 What bad things shouldn't get
12 Fritz's 1984 running mate
13 Poetically ajar
14 Baseball's McCarver
15 1988 film "Rent-___"
16 "Starring in 'Who's the Boss?' was a breeze," said ___
17 Ultimatum
18 Ball stars
20 ". . . ___'clock scholar"
23 Le Carré's "___ People"
28 Put on
32 Pop singer Ian
33 "Punk rock is cruel," said ___
36 "I was no wallflower in 'Vanity Fair,' " said ___
37 "I fear watching my own films," said ___
39 Undiluted
40 Limousine
42 Mystery novelist Cross
43 More than medium
45 River to the Rhone
46 Part of 35-Across
50 Cruising
51 Nuts
52 "I'll do my Hepburn imitation in a minute" said ___
54 Annoyed
56 Sends
57 Like a fugitive
58 "Drat!" magnified
59 " 'The Sound of Music' would make a good movie," said ___
60 Lost
63 Japanese-American
65 Patient's cry
68 Belgian waterway
72 Part of a stable family
73 Director Wertmuller et al.
74 Words with "stone" or "the matter"
76 That girl
77 Finished, in a way
82 In ___ (stuck)
83 One who vituperates
84 Evidence of lack of empathy
85 Has the con
86 It's a tight fit
87 ___ Tomé
89 A.B.A. members
93 Cast out
94 Confrontation
95 Dallas suburb
96 Steps
98 Security item
100 ___ Paradiso in the Alps
103 10% of DCX
104 Former Sec. Aspin
106 Org. the Surgeon General addresses
107 Grammy category

by Randolph Ross

ACROSS

1 Pro ___
4 Singer Khan
9 Stately
14 Jimmy of "NYPD Blue"
19 Japanese admiral Yuko
20 Was moribund
21 Ne plus ultra
22 U.S. Chief Justice, 1936–65
23 Tom, Dick and Harry
27 Strips
28 Battery inventor
29 Just conclusion?
30 First name in skating
31 Telephone man
32 Cartoon dog
33 Turkish honorific
35 Part of N.B.
36 Buckets, perhaps
40 Tom, Dick and Harry
46 Ye ___ Curiosity Shoppe
47 Irish actor Patrick
48 Nay sayers
49 Christian ___
50 Apollo component, for short
51 Forearm parts
52 Flexible
53 Redhead?
55 One at the start
56 In view
57 Battery type
58 Admission requirements, informally
59 Tom, Dick and Harry
68 "___ est celare artem" (Latin proverb)
69 Council member: Abbr.
70 Grease monkey's task
71 Mouths, anatomically
72 Dental restoration
75 Cornerstone features
77 Novel forms
78 Small songbird
79 Duffer's dream
80 Opposite of remove
81 1928 Fritz Lang thriller
82 Thorn, for one
83 Tom, Dick and Harry
88 Enough
89 Gaming table equipment
90 Churl
91 Fontanne's partner
92 Weeping
93 Bank holdings: Abbr.
97 Burial markers
100 They can always be counted on
102 Where Medicine Hat is
104 Tom, Dick and Harry
108 "Count ___!"
109 Star in Orion
110 Norse pantheon
111 Forty-niner's need
112 Trattoria topper
113 Cup, in Caen
114 Projecting part
115 Guinness suffix

DOWN

1 Shakespeare's mad general
2 Prefix with centric
3 Bewail
4 Simoleons
5 Scene of busyness
6 "___, my Love! ye do me wrong"
7 Baseball's Griffey Sr. or Jr.
8 Make sense, with "up"
9 Composer Rimsky-Korsakov
10 Digger ___ of "The Life of Riley"
11 Recipe instruction
12 "Peyton Place" actress Wood
13 Old age, in old times
14 More poker-faced
15 Actor without lines?
16 Actress Swenson
17 Socials
18 Auld lang ___
24 Needles, Calif., locale
25 Mimieux of "Where the Boys Are"
26 Central positions
31 Is wearisome
32 "Do ___"
34 Ornamental bands
35 Japanese city, host of the 1998 Winter Olympics
36 Cambridge student
37 Flower: Prefix
38 Govt. agents
39 Madras garb
40 Soil layer
41 Nicholas Gage book
42 Mingle with
43 "Olympia" painter
44 Young dragonfly
45 A Bobbsey twin
51 Shylock's terms
52 Hauls in
53 Thomas Hardy's "___ Little Ironies"
54 Skeleton starter
58 Hot sauce
60 Pasture cry
61 Kind of son or American
62 Coeur d'___, Idaho
63 Skater Zayak
64 Went downhill fast?
65 Still in bed
66 Singer Lopez
67 Finished dinner
72 Western Hemisphere treaty grp.
73 Tourn. sponsor since 1939
74 Satyric
75 Gold coin
76 Rat ___
77 Talked, old-style
80 Trimmed
81 Bowl locales
82 Traveled à la Heyerdahl
84 Not wait to be called
85 On a par with
86 Hardly a torrent
87 Site of early Beatles gigs
92 Goods
94 Beef
95 Lab burners
96 Virtuous one
97 Corn porridge
98 Place for a small house
99 Slaughter in baseball
100 Inter ___
101 Luggage
102 Charlie Chan comment
103 Beef cut
105 PC monitor
106 Fuzz
107 Van ___ Waals forces (physics topic)

by Fred Piscop

ACROSS

1 Undergrad degrees
4 Crow
9 First observed asteroid
14 Martinique and others
18 Bank I.R.A., e.g.
20 Film producer Hal
21 Byrd book
22 British general of 1775
23 Give up gardening?
26 Goad
27 Congressional committees have them
28 Club used in traps
29 Large wine bottle
31 Actor O'Brien
32 ___ Hawkins Day
33 With complete accord
34 Refusals
35 Nev. neighbor
36 Howell Heflin, for one
39 Cartoonist Groening et al.
42 Place for notable artists?
44 Man/mouse link
45 HELLO! . . . Hello! . . . hello . . .
46 Illicit leaves
47 End in ___ (come out even)
48 Prompted
49 Live
50 Squeaky-clean smile?
54 Western mining center
55 A woman can see through this!
57 Street show
58 Oilman's boon
59 Badger's cousin
60 Timeline points
61 Spy in Canaan
62 Dumbfounds
64 Lawyer Becker of "L.A. Law"
65 "The ___ of the Breakfast-Table"
68 "The Highwayman" poet
69 Water survey?
71 Bon ___ (cleanser)
72 Whitney contraptions
73 Cozen
74 These are always dubbed

75 Boris Godunov, e.g.
76 Hindu Mr.
77 Parade ground predicament?
81 Discernment
82 Copper mineral
84 Wouldn't hurt ___
85 Beard of grain
86 Scratch out
87 Word before head or mint
88 Official measuring of contents
92 Will matter
94 Agile swimmer
95 Sills and Moffo
97 Been in bed
98 Prudish trio?
101 "Shake ___!"
102 Yarns
103 Raincoat
104 Lotion ingredient
105 ___-majesté
106 Luxor's land
107 Necktie, of a sort
108 City trains

DOWN

1 Wash
2 Was sore
3 "Git!"
4 Dances suggestively
5 "The Kingfish"
6 Treat for Count Fleet
7 Alas, in Aachen
8 Former Berlin divider
9 Town known for a "giant" hoax
10 Funeral oration
11 Poet laureate Nicholas
12 Wind dir.
13 Identical
14 Galápagos critter
15 Talkative generals?
16 Waffle brand
17 Spotted
19 '93 World Series champs
24 People who make too many port calls?
25 Boredom: Sp.
30 Earring site
32 Diet dish for Dieter
33 French actor Delon
35 Private hoard
36 Shaw of swing
37 Mountain ridge
38 Public Interest Research Group founder

39 Like Dickens's Murdstone
40 It can be a lot
41 Dreary decade?
42 Hailey novel
43 Business for taxis
46 Old elevator cars
48 Unit of flow
50 Falls for
51 Heavens: Prefix
52 Dyeing technique
53 She wrote "The Female Eunuch"
54 Claus von ___ ('82 defendant)
56 Vegges out
58 Microsoft chief Bill
60 Waggish
61 To cook for Pierre
62 Inner turmoil
63 Op Art pattern
64 Have ___ to play (be of use)
65 Spanish province
66 Latin 101 word
67 It may have bias
69 Nightclub
70 Glacial ridge
73 Fringe of curls

75 Trumpet blast
77 "Oh, fudge!"
78 Part of some health checkups
79 "___ Fine" ('64 Beatles hit)
80 Battle call
81 Nerd
83 Food that comes in slices
85 Unit of current
87 Pricey
89 Old-womanish
90 He wrote "Dead Souls"
91 Lisper's bane
92 Airline to Ben-Gurion
93 Post-Christmas event
94 Air France lands there
95 W.W. II battle site
96 Sounds from a plaza de toros
99 Witch
100 Pedro's uncle

by Joanne W. Edwards

ACROSS

1 Stretch
6 Adventure story
11 Understands
17 Event at Lillehammer
18 Dazzle
19 Variety of hornless beef cattle
21 Nathan after sunbathing?
23 Sideshow collection
25 Garfield's middle name
26 Ending with talk
27 Like Lorraine, of song
28 Certain child: Abbr.
29 Elvis's record label
30 Fair offering
31 Worked on pumps
32 Retail
33 A person
35 Exhortation to a tailor?
37 One from the heart
38 Cologne crowd?
39 Historic caravel
40 Yahoo
41 1919 Peace Nobelist
42 Begins to brighten
44 Econ. yardstick
45 Soapstone constituent
46 Drop-leaf table feature
49 Expected
50 Stay away from
52 Book after Joel
56 Cleared the tape
57 Scissors alternative?
59 Pusher catcher
60 Musicians Jackson and Puente
61 Deflect, with "off"
62 Bring down the house
63 Not so important
64 Bomber letters
65 Backpacker's slogan?
67 City near Milwaukee
68 Salon treatment
69 Red in the middle
70 Citrus cooler
71 Dependable source of income
72 Rather
74 Prior to, in poetry
75 "I've ___ Be Me" (1969 hit)
76 Some kibbutzniks
79 Firm
81 Ocean flier
82 Walkway for Plato
86 School
87 Pebble Beach bunker material?
89 Gardening sci.
90 Straight: Prefix
91 Strips for breakfast
92 "Wishing will make ___" (pop song lyric)
93 Poke fun at
94 Cambridge campus
95 Peppermint candy
96 Made holy
97 Spasm
99 South Carolina tree
101 Cobbler's slippery problem?
103 Morocco, e.g.
104 First name in dance
105 Ice-cream cone, in Britain
106 Fleet
107 North Sea feeder
108 Intense desires

DOWN

1 Part of the Super Chief
2 Harried routine
3 ___ Longa (ancient city)
4 "Cheers" character
5 Comic Philips
6 Blue wildflowers
7 Spiny anteater
8 Worked like a dog
9 Spun yarn
10 Time for les vacances
11 Cur
12 Turn in
13 Supplementary
14 Polish partner
15 Kitty
16 Fox sci-fi series
17 In a trap
20 Shed
22 Distorting
24 Nubian Desert locale
27 Carnaby Street locale
31 It may be full
32 Dish akin to three-alarm chili?
34 Tanner's monthly supply?
35 Single
36 Doubleday of baseball
37 Have a bug
41 Peter out
43 Round at the Duck and Drake
44 Sacagawea, for one
45 Play "My Dog Has Fleas"
46 Outfit
47 Leave the depths
48 Siberian native
49 "___ schön"
50 Quench
51 Harass the pledges
53 Hyperactive
54 Home of the Black Bears
55 Turnkey
57 Leave it to him
58 Fall preceder?
61 Lacking fizz
63 It's rigged
65 Flower of one's eye?
66 Roaring Camp creator
67 M.P.A.A. approved
71 Imply
73 Cry of contempt
74 N.F.L. broadcaster
75 More lush, in a way
76 Bristol dance
77 Kind of photography
78 Much of the "Iliad"
79 Plant
80 Chinese island now called Xiamen
81 Getty or Parsons
83 Spate
84 1983 World Series champs
85 Optimally
87 With a lid on
88 Moon valleys
91 Use a Jacuzzi
95 Best of the Beatles
96 Fictional Adam
97 Grand
98 Linen marking
100 Tour book feature
101 Shoot the breeze
102 Seventh-century date

by Richard Silvestri

142 IN 1945

ACROSS

1 Ethan Frome's home
5 Call ___ to (stop)
10 Part of a spur
15 Finished
19 Tubular instrument
20 Shade of brown
21 Ancient superintendent
22 Lui's counterpart
23 Actress born in 1945
25 Drug introduced commercially in 1945
27 Chip, for one
28 Football Hall-of-Famer Greasy ___
30 W.W. II wolf pack
31 One of Perry's reporters
32 Gathering storm
33 Outlay
34 Galley arrangement
37 Italian city liberated in 1945
38 Piranha, e.g.
42 Carrara cash
43 President in 1945
46 ___ Islands, near New Guinea
47 Make ___ of (botch)
49 Motorcycle, slangily
50 Nautical heading
51 Year in Nero's reign
52 Curler's target
53 Organization founded in 1945
60 Sibs
61 Best-selling vet
63 Wind-borne
64 Bit of machine maintenance
66 Computer programming phrase
67 Warbucks ward
68 Northern constellation, with "the"
69 Party lines
71 ___ perditae (lost skills): Lat.
72 Demonstration halter
75 Tank supply
76 World Series champs of 1945
80 Lunch order
81 Harry James' "___ My Guy"
82 Inlet
83 Zilch
84 Non-Polynesian
86 Lance of justice
87 E.B. White classic of 1945
93 Transvaal settler
94 Big blazes
96 Peoples
97 Come to
99 Poet Coolbrith et al.
100 Printer's apprentice
101 Now, in triage
102 ___ Stone, Chief Justice in 1945
105 Type of type
106 Kind of cap
110 Earthshaker of 1945
112 Winning general in 1945
114 Cross-country gait
115 Salon support
116 Division of Germany
117 "To Live and Die ___"
118 Made tracks
119 Ghost
120 Artist Andrea del ___
121 Alphabet run

DOWN

1 Harvard art museum
2 Peek-___
3 P-51 maneuver
4 Fruit growers' worries
5 Like some hands
6 Belly shakers
7 No room to swing ___
8 Depressed
9 Where pigs become pigskins
10 Touch up
11 Children's author Scott
12 Rioja, e.g.
13 Bulldog
14 "Jungle Drums" composer Ernesto
15 Jai alai ball
16 "It was ___ mistake!"
17 Lance
18 X's
24 "This one ___ me"
26 "The Wild Duck" dramatist
29 Pantheon troublemaker
32 Get rid of
33 Brief appearance
34 "Ariel" poet
35 Evangelist Sister ___
36 Top female box-office draw in 1945
37 Kentucky Futurity event
38 It usually has a key
39 Recording item launched in 1945
40 Watergate Senator Sam
41 Sorry
44 Take ___ on (inhale, as drugs)
45 Double a knot
48 Appropriate
54 Choker
55 Tooth: Prefix
56 Chamber group, maybe
57 What Santa makes
58 Punch in the face, old-style
59 Backwater college
62 Go bad
65 Household spirit
67 Loud
69 Master, in "The Raj Quartet"
70 Deceive
71 1987 Peace Prize winner
72 Snitch
73 Stuttgart street
74 Rudder locale
77 Sets straight
78 Computer giant
79 Beats it, in dialect
85 Upton Sinclair subject
87 Where Moses got the Word
88 Medium states
89 Quake
90 Kind of flow
91 Remove
92 Corrode
95 Shot
98 Drawers on a line, e.g.
100 Like St. Peter's
101 Forehead beads
102 "The Jolly Toper" painter
103 In a superior position to
104 Velvet barrier
105 Sub ___
106 Mogul
107 Admits, with "up"
108 Porkpie material
109 Fritz's missus
111 Scroogian expletive
113 "Give ___ go"

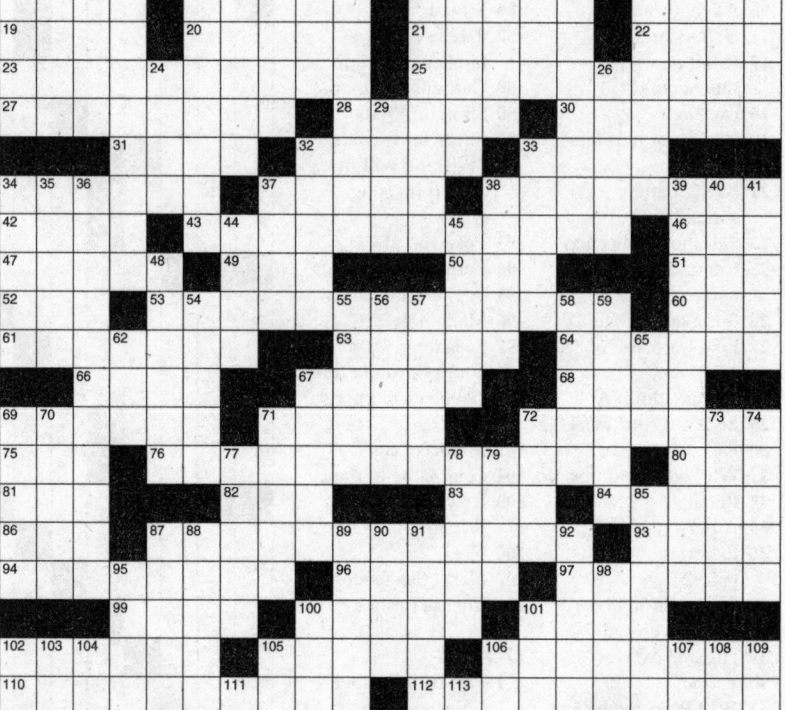

by Fran and Lou Sabin

ACROSS

1 Subject of the film "Sweet Dreams"
6 Nonpoisonous
10 Showed contempt
14 Move, in a way
17 Facilitated
18 Encumber
20 Colin Dexter's inspector
21 Grazing ground
22 Why Mr. Martin isn't popular on Memorial Day?
25 Fish with long jaws
26 Coach
27 Drift
28 "Maisie" star
30 Successfully persuade
31 Michaels and McGuire
33 Hoglike critters
35 Mountain home
36 Pro
38 Plantation homes
40 "Hogwash!"
41 Impolite goodbye
45 What the quality control chief did at the Japanese auto plant?
48 Allan Folsom's "___ After Tomorrow"
50 "The King" portrayer
51 Some cocktails
52 ___ scale
54 Arthur Murray lesson
58 Brit. honorary initials
59 Where "Hatikvah" is sung: Abbr.
62 Bonne ___ (clever thought)
63 Disparity
65 Impends
67 Vice President John ___ Garner
69 Why Mr. Beatty's fragrant herbs get trampled?
74 Esurience
75 Vogue
76 Jihad
77 Dryer residue
78 Radiator sound
79 "___ now!"
82 Romance scene
84 Pink
86 Take in
88 W.W.I inits.

90 Person in a circle, maybe
91 What the tipsy Oscar artist couldn't do?
98 Infers
99 Ethnic music
100 Agnew and others
101 City west of Manchester
103 Oven brand
105 Magnet alloy
107 Stowe's Little ___
108 Shot
112 Shine
114 Uneven
116 Extra
118 "A Spy in the House of Love" author
119 Why the Burbank train derailed?
122 Nav. rank
123 "___ you glad . . . ?"
124 Go smoothly
125 Adm. Byrd book
126 Eastern holiday
127 Soft drink
128 Soft drinks
129 Arms supplies?

DOWN

1 Signature sites
2 Petrol quantity
3 Pinnacle
4 Novelist Shute
5 Old New York tourist site, ___ Musée
6 Showing deep embarrassment
7 Inlet
8 "Spartacus" author
9 Ant
10 Supreme ruler: Abbr.
11 Part of the White House
12 Regarding
13 Seed cover
14 Berber's home
15 Not as energetic
16 Pledge money, at law
19 Summer hat
20 Fine yarn
23 Hindrance for Superman
24 Pitcher Steady Eddie
29 Subsidizes
32 Still active
34 Orbison and Rogers

36 Latin I verb
37 Elementary particles
39 Proof of purchase, maybe
41 "Elevator music" music
42 Faultfinders
43 Abates
44 Stick
46 Filofax
47 Bout locale
49 Old-fashioned criminal
53 Actress Charlotte
55 A successor to Gompers
56 Shop tool
57 Biblical lion
59 Archeologist Jones
60 Like some candles
61 Share-croppers
64 "Hey!"
66 Compass dir.
68 Actress Francis
70 Turkish city
71 N.Y.C. subway
72 Canal site
73 Mushroom

80 Hall-of-Famer Hubbard and others
81 Used a surgical saw
83 Ship-builder's choice
85 King
86 Spenser's birds "of goodly hue"
87 Kind of eye
89 Exempt
91 Fishing device
92 Nautical rope
93 Facing
94 English poet Dowson
95 Nantes's river
96 Annual racing events
97 Allocates
102 Pew locale
104 Africa's ___ Mountains
106 City known for its puppet theater
108 Comical
109 Wouldn't stop
110 Satellite launcher
111 Brawl

113 Architect Saarinen
115 "Holy moly!"
117 Genesis name
120 Three ___ match
121 Had

by Janet R. Bender

ACROSS

1 Waste
5 "Catch!"
9 Pure
15 Canine greeting
18 Stevenson character
19 Sharp
21 Corrida participant
22 Early August arrival
23 "Quanto è bella," e.g.
24 Weather forecast
25 Only Illinois-born President
26 Defile
27 Speaker of this puzzle's quip
30 Soothe
32 Knotted up
33 Petition
34 Wins over
35 Noted writer on poker
38 Foundation
39 Stage planning
40 Part 1 of the quip
45 Island transportation
49 Semi-conductor giant
50 Actor's direction
51 Slick
52 Dodge
53 Rock and Roll Hall of Fame architect
54 Kind of movie
55 Remote button
56 "Eat!"
57 Tangle
59 Many a Michener novel
60 "Impression: Sunrise" and others
61 Part 2 of the quip
67 "Britannicus" playwright
68 Be bereft of
69 The Louvre's "Venus d'___"
70 Battery end
71 Reference
72 Betting game, informally
73 "Deep Space Nine" changeling
76 Kim Philby and others
77 Gossip
78 Stitch together
79 Rocky Mountain town
81 Sci-fi writer Anthony
82 Part 3 of the quip
85 Disheveled
87 Facilitate
88 Hobo's lodging
89 Younger son of a Spanish monarch
92 Christmas staple
93 Perspective
95 Reward
96 End of the quip
102 Street of film
103 1965 Yardbirds hit
105 Nicholas Gage book
106 Leading ___
107 Wolfed
108 On now
109 Australian sheep menace
110 Capacity
111 Club ___
112 Commercial papers
113 First place
114 Kind of dog

DOWN

1 Bygone ruler
2 Prop for Orpheus
3 Frigg's husband
4 Part of a "Twelve Days of Christmas" gift
5 Carriage horse
6 Psychologist Havelock ___
7 Pee Wee of Cooperstown
8 Christian and others
9 Threshold
10 "Waiting for the Robert ___"
11 Gertrude Lawrence film bio
12 Coat, in old slang
13 Like 1, 2, 3
14 1986 Pulitzer novel
15 Place of worship
16 Sphere
17 Return parts
20 Cut into thirds
28 Streisand film
29 Fully exposed
31 Comedy club on cable TV
34 Stand up to
35 Fragment
36 Movie prefix
37 Hostile to
38 Nancy, in a Sir William Gilbert song
39 ___ Food Company
41 Pioneer bacteriologist J.R.
42 Deify
43 Treat with nuts
44 Pre-Jet New York footballer
46 Sound of Washington
47 "Dombey and Son" wife
48 Compact
54 Clearance
55 Mt. Katahdin's locale
57 Peter Parker's alias
58 Superfluous
59 Blister
60 Adjective in cigarette ads
61 "My Three Sons" dog
62 Former enemy capital
63 Molière's "L'___ des femmes"
64 First two words of "Dixie"
65 "Fie, thou dishonest ___!": "Twelfth Night"
66 Complainer
71 Slicker's home
72 Acorn, e.g.
73 Outdoors
74 Small progress
75 "I'm ___ you!"
77 Two pills, e.g.
78 Rousted
79 Bowl
80 Sows
83 S.C. Johnson brand
84 Rapture
86 Perplex
89 Girder
90 "Extreme Prejudice" actor
91 Got angry
92 Large canines
93 Outlay
94 Knife wielder's move
96 Contemporary novelist Martin
97 Curse
98 Writer Wiesel
99 ___ worship
100 Check out, so to speak
101 Desideratum
104 Coach Parseghian

by Michael W. Perry

ACROSS

1 Lindstrom or Zadora
4 Wand waver's word
10 Starting
14 Gazelle hound
20 Du Maurier's "Jamaica ___"
21 Lean against
22 Windsurfers' mecca
23 Confidentially
25 Part 1 of a quote
29 Sharif-Andrews movie "The ___ Seed"
30 Notices
31 M-G-M founder Marcus
32 Napkin holder
33 Guardian Angels founder Curtis
34 Looks pooped
36 Summer theater, sometimes
37 Nauru export
39 Quote, part 2
45 Horrified
46 Housman's was from Shropshire
47 Jawbone source
48 Withdraws, with "out"
52 Clanton foe of 1881
53 1974 McCartney/Wings hit
55 Save
60 Author of the quote
62 Someone else
65 Valiant mate
66 Cairo in "The Maltese Falcon"
67 Quote, part 3
70 Know, somehow
72 Provider of sound bytes?
73 Little wise one
74 Supercilium
76 Hot time in Chile
78 Engage in vote-swapping
84 Where to take a load off
87 Totaled
90 Sartre novel
91 Quote, part 4
98 Lost City of the ___
99 Ypsilanti's river
100 Albertville abodes
101 Quote, part 5
103 Catch
105 Auto racer ___ Fabi
106 Opulence
107 Electronic monitors, for short
108 A little butter
109 Carl Icahn company
111 Buck
113 Quote, part 6
122 Prop (up)
123 Start of a child's rhyme
124 Toll rds.
125 It means "high woods"
127 Single layer
128 Fourth-down option
129 Whodunit writer Grafton
130 Criticize vigorously
133 End of the quote
139 Steroid, for instance
140 Ballet bend
141 Plumbiferous
142 Selected at random
143 Columbus, e.g.
144 Attacks a sub?
145 Camisole size
146 Govt. code grp.

by Manny Nosowsky and Bob Klahn

DOWN

1 "The Gale Storm Show" co-star
2 Bisected
3 Iron deficiency problem
4 By share
5 Do-fa filler
6 Cable staple
7 Draw alternative
8 Sandbox set member
9 Last word of "A Christmas Carol"
10 In the thick of
11 Guff
12 Paris accord
13 Where Sibelius made his markkaa
14 1994 Elle Macpherson film
15 De novo
16 Cornwall co.
17 Lake of Lucerne canton
18 Genghis' grandson
19 Gas-pump platform
24 Tit for tat, perhaps
26 Ravens' ravin's?
27 Madras music
28 Classic '30s auto
34 Hang
35 Cunning
36 Pastoral plaint
37 Austrian painter Klimt
38 College in East Orange, N.J.
40 "The Morning Watch" author
41 Bewitch
42 Carson's swami
43 "Rocket Man" John
44 World chess champ, 1960–61
48 Burr Tillstrom puppet
49 Hoosier state flower
50 Eggy cake
51 Hit the dirt?
53 Husband of Medea
54 Count
55 Unload, so to speak
56 Sylvia Plath title
57 Flycatcher?
58 N.F.L. city: Abbr.
59 "Whoopee!"
61 Charles, to Elizabeth
63 Oilman ___ Pickens
64 Fell
68 Easily angered
69 Henry VI founded it
71 Shute's "A ___ Like Alice"
75 Slap hard
77 ___ Rizzo of "Midnight Cowboy"
79 Writer Godwin
80 Like the futhark alphabet
81 Peace Nobelist ___ Arias Sánchez
82 Inclined
83 Doesn't wear out
85 Long
86 Elvis' record label
88 Moses' burden
89 Torrent
91 "___ nuff!"
92 1964 Murray Schisgal play
93 Get a lode of this
94 Sterile bee
95 After a while
96 Price twice
97 Popular Civil War song
102 In case
104 Miss Clare of "Bleak House"
109 Old photo
110 Technique
111 Washington's ___ Stadium
112 Like most highways
113 To Sandburg, it comes on little cat feet
114 French painter Daumier
115 National Cartoonists Society award
116 It's put before Descartes
117 Chopin's "Twelve Grand ___"
118 "Well"-financed grp.
119 Final notice
120 Heraclitus, e.g.
121 Authors Anya and Ernest
122 Persian pooh-bah
126 Raskolnikov's love in "Crime and Punishment"
128 Baseball's Alejandro
129 Huff
130 Hightail it
131 Autobahn auto
132 "___ a song . . ."
134 D.D.E.'s Veep
135 Bill's companion
136 1941 Pulitzer winner Winslow
137 The Eiger, e.g.
138 "To Kill a Mockingbird" author

ACROSS

1 Language from which "bog" is derived
7 Peer Gynt's Arabic love
13 Begin a losing streak
19 Part of the iris
20 Fish that spawns at high tide
21 Galileo's muse
22 "Noises Off" and others
23 Phantom
24 Shred
25 Unexpected hitch
28 Commercial ___
29 Little terror of children's literature
30 "Little Rascals" creator Hal
32 Car ad abbr.
35 Cubemeister Rubik
36 Fold
39 German metaphysicist
43 Brooklyn Bridge engineer
46 Intended
47 "All systems ___!"
48 Secures
49 ___-weenie
50 Activities
51 1983 Michael Jackson hit
52 "America's Most Wanted" info
53 Fever
54 Pearl Harbor tributes
55 Arrest
58 Judicial writ
60 Adds spice to
62 Rock group with a blissful-sounding name
64 Hairlike
68 Spiff up
70 "Green Mansions" novelist William Henry ___
72 Crossword bird
73 "Chilly Scenes of Winter" author
76 In ___ (unborn)
78 Three times
80 Robin Hood, e.g.
81 Toast to one's health
82 "Man of ___"
83 Track athlete
84 "A Girl Named ___" (1962 film)
85 Fakery
86 Kind of tank
87 Agreement
88 Head material, perhaps
89 Your: Fr.
90 On the mother's side of the family
92 East Indian sailor
94 Seed covering
97 Clumsy one
105 Freshwater minnow
107 Crescent-shaped window
108 Levi Strauss rival
109 Tenor Jan
110 Type of afferent nerve
111 ___ Institute (self-improvement group)
112 St. George, for one
113 Casino employee
114 Not uniform

DOWN

1 Kind of sail
2 Asian sea
3 Spine-tingling: Var.
4 Points
5 Actress Graff
6 Impossible dream
7 Recitative song
8 Blue picture
9 Sharing, as a secret
10 Type of steering
11 Ship cabin
12 "The Vampire Lestat" writer
13 Architectural drop
14 Jody's mother in "The Yearling"
15 Best seller of 1951, with "The"
16 Aware of
17 Emulated Ananias
18 Throw down the gauntlet
20 Turning right
26 Brass
27 Score unit
31 In disarray
32 Fit for farming
33 Irish moonshine
34 Sears specialty
36 High hopes
37 ___ Lang (Superboy's girlfriend)
38 Aromatic seed
40 Kind of pool
41 Shirred items
42 Destruction
44 What crazy people have
45 Weeks per annum?
46 Name of four Popes
49 Chess champ Mikhail
50 Selfish one
53 Lifesaver
56 Buy into a poker game
57 Apply
59 O.T.C. grads, perhaps
61 One who's seen combat
63 Antique shop item
65 Get situated
66 If
67 Some lawn mowers
69 "The Flying Finn"
71 Telegraph bit
73 Sounds of impact
74 Lexicographer Partridge
75 Defendant's friend, often: Abbr.
77 Words after "hop" or "get around"
79 Angry, with "up"
81 Like a den, often
82 Actress Lords
84 "Swan Lake" garb
85 More extravagant
88 Five to ten, e.g.?
91 Yokum boy
92 Milk, in Milano
93 Mrs. Gorbachev
94 Dadaist pieces
95 Projectionist's need
96 Inkling
98 Elegance
99 Quechua ruler
100 Buzz's lunar partner
101 Bellows painting "___ at Sharkey's"
102 Guard's cry
103 Eminently draftable
104 Pioneering video game
106 The rocks in "on the rocks"

by Raymond Hamel

ACROSS

1 Fruit beverage
6 Nap
10 Muddle
14 Contorted
20 "What's in ___?"
21 Classification in human evolution
22 Finely ground quartz used as paint filler
23 Intended
24 Spoiler
27 Two-time Pulitzer-winning journalist
28 Dentist's target
29 Discomfort
30 Went beyond
32 Atty.'s org.
33 Using for substance
36 Boorish
37 Biblical suffix
38 A or B, e.g.
40 Marketing ploy
43 Advantage
44 Bona fide
46 Incline
47 Bulgarian monetary unit
48 Golf shot
49 Rambler, for one
51 Hunk
54 Ruin
55 Overseas network
58 Without planning
63 Auto industry regulator: Abbr.
66 Mt. Blackburn locale
68 Egg-hatching elephant of children's lit
69 Waterproof: England:: ___: U.S.
71 O.J. Simpson, once
72 Sen. Hatch
73 Features
75 ___ importance
76 Some radioactive electrons
77 Asparagus unit
78 Expands
79 Thick waterproof fabric used in cold climates
80 Love, overseas
81 Fat Albert's creator
82 Plant appendage
83 Schoolmaster's rod
84 First president of the Continental Congress
86 "Johnny Get Angry" singer Sommers
87 Cobbler's tool
88 "Wheel of Fortune" purchase
89 Whatever it takes
93 QB's try to get them
94 Goblet feature
96 Party concerns
97 More than impressed
99 Modeler's medium
100 Evidence in a paternity case
101 Poker holding
104 Arp's movement
107 Plain of Jars locale
108 Prepare for unpleasantness
114 "Edward Scissorhands" star
116 Mtn. stat
117 First name in choreography
118 Dressed to the nines
120 Dernier ___
121 Currently
123 Mania starter
125 Bungle, with "up"
127 Alarm respondent
128 Matt Dillon, e.g.
132 1963 N.F.L. passing leader
133 Broadway aunt
134 Actress Thurman et al.
135 Register
136 Bounced back
137 Procter & Gamble brand since 1947
138 Subject
139 Puts back

DOWN

1 Full-length garment
2 Expecting momentarily
3 Contractor's quote
4 Let off
5 Kind of artery
6 Library sound
7 Weed
8 Is equivalent (to)
9 Attacking
10 Turns down
11 Opposite of a weather
12 Kind of master
13 Wrest by force
14 From the top
15 Stadium divisions
16 Ted of TV's "Blossom"
17 While officially working
18 Climb like a squirrel
19 Metric increments
22 Position
25 Tampa paper, familiarly, with "the"
26 Brightly colored
31 Payroll record abbr.
34 Restaurant employee
35 Jr.'s Jr.
36 Like some responsibilities
39 Attention
41 "Backyards, Greenwich Village" artist
42 Traveled
43 Campus letter
45 Empiricist John and others
48 Didi of "Grease"
50 River to the Moselle
51 Up and about
52 Raid alternative
53 More astute
54 Honoree's spot
55 Santa ___
56 Off Broadway's ___ Group
57 Join, for better or worse
59 Car thief's destination, often
60 Biblical peak
61 Lineup
62 Engine parts
64 Covered, in a way
65 Former sinners
67 Fragment
70 The Rockies' ___ Field
73 O. Henry technique
74 Picker-upper
77 College student, for short
78 Takes without warning
79 Got out
81 ___ Yeobright (Hardy's native)
82 Divide
83 Run
85 Word from a hypnotist
86 One with quite a fish story
90 Bygone
91 "Kritik der reinen Vernunft" author
92 Sculled
95 ___ in tango
98 Pop
99 Like French fries and ice cream
101 Retreat
102 1984 Steve Martin film
103 Quèbec's ___ d'Orléans
105 Keep secret no longer
106 Brandy flavoring
107 Woolly
108 Was loud
109 Brown, e.g.
110 Nursery rhyme word
111 Lawn-care equipment
112 Old English Christmas dish
113 Narrow conduit
115 Image components
117 40's-50's actress ___ Mara
119 Religious leaders
122 Regarding
123 Pinochle play
124 Foil relative
126 Advanced
129 New Haven collegian
130 Assess
131 Presidential monogram

by Rich Norris

ACROSS

1 Fountain sales
6 Make ___ at
11 Château Lafite products
18 Used a plane
20 Angle measurement
22 Gone
23 Mama bird
24 Like the toughest part of the race
26 Pod preceder
27 Gordon of "Oklahoma!"
29 Year in the Yucatán
30 Greek dialect
31 Homely fruit
33 W.W. II woman
34 Guns
36 Workout count
37 Ran hard in the marathon
43 "Star ___"
44 Start for center
45 Boxer Griffith
46 Calendar abbr.
49 ___-Rivières, Quebec
52 Like a marathoner
55 Jog through old-fashioned streets
60 ". . . and the fourth for mine ___": Addison
61 Largely
62 Nuclear force elements
65 Work at the post office
66 Vlad the Impaler, e.g.
68 Upgrade the factory
72 Nutty
76 Switch suffix
78 Kept healthy
83 60's British invasion band, with "The"
87 Doing poorly at the marathon
89 Did well at the marathon
92 Land at Orly?
93 Eye sore
94 Habituate
95 TD's are worth 6 each
97 Cruising
99 Signed up for the marathon
105 W.W.II adversary
108 County below Broward
109 Correct copy
110 Use an optical reader
111 "___ my case"
113 Fathers and sons
114 Thicket trees
116 John Gunther topic
117 Overdo it at the marathon
121 Minute
123 International accord
124 Duke of the Dodgers
125 Obvious
126 Honey ___
127 Horned creatures
128 Things to avoid

DOWN

1 Parodied
2 Exceed
3 Ball's production company
4 Hill builder
5 Look
6 Turkish landfall
7 Verve
8 Musically together
9 Suck up
10 Clive Cussler best seller
11 Piece of animation
12 Chem. classroom
13 Small amount
14 Answer
15 ___ deux
16 Dutch still-life subject
17 Project details
19 Chest part
21 Assyrian capital
25 Title words before "Do" and after "Do You"
28 Heels
32 Accepted by
35 Put on a happy face
38 Extinguished
39 Miniseries, maybe
40 Fox hunter's coat
41 Southern religious school
42 Hawaiian state bird
46 Cold, in Caracas
47 Sorry soul
48 Research facility: Abbr.
49 Summer weather stat.
50 "Oysters ___ season"
51 Giant slugger
53 Ivan or Peter
54 Baseball execs, for short
56 Glasgow uncle
57 First degrees
58 Ready to eat
59 With 69-Down, a pet's choice
63 Software listing
64 VCR button
67 Three-time skiing gold medalist Sailer
69 See 59-Down
70 Incan treasure
71 Conversation starter
72 Dickensian expletives
73 Gray's subj.
74 A ___ sum
75 Little, to a lassie
77 Get-up-and-go
79 Tribal weapons
80 Part of H.R.H.
81 Auction conclusion
82 He ran with R.M.N.
84 Money-changer's profit
85 Burt's ex
86 In good health
88 Head of Le Havre
90 Imagined
91 Hay drying machines
96 Prepared shrimp
97 Suisse sweetheart
98 Ancient Persian governor
99 Kids
100 Kind of farmer
101 Sources of milk
102 Sharpness
103 Clams ___
104 Passes
105 Symbol of ferocity
106 Home of the Black Bears
107 Volkswagen model
112 Caterpillar construction
114 It ends at the Temple of Vulcan
115 The Man
118 Baseball season in Montréal
119 Marked a ballot
120 "O sole ___"
122 Oklahoma tribe

by Randolph Ross

ACROSS

1 Strands
8 Hopi home
14 Finish with a flourish
20 Antiquated
21 Gain
22 Maestro Toscanini
23 BAILEY, BUCK, WHITE
25 They may be dental
26 Visit
27 "___ life!"
28 Arctic traveler John
29 Betsy and Diana
30 BUCHWALD, CARNEY, GARFUNKEL, LINKLETTER
35 Half a fly
36 Bake, in a way
40 Anatole France novel
41 ___ del Sol (region in Spain)
43 Dome-shaped jellyfish
46 Honest ___
47 The least bit of concern
49 A party to, as a secret
52 Trojan War figure
53 SIMMONS, STAPLETON
56 Writer Buchanan
57 Scam
58 Hunting dog
59 Pismires
60 Peeping Tom
61 First-aid ___
62 Common test answer
63 Needle holder
64 Talkative
65 Give a ticket to
67 LEONTYNE, RAY, VINCENT
72 Actress Swenson
73 Actor Willem
74 Like McCuller's cafe
75 Kitty
77 Luck of the draw?
79 Brownie-to-Girl Scout ceremony
80 Teen hangout
82 Scales
84 Patriot's end
85 Kind of joint
86 DENNIS, DORIS
88 Bridge player's goal
89 January 1 word
90 Hot times on the Riviera

91 Subjoin
92 "Carmen" setting
94 Adapts for special use
96 Burger King offering
98 Miniature map
99 Farragut, e.g.: Abbr.
101 CHARLIE-DOROTHY, ELEANOR-FESS
106 Old salt
108 Long time
109 Brainchild
110 Corp. biggie
113 "Boom" preceder, in song
114 CAREW-MCKUEN-SERLING-STEIGER-TAYLOR
119 Short sock
120 Shows reverence
121 "I Was a ___ Werewolf" (1957 flick)
122 Live
123 Nicole Hollander comic strip
124 Stupefies

DOWN

1 Striped fish
2 Artist de Tirtoff, professionally
3 Subdivision subdivision
4 Fraternity letter
5 Airport features
6 Eastwood's "The ___ Sanction"
7 General called "Old Fuss and Feathers"
8 Drivel
9 Language related to Aztec
10 Flight abbr.
11 Ballet-practice fixtures
12 New Hampshire's state flower
13 Start
14 They grow down
15 Some fabrics
16 School orgs.
17 BRADLEY, CLINTON, COSBY
18 Manumits
19 "Cabaret" director
24 Item for Sgt. Friday
31 Midwest hub
32 Important political bloc
33 Gladly

34 Pictures on monitors
36 Sign of love—or hate
37 With valor
38 HAMILL, HARMON, MESSIER, SPITZ
39 Neighbor of Ukr.
42 Haberdashery accessory
44 Rich Little, e.g.
45 Showed surprise
47 Painter Rousseau
48 Haggis ingredient
50 Frenzied store event
51 Not any
54 Anatomical passage
55 "Go directly to ___"
58 Declivitous
60 Ham go-with
63 Rate setter, with "the"
66 "Dome doily"
68 Mallorca and Ibiza, e.g.
69 A little lower?
70 Tater

71 Albacore and bluefin
73 U.S.A.F. awards
76 Eye problem
78 Irish patriot Robert
80 Taiwan Strait island
81 Roll-call response
82 News conference attendees
83 Direct
86 Belittle
87 Weather protector
88 Kind of tax
93 Grim-___ (stern-faced)
95 Beloved
96 Relative of parsley
97 Revue segment
99 "___ Fell Out of Heaven" (1936 hit)
100 1776 patriot Silas
102 Heineken rival
103 Bonkers
104 Censors
105 "Walk Away, ___" (1966 pop song)
107 Buñuel collaborator
110 Chesterfield, e.g.

111 Keenness, as of appetite
112 Suffixes on candy wrappers
115 Ida. neighbor
116 Ransom ___ Olds
117 The Grays' side: Abbr.
118 Genetic letters

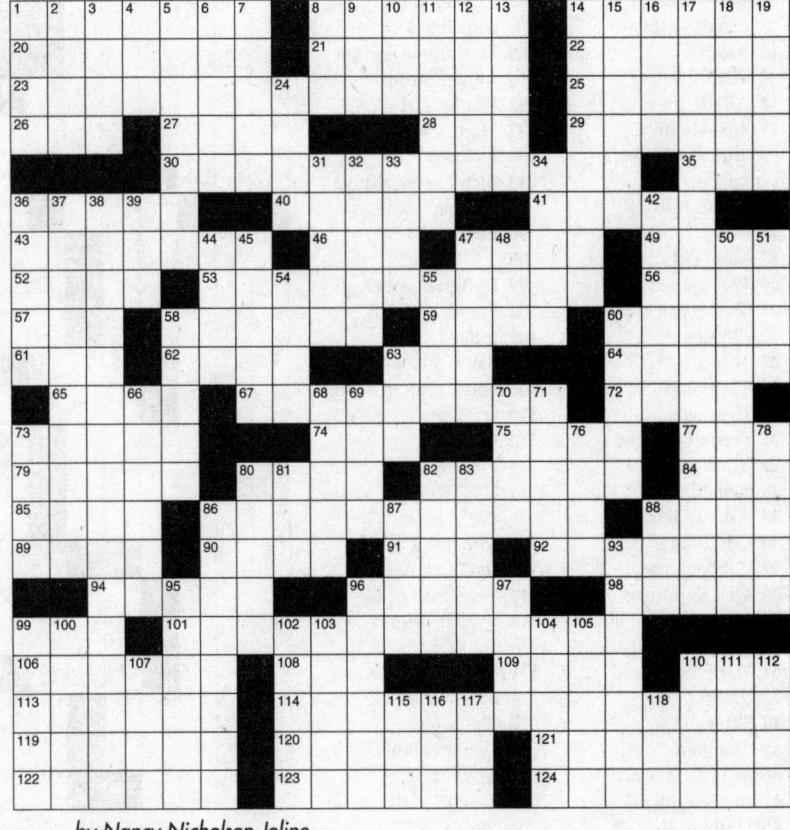

by Nancy Nicholson Joline

ACROSS

1 Sage
7 Circus surface
14 Ask for identification
18 Alfalfa
19 For whom appearance is important
20 Heretofore
21 Best
23 Monopoly property
24 1966 movie or song
25 Graveyard shift physician
27 "I'm ___!" ("Ta-ta!")
29 Capp and Capone
30 Heartsick
31 Prefix with gram
32 X
33 Remedy
34 Apr. 15 harrier
35 Conditions
37 Cabbage
39 One that turns either way?
40 Wade opponent
41 "Jane Eyre" girl ___ Varens
44 Skillful
45 Sparklers
46 Mikhail, for one
47 Reb's anthem
48 Hightail it
49 ___ on (spoil)
50 Families living on chicken feed
52 Drive away
53 Curtain fabrics
55 Musical phrase
56 Follower's end
57 Mustangs of coll. football
59 Rated NC-17
60 More sharp
63 Interest group, with "the"?
64 Elk
68 "Say again?"
69 Concerning Comanches, e.g.
71 Shenanigan
72 Nile biter
73 Vanity case?
74 Car's steering option
75 Kind of class
78 Hurt
80 Drops drops
82 ___ Hood, Tex.
83 Series end
84 Unpiloted plane
85 Kind of ball or hall
86 Angled pieces

87 Stuff
88 Circled items, sometimes
89 Directional ending
90 Judges' group
92 Beatles girl
93 High school class
94 Inclined
95 Blank verse rhyme scheme
96 Embargo
97 ___-Magnon
99 Postgraduate deg.
102 Friend of Pooh
103 Indeed
104 Pawn a newspaper
108 Short putt, in slang
110 ___ rice
112 Ran
113 Employment
114 U.N. member since 1991
115 Underling
116 1987 Costner role
117 Frankfurter piece
118 It's left behind

DOWN

1 McIntoshes, e.g.
2 The beginning
3 Cast a ballot
4 Fervent
5 King of early comics
6 Clues for detectives
7 Wheeled around
8 Time piece
9 Confidential statistic
10 Where many Indians live
11 Kind of price
12 Go down
13 Auditions
14 Eagle wearer: Abbr.
15 Sexy trysts
16 Steamroller
17 Chiffoniers
20 Less hairy
22 Cut
26 Fruit snack
28 Return swing
33 Awakens
35 Nasty at court
36 Suffer embarrassment
38 Naples's Castle of St. ___
39 Give old news
41 At the current's mercy
42 Faster
43 Trip back for Thanksgiving, maybe

44 Autograph ___
45 Get separate checks
46 Protein source
49 Marcel Duchamp, e.g.
50 Crows
51 Oriental workplace
54 Just Plains folks
58 Goes soft
61 Poet Field
62 Big statue isle
65 Stuck
66 Wrap up
67 Shuffle
70 "Show Boat" tune
76 Nut's best part
77 Stick
79 Learn in a hurry
80 Diver's weapon
81 Navy trainee
86 Fully packed
87 Becomes evident
90 One who's got it coming
91 Tall prez, for short
92 Molière rival
93 Yankee followers?
96 Sonny and Cher, once

98 Public regard, informally
99 Baroness von Trapp
100 Reply sheepishly
101 Befuddle
104 Rug covers
105 Just one of those things
106 Lambies' mammies
107 Let
109 Small sports cars
111 ___ particle

by Harvey Estes

ACROSS

1 Mosaic tile
9 Flowery perfume
14 Where Nejd is
20 Almost
21 Kentucky county
22 Calls, in a way
23 The King
25 Sings lullabies
26 Opposite of sans
27 The King's Head order
28 Old-time journalist Bugs
29 Weak English king
38 Article on a rack
41 Fish of the carp family
42 Lunchbox item
43 Blackthorn fruit
44 Kind of wood
47 Bother, with "at"
50 Immemorial
51 Mel of the diamond
52 Skyscraping center?
55 Kansas city on the Santa Fe Trail
59 Bristly
60 Important interval
61 Even
63 Chemical suffix
64 "___ Little Teapot"
67 Simply because of that
69 1923 Wallace Beery portrayal
76 Ballot-related
77 Put in one's ___ (meddle)
78 Laugh syllable
79 Île St.-Louis native
81 Bard's contraction
83 Punctilio
86 Clare of ___
87 1959 #1 song
90 Symbol of safety
91 School org.
93 Aisne tributary
94 Bacon work
95 Exploit
97 Soothsayers
100 122-Down − 2
102 Félicité, e.g.: Abbr.
103 First king buried in Westminster Abbey
109 Slog (through)
110 Pester
111 Like most colleges
113 Primitive conveyance
116 Last of the Hebrew prophets, in Christian belief
123 Spoon-bending psychic
124 Inception
125 Colander
126 They're not serious
127 Peace Nobelist Williams
128 City east of Montgomery

DOWN

1 Stun
2 Author Kaufman
3 Edison's middle name
4 The "C" in C.S. Lewis
5 Still runny
6 Soapberry's kin
7 "Phew!"
8 Word for a lady
9 White poplar
10 Glass Capital of the World
11 Hasidism founder Baal Shem-___
12 Black cuckoo
13 ___ judicata
14 Esoteric
15 Harder to find
16 Has a crush on
17 Who's Who piece
18 Kind of storm, in sci-fi
19 Plow puller
24 Shoot as expected on
28 Hacker's headache
30 Lip
31 Microscope part
32 Ending with fox or dog
33 Shakespearean prince
34 Wind up
35 Hello or goodbye
36 Lavishes care (on)
37 So far
38 Mooring rope
39 ___ generis (of another kind): Lat.
40 Ancient Mexican
45 W.W. II abbr.
46 Rds.
48 Supped
49 In better fighting shape
53 Fortune hunter's catch?
54 City ESE of Buenos Aires
55 Siouan tongue
56 Lake of the Four Forest Cantons
57 Official records
58 Marvel Comics superhero
61 "Barney Miller" actor
62 ___ concern
65 Year in Elizabeth I's reign
66 Heine poem "___ Troll"
68 Glass component
70 Towel word
71 Et ___
72 Sugar pie
73 TV actress Brooke
74 Emulate Sprat's wife
75 Sign of impassiveness
79 Skinned
80 Cockeyed
82 Kind of jump
84 Tina's ex
85 Brain and spinal cord: Abbr.
87 ___ Antony
88 Align
89 Some party attenders
90 "Fables in Slang" author
91 The Steel City, for short
92 Calendar abbr.
96 Loiter
97 Vipers
98 Shoshonean
99 Spenserian work
101 Star's statuettes
104 Fuming one
105 Dapper
106 Alphabetic sequence
107 Black tea variety
108 Make the knot tighter
112 Dent
113 Pepper, e.g.
114 Sign of a leader, it is said
115 Tarzan portrayer
116 "Get a ___"
117 Self starter
118 Inits. of 1948
119 '70s training
120 Heat measure
121 Comprehend
122 100-Across + 2

by Frank A. Longo

ACROSS

1 Key state: Abbr.
4 Ending for mom or dada
7 Calculates astrologically
12 Keeps expenses low
18 Take another sip
20 Intense dislike
21 Indy problem
22 One more
23 It's hit on the head
24 Sophisticated
25 Why crows band together?
27 Nabisco treat
29 Rebel follower
30 Running amok
31 Charlemagne's dom.
32 Bugs
35 Female ruff
36 Instant
37 Sheep-shearing spot?
39 Has a yen for
41 Lost one's balance?
43 Items in a march?
44 Trodden way
45 Heartfelt
48 Swamp critter
49 Filling fellow
52 Swells
53 Units of loudness
54 Maneuvered
55 "In Cold Blood" star
56 Pigeon-killing blow?
58 Airline to Oslo
59 Script addition
60 Bakery product
62 ___-majesté
63 North and south: Abbr.
64 Spots on TV
65 Cat on the stage?
69 Sunday singers
71 Talks
73 Leave off
74 Beehive, for one
75 Sticks
76 Laurel and Lee
77 Put off
78 Opposite of flunked
79 A lot
80 The Little Mermaid
81 Bank robber's secret
83 Hollywood cow?
85 Chest protector
88 German I
89 Strudel kin
91 Bit of work
92 Early mall
94 Precious

96 TV's "___ Three Lives"
97 Negative horse?
99 Enduring
101 Conclude
104 Private's privy
105 They often lie
106 Leader of Herman's Hermits
107 Goes by
108 Spanish philosopher ___ y Gasset
109 Von Stroheim epic
110 Cry out loud
111 T.E.D. defeater

DOWN

1 Scrap
2 "Raven" maiden
3 Minute
4 1974 hit "___ the Sheriff"
5 British gun
6 Shopkeeper
7 Bit of haunted-house décor
8 Flaps
9 Sermon subject
10 Drawer of ships
11 Less bumpy
12 Animal trail
13 White wine aperitif
14 Deeply
15 The story of snakes, updated?
16 Coop youngster
17 Coifs
19 Sphere starter
21 Lottery, for short
26 What the suspicious smell
28 Platonic P's
32 Badgered
33 Absorb gradually
34 Jolson song
37 Mamie's predecessor
38 Hersey locale
40 A.B.A. members
41 Moccasin without laces
42 Sneaky guy?
44 Change at Oxford
45 A drop in the ocean?
46 Referred indirectly
47 Inkblots for lions?
48 Explode
49 "Buenos ___"
50 Tidewater
51 N.F.L. scores
53 Marks for life
54 Jacques, in the round

57 Daly's onetime co-star
60 Drew
61 Rock group
63 Medicine bottle
64 In the manner of
65 Uses the blender
66 Do to do
67 Enter data
68 Parson's home
69 Rock musician John
70 Staff associate
72 Georgia ___
74 He succeeds
76 Chewing out
77 Trails along
79 Boot bottom
80 Longfellow's bell town
81 Roman orator
82 More critical
83 Gangland gals
84 Get mad
85 Engagingly innocent
86 Cara and Ryan
87 Least cluttered
90 Pageant prize
92 Take ___ at
93 Irving hero

95 Art Deco illustrator
97 Hawaiian honker
98 Light headwear?
100 Pos. canceler
102 Hide-hair connector
103 Adversary

by Richard Silvestri

ACROSS

1 Clog (up)
4 Venue for political coverage
9 Sharp
14 Range
19 It has a head and hops
20 Kind of cuisine
21 Like some caps
22 Shiraz native
23 TV show on delayed broadcast?
26 Lloyd George contemporary
27 Beef cuts
28 Absolute Truth
29 Worn
30 One of the Pointer Sisters
31 Kind of deck
32 Surrender specifics
34 Kissers' interference
35 Somewhat
36 Part of a pound
39 Actress Merkel
40 Like a good cake
41 Run through
43 "Sesame Street" setting
44 Former Bills coach Levy
45 State name preceder
48 Dolt
49 "The Waltons" character
51 ___ siècle
52 One in a wool coat
53 "Billy Bathgate" author
54 One of three Indy winners
55 "What did I tell you?"
56 Out of control
58 First name in autocrats
59 Parent
60 German-Polish border river
61 Steady high
63 It's south of Eur.
65 Girls' shoes
67 Work
68 Vienna transport
70 India's first prime minister
72 Does field work
73 Folks
74 "Who's there?" reply, informally
75 50's TV actress
77 Expiration
78 Raiders leader
79 Feudal state
80 Had been
83 Van Owen player on "L.A. Law"
84 Look over
85 New York City highway, with "the"
86 Melodramatic parting
88 Chance
90 Word with water or wall
91 Slangy greeting
92 Tennis's Nastase
93 Does "Jingle Bells"
95 It precedes "Remember" and "Forget" in song titles
97 Wasted time
98 Mohawk Valley city
99 City sacked by Tamerlane, 1395
101 Scurrier
103 Untrained
104 Assassination victim of 1981
105 Rain date for a big sports event?
109 Academy founder
110 Draw ___ in the sand
111 Aloft
112 ___ Aztecan (language group)
113 Less straight-forward
114 Kind of knife
115 Shocks
116 Intl. writers' org.

DOWN

1 Anesthetic
2 Loudly laments
3 Places for December lights
4 Stadium sound
5 "___ who?"
6 Subject of a Swift essay
7 Working tirelessly
8 Undo
9 To the point
10 Newspaper reportage
11 Dido of Carthage
12 Speak deliriously
13 Raised
14 It joins the Colorado near Yuma
15 Stadiums

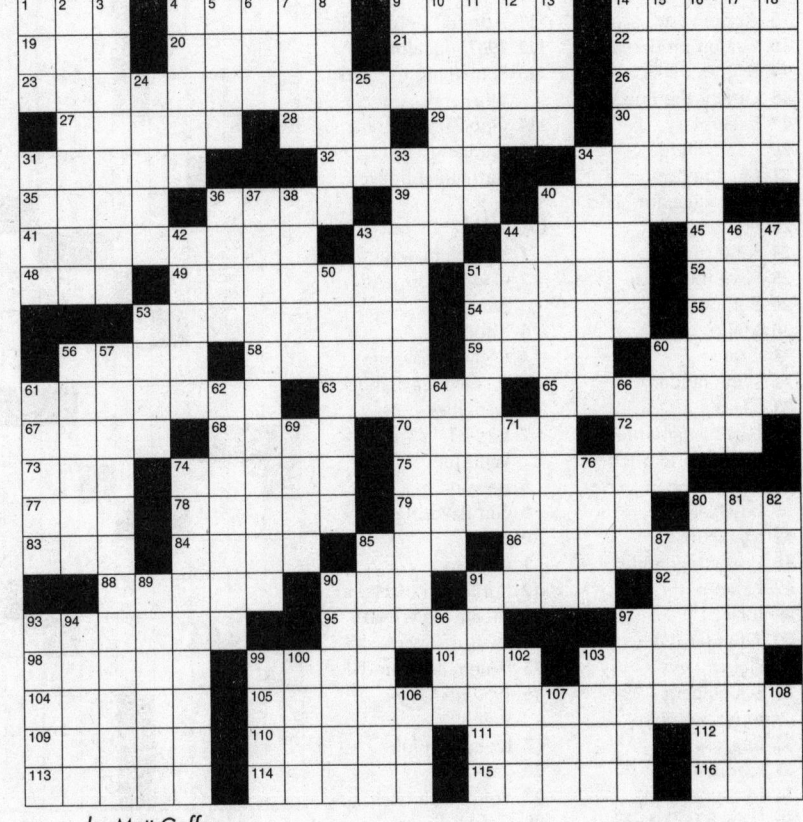

by Matt Gaffney

16 1986 pop hit released behind schedule?
17 Link
18 Brown and Turner
24 Semiconductor device
25 Clod buster
31 Mitchell place
33 Mick Jagger's late girlfriend?
34 Treaty subjects
36 Gator cousin
37 Second day of Lent?
38 Columbus's home
40 Tardy employee?
42 "What ___!"
43 English port west of Bournemouth
44 It gets the shaft
46 Publishers Clearinghouse contests
47 Sibyls
50 Cup filled to the top
51 More advanced
53 Popular pencil and paper game
56 Skiing event
57 Postponed religious event?
60 French- and Arabic-speaking seaport
61 Nudged
62 Goes after
64 "If ___ see you . . ."
66 Week of tomorrows, herein
69 "Agreed!"
71 One-named children's singer
74 Porcelain, e.g.
76 Celebrated Freud case
80 Formed, as tears
81 Drive away
82 Racing vehicle
85 Impassioned
87 Ream
89 Pinpoint
90 "Quit bothering me!"
91 Phi Beta Kappa and such
93 Architectural decorations
94 To any degree
96 Picked-up item
97 Best Actor of 1990
99 P.D.Q.
100 Inkatha Freedom Party supporter
102 Ridicule
103 Feds
106 King of Spain
107 Baton Rouge sch.
108 Over there

ACROSS

1 Liquor shop order
5 Apple variety
10 Carson predecessor
14 Bag, in dialect
18 One of the Bowls
19 Exemplary
20 "___ when?"
21 Final notice
22 Nest eggs, for short
23 Softly
24 Kind of dish
25 Give the slip to
26 Potholes
30 Makes one
31 Grays
32 Wine holder
33 Claims
36 Part of the familia
37 Addition to a letter
41 First name in hotelkeeping
42 Manicurist
46 Projecting angle
47 Lasso parts
49 Iota
50 Thunder Bay locale: Abbr.
51 Schoenberg's "___ to Napoleon"
52 Engross
53 Exfoliate
54 Idiosyncrasy
56 Parachute attacks
61 Store fodder
62 Sushi offering
63 Shaky start?
67 Wristwatch
74 Ornery fellow
76 Heart-to-heart
77 Indispensable
78 Literary initials
79 What "+" means: Abbr.
80 "Easy to Be Hard" musical
81 Webster, for one
83 Roman ethicist
84 Utility bill
88 Timekeeper, of sorts
89 Encroachments
90 ___ Brainard, the Absent-Minded Professor
91 Intellectualizes
93 Bus depot abbr.
94 Belt
96 Detects
98 Dust
105 Hatcher of "Lois & Clark"
106 False front
107 Hearing enabled
108 Plant pod
109 Cereal choice
110 Over
111 Admiral Byrd book
112 1967 folk album
113 Something to break into
114 Opposite of alway
115 Nudges
116 Individual figure

DOWN

1 Minimum wager
2 Goddess of gentle winds
3 Tito, e.g.
4 Right of passage
5 It comes as a shock
6 Activities
7 Early TV's "___ With Judy"
8 Repairs
9 Gin flavoring
10 Slice
11 Pro's foes
12 Port north of Haifa
13 Create the wheel?
14 Tactful
15 Penetrating wind
16 1930 hit "The ___ Waltz"
17 It starts in juin
20 Tap
27 Prefix with dose
28 Goes belly up
29 Muslim judge
33 Bookcase site
34 Heavy
35 Hardly partygoers
36 Secure
37 Kind of dog
38 Regulus' constellation, with "the"
39 Thin
40 Hill dweller
42 Author Behn
43 Spumante source
44 Juice server
45 "Good night, ___" (old TV sign-off)
47 Comparatively likable
48 Follicles have them
52 Vexes
53 It gets a tanning
54 Pay obeisance
55 "The doctor ___"
57 Rewards for waiting
58 Without water
59 French preservative
60 Sesame Street dweller
64 Prefix with sphere
65 Overcoat material
66 Bean and others
68 Bushels
69 Home to 18 Congressmen
70 Pusher's pursuer
71 Sculptor Mestrovic
72 Fly catcher
73 W.W. II area: Abbr.
74 '40s boxer Billy
75 Word with friendly or fee
79 Ieoh Ming ___
80 #1 on a table
81 Physics particle
82 Flushed
83 Winter melons: Var.
85 Brisk, as business
86 Uniforms
87 Having a single foot
88 ___ State (David Letterman's alma mater)
91 Fresh
92 Escapes
94 Nasty
95 North Sea feeder
96 Warmed-over
97 Some Surrealist works
98 Pertaining to flight
99 Neighbor of Armenia
100 Ancient writing
101 Come by
102 Suit material, perhaps
103 Miss Cinders of old comics
104 Groove
105 Cable network

by Alex and Victoria Black

ACROSS

1 Vulcan's workshop, in myth
5 Movement begun by Tristan Tzara
9 Digs into
14 Parliamentarian's call
17 Fritters away time
19 Joie de vivre
20 Pass
21 Legends
23 Heavy-duty farm machine
26 ___ mater
27 When D.S.T. ends
28 Hilo mementos
29 Honors with style
30 "Rinaldo" and others
32 Vacillate
34 Call by intercom
35 Signify
36 Wall Street order
37 Playing the toady
42 Fictional dog
43 Bar orders
45 Orangish food
46 Item of kabuki apparel
47 Ballot abbr.
49 Seurat, e.g.
52 "This must weigh ___!"
53 Sails close to the wind
56 "Hey!"
59 "A Dissertation on Roast Pig" writer
63 Serving dish
64 N.C.A.A. participant: Abbr.
65 Writer Murdoch
66 60's B-ball champs
67 Patent medicine
69 Certain clipping
71 Rugby get-together
72 Yielding
73 Start of a Harper Lee title
74 "Pardon me!"
75 Hide
76 ___ française
77 "A Summer Place" star
78 Newspaper employee
82 Ring rock
83 She played Jane to O'Keeffe's Tarzan
85 Yahtzee equipment
86 Grasp
88 ___ rule
89 It's north of Minn.

90 Police sch.
92 Drains
95 Ma Bell
97 Rodgers-Hart show
101 Besides
103 Dreaming, to Hamlet?
105 Dusks, to Donne
106 Least clever
109 Smoothly, to Solti
110 Flavorless
112 Logical start
113 Dian Fossey subject
114 "Unto us ___ is given"
115 Fields-West film
119 Frangible
120 Lindsay's successor
121 Issue
122 Correct
123 34th, Elm, etc.: Abbr.
124 Cavalry weapon
125 First name in New York City politics
126 Apposes

DOWN

1 Jostles
2 Faith healer, perhaps
3 One way to dress
4 Sternward
5 Just said no
6 "___ fair . . ."
7 "Life with Father" writer
8 Gift for a budding entomologist
9 Hammered
10 In the old days
11 "Phooey!"
12 "Foucault's Pendulum" author
13 Walked purposefully
14 Mayflower Compact signer
15 Where to pack troubles
16 Slips
18 Ego
22 Buffered
24 Presb. or Epis.
25 Co-host of morning TV
31 Agatha Christie's "___ at End House"
33 Hightailed it
34 Oyster catch?
38 Sentinels
39 Robin's hangout?
40 Organ stop
41 Hollywood crosser

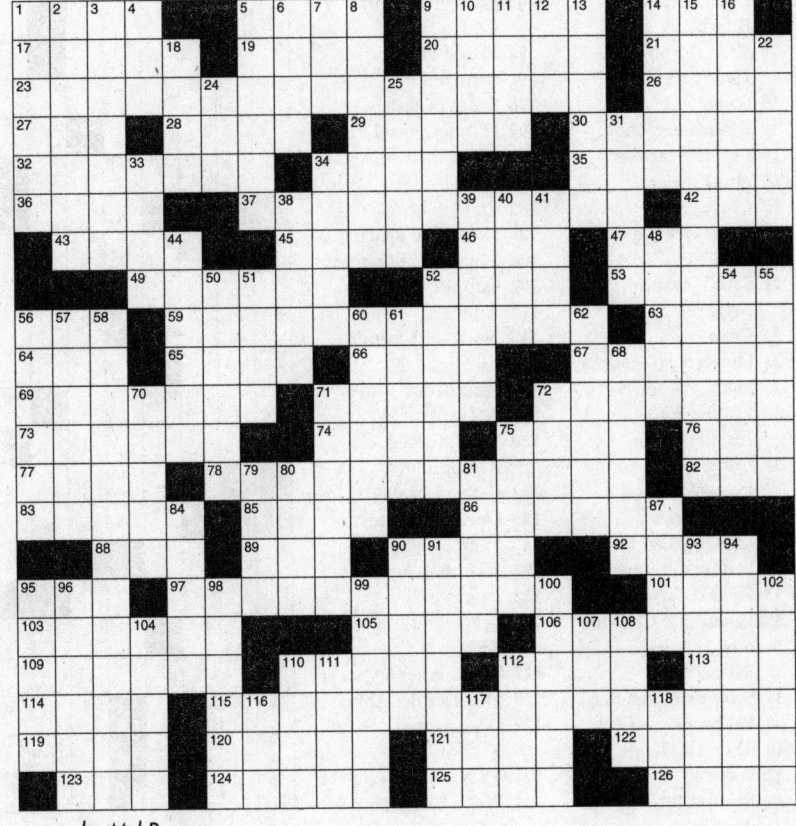

by Mel Rosen

44 Gregarious
48 Ancient Red Sea kingdom
50 Send
51 Bedog
52 In ___ (batting poorly)
54 Ribbed silk fabric
55 Parade
56 Praised, in a way
57 Filmland's Joe Besser, e.g.
58 Pat Morita film
60 Swindle
61 Rocky debris
62 Bit of ammo
68 Petrol amounts
70 Striped yellow balls, in pool
71 Retreats
72 Fido and Fluffy
75 Madrid landmark
79 Rock's Billy
80 Word from a pen
81 Sheik Rahman et al.
84 Dead
87 Entertains like Hammer
90 Catalyst

91 Egg tester
93 Was appealing?
94 Defer
95 Attorney ___
96 Luther's postings
98 "Fat Man" and "Little Boy" of 1945
99 More in order
100 Marvel
102 Arabs, perhaps
104 Puts in order
107 Ballad ending
108 Knob
110 Sing
111 Soil sweetener
112 Footnote note
116 Voice vote
117 Bird in a herd
118 G.P.'s org.

VAMPIRE'S DELIGHT

ACROSS

1 One of the Brady Bunch
7 "___ Darlin' " (Neal Hefti song)
10 Some W.W. II service personnel
14 Public relations effort
18 Consecrate
19 River or reservoir in Hesse
21 Saudi Arabia neighbor
22 Corn ___
23 Showed no emotion
25 "Dracula" miss
26 Epithet for Adenauer
27 Daughter of Teddy Roosevelt
28 Natterjacks
29 Like chicken fingers
31 Hanukkah item
33 Singer Garrett
35 Where the Clintons met
36 ___ de coeur
37 Sculpture material
38 Pakistani river
40 Sister of Helios
42 Fortress parapets
47 Related through the mother
50 90-Down's land
51 Crocus and gladiolus
52 Whit
54 Broadway belter
57 Wrongs
58 Valse, e.g.
59 Southern capital
61 "The Hundred Secret Senses" author
62 Movie theater
63 Pro ___
65 Riot
67 Mexican President, 1946–52
69 Allowance
72 Painter Childe ___
74 Some undercover operations
76 Make
77 List ender
79 Verdi's "___ tu"
80 Leave
82 Tallinn natives
84 Disturb
85 Word with buddy or binary
86 Kind of prize
87 Spa feature
88 Con game
91 Daughter of Juan Carlos
94 Prince Philip's surname
96 Sense of taste
99 Hat designer Lilly
101 Water channel: Abbr.
102 Partook of
103 Like outer space
106 Stage telephone, e.g.
107 Coppice
112 Attempt
115 North of Virginia
117 Task
118 Rick Blaine's love
119 A Turner
120 1992 Michael Keaton film
122 Barbary beasts
123 One of Chekhov's "Three Sisters"
124 Like Rioja wine
125 Execrate
126 Beverage from une vache
127 Vegas night sight
128 Boxer's title: Abbr.
129 Deals with

DOWN

1 Word heard in fine stores
2 Old-womanish
3 "Le Penseur" sculptor
4 Mexican holiday ___ de Mayo
5 Lulls
6 Up
7 Big star at night
8 Don Quixotes
9 Rembrandt's birthplace
10 Aussie marsupial
11 "Jaws" setting
12 Former capital of Crete
13 Tangles
14 Bicker
15 Keeps up the beat?
16 "ER" extras
17 More strapped
20 Live
24 Demosthenes, e.g.
30 Charge
32 Point of no return?
34 Amusing
39 Polynesian tongue
41 Fencer's movements
42 Castro predecessor
43 Bar events
44 Old World finches
45 MS. vetters
46 Pitches
48 X rating?
49 Messes up
53 Forward pass, in football
55 Some ice cream orders
56 Acoustic
58 Airheads
59 Secured with "down"
60 Let go tactfully
62 Critic Vincent
64 Lender's letters
66 Iwo Jima flag raiser
68 Toxic atmosphere
70 Made a yoke
71 Part of a "Star Wars" name
73 Where to see "The Last Supper"
75 Venue
78 Spacecraft part
81 Cartoonist's transparency
83 Here or there
84 African capital
87 More rigid
88 Dimensional
89 Tree with white flower clusters
90 Comrade Kosygin
92 Pile
93 Tumblers, e.g.
95 Utmost
97 Wilson Dam org.
98 "For Your Eyes Only" singer, 1981
100 Fictional mastermind
104 Fence feature
105 Albéniz's "___ in D"
108 Amusement park attraction
109 Park land?
110 Artist Max
111 Dips one's toe in
113 90°
114 Wayne film "Back to ___"
116 A party to
121 Summer hours in D.C.

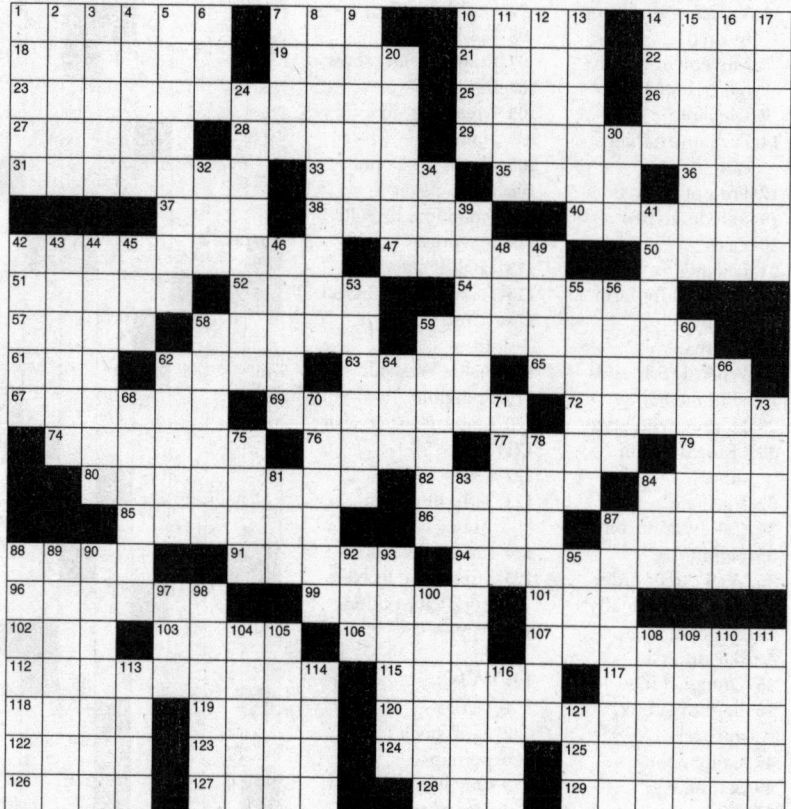

by Nancy Nicholson Joline

ACROSS

1 Problem for the wheelchair-bound
6 Dread
10 Cry of dread
14 ___ a pig
19 Most common inert gas
20 Zhivago's love
21 Intensity
22 "___ Wanna Cry" (Mariah Carey hit)
23 LABOR ACTIVIST
25 GOVERNESS
27 Pattern of behavior
28 Mountain transport
30 Idle
31 French 101 verb
32 Clear as mud
33 Urgent message
34 Do in the evening
37 Periphery
38 Embassy need
42 Indy winner in 1992 and '94
43 PIANIST
45 Relative of arian
46 Guide on the dance floor
47 Enticement
48 Snooty attitude
49 Sore spot
50 Transportation Dept. agcy.
51 TAXI DRIVER
55 Competed in the Tour de France
56 One of the Aleutians
58 Felt off
59 Persistent pest
60 Reunion goers
61 Paths to success?
62 More steady-handed
63 Mr. C. portrayer on "Happy Days"
65 Ancient British monument
66 Break in a baseball schedule
69 Oratorio solos
70 JAZZ DRUMMER
72 Brady Bill opponent
73 Lens holders
74 Things to eat
75 Airport counter name
76 How a fool and his money are parted
77 Hiss partner
78 NURSE
82 Clear, in a way
83 Bills
85 Magic star
86 Zoo denizens
87 Russian pancake
88 Historical record
89 Butch's "Our Gang" pal
90 The Scourge of God
93 "God ___"
94 Conservatives
98 SCHOOL MASTER
100 LANDSCAPE PAINTER
102 Old wine ___ bottles
103 Nightclub number
104 Elbow grease
105 Like some clothing styles
106 Yarn
107 Put to work for oneself
108 Understanding
109 Westphalian city

DOWN

1 Get smart with
2 Poker card
3 Alaska's first governor
4 Mulled over
5 Doozy
6 Sweetheart
7 Life of Riley
8 "All the Things You ___"
9 L.B.J. mentor
10 Northern Arkansan
11 Shakespearean king
12 Second start
13 Flamenco shout
14 Telephone pole source
15 Honored
16 Kind of poem
17 Six-footers
18 Retain, in a way
24 James Farmer's org.
26 Scots' tots
29 Itch
32 Conductor from Bombay
33 Dizzying itinerary
34 Antibiotics' ancestor
35 When "S.N.L." ends, in most places
36 BIOCHEMIST
37 "And there you are!"
38 Tackled moguls
39 JOCKEY
40 Mrs. Mertz
41 Like some marshes
43 Openers, at times
44 Relievers' rewards
47 Nuts
49 Gave a hand to
51 Tarzan's transportation
52 Speak boastfully
53 Elbow, essentially
54 "Luck and Pluck" writer
55 Old dance sites
57 Pantomime dances
59 Calvin Klein competitor
61 Magazine's exhortation
62 "For Whom the Bell Tolls" setting
63 Singer Benton
64 Where Rigel is
65 Smarts
66 50's governor Faubus
67 Swift's "A Modest Proposal," e.g.
68 Furniture designer Charles
70 Second-century physician
71 Anwar's predecessor
74 Salon job
76 Navigation units
78 Tall and graceful
79 Dulcet
80 British legal societies
81 Restaurant services
82 Synge title character
84 ___ dictum
86 Combatant of 1899
88 Byrd book
89 Moby-Dick
90 Author Ahmed and others
91 Part of a backpacker's pack
92 "___-Bungay" (Wells novel)
93 Cooling capacity
94 Artemis, to Apollo
95 Comes by
96 Chinese calendar animal
97 Video-game film of 1982
99 Queue after R
101 Edmond O'Brien classic

by Stanley Newman

158 OVERCROWDING

ACROSS

1 500, e.g.
5 Hubby, in Paris
9 Mountain in Turkey
15 Rifle peephole
19 21 or over, liquorwise
20 Revises
22 Dress part
23 Mr. Penzler of mystery fiction
24 Actress Massey
25 Leave
26 Newsman in the Sahara?
28 Canal Zone film favorites?
31 Answer to "Who's there?"
32 Thrice a day, on prescriptions: Abbr.
33 Nastase of tennis
34 Oscar nominee for "Exodus"
35 Apportions
36 TV's "___ with a 'Z'"
37 Scale syllables
38 Fuzz
39 "Silkwood" actress
41 It was first conquered in 1953
43 Used up
44 Dart
46 Ink
49 Harass
50 Actor who craved goulash?
54 Boxing legend
55 Holds
57 Winter air
58 Sister of Euterpe
59 Feminist Bella
61 19th-century sea novelist
64 Prunes
66 Dining table decoration
67 Pilot
68 North Carolina college
69 Aries or Taurus, e.g.
70 Workers' ___
71 Revisionist
72 See 88-Across
73 Singer on a South American gig?
77 1-___ (way to guard)
78 Withdraws
80 Soon after
81 Yearn
82 Melody
83 Dodged
84 Bush Secretary of State
86 Title holder
87 "Confessions of Felix Krull" author
88 Band instrument, with 72-Across
89 Hawthorne locale
90 Vaunt
91 Match, in poker
93 Suffix with dull or drunk
94 Actress with an arty affectation?
98 Take out
102 Tolkien's "The ___ of Beleriand"
104 Clear of vermin
105 Uninspiring
106 Does a brake job
108 The Windsors, e.g.
110 Fr. holy women
111 Parenthetical comment
112 "Jellicle Ball" musical
113 Pat and Debby

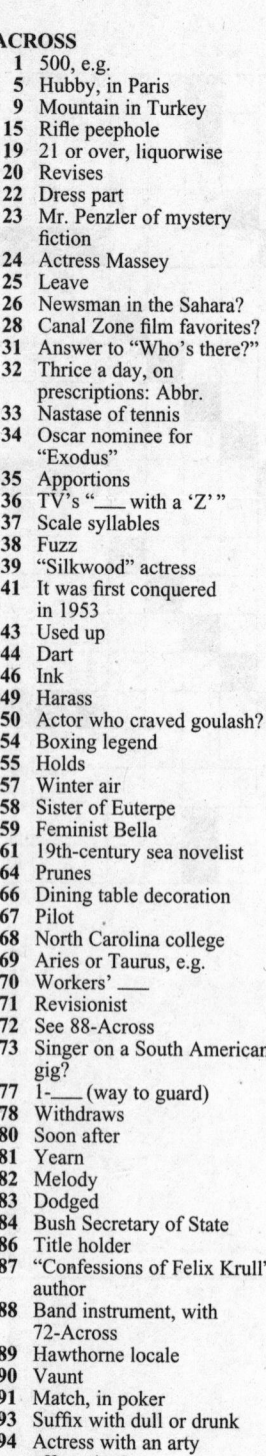

by A. J. Santora

115 Ex-Met Rusty
117 Finely appointed
118 Some PC's
119 In with
120 Singer with a Latin beat?
125 Washington V.I.P. in Dakar?
127 Assayer's container
128 Sportscaster's details
129 "___ the picture"
130 Frog
131 First name in college football
132 Santa ___
133 The opposition
134 Wool garments
135 Recognize
136 Angora notables

DOWN

1 Proportionate
2 Struggles (over)
3 "The Country Girl" up north?
4 Susa's country
5 Building block
6 Hunk
7 ___ Janeiro
8 Live ___ (enjoy the good life)
9 Without
10 Way to go
11 Supplement
12 Irani money
13 Benzoyl peroxide target
14 Artist Gerard ___ Borch
15 Carboys
16 Singer actress in Africa?

17 1946 Bikini event
18 L.B.J. chronicler Kearns
19 Edge
21 Lasting
27 French wing
29 Intentions
30 Home run hitter of the 40's
35 Commedia dell' ___
36 Neighbor of Isr.
38 Boxes
39 Blackish
40 ___ Gigio ("Ed Sullivan Show" regular)
42 Touchdown abbr.
43 Early astronomical instrument
44 Screenplay
45 Ember
47 Protein in Wheaties
48 Hakeem Olajuwon, e.g.
51 Weld
52 ___ of the guard
53 Lunatic
56 Looked wide-eyed
60 Hopper
61 Papal letter
62 Lotion ingredient
63 "60 Minutes" D-Day reporter?
65 Toupees
66 Red Cross hero
67 Dubai leaders
70 Flicks
71 Novelist Tyler
73 "God is ___": Fuller
74 Absorb abuse

75 Acclivitous
76 1964 Lorne Greene song hit
79 "___ you know the muffin man" (children's lyric)
82 Reluctant flier at home?
84 Bugs and Buddy
85 ___ mater
86 Gold braid
89 Artist/author Silverstein
90 Dramatic fashion look
92 Long fish
95 Sultanas' rooms
96 Ignes ___ (marsh lights)
97 Handcuff, in slang
99 Asiatic Turkey
100 Two-handed hoop attempts
101 Double twist
103 Browning works
107 Come back
109 Peterman
110 People of interest?
111 1976 rebellion site
113 Sink
114 The end
115 Hillside
116 Trite
117 Enliven
120 Muffed
121 Arch molding
122 Superior ones?
123 Final Four org.
124 Washington power grp.
126 Inclined (to)

ACROSS

1 Sports surprise
6 Rather
10 Supply with merchandise
15 Executes
19 It's measured in watts
20 "Nonsense!"
21 Tonkin city
22 Opposite of exo-
23 Gig for Domingo
24 Eddie Rabbitt hit?
27 Before marriage
28 "Let's Make a Deal" option
30 Entangle
31 Longtime Susan Lucci daytime role
32 His and her
34 Like a horse
35 Fraternity unit
37 Beleaguer
39 Purple with anger
40 Shpoke like thish
41 Treat with contempt
42 German spa
43 Old radio's "___ the Magician"
44 Radio format
45 Snoop Dogg hit?
47 Scuttlebutt
51 You can dig it
52 Marketing data
53 Meditation system
54 Victors' cry
55 One-millionth of a meter
57 Mom-and-pop enterprise
59 Expired
60 Persian Gulf country
61 Use the bean
62 Brawn
63 Pablo of musical fame
64 Fall in folds
65 Conviction
66 Of service
67 Fact finisher
68 Unseasoned
69 To a great extent
72 Eat like a bird
73 Byrds hit?
77 Asian expanse
78 Region of Greece and Turkey
80 Rochester's boss, in old TV
81 Instrument for 63-Across
82 Augment
84 Middie opponent
85 Straw bed
86 Record holders
87 Polite refusal
88 Green sauce
89 Swift's "___ of a Tub"
90 Cobbler, at times
91 Butter
92 Org. for Tyson
95 Monkees hit?
99 Significant person?
101 Mars, in combinations
102 Hardhearted
103 Manitoba native
104 Barely audible
105 Forsaken
106 Easily confused
107 Look after
108 Exhaust emanation

DOWN

1 Topping
2 John, Paul or John Paul
3 Country Joe and the Fish hit?
4 Perpetually, poetically
5 Car price factor
6 Execrate
7 Hog wild?
8 Leb. neighbor
9 Poem mentioning "the lost Lenore"
10 More than jostled
11 Broke, in a way
12 "The ___ lama . . ."
13 Popular comedian, briefly
14 Young beaver
15 Corey Hart hit?
16 Kind of inspection
17 Brought out
18 Sub detector
25 Singapore punishment
26 Got wind of
29 Driveway stain
33 Listen
34 Some skirts
35 MacGregor, for one
36 Put up
37 About
38 Vaccination reminder
39 Weighed down
40 Stand out
42 One way to choose
43 Bob Cratchit, e.g.
45 Homer hero of '61
46 Stratosphere layer
48 Los Lobos hit?
49 Libertine
50 Charge letters
52 Do to do
54 Stayed at home
56 Cat Stevens hit?
57 Elm offering
58 Dope on a horse
59 Wielded the scepter
60 Jackson or Smith
61 Chief's followers
62 Word of choice?
63 Eight fluid ounces
64 "Vita" describer
65 Main force
68 Dead duck
70 Skillful
71 Haymarket Square event
73 English Channel feeder
74 G.I. Janes
75 Put-down artist
76 Change the course of
77 Shekels
79 Noted writer-statesman
81 Thrown away
82 La corrida combatant
83 More imminent
84 Without emotion
85 Podded plant
86 "Married . . . With Children" co-star
87 "The Highwayman" poet
88 Set forth
90 Blue books?
91 Feds
93 Pop music's ___ King
94 Liberal pursuits
96 Calculator part: Abbr.
97 Model for filmdom's "The Greek Tycoon"
98 Auxiliary verb
100 Cross type

by Richard Silvestri

STREET TRANSLATIONS

ACROSS

1 Certain reporters
5 Slip
10 Nickname for Haydn
14 Monastery manuscript
19 Kind of arch
20 Religious author Philip
21 "___ blue as I can be . . ."
22 Ocher green
23 Pain?
26 Sheltered, as bees
27 Nationality since 1948
28 ___-eye (tinstone)
29 British Labor leader Ernest
30 Heavy farm cart
31 Prefix with active or grade
32 Pyromaniacs' delights
33 Dead Sea fortress
36 Toned down
37 Party clothes and such
40 Fragrances
41 Mayan?
43 Writer ___ Winslow
44 Plangent
45 Corrida performer
46 The Great Commoner
47 Nabokov book, 1957
48 Prince Valiant's eldest
49 Please?
53 Intoxicate
54 Spring harbinger
56 Sea arm
57 Explorer of Florida, 1539
58 Poetic feet
59 Part of M.O.
60 ___ Galilee
61 Pioneer of Dadaism
63 Conductor ___ Maazel
64 U.S.S. Enterprise, e.g.
67 Bach music maker
68 Lunges?
70 "A Chorus Line" song
71 Conference start
72 Ship plank
73 Came down
74 Tallow source
75 Opposite of "là," in French
76 Leis?
80 ___ Haute, on the Wabash
81 Ersatz art
83 Buddies
84 Dines à la Lucullus
85 Make an effort
86 100 groszy
87 Auto racer Graham
88 Like many interviews
89 Rears its ugly head
90 Had a life
94 It can be cured
95 Pals?
98 Came up
99 ___ cheese
100 European dormouse
101 Gossip column squib
102 Airport center
103 Nurse's ___
104 Blackmore's Lorna
105 See 38-Down

DOWN

1 Mozart's "___ fan tutte"
2 Grunts of distaste
3 Suds
4 Harrison Ford's "Fugitive" co-star
5 Iago's wife
6 Made a collar
7 Toupee, informally
8 Conquistador's quest
9 Send by a designated path
10 Historical French region
11 Writer Jorge
12 Head-'em-off site
13 Shade of blonde
14 Sticks
15 1963 Broadway smash
16 Mince?
17 Uniform
18 Struck out
24 Police hot line calls
25 Schlepped
29 Big name in I.Q. tests
31 ___ the green (links luck)
32 Dukes
33 Wisdom tooth, e.g.
34 Put on a pedestal
35 Moon?
36 "Anyone who disagrees with me," in a saying
37 Send come-hither looks
38 With 105-Across, a Kevin Costner role
39 ___ Domingo
41 "___ the Hour" (1948 Crosby hit)
42 Fencing equipment
45 Brindled cat
47 Peons' pay, perhaps
49 Miller's salesman Willy
50 Icy waterway: Var.
51 Ashley Wilkes sister, in "G.W.T.W."
52 Bobbin lace
53 Baylor athletes
55 ___ aves (nonpareils)
57 Gave everybody a hand
59 Calvin Klein employee
60 Splotch
61 Recurrent melody
62 Tropical palm
63 Trills lightheartedly
64 1991-92 U.S. Open tennis champ
65 Sluggish
66 "For ___ sake!"
68 "Olympia" painter
69 Jolson song subject
72 Grotesque
74 Eskimo's wrap
76 Less trained
77 Pastoral poem
78 Defeat, and how!
79 Peddled better than
80 Purposive
82 Blow the whistle on
84 Get stuck (on)
86 Like city real estate
87 Cousin of the egret
88 Tropical tuber
89 Caron film, 1953
91 Place for a chapeau
92 Noisy-le-Sec summers
93 Mil. awards
94 Casey's club
95 Cops' org.
96 Classic prefix
97 ___ Harlem Brundtland (Norwegian leader)

by Frances Hansen

ACROSS

1 Olive's cousin
4 Lets down or out
10 A little night music?
14 Improvisation with leftovers
18 Ref's ring decision
19 "Do you really ___?"
20 Kate Nelligan title role, 1985
22 Land in the water
23 Arctic newspaper?
25 A quarter of Paris
26 Speed
27 It may be on a roll
28 Hades newspaper?
31 Pole, e.g.
32 Anatomize
34 Gable's "G.W.T.W." costar
35 Dynamic beginning
37 Discovery cries
39 Sad, to Sade
43 Hoteliers' newspaper?
49 Rocket flight event
50 Abates
51 Horse hair
52 Middle March
54 Tackle
55 Scrap of scrapple
56 Get the lead out, in a way
58 Agnus ___
59 Hammett hero
60 Journeys
62 Courthouse newspaper?
65 Result of riddling
66 Fodders for mudders
68 Start of a Faulkner title
69 Spots
71 Part of N.L.R.B.
74 Hairdressers' newspaper?
79 Wee bairns
83 Señora's sayonara
84 Author Levin
85 Sounder
86 Excusez-___
87 Not on the rocks
88 Filling for a taco
89 Dough for a taco?
90 Hit man's "icing"
93 Thickness measurer
95 Photographers' newspaper?
98 Donahue of "Father Knows Best"
99 Tatum's dad
100 A Bates
101 Must, slangily
103 Tee-hees
107 Terribly urgent
111 Disk jockeys' newspaper?
115 Macmillan's predecessor as P.M.
116 Philosopher from Königsberg
117 Union platform?
118 Financial newspaper?
122 Movie Chase
123 Alabama city on the Alabama
124 Slicker
125 Expert
126 Earth's shape
127 Tight closure
128 Oktoberfest souvenirs
129 Eng. Inc.

DOWN

1 A Musketeer
2 Head of the anatomy class
3 Prophetic son of Beeri
4 First name in etiquette
5 Book after Exod.
6 Lao-tzu's universal
7 Bagnold and Markey
8 Mushes, as potatoes
9 Rock singer Tyler
10 "To ___ Truth"
11 Sighing word
12 Corolla components
13 Cutting
14 Nuptial newspaper?
15 On the briny
16 Blind piece
17 Now partner
21 Come-ons?
24 Muriel cigar pitchman of the 50's
29 Caesar's "veni"
30 Folklore fiend
32 Stops in
33 Debtor's letters
36 Richmond, Ky., coll.
38 Out of the way
40 Bargain for a burglar?
41 NASDAQ transaction
42 A Brontë heroine's family
43 Stop up
44 Lunch order
45 Luncheon finisher
46 Phony bill collectors
47 Soft mineral
48 Because
49 Put out a new edition
53 ___ Moines
57 Mark of the N.H.L.
59 The lass
61 Western outlaw's newspaper?
63 Omega preceder
64 Gets the suds out
67 Horace's "___ Poetica"
70 Registers
71 Uhlan's weapon
72 Hall's "Let's Make ___"
73 Bagel alternative: Var.
75 Rather than, to Cowper
76 Challenge for denture wearers
77 Big cut
78 Elitist, in a way
80 Leave out
81 Author Morrison
82 Omen or "Open," e.g.
88 Wide, lacy collars
89 Riot of a kind
91 Sunshine St.
92 Wheel guard
94 Tigger's friend
96 A pass that isn't forward
97 Nasser led it: Abbr.
99 Fluster
102 Scrabble squares
104 Stirs
105 Quality
106 Roman official
108 Perfect
109 Respond to a provocation
110 Brought to a close
111 Leave out
112 Bull, cob or tom, e.g.
113 "Diana" singer
114 Sita's husband, in myth
119 Weeks per annum
120 Hankering
121 Condo-ad abbr.

by Cathy Millhauser

ACROSS

1 Fix firmly
6 Galileo's birthplace
10 Part of a communications company's 800 number
13 Moolah
17 Focal point of the Reformation
18 Uncomplimentary comments
19 Libertine
21 Mideast title
22 "Gimme ___"
23 FLORIDA
26 KANSAS
28 Items in Gray's country churchyard
29 ___ blanco (polar bear)
30 Check
31 Clerical error?
32 Pilot's heading
33 Follow
35 Member of the wedding
40 MASSACHUSETTS
48 Anna of "Nana"
50 Going in the right direction
51 Enveloping glow
52 Patently amazed
56 Tipped off
57 Horner's find
58 Datum for an economic indicator
59 Many Muslim men
60 OHIO
63 NEVADA
71 Joie de vivre
73 Half-cocked
74 Spy in '94 headlines
78 They're found on reservations nowadays
81 Hamlet's mother
82 Neighbor of Sonoma
83 Bags more game than
85 Southeast Kansas town
86 ILLINOIS
91 Shine
92 Dismissive visage
93 "___ My Party"
96 H
99 Frankfurt's river
103 Business letter abbr.
104 Home to billions
105 MISSOURI
111 MINNESOTA
112 Cover stories?
113 M-G-M founder
114 Ocean flier
115 Hirschfeld's girl
116 The absolute minimum
117 ___ buco
118 Banking convenience
119 Sentence
120 Chicago's ___ Tower

DOWN

1 Rises up
2 Where to do as others do
3 Some execs
4 Assessment: Abbr.
5 "Here..."
6 Expand, as the chest
7 Beach Boys' "___ Around"
8 Peacock Throne occupants
9 Plus
10 1954 show tune "___ in Bloomsbury"
11 Vegetarian staple
12 Campus in Medford, Mass.
13 Apteryx
14 Cry from the flock
15 Fat
16 Mommy's triplets
17 Rubbernecks
20 K-12, scholastically speaking
24 Literary monogram
25 Confess
27 Greek peak
33 Papa's real name
34 Funnyman Philips
36 Blow
37 Cargo
38 Hosiery shade
39 Stationer's order
40 Medieval rival of 6-Across
41 ___ toot
42 1995 N.C.A.A. basketball champs
43 Carols
44 First capital of unified Italy
45 Lied
46 Real ending in London
47 Sparks on the screen
48 Bar order
49 Convey
52 GQ, e.g.
53 Yevtushenko's "Babi ___"
54 Samuel's mentor
55 Takes away, in law
61 Root of diplomacy
62 Incurred
64 Trouble
65 Hub: Abbr.
66 More bohemian
67 Descamisados' leader
68 Epistle apostle
69 Audrey Hepburn's real first name
70 Processed food additive
72 The absolute minimum
74 Do this if you want to get a hand
75 "Capital" fellow
76 Of enormous import
77 Kemo ___
78 Cote quote
79 Strauss's "Ariadne ___ Naxos"
80 Orch. section
84 Spanish ayes
87 Kate Nelligan title role
88 .035 ounce
89 Kevin's co-star in "Tin Cup"
90 Holy City populace
93 Front line
94 Marketing ploys
95 Fresh
97 Vocal quality
98 Network employees' union
99 "___ Golden Slippers"
100 Condensation
101 Largest living antelope
102 Cosine or secant
104 "West Side Story" role
105 Fight enders
106 Court cry
107 Tax filer's form
108 Oxygen ___
109 Seat of Washoe County
110 Burn treatment
111 Sign of caution

by Randolph Ross

ACROSS

1 Siren
5 Desert
12 Gathered
19 Dieters' choices
21 Colleague of Placido
22 Kind of language
23 Pictorial card
24 Outcomes other than expected
25 1 + 76
26 Engraves
28 Understanding
29 Socks and Millie, e.g.
30 Grill's go-with
31 Juan Carlos I, e.g.
32 University of Georgia home
34 Shiraz native
36 Italian noble house
37 Robin of old ballad
38 Clinton aide Panetta
39 ___-de-sac
41 Some radio shows
44 Art ___
45 Party items that get broken
49 Gave a keynote
50 Debonair
52 91 + 66
53 Diamond Jim's opposites
54 Caen's river
55 Outdo
56 Half of "The Odd Couple"
57 Dickensian exclamation
58 Line in a forecast
60 Uh's cousins
61 Snuggeries
62 Zoo snack, maybe
64 They go in parentheses
66 Clock parts
69 Retreat
70 Calm
72 Kind of dog or horse
75 Lab culture mediums
76 Choler
77 Nursery school item
78 98 + 6
81 Gives back
83 The English
84 Wake up
85 Puts out, as a batter
86 Frostbite sites
87 Covered (for)
88 Honor society letter
89 Boast
90 Carried
91 Some are south
94 The Shadow's cover
96 Paged
98 Swiss accompaniment
101 ___ Miss
102 Charon's river
103 Spirits
105 "Porgy" author ___ Heyward
107 55 + 62
109 Shakespeare's "lean and hungry" character
111 Plains Indians
112 Group within a group
113 Some coats
114 Film maker Coen
115 Brings on again
116 It's spotted on kids
117 Without

DOWN

1 Booth occupant, perhaps
2 Winged
3 Old-fashioned exclamation
4 Famous corner in literature
5 109 + 77
6 Rehnquist's predecessor
7 Furniture finial
8 They're hidden in Hirschfeld drawings
9 Seat of honor locale
10 Alternative to a bikini
11 Two-year-olds' utterances
12 Elizabeth or Eve
13 Addams Family member
14 Part of conjugation practice
15 Mil. defense grp.
16 Rebuffs
17 Display of pomp
18 "The Wreck of the Mary ___"
20 Less rocky
27 Substitutes
29 Certain camera shot
33 "___ Way" (Sinatra bio)
35 Aussie hopper
36 Passes
37 Der ___ (Adenauer)
38 89 + 30
40 Ruined
41 Search thoroughly

42 Piece for 21-Across
43 Tie
44 Comic Carvey
45 Stomach enzyme
46 Tic-___ (popular candies)
47 Gray area: Abbr.
48 Lat. and Lith., once
50 11-time Orange Bowl champs
51 Sophisticated
52 Big Band brothers
55 Claw
59 Girl-takes-boy parties
62 Wodehouse's Wooster et al.
63 Classify
65 Excluded
66 Jamie of TV's "M*A*S*H"
67 Writer-critic James
68 Players
70 Twist
71 Yalies
72 Censor's target
73 Proficiency
74 Got a top mark on

79 Wellington nickname, with "the"
80 Out
82 Not taking the lead
83 Where to get a volume discount?
86 Musical syllable
87 89 + 41
89 Tricia Nixon now
90 Take care
91 Log roller
92 Dress style
93 Country lass
95 Director Adrian et al.
96 Nabs
97 One of the Saarinens
98 Hullabaloo
99 City south of Luxor
100 Money
102 Box
104 Greek peak
106 Computer units
108 The, in Torino
109 Diploma word
110 Natl. registry grp.

by Nancy Nicholson Joline

ABOUT MISS DAW

ACROSS

1 Harass
7 A knight to remember
14 Celebrated
19 Beethoven's Third
20 Scrutinize
21 Give up occupancy
22 Start of a verse
25 Certain playing marbles
26 Tenor Peerce
27 Apollo's twin
28 Hall of Famer Mel
29 Wear with an air
31 Hoop group, for short
32 Cozily warm
36 Thackeray's "___ Lyndon"
37 "To a Skylark," e.g.
38 Sacred bull of Egypt
42 ___ Rios (Jamaican resort)
43 Swiss river
44 Privy to
45 Chianti, e.g.
46 More of verse
52 Comparative suffix
53 Sgts. and cpls.
54 With full force
55 Seafood serving
56 Judas
58 "Canterbury Tales" inn
60 Kvetched
61 "___ the Brave" (1965 Sinatra film)
63 Usher's concern
65 Quakers
68 Stationary
70 Assailed
74 Language from which "kiwi" comes
75 ___ de Guerre (French award)
76 Test giver's call
77 Pay dirt
78 More of verse
83 The "limp watch" painter
84 Minus
85 Busy as ___
86 Sister of John-Boy Walton
87 Old Greek theaters
88 Table scrap
89 Trick
91 Admiral nicknamed "Bull"
93 Eastern title
94 Wherewithal
95 Tufted bird
96 Cousins of the guinea pig
100 Seine sight
101 Football formation
106 End of verse
110 Decorative band
111 Quiet, now
112 Belgian ___
113 Entreat
114 Breviary contents
115 Gets smart with

DOWN

1 Haw's partner
2 Part of Q.E.D.
3 Part of the Earth
4 Buster Brown's dog
5 Leopardlike cat
6 Hen's tooth, e.g.
7 They have their settings
8 Bad ___, Mich.
9 Opposite of long.
10 Key of Beethoven's Seventh
11 Saint ___ of Poitiers (French bishop)
12 Concerning
13 RR sta.
14 Statements in a legal case
15 Yearn
16 "Yes, ___!"
17 Needle case
18 Trophy rooms
21 Fragrant garden plant
23 So soon
24 Stopped ticking, as a clock
29 Robe
30 C.E.O.
32 Specifically
33 Paint pigment
34 Now, in the barrio
35 1975 Abba hit
36 "A Christmas Carol" cries
37 New York Indian
38 Garden-variety
39 Galileo, e.g.
40 Worshipful (of)
41 Audio
43 "O come, let us ___ Him" (carol lyric)
44 Turkish hospice
47 Merchant of Venice
48 Emblems
49 Apprehend
50 Pile up
51 Freeloads
57 Sluggishness
58 Coaches
59 Hotel lobbies, often
60 Orange Bowl locale
62 Smallest in amount
64 37 Down, en masse
65 Brazilian novelist Jorge
66 Word with oil or plate
67 Dr. Jekyll's servant
69 Not a local: Abbr.
71 1991 Val Kilmer film, with "The"
72 Palmer, to his "army"
73 Wee
75 Cling fondly to
76 I.R.S. agents
79 One who makes arrangements
80 Loll about
81 Observe
82 Become set
89 Piña ___ (rum drink)
90 Not round
91 Shows disapproval
92 Odysseus's adviser
93 Silver, for one
94 Silas Marner, e.g.
95 "Turandot" slave girl
96 "Rush!"
97 Miss
98 "This one's ___!"
99 Pac 10 team
101 Bankrolls
102 Hospital capacity
103 Medical suffix
104 Where the congregation congregates
105 Farm mothers
107 Geller's forte, for short
108 Summer in Savoie
109 Sun. talk

by Frances Hansen

by Cathy Millhauser

ACROSS

1 Sweetly, in a suite
6 Jambalaya, for one
10 Very shortly, shortly
14 Put one past
18 Provinces
19 Like L'eggs containers
21 Count, in England
22 Blues singer Big ___ Thornton
23 What's your favorite opera?
26 Side in a 1980's war
27 Japanese cult leader Shoko
28 Part of a "Mikado" refrain
29 Famous 12-book story
31 How do I get these tablets out of the bottle?
35 Clueless
39 The Way
40 Loci
41 Logic truths
44 Candied
48 Staff of Life
53 In what state are many of your customers?
57 Ragtime's Blake
58 "Alfred" poet Henry James
59 Guy Fawkes Day mo.
60 Famed baseball family
61 Helen of Troy's mother
62 Uncut
64 What's your favorite old TV show?
68 New York and New Jersey river
70 Offs
71 What should I keep locked in a cabinet?
77 Numb
80 Mr. Trebek
81 Loewe output
82 Civil War combatant
83 Mead
85 Fossil, e.g.
87 Which Wharton novel would you recommend?

91 Deliverance
93 Game with a 40-card deck
94 Epoch in the Cenozoic Era
95 Tiff
98 Mike Hammer, for one
100 Jejuna neighbors
101 What would you cry if you found some pills in your mixed vegetables?
110 Melodious
111 Pope John Paul II, originally
112 Layette pair
117 Disney's Simba or Nala
118 Where's the other pharmacist?
122 Enraptured
123 Listerine target
124 Stand in some studios
125 Frill
126 Word of regret
127 Homeric H's
128 Salad plate scoopful
129 Dauntless

DOWN

1 Man Ray's art
2 Hockey's Bobby et al.
3 "Star Wars" role
4 Change, e.g.
5 Founded: Abbr.
6 Audible
7 New Deal agcy.
8 Unspecific duration
9 Furniture measurement
10 Greek god of the winds
11 Sub stratum
12 Suffix with drunk
13 Gratified
14 Part of PABA
15 Seven-time A.L. batting champ
16 Alternative to the post office
17 Splendiferous
20 Pressing
24 Neighbor of Scorpius
25 Exam for the U.-bound
30 Stage actress ___ Janis

32 Enraptured
33 Exaction
34 Anna of "Nana"
35 Northern nomad
36 Small round window, in architecture
37 Wailer
38 Crown
42 Servile
43 Kind of relationship
45 Key to Mozart's 21st: Abbr.
46 Caffeine source
47 Kind of jacket
49 Green Wave's school
50 Observe
51 Lift
52 Cauterize
54 Eye parts
55 TV newsman Hughes et al.
56 Analogy words
63 "Hi and Lois" baby
64 Italian ball game
65 The Supremes' "I ___ Symphony"
66 Ancient mystic

67 Spanish port
69 Word on a door
71 Actress Felicia
72 Out of the wind, on windjammers
73 Pell ___
74 Range
75 "Tantum ___" (hymn part)
76 Youth magazine
78 Architect Saarinen Sr.
79 Tubular pasta
84 Not on land
86 Sheathes
87 Actress Hatcher
88 One of the Ringling Brothers
89 Podia
90 Third-century date
92 Miser
96 Capital of ancient Galatia
97 Job follower
99 Occult doctrine
101 Model wood
102 An archangel
103 Actress Fullerton
104 Church receptacles

105 Suffix with press
106 Little bay
107 Footing facilitator
108 Cry in gasps
109 Hydrant hookups
113 Sermon's basis
114 Dividend preceder
115 Sandy shade
116 Ticket specification
119 Snood
120 Columbus sch.
121 Swamp

ACROSS

1 Played for a stake
6 Drive up the wall
12 Breathe fire and fury
18 Verdi opera
19 Immature pigeon
20 Secret places
21 Lass with good business contacts?
23 Capture
24 Murder, in mob talk
25 Suffix with defer or confer
26 Hank of the 50's Yankees
28 ___ supra (above-mentioned)
29 Western rain attire?
35 "Give ___ rest!"
37 "Sounder" director Martin
38 Five-centime piece
39 Home of Zeno
40 Mobster's piece
41 Simple baskets
44 Shivering fits
47 Lecturer
49 Wide-eyed
50 Think better of
52 Piquant
53 Informal information
54 One-sixth of a drachma
56 Heavyweight champ Willard
59 Lap of luxury
60 Sister Sledge's "We ___ Family"
61 Wake?
65 Computerized playgrounds
67 Up positions, usually
68 Eggbeaters
70 Shoe store mannequin's complaint?
73 Comparative ending
75 Business basis
76 Nieuport's river
77 Montgomery's "___ of Green Gables"
78 Actress Purviance
79 It's found in a stack
80 Harry Bailly's inn
83 Consecrated
84 John ___, president of the Continental Congress
87 Six Day War hero
88 French family members
89 Bug-eyed monsters, for short
90 Learned book
92 Grand Union, e.g.: Abbr.
94 Exuberance
95 Supermodel Carol
96 Secondary-school club?
103 Writer Levin
105 Surgeon's intro
106 Opposite of manual
107 Cleveland athlete, for short
108 Brand-new
110 Christmas dinner for a don?
115 "Just Another Day" singer Jon
116 Swimmer Gertrude and family
117 Primitive artist Ralph et al.
118 Scotland's ___ Islands
119 Holdups
120 Spoiler, perhaps

DOWN

1 "Manolete" dancer José
2 Put in the pot
3 Hillbilly mother
4 Rock's Brian
5 Engineers
6 Darlings
7 Std.
8 Not spec.
9 Cover story
10 Glacial peak
11 Columbia University hospital
12 Disfigured
13 Barber's obstacle
14 Beige
15 Experienced, if overweight, equestrian?
16 Fence-sitting
17 Erhard's teaching
18 Tennyson heroine
19 Ref. work
22 Grow together
27 Sushi dish
30 Squawk
31 "___ kleine Nachtmusik"
32 Billy Crystal TV series
33 Lillehammer event
34 ___ Miguel, Azores
36 ___ Gen.
41 Vocal imitation of a fanfare

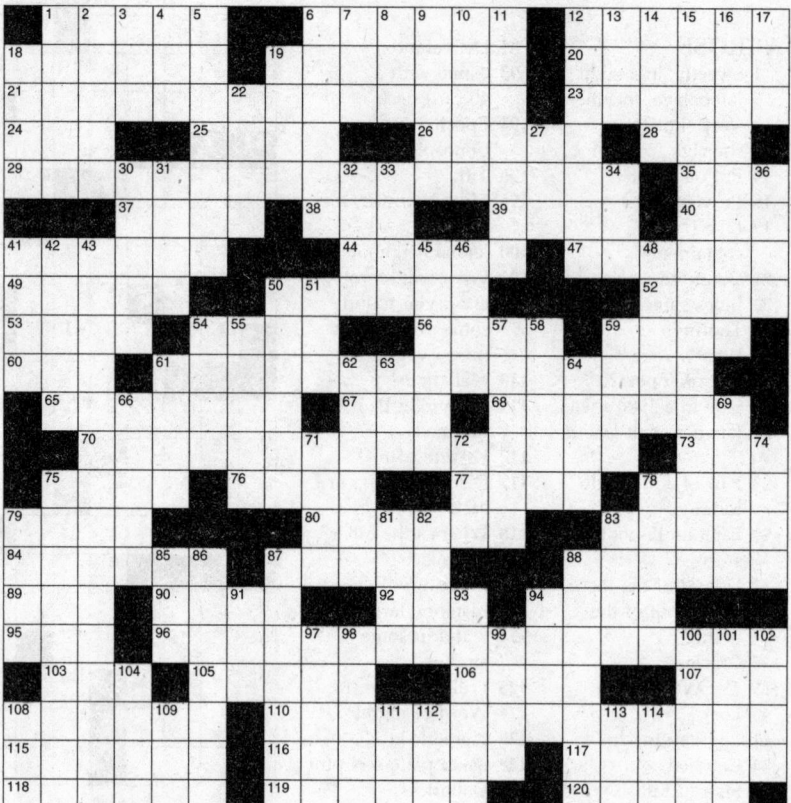

by Alex K. Justin

42 Classical mall
43 Halloween cutout smacked?
45 Wrong
46 Somme summers
48 Orange box
50 Ribs or ribbings, maybe
51 Neigh: horse:: bugle: ___
54 Word before shoppe
55 Stout
57 Back up
58 Neck
59 Folies Bergère designer
61 Latvian, e.g.
62 "___ for Hollywood"
63 Warbler Yoko
64 Chancel neighbor
66 Closed sacs
69 Acumen
71 Goat cheese
72 Dancer-choreographer Lubovitch
74 "Phooey!"
75 Winter garment insert
78 Kate Nelligan film role
79 1969 World Series stadium
81 Big do
82 Con
83 Bric-a-___
85 Like some stocks, for short
86 Meridian, now
87 Overrun
88 Bowled over
91 Skiing gold medalist Tommy
93 Migs' relatives
94 Italy's Isabella d'___
97 Undercut
98 Mountain air
99 Expressions of disbelief
100 Professeur's site
101 Stun gun
102 Director Allegret
104 Strong-ox link
108 Kind of show
109 Gelderland city
111 Mozart duet "___ gli amplessi"
112 Khan who married Rita
113 Fed. watchdog agcy.
114 Fido's find

ACROSS

1 Cheese in a mousetrap
5 Rider Haggard romance
8 David Stockman's dept., once
11 Dickens alias
14 Cheerless
18 "Moses" author, 1951
19 Circle
21 One who has the hives
23 "In the evening when I sit alone a-dreaming . . ."
25 Arm of the sea?
26 Kind of tea
27 "Oh, give me land, lots of land . . ."
29 Bruiser
30 Beethoven dedicatee
31 Org. for the 20-Down
32 Excel
35 Landslide detritus
37 Carve across the grain
41 Lincoln in-law
42 Selects
43 Popular sports car
44 Like versatile appliances
48 Each
49 Call it ___
50 Tax evaders' bugbears
51 Turn about
52 Noted castaway
54 Iranian desert
55 Handbills
57 Gulf north of Somalia
58 Mummer, at times
60 Start, in a way
61 Trifled
63 Top dog at the zoo
64 Some canines
65 ___ cropper
66 Bracelets
67 Spring
68 Seconds
70 M.I.T. grads, perhaps
71 Least clear
75 Gallimaufry
76 Spray alternative
78 Nut cases?
79 Wipe out
80 Cult film" ___ 9 From Outer Space"
81 Protective rings
82 Where eagles gather

83 Kids' stuff?
84 Not well
85 Paid (up)
86 Hamlet's father, e.g.
87 Composed
90 Milk: Prefix
92 Where to go for a spell?
93 "Trailer for sale or rent . . ."
97 Salad bar item
101 Introductory offer
102 "Alas! My love, you do me wrong . . ."
105 Court official
106 Anomalous
107 Legendary gunfighter
108 They've earned their stripes: Abbr.
109 German spa
110 Common pluralizer
111 Stephen Foster's Nelly
112 "Let us ___"

DOWN

1 Do
2 ". . . ___ forgive our debtors"
3 Petit four finisher
4 "Casey would waltz with a strawberry blonde . . ."
5 Map info
6 Bricklayer's burden
7 Printemps follower
8 1983 World Series champs
9 Paul Bunyan's wife
10 Borscht base
11 Restrain
12 U.S. ___
13 Wurtzite ingredient
14 Playhouse fare
15 Kitchen gadget
16 Have ___ of the tongue
17 One of a vitamin complex
20 Seniors, with "the"
22 Special forces unit
24 End of the race
28 Malodorous
32 Kind of horn or line
33 Snake dancers
34 Pop star
35 Nubian Desert locale
36 Family
38 Prospective taxi fare
39 Out-and-out
40 Tabula ___
42 Pent up

43 Changes
44 "Stormy the night and the waves roll high . . ."
45 Anti-slip device
46 Reagan nickname
47 "___ á rire" ("It is to laugh"): Fr.
50 "As the blackbird in the spring . . ."
53 Flawless
54 Gifts
56 Kind of accident
58 Groaner
59 Computer software abbr.
61 ". . . and ___ a goodnight!"
62 ___ vincit amor
63 Informal
64 Laconic
65 Hatchet job?
66 Sit on
67 Like supermarket tabloids
69 Madame Bovary
71 Entomb in a wall
72 Dollar prefix
73 Car-roof items

74 Words
77 Vogue
78 Happens to
82 "Invincible" victim of Hercules
84 Dries, in a way
85 Nuts
86 Personality determinant
87 Kind of duty
88 ___-trump
89 Monsters
91 Bicker
92 Food processor
93 City south of Düsseldorf
94 Rage
95 Stratford streetcar
96 Plymouth Rocks, e.g.
98 Basso Andresen
99 Actress Miles
100 Spot
103 Crux
104 ___ ammoniac

by R. M. Hopkins

ACROSS

1 Of a leg bone
7 Gardening device
14 Slave driver's exhortation
20 "Romanian Rhapsodies" composer
21 Change the dimensions of
22 Drag
23 More sore
24 New addition to one's address book?
26 ___-mo
27 Kind of dog
29 Smooth
30 Galsworthy genre
31 Blunt
33 Casting out ___ (math procedure)
35 Son of Judah
36 Memory unit
37 Extra
39 Projected amount in a business forecast?
42 Jubilant gaiety
43 Ponderer's phrase
45 ___ maison (indoors): Fr.
46 Pungency
48 F
49 City once named Eva Perón, with "La"
51 Boito opera
52 Suburbs?
56 "Search for Signs . . ." Broadway comic
60 Butt
62 Faint
63 Inner, in anatomy
65 Bullyrag
66 "A pity!"
68 Tempter
70 Wingdings
72 Town of July 1944 fighting
73 Man with a famous lap
75 Rolls dem bones
77 Films
79 Post-dusk
80 Video image units
82 The top of Bald Mountain?
85 Screenwriter Jack ___ Jr.
87 Idyllic spots
88 Dances in 4/4 time
91 Demand in court
95 1970 Jagger film "___ Kelly"
96 Paris's Place de la ___
98 "Tarzan" extras
99 Brooch watch?
102 Scrape away at
103 T-shirt size: Abbr.
104 Cooped (up)
105 Legislative postscript
107 Marketed
108 Puccini's "Vissi d'___"
110 New sitcom star of 1988
111 "American Psycho" novelist
113 Buddy
114 Where the Politburo members studied?
119 Via ___ (Roman thoroughfare)
121 Conceive
122 Renowned Big Apple restaurant
123 Adviser in Roman myth
124 Looked
125 Craft
126 Forswears, in short

DOWN

1 "Let It Be Forgotten" poet
2 Comprises
3 "Ecce felis!"?
4 "It ___" (reply to "Who's there?")
5 Easily passed
6 "The Millionairess" star, 1960
7 Apprentice
8 It's automatic
9 Country with a blue and white flag: Abbr.
10 Sprint rival
11 Pearl Bailey's middle name
12 West Coast weather factor
13 New version
14 A Mickey
15 Not to mention
16 "___ the One" (1996 movie)
17 Duty-bound?
18 "Adonais" and others
19 Corrects, as archeological records
25 Like some Greek islands
28 Creeper
32 Folk music historian John
34 Buy time
35 Panegyrics
38 "___ to you!"
40 Come in second
41 Waste allowance
42 Garden figures
44 Gushes
47 Bring (out)
49 Ornamental plume
50 Campaign tactics
53 Kind of test
54 Untagged, in tag
55 Bill Clinton, once
57 Rubber underclothes?
58 Key
59 Storefront item
60 Horseshoer's tool
61 Asia's ___ Mountains
64 Coast, for example
67 Precipitous slopes
69 Don't have to
71 Splitting points
74 Rival rival
76 Mean mien
78 Flood
81 Work-order detail
83 Slashed words?
84 OPEC leaders
86 Respond to testily
89 Language in an etymology
90 Aril
91 Pizzeria supplies
92 Stay current, computerwise
93 Hive location
94 Punishes with arbitrary penalties
96 Like an empty hospital
97 Jump with a twist
100 Sign up
101 Feudal lords
106 Split
109 Checkup
110 Teacher's deg.
112 Kind of lily
115 Devotee's suffix
116 Establish
117 Vietnam Veterans' Memorial designer Maya
118 From La. to N.C.
120 Born

by Wayne Robert Williams

ACROSS

1 Gruesome
7 Appeal
11 Mount for Abraham
14 Cut
18 Lawrence of Arabia portrayer
19 Résumé entry
22 New Rochelle college
23 Creedence Clearwater question, 1970
25 Skier's aid
26 "There, there," e.g.
27 War room fixture
28 Moss Hart's autobiography
30 Prominent legal celebrity
31 "Cat on ___ Tin Roof"
33 Blocked
34 Sonny and Cher question, 1966
40 1813–14 Vice President
41 Sought congers
42 First manned mooncraft
43 Maj.'s superior
44 Sound exasperated
47 False god
48 Off track
50 Minnesota appellation
51 Mauna ___
52 Exaggerated
54 1973 Vidal novel
55 Extend, in a way
57 Slavic hero
58 Prophet in I and II Kings
60 Uneven
61 Kind of panel
64 Press
67 Not so many
68 Holiday hanging
69 Degrades
70 Sci-fi film of 1954
72 X-___
73 Damask, for one
74 Speaks tersely
79 "___ been real!"
80 Immerse
81 Common answering machine message
83 Compact
84 Phone or cycle preceder
86 Montana call
87 "Cheers" character
88 Visit again
89 Liquid fat
91 Young Rascals question, 1967
94 Gave consent
96 "My Way" songwriter
97 Jiff
98 Speed
99 Patient's need
100 Arctic habitats
106 One ___ (ball game)
107 Bobby Freeman question, 1958
111 Source of confusion
112 Michael Jordan, e.g.
113 L.A.'s ___ Boulevard
114 Hopalong Cassidy portrayer
115 Legal things
116 Carry on
117 Ready for typesetting

DOWN

1 Cuts
2 First-century Roman emperor
3 Rafter's locale
4 Flee
5 Proverbial bringer of misfortune
6 Nash competitor
7 Cattle ___
8 Exercise units
9 Behind
10 Slangy assent
11 Freshen, as milk
12 Hike
13 School subj.
14 They usually work evenings
15 Peter and Gordon's answer to 23-Across
16 Nutty
17 Trimmed
20 Take out
21 Paint store choices
24 Think, old-style
29 E.M.T.'s procedure
31 Bit of Chlorophyta
32 Sacrosanct
33 Gershwin's answer to 107-Across
34 Entanglements
35 Make simmer
36 Winglike
37 Coded wire transmission
38 Apportion
39 Large quantity
43 200 milligrams
45 Specklebreasts, e.g.
46 One who hesitates
48 Behave
49 The Miracles' answer to 91-Across
50 Honshu peak
53 Out of gas
54 Some ballpoints
55 Send (to)
56 Solitary ones
58 Choice word
59 George Washington no-no
61 Open-weave fabric
62 Emulate Webster
63 Prince's answer to 34-Across
65 Sinker of sorts
66 Luxuriate
71 Toolshed item
74 "... and to ___ good night!"
75 Approach
76 Actress Pitts
77 Like certain profs.
78 Maximilian von ___
80 Badges
81 Opaque barite
82 Ancient strongbox
85 Cautioned
87 Agree
88 Withdrew
90 City east of Utrecht
91 Nimbi
92 "They laughed when ___ ..."
93 "Could This ___?" (1990 song)
94 Invention of 1945
95 Kind of bean
99 A or O, e.g.
100 Catch
101 French 101 verb
102 Hindu royalty
103 Monogram part: Abbr.
104 ___ signum
105 Spring purchase
108 Part of S.O.S, supposedly
109 Vane dir.
110 ___ loss

by Rich Norris

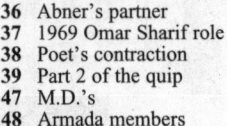

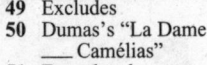

by Trip Payne

ACROSS

1 Truman's birthplace
6 Pass over
10 Cutesy farewells
15 Get to the point?
20 Garment cut
21 Dieter's spread
22 "Your papers ___ order"
23 Bartender's stock
25 1982 Barry Levinson film
26 Bragg or Lee, e.g.
27 David Copperfield's mother
28 Take the wrong way
29 Start of a quip by stand-up comic Brian Kiley
33 Lived
35 FDR mentor
36 Abner's partner
37 1969 Omar Sharif role
38 Poet's contraction
39 Part 2 of the quip
47 M.D.'s
48 Armada members
49 Excludes
50 Dumas's "La Dame ___ Camélias"
51 Ear-related
53 Farmland unit
54 Fortune profiles
55 Martina's rival, once
57 "Hogan's Heroes" setting
61 Boat on the Seine
63 Part 3 of the quip
67 Liqueur word
68 Election Day victors
69 See 111-Across
71 Incapacitate
72 "Addams Family" nickname
74 Go to pieces
75 Critic Huxtable and others
76 One held in thrall
77 Regular hangout
79 First name in fashion
80 Part 4 of the quip
86 Driver's seat
87 Alphabetize, e.g.
88 Plate watchers
89 Son of Aphrodite
90 Self expression?
91 Golfer Norman
92 Harness race
93 Author Lustbader
94 Hay area
97 Pied-billed bird
99 Part 5 of the quip
103 Neville Brand TV western
105 West End street, with "The"
107 Baptism and confirmation
108 ___ en scène
110 "Like ___ lump it"
111 With 69-Across, Requiem hymn
113 Frequent Powell co-star
114 Royal George
116 Synagogue, in Yiddish: Var.
117 Xanthippe
120 Part 6 of the quip
124 From the U.S. of A.
126 Just like
127 Add-on
128 Start of three John Wayne titles
129 Draft-card issuer: Abbr.
130 End of the quip
138 Overrun
139 Parlance
140 Performances for one
141 Wise guy
144 Start of a carol
145 Colorful aquarium fish
146 Author Sarah ___ Jewett
147 Qum resident
148 Three-time Masters winner
149 "I Left My Heart ___ Francisco"
150 Cape ___, N.C.
151 One of the Barrymores

DOWN

1 Literary collie
2 Benazir's father
3 Little attire?
4 All over again
5 Starts back at page one
6 Tap alternative
7 Boy gets/loses/gets girl, e.g.
8 Prefix with gram or train
9 Just some
10 Puget Sound city
11 Woody's boy
12 Common office décor
13 They may be put on
14 Grab
15 Gullywashers
16 On the safe side
17 Galileo, for one
18 Tied
19 Hand over
24 Moves a muscle
30 Catch
31 Loafers
32 Football Hall of Fame locale
33 Mustard plant
34 Prendergast's school
40 Sport in which players wear metal jackets
41 Gush
42 Birthday-party tradition
43 Book about Nineveh's fall
44 1970 Brando movie
45 Script word
46 Leave in the lurch
52 Jam ingredient?
54 Gallery employee
55 Hairdressers' creations
56 Play matchmaker
58 Poet Jones
59 Texaco rival
60 Mount
62 Igor, to Frankenstein
64 Sheik's peer?
65 Runner Lewis
66 Hair salon worker
70 "Every man . . . can tame ___ but he that hath her": Burton
73 Germfree
75 Branch
76 Weathervane abbr.
77 Seven, in compounds
78 Martino and Molinaro
79 Pennies: Abbr.
80 Victors in 1840 and 1848
81 "Damn Yankees" hit
82 Cartoon hunter
83 Award for Ngaio Marsh
84 Some medical plans, for short
85 Caesar's partner
91 Guardian spirits
92 "I thought ___ never leave!"
93 Author Wharton
94 6½-quart bottle
95 Nonalcoholic brew brand
96 Provinces
98 Deleterious
100 Storage site
101 Plane on an aircraft carrier
102 John Ciardi's "___ a Man"
104 "Little Caesar" role
106 Like some milk powder
109 More bespangled
112 Bank deposit?
114 Literature Nobelist Heinrich
115 "Robert's ___ Order"
116 Kurtz of TV's "Sisters"
117 Gymnast Comaneci
118 Straightens out
119 Media mogul David
121 Papeete's land
122 British farmer
123 Hint from Heloise
125 "Don't You Know?" singer, 1959
131 Nora's pooch
132 Paradise paradigm
133 Algonquin Round Table members
134 Celebratory dance
135 Study
136 Radius neighbor
137 Catalogue
142 Small number
143 Less than 142-Down

ACROSS

1 Deception
5 "This Gun for Hire" star, 1942
9 Fires
13 Story, sometimes
18 White-spotted rodent
19 "O.K."
20 Cowboy's lasso
22 Bringing ruin
23 Compliment for Ken Griffey Jr.?
25 Killer whales
26 Bigger than big
27 Volunteers' words
28 Air conditioner abbr.
29 Compliment for Mickey Rooney?
31 Compliment for Frankenstein's monster?
34 Disinclined
35 Unsteady on one's feet
36 Not beyond
39 School founded in 1440
43 Dig in
45 Missile launcher
47 First name in TV comedy
48 Brief
49 Classical meeting sites
52 Block houses?
54 Pacify
57 Board game from India: Var.
60 "At Seventeen" singer Janis
61 10-stringed lyre
62 Kind of center
63 Attack
64 Expect
65 Sum total
67 Compliment for Wyatt Earp?
70 Noted Corsican family name
73 "The Crying Game" actor
74 Bartender's supply
76 Mirror
77 "___ the calmly gathered thought": Whittier
78 "Roll ___ bones"
79 Capable of changing
82 Queen's Cup, e.g.
84 French wine center
86 Rush hour shortage
87 ___ Fox
88 ___ Japanese War
90 Hamelin helper
93 Kind of brain
94 Reliever's goal
95 Computer access code
97 The time being
100 Testifies
102 Compliment for E.T.?
106 Compliment for Alessandro Volta?
111 Hotel ending
112 Early TV drama sponsor
113 Father-in-law of Jacob
114 "The Wild Duck" dramatist
115 Compliment for Steffi Graf?
117 Public enemy No. 1, 1933
118 Rose and others
119 Otherwise
120 Biol. subject
121 "What ___!"
122 Libertine
123 "N.Y.P.D. Blue" offs.
124 Eyelid problem

DOWN

1 Indulge
2 "___ talk?" (comedy line)
3 Chemical catalysts
4 "The Song of the Earth" composer
5 Canadian pol. label
6 Clear ___
7 Fourth in a series
8 Fooling
9 Puts pressure on
10 Yorkshire river
11 Ocean compound
12 Played for time
13 Under way
14 Debut at Turin, 2/1/1896
15 Particular
16 Low
17 TV's "___ Three Lives"
21 Compliment for Mary Lou Retton?
24 Glamour rival
30 W.W. II heroes: Abbr.
32 Men
33 Spin
37 Caddie's offering
38 Composer ___ Prés
40 Miss topper
41 Attack
42 Family reunion member
43 Psychic's field
44 ___ standstill
46 Name add-on
50 ___ part (role-plays)
51 Olympics event
53 Ribbon holder of song
55 Bassanio's love
56 Take for oneself
58 Off-base
59 Compliment for the Marquis de Sade?
61 Before the present
64 Archeological datum
65 "So!"
66 Actress Scacchi
68 "Am ___ blame?"
69 Minor-league, maybe
70 Zingers
71 Milieu of 99-Down
72 Israeli region
75 Sales tax in some states
78 Lateen-rigged boat
79 Its scientific name is Naja haje
80 Go (for)
81 That: Sp.
83 Sunken spaces
84 Hosp. personnel
85 Assisted, in a way
89 Practices teetotalism
91 Commit
92 Down Under bounder
95 ___ favor
96 Hans Christian Andersen's birthplace
98 Litter-free
99 "Master Class" subject
101 Sells by machine
103 Fraser of 50's–60's tennis
104 ___ nothing of
105 Dispatch
106 Code word for "A"
107 Conceal, as a card
108 Kind of pipe
109 Racketeer's org.?
110 Request
116 Nice article

by David J. Kahn

ACROSS

1 Bibliographical abbr.
5 Look
9 Elbow
15 Put away
19 Tone down
20 Forearm part
21 Puck's master
22 Peacock in the sky
23 Chinese restaurant offering
25 Reagan chief of staff
27 White-tailed bird
28 Formosa Strait island
29 Ship's course
30 Two-wheelers
31 Boot camp fellow
33 Hood's heater
34 Newsman Bernard and others
35 Gain a lap
36 Directs
37 A Fodor's volume
39 Peaceful pause
41 Royal pardon
44 Ran rings around
45 Shirt shade
48 Recipe approximation
49 Cossack chiefs
51 Arab chief
53 With flexibility
56 Glassmaker's oven
57 Crumple
60 Cousin of the raccoon
61 Like smarting eyes
62 Musical direction
63 "These ___ the times . . ."
64 Adds a rider
66 Rising star
68 Apparition
70 Bakery purchase
71 Tough laundry problem
73 TV teaser
75 Tedium
76 Wind up
77 Actress Thompson
78 "Casey at the Bat" writer Ernest
79 Get extra value from
80 Without exception
82 Sunshade, of a sort
84 Tours summers
85 Foxfeet and sphagnum
88 Washington, D.C.
92 Country's best at the Olympics

93 First name in French literature
94 Use intimidation
98 1969 Broadway hit
99 Check writer
103 Furthermore
104 Step-by-step
105 Mend metal connections
107 Laughingstock
108 "The Battle of Eylau" painter
109 Small ones
110 Presidential also-ran
112 Marsh growth
114 Nobelist Wiesel
115 Shed
116 Hooked on
117 ___ vera
118 Juiceheads
119 Ancient mystic
120 Quintessence
121 Chateaubriand novel

DOWN

1 Ashes-to-be
2 Rotating emplacement
3 "Now!"
4 Author Wallace
5 Engaged in conjecture
6 "Gerontion" poet
7 Ref. set
8 Common female middle name
9 Frequent court "figure"
10 The duck in "Peter and the Wolf"
11 Put in stitches
12 Severely pan
13 Spanish poet Federico Garcia ___
14 Provide with income
15 Word fight
16 Consumes
17 Not neat
18 Like some suits
24 Micronesian land
26 Paul Revere
29 Standard
32 Avenge
33 Hurry-hurry
34 Fringe group
37 Follow
38 Request fervently
40 Old-time bandleader Edmundo
42 Manhattan flank

43 Manchurian border river
44 Actress Christine
45 Way out
46 "Sonata in B minor" composer
47 Acquired
50 Brilliant
52 Solomon's project
54 Old hand
55 Coagulable fluid
57 Gunstock wood
58 Stir up
59 Says "No way!"
62 Homer
65 Exclamations like "Phooey!"
67 Proposal of 3/22/72
69 Like some jacks
72 Artist Chagall
74 Country singer Travis
78 Thsi, e.g.
80 ___ Today
81 "The Wizard of Oz" co-star
83 Ultrasmall photo
85 Gordon and Meredith

86 Board game like reversi
87 Chooses
89 How the Old Woman lived
90 Oodles
91 Words before a drink
95 Frill
96 Smoker's purchase
97 French palace
100 Confuse
101 Agreements
102 "Aunt ___ Cope Book"
104 Actress Scacchi
106 Galena and mispickel
107 Envelope abbr.
108 Kind of therapy
111 Suffix with serpent
112 Hub's opposite
113 Coalition of 1958: Abbr.

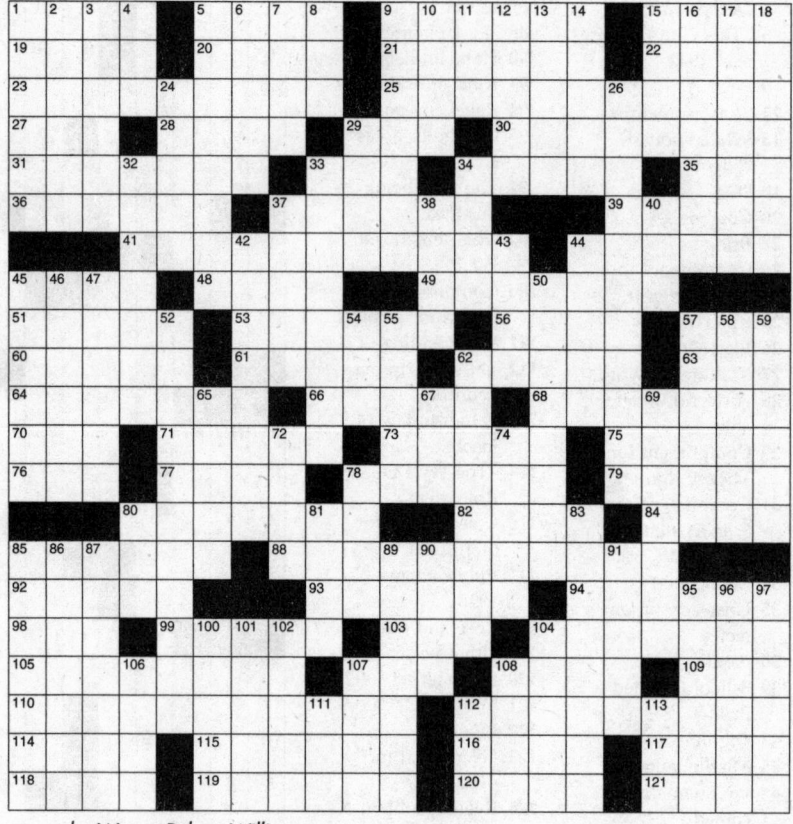

by Wayne Robert Williams

ACROSS

1 Nursery
7 Ointment
11 Former occupant
18 Gas fuel
19 Microgrooves
21 The scholarly life
22 Fast writers
23 Lillian Hellman title from The Song of Solomon
25 Call to the U.S.C.G.
26 "Domani" singer, 1955
28 Worst
29 Calendario period
30 Flightless bird
31 King of comedy
32 Swedish currency
34 Rival of Hires
36 Lacking
38 Irwin Shaw title from Psalms
41 Its HQ is in Brussels
43 Jupiter, e.g.
44 Set the pace
45 Medical suffix
49 Zhivago's love
51 In
54 Meaning
56 Guinness superlative
60 Basin adjunct
61 Arab League member
62 Pearl Buck title from Mark
65 Long opening
67 Golden time
68 Bore
69 Exactitude
70 Mazda model
72 One ___ (ball game)
73 Number of Disney Dalmatians
74 Penultimate letter
75 Upton Sinclair title from Matthew
78 Spiteful
80 Writing on the biblical wall
81 Late afternoons in Kensington
82 Starts of 29-Across
84 Some simians
87 Bathe
88 Sinclair rival
89 Lodge
91 Primary source: Abbr.
93 Lord's worker
95 John Hersey title from Psalms

101 Something to follow
103 Model material
106 French seaport
107 "My People" author
109 Plane heading
110 Philanthropist Lilly
111 Pass, as on the golf course
113 Convenient
115 Repose
116 William Faulkner title from II Samuel
119 University of California campus
121 Mosaic piece
122 Razes
123 Manifest
124 Enters by osmosis
125 Some tests, for short
126 Papyrus plants

DOWN

1 Nobel physicist Victor et al.
2 Living room piece
3 Ernest Hemingway title from Ecclesiastes
4 Exception
5 ___ Gay
6 Make ocean water drinkable
7 Escape
8 Need a doctor
9 Covered, as with paint
10 Parceling (out)
11 1980's sitcom
12 Bullets
13 Beach cover-up
14 ___ Annie of "Oklahoma!"
15 Ross Perot, e.g.
16 Tinker with the text
17 Plant again
19 High
20 Fractional suffixes
24 Fisherman, perhaps
27 Fan's encouragement
33 Cursory
35 Unanimously
37 Liberty Island attraction
39 House vote
40 Surplus
42 Vein contents
46 James Jones title from Mark
47 Echo
48 Places for whips
50 Murphy Brown's baby
52 "You ___ one"

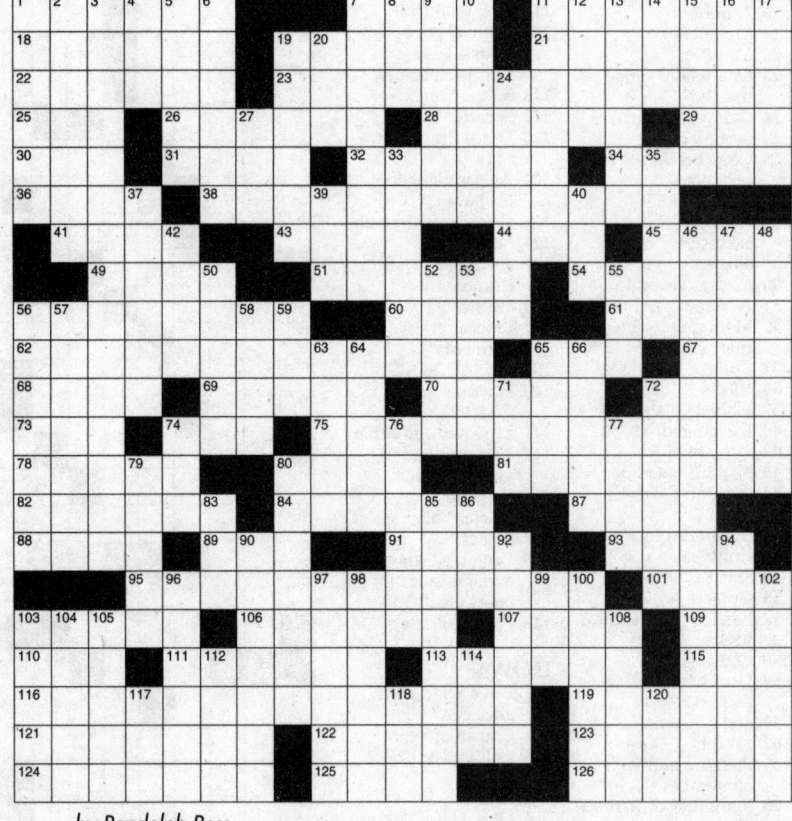

by Randolph Ross

53 Middle fingers
55 Watch
56 Special performance
57 Glenn and Metzenbaum
58 Mrs. Paul Simon
59 Fix
63 He swears
64 One of Chekhov's "Three Sisters"
65 Kitchen extension
66 1986 Indy winner Bobby
71 Nova Scotia hrs.
72 Statistical graphs
74 Casper's st.
76 Afresh
77 Sched. info
79 Part of a French countdown
80 Flamenco guitarist Carlos
83 Watch junior
85 Particles
86 Part of R.S.V.P.
90 "God is ___, that he should lie": Numbers
92 Sparkles

94 Bankroll
96 City near Vesuvius
97 Telescope name
98 Chirac's home
99 "Cabaret" lyricist Fred
100 Crimson rivals
102 Prairie homes
103 Rhythms
104 "Tiny Alice" playwright
105 Gauze fabric
108 Moxie
112 Actress ___ Singer
114 Mr. Sun
117 Daddy Warbucks henchman, with "The"
118 Part of e.r.a: Abbr.
120 Kid-___ (children's TV)

ACROSS

1 Shells and elbows
6 Taught
14 Miscellany
22 Carts
23 One who's joined the club
24 Gateway Arch designer
25 Chesebrough-Pond's products
26 "LETHARGIC"
28 Annotate excessively or absurdly
30 Liz has several
31 Averred
32 Montgomery bus rider Parks
33 College knowledge
34 1960's TV lead
37 Pianist Gilels et al.
40 Exchanged words
42 Type of eng.
43 N.Y.S.E. neighbor
44 "Ode to Psyche" poet
46 Celebrates in song
49 Cultivate
50 "SICKENING"
55 Guns
57 Barrie's "___ Licht Idylls"
58 CBS logo
59 Jerusalem's ___ Dolorosa
60 Some gowns
62 "WILD"
69 Fleming and namesakes
70 Reminder of Rennes
71 Crop up
72 Casas grandes
73 Exuding, old-style
75 Dispossess
77 Long Island town, home of William Cullen Bryant
78 Common computer
79 Amerada ___ (oil giant)
80 Contest entry encl.
81 Horsefeathers
82 Old film letters
84 Occult matter
86 Site of Mark Twain National Forest
89 John Doe, maybe
91 One of the Society Islands
92 Bellowing
93 See 117-Across
95 Matthew Arnold's "Empedocles on ___"
96 "WONDERFUL"
99 Pot
100 "Shiny Happy People" band
101 Not non
102 Supercomputer maker
103 "I'll be!"
104 "BEAUTIFUL"
112 It's just a waste

115 Start of a Carroll title
116 Pick wild fruit
117 With 93-Across, assassinated European leader
118 Singer Sumac
119 Sorority letters
120 James Brown hit "My ___"
122 Ancient kingdom of Jordan
123 Certain moviehouse
124 "What ___!"
127 Any chapter of the Koran
129 1988 country album
132 Biblical priests' garments
134 "DISASTROUS"
140 Haydn's "___ Quartet"
141 21-Down and others
142 Underground vegetable, in England
143 Silicon Valley giant
144 Honest
145 Language whose name means "perfected"
146 People: Prefix

DOWN

1 Peter Schickele's alter ego
2 Cousin of veno-
3 "VENERABLE"
4 Errata
5 Adjt.
6 Like Abner Yokum
7 Alfonso XIII's queen
8 Evaluated, with "up"
9 River of Hell
10 River of France
11 Ad ___
12 S.A.T. company
13 Narc's employer
14 Letters before Titanic
15 Active Philippine volcano
16 Emergency room case
17 Mesozoic, e.g.
18 Shanty covering
19 Prefix with plasm
20 Classic cars
21 Ruler of Russia, 1730–40
27 Kings' grp.
29 September TV special
35 Agent
36 Wears out
38 N.Y.C. subway org.
39 Country est. in 1948
41 Dwight Gooden moniker
43 Dune buggies, for short
44 Garbed, as a Glaswegian

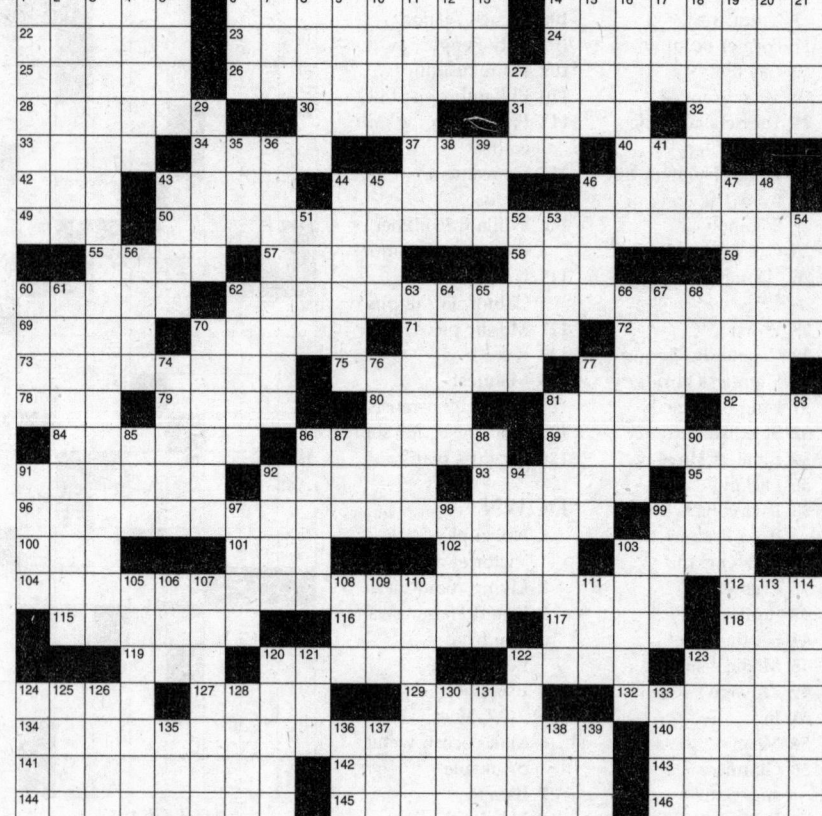

by Martin Schneider

45 13th-century literary work
46 Heaven, in Le Havre
47 "ENCHANTING"
48 18 million Asians
51 Dislodge
52 Brewer's need
53 "Here Is Your War" author
54 80's sitcom "My Two ___"
56 Start with while
60 Per ___
61 Play on which "Cabaret" is based
62 The brainy bunch
63 Old Iberian kingdom
64 Rosetta stone language
65 Cheer start
66 DeCarlo of "The Munsters"
67 Whitewater prosecutor Robert
68 "___ say!"
70 Land
74 "The Air ___ Breathe" (1974 hit)

76 Biblical forebear
77 Sot
81 Hype
83 Wood sorrels
85 Commerce, colloquially
86 Hatch on the Hill
87 Ending with proto-
88 Gyrocompass inventor
90 Sun. speeches
91 Court protection
92 It gives you fits
94 "___ for Man, so stealthily betrayed": Millay
97 Quadrennial conventioners
98 Former Chrysler offering
99 Pro-am game
103 Orb
105 Longtime Giants owner
106 Fort Worth inst.
107 Acting the sycophant
108 Draft org.
109 Daily financial quote

110 Suspect in the game Clue
111 Camellia State: Abbr.
113 Bit
114 Role that made Ford a star
120 Rendezvous
121 Uris book, with "The"
122 Batman's home
123 U.N.'s U ___
124 "Julius Caesar" has five
125 "___ thou eaten of the tree?": Genesis
126 Winged
128 Sundance Film Festival local
130 Newts
131 Jurist Robert
133 Ballet movement
135 Turn-of-the-millennium date
136 Crunches work them
137 Org. in the Mapplethorpe flap
138 "How ___ love thee?"
139 Lawyer: Abbr.

ACROSS

1 Play the stock market
7 Name in a directory
13 Word of caution
19 Woodsy shelter
20 Joins
21 Taxco wraps
22 Slapping webbed feet, doing backflips into a stream, etc.?
24 Stalls
25 Assault the nostrils
26 Pain in the neck
27 Edgar-winning mystery writer
28 ___ d'amore (baroque instrument)
30 Put up with
32 Dweller along the Morava
33 Killer whale
37 The Wildebeest Weekly, e.g.?
39 Old-time leading lady Dolores
41 Neighbor of China
42 Poetic contraction
43 Noted name in I.Q. testing
45 Christians' ___ Creed
47 Coach
48 Strand
51 Rephrased
53 Altar part
55 Act mawkishly
57 Hall of ___
59 Defunct council
60 Egyptian judge of the dead
62 Fishing equipment
64 In-class work
65 Cpl.'s inferior
66 Pull up
68 Ancient meeting place
70 Change: Abbr.
71 Closefitting hat
73 More than irk
77 Share the marquee
79 Toughened
81 "___ Pyle, U.S.M.C."
82 Bush's predecessor
85 Terry Bradshaw was one
87 Ladies
90 Blotto
91 Cultivate
92 Add zing to
94 Papal headdress
96 Decline
97 Gossip queen Barrett
99 Gauchos' gear
101 Hit that causes the fans to roar?
104 Moment: Abbr.
105 Nautical twist
106 Roman naturalist
108 Habitual procedure
109 Fish, in a way
111 Gist
112 Kunta Kinte portrayer John
114 ___ Islands (Guam and others)
117 Halloween light that's a howl?
122 Faculty
123 Familiarize
124 Seesaw
125 ___ Day (July 1)
126 Uses, as influence
127 Slips

DOWN

1 U.N. agency
2 Capture
3 Vintner's need
4 Summer months in Argentina
5 Best Actress of 1982
6 Color quality
7 Novelist Deighton
8 Motivated
9 Bucephalus, e.g.
10 Made taut
11 Formerly, once
12 Language suffix
13 Den meal leftovers?
14 Sins
15 "Brillo Box" artist
16 Friend of Fossey
17 Meth. or Luth. teaching
18 Weaver's path
21 Less tame
23 Safari sighting
27 Hired soldier, in slang
28 1993 N.B.A. Rookie of the Year
29 Slow-moving New York City transportation?
31 ___ facta (brave deeds): Lat.
32 Curve balls
34 Bus that makes short hops?
35 Deep gulches, out West
36 Financial report heading
37 Esteemed ones
38 The Yokum boy and others
40 Kind of fire
44 Spat
46 George Orwell's alma mater
49 "Jude the ___"
50 Kimono sash
52 1960–61 chess champ
54 Salad ingredient
56 Ceremony
58 Campus org.
61 It comes in bars
63 Condemn
65 Bridge type
67 Advertise
69 Kyushu volcano
71 Hebrew month
72 Spitchcocks
74 Name in appliances
75 H.S. proficiency test
76 Part of Q.E.D.
78 Cable channel
80 Start of a Christmas letter from Rudolph?
83 Skiddoo
84 Honer's target
86 Funicular
88 Contentious
89 Johnny of the '40s Braves
93 Author Bellow
95 Queenly
98 Loser at Châlons-sur-Marne in 451
100 Coined money
102 Boring speaker
103 Roll
107 Nonmaritime ship
110 Harpers Ferry event
111 "Das Kapital" author
113 Friend Down Under
114 Bud
115 Coarse fabric
116 ___ Tin Tin
117 Average fellow
118 O.C.S. grads
119 Letter from Greece
120 Emeritus: Abbr.
121 3-million-member sporting grp.

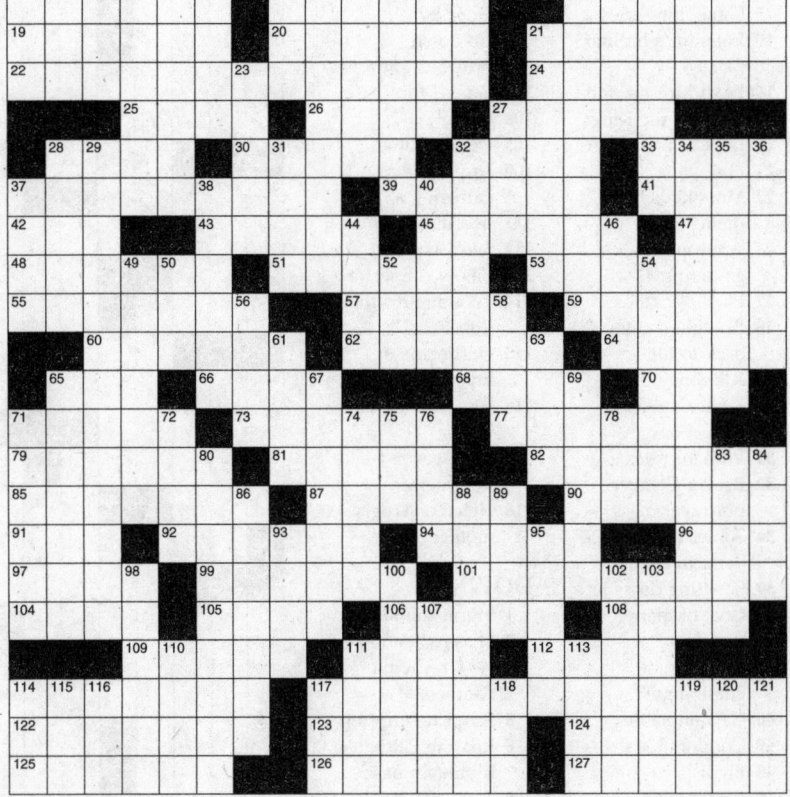

by Warren W. Reich

176 GATHERINGS

ACROSS

1 Scrooge's sign?
5 Some miniseries
10 Polonius's hiding place
15 Pearl Mosque site
19 "City of the Kings"
20 Lack of harmony
21 Flirt
22 Monokinis lack them
23 Appropriate gathering #1
27 Playbill names
28 Brought a cigar back to life
29 All gone
30 Yemen's second-largest city
31 Walking stick
32 Beaver Cleaver portrayer
34 Amiens's department
37 Smelting dross
38 Goal of many travelers
39 Appropriate gathering #2
46 Gawain's title
47 Comfortable dress
48 Bigot
49 Person with a whistle
51 Word with ware or winder
53 "Stride Toward Freedom" author
54 Peal of laughter
55 Bookcase site
58 Minister
60 Got off
61 Infamous mosquito
62 Appropriate gathering #3
69 Kapellmeister's group
70 Billy of show biz
71 Home
72 Photographed again
74 Jihads
75 It has a head and hops
76 "Oklahoma!" prop
80 U.K. award
81 "Maria ___" (1941 hit)
83 Turkish palace
84 Impresario Hurok
85 Appropriate gathering #4
91 ___-arms
92 Marriage, e.g.

93 ___ mutantur (all things change)
94 Gone by
97 Go down
99 Browbeat, in a way
101 Go ___ for
102 Ridge
103 Devil's home
107 Appropriate gathering #5
111 Becomes definite
112 Stereotype
113 Elbow connectors
114 "Waiting for the Robert ___"
115 First name in mysteries
116 Safe deposit box item
117 Floor covers, informally
118 Helen of Troy's mother

DOWN

1 Storm sound
2 "Lasher" writer
3 '44 Crosby hit
4 Soothers
5 Script description
6 Road to Fairbanks
7 Mountain pass
8 "___ was saying . . ."
9 Deficit
10 Lagoon locale
11 Make ready for use again
12 Absorbed
13 Hebrew for "healer"
14 Like zinfandel
15 Oscar winner for "Amadeus"
16 Danger for high heels
17 Judge
18 Orgs.
24 Deposits
25 Dobbin's vote?
26 Fore-and-aft rigged vessel
31 Cast
32 Slight
33 Capital east of Abidjan
34 Teen talk?
35 Cut out
36 Dream, in combos
37 Literally, "way of the gods"
38 Trombone device
40 Hard, in a way
41 Spirited dance

42 Two-wheeled carriage
43 Stops
44 Lose support
45 1985 hit by Heart
50 Actor Parker
52 N.H.L.'s Lemieux
54 Salinger family
56 "This Gun for Hire" star
57 People Weekly profile
59 Copter kin
60 Away from the mouth
62 Kind of phobia
63 Inge puppy
64 Clan symbol
65 Ball-park dinner
66 Denmark's ___ Islands
67 Skyscraper support
68 Andrea ___
73 City on the Ashuelot
74 Filling
75 1981 Higham film biography
77 Slippery ___ eel

78 Points
79 "Lohengrin" heroine
82 Burden
83 Vindictive
86 Full stop
87 Tree houses
88 One of Zeus's daughters
89 Bellini opera
90 Form a jury
94 French story
95 Homebody, perhaps
96 Have ___ (frolic)
97 Van Gogh's "Bedroom at ___"
98 Stendhal's real name
99 Chocolate source
100 Some fertilizer
102 Israel's Eban
103 N.C. neighbor
104 Christie murder locale
105 Froze
106 Drifting
108 Old cloth measure
109 Fannie ___
110 CDXLII + DCIX

by Arthur A. Verdesca

ACROSS

1 Use a juicer
5 Kind of polish
9 With a bow, to Stern
13 Ill-suited
18 Laura's lover in "La Gioconda"
19 Turkey neighbor
20 Tom Arnold's in-laws, once
22 City on the Arkansas
23 Francis Bacon question to Shakespeare?
26 Doctor
27 Long-winded speeches
28 Utensils for overgrilled steaks?
30 Hägar the Horrible's wife
31 Captain once played by Omar Sharif
32 H.S.T. was one
33 Thalia and sisters
36 Items to be cut
40 Space for a ship
43 Bette Davis's era?
47 South American ostriches
49 Provoke
50 Casts
51 "Up, up and away" company
52 Knack
54 Bluefin et al.
56 Elm City collegians
57 One of TV's Mavericks
58 What "-vore" means
59 Regarding
60 Train, as some sheep?
63 Kind of couch
64 E.R. cases
65 They loop the Loop
66 Cinque follower
67 How some vaccines are given
71 Orchard worm's average diet?
79 Decided collectively
80 Sal of "Exodus"
81 Violinist Leopold
82 Blacktop
83 "Dallas" mom
84 "Pomp and Circumstance" composer
85 Year in Leo IX's reign
86 1966 Tony winner for "Marat/Sade"
87 Model T contemporary
88 English actor Davenport
90 Niagara barrel-rider's reaction?
92 Puppet
94 Emits powerful beams
96 Models
97 Dropped in the drink
99 1939 film site
101 King Arthur's father
105 Farmers' specialty group?
110 Maligned
112 Beauty parlor procedure
113 Black-and-blue Scot of yore?
116 Extra
117 Simon Legree's creator
118 Carry on
119 Abound
120 Disheveled
121 Hankerings
122 Poet translated by FitzGerald
123 "___ perpetua" (Idaho's motto)

DOWN

1 "Curious George" co-authors
2 Cain raised him
3 Blue shade
4 Truffle relative
5 County of eastern Ireland
6 Tax-deferred svgs.
7 Manner
8 Wechsler test figures
9 Pianist Chasins
10 Muzzle loading aid
11 Tot spot
12 Caen's river
13 Voice
14 I.V. league?
15 Like some dogs' coats?
16 The Beatles' "___ Her Standing There"
17 Makes lace
21 Like Chianti
24 Fleming and Guggenheim, e.g.
25 Bigger than big
29 ___-daisy
31 Wipe out
34 Nolan Ryan team
35 Emulated a raven
37 One of a mythical ennead
38 Powhatan, e.g.
39 The Galloping Gourmet
41 Afghani's neighbor
42 Linguine topper
43 1969 Oates novel
44 Work off some poi, perhaps
45 Swedish poet Karlfeldt
46 Differently
48 Inactive
52 Have empathy with
53 Noosecaster's need
55 50's Burmese P.M.
57 Wine or hair quality
61 Destined for success
62 "If I ___ Rich Man"
63 Mystic
66 Aussie lassie
67 Manifest
68 Lumberjacks' contest
69 In the rear of some johns?
70 Wahine's accessory
71 Naps
72 Perspective
73 Sheraton competitor
74 Meshy material
75 Libran's stone, maybe
76 Tabla player's music
77 By any chance
78 Come across as
80 Start of something big?
86 Perfect
89 Actress Chase
90 Walk destination
91 Dormancy
93 Backslides
95 Scattered
98 Sans resources
100 ___ ski
102 Champagne "high"
103 Some native New Yorkers
104 Bowling alley button
105 Roosevelt Island transport
106 Tanning target
107 A.A.R.P. members
108 Perfumery name
109 Shawm descendant
110 Nintendo rival
111 Take it out for a spin
114 Afternoon hour
115 Prosciutto

by Cathy Millhauser

ACROSS

1 Rod with a bat
6 Switchblades
11 It's not wanted
19 English architect Jones
20 "Clueless" star Silverstone
21 #1 Helen Reddy hit
22 Classic Whitman poem
24 Fourth-century pope
25 Franklin Mint ware
26 Bulldozer, in Brighton
28 Burgs
31 Manhandled
32 Bull, of a sort
35 Hydrosphere components
36 It's catching
38 Snaffle bit
40 Supermarket check
41 Process of mountain formation
43 Scottish Gaelic
44 "I didn't know that!"
45 Fifty past
47 1955 song "Fifty Million Times ___"
48 Crimson rival
49 Mikhail's wife
51 ___ (Kookie) Byrnes
52 New London-based org.
54 Former First Family
57 Clink
58 Eagle, e.g.
59 George Meredith novel
62 Some martinis
64 Film character with the voice of Frank Oz
66 Upkeep
68 Kind of hand, in euchre
69 Confers
72 "Hannah and Her Sisters" star
74 Campers
77 Curriculum range
78 Tyke
80 N.C.A.A. regional
81 Piece
82 Early summers
84 Fleur-de-___
85 Hua's successor
87 Convex molding
89 ___ grass
90 Site for a seat of honor
92 Curtailed cone, in geometry
95 Abecedary phrase
96 Doubly
98 Taken care of
99 Charge
101 Peachy-keen
102 Red Sea republic
103 Hangdog
104 Well-thought-out
106 "Adam's Rib" co-playwright ___ Kanin
108 Examination
111 Louis XIV affirmation
116 Pavarotti encore
117 Radar blips
118 Jean Renoir film heroine
119 Some night life
120 Pizzazz
121 Lycra cousin

DOWN

1 Successor to the U.S.S.R.
2 "It's ___ win situation"
3 ___ Tin Tin
4 Shade of purple
5 Providing warmth, perhaps
6 Roy Rogers a k a Leonard ___
7 Boo follower
8 Protection money, in slang
9 Heavy
10 A&P competitor
11 Had something the matter
12 Finalize, with "down"
13 Strollers
14 More outdoorsy, as fashion
15 Abominable
16 Longtime record label
17 When repeated, a Kenyan revolutionary
18 Years, in Thiers
20 Lbs. and qts., e.g.
23 1980 Dom DeLuise film
27 Check for accuracy
28 Traveler's stop
29 Give in
30 Old Ted Lewis standard
31 Game in the woods?
33 Descartes axiom
34 Walks oddly
36 Registers, as a complaint
37 ___ Khan
38 Get, pricewise
39 Verges on
42 Heat
43 "Telephone Line" rock grp.
46 Top
48 Newsy's special
50 Club: Abbr.
53 Early woodwind
54 Almost catch, as the heels
55 "Time ___ the essence"
56 Outbuildings
60 Forrest's folks
61 Ron Howard TV role
63 Honor, in a way
65 Suffix with psych-
67 City in northern Italia
69 1991 Disney prince
70 Acts pushy
71 Cubic
73 Saucy name?
75 Carry-on item
76 Ripped
79 Mathematical constants
83 Devotee
85 Comedienne Nora
86 70's teaching
88 With an empty expression
91 Unsurpassed
92 Cows and sows
93 Opposite of send packing
94 Pool shot
97 Punishing rod: Var.
98 Hatfield or Coats, e.g.: Abbr.
100 On the A-list
102 Ninnies
103 Meteors' paths
105 Orig.
106 "The Ballad of Reading ___"
107 To ___ (precisely)
108 Part of ASCAP: Abbr.
109 1860's abbr.
110 Fleece
112 "___ will be done . . ."
113 N.F.L.'s Blount
114 "Sail ___ Ship of State!"
115 Author Fleming

by Dean Niles

ACROSS

1 Corrupt
6 Dupe
11 Rope materials
16 Measures
21 Li'l one
22 San Antonio attraction
23 Profit
24 De Valera of Ireland
25 Creature not yet found?
27 Celebrated tightwad of old
28 Meander
29 Zurich's and Zug's locale
30 North Carolina college
31 K follower
32 "West Side Story" girl
33 Actress Thompson
34 Meat, fruit, honey?
40 Wall fixture
41 It may be dead
42 TV's Dame ___ Everage
43 Up-to-the-minute
44 Photo add-on
45 Gets an A
46 Escort
47 Sailor's interjections
48 De Brunhoff's pachyderm
49 Spiritualist's device
51 Sequel title start
53 Cluck, crow, gobble, peep?
56 Poop deck's place
59 Tool handle wood
61 Forfeit
62 Directional suffix
63 Fixed
65 Pharisees, e.g.
68 Not nearby
70 Rings
73 Some game pieces
74 Yups' opposites
75 Workman's wheels
76 Sardines players
78 Kind of call
80 Ear: Prefix
81 Crystallize
82 Misbehaving antelopes?
83 Galena, e.g.
84 Scratch (out)
85 Auto summonses?
87 They hardly give a hoot
88 Defect
89 Still-life subject
90 ___ Gay (W.W. II plane)
91 Lamb products
93 Kind of bread
94 See 58-Down
95 "The ___ Class" (O'Toole film)
97 "___ on parle français"
98 One-on-one sport
100 Easter preceder
102 Hot-tub locale
103 Uninvited swine?
107 Daily index, with "the"
109 Cleric, e.g.
111 Spreads
112 Oda ___ (Whoopi's role in "Ghost")
114 Hoo-ha
117 Nautical heading
119 Followers of printemps
121 Jurist Robert
122 Piquancy
123 Stole
124 Cougar
125 Biting, chest-thumping, roaring?
128 Brother
129 Choreographer Moiseyev et al.
131 Track competition
132 Ship sailed by Tiphys
133 Rock 'n' roll pioneer Freed
134 Former "Masterpiece Theatre" host
135 Keys in
137 Ranching that's growing by leaps and bounds?
140 Advantages
141 Hilly districts, to Brits
142 Saw
143 Al ___ (way to cook pasta)
144 Bank claims
145 More than big
146 Reach
147 Pundits

DOWN

1 "Hot" ones
2 Chisholm Trail stop
3 Without restraint
4 Capone foe
5 Chemical prefix
6 Loose overcoats
7 Cave temple site in India
8 Golfer ___ Stewart
9 Presidential monogram
10 Near miss in tic-tac-toe
11 Aria for Carmen
12 Six-time U.S. Open tennis champ
13 Praying one
14 A.T.M. access
15 Vulpine
16 Fashion line
17 South Florida city
18 Cuddly farm animal?
19 "Every Breath You Take" group, with "the"
20 Dastards
26 Impoverished
31 ___ detector
34 The slightest amount, informally
35 Deli dishes
36 Marten
37 Adjust
38 Actress ___ Flynn Boyle
39 Some parties
48 Churl
50 Irritate
52 Toasted ___
53 Spanish dessert
54 Political family of India
55 Flagrant
57 Spotted
58 Canopies for 94-Across
60 First president of the Czech Republic
64 Distress
65 Sleep disturbers
66 Consumed
67 Brown ruminant?
69 Bogus
70 Bounds
71 Minimal change
72 Reconnoiter
76 Michener novel
77 Without forethought
79 It has many stops
81 Ricochet
82 "The Garden of Earthly Delights" artist
86 Clay today
88 Catafalque
89 Zaragoza's river
92 Carrie, for one
93 Pierre's pois
96 "Peer Gynt" composer
98 Film critic Roger
99 Sprite of Irish folklore
101 "The Country Girl" playwright
104 Concerning
105 ___ oblige
106 Show smugness
108 Equivocating
110 Give heed
112 Simenon sleuth
113 Giant automaker supplier
115 He said "Everybody wants to get into da act"
116 Sevilles, e.g.
117 Of a summit
118 "The Count" biographee
120 ___ Simon
122 Italian liqueur
126 Yorkshire city
127 Gem weight
130 Units for Sampras
133 Perplexed
135 "Sophia Loren's "___ Women"
136 London lout
137 Harridan
138 Juice drink
139 Driver's lic. and others

by Nancy Nicholson Joline

ACROSS

1 Hoops
8 Kind of hunting
15 "Star Wars" director
20 Mark Antony's first wife
21 Fine
22 Kind of layer
23 With 117-Across, what the answers to the italicized clues have in common
25 "Chapter Two" playwright
26 Shot
27 Former capital of Nicaragua
28 Novelist Rand
29 Luna's counterpart
31 Knock-knock joke, essentially
32 Protrude, in a way
34 Connective tissues
36 *View along the highway*
40 Make one two
42 Stevie Wonder's "My Cherie ___"
43 Atheist leader
45 Ballot marks
46 The All-wise, of myth
48 Steakhouse orders
50 Madonna album
52 Exhausts
54 M.D. spots
55 Eponymous Dutch town
57 Recital pieces
59 Schoenberg's "___ to Napoleon"
60 Speech help
63 Free TV commercials, for short
64 "Rescue 911" host
67 Grammy winner Etheridge
69 Makes straight
71 Flambé
74 Milk product
76 Cultivated
80 Actress Hagen
81 Car front
83 Mantel piece
84 Cole Porter, collegiately
85 Noted Big Apple restaurant
88 Time for "Today"
90 Paint variety
93 Farmer, sometimes
94 Painter Gerard ___ Borch

95 ___ Strait (waterway bordering Japan)
97 As good as new
98 Cuban resort city
101 *Mountain demarcation*
103 Month's start
105 Kind of advice
107 Snitch
108 It may be used in a rubout
109 Chemical suffix
110 Rise
111 "Ooh" follower
115 Oval
117 See 23-Across
121 Construction support
122 Racing, as pacers
123 Catherine the Great, e.g.
124 "The Glass Bead Game" novelist
125 Handout sign
126 Prokofiev's "War ___"

DOWN

1 This and that
2 Hurting
3 Process part
4 Floor
5 Adolf's mistress
6 Bar on a boat
7 City near Pompeii
8 High-tech prosthesis
9 Du Maurier's "Jamaica ___"
10 Reached
11 More bleak
12 Court situation
13 Chaps
14 German theologian Thomas
15 *"La Bamba" band*
16 Israeli weapon
17 *Likening*
18 Have ___ (be able to escape)
19 Plant yielding a cathartic drug
24 Classic "S.N.L." characters
30 Agatha Christie's "N ___?"
32 Present
33 Sony co-founder Morita
34 Three-time Masters winner
35 Subject of Cyaxares
36 Boca ___

37 ___ Latin (ancient Italian)
38 Plug
39 Cookout item
41 Let go
44 Itinerary segs.
47 Fully exposed
49 Steadiness, in a way
51 "Try ___ see!"
52 Led (in)
53 A shot
56 Less interesting
58 "Cómo ___?"
61 Popular record label
62 Disney collectible
63 Pope, 1605–21
65 "So?"
66 China's Lao-___
68 Cornea neighbor
70 Trojan War king
71 Au ___ (menu phrase)
72 Karl Malone's team
73 *Instruments with aneroid cells*
75 Stench
77 "Forbidden Paradise" star, 1924
78 ABC sitcom

79 Electron tube type
82 Jolson's "___ My Wife to the Thousand Isles"
83 Marbleize, e.g.
86 Kind of ear
87 *Water*
89 Denial of a sort
91 "___ in the Dark" (Streep film)
92 Gertrude's 1951 Broadway co-star
94 Envision victory
96 Kidnaps
99 Where a pct. of one's income may go
100 Famous
102 Westernmost Texas county
103 Criticize severely
104 "Ah Sin" playwright
106 Glossy proof
109 Baghdad's land: Var.
111 Italian cabbage
112 Working
113 Turner of the screen

114 Lament for Yorick
116 Greek consonants
118 Spanish article
119 Seemingly forever
120 Long shot?

by Matt Gaffney

ACROSS

1 Bearded world leader
7 "___ Poems" (Sandburg's first book)
14 Overstate one's case
18 Vatican II pontiff
19 Unpleasant sentiment
20 One of the Horae
21 BAY
23 An Allman brother
24 "... ___ o'clock scholar"
25 Boot one
26 "Unbelievable" rock band
27 1992 Clinton rival
29 Like most music sold nowadays
31 ___ marshal (British officer)
33 Tons
35 Effortlessness
36 Rear, informally
38 Twisted, as a bulb
41 "Encore!"
44 DOUG
46 Asian coin
49 Statement
51 In the wee hours
52 Really nice
54 Re religious meetings
56 Norman Chandler's paper, briefly
60 Controversial execution of 1927
61 Some Spanish religious paintings
63 Assyrian capital
65 Token
66 Soundhole shape
67 Rap star/actor
69 Dotty
70 German article
71 Free-trade measure of '94
72 Straight for
76 Stupor
79 Meanies
81 Nods
83 ___ support (alimony)
84 Coat materials
86 Some tides
88 Altogether
89 Men
90 MARC
95 Graycoat
96 Lucy's love, in the comics
98 Italian opera house
100 Zoophilist's org.
102 Bugs
103 "Raiders of the Lost Ark" creatures
104 Pronto
107 Scarring events
109 TV schedule letters
111 Sault ___ Marie
113 Sudden noise
115 Dissect, in a way
116 PERT
121 "Doe, ___, a female..."
122 Connected
123 ___ Australia (southern constellation)
124 Tops, e.g.
125 Colleague of Calliope
126 Scarlet letter wearer

DOWN

1 Samoan capital
2 Sought support from
3 Frost contemporary
4 Draw back
5 Rock video award
6 Spearer, of sorts
7 "All-American Girl" star Margaret
8 "A Private View" playwright
9 Entry
10 Writer who co-founded Random House
11 "Atlas Shrugged" name
12 Muck
13 Play set in Grover's Corners
14 Country on Borneo
15 BUS
16 Trollope lady and namesakes
17 Simpletons
19 King Arthur's mother
20 Familiar vow
22 Sphere of struggle
28 Mount
30 Infamous French soldier
32 Splendid
33 Mannequin part
34 Felis ___ (lion)
37 Backdoor
38 Long-time Windy City orchestra leader
39 "It's a ___ shame"
40 Salon supplies
41 Groundwork
42 Kind of education
43 MARIA
45 QB Tarkenton
47 Denounce harshly
48 Vegas gas
50 Beat
53 Arrayed
55 Shade of brown
57 One of the "Little Women"
58 Welsh "John"
59 Not Nintendos
62 Ices, with "up"
64 Angel, perhaps
68 Helpers of profs.
71 "Holy cow!"
73 Spanish railway company
74 Kiev's river
75 Guiding light?
77 80's guerrilla
78 Bachelor, stereotypically
80 Third son of Adam
82 Descries
85 Neighbor of Turkey
87 Accelerates
91 Fast wheels
92 Cry of alarm
93 Has too much, informally
94 Some bridge players
97 Subjects of investigations
99 Spring event
100 March 17 honoree
101 It has many 61-Across
103 Grocery chain
105 Set aside
106 "Common Sense" pamphleteer
108 ___ des Caraibes (Martinique locale)
109 Young'un
110 Oktoberfest serving
112 Work like Dürer
114 Comic Jack
117 Bettor's note
118 Young'un
119 Consonantless German city
120 Wade opponent

by Matt Gaffney

182 HUSH!

ACROSS

1 Waltzed
7 Unrefined petroleums
13 Overshadow
20 One of the Dionnes
21 Famous flight, A.D. 622
22 Took turns
23 Ashtray emptiers
25 Wall Street worries
26 Think of it!
27 Step 2 for a marksman
28 Citizens: Suffix
29 Kingdom's worth, to Richard III
30 Shaving mishap
32 Bassoon, e.g.
33 Stopped talking, finally
36 Cabalist's caution
40 "From Here to Eternity" author James
41 Steam
42 Duelers' equipment
43 Dashboard reading, for short
44 Kind of cross
45 He wrote "The Postman Always Rings Twice"
46 Actor Beatty and others
47 Part of Longfellow's forest primeval
53 Magician's name suffix
54 Police support org.
57 Revolutionary Trotsky
58 Kind of geometry
59 Byron's "calculating" daughter
60 Twaddle
61 Old Mideast inits.
62 Sorry folks
65 Beatles lyric of 1964
71 Merchants
72 Much of "Deck the Halls"
73 Supreme ruler: Abbr.
74 Status follower
75 1960 NASA launch
76 Microscopic organism
77 Baseball's Cobb and others
78 Dièci minus nòve
79 1942 Joe E. Brown comedy
84 River isles
85 Word before and after "against"
86 Border
87 Colorful moths
89 Stop, in Québec
90 Double twist
91 Masquerades
94 Kitchen contraptions
97 Court player
99 Loudness unit
100 160 square rods
101 Calibrate
102 Ersatz bankers
103 Kind of lamp
104 Ethnic music
108 Jot
110 1955 Graham Greene novel, with "The"
113 Terrestrial
114 Not close, once
115 In disgrace
116 Nash contemporaries
117 Pronto
118 Alone

DOWN

1 First name in TV comedy
2 During
3 "Cleopatra" setting
4 Scours
5 "A" as in Aachen
6 Separate
7 Playmate
8 Emeritus: Abbr.
9 More hostile
10 Followed the Pritikin plan
11 Made slips
12 Be disrespectful to
13 Imp
14 Full of tiny holes
15 Blasts off
16 Café order
17 Pericles or Socrates
18 Right command
19 Actor Harris and others
24 Hell's Angel
31 "___ So Easy" ('77 pop hit)
32 Wolf boy?
33 St. ___ (Missouri native)
34 Enemy of the Iroquois
35 Libraries
36 Servant
37 Capsized
38 Settle
39 Typist's speed: Abbr.
40 Cookie ___
44 Cask
45 It may be hard or sweet
48 Bring in
49 Sour cherry
50 Answer to "Are we there?"
51 Like Poe settings
52 Barracks items
54 Heat, of a sort
55 Big Apple area
56 Pulsating
63 Lack
64 Stroll
66 Photo option
67 Clowns around
68 Prego competitor
69 "There ___ and place for everything"
70 Sleeping spots
76 Bit of gear for a rock tour
79 Queens stadium
80 Party fellow
81 In the brain, so to speak
82 Dogfaces
83 Play ___ with (make trouble for)
84 Major, as a road
88 Throng
89 Auto option, informally
91 Brainy
92 Boxing trainer ___ Dundee
93 Bruce and others
94 One in line for a fall
95 Invisible
96 Public ___
98 "You're never too ___ learn"
99 Evel Knievel act
102 A pastel
103 Bern's river
105 Ne plus ultra
106 Highlander
107 Humorist Rooney
108 But: Lat.
109 Investor's Ginnie ___
111 Middle X or O
112 Fraternity letter

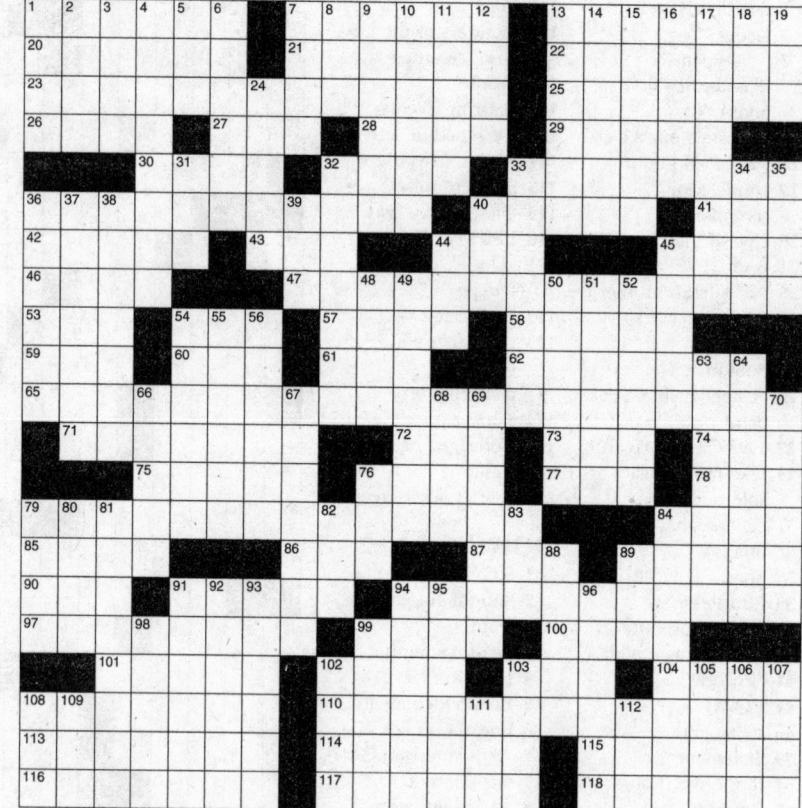

by Ralph G. Beaman

GAINING MOMENTUM 183

ACROSS

1 Crockett's partner on "Miami Vice"
6 Turquoise
10 1982 best seller on sexuality, with "The"
15 In-tents experience?
19 To smithereens
20 Crescent
21 Freedom, in Swahili
22 "Jewel Song," e.g.
23 Codicil
24 Monkeyshine
25 Table game for brooders?
27 Symbol on French V.I.P.'s cars?
30 Ascribe
31 Hard-rock connection
33 Elvis's "A Fool Such ___"
34 Umbrella part
35 Social worker
36 One of the family
37 Dish in a cream sauce to remember?
43 He follows the news
44 CH₃
45 ___ Tin Tin
46 Mideastern jambalaya
47 Snappish
48 Like some textbook publishers
49 Name in a Salinger title
51 Dispatch
52 On one's ___
54 Angel hair, e.g.
56 Early South African P.M. Jan
57 Coins in a Spanish treasure
61 Affianced
64 Watered down
65 Japanese emperor beginning 1989
66 Scuttlebutt
67 Bit of dew
70 Very, to Verdi
71 Habitual liar
73 Harness part
74 Situated along a river
76 "The Look of Love" pianist, 1968
77 Sported
78 Fear
79 Emerson's "jealous mistress"
80 Battling
81 Secures
82 Stinky
86 Some game
89 Baseball's Little Colonel
91 NBC prog. since 1975
92 Marbles, so to speak
94 Ron Howards' first TV role
95 Fashion designer who loves an old Ford?
98 Cartoon Chihuahua
99 Complete
100 Horned Frogs of coll. football
101 Coddled item
102 Jupiter or Saturn
103 Long-distance auto race
105 Hit song by a Beatles janitor?
110 Cat's mealtime lament?
112 Malaria symptom
113 What a dhoti covers
116 B, gradewise
117 Molière miss
118 Literally, "injured"
119 "The Untouchables" composer Morricone
120 Ustinov in "Quo Vadis?"
121 Hurried over?
122 Fleet fleet
123 Doer of good deeds

DOWN

1 Seafarer
2 Name in the news
3 Treachery
4 "If We Only Have Love" composer
5 Unevenly colored
6 Buzz in space
7 Piccadilly pound
8 Be the basis of
9 Wind-blown
10 Judy Garland's real last name
11 Wave away
12 Small boxers
13 Mouth: Prefix
14 Utensil of note
15 Fearless Fosdick's creator
16 Fired up
17 Moneymaking operation
18 Shoulder-length do
26 Prime meridian std.
28 Like a fifth wheel
29 "Think" tank?
31 Crown
32 Satirist Silverstein
35 Japanese airline
38 Cartoon about a Veep?
39 Loss of 1588
40 High spot?
41 Good working condition
42 Reformers' targets
43 Stimulating jazz singer?
50 Cassoulet and others
51 Where a groundhog shops?
53 Goethe National Museum site
55 Better ventilated
56 Stabilizer
58 Film on which "Carnival" was based
59 Sundance's heartthrob
60 Gershwin song of 1930
61 It's pushed in Hyde Park
62 Viking character
63 Mideast's Gulf of ___
65 Make ___ of money
68 Irving Berlin's "___ Good Girl"
69 Magic 8 Ball, e.g.
72 Celsius, for one
75 Paragraph, perhaps
77 Middle of a Latin trio
81 Caters to
83 "Little tongues"
84 "Do ___ Me" (1992 #1 hit)
85 Couple
86 Unfamiliar
87 Shoe style
88 Saxe-Coburg and Gotha, since 1917
90 Needlepoint?
91 Teas
93 They may have a pair of diamonds
96 Washington, McKinley et al: Abbr.
97 Overflow controls
99 Treasure of the Sierra Madre
104 Destroy
105 Sierra Club founder John
106 Peak in myth
107 Spherical striker
108 Boot
109 Chaplin's widow
111 ___ Miss
114 "House of Incest" author
115 One who can't pass the bar?

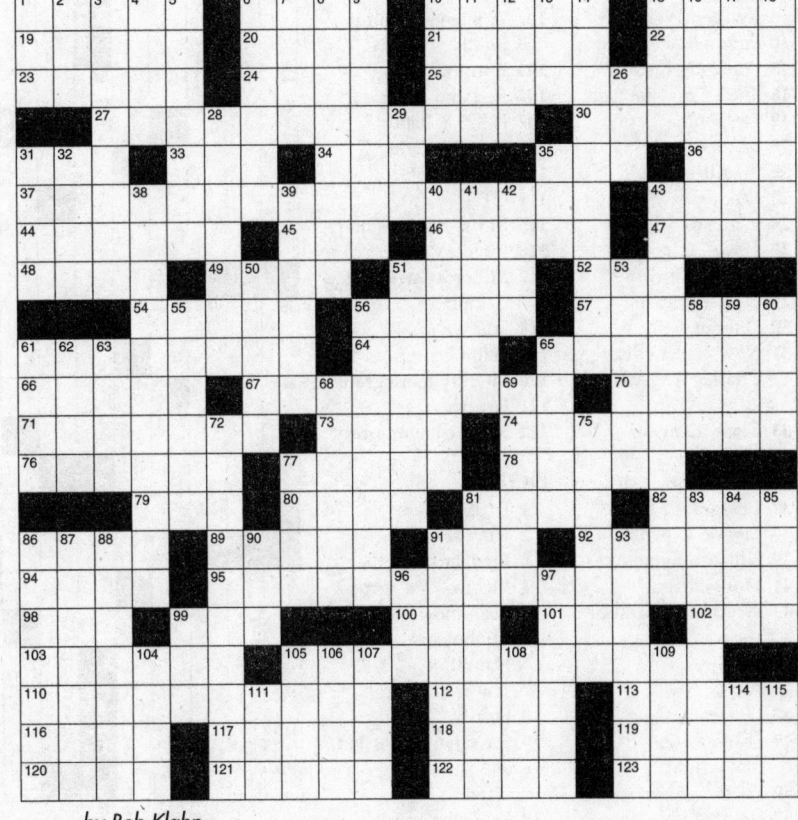

by Bob Klahn

ACROSS

1 Kitchen pest
6 John, in Wales
10 Any fellow
13 Some are historic
18 "L.A. Law" lawyer
19 Desperate
20 Pequod captain
22 "Fiddlesticks!"
23 OY
26 Winged
27 Have ___ at
28 Sulking fit
29 Newel shapers
30 Dugout
31 Newspaper editor Charles Anderson ___
33 Class that uses 29-Across
36 Marks out
37 1990 movie "___! Tie Me Down!"
39 Hill and namesakes
41 More current
43 Word with Band or Farm
44 Followers
45 AY
47 Like some vins
49 "Rhinoceros" playwright
50 Food flavorer
52 Custard base
55 Menacing
58 Like Mozart
60 Way to go
62 Blew in, so to speak
63 Candy brand
64 "___ life!"
65 Pampered
67 One at Orly
68 EN
71 Itinerary portion
72 They're plucked
74 Selene's counterpart
75 Sight: Fr.
76 1989 Literature Nobelist
77 Extend
78 Walker of football
80 Bacchus attendant
81 Clarifying words
82 Palindromic time
83 Not as timely
85 "Over my dead body!"
87 EY
91 Jazz theme
94 Wheat stalk part
95 Skiwear
96 Not so strict
97 Recruits
99 ___ pump
100 Literary homophone for 99-Across
102 70's tennis champ Smith
103 Burning
104 Red and silver, e.g.
107 N.Y.S.E. listing
109 Swedish cents
110 British cents
111 OT
115 In the beaver state?
116 Pinlike
117 Milton's "sweetest nymph"
118 Survive
119 Habit
120 Literary monogram
121 Drudge
122 Shaw contemporary

DOWN

1 Park shelters
2 Stew seasoning
3 Prospero's brother
4 McLean, Va., grp.
5 Teen movie of 1965
6 Mythologist Hamilton
7 Tracer of note
8 Fortify
9 Screenwriter Jordan of "The Crying Game"
10 One who's up
11 Casual noes
12 Venture
13 Leeway
14 AH
15 Scottish chieftains
16 Leave the kitchen
17 Important TV period
21 "Hush!"
24 Moderate
25 Graph lines
32 Costume
34 It fits all
35 60's catchword
38 Social reformer Wells
40 "Hey there!"
42 Motorist's goof
43 Having the stuff
46 Thermometers measure them
48 Square
50 Vocal opponent
51 Caesarean section?
53 Esophagus
54 Stalwart
55 Gear type
56 "O" follower
57 What former foes make
59 Some Plymouths
61 Literary award
63 Pizza
65 Hopeful plea
66 "___ to Psyche"
68 "Death Be Not Proud" poet
69 Singer Laine
70 "Gray's Anatomy" feature
73 Y
76 Mexican novelist Fuentes
78 Saddle part
79 Ex-Aussie P.M. Bob
80 Utah's state flower
82 Guy with a deadline
84 Miniature harbors
86 Kilmer of "Top Gun"
87 Ecdysiast
88 Columbia River port
89 Directions-inquiry word
90 Conductor Ansermet et al.
91 Brought in
92 How some people live
93 Extreme
95 Northwest workers
98 Certain looks
99 Shock
101 Babbled
105 Parodist
106 Procedure part
108 Community center, for short
112 Chill
113 "I get it now!"
114 Can

by Matt Gaffney

ACROSS

1 Wetland
6 Shawl
11 Close down
15 Lose it
20 Soap plants
22 Stave off
23 Sported
24 "___ my doubts"
25 Leave the junk
26 Jackie Gleason biography
28 Kids around
29 Old distiller's vessel
31 Moviemaker
32 Cable channel
34 "___ tu" (Verdi aria)
35 Russian space station
36 Warhol genre
38 Fall sound
40 Think over again
42 Takes a loss on, in slang
44 Cash in
46 ___ tie
48 Part of B.T.U.
49 Hydromassage facility
50 Pics
51 From ___ Z
54 No-goodniks
56 May and others
58 Injustice
60 Cosmetician Arpel
61 V.I.P. in magazine publishing
63 Lady of Livorno
65 Cambodia's Angkor ___
66 Hardly flexible
67 Dog in astronomy
68 Lamb's name
70 Tropicana and Minute
   Maid, e.g.
73 Defeats
74 Try to open, in a way
75 Priggish
77 Pro ___
79 Foul up
80 Look-alike
82 Fast
83 Goat-man
84 Not grades to brag about
86 Conjecture
88 Bandleader Alvino
89 Recently
92 Kind of "Fingerprint"
93 City near Sun Valley
94 Eminent
96 Actor Everett and others
97 ASCAP rival
99 Passage between buildings
101 Now
102 Economize
105 "La vita nuova" writer
106 Oily disinfectant
107 Prove
109 Brazilian port
110 Consolidates
111 Pouch
113 Lustrous black
114 Latticework strip
116 A wood stain
118 Enero-to-diciembre periods
120 Kind of mobility
122 Shoreline indentation
125 Snitched
127 Caterina's three
128 Olympics participant: Abbr.
129 Gasthaus cubes
131 Alternative to pj's
133 Filled (with)
136 Noel ___, 50's Lois Lane
138 Best Actor of 1957
141 How the villain looked?
142 All, in music
143 Have a blintz, maybe
144 Artist's preparation
145 Obtain free
146 "Give it ___!"
147 Responsibility
148 Attempt
149 Goose genus

DOWN

1 "___ X" (1920's play)
2 Bloomer and others
3 First U.S. poet laureate
4 Bridge feat
5 Spearmint, e.g.
6 ___-jongg
7 Salad fruit
8 A. P., Reuters, etc.
9 ___ et quarante (card game)
10 Fit conclusion?
11 Perfect basketball shot
12 Body relaxer
13 Sch. south of Providence
14 Former "Entertainment
   Tonight" co-host
15 W.W. II enlistee
16 Gloater's cry
17 Sounds reasonable
18 Dislike
19 Stops
21 Jump
27 Do a handicraft
30 Pedimental ornament
   over a door or window
33 Namath milieu
37 Role in "The Robe"
39 Wingdings
41 One who keeps work
   in balance?
43 Alternatives to Viceroys
45 Edge
47 Mauna ___
50 Turku people
52 It can be inflamed
53 Plastic ___ Band
55 Gun lobby
57 G.P.'s expertise
58 Carry the day
59 Jealous
61 Gossiped
62 Showered with love
63 Turn down, with "to"
64 Calm
67 Popular puzzle
69 ___-advised
71 Garden party decorations
72 ___ Island ferry
74 Joint meetings
76 Comedian Irwin
78 "___ of robins in her hair"
80 Prompt
81 Verdi opera
85 Hepburn title role, 1954
86 Prince Rainier's family name
87 Defer (to)
89 Dairy section purchases
90 Dandies
91 Arthur Godfrey regular
95 ___ kwon do (martial art)
96 Protect
98 Central
100 Hearing aid
101 Rainbow fish
102 Hitchcock classic
103 Emmett Kelly makeup
104 School org.
106 Napoli noblewoman
107 Hindu philosophy
108 Lister's abbr.
110 Unadorned
112 Procession
115 Candid
117 Shaw and others
119 Farm machine
121 Ended the blackout
123 Mineral water
124 Source of facial
   embarrassment?
126 Country singer Reeves et al.
130 Smooth
132 Tremendous
134 Rap group Salt-N-___
135 Clinton aide
137 Mil. officers
139 Baseball's Piniella
140 Kind of bean

by A. J. Santora

PUZZLE OF THE FUTURE

ACROSS

1 Dove home
5 Futuristic genre
10 Sweet
16 Heart hurt
17 "Is Paris Burning?" co-star
18 "Who controls the past controls the future" book, with 22-Across
20 "Future Indefinite" autobiographer
22 See 18-Across
24 Quiz feature: Abbr.
25 Put ___ to (squelch)
26 1958 Ritchie Valens hit
27 "We ___ please"
28 Did salon work
30 Castle strongholds
32 Does hand shuttle work
33 They can give you fits
34 Utah park
36 Alpaca's home
38 Nevada county
39 Jai ___
40 The Mariners' airport
42 Night sight
44 She wrote "The Wave of the Future"
47 Kind of lighting
50 Soft palate extensions
54 Overly
55 S. C. Johnson's Future, for one
57 "The Once and Future King" setting
60 To fly on Alitalia
61 1945 conference site
62 "Do Ya" rock grp.
63 "Future noir" film of 1982
67 Sheet music abbr.
68 The bucking stops here
71 Opts
72 "The future of law enforcement"
75 "He's a little worried about his future"
77 Having magnitude only
79 Pacific islander
80 6 on your dial
81 Futurity
84 Dove home
86 Flat friend
88 Colombia city
90 Egypt's ___ Simbel
93 Pot emission
96 Not be discreet
97 Classic Burris-Smith song "___ the Jack"
99 Greeting for Legree
101 Reason for an identity crisis
103 Relates again
104 Certain berth
106 Cove
107 Southernmost city in Illinois
109 Canine command
110 They released "Days of Future Passed" in 1967
112 "Back to the Future" figure
114 Author of "The Army of the Future"
115 Will Durant's wife
116 Question session
117 Future et al.
118 Reunion group
119 Ex-"Ellen" actor Gross

DOWN

1 Double-deck game
2 Big Band singer Helen
3 Fought-over peninsula
4 Orinoco shocker
5 Muffin alternatives
6 Fulfilled a crowing need
7 Where Qum is
8 Futura maker
9 Party outsider: Abbr.
10 Enlist
11 Takes one's mitts off
12 Lay one's mitts on
13 "Comin' ___!" (3-D western of 1981)
14 Attach anew, as lug nuts
15 Navy enlistee
18 Black-clad mercenary
19 Bats
21 Crunch's rank
22 Awfully long time
23 White House bud, in the future
26 Lady of Brazil
29 Grosse ___, Mich.

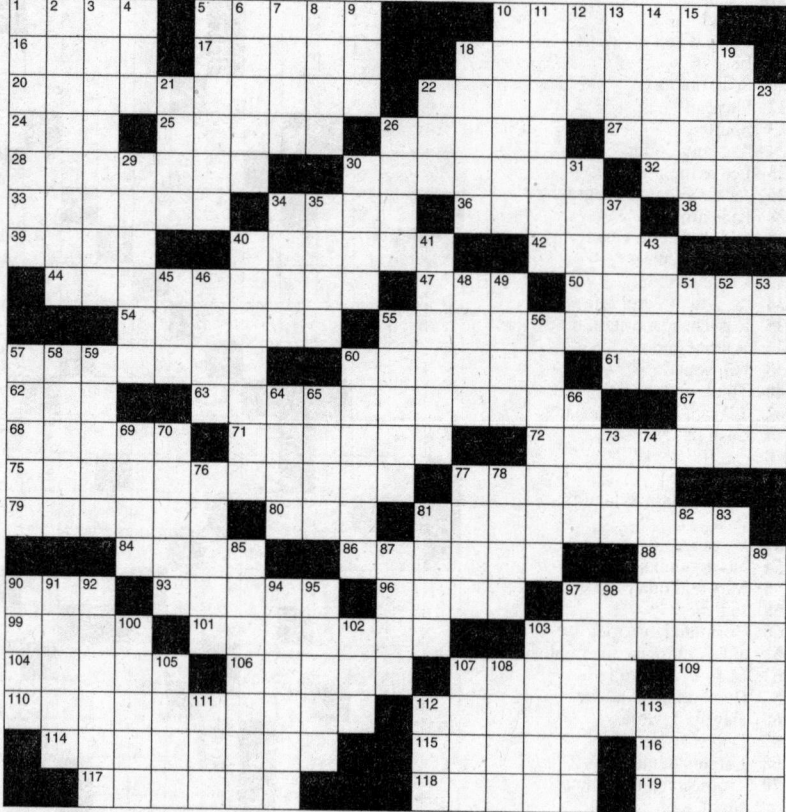

by Merl Reagle

30 "The lady ___ protest too much": Shak.
31 Trap
34 Today's dodo count
35 Literary plotter
37 Old Italian royal house
40 Alit
41 It's hard, on your feet
43 Actress Lenska
45 Abbr. at an exchange office
46 Chucklehead
48 Horse color
49 "Hee Haw" fodder?
51 Cousin of Corinthian pink
52 105-Down, notably
53 Tacky?
55 Long suit
56 Wipe out again
57 Popular mints
58 Isle be seeing you?
59 On-line need
60 Missile's heading
64 Reuniongoer
65 Admissions post
66 Character
69 They may clash on the set
70 Future doctors' test
73 No, in circular signs
74 Future teller
76 A Pointer sister
77 "Brave New World" joy juice
78 Manger upgrade
81 Hidalgo hi
82 Summons
83 Maker of Darvon and Prozac
85 "Fall River Legend" choreographer
87 Passing piece
89 Chic
90 Extremely busy
91 Two-legged rifle mount
92 e.e. cummings, e.g.
94 Invalidates
95 Soccer game outcome?
97 Greenish blues
98 Pile particle
100 Papyrus's family
102 French possessive
103 Standard practices
105 Strikeout king
107 Journalist Bernstein
108 "Turandot" tune
111 Airport shuttle
112 Bud
113 Spreadsheet pro

ACROSS

1 Melba and Moore, e.g.
6 Roast-masters
9 Thick serving
13 Consoling word to a loser
19 Medium
20 1978 Linda Ronstadt hit "___ Baby Baby"
21 Made tracks
22 Controversial Reagan adviser
23 Words by 7-Down
27 Place of bestial debauchery
28 Actress Talbot
29 Light
30 Decoratively painted metalware
31 Radio, for one
32 Minor matter
35 Flat bread?
36 Take the wind out of
40 Saskatchewan native
41 Trial locale
43 Its in French
44 See 73-Across
46 Singer LaBelle et al.
49 "Same Time, Next Year" playwright Bernard
50 They're Red, White . . . and blue
51 See 73-Across
54 It may be cocked
55 Realm of King Rama
56 Pop
57 Topped, in a way
59 Royal assistant
62 Cabinet member Federico
63 "Sleuth" actor
64 Key title
70 Wife of Abraham, originally
71 Bandleader Columbo
72 Temporary holder of property
73 With 44- and 51-Across, words by Francis Bellamy
75 Curly-leafed vegetable
76 Divided
77 Cry of mock indignation
80 With 86-Across, words by Katharine Lee Bates

82 Anklebones
83 Composer Saint-___
85 Like streets of Victorian London
86 See 80-Across
88 Yacht appendage
91 French seasoning
92 Van Gogh's "Letters to His Brother ___"
94 Bonds, in a way
95 Book in the Book of Mormon
97 Some ladies' garments
101 Stipulations
102 Cast
104 Fits with new sails
105 Noggin, to Brits
107 "___ on Indolence"
110 More words by 7-Down
114 Lined up
115 Nothing, in Nantes
116 Speaker's site, for short
117 Solzhenitsyn, in 1953
118 Spartan workers
119 Discounted by
120 Computer software letters
121 Macnee's 60's TV role

DOWN

1 Smidgens
2 Jim Croce's "___ a Name"
3 Exceedingly
4 Reinking of "Pippin"
5 Neolithic period
6 Nobel physicist Sir Nevill
7 Actor, dancer, playwright, singer and songwriter
8 ___ devil
9 Corona, e.g.
10 Relax
11 Sure alternative
12 1981 film biography
13 Commotion
14 Forsaken
15 Like some parties
16 Seedlets
17 Diana's Greek counterpart
18 Rendezvous
24 Bruce Gordon TV role
25 Worsted threads
26 Hygienist's concern
31 Kind of dog

33 English philosopher William of ___
34 Slangy goodbye
36 T, in code
37 Poet ___ Wheeler Wilcox
38 Lickspittle
39 Lighter
42 Type of lens
45 Converges on
46 Of the foot
47 ___ price (dearly)
48 Actor Everett
51 Deliveryman's device of yore
52 1986 Blake Edwards film spoof
53 It builds character
55 Union, e.g.: Abbr.
56 Smarts
58 "___ Rosenkavalier"
60 One way to be sick
61 Badges of infamy
62 São ___
64 Child's meas.
65 Moiety
66 Brooklyn institute
67 Levi's "Christ Stopped at ___"

68 Foolhardy
69 Crib
74 Mississippi has four
75 Trombonist Winding
76 Resort lake
78 Basie's "___ 'Clock Jump"
79 "This ___ outrage!"
81 First name in mysteries
82 Nagana carrier
83 Whines
84 Lifetimes
87 It's a long story
88 Fixation
89 Smoke
90 Part of "snafu"
92 Toys "R" Us goods
93 Actress Jean and others
96 Knock-down-drag-out
98 Rock's ___ Jam
99 "L.A. Law" lawyer
100 Play viewer's aid
103 Stimulate
106 All-thumbs apology
107 Tony's cousin

108 Senate V.I.P.
109 Leered
111 Copy workers: Abbr.
112 Family V.I.P.
113 Part of a telephone no.

by Alex K. Justin

ACROSS

1 Quite the rage
5 "Throw ___ from the Train"
10 Abbr. in car ads
13 Gilt
19 Top of the line
20 Ne plus ultra
21 Associate of Tigger the Tiger
22 One of the Beverly Hillbillies
23 1990 Craig Lucas play
26 Rich fabric
27 Go with
28 Old-fashioned
29 Galatea's beloved
30 Agathe and others: Abbr.
31 Lofty perch
32 Onetime Hershey's rival
35 Contributing ___
38 "It is a nipping ___ eager air": Shakespeare
39 Location of many bars
42 Side petals of a flower
43 1966 Wilson Pickett hit
46 Anderson's "High ___"
47 Skedaddles
48 ___-disant (so called)
49 Good-sized
50 Sphinx site
51 Sample
52 "Hurts So Good" singer
57 Dred Scott Justice
58 Purpose
59 Robt. ___
60 Worker, informally
61 Disposes of evidence, in a way
62 Colorful perennial
64 Sculptor George
65 Stone heap
66 One of the twins in "Twins"
68 ___-ski
69 Caramel-topped dessert
70 Literary monogram
73 Copacetic state
74 Shelley work
76 ___ glance
77 Criticized
78 L.B.J. biographer Robert
80 Propeller
81 France's ___ de Glénans
82 Sorority letter
83 1954 Kurosawa classic, with "The"
88 Give way
89 Boost the battery
91 Cache
92 Let down one's guard
94 Tilts
95 Person with a mission
96 ___ cosa (something else): Sp.
97 Small airport craft, for short
99 First woman in the British Parliament
100 Places for doctors' strikes?
104 Author Raymond
107 Oklahoma group
109 News interruption
110 Chess champ Mikhail
111 Certain addicts
112 Actress ___ May Oliver
113 Fit
114 Rte. 66, e.g.
115 Feminist Lucy
116 Baritone

DOWN

1 Bullfighter's red cloak
2 ___ de combat
3 ___ de Castro (Spanish noblewoman)
4 Piano pedals that mute the strings
5 College test
6 "Waiting for Lefty" playwright
7 "Take ___ your leader"
8 Much-quoted luminary
9 San Francisco suburb
10 Stemming
11 Group on horseback
12 Looking up
13 Nightwear, for short
14 Wildflower site
15 Onslaught
16 Hammett character
17 "... ___ saw Elba"
18 Capos
24 Golden-rule word
25 It starts "In the name of Allah ..."
31 Prank
32 Not shrinking
33 Paris destination
34 Piggery
35 Disloyal
36 Novelist Robbe-Grillet
37 Carter compact
38 Collectively
39 Laissez-___
40 Displayed, as charm
41 Dentist's shots
44 House of Poe
45 Stop running
50 "Mr. Mom" co-star, 1983
52 Overhang
53 Low-fat alternative
54 "Yolanta," e.g.
55 Presses
56 "___ Alice" (antidrug film)
57 "Just ___!"
61 Mosel feeder
63 Spot
64 Scoop (up)
65 David Copperfield's mother
66 Adventurous one
67 Gush
68 Up ___ (stuck)
69 Distress signal
71 Publisher Hoffenberg
72 Let up
75 Porter's "___ Got That Thing"
78 Legal writ from an appeals court, briefly
79 Middle amts.
81 Influenced
83 ___ Bruno, Calif.
84 First word of "Ulysses"
85 Fire
86 Times hence
87 High-powered
90 Honeyed Turkish confection
93 Range of expertise
95 "Fiddlesticks!"
96 Tie ___
97 Lowlife
98 Runner's goal
99 Pituitary hormone, for short
100 Vegas attraction
101 Man Friday
102 Corn cake
103 Cereal sound
105 When Paris sizzles
106 Raw
108 Do-it-yourselfer's start

by Dean Niles

ACROSS

1 Work well together
5 Virgil genre
9 Ill-gotten gains
13 "___ not amused"
18 "Now ___ me down to sleep"
19 Chute opening
20 Tashi's superior
21 Crowns
22 Stir up
23 Boardwalk purchases
24 Vic Damone's "___ But One Heart"
25 Perlman and others
26 Shakespeare's lament upon crashing? ("Henry VIII" I, 1)
30 Many a "Star Trek" alien
31 Like
32 Code carrier
33 Interjections of doubt
34 Cowpoke
37 It's far above Cayuga's waters
42 Shakespeare reviews hypertext? ("Othello" III, 4)
47 Astrological aspect
48 Word with first or foreign
49 Old film studio
50 Less than regular
51 Düsseldorf dog
52 Bargain
54 Wife of Constantine the Great
57 "Brave Men" author, 1944
58 21st, e.g.
60 Foray
62 Soupçon
64 Shakespeare's cry when he can't click an icon? ("Twelfth Night" I, 5)
71 Wings
72 Heaven, to Henri
73 Fortuneteller's aid
74 New Mexico's Enchanted ___
78 Rock's ___ Brothers
80 Characteristic property
82 Carry (away)
83 School on the Seine
85 ___ Schwarz
86 Writer ___ Louise Huxtable
87 Actress ZaSu
88 Why Shakespeare logs on at night? ("The Two Gentlemen of Verona" III, 1)
94 Intl. humanities agcy.
95 Boo-boos
96 Kind of wheels
97 "I ___ Rock"
99 LP's center?
100 Odd couple
105 Shakespeare on planting a virus? ("All's Well That Ends Well" III, 3)
112 Sixth-century B.C. author
113 1909 Physics Nobelist
114 Table d'___
115 One that gets a leg up?
116 Ship to remember
117 Springy
118 One on-line
119 Hightails it
120 Queue
121 Sawbones
122 Caves
123 Grease, as one's way

DOWN

1 Great amusement
2 Mr. Yale
3 Peabody Museum site
4 Laughing one
5 Typification
6 Game with a cross-shaped board
7 Companion of Artemis
8 Lip
9 Iranian royal name
10 Israeli airline
11 Lap against, as the shore
12 Brute
13 Military courses
14 Early satellite
15 "Indeed!"
16 Printer's ___
17 Start of North Carolina's motto
20 Scripts, mostly
27 Habituate
28 Its symbol is F
29 28-Down, e.g.
34 Youngest son of Ivan the Terrible
35 Beige
36 Old Oriental vehicle: Var.
38 Kentucky product
39 Kind of game
40 Tiny room
41 Up to it
42 Cape Cod resort town
43 Brahmanist
44 "The ___ near!"
45 Former Neb.-based defense org.
46 Disfavoring
47 ___ McAn shoes
52 Saint Francis of ___
53 That is hay
54 Assimilate
55 Together, musically
56 Goose genus
59 Teachers' org.
61 Old treasure chest
63 United competition
65 Having a curtainlike membrane
66 Aquatic plant
67 Rodrigo Diaz de Bivar
68 Gaucho's necesidad
69 1955's Best Picture
70 Young newts
74 Dishes
75 College major, slangily
76 A portion
77 "Oh, woe!"
79 "Silent Night" writer Joseph
81 County officials, for short
84 Settled
86 Follow, as an impulse
87 Miniature
89 Very comfortable
90 Two-year-olds, generally
91 Husky, e.g.
92 Bewitched
93 Severe critics
98 "___ as things may seem . . ."
100 Bucolic bugler
101 Lit
102 Shinbone
103 Film showings
104 "Siddhartha" novelist
105 Certain foot
106 Syrup flavor
107 Govt. publicity grp.
108 Author Morrison
109 As a result
110 Churchgoer
111 Bomb's sound

by James Savage

ACROSS

1 Muezzin's call at a mosque
5 Bottomless pit
10 Escapade
14 Cutlass cut
18 Hitachi competitor
19 Give a price
20 Unsteady on one's feet
22 One of the Furies
24 TV knob
25 Proponent
26 Nun, e.g.
28 Demographic datum
29 Captain of the Sáo Gabriel
30 Earth-moving equipment?
31 ___ publica
32 Cinnabar and barite
33 Overrefined
35 Speakeasy customer
36 Joey ___ and the Starliters
37 Burns' "___ Mouse"
38 Laugh: Fr.
39 Start of a laugh
40 Hindu gentlemen
42 Kind of timer
43 "Enough, Giuseppe!"
45 Foreshadow
49 Ancient Roman priests
51 "All ___!" (court phrase)
53 Nightmare
55 Broadcast
56 Gate-crasher?
59 Ivan, e.g.
60 "Ben-Hur" studio
63 Exams for would-be workers
64 People with lists
65 Sale-price abbr.
66 Noted spokestuna
67 Social hangers-on
68 Cherished one
69 Computer company
70 Geom. figure
71 Bambi's aunt
72 Barker and Kettle
73 South China, e.g.
74 Balancer, of sorts
77 1958 song "___ Blu, Dipinto di Blu"
78 Handel's "___, Galatea e Polifemo"
79 Celtic Neptune
80 1995 House chant
81 Greek
83 Kind of cross
84 "Odyssey" fruit
87 1960 John Wayne movie
89 Ernie of the P.G.A.
90 Match king Kreuger
91 Patsy?
92 Printer's daggers
93 Smash hit
94 Case worker: Abbr.
95 Like a drunk's speech
97 Professional soc.
98 Song of joy
101 Auto ad abbr.
103 Hypnotic ingredient in medicine
104 QB's goals
106 "Oranges & Lemons" rock group
107 Telecommunications corp.
108 "We Do Our Part" org.
109 Darker than chestnut
111 Jellyfish
115 Fortune
116 Years and years
117 Sidling arachnid?
120 Pieces of pieces of eight
122 Phone dial trio
123 Lorgnettes
124 Loses vigor
125 Clock hour
126 Conspectus
127 First name in silents
128 Atlas picture
129 Verb type: Abbr.
130 Jocular Johnson
131 Otherwise
132 Has to have
133 Architect ___ van der Rohe

DOWN

1 Aphrodite's Semitic counterpart
2 Re the science of animal distribution
3 "Patriot Games" actress?
4 Humorist Bill
5 Locales for swordtails
6 "1985" novelist
7 Meditative methods
8 Check
9 Shawl for siestas
10 Actress Christine
11 Tracts
12 Picture puzzle
13 Dairy cattle breed
14 Tenor sax great
15 Followed, as a tip
16 Sound investments
17 Engine power, informally
21 100 bani
22 Brilliant orange star of the northern sky
23 Circus stars?
27 Storm heading
29 June bug
34 Breaks violently again
39 Measures for punts
41 Bunk
44 Trident feature
46 Final notices
47 They're often paid
48 Pluralizer
49 Aspect
50 1929 Gershwin song
52 To-do
54 Shaw's "___ and Cleopatra"
56 Berrylike
57 Havoc
58 "The very ___!"
60 Diamond club?
61 Superman's bane
62 Bald man of advertising
64 Poisonous mushrooms
68 Kin of silverware
73 Ancient marine "hazards"
74 Whack
75 Bergamot, e.g.
76 Leagues
79 Attention-grabbing
80 Linguist Chomsky et al.
82 Milk: Prefix
84 Gymnastic apparatus?
85 Baggy, as clothes
86 Scheherazade's recital
87 Mil. members
88 Lake from which the Blue Nile springs
91 Akihito's temple
92 Unconscious
95 Windshield clearer
96 Least fat
99 Noble
100 Gives proof
102 "La Loge" and "La Grenouillère," e.g.
103 Mooring for a Spanish galleon
105 Noted naturalist
110 Designer's monogram
111 ___-Mokwa ("Hiawatha" bear)
112 Corsair or Ranger
113 1936 Cooper role
114 Alpha ___ Minoris (Polaris)
115 Counterfeit
118 Rock's Mötley ___
119 Perfectly
121 Article written by Nietzsche
125 Get-up-and-go

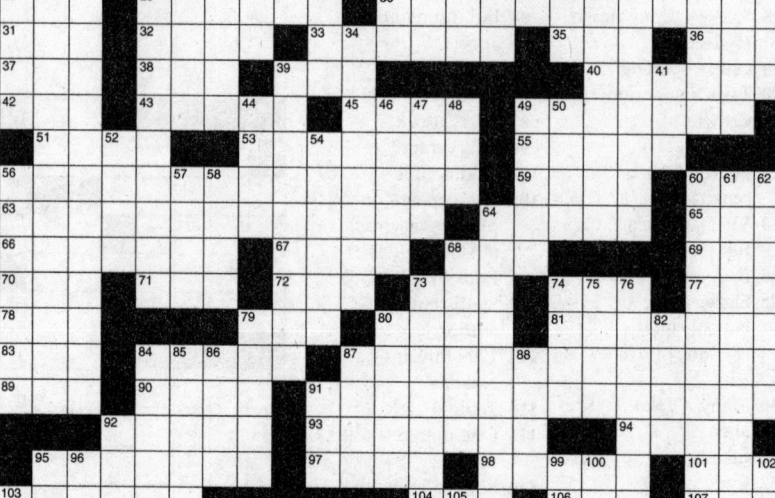

by Bryant White

ACROSS

1 Site of the Shandong Peninsula
5 "Closer to Fine" singers
11 Capital near Lake Tuz
17 MasterCard rival
19 Petrarch works
21 Took it easy
22 Swami routine of the old "Tonight Show"
23 Interminable
24 Some are French-cut
25 "The African Queen" scriptwriter
26 Bud, eventually
28 River to the Caspian
30 Polish writer Stanislaw
31 1961 Pulitzerwinning author
32 Orson's planet in 70's TV
33 TV show about agents Robinson and Scott
35 Makes, as a living
39 Horned vipers
41 Average grade
42 Pitcher Young and namesakes
43 Exploits
44 Judo level
45 Grill
47 Lose control on the road
49 Srta., across the Pyrenees
50 Retsyn-filled mint
51 Trinkets
55 Nighttime's start, in poetry
56 Verdi opera
58 "Bird ___ Wire"
59 Salon works
60 Name of 16 popes
62 Nora Helmer's creator
66 1968–75 Norris Trophy winner
67 Dept. of the Treasury div.
68 Luke was his disciple
69 Make a big effort
70 Table linen, often
72 After-shower scene
75 Doctor
76 Toxic defoliant
77 Lover of Aphrodite
78 Flight board abbr.
79 Edison, e.g.: Abbr.
80 Tanzanian coins
81 Coquette
84 Actress Zadora
85 Kind of ball or card
86 Basketball ploy
88 Cell stuff
89 Lures into wrongdoing
91 "I hear you," to a CB operator
94 Fermented
95 Years and years
97 Josh
98 Coach Parseghian
99 It's shocking!
100 Poivre's partner
101 One-fifth of MMV
103 Shoe coverer
107 Most colored by the sun
109 Tad
110 ___ Tin Tin
111 Louisville Slugger material
112 Douglas, for example
113 Sale place
115 Mao successor
116 Hugh Hefner prop
117 Negatively charged atoms
120 Where to see 72-Across
123 1986 Spacek/Kline flick
125 Algiers's old quarter
126 Run-scoring bunt
127 Vonnegut's "The ___ of Titan"
128 Name of two English kings
129 Made an MRI picture
130 Letter opener?

DOWN

1 It might have the heading "Vacuum-Van"
2 Silkwood portrayer
3 "___ kleine Nachtmusik"
4 Doogie Howser's org.
5 They prey on small mammals
6 Boo-boo
7 B&B
8 Hosp. workers
9 Pauses
10 Floor
11 "Let's Stay Together" singer
12 They always have titles
13 Some MOMA paintings
14 Dessert option
15 Stimpy's buddy
16 Commercials
17 Central Florida city
18 Novel that features the language Nadsat
20 Health club
27 Before, to Byron
29 Stahl of "60 Minutes"
33 More frigid
34 Actor in "The Maltese Falcon" and "Casablanca"
36 Hull attachment
37 Old Mideast inits.
38 Explosive stuff
40 Wilt
43 Kind of lamp
46 Cruel
48 College party essential
49 Song also recorded as "Harlem Footwarmers"
50 Army attack helicopter
51 ___ gold
52 Incense
53 Soldiers
54 Draft org.
57 Intellectuals
61 Michigan Wolverine cheer
63 Glass ingredient
64 Tie
65 Anxiety
69 Self-effacing people
71 Uneasy
72 Bridge situation
73 Curaçao ingredient
74 Less brave
78 Imitate
81 Allegiance
82 ___ Gay
83 Kurosawa's "King Lear"
87 Greek letters
90 Rural rtes.
91 Socks, e.g.
92 ___ pro nobis
93 Perch, for example
96 Fastened with threads?
99 Springy
100 It explodes when wet
102 Racket
104 Sock sorter
105 Fluttering trees
106 Despondency
108 Tantalus's daughter
109 Kirkuk native
114 "___ magna" (anagrams, appropriately)
115 Nap
116 ___-mutuel
117 King's superior
118 Actor Pendleton
119 Bit
121 Teachers' org.
122 Petition
124 Family girl

by Peter Gordon

ACROSS

1 Mountain lion
5 Kind of jet
9 Slangy thrill
13 Dishearten
19 Buckinghamshire town
20 "Casablanca" actress Gruning
21 Friend to Colette
22 Eyepiece, in jargon
23 Where to find pay dirt
26 Guardian spirits of ancient Rome
27 Lonely place
28 Ford of old
29 Customized
30 Nation of citrus addicts?
34 Dried up
35 Measure marker
38 U.S.N. division
39 Turkish inn
41 Uttered a taradiddle
43 Chassé
48 M-G-M motto start
49 The "id" in "id est"
52 Loathing
54 Arithmetic teacher's announcement?
58 Boozing musicians?
60 Powering force
61 La Scala locale
62 Levene and Levenson
65 More flashy
66 W.W. II Brit. group
70 Saint a.k.a. Apostle to the Slavs
72 Birth-related
74 Bollix (up)
75 Mistreat
77 Rip off
79 Back, to entomologists
81 Sheer fabrics
82 Bunch of steamed-up hobos?
88 Bottom of Miss Riding Hood's cloak?
92 Fifth-century invader
93 By and by
94 Balderdash
95 Hebrew letter before koph
96 Grammy-winning Braxton
97 Hat with a creased crown
99 Ella or elle

102 Arrested Development offering
103 Union betrayer
106 Words to a charades-playing woman?
113 Firms, as abs
115 Ancient Greek colony
116 Offensive, in a way
120 Historical records
121 Warped?
124 Dorm mate
125 Not crumbly
126 "The NeverEnding Story" writer
127 Grand
128 Guarded get-togethers
129 The middle son, on 60's TV
130 Ostiary's post
131 TV actress Dietrich

DOWN

1 Nudnik
2 Delta Center team
3 Actuate
4 One of the Pointer Sisters
5 "Peanuts" character
6 Dr. Jekyll's creator, for short
7 Giraffelike beast
8 Stampede stimulus
9 Sled dog of a 1995 film
10 O'Neill's "___ for the Misbegotten"
11 Actress Long of "Boyz N the Hood"
12 Cat's-eye
13 One of Santa's team
14 Neighbor of Peru: Abbr.
15 Avoids a sticky situation?
16 In crowd
17 Chair fixer, perhaps
18 Part of Nafta
24 Pitcher Hideo
25 Forensic letters
29 Pile up
31 With justice
32 Neeson of "Nell"
33 50's Hungarian leader Nagy
35 Out-of-focus picture
36 Opera set in Memphis
37 Control
40 People: Prefix
42 Bomb

44 "Paganini" composer Franz et al.
45 Pacific
46 Wagner's "___ Fliegende Hollaender"
47 French coins of yore
50 Digression
51 Medley material
53 Pop idol?
55 Mideast's Gulf of ___
56 Roman earth goddess
57 Bodies of eau
59 Most like Nelly
63 La ___, Spain
64 Kept in the attic
66 Two-time skating gold medalist
67 Hello or goodbye
68 Exotic
69 All smiles?
71 Lion of Hollywood
73 Particle-based philosophy
76 Rouen's river
78 Champagne name

80 Ed.'s trayful
83 Receivers make them, for short
84 Be up
85 Pompeia, to Caesar
86 Pulitzer poet Van Duyn
87 Impudent imp
89 Tread heavily
90 Loughlin of "Full House"
91 Greek letters
98 Drenches
100 Cat, at times
101 Oscar-winning Thompson
103 Tee off
104 Irish author/diplomat O'Brien
105 Tee off
107 Tees (off)
108 Actors Calhoun and O'Brien
109 Granddaughter of Queen Victoria
110 Judged, with "up"
111 Refuse
112 Caught congers
114 Incision

117 Relaxed gait
118 Chop cut
119 1978 Village People hit
121 Innsbruck interjection
122 Francisco or Paulo lead-in
123 Bustle

by Cathy Millhauser

ACROSS

1 Dance half
4 It comes in a case
9 Sudden activities
15 Some change: Abbr.
18 His Veep was George
19 Late Swedish P.M.
20 Sung story
22 Part of 59-Across
23 Ford portrayal
26 Alice's boss on "Alice"
27 Gathers on the surface, chemically
28 Prefix denoting equality
29 Inculcate, as suspicion
30 Time Inc. magazine
32 Big night for teens
33 Musical notes
35 Words to a traitor
37 ___ dogs (lab experiment subjects)
38 60's war site
39 Subcontinent language
41 Medical school subject
42 Prior to
43 Roy Orbison's "___ Over"
44 Author who served as U.S. minister to Spain
47 Funny Caesar
48 Mazda offering
50 Serengeti roamer
51 "Put ___ my bill"
52 Volvo rival
54 Segovia medium
57 Lotion ingredients
59 Note in a poker game, e.g.
60 Botanical seed
62 Unexpected blessing
64 Bird on a Canadian dollar
66 Girl of a 1925 song
71 Dessert maker's equipment
72 Captaincy
73 Major force in chess
74 Bachelor's home
75 Moore co-star on 70's TV
79 According to law
81 Supermarket checkers do it
85 Gaslight and others

87 Shaped (up)
89 Takes home
91 Woodcutter in a children's story
92 Author in the Bloomsbury Group
96 Noted judge
97 Pro Bowl team: Abbr.
98 1983 World Series champs
99 Gained
101 Casual negative
102 Kind of letter
103 Contrary one
104 Neither's partner
105 Picasso contemporary
106 Prepare for slumber
107 Shriver of tennis
108 "Caught you!"
110 Encyclopedia Brown creator
111 Just fine
112 Two-time Pulitzer-winning playwright
117 Title on a Fr. envelope
118 Like some coastlines
119 Contact, in a way
120 Turn-of-the-century Pope
121 ___ favor
122 Pregame events
123 Declining, as a fire
124 Heir, sometimes

DOWN

1 Potato chip quality
2 Appearance moneys
3 Wife of Perseus
4 Karlovy Vary and others
5 Spank
6 Menu phrase
7 Full of mischief
8 Old autos
9 Poly ___
10 Twiddle one's thumbs
11 Neighbor of Bretagne
12 Pack
13 "Wow!"
14 Make way
15 20-Across, e.g.
16 Redundant time
17 Graf rival
21 Letter closing
24 Apple foe
25 Trompe ___ (optical trick)

31 Legendary Norwegian king
33 Marathon problem
34 It often comes with a battery
36 Shot
37 Jane Campion film, with "The"
39 Korean surname
40 Keep guard
41 Push-button alternative
45 Insider of a sort
46 Endangered animal
49 "___ yellow ribbon . . ."
53 Get spares, perhaps
55 Having the power
56 Explorer Amundsen
58 Wild plum
61 Sacred Hindu text
63 "This one's ___"
65 Admits (to), with "up"
66 Thin snack
67 Cast
68 Crayon color
69 Sonora snack

70 Type in again
71 Name in Democratic politics
74 Apiece
76 Ritzy contraband
77 Three trios
78 Some eligible receivers
80 Bridges or Daniels
82 "Robinson Crusoe" extras
83 Popular sports car
84 Joker portrayer
86 Evade
88 Neurotransmitter of note
90 Earth
93 Illinois city
94 Hockey Hall-of-Famer
95 Like a boy scout
100 Possibly
102 34-center
103 Song thrush
105 "Li'l ol' me!"
107 Many college profs.
109 Drove
110 Toil
113 ___ Canals

114 Gridiron positions: Abbr.
115 ___ Amin
116 Mao associate ___ Piao

by Matt Gaffney

ACROSS

1 Made creases
7 Brooklyn institute
12 Filled in holes
17 Stomach soother
21 ___ Islands, British protectorate until 1965
22 She played the woman in "A Man and a Woman"
23 Fall off
24 Give off
25 Avocado
27 Opening of 1914
29 "Ministry of Fear" director
30 "Our Miss Brooks" actress
31 Spoil
33 Disinclined
34 Business V.I.P.
35 Temptingly tasty
37 Thirsty
38 Sound from Sandy
41 Roles for Oland and Toler
43 Site of Jesus' first miracle
44 Belief
48 Achieved
50 Gather
52 Herds of whales
53 "The Diamond Queen" actress
54 Imperfect
55 Visitor of 1986
57 Skater Babilonia
58 ___ one
59 Foreshadows
60 Compelled to go
61 Tee, e.g.
63 Basslike
64 "___ Le Moko," 1937 film
65 Dog, in a way
66 Foil
67 Train station abbr.
68 Producer of motion pictures?
72 Family name on TV's "Alf"
73 Rascal
75 Peter of cable's VH-1
76 Alternative to waffles
77 Mother-of-pearl source
79 Western wear
82 Cleaner, for short
85 B-29
86 Pulled into
87 Honker
88 Founder of the Stoics
89 Peter Mansfield book, with "The"
90 Mediterranean shipping center
91 Was inattentive
93 River to the Caspian
94 ___ Marino
95 X, for example
98 Western capital
99 "Holy smoke!"
101 Night times
102 Architect Jones
103 English game played with horse chestnuts
104 Returned-mail notation
106 Sweetheart
107 Singer Judd
109 Literary inits.
110 Stand
111 Shakespeare's "fairy favours"
113 1965 Ursula Andress film
114 Deposed
117 90's parties
118 "Tiny Alice" playwright and family
120 Canvas
124 Captain's superior
126 Slow method
129 Word of woe
130 Supporter of the arts
131 Window shades of a sort
132 Turn on
133 Thérèse and others: Abbr.
134 Red and spotted, e.g.
135 Darling
136 Gossips

DOWN

1 Insignificant
2 Greenhouse bloom
3 Frigg's husband
4 Co-star of "The Avengers"
5 "Uncle Tom's Cabin" girl
6 Impartial
7 Inmate's wish
8 Ready
9 Fix
10 ___ service
11 Of third rank
12 Per ___
13 Erie Canal city
14 "Critique of Pure Reason" author
15 Letter in a fraternity name
16 Actor William
17 Withdrew
18 Early astronomer
19 Noises
20 Start of a Dickens title
26 Greek nymph
28 Keen
32 Record
36 Farmland
37 Pistol-packing
38 Loser of 1588
39 Lector
40 Popular weather forecaster
41 Mr. Huntley
42 Burnt
44 Kind of back or hair
45 Movie starring "King"
46 Accusation
47 More noble
49 Los Angeles gang member
51 Hurrah!
52 Rangers' defense
55 Noted potters
56 Hitching post?
59 "Out of my way!"
61 Tee off
62 Practice, so to speak
64 Four-time Masters winner
65 Harmonizing
66 Strip, for one
68 Actress Carol et al.
69 Kind of show
70 Unit of loudness
71 Part of the works
74 Batting wonder, 1905–28
76 Prattle
77 Belittled
78 Blue-flowered European herb
79 Byes
80 Titania's husband
81 Neighbor of Tibet
83 Tees off
84 Vulgar
86 Still
88 Knock out
90 Van line
91 Snap request?
92 Cabriole
93 First of an ancient trio
95 Sowed again
96 Daughter of Tantalus
97 Like some numbers
98 "___ Book," circa 1086
100 Leaves
103 Comedian Myron
105 Leontyne Price role
106 Robert and Shelley
108 ___ as ABC
111 More collectible, maybe
112 Juices
114 Mountains south of the Kara Sea
115 Groomed
116 Official's staff
117 Mezzo-soprano Stevens
119 Farm worker
120 1982 Disney film
121 In ___ (stuck)
122 Sub ___
123 White House abbr.
125 She played W.C.'s "chickadee"
127 "Norma ___"
128 Long intro

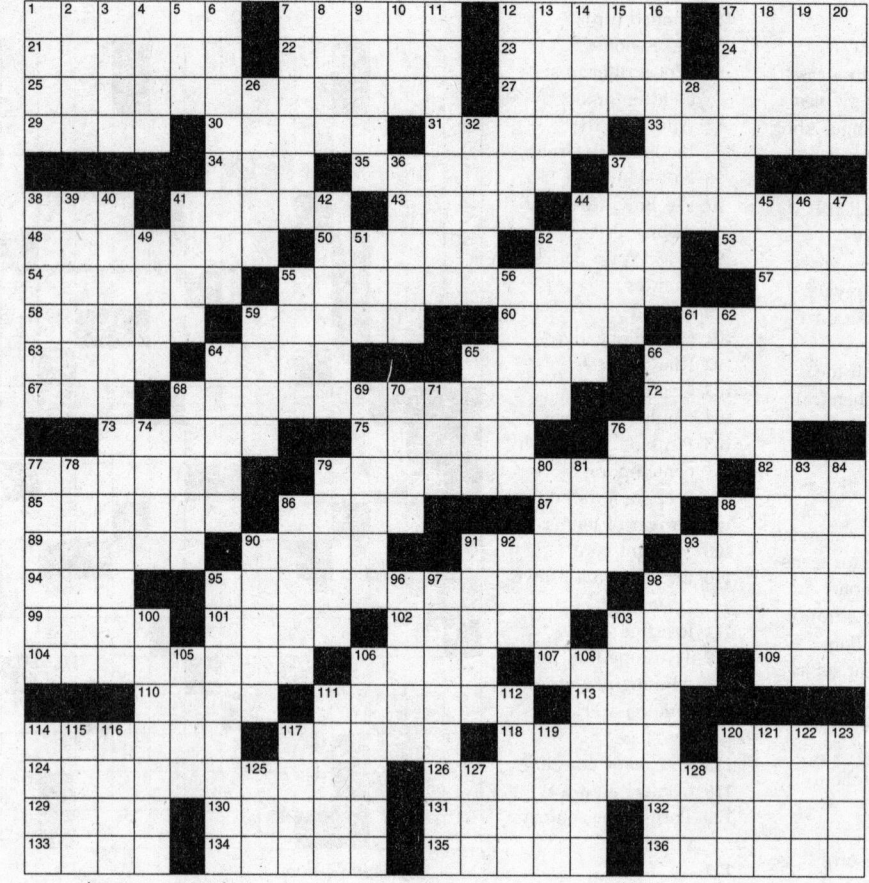

by Bette Sue Cohen

ACROSS

1 Innocents
6 Small heavy ropes
13 Part of a Mayberry address
16 Ordinarily
18 Apply, as enamel
19 Bank deposits
21
23 Bonaventure, for one
24 Ivy Leaguer
25 Pat Riley, once
26 ___ Canals
27 Account amount
29 Tyke watcher
31 Ticks off
33 Discothèque feature
35 Continental prefix
37 Handrail post
39 Equine vote?
40 Outer coat of a pollen grain
41 Routine
43 Neurological point
45 Grain supplies
46 Word with screen or teen
48 Mon ___
49 "Mon Oncle" star
50
56 Discriminators of a sort
60 Corona, e.g.
61 Bedtime for some
62 Comforts
64 Very stylish
65 "Flash Gordon" creator ___ Raymond
66 Lineman
68 Hobo transportation
69 Entangle
70 Door word
71 Olden warriors
73 "___ on parle . . ."
74 Windy home
75 Small talk
77
80 Electric units
81 Room for expansion
82 Biblical verb
83 Young runners
86 Dos Passos's Annabelle et al.
90 Fine-quality paper
94 Life and others
95 Long-jawed pike
96 Forms of address
98 Singer ___ Marie
99 Develops fully
102 Criticizes, with "down"

104 More than "phooey!"
105 Using two musical keys
106 Manuscript encl.
108 Island off Scotland
110 Holiday party serving
111 College major, informally
112
116 Barbecue order
117 Cosmetic
118 Buttons, thread, ribbons, etc.
119 Fleur-de-___
120 Helmsman
121 Short pants

DOWN

1 Thin sheets
2 Wall St. dealer
3 "Fernwood 2-Night" star
4 Bedim
5 Pianist Peter
6 1040 worker
7 Some notices at LAX
8 Hound
9 Snorkeling locales
10 Author LeShan
11 Spirited lass
12 "Golf Begins at Forty" author
13
14 Last Holy Roman emperor
15 Ancestry
16 Solicitors
17 Kind of cap
18 Off the wall
20 Cordwood measures
22 Tennis star making a return?
28 Son of Polonius
30 Avoiding duties?
32 French assembly
34 Leave: Scot.
36 Meal with wine
38 "Final Impact" star
42 Soft shoe
44 Stacker
45 Light green plums
47 Calif. paper
49 Agreed
50 Rogue
51 Worker on hands and knees
52 Rocket stage
53 Where the Amazon arises
54 Naturally sluggish

55 Coffee spot
57 Bake in a shallow dish
58 Decorative Japanese gateway
59 Immerse
63 Twitches
66 Climb the ___
67 Upbeat critic
69 Like some water
71 J.R. headgear
72 Fakir's faith
74 Goodwill, e.g.
76
78 Forelimb bones
79 "Mazel ___!"
83 Soprano Eleanor
84 Spiral-shaped
85 Convention activity
86 Squatted
87 Valley span
88 Star cluster
89 Sting
91 Sheds
92 Like high hay, e.g.
93 Juicy fruits
95 Small trading vessel
97 Leaving time?

100 Life-saving equipment
101 Announcer
103 Navigators Islands, today
107 Villa d' ___
109 Mosquito protection
113 Shakespearean exclamation
114 Kind of verb: Abbr.
115 Taste, as soup

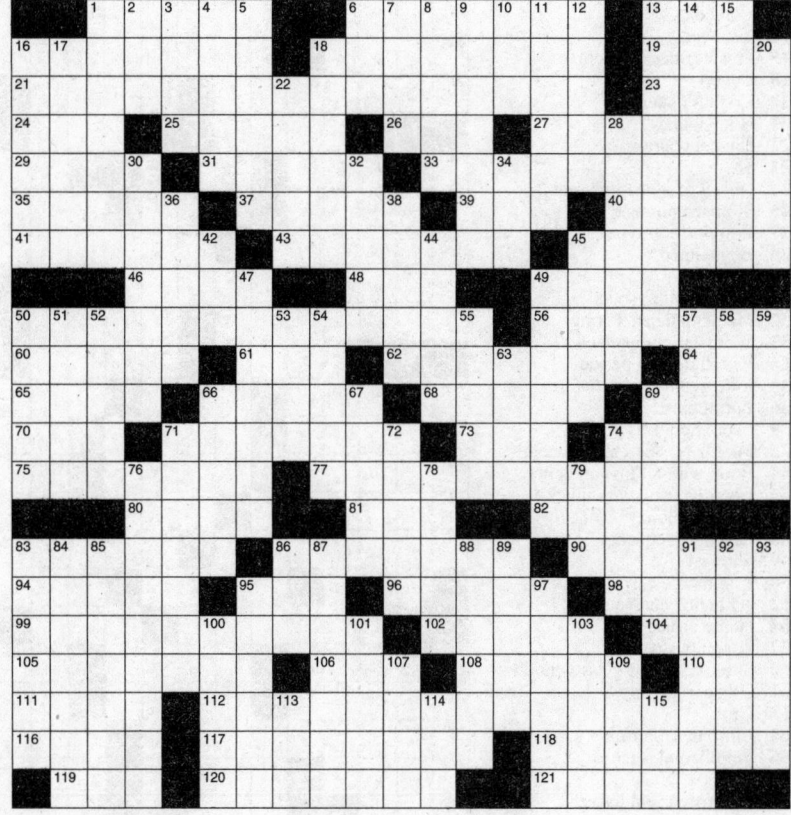

by Jim Page

ACROSS

1 Biblical transport
4 Comedians, often
11 ___ War
15 Fresh Prince medium
18 Covert
20 Couldn't stand
21 Hoof sound
22 Handel opera
23 So
24 Object of a onetime search
25 Stomach ailment
27 Composition type
29 Be inclined
30 Due
31 Euro meeting spots
32 Mathematician Turing
33 Words of comparison
34 Revolutionary period
35 Like gymnasts
36 Barrel part
39 Econ. figure
42 First U.N. Secretary General
44 Book with a Mass audience
46 Communicate with quickly
47 Modern money
48 Alphabet sequence
49 Showy
50 And more
52 "Othello" character
54 Home project
57 Aspen business
60 Site for stained-glass windows
61 70's pop greasers
63 Grok
65 Einstein or Fermi, e.g.
66 Pulp fictionesque
68 Allege
69 Newspaper publisher Chandler
71 Betelgeuse's constellation
72 ___ mouthful
73 One looking for a match?
74 Shah name
75 Mercury project hero
76 Up to this point
79 Part of many E-mail addresses
81 Across the street from: Abbr.
83 ___ Kan pet foods
84 QB John
85 Fad doll of the 90's
86 Basis for financial aid
88 Collegians' extracurricular activity
90 Hawks' arena
92 Like some bars
93 Aspirin target
94 Galba's successor
95 Life jacket
99 Ancient documents
101 "___ De-Lovely" (1937 hit)
102 Modem requirement
104 Tresses, in Dresden
105 Massaged
107 Proverbial last-place finishers
109 Not right
111 Novel subtitled "A History of Adventure"
112 Tiller's start
114 Legendary Latin hero
115 Royal Dutch Airlines
117 Little amount
118 "Here . . . !"
120 Neighbor of Russ.
121 Main
122 They come with bows and beaus

123 J. D. Cameron book series
125 Manx's lack
127 It can come as a shock
130 "Phooey!"
132 City on the Rhine
133 First Bond flick
134 Like 50's LP's
136 Nestlé bar
140 1912 Peace Nobelist
142 Stuffing for olives
144 It's a laugh
145 Repro
146 Kind of soup
147 Best Actor of 1992
148 Rank
149 Cochlea's locale
150 Fuss
151 Lugs
152 Young fellow

DOWN

1 Actor Guinness
2 Geena Davis sitcom
3 Speak with the hands
4 Hodgepodge
5 ___ guard
6 Phlebitis problem
7 Divided land
8 Photographer Walker ___
9 Advance in business
10 Hit letters
11 Former NBC newsman Frank
12 Where Forrest Gump grew up
13 Flared items
14 Choose
15 Schwarzenegger wannabe
16 Shakespearean sprite
17 Range group
19 Transportation for Charlie, in a Roald Dahl book
20 White cheese
22 Former rebel cry
26 Some TVs
28 Grandson of Catherine the Great, informally
30 Colorant
36 Hearty entrée
37 Musical speeds
38 Select group
40 March Madness org.
41 ___ Fell" (Beatles song)
43 "___ Fell" (Beatles song)
45 Benefit
48 Moolah
49 Like 70's inflation
51 Mexican beer brand
53 Needing a tan
55 One of the Monkees
56 Pervasive atmosphere
58 "Your Show of Shows" name
59 Kind of weight
62 Pack animal: Var.
64 Sphinx site
67 Five or six people, say
70 Biblical dancer
76 Quantity of poker chips
77 Vital ___
78 Make lots of noise

80 Metric prefix
82 Vichyssoise, e.g.
87 Mr. Arnaz
89 Drive-___
91 Japanese merchant ship
96 Brings home
97 Impertinence
98 Newspaper sources
100 Architect Saarinen
103 Vacation spot
106 "Stop!"
108 Injection amts.
110 Direction suggested by this puzzle's theme
113 Yellowish-pink flower
116 Strands
119 Asian border river
120 Jeff Lynne band
123 More than pudgy
124 Its capital is Valletta
126 Under one's charge
128 Zip
129 Shaq
131 Comment from Mr. Moto
135 Fairy tale start
137 Catch red-handed
138 Wife of Cronus
139 The "y" in Nimby
141 Y offerings: Abbr.
142 ___ allé (ballet move)
143 15%, maybe

by Matt Gaffney

ACROSS

1 Actress Moore
5 Some are giant
11 Physicist Ernst
15 Muddle
19 Little archer
20 "The Night of the ___"
21 Model-filled magazine
22 Pastiche
23 Novel about an aging tennis star?
26 Hockey position
27 Push ahead
28 Follow one's feet
29 Hole worlds to explore
30 Play based on a "Wild Kingdom" episode?
35 Basic question
36 Pulver's rank, in film: Abbr.
37 Overseas stop
38 Scholarship consideration
39 Amber, for one
41 Resigner before Richard
42 Boss
43 Minnesota poet Robert
46 Story of a tough town in Africa?
49 Ring around the castle
50 Gin fruit
51 Weevil, for one
52 Orinoco shocker
53 Grab (onto)
55 One home of 5-Across
56 Night predators
58 Exposé of airline pricing?
62 Chubby Checker's autobiography?
64 Play about a singer's army years?
65 Like Nash's lama
66 Like Seattle
67 Cyan
68 Fatherhood-testing info
69 Small amount
73 Jackie's dresser
74 Wind gust
76 Sequel to "Madame Bovary"?
79 Author Kaufman
80 Proud, energetic, domineering ones, they say
81 Musket's name, often
83 An archangel
84 Arizona city
85 Crème-filled munchies
86 Damage
88 Mr. Turner
89 Trashy best seller?
94 Big Schott
95 Stuff
96 More work
97 Famous words of accusation
98 Fashion book that will make you look like a million bugs?
104 Mighty god
105 Teeny bit
106 Washington airport
107 French theater
108 Faxed
109 Algerian port
110 Agree out of court
111 Jazz singer Anita

DOWN

1 3, on a phone
2 Newsworthy time
3 Way an organism develops
4 Grenoble's river
5 Frisbee forerunner
6 Shoelace tips
7 None: Prefix
8 Equine mother
9 Even the slightest
10 Type of acct.
11 Giant slugger
12 Kareem's God
13 Mozart's "La ___ di Tito"
14 John Madden sentence starter
15 Author Fast
16 Piers Paul Read thriller
17 Tendon
18 Sloppy eaters
24 ___ studies (college major)
25 Gluck hero
29 One-name star
30 Kind of song or park
31 Scruff
32 Determination
33 Three-time Hart Trophy winner
34 Plane reservation
35 Present coverage
40 Chanting
41 French seasoning
42 Snug
43 Guided only by instruments
44 Like Chandler's "Goodbye"
45 Term of endorsement
47 "Family Matters" actress Hopkins
48 Change to 000
49 Early synthesizers
50 Protector
53 Solemn
54 Director Riefenstahl
55 Cell suffix
57 Not straight
58 Place to play
59 Due process championer, familiarly
60 Air-mass boundary
61 Island veranda
62 One of the Durants
63 Picture poser
64 Seem trivial
66 "Knock over"
68 Letters after Clinton's name
70 Lysine or tryptophan
71 Ruin, as calligraphy
72 Stoppage
74 Partly
75 Chung or Rather, e.g.
76 It's little matter
77 Space race participant
78 Moon of Jupiter
80 Heartthrob Perry
81 Upset solver?
82 Poet's contraction
84 Healthy lunch
85 "The true measure ___ ..."
86 Barbie maker
87 Words after "loose as" or "silly as"
89 Shaping tool
90 "Loot" playwright
91 Actress Scacchi
92 Erected
93 70's "in" spot
94 "Miracle" group
98 Monterrey uncle
99 Radical 60's grp.
100 Whom: Fr.
101 Nth: Abbr.
102 ___ roll
103 "Brat Farrar" author

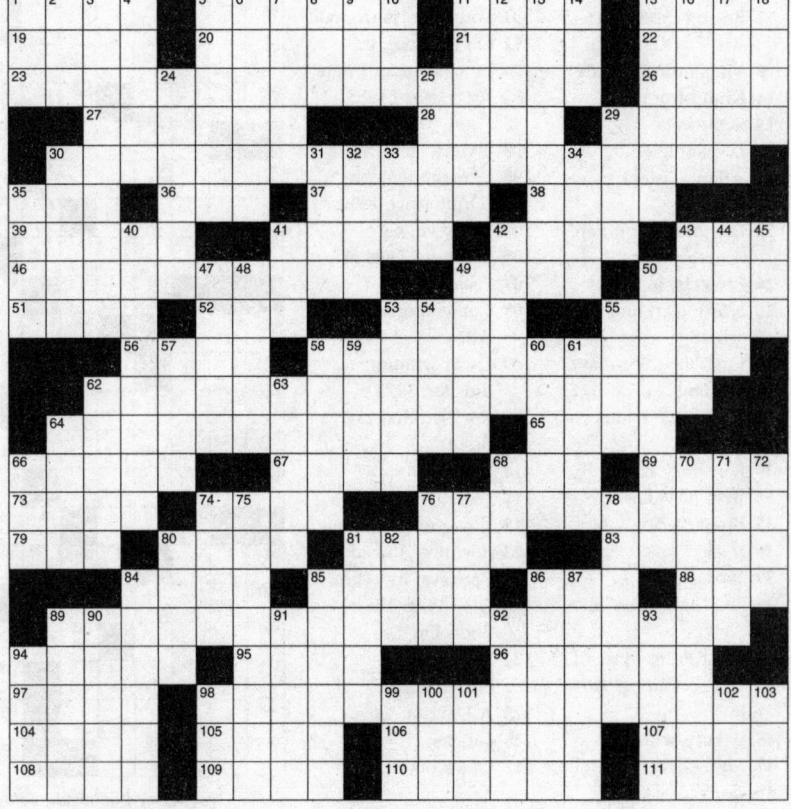

by Merl Reagle

Note: Answers to the asterisked clues have something in common

ACROSS

1 Boeing headquarters site
8 Midshipmen rivals
14 Kind of orange
19 Some cats
20 Unparalleled
21 Atlantic islands: Var.
22 *Harold Macmillan contemporary
24 Protects, in a way
25 North Carolina school
26 First U.N. Secretary General
27 Like some bands
29 Border
30 Lansbury role
32 Item of value
34 Broadcasting worry
36 *Flee
39 *Froufrou
42 "N.Y.P.D. Blue" title: Abbr.
43 West Point byword
44 "It ___ Fair" (1950 hit)
46 Bakery selection
47 Mini-spacecraft
49 Core
51 Wiped out
53 Lawn item
56 Multitude
57 "___ Help" (1974 song)
58 Ancient Persian teacher
60 Rod
63 *1919 children's classic
66 Like some records
67 Neighbor of Leb.
68 A little of this, a little of that
69 Verdi's "___ tu"
70 Censor's target
71 Jazzman Dickenson
72 Not moving so much
74 *Uninhibited school
76 Superlative ending
77 Brief fashion
80 Edible seaweed
81 Lettuce arrangement
84 Windows with more than a 180° view
85 Catches, in a way

87 Figures in capes
91 Forensic science tool
92 On the hoof, in lunch counter lingo
93 Agcy. since 1958
95 Plain
96 Swimwear item
98 *Stream denizen
101 *Drink since 1890
103 17-Down, e.g.
105 Hunt of "Twister"
107 Feeler
108 Contemporary of Bjorn
109 Oscar-winning director, 1974
112 Rock producer Brian
114 Prong
117 Form a connection
119 *Long time
122 Borrower's need
123 Portrayal in "They Died With Their Boots On"
124 Famed bacteriologist
125 A Davis
126 Guides
127 Gluck opera

DOWN

1 Benefit
2 Chemical compound
3 Nicknames
4 Important weather news
5 La preceder
6 Dished out
7 Actor Morales
8 Signal
9 Two of six for Henry VIII
10 Called
11 Some circles
12 Calendar abbr.
13 Barcelona-born architect
14 Bump hard
15 Having a heater
16 *MSG, e.g.
17 Tabloid favorite
18 Express
21 Veneered
23 Mergers and buyouts
28 Muckraker Tarbell et al.
31 Battle site of 1918

33 "What fools these mortals be" writer
35 Hard-top
36 1994 Harry Connick Jr. album
37 Flattens
38 Stop working
40 Court cry
41 Finger: Sp.
45 Trafficked
48 Hop-drying kiln
50 Talk-show features
52 Cold-weather garb
53 Familiar raincoat wearer
54 Wimbledon sections
55 Raise
57 Witness's words
59 Some butters
60 Doohickey
61 Up
62 *West Indies residents
64 Concession attachment
65 Creasey's Scotland Yarder
68 Arsenic accompaniment

70 Spoonful
73 Bank claim
75 Strasbourg's locale
78 Deli dish
79 Quartz variety
82 Fall off, as support
83 Overwhelm
86 Fish that can twine its tail
87 Thrash
88 Water conditions toxic to shellfish
89 Eight-time Norris Trophy winner
90 Dump, so to speak
92 "Hair" co-lyricist
94 More judicious
96 Scratch pad?
97 Counts
99 It's kept on track
100 Expunge
102 Not keyed
104 Fictional orphan
106 Aussie tennis great
110 Subordinates to cpls.
111 Fit of pique
113 Western wine center
115 Cosmo follower

116 Brontë heroine
118 Notice
120 Hems' relatives
121 Mil. medal

by Nancy Nicholson Joline

ACROSS

1 60's labor leader
6 Aristotle treatise
12 They're no gentlemen
16 Filmmaker's special effects shot
21 TV comic DeGeneres
22 Fit to till
23 Mule Sal's canal
24 Literature Nobelist Canetti
25 Headline of #36,683 (July 1, 1958)
28 Explosive liquid
29 Motley
30 Nightclothes, informally
31 Fragrant compound
32 Gym wear
33 Controversial James Lovelock book
35 Marks left
36 Proust hero
37 Headline of #6,256 (Oct. 9, 1871)
43 Holiday stamp
44 Language suffix
47 Eared seals
48 Proboscis
49 Be gracious to
50 Ancient Chinese dynasty
51 Sang like a crow
52 Bull: Prefix
54 It has many feet
55 Assault
57 Headline of #31,545 (June 6, 1944)
62 Slowpoke
63 Part of L.A.
64 "The Cocktail Party" playwright
65 Roofer's concern
66 Alters
68 They can be grand
69 Where clothes spin
70 Ziegfeld, to pals
71 Hootchie ___
72 Baseball historian Burns
75 Vandals
76 Tiny openings
77 Song sung singly
78 Variety show since 1975: Abbr.
79 Uganda's Amin
80 Dortmund dessert
81 Pipe root
82 Point count bidding pioneer
83 Socials
85 Anthony or Elmo, e.g.
86 Dolphin sense
87 Alphabet trio
90 Mellow Mel
91 Headline of #48,377 (Oct. 3, 1990)
95 Party line
96 Iran's Bani-___
97 Hardly trustworthy
98 "All right"
99 Eight-time Norris Trophy winner
100 Cooper's Bumppo
102 Box
104 Comic strip originally called "Li'l Folks"
106 Mao follower
107 Swing around
108 Headline of #26,212 (Oct. 30, 1929)
111 Biological bodies
113 Unwilling
114 Hit obliquely, as a nail
115 Stage actress Martin et al.
117 Malaysian export
118 Comet's path in the sky
119 Eras
125 "Ragged Dick" writer
126 Headline of #27,710 (Dec. 6, 1933)
129 Kind of boom
130 "Beloved" author Morrison
131 Actress Dorothy
132 Olga's successor
133 CBS exec Laurence
134 Church part
135 City on the Willamette
136 With it

DOWN

1 Learn via the grapevine
2 Stew
3 Ross national product
4 Song or slug follower
5 "Puppy Love" singer, 1960
6 Sup
7 Capricorn, e.g.
8 Palindromic Yemeni city
9 Nigerian people
10 Year in Ptolemy's life
11 Iroquoian Indians
12 Il ___ di gravità
13 Bygone Dodge
14 New Look designer
15 D.C. V.I.P.
16 Headline of #40,721 (July 21, 1969)
17 Highly unusual
18 Headline of #19,806 (April 16, 1912)
19 Not bland
20 Those, in Tegucigalpa
26 Texas A&M player
27 Grammarian's topic
32 Ugly Duckling, actually
34 Reply: Abbr.
35 It may be tied
36 Tuxedo junction
37 The "f" in f-stop
38 ___-Turkish War, 1911–12
39 Singer Lou
40 ". . . ___ saw Elba"
41 Up-down connector
42 Eskimo people
43 Wood stock sites
45 Author Sidney
46 Diamond datum
49 Color tester
52 Cuts away
53 "My Michael" writer ___ Oz
54 Smooths the way
56 Not, to a Scot
58 "Cannonball Run" co-star
59 Mathematician Turing et al.
60 Put teeth into
61 Productive hen
62 They've got the goods
67 Monetary unit of Peru
68 Headline of #4,110 (Nov. 25, 1864)
69 "What's ___?"
70 Brief incursion
72 Kipling youth
73 Copyholders?
74 Headline of #42,566 (Aug. 9, 1974)
76 Rap sheet info
77 Any lad
81 Off-color
82 Ideal
84 Energy unit
85 Washington ___
86 Brat's look
87 Equip
88 Proofreading marks
89 To the point
92 European freshwater fish
93 Caspian tributary
94 Pop singer Hendryx
95 Rustic house
96 Actor Erwin et al.
101 "Woe is me!"
102 "First ___ see . . ."
103 Drink
104 "Israfel" writer
105 Senior Mormon
108 Meryl Streep's 1982 title role
109 Comfortable gait
110 Caterpillar's quarters
112 Type of acid
113 Grebes' cousins
115 Z-like
116 "The Time Machine" people
117 Cut short
118 Give ___ (pull)
120 Catcher Tony
121 Solitaire item
122 Turn over
123 Bangs, e.g.
124 Chair support
126 Educ. grp.
127 Cash alternative
128 From N.M. to N.D.

by Charles M. Deber

ACROSS

1 Having dogpaddled
5 Tax lowerer
11 Witticism
16 Glancing blow
17 Yucatán's capital
18 Taft, for one
20 A: Yale. Q: What do they call a ___?
22 Like St. Petersburg in 1991
24 Yarn
25 Renowned Bears coach George
26 French river or department
28 Buster Brown's dog
29 Aardvark snack
30 A: 9-W. Q: Wolfgang, do you spell your name ___?
33 Neb. neighbor
34 Toot
36 Talese's "Thy Neighbor's ___"
37 Bacchus worshiper
39 Women's suffrage leader
40 Calm
42 Wear
43 Flabbergasts
45 One point of eating?
46 Happy one
47 Play part
48 Incensed
51 A: Seven drachmas a day. Q: What's a ___?
54 Caress
57 Teed off
58 Ghost costume?
59 Nigerian city
60 "___ Believer" (Monkees hit)
61 Wobegon, e.g.
62 Celebration
63 Of bees
64 Boo-boo
65 Seine sight
66 Beanstalk dweller
67 "___ needs a good memory" (old maxim)
68 Oar fulcrum
69 Smoking flick?
70 A: No strings attached. Q: How do you describe ___?
72 Tarried
73 Creeps
75 Johnson of "Laugh-In"

76 Laze
77 Keep tabs on it
79 Perseus's mother
81 Anadems
85 Rock-___-baby
86 Lathered up
88 "Lélia" author
89 Winter fall
90 Near empty
91 A: Dr. Livingstone, I presume. Q: What is your full name, ___?
93 I.R.S. challenger
94 "The King and I" locale
96 Tennis's Sampras
97 Court event
99 The old sod
100 Fine homes
102 A: Annie Laurie. Q: What is the indefinite English ___?
106 Wyoming peaks
107 Compelled
108 Unrefined
109 Mary Richards's TV neighbor
110 Depositors
111 Big ___ conference

DOWN

1 Feel the heat
2 Not on target
3 A.P. competitor
4 What gears do
5 Provide details
6 Scold
7 Come up
8 Notes
9 Tokyo, once
10 Exceeded
11 Eye part
12 Korean statesman
13 Rhone tributary
14 Blazer
15 A: Chicken Teriyaki. Q: Who is the sole surviving ___?
16 Al Jolson hit
19 Nullify
20 Uses a dirk
21 Grandson of Noah
23 Body shop jobs
27 Patronize Avis
31 Collision
32 One of the Judds
35 Dress size
36 Hockey position
38 Fabric invented in 1941
39 Fire

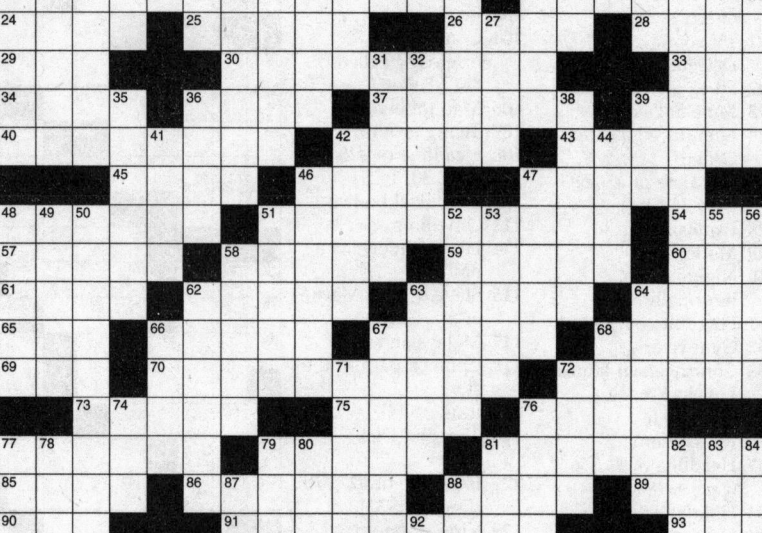

by Tom Underhill

41 1982 Tommy Tune show
42 Postman's challenge
44 Clothing department
46 Summits
47 Result of raising cane
48 Daughter, to Cato
49 Eurasia divider
50 A: Boil the hell out of it. Q: How do you ___?
51 Accra's site
52 Skiing event
53 Water nymph
55 A miss's equivalent
56 Not live
58 Old catalogue issuer
62 Many phone lines, nowadays
63 Winged
64 Scam accomplices
66 Stare
67 Wear away
68 Sprinkle after a shower?
71 More logical
72 News

74 "___ to Billy Joe"
76 Not 2-D or 3-D
77 Test answer
78 Chamber ensemble player
79 Flit
80 Attaches
81 Military trucks
82 Form a hard surface
83 They're open to discussion
84 Oh, so elegant
87 Black Sea port
88 "Swell" guy?
92 Singer Winwood
95 Number crunching
96 Hang fire
98 Chantilly ___
99 Epochs
101 Overly
103 Altar in the sky
104 Twice DII
105 Refrain syllable

ACROSS

1 Competition involving legs
6 Give a free pass
10 "My Name Is Asher ___" (Chaim Potok novel)
13 Run-in
17 Memorable mission
18 They're off-base
20 Warren ___, 1999 N.F.L. Defensive Player of the Year
21 It has Swiss banks
22 Description of 120-Across and 40-Down
25 Senior event
26 Ending with real in London
27 Took the cake, say
28 Oscar Wilde genre
29 Add
30 Snootiness
32 Indivisible
34 Art photo
35 "___ my case"
36 Roving eyes on an exam, e.g.
37 Description of 82-Down and 27-Across
41 From, in France
42 Comics canine
44 Football Hall-of-Famer ___ Hirsch
45 1933 Physics Nobelist Paul
47 It may be legal
49 Perform high-tech surgery
51 Brilliant maneuver
54 Long operatic solo
56 Comet's partner
59 Made with garlic and butter
61 Oil-rich land
63 Jipijapa hats
65 Adrien ___ skin care products
66 Funny Philips
67 Description of 25- and 26-Across
70 Common request for Pat Sajak
71 Shock: Var.
73 Bill blockers
74 Transmits twice
76 Was out for a bit
78 Dustin Hoffman title role
79 Saint ___ University of Minnesota
80 Pirate sticker
81 Computer programs, for short
83 Lofty groups?
86 Popular Yale major
88 Place to kick something
90 ___-off (shortened)
94 Arles article
96 Description of 10- and 111-Across
100 Where the whale is?
101 They're non-PC
103 Easily taken advantage of
104 Visitors from afar, briefly
106 Cipher
107 Sensation
108 Ballet rail
109 "___ questions?"
111 Two-time U.S. Open champ
112 One in charge of discipline, maybe
113 Description of 51- and 94-Across
118 Sen. Stevens and others
119 Draft selections

by Randolph Ross

120 True
121 Static, e.g.
122 Bone in Rome
123 Global positioning fig.
124 Subject of King Cyaxares
125 Daly's TV co-star

DOWN

1 Angle measures
2 Jack-o'-lantern feature
3 Half of an old sitcom duo
4 "Where ___?"
5 Sage of sci-fi film
6 Rhythmic
7 Hogwarts postal carrier
8 Sound heard by Old MacDonald
9 Thickness
10 Nonclerical
11 One-on-one sport
12 Some corp. execs
13 Sweetness or sourness
14 Description of 6- and 109-Across
15 Stir
16 Beguiles
19 This should come first, it's said
20 Narrow groove
23 D.D.E.'s command
24 Reindeer raiser
29 Factor in ticket pricing
31 Post office machine
33 Reese's role in "Legally Blonde"
34 Bay Area airport letters
38 Slip
39 Pop-ups, e.g.
40 Connections
43 Like a sound argument
46 Rent-___
48 Dipilatory brand
49 Frequent airport sights
50 First mate?
52 Flips
53 Lots
54 Hong Kong harbor craft
55 Description of 113- and 39-Down
56 Basic reading
57 Let loose
58 Turn aside
60 Vegas venue
61 Slightest amount, informally
62 Mo. containing Guy Fawkes Day
63 For whose sake?
64 Paul McCartney title
68 Food for sea urchins
69 Final preceder
72 Mimic
75 Unreal
77 Requiring more time in the dryer
82 Goombah
83 "Evita" role
84 Hardy
85 Problem to be overcome
87 No. 2: Abbr.
88 Give away
89 First mate?
91 Cyclist's stunt
92 Like some seals
93 Waste products
94 Intentionally threw off
95 Runs the show
97 Peeved
98 Skater Lipinski and others
99 One way to Southampton: Abbr.
102 Response to a playground challenge
105 ___-Caps (candy)
108 Gymnastics coach Karolyi
110 Egg foo ___
113 Bando of baseball
114 ___ turkey
115 Batter's asset
116 Pop
117 Campaigner, for short

ACROSS

1 Short-legged horses
5 ___ Ababa
10 Drop heavily
14 Broadway's Jane
18 "___ the Great," E. Dumm cartoon
19 Early or late Crawford
20 Vibrant
21 Piece of Marilyn Mims
22 WHERE'S THE STATION?
24 WHERE'S THE SECOND?
26 He caused earthquakes
27 Unpleasant sound
29 Capricious indulgences
30 Month, in Milano
31 Pub drink
32 Skin or slick preceder
33 Cozened
36 Sheppard-Turpin guns
37 Elongated, as a spheroid
41 Month before Nisan
42 WHERE'S THE FINDING?
46 Like "cats" in the 40's
47 Rock group
48 Letters
49 Harness
50 Heraldic design
51 Kelep
52 WHERE'S THE ARIAN?
56 Scenic view
57 Swear anew
60 Viracocha worshiper
61 Iraqi neighbors
62 Kind of dropper
63 Ancient Greek city-state
64 Five of trumps
65 Grading systems
67 Amenhotep IV's god
68 Earlier bid
71 Construe
72 WHERE'S THE TILL?
74 Part of TNT
75 Stratum; level
76 Former Chinese leader
78 The life of Riley
79 A Sinatra
80 And the rest: Abbr.
81 WHERE'S THE SHOPPING?
85 Presage
86 Belittle
88 Designer Oscar de la ___
89 Usurp
90 It's between the U.S. and Eur.
91 Bourrée or forlana
92 Quality; nature
94 "I did but ___ little honey . . .": I Sam. 14:43
97 Twofold
98 Injured a joint
102 WHERE'S THE WAVE?
104 WHERE DO WE GET LACE?
106 Couple
107 Parts of pumps
108 Strand
109 Space on the face of a bird
110 Commits a bull
111 Kin of a hydria
112 One of the Dryads
113 Assyrian war god

DOWN

1 Quibble
2 Potpourri
3 Petitions
4 Intrigants
5 Footless ones
6 "An Essay upon Projects" author: 1697
7 Cockcrow
8 City in Peru
9 He practices pettifoggery
10 Flat double fold in cloth
11 Heeltap
12 Ab ___ (from the start)
13 Of necessity
14 Fishing fly
15 Battle of ___ July 3, 1940
16 Playwright Sir Arthur ___ Pinero
17 The Four ___, singing group
20 Reddening
23 Litigated
25 "Cats" libretto author
28 Paris's ___ Neuf
31 Roman burial stone
33 Senegal's capital
34 City NW of Trieste
35 WHERE'S THE PITCH?
36 Pack tightly
37 Dawber or Shriver
38 WHERE'S GREENWICH?
39 Beats, to Puccini
40 Flèche weapons
42 Ammonia derivatives
43 Sharp projections
44 Alcohol heaters
45 Falstaffian
50 Skin exfoliation
53 Runs amok
54 Table bay is one
55 Currants, e.g.
56 Javanese carriage
58 Four-time Wimbledon winner
59 Perpetually
61 Farm machine
63 Half a Samoan island's name: Var.
64 Cues in group singing
65 Commended for gallantry
66 Colligate
68 End of Mont.'s motto
69 Pelagic raptors
70 Cheerful
72 Bank abbr.
73 "Festina ___" ("Make haste slowly")
76 Of a lower social order
77 Triton
79 Mexican baker's product
81 Anon
82 Ancient Germarie people
83 Triclinium meal
84 Put a fence around
87 Teachers, at times
89 Swaddle
91 Reno roller
92 Rollick
93 "___ ed Euridice"
94 VCR insertion
95 In the distance
96 Rustle
97 Clay used as a pigment
98 Kin of a parvis
99 Ancient temple
100 Raw-silk shade
101 Sambar
103 Quo modo
105 Clock, in Kölin

by Jack L. Steinhardt

ACROSS

1 Esparto grass
5 Treasury worker
9 Decline
14 Join into a whole
19 Unable to decide
20 Broadway actress Mary
21 Waugh's "The ___ One"
22 Agatha's award
23 Sulky's driver's dessert?
25 Game warden's dish?
27 Jackie's second mate
28 One touch of Venus
30 Estuary
31 Wood ibis
32 Goes over old ground
34 Detect and expose
36 Dot, in Lisbon
37 Freshens
38 Start of a D. H. Lawrence title
39 Night crawlers, e.g.
40 Unctuous speech
43 Property held for others
45 Banker's breakfast?
47 Cairo lizard
48 After
49 Ormoc's locale
50 Plumber, at times
52 Habituates
54 Like many a hoopster
56 A.F.B. in Texas
57 Mies van der ___
58 The Greatest
59 RR train
60 Secret explosions
61 Croupier's comestibles?
66 A Siouan
71 Call from a columbary
72 Rain and snow mixt.
73 Use a letter opener
77 Baseball's Banks
78 Change a bit
80 Ancestral link
82 Beatty, for one
84 Editing mark
86 Lexiconizing physician
87 Stickiness
88 Complaint manager's meal?
90 Naught, in Nottingham
91 Put it to
92 Ganges platform
93 Holy statue
94 Aspect
95 "___ hell": Sherman
97 Tricolore part
98 Singer Natalie's side dish?
101 Enter, as a crowd
103 Grand ___, Nova Scotia
104 Zanuck
106 Where Tell did his thing
107 Violinist's veggies?
110 Sanitary engineer's treat?
112 Pyromaniac's crime
113 TV role for Linda Lavin
114 When Casca struck
115 Porgy
116 Shoddy
117 Doctrine
118 Opera by Handel
119 People generally

DOWN

1 Stock term
2 Peter of "Casablanca"
3 Boxer's beverage?
4 Blyth
5 Hard blows
6 U.S. slalom greats
7 First sign
8 Siestas
9 Zermatt sight
10 Like Stanley Kowalski
11 Make use of
12 Mexican Indian
13 Dead letter
14 Bluestocking
15 G.I.'s dog tag
16 Psychiatrist's supper?
17 Bingo device
18 Whilom
24 Old card games
26 He has "I" trouble
29 Muzzle
33 Deliverance
35 Padre's pastry?
36 ___ Mink, Hawaii's first Congresswoman
38 Certain legumes
39 Poppycock
41 Explanatory phrase
42 Penates' partner
43 White Russian ruler
44 Petrocelli of Red Sox fame
45 Resign
46 Beethoven's last symphony
47 Not aweather
49 Tibeto-Burman group
51 J. S. Copley's forte
53 Bark cloth
55 Circle segment
60 Concerning
62 Astringent
63 Fashion
64 Cut off, in a way
65 Novelist's need
66 River triangle
67 Court star
68 Critic's snack?
69 Message from the pen
70 Lunar New Year in Vietnam
73 Klammer's arena
74 Electrician's repast?
75 Curare's cousin
76 Four: Comb. form
78 Hog plums
79 Gist
80 Cleanse of oil
81 Battery type
83 Heartsore
85 Not sotto voce
89 Golden intangible
90 Belafonte's forte
92 Like the Cheshire Cat
94 Previous
96 Out of control
97 Smart one
98 Unfinished
99 Contend
100 Nebulous
101 H.S. junior's exam
102 Norwegian river
103 He kicked to conquer
105 Tennis term
108 Lost weekend
109 Young plant
111 Adherent

by Tap Osborn

204 BOGIE

by Barbara Lunder Gillis

ACROSS

1 Judge's bench
5 Fille's mother
9 Open to all
13 Pivoted bolt
17 Daughter of William the Conqueror
19 Juniper
20 Capital of Latvia
21 Repeat
22 Novel about Harry Morgan
25 Junket
26 Deductive
27 Estimate
28 Elf
30 Kind of point
32 Fulmars' kin
34 Seconds for Holmes
35 Florida island
38 Home street, to a gang
40 Piebald
45 Dessert
46 "___ Fair," 1953 play
49 Hello, in Hilo
50 Spur
51 Aft's antithesis
52 Port Pat side when sailing south
54 Young hare
56 "Beau Gest" locale
59 Bohemian dance
61 Piedmont city
62 Antarctic base
64 Bronowski's "The Ascent ___"
65 Governor of N.Y.: 1869–71
68 Resource
70 Encircling
72 City in Portugal
73 Sight at a marina
75 Arab prince
76 Like some causes
78 Locale of the Pindus Mountains
81 ___ bullet
85 Record
86 Gula
88 Turkish regiment
90 Benevolent Chinese spirits
91 Blind alley
93 Type of car or hall
95 Fumes
96 Honshu city
97 "Barefoot" lady
99 Baghdad native
102 Admonishes
104 Radio signal term
109 A Gorgon
111 Dance for Washington
114 Smooth flounder
116 Tony's relative
117 Hammett book
120 Unaspirated
121 Batman's creator
122 Plant of the lily family
123 "___ Promise," Dawson poem
124 First name of 125 Across
125 "M*A*S*H" star
126 Residue
127 Peace Nobelist Cassin

DOWN

1 Seaport in Guinea
2 Choose and take
3 Free India's first P.M.
4 Debussy's "___ de Lume"
5 Hands
6 Mussolini's daughter
7 Stadium sounds
8 Puzzlers' tools
9 City where they're raisin' raisins
10 Washer cycle
11 Caesar's "___ ipse"
12 Sign that could stop a truck
13 Sherwood play (with "The")
14 Pungent
15 Whizzer or E.B.
16 Davey of baseball
18 Severn feeder
19 Wouk novel (with "The")
23 Composer Satie
24 Border
29 Young salmon
31 City in Hungary
33 Nova, e.g.
36 Pulls
37 Cruising
39 "Deutschland ___ alles"
40 Crony
41 ___ du Diable
42 Scorpio-Sagittarius mo.
43 Forester book
44 Henley competitor
46 Emulate a lark
47 Famous mother-in-law
48 City on the Nile
51 Worry
53 Savor
55 Kennedy initials
57 Dispatch
58 Kin of kvass
60 Flint implements
63 Chandler book
65 Ziegfeld's first wife
66 Shaped like an avocado
67 "Dancin'" director
68 Brazilian boundary river
69 Andress film
71 Friend, in Falaise
74 Elderly
77 Migrant
79 Jargon
80 Critic Faure
82 Bond
83 Fell
84 U.S.N.A. grad
87 Chew like beavers
89 Looped handle
92 Footpace
93 Reed or Mills
94 Affronts
97 Soviet peninsula
98 Hebrew letter
99 Bolognese painter: 16th century
100 Arise
101 Donizetti heroine
103 Improve
105 Map
106 More competent
107 "Le ___ du Printemps"
108 Disdain
110 Aleutian island
112 Small case
113 Swiss patriot
115 Joint
118 Producer Wallis
119 Win at musical chairs

ACROSS

1 Flower arrangement
6 Unruly child
10 Taj ___
15 Viola da ___
20 Investigate thoroughly
21 Decoy
22 Fearful: Fr.
23 "___ Indolence": Keats
24 Just deserts, in Iran?
26 Rx for a hangover
27 Sting
28 Enthralled
29 D.D.E.'s domain in W.W. II
30 Cloning in Malaysia?
33 Palanquin
35 Scents
36 Allowance for waste
37 "Mayday!" cousin
40 Recreation vehicle
41 Cancel
43 Iranian coin
44 Three-toed sloths
47 In attendance
49 How Irish tea was once served in China?
52 Former stage luminary
53 Quantity
54 Set
55 A tooth
56 Tasso's patron
57 Gloomy
58 Seed coverings
60 Lambastes
61 "___ a Hot Tin Roof"
62 Building extension
63 Boring, in Lebanon?
66 Isl. W of England
67 Judeo-Spanish
68 Provide a new sound track
69 Is of consequence
70 Flynn of films
72 Large gully
73 Widened a gun bore
75 Church dogma
76 Having rhythmic flow
77 Verse form
78 Edible mushroom
79 Boring tool
80 Police release, for short
83 Make more substantial
84 Noted archeologist: 1840–1909
85 Creeping anger in Switzerland?
87 It precedes la-la
88 Plant insect
89 Sagan or Jung
90 Earthen water jars
91 Food regimen
92 Dyeing vat
93 ___ play (snap)
95 Lair
96 Press flat
98 As to
99 Pests in Vietnam?
102 Law
103 In medias ___
104 Column part
105 Hoods
106 Prefix with angle
107 One of the Chaplins
108 Thespian's delight
109 Cremona violinmaker
111 Tropical creeper
113 France's favorite TV show?
117 Astern
118 Eight furlongs
122 He succeeded Nasser
123 Relief
124 Pretentious, in Israel?
127 Aromatic herb
128 Baseball boo-boos
129 "Judith" composer
130 Very: Mus. dir.
131 Grimes of opera
132 First U.S. diplomat sent abroad
133 "I've ___ to London . . ."
134 Vandyke, e.g.

DOWN

1 Senate and people of Rome: Abbr.
2 Indonesian boat
3 Frolic
4 Touches upon
5 Slangy assent
6 Obtrusive
7 Kind of sentence
8 Trefoil shape
9 "Così fan tutte" trio
10 Of small organisms
11 Moslem prince
12 Vagrants
13 smell ___ (be suspicious)
14 Diplomatic missions
15 Evangel
16 Own up
17 Ignoble
18 Tennis great
19 Pismire
22 Busy
25 Formalist in teaching
31 Anchor rings
32 Incensed
34 Level
37 Dug
38 Imitation gold decoration
39 Kindred spirits in S. Korea?
41 Smelting product
42 Rostropovich's instrument
43 Variety of white wine
44 Showy in Texas?
45 Chant
46 Pool person
48 It's Big in Calif.
50 Reformer Carry
51 Growl
52 Intro
54 Avarice
58 Soviet workers' cooperative
59 Daub
61 Underground chamber
63 Swapped
64 Chinese official's residence
65 Pelagic predators
67 One in a leaking boat
71 Norse Chieftain: 860–931?
72 Furors
74 Undivided
75 "___ Leave You?": 1971 song
76 Kind of heel
77 Plunder
78 Phil's mate
79 Without fear: Var.
81 Like many a model
82 Took to the tub
83 Hindu beggar
84 Feb. 15, 1898, headline word
86 Of a bygone era
89 Punished
91 Marriage portion
93 Kind of beet
94 Indian chief
96 Layers
97 Principal
100 Observers
101 Coconut fiber
102 Become less flexible
104 Playful teasing
108 "___-porridge hot . . ."
109 Port city of Ghana
110 City in France or Georgia
111 "Mule Train" singer
112 Divert
113 Walking stick
114 Mine entrance
115 Last, long ago
116 King of Israel: ninth century B.C.
119 "___ girl!"
120 Ananias
121 Okla. city
122 Weaken
125 Exist
126 M.I.T. room

by Jeannette K. Brill

ACROSS

1 Bit part
5 Parka piece
9 Intrigue
14 Whipper-snapper?
20 Blockheads
21 Ivy League school
22 Allan-___
23 Monte Carlo number
24 "Don't throw bouquets ___"
25 Nanny's carriage
26 Short ___ (little attention)
28 Pencil "helmet"
29 Greek letter
30 Film from a biblical phrase
33 Foiled the posse
35 Chili con ___
36 Naval off.
37 Jerky, e.g.
38 Ruins
39 Manual arts
41 Ex-constellation
42 Inventor of a sign language
43 Portly
44 Placed in a heavenly area
46 Consecrate
48 "___ Dei" (prayer)
50 "But ___ begin": J.F.K.
51 Orale
52 Cara or Papas
57 "...grow too ___ dream"
58 Sponsorship
59 Sugarless item
60 One leaving a will
62 Slipper
63 "Am" for two
64 Fine wool
66 Root and 21 Across
67 Three, at the Trevi
68 Houston org.
70 With "The," film from a biblical phrase
72 Writer Rand et al.
74 Abrogate
76 ___ of (addressing term)
77 Whilom
81 Film based on a biblical phrase
84 ___ Halaby (Jordan's Queen Noor)
86 Cry of pleasure
87 "...baked ___"
90 Actress North
91 Mideastern org.
92 Tally
94 Site of Stanford U.
96 Capek classic
97 Boat-bottom timber
98 Less apt to bolt
99 "___ Like I," Loos autobiography
100 Frequently
102 Wait on
103 Sultan's decree
104 In the attic, e.g.
106 Brief
108 Giant Hall of Famer
109 Hot box
113 Laugh, in Lyon
114 Condiment
115 "___ Way," Cahn-Van Heusen song
118 Prometheus's theft
119 "Life ___ jest...": Gay
120 Worthless talk
121 Flood
122 Film from a Donne phrase
127 Crock or trick ending
128 Overjoyed
129 Croaky
130 Call at sea
131 Power source
132 Ripped again
133 Gives forth
134 Sanction
135 No great shakes
136 Grand places?
137 Strikes out
138 In ___ (completely)
139 In business

DOWN

1 In a lather?
2 Film from a phrase in Gray's "Elegy..."
3 Film from a Burnsian phrase
4 Half a fly
5 ___
6 Sculled
7 Norwegian saint
8 Show car
9 Rippling folds
10 Stuck
11 Cuts of beef
12 "What ___," 1939 film
13 Portside
14 Autry's hat
15 Indonesia's ___ Islands
16 Chicken Little's cry
17 Conforming

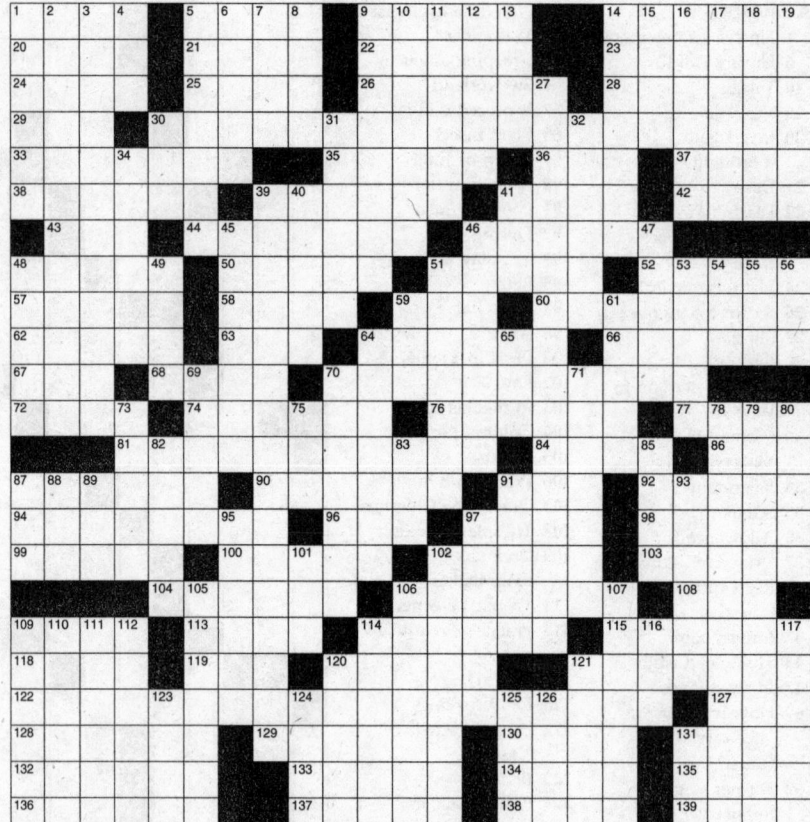

by A. J. Santora

18 Old headstones
19 Cylindrical
27 Film from a biblical phrase
30 Meas. of revolutions
31 Second flyer
32 Donkey, e.g.
34 Sagacious
39 Film from a Julia Ward Howe phrase
40 Get even again
41 ___-Margaret
45 Satisfies
46 He wrote "Now We Are Six"
47 Lord or Sir, e.g.
48 Blood line
49 Forthwith
51 Stealthy
53 Bump, in poker
54 Numerical ending
55 ___-Turn (road sign)
56 Ending for 76
59 Fetch
61 Male and female
64 Average
65 Required: Abbr.
69 A moon of Uranus
70 Having strata
71 Ripken's cohorts
73 Flavor
75 Monogram of the author of "The Killers"
78 Film from a Daniel Webster quote
79 Film from a FitzGerald phrase
80 Voilá!
82 Omani money
83 Neath's opposite
85 Vino center
87 NW Argentine group
88 Fishwife's cousin
89 Man with 40 men
91 Nez ___ (American Indian)
93 Old round dances
95 Me-___ (coattails policy)
97 Doghouse
101 Ball prop
102 Like some birds
105 Electron tubes
106 Actress Holm
107 "___ bed..."
109 Bids
110 Bloomer girl?
111 Typos
112 Unit of force
114 Small thread
116 Bandleader Brown
117 Root word
120 Former N.Y.C. mayor
121 Raft
123 Remuda
124 Weeded
125 Big name in 126 Down
126 Where Ashtabula is
131 Japanese national park

ACROSS

1 Gaiters
6 Zounds!
10 Duct
14 "___ Thirteen": Faulkner
19 Stash
20 Fifth-largest desert
21 A wife of Esau
22 "Kitchen" of Manhattan
23 "___ Grows in Brooklyn"
24 The color purple
26 Islamic devil
27 "___ on the Drina": Andric
29 Isak Dinesen book
31 Uncanny
32 Kobo and Burrows
33 Tessera
34 Leaf beets
37 Rich man in Luke 16, Vulgate version
39 Mountain ashes
43 Remedy
44 Frost book
48 Fermi or Caruso
51 Pluck
52 Was off base
53 Dactyl, e.g.
54 Demeter's dad
55 Hebrew letter
56 Employed busily
57 "The Seaman's Friend" author
58 Monarchy
60 Aerie components
61 Swimmer Weatherford
62 E.M. Forster novel
66 MX and Sickle
69 Herrick's creation
70 Dark period in a Koestler book
74 Give a hang
75 Many a "Brother Rat" character
76 In academia a 4.00, e.g.
78 Muslim messiahs
79 Levin or Wolfert
80 Criterion
81 Fulminate
82 Shell-game decoys
83 Graham Greene novel
86 Orange-neck goose
87 Soprano Resnik
88 Throws off
90 Books, to Zola
92 ___ Ifni, Morocco
94 Fed
95 Al-Qahirah, to Flaubert
97 Isaak Babel book
101 James Joyce book
105 Result of a wedge shot
106 Place to write letters
108 "Land of cotton"
109 Running: Comb. form
110 Cape of Chile
111 Large kangaroo
112 Moliére's "L'___ des maris"
113 Tip
114 Of French rock music in the 60's
115 ___ Mawr
116 Passover feast

DOWN

1 Vamoose
2 It's often beaten
3 End of an E. Caldwell title
4 Deighton book
5 Be angry
6 Islands off Sicily
7 Overcharged
8 Author Prevost
9 Cube with 21 spots
10 Most ambiguous
11 Emulates Robert Giroux
12 Minute: Comb. form
13 A purloining
14 A rainbow followed this
15 New Testament book
16 She outwrestled Thor
17 Bankrupt Federal org.
18 She, to Soldati
25 Poet Service
28 Org. that audits
30 Springless mattress
32 Get around
34 Tab
35 Novelist Barbusse
36 Role in "Green Pastures"
38 It's worn on an obi
40 Fragrance
41 Kern's "___ But Me"
42 Kind of preview
45 Light: Comb. form
46 Inventive
47 City SE of San Jose
49 Pointed ends
50 ___ Peak, N.M.
51 Romany realm
56 Small part of an oz.
57 Thomas Mann novella
59 Bensalem is one
60 Gumshoe
61 Alice's cat
63 The Salt Palace, e.g.
64 Shoo!, in Dogpatch
65 Benedictine titles
66 Less amicable
67 "Daybreak" director
68 Fort in N.C.
71 Fainéant
72 Eeyore's creator
73 Squiggles
75 Homeland of 25 Down
76 Street urchin
77 Painter Mondrian
80 Container for coffee
81 Group anew
84 Supple
85 Estate
89 Scamper
90 "___ Liza Jane," 1916 song
91 Fleurs-de-lis
93 Antsy
94 Celebrity
96 Minor judge in Judges
97 Chances
98 Tittle-tattle
99 Bacchic shout
100 ___ Islands, off New Guinea
101 Gloomy
102 O.T. book
103 Ruffle
104 Melampus or Mopsus
107 "Charlotte's ___"

by John M. Samson

ACROSS

1 Hold
5 Part of T.A.E.
9 Final part of a pas de deux
13 ___ pudding
18 Daredeviltry name
19 Manicurist's charge
21 Prognostic
22 Brutus's burdens
23 Actress-novelist match
26 Stair post
27 Actress Stritch
28 Kind of jaw
29 Bunyan's Babe, e.g.
30 ___ de guerre
31 Cooking banana
33 For shame!
34 Progenitor
35 Fine point
37 Comedian-actress match
40 Parallel passes
42 "It's ___ than you think!"
43 Migrate
45 Loren's birthplace
46 Surfeit
47 Candied items
51 Biblical book
53 Deadened
55 Excited
57 Loser to Braddock: 1935
59 Punty
60 36th U.S. Pres.
62 He's below a marquess
64 Dreamy composition
66 Call ___ day
67 Actress-tennis star match
70 Yelp
71 Prufrock's air
73 Speck
74 Aristotle's Aurora
75 Low
76 Director Buñuel
77 Terra ___
79 It's made backwards?
81 Novae, e.g.
83 Rec. measures
85 Boxer O'Grady
86 500 sheets
88 Highlands language
89 More frigid
91 Most mirthful
93 Actress-painter match
98 Implant
100 Mr. Bones
101 Apt. particulars
102 Makes hay, in a way
103 Homophone of neigh
105 Aramaic translation of the Old Testament
106 Main
109 Themes
111 Anew
112 Comedienne-camera bug match
114 Sledded at Lake Placid
115 Taxi
116 Seasons lumber
117 Countertenor
118 Looks of a rake on the make
119 Malts
120 New England grid team
121 Swill

DOWN

1 Herculean ones
2 Arthur's island paradise
3 Actress-jazz musician match
4 She out-wrestled Thor
5 Echidna or pangolin
6 ___-de-dah
7 Stringed instrument
8 Soprano Gluck
9 End of an O'Neill title
10 Bongo of Gabon
11 For, in Frankfurt
12 Actress Sheridan
13 Type of degree
14 On ___ keel
15 Needlework
16 Vingt-neuf follower
17 Mythical beast
20 World's greatest coffee port
24 Start
25 Ticket part
29 Bundle
32 Pianist-singer match
34 Ballplayer-entertainer match
36 Word before walk or mix
37 Mame's critic
38 Norway's patron saint
39 Eucharistic plate
41 ___ Darya, Asian river
43 Delight
44 Dig up
46 West Point greeting
48 ___ Dhabi, Mideastern land
49 Actress-comedian match
50 Privileged students
52 Sunday clothes, for some
54 West role
56 Imitator
58 Rest
61 "___ good cheer . . ."
63 Greek letter
65 Mrs. Tracy
68 "Sing all ___ willow": Shak.
69 "When the ___ Robin . . .": Woods song
72 Geller's gift
78 Where trades are made
80 Gas: Comb. form
82 Assay
84 Freudian names
87 Foolish
90 Stuff
91 Unlike a rolling stone
92 Industrial hub of the Ruhr
93 It may be major or minor
94 Madden
95 Less at ease
96 Destroys
97 Atlanta arena
99 Shed
102 Actress Shire
104 Prohibit legally
105 Lofty
106 Nuncupative
107 University in N.Y.C.
108 O.K. Corral fighter
110 Arts degs.
112 Borrioboola-___, locale in "Bleak House"
113 Service call

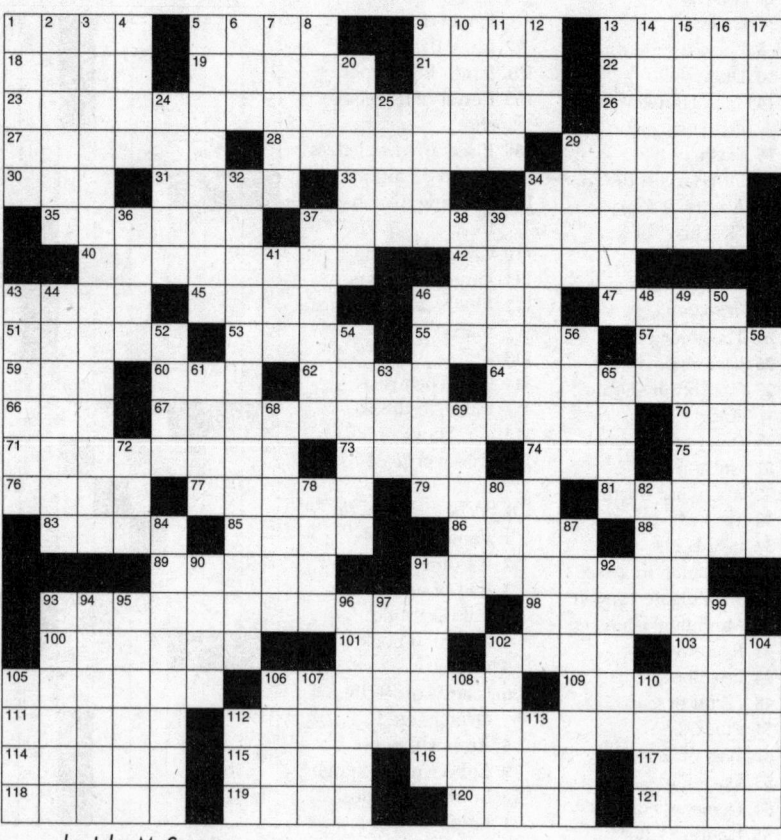

by John M. Samson

ACROSS

1 Refrain start
6 G.I.'s weaponry
10 Furtive whisper
14 Mad or red follower
17 Fix the lawn
18 Liquid part of fat
19 Novelette
21 Ethiopian town
22 Tune for author Hesse?
26 L-P connectors
27 Word on a bottle of "snake oil"
28 Concerning
29 Play the Old Vic
30 Smell that may cast a spell
32 U.S. humorist Finley Peter ___
34 Walking ___ (euphoric)
36 Cry of vindication
37 Treat for Cheeta
38 "Dialogues of the Gods" author
40 Thurible contents
43 Shamir's words to Peres?
46 Actor Delon
47 Foreman's opponent in Zaire
49 What wreckers do in Soho
50 Gold, in Genova
51 Mechanic's garment
53 As guilty ___
56 Legendary Irish king
58 Soprano Marton
59 Some desk trays
60 Unlikely
62 Philippine vine
63 First loyalty, to Polonius
65 Remark from Mrs. Guinness?
68 Arizona artisan
72 Run up bills
74 Marilu ___, "Taxi" actress
75 Yarn measure
77 Muffler mangler
78 "I ___ dream": King
81 Typewriter of sorts
82 Moriarty and J.R.
85 Candlenut tree
86 Proceed; act
88 Clock-radio button
89 With caustic humor
90 'Bye, Godfather?
96 Dwells
98 Longfellow subject

99 Shirley in "Terms of Endearment"
101 Speak softly
102 Goddess who knew her oats
103 Podium prelim
104 Upset on a jet
108 Puppeteer Lewis
110 Historian's subject
112 ___ gai pan (Chinese dish)
114 Antonym's antonym: Abbr.
115 Paint Goya out of the picture?
119 Fogeater
120 Sheer woven fabric
121 Fishhook line
122 Was reverential
123 Indeed
124 Chimney on das Haus
125 Ocean motion
126 Linus and Elihu

DOWN

1 Bird of passage
2 See old schoolmates
3 About
4 Kind of blow
5 Be short with Toulouse-Lautrec?
6 Judd Hirsch TV role
7 Capital of Yucatán
8 Incomplete metal castings
9 Indivisible
10 Fasten in advance
11 Made ecstatic
12 Educator in the Middle Ages
13 Stalemate
14 Note Novarro's comings and goings in Italy?
15 Country cousin of ain't
16 Emulate Echo
18 Garfield's friend
20 SPECTRE specialty
23 Virtuoso Mischa
24 Co-creator of "The Flintstones"
25 When Prince William will be 21
31 Prima ___ evidence
33 Slangy refusal
35 Nut, in Nürnberg
37 Liberty, for one
39 Writer Ephron
40 "___ thy rocks and rills"
41 Describing some stores

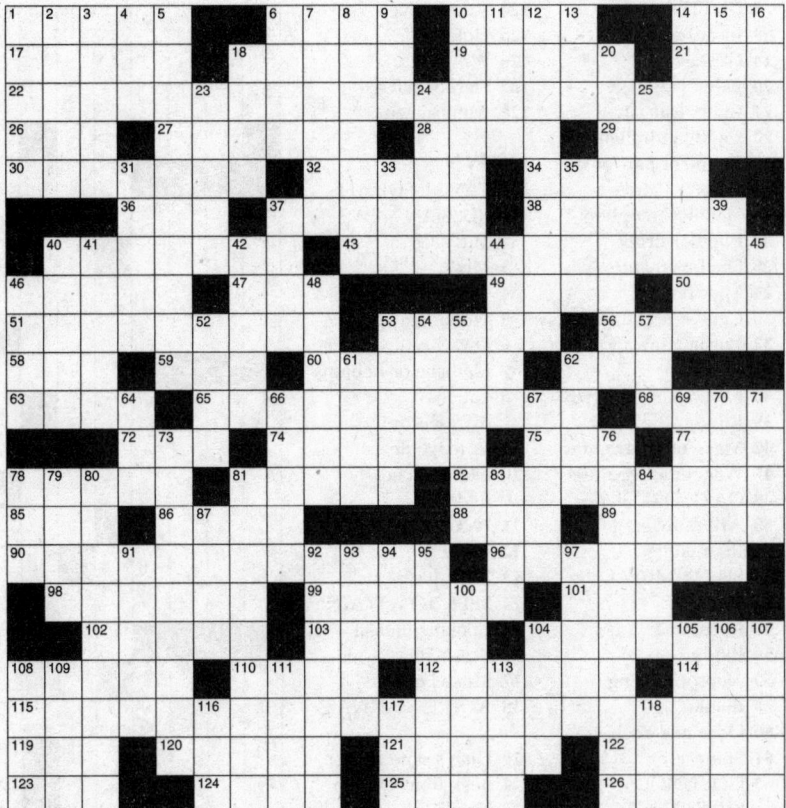

by Charlotte Shore

42 Latin-style dance music
44 A college at Oxford
45 No, in Noisy-le-Sec
46 Dice throw
48 ___ Baline (Irving Berlin)
52 Poker pittance
53 "I don't care . . . ___, or a Sphinx": Dickens
54 Achy
55 Looks fixedly
57 Kin of "Wow!"
61 Peon of yore
62 It's SE of Gmld.
64 Cheyenne, to a Pawnee
66 Letter after eta
67 Choice
69 "What immortal hand ___": Blake
70 Some knitting stitches
71 Bitsy's partner
73 Admirer of the composer of "Rienzi"
76 Farewell Stallone?

78 Experiences
79 Love, in Latium
80 Caesar's words to his first assailant?
81 Millenniums and minutes
83 Ship of "Ship of Fools"
84 Desert region in China
87 Grimm villain
91 Not underhanded
92 Pear-and-quince preserve
93 Stars of "The Visit": 1958
94 Alley cat's scrap
95 Mabel of the silents
97 Shoot cut for grafting
100 Like Seattle's Kingdome
104 "I've Got ___ in Kalamazoo"
105 Basketballer Dan
106 Recurring pattern
107 Hitches and slips
108 Logger's locomotive

109 Aesopian smart aleck
111 Macao money
113 Airfield near Paris
116 Prevaricate
117 Monogram of "The Waste Land" poet
118 Claire or Balin

START MAKING TARTS

ACROSS

1 CUTTING
9 Incensed
14 Gushes
20 Baltic language
21 Calyx leaf
22 Caddoan Indian
23 Pertinent part of the "Gloria Patri"
26 Halloween option
27 Popular drink
28 Duel memento
29 Middling
30 Causes resentment
32 Waste allowance
34 Brandish
38 NAUTICAL CHAIN
39 Rime
42 Make effervescent
47 Wagnerian goddess
48 GAZE FIXEDLY
50 Ark numbers
52 Roof edges
53 SHINY METAL PLATES
55 Decorated
58 Binds
59 Nap-producing plants
60 Odes and such
61 Shine
63 GLUTINOUS SUBSTANCE
65 Changed the hue
66 State positively
70 Resistance to change
73 Some moths
74 Inexpensive tires
76 Item
78 Foot lever
79 Fashions
81 Mercenary
86 Partners of haws
87 Domesticates
89 Important court action
90 Vacant
92 Buffalo's county
93 Recoils
95 WISE
96 Like a clarinet
98 Atlanta arena
100 HAVE DINNER
101 Celebes oxen
102 Globule
104 HASTEN
107 Crime boss
111 Goddess of discord
113 Jannings or Ludwig
114 Giant grass
118 Pertinent words from La Fontaine's "Fables"
123 FRIGHTENS
124 Atka native
125 Hotel fee
126 Wrong
127 Sightly daft
128 Autobahnen

DOWN

1 TAVERN QUAFF
2 RUSSIAN NEWS SERVICE
3 Mix
4 Table d' ___
5 To the center
6 Dwarf-cattle breed
7 Methane or helium
8 Laughs disrespectfully
9 Cordage fiber
10 Old story newly told
11 Wou-wou, e.g.
12 PIERCE
13 Negative particle
14 SEEK TO ATTAIN
15 Cooking utensil
16 PLANTED
17 Mussel genus
18 ACTRESS ANNA ___
19 Utah's state flower
24 Nick from Omaha
25 Needlefish
31 Province of Mozambique
33 NICE HOT TIME
34 Sobbed
35 Dies ___
36 Writer Ferber
37 DROSS
40 EXPLORER DE ___
41 Distorted
43 AU ___ POTATOES
44 Fly a plane
45 Wobble
46 TAXED
48 Warning device
49 Rhone tributary
51 DANISH WEIGHTS
54 Looked askance
56 Humiliate
57 Sine die
60 Fasten
62 Assimilate
64 "My Country ___ . . ."
65 A GERSHWIN
66 Garfield's follower
67 Placid
68 Addison's co-author
69 Rubbed out
71 Lock
72 POSE
75 PARADISE
77 Photographer's word
79 Mangle
80 ALASKAN CITY
82 Peruse
83 Shakespearean villain
84 On the briny
85 Headland
88 Figurative
89 GRAPHIC ARTS TOOL
91 Spread hay
94 Damp and hot
97 Stylish
99 Frosts, as a windshield
101 Respiratory disorder
103 ROCKY PEAK
105 Friendship
106 Helicopter part
107 Comedienne Imogene
108 CAPITAL OF YEMEN
109 Saucy
110 CITY OF SEVEN HILLS
112 Alone
115 EARLY IRISH TENANT
116 Oolong and pekoe
117 Grafted, in heraldry
119 EUR. COUNTRY
120 SINGLE
121 Decay
122 Study

by Ernst Theimer

ACROSS

1 Singer Franklin
7 Burghoff role
12 Swedish explorer Hedin
16 Arrow-poison tree
20 Lewd one
21 Act, in a way
22 Wing: Comb. form
23 Part of TV
24 Herb's promise for kids?
27 Kemo ___
28 Acts dreamily
29 At ___ (free)
30 Takes forty winks
32 Chew the ___ (ponder)
33 Deficiency: Comb. form
34 NASA cart
35 Dill of the Bible
36 Honors
38 Jim Lawrence's advice to teetotalers?
44 Stadium surface
45 Diseases of rye
46 Orient expresser
47 Buffalo Bill
49 Upgraded trail
52 Tyke protector
54 Encapsulate
57 Sticky stuff
58 Shield border
59 More demure
63 Tops
65 Fake goldleaf
67 Agitate
68 Bonkers
69 Covered
70 Heap of stones
72 Part of the U.K.
74 All-purpose trk.
75 Fillings after drillings
77 Make a collar
79 Grandpa on "The Waltons"
81 More osseous
82 Start of Julius's phrase for a carpenter?
85 Cradle tenders
88 ___-do-well
89 Colima cover-up
90 Frightful
92 Thai's neighbor
94 Anil, e.g.
96 Challenger
97 Legal claim
98 Radiate
99 Prefix with chord or meter

101 Cabot Cove's Jessica
103 Cows, to Cowper
104 Ask repeatedly
105 Apex
106 Hoopster Manute ___
107 Bacon products
110 Kind of bear
112 Brain passage
113 "The jig ___!"
115 Smell ___ (be suspicious)
116 Marina sights
121 Burbot
123 Harry's phrase for a goalie's crease?
128 Certain summaries
131 Kind of surgeon
132 Libation station potation
133 Smeltery pile
134 He wrote "The Brave Bulls"
135 Partner of Old Lace
137 Mouth, to a zoologist
140 Actress Massey
141 Feedbag filler
143 René's words for a lurker?
146 Soft cheese
147 Mixers' frozen assets
148 Tushington and Moreno
149 "Bridget Loves ___"
150 Koko's weapon
151 New Zealand parrots
152 About
153 Old lemons

DOWN

1 Thin silk for hoods
2 Change a shade
3 Parrot's activity
4 "... men have found a ___ love": Chesterton
5 TV's Ramsey et al.
6 Ham saver
7 Dub over
8 Arabian commander
9 Tintinnabular sound
10 To ___ (exactly)
11 Race a motor
12 Astringent
13 Last-word power
14 Notched, as a leaf
15 Horace's good news for a student?
16 Old musical syllables

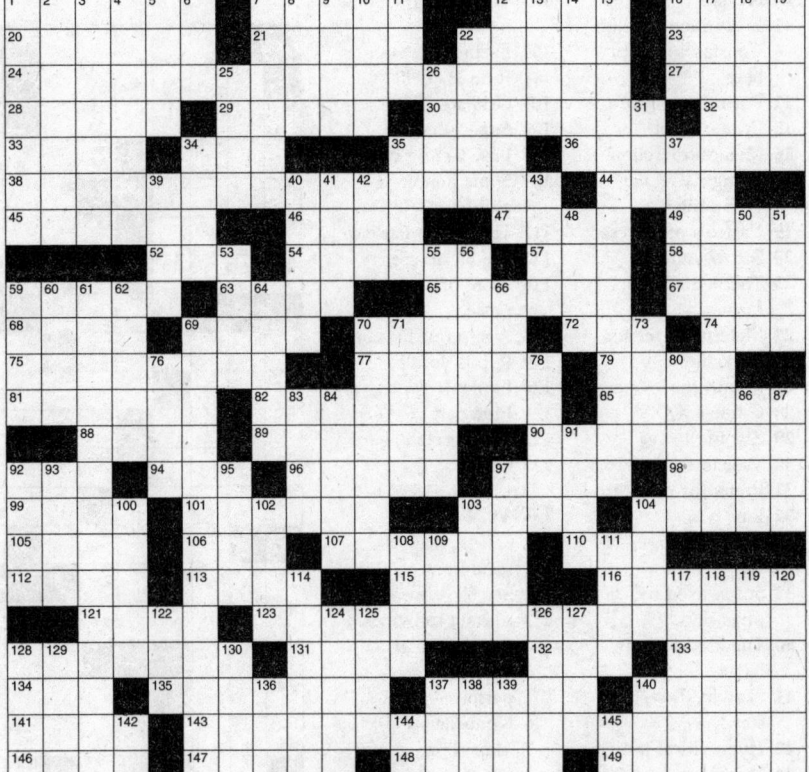

by Robert H. Wolfe

17 France's wish for Marcel à la Neville?
18 Photo collection
19 Uses a gin
22 Gloat
25 Everest stat.
26 One with eagle eyes
31 A memorable Erwin
34 Actress in "Signore e Signori"
35 Hailing call
37 Fielder's boot
39 Most of the U.K.
40 Topple
41 Corn bread
42 Forte of a good hosp.
43 Kind of stick
48 Bush rival in 1988
50 Touched down
51 Galley mark
53 Gilead's lack
55 More contrite
56 Kilmer opus
59 Hunk
60 "Ecce ___," Titian painting
61 George's retail-failure admission?

62 Isole ___ (isles off Sicily)
64 Desert relief
66 Cartouche
69 T.R.'s advice to a strong mason?
70 Elm fruits
71 Thin pancake
73 Tackle
76 Opposite of hawed
78 Two, once
80 Species of wheat
83 Grant
84 Papal vestment
86 Flavoring for a Cannes cordial
87 Some NCO's
91 Sediment
92 Places
93 ___ above (better)
95 Author-lecturer Mills
97 Site of knights' fights
100 A certain fool
102 Flood
103 A tippy canoe?
104 Pod denizens
108 Author Bellow

109 Cometic path
111 Hoopla
114 Imposters
117 Wraths
118 Juliet or Cordelia
119 Shipbuilding peg
120 Tropical, herbaceous plants
122 U.S. flight org.
124 Moran and Gray
125 Lobo group
126 Most domestic
127 Minn.'s St. ___ College
128 Messy ones
129 Pine
130 Progeny
136 Exile isle
137 Leg part
138 Mal de ___
139 Algerian port
140 Angered
142 Bishopric
144 Between, in Bologna
145 Eng. title

ACROSS

1 Encourages a felon
6 Constantine slept here
11 Portrait sculpture
15 Printer's dot
16 Musical direction
17 "King ___ Road," 1965 song
19 Castro's predecessor
20 See 67 Across
23 Toothed: Comb. form
24 Maternally related
26 Yorkshire city
27 Month for lovers
28 C times XXXV
29 Zwei follower
30 Vesicle
31 Prefix for puncture
32 Ray
33 See 67 Across
38 Con
39 Suffix used by physicists
40 The 23rd Hebrew letter
41 "Fawlty Towers" star
42 Hypocritical talk
44 Melody
46 Spinning devices
47 Backward, nautically
50 Duroc's home
53 Tibetan monk
55 City on the Loire
58 Scrooge word
59 Wind of S. France
62 Ego
64 Former Spanish enclave in Morocco
65 Kind of sch.
67 Heart of the matter
69 Dispatch
70 Star's car
71 Greet
72 Dolt
74 Sign of triumph
75 Scaly crust
77 Buddies
79 Carrie or Louis
80 Playground time
82 Jazz dance
84 Ursula Andress film
86 Isinglass
87 Gun aimed at a bomber
89 Capp and Capone
91 Daisy ___ Scraggs
92 Mezzo Stevens
96 See 67 Across
101 Perfume measure
102 Bridle part

103 Wine experts' comb. form
104 Earthquake site: June 21, 1990
105 Grimace
106 Super serve
107 Base Gehrig covered
109 Some Renoir paintings
111 Thrice minus twice
112 See 67 Across
116 More drippy, as paste
118 A sister of Eunomia
119 Pupils' locales
120 Jubilant
121 Pipe part
122 Ethyl acetate, e.g.
123 Gulls

DOWN

1 Self-service restaurant
2 See 67 Across
3 Certain railways
4 Parisian head
5 Top-notch performer
6 Nonbeliever
7 Map abbr.
8 Sitter's feature
9 One of the Waughs
10 Least batty
11 Movie Messala
12 Sky sightings: Abbr.
13 P.O. item
14 See 67 Across
15 Outlaws
16 Paravane
18 Puts up
19 Pump, in Peru
21 Meadowlands team
22 Obloquy
25 Calla, e.g.
30 Kind of servant
33 Language of Helsinki
34 Motorists' org.
35 Like a street after sleet
36 Worker's rights org.
37 Part of Asia Minor
43 Branch
45 How madcaps act
46 Corolla part
47 Actor Walter and family
48 Of a Frankish people
49 See 67 Across
50 Narrow furrow
51 Joan Sutherland specialties
52 Gab

54 Ballerina Park
56 Writer of suspense tales
57 Teams
60 Olivia of the Met
61 Guided
63 Harbor sights
66 Human
68 Large cask
73 Ten: Comb. form
76 Centers of attention
78 Plumed hat
81 See 67 Across
83 Trading place: Abbr.
85 Big name in New Haven
86 Affected
87 Facing the pitcher
88 Pretentious
90 Brandy-based cocktail
91 Hoover Dam's lake
93 Satires' cousins
94 Tipsy
95 Eastern V.I.P.
97 Legal wrong
98 Nielsen or Uggams
99 Comes onstage

100 Bind tightly
107 Exquisite
108 Gossip tidbit
110 Sea in the W. Pacific
113 Permit
114 Fruit center
115 Expert ending
117 Carpet feature

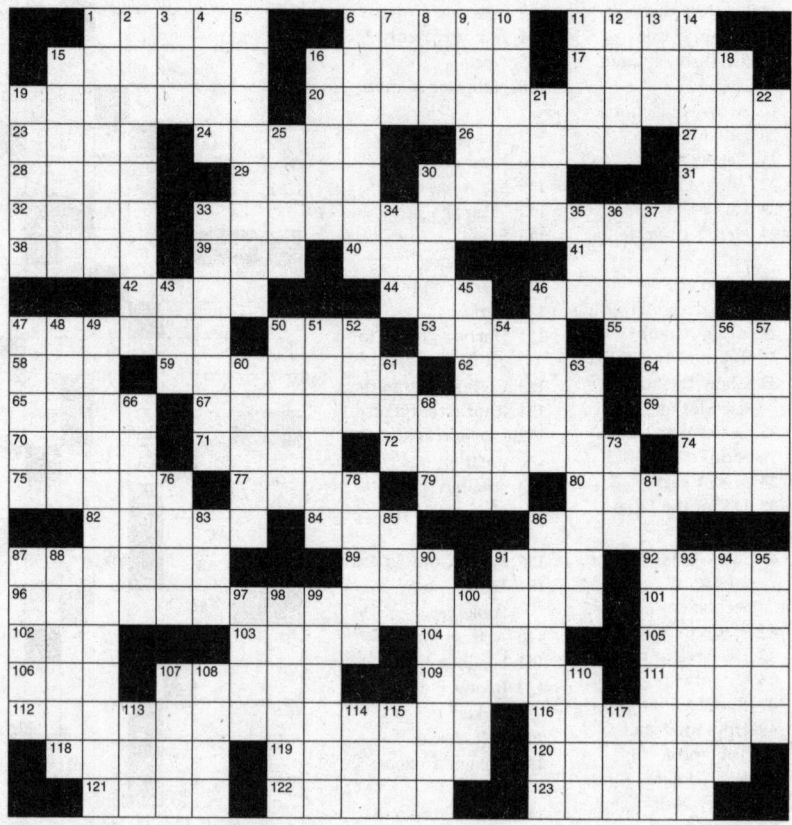

by Nancy Scandrett Ross

ACROSS

1 Feast at Waikiki
5 Cook on a grill
10 Florida city
15 Portmanteau word
19 Elec. units
20 Viking chieftain
21 Italian "Cleopatra": 1954
22 Setting for Leigh and Gable
23 Charles Boyer: 1938
25 Clint Eastwood: 1971
27 With 48 Down, Sinatra film: 1957
28 Always
29 Surgical instrument
31 Plant of the parsley family
32 Enthusiastic
34 Request
35 Like some screens
36 Soviet news service
37 Think
39 Lamb stew
42 Bearded, as barley
43 Biographer Leon
44 Piquant
46 Merkel of films
47 Mount climbed by Moses
48 Robert Duvall: 1972
50 V.P.'s boss
51 "___ Love You"
52 G.I. on French leave
54 Looked cheerful
55 Developed motion-picture film
56 Most vaporous
59 Sheep genus
60 ___ vivre
61 Like some R-rated films
62 Loss of breath
64 Tape erasures
65 Complain
68 Rosebud of "Citizen Kane"
69 Guest at the club
74 "___ New York"
75 Ravel hit
77 "Rosemary's ___"
78 Prefix with spore or sphere
79 Field mouse
80 Cary Grant: 1946
82 ___ Bell (Emily Brontë)
84 "Knute Rockne, ___ American"
85 Fashion-show attendee
86 Jacks of clubs

87 Barbra Streisand: 1969
88 Like a wedding cake
90 Follower of knock or weak
92 Curved arch
93 Bad guys in W.W. II films
94 Allot
97 Deep void
99 Provide
101 Mail
102 Chemical suffix
103 Beige's kin
106 Gert Frobe: 1964
108 Rosalind Russell: 1958
111 Kind of club
112 Newman-Redford film, with "The"
113 Meetings
114 Syria, once
115 Compound
116 Scuffle
117 Notched, as a leaf
118 Thereabouts

DOWN

1 Arctic nomad
2 Swedish port
3 Bette Davis: 1961
4 Kind of tax
5 Musical note
6 Doc Holliday: 1939
7 Swan genus
8 Type
9 Laxity
10 Silent film, e.g.
11 Spirals
12 Word on a Montreal stop sign
13 Baltic citizen
14 Some of a sum
15 Locus ___ (right to be heard)
16 Greer Garson: 1943
17 Stowe's "The Pearl of ___ Island"
18 Marvin of recording fame
24 Ray Danton: 1960
26 Comous
30 Bob Hope: 1951
33 On the Celebes
34 Contract proposals
35 G.I. Janes of W.W. II
36 Jackie Coogan: 1922
38 Strips
39 Colored
40 Upright
41 Art appreciation
42 Kin of daboias

44 Of a Frankish people
45 "Peyton Place" denizen: 1957
48 See 27 Across
49 Hipster's patter
50 Polyhedron
53 Litz, e.g.
55 Gene Hackman: 1971
57 Nimble
58 More up in the world
60 Door-frame piece
63 Coop sound
64 Growl
65 Compete with
66 ___ Gay, famed plane
67 Shelley Winters: 1964
68 Fish entree
70 Like Arbuckle
71 Jane Russell: 1951
72 Banishment
73 Cheerful
75 Hopalong Cassidy: 1935
76 Soft drink

80 What directors give
81 Agents, in some films
83 Firewood
85 Like a trailer from Hollywood
89 Oozed forth
91 Robert Donat: 1934
94 Potter's clay
95 Film shot
96 Title for Silvers in "You'll Never Get Rich"
98 Capital NW of Salt Lake City
99 Like omelets
100 Lopez theme song
101 Pay for a hand
102 "Journey ___ Fear," 1942 film
104 Latin lover's word?
105 James Mason: 1954
107 Doctrine
109 Erstwhile Arab rep.
110 Little Red Book author

by A. J. Santora

UN-STABLE BELLE

ACROSS

1 Last Egyptian king
6 Limerick foot
13 Pat by a bishop at confirmation
18 Golonka or Francis
19 Hawthorne's "The Blithedale ___"
20 "Nothing doing!"
22 Verse: Part I
25 Afternoon ballroom event
26 Charged particle
27 Battologize
28 ___ volente
29 Coffer
31 Deg. Wilson earned
32 He gives a dam
36 Divvy up
37 "Lord, is ___?": Matt. 26:22
38 Jamboree gp.
41 Abruzzi cathedral town
42 Do out of
43 "Chacun ___ goût!"
44 "In the Boom Boom Room" playwright
46 Verse: Part II
52 Bridge reversal
53 Southwestern plowed land
54 Enduring ennui
55 Admitted
56 A dancing Powell
58 Jeopardy
59 "The ___," Nevin song
60 ___ Kemal, Turkey's first president
63 Natives of Valletta
65 Dean Martin 50's hit
68 Western cutthroat trout
70 Bennett's order to flag viewers
74 Cake embellishment
75 Usher's beat
76 Duck around
78 Heavenly letters, to angels' eyes
79 Verse: Part III
83 Wild water buffalo
84 Agile
85 "Three men in ___"
86 All there
87 Triple this for a white wine
88 Quaker possessive
89 Executed a gainer
91 Spirit of St. Louis?
93 Mexican Mrs.
94 Skywalker's father
95 Yoko
96 Rib-tickling
100 Trappist cheese
101 Occasioned
106 End of verse
110 One of England's Days
111 European bunting
112 Hall of Famer Brimsek was one
113 Washer cycle
114 Man of the soil
115 Kaput

DOWN

1 Cleaving tool
2 Soprano Gluck
3 Clarinet, for one
4 Like some beds
5 More acute
6 Prado offering
7 ___ de plume
8 Mrs. March's youngest
9 Mâché material
10 "La Vie ___," Piaf hit
11 Whiff
12 Asian holiday
13 Aught
14 Swung along easily
15 Month before Nisan
16 Type of type
17 Vinegar: Comb. form
18 Take steps
21 Prior to, poetically
23 "The Name of the Rose" author
24 Teetered through the tulips
29 Slow boat destination
30 Knack
32 ___-Terre, Guadeloupe's capital
33 One of the Waters
34 Mountain ridge
35 Brit. title
36 Lose traction
37 "War ___": Sherman
38 Reads randomly
39 Finnish bath
40 First name in Dogpatch
42 Dark-complexioned, to Shakespeare
43 Roman courtyards
45 Swirl of water
47 Pantagruel's companion
48 Came up
49 Honest one
50 The Velvet Fog
51 Barnyard strutter
57 "___ on a rock...": Proudfit
58 Actress Prentiss
59 Aptly named author
61 Things go hummingly here
62 Like a tale of "the one that got away"
64 Tiny Tom
65 Tourist's entry permit
66 Pigment for Constable
67 Mortgage claims
69 Kind of strike
71 Felix's "odd" friend
72 Mirella of the Met
73 Woods, in Wassy
75 Sidewalk surface
76 Poly follower
77 Clamorous
80 Alienate
81 Brubeck or Garroway
82 Cleo's bosom buddy
89 Crow's relative
90 Big baking potatoes
91 Put behind bars
92 Lose enthusiasm for: Colloq.
93 Does some meter reading?
94 Word in a French toast
95 Low rating
96 Hack
97 ___ about (approximately)
98 1511, to Fabius
99 "Heads ___, tails you lose": Croker
101 Wonder's "___ She Lovely?"
102 Tobacco, for one
103 Hoyle decision
104 Writer Bagnold
105 Ike
107 Bribe for Cerberus
108 Wave, to Juan
109 Bled in the laundry

by Frances Hansen

ACROSS

1 Leave out
5 Nero's successor
10 Place
15 "The ___ Rig": Burns
18 Columbus' port
20 Book by André Maurois
21 Seats splitter?
22 Ancient
23 Line of cliffs
24 Orozco work
25 Break time, for some
26 Aitch preceder
27 Actress turned adjutant?
31 Confirmed
34 Hamartiologist's topic
35 "Rats!"
36 Nostalgic singer?
42 Endures
43 Lay ___ (flatter)
44 Marine flier
45 Counterfeiter's nemesis
49 City in S. France
50 Large parrot
52 Terrible
54 Author of "Hard Cash"
55 Koppel or Turner
56 Allotheist, e.g.
57 Where Fez is
59 Like steak tartare
60 Singer with medical training?
63 Smelting residue
66 "___ Blue?," 1929 song
67 Della and Pee Wee
68 Actor who comes for breakfast?
75 Peak in 30 Down
76 American songbird
77 Some tests
78 Top bowling score for Brutus?
81 Hari et al.
83 Fateful date
84 "Für ___," Beethoven opus
85 Mitchell estate
86 Going before: Abbr.
87 Title for Thérèse
88 ___ Bator
89 Raring to go
90 Balanced actor?
96 Part of a buttercup
99 Break bread
100 On in years
101 TV star who cleaned up his act?
107 Pro ___ (for the time being)
108 Hungarian hero
109 Kind of nest
110 Main artery
114 Author LeShan
115 Celebrate Alumni Day
116 Francis of the N.H.L.
117 Board members?
118 With 95 Down, a Tarzan
119 Terror
120 Deceives
121 Kidnapped

DOWN

1 Harvest goddess
2 Singer Davis
3 Dockers' org.
4 Hard rains
5 Reproductive cell
6 Cuckoopint
7 Calabrian currency
8 Smokey, for one
9 "Little Women" actress: 1949
10 Very smooth
11 Even
12 Slave of old
13 Fictional lamp owner
14 Reduce in dignity
15 Boston landing spot
16 Fragrant resin
17 Skillful
19 Frightens
28 ___ generis
29 Cause of inflation?
30 Where Suda Bay is
31 Musical term
32 Cape for John Paul II
33 Brought down the house, abroad
37 ___ Torrance, "The Rifleman" Marshal
38 Mythical flier
39 Part of a barn
40 Dormouse
41 Betel palm
46 Famed teammate of Mantle
47 "___ With Judy," 1948 film
48 Tritons
50 Gourd-shaped rattle
51 Actor's rep
52 Andrea ___
53 That 4/15 org.
54 Cowboy shindigs
56 Emulates Wyeth
57 Mythical Norse giant
58 Social group
60 Silkworm
61 Backs a dicer
62 Barbie's boyfriend
63 Be sparing
64 ___ of Lebanon
65 Rounded
69 One of the Pointer Sisters
70 Horowitz contemporary
71 ID datum
72 Ryan of mound fame
73 Sea water
74 ___ in apple
78 N.B.A. player
79 Angler's basket
80 Are her songs Simon-ized?
82 Agonized
84 Guido's high note
85 Become settled
87 One under oath
88 Feral
89 Make beloved
91 Straight ahead
92 Conveyed legally, as an estate
93 River blade
94 They're often metered
95 See 118 Across
96 Miller's "___ the Fall"
97 Can you believe this?
98 Dolph Lundgren role
102 Mold overflow
103 Mandlikova of tennis
104 Whale in a 1966 film
105 Twerp's cousin
106 Strike order?
111 Friend of Milne's Tigger
112 Part of Ali's rec.
113 Invite

by Joel D. LaFargue

ACROSS

1 Fiery felony
6 ___ law (Germanic code)
11 Type of herring
16 Residue
19 Stiller's wife
20 Bandleader Louis
21 Enforcement powers
22 Watering hole?
23 Ait
24 "The Shield of Achilles" poet
25 Decathlete Johnson
26 Darn
27 Wrestling holds
29 Fernando's fast food
31 Is under new management
33 Yoko
34 Elec. units
37 Fill this puzzle
39 Quail
40 Syndicated columns?
44 Bury
45 Smith and Capp
46 Bucolic
47 Eschew
49 Tex. battle site
52 Memorable stutterer
53 "___ thee late a rosy wreath": Jonson
54 Halfway-like
57 Out of the race
59 Dublin or nothin'?
62 Cool quaff
63 Kind of frost
64 Aesopian finale
65 "My Fair Lady" lyricist
66 Wilbur works
68 Muslim wise man
69 Greek letters
70 Nod off
72 Scolded
73 Pseudologist
74 Stalemate
77 Hiked through camp-grounds?
79 Librarians' clientele
81 Article
82 Physicist Bohr
83 Soviet sea
84 Merchandise
85 Group of badgers
86 Brilliance
88 Ens' followers
89 What Salk conquered
93 Beer foam?
98 Carry out
100 Wildebeest
101 Vend

102 Symbol of strength
104 He dyes for a living
105 Cartoon tiger
107 Dickens's Madame ___
110 Bern's river
111 Pepper pot ingredient
113 Capitol Hill body
116 Building projection
117 Racket
118 Kovacs
119 Depside is one
120 Arabian gazelle
121 Silly pair
122 Stormed
123 Facients
124 Après-ski drink

DOWN

1 ___ acids
2 Take umbrage
3 Jaundiced
4 Mine finds
5 Brussels-based org.
6 Bursts of energy
7 Indonesian island group
8 Palpebra
9 "___ a man who wasn't there"
10 Rummy game
11 Promenade
12 Green or jacket
13 What a pause does
14 Fit to ___
15 Advice to an inept gardener?
16 Agreement
17 Londoner's pantry
18 Mooring rope
28 Scots' negatives
30 Anthracite
32 Barrette
35 O. Henry
36 Swung around
38 Craft
41 "___ Camera"
42 Moths' meeting?
43 A.M.A. members
48 Muddied
49 Third king of Judah
50 Statistician's Abbr.
51 "I long for ___ . . .": Wordsworth
52 Discovery sounds
53 Mosque priest
54 Cathedral
55 Jewel thief's loot
56 German article
58 ___ Française (French national theater)
59 One-liners, e.g.

60 Jejune
61 Sixty minutes, in Siena
64 Dillon of "Gunsmoke"
67 Sounds from tack-sitters
68 Brinker of fiction
69 Spin a log
70 Agr. is one
71 Fall call
72 D.S. Freeman book
73 Abominate
75 Wrath
76 Ar's chaser
78 Attaching ropes
79 Churlish children
80 Porter's "DuBarry ___ Lady"
83 TV sitcom
86 Ferber or Millay
87 Gave reluctantly, with "up"
88 Make eyes at
89 Dressage maneuver
90 Soup ingredient
91 Ascertains
92 Here, in Haiti
94 Made a pact

95 Church officials
96 Vile
97 Lost muscle tone
99 ___ incognita
103 Singer Smith
106 Mediocre
108 Soho pad
109 Baltic island
112 Nesselrode, e.g.
114 Actress Christensen
115 Sun. discourse

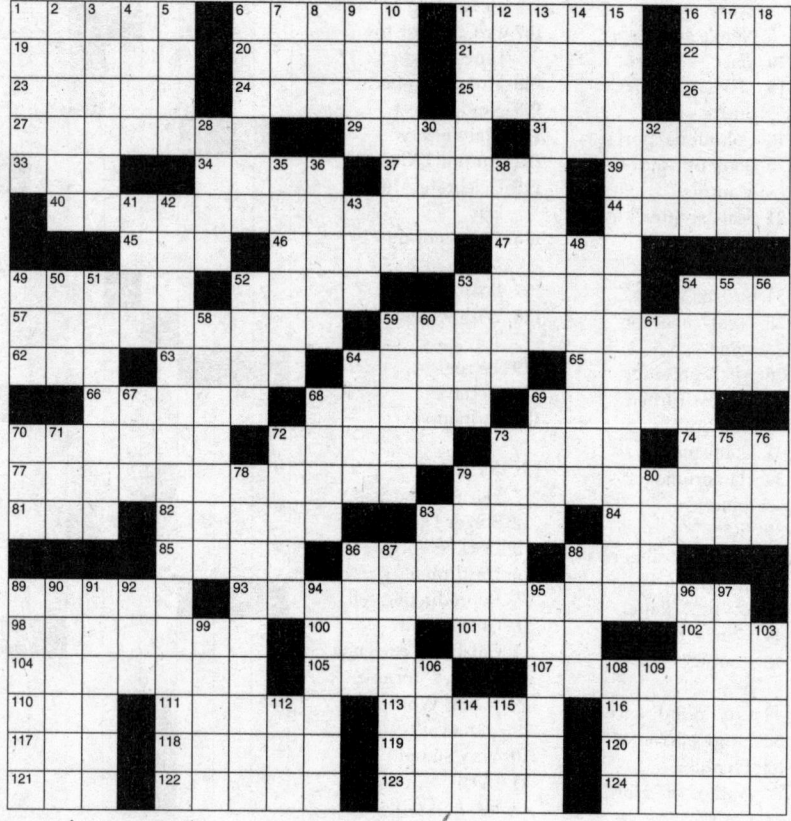

by Jeanne Wilson

by Patrick Merrell

ACROSS

1 Some grad sch. requirements
4 Auctioned auto, often
8 Low-level workers?
14 Monthly bill
19 Cup filler
20 Stream of literature
21 Jarring, musically
22 Continental divide?
23 Most pricey
25 Focal point
26 Like some old alphabets
27 TREASURE HUNT STEP 1: Where to start
30 Sensational
31 Jay watched by owls
32 Green-lit
33 Lead-in to while
34 Jurist Black
35 Constitution writer
38 They're stuck in I.C.U.'s
41 TREASURE HUNT STEP 2 (include black squares)
45 Wrap
49 Drills
50 Greeter's greeting
51 Break
52 AOL Time Warner division
54 Where cc's might be given
55 Bite-size snacks
56 Look
57 Certain hospital case
60 XXX
61 TREASURE HUNT STEP 3
68 Amidst, briefly
69 Made
70 Events at which people may wear gloves
72 Poetic pocketful?
75 French possessive
78 Worked (up)
79 "Is that so?!"
81 Dumas swordsman
82 Entertaining
84 Anatomical cap
85 TREASURE HUNT STEP 4
89 Hanoi holiday
90 ___ Pieces
91 Galatea's love
92 Drove, with "off"
96 Graybeard
99 Electric discharges
100 Blip displayer
101 TREASURE HUNT STEP 5: Read these (starting east) . . . and congratulations!
106 Brownish yellow
107 Tritt who sang "T-R-O-U-B-L-E"
108 Wacko
109 Matches, as tracks
110 Least threatening
111 Bring in
112 Kind of shot
113 Button that replaces pins
114 Treats for horses
115 Misses a fly, say
116 Mock, in a way

DOWN

1 Stir
2 1981 Moore/Minnelli film
3 Shows displeasure, in a way
4 Galloping
5 Paid in full
6 Musical piece at the end of a church service
7 Moving
8 Bette's "All About Eve" role
9 It led to ancient Rome
10 Innocent's claim
11 Home of Vance Air Force Base
12 They might cut and paste letters
13 Relaxes
14 Groan-inducing, perhaps
15 Less than right
16 Late-marrying men
17 Inner sanctum
18 Letter accompanier: Abbr.
24 It might be shown to one who's seen it all
28 Sufficient, once
29 Pitcher parts
34 Colts can be kept in them
35 The Seminoles, for short
36 Queens's ___ Park
37 State
39 L.B.J. or R.M.N., once
40 Former union members: Abbr.
41 Mdse.
42 Model Campbell
43 Reason for insurance
44 Liqueur
45 Yearbook sect.
46 Tear up
47 Pete Sampras, sometimes
48 Bad career move
52 Fooled
53 Work on tables
55 Cheese selections
58 Royale of old autodom
59 Cutter
60 Compadre of Fidel
62 Silver holder
63 "The Godfather: Part II" setting
64 Find for 8-Across
65 It may be brought to a razing
66 Finger, perhaps
67 Farfetched
71 Grp. famously involved in bank robberies
72 Diplomat's goal
73 Plains dweller
74 Closings
75 Cop's hangout
76 Sinuous creatures
77 Old blade
80 Suffix with Capri
82 Lehár work
83 VCR attachments
84 Aunt in "Arsenic and Old Lace"
86 Russian river
87 Raider?
88 "The Virginian" actor
92 Word with ghost or boom
93 "Hmm?" inducer
94 Relax
95 Change channels?
97 Scale mark
98 Rendezvous
99 Support staff: Abbr.
100 Is happy-footed
101 Alice of old musicals
102 Pat
103 Daredevil Knievel
104 Angry reaction
105 Blacken
106 Dungeons & Dragons game co.

ACROSS

1 These may be bald
6 Three, to Tomás
10 A language in Bangkok
13 Vivaciousness
19 Expiate
20 What flattops carry
22 Stipend
23 Venezuelan instruments?
25 Inquiry into lost goods
26 Worldwide workers' org.
27 Hwy.
28 Admission
29 Liqueur ingredient
30 Doral sight
33 Certain wise men
34 Table fowl
36 Like certain sports
37 Italian metal?
40 Twilight
43 Situation
44 So
45 Site of Honolulu
46 Largest of the Truk Islands
47 ___ de mer
48 Max, Buddy or Bugs
49 Austrian author Marie von ___. Eschenbach
50 Toltec capital
51 South African headgear?
55 Shawl
56 Regimental commander
59 Ellipses
60 Xenophobe's fear
62 Disposed to love
63 Jar for oil, etc.
64 Mercury or Mars, in Marseille
65 Scold
66 Ancient Greek council
67 Brought into agreement
68 Shake ___ (high-tail it)
69 Southwestern manor?
72 "...ye better reck the ___": Burns
73 Drug fighting infections
74 In a skillful way
75 Concorde
78 W.W. II post for Ike
79 "Questa o quella," e.g.
80 Nobelist in Chemistry: 1934
81 Dull finish
83 Quiet!
84 Some New York traffic sounds?
87 Fruitless
88 Root used in perfume
90 Cleopatra attendant
91 Alighieri admirer
92 Man's slipper
94 Miller's "___ the Fall"
96 Switz., Ger. et al.
97 Ending for function or budget
98 Captivate
100 Island sleepwear?
104 Announcement
105 Belief
106 "___ Psyche": Keats
107 Pledges
108 Sun. talk
109 A ruminant
110 Bridge expert

DOWN

1 Quaker tenet
2 Legendary Greek heroine
3 Doughnut-shaped
4 Former Spanish queen
5 Dry, as champagne
6 Toothsome
7 Coleridge creation
8 Period
9 Yells
10 Strategy
11 At a distance
12 ___-bitsy
13 Part of i.e.
14 Mexican's woolen blanket
15 Flat: Comb. form
16 Midwestern soup bowl?
17 Angers
18 Londoner's radial
21 Scope
24 Sandarac tree
31 Decay
32 Misfortune
33 Grieve
34 Comedian Myron
35 Sino-Russian border river
37 S.A. ostrich
38 Limp
39 Hindu princes
41 With light rapidity, in music
42 Slipped by, as time
44 Board
48 Judicial writ
49 Cancels
50 Moral pang
51 Feeble, childish condition
52 Single quantity
53 Yeastlike fungus
54 Palate part
56 Nightclub
57 Brunch dishes
58 Texas beefsteak?
60 Relieve
61 Secular
63 Grant's first Vice President
64 Adjective for buddies
66 Actress Ina
69 Spanish coins
70 Hyde and Regent's
71 Vigoda et al.
73 Item for Indira
75 Banner
76 An ester used in ointments
77 "Idylls of the King" poet
80 Without protection
81 Staff
82 Bonsai or origami
84 Ornamental pin
85 To this place
86 One of Pan's companions
87 Theda of silents
89 Put off
91 Miami's super receiver
92 Schism
93 ___ about (time-setting phrase)
94 Rudiments
95 Subway token
96 Verb suffix
99 Legal matter
101 Chemical ending
102 Emulate James F. Fixx
103 Stir

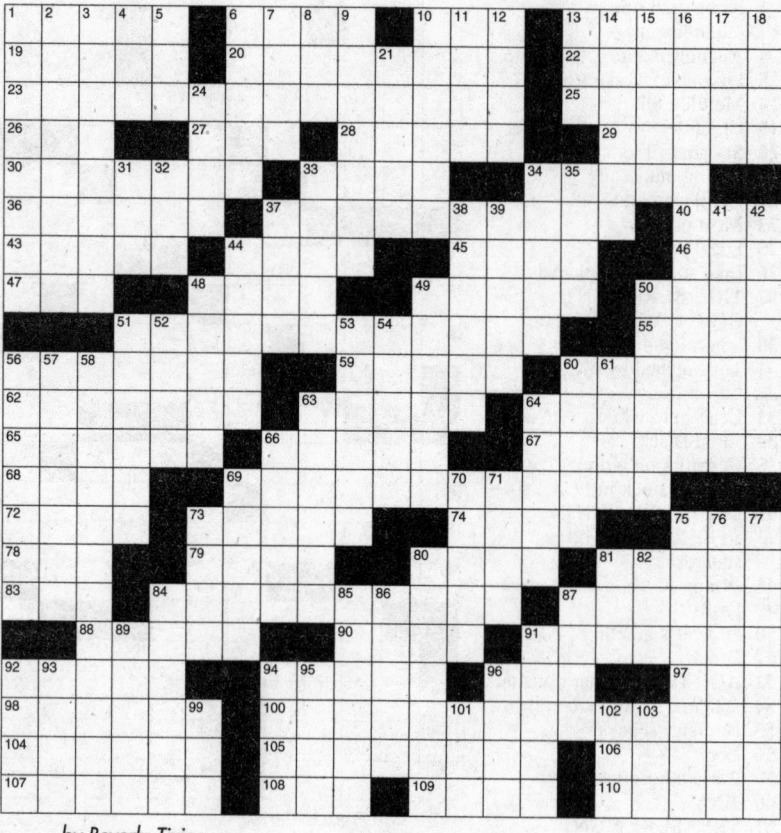

by Beverly Tivin

ACROSS

1 W Afr. republic
4 Awed chap
9 W.W. I plane
13 Applies
17 Maui or Molokai
19 Where Black Bears study
20 Audience response
21 ___ nous
22 Kindergarten hazards?
25 Exhaust, as strength
26 Taurus cluster
27 Nautical home
28 Pullulated
29 Puts in order
30 Inclinations
31 Plat anew
32 Louganis score
33 Bald eagle's cousin
34 Greene or Shatner
37 "My Name Is ___ Lev": Potok
40 Wee picnicker, after tasting spilled rye?
42 Blue Eagle monogram
43 Winter headwear
44 Golfer Peete
45 Blame
46 Composer of "Happy Days Are Here Again"
47 Wing that can't fly
48 Haylift?
52 Hasso of films
53 Calm
56 "Stormy Weather" composer
57 Dress fabric
58 Reflection
59 Manifest
60 Brief role
61 Loses control
63 ___ mind (considered)
64 Kind of Congressman
67 Perspective
68 Buck going out with doe?
70 Teacher's org.
71 Cry of alarm
72 Filly's brother
73 Elec. unit
74 Passover feast
76 U.N. member
77 Don Juan's prize?
81 "Rinaldo" poet
82 Favorite boutique?
85 Young or Hale
86 Where to see olas
87 Salad days
88 Horace, e.g.
89 Golfer Willie or Jimmy
93 Unwilling
95 Fire starter
96 Holes in space?
97 Thierry's topper
98 Crowds of typographers?
100 Singer Ross
101 Roof section
102 Scandinavian
103 Bulrush
104 Over and above
105 Zees' forerunners
106 Asa and Thomas
107 Gormandize

DOWN

1 Speech defects
2 Weaver's fiber
3 Plant with four-lobed flowers
4 Kind of mean
5 Zodiacal sign
6 Lyrical Lily
7 Siamese twin
8 Highway ___
9 Abbreviate
10 Covenants
11 Egyptian key of life
12 Shingle letters
13 Illiterate
14 Post office?
15 N.Y. canal
16 Convey
18 Shed
21 Plant problem
23 Plantation crew
24 ___-Lenape (Delaware Indians)
28 Jamboree units
30 Lawyer Melvin
31 Hoisted, as a flag
34 Decree
35 N.B.A. site
36 Breathing passages
37 Attention-getter
38 Han of "Star Wars"
39 Wrestlers' methods?
40 Diminish
41 Bridge master
44 Refer to
46 Played the paraclete
48 Shipment to a paper mill
49 Nita of the silents
50 Silo filler
51 What limpets do
52 Ditto
54 Rousseau boy
55 Event for Atalanta
57 Ball role
59 A Reagan daughter
60 Something to break
61 Settle accounts
62 Aromatic herb
63 Split
64 Mine gear
65 So-so grades
66 N.Z. shrub or tree
68 Swinging things
69 All bones
72 Reasonable facsimile?
74 Antithesis of surfeit
75 Serious
78 Author Gordimer and singer Conner
79 Flash
80 Studio department
83 Tranquil
84 Snappish
86 Guillemots
88 Oil source
89 Half crocked
90 Follow
91 Inscribed pillar
92 Resource
93 Fit
94 Meat order
95 Melee
96 Site of Shah Jahan's memorial
98 Pepe Le ___ of cartoons
99 Easter preceder

by Louis Sabin

220 CAPITAL GAINS

ACROSS

1 Censure savagely
7 Record holder
13 Author Carroll
18 Here
20 Kind of power
22 ___ del mar (arrow crab)
23 Ark. gala?
26 Infuriated
27 ___ en point: Her.
28 Hartebeests
29 Salty sauce
30 Set of three
31 Declivity
33 Author of "One World or None"
34 Peanut, to Pedro
35 Orly speed demon
36 Investigative object
37 W.W. II Greek underground
39 Stored the stores
41 Most like Babar
43 Borecole
44 Biblical verb endings
45 Had a wordy wrangle
48 Extol
50 "___ be true..."
53 Condiment containers
54 "___ poor Nelly starve": Charles II
56 Seven-candles holder
59 French trace
60 First name in fashion
61 Frigga's spouse
63 Angel's delight
64 Bank abbr.
65 Canine at a Portuguese conflagration?
70 Building wing
71 Penultimate Greek letter
72 Episcopates
73 About
74 Hamstrung
76 Contiguous
79 Bed adjunct
81 Elizabethan court dance
82 Way in or out
84 Tone: Comb. form
85 Man before the mast
86 Patron of Roman husbandmen
87 Hebrew letter: Var.
89 Covered collections
91 ___ seed (deteriorated)
93 Alter course
94 First site of the Olympic Games
95 It's the word
98 A King
99 Strawberry's patch, once
101 Complained
104 Capital of Yemen Arab Republic
105 Wire measurement
106 Appropriate forcibly
107 What Polly Flinders was warming
108 Arch preceder
109 Serbian educator?
114 Mountain nymph
115 Salary
116 Kind of service at Easter
117 Where Tacloban is
118 Gins
119 Cures by smoking: Scot.

DOWN

1 Flattens on impact
2 Crow and Fox
3 Cutting comeback
4 Actor John from Baltimore
5 Hew
6 Compass pt.
7 Anglo-Saxon lawsuit
8 Jerry West was one
9 Saharan region
10 Bambi's aunt
11 Notably effective
12 Gave sanction to
13 Sitting formations
14 Memorable time
15 Polish buck rider?
16 Chants
17 Title for a noble Moslem
19 Braided
21 "American Gigolo" star
24 French weights
25 Refusals
31 Opera's Emma
32 Chinese croaker cookout?
34 Words to live by
36 OPEC, e.g.
38 Composer Edouard
40 Typical college freshman
41 Weight allowance
42 A. Conan Doyle's" ___ World"

45 Handwriting
46 Press, in Palma
47 Tex. music center?
49 Sun disk for Amenhotep
51 Surrounded by
52 Unhitching post
54 Uvula
55 Flux
57 Francis from Boston
58 Tenant
62 Does, e.g.
66 Berlin's "Say It ___ So"
67 Bristle
68 ___ thin air
69 Looks daggers at
75 Rara ___
77 Bridge expert
78 Formerly, formerly
80 Fleuret's relative
81 Showing fear
83 Young hares
85 Harasses
86 Tartuffe's creator
88 "And the wild cataract ___ glory": Tennyson
90 Drive back

91 Frolic
92 Greek peak
95 Johnny of song
96 Disquiet
97 Hotel de ville bigwigs
100 Hulls of Yorkshire berries
102 In accord
103 Sylvan area
104 Holy, at Lourdes
106 Heraldic anagram for rude
108 Gem facet
110 Channel
111 I.R.S. employee
112 L.B.J. beagle
113 A cont.

by Elaine D. Schorr

ACROSS

1 Neglect
7 It may be called
12 Suffix with problem
16 Mo. of George W. Bush's birthday
19 Isolate
20 Plunder
21 Drive-___
22 Methyl or ethyl follower
23 Restaurant options #1
26 Author LeShan
27 Tested, as duds
28 Guileless
29 Subject of the lyric "A horse is a horse, of course, of course"
30 Elates
31 Detectives' aids
36 Tire meas.
37 Sibyls
38 "So what?!"
40 1948 Bogart/Bacall film
42 Restaurant options #2
47 Serves at a restaurant
48 Restaurant options #3
50 ___ Blount in the Football Hall of Fame
51 Sequentially
52 Marshal at Waterloo
53 Oman man
55 Crucifixes
59 ___ la la
60 Bekaa Valley locale: Abbr.
62 City SW of Ithaca
64 Opposite of sans
65 Western lily
67 Restaurant options #4
71 Occupy
72 Prophet's reading
73 Oil source
74 12/24, e.g.
76 Domingo, for one
77 Some etiquette rules
79 Fashion craze
80 ___ clip
83 Swamp
85 Cousin of a mandolin
87 Restaurant options #5
90 Tony-winning writer of "Evita"
94 Restaurant options #6
95 Like most tutoring
97 Cylindrical totes for sailors' gear
98 Broadway fare
99 Take, as tea
101 TV's Morgenstern
102 Toxin combatant
107 One may be placed before a king
108 Serious fan groups
110 Popular Web service provider
112 "Prince ___" ("Aladdin" song)
113 Restaurant options #7
118 Former TV dog
119 Renaissance musicmaker
120 Push off
121 Recipients
122 Physics unit
123 Chinese calendar animals
124 Praise
125 Fleet

DOWN

1 Figures shown in red
2 Habituate
3 Cause of some arrests
4 You, in the Yucatán
5 Makes tracks, in a way
6 Architect Saarinen
7 Arctic interjection
8 Fleur-de-___
9 Aerial anomaly, for short
10 Sneeze's cause, perhaps
11 Plant with fiddleheads
12 In harm's way
13 Popular morning talk show
14 "Dies ___"
15 ___ laude
16 Vocal opponents
17 Experience
18 Entices
24 Wired
25 Limit
29 Home-style entree
32 Incite
33 Revere
34 Chaplin's chapeau
35 Arabian capital
37 Less straightforward
38 Immensity
39 Townsfolk
41 Starchy food
42 City east of Monaco
43 Radiation, e.g.
44 Buckeyes' sch.
45 Jazz's Malone
46 Early actress Talmadge
48 Squelches
49 Digital protection
54 Mill Hole ___ (home for Robert Burns)
56 Egg conveyor
57 1949 title role for Hedy Lamarr
58 Scrape the ground with a golf club before hitting the ball
61 Orange Free State settler
62 "That will be ___ the set of sun": "Macbeth"
63 Hither and yon
66 1990's sitcom starring a real-life rap/R & B family
68 Companion of the Natl. Guard
69 Actress ___ Brewster
70 Some sorority women
75 Prefix with skeleton
78 Hides
80 One who's much praised
81 Modern workout system
82 Rachel Field verse "___ Might Lead to Anywhere"
84 Auto introduced in 1989
86 "The Island of the Day Before" writer
88 "Deutschland ___ alles"
89 Prefix with genesis
90 Beyond what's necessary
91 Nicotrol device
92 Cat's activity
93 As part of a set
96 Ford of fashion fame
100 Liq. measures
102 Sharpener
103 Mag published without paper or ink
104 Soprano Fleming
105 Pushed
106 Antiquated
108 Essence
109 Disgruntled
111 "Tight" ones
113 Mrs. Andy Capp
114 Leader in old Rome
115 Go (for)
116 Start of some art movement names
117 Not in the pink

by Michael Grudzielanek

ACROSS

1 Like the acid in apples
6 Neckline?
11 Deserving a thumbs-up
15 Certain cookie
19 Idealized view of a parent, say, in psychology
20 Oil-well capper Red ___
21 Morales of "La Bamba"
22 What an imp never wears
23 ___ chairman
24 Hero after whom eight U.S. counties are named
25 ___ the Great, juvenile detective
26 Ties around the middle
27 "The nerve!"
29 High-level course planners?
32 General assembly?
36 Alice who won an Emmy for "Bewitched"
37 Waggle dancer
38 Nutritional info
40 Trinity component
41 Dramatist Fugard
45 William Kennedy Pulitzer-winning novel
48 Coin with the image of St. George the Warrior
53 Servant
55 Take care of
57 Prefix with lateral
58 East Indian sailors
59 Sulphur Island, for short
60 Makes flush
61 Dilutes
62 One attacking a colony, maybe
67 Taliban mullah and others
68 Metric liquid meas.
69 It may have big ears
70 Mine
71 Swiped a mink?
73 English court
74 Port in the Punic Wars
76 Kind of probe
77 Feel queasy, e.g.
78 Dwellers along the Bay of Biscay
80 Encourage, in a way
81 1904 Olympics site
85 Thief
86 Superlatively festive
88 Envelope stuffer
90 Lies
91 Meyers of "Kate & Allie"
93 Los Angeles suburb next to Torrance
95 Get battle-ready
98 "You ___!"
101 One who can't cope
106 A small price to pay
109 Like many fish and mountains
110 All over the media
111 ___ soi (at home): Fr.
112 "Alice" director, 1990
116 Zoo critter
117 List part
118 On earth
119 Satisfy, in a way
120 Blockheaded
121 Like some football passes
122 Flanders river
123 Overblown
124 Some curlicue parts

DOWN

1 Take off on
2 Company named after its hometown
3 Put on
4 "___ at the office"
5 Rival of Ajax
6 The Clintons' Buddy, e.g.
7 Flap
8 ___ Tiago (one of the Cape Verde islands)
9 Old jug
10 Certain cookie
11 Rap or country
12 Noted cave-dweller, informally
13 "Colorado Serenade" and others
14 "Just for the taste of it" sloganeer
15 "Git!"
16 Bigwig
17 Correspondently
18 It might be mounted in the West
28 Widescreen choice
30 In turmoil
31 Recent: Prefix
33 Jumbles
34 One of the Kennedy clan
35 ___ Tour
39 Milk supplier
41 Sports org. with the Calder Cup
42 Just so
43 Counterpart of a speaking fee?
44 Swing
46 Daily V.I.P.
47 Woman's marriage gift: Var.
49 Tavern owner, e.g.
50 Algebra work
51 Stage assistant
52 Rodin sculpture, with "The"
54 Abbr. in real estate ads
56 Norse goddess of fate
60 It's classified
62 For a bit
63 Kevin of "S.N.L." fame
64 Toe count
65 Hidden element in this puzzle's theme
66 It gets to the point quickly
69 "Git!"
71 Refuse to get rid of
72 Band member
74 Two-time Art Ross Trophy winner
75 Turn ___ profit
78 One Israel party leader
79 Yearbook inkers: Abbr.
81 Elastic
82 Bruin athlete
83 Pier grp.
84 Salt pork
85 Digital-display types
87 Kemo ___
89 White stuff, in Dundee
92 They're produced by hives
94 ___ Cayes, Haiti
95 Greenfly, e.g.
96 Way to go
97 John D. MacDonald sleuth Travis ___
99 Like une amie
100 Stereotypical fraternity member
102 Troubles
103 Philosopher Watts and others
104 Pick up
105 Head starts
107 Shawn of the N.B.A.
108 Band-Aid site
113 Baby seat?
114 Just make, with "out"
115 Nascar racer Jarrett

by Jim Page

ACROSS

1 Risky biz
5 Tyrian contemporary of Solomon
10 Philadelphia suburb
15 Anjou or Bosc
19 Dolphin's predator
20 Writer Rogers St. Johns
21 Dynel relative
22 River to the Laptev Sea
23 Arlene's puppets?
25 Disney's dance?
27 Impassive
28 Protozoan
30 Singer-actress O'Shea
31 Broadway musical
32 London lane
33 Author Stoker
34 Hoople's rank
37 Personal assurance
38 Four-in-hand kin
42 ___ Dhabi, Arab emirate
43 Composer's coins?
47 Peppery
48 ___ Aviv
49 Psalm ending
50 Elizabeth II, to Lady Sarah
51 Lay at anchor
52 Type of eng.
54 Lew's lilts?
58 Symbol of a sort
59 Asset
61 Gore
62 Bigwig in Kabul
63 Violinist Laredo
64 Debussy's "___ de lune"
65 Nicholas and Alexander
67 Furthers
69 Star of "The In-Laws"
70 Laments
73 Lapwing
74 Madison's makeup
76 A Copperfield
77 Mars, to Menander
78 "Comus" composer
80 ___ prosequi
82 Short word after long
83 Doing poorly
84 Sprite's sensors?
88 January on the links
89 Breathes
91 Carthaginian
92 Dough

94 English architectural style
95 Best seller in 1924
96 Hershfield's "agent"
98 One of six Vatican leaders
101 Pivots
102 Drew or Lester
106 Harlow's heritage?
108 Sin of one of the Finns?
111 Peak
112 Storehouse
113 Glorify
114 Scenery changer
115 Antarctic sea
116 Univ. divisions
117 Strikes out
118 Gives the once-over

DOWN

1 Repairs the lawn
2 Low trick: Scot.
3 A feature of this puzzle
4 Printed cotton
5 Attacked
6 Fans' favorites
7 Electrical unit
8 "___ These Women," 1964 Bergman film
9 First president of Czechoslovakia
10 ___ attorney
11 "The Sheik of ___"
12 Pot, in Potosi
13 Oft-drawn item
14 School
15 Transfusion infusion
16 Fish dish
17 Prefix for septic or social
18 Demolish
24 Mufflers
26 Whip marks
29 Rumple
32 Chapeau designer Lilly
33 Beethoven's birthplace
34 "Stabat ___"
35 A poplar
36 Massenet's marquises?
37 Springe
38 Gounod opera
39 Cecil's streets?
40 Sidestep
41 Cowpoke's charge
44 Fortify again
45 Type of clover
46 Less common
51 Muzzle stuffer

53 Mexican tree dwellers
55 Describing armozeen
56 Author Nin
57 "Of Thee ___"
58 Jezebel's god
60 One of the Hebrides
64 Unrelenting
65 Edison contemporary
66 Hex
67 "___ of star-cross'd lovers": Shak.
68 A Milton who found paradise in TV
69 Choreographer de Mille
70 Chemical suffix
71 Cereal blight
72 Rhone feeder
75 Strip a ship of tackle
78 Put in order
79 African's leather thong
81 Sighting
84 Roles for sopranos

85 Consorts
86 Champagne department
87 Isolated
90 Tom and Robert Treat
93 Charge with gas
95 Was dormant
96 Sweeting, e.g.
97 Surpasses
98 Open a bit
99 Art ___
100 L.A. team
101 Pushover
103 Agile
104 Baritone Hawkins
105 Fiber clusters
107 Summer, in Saumur
109 "Whacks-work"
110 Buddy

by Mary Virginia Orna

ACROSS

1 Griddle offering
8 Black-tie accessory
12 Military advance
20 Crane
21 Egg on
22 Fragrant
23 Yell about owning beard softener
25 Meat found in dessert at shore outing
26 Spread seeds
27 Chinese official's office
28 Degrees of merit
29 Aboriginal Chinese people
31 Pierced repeatedly
33 Ukr. was one
34 Humiliate
38 Top-notch
39 Sun ___ of China
43 Legal right
44 Fugard's "A Lesson from ___"
46 Play quoits
48 Rock elm
49 Compass pt.
50 Outside range, sandwich is least tasty
52 Finished
54 "___ was saying . . ."
55 Suffix for certain acids
56 Noah's units
58 Myrna
59 ___ Tinto, city in Brazil
60 Slothlike
62 Nastase
64 Macadamize
66 Spanish landladies
67 Wireless
69 Plates are reordered anew in shop
71 Whittle down
72 Same, to Seneca
73 Brother of Moon Mullins
74 Orch. section
75 Have a gabfest
76 Military decoration
77 Tailor's goal
78 Comportment
80 Storied upset runner
82 Many lbs.
85 Litheness
87 Bird takes family inside to make a coat

89 Becker boomer
90 Flaxen fabric
91 ___ Shah Pahlevi
94 ___ rye (deli order)
95 Corrode
96 Tenets
98 Wooden blocks
100 Aleksandropol, today
102 Tor. locale
103 Holdup man
105 Have the flu
106 Guinevere's lover
109 Astronaut's milieu
111 Michael Jordan, for one
115 Storekeeper is one who complains about hit movie
116 Search results when certain barbarian breaks up treat
118 Widespread
119 Austrian title
120 Church discipline
121 Top hit man
122 MI
123 Fund-raisers' rewards

DOWN

1 Kettle emission
2 Dos x cuatro
3 January warm spell
4 B.C., e.g.
5 Resident
6 Part of a Heyerdahl craft's name
7 Up-tight
8 Conjectured
9 Wooded
10 Kampala is its capital
11 L.B.J. was one
12 Pinball sites
13 Mistress Quickly
14 Fresh as ___
15 War cry spotted in Indian city
16 Canadian Ladd Parks inside
17 Scorch
18 Puts into law
19 Sault ___ Marie
24 Child in autoMobile gets capital
28 Recent: Comb. form
30 How some exams are given
32 Bingo relative
34 One of the pride of Joy
35 Fan

by Derrick C. Niederman

36 Existing around author is confusing
37 Turkish regiment
40 Smelled Woody inside armored vehicle
41 Eternal
42 Knobby
45 Recessed
47 Ointment
50 Galoot's cousin
51 Popeye's kid could cry in the ocean
53 Dactyl or hallux
57 Bandy words
61 Archery requisite
63 Impend
65 Greek war god chimed in
66 He was a thriller in Manila
67 Coarse
68 Ballet duet
69 Bacchus attendant
70 Strumpet
71 Sigh sound
73 Little fox
75 Skulls

77 Tycoon found in more lavish surroundings
79 Adult insect
81 Soon
83 Sponsor of a court tourn.
84 Like a baseball's seams
86 Drink made from simple organism, in general
88 Bushman's milieu
92 Put teeth in a law
93 Suit type
95 Grail retriever
97 Sailor's guide
99 Hi-fi must
101 Christian creed
104 Wing: Comb. form
106 Saber más que ___ (to be wide-awake)
107 Keep ___ (persevere)
108 Floral wreaths
110 Adolph of coaching fame
112 ___-ho
113 Suffix with defer

114 1 and 66, e.g.
115 Fabric for ties
116 Sulfurous: Comb. form
117 Epis., e.g.

ACROSS

1 Airy creature
6 Joint
10 Sacrifice
14 Nightingale's device
18 Papal adornment
19 "___ the alien corn": Keats
20 Marketing pro
22 "Dies ___"
23 Window skirt
24 Mammoth sight, in Ky.
25 Dough or bread
26 Learner
27 Feather
31 Fawning
32 Radar and Hawkeye, e.g.
33 Youngman from Liverpool
34 Sound of disapproval
37 Former French province
41 Tomato blight
43 Bear witness
45 See 39 Down
47 "A Clock-work ___," Burgess book
52 Letter
56 Lowell or Alcott
57 Chemical suffix
58 "Honi ___ qui mal y pense"
59 Start of a Remarque title
60 Asian deer
61 Emulate Gwinnett
62 Bodkin's cousin
63 Mantises seemingly do this
64 Writer Morrison
65 Allow to enter
68 Sea birds
70 Leave a lover in the lurch
71 Beau ___
72 Impetuous ardor
73 Put into service
74 Chess-set components
75 Walked heavily
77 River at Leeds
78 Soak hemp
79 Parisian green spot
80 Immeasurable period
81 Grad. degree
84 Game
89 Hungarian cavalryman
90 Kindred
91 Takes a hike
92 Fortified frontier
95 Make beloved
97 "Portnoy's Complaint" author
98 "Tiny Alice" playwright
102 Pasty
104 Pair
106 String
114 Tolstoy character
115 Devoid of sense
116 Part for O'Brian
117 Mental deficiency
118 Posthaste, to a doc.
119 Dueling maneuver
120 Glassmaker's mixture
121 "Jonah" painter
122 Concavity
123 Church offering
124 Hamilton adorns these
125 Use muscle power

DOWN

1 Pink
2 Cry out sharply
3 Embellish
4 Made a suggestion
5 Capital of Vietnam
6 Metrical foot
7 Moslem priest
8 Oxford oral, exam
9 Greek resistance org. in W.W. II
10 Part Hitchcock often took
11 Like carbon monoxide
12 Cured, in a way
13 "Honor Thy Father" author
14 Supple
15 Indo-Iranian, formerly
16 Memorable painter of Me. seascapes
17 Showy bloom
21 Anti's vote
28 Roof material
29 Girl Scout emblem
30 Cautious
34 Sunken fence
35 ___ veto (gubernatorial power)
36 Spar rope
38 Tchrs., milieu
39 With 45 Across, kids' activity
40 Bermuda petrels
42 Ms. Bloom
44 Done in
46 "The Boy King"
48 Let up
49 Largest of the Cyclades
50 Inkling
51 Advertising bovine
53 Beginnings
54 Fatha Hines
55 Butter up
61 Source of vigor
63 Economized
65 Trio, as of hounds on a hunt
66 Yale or Root
67 Tropical food plants
69 Plexus
70 Sleeveless jacket
71 Dead duck
73 Arrow poison
74 First name of "The Blue Angel" star
76 Speaker's spot
79 Ger. neighbor
81 Nerd: Var.
82 Egyptian Christian
83 Interlock
85 Diplomat Cushing: 1800–79
86 Launderers' concerns
87 "___ to Duty": Wordsworth
88 An August birthstone
93 Type of opus
94 Home, to Joan Miró
96 Accommodates
98 Disconcert
99 Slowly, to Solti
100 Hackneyed
101 Mother's cousin, e.g.
103 Fencing swords
105 Mindful
107 Have the pip
108 Dexterous
109 Like certain books
110 Hibernia
111 Took a cab
112 Recliner
113 Dan Cupid's missile

by June A. Boggs

FRACTURED POLYSYLLABLES

ACROSS

1 Certain secants
7 Cried loudly
13 Border river in 104 Down
17 Prohibit
20 Charm
21 Each
22 Assert
23 Match king Kreuger
25 OPPOSED TO A BANNER SHARE
27 AWAY, SORROW!
29 Forum garb
30 European carp
31 Distort
33 Britain, poetically
34 Plow sole
35 Run, as a dye
37 DEDUCE A REFUSAL
38 Lay a lawn
41 Fondles
42 Suspicious
43 Foreign
44 Hedge shrubs
46 Hall in a casa
47 Son of Seth
48 Agnus ___
51 Atlas items
52 Ni
55 Flowerless plant
56 Speeds
57 Recess ramp
58 Capital of Guam
59 Apportion
60 Over
61 Marry in haste
62 Skipper's "Stop!"
63 European sea bream
64 Author Deighton
65 LOUGANIS'S CHARGED PARTICLE
67 Pipe repairman
68 Placid
71 Flightless bird
72 Race horse: Slang
73 Like fanatics
75 STREAKERS TOP NOTES
78 Gypsy boy
81 Fragrant blooms
82 Australian tennis great
84 East Indian woody vines
85 Elephant's-ear
86 Basketry grass
87 European finch
88 Come up
89 Wreck completely
90 "Prince ___," R.L.S. work
91 SEAFOOD VENDOR'S STALL
93 Quarter ___ (8:45)
94 Enemy
95 Executioner in "The Mikado"
96 Nominate, in Scotland
97 Crowds
98 Small napkin
100 Brainstorms
102 Very proper
103 Obtain
104 Supplements
107 Curl the lip
108 Solo
109 Appeared
110 Color
111 Imbibed
112 Turkish regiment
116 CONTRACT DEBT CHITS
118 HOW TO MAKE MEN TAT
122 Suffix with comment
123 Sisters
124 Navy engineering corpsman
125 Write symbols
126 Hurricane center
127 Ashen
128 Makes croutons
129 Soho cig

DOWN

1 Covenant
2 Melville novel
3 Respiratory organ
4 Esparto
5 Electrical unit
6 Hollywood hopefuls
7 Pressure units
8 Speedily
9 Accompanying
10 Wahine's wreath
11 Italian writer
12 More compact
13 Deviated from course
14 Own
15 Shelter
16 Franciscan nun
17 London attraction
18 To have: Fr.
19 Kept talking
24 City with lots of slots
26 Fall guys
28 Sprite: Fr.
32 Pitch
34 Small barracudas
35 Misrepresent
36 Page
37 Actress Massey
38 Helix
39 Overly frilly
40 BEEF ABOUT 3 A.M. RECORD PLAYING
42 Stocking run
43 Concerning
45 Barkley was one
46 Marsh bird
47 Epochs
48 PANNING THE COLD CUTS SHOP
49 Irregular
50 Bury
52 "___ Lucy"
53 Churchill's good will
54 Actor Richard
55 Blaze
57 David's weapon
59 Snug as a bug in ___
61 British noble family
62 Rifleman, at times
63 Sanctify
66 ___ clock (six bells)
67 "The Old Wives' Tale" dramatist
69 Poetic Muse
70 Sake source
72 Grind one's teeth
73 IT CONSISTS OF 592 TCHASTS
74 Same
75 "Amores" poet
76 Conservatives
77 Pindar, for one
79 Bergamot or mandarin
80 Harass
82 Pervious
83 Tuscan river
85 Wells's "___-Bungay"
87 Roman cloak
88 Frighten: Dial.
89 The Velvet Fog
91 Problem on an icy road
92 Run away
93 SVELTE MONARCH
97 Mineral found in dried lake basins
98 Decorous
99 Unique person
100 Hostel
101 Hate
102 Home bases
104 Largest continent
105 Spaghetti al ___
106 Lure
107 Actress Spacek
108 Court decree
110 Albacore
111 Noted Socialist
112 Danish counties
113 Jump
114 Feed the kitty
115 Brain passage
117 Start of the Lord's Prayer
119 Modernist
120 Chinese pagoda
121 Common, in Hawaii

FURTHER CLUES

25 A-37 A
52 A-116 A
65 A-118 A
27 A-40 D
48 D-93 D
73 D-91 A

by Ernst Theimer

ACROSS

1 ___ Dhabi, emirate
4 Republican monogram
7 Hexahedra
12 Recon aircraft
17 Celebration conflagration
19 Cropped up
20 Bishop, for one
22 Clad
23 Beethoven's "___ solemnis"
24 Strike callers
25 It's not a moving picture
27 WKRP or WJM-TV
29 Model Macpherson et al.
30 Adorable
32 Give in
33 Visit
34 Drops in the morning
35 Marzipan ingredient
37 C.I.A. predecessor
38 Bucknell mascot
40 Clinch breaker
43 Evidence
45 Party pro
46 "The Haj" author
47 Agitate
48 Strike makers
52 Worked on soles
55 Marching-band glockenspiels
58 Property claim
59 Auditorium
60 One of the Jacksons
61 Makes airtight
62 Eight, in Ancona
63 Bass-baritone Scaria
64 Maxilla, e.g.
65 Make eyes at
66 Canton's state
67 ___-majesty
68 Doctoral hurdles
70 A foe of Pan
71 Hold on to
72 "Dianetics" author Hubbard
73 Popular
75 Puppeteers Bil and Cora
77 Bodega quaff
79 Hibernia
80 ___ diagram, in symbolic logic
81 Ballet point
82 "Barbarella" director
84 Joy
87 Suitable position
90 Bro, e.g.

91 Tridents
93 "___ pro nobis"
95 Free throw's value
96 Objectives
98 Mortar ingredient
99 "___ Dei"
101 La. senator: 1948–87
105 Clumsy
107 Enmesh
108 Superlatively bad
110 Keyboard instrument
111 Tess, to Hardy
112 Clear the slate
113 Speaker component
114 "Ballet Class" painter
115 Postpone
116 Radical org. in the 60's
117 Thus far

DOWN

1 Demeaned
2 Canner's kin
3 "___ meet again!"
4 Little women
5 Pitcher Hershiser
6 Zoological stalks
7 Revived
8 Spoon-bender Geller
9 Bartlett relative
10 Repplier work
11 Otary
12 Packing a rod
13 Shed tears
14 Landed
15 Loving touch
16 Mono improved
18 Dossier
20 Yanks
21 Ruhr city
26 Seethe
28 Not so much
31 Store fodder
35 Droughty
36 Pickle type
38 Acknowledge applause
39 Sinister or ugly
41 Kind of mirror
42 Afore
44 Solidifies
45 Oater group
47 Narrate anew
48 Ball star
49 Choice word
50 Tightened the shoelaces
51 Busybodies
52 Cioppino leavings
53 M. Atget's companion
54 Author Lurie

55 Unoriginal
56 "The ___ of the Guard": G. & S.
57 Spread unchecked
60 "M*A*S*H" land
64 Knife man
69 Coaster
70 Keeps costs low
74 State flower of Tenn.
75 Units of loudness
76 Black cuckoo
78 Caviar
80 Court decisions
82 Schnitzel meat
83 Gave permission
84 Moist and chilly
85 Quality Ananias lacked
86 Fiduciary
87 Realm of Boreas
88 Adapted to rigors
89 Borgia or Siepi
90 Esther of "Good Times"
92 Pasch
94 Postulate
96 Secluded valleys
97 Stertorous sound

99 "Deutschland über ___"
100 Merriment
102 Portmanteau word
103 Blood state: Comb. form
104 Navratilova rival
106 Salacious
109 Calais-to-Paris dir.

by Richard Silvestri

ACROSS

1 Kiddie's foot
7 Oodles
12 Cases for small articles
17 Sagan or Sandburg
21 Hangnest
22 Commandment verb
23 Traffic sign
24 Margarine
25 "___ Talk," Doris Day film
26 Board for a medium
27 Roi's mate
28 Marquand's sleuth
29 Words by Edward Caswall
33 Mass. cape
34 Kind of glass
35 "Betty ___," 1930 song
36 Three-legged stand
37 Labels
39 Check
41 Grand ___ (Rocky Mt. peak)
43 Grovel
44 Granted
47 Ninth Islamic month
49 Attracted
53 Like a bull
56 Colorless
58 Composer of "The Seasons"
60 Former U.S. agcy.
61 Possessing
62 Dodge
63 "___ armes, citoyens!"
64 Of milk
66 U.S.A. member
67 Chaplin prop
69 Fiddle with a guitar
71 "___ Road," Caldwell novel
72 Atlas abbr.
73 Alecto, for one
75 Punch
76 Enjoy
77 Words from a Czechoslovak carol
84 Old calculators
85 Shubert or Strasberg
86 Kind of pace
87 MOMA offering
88 "He that ___ his rod...": Proverbs
91 Zero
93 Sole
94 Cheer
95 Ancient scrolls
96 Explosive
97 Pitchers
99 Basswood
102 Actress MacGraw
103 Gemstone
105 Monastic
106 Painter of "Guernica"
107 Fling
109 Some colonists
112 Calms
114 Gone
116 City on the Missouri
118 Fast time
119 Dostoyevsky's "___ Youth"
123 Ancient Italians
126 Have ___ for (wish evil to)
127 A Dumas
129 Topsy's playmate
130 Words from a Sussex carol
137 Connect
138 Manlike ape, for short
139 Early father of twins
140 Wife abandoned by Paris
141 All the same: Fr.
142 Remove a ship's upper deck
143 Scandinavians
144 Adjective for intransitive verbs
145 Over
146 Long for
147 Punkies
148 Some Fords

DOWN

1 Formal wear
2 Epithet for Elizabeth I
3 Lubrication
4 Kind of booth or bridge
5 Slow animal
6 "___ now proclaim Messiah's birth"
7 Scrubbed
8 Autosuggestion pioneer: 1857–1926
9 Tel ___
10 Dishearten
11 Words from a Polish carol
12 Eden's domain
13 Bumbo or cacao
14 "Exodus" author
15 Charged particles
16 Words from "Song of the Crib"
17 Order
18 Throw for ___ (flabbergast)
19 Type of rocket
20 Bats
30 Eccentric
31 Greek letter
32 Mountain ___ (moonshine)
38 Draped garment
40 Potpourris
42 Book of the Bible
43 Fairy
45 Prevail
46 Actress Joanne
48 French spa
50 Campus org.
51 Heroic
52 Site of Baylor U.
53 Namely
54 Overflowing
55 Family member
57 Certain personals
59 Gomer Pyle's real name
62 This is not joie de vivre
63 Kissel and Marmon
65 Singer Vikki
68 Gee follower
70 Edge
71 Dravidian language
73 Colo. peak
74 French greeting
76 Nixon's first Sec. of Commerce
78 Not one, country style
79 Triangle side
80 Breather of a sort
81 Compounds
82 Highlanders' hillsides
83 Race: Comb. form
88 Lovers' quarrel
89 ___ Alto
90 Bee genus
91 Beachhead of W.W. II
92 Word with step or time
96 Young one
98 Naval off.
100 Rosalynn Sumners's milieu
101 Space org.
104 Half a motor-boat sound
106 Kind of button
108 Scintillate
110 Little bit
111 Bye-bye
113 Mars
115 Some
117 "Dombey ___"
120 Far off
121 Family name in Scott's "The Monastery"
122 Baseball's Big and Little Poison
123 Flirted, in a way
124 Irish county
125 Middle name of author Doyle
128 Charger
131 Anglo-Saxon coins
132 Where Samson died
133 Standout
134 State of Brazil
135 Cardinal point
136 Obligation

by Anne Fox

ACROSS

1 Playwright Connelly
5 Talisman
10 Tots
14 Spectral type
19 Opposite of apterous
20 Abode of the Muses
21 Orenburg's river
22 "Lake ___," Sargent painting
23 Talented actress?
25 Actress Rowlands
26 Electronic device
27 Cordial flavorings
28 Capricious actor?
31 S. Lewis's "___ Timberlane"
32 Calls, in poker
33 Banker's Sallie ___
34 Eaglewood
37 Actress Granville
39 Small amount
43 Brickmaker's need
44 Dawdling Opry singer?
47 Chemical suffix
48 Monogram pt.
49 The Cat Nation
50 Barrie's dog-nurse
51 He wrote "Brave Men": 1944
52 Ariz. neighbor
53 High-strung actress?
57 Oboist's purchase
58 Like some movies
60 They're knitted at times
61 Sudden movements
63 Hogarth's "The ___ Progress"
64 Apprehensions
65 Estonian city
66 Groves on prairies
68 What shalom means
69 Outlanders
71 "___ may look on a king"
72 Underworld actor?
75 Eureka!
77 A famous Virginia
78 Actress Deborah
79 South African settler
80 Slender shoot
81 City off.
82 Give-and-take actress?
86 Lagomorph
87 Dance center of a sort
89 Consolation
90 He wrote "The Seven-Percent Solution"
91 Photographer's abbr.
92 Japanese monastery
93 Hilum
95 Note-taking actress?
101 Vacation site
105 Junctures
106 Lamb who wrote about a pig
107 Truthful actor of yore?
109 Certain rerun
110 Zest
111 Vitiate
112 Pickerelweed
113 Fuels
114 Heraldic term
115 ". . . ___ Danaos . . .": Virgil
116 Put away

DOWN

1 Goya subject
2 Astronaut Bean
3 Gypsy lady
4 Turkish symbol
5 Contents of urnes
6 Parts of ships
7 Collections of sayings
8 Venezia's canals
9 "Lili ___," old song
10 Masters' local
11 German three
12 Rather and McGrew
13 Side dish
14 "___ Soul," song hit of 1930
15 ___ up (appeared)
16 Old Irish capital
17 Sandarac tree
18 Strip of shoe leather
24 Sunglo and gowiddie
29 Trompe-l' ___ (illusion)
30 Diva Lucine
32 Cobbled
34 Related
35 QE2, e.g.
36 Late actor?
37 Soft cheese
38 Family of a well-known Baltimorean
39 Fictional skater
40 Missing actress?
41 Like some apartments
42 Yorkshire city
44 A Revolutionary officer and a Civil War commander
45 Birds of merit?
46 Lad, in Lyon
51 Jabber
53 Hunky-dory
54 "___ up the pillars . . .": Psalm 75
55 Austin of tennis
56 Biblical mountain
59 Certain photo finish
61 Compensation
62 One of triplets
64 Famous U.S. engineer
65 Toned down
66 Term of address
67 Fla. city
68 Averages
70 English draft horse
72 ___-majesté
73 Rope fiber
74 Lost
76 Composer of "Ain't She Sweet?"
78 Shade of green
80 "The force . . . that blasts ___ of trees": D. Thomas
82 Bobby, Tom et al.
83 Sight at 101 Across
84 Not windward
85 Wimpole St. name
88 License
90 Raincoats, for short
93 Catcher in the Rhine?
94 Ezra Pound product
95 Wet
96 African river
97 Art genre
98 Ballet leap
99 Luise Rainer role
100 Hue
101 Sink's alternative
102 Part of été
103 W.W. II battle site
104 Muscle
108 Bao ___, former Vietnamese emperor

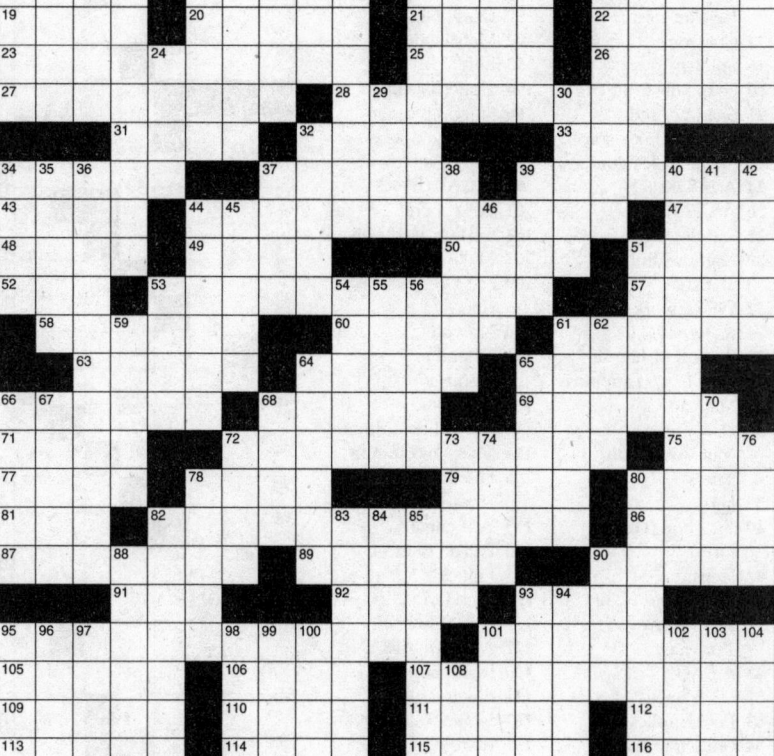

by Mary M. Murdoch

ACROSS

1 A VIRGO
6 TV role for Kate Jackson
12 Confront
16 Splotch
20 Soap substitute
21 Shade of red
22 Robert Alda's son
23 Name in fashion
24 A SCORPIO
26 A GEMINI
28 R.W.R., e.g.
29 Night sound
30 Statistic
32 Wickerwork material
33 It's full of hot air
34 Two-legged support
35 Madcap
36 D.C. group concerned with prices
39 Hgt.
40 ___ rima (verse form)
42 Jeeps
45 "Her eyes ___ of silent prayer": Tennyson
48 A SAGITTARIAN
51 ___ glance
53 Puerto follower
54 Contemptible person
56 Occupations
57 Vestige
58 Word after iron or ethyl
59 Fool
61 Grown old
62 Pilsener
63 Quannet
64 Brawl
65 Alleviated
67 Bribery of sorts
68 Mo. when 127 Across was born
69 A PISCES
71 Long, hooded cloak
72 More insipid
74 Women's ___
75 Duty
76 Upset the iron horse's course
77 AN ARIES
81 Where to become an off.
84 Islands of the Bahamas
85 Free, in Marseille
86 Place for a buttonhole
87 Four rows at the Palace
88 Like Harvard's walls
89 Bowery denizen
90 Used a lighter
92 Metric unit
93 Lofty
94 Singer Easton
96 Snick's partner
97 Peace goddess
98 Photog's blowup
99 A CANCER
101 Took a poll
104 Certain Madrileñas
107 Make into law
109 ___ Dee, Carolina river
110 No vote
111 Emend a manuscript
112 Electronic navigational device
114 More uncommon
116 Hitchcock's "Strangers on ___"
119 Pub game
120 Patron saint of France
121 ___ Hari
125 A CAPRICORN
127 AN AQUARIAN
130 Irish patriot
131 B'way group
132 Grand Tour site
133 Extreme
134 Close to
135 End of a hammerhead
136 He's no nudist
137 A LIBRA

DOWN

1 Finn's neighbor
2 Sharif or Bradley
3 Mantle
4 Building extensions
5 Prefix with Impressionism
6 A mile ___
7 City in Ga.
8 Mountain in Turkey
9 Reporter's asset?
10 ___ Passos
11 Subject to electrolytic action
12 Ipso ___
13 Orally
14 Storm preceder
15 Opp. of WSW
16 Big ___ (W.W.I cannon)
17 Native of Riga
18 A first-floor appartment
19 Swiss canton
23 Gasconade
25 Sacred song
27 Gambados
31 Independently
33 Rhone feeder
34 Godden's "In This House of ___"
35 Tore
36 Distant
37 Ed Norton's wife
38 A LEO
41 Walking on air
42 Sojourned
43 A TAURUS
44 TV's "Remington ___"
46 Angle, in geology
47 Resembling a pillar
49 Key on some typewriters
50 "Dirty Dingus ___," 1970 film
52 Taj Mahal site
55 To dare, in Dijon
57 ___ Atonement
59 Highly esteemed person
60 Works on a chesterfield
62 Rabbit fur
64 Year in Edward VI's reign
66 Eban of Israel
67 Word of mouth
69 Dik-dik's big cousin
70 Winglike
71 Boxed
73 One of the archangels
75 Kin of wickiups
76 Oriental royal councils
77 Eatery
78 "___ and Ivory," 1982 song
79 Facility for outpatients
80 Sound
82 Eye part
83 Quick
84 Take the bait
85 Mortgages
87 Bog
89 ___ germ
91 Thai, e.g.
92 Chopped ___
94 Lourdes attraction
95 Prevent
100 Agitated
102 Insurgent
103 A.F.B. in Tex.
105 Less messy
106 Pindar was one
108 Seismograph recording
112 Beatrice's adorer
113 Spleen, e.g.
115 "Is man ___ or an angel?": Disraeli
116 TV sitcom
117 What Kate became
118 Italia's capital
119 Where to see sea oats
120 "___ Maar Seated," by 24 Across
121 Factory
122 ___ spumante
123 Cowfish
124 Med. subject
126 Open a barrel
128 Former capital of Annam
129 Proper

by Bette Sue Cohen

ACROSS

1 Scriptures reading
7 1970's–80's singer Ronnie
13 "You just missed!"
19 Adjust
20 Colored ring
21 Wet
23 British isle's textiles?
25 Ancient strategy game played with stones
26 Like many a parting
27 Food, plates, silverware, etc.?
29 Muppet who's tickled
30 Renaissance artist Guido ___
31 Wide-mouthed comic Martha
32 Puppet ending
33 Author/illustrator Silverstein
35 European carrier
37 Encircle
39 Hardly a mark to be proud of
42 What avid auctioneers have?
46 Modem speed measure
48 Take in the mail
49 Expend
50 Proper name in Masses
51 Food-swapping at a rooming house?
55 Hollywood display
57 Spiraling part
59 "Babes in Arms" star, 1939
60 Songs for one
61 British poet laureate Tate
62 Cut corners
64 Fishy idea?
69 Surfeit
71 Artificial, after "in"
72 Morales in movies
76 Evangelist's imperative
77 Word with big or blue
79 Sticks in pits
81 What a brass band has?
84 Milldam
86 Factor in protein synthesis
87 Twiz candy maker
88 Barre room bend
89 When the prisoners will escape?
92 Short
93 Moving targets?
95 St. Louis sked abbr.
96 "The Simpsons" saxophonist
97 Sob syllable
98 Jazz singer Anita
101 Bust, of a sort
103 Immediately
107 Pencil-sharpening problem?
112 Part of a black suit
113 Like the music in "Turkey in the Straw"
114 Flute competition, e.g.?
116 Popular modern exercise system
117 Ordered group of numbers in math
118 Driving areas
119 Choral group
120 Approvals
121 Wool source

DOWN

1 Supply for a cappuccino machine
2 "I Love Lucy" role
3 Cooking method
4 C12H22O11
5 As recently as
6 Opposite of paleo-
7 Capital of Minorca
8 One who uses words in ways opposite of their literal meaning
9 Southpaw's side
10 Actress Suzanne
11 Actress Stewart
12 Undergarment
13 It flies through barrels
14 Slip-on shoe
15 Made, as money
16 ___ fever (annual February/March phenomenon)
17 Attempt
18 Show's partner
22 Scottish refusal
24 Immune system lymphocytes
28 Smooth transition
30 Direct elsewhere
34 Chain hotel, for short
36 Walking like a peacock
38 Line before a reception
39 Silas of the Continental Congress
40 Follower of lop or dog
41 Water whirl
42 Hauls
43 Winter Olympics site after St. Moritz
44 Some white meat
45 Power overload result
46 Sheep's "Sheesh!"
47 Insert
48 Tiny plant part
52 Cartage company, e.g.
53 Cold, in Colombia
54 Pro ___
56 They may be seen with snowballs
58 L.B.J.'s veep
61 Eccentric
62 Eccentric
63 Even if, briefly
65 Charades gesture, e.g.
66 Like Cheerios
67 Ogres
68 Fleet, Wall, etc.: Abbr.
69 Psalms interjection
70 Mocking behavior
73 Resentful
74 Wife in "Finnegans Wake"
75 Author Dinesen
76 Tach readings, for short
77 ___-Town (Midwest hub)
78 Furrow maker
79 Having two equal lobes
80 Financial wheeler-dealers, briefly
82 Unstop, poetically
83 Take, as an airline
85 Crude stone artifact
90 To a small degree
91 Hoarse
93 Vichyssoise ingredient
94 Computer networking device
95 Locale of U.N. peacekeeping forces, 1964
97 Virile one
99 Soft
100 Suffer ___ worse than death
102 New kitties?
104 Letter after sierra, in radio lingo
105 Viper
106 "The Gondoliers" girl
107 Afternoon treat, maybe
108 "Let me sleep ___"
109 Stir
110 One of the friends on "Friends"
111 Unwelcome word from a surgeon
112 Whooper, e.g.
115 Grand time

by Cathy Millhauser

ACROSS

1 "I Loves You, Porgy" singer
5 How some stocks are sold
10 Rat-___
14 Intimate
19 From scratch
20 Ready to read the riot act
21 "A Treatise of Human Nature" writer
22 Mojave plant
23 Many a homestead spread
24 Reservists
26 Bank that may be created by the government
27 Radiance
29 Part of Florida
30 Creepy looks
31 Chant
32 Where a newspaper index often appears
33 "Married filing separately" on an I.R.S. form 1040
35 Lady of la maison: Abbr.
36 Unconvincing
37 Annex
38 Actor Keach
39 Salt shaker?
40 No longer sharp
41 Have a canyonlike effect
44 Gossips
46 Greek theaters
47 "Bingo!"
50 Places with a bird's-eye view
52 Miniseries segment
54 Rest
57 "Thumbs up" response
59 Like some internships, in length
60 Howard ___, "Mayberry R.F.D." character
62 Packing
64 Raipur raiment
65 "Evil Woman" grp.
68 With 69-Across, bygone phone message
69 See 68-Across
71 Cook's abbr.
72 Brown & Williamson brand
74 Shows inconstancy
75 Some opening night theatergoers
77 World Series finale
79 Tempe inst.
80 Women's dress sizes
81 Skittles
85 Minnesota twin?
87 It may be balding
89 Sculpture student's subj.
90 Big name in book publishing since 1818
92 "My Eyes Have Seen" singer
96 "Veni . . ."
97 Hardly likely to streak
98 Certain 111-Downs
101 Discount rack abbr.
102 Repeated cry while waving a hand
103 High ball?
104 Entry in a spaceship log
105 Low visibility figure
107 Hits repeatedly
108 It may arrive with attachments
110 One may be picky about these
112 Skater Hughes
114 Style
115 Fortuitous
117 Cops and robbers, e.g.
118 Hollywood family
119 Lot
120 Cold shoulder treatment?
121 Egyptian solar deity
122 Causes dissolution of cells
123 Apportion, with "out"
124 Wished
125 Mouth, so to speak

DOWN

1 Pastoral sounds
2 "Big" one
3 One who sings to the balcony
4 Sugar-covered nuts, bonbons, etc.
5 Ambition
6 Fall guy?
7 Pub order
8 Like skin, after a facial
9 Tighten one's laces, say
10 Sounds of discoverers
11 Kerfuffle
12 Title woman in a Joni Mitchell song
13 Holding of land
14 Call that may complete a full count
15 Curved molding
16 Latecomer's plea
17 Dominates
18 1980's attorney general
25 Halved
28 "Thanks, but don't bother"
34 Observer
38 Soak
39 Tucks (away)
40 Fashion plate
42 Fishing baskets
43 R & B group with the 1991 #1 hit "I Like the Way"
45 Carbon, to a lab worker: Abbr.
48 Zimbabwe's capital
49 "Laugh-In" regular on old TV
51 LP flaw
53 Tea time, maybe
54 Small drum
55 Discriminating person
56 Civilization, to Hesse
58 Ancient Brits: Var.
61 W.W. II heroes: Abbr.
62 Bow (to)
63 Agnus ___
65 Ticker tapes?
66 In an offensive way
67 Oktoberfest entertainers
70 Big jet
73 60's guru
76 "Star Wars" and the like
78 Old "You like it, it likes you" sloganeer
80 Year that Augustus exiled Ovid
82 Juliet, to Romeo
83 Cooperate with the feds, say
84 Québec map abbr.
86 Make advances?
88 Aurora's counterpart
91 Corot painting style
93 Connect with
94 Place with a bird's-eye view
95 Picture show?
96 Shuts up
99 Right this minute
100 Garfield, for one
103 Kind of advice
104 Completely black, in a way
105 Focused (in on)
106 Word said with a slap
109 "Dies ___"
111 Beachcomber's concern
113 ___ teeth
116 Outranked

by Elizabeth C. Gorski

ACROSS

1 Carpenter's friend
7 Like fattening foods
14 Second-largest Syrian city
20 "___ Necessarily So"
21 Done with
22 Club soda, branch water, etc.
23 !PU SMOTTOB
26 Use a wiretap
27 High dudgeon
28 Spring bloomers
29 Norm: Abbr.
30 Bundle of sticks
32 Not gross
33 Cloister head
37 Storage problem
38 Save
39 Mine car
43 King Hussein's wife
44 Popular pickle
45 Seemly
46 Chaplin's widow
47 !PU SMOTTOB
53 "___ was saying . . ."
54 Architectural style
55 Flying prefix
56 Billiards shot
57 Hat for J. R. Ewing
59 Repute
60 Dreiser's Carrie
61 Tenor role in "Don Pasquale"
65 Street game
67 Jolson hit
70 Six: Comb. form
72 Tagged
76 Poet H.D.'s first name
77 Price addenda
78 Moonshiner's device
80 Soul of St.-Cyr
81 !PU SMOTTOB
86 "___ Do Is Dream . . ."
87 Peak of perfection
88 Auld lang syne
89 Minute amount
90 Stable pet
91 Jersey or Manhattan trailer
92 Boss, in darkest Africa
94 Dry table wine
96 Arafat's org.
97 Ship to remember
98 Writer Brofeldt's pseudonym
99 Lax little shepherdess
102 007, e.g.

103 Shallow-water transport
108 !PU SMOTTOB
112 Samantha's mother on "Bewitched"
113 Pep up
114 Lassie, for one
115 Tempest container
116 Mean, cowardly cad
117 Make beloved

DOWN

1 Heir's concern
2 Thine, in Noisy-le-Sec
3 Prince Souphanouvong's land
4 Schism
5 Provided
6 Is frugal
7 ___ Andy of "Show Boat"
8 One ___ time (singly)
9 New Guinea seaport
10 In heaven
11 Certain rockets
12 Map feature
13 B-F connection
14 Little cherubs
15 On the up and up
16 They've been "Renovated"
17 Marquette, e.g.
18 Corp. head
19 Kirghizian oblast
24 Disencumber
25 Stately court dance
30 Kind of acid
31 Tamarisk salt tree
33 Writer Seton et al.
34 Blow one's own horn
35 Alamo name or knife
36 Suffix for trick or witch
37 Rodolfo's love
38 In front
39 Go ___ (become worthless)
40 Shake out of bed
41 By ___ (barely)
42 Louis B., the "star-maker"
44 "Go and catch a falling star" poet
45 City in Argentina
48 Interpret wrongly
49 Not a soul
50 Leader of the Long March

51 Go back to the drawing board
52 Good-natured
58 Plant's clinging part
60 Milan's La ___
62 Doubting Thomas's demand
63 Up-tight
64 Former name of the Amu Darya
66 Like peas in a pod
67 Bundle of stalks
68 ___-the-wisp
69 Spurious wing
71 G.I.'s address
73 One of the Days
74 Ham it up
75 Coup ___
78 Tea accompaniment
79 Neighbor of Twelve Oaks
82 Reviled
83 Denizens of the deep
84 Tatum's father
85 Inlet
92 They're locked in with lox
93 Hip

94 Risk
95 Relief for dishpan hands
96 Rock: Comb. form
97 ___ Carta
98 High-school math
99 Cause of distress
100 Strange-sounding Norwegian canton
101 A deck
103 Part of UNICEF
104 Forward
105 Make eyes at
106 Author Lieblich
107 Stadium feature
108 As ___ (until now)
109 Buttons
110 Tenn. power project
111 For each

by Frances Hansen

234 WACKY WEATHER REPORTS

ACROSS

1 Denture arm
6 Walton's fling
10 Gasconade
14 Fen fuel
18 Capital of Flanders: 17th century
19 Norse goddess
20 Section of Warsaw
21 Heroine of Conrad's "Victory"
22 "For want of ___..."
23 Juvenal's journey
24 Swiss composer: 1852–1921
25 Solans' kin
26 Puzzle
28 For Americans, Jan 17, 1893?
31 Hershfield's "agent"
33 Practiced extortion
34 ___ Cruces, N.M.
35 Water-rooted plants
40 Anecdotal collections
42 May or Stritch
46 For El Salvador?
48 Cabinet-maker's tool
49 Org. for Tilden or Budge
50 "Cows ___ my passion": Dickens
51 Furnish a lining
53 Peculate
54 Egyptian deity
55 Oppose
58 Bounty man
60 Item from Iraq
61 Make lace
62 Dr. Dolittle's Gub-Gub
63 Poet Mark Van ___
66 Shabby abodes
68 Gunlock hammer holder
69 Resin used in printing ink
70 Mind
71 Testator's largess
73 Gained a championship again
74 Soak timber
75 Pend.'s pal
78 Whine
79 D.A.
81 Vascular plant parts
83 Vedic ritual drink
84 Kind of artery or vein
86 One of last year's frosh
89 M. Levin novel
90 Kind of battery
91 Naval vessel
93 For Texas ranchers?
97 Branch of the Campbells
98 Healthy, in Honduras
99 For golfer Irwin?
100 Worthless horse
101 Can. law enforcers
103 Duplicate event
104 For an ailing prince?
110 Venomous snakes
115 A pope who became a saint
116 Chemical compound
117 Director Fritz ___
119 Jinx
120 Word that stuck in Macbeth's throat
121 Large, coarse seaweeds
122 "Martha" melody
123 Fla.'s Marion County seat
124 Raft's gats
125 Within: Comb. form
126 Fierce
127 Stern purchase

DOWN

1 Group of families
2 Folkestone floor covering
3 Actor Badel
4 Knitting stitch
5 Disease caused by niacin and protein deficiency
6 Style of cooking
7 Hockey's ___ Ross Trophy
8 Stalk of bananas
9 Beat
10 Former Olympic V.I.P.
11 Nobelist in physics: 1944
12 Town on the Garonne
13 Mouthwashes
14 For smiling Susan?
15 Hitchcockian
16 A Hathaway who had a way with Will
17 Ivan's news source
20 Mental
27 Above, in Aachen
29 Hawaiian lizard fish
30 Papa Bear
32 Lab burners

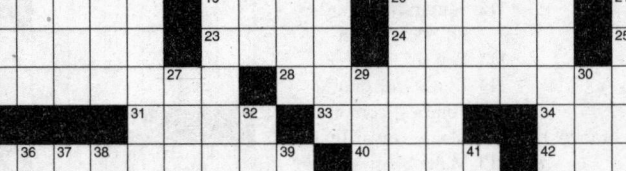

by Maurice J. Teitelbaum

35 Vesuviate
36 Flower into the Aegean
37 Publicity
38 Sultan of Swat
39 Water ___ (long-legged bug)
41 State of agitation
43 Model
44 ___-foot oil
45 Dashiell contemporary
47 Put new platforms on platforms
52 City in NE Pakistan
55 Lariat
56 Plumed birds
57 Trousers worn under kilts
59 Galabias
62 Type of shooter
64 Emulated William Gillette
65 Assyrian capital
67 Doc for Dobbin
68 For Churchill Downs?
71 Great Swiss mathematician

72 First-aid contrivance
75 Propelled a gondola
76 Town on the Tigris
77 Behindhand
78 Century plant
80 Adds up
82 "___ Theme"
83 London district
85 Lass in "As You Like It"
87 Larynx's neighbor: Comb. form
88 Jostles
90 Army officer, somewhat abbreviated
92 Mend armor
94 Alaskan cape
95 Adjective for a speak-easy
96 Patricia from Ky.
102 Rice dish
104 Suffix with cell
105 James Mason role
106 What Markham's man did
107 D.C. agent
108 Soupçon
109 Like a royal flush

111 Somewhat, to Mehta
112 Balin and Claire
113 "Persistence of Memory" painter
114 Mongoloid people of Asia
118 "___ desperandum": Horace

ACROSS

1 Poet Nicolson
6 Dolphin's cousin
13 ___ Lama
18 Pliant
20 Reaches
21 Pattern
22 Start of a four-line verse
25 Accumulated
26 Santa ___
27 Inuit or Yuit
28 Understand
29 Chuck's follower
31 French soul
32 Tongs' partner
36 Ceremonial acts
37 Saharan
38 Lummox
41 Length times width, e.g.
42 Part of être
43 Galatea's lover
44 Model Macpherson
45 Second line of the verse
51 "A ___ cara," Bellini aria
52 Court allegations
53 Despicable
54 Teheran native
55 Caravansary
56 Bluewing
57 Group of six
58 Three sheets to the wind
59 Choreographer Michael
60 Vetches
61 Mend
62 Edit film
65 Judges' garb
66 Marine flier
67 Summer quaff
70 Living teddy bear
71 Of a hypothetical unit of living matter
72 Veranda
73 Pedro's aunt
74 Third line of the verse
79 Mind, to Marcus
80 Paris airport
81 "An apple ___"
82 Winged
83 Opposite of post
84 Off-Broadway award
85 Pipe
87 Mower
89 Wheat, in Grenoble
90 Brands
91 Neckpiece
92 Kind of path
95 Word with kin or nip
96 Ode
101 End of the verse
105 Represented as flying, in heraldry
106 Was a diarist
107 Strip a whale's blubber
108 Clio or Edgar
109 Certain motel fee
110 Tallinn natives

DOWN

1 Brouhahas
2 Mama's imperative
3 Repeat
4 Storyteller
5 Purport
6 Stare open-mouthed
7 Map abbr.
8 Munched
9 Run
10 Instruments for Ax and Watts
11 Deprive, in a way
12 Compass pt.
13 Adorned
14 Holly of Dixie
15 Writer O'Flaherty
16 Comfort, in Calabria
17 Neither Rep. nor Dem.
19 Church official
21 Fire
23 Ump's cry
24 Hon
29 Bowery figures
30 Aleutian isle
32 "Katie Went to ___": C. Porter
33 "Stormy Weather" composer
34 Casaba
35 Army off.
36 Queenly
37 Yearned
38 N.Y. city
39 Coeur d'___, Idaho
40 Malodorous
42 Sam of links fame
43 World supporter
44 Flynn of flicks
46 Kind of illusion
47 ___ la Cité
48 Ham it up
49 Puts thumbs down
50 Immense
57 Sacred: Comb. form
58 Oriental hostelry
59 Prevents publication of
60 Hot drink
61 Unit of inductance
62 Cut corners
63 Capability
64 Woolen cloth
65 Legal paper
66 Turkic language
67 Inclining
68 Alice's cat
69 Tidal flood
72 Namesakes of Clytemnestra's mother
75 "This was the ___ Roman . . .": Shak.
76 Help to adjust
77 Long-running Broadway musical
78 Round Table knight
84 Deaden
85 Star of "Shampoo"
86 Cronkite successor
87 What "Mac" means
88 Guernseys
90 "Aïda" segment
91 Leatherwing
92 Cuff
93 Singer Logan
94 Discordant
96 Surrender formally
97 Piques
98 Copper
99 Castigate
100 Vous ___
101 Marsh elder
102 Partner of board
103 Roman or Christian
104 Macerate

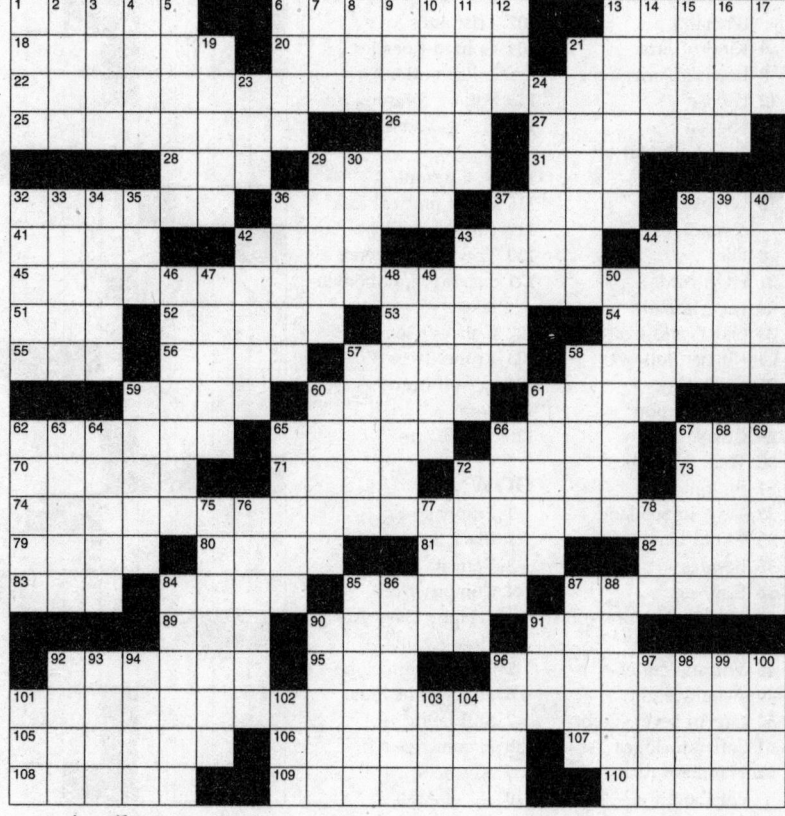

by Alfio Micci

ACROSS

1 Germany's Otto ___ Bismarck
4 Kind of prof.
8 Lewis's Timberlane
12 Excuse
16 Shaped
17 "___ Kick Out of You"
18 "Gypsy Love" composer
20 File
21 High cards
22 ___ Marmara
23 Old World lizard
24 Kitchen follower
25 Stone-Day collaboration?
29 Coarse silk
30 That, in Cannes
31 Inhibit
32 Tiny, in Scotland
33 "Auld Lang ___"
36 Besides
38 Elsa, e.g.
42 MacDonald-Graves collaboration?
46 Volcano crater
49 Asian weight
50 One of seven: Abbr.
51 Saharan ridges
52 Hamilton-Rice collaboration?
58 Sophia or Isabel
59 Actress Alicia
60 Wilder's "___ Town"
61 Keddah, e.g.
65 Warren-Kingsley collaboration?
72 North Sea feeder
73 Long time
74 "High ___": M. Anderson
75 One Muppet of two
76 Saint-Exupéry-Borodin collaboration? (with "The")
82 Russian mountains
87 Mouths
88 Arabian V.I.P.
89 Pokey dwellers
90 Wouk-Tolstoy collaboration? (with "The")
96 "___, Lover!," 1954 song
97 Henri's soul
98 "...Cupid ___ longer an archer": Shak.
99 Bearish period
102 Vedic god's thing

105 "___, That Kiss," 1931 song
107 Tristram's love
109 Conrad-Koestler collaboration?
115 Square column
116 ___ and sometimes Y
117 In a tumult
118 Use a musical fork
119 Rock star Billy ___
120 Town in Provence
121 ___ Sap, Cambodian lake
122 Galatea's lover
123 Prunes trees
124 ___ off (irate)
125 Hem
126 H.H.S. arm

DOWN

1 Empty space
2 Black Sea port
3 Retreats
4 Composer of "Happy Days Are Here Again"
5 Close an envelope
6 Follower of Zeno
7 Stiff fabric
8 Hammer part
9 Auspices
10 ___-al-Arab
11 Euphemism for "hell"
12 So-called, in Provence
13 Plaster holder
14 Tasso's patron
15 Mimic
16 Brewers' needs
17 Rainfall-chart lines
19 Basket fiber
26 Trouble, in Ayr
27 Orwell's school
28 Not in a whisper
34 Orderly
35 Hungarian city
37 Harem rooms
39 "___ Heidenleben": R. Strauss
40 Petition
41 Draft org.
42 Rivers in England and Ontario
43 Collect, as grain
44 World banking org.
45 King of Thebes
46 Corday's victim
47 Anoint, old style
48 Spry
53 ___-di-dah
54 H.S. subj.
55 Flavor

56 Rapa ___ (Easter Island)
57 Sea eagle
61 Threefold
62 Beatles' Starr
63 Suffix with form or reform
64 Equals
66 Moray
67 Japanese carp
68 Under one's control
69 Swab
70 Bungled
71 ___ Willie Winkle
77 Musical syllable
78 Pasternak girl
79 Body of African warriors
80 She wrote "Seven Women"
81 Having a skull
82 Hole maker
83 Trygve of the U.N.
84 Explosive letters
85 Nimitz and Byrd
86 "___ thee late a rosy wreath": Jonson
91 Group of eight
92 Fine

93 In a violent rage
94 Infant under one month
95 Price
99 Loafer
100 Persephone's love
101 Chromosome parts
103 Verona's river
104 Rhone feeder
106 A king of Judea
108 Ready for action
109 Multiseasonal pelter
110 Inner: Comb. form
111 Upon
112 Regretted
113 Trill or troll
114 Shoe part

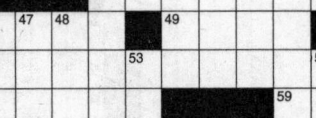
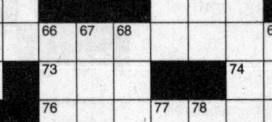
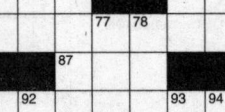
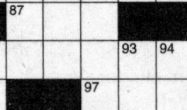

by Joy L. Wouk

ACROSS

1 It's held during an opening
5 Family sitcom role
8 Tooth care grp.
11 Chariot rider of myth
14 Test section
18 Popping up all over
19 Past
20 Stocking material
22 Western New York county
23 Part of a neuron
24 Travel service started by a Spanish-born actress?
27 Hard drive item
28 Ritz shelfmate
29 Wistful comment, after "a"
30 Little contraption
31 Studio started by a TV actor?
35 "What's ___ for me?"
36 Villain in "David Copperfield"
37 "Stand" band
38 Five or ten gallons' worth
41 Small flowering tree
44 Gelatin substitute
46 Astronomer who discovered Uranus
48 Little piggies
49 "Te ___" (hymn)
50 Mating game
52 It has curved arms
53 Fancy grocery started by a nightclub singer?
56 Meir's successor
57 I.R.S. deadline mo.
58 Cat call
59 Disney's "___ & Stitch"
60 Heavy drapery fabric
61 Transportation agency started by a fashion designer?
66 Subordinate
68 Noisome smell
69 "Gangs of New York" actress
70 Army E-3
73 Passing with ease
74 Orphanage started by an Oscar-winning actress?
78 Win margin
79 "The Metamorphosis" character Gregor ___
80 Guitar forerunner
81 Collectible plate holder
82 Gen. Garibaldi
84 Parts of un livre
85 Curtain froufrou
86 Roll-___
87 ___ culpa
88 Meister ___ (beer brand)
90 Sets (on)
91 Plant nursery started by a football Hall-of-Famer?
98 Tintoretto's "The Miracle of ___ Freeing the Slave"
101 Didn't have enough
102 "Zounds!"
103 Orsk's river
104 Pastry shop started by a televangelist?
107 Lean
108 "One-touch" sport
109 Treaded sneaker part
110 Make sure
111 Sound effect
112 It underwent the Enlightenment, with "the"
113 "Cimarron" studio
114 Starr of song
115 Stadium stirrers, for short
116 Comparative word

DOWN

1 Old "Television Theatre" sponsor
2 Water sprite
3 Gone by
4 Pope during the siege of Rome by Lombards
5 Genus of crustaceans named for a classical nymph
6 One without proper respect for elders
7 "Tiny Bubbles" singer
8 Samuel Gompers's org.
9 Unit of refractive power of a lens
10 Aim
11 Multivolume ref.
12 Poetic preposition
13 Diligent pupils
14 It might get a thumping
15 Dry
16 Media honcho Brown
17 Follow
21 In a flutter
25 Long time
26 Speeds
32 Liqueur flavoring
33 It causes redness
34 Lock
38 Mountainous route once used by Alexander the Great
39 Unnatural
40 Close on stage
41 Neighborhood
42 Dutch landscapist Aelbert ___
43 Name in a Shakespeare title
44 British landing field
45 Plants known as "sticky-heads"
46 Good-time Charlies
47 Santa ___
49 Active sort
50 Fiber made from coconuts
51 Putted successfully
54 Gangster follower
55 Come off, as paint
56 Big bird
60 Windy locale?
62 Goes kaput
63 Minor functionary
64 Sci-fi princess
65 "Soap" family name
66 Tropical fruit
67 Isolate, possibly
71 Remove from isolation
72 Modern phone
74 Black varnish
75 Fine meal
76 Get to
77 White-bean dish of France
79 Represent
83 It may be at your fingertips
84 Birthplace of a biblical Mary
85 Decorates 60's-style
88 Old radio's Major ___
89 Nike competitor
90 Got unexpectedly
91 "State and Main" director, 2000
92 "___ the World"
93 Mock-scared cry
94 Discharge
95 Star of TV's "Vega$"
96 Popular English doll
97 John knighted in 1998
98 77-Down, for one
99 Race finish
100 "Dangerous Liaisons" ladies: Abbr.
105 North Sea diver
106 Essential

by Patrick Berry

ACROSS

1 "Choice" fellow
7 Bos. or N.Y.
10 Memorable Belgian musician
14 Reckless
18 Boo-boos in a book
19 Parseghian
20 Legal
22 Scat singer
23 Pride member
24 Admiral's nightmare?
27 He raised Hel
28 "... ___ her curds and whey"
29 Regatta and poet William E.
30 Engineer's downfall?
34 Reverse of verso
35 African lake
36 Tomato blight
38 Scents
42 Bowl call
44 Quagmire
47 Bad time for an auto mechanic?
49 French saint: Dec. 1
51 Buttons on dryers
53 Lair for Leo
54 Marie or Anne: Abbr.
55 Kind of ray or globulin
57 Snide remark
58 Referee's predicament?
63 Haberdasher's headaches?
65 Andrea ___
67 Type of sleeve
68 "Tribute" playwright
70 Reuters' rival
71 Northern forest
72 Shipment to Kennedy
74 Set starter
76 Peril for a veterinarian?
80 Mattress salesman's affliction?
83 Sprite
85 Prepared
86 Chip off the cold block
87 Mouths, to Marius
88 Incantations
91 Pickle spice
92 Plumber's fantasies?
97 Guarantee
99 Peggy or Pinky

100 Wonder of songdom
101 Whale spray
103 Baseball's Rusty
105 Follow
107 Electrician's worry?
112 Comes forth
115 Type of type
116 Doer: Suffix
117 Watchmaker's woe?
119 Darcel or Levertov
121 Burden
122 Witnessing clause, in law
123 Huxtable or Rehan
124 Dangerfield
125 Robin's residence
126 Flagmaker
127 Belgian-French river
128 Prevailing procedures

DOWN

1 Cry of surprise
2 Celestial hunter
3 Problem for a real-estate agent?
4 Mental health
5 Suffix with Capri
6 Author Hentoff
7 Hebrew letter after nun
8 Famed Trojan
9 Most delectable
10 Bridle flap
11 Where socks are exchanged
12 Hosp. test
13 Limber
14 Perennials do this
15 Maguey's relative
16 Do in
17 Toppers
21 "My Mother ___," TV series of yore
25 Pakistani region
26 ___ nous
31 Batter or butter
32 Hebrew lyre
33 Was solicitous
34 Judges
37 Middle: Prefix
39 One-time Perle of society
40 Chekhov
41 "That's one small ___ ..."
42 Mil. group
43 Jai ___
45 Dramatic device
46 Perennial herb
48 Prefix with mural or muscular

50 "___ will, I can ...": Sheridan
52 Petty thieves
56 "A man, ___ ..."
59 Pelage
60 Secular
61 Actress Samantha
62 On the schedule
64 Emulated Stratas
66 Trick
69 Crusoe's creator
71 Legendary Uri family
72 Footnote abbr.
73 Pancake
75 Victory signs
77 Carpenter's bad habit?
78 Inactive
79 Gomer or Howard
80 Drinks a little
81 Rub out
82 Bara role
84 Poker hand
89 Fatherly
90 Mlle., in Madrid
93 Bleak peak
94 Dog found in the Outback

95 Take offense
96 Calms
98 Handle
102 Eye part
104 Kampala is here
106 Member of the wedding
108 She is "Woman"
109 Things, en casas
110 "Long time ___"
111 Zane and Jane
112 School Shelley attended
113 Golconda
114 Big birds
115 Concordes
118 Prefix with bar or graph
119 Actress Joanne
120 Dawn goddess

by Charles M. Deber

ACROSS

1 Bussed audibly
8 Family member
13 Attacks
20 "___ child are doing well"
21 Bucolic
22 Kerchiefs
23 Disrupt; perturb
24 Sluggish
25 Spark-plug spacings
26 Ermine, at times
27 Co.'s arm for investigation-growth
29 Cry at Bonn
30 Cherbourg cherub
31 Ozark individuals
32 V.I.P.
35 Milk: Comb. form
39 Toward sunrise
41 Line on a letter
42 Headland
44 Kind of plexus
45 In broad and noble style
48 Mouths
49 Lecture material
51 Air-quality org.
52 "___ do thou likewise": Luke 10: 37
53 Word with ears, heart or thumbs
54 Speech part
56 ___ forth
57 Crossed out
58 Sledder's gear
61 Reduces speed
64 Wicked wax
65 Witness
67 Jam
68 Sun: Comb. form
69 Frankfurt an der ___
71 Solution strength
73 Sends back to a lower court
75 Algerian port
76 Enclosures
77 Domingo is one
79 N.F.L. team
81 Give off
82 Bridge gaffe
84 Offspring
87 Opposite of pos.
88 Off ___ (occasionally)
89 Obstacle
91 Bad ___ German spa
92 Trivial bother
93 A hardwood
94 Mr. ___ (Prince Charming)
97 W. African language branch
98 Tiered centerpiece
100 Job for an emcee
102 "A Boy Named ___"
103 Preppy town in Mass.
105 Kin of etc.
106 Excise
108 Four-flusher
110 ___-fi
111 Barbershop song
113 Midianite king
114 Stoolie
116 Like certain bombs
119 Hash house
122 Ragout of game
124 In a wrathful way
126 Deadlock
127 Briefs
128 Fit for drinking
129 Foreigner
130 Dish up
131 Althing member

DOWN

1 Insts. in Tex. and Mass.
2 ___ Blanc in the Alps
3 Collection of tales told by Scheherazade
4 Vino at Harry's Bar
5 Clark and Rockwell
6 Work unit
7 What some get up when mad
8 Refrigerator's milieu
9 Emulate Cram or Ovett
10 Calif.'s San ___
11 Twain portrayer: 1944
12 Brasses member
13 Rhyme scheme
14 Prepaint work
15 Sea east of Bermuda
16 Deputy in "Measure for Measure"
17 Frost's "___ Vale"
18 Pass at Indy
19 Draft initials
28 "Eat, drink ___ merry"
33 Copters' kin
34 Yellow River feeder
36 Golden oldie: 1911
37 Giant star in Auriga
38 Part payment, at times
39 ___ Benedict
40 "East of Eden" character
41 Entreaties
43 Shirley Temple film: 1934
46 Malt kiln
47 S. African gulch
50 Clairvoyance, for short
55 Black, in Brest
59 Best
60 Heads of France
62 Emulate Niobe
63 Poisonous plant
64 Keyboard combination
66 Tear
69 Alfresco
70 Estate
72 Anonymous Richards
74 Economize
78 Private or corporal
80 Otherwise
82 Me, to Miss Piggy
83 ___ Moses (Pentateuch)
85 Author Ferber
86 December word
88 "___ the Lion"
90 ___ to (brought about)
95 Focal point
96 Planned progress
99 Dance concert
101 Kingly
104 Historic time
107 Pithy
109 Conserve of grapes
110 Express
112 Looker
115 "___-Tin," 1938 song
117 Paris magazine
118 Alizarin user
119 Résumé
120 Rhea's cousin
121 Inclined
123 CDI quintupled
125 Bird in 3 Down

by Ralph G. Beaman

EXCUZE MY SPELLING

ACROSS

1 Waistband
5 Musical family
10 Autumn tool
14 Belabor
18 "Women and Love" author
19 Knock for ___ (stun)
20 Brazilian novelist Jorge
22 Actor Julia
23 PREADULT-HOOD
25 CREAMY SALAD DRESSING
27 Distinguishing feature
28 Fad
30 "___ Fideles"
31 Waistband
32 Certain electron tube
33 Middle East trouble spot
34 Tijuana Brass trumpeter
37 "Oh ___ Beautiful Mornin' "
38 Gold rush region
42 Itsy
43 ROSTROPOVICH'S INSTRUMENT
45 Male gypsy
46 Biting
47 Pinball goof
48 Actual
49 Author Stoker
50 Doctrine
51 SOLEMN PLEDGE
55 Open-weave fabric
56 Taiwan divides it
58 Gathers the sheaves
59 Prized Himalayan cedar
60 Largest country in Africa
61 Art style
62 "Death, Be Not Proud" poet
63 "___ Rides Again"
65 Witches' get-together
66 Ava played a barefoot one
69 Send the spirits soaring
70 HURTFUL
72 Is able to
73 Shropshire simpleton
74 Location
75 "___ It Romantic?"
76 William or Sean

77 Expanse east of N.A.
78 AMASS
82 "La Plume de Ma ___," 1958 Broadway hit
83 Covers one's sword
85 Skating champ Rodnina
86 Highest point
87 Kind of poker
88 Wild goose
89 Bamako is its capital
90 The Big Apple
93 Platform part
94 Willy Loman, for one
98 DISCONCERTED
100 SUFFOCATE
102 Wander about
103 ___ hot (middling)
104 Prods on
105 Black Sea arm
106 What less is?
107 "Red" initials
108 Comedian Murphy
109 Slangy dissent

DOWN

1 Pahlavi's title
2 Amonasro's daughter
3 Acronym for a certain plane
4 Dead set (on)
5 Igneous rock
6 On the qui vive
7 Bop on the head
8 Hic, haec trailer
9 Unique
10 Islamic fasting month
11 Astonish
12 Danny or Sammy
13 Conductor de Waart
14 Quaker
15 Highlands girl
16 Give the boot to
17 Hilarity
21 Enjoying a winning streak
24 Manicurist's board
26 Major Joppolo's post
29 French roast
32 Gandhi's loincloth
33 ___ ease (uncomfortable)
34 Top story
35 Rover's restraint
36 SANCTIONED
37 Fred Flintstone's wife

38 Laments loudly
39 NACREOUS
40 Down under eucalyptus eater
41 Hard red wheat
43 Flexible shoot
44 Thin pancake
47 That is ___ (so to speak)
49 Daniel or Debby
51 Staff officers' group
52 Rome's famous fountain
53 Belief
54 Château-Thierry's river
55 Wall outlets
57 Like a fruitcake
59 It goes with a cup of java
61 Robot of Jewish folklore
62 Blackmore's Lorna
63 "Prima Ballerina" painter
64 Israeli seaport
65 Whale in the sky
66 Old Roman receptacle

67 Word in a French toast
68 Building afterthought
70 Used the gaming tables
71 Laughing
74 French prime minister: 1947–48
76 Montmartre resident
78 Rose distillation
79 Oriel
80 Monitor lizard
81 Hookup
82 Communications device
84 "That's ___" (too bad)
86 Carry-on luggage
88 Consecrate
89 Moslem Messiah
90 Spore
91 "Typee" sequel
92 Ski lift
93 Attention-getting hisses
94 Mining nail
95 Author de la Roche

96 Over
97 Field of glacial ice
99 Trifling amount
101 Do a lawn job

by Frances Hansen

ACROSS

1 Wrongly
6 Runs in neutral
11 A light: Slang
15 Collegian's pad
19 Saltarello, e.g.
20 Nantes's river
21 Rene's laughter
22 Fencing tool
23 CONSTITU-
TIONALS?
26 Enclosed trucks
27 Hitchcock movie:
1964
28 Some amplifiers
29 Wraps up
31 Prima ballerina
32 Heredity factors
33 O.T. book
34 Summits, in Siena
36 Heretofore
38 Dike
42 Silly person
45 Watch over
47 Ranks of nobility
50 MORNING
SHOWER-SHAVE
RITUAL?
55 Morocco, to Marcel
56 Rim
57 Spanish river
58 Pintail ducks
59 Tex. shrine
60 Bridge expert
Culbertson
61 Test photos
64 Backward
66 Plant also called
avens
68 Abel Janszoon ___
69 Univ. in Dallas
70 J.F.K. Abbr.
72 Asian wild ass
76 Rama I's domain
78 "Iliad," for one
80 Ancient Greek
geographer
81 Singer Tillis
84 Lasso
86 Slatterns
88 Dupe
89 Japanese sash
90 Limpid
91 BOGART TWIN
FEATURE?
94 Lowered in social
position
96 North Korean river
97 Ar chaser
98 Driving hazard
99 Insect's lower lip
105 Muscovite
107 Summit

110 City NE of Rome
111 Humorous
115 Stored away
118 Tropical bird
120 Zoroastrian sacred
writings
121 Whip
122 HIRED GUN?
125 Commedia dell'___
126 Khayyám
127 Like some walls
128 Former county in
Scotland
129 Kern's "Very ___,
Eddie"
130 Rink feature
131 Mother-of-pearl
132 Bean and Shepard

DOWN

1 ___ a dozen
2 ___-arms (soldier)
3 Prefix for mission
4 Picturesque
5 Old-age infirmity
6 Chinese river
7 Condemn
8 Editor's concern
9 Utensil on a pencil
10 Moon goddess
11 Late governor of
Conn.
12 West role
13 Vexed
14 Legal term for
"middle"
15 Ardent
16 Oct.'s gem
17 Tear apart
18 Army meal
24 Poured
25 Church architect
30 COMPLETE
NOBLEMAN?
35 Biblical patriarch
37 Welfare of the
community
39 Short-tailed rodent
40 Author Ludwig
41 Glimpse
42 Skilled
43 Native-born Israeli
44 Aegean island
46 Dantès's creator
48 "To ___ and a
bone . . .": Kipling
49 Men's house
slippers
51 Impends ominously
52 Tarnish
53 Slacken
54 Suffix with journal
55 Loose robe

62 HONORABLY
WON SWEET-
HEART?
63 Escargots
65 Duplicate, for short
67 Actress in
"Winterset"
71 A singing Boone
73 Measure
74 Muslim Satan
75 Functions
77 Murray and Marsh
79 Peculiar
81 Seed containers
82 Genesis man
83 Nursery-rhyme trio
85 Asian weight
87 Critic's disapproval
92 Chariot-of-fire
prophet
93 Rumanian region
now shared with
the Ukraine
95 Restrained
100 Garb
101 "Lulu" composer
102 "___ the water shall
float" (old English
saying)

103 Quebec bay
104 Causing excessive
pupil contraction
106 Perfumery
compound
108 French wine region
109 Water swelling
112 Port city for
Pompey
113 Harsh
114 Merits
115 Metal dross
116 Arum plant
117 Concerning
119 Not ever, to Blake
123 Droop
124 E.T.O. head

by Edward Marchese

ACROSS

1 Popular side
5 Fingers
11 Andrews, e.g.: Abbr.
14 Coors competitor
19 Island wiggle
20 Captivate, in a way
21 Mallorca Mrs.
22 Gaucho's turf
23 The bakery worker ___
26 Pop singer Neville
27 Professional headgear
28 Mies van der Rohe's motto
30 Arcade favorite
31 The spendthrift ___
35 Wrap artist?
37 Is down with
38 The gardener ___
46 Fly catcher
49 Berated loudly
50 Super
52 Arabian peninsula city
53 Mother of Helen
54 The enterprising musician ___
58 Ladder company?
62 Stable particle
63 Identify, in a way
64 Drain, in a way
65 Dork
68 Commercial prefix with Cat
69 Isolde's love
74 Stutz contemporary
75 Barbecue setting
80 The short-tempered fellow ___
83 Like slander
84 Caught flat-footed on a tennis serve, maybe
85 Medicinal plant
86 Lincoln and Madison
90 Michael Stipe's band
91 Aladdin ___
95 Simile's center
98 From humble beginnings
99 The shopper ___
106 Trattoria bottles
111 Past masters
112 Emergency delivery, maybe
113 Better trained
114 The unambitious worker ___
119 Start of a legal conclusion
120 Many moons
121 "Bewitched" witch
122 Words with instant or uproar
123 Fits in well
124 Get the drift
125 Prepare for the new model year
126 Hoopster Thurmond

DOWN

1 Go from second to third, say
2 Port St. ___, Fla.
3 Argus-eyed
4 Egret, e.g.
5 Kicked around some more
6 Working without ___
7 One X
8 Mustangs' sch.
9 "Alley ___!"
10 A.E.C. successor
11 Didn't hold back one's curiosity
12 Deserving a slap, perhaps
13 Low men
14 Bank holding?
15 Los ___ (nuclear site)
16 Peer
17 Dorm annoyance
18 Cruiserweight boxing champion James ___
24 Old talk show name
25 It may be bitter
29 "Kinda" suffix
31 1984–88 skating gold medalist
32 Havana residue
33 ___-Foy, Que.
34 Road help
36 Nutritional fig.
38 Noah of "ER"
39 No-goodnik
40 Designer Gucci
41 Mark time, in a way
42 Bloke
43 Fraction of a joule
44 It's been done
45 Cruel one
46 City where Dr Pepper originated, 1885
47 Goals
48 Slider's goal
51 Early aristocrat
52 Fig. with two dashes
54 Okra unit
55 Bar topic
56 Prenatal care centers?
57 Operatic prince
59 Book after Neh.
60 Hard-to-find cards, to collectors
61 Spreading device
66 Bard's nightfall
67 Wetlands area
69 Whaler's direction
70 "Dirty" dish
71 Agenda part
72 Usual: Abbr.
73 Answering machine offering, sometimes
76 Some schoolwork
77 Galway Bay's ___ Islands
78 Cartel city
79 Different
81 Having five sharps
82 Maze site, maybe
86 Tinker, Evers and Chance
87 From ___ Z
88 Wagner opera
89 Tune out
92 Assist, to Eliza Doolittle
93 When said five times, a 1974 Rolling Stones hit
94 Part of B.Y.O.B.
95 Best suited
96 Trivia category
97 ___ Lingus
99 Part of a power saw
100 Cuba ___
101 Getaway spots
102 Dutch sights
103 Vacation rental, maybe
104 Two-___ (court situation)
105 O.J.'s team
107 Novelist ___ René Lesage
108 Actress Lisi
109 Black key
110 "Funny Girl" composer
112 ___-Cuban music
115 Plunk preceder
116 Hydrocarbon suffix
117 Banned pesticide
118 Hugs, symbolically

by Fred Piscop

ACROSS

1 Capp's ___ Iggle
5 Wild goat
9 Bay State town
14 Cogwheel item
19 Lulu
20 "It's ___!"
21 TV's ___ Na
22 Shade
23 HARRY
26 A Peace Prize winner in 1908
27 "Etude ___": Swinburne
28 Amsterdam
29 Uriah
30 Rumanian coin
31 Trunks
32 Glacial mass
35 European thrushes
38 Danton colleague
39 Sylvan
42 Mortimer of radio fame
43 SUE
45 Fatima slept here
46 Call it ___
47 Locale
48 Phoenician letters
49 Out yonder
50 Comprehend a joke
51 FRANK
55 "Thus with a kiss ___": Romeo
56 Citizen of Asmara
58 Annapolis inst.
59 Kraits
61 Family of dynamite's inventor
62 Derisive interjection
63 More cunning
65 Used a ketch
67 Aggrieved
68 Neglecting
71 Love song
72 SALLY
75 Antiaircraft missile
76 Signet
77 ___ Raton, Fla.
78 European linden
79 Auspicious
80 Utter
81 BOB
85 Cathedral section
86 Toward the center
88 Zeena's mate in a Wharton book
89 Voguish
90 Sent to Elba, e.g.
91 Minor prophet
92 Highly timely
93 Four noggins
95 Support for Manet
96 Copper smelting center
101 Reach an ultimate point
103 JEAN
105 Sand did this
106 Even
107 Father of Ahab
108 News, for short
109 Conduit
110 Professed opinion
111 Kringle's, burden
112 Sheep shelter

DOWN

1 Adonis's killer
2 Last Stuart ruler
3 Harold Teen's leaping car
4 Whimsical humor
5 St. Paul's birthplace
6 Sanction a crime
7 Expectancy
8 Deli choice
9 Elaine's bailiwick
10 "... that serveth ___": Num. 3:36
11 Pluto
12 Just
13 Minstrel's offering
14 Place for three men
15 Sioux
16 MARK
17 Ailanthus, e.g.
18 Part of a lamp
24 Harvest
25 Love, in Lucca
31 Overdoes it on the beach
32 Fathom
33 Goofs
34 Soak hemp
35 Inedible orange
36 D. Thomas's "___ Milk Wood"
37 CAROL
38 Morning prayer
39 Pâté de ___ gras
40 Robin of balladry
41 Galba's ghostly guardians
43 Kind of basin
44 Soprano Lisa Della ___
47 Golfer Ed
49 Brass helpers
51 The City, Rome: It.
52 Geologist Arnold: 1807–84
53 Shark's crime
54 Printer's roller
57 Kind of loss
59 "It's ___!"
60 Record
63 Inducement
64 Forcefully, in poesy
65 Cheek and Foldi
66 City on the Allegheny
67 Corset part
69 Prosaic
70 Grinding substance
72 Humanity
73 Cloyingly sweet
74 Besides, to Brutus
77 Eliot hero
79 Bombast
81 Monogram of the author of "The Biglow Papers"
82 Afflicted with rubella
83 Moor who suspected amour
84 Greenland air base
85 Italian philosopher: 1866–1952
87 Wily
89 Id est
91 Ingenuous
93 Seats for parishioners
94 Concerning
95 Pitcher
96 Weapons, for short
97 Not any, in Dogpatch
98 Lad, in León
99 Bonkers
100 Drug-yielding plant
102 Through
103 What an R.N. gives
104 Punctum

by June A. Boggs

ACROSS

1 Precipitate
5 Long, long follower
8 Music from a subcontinent
12 Its lawgiver was Lycurgus
18 P. Mason or C. Darrow
19 Wool dress fabrics
21 More lighthearted
22 Born's partner
23 High-finance football team
26 Spinning sound
27 Steel-mill employee
28 "... the way of a man with ___": Proverbs
29 On ___ (gossip's morsel)
30 Hawaiian plantation foremen
32 Sensory stimulus
33 Swim spot for oreads
34 Padua pronoun
35 Uprising
37 Mil. trials
38 Kind of boss or bull
39 Structure on a predella
40 Triangular sail
42 Party-going football team
45 Germinative
48 Zona Gale's Miss Lulu
50 Got the drift
51 ___ plaisir (gladly, in Gard)
52 Conway of the silents
54 ___ Gabelhorn, Swiss Alpine peak
56 Galileo's home town
60 About 1.057 quarts, in Quebec
62 Name on a '45 plane
63 Held in awe
65 Floral fragrances
67 Handyman
69 Member of a Hebrew tribe
70 Dog properly named Spot
72 Tom's bar partner
74 Accipiter's dive
75 Grieg's "___ Death"
76 1 and 95, e.g.
77 Willingham's "___ Man"
79 "Diamonds and ___," Baez song
80 Number of cards in a "pons" deck
81 Island occupied in '42, retaken in '43
82 Lobsters' sheddings
84 Peripatetic football team
90 More spectral
92 Van Gogh painted here
93 Football Hall of Famer Parker
94 Org. for Bird and Birdsong
95 Algerian horse troopers
99 Lobscouse
100 Author de la Roche
102 Then, in Rennes
103 Where the Ghibellines held forth
104 Acapulco aunt
105 Copland's "El ___ Mexico"
106 Noblesse chaser
109 Adm. Farragut's imprecation
110 Handy Andy's football team
113 ___ escolar (school age, in Sonora)
114 Ida from London
115 Bull Run, to the C.S.A.
116 Tobin or Kyle of football
117 City on the Moselle
118 Favorable expressions
119 Taoist Lao-___
120 Prune, to Jackie Stewart

DOWN

1 Canaille
2 Sitting room
3 Shandy's creator
4 Water-pumping football team
5 Take ___ view (frown on)
6 Wilder who's often wild
7 Companion for arsenic
8 Flight components
9 Sinus cavities
10 Once-divided Eur. nation
11 His area is about 17,000,000 sq. mi.
12 Certain Moslem group
13 ___ a poke
14 Jejune
15 Minor waterway
16 Looks after
17 Anagram for Sinatra
20 Fashionable football team
24 Nicola of Cremona
25 Merak and Mizar
31 Freberg of TV commercials
34 Lilly of pharmaceuticals
36 Californie, par exemple
38 Fishing trap
39 Precursor of trig.
41 "Waiting for the Robert ___"
42 Turbine-operating football team
43 Capital of South Yemen
44 Attracted to a coachman
45 Salt-covered plain of the Southwest
46 Patti LuPone and her role successors
47 Spirit; courage
49 Contemporary of Della and Sarah
53 Celestial handles
54 Indigent football team
55 Three-time American League M.V.P.
56 Overweight football team
57 Advent or fact ending
58 Like a hedgehog
59 Those with expertise
61 Proposed Const. amendment
64 Cousin of a ness
66 Pilaster fillet
68 ___ up (confined)
71 Follower of Ham or Shem
73 W.W. I river of contention
78 Galatea's unlucky love
80 D.J.'s offerings
81 Modern art
83 Chester and Festus, for short
84 Matting fibers
85 Contract component
86 Make orderly
87 Long Island's ___ Gardens
88 Tot's musical instrument
89 Beryl Sprinkel's concern
91 Least onerous
94 Knitted shoulder scarfs
96 Frontal
97 Beadsman, for one
98 Polished, in a way
100 Windfall
101 Perfume ingredient
102 Where the temple of Parvati is
105 Being, in Bonn
107 Mardi or foie follower
108 Start of the N.C. motto
111 Roof piece
112 Mystery writer Foley

by Bert Rosenfield

ACROSS

1 Molten-metal carrier
6 Memphis god
10 Parts of dols.
13 Danish cape, with "The"
17 Of oil
18 Hall: Ger.
19 Snapshot
21 Londoner's subway
22 Third of a series
23 Pass receiver Collinsworth
24 Kind of quarter
25 Corrida sounds
26 Presley vending song: 1963
30 One of the Hebrides
31 Backer
32 Glacial ridge
33 Presley estate
37 Unfruitful
39 Peruvian clothing
40 Latin conjunctions
41 Anthropologist Margaret
42 She wrote "Delta of Venus"
43 Fannie follower
46 Colonel North
48 Legendary British king
49 Ecdysiast's covering
51 Rueful Presley song: 1961
54 Abdul-Jabbar's gp.
57 Takes care of
58 "Pagliacci" role
59 Got on
61 Perfect
63 Hopeful Presley song: 1968
65 Autonomous region of NW Italy
70 Indo-Iranian
71 Weighs or weights
76 Teem
77 H.S. V.I.P.s
79 Presley avowal song: 1966
81 Excellent
83 Radio amateurs
85 Product resulting from cracking petroleum
86 Enzyme suffix
87 Ending denoting origin
88 Champagne town
89 Brazilian border river
91 Utah resort
92 Made ineffective

94 Giving-up Presley song: 1961
96 Algerian cavalryman
100 Conscious
101 Qum native
102 Presley thoughtful-question song: 1960
109 Rich source
110 Wimps' cousins
111 Strigiformes sound
112 Sister, to Cato
113 Tied
114 Key
115 Defoe heroine
116 Battery terminal
117 Louis L'Amour's "The Haunted ___"
118 Dutch commune
119 Barrie pirate
120 Billiards stroke

DOWN

1 Trademark kin
2 Senator Cranston
3 Attica division
4 Tamarack part
5 Card game for two
6 Rodent robber-hoarder
7 Soup vessels
8 Brought into agreement
9 Diner order
10 What the Light Brigade did
11 Walk like a two-year-old
12 Oppressive
13 Facing a glacier
14 Farmer opposed to Soviet collectivization
15 White poplar
16 Hameln's river
19 Banana plant
20 Yoko ___
27 Edmonton hockey team
28 Studio feature
29 Come in again
33 Intersecting vaults' edge
34 Pocahontas's spouse
35 On foot, in Paris
36 Hollowed out
38 Supple
41 Jason's first wife
43 ___-en-scène
44 Leaf cutters
45 Selves
47 Guido's note
48 Commuter's delight
50 Sis, e.g.

52 Some switch positions
53 Lures
55 Emerald and aquamarine
56 Of a region
60 Genetic material
62 Rave's partner
63 Treat with a certain antiseptic
64 Small amounts
65 Cow, in Vigo
66 Down with: Fr.
67 Long, swinging stride
68 Motorist no-no, for short
69 Violinist-composer Vivaldi
71 Toque or cloche
72 Patriot Allen
73 Kind of goal or trip
74 Pierre's aunt
75 Besmirch
78 Most transparent
80 ". . . ___ evil"
82 Court jargon
84 Vicuña's milieu
88 Met zealot

89 Halo
90 Babble
93 Kissinger's "___ Restored . . .": 1957
94 African desert wind
95 Lonely, in Ems
96 City in India
97 Try out
98 Yellow-fever vector
99 Wolflike carrion eater
103 Prefix with form or cycle
104 Electrical resistance units
105 New Rochelle college
106 ___ de Londres (ribbed silk)
107 Coal scuttles
108 Shoe insertion

by Joy L. Wouk

ACROSS

1 Constitution
8 "___ 70's Show"
12 Operating
17 "How dare they?!"
18 Darn it
19 Uranium-exporting country
20 Infinitives . . . it's ___
23 Word we share
24 Daily Planet worker
25 Reach
26 Beverage served with le dessert
27 More, in music
29 Big fish, to a fisherman
31 Paleontologist's discovery
32 Frat party detritus
34 The passive voice ___
38 Agcy. once involved with fallout shelters
40 Carrier with HQ in Tokyo
41 Gift on "The Bachelor"
42 N.F.L. linemen: Abbr.
43 Ambiguity ___
49 Trip planning org.
51 Pub order, maybe
52 Rhetorical questions . . . ___
57 Fantastic
58 Author's desire
59 Pope after John X
60 Org. that rates members of Cong.
61 C-worthy
64 Cold capital
66 Latin foot
67 Meshlike
70 ___ Life ("Porgy and Bess" character)
74 1997 title role for Demi Moore
77 Subject-verb agreement ___
79 One in the fast lane?
81 Deface
82 Contractions ___
84 Show whose theme song is "Who Are You"
86 Shortstop Chacon of the 1962 Mets
88 Malodourous room?
89 84-Across airer
90 Prepositions are not good ___
97 Sad poets
98 Creator of "All in the Family"
99 Mule alternative
103 Outworn
104 Scratch (out)
105 Not much
106 Daydreaming, say
108 Word said with a salute
109 Exaggeration is among the ___
114 Put back at zero
115 Ticked
116 Toughened
117 Macho types
118 Proceed slowly
119 Reporter's purchase

by Randolph Ross

DOWN

1 Vacuuming, e.g.
2 Setter
3 Perspectives
4 Comeback
5 Adviser of Capt. Picard on "Star Trek: T.N.G."
6 When to call, in some ads
7 M.L.K. Jr., e.g.
8 Seat of power
9 Inexpensive place to stay
10 Brand in a can
11 Bus. card info
12 Ahead
13 Bistro, informally
14 "I don't like it"
15 Overlook, as someone's weaknesses
16 Fine furs
17 Steadfast
20 Bowl-shaped pan
21 They may be stroked
22 Receipt listings
28 Mt. Rushmore State sch.
30 Apparel company Evan-___
31 Round end?
32 Part of a talk show staff
33 Work for a museum
35 Spanish eyes
36 Restaurant waiting areas
37 Lecture badly
38 In pieces

39 Abu Dhabi, e.g.
43 Creature in a Tennessee Williams title
44 Cellular stuff
45 Elusive swimmers
46 Member of the flock
47 Doo-wop syllable
48 Piece of property
50 Communication for the deaf: Abbr.
53 Night school subj.
54 Not hoof it, perhaps
55 Planes
56 Lowest state?
58 Tree trauma
62 Jardin zoológico attraction
63 Trainers treat them
65 Meanie
68 Comic's asset
69 Singer Sumac
71 "The Facts of Life" actress
72 Spike TV, formerly
73 Cousin ___ of "The Addams Family"
75 Collection agcy.
76 Heifetz heard at Carnegie Hall
78 Media handouts
79 Big suits
80 "Don't have ___!"
83 Pgh. Pirate, e.g.
84 Nabs
85 Tiny start

87 Wings hit "___ in"
90 Formula One driver Fabi
91 Lost on purpose
92 What a picador pokes
93 Got warm
94 Bad boyfriends
95 "Perhaps"
96 Do some fancy footwork
100 Counterfeited
101 Spotted
102 Hi-___
105 What a soldier shouldn't be
106 "___ Angel" (Mae West movie)
107 Force
110 Baton Rouge sch.
111 Medium ability?
112 Whip
113 ___ king

ACROSS

1 Country that won its first Olympic medal in 2004
8 1959 Ricky Nelson hit
15 Summons
20 Nay sayers
21 Tennis star Zvereva
22 Essence
23 Shady accountant's April 15 work?
25 Allied (with)
26 Saxophonist Al
27 Racer Al
28 Director of "Chicago" and "Dancin'"
30 Hula hoop
31 Connects with
34 Chinese "way"
36 Smash hits
38 G.R.E. takers
39 Caroler's reward?
44 Kind of D.A.
45 Rolodex no.
46 Pad site
47 Handy-andies
49 Unsmiling
51 Slip in a pot
53 1940's–50's All-Star Johnny
55 Pilot announcements, for short
57 "Little Shop of Horrors" dentist
58 Persistent photographers?
61 Sorority letters
63 Main entrances?
65 Wisecracker
66 Analyze
68 Turkey part
69 Mischief makers
73 Deep Throat, e.g.
74 Owls
76 Vandal
77 Comparatively small
79 Late 80's sitcom
80 Unfolding view for a hapless hang-glider?
84 Summer cooler
85 Summer coolers
87 Art containing 4-Down
88 Elvis or Madonna
89 Honeyed drink
90 Tens, e.g.
92 Cry of eagerness
94 Et ___ (following)
95 Asunción assent
97 "Faucet drips ahead"?
101 Nutrition info, for short
104 Graffitist's addition to a face
106 Org. that drafts guards
107 School zone requirement
109 Goals in 106-Across, quickly
110 "Cool!"
113 Runner
116 Served past
117 Dull
119 Roller coaster inventor?
123 Top guns
124 Waist reducer, perhaps
125 Current contraption
126 Comic Lewis
127 Sits atop
128 Fancy parties

DOWN

1 Puts out
2 "La Loge" artist
3 Feels irritated
4 Kids' TV staples
5 Like some sleep, for short
6 ". . . ___ he drove out of sight"
7 Not dull
8 "Need You Tonight" group, 1987
9 Weight allowance
10 Catch off-guard
11 Ontario, par exemple
12 Request
13 Dutch filmmaker ___ van Gogh
14 Packs away
15 Old Toyota
16 Jackie's "O"
17 Concern for Rev. Falwell?
18 Gulf State V.I.P.'s
19 Tormentor
24 Soon
29 Sports venue seen from the Grand Central Parkway
32 Twosome
33 Kings' org.
35 Hairy Halloween costume
37 Fountain order
40 30's migrant
41 M.D.'s who may cure snoring
42 "Got it"
43 Like city land, usually
45 Soldier's helmet, slangily
48 Instruction unit
49 Nutritious nosh
50 Where the ice skater fell?
51 "Evita" narrator
52 English pianist who was made a dame
54 Works of Michelangelo
56 Follow
57 Hold 'em variation
58 Mild cigar
59 Part of the 1992 Olympic Dream Team
60 Knolls
62 Metric measure
64 ". . . and I mean it!"
67 1968 hit with the lyric "I like the way you walk, I like the way you talk"
70 Dr. ___
71 Shoos
72 W.W. II site
75 Projecting part at the foot of a wall
78 Dark time in poetry
81 City south of the Salt River
82 Stylish gown
83 Yearn
86 Get to work on Time?
89 29-Down team
91 One way to turn
93 Rural valleys
94 Liverpool-to-Plymouth dir.
95 Military V.I.P.
96 Halogen salt
98 Comic Don
99 Staff leader
100 Main lines
101 Say poetry, say
102 Political pundit Myers
103 Puff ___ (Old World menaces)
105 Other side
108 Kitchen implement
111 Way off
112 Yarn
114 Chocolaty treat
115 No-no on office computers
118 Salt
120 Plenty steamed, with "up"
121 Wellness grp.
122 Recording giant

by Ashish Madhukar Vengsarkar

ACROSS

1 Stillage or spillage
5 Con man's ploy
9 Roe source
13 FATHER OF ONE-EYED SONS
19 Statue by Polyclitus
20 One of the Guthries
21 Do port work
22 Cocktail-party item
23 Forbear
24 Trumpet
25 Hussein, for one
26 Up
27 WEILL MUSICAL
31 Paramour in Paris
32 Posher
33 Screw pine
34 N.K.V.D. antecedent
36 Robert or Alan
37 "Student Prince" prop
38 Indian groom
41 Notation in an M.D.'s book
43 Hunk of pie
45 METEOROLOGY OR GEOPHYSICS
51 Biblical verb ender
54 Ship's berth
56 Electrician
57 General Eaker
58 Worm of Assam
60 "Of Thee ___"
63 Tappet mover
64 Tizzies
66 Leo, for one
67 Virgilian opus
69 FINANCIAL MOGUL
71 Bd.-of-director's head
72 Renowned Met basso
74 Make lace
75 RODGERS-HART OPUS
78 Entire membership
80 Amos of baseball
82 Eyepiece
83 Abet's companion
85 Canonic mark
86 "Le ___," Massenet aria
87 European salamander
88 ___ the Admiralty (U.K. naval brass)
91 Shipment to a hospital
93 Aberdeen's river
94 NORTH AMERICAN WHELK
97 U.S. mil. decorations
99 Where Sikkim is
100 Port ___, Egypt
102 Potsdam pronoun
105 Minn. neighbor
108 Rowing gaffe
111 Have being
113 Sulky
115 ___ in (receptive)
117 CALOMEL
121 Grape seed
123 Worms get-together
124 Ab's follower
125 Partaking of
126 Soirs' antitheses
127 Ferber
128 Fad
129 A billionth: Comb. form
130 Kent's Daily ___
131 Time's Thomas
132 Anne and Cécile: Abbr.
133 Kind of plaid

DOWN

1 New growth
2 Aegean island
3 ___ Express
4 Little pies
5 WINGDING, ROMAN STYLE
6 Zambezi denizen, for short
7 Hilo hello
8 Traverses the turnpike
9 Serb or Croat
10 Pika's cousin
11 Hersey's W.W. II town
12 Spray a vine
13 Fiddler-crab genus
14 ___ avis
15 Do a Disney job
16 Twangy
17 Topple
18 "Flying Dutchman" soprano
28 ___-de-boeuf (oval windows)
29 Alice of films
30 Burst of energy
35 Directed aloft
39 Cornfield sound
40 Sevareid
42 Tex's mount
44 Split a circle
46 ___ John of TV
47 Ups and downs of fashion
48 Treated chemically
49 Ingenious
50 Shrine Bowl team
51 M.I.T. degrees
52 Type of landing gear
53 L.A. event in 1984
55 Small minnows
59 Invalidate
61 Rather miserly
62 Hodges or McDougald
65 Plummer, e.g.
68 Short swim
70 New
73 Nadelhorn, for one
75 Jovial
76 Stake, to Sulla
77 Wry
79 REVERSIBLE COTTON FABRIC
81 Match the bet
84 Sylvan denizens
89 Build up matériel
90 Ala. neighbor
92 ___ acids
95 Gulled
96 Mendacious one
98 Employing a springe
101 Basement appliances
103 Town on the Moselle
104 Fixed over
105 Act of 1765
106 Almost princely
107 Singer O'Day
109 Dangerous mosquito
110 June walker
112 Dash
114 Wood-joint component
116 Cape Cod feature
118 Copper, once
119 Its motto is "Industry"
120 Titanic
122 Orly-Dulles transp.

by Bert Rosenfield

ACROSS

1 Curve part
4 Snoop
9 Dillon or Houston
13 Less ruddy
18 Cry of disgust
19 Rounded script
20 Penumbra
21 Cactus used as a drug
22 Title of Statue of Liberty poem
25 Female ruffs
26 India's monetary unit
27 Lessens
28 Place between
29 Dutch cheese center
31 Foot: Comb. form
32 "___, Ernest...": 1922 song
34 "___ nation, under God..."
35 Where the statue stands
40 Summarized
43 G.I. dog tags
44 ___ vie (brandy)
45 Most favorable
47 W.W. II boat
48 Craze
50 Spectrum producer
53 Unstable
58 With 80 Across, the statue's sculptor
61 Nectar collector
62 Love affair
63 Go to class
65 At some other time
66 Printing measures
67 Southwestern oaks
69 Bohemian to an extreme
71 Rubble
73 Mount where Aaron was buried
74 Farrow and Slavenska
76 Oil transport
78 ___ Lehmann, memorable soprano
79 John Duncan was one
80 See 58 Across
82 Analyzed
84 "All that is and ___ be": Sophocles
86 Restraints
87 School org.
88 Without neckwear
90 Sainted English scholar: 673–735
92 Org. for Miller and Barber

95 Heavenly bodies
97 "...my lamp beside ___": Lazarus
102 Tot's "piggy"
103 City SW of Brussels
105 Footnote term
106 Colonist's greeting to an Indian
107 Trumped
110 Infallible adviser
112 Void
114 Reach a goal
115 The statue's other name
119 More penetrating
120 Blunted fencing weapon
121 Express a view
122 Building wing
123 Noble British family
124 Pete Rose's team, once
125 Japanese alcoholic drinks
126 Shade of blue

DOWN

1 Appropriate
2 College cheer
3 Little innocents
4 Make ready
5 Schoolboy ___, former Detroit pitcher
6 Ralph ___, 20's leading man
7 Former name of Tokyo
8 Backslide
9 Ancient Jewish stronghold
10 Author of "Emma"
11 Faithful
12 "Jerusalem Delivered" author
13 Hammer part
14 Votes in favor
15 "Our reliance is in the ___": ... Lincoln
16 For all time, in poesy
17 Slept
21 A ___ (deductive)
23 Modigliani's "The Rose ___"
24 Ancient Greek coin
29 ___ Stati Uniti
30 Suffix with aster
33 Acquire
36 Ankle bones
37 Spanish dagger, e.g.
38 First name of a Ugandan exile
39 Completed

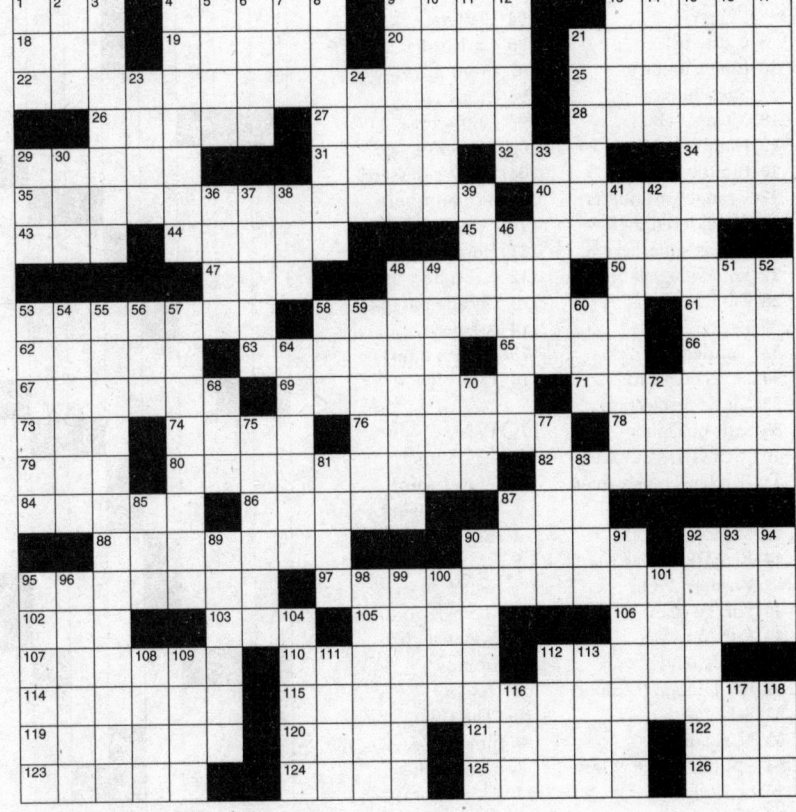

by Edward Marchese

41 Calls a jury
42 Corn spike
46 Lafitte was one
48 Servants
49 Quantity to be appended
51 Descendant of Shem
52 Bungled, with "up"
53 Jutland seaport
54 Unwrinkled
55 "...huddled masses yearning ___": Lazarus
56 Flute: Comb. form
57 Shaker
58 W.W. II plane
59 Olympics heroine: 1984
60 North Atlantic fish
64 These cannot be disputed
68 Pueblo Indian
70 Wedel
72 Long, fluffy scarf
75 Check
77 X follower
81 Sound seeking attention
83 Vic's radio partner

85 Fabulize
87 "___ Joey"
89 One who faces the music
90 Spanish dances
91 Auxiliary buildings
92 Large drinking vessels
93 Mawkish drivel
94 Leading Dadaist
95 Ship's planking
96 Decanted
98 Inflamed
99 What an aquafortist does
100 Forceful outburst
101 Arnaz
104 He painted "Maine Coast"
108 Sibelius was one
109 Arden and Queler
111 Lasso
112 SE Nigerian
113 Part of a chromosome
116 W.W. II org.
117 Wawaskeesh
118 Wily

250 TITULAR TITTERS

ACROSS

1 Kind of post or lighter
5 Cattle breed
10 Elbe tributary
14 Speechless
18 Moslem chief
19 Damp
20 Bundle
22 Evangelist Roberts
23 Bewildered fish?
25 Midas's marker?
27 French legislature
28 Biblical plants
30 Le ___ Soleil
31 Slander
34 Noted ennead
35 Musical selection
39 Luft or Doone
40 Rich German cake
41 Belgian-French river
42 Owns
43 Monogram pt.
44 Remark at a Western P.O.?
48 Forage plant
49 Puts up
50 Dail's land
51 Ivy League member
52 Selvage
53 N.Y. subway
54 Epithet for Orville or Wilbur?
58 English river
59 They give confidence
61 Egyptian Christians
62 "___ Amore," Dean Martin hit
63 The Joads, e.g.
64 Dumas character
65 "Robin ___" (old song)
67 Parlor pieces
69 Relating to oil
70 Got ready to spring
73 Switch positions
74 Remark at a geranium nursery?
77 French article
78 Siouan
79 Egyptian skink
80 Electrical units
81 "The Kink ___," film with a twist?
82 No soap
83 Crusoe and Friday?
87 Mail: Abbr.
88 Scot's uncle
89 Licensed brand: Abbr.
90 "The Son Also ___," family film?
91 An Alaskan
92 Do a movie scene over
94 Platters
95 Carlsbad ___
97 From ___ Z
98 ___ Rica
99 Golf score
100 Jouster's steed?
104 Eloise's dessert?
109 Sicilian resort
110 Of blood
111 Horner or Sprat
112 ___ code
113 Decade part
114 Assay
115 Correct a text
116 Tale

DOWN

1 "___ Girls"
2 Latin I word
3 Wire measure
4 Puts on
5 "___ home is his castle"
6 Juvenal's jottings
7 Essential part
8 Employ
9 Height
10 "The Coin ___," film re numismatists?
11 Parts of brake mechanisms
12 Congers
13 Half a diam.
14 ___ Gillis of TV
15 Neighbor of Arg.
16 Name in Communism
17 Robert ___, modern poet
21 Charon's colleagues
24 Antitoxins
26 Cacophony
29 Italian wine center
31 Ballerina Markova
32 Devices on destroyers
33 Hunt-club wall décor?
34 Edible mushroom
35 Ancient Greek war cry
36 Singles-bar patron?
37 Type of practice
38 Rate
40 U. of Md. team
44 Giggle
45 Yesterdays: Fr.
46 Methods: Abbr.
47 Machine parts
52 Set of values
54 Baseballer Speaker
55 Emulated Bernhardt
56 Type of baseball game
57 Notable period
60 Autocratic order
62 Greek letters
64 ". . . ___ and hungry look" Shak.
65 On ___ (going strong)
66 Search for water
67 Oklahoman
68 Start of a Wolfe title
69 Church calendar
70 Salad ingredient
71 Football play
72 Certain believers
74 Serrate
75 Tooth:Comb. form
76 Tribe whose name means "long tail"
81 Urban passage
83 Fidelity
84 Divide into three parts
85 Sound seeking attention
86 Jailbreak participant
91 Sts.' kin
93 Horrible one of comics
94 Mother of the Nereids
95 Beguile
96 Henry ___ Wallace
98 "Some ___ Punning," witty book?
99 Moderate
100 Reef
101 Compass dir.
102 Actress Claire
103 Bonilla, e.g.
105 Hood's exit
106 Mayan or Roman
107 Perpetually, to Poe
108 Thrash

by Mary R. Murdoch

ACROSS

1 Video session
7 Identified
12 Pitcher, of sorts
17 Bore
21 Kitchen gadget
22 Ancient Greek coins
23 It flows into Lyons
24 European state
25 Gershwin folk opera
27 What can be said of a Gershwin tune?
29 Gaelic
30 Knob
31 Twit
33 Slew
34 Itinerary abbr.
35 Most attractive
37 Charitable giving
38 Culture lead-in
40 Like shoes
41 Typeface imitative of handwriting
43 Tyke's transport
47 California city
50 Two-step, for one
51 Kind of stage, in human development
52 Before, to Byron
53 Shorebird
54 1925 Gershwin premiere
56 Jot
57 Ol' Man, e.g.
58 Gymnastic equipment
59 Directional suffix
60 Belle's partner in film
61 Affirm
62 Language of Iran
63 Arrives impolitely, with "in"
66 Jackie's predecessor
67 Rocket's deviation
68 Song from Gershwin's "Girl Crazy"
70 Cut into three
72 Some are red
74 Baseball's Preacher
75 Yalta's locale
76 Unhand
78 Song from Gershwin's "Rhapsody in Blue"
82 "My mama done ___ me" (song lyric)
85 Called on
86 Phobias
88 Shade of green
89 Tournament org.
90 You might have to eat this person's words
91 "___ now . . ."
92 Repent
93 British P.M. during Nixon's Presidency
94 American paters
95 Gershwin satire on politics
99 Pen name
100 Prefix with dermis
101 Subway riders
102 Writer Jong
103 They make cameos
104 Drawn
106 Use a lever
107 Full of idle talk
108 Bounce
109 Cruise ship freebies
110 007 foe
112 It's a waste
115 Piano's opposite
118 Having better sense
119 Pulitzer author Buchanan
120 Feminine name suffix

121 Another song from Gershwin's "Girl Crazy"
124 Gershwin song in a 1924 Astaire musical
128 Palindromically named magazine
129 Lariat
130 "___ Ben Johnson!"
131 Use as support
132 Oats
133 Audited a class
134 Republic of 1836
135 Named à la Spenser

DOWN

1 Sot
2 To the left
3 By itself
4 1953 Pulitzer dramatist
5 Marshal in Napoleon's army
6 Like some sugar
7 Erred through oversight
8 Religious men
9 1994 skiing gold medalist
10 Noisy transports
11 Outdo
12 Postulate
13 Eighth word of "The Star-Spangled Banner"
14 Debatable
15 Massachusetts cape
16 TV's "___ and Stacey"
17 Wreck
18 Songwriter's starting point, maybe
19 In ___ (stymied)
20 Sets
26 Big-name

28 Children's author LeCain
32 Tree in a thicket
35 Secret device
36 Kind of visa
38 Envelope abbr.
39 Match for Seles
40 Cleave
42 Previously
43 Fishing net
44 Title song from a 1933 Gershwin musical
45 Like Ovid's "The Art of Love"
46 Have a second session
47 Flower display
48 Three-time A.L. batting champ
49 Gershwin ballad from "The Goldwyn Follies"
50 Prefix with lateral
51 Progress steadily
54 Hikers' woes
55 Office time
56 Demean
58 Protected from the sun
62 Fitch and muskrat
63 Good times
64 Field
65 Tried hard
66 The silent type
68 Droplet
69 Mr. Rogers
71 Split
73 Unwanted looks
75 Stick
76 Wall Street villain
77 Getaway
78 Some schools
79 Milton's "Immortal ___"
80 Takes in

81 A Massey
83 Many a John Wayne film
84 "The Wizard of Oz" actor and family
87 Made the grade
89 Hardly shy
92 With defects and all
93 Unsparing
95 Trireme gear
96 Stew
97 Chilling
98 Perfume ingredient
99 Somewhat
101 Eis's opposite
103 Ferris wheel operator
105 Like some lines
106 Copyist
107 Actress Barbara Bel ___
109 "Chicago Hope" actress
111 Half a famous comedy act
112 By oneself
113 Fore-and-after
114 Was without, briefly
115 Feudal estate
116 Get a load of
117 Position to fill
118 R.B.I. or E.R.A
120 Even, to Yvonne
122 Many mins.
123 Verily
125 Otto I's domain: Abbr.
126 Calif. touchdown site
127 Intl. trading assn.

by Jeanette K. Brill

RETRONYMS*

*More descriptive names to differentiate old things from their new forms

ACROSS

1 Relative of "oy"
5 Early poet laureate Henry
8 Mine vapor
12 A lot
17 Pitcher's stat
19 King Duncan's resting place
21 Mixed bag
22 "My Fair Lady" locale
23 The press
26 Animal track
27 Attempt to escape
28 "Beetle Bailey" dog
29 Fill in (for)
31 ___ supra (where mentioned above)
32 Singer Stevens
33 Reuben's base
34 "Billy ___" (Keith Waterhouse satire)
35 Bar intro?
36 Pathetic
37 Undershirts
39 Coffee additive
42 Words before cuff or record
45 Speak in a high voice
47 "Woe ___"
48 Supermarket department
49 Traveled with the Tlingit
52 Postal service, once: Abbr.
55 "___ was saying . . ."
57 Be silent, in music
60 Defenseless
62 Durable wood
65 Quell, as rioters
67 Dishes (out)
68 Juice extraction device
70 Ballet star
71 Dallas inst.
72 Popular sporting event
74 Business inits. since 1920
75 Early clock
78 Sign of spring
79 "A Garden of Earthly Delights" novelist
81 Think through
82 Wined and dined
83 Going price
85 Fargo's partner

86 Rather than
88 Census detail
90 Refuses to deal with
91 "Très ___!"
93 Killer whales
96 Big Sky conference team
98 Big name in Gdansk
100 Slalom participant
103 Win at cat-and-mouse
107 Latin 101 verb
108 ___ dancing
110 Group of badgers
111 California has a big one
113 Southern Australia's ___ Bay
114 George's predecessor
115 Ardor
116 60's–70's pitcher Jim
117 Moorish castle
119 Papyrus' family
121 Communications device
124 Crosswise to the keel
125 Pointed stick
126 Mattress support
127 Looks after
128 Mud nesters
129 Out of action
130 Podium pauses
131 Gist

DOWN

1 Air
2 Young insects
3 Fly
4 D.C. figures
5 Show the way
6 "___ Send Me" (Sam Cooke hit)
7 Join up
8 Colorado tributary
9 "Rope-a-dope" boxer
10 Is too soon or too late
11 Apples and pears
12 Closer
13 Clairoyant's claim
14 Singer's accompaniment
15 Bureaucratic bigwig
16 Unit of progress
18 Child's order?
20 Bit of buffoonery
24 Reckless act
25 Nintendo forerunner

30 Mind-set
38 Achieve
40 Eliot's "cruellest" mo.
41 Asian nurse
43 Greek cheeses
44 Broaden
46 Lines of fashion
49 Gratuity
50 Buttercup family plant
51 Many Scandinavians
53 Extra weight
54 Undermine
56 Leaning to the right
58 ___ diamondback (venomous snake)
59 Glossinidae members
61 Sugarcoated medication
63 Bowler's button
64 Thick liqueurs
66 Photo abbr.
69 Size up
70 Judo degree
72 Crate qty.
73 Remain

76 One in a fine mess?
77 Recedes, diseasewise
79 Mus. ensemble
80 Like the game, to Sherlock
82 Moonwort, for one
84 Chiefly
87 Decorative furniture veneer
89 Top-of-the-watch number
92 Execute perfectly
94 Decorative knot of ribbons
95 Kind of word
97 Makes potable, in a way
98 1939 invasion site
99 Simple creature
101 Holds back
102 Mother's whistler
104 Make a board decision
105 Plummer of film
106 Most perfect
109 Pembroke pooch
112 "Bill paid" paper: Abbr.

115 Beauts
118 Sound of a break-in?
120 Interstice
122 Mikhail of chess fame
123 Flair for music

by Mel Rosen

ACROSS

1 Hercules feats
7 Alphonse's friend, in the comics
13 Legendary name in bridge
19 Turkish hospice
20 Merlin's stock-in-trade
21 European airline
22 Start of a verse
25 Informer, informally
26 "___ live and breathe!"
27 Cars with Teletouch transmission
28 Means of enlightenment
29 Specifically
31 Undergrad degrees
32 Baking potatoes
36 Greenland air base
37 Of city govt.
38 Gasp of delight
41 Allgood of stage and screen
42 Husband of Ruth
43 Shape
44 ___ Domini
45 More of the verse
51 Kind of dye
52 Site of the first Olympics
53 Clearance
54 Symbol of hardness
55 Thin white linen fabric
57 Old Blood and Guts
59 Sportscaster Vin
60 Greenhorns
62 Moil and toil
64 Shipping route
67 Enlivened
69 Trollope's "The ___ Diamonds"
73 Presses
74 Colorful fish
75 First name in folk music
76 Mimi's dissent
77 More of the verse
83 Arms recipient, maybe
84 On ___ with
85 Architect Mies van der ___
86 ___ jet
87 Madrigal
88 Women's grp. since 1890
89 Repeat oneself, in a way
91 "Tristram Shandy" author
93 Hang out
94 Piqued
95 Scandinavian actress Aulin
96 In ___ res
99 Untried
100 Neighbor of Oakland
104 End of the verse
109 Verdi opera, 1887
110 Apportion
111 Football unit
112 Facade
113 Goes all out
114 Forwarded

DOWN

1 French flower
2 Conjugation bit
3 Switch's partner
4 Church calendar
5 Señora's long scarf
6 Stone pillars
7 Maudlin sentimentality
8 Usher's offering
9 Write badly
10 Comedienne O'Shea
11 Circle
12 Comic author Bill
13 Hunky-dory
14 1989 underwater thriller, with "The"
15 Grant
16 City south of Moscow
17 It's not fair!
18 Maneuverable, as a ship
20 Jeanne or Bernadette, e.g.: Abbr.
23 "A Spy in the House of Love" author
24 Mount Palomar sighting
29 "___ said, . . ."
30 Anise-flavored liqueur
32 Shorthand inventor Pitman
33 Tony of "Who's the Boss?"
34 Woolf's "___ of One's Own"
35 Beaver, for one
36 Eight-six
37 Pavarotti's birthplace
38 Newsman Roger
39 Start for fours or sides
40 Heavy and awkward looking
42 Third little pig's material
43 Old servant's phrase of address
44 To ___ (excessively)
46 Valor
47 "The Cocktail Party" poet
48 Alphabet trio
49 Paint choice
50 Canine's neighbor
56 Snifter's contents, maybe
57 Bombard
58 Flu type
59 Waterfall
61 Front line?
63 Prophetic writer
64 Cordage fiber
65 Skipping syllables
66 Turbulent
68 Windy City, breezily
70 Displease
71 "Twenty Years on Broadway" autobiographer
72 Among: Fr.
75 Wimbledon winner, 1975
78 Heater
79 Scattered
80 Hanover Stake, e.g.
81 "Last Days of Pompeii" girl
82 Seine sight
89 Father
90 Person with unwashable briefs
91 Pitchman
92 Steamed dish
93 Bride's best
94 The Dow, e.g.
95 Draper's measure
96 Speck
97 Gershwin biographer David
98 Hill's opposite
100 Back
101 Makes do, with "out"
102 Bathyspheric mission
103 Ancient sun disk
104 "Mazel ___!"
105 1952 hit "Botch-___"
106 Caught
107 Suffix with rigor or vigor
108 Tolkien tree-man

by Frances Hansen

ACROSS

1 Apples, informally
5 Short intakes
10 Stringent
15 Diplomacy
19 Noted Mideast diplomat
20 Red as ___
21 Silk-stockings
22 First name in folk
23 1947 adventure sequel
25 "I Can Get ___ You Wholesale"
26 Part of a knight's insignia
27 First president of Bolivia
28 AT A
31 Vingt-___
33 Masters subject
34 Like bell-bottoms
35 Five-time Rose Bowl winner
37 Coleridge's "sacred river"
40 Poll amts.
44 Actor Markham et al.
45 Leather-to-be
46 It may be rigged
47 Boodle
48 First name in despotism
49 "___ Slew-Foot" (1961 country hit)
50 Licentious one
51 Melville novel
52 Endangered swimmer
56 Recurring marine phenomenon
58 I and II Timothy, e.g.
61 A.C.C. school
62 Use an S.O.S.
63 Holiday abroad
64 Port intro
65 Juillet times
66 Calendar abbr.
67 Marlon Brando's birthplace
70 Lloyd George contemporary
71 Orch. group
72 Loading site
73 Opening between montañas
74 Actress Courteney
75 Egg white
77 Part of XXX
78 Peevish
80 Des ___
82 Base
85 Opposite of a wrinkle remover?
86 Fix, as the sails
88 Moo goo ___ pan
89 "Glass Bell" writer
90 Whaler's direction
91 Noted paperback publisher
92 It builds int.
93 Broadcast preparation
96 To be, in old New Orleans
97 Hogshead
98 Flyspeck
99 Beethoven dedicatee
100 Slimeball
102 Ending with road
104 AFORE-THOUGHT
112 Late Ford
115 "Pogo" character Wiley ___
116 "L.A. Law" lawyer
117 Most gracious
119 Part of C.C.U.
120 Gin drink
121 "You're ___ talk!"
122 Suffix with Dixie
123 Children's author Howard
124 Lucy's colorer
125 Plus
126 "___ silly question . . ."

DOWN

1 Grunt's chow
2 Arab name part
3 OUT TIME
4 Show contempt for
5 Ref. book
6 "Take ___" ("Congrats!")
7 Evening at La Scala
8 IT'S THAT COUNTS
9 Franklin, for one
10 Murder mystery suspect
11 Start of some cloud names
12 Jazz phrase
13 Hold back
14 Goethe title
15 Island south of Wilson's Promontory
16 Stephen Dedalus, in a Joyce title
17 Parsing subject
18 Mel and family
24 Coup de ___ (gunshot): Fr.
29 Hero's tale
30 Work of Horace
32 BRAND
35 Vote ___ down (decide by ballot)
36 Not earthbound
38 After 11 P.M.
39 Con Ed watchdog
41 Nav. officers
42 AND A FOR A
43 Hot
44 CUFF
50 Brooklyn sch.
53 FOUR OF THE EARTH
54 Get hysterical
55 Isn't now
57 Get the show on the road
59 Hailstone size
60 Michael Costa oratorio
65 Morales of "La Bamba"
68 West of Brooklyn
69 In ___ (het up)
70 Actor Chaney
72 Grp. for Mr. Novak
74 Actress Barbara
76 Don't keep up
79 Role for Gielgud
80 Cons' cons
81 Locus
83 Cordial
84 Closet items
87 "The Loco-Motion" girl
92 Whence the line "Let freedom ring!"
93 Service component
94 It's named for the Duke of York
95 Seed bearer
101 "The ___ Hour" (50's drama series)
103 Start of some Israeli place names
105 Make liquid, in a way
106 First name in courtroom drama
107 "Come ___!"
108 Huckleberry or Mickey
109 Prefix with phone
110 Signals
111 Collectible illustrator
113 Author Dinesen
114 Singer James
118 Dram of liquor, in Britain

by Robert H. Wolfe

ACROSS

1 Flagrant
6 Bradley cohort
11 N.B.A. statistic
18 Cover up
19 Radioactivity unit
20 Food grouping
22 Boat or boy
24 Conscious
25 Sit-ups improve them
26 Dark brews
27 Object of disgust
28 ___ precedent
29 Bud Fisher cartoon character
31 Breaker or zone
34 Hitch
35 Censor's sound
37 Consonant (with)
38 "This man is now become ___": "Julius Caesar"
40 Martian ET's
43 ___ Miss
44 Where seeds are sown
47 Monopoly quartet: Abbr.
48 Have more firepower than
51 Fighting force
53 Chosen number
54 Berlin's "___ Lovely Day Today"
55 U.S.O. audience
57 Audited
58 Singing syllable
59 Baubles
61 "Maria ___" ('40s song)
63 Roast repartee
65 :50
66 Fix and cut
68 Smog cause
69 Tower of Pisa, e.g.
71 Words on a Wonderland cake
72 Cav competitor
73 Tokyo, once
74 Rednecks have red ones
76 Equine mother
77 Alternative to wax
78 Mantelpiece piece
79 Cry of success
81 Pax ___
83 Partisan
86 Stuffs
88 Unfamiliar
90 Nathan Detroit's doll
92 1939 Bolger co-star
93 Understands
96 Soprano Berger et al.
97 Told, as tales
99 Belly or barrel
103 U.S.N. V.I.P.
104 Fresh words
105 Pair
106 Like some suckers
108 Sports car of old
109 H_3PO_4 and others
111 Goer or maker
114 Primitive time
115 1936 Olympic hero
116 Stream migrators
117 Pump pads
118 Frozen mountains
119 Oboes and bassoons

DOWN

1 Like beads
2 Wharf workers
3 Fifth qtrs.
4 Mother and daughter
5 Amish and Hasidim
6 Using elbow grease
7 St. Edward's University site
8 Pats down
9 Prussian pronoun
10 Bylaw, for short
11 Part of N.A.A.C.P.: Abbr.
12 Knife type
13 Dudevant's pseudonym
14 N.Y.C. subway
15 Cut out
16 Keeper or saver
17 Actress Berger
18 Star ___
21 Without women
23 Sodom survivor
27 Comes to a point
30 Hanoi holiday
32 D.D.E. sphere
33 Gymnastics coach Karolyi
36 Graph or copy
38 Murphy with medals
39 Stand or mother
41 Tousle
42 Sched. approximation
44 Trio of destiny
45 Film director Herzog
46 Some window treatments
49 Unattractive fruit
50 Maria, to Ted
52 Skin problem
54 Favorite
56 Three-time P.G.A. champ
59 Nerve cell parts
60 Law or let
61 Acted humanly
62 Flower oil
64 Sumptuousness
65 Jam
66 King called "The Short"
67 BB's
70 Rock bottom
72 Anti-nuclear testing org.
75 Not quite burned
77 Walletful
80 Map abbr.
82 Like pure energy
83 Schemed
84 AC/DC gadgets
85 Wise counselors
87 The Doles, e.g.
89 B.Y.U.'s league
91 Crescent line
94 Tyke
95 Yard fence
97 Heathrow sights
98 Serial opener
99 Tennis legend Don
100 Lets up
101 D.C. clock setting
102 Not so well done
105 Numbered circle
107 Where the Clintons met
110 Business V.I.P.
111 Whom Antony addressed
112 Be in for
113 "___ got it!"

by Randolph Ross

ACROSS

1 He was Sonny Corleone in "The Godfather"
5 Swanky
9 Tuscany town
14 Václav Havel's home
19 Official language of Pakistan
20 Site of Hickam Air Force Base
21 In command
22 Kidney-related
23 Lazy person's racquet sport?
25 Physician in "Jurassic Park"?
27 Was emphatic
28 ___-Litovsk Treaty, 1918
29 Ewes look up to him
30 Precipitate
31 Winglike
32 Attacked
34 Poolside shelter
37 ___ Wars (Rome-Carthage conflicts)
39 Sheer fabric
43 Mine entrance
44 "You put up the tent, I'll get the wood"?
48 January, in Juárez
49 Parallel to
50 Gun moll's gun
51 Still-life subject
53 Bearded animals
54 Malcolm X profiler
55 Believer in plant parenthood?
61 Angle or pod preceder
62 Night sky marvels
64 More put-out
65 Pier support
67 Eau de Paris
68 Up
69 Hospital supply
70 Sierra ___
72 Porter's "___ Kick Out of You"
73 Lunatics
76 Exchanged words
77 Expert on students' rash behavior?
81 Important D.C. lobby
82 Take five
84 Flash Gordon serial site
85 Doublet
86 Card catalogue abbr.
87 Departments
89 Workplace for a short order cook?
94 Org. with a mission
95 Feeling
97 Russian skater Rodnina
98 Pitched
100 Harvard, Brown, Princeton, etc.
102 Epochs
103 Ms. Lollobrigida
104 Perseus's mother
106 Del ___ of the 50's Phillies
108 Marks off
112 Fruit that's hard as a rock?
114 Early meat eater?
115 Bearing
116 Standout performances
117 Wave maker
118 Pop singer Brickell
119 Outfit
120 Ain't polite?
121 Dashed
122 Major employer in Hawaii

DOWN

1 Where the conga originated
2 Lover of Aphrodite
3 Supplements
4 List in detail
5 Ottawa chief
6 Grainy
7 Did blacksmith's work
8 Marauder
9 Voice from on high
10 Provisional
11 Dijon dog days
12 Arctic
13 Address abbr.
14 Apportion, as costs
15 Not adlibbing
16 Up-front amount
17 ___ office (old Hollywood code group)
18 Aggregate
24 Land on the Caspian
26 Some MOMA works
28 Obfuscate
31 Datebook listings: Abbr.
33 Crosswise, nautically
34 Greenhouse bloom
35 So long
36 13 motorcycles?
38 Hard-to-read writing
40 Doting on shiny coins?
41 Cape Cod resort
42 Red dye
45 Go along (with)
46 Tennyson's "The ___ Queen"
47 Geomancer
52 TV western star of the 50's
55 Yowled
56 Victorian taxi
57 Holding
58 "___ worry..."
59 Balloon, perhaps
60 French Revolutionist Jean Paul
63 Opposite of neath
66 ___ Sawyer of the comics
68 1992 Wimbledon champ
69 Heir or heiress
70 Kind of touch
71 Idolize
72 Hungarian patriot Nagy
74 Wipe off
75 First course, maybe
78 Street show
79 Others, on the Orinoco
80 D.C. campus
83 Facility
86 Blew up
88 Goths and Vandals
90 1776 battle site
91 Most open
92 Merkel and O'Connor
93 Cut slightly
96 Level
99 "The ___ Love" (Al Jolson tune)
101 Mister, down south
103 Sparkly collectible
104 Way out
105 Chère woman
107 Where Moses rafted
108 Faucet fault
109 ___-China
110 Sweat (over)
111 Snick-or-___
112 Mail-order abbr.
113 Botanist Gray
114 Coppers: Abbr.

by Charles M. Deber

ACROSS

1 Lord Byron poem
5 Loopy
9 "Uncle ___" (Paul McCartney hit)
15 Boom causers
19 "Absolutely!"
20 Mighty mite
21 1976 De Palma shocker
22 Tennis stroke
23 Flan
24 Royal pastime
25 Reservations
26 Recherché
27 Kind of planning
29 Legislators
31 Phoenix suburb
32 Kind of question
33 Plane's right
34 Paged
35 Kenneth Grahame character
38 "I cannot tell ___"
39 Figures out at the beginning?
41 Abounding
44 Sliver
46 Second servings
48 Flynn portrayal
49 Record producer Brian
50 Program since 1965
52 "___ may look on a king"
53 Summer of 1980 question
56 Madrid museum
57 "Yeah, sure"
61 To some degree
62 Magazine contents
65 Procrastinator
67 War story
68 It's depicted by parts of today's puzzle
71 Polynesian tongue
72 "Locksley Hall" poet
74 Hope and Crosby, often
75 Mickey's partner
76 Beat (out)
77 ___ 6
79 Lampoons
82 Slack-jawed
83 Most likely
85 ___ deus in nobis (there is God within us)
86 Remove
90 Part of a 1995 reunion
92 The ___ of the land
93 Ancient goddess of fertility
94 Today's soldier, e.g.
96 Bass ___
98 Tom Clancy hero Jack
100 Noisy gulps
101 Plesiosaurlike reptile, familiarly
103 "The Taming of the Shrew" setting
107 Author Ken
108 Salespeople push it
110 Wondrous
111 Bye
112 Thus
113 Magwitch of "Great Expectations"
115 1979 disco hit
116 Kind of rack
117 Shop's replacement
118 Mooring site
119 Bed piece
120 Forward
121 Early English poet laureate
122 Major hit
123 Bang out, in a way

DOWN

1 Half a 1980's TV duo
2 Get a smile out of
3 Race do-overs
4 How to play "Loch Lomond"
5 Breach
6 From ___ Z
7 Classroom reward
8 Slide sight
9 Familiarize
10 Artist Toulouse-___
11 Form a queue
12 Perry's creator
13 Net supports
14 Parisian possessive
15 Brake sound
16 Movie for which Lee Grant won an Oscar
17 Sink
18 Went 80, say
28 More than enough
30 Traveler's guide
31 Leaves in the pot
34 Words in an anthology title
36 More than disdain
37 Japanese assembly
39 Tilting building?
40 Gentle ___ (Miss Manners salutation)
41 Newspaper's ___ desk
42 Had an inspiration
43 Foundation
45 Atlantic City resort, with "the"
47 Item in a lock
51 Downer
54 Classic film set in Wyoming
55 Delilah in "Samson and Delilah"
56 Madonna, for one
57 Mideasterner
58 Military decoration
59 Most like a ghost
60 Europe's Gulf of ___
63 Year in Louis XIV's reign
64 "O Sole ___"
66 Foreign title
68 Get down, so to speak
69 Chant
70 "Over here!"
73 Brainpower
75 Fictional Walter
78 Baker's need
80 W.W. I grp.
81 Peter, once
83 George Cukor classic
84 Unversed?
86 Windows work area
87 Officially not working
88 Psych out
89 Southern stinger
91 Quarterback
93 Financial page figure
95 Kind of satellite
97 Perfume dispensers?
99 Classified ad abbr.
101 Very much
102 Pasta shape
104 Not very intelligently
105 Open, in a way
106 Talismanic stone
108 French Christian
109 Green light
110 Ingénue, perhaps
112 Honorary law deg.
114 "Uncle Tom's Cabin" girl

by Eric Albert

ACROSS

1 Rolls
6 33-million circulation magazine
12 Hannibal of "The Silence of the Lambs"
18 ___-Detoo ("Star Wars" android)
19 People of great interest
21 Lawrence of Arabia portrayer
22 Stretch . . .
25 1978 Fosse musical
26 Settles
27 Outcry
28 With 47-Across star of "Heartland"
29 Perfect shot
31 Causeway
32 Ligature
33 Dim ___
34 Arith. process
35 Ian Fleming, e.g.
37 High rating
38 Lift . . .
41 ___ of Christ (the Pope)
44 First name in cosmetics
46 Stick up
47 See 28-Across
48 North of Virginia
49 Expel
51 "Horrors!"
52 Equality
54 S.A. country
55 Semisheer fabric
57 Jog . . .
60 Six-yr. V.I.P.
61 Mitigate
62 Old-fashioned learning, in a way
63 Dudevant's pen name
64 Tyrant Amin
65 Renowned toymaker
66 Jalopy feature
69 Bust
71 Showroom model
73 Churl
74 ___ loss
75 Quahog
77 Acapulco aunt
79 Without guile
81 Yak
82 Run . . .
85 Certain cycle
86 Country music's Diamond ___

87 Part of a bray
88 Hoover, e.g.
89 Memo word
91 Conductor Rodzinski
93 Kensington Gardens sight
95 M-G-M rival, once
96 ___ Park, Colo.
100 Paris tube
101 Bend . . .
105 Cookbook phrase
106 Boxy, overstuffed sofas
108 Punishment, metaphorically
109 Madrid replies
110 Scale notes
111 Word of agreement
113 Admiral Benbow, e.g.
114 Kind of bag or sac
115 Inclement
116 Hankering
117 More suggestive
119 Punch . . .
123 "Home to Harlem" author McKay
124 Hat parts
125 1970s New York governor
126 Aussie tennis coach Harry
127 Itty-bitty
128 Fools

DOWN

1 Gear for a newborn
2 Opposite-of-expected outcomes
3 Kind of body
4 Peaks
5 Spain's Costa del ___
6 Color also called "eureka red"
7 Result of burnout?
8 Setoff chapter heading
9 Attain fame
10 Benchley best-seller, with "The"
11 Roman, for one
12 Heavy coat fabric
13 Secret-society letter
14 Transportation giant
15 Jump . . .
16 "Dream Children" essayist
17 Tear
20 Bonnie Blair, e.g.
23 "No way"
24 Every teléfono has one

by Nancy Nicholson Joline

30 Southern bread
33 Terry Bradshaw, notably
34 One with obligations
35 Calls up
36 Procter & Gamble brand
39 Calhoun of "The Texan"
40 Dating stars, perhaps
42 Black and tan
43 Undo a breach
45 Make a long story short
50 Fudgelike candy
51 Corrigendum
53 Philly suburb
55 Francois Marie Arouet
56 Twist . . .
58 Samovar
59 Unbalanced
61 New York's ___ Building
67 Puts off deciding about
68 Start of an Atlantic

City name
70 Show ___
72 They express views
76 Household heads
78 Blue, poetically
80 Tolkien's forest giants
82 Afghan
83 Showed up
84 Bothers
90 Attacks
92 Pitchblende ingredient
94 Singer Milsap
97 Ill-tempered ones
98 Chosen one
99 Walks self-importantly
102 ___ Park, Baltimore
103 Greg of golf
104 Assistance provider
107 Lorelei, e.g.
111 Mischievous
112 St.-___, France
114 Port seized by the Crusaders, 1191
115 Not free
116 Actress Kaminska et al.

118 Author LeShan
120 A Turner
121 Letter ender, for short
122 45 r.p.m. introducer

ACROSS

1 Separates for the wash
6 Fashioned
10 Puts up
16 "Second Chorus" star
18 Polio was his target
19 Brigham Young's settlement
21 Shopper's convenience
23 Punish, in the lockup
24 World chess champ, 1960–61
25 ___ Lawrence College
26 The Bounty's anchorage
28 Beer order
29 1958 Oscar winner for "The Big Country"
31 Scare off
33 Wyandot Indian
34 Point on a radar screen
35 Life ___ (emergency gear)
37 Muster out of the R.A.F.
39 Rev.'s offering
40 Coeur d' ___, Idaho
41 Kind of planning
43 Part of R.S.V.
45 King during W.W. II
46 Vincent Lopez's theme song
48 Chemical endings
49 ___-a-brac
50 Itinerant minister
55 Bending
59 So far
60 Boater or stovepipe
61 Scene
63 Ovett track rival
64 Some M&M's
65 Hullabaloo
67 Slav in the news
68 Vandyke place
69 Italian countdown word
70 "Gigi" actress
72 Closure
73 Electrical problem
74 Herpetologist's pets
76 Bargain centers
79 Ripe for drafting
80 Classmate, e.g.
81 Kind of hand
82 Braggart
85 Colonel on the board
88 Won skillfully
92 Dijon dreams
93 Julie Andrews comedy, 1981
94 Sweethearts' electricity
96 Winter wear
97 "Happy Days Are Here Again" composer Milton
98 Leave angrily, with "off"
100 Jane Campion film, with "The"
102 Yield
103 Common butt of jokes
104 Feeling a loss
106 Amphion's wife
108 First-rate
109 Add spice to
111 What's going on
114 Forestalling, with "off"
115 Energy sources
116 Russian political oddity
117 Quick
118 Word
119 Medicinal herb

DOWN

1 Most outdated
2 Pulwar puller
3 Truck stop stoppers
4 "Don't ___ on me!"
5 Cauterized
6 Red Book author
7 Touch
8 50's singer Washington
9 Bubbles over
10 Masthead heading
11 Plastics base
12 That, in Toledo
13 Part of a pen
14 Bloodhound
15 Play layout
16 On the go
17 Removes a layer
18 Connive
20 Brave retreat?
22 Do a banquet
27 Drove up the wall
30 Positions
32 Peregrinated
36 Robust
38 Noted name in I.Q. testing
40 Y's associates?
42 "L.A. Law" lawyer
44 Glacial ridge
45 Old English coin
47 Falcons' nest
49 Spaciousness
50 Hauls
51 Val-d' ___ (French resort)
52 Winona from Winona
53 Olympics logo
54 One's own: Prefix
55 Look-alike
56 Apollo's blood
57 Bête ___
58 Words on some doors
62 Entertaining Jacques
65 Clementine's father, e.g.
66 Spiny-leafed plants
68 Beethoven's Ninth
70 Subject of biotech study
71 1993 Sinatra album
73 Bilked
75 Prelude to an airplane bombing
77 ___ Family Singers
78 Offshore A.P.B.
80 Tavern keeper
82 Rubbernecks
83 College board
84 Waste cause
85 Punster's reward
86 Batting champ Tim
87 Sink necessity
89 Wallachia and Moldavia, today
90 Boots
91 Execrate
93 Tight
95 Don who played Barney Fife
98 Splurge
99 20's "All American"
101 Like Jabba the Hutt, of "Star Wars"
105 Swell
107 Author Hunter
110 Play the game
112 Rental sign abbr.
113 Part of a crossword aviary

by Louis Sabin

ACROSS

1 Headed downward
5 "Forever" girl
10 "Not guilty," e.g.
14 Movie moguls
19 Sportscaster Rote
20 Nursery rhyme vegetables
21 Sentry's cry
22 Man of many words
23 Sans ornamentation
25 Bestseller of 1944
27 Côte d'Azur resort
28 Kind of service
30 "I Write the Songs" singer
31 Charlie Brown's belligerent friend
32 Drug-yielding plants
33 Chico's aunt
34 Island off the west coast of South America
37 Lumberjack's tournament
38 Like some garages
43 Grier of sports and TV
44 Stag line's favorite
46 Joseph Lincoln book "Cap'n ___"
47 Eastern title
48 Golf champ Ballesteros
49 Flag
50 Fly in the ointment
51 Benevolent monopoly, once
52 In a narrow escape
56 Start of a book
57 Exit on the sly
59 Checks
60 Whitewater rafting site
61 Dress cut
62 Mercutio's friend
63 Wood hyacinth
64 Frederick Ashton ballet
66 Many a Hitchcock performance
67 French director Tavernier
70 Foreign dignitaries
71 Amaryllis
73 Space station name
74 One of a Latin trio
75 Kipling's Rikki-Tikki-___
76 Desperate
77 Start of a volume I label
78 One with a habit
79 Insurrectionism
83 Italian holy man
85 Supreme Court, e.g.
87 Carols
88 Persian treat
89 Ballot abbr.
90 Shaded walk
91 Kind of land
92 Oblique
96 Taylor's third
97 Leprechaun locale
101 "Cautionary Tales" writer
103 Pre-World War I period
106 Mountain ridge
107 Bop on the head
108 Remove chemically
109 America West Arena team
110 Household appliance
111 Sees red?
112 Rum, to some
113 Was the ruin of

DOWN

1 Gull-like bird
2 Boston suburb
3 "___ the Stars Get in My Eyes" (1953 country hit)
4 "Oklahoma!" choreographer
5 Per
6 Chaotic
7 Cousin of "Phooey!"
8 Wyo.-to-Mo. direction
9 Cousin of the coyote
10 "Aida" figure
11 Singer Patti et al.
12 Puck
13 Mote
14 Of the skull
15 Lion's or bull's place
16 "I've Got ___ . . ."
17 MGM Grand site
18 Pack
24 Audible navigational marker
26 Disconcert
29 Rapper with the group Body Count
32 Whispered sweet nothings
34 Wedges (in)
35 Actor Paul
36 "Camille Claudel" actress
37 Strengthen, as a levee
38 "___ Irish Rose"
39 Writer Ida
40 "Kings Row" author
41 Sappho's Muse
42 "Eat hearty!"
44 Largest U.S. city hospital
45 Race: Prefix
48 Mâcon's river
50 Not so zany
52 Drums, slangily
53 Headache remedy
54 Where Mocha is
55 Attach, in a way
56 Wingding
58 A con artist may go by it
60 "Sunrise Serenade" composer Frankie
62 Beachgoer's item
63 Murder mystery suspects, often
64 Praying figure
65 Belgian province or its capital
66 Nitpick
67 Ecstasy
68 "The Untouchables" villain
69 Wilt
71 Indian of British Columbia
72 One of the Astaires
75 Compassionate
79 More stunted
80 Opens
81 Sign at an antique shop
82 Twitted
83 Starchy tuber foodstuff
84 Confounded
86 Growing in pairs, botanically
88 Lurch
90 United
91 Stay fairly stationary, as a ship
92 Major Barbara's creator
93 Foreign currency
94 First name in TV emceeing
95 20's look
98 Marine shade
99 Former Senate Armed Forces Committee head
100 Secretary, e.g.
102 Roar
104 Falstaff's quaff
105 Activity for Caesar

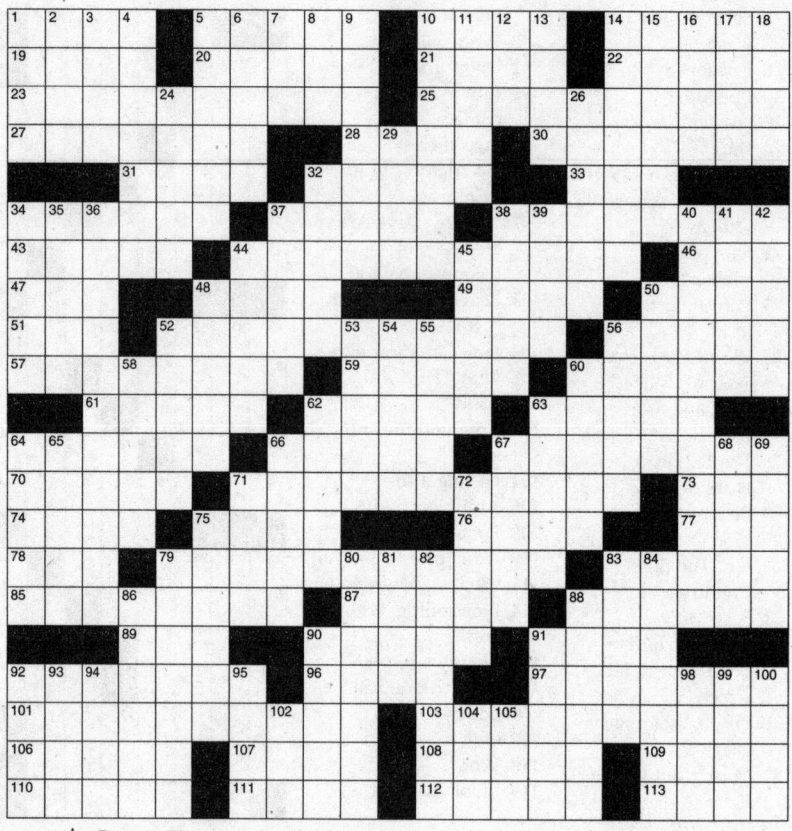

by Frances Hansen

ACROSS

1 Studied intently
6 Villa features
11 Hunt
16 "Rather!"
21 Cultural prefix
22 Crazies
23 Anthropoid's cousin
24 Drugged
25 Scientist featured in an adventure film?
28 For the birds
29 Long-necked distilling vessels
30 Mullah's text
31 Snow vehicle
33 Superficially cultured
34 Telecommunications inits.
36 Major oil corp.
38 Backscratch, politically
42 Liberal one
45 Fore-and-after
48 Number five iron
49 "___ first you . . ."
52 With lines
54 Prefix with angle or borough
55 Austen title
56 "Quo Vadis?" figure
57 Otherwise
58 Yuletide
59 Decorates over
61 Scientist featured in a Southern novel?
66 Pulitzer author Russel
67 It's across the strait from Singapore
68 Guru's home
69 Celestial firework
71 "___ live and breathe!"
72 Number of dresses?
74 Type of shirt
75 Mountain where Dionysus was hidden
77 Space, to poets
80 Bona fide
82 By
83 B.&O. and others
85 Sun
87 Prototype, for short
88 Six-time Emmy-winning actor
90 Word with Georgia or high
93 Stop on some art tours, with "the"
95 Gall
97 Johnny ___
98 Religious rationalist
100 Caribbean capital
102 Tropical drinks
104 Typist's stat.
106 Scientist featured in a cliff-hanger series?
110 Golden years
112 Miss Horne
113 Beckett's homeland
114 Cherub, at Notre Dame
115 Move laterally
116 "What's the ___?"
117 A Patriarch
119 Resident suffixes
120 Rubber
123 Gilder's undercoating
126 Grinding tool
128 Alluring girls
130 Except
132 Eur. airline
133 Stimulating shrub
137 Urban subsection
140 Tool for Archimedes
143 Sits with bad posture
145 Bouquet ___ (chef's bundle)

148 Scientist featured in an X-rated film?
151 Nahuatl Indian
152 Chosen
153 Endangered bird
154 Assemblies
155 British foes, 1899–1902
156 Pick up on
157 Amateurs
158 Like some cereals

DOWN

1 Edomite capital
2 Alternative
3 Role for Clark
4 Waiter's exclamation
5 It comes with a catch
6 Kind of cast
7 Low digit
8 Dupe
9 Dope
10 Second word of Kansas' motto
11 From that place
12 Series
13 "Lucky Jim" author
14 Cellular response?
15 Kowtow (to)
16 Ancestral zebra
17 Inexperienced
18 Uganda's Amin
19 Leaves in the cup
20 Directional suffix
26 Mormon refuge
27 Refer, with "back"
32 Champagne title

35 More bona fide
37 Hassock
39 Scientist featured in a cowboy tune?
40 Overseas sailor
41 Business owner's paper
42 Brewery products
43 Allure competitor
44 Give a new pew
46 Peanut butter choice
47 To the ___ (maximally)
49 Steeps
50 Scientist featured in a romantic ditty?
51 Section
53 More opaque
58 Easter preceder
59 ___ Speedwagon
60 Salinger heroine
62 Nerd
63 Newspaper
64 Insulating
65 Wind instrument
67 Title sister in an Eastwood film
70 Schedule abbr.
73 Before
76 No-good bum
78 Is revealed
79 Rolls, so to speak
81 "School Daze" director
84 Karate instructor
86 Conts ___ (fairy tale): Fr.
89 Miss Hayworth
91 Snap comment?

92 Take control of
94 Eastern philosophy
96 Bakery goodie
99 Timid
101 ___ Dolorosa (Christ's path to the Cross)
103 Shade
104 Potter's aid
105 Five of trumps, in card talk
107 Advertisement
108 Lady of the Haus
109 Carillon sounds
111 Klein or Claiborne, e.g.
118 Marxist groups
121 Law school course
122 Actress ___ Dawn Chong
124 Pay homage to
125 Beyond
127 Wordsmith Willard
129 Porcine locales
131 Dispossess
133 Arum lily
134 Baby bird
136 Duplicate
138 Dam site
138 "Peter Rabbit," for one
139 Sign
141 Unnerving: Var.
142 Surf sound
144 "___ Man" (Estevez film)
145 Jaw
146 ___ dye
147 Map abbr.
149 Injection units
150 One of the Spanish

by Naomi Geller Lipsky

262 'SPLAY

ACROSS

1 Ancient Yemen
6 Domain
11 Basic wage
16 Closes the gap?
21 Certain angler
22 Mrs. Banks of "Father of the Bride"
23 Red dye
24 Prohibit
25 House of the Seven Gables site
26 Imitate Crosby
27 Scholia
28 Like caramel
29 'Smiler's goal?
31 'Smothering?
33 Pinfold residents
34 Blond
35 Is forthcoming
39 Goggle boxes, so to speak
42 Scudded
43 Demesne
46 Born
47 Compass dir.
48 Knolls
51 Details handler
52 Like a rainbow
54 "Dreams and Projects" author
55 Galahad's mother
56 ___ spout (house part)
58 "Eight Days ___"
59 Bikini part
60 Stuck (to)
61 'Swine enthusiast?
64 Spain's ___ del Sol
66 Emilia's husband
67 Let out, perhaps
69 Like ___ of buffalo
70 Pierced
71 Mountain ___
72 Sweetheart, in Savoie
73 Sagacious
75 Proofs
76 Dowers
79 Unified
80 Most dolorous
82 Cleopatra's Needle, for one
84 Running, but not getting anywhere
87 Catches
88 Uffizi contents
91 Pulitzer-winning composer George et al.
92 Parisians think of them
93 Up the bet
95 Part of a Civil War signature
96 Contemporary author Canin
97 'Slavish account?
99 Ancient Roman gown
100 Dale's favorite cowboy
101 Lightens up?
103 Stake
104 They can be mental
105 "Hey ___!"
106 City on the Rhone
107 Belted
109 Firm
111 Diminutive suffixes
112 Centennial State: Abbr.
113 Actor James
115 Noted Warhol subject
116 Tee neighbor
117 Cabbie's query
119 Verily
120 Tenure of John Paul II
123 'Slug off?

125 'Smart money?
130 Onetime Clinton cause
133 Ammonia compound
134 Ship's shipment
135 The Supremes' "___ a Symphony"
136 Nearby
137 Twerps
138 Test
139 Standards
140 Chutzpah
141 "Swell"
142 Words between Friends
143 Graylag or specklebelly

DOWN

1 Mtg. of Congress
2 Make whole
3 Singer Fitzgerald
4 Warning sounds
5 Eagle flier
6 Start a Model T again
7 One of the Jetsons
8 Burns poem "To ___"
9 Symbol of St. Mark
10 Patch
11 Having esthesia
12 The ___ Monster
13 Up and around
14 Claim
15 Settle snugly
16 Ordained
17 Visibly frightened
18 Map abbr.
19 Immediately
20 Bond, for one
30 ___ to the finish
32 Sneak ___
34 Rage
36 'Scornful book?
37 Not G, PG, R or X
38 Life
39 Spook house?
40 Country homes
41 'Shah's palace?
44 Relishes
45 Row
49 Prefix with type
50 Sonnet's end
52 Kind of ceremony
53 Tear
57 Siamang, e.g.
58 "___ Good Men"
59 "Treasure Island" captain Billy
62 Besmirch
63 Polish
64 Burdens
65 Blurbs
67 Make ___ of (muddle)
68 7.92 inches
70 Overhang
72 Tabloid cover topic, maybe
74 Golfer's goals
75 Vitamin amts.
77 Mollify
78 Moves furtively
81 Patient one

82 Unsealed, in poesy
83 Affiance
85 ___ ex machina
86 Lowly laborers, in slang
89 Fills a vacancy
90 Ribs
92 Key
94 Colony member
95 Collective abbr.
98 Diet
99 Some amorousness
101 Prefix with type
102 Permissive
104 Spanish composer Albéniz
105 Ground hemlock
106 Cellophane substitute
107 Most griseous
108 Auberge
110 Puts to good use
113 Actress Blake
114 Uncrowded
118 Queue after Q
119 Hawn film "Bird on ___"
121 Spirogyras
122 Bumpkin
124 New World Abbr.
125 Specialty of 3-Down
126 Pound
127 "Camelot" co-star
128 Herds of humpbacks
129 Celtic tongue
130 Actress Grey
131 Basketball's Saperstein
132 In favor of

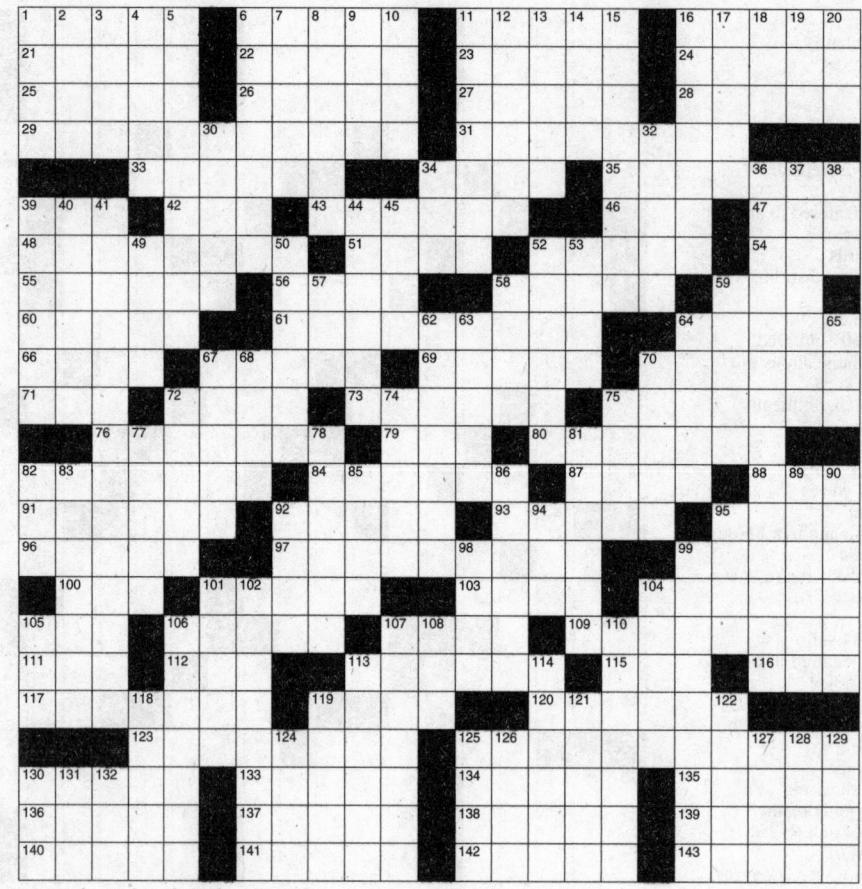

by Deborah Kathryn Tromley

ACROSS

1 Club name since 1802
7 Leave ___ for (give room)
13 Venice's Ponte di ___
19 Stabilize
20 Bronze
21 Magazine
22 1959 Johnny Mathis hit
25 Small rock combo?
26 Riga native
27 Habituate
28 Emmy-winning TV host of 1949
30 Reception
31 Approving sound
32 Land ruled by Sargon
33 Genetic transmitter
34 Jungle weather phenomena
36 HBO alternative
38 Whip but good
39 Shakespearean comedy
42 Pen
45 Leave on shore
47 Waiver
48 VCR button: Abbr.
49 Winter time
51 Rockefeller, for one: Abbr.
52 Line div.
53 Pro ___
54 Pair connector
55 Thomas Hardy novel
60 New Deal org.
61 Merkel of the movies
62 Half-soled shoe
63 Some chasers
66 Trifler
68 Actress Clarke of "The Front Page"
70 Signs, sort of
72 "Some Like ___"
74 Cut off from the mainland
76 Seed coatings
80 L.A. clock setting: Abbr.
82 Show one's humanity?
83 1967 Newman film
86 Slew
87 Mil. titles
90 Self starter?
91 70's discipline
92 Hibernia

93 Sir ___ of Arthurian legend
94 Rubbers
97 Listing
99 Important points in a legal case
101 Early Eastwood film
104 Subject of psych. research
106 Cartoon canine
107 Some are tall
108 Forester opera
109 Cock and bull
111 ___-Cat
113 Potash
114 Capriccio
116 One of the Carolines
117 Enter, in a way
119 Baseball rarity
121 1992 Best Picture nominee
124 Bright
125 Work of Ovid
126 "The Fugitive" lieutenant
127 Marx collaborator
128 Gone
129 Covered

DOWN

1 Breeze (along)
2 Put under
3 Hit 70's-80's sitcom
4 Beats
5 Take
6 One of the bold ones?
7 Like some obligations
8 Component of synthetic rubber
9 Cat, at times
10 From ___ Z
11 Check
12 Marine abode
13 Latest
14 Kind of verb: Abbr.
15 Affectionate
16 Parlor piece
17 Monograph
18 Olive ___
23 Hardware item
24 Bond adversary
29 Big name in fashion
34 Elem. particle
35 Florist's unit
37 Wizard
39 Had a part (in)
40 Show uncertainty
41 Toys since the 1940's
42 Brooklyn's ___ Institute

43 Expulsion from a country
44 Parser's concern
46 Result of a strain
50 Cocktail party offering
52 ___-Ball
56 Suit fabric
57 Put the kibosh on
58 Tide component
59 "Just kidding!"
64 Hammett novel
65 Angry with
67 Seasonal worker?
69 Working hard
71 Instigate
73 Waiter's weights
75 Frank document
77 Wind ___
78 Delectable
79 Con
81 Look at the highlights
84 Well driller's joy
85 Frees
87 Unused
88 Test
89 Setting out
95 Skyline sight

96 Words from gramps, maybe
98 Some upholstery
100 Bring back
102 Gardner and others
103 Riotous spree
105 Loot
109 Software convenience
110 Steel impurities
112 Albers's "Homage to the Square," e.g.
114 Apple polishers
115 Word from Tonto
118 Prefix with scope or spore
119 Poetic monogram
120 Diamond gal
122 Nice name
123 Like some hours

by Rich Norris

ACROSS

1 Sits too long
6 Exasperates
10 Insects' sense organs
15 Resistance unit
18 From Korea
19 Flood engineer?
20 Takes ___ on (wears)
21 Any minute
23 With 43- and 48-Across, a barb to 14-Down
26 Diva Moffo
27 Kind of nut
28 American symbol
29 Couriers' deliveries
31 Reach over
33 Grand Ole Opry founder George
34 Ho Chi Minh Trail locale
35 Travelers' stops
36 Swelled heads
38 More zany
42 Ditty syllable
43 See 23-Across
47 N.Y.C. highway, with "the"
48 See 23-Across
50 Wise about
51 Kind of ink
53 One-named folk singer
54 "___ you sure?"
55 Clear
57 Sees just the highlights
58 Hilo dish
61 Mother ___
63 Laceless shoes
65 Gave it a whirl?
66 Forestalls, with "off"
67 With 84-, 88- and 111-Across, 14-Down's retort
68 Roles in "G.W.T.W." and "Scarlett"
70 Residents: Suffix
71 Italian magistrate
72 Enclosing rim for a jewel
73 100 yrs.
74 Capital of ancient Ethiopia
75 Kind of garage
78 Like no other
79 Spa features
81 5 point type
83 The others
84 See 67-Across

87 Painter Gerard ___ Borch
88 See 67-Across
90 Ending with beat or refuse
91 Permissible
93 Northern apples
94 "From Here to Eternity" actor
96 Woes
98 ___ Lilas (Paris suburb)
99 Overwhelm
103 Greek
106 They sit on a bench together
109 W.W. II address
110 First name in mysteries
111 See 67-Across
114 Club revenue
115 "The Barrel-Organ" poet
116 Kind of corner
117 Observant
118 Ultimate
119 Build ___
120 "You ___?"
121 Position

DOWN

1 Tracks
2 Consume
3 "___ song of sixpence . . ."
4 Atlantic City resort, informally, with "The"
5 Kind of appeal
6 Stiff
7 Actor McDowall
8 "Swing and away" star
9 Sand bar
10 Buckingham room
11 Under the most favorable circumstances
12 Forfeit in a card game
13 Sitting-down sound
14 Actress Chase
15 City near Kobe
16 1979 Billy Joel hit
17 Spanish hunter's cap
22 Bahamas stop
24 Boor
25 British Commonwealth member
30 "Danse des nymphes" artist

32 Witch's brew ingredient
37 Complains
39 Assisting, with "over"
40 Particulars
41 Young 32-Downs
43 "___ the use!"
44 Dissenter
45 Make the cut?
46 Certain photo: Abbr.
47 Biblical fruit provider
49 Mountaineer's descent
52 Back-to-back, to Braque
53 Pat O'Brien W.W. II film
56 Nose: Prefix
57 Burleigh Grimes pitch
59 Attitude
60 Vehement
62 In spite of that
64 U.S. Open golf champion Ernie
65 Anon

67 The Swordfish, to astronomers
68 Victor corp.
69 Charger
71 Kind of colony
74 Think (over)
76 Direct finish
77 Cooping up
80 It may be used in a game of miggles
81 Hawker
83 Greet uncivilly
84 Progressed slowly
85 Distance event
86 Frying pan
87 Bony fish
89 Disarrange
92 Tough, flexible twigs
95 Nylons shade
97 Blacken
98 Weighed down
100 Ply
101 To the left
102 Adolescence
104 1945 Noël Coward song
105 Thames school

107 Peggy Wood TV role, 1949–56
108 Try
112 Pipe joint
113 ___ Miss

by A. J. Santora

ACROSS

1 Harbor
6 Fluid part of blood
12 Slangy refusal
18 1990 movie "Home ___"
19 Chap
20 Blackboard adjuncts
22 Fitting name for a baseball pitcher
24 Catches a misdeed
25 "Exodus" hero
26 "La Plume de Ma ___"
27 Essence
29 TV Guide listing
30 Noisy fight
32 Solid unsaturated alcohol
34 ___ Rio, Tex.
35 Former name of radon
36 Fitting name for a prison warden
40 Govt. flight regulator
43 Nibbles
44 Creepy 1976 film, with "The"
45 Tosspot's problem
46 Small islands
47 Show infatuation with
48 Israel's Eban
49 English poet Matthew
51 Exclamations of inquiry
52 Fitting name for a golfer
55 River in northern France
56 Stashed away
60 Alda and Paton
61 Gardener, at times
62 Not given an audience
63 Dr. Fu Manchu player of 1929
64 Israeli Prime Minister, 1953–55
65 Meager
66 Earthen container
67 City where Henry IV was crowned, 1594
68 Severs
69 Fitting name for a Congressman
71 Sunny vacation spot
72 Goodbyes
73 Toothy tool
74 Big name in 60's folk music
78 Epitome of thinness
79 White House moniker
80 Word with soul or help
81 Primp
82 Masthead listings, for short
83 Fitting name for a golfer
87 Ordain
88 Soldier of 1861
91 Inscribed stone markers
92 "___ Lady" (Willa Cather novel)
93 Conservationists' ___ Club
96 To dare, in Dijon
97 Insects' sensory organs
100 ___ generis
102 Throwback
104 Fitting name for a tennis player
107 Reconcile
108 Refuges
109 ___-ski
110 Enzyme in milk
111 Big name in candy
112 Strapped

DOWN

1 Mexicali locale
2 Frightful
3 Relating to people at large
4 Sign
5 Makes trim
6 Mail
7 Accompaniment for a pavane
8 Farm-related: Abbr.
9 Photography sessions
10 Botanist Gregor
11 Sweater material
12 "High Noon" composer Washington
13 Vein contents
14 Out
15 River to the Rhone
16 Fitting name for a baseball player
17 Collectible modern illustrator
19 Presidential monogram
21 Draft agcy.
23 "The Facts of Life" star
28 Not the quiet ones
31 Actor Rob
32 Original ___
33 Divulge
35 Ex-Vietnamese leader ___ Dinh Diem
36 Aimed high?
37 Set firmly
38 Have on
39 Obsolete map abbr.
41 Olympian
42 States positively
46 Have ___ (be kind)
48 "Here Comes Santa Claus" singer
49 Mischievous
50 Split apart
52 Preliminary races
53 Vultures have them
54 Candied, as fruits
55 Bit of excitement
56 Sigh
57 Covered completely
58 Fitting name for an author
59 Let
61 Classic western
63 Odd, to a Scot
64 Dinner table item
66 Serve specially
67 Jalopy
69 Raisin cakes
70 Become raveled
72 Nickname
74 Peter the cartoonist
75 Give comfort to
76 Rebuked at length
77 Its cap. is Toronto
80 Al Capp's Daisy ___
81 Avian bigmouth
84 Toady
85 Word repeated before "Me" in a Beatles hit
86 Bird and King
89 See 93-Down
90 Skater Boitano
92 Inclined
93 With 89-Down, a past Senator from North Carolina
94 Brain passage
95 ___ spumante
97 Novelist Theroux
98 French weapon
99 Bandleader Brown
101 Small beginning?
103 Decamerous group
105 Gold in color: Abbr.
106 Unfold, poetically

by Jeanette K. Brill

ACROSS

1 Labor party, in England
8 Not as outgoing
13 Cut
19 Upper jaw
20 Somnolent state
21 Filmdom's Peter
22 "Nobody wants justice"
24 New version
25 Passport datum
26 Kitchen finish
27 Puppet
29 Let go
30 "You can get a lot more done with a kind word and a gun than with a kind word alone"
33 Dime ___
35 More divine
38 Work unit
40 Aristocratic beliefs
44 It's said to be not as lovely as a tree
45 Comparative words
47 Grayish green
49 Excuse
50 "By the time we've made it, we've had it"
54 British parent, familiarly
55 Open school grp.
56 Add-on
57 Reddish-brown gem
58 Squealer
59 Walk like a vamp
61 Honda rival
64 Out of port
66 Get but good
67 Word with ticket or rail
68 "I used to be Snow White, but I drifted"
70 Dawdle
71 Ring contents?
72 Fawn-colored antelope
73 Salvador's country, to Salvadorans
75 Act of law enforcement
78 Suffix with expert
79 Ho Chi Minh trail locale
80 Bill in the till
83 Social worker?
84 Constellation next to Scorpius
85 "It's not easy bein' green"

89 Start of a volume I heading
90 Broadway's fate?
92 Some promos
93 Simpletons
94 Italian noblewoman
96 Georgia, once: Abbr.
98 Supermarket device
100 Composer Bruckner
101 "Start every day off with a smile and get it over with"
104 Quite a nose
107 Kind of kick
110 Song syllables
111 Curator's degree
114 Be pregnant
116 "If I were two-faced, would I be wearing this one?"
120 Magazine illustration
121 Spree
122 Broke out
123 Treeless tract
124 Impurity
125 Purchase incentives

DOWN

1 Govt. agent
2 Ring to wear
3 Midyear, e.g.
4 Author ___ Yutang
5 Years ago, years ago
6 Overcharge
7 Dentist's target
8 Angel's wish
9 Nautical rope
10 Monogram feature: Abbr.
11 Prefix with -morphic
12 Gerrymanders
13 "Every time a friend succeeds, I die a little"
14 Bothered, with "at"
15 Iman, at birth
16 Imposture
17 Sommer of film
18 It's done
20 One of TV's Huxtables
23 Indy 500 advertiser
28 Automatons
30 Actor McCowen
31 Wheels for wheels
32 Handy to
34 Light cotton fabrics
35 Foxes, e.g.
36 Fire ___

37 "You'd be surprised how much it costs to look this cheap"
39 Bribed, so to speak
41 "Everything you see I owe to spaghetti"
42 In an unspeakable way
43 Talented one
45 House support
46 Do lawn work
48 Adlai's 1956 running mate
51 Grueling 3-Down, for short
52 ___-jongg
53 Comparatively tanned
60 Ankles, anatomically
62 Der ___ (Adenauer)
63 Wrong
64 Some wedding gifts
65 Diamond stats
67 The way of the gods
69 Equally
70 Track event
74 Twaddle

75 W.W. II participant
76 "Wit is educated insolence"
77 Judge
79 Stopper
81 Detecting ability
82 Elbe tributary
86 Dramatist Connelly
87 Mild oath
88 Peaty areas
91 Roof type
95 Fill
97 Workout garb
98 Popular product
99 1948 Oscar winner Trevor
102 Bakery offering
103 Cartesian words
104 Drinks: Abbr.
105 Kind of poll
106 Place for a vault
108 Construction piece
109 Fleming villain
111 Early feminist Lucretia
112 Vamoose
113 Common conjunctions
115 Climax

117 Owns
118 Gist
119 Tax consultant, often

by David J. Kahn

ACROSS

1 Check
7 Fast time
14 Baked desserts
20 Put through a strainer
21 It's much thanked in March
22 Jinx
23 Start of the epitaph
26 Seventh-inning ritual
27 Type of whale
28 These can be lucky
29 Overly
30 One with a pitchfork
32 Nevada town
33 Start of a well-known hymn
37 Painter of waterlilies
38 Symbol of electric flux
39 Obtain
43 Down-home entertainment
44 Late great Grant
45 "___ oui!" (certainly): Fr.
46 Gottfried's sister, in opera
47 More of the epitaph
53 Tiverton river
54 Pumped-up body
55 Rough, as a road
56 Simon and Diamond
57 Stare at
59 Beaut
61 Ally of "St. Elmo's Fire"
62 Sites for bookcases
64 Having chairs, maybe
66 Skullcap
69 How to draw an egg
71 Behan's "___ Boy"
75 Violinist Mischa
76 Connaught county seat
77 Japanese sandal
78 Coded matter
79 More of the epitaph
84 Hospital supplies
85 Be held in esteem
86 Forbes profilees
87 Years ago
88 "___ bien!"
89 Pacino and Gore
90 Boxer with a 90-9 career record
92 Wasn't serious
94 Puppeteer Baird
95 Steven of Aerosmith
96 Half a sawbuck
97 Aware of
100 Cricket sides
101 Move
105 End of the epitaph
110 Less fleshy
111 Regrouping tactic
112 1992 Wimbledon winner
113 Takes it easy
114 Computer memory
115 Hardy novel locale, usually

DOWN

1 Kabibble of Kay Kyser's band
2 Architect ___ van der Rohe
3 Natty
4 At all
5 Kind of key
6 Life support?
7 Multitude of occurrences
8 Take steps
9 ___-jongg
10 Carol starter
11 Master
12 With full force
13 Falstaff's rascally crony
14 Ill-natured
15 Football's Grier
16 "Bridges of Madison County" setting
17 Neighbor of 16-Down: Abbr.
18 Big winnings
19 Boozehound
24 "Apocalypse Postponed" essayist
25 Tub's problem
30 Teed off
31 Novelist Seton
33 "Long time ___!"
34 Adhesive
35 Paris' Musée de l'___
36 Jewish ___
37 The "M" in M-1 rifle
38 Encouraged, in a way
39 Tries again to make rain
40 "Dallas" miss
41 ___ as the hills
42 Sucker
44 Food wrapping, informally
45 Rebel
48 Good beating
49 Actor Tom of "Amadeus"
50 Buddy
51 European blackbird
52 Be left
58 Bats
59 Work out
60 Lake of the Ozarks tributary
61 Avowed
63 Triptych side panels
65 Cousins of musettes
66 Half of a Disney duo
67 Inventor Sperry
68 Dean Martin subject
70 Truncate
72 E.C. Bentley detective
73 Within ___ of (near)
74 Filled a hold
76 Hardly intellectual
77 Site of King David's royal residence
80 Rats
81 Farm unit
82 Well up
83 Some fashion tips
90 Go-getter
91 Lough Erne location
92 Common card-table project
93 Incense
94 "John Brown's Body" poet
95 Namely
96 "For shame!"
97 Owl's question?
98 Gaels of college athletics
99 Nordica products
101 Little bit
102 Puzzle solvers' cries
103 1994 title role for Shirley MacLaine
104 Facility
105 Pugilists' org.
106 Relatives of aves.
107 Shelley's "___ Skylark"
108 Schlep
109 Fort ___, N.J.

by Frances Hansen

ACROSS

1 Kind of court
6 Like good cheese
10 Noncom: Abbr.
14 Secret scheme
19 Deflate
20 Cleave
21 It may come in pats
22 Redolence
23 Author's dream
25 Farmer's dream
27 Levied
28 Workshop fixtures
30 They can knock you out
31 Goes to waste
32 Handles
33 Without plans
34 Endorse publicly
37 Riveting name?
38 Proverbial starting point on the corporate ladder
42 Part of a French countdown
43 Prospector's dream
45 Govt. seed agcy.
46 "___, Our Help in Ages Past" (old hymn)
47 Venetian magistrate
48 "The College Widow" playwright
49 Formula One car
51 Art style
52 Scientist's dream
56 Pollute
57 "Hurry up!"
59 Ancient symbol
60 Yens
61 Honey badgers
62 Coach Parseghian
63 Social strata
64 Stress, in a way
66 Kenton of jazz
67 Quack: Var.
70 Matriculates
71 Politician's dream
73 In the manner of
74 Tusks, to a bounty hunter
75 Any ship
76 Smell ___ (be suspicious)
77 British automatic
78 Noted rights grp.
79 Prosecutor's dream
83 Intimidate
84 Word elisions, as in "forecastle" to "fo'c'sle"
87 Ethos
88 Corpus header
89 Tuneful pipe
90 Celerity
91 It's often held in diners
92 Dispenser
95 Climb
96 Practical jokers
100 Optimist's dream
102 Solver's dream
104 Good on one's feet
105 Isn't colorfast
106 Anthony or Barbara
107 Professional negotiator
108 Old hat
109 Cigar tip
110 20's tennis champion Lacoste
111 Musical marks

DOWN

1 Sunscreen ingredient
2 Playwright Burrows et al.
3 Ticket
4 Belt type
5 Studies
6 City on the Rhone
7 Decorate, as a book
8 "___ of Destruction" (1955 hit)
9 Muslim ascetic
10 Person with a racket
11 Turns
12 Ring highlights?
13 Zenith
14 Business bloc
15 George of the Senior P.G.A.
16 Yawn producer
17 Cupid
18 Children's seats
24 Abbr. on company letterheads
26 Weird
29 Netman Nastase
32 Concierge's place
33 Dim
34 Subway stations
35 Grass fungus
36 Baseball player's dream
37 Book next to a dictionary
38 Method
39 Actor's dream
40 Too plump
41 Stable residents
43 Ambulatory
44 Loaf
47 ___ Basin (Ukrainian coal region)
49 Journalist James
50 "___ Irish Rose"
52 Legal clerk
53 Chatter
54 Pastoral
55 Silly
56 Tyrant
58 Plymouth pop
60 Physician's patron saint
63 Lemon, e.g.
64 Means of control
65 Messenger
66 Search
68 Turgenev heroine
69 Harangues
71 Greek letters
72 Incarcerated
75 Hook's henchman
77 Deliberately gum up the works
79 Good-natured fellow
80 Deadlock
81 Coward of films
82 More inexperienced
83 The sun
85 Twosome
86 Complied with
88 Halloween figures
90 Tracker's guide
91 A ship to remember
92 '56 song "If ___ My Druthers"
93 Heroic narrative
94 BBQ rod
95 Indecent literature
96 Hoover's force
97 Supplements, with "out"
98 Torn
99 Fast fliers, briefly
101 Choler
103 Lyrical poem

by Joel Davajan

ACROSS

1 Actress Thompson
5 Punk
9 Peggy Wood title role on early TV
13 Static
18 Carolina ___
19 Oh, what a relief it is!
20 King Harald's predecessor
21 Tee off
22 Assist in malfeasance
23 Powerful voting bloc
24 Loll
25 Floorer
26 Picket line
30 Brendan Behan's home
31 Side in an all-star game
32 Horse of a certain color
33 Chances
34 Something to build on
35 Style
36 Horse of a different color
39 "His face could ___ clock"
42 Modern kind of room
43 "Them" of the 40's
44 Bingo-like game
45 Transportation line
50 Dollar alternative
51 Clerihews, e.g.
52 Spot
53 Words on a Wonderland cake
54 Bled
55 Goofus
56 "___ fan tutte"
57 Prince Valiant's eldest
58 Reception line
67 Colonist
68 Bridges of Hollywood
69 Sounds of indecision
70 Tractor-trailer
71 Dr. or Mr.
74 Henry VIII's sixth
75 Row
78 Council city of 1409
79 Telephone line
83 Appropriate
84 First place
85 Model
86 Buenos ___
87 Prelude to a kiss
88 Years on the Yaqui
89 Hairsplitting
90 Greenpeace subj.
92 Smidgen
93 Pigeon pad
94 "Raging Bull"
98 Clothing line
104 Hawk's home
105 Sweat and strain
106 1978 Broadway revue
107 Tennis event
108 "___ Love Song" (1929 hit)
109 Deco doyen
110 "A Lesson From ___"
111 Kind of bog
112 Better
113 Library poster message
114 Marshy lands
115 Bretons, e.g.

DOWN

1 Pundit
2 Shady spot
3 Corporation headquartered in Moline, Ill.
4 Bushbucks
5 Consumer selections
6 Leaf part
7 Fukien seaport
8 Early trolleys
9 In the dumps
10 Storm posting
11 Captain's ___ (shipboard hearing)
12 Edgar Cayce topic
13 Detroit from New York
14 Bretonne sauce ingredient
15 Ice house: Var.
16 Psychic networker
17 Goes wrong
19 Strawberry ___
27 Not happy with
28 "Plain Language From Truthful James" writer
29 Outdoor dinner
34 "Excuse me"
35 Rarely seen
36 Kind of financing
37 One of the U.S. coins
38 Investigate, with "around"
39 Natty
40 Actress Feldshuh
41 Ewelike
42 Revolutionary name
43 Get ___ out of
44 Actor Reeves
46 Modern designs
47 Guzzle
48 Beginning
49 Deli offerings
55 General Foods product
56 French vineyard
57 Cause for a blessing, maybe
59 Stars & Stripes, e.g.
60 Moderates
61 1996 Madonna role
62 Holliday companion
63 Tarlatan skirt
64 Westminster Abbey poet
65 Hosiery thread
66 "Holy smokes!"
71 ___ Valley, Calif.
72 Argued, as a claim
73 Innkeeper's spread
74 It picks up the pace
75 Unhearing
76 Governess of Thornfield
77 Nursery rhyme boy
78 Diderot or Voltaire: Var.
80 Mean words
81 Rightmost column
82 Campbell of fashion
88 Wait on
89 Villain's lament
90 Holmes girl and others
91 Brewery output
92 Like the yak
93 Tony-winning Rivera
95 Like some personalities
96 "The better ___ you with"
97 Some female reuners
98 Video
99 Chew out
100 Prompt
101 Went lickety-split
102 Decree
103 Sable

by Fran and Lou Sabin

ACROSS

1 "Little" person
7 Qualifies
15 Calyx division
20 To land
21 Brownish-yellow to the extreme
22 Astronaut Schirra
23 "I may be ___, but . . ."
24 Captain Kirk
26 Excommunicates
27 Binders
28 Say it's so
29 Whole
32 Peter of rock's Kiss
34 Clever remark
36 Ancient X
37 San ___, Italy
38 Cookout fare
39 Other
43 Captain America
48 ___-flow turbine
49 Suffix with magnet or meteor
50 Grew aware of
51 Once more or no more
52 Lick
53 Common side dishes
55 Waiting period, seemingly
56 Captain Bligh
58 Moon phenomenon
59 Novelist ___ Easton Ellis
60 Scratches (out)
61 "Old MacDonald" syllables
62 Kind of name
64 Happy as a lark
65 Less happy
69 Nanny's charge
70 Green scene
72 Hires a crew, perhaps
74 Linen hue
75 Captain Hook
79 Health care lobby, for short
80 Aunt Jemima or Uncle Ben's, e.g.
81 Subject of "The Last Command"
82 Put up
83 Brio
85 Not dawdle
86 ___ Orbiter (1960's craft)
87 Captain Nemo
90 Barbra's "Funny Girl" co-star
91 So-so
92 Sports org.
93 Bundle of money
94 Be behind
96 Days-old
97 Muffs
101 Less of a struggle
104 It should be even
105 Pocket liner
106 "Captain Blood"
111 Manifest
113 Docked, in a way
114 Without a doubt
115 Bygone flag symbol
116 Keeps in
117 "Mean Streets" director
118 Whole bunch

DOWN

1 Browning's "___ Ben Ezra"
2 Flu variety
3 Obsolescent contraction
4 Famed horseman
5 "Be" conjugate
6 Forewent
7 Connections in old Rome
8 Fluff
9 Cheated on
10 Denture part
11 Tots: Var.
12 Take away, in a way
13 Double-hook shape
14 Erwin of old TV
15 Fab
16 Captain Cook
17 Balletic bend
18 Sleep like ___
19 Swan's neighbor, in the night sky
25 Is friendly, with "around"
30 1988 Tim Rice musical
31 It comes after Easter
32 Fictional mariner from York
33 Word in a street-corner sermon
34 "The Divine Comedy" creatures
35 "Stop it!"
38 Vaudeville offering
40 Manchurian river
41 Settled
42 Actress Sommer
43 Baryshnikov, to friends
44 Road ___
45 Shuts up
46 Mortimer the dummy
47 It's never played in school
48 Of equal size
54 Captain Queeg
56 Schnozzes
57 Cravings
59 Early English historian
63 Student's declaration, maybe
64 "Good ___!"
65 Cost ___ and . . .
66 Airline exec Carl
67 "Sesame Street" regular
68 More of a boor
70 It may be mechanical
71 About
72 Repairman's reading
73 Marine biology subject
75 Stick: Sp.
76 Styptic substance
77 1934 film seductress
78 Kenyan native
80 Lord of poetry
83 Step up
84 Breaches
88 "ER" sights
89 Emphatic type
91 Croft
95 Splits
96 Passover feast
98 Stoolies
99 Tom or Sam, e.g.
100 Bluish-gray
101 Report card woes
102 Got off
103 Auld lang ___
104 Instrument with 13 strings
107 Mini-albums, for short
108 Varnish base
109 Metric volumes: Abbr.
110 "Yes, sir!"
111 Wordless communication
112 Through

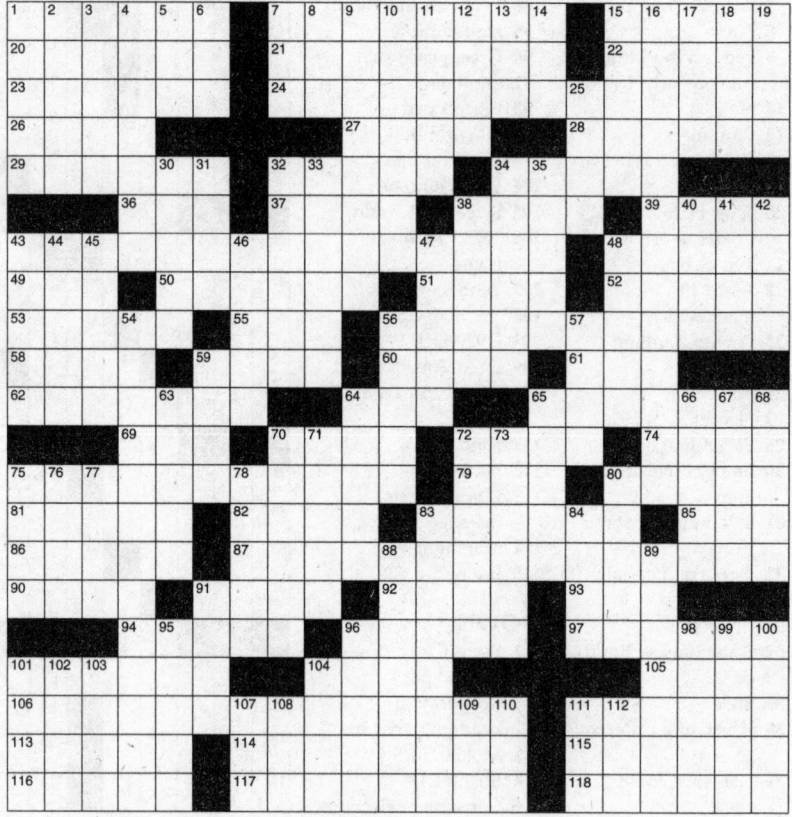

by Coral Amende

The 10 unclued answers in this puzzle are familiar phrases presented literally. When the puzzle is completed, the 12 circled letters—reading in order from top to bottom—will spell an appropriate phrase.

ACROSS

1 "My Life as ___" (1985 film)
5 Mandela's org.
8 Ultraviolet light protector
12 Refinement
17 Louise of "Gilligan's Island"
18 50's war zone
21 1977 Scott Turow book
22 Slowpoke
23 See instructions
25 See instructions
27 Steve McQueen's TV horse
28 Rights org.
30 Hot clue
31 Like the White Rabbit
32 See instructions
37 "___ evil . . ."
38 Sight from Albertville
39 Puccini's Floria
42 Spitfire fliers: Abbr.
45 Sought by bibliomaniacs
47 "Give ___ rest!"
49 Pertaining to medicine
51 Some nest eggs
53 See instructions
57 Pop music's Plastic ___ Band
58 Say it again?
60 Transcript figures, for short
61 Kinfolk
62 Slob's home
63 Actress Sally of old Hollywood
64 Be an appetizer for
65 Follows
68 ___ store by
69 Gives excessive care to
72 Bead material
75 From a spring
77 Legendary Wildcats coach
78 Made a whirring sound
79 Battery size
81 Reagan Secretary of State
83 Journal's end
84 Printer's ems
85 Bug
86 See instructions
89 Bone: Prefix
90 Creditor
92 Big Band ___
93 Word between up and down
94 Gal of song
95 "___ far, far better thing . . .": Dickens
96 "Shame!"
98 "Cheers!"
101 See instructions
109 Professional org.
112 Co-star for Marlene
113 Van ___
114 Buddy, in Bologna
115 See instructions
118 See instructions
121 Anklebone
122 Plenty, to a bard
123 Miniature kangaroo of Australia
124 Teen bugbear
125 Classy horses
126 Cooked
127 Brillo rival
128 Sparks and namesakes

DOWN

1 Arcade name
2 Start-of-meal comment
3 Upright
4 Allahabad's river
5 Rap-sheet letters
6 Fireside drink
7 Architects
8 Teller of tales
9 Invigorating
10 Deck out with jewels
11 8-Down's middle name
12 Literary initials
13 Shrink
14 It's a long story
15 Show bias
16 Robt. ___
19 Reference work: Abbr.
20 Gudrun did him in
24 Volume
26 First ones are special
29 Merkel of the movies
33 Jitters
34 Where bombs burst, so we sing
35 Sixth-century date
36 Bring ___ end
40 See instructions
41 Temptations' "___ Too Proud to Beg"
42 Escalates
43 Auerbach of "The Jack Benny Show"
44 See instructions
46 Skating maneuver
48 Fast ___
50 Holding back, in a way
52 Person in a pool
54 Unrolled
55 Good-___ (amiable)
56 Johns, in the Highlands
59 1982 Jeff Bridges film
64 ". . . but we know what ___"
66 Military squad
67 ___ the ground
69 W.W. II miss
70 Chicanery
71 Goggles
73 ___-car
74 Detroit's Corsair or Citation
76 Site of a Marx Brothers movie
78 F.B.I. center
79 Denver's Lowry, e.g.: Abbr.
80 Et ___
82 Arctic bird of prey
84 French wine center
86 Offspring: Abbr.
87 Classic play based on a Maugham tale
88 Galleys
91 Circus young 'un
97 Heart printout, for short
99 Body shops?
100 West coast Floridian
102 Called the game
103 One grand
104 Eddie ___, The Walking Man of baseball
105 Old Russian secret-police org.
106 Part of a family tree
107 "___ Company" (Namath film)
108 Couples
109 Movie pooch
110 Argue
111 Hacienda division
116 Pluralizer
117 Shropshire she
119 "Give it ___"
120 Flattens

by Ernie Furtado

ACROSS

1 Place for a heeler (or a healer)
5 Understanding
10 Condo ad abbr.
13 "Northern Exposure" setting
19 Art forger's aid
20 Bluffs
21 Gobble
22 Prepared horses' hooves for shoeing
23 F IDE LIT Y
26 Like a dame
27 Takes up
28 Bomb vestige
30 Colorless people
31 Yields
32 Jazz trumpeter Baker et al.
33 Wooer of Merope, in myth
35 Generous and strong-willed one, supposedly
36 Nightclub
37 Bulwark
40 Donkey's uncles
43 A CTO RS
45 Hurricane heading
46 Schubert composition
47 Algid
48 Part of a three-weapon competition
49 Counterpart of a Mlle.
50 Weisshorn, e.g.
51 SA LL Y
55 Decathlete Johnson
56 Procrastinators
58 Flee with a flame
59 Grinders
60 Disturb
61 "Skedaddle!"
62 Parisian puffing stuff
63 Percussion sticks that accompany dancing
65 San Diego founder Junipero
67 New Jersey governor Whitman
70 Redirect
71 FIL T ER
73 Tick off
74 He KO'd Carnera, 6/14/34
75 To ___ (precisely)
76 "ER" medic
77 1935 Rodgers and Hart song
78 Question in a defensive reply
79 C LI NCH
83 Backside
84 "Stag at Bay" painter
87 Sayyid's subjects
88 Spare unit
89 Leave off
90 Hornless cow
91 Part of Jesus' attire
95 Wear
97 Transfer
99 Maine symbol
100 Mailer's "The ___ of the Night"
102 FA NT AS Y
104 Den box
105 Perfect, in a way
106 École-ite?
107 MCI and CCC
108 Monk of yore
109 Light conditions
110 Closer to maturity
111 Puppy pleasers

DOWN

1 Ibis, e.g.
2 Twinkle-toed
3 Live it up
4 Talked childishly
5 Isolated area
6 Luna Park attractions
7 "___ right with the world!": Browning
8 Road alert
9 ___ Friends Network
10 Familial
11 Dillon and others
12 Ocular woe
13 Bach's "The ___ of the Fugue"
14 Stored
15 Lone Star pros
16 CLI Q UE
17 Castle section
18 Dubs in
24 Ophelia and Laertes
25 Geological feature
29 Peregrinated
32 ___ Nast
34 Shine's partner
36 Scams, in a way
37 Common street name
38 It has a yellow disk
39 Vineyard data
40 Gloomy Gus's expression
41 Delta builder
42 SA LA RIES
43 "Roger & Me" creator Michael
44 Smarmy Dickens character
47 Peppery greens
49 Palacio divisions
51 Further down?
52 Pola of the silents
53 Mischievous miss
54 Bits
55 Falstaff's page in "The Merry Wives of Windsor"
57 One in St. Valentine's care
59 Parts of stable families
62 "___ Foolish Things"
63 Conspiracy
64 Zoo animal
65 Fish in a way
66 Volta's subj.
67 Swamp swimmers
68 Part of a multivitamin
69 Counter's opening
71 1979 and '82 Oscar winner
72 Plagiarizes
75 Blackjack bases
77 Bogey territory
80 Amelia Earhart and Mort Walker, e.g.
81 Crop problem
82 Intimidating sort
83 Let off easy, maybe
85 Infer
86 Lustrous fabric
88 Cater (to)
90 Looking scared
91 Not much of a blockade
92 Circus site
93 Canted
94 Tourney stage
95 Fill
96 C.E.O.
98 Regarding
99 Attend Andover, e.g.
101 Meet a raise
103 Cantab's rival

by Fran and Lou Sabin

ACROSS

1 Auto accessory
6 Britannia
12 Country music's Axton
16 Hansom
19 Part of "I, Claudius"
20 Treat, as per a famous rule
21 Remedy for dry toast
22 First president of Korea
23 Event at which people have a ball
27 Sanctions
28 Cousin of a gimlet
29 Prefix with masochism
30 It's all downhill from here
31 Barely contain one's anger
33 Joplin tune
35 Madrileño, e.g.
38 Dismay
39 Land
40 One of the Maunas
42 "Get off ___!"
44 Hearty quaff
45 Jazz's Kid ___
47 Laugh-a-minute
49 Tenth of a joule
51 Ruby anniversary
55 Flaming Gorge Reservoir site
57 Opinion
58 Like Haydn's "Surprise Symphony"
60 "Jake's Thing" author
61 Whence Jackie got her O
62 Full of holes
64 Hugger-mugger
67 Stimpy's pal
68 Spiral-shelled snail
70 Additionally
71 Madrileño's moolah
72 Plankton components
74 Our wish to you
78 Three-___ (multipurpose)
79 Sink
81 History chapter
82 Traffic jam
84 Army
85 Thickset
86 DeNiro's "Mean Streets" co-star
89 Stack of oldies, maybe
90 Greek consonants
91 180 degrees from norte
92 One of the Vanderbilts
94 First name in architecture
95 Not one to go solo
97 Cornstalk strands
100 "Understood"
102 Dude
103 Bridle's mouthpiece
105 Singer Carey
107 Adolphe ___, musical instrument inventor
108 Shaped like an inner tube
112 Tony nominee for "Mass Appeal"
114 She's unarmed
116 Beak
118 Neat
119 Titular tenor in a Verdi opera
121 Where heros are made
123 "I ___ saw . . ."
125 Pa. neighbor
126 Timely opening words
131 Improbable
132 Bond foe
133 What it is
134 Sans smog
135 Par: Abbr.
136 Revue piece
137 Esurient
138 Mythical monster

DOWN

1 Harass publicly
2 "See what I got!"
3 Comedian
4 Former White House inits.
5 Subject of a 1917 execution
6 Work like ___
7 Drop
8 Japanese puppet theater
9 "___ moment"
10 Baseballers Ed and Mel
11 "___ a Stranger" (1955 film)
12 Waits for weights
13 Flamenco accolade
14 "Owner of a Lonely Heart" band
15 Go for a ringer
16 New Year's welcome, frequently
17 You may see it on TV
18 Semiantique car
22 Beef cut
24 Awaited
25 The same
26 It can move mountains
32 Brings (out)
34 Outfit
36 Not merely pudgy
37 Sitarist's rendition
41 Kind of pilot
43 Psychic author Edgar
46 "Sure!"
47 Refrigerate a Tex-Mex dish
48 Leaves the ball
50 Torn
51 Capacitance units
52 Frittatas
53 Leaves the past behind
54 Tire pattern style
56 Deride the foot
59 Babysitter, perhaps
63 Quiet word in the Garter motto
65 Soviet poet Mandelstam
66 Soporific sucker
68 It'll last for days
69 Swiss abstractionist joint
71 Readies quick looks
73 Gulf of Guinea port
75 Cheese city of Pennsylvania
76 One who devours a spud
77 Fuel ship of a more offensive nature
80 Lake Malawi's old name
83 New London grp.
86 Australian novelist ___ Tennant
87 Piccadilly Circus statue
88 J.F.K.'s Boston counterpart
90 "Stir Crazy" star
93 Erstwhile talk-show host
96 Surpass Nolan Ryan
98 Lowercase
99 Setting for a diamond
101 Do
103 Promotes
104 "___ All There Is?"
106 Shaded
109 Female stand-up star
110 Glossy cover
111 Stick in the salad
113 Lead-in to Tishri
115 Word on the street
117 Spoke sheepishly
118 D.C. V.I.P.
120 Tote board tally
122 Writer of "Happy Birthday"
124 Boglike
127 Refuge
128 Numerical prefix
129 "___ pasa?"
130 Emulating

by Henry Hook

ACROSS

1 Blacksmith's tool
5 Easter Island head, e.g.
10 Sacred symbols at Thebes
14 Nutmeg's sister
18 "___ you!" (words in a tot's game)
19 Kafka novel, with "The"
20 Medicine Nobelist Severo ___
21 Impulse carrier
22 N.F.L. lumber?
24 N.F.L. pumpernickel?
26 Outstanding feature
27 Football-like
29 Exercises
30 Ontario native
31 Make challah
32 Bandleader Kenton
33 Brownie ingredients, sometimes
36 Not slick
37 Laptop, e.g.
41 In agreement
42 Supreme Court Justice from the N.F.L.?
44 Foreign article
45 Words of wisdom
46 Mountain pool
47 Memo sign-off
48 Cosmetics applicator
49 It may have a ring
50 N.F.L. recruiters?
54 Artist Andrea del ___
55 Plenty
57 Copper source
58 It sounds the hour
59 Words
60 Painters' needs
61 Contend with
62 Juntas
63 "___ the Conqueror" (1988 Best Foreign Film)
64 Devoted swain
66 Do penance
67 N.F.L. transportation?
69 King Arthur's steward Sir ___
72 Laugh-a-minute
73 Bit of saltwater?
74 Ill-favored
75 Queen of the heavens
76 Suffix with consist
77 When an N.F.L.er is feted?
81 Go by car
82 Some flower beds
84 Antibacterial virus
85 Chap
86 "Buffalo ___" (old song favorite)
87 Like a flophouse
88 Gives the heave-ho
89 Annual report listing
92 Put on the line
93 Film holder
97 Cuddly N.F.L. mascot?
99 N.F.L. subduers?
101 Roberts of "Star 80"
102 Reggie and Michael Jackson, e.g.
103 Dropping the ball, e.g.
104 Trapped like ___
105 Just say no
106 A canonical hour
107 Actor Aiello
108 Bering Sea port

DOWN

1 Cookout fare
2 Minor place
3 Deal in
4 Christian symbols of charity
5 Diamonds
6 Harness strap
7 Brian Friel's home
8 Stripling
9 Slowpoke
10 Biting
11 Like show horses
12 Explosive sound
13 Hazard
14 Daughter of Pericles, in Shakespeare
15 Double or triple feat
16 Welsh product
17 They're sometimes loose
20 Orchestra member
23 Copyright treaty city
25 Katzenjammer Kids, e.g.
28 Like all outdoors
31 Pickling agent
32 Biological bodies
33 Yesterdays
34 The Bible's "hairy one"
35 N.F.L. footwear?
36 Van Doren and Van Vechten
37 It goes par avion
38 Where some N.F.L.'ers shop?
39 Door frame
40 Soothsayer's home
42 Solomonic
43 Moves by rail
46 Powders
48 Put aside
50 Ancient magistrate
51 50's actress Gia
52 Kind of beans
53 Exxon Valdez, e.g.
54 "Rocky" co-star
56 Praying figure
58 Back-room fellow
59 Barrio resident
60 Bacteriologist J.R. ___
62 Thoughtful soul
63 Compote ingredients
64 Fish food
65 "What's My Line" host John
67 Leaps for Peter Martins
68 Not thin
70 Buck add-on
71 Tall one
73 Pilot's danger
75 Quartet member
77 Whitney's business partner
78 Covent Garden offerings
79 Pat Boone's "___ I Love"
80 Ready to be ridden
81 The brainy bunch
83 Reuters, for one
85 Turnover
87 Edge
88 Paternoster preceder
89 Fossilized
90 Stable parent
91 Pitcher Johnny
92 Not right now
93 Skier's snow
94 Mr. T's last name
95 Amusement park transport
96 Villa d'___
98 Trouble
100 It can be in C.D.'s

by Louis Sabin

ACROSS

1 Pirate's punishment
7 Container for liquid nitrogen
12 Thrown away
19 On the beach
20 Computer function
21 God
22 Wine connoisseurs at dinner?
24 Pond denizen
25 "Je ne ___ quoi"
26 Small vol. measurement
27 Taken (with)
29 Exuberance
30 Bug
31 Get on
33 Bit of color
35 Digital watch part: Abbr.
36 N.T. book
37 Expire
39 Cornerstone abbr.
40 Recesses
42 Calendar abbr.
44 Big scissors from the Big Apple?
48 Butcher's order
49 Nerdy attire
50 Vladimir Nabokov or Jerzy Kosinski
54 Fix up
56 Packs, as sardines
57 Game sometimes called "bucking the tiger"
59 Like an old gen.
60 Snappy comeback?
61 Bait
63 Home of the Visconti and Sforza families
64 It can heat up Brie
65 L'Abbaye-aux-Hommes locale
66 Goes on a diet?
68 Ice cream thickener
69 Prefix with athlete
70 Turn down
71 Goiter sufferer's need
72 Louis d'or, e.g.
73 Where TV's Mindy honeymooned
74 Finnish skiing gold medalist Maentyranta
75 Moore of "Striptease"
76 "Look Back in Anger" playwright
78 Do a cobbler's job
80 Religious center

82 Goddess who sparked the Trojan War
83 Sheriff's grain harvest?
86 First name in tennis
87 Wallpaper design
90 ___-disant (self-styled)
91 Went through and robbed
93 White House grp.
96 Sounds at a doctor's office
97 Walk ostentatiously
101 Journalist's workplace
102 ___ Canals
103 Word in a hymn
105 Burst in
107 Unkindly
108 Impulse
109 Traveling
111 Bit of paper company stock?
114 Rootless one
115 Smits's "N.Y.P.D. Blue" role
116 Makeup artist?
117 Supposed aphrodisiacs
118 Limited
119 Takes a little bit

DOWN

1 Female lead played only by males
2 B flat equivalent
3 Like some Arabs' conversations?
4 ___ de combat
5 Mismatch, e.g.
6 Grant's 1868 opponent
7 Rosa Parks Day mo.
8 Club with a clock on its emblem
9 Originator of the Washington/cherry tree myth
10 In position, as a sail
11 Fidgety
12 Mendelssohn work in E flat major
13 Garçon's tip, maybe
14 Angry, with "up"
15 Seaside setting
16 A lot of Micronesia
17 Take away the pain
18 Style news
20 Strip
23 Syllabus
28 Nonsense, in England

31 Carroll's "Sylvie and ___"
32 Eclipse statistic
34 Football great nicknamed "Old 98"
38 Refreshers
41 Kind of particle
43 Try to pick up
45 Notable anniversary
46 Makes one's mark?
47 Clears out, in a way
48 "A Murder of Quality" author
49 Film with 8,000 extras
51 Monastery no-no?
52 Engages
53 "Open thine eyes ___": Keats
54 College official
55 Correct a typo
57 Poodle's name
58 It has 12 steps
62 Picador's target
63 Great Society measure
67 More comfortable
68 Cupped fruit

70 Wish "bon voyage!"
75 "Law & Order" characters
77 Like suspicious eyes
79 Commercial prefix with lady
80 Lacking ore, as a mountain
81 Liaison d'amour
84 Glucose and galactose, e.g.
85 Revolution result, possibly
86 Shrew
87 Coped
88 Annual literary award
89 Trouble, in Yiddish slang
92 "Darling ___" (Hudson flick)
94 Evening gala
95 Stars-to-be
98 Bottle size
99 Case for a vet
100 Plant problem
104 Like some ice cream
106 Nobel Prize category: Abbr.

108 "___ there?"
110 Chief Ouray, e.g.
112 USA competitor
113 Timetable listing: Abbr.

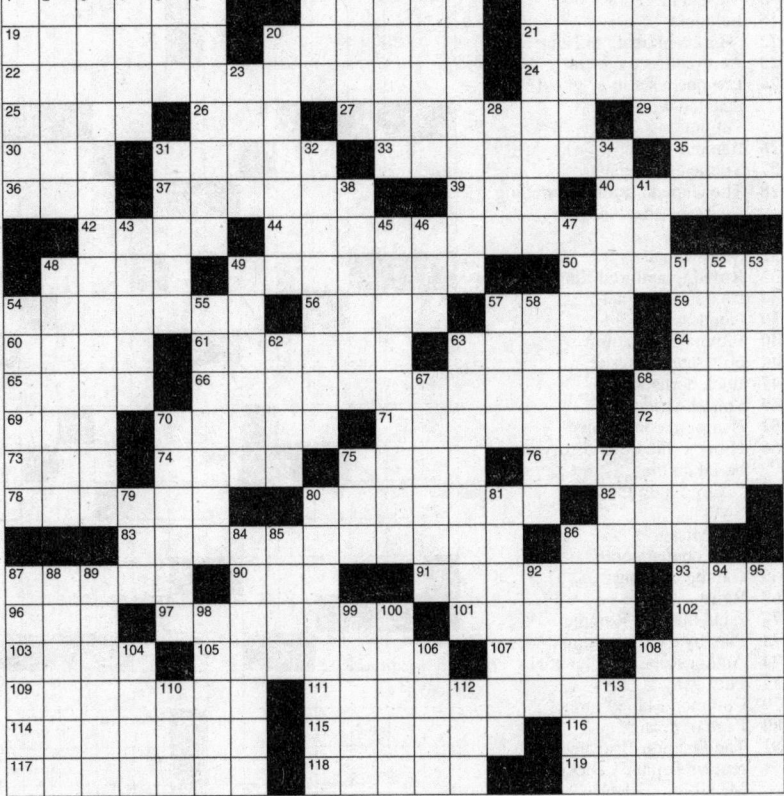

by Dave Tuller

ACROSS

1 Actor Cage
8 Mosaic piece
15 Belabors
22 "Hubba-hubba!" to Henri
23 Accepted as payment
24 Poe poem set in a "ghoul-haunted woodland"
25 Put out
26 Ran out
27 To the extent that
28 The German troops' marching song was adapted from ___
31 Purposive
32 Miss-named
33 Rose hip and Red Zinger, e.g.
34 Chekhov's "Uncle ___"
39 Goddess of night
40 Province of Latium
44 60's satellite series
47 Lock horns with
49 Poison antidotes
52 Bedroom community
56 Hitler's blitzkrieg theory was based on the ___
62 "___ go, into the . . ."
63 Switch
64 ___ Miss
65 Bara contemporary
66 Gaping opening
69 Ruins
71 Field marshal Rommel
73 Play by e.e. cummings
74 Author Robbe-Grillet et al.
77 Puts away
79 Common Market money
80 Page of music
82 The first non-Britisher to receive Britain's Dickin Medal for Gallantry was a ___
87 Din
88 Glamour competitor
89 Hooks up
90 Leaning
91 Solecize
92 Model's makeup, often
94 One who neatens a bed
97 Ottoman V.I.P.
98 Quarter back
101 Letter from Athens
102 Red letters
104 Author James and others
107 Negotiations leading to the surrender of German troops in Italy ___
114 Plenty angry
115 "CHiPs" chap
116 Capital on the Tanshui River
117 Okinawan seaport
120 Blue hue
121 White pages abbr.
124 1976 Beach Boys tune
125 Refuges
129 "Prince ___" ("Aladdin" song)
131 Pretend to be
133 The BBC promoted V-for-Victory in musical Morse code by frequently broadcasting ___
145 Pennsylvania Railroad city
146 Flower petals, collectively
147 60's TV western
148 French auto
149 Biblical liar
150 Blue books?
151 Here and there, to Pierre
152 Nerve impulse point
153 Fishermen's patron

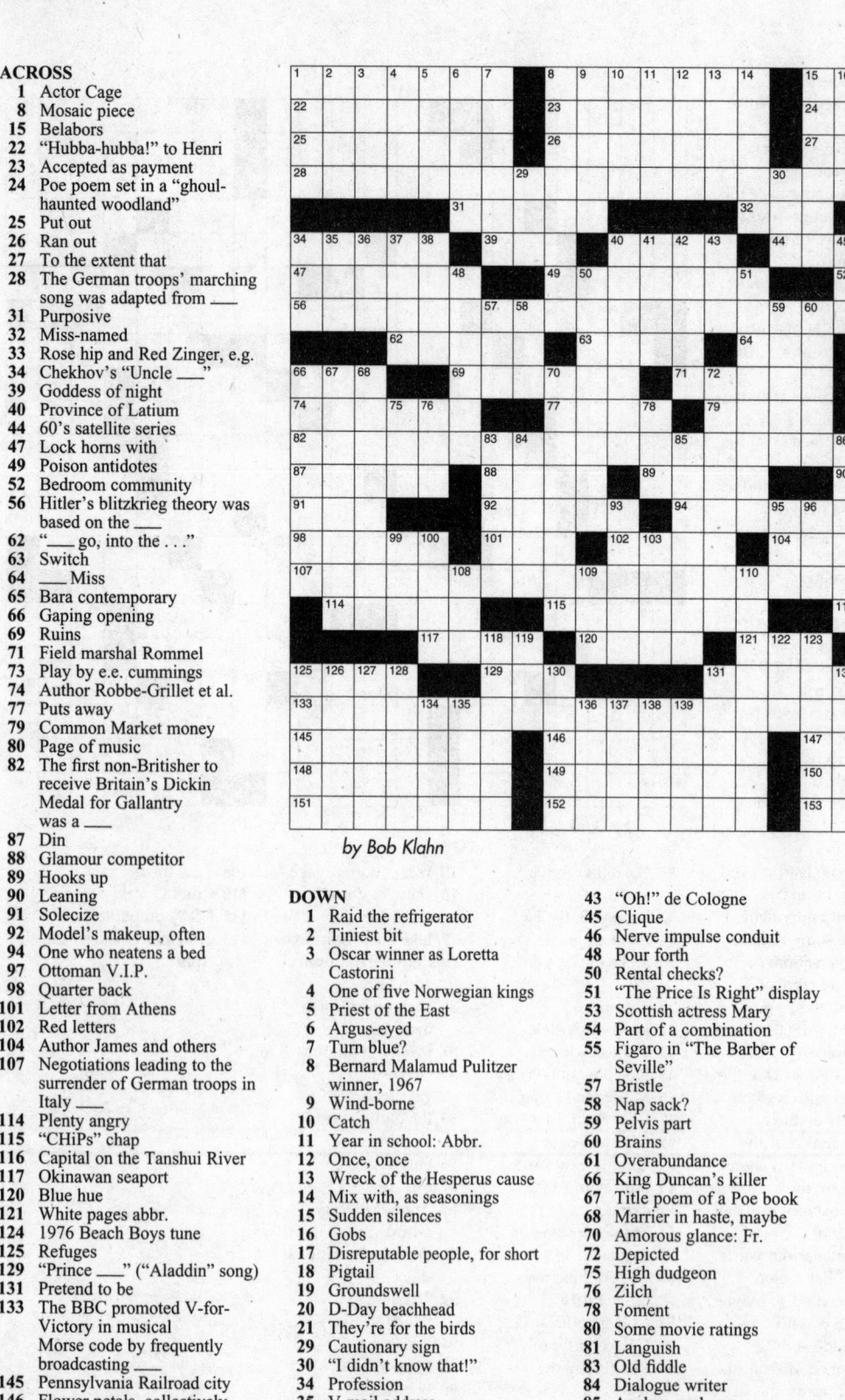

by Bob Klahn

DOWN

1 Raid the refrigerator
2 Tiniest bit
3 Oscar winner as Loretta Castorini
4 One of five Norwegian kings
5 Priest of the East
6 Argus-eyed
7 Turn blue?
8 Bernard Malamud Pulitzer winner, 1967
9 Wind-borne
10 Catch
11 Year in school: Abbr.
12 Once, once
13 Wreck of the Hesperus cause
14 Mix with, as seasonings
15 Sudden silences
16 Gobs
17 Disreputable people, for short
18 Pigtail
19 Groundswell
20 D-Day beachhead
21 They're for the birds
29 Cautionary sign
30 "I didn't know that!"
34 Profession
35 V-mail address
36 "All Things Considered" network
37 Julian's stepmother
38 Starting
40 Try, try again?
41 Safety elevator inventor
42 ___-Mokwa ("Hiawatha" bear)

43 "Oh!" de Cologne
45 Clique
46 Nerve impulse conduit
48 Pour forth
50 Rental checks?
51 "The Price Is Right" display
53 Scottish actress Mary
54 Part of a combination
55 Figaro in "The Barber of Seville"
57 Bristle
58 Nap sack?
59 Pelvis part
60 Brains
61 Overabundance
66 King Duncan's killer
67 Title poem of a Poe book
68 Marrier in haste, maybe
70 Amorous glance: Fr.
72 Depicted
75 High dudgeon
76 Zilch
78 Foment
80 Some movie ratings
81 Languish
83 Old fiddle
84 Dialogue writer
85 Anchor, perhaps
86 "___ Thou Now O Soul" (Whitman poem)
93 Unc's mate
95 Patriotic org.
96 Maniacal leader
99 Former Ford
100 Opposite of seek

103 Hall and Oates' "___ Smile"
105 Morales of "La Bamba"
106 "M*A*S*H" Emmy winner
108 Fuel efficiency rater: Abbr.
109 Helpful PC key
110 Clichéd climax of a movie thriller
111 Photo ___
112 Stutz Bearcat contemporary
113 Cartoonist Browne
118 Morro Castle site
119 Brighton brew
122 Visitors from afar
123 "Eight Men Out" director John
125 They're to be counted on
126 Collector's item
127 "Look Homeward, Angel" dramatist ___ Frings
128 Accumulation
130 Kon-Tiki worshipers
131 Oversized library volume
132 Like some bombs
134 Laugh and a half
135 Scott Turow book
136 Company co-founded by Akio Morita
137 Ollie's biggest friend
138 Hebrides island
139 Impertinent
140 Plaything
141 "I have seen war . . . I ___ war": F.D.R.
142 Strike out
143 Congenial
144 1945, for one

ACROSS

1 "The Virginian" star
5 C.I.A. mole, perhaps
10 Yankee home-run legend
15 Blackmailer's meeting point
19 Defendant's friend, often
20 Delivers a philippic
21 Practice piece
22 New Rochelle college
23 Start of a quip
27 Start of an ode's title
28 One of 12 popes
29 Redding of 60's soul
30 Lists
31 Writer Quentin
33 Stop on a European tour
35 Secretly take
37 To land
39 Mata ___
40 Leaves
43 Quip, part 2
48 Ending for silver or glass
49 Rubbernecked
50 They may be wee
51 Wander
52 Unwitty comebacks
53 Board
55 Like Windsor wives
56 Actress Belafonte
58 "M" star of 1931
59 Miss Piggy and others
60 Untrustworthy sort
61 Quip, part 3
67 Electron collectors
68 Aware of
69 Notre Dame faithful
70 Lucky ___
71 Kind of acid
73 Meanness
74 Blubber
77 Food additive
78 Stories
79 Circuit component
80 A lot of lot
81 Quip, part 4
87 Goddess of righteous anger
88 All over
89 Filmdom's Mr. Chips, 1969
90 Governor Wilson
91 Sunbathing, reading, etc.
93 Pad type
94 1979 Weaver film
97 El ___
98 Stuff
99 Burn cause, perhaps
102 End of the quip
108 Genesis brother
109 Donnybrook
110 Weak poker hand
111 Rats!
112 African rulers
113 Gets slick on top
114 Insults
115 Wonders aloud

DOWN

1 V.I.P. in woman suffrage
2 ___ Rios, Jamaica
3 Stands
4 Bribe
5 Stroked
6 Short shot
7 Colony members
8 Utmost
9 Mao ___-tung
10 Bombay-born conductor
11 Had a quiet dinner
12 Ingredients in presidentes
13 Infamous dictator
14 "Wait a ___!"
15 Catch-22
16 Parks of Alabama
17 "Come ___, the water's fine!"
18 One-star ratings
24 Hubert's successor
25 General Powell
26 "All praise to ___"
32 First film in CinemaScope, with "The"
33 Flicka and others
34 Angry
35 Raymond's lawyer role
36 Statutes
37 Part of a Welk intro
38 Toppled leader of 1979
39 Mills of Hollywood
40 Grim
41 Pretty follower
42 Light brown
44 Pine
45 "Tommy" band
46 Not so good
47 Vibrato sound
53 Saunter
54 Times to remember
55 Words of wisdom
56 Brainpower
57 Doth possess
58 Munroe of "Charlie's Angels"
59 Browning work
60 Hold on
61 Like nice weather
62 Perfect accord
63 Word with tie or lash
64 Teary
65 Wood cutter
66 Colonial newscaster
71 70's sitcom
72 Stockyard sounds
73 Tenant tender
74 Cause of some halted traffic
75 Nuncupative
76 "La Belle et la ___" (Cocteau film)
78 "Ahem!"
79 ___ off (repel)
80 Like ___ of bricks
82 Momentum
83 Adults-in-training
84 Capital near Bac Ninh
85 Is unsteady
86 Foundry product
91 Dragged, in a way
92 ". . . ___, dust to . . ."
93 Indian V.I.P.
94 Passed easily
95 Make a successful getaway from
96 Britisher's exclamation
97 Influence
98 Head the cast
100 Big Apple namesake
101 Eagles
103 Govt. money overseer: Abbr.
104 "Cry ___ River"
105 Computer key
106 Nautilus habitat
107 Nabokov heroine

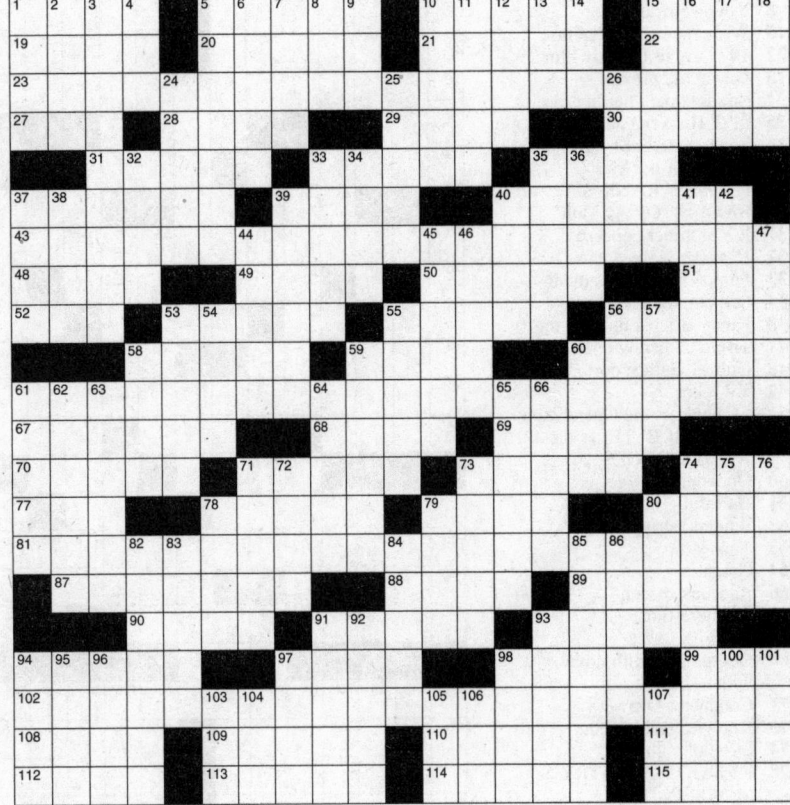

by Harvey Estes

ACROSS

1 Breath protector
8 Young chicken
15 Write mediocre literature
22 1979 Caine-Ustinov film
23 Day at the movies
24 Strauss opera heroine
25 "T.J. Hooker" star
26 Song heard at Sky-Dome
27 Munsel of the Met
28 HIS NEW RANK'S SAME: "TOP ACTOR"
31 It's of miner concern
32 Has a bawl
33 Pumpernickel ingredient
34 Serpentine nickname
38 Fanny Brice's theme song
41 Triple Crown winner, 1937
48 Gulf of Guinea port
50 TV joker
52 "A Night at the Opera" tune
53 OH-H NICE! TELL ARISTIDE FOES . . .
60 Occasional
61 Harmful
62 Raiders' strikes
63 Tickles
64 Green
66 Raucous speech
67 Uninteresting
68 Stinging
69 George Meredith novel, with "The"
71 Conductor Ozawa
73 Knowledgeable about
74 Piece of eight
78 I'VE GOT COUNTRY'S MIND SPLIT
83 Eighty-six
84 One with will power?
85 Succeed
86 Snobs' looks
87 Ancient Persian
88 Sought office
89 "Buffalo ___" (old song)
92 Patois
93 Stuck
97 Jack of clubs
98 "Paper Chase" subject
100 Man with an alibi
101 CALAMITY! I SHOOK, SHATTERED
105 In a huff
106 Poet-novelist Wylie
107 Japanese porcelain
108 Scotch and Drambuie drinks
111 Feel nostalgic
114 Foreign correspondent?
118 Lily Tomlin's Edith ___
119 Lets touch them
121 Contemporary art
122 PULL BIG STREAK! O'S CHEERING
135 Excitement
136 Tough guy of filmdom
137 Island on which Father Damien worked
138 Birthplace of grunge rock
139 "Annie" choreographer Peter
140 Buddy
141 Transports for Holmes
142 Australian hobo
143 He 88-Across and 88-Across and 88-Across

DOWN

1 Half an early comics duo
2 Having missed the boat
3 Mortifies
4 High school requirement
5 & 6 "Nana" actress, 1934
7 Douglas and Cameron
8 Auto engine leakage
9 Bigotry
10 Algerian port
11 Scottish playwright Hay et al.
12 Makeup artist?
13 "Momo" author Michael
14 Cut the mustard?
15 Exotic punch flavor
16 Waxed eloquent
17 Jackson 5 member
18 Lush settings?
19 Pindaric
20 Machu Picchu native
21 Sideways look
29 Gulf of Aden abutter
30 Cedric ___ of "Little Lord Fauntleroy"
35 Gained a lap
36 Chill
37 Bounce back
39 Pound's sounds
40 Easter starter
41 Overgrown
42 Homer's "scourge of mortals"
43 Dovetailed
44 Pelvis parts
45 Hoppers
46 Mrs. Shakespeare
47 Off
49 Classic theater name
51 Science of poetic rhythm
53 Square
54 Love-duet sequence in ballet
55 Eat crow and talk turkey, e.g.
56 One with a rod
57 Top-drawer
58 Center of Florida
59 Holds tight
65 Honchos
67 Islamic folklore figure
68 G.I. address
70 Under control
72 Think tank member
73 On pins and needles
74 Berth place
75 Creditor's writ
76 Flatter
77 Pearl harborer
79 "Pagliacci" soprano
80 Do battle
81 Pull on
82 In the dark
87 Cereal eater of old ads
88 Harold of "Ghostbusters"
90 Guided beyond the threshold of
91 Twiggy
93 Calaboose
94 Kind of street
95 Endorsements
96 Rock's ___ the Hoople
97 Campaign aid
98 Wax-glazed fabric
99 Now!
102 "Die Lorelei" poet
103 Playfully noncommittal
104 Peccancy
109 It's incendiary
110 Footholds?
112 Cochise player on 50's TV
113 Trust
115 Winter coats
116 French satellite launcher
117 Innumerable
120 Drainage sites
122 Fives and tens, e.g.
123 Side by side figure?
124 Kind of office
125 Channels
126 Colon, in analogies
127 Emulates Xanthippe
128 Squandered
129 Mystery writer Buchanan
130 Dance partner
131 Car on rails
132 Satyr, in part
133 "A Chapter on Ears" essayist
134 Brother of Little Joe

by Bob Klahn

ACROSS

1 Duel tool
5 Plant bristle
11 24-hr. service
14 Barbarians
19 Big bargain
20 One of a religious trio
21 Revolutionary name
22 Outlying, in a way
23 Powerful pitcher? (1975)
25 Runabout
26 "___ to bury Caesar . . ."
27 ". . . lamp ___ my feet"
28 Dull and dreary
29 Attempting to score? (1978)
31 "___ the loneliest number"
32 Song
33 Rugged ridge
34 Punch
35 Pageant title
36 Dig
37 Finishes a flight
39 Players
42 Veteran slugger comes out of retirement? (1992)
45 "Any ___?"
46 Anesthetic
47 "Baked in ___" (nursery rhyme phrase)
48 Smelly
49 Plant anew
52 Medicine cabinet item
53 Opposite sides
56 Gymnastics coach Karolyi
57 Unassisted
58 Ump's strange calls? (1984)
60 ___ it all
62 Swimmer's path
63 Lifesaver, maybe
65 Stews
66 High pop-up? (1972)
68 Terrific
69 Shoot in the foot?
70 Chinese flower
71 Author Bates et al.
72 Final word
74 Not absorbed
75 Court plea, briefly
76 Earth covering
77 Soldier's lodging
79 Defensive woes? (1967)

85 "Gunsmoke" star
86 Ocean
87 "She loves me ___"
88 Medical prefix
89 Like the O.G.P.U.
90 "Pudd'nhead Wilson" writer
92 What's more
93 There's nothing like this, in song
94 Batter's new strategy? (1984)
97 Plug up
98 Impolite remark
99 1948 Tommy Dorsey hit
100 Supermodel Carol
101 Base runner's shining moment? (1949)
104 Reagan Cabinet member
105 Begin, with "off"
106 Apollo site
107 So
108 One of the Foys
109 Tack on
110 Zoo showoffs
111 Brit. mil. awards

DOWN

1 Co. founded by Perot
2 Funnel-shaped flower
3 Sincere
4 Snobbery
5 Hotshot
6 Give-away emcees
7 Fence off
8 Fine mist
9 White lie, perhaps
10 A verb for you
11 Grants
12 Parliamentary prospect
13 Kind of scholarship
14 Lively person
15 Response to a jerk?
16 Ticket dispenser
17 Hits the nail on the head
18 Reposes
24 Wallops
29 Film festival site
30 Vetoed
31 Govt. book balancers
36 Plague, with "at"
37 "Evita" Tony winner
38 Proceed (from)

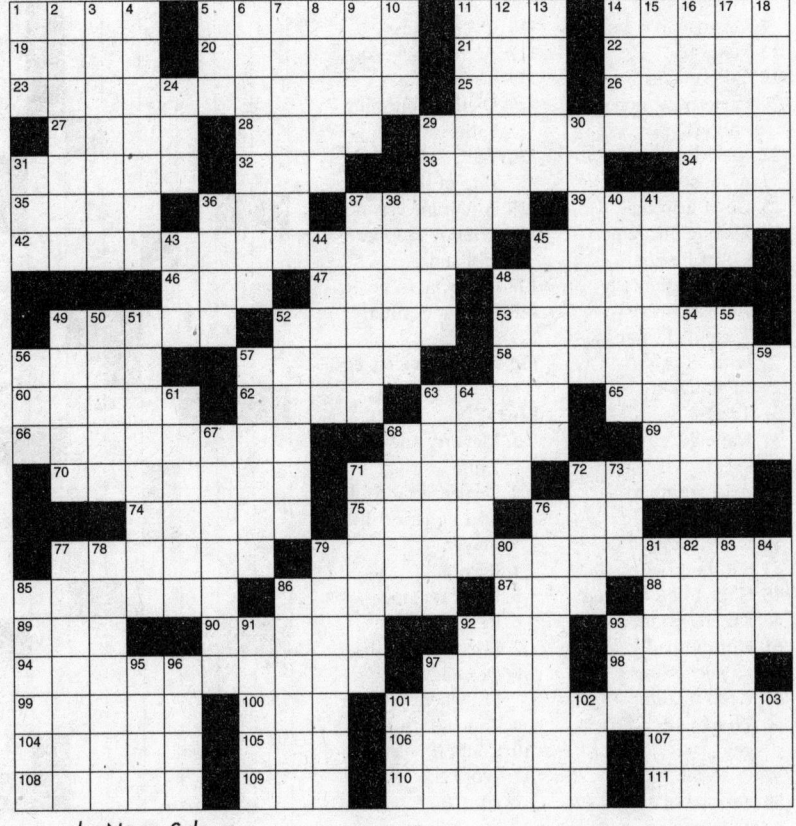

by Nancy Salomon

40 Like the arms in exercise class, at times
41 Toward the center
43 Gone by
44 Draw pile, in cards
45 Take care of
48 Invests with land, in olden times
49 Shoot down
50 Have wedding bells sans wedding bills
51 Not yet completely lost
52 Whipped
54 Inventor Howe
55 Replay feature
56 Many college grads
57 Ready
59 Vane dir.
61 Flynn and others
63 Elapse, as years
64 "What ___ Believes" (Doobie Brothers hit)
67 Woodlands
68 Journalist Heywood
71 Consecrate
72 Lot

73 Hornet's nest
76 More stuffy
77 Sautéed
78 On the guest list
79 Lacked purpose
80 Exalt
81 Like some ancient manuscripts
82 Some check payees
83 Back pain
84 Afore
85 Take on
86 Saved, with "out"
91 "___ way to go!"
92 All-points bulletin
93 Sit-ups toughen them
95 Decree ___ (legal term)
96 Euphoria
97 Heart-to-heart
101 In spite of, in short
102 Baseball execs
103 Article for Cervantes

ACROSS

1 Yacht spot
7 Greenspan's domain
13 Haifa hi
19 Coordinates
20 Eastern European nation
22 Mexican state south of Jalisco
23 Get a grip on
24 Dieting Supreme Court Justice
26 Telly on the telly
27 Aesir member
28 Springfield family, with "The"
29 Radio choice
31 Teach
35 Damage, so to speak
36 Add aroma to
37 Hardly art
39 River through Leeds
43 Set the price
45 Gaps to be bridged
48 Dieting comic
51 Not too badly
53 Physicist Georg
55 April mailing
56 Word with ad or gay
57 Pedestal figure
58 Festival of deliverance
60 On ___ with
61 Nationality suffix
62 Amandine Dupin's pen name
63 Mother of Salome
66 No good
68 Dieting industrialist
72 Sucker seeker
75 Officially, Alcatraz had none
76 Cubemeister Rubik
80 Live
81 1935 Cagney film
84 Miss Webb of "Our Town"
85 Speaking role for Rocky Lane
86 Fisher's gear
87 Virgil hero
90 Manuscript encl.
91 Big rig
92 Dieting actor
95 March honoree, for short
99 Part of Italy
100 Individual
101 Recorded
103 Greek god's blood
105 Wear out
108 Some type: Abbr.

110 Winter Olympics sight
113 Overwhelms
117 Actress Swenson
119 Cassette top
120 Dieting Founding Father
124 With 114-Down, ship of song
125 A hairline can do it
126 "Happy Hooker" Hollander
127 One way to lie
128 Ross and others
129 Socialites
130 Miss Universe, e.g.

DOWN

1 McLarty and the Knife
2 Dispense carefully
3 Dieting baseball player
4 Born
5 Bit of romance
6 Refuse
7 Like taken paths
8 Denzel "St. Elsewhere" co-star
9 Touches up
10 Cool off
11 Word before and after "to"
12 Do alternative
13 Jerk
14 Basketball, slangily
15 Selected athlete
16 Fancy wheels
17 Dodona message
18 Physics calculation
21 Michaels and Martino
25 Laps
27 Scott Turow book
30 Midwest megacampus: Abbr.
32 German pronoun
33 "Dona ___ and Her Two Husbands"
34 Knight time
38 Govt. program for the unemployed
40 Unemployed
41 Hike
42 Lay (in)
43 Sale condition
44 Kind of water
46 Quartets
47 Tuesday type
49 Heartthrob singer Randy
50 Matriculate
52 Former
54 Touchy one

58 Little: Fr.
59 Kind of meat
63 Where Gott resides
64 "Careless Love" novelist Alice
65 Art photos
67 New couples
69 Indiana Senator Richard
70 Got a new roomer
71 Bygone notable
72 Start of a Victor Herbert title
73 Revolted
74 Revolter
77 Dieting Prime Minister
78 Nobody, in ancient Rome
79 Garfield's pal
82 Benefited from
83 Bright, colorwise
88 Nay sayer
89 Pants part
93 Adds on
94 Karlovy Vary is one
96 City north of Livorno

97 Cry of horror, in the comics
98 1989 Paul McCartney song
102 Ruling groups
104 Algonquian language
106 Set
107 "___ of God"
109 Insomnia cause
111 Kind of system
112 Barbecued item
113 Biting comment
114 See 124-Across
115 Branch
116 Driver's license info
118 Relative of the midge
121 Onetime Indian government
122 "___ got it!"
123 Aflame
124 Kid

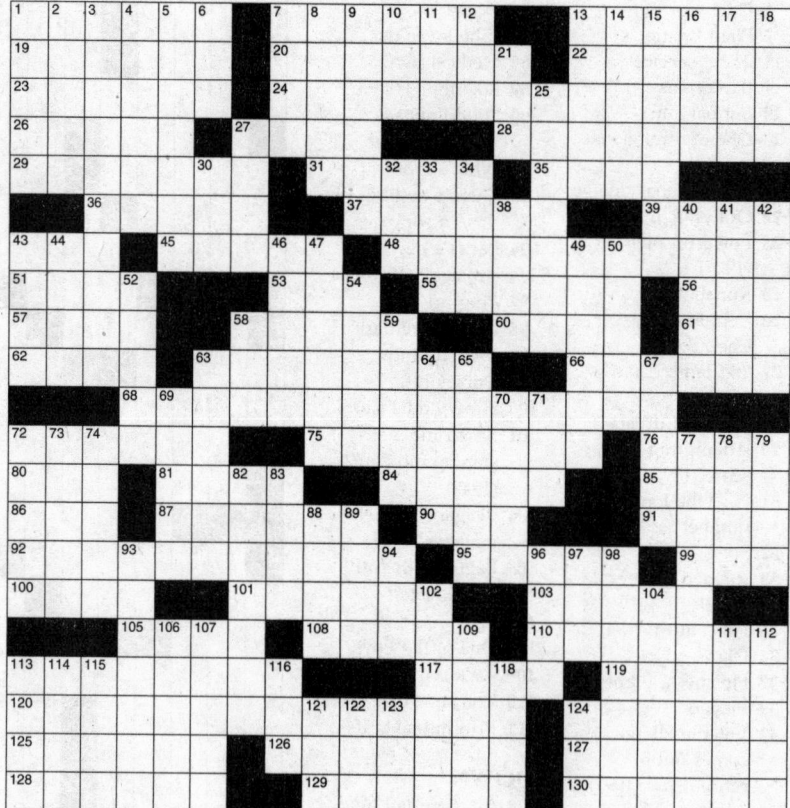

by Matt Gaffney

ACROSS

1 W.W. II female fliers
6 Rice dish
11 Sub sinker, maybe
15 Equestrian need
19 Fully up-to-date
20 Answer to "Who's there?"
21 Grounds
22 Symbol on Pakistan's flag
23 SC★
25 CL★
27 Ones going to court
28 Alternative to Prell
30 Relative of the zebra
31 Has consequences on
34 ___ time
35 "___ With Love"
37 Basque port
38 B★
40 K.C. zone
43 Artist Steinberg et al.
44 "You Don't Mess Around With Jim" singer
45 Urban scavengers
47 Prize for Oprah
48 Surf
49 Things tied up in knots?
50 "Present"
51 Penpoint
52 UNC★H
55 ___ were
56 Key
58 "Stagecoach," e.g.
59 Where some drives end
60 Dakota Indian tribe
62 Horror film staples
64 Stowe villain
65 Beat by a nose
66 Scandinavian gods
67 They may be shafted
68 Noose maker
69 R★ES
72 Typewriter key
75 Asia's ___ Sea
76 Icelandic literary works
77 Squeezes
78 Like some orders
79 Year-after-year
81 "Come back, ___" (1953 movie line)
83 Barbecues badly
84 Presidential inits.
85 Y★H
87 Intergalactic distance
88 "Awake and Sing!" dramatist
89 River past Interlaken
90 Grants
91 Throat soother
94 Word with look or back
95 Large halls
96 DEV★
99 C★URE
104 Take off
105 Architect's curve
106 ___ the line
107 Brief
108 Actress Austin
109 Board go-with
110 New Hampshire town
111 "Got ___ With an Angel" (1931 song)

DOWN

1 "The Red Badge of Courage" topic
2 Paralyze, in a way
3 Pouch
4 Not for sure
5 Iroquoian people
6 Epithet for Louis I, with "the"
7 End of an affliction
8 Eng. course
9 Hospital-clean
10 Home of the Medicis
11 Fish food
12 Directional suffix
13 Officiate
14 Snow shoes
15 Remove trees from
16 Pealed
17 How some cousins are removed?
18 Duke, e.g.
24 Kind of forces
26 Kwanzaa principle
29 Eggs
31 "The Master Builder" playwright
32 Super Bowls VII and VIII champs
33 SP★
34 Spice, e.g.
35 Farmhands
36 Closely observed
38 Buggy
39 Comparatively cloudless
40 CR★ON
41 Magnetic card feature
42 Trypanosome carrier
44 .45, e.g.
46 Bugle's signal
48 Disappear
49 Coin takers
52 Early TV's "___ Three Lives"
53 Ruckuses
54 It's the pits
57 Brosnan TV role
59 Jacks take them
60 Milton's Abdiel, e.g.
61 Likes a lot
62 Flip-flops
63 Fleur-de-lis feature
64 Fabrications
67 Bank deal: Abbr.
69 Dolt
70 Clan head, of old
71 Reuniongoer
73 Square (with)
74 Certain pears
76 Undertaking
78 Clobbered
80 1996 third party organizer
81 Blistered
82 Anne of Green Gables, e.g.
83 Game with 12 wild cards
86 ___ Lorenzo
87 Vamp Negri
88 Actress Cheri of "Saturday Night Live"
90 Fast-talking duck
91 Central computer
92 ___ d'amour
93 Mikhail, e.g.
94 Paragraph
95 Renowned restaurateur
97 "Give it ___"
98 Revivalist, of sorts
100 Former Warsaw Pact member: Abbr.
101 C.P.A. recommendation
102 German direction
103 Born

by Charles M. Deber

ACROSS

1 Auto's high and low
6 Just ___ (not much)
10 Biographer's item
14 Work period
19 ___ in the right direction
20 Reply to the Little Red Hen
21 N.F.L. kicker Matt
22 Novelist ___ Vargas Llosa
23 Where accommodations might give trouble
25 Half of a pop duo
27 Unearned
28 Ruth's land, in the Bible
30 Applauded
31 Like some hair
32 Of the shinbone
34 Wall Street worker, for short
35 Like "sequoia," letterwise
38 Charles Perrault tale
40 Off yonder
44 "___ it!" (gleeful cry)
45 Actress Turner
46 ___-jongg
47 Home of the oldest university in the Americas
48 Big Ten's ___ State
49 Dirty digs
50 Ancient monument
52 Time to attack
53 Blemishes
56 Moving packs
57 Ballet bend
58 Rome's ___ Wall
59 Super
60 Addict
61 Part of an inning
62 Coiffures
66 Chump
67 Yuks
69 Counting method
70 Blank spaces
73 Kind of mitt
74 Stand
77 Virgin, in a way
79 Lacerate
80 Smears
81 Big name in cosmetics
83 Kind of sermon
84 Throw for ___
86 Treatment
87 One with no standing?
88 Marketer's start
89 Drama critic John
90 Some dives
94 Frost lines
96 ___ witch hunt
98 French rocket
99 End piece
100 Whip up
104 Res ___ loquitur
105 Get ready for dinner?
109 Tasty pie filling
111 Noted English diarist
113 Saw
114 Domestic slave
115 Murder
116 Princess' need
117 Five Felipes
118 It's an imposition
119 Chip, maybe
120 Veers

DOWN

1 Bust-up
2 Ice star Phil, to friends
3 Egyptian sun disk
4 Aged
5 Aeronautical maneuver
6 Worked up
7 Beer mug
8 To ___ (exactly)
9 Ouster
10 Secure
11 Thick-trunked African tree
12 German pronoun
13 Public embarrassment
14 Soil
15 Invader of 218 B.C.
16 You can see through it
17 Donizetti's "La ___ du Régiment"
18 Digital
24 Dark blue
26 Wrecks
29 Sash for Cio-Cio-San
32 Air
33 Was imminent
35 Big guns, for short
36 "The Country Girl" playwright
37 Adventurer with Robin
38 Stately dance
39 It's hard to believe
41 Fusses
42 With force
43 Shone
45 Indian water pot
49 Japanese yes
50 Volume units
51 Lock
54 Grumble
55 Biggest stars, briefly
56 "One for My Baby" singer
57 1993 Holly Hunter film, with "The"
59 Abaci
60 Lou Gehrig's number
63 "Three men in ___"
64 Dodges
65 Less frantic
67 Like clock chimes
68 Saint Theresa's birthplace
71 Box: Abbr.
72 Activist Bobby
74 Train
75 Grp. behind Magellan
76 Chaperon
78 Historian Russell and others
81 "Crimes and Misdemeanors" star
82 Moon valley
85 Ward
88 Anguish
91 "Mysterious" place
92 Comedian Russell
93 First degrees
94 Tennessee players
95 Ukases
97 Local screens
99 Ship in a 1951 best-seller
100 Emulsifying agent
101 Former Philly mayor Wilson ___
102 British exclamation
103 Missed the mark
105 Houlihan portrayer
106 Pianist Claudio
107 Made tracks
108 Greece, to modern Greeks
110 Terre Haute sch.
112 Many lifetimes

by Alfio Micci

ACROSS

1 Pops
6 Cards left over from a deal
11 Invited a ticket?
15 Born's partner
19 Parts of villas
20 Handel bars?
21 The Ponte Vecchio crosses it
22 Dalai ___
23 Genius's residence
26 Michele's area of study
28 "___ do" (old hello)
29 State of being late
30 Pan's opposite
32 Site in "Julius Caesar"
33 Sawyer and others
34 Lighting problem?
35 Like many doorways
36 Baby food
39 Sty matriarch
40 Considerably
41 Happy hour order
42 Affirm
44 Bentsen's dental device
50 Defective
53 Size 5 women's shoe
55 Enlists again
56 Asia, with "the"
58 Balzac novel "Le ___ Goriot"
59 Wind: Prefix
60 Women's auxiliary
   of 60-Down: Abbr.
61 Bird back from near
   extinction
63 Testify
64 Start of many horror titles
65 Outhouse site, perhaps
68 Thinly
70 "Owner of a Lonely Heart"
   rock band
71 Having a golden touch
72 Merriment
73 Terrorist cell
74 Stephen King best seller
77 Marriage locale
78 Hebrew for "house of God"
80 Rumble
81 Robber's take
82 It's north of Okla.
83 Mos. and mos.
86 Worse than feeble
89 Shula's shoelace problem
91 Confused
93 Thumb-twiddling
94 Seth or Clarence
96 Spare parts?
97 Desires
98 Admissions chief
99 Bach violin sonata, e.g.
100 22-Across's capital
102 Shinbones
103 Site of semicircular canals
104 With whom Backus quarreled
108 "I cannot tell ___"
109 Nice friend
111 Hatchery sound
112 One who wears stripes
114 Law degree
115 Gypsy
119 Hobo's home
121 The "R" in CORE
124 City north of Lisbon
125 Nursery color
126 Filled
127 Party girl
130 Where a Muppet strolls
132 Sondheim's secret from
    the Feds

135 Noted Harper's Bazaar
    illustrator
136 Words of comprehension
137 One way to be cast
138 Mount
139 During office hours
140 "Mask" star
141 Have the ___ on
142 Married, in a way

DOWN

1 Part of an officer's uniform
2 Emperor of A.D. 69
3 Keene sleuth
4 ___ Jordan
5 Bar-made items?
6 Keepsake
7 Vase handles
8 Cowardly Lion actor
  and family
9 Siouan Indians
10 60's service site
11 One discharged from
   the Navy?
12 Primp
13 Wind dir.
14 Chancel cloth
15 Mont ___
16 Indian prince
17 Overact
18 Adventured
20 Doctor's note?
24 Player at Camden Yards
25 Box score component
27 Sea, in old verse

31 ___ spumante
34 Clerical garb
36 Roman rule
37 New York's Columbus
38 Apostle's wine storage area
40 Venomous viper
41 Moral man?
43 Opposite of hubs
45 ___ of Zeus at Dodona
46 Brewing aid
47 Rump
48 Thieves' locale
49 Wanders
50 Part of actress Garland's
   window
51 Have ___ to play (be of use)
52 Moist, perhaps
54 Piggie
57 Religious essays
58 ___ deux
60 See 60-Across
61 Shoe "treads"
62 Czech river
66 Northern hemispheres?
67 Singer/songwriter John
69 Cheer
71 Says hi
75 Intro for stock or horn
76 Electrical unit
77 "Sweet Liberty" star
78 Tropical African tree
79 Tolkien creatures
80 Euripides tragedy
82 Fried snack
84 Kind of outlet

85 Talked back
86 Ensconce
87 Japanese sliding screen
88 Sun: Prefix
90 1800's U.S. Army rifle
91 Champion crowned 10/30/74
92 Part of a marching band
95 Tattoo dedicatee
100 Kind of soup
101 Very fashionable
102 Candies
105 Link
106 Peninsulas
107 ___ Express
109 They take to the hills
110 Having Coke-bottle glasses?
113 Plump
115 In judicial attire
116 Threepenny entertainment?
117 Mickey Mouse nephew
118 Johnson and others
119 Shopping ___
120 Outdoorsman, perhaps
121 Not an original
122 Farm pest
123 Staff leaders
126 Write over
127 Actor Bogarde
128 Otherwise
129 Blackmailed
131 Firewood choice
133 Make out, in baseball
134 Overmuch

by Brian G. Tyler

284 MYSTERY THEME

The answers to the 22 asterisked (*) clues all have something in common. Can you state what it is?

ACROSS

1 United nations
5 As loud as possible, in music
8 British P.T.A. members
12 Brewer Frederick
17 Gymnastics coach Karolyi
18 Prodigy rival
19 At the bottom
20 Freshen, in a way
21 *Seamy locale
23 Jimmy Dorsey's "Maria ___"
24 *Fruit juice
25 Circulation aid
26 Enriches
27 Dumas duelist
28 Thirds in series
31 Neth. neighbor
33 Sudden bolts of lightning
35 *Gray-brown goose
36 Not miss ___
37 Wiped out
39 Top vaults
40 Stowe tow
41 Hosp. printouts
42 Stranger
44 Projecting angles
46 Twain family name
47 Rival
52 Clear, as tables
53 Surprise hit?
54 Destined for the playoffs
55 Irk
58 *Building ___
59 Finis, in Frankfurt
60 Hwys.
61 *Popular Florida theme park
63 *Pac-Man, e.g.
65 Smelly
66 *Peel
67 Lincoln and others
68 "Wayne's World" co-star
69 Honor
71 Amphorae
72 First word of Burns's "To a Mouse"
73 Any of the Trucial States
74 "I Spy" co-star
75 Shore creature
80 Public image
82 Surrounded
83 Overly adulatory
84 Smooth, as a road
87 Squire
89 Half of "The Odd Couple"
90 ___ world record
91 *Inter follower
92 "Kill ___ killed"
93 Let out
94 Now
96 British biscuit
98 Start of many Spanish place names
100 *Calling a spade a spade
101 Atmospheric probe
102 *Monument
106 Like some old joints
107 Margarine fat
108 "___ we there yet?"
109 Inflict on
110 In singular fashion
111 Picnic hamperer
112 Au contraire, in slang
113 "The tax which all distinction must pay": Emerson

DOWN

1 English channel
2 Composer Delibes
3 Slangy suffix
4 *Italian dish
5 Science events
6 Set of letters
7 Hardly four-star hotels
8 *Alcoholic product of Spain
9 Patron
10 *Bureaucrat
11 Gory film figure
12 One of the elite
13 *Secret
14 Michael Keaton and others, filmwise
15 Laundry woes
16 In telegraphese
19 Poe poem, with "The"
20 Collector's items
22 It may hold the fort
28 Roscoes
29 With 45-Down, author of "My People"
30 *Grist
32 Ogee's outline
34 Last-minute writings
37 Flushing Meadows team
38 Copper
39 Constant
41 Specify
43 Fixed insertion
45 See 29-Down
46 "Merrie Melodies" name
48 Egg classification
49 Essence
50 Swarms
51 First word of Massachusetts' motto
53 Covenant
54 Family members, informally
55 "The Crucible" locale
56 Singer Lopez
57 Duck down
58 *Punish severely
59 Takes the primrose path
61 Cop's order
62 Like some meanings
63 Over-50 org.
64 Word with eagle or bug
67 *Tangerinelike Philippine fruit
70 Rembrandt's "___ of Ganymede"
71 D-Day beach
72 Guarded
74 *Product once advertised as an "esteemed brain tonic"
75 Court official
76 *Transportation provider since 1976
77 *European capital
78 Give ___ up
79 Yorkshire cow shed
81 Snip
82 Jaw
84 Early explosive device
85 Made up
86 *Graffiti artist, e.g.
88 Fuss with feathers
89 "For ___ us a child is born"
90 1921 murder defendant
91 Lofty, as a mountain peak
93 Not satisfied
95 *Like some furnace fuel
97 "The ___ Love" (1987 R.E.M. hit)
99 30's auto
103 Physicist's concern
104 Relative of a dune buggy, for short
105 "The Best Years of Our Lives" co-star

by R. M. Hopkins

ACROSS

1 A Marx brother
6 Orpheus, Heracles et al.
15 Pronunciation symbol
20 Silver companion?
21 Role
22 Defense motions
23 Boat for a tipsy crew?
26 Needles
27 Control tower datum: Abbr.
28 Eur. land
29 Noted family in philanthropy
32 Certain radio stas.
34 70's–80's music genre
39 Bolger co-star
40 In a big way
44 Prize for Toni Morrison
45 Strike out
46 Word between Friends
47 Head honcho
48 Without company
49 Be beholden to
50 "War of the Worlds" base camp
51 Flop
52 Kid's ammo
53 Hoskins role in "Hook"
54 In ___ (going nowhere)
55 Size up
56 Atomic bomb trial, briefly
58 Leaf vegetable
59 Put the cuffs on
60 Related (to)
61 Microsoft product
62 Chickens to cook
64 Fall
67 "Gee" plus
68 From Bratislava
69 Podium-pounding speech
70 Gibson of "Braveheart"
71 Aachen abode
72 Tricked
75 Three-time Presidential nominee
76 Biblical monarchy
78 Author Rand et al.
79 ___-mutuel
80 Unimagined
81 Meter-watcher
82 Russia's St. Alexander ___
84 They pass bills
85 Business magazine
86 Daughter of David
87 Witch
88 Rhône / Saône city
89 Imprecise ordinal
90 Kind of driver
91 Write, as computer programs
93 Penthouse reader
94 Prepare
96 That, to Pedro
97 Brit's word of surprise
99 Baseball's Master Melvin
100 ___ stretch (serve time)
102 Forbidden fruits, e.g.
105 Diagram error at a naval museum?
114 Norelco competitor
115 Old office group
116 Black Bears' town
117 Captain of the Caine
118 One who goes along
119 Gettysburg general George

DOWN

1 F.D.R.'s successor
2 German "alas"
3 Potential perch
4 Scotch
5 Not yet named
6 Bridge honors
7 50's South Korean leader
8 Cheesecake feature
9 ___ pro nobis
10 Not wide: Abbr.
11 Take the role of
12 Gas or elec. co.
13 Canvas stretchers
14 Asian honorific
15 Diamond play?
16 Crossword maker, at times
17 Coop dweller
18 Female enlistee, once
19 Bit of air pollution
24 Ill-considered
25 Bedding
29 "M*A*S*H" director
30 Most of Libya
31 With 36-Down, gem of the Persian navy?
32 Caen cop
33 Naval expression of regrets?
35 Bad news for twin middies at Annapolis?
36 See 31-Down
37 Crows
38 Fouled, in a way
41 Petty officer's petty remark?
42 Au ___ (menu phrase)
43 "Barnaby Jones" star
44 Turtlenecks hide them
51 Mountebank
53 Met home
57 Service station service
58 Weeks in duo anni
63 Dr. Michael of "Peyton Place"
65 Russia's ___ Mountains
66 Beat soundly
67 Fly trap
68 Refuses
69 Twice quinze
70 Scotland yard?
71 Devastation
73 Biological ring
74 Theme park name
75 Deliver
77 Industrial strength
79 Handyman's work?
81 Taste
83 Mr. Rubik
86 Mao follower
92 Black
95 Lawn game played with mallets
96 "...could ___ lean"
98 Commercial eye-catchers
101 Crude group?
102 Occupational deferment category in the 60's draft
103 Schoenberg's "Moses and ___"
104 Cloth measure
105 Letters on a charcoal sack
106 ___ Islands, southwest of New Guinea
107 ___ Dawn Chong of "Quest for Fire"
108 Snake sound
109 50's dance
110 N.T. book
111 Soldier for 7-Down
112 Chemical suffix
113 Sister of Selene

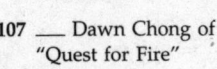
by Manny Nosowsky

ACROSS

1 Soprano Teresa
8 Relieves
14 Jalopies
20 Get along peacefully
21 Common sweetener
22 Oust
23 Trattoria serving
25 Choice word
26 Stephen of "The Crying Game"
27 Pied-à-___
28 Die ___ (German elite)
30 Bambi's aunt
31 "___ right with the world"
33 At least R-rated
35 Inoperative
36 Kind of joint
37 Nightclub
39 1955 Disney dog
40 Cheviot sounds
41 "When We Were Very Young" writer
42 Shaped roughly, as stone
44 Laws-to-be
46 Prison camps
47 Out for the night
48 Ballet move
49 ___ the saddle (proud)
51 Site of the Piltdown man hoax
54 Cliché-in-the-making
56 Chinese porcelain
59 Highlander's pattern
60 Word among Friends
61 Waistbands
63 Buddy
64 Part of I.L.G.W.U.: Abbr.
65 Everglade
66 Novel conclusions
67 Hustler from Minnesota
68 Dept. of Transportation agcy.
69 Stand for
70 Things to pay
71 Java flavoring
72 Olympics event since 1896
74 John Wayne productions
76 Starter of a sort
77 Brutalize
79 On the qui ___
80 Outfit
81 Vehicle stickers, e.g.
83 Tractor name
85 Certain acid salts
89 Widely sighted figure
90 "___ for All Seasons"
91 Sports org.
93 Shumagin islander
94 Part of A.F.L.-C.I.O.: Abbr.
95 Sorority letters
96 Kind of humor
98 To be, to Babette
99 June bug
100 Railroad mechanism
102 TV workers' union, for short
104 Step on the gas
105 Store fodder
107 Popular dessert
110 Help around the office
111 Ogata Korin painting
112 Tutsi or Hutu national
113 One who's quizzed
114 Tardy arriving
115 Man-becomes-cobra flick of 1973

DOWN

1 Egyptian symbols
2 "Wild Thing" rapper
3 Royal duds
4 Jack's tool
5 Pinball goof
6 Residue
7 All shook up
8 Difference between prices bid and asked
9 High point
10 60's tripper Timothy
11 Amphora
12 Summery
13 Littoral
14 Something to believe in
15 Harness part
16 Quantity: Abbr.
17 1955 Audie Murphy flick
18 Prime-time time
19 Shawls
24 "___ the news today, oh boy" (Beatles lyric)
29 Welcome words
32 Fourth-century church father

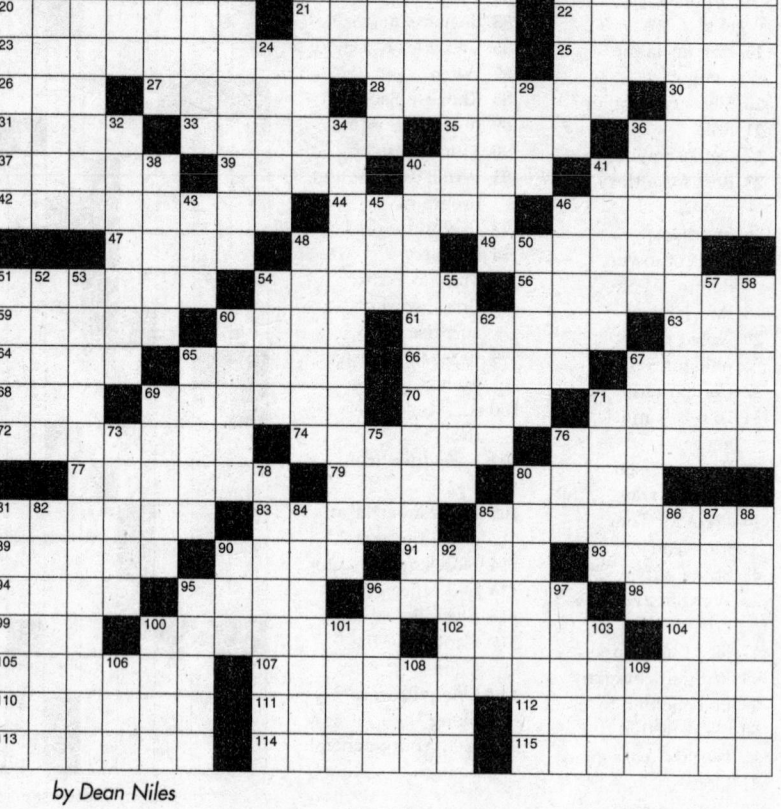

by Dean Niles

34 Gene Austin's five-million-seller
36 Eyelashes
38 Fell off
40 Birth, so to speak
41 Meditates
43 Superman foe Luthor
45 Three, of a kind
46 Chorus songs
48 "Shazam!"
50 Feels (for)
51 Neaten, with "up"
52 Forearm bones
53 1989 best seller, with "The"
54 "Comin' ___ the Rye"
55 Full-fledged
57 One ___ other
58 Have ___ in the matter
60 Strong flavors
62 Starts of many Québec place names
65 Screen lists
67 Moving words
69 Particular pickles

71 Source of igneous rock
73 Filmmaker René ___
75 French shooting match
76 Whisper sweet nothings
78 English king called Ironside
80 Quislings
81 Least exciting
82 Los Angeles suburb
84 American rival, once
85 Rocky Mountains park
86 Double duos
87 Some vacuum cleaners
88 Ginsburg colleague
90 Sports org.
92 Gliding step
95 "___ Dreams" (1986 pop hit)
96 1974 pension provision: Abbr.
97 Plains people
100 ___-eyed
101 Infamy

103 Nabokov heroine et al.
106 Savings acct. abbr.
108 Permit
109 Brain and spinal cord: Abbr.

ACROSS

1 Ball
4 Handouts
7 "Like, stupid!"
10 Reprimand viciously, in slang
16 Make suitable for family viewing, e.g.
18 Close-fitting clerical garment
20 Chest
21 70's White House name
22 Less compromising
23 Kickback
24 Crazy bird?
26 Tied article of apparel
28 "Happy Birthday" writer
29 Doesn't forgive and forget
30 Concluded
32 "___-ce pas?"
33 Computer interface jack
34 Forecast info, for short
38 Attendance notation
40 Silver or blue follower
41 Belly
42 "Butterfield 8" author
46 Geronimo and kin
50 Hudson Bay settlers
53 Brash
54 Secure by tying down
55 Recorder abbr.
56 Mister abroad
57 Play period
58 Barbara, to friends
59 Dressing ingredient
61 Kama ___
62 "Bummer!"
63 Bird's privileges?
66 Kind of test
69 Nubs
71 Election results
72 Numbskull
73 Outdo
75 The Andrews Sisters, e.g.
77 Part of an Egyptian headdress
78 Colonial suitor
79 Subjects of New Age study
80 1989 Winona Ryder movie
82 Comic John
83 Marquises, e.g.
84 Jackie's second

85 "The ___ Tale" (Chaucer segment)
87 Pines
89 Car with Teletouch transmission
90 Polish's partner
94 Schlep
97 Duplicity
100 The sea personified
102 Kind of game
103 Spanish bear
104 Cultural bird-geoning?
108 Like some reasoning
110 Helped
112 Perthshire pattern
113 Vocalize
114 Was excited
115 Fairy folk
116 Reps
117 Convened
118 Personal ___
119 Ile surrounder

DOWN

1 "Food, Glorious Food" musical
2 New-sprung
3 Since, colloquially, with "as"
4 Grp.
5 Trace
6 Something one can't do
7 Step lively
8 A, as in Arles
9 Dueling bird?
10 Sort
11 "What ___ . . ." (cry of surprise)
12 Dating a young bird?
13 "It's ___ to the finish"
14 Clotho, Lachesis and Atropos
15 Push
16 "Superb!"
17 Artist's range of options
19 Speaker of baseball
21 Police operation
25 ___-friendly
27 Arrests
31 Reno transaction
35 Measuring (out)
36 Shopper's burden
37 Relative of reggae
39 Multipart composition
40 Short
43 Prefix, of sorts

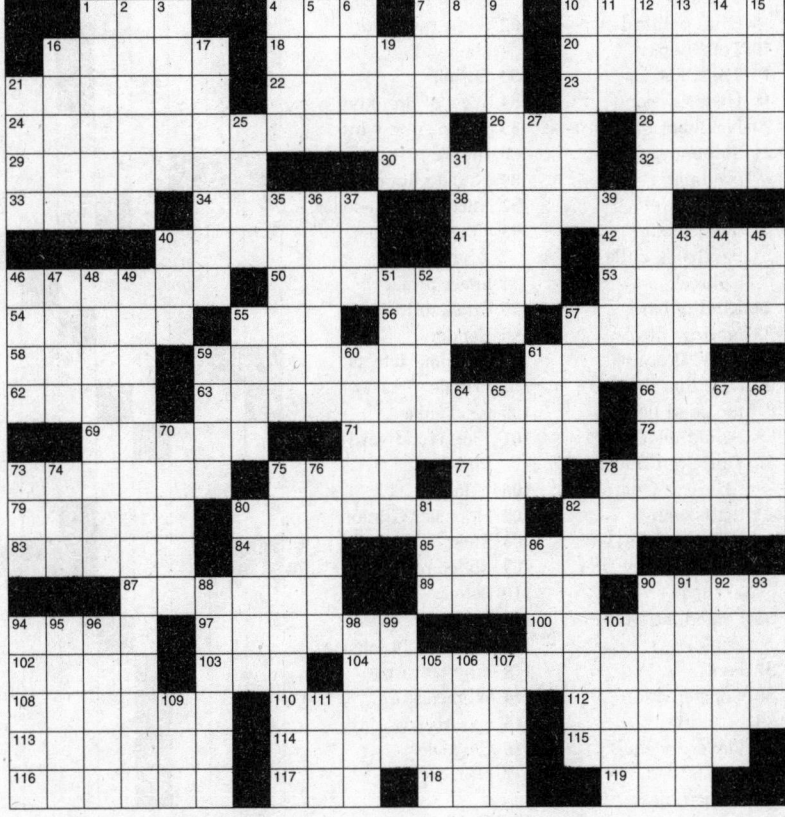

by Norma Steinberg

44 Vacation homes, for short
45 Old-style exclamations
46 Group that did "I Do, I Do, I Do, I Do, I Do"
47 Knell
48 Long-finned tuna
49 What a suspicious bird will do?
51 Ruler in Exodus
52 Cause of worry
55 War statistics
57 Old bandleader Morgan
59 No. 2
60 Understand
61 Part of a process
64 Expressed anger, in a way
65 Villain's earful
67 March time
68 Ready to eat
70 Ballet ___
73 It runs in the woods
74 Vietnamese city
75 Treacherous birds?
76 Hike

78 TV's Bundy and others
80 Symbols of speed
81 Prior to
82 Madame ___, French dancer of old
86 Start of Caesar's boast
88 Flips over, so to speak
90 More than fast
91 Special team member, in football
92 Conquerees of 1533
93 YM competitor
94 Actress Shire
95 Due (to)
96 French relation
98 "___ my Maypo!"
99 High school math
101 Song of David
105 First name in jazz
106 Impecuniosity
107 Puts on
109 Certain soldier
111 Trajan's way

288 FULL MARKS

ACROSS

1 Supreme
5 Ohio political clan
10 Tots' pops
15 Thus: Lat.
18 Historic island
20 Neighbor of Taurus
21 Sorbonne, par exemple
22 Thoughtful interjection
23 Baseball's Little Colonel
24 Kind of bar
25 Narrow furrow
26 W.W. II org.
27 "___ that this too too solid flesh would melt"
30 Paul Scott novels "The ___ Quartet"
31 Staffs anew
32 Met tenor, 1941–66
33 Allied victory site, 7/18/44
34 Dotted, as a coat of arms
37 Fool
38 Consternation
39 ___ torte
41 Player for the angels?
43 Three-time American League M.V.P.
44 Old college, e.g.
45 Syrian chief and namesakes
46 ___ favor
47 Sixth-century date
50 "Fantasia" dancer
53 Sleep: Prefix
54 Had not been
58 Food whose name means "lightning"
60 Cabinet dept.
61 Cries of surprise
62 Inventory abbr.
63 Playwright Christopher
64 Column ending
65 Overseas denial
66 Part of overalls
67 Some clinic workers: Abbr.
68 Skater Babilonia
69 Half of sechs
70 It's often cast
71 Comeback
73 "Repeat the name, please"
77 "That's ___ question"
80 Make sense
81 O'Hara's "___ North Frederick"
82 Some cards, for short
83 Shrink
84 West of Brooklyn
85 Breaks, in a way
88 Induce
89 Noted puppeteers
92 Michener best-seller
93 "You know what . . ."
94 Space prefix
95 Ethel, to John Jr.
96 Render
98 Old-time actress Pringle
100 ___ Lanka
101 1968 Woodward film
106 "Mazel ___!"
107 Hoopster Gilmore
108 Burst
109 Rodeo rope
110 Before
111 Implied
112 Discombobulated
113 Tiny tantrums
114 Women's org.
115 ___ Ababa
116 Clientele
117 Near-rapture

DOWN

1 Much-admired sandwich?
2 Riverboat Robert ___
3 Michael in "Family Ties"
4 Bankbook balancer's problem
5 Part of a fore-and-after
6 Parliament chasers
7 Formal orders
8 Singer Basil
9 Spy
10 Outlaw
11 Hunt and Peck
12 Alternative to Corinthian
13 Puts straight
14 Hassock
15 Like some missiles
16 Stick
17 Key of Sibelius' Symphony No. 7
19 Bosox pitcher Aaron
28 Roll up
29 About
33 Collectible money
34 Former potentate
35 Good-tempered
36 Wyler film of 1942
38 1976 Abba hit
40 Greece's Mount ___
42 Poster subject
43 Jackson and others
46 In sections
48 Lines from Willard Scott
49 Postulate of 1637
51 Strokes
52 Financial page abbr.
54 Most sapient
55 1949 Doris Day hit
56 Incubator babies
57 Knocks over
59 It follows a million
63 Saudi king
67 Mortgage holder's action
68 United rival
69 Flimflammed
72 African board game
74 Oil can, maybe
75 Fascinations
76 Spots
78 Soviet scientist Kurchatov
79 Gambling haven
83 Actor Jon
86 Skating pioneer Paulsen
87 Creator of the character Bip
88 Tropical trees used in golf ball manufacture
89 Helped brown the turkey
90 Light show
91 Gaped
92 Sesame seed paste
93 Smirk
97 Outward, to an anatomist
98 Divert
99 Up to one's ___
101 Hindu epic hero
102 The makings of a stew
103 Rain hard?
104 Wagon add-on
105 Emit coherent light

by Robert H. Wolfe

ACROSS

1 Panchen ___ (spiritual leader)
5 Overload
10 Fail to mention
14 Short end of the stick
18 Spirit
19 Locked passageway
20 Mr. Agnew
21 Diminish
22 Which came first, the chicken or the egg?
24 Subject of 1962's Best Picture
26 Lowered
27 Bird hunter's shelter
29 Intensify
30 ___ generis
31 Writer O'Faoláin et al.
32 "Sorry, I can't come"
33 Spicy cuisine
38 Experiences
39 Grow accustomed
40 Noted war story
41 Pet rocks, once
42 Extinct bird
45 Warship of old
46 Property may have these
47 Lawn care product
48 Curse
49 Out of favor
53 End of a fitting phrase
55 Hash
56 More cowlike?
57 Convenient
59 Provoked
60 Persisted
63 Castigates
65 Overhead
68 Some parties
70 Crusades combatant
74 Sir Freddie of Skytrain
75 Kudzu, e.g.
76 Zap
78 Open slightly
79 Third man
81 Golfer Calvin
83 Northernmost city of ancient Palestine
84 Right to decide
85 ___ tectonics
86 Record
87 "Kiss an Angel Good Mornin'" country singer
89 Enjoys, with "in"
90 Takes to heart
92 ___ Springs, Colo.
95 Histrion
96 ___-o'-shanter
97 Click beetle
98 Geometrical solid
99 Emulate Voltaire
104 Gainsay
106 Flabbergasted
108 It needs to be broken
109 Polite refusal
110 Some cheeses
111 Miracle site
112 Distantly
113 Flowering shrub
114 Coup ___
115 Scout's handiwork

DOWN

1 Impart
2 Ship's direction
3 Impair
4 Kicks in, initially
5 Suitable for a postcard
6 Sale item
7 It was given by St. Nicholas
8 Staff, in a way
9 Common
10 Bids one club
11 Temperate
12 A Gershwin
13 Allergy victim's fate
14 Asseverates
15 "La plume de ma ___"
16 Intact
17 Page noises
20 Abscam, for one
23 Frequent
25 Groove for a sliding door
28 Orbiting photographer
31 One who gets a lift?
32 Clear of debris
33 Antilles native
34 "A Bell for ___"
35 House supports
36 Crude container
37 Mélange
38 One response to a challenge
41 Scrub
42 Flash Gordon's foe
43 Previously
44 Canceled
48 Puzzle type
50 Letter closing
51 Nostalgic film of 1982
52 Multivolume ref.
54 Tommy Dorsey's "___ Is It"
55 Transport to the Tuileries
57 Gulf of ___
58 Make out
61 Fixes firmly
62 Baby Doc Duvalier, e.g.
64 DeSoto or Hudson
65 Sadly
66 Californian's vacation spot, informally
67 Approve
69 Thinks better of
71 Port NW of Gibraltar
72 Get clear of
73 Barcelona babies
76 Foot pattern?
77 Passage
79 Losers
80 Kasparov's birthplace
82 Holed up, in a way
85 Dad
87 Black Watch, for one
88 Canyon's edge
89 Acrimonious
90 More slippery
91 Corroborate
92 Hajj objective
93 Cool
94 ___ Devi (second-highest peak in India)
95 Football Hall-of-Famer Herber
98 Coin of Chihuahua
99 Kind of team
100 Heroine of Tennessee Williams's "Summer and Smoke"
101 Mr. Lendl
102 Paradoxical philosopher
103 Part of Q.E.D.
105 TV knob abbr.
107 Jonson wrote one to himself

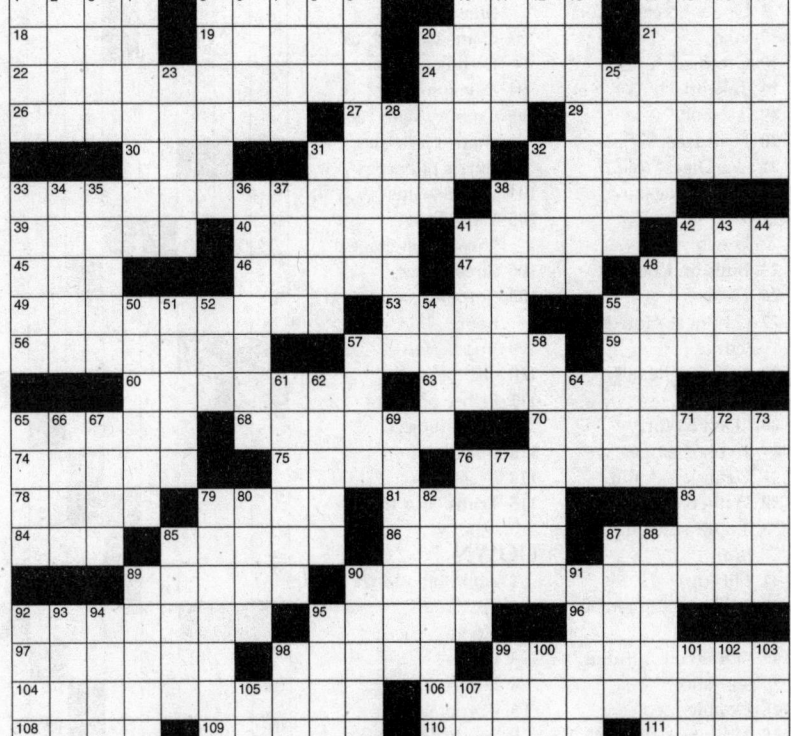

by Ted Fulton

ACROSS

1 Mel Tormé piece
5 One who can take a joke
10 Gratified
14 Takeoff
19 ___-poly
20 Fruit tree
21 ___ Digest (old flying magazine)
22 The "C" in C.S. Lewis
23 Bulls and Bears
26 Havens
27 City near Horseshoe Curve
28 Follows illegally
29 Clear
30 "Don't Worry Kyoko" singer
31 Uganda's Amin
32 Withered
33 Triple witching hour
41 Fill (up)
45 Ballet's ___ marché
46 Spurious
47 "Orfeo ed Euridice" soprano
48 Double-reed
49 Mountain-climbing challenges
52 Symbol of noncaring
53 Abecedarian phrase
54 Starting point
55 Stockholder
59 Act rudely on the dance floor
60 Amphitheaters
61 "___ Johnny!"
62 Hens, in a way
63 Pants material
64 Illustrious
65 Intensive care conditions
66 Throughout, in music
68 Lowly ones
69 Partner of won
70 "___ Muchachos" (1932 song)
71 Watered stock
76 Kind of help
77 Downwind
78 Facilitation
79 Come out the same
80 Eurasian duck
81 Fortas and Burrows
82 Villa features
84 Bibliographical suffix
85 Maneuverable
86 Book value

91 Start for "Around" and "Ideas" in song titles
93 Comedian Bill, to friends
94 Raven maniac?
95 Country with its shape on its flag
98 Bursts of energy
101 Like Sibelius
105 Words never "heard" on stage
106 Street name
108 Certain secondhand items
109 Impression
110 Off the wall
111 Prince of opera
112 Code subject
113 In the vicinity
114 Privations
115 Trims, as a tree

DOWN

1 Abbr. on a letter to Spain
2 Hood
3 Loads
4 Forbes 400 sort
5 Corporate split
6 South American rodent
7 1940's inflation fighter: Abbr.
8 Poverty, so to speak
9 Double-cross
10 Manx language family
11 Reporter's news source
12 Treaty subject
13 Computer acronym
14 Ransack
15 Spot market
16 Compiègne's river
17 Hot spot
18 Event suffix
24 Fine-tune
25 Vocal fanfare
29 Old-time comic Lew
32 Go piece
33 Juvenile protection grp.
34 Dear, in Tuscany
35 Comic dictionary compiler Evan
36 Chance happening
37 Musical medleys
38 Prelate's title: Abbr.
39 Like juicy turkeys
40 1964 Disney boy and others
42 Slows down
43 Private reply

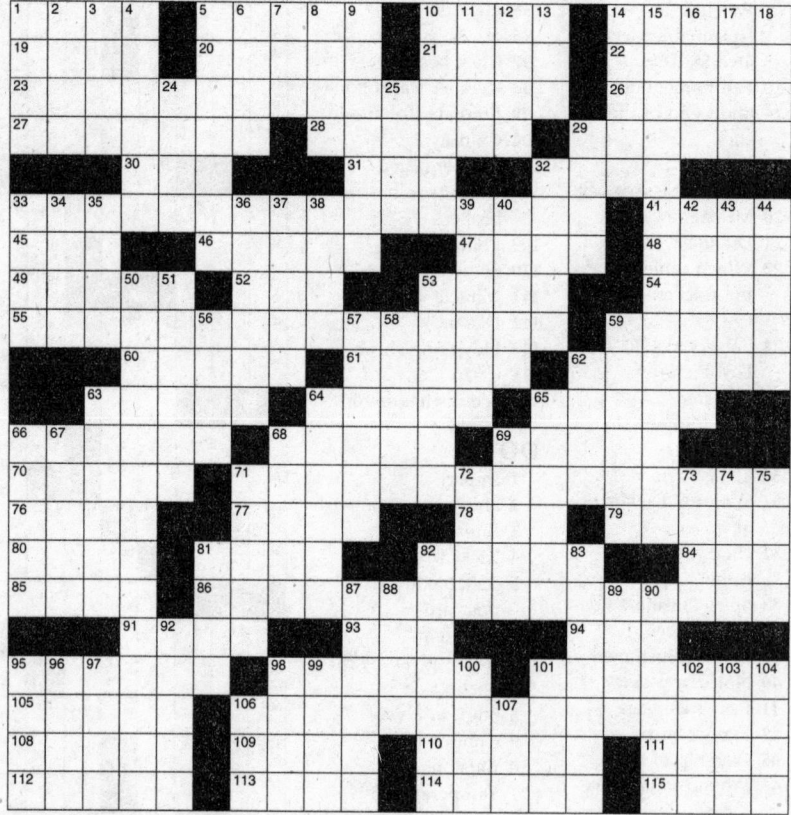

by Norman S. Wizer

44 Wails
50 Odd lot
51 Bank patrons
53 Still
56 Fill a hold
57 Don't sit on the fence
58 Prudential competitor
59 Brownie
62 Spoils
63 Happy face
64 Most up-to-date
65 Help revise
66 Nickname for Sarah Vaughan
67 Puffiness
68 Explorers' destinations
69 Fan sounds
71 Bruce ___, Fay Wray's "King Kong" co-star
72 Site of some Sargent paintings
73 River to the Caspian
74 Barry of "Bat Masterson"

75 Audition
81 Whizzes
82 Sit on one's hands?
83 Has dreams
87 Eyepiece, in jargon
88 Mold
89 Years on end
90 Progresso soup variety
92 It can be wild
95 It can be wild
96 European river that connects a network of canals
97 Mouthpiece?
98 "No Ordinary Love" singer
99 Appeal
100 Kind of curve
101 Affectionate
102 Othello's ancient
103 Knock off
104 For the lady
106 Success
107 Scottish dissent

ACROSS

1 Jackson 5 hit of 1970
4 Mexican dictator Porfirio
8 Get with the tines
13 Ernie Banks' team
17 Exclamations from Ebenezer
19 Oxford's "Gloomy Dean"
20 Lamented
22 ___ were (so to speak)
23 Every morning the klutz ___
26 California wine region
27 Cite
28 Got down
29 Address
31 Drink rudely
33 At dance marathons the klutz ___
37 Holdup
38 Hardly feisty
39 Looped crosses
40 Work on a submarine
41 Rotund plus
43 Book with St. Paul's story
46 Average
49 One by one the klutz ___
55 Suffix with fail
56 Application
57 Press
58 Decked
60 Comedian Mort
63 As a day-care worker the klutz ___ . . .
68 Faultily
70 Chow mein chaser
71 Foreign market, for short
72 Florida city
73 . . . and in so doing the klutz ___
79 Sanction misdeeds
80 Mosaic piece
81 Whit
82 Music center?
84 Poetic preposition
85 On the way home the klutz often ___
93 But: Lat.
94 Ones: Abbr.
95 Opponent of Tom and Harry in 1948
96 Eggs
97 Wagon alternative
101 Color of le ciel
102 Dogpatch denizen
104 At surprise dinners the klutz ___
110 Freetown money
111 "Guernica" painter
112 Epithet of Athena
113 Peeping Tom
115 Café addition
116 In a final desperate move the klutz ___
122 Archer of film
123 Become understood
124 Mauna Loa locale
125 Mr. Rubik
126 Threads
127 "Bells Are Ringing" composer
128 Bollix (up)
129 "Sure!"

DOWN

1 Tummy muscles
2 Cotillion: Fr.
3 Little boy, in Barcelona
4 Losing proposition
5 Obliged
6 Past
7 Satori-seeking sect
8 Canine show?
9 Assume as fact
10 Her day is April 22
11 It ends in diciembre
12 Like some Christians
13 Unfinished Pound epic
14 Allegheny, today
15 Rifle stand, e.g.
16 Athletes Mikita and Musial
18 Incites
21 Moore's "10" co-star
24 Ring tab successors
25 Cod kin
30 "Alas," in Augsburg
31 Get rid of
32 Cordelia's father
34 Impulsive
35 Buddhists' sacred peak
36 Lessen
42 Complain
43 Place for a pick
44 Brag
45 Plated, in a way
46 State of India
47 Anatomical ring
48 Certain chiropter
50 Beats
51 Rock's ___ Vicious
52 John ___ Garner
53 Banned insecticide
54 Noted art district
59 Phrase in an entirely new way
60 Stir-fries
61 Volt-___ (watt's equivalent)
62 Sounded angry
64 Revolutionary Allen
65 Shelter, on ships
66 Shoestrings
67 National anthem contraction
69 Suffix with trick or prank
74 Song syllable
75 Off-Broadway's "___ Baltimore"
76 Skater Midori et al.
77 ___-di-dah
78 Stout's sleuth Wolfe
83 1990's peacekeeping site
86 "___ It a Pity?"
87 Mallorca, e.g.
88 Filmdom's Anna
89 Vegetable capital?
90 Like some memberships
91 Fair
92 One-in-a-million
97 Schedules
98 Chicago Loop group
99 They get into rows at school
100 Aphrodite's beloved
101 Droplet
103 Pioneer bathyspherist William
104 Water balloon sound
105 It provides a sounding board
106 Aeronautical worry
107 ___ Sack (beanbag toy)
108 "The Magic Kingdom" novelist Stanley
109 Designer Geoffrey
114 Specialists
117 Mich. neighbor
118 Resistance unit
119 Contend
120 Compass point
121 Bests, in bouts

by Cathy Millhauser

ACROSS

1 Tess Durbeyfield's seducer
5 In a good lookout position
9 Game saver, at times
13 Word of woe
17 Beans
19 He played Ugarte in "Casablanca"
21 Word ending a radio announcement
22 Mona ___
23 REAGAN, TO BUSH
25 ARMY CRITTERS?
27 Persevering
28 Shaggy-maned mammal
30 Gaucho's home
31 Booty
32 Mickey and Mighty
33 Fluff
34 Milton hero
37 PARTS
40 Taj Mahal city
44 ___ mode
45 Almost
47 Reinforcement
48 In medias ___
49 Festival
51 Tom of the T-M Bar Ranch
52 Logo
55 ___ blanche (sword)
56 CLEANING-RELATED
60 Comets' heads
61 It often comes with a twist
63 Onetime Dodge model
64 1983 Michener best seller
65 Signs of boredom
66 Barbershop sounds
67 Dumas's "The Black ___"
68 Mugged, maybe
70 Jim Backus provided his voice
71 Kids' board game
73 One who's starstruck
74 TUNA SALAD STAPLE
76 Vituperates, with "into"
78 Traveler's aid
80 Consoles, perhaps
81 Flappers?
82 Printers' measures
83 Casino equipment
85 Most parched
88 Court matter
89 Retardant
91 QUADRENNIAL EVENT
93 Rubs out
95 Some banks have them
97 Chop-chop
98 Cordon ___
99 Equus hemionus
102 Prearrange
104 The Yankee Clipper
108 JUST-IN-CASE CRAFT
110 FIX-UPS
112 Quotation notation?
113 Shoo, to Socks
114 Working stiff
115 Conductor Koussevitzky
116 Monster's home?
117 Novel ending
118 Fox hunt cry
119 Summer shirts

DOWN

1 Sacred serpents
2 Tradition has it
3 Gazed upon
4 BAYOU RESIDENTS
5 Alaskan people
6 Start of a bowl game
7 Heraldic golds
8 Rectitude
9 ___ avail (fruitless)
10 Stratford stream
11 Increase the r.p.m.'s
12 Said "Let's wed"
13 Wellesley grad
14 Speaketh?
15 Drifting
16 Smart talk
18 Gunfight site, in films
20 Longtime Susan Lucci role
24 Singer Peter
26 Rabbit's foot
29 Milosevic, e.g.
32 Year in the reign of Louis VII
33 Transferable print
34 "Lonesome Dove" genre
35 Wake-up call
36 VERBAL BLUNDER
37 African antelope
38 Bandleader Shaw and namesakes
39 1962 film "___ Bulba"
41 TENSE STUDENTS?
42 Did not premiere
43 "You ___ For It" (old Art Baker show)
46 Approvals
50 Bubbly
53 ___ des Beaux-Arts
54 "Le Misanthrope" author
56 Lucky strike
57 Arthur Murray lesson
58 Rigel's locale
59 G.O.P. birthplace
62 Poetic contraction
64 All-natural
66 Skater David
67 Cup of café
68 Goaded, with "on"
69 Volcano's opening?
70 Colognes
71 Mannerly
72 Berlin's river
74 Rivers and others
75 Walk into ___
77 J.F.K. drop-ins
79 Cowslip
84 Tiff
85 Curtains
86 Onetime march site
87 Dog rewards
90 Heathens
92 Seize the throne
94 SHAKESPEAREAN LASS
96 Thrice, in prescriptions
98 Pull-up assister
99 Wang Lung's wife
100 Diamond group
101 Judean prophet
102 Immediately, to a surgeon
103 Ferrara family
104 Avant-garde writer Floyd
105 Al from Tennessee
106 "The Dark at the Top of the Stairs" playwright
107 Sugars
109 Don't just sit there
111 A deer, a female deer

by Charles M. Deber

ACROSS

1 "Class Reunion" author
6 From head to foot
13 Mild cigar
18 Operatic barber
19 Immediate
20 Saudi king, 1964–75
21 Start of a verse
24 Behind
25 One of the Germans
26 Makes a collar
27 Storm heading
28 He drew laughs from his "Well!"
30 Layer
31 Subject of medical advice
35 "The Prisoner of ___"
36 Marryin' ___ of "Li'l Abner"
37 ___ uproar
41 Plenty, to FitzGerald
42 Comic Sahl
43 Antique description
44 "Peter Pan" dog
45 More of the verse
51 Filmdom's Alastair
52 Where to see Gérard Depardieu
53 "X-Files" extra
54 Davis of "Evening Shade"
55 Bridge type
57 "Phèdre" playwright
59 Pollen bearer
60 Eagle wearer
62 Solidly based
64 Brightly colored wrap
67 1963 Broadway hit
69 British aristocracy
73 Month of the año
74 Pundit
75 Norway's patron saint
76 "That makes me mad!"
77 More of the verse
82 Greek oil-flask
83 Let up
84 Stiff in the joints
85 ___ European
86 Glamour founder
87 Julienne, e.g.: Abbr.
88 Pitches, as hay
90 Late, great saxophonist Gordon
92 Erwin of early TV
93 Immediately
94 ___ of ale

95 More wan
99 Oviform : egg :: dolabriform : ___
100 Fell back
105 End of the verse
109 Morning prayer
110 Grevious, to grandma
111 1990 Stanley Cup champs
112 Kind of theater
113 Makes effervescent
114 Song of triumph

DOWN

1 Foolin'
2 Teen follower
3 "M*A*S*H" co-star
4 Kind of pan
5 Tertiary Period epoch
6 Wax-glazed fabric
7 Black cuckoo
8 Letter addenda
9 Come to
10 "The Magic Flute" heroine
11 ___ case
12 S.A.T. company
13 Stone landmark
14 Bowl of cherries, maybe
15 Store warning
16 Carry on
17 Cutlass, e.g., informally
18 Certain investigator
20 Panel heads
22 Historic Eur. inits.
23 Arid
28 Chip off the old ice block
29 Tolkien tree-men
31 Believer in one God on rational grounds
32 Broadcasting
33 Amiens's river
34 Hardware item
35 Taxi map division
36 Shiny material
37 Juli of the L.P.G.A.
38 J. Carrol ___, TV's Charlie Chan
39 Poe poem "For ___"
40 Raider Ralph
42 Sal ___, the Switchblade Kid
43 Emmy winner Rob
46 Paper nautilus, e.g.
47 ___-de-Paris, France
48 W.W. II enlistee
49 Blue bloods
50 Brian of "Beau Geste"

56 Sin color?
57 Pertain
58 Go out on ___
59 Shipboard position
61 Not at all
63 Marquand's late George
64 Attach, as a button
65 "Waterworld" girl
66 Enlists again
68 Fight (for)
70 Envoy
71 Year in school
72 Slip
74 Height
75 Noted newspaper publisher
78 Home makers
79 Japan's first capital
80 Repugnant, to Junior
81 Fort near Trenton
88 More shrewd
89 Classic Bee Gees album
90 Whipped cream serving
91 And others

92 Tuscany tourist locale
93 Western lake
94 Pellet
95 Fine cotton
96 In the distance
97 Where it's at
98 Certain movie theater
100 Bartender's bottles
101 1944 Pulitzer journalist
102 "Did you ever ___ lassie . . . ?"
103 Gross, so to speak
104 No and Dre, e.g.
106 USAir rival
107 Cousin of "huh?"
108 Soul, in Sens

by Frances Hansen

ACROSS

1 Card game with four jokers
8 Lovebird's phone question
14 Spinning
20 70's tennis star from Spain
21 All the same
22 Short-skirted garment
23 White or gray mineral
24 Longhorns
25 Ivanhoe's love
26 ___ Alamos
27 Part of a shuffle and three steps
28 Monopoly landings: Abbr.
29 Subsidy
30 Dallas player, for short
31 Spring ___
33 What Lola did in "Damn Yankees"?
38 Rehearse stand-up comedy?
41 Dry up
42 Feeling unworthy
43 Swell on el océano
44 Pulled a lever, maybe
45 Small number
48 Milk cow
50 Janis Joplin, to her fans
52 Believer of spirits in plants
54 Ad ___
55 Old infantry soldier
59 Friction
60 Took notice
62 Precious
63 "Chances ___"
64 October alternative
65 Model
66 Big hand?
68 "Missing" locale
70 Command ending
71 Annoy
72 Kind of copy
74 Ready to spring
75 House transactions
78 Pencil partner
79 Sensible
80 Hugo play "___ s'amuse"
82 Exhibitor's place
84 Old car make
85 Comedy writer Pat ___
87 Čapek play

89 Protective sheet for artwork
91 Kind of stream
92 How to use excess cotton or silk?
97 Attracted to the wrong men?
99 "Do I ___ Waltz?"
100 4-point Scrabble tiles
101 Marching cadence word
102 Neighbor of Ger.
103 With 16-Down, old TV show
105 Together: Prefix
106 Math figures
108 Bolivar and Legree
111 Resembling a birthstone
113 Texas wildcat
114 Peevish
115 Colosseum officials
116 Actor Jacobi et al.
117 Picked up on
118 Finisher of a sort

DOWN

1 Word with white or dog
2 Botanical space
3 Queasy feeling
4 Mandela's polit. party
5 Work period in a glue factory?
6 Ninth Hebrew letter
7 Not landbound
8 "No ___!" (Spanish boxer's cry)
9 Communications corp.
10 Auto option
11 Subsidiary of 9-Down
12 Bring together
13 S.A.T. company
14 Pungent
15 Angst-filled movie?
16 See 103-Across
17 One way to reduce taxes
18 Like Saigon, today
19 Raise, in a way
29 Know-how
32 Oklahoma town
33 Beauties
34 Franklin et al.
35 High-tech communication
36 Put ___ on (limit)
37 Boxer's quest
39 More than that
40 Sentry's cry

44 Full of oneself
45 "Step on it!"
46 Menu item
47 Electricians
49 Hosp. area
51 Narrative poetry
53 Frank's third
56 1980 Pulitzer novelist
57 Longtime "What's My Line" name
58 Must
60 Either of two A.L. teams
61 Minesweeping device
62 Spell
65 Devalued currency
67 Legal add-on
68 Local politicians?
69 Camouflaged
71 Green, in heraldry
73 Car-emissions agcy.
74 European in the news
76 Vocally
77 Tricky Sandy Koufax pitch?
79 Core

81 Latin hymn word
82 Like the Mesozoic Era
83 Mr. Diamond
85 Introduction
86 Friars Club member, often
88 Lira: Italy:: karbovanet: ___
90 Classified ad inits.
91 This may be spared
92 Sports award
93 Descriptive of some fables
94 Uncomplicated
95 Homemaker, sometimes
96 Least feral
98 Removes
103 50's Davis Cup player
104 Abbé de l'___ (sign language pioneer)
107 Seine sight
108 Family member
109 Society page word
110 Car size abbr.
112 Flower on a French shield

by David J. Kahn

This puzzle is dedicated to the memory of Eugene T. Maleska, who created the first Stepquote.

ACROSS

1 Put in piles
5 Feudal status
14 Enervates
18 Bend
20 Roman title of honor
21 Not portbound
22 Of base eight
23 Crossing lines
24 Alex Haley epic
25 Stepquote [beginning across and making six turns down the grid]
26 Threefold
27 Compensates
28 Blotto
29 Group of quail
31 Author of the Stepquote
35 Lower
37 Snobbish ones
38 Demand
41 Boy who takes a bow?
42 1988 Tom Hanks comedy
45 "My People" author
49 A.M.A. members
50 City south of Gainesville
52 Test site
53 ___ Muslims
54 Federal farm subsidy plans
56 Regan Secretary of State
60 Rational belief in God
62 Church of St. Maclou's site
63 Star in Scorpius
65 Messy abodes
67 Stanzas and Pathfinders
71 Sound equipment
73 Singer-actress Susan
75 Establishes
76 Old West transports
80 Titan's "___ and Cupid"
82 ___ du Diable
83 Out of the way
84 James Woolsey's org.
85 Bathroom sprinkle
86 She has a ball
87 Statuesque
88 Without any changes
90 Thin tangles of cell chromatin
94 Conk out
97 Source of the Stepquote, with "The"
101 Refrigerate
102 Show appreciation for
104 Habituated
105 Plant with arrow-shaped leaves
108 Courtyards
109 Photo equipment
113 Hearsay
114 Computer command
115 Racecar, usually
116 Has meter, as poetry
117 Spiritual, e.g.
118 Stinking vermin
119 Kind of cap or jerk

DOWN

1 Scrooge's look
2 Light purple
3 Go through cycles
4 Perfectly
5 Kid-___ (TV for children)
6 Peace
7 Mineral name ending
8 Playoff rounds
9 McNichols and Market Square, e.g.
10 ___ the day (near evening)
11 Nibbled
12 "By ___!" (minced oath)
13 Hesitation sounds
14 Condescends
15 Unanimously
16 Playwright Shaffer
17 Fresh
19 Noted name in cat caricature
21 Conductor Rodzinski
27 x, y and z
30 Phlebotomists' targets
32 Privations
33 Hitchcock forte
34 Gradual deterioration
36 Hamper
39 Betting game, informally
40 Fork prongs
42 Secret rival
43 Genre
44 Tankful
45 Wagner girl
46 Road to the Rhein
47 Stand side by side
48 Soul singer Baker
50 With lots of rolls?
51 Biblical verb
55 Pitcher Tiant
57 Limping, perhaps
58 Overdone
59 Cowardly Lion's name
61 Is parsimonious, with "out"
64 Australian food fish
66 Actress Braga
68 30% of the world's land
69 Zero
70 Investor's work, for short
72 Happy sort
74 Gists
76 Worked up
77 "It's no ___!"
78 Women's ___
79 Ragout of partially roasted game
81 Northwest Irish port
85 Lao-___
87 Even
89 Clock watchers
90 Necklace
91 Double fold
92 Box
93 Bogeyman
95 Tarzan
96 Popular TV news magazine
97 Performs entrechats
98 Start
99 City on the Po
100 "The Dream of Geronitus" composer
101 Inverted V
103 Elliptical
106 "___ smile be . . ."
107 Vacuum (up)
109 Daughter of Hyperion
110 Vane reading
111 Author Wallace
112 Some name suffixes

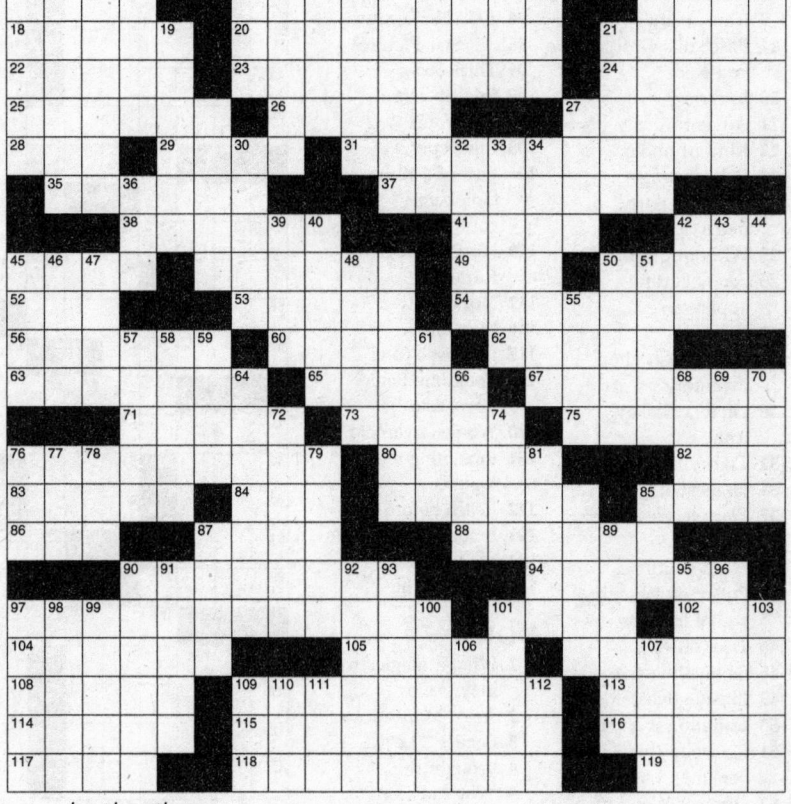

by Alvin Chase

296 CHOICES, CHOICES

ACROSS

1 Medical chart info
7 Jeans, restyled
14 Baseball's George and Ken
20 In error
21 Adventurously
22 Kind of photo
23 Pyle portrayer
24 Birthday party items
25 Without question
26 Screw-cutting apparatus
28 Neuters
29 Auto repair shop inventory
30 Ottawa hockey team
32 Clarifying words
34 Highest stage
37 Place to wear a fez
38 Fortune
39 "God's Little ___"
43 Policy of achieving a goal in steps
46 Take down ___
48 Be busily active
49 Elusive one
50 Common worker
51 ___ bono (for whose benefit?): Lat.
52 Director Wenders
55 Onetime butterfly-bee analogist
56 Machine gun noise
58 Nasal sound
60 Seraglio room
61 Tree member: Abbr.
62 Tennis overhand
63 Pay ___ goes
64 Child's delight
66 Symbol of mourning
69 New Deal proj.
70 Inactive one
71 Will Rogers trait
74 Of the back, anatomically
76 Gamut
80 Last poker bet, sometimes
81 Brillo rival
82 Exercises outdoors
83 Well-formed
85 O.T. book
86 Cable network
87 Sampras objective
88 ___ Girl (Clara Bow)
90 Sorrow
91 Seventh in a series
92 On ___ (anxious)

94 Political cause of the late 1800's
96 1978 Yankee hero
98 ___ Star Pictures
99 Thick jar
100 English refs.
101 Bankrupts
103 Innkeeper
106 Part of a Rube Goldberg contraption
109 Northern highway, formerly
112 Not imitative
116 Mess up
117 Domestic fowl
119 Longtime Peter Lorre role
120 Woolen overcoat
121 Inhabiting elevated regions
122 Reach before
123 Extorts from
124 Made hard
125 Ray of light

DOWN

1 What a magician may wave
2 Actor Morales
3 Beatles' "Let ___"
4 Brought in
5 "The Luck of Roaring Camp" writer
6 Ring leader?
7 1988 Tom Cruise movie
8 ___ de gato (Western shrub)
9 Chinese geometric puzzle
10 Most peculiar
11 Suffer defeat
12 Baretta's cockatoo
13 Attached by the base, botanically
14 Long-eared breed
15 Enlists again
16 Editor's compilation
17 Category
18 Report
19 Stallone and Stone
27 Mustang corral?
31 Haunt
33 Missouri's state tree
34 Certain paint processors
35 Word with puff or soda
36 It became independent on 9/21/64
40 One-named actress

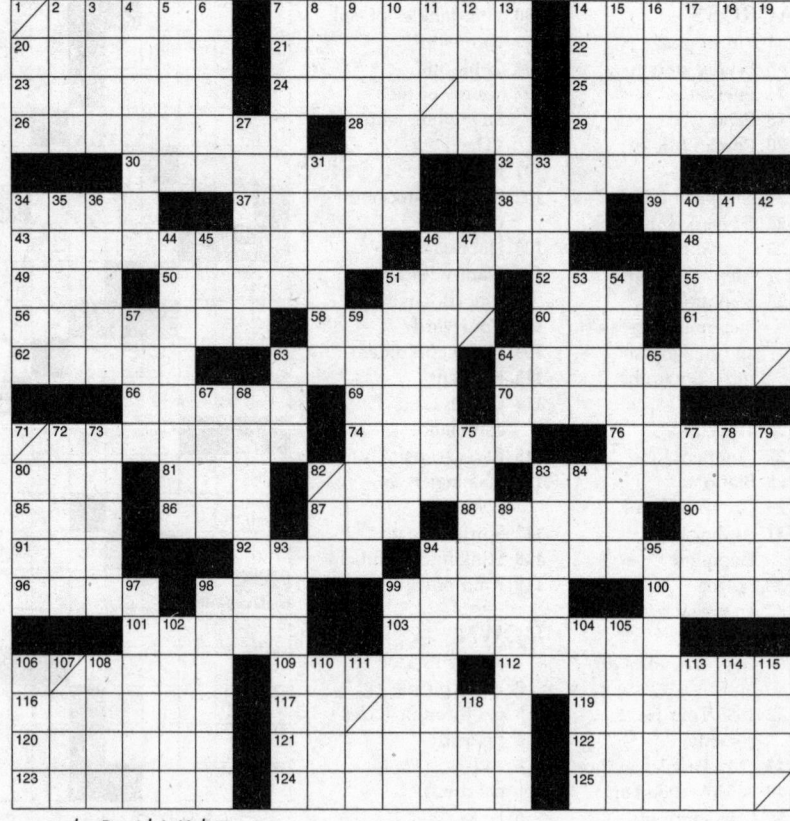

by David J. Kahn

41 School tool
42 Noted first name in literature
44 Rocket motion
45 Blue-and-yellow macaw
46 Golden
47 Cherry ___
51 Call together
53 Pastoral poem
54 Stylish Italian auto
57 Yiddish writer Sholem
59 Unpleasant
63 ___ Lingus
64 Pop group ___ Tuesday
65 Golf impediment
67 ___ Goeth of "Schindler's List"
68 Private entrance
71 Treated to a night out
72 Divert, in a way
73 Arizona native
75 Houston pros
77 Chutzpah
78 Fixed on, with "to"
79 Intent watchers

82 Slovenly woman
83 Jason, e.g.
84 Greetings
89 Bullied
93 Wins over
94 Direct
95 Big name in TV production
97 Melancholy
98 1984 World Series champs
99 Pure
102 Lacking guidance
104 Extensions
105 White-plumed heron
106 Part to keep
107 It's collected at a booth
108 Subterfuge
110 1966 Joe Orton play
111 Word with sugar
113 Observe
114 Start of a cry of encouragement
115 Appear
118 Chemical suffix

ACROSS

1 Thickness, as of a tree
9 Imagined
15 Rip-off
19 If
20 Kind of stamp
22 March ___
23 One with no work grievances
25 "The King and I" role
26 Major suffix
27 Basilica parts
28 Did wrong
30 Beethoven's "___ Overture"
34 Test
35 Accessory for Robin
38 Reliable hearsay
43 Bud holder?
46 National competitor
47 Kids
48 Give some slack
49 Pot starter
50 Bark
51 Pop group Boyz II ___
52 Frequently lost item
53 1957 Cy Young Award winner
54 Sunny skies
58 Worker at a temp agency
59 Bother, as a problem
60 "If ___ Your Woman" (Gladys Knight hit)
61 Fetter
62 In an underhanded way
64 Distress
67 Dirt road hazard
70 Consider, with "on"
71 Fennel and lovage
75 New York lake
76 Unpredictable outcome
80 Scrabble rackful
81 1967 song "___ Groovy"
82 Garnet
83 Lad
84 See 12-Down
85 Irony
86 Ancient strongbox
88 Music box, informally
89 Johnny ___
90 Good manners
92 Takes after
93 Slightest
95 Edward VIII's love
97 Is furious
99 "___ luego" (Spanish goodbye)
102 Côte d'Azur city
105 Kimono ties
106 Intentional flub
113 Borge, for one
114 Double agent
115 Go (to), by car
116 Asylums
117 Scattered
118 Popular summer job

DOWN

1 Appreciate, slangily
2 About
3 ___ above (superior to)
4 Covers
5 Helena competitor
6 ___ Aviv
7 Want ad abbr.
8 Country mailing addr.
9 Muted
10 Attacks, with "into"
11 First name in mysteries
12 With 84-Across, Kansas City Royals star of the '70s
13 "I" preceder, in a kids' game
14 Overtime cause
15 Author ___ Alexander
16 Normal ability
17 "Rule, Britannia" composer
18 Pasture, to Shakespeare
21 Moral
24 Makes
29 Land on the Med.
31 Time and again
32 Midday
33 Shopping, maybe
34 "I completely agree"
35 Edgar ___, The Sleeping Prophet
36 1954 A.L. batting champ Bobby
37 Lab tube
39 Cream
40 Biblical verb
41 Uncreative education
42 Pusher's target
44 Lucy's best pal
45 Sci-fi or suspense, e.g.
49 Cochise and Geronimo
51 Approaches
52 Sister of Lazarus
53 Drastically reduced
55 Five-irons
56 Teens conflict: Abbr.
57 Conger
58 Key letter
61 Law and order hero
63 Imitative words
64 Josephine Tey investigator ___ Grant
65 Wyo. neighbor
66 Firm up
67 Travel, in a way
68 Bring together
69 It's easily erased
70 Agassi rival
72 Refresh one's memory of, in England
73 Chap
74 Ocular irritations
76 Like a Poe tale
77 Make or break
78 Netman Nastase
79 Raises
81 Piano hammer material
85 Chide, colloquially
86 Birdlike
87 Kind of shot
88 Custodian
90 Crash into
91 Opposite of ahead
94 Makes tolerable
96 Dawning
97 Word with cream or ice-cream
98 Skier's aid
99 Murder suspect, often
100 Ruth's "Laugh-In" tormentor
101 Put away
103 Fall (in)
104 Gets by, with "out"
107 No and others
108 Industrial container
109 Credit info corp.
110 "Mamma ___!"
111 Dictator Amin
112 Hesitant sounds

by Rich Norris

ACROSS

1 Mozart's alleged poisoner
8 In jeopardy
15 Itsy-bitsy bits
20 Part-time reporter
21 Stimulate
22 Text for public reading
23 Election pledges?
25 "Mefistofele" composer
26 Noted Washington couple
27 Oilstone
28 1982 World Cup site
29 Place for props?
30 Talked into
31 Lapwings
33 Joseph Smith's grp.
34 Tittle
35 Comeback victor of 1974
36 Daffy Duck's voice
37 Reason for sudden death
39 "Le Coq ___"
40 The Wild Man of Africa
41 Termite's medium
45 Election victory celebration?
49 Last place?
50 Rockefeller and others
52 Not playing around
53 End of ___
54 Former French Sudan
55 Subject of the movie "Sweet Dreams"
56 Mussolini's son-in-law
60 Political therapists?
63 Hubble component
64 Winston Cup sponsor
65 Gold source
66 Lawyer Dershowitz
68 Highest degrees
69 With 74-Across, devious skill in politics?
74 See 69-Across
78 Ford's press secretary
79 Lane-Lerner's "On ___ Day"
80 Words from Caesar
81 Informality
83 Bear hugs
84 Louise or Victoria
86 House whips?
93 Pan-fry
94 Warlord in the news
95 ___ off (beside oneself)
96 Actor Delon
97 Triathlon athletes
99 English composer
101 Excite
102 Prosperous political outing?
106 Gut response
107 "Give it ___!"
108 Social hanger-on
109 Arctic explorer
110 Largo, e.g.
112 Gulager of "The Virginian"
113 Comment from the byre
114 Society event
116 Post-office pane
118 Meanders
122 Add, as a rider
124 Set on fire
126 ___ de capo
127 "The Frog and the Ox" writer
128 Jaeleel White TV role
129 Bowing to a Presidential veto?
132 Contract negotiator
133 Leader of France?
134 Diving gear
135 Resulted in
136 Mrs. Bob Hope
137 Yea votes

DOWN

1 Filibuster
2 Type of conflict
3 Ruby items
4 ___ sense
5 Highbrow
6 Celebrity
7 Pacific
8 Air traffic controllers' sys.
9 Relative of Wm. or Robt.
10 "Home Sweet Home" site
11 Three-note chord
12 Point in orbit
13 Poignant
14 Annapolis grad.
15 Up
16 "Tummy Trouble" character
17 Paperwork?
18 Mary of "Equal Time"
19 Bracing
20 "Off you go!"
23 I.R.A. investments
24 Dearie
29 Mob
31 Graph
32 Maneuver
34 "Go and Catch a Falling Star" poet
36 Maverick Idaho Senator
38 Evaders' enemy
39 Sews up
40 See 48-Down
41 Dead heat
42 Hebrew name meaning "joy"
43 W.W. I battle site
44 Promise
45 Eshkol's successor
46 Soviet dissident Bonner
47 Get ahead
48 Houdini et al., with 40-Down
50 Well-founded
51 Nicholas Gage book
54 Clarke of "The Public Enemy"
55 Button one's lip
57 Handel's "___ and Galatea"
58 Big shot
59 Algerian port
61 Middle of a famous trio
62 Saved with "away"
64 "___ taxes"
67 Stock holding
69 Pouches
70 John Wooden's school
71 Blue in Berlin
72 Appear before a House committee
73 Dukas ballet
75 ___ duck
76 Harvest goddess
77 Director of "Breaking Away"
82 A Chaplin
84 Brink
85 ___ of thieves
87 "Take ___ from me"
88 Oprah's production company
89 Jesus, for one
90 Net lining in a woman's hat
91 Philematologist's study
92 Old knife
94 Ellerbee's "___ It Goes"
98 Salad bulb
99 Car-front cover
100 "Fairy tales"
101 Music enhancers
102 Sure-enough
103 Loose
104 Hauled
105 John Deere product
106 Repercussions
110 Pacific battle site of 1943
111 Herzog and Zola
113 ___ allegro (very quickly)
114 Pitched
115 One of nine
117 Randy's skating partner
118 Understand
119 Small helpers
120 John and Jane
121 Rudolf Abel, e.g.
123 Artist Rockwell
124 "A ___'clock scholar"
125 Patch site
127 Give ___ for one's money
129 Triste
130 Latin thing
131 Deal with

by Alex K. Justin

ACROSS

1 Make sour
9 Finished perfectly
13 Ring rating assn.
16 Unseldom
19 Deprives (of)
20 Boisterous party
21 Rubout
23 Scrawling ceramicist
25 Poured wine, ceremonially
26 Up
27 Penning pastry chef
29 Chinese soup ingredient
32 Kind of light
33 Palm feature
34 Yoga type
35 Start of an ode's title
36 About 5% of Europe
37 Blotter letters
39 Old-fashioned buckle
41 White House advisory grp.
43 Bad: Prefix
44 Mountain overlooking Troy
47 Oprah alternative
49 Result of a firing?
51 Where any two diams. meet
53 Marion Cunningham, for one
55 Supplements
56 Alphabet run
58 Japanese-born conceptual artist
60 Hospital instr.
63 ___ jure
64 Composing caskmaker
69 Writing redcap
71 Typing tenor
73 Title fellow in a Beatles song
75 Inlet
76 Medit. nation
77 Sign of triumph
78 Rectangular pilaster
79 "I never ___ much in my life!"
81 Sodom refugee
83 Any ship
85 Patron of Venice
87 Hankering
88 Toupee
91 Stake
93 Last Supper question
95 Stocking stuffer
96 Synodic decrees
98 Gator or orange follower
100 Small anchor
102 Like some verse
104 Roman household god
105 Olympic sport
106 Sonnetizing servant
108 Not exact
112 Court sport
113 Scribbling sculptor
117 "It's probable . . ."
118 Second coming?
119 North-ern exposure?
120 "You bet!"
121 Postal abbrs.
122 Directly
123 Asian capital

DOWN

1 Pop group in "Muriel's Wedding"
2 2.0 grades
3 He was, in Rome
4 Wrinkle remover
5 Hair clasp
6 Bird: Prefix
7 S.E. Hinton novel
8 Telepathist's gift
9 Conductor Toscanini
10 The very picture of health?
11 Times in classifieds
12 Vagrant
13 Robust
14 Abscam crime
15 Mystical scholar
16 Extinguish, in dialect
17 Jacques of song
18 Alaska's Sen. Stevens
22 Egyptian waterwheel
24 Emulates Webster
28 Word in political movements
30 ". . . you ___ your God": Leviticus
31 The second X in XXX
34 Attendant
37 Key of Beethoven's Symphony No. 7: Abbr.
38 Rochester-based company
40 Elephant man?
42 Snobs
44 Fertilize
45 Items on a list
46 Part of a Latin conjugation
48 Jungle menaces
50 Real estate offering
52 Doesn't serve
54 ___ Memorial
57 Word of thanks
59 ___ ark
61 Thicket
62 March, in a way
65 ___ Na Na
66 Claire of "Ninotchka"
67 Part of S.A.S.E.: Abbr.
68 Longtime Mex. ruling party
70 Fashion type
72 Search thoroughly
73 Noisy bird
74 Western Atlantic Conference player
80 Solemnly prophetic
82 Masks
84 Westernmost of the Canaries
86 Beach
89 Like good children, traditionally
90 Blockers
92 Word to a hound
94 One of the Turners
96 Deep sleeps
97 Quill tip
99 Inferior deity
101 Former magazine of John F. Kennedy Jr.
102 18th Hebrew letter
103 Speakeasy occurrences
107 ___ Bell
109 Track figure
110 The fourth man
111 ". . . ___ saw Elba"
112 Euphoria
114 Acquaintance of Henry Miller
115 Rap's Dr. ___
116 Farm sound

by Martin Schneider

300 FROM STOVE TO VOTES

ACROSS

1 French dessert
6 Desktop buy
10 Percussion instrument
14 Tender
19 Race form
20 Race form
21 Bar at the dinner table
22 Nord department capital
23 Feeling for Tosca
24 ___ Lee
25 Dressage factor
26 Crammer's headaches
27 Start of a verse
31 Mlle.'s pen pal, maybe
32 Kilmer of "Batman Forever"
33 Minerva's symbol
34 Tahini, e.g.
35 Unearth, with "up"
37 Taro dish
38 Rorschach test image
40 Jejuna neighbors
43 Line 2 of the verse
49 Pulitzer biographer Winslow
50 Plus
51 Headlight?
52 Cold-shoulders
53 Support meeting
55 Bert Lahr's sign
57 First woman Supreme Court Justice, ___ Day O'Connor
60 Straw product
61 Floor piece
62 1-Across, literally
64 Polaris bear
66 Anne Lindsay's "___ Robin Gray"
68 Measure marking its 75th anniversary on 8/26/95
74 Iditarod sight
75 Yours, in Tours
76 Flushed
77 Some are blue
79 Use carets
82 Women's rights advocate Bloomer
84 Writer Deighton
86 Euripides drama
87 Swallow perch
89 Annual Epsom race, with "the"
91 Do the hustle
94 Bother

95 Line 3 of the verse
100 D-Day river
101 Till's bills
102 Women's rights periodical of 1853
103 Department
104 Pigment from cuttlefish
106 Jan. 15 honoree
107 Simpson judge
108 What Lucy Stone kept at her 1855 wedding
112 End of verse
117 Cabal successes
118 Vacillate
119 Part of SEATO
120 Ward off
121 First name in cosmetics
122 Slangy timetable
123 ___-Ball (pay-to-play game)
124 Use a pen or sword
125 "Paganini" composer
126 Hardy girl
127 They demand an expiation
128 Unexciting bridge holdings

DOWN

1 Bamboo, for one
2 Nocturnal primate
3 Up
4 Cost of a ride
5 Checker of a sort
6 City near San Jose
7 Advantage
8 Snickers company
9 Troop group
10 "Taras Bulba" author Nikolai
11 Patron Saint of Norway
12 Harris of "Doggie Howser"
13 Deteriorate
14 Cosmonaut Atkov et al.
15 Obsession
16 Whiplike cell part
17 One of the Muppets
18 Legal matter
28 Owns
29 Rustling sound
30 Defense grp. since 1949
36 Jazz singer Anita
37 St. ___ (vacationer's mecca)
38 Biblical prophet on a mount

39 Mount Holyoke founder Mary
41 Island east of Corsica
42 Second: Abbr.
43 Left on board?
44 French actor Delon
45 "Grease" singer
46 Row
47 Christmas spirit?
48 Hymn
54 Cataract site
56 Film cut
58 Claudius subject
59 Late newsman Hughes ___
62 People tidbit
63 Sign away
65 Fraternity letter
67 Take a letter?
69 Cheer
70 Aquatic nymphs
71 Banks of Chicago
72 Gymnast Comaneci
73 Dweeb
78 Advantage
79 Big-bang physicist Penzias
80 Kind of prize

81 Where some Yankees winter
83 Unattended
85 Early work of mythology
86 Jazz pianist Allison
88 Climbing legume
90 Row
92 Legal references
93 "Orphée" painter
96 Susan B. Anthony is on one
97 Panel expert
98 Out of the blue, perhaps
99 Dartmouth site
105 Riddle
106 Verbs and people have them
107 "Rosmershohn" playwright
109 Coeur d'___
110 Dobbs Ferry college
111 1956 ticket name
112 Tracking power
113 Hook up
114 Deli selections
115 "The Square Egg" author

116 Piece of toast, in dinerese
117 Animation unit

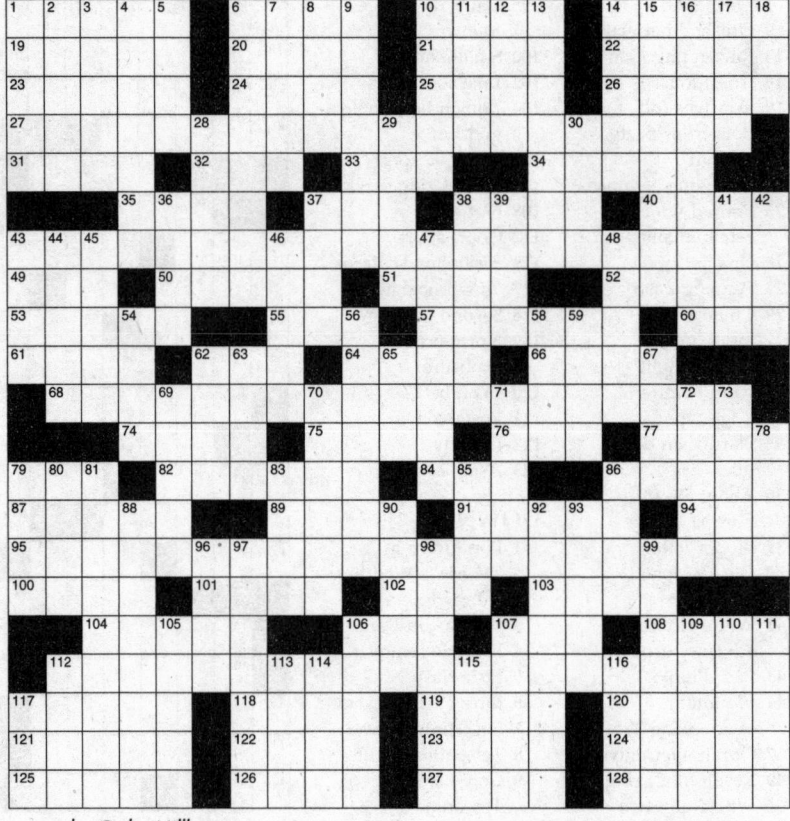

by Cathy Millhauser

ACROSS

1. Chip on chip on chip
6. Phonetic elision
10. Theater booth
14. Companion of Paul
19. De Valera
20. Type of space
21. Latin greetings
22. "Mother ___": Kipling
23. DOSTOYEVSKY NOVEL
26. Chief Etruscan god
27. Italy's golden age
28. New Orleans pro
29. Jewish village
30. Atlas was one
31. Phoenix's N.B.A. team
32. Weaver's reed
33. Valuable Brazilian tree
36. Author Mazo ___ Roche
37. Levant vessel
38. LEARNED MAN
41. Mire
42. DELIGHTED
45. ___ de Queiroz, Portuguese novelist
46. Property charge
47. Earth goddess
48. Otherwise
49. Ratite bird
50. Yerby's "A Rose for ___ Maria"
51. IN A POLYPHONIC WAY
55. Like a nobleman
56. WILL ROGERS'S HUMOR
58. Rich cake
59. Curved swords
60. Mus. mark
61. ___ Zagora, Bulgaria
62. Certain driver's warning
63. Climbing palm
66. Mme. Gorbachev
67. Kicker's nightmare
71. Detest
72. TARDINESS
74. Gullet
75. Hera's mate
76. Pants section
77. Obligation
78. Whodunit item
79. This might be slippery
80. Flats
84. His law relates to thermodynamics
85. Neighbor of Syr.
86. Fox hunter's shout
87. Soprano Berger
88. Impignorated
89. Spanish river
90. Cousins of 49 Across
91. Critter for Tex to tame
93. American cat
96. Like Daffy Duck
97. Excel
101. Crossbill's genus
102. "WHEN THE ___": RILEY
104. "Enigma Variations" composer
105. Photographer Morath
106. Tintinnabulate
107. Noted conductor from Genoa
108. Erect
109. Digitate
110. Wyes' predecessors
111. Ars' followers

DOWN

1. Parsees, e.g.
2. Wyndham Lewis novel
3. Fifi's friend
4. GUILT FEELING
5. Wrestler's ploy
6. Subject of a famed 1897 editorial
7. Tempted
8. Tell's canton
9. Antarctic waterway
10. Layers
11. Calcars
12. PIQUANT
13. "Iacta alea ___"
14. BEAT ___ (HIT FIRST)
15. FREEDOM FROM HARM
16. Prong
17. Monad
18. Phocid
24. Date preceder
25. Exerts traction on
29. Poor golf shot
32. Impertinent
33. Psalmic pause
34. Type of acid
35. Reinforced support
36. Costly
37. Maison section
38. Use antifreeze
39. FIRST ___: 264–41 B.C.
40. Caudal parts
42. Type of button
43. Baltic native
44. The Nile has one
47. English daisy
49. Baseball's Rookie of the Year: 1957
51. Certain luminary
52. Garret
53. Skoal, e.g.
54. Pianist Claudio from Chile
55. Austen character
57. Spanish deictic
59. Fuliginous
61. "À votre ___!"
62. Imitates Tinkerbell
63. FAIRY-TALE GIRL
64. White poplar
65. Tom, the General
66. Howard ___ in "The Fountainhead"
67. Type of law
68. Playwright Williams ("The Corn Is Green")
69. River or town in Ecuador
70. Soft fabric
72. Type of surgeon
73. Spanish port NE of Gibraltar
76. Sudden fright
78. CATTLEMEN
80. GAMBLING DEVICE
81. Transferred, as sovereignty, by death
82. Word on a penny
83. What Muses do
84. Keener from Kerry
88. A size of paper
89. Of Lamb's writings
90. Encomium
91. Wilderness Road traveler
92. Ladder steps
93. Pseudo butter
94. German city
95. OBLITERATE
96. Italian river
98. Newsmen Pappas and Seamans
99. Nest of pheasants
100. Compass dirs.
102. In good shape
103. Ice-hockey team

by Emanuel Berg

ACROSS

1. Part of a dart
6. Fuddy-duddies
11. Author of "Two Years Before the Mast"
15. Hari or Hale
18. Usher's milieu
19. A son of Midian: 1 Chr. 1:33
20. "Iliad," e.g.
21. Like Willie Winkie
22. Gaze with malicious pleasure
23. Sicilian code of silence
24. Primer dog
25. Altar on high
26. Blue Frost subject?
28. Keeve
29. Product of a lorimer
30. Infuriated
31. Most ironic
33. Yellowish-brown European?
37. Zodiacal sign
38. One of a Michelangelo trio
42. Prod
43. Begley and Asner
44. Red onlooker?
47. Victoria's consort
49. Actor Vidov
51. Old Faithful's activity
52. Let
53. Some putti
55. Kind
56. ___ Paulo, Brazil
57. Greek port
59. Labor leader Conboy: 1870–1928
61. Que. neighbor
62. Bluish-green chiefs of an armed forces branch?
68. With, to Cato
69. Titi or sapota
70. Truck-stop sights
71. Cover
72. Hasten
73. ___ Fair (N.Y. 1939 event)
74. First Indian ruler to embrace Buddhism
78. Grounds for belief
81. Sea east of the Caspian
82. Cheap: Slang
83. Yellowish-green, foolish oldsters?
85. Bern's river
87. Catholic tribunal
88. Incline
89. Number before sette
90. Deep-red gadfly?
93. Extents
96. Judge
97. Buffoon
100. Peer Gynt's mother
101. Bright-green municipal officials?
106. Eggs, to Caesar
107. Preside at tea
108. Oily hydrocarbon in petroleum
109. Pale yellow
110. Fall mo.
111. Of an epoch
112. Attentive one
113. Turn ___ new leaf
114. Lamb's dam
115. Sly
116. Heraldic borders
117. Of the kidneys

DOWN

1. Droops
2. Seed scars
3. Wet
4. Hullabaloo
5. Leash
6. Humbles
7. Irritable
8. Roof window
9. Group of eight
10. A Tai language
11. Ruins
12. Support, in Sedan
13. A queen of Thebes
14. Play part
15. Barter
16. Alpaca's habitat
17. Oenologist's concern
19. Abominable
27. Estuary
29. Limit
31. "Charlotte's ___": E. B. White
32. Glowing bit
33. Bedouin headband cord
34. Breakwater
35. ___ ghanouj (Middle Eastern salad)
36. City WNW of 57 Across
37. Drags along
39. That Menlo Park man
40. Lessee
41. Jargons
44. Blue-pencil wielders
45. Helices
46. New Orleans institution
48. Extract juice from
49. Suggest
50. Cotton to
53. Emend
54. One-horned fish
58. Hispanic-American
59. In a state of parvitude
60. Surrounded by
62. Believe in
63. Be tremulous
64. Diamond figure
65. Odd, in Oban
66. Limn
67. Classify
72. Gabler or Hopper
73. Dry watercourse
75. Payment for Charon
76. Forked-tailed hawk
77. Opera by Salieri
79. Dismal
80. Describing winds from the Orient
82. Cornered
84. Legal thing
85. French-built rockets
86. Stag adornment
90. She pulled a switch on a witch
91. Rub off
92. Earthquake feature
94. Soprano Kiri Te Kanawa, e.g.
95. Commonplace
96. "Abdul the Bulbul ___"
97. Region
98. Say it is so
99. Cathedral part
101. Dali's "Nostalgic ___"
102. Rant's partner
103. Appearance
104. Hebrew prophet
105. Colzie of the N.F.L.
107. "Treasure Island" character

by Joy L. Wouk

ACROSS

1. Strait outlet?
6. Ponderosa apparel
11. Librarian's device
16. What it costs nothing to be
17. Ho's partner
18. Creature with 14 legs
20. I AM A CAD, MA
22. Like Shelley's works
24. Davis's "Yes ___"
25. Hegel's forte
26. It carries a lot of weight
28. Hebrew Bible reading: Var.
29. Guitarist Lofgren
30. Work in a smokehouse
31. Flora and fauna
32. Avian chatterbox
33. Half of 11?
34. Daughters of Zeus and Themis
36. River to return as 33 Across?
37. He made a pile for Nabors
38. STONE'S DAD
41. Places for races
42. "___ Song Go . . ."
43. Exploits
44. Like Monday's child
45. Sudra and Vaisya
48. When overturned, is it a bucket seat?
49. Gets it all together
53. Quaker in a grove
54. UNSET
57. Chit
58. Landlocked country
59. Saarinen
60. Fit for the job
61. Evans or Carnegie
62. Navy's C.I.A.
63. DRAW A BOY
67. Paint-factory employee
68. Showy fan palms
70. The rite things to say
71. Beard erasers
72. Any time at all
73. Like a rugged bug?
74. Luigi's love
76. "The Kiss" sculptor
78. B. A. DONNA
84. TV's "Green ___"
85. "Stop, Pierre!"
86. This answer has three
87. Leandro's amorosa
88. Modernists
89. "___ Age," book by Comfort
90. Flavoring for a Cannes cordial
91. At a distance
92. Roscoe
93. A computer language
94. Huesca houses
96. French wines
97. Dub
99. FINGER
103. Shut tight
104. Don's January
105. Ups the ante
106. Cacophonous
107. Sole provider?
108. Team that's almost bare?

DOWN

1. Settings
2. King and Ladd
3. El ___, Heston role
4. This could a tale unfold
5. Tom cared about this voter?
6. Presided over
7. From this time
8. Amateur-sports gp.
9. Sgt.'s underling
10. Freud's appointments
11. Widened
12. Places of safety
13. Sped
14. Finial
15. MACARONI
16. Serpico on the screen
19. Rye grass
20. Heavy weight I'm lifting in N.D.?
21. Creature with a black-banded tail
23. Kind of poker
27. Etna feature
31. How Godiva rode!
32. It's for reel!
34. Moody tennis player?
35. Keats feats
36. Lass whom Cantor knew
37. Gretzky's stats
39. Developers' interests
40. Master, in Malaysia
44. Absquatulate
45. Close-fitting cap
46. Yoga squat
47. OLD PIES
48. On one's uppers
49. ___ sugar (lump for Castro?)
50. This and no more
51. He portrayed Chan after Oland
52. Litigious people
54. Felt silly?
55. Round figures
56. Shooting marbles
59. ___ effort
61. Dirty group out of Hollywood
63. Some tournaments
64. Hogged the conversation?
65. Fully grown
66. Italian magistrate
67. "___ Bulba"
69. Campus climbers
71. Wapner's wrap
73. Curled, as a Torah
74. St. Francis's bailiwick
75. Total wipeout
76. A to Z, for one
77. Where to paddle canoes?
78. Spacek's "___ Man"
79. Buck finisher
80. Ranger, before 1972
81. What de speeders pay?
82. Sumatran primates
83. From Oslo
89. "Deutschland uber ___"
90. Without ___ in the world
91. Dispatch vessel
93. Gudrun's mate
95. Tunisian city ('tain't photocopy!)
98. Honey-eating bird
100. Numero ___
101. It's east of Calif.
102. "As you sew, so shall you ___"

by Joel D. Lafargue

ACROSS

1. Heavyweight Max
5. Kind of lily
10. Harts
15. Addis ___, Ethiopia
20. Melville book
21. Anonym
22. Francis of "What's My Line?"
24. Festivals
25. Mythic coffer
27. Entertainer Kazan
28. First Family of Alaska in the 60's
29. Takes the helm
30. Craggy crests
32. Callowness
34. Serling of TV
35. Capita preceder
36. Trident prongs
38. Cays
39. Podded plant
41. Chisholm Trail town
43. What Nichols makes
44. Lets
46. Chg. for a loan
47. Perlman or Howard
48. Ms. Shire of "Rocky" films
49. Floating ice mass
50. One connected with: Suffix
53. Emulated Maxwell Perkins
55. Roger Clemens's team
57. Vanuatu's former name: Abbr.
59. Murmured fondly
60. Horehound and mad-dog
61. A Sedgwick
62. Enshrine
63. He fought Joe Gans
64. Avernus
65. Stowed cargo
67. Finally
68. Person from Ponca City
70. One of the Bears
71. Infant's garment
72. Certain airline initials
75. A courtroom procedure
80. Last year's jrs.
81. Satiated
83. Felt remorse
84. Cater basely
86. Birds' "thumbs"
87. "Robin ___," old Irish song
89. Absurdly eccentric
90. Hither
94. Tamarau's relative
95. Cabal
96. Nelson and Springfield
97. Spurn
98. Lead-pipe cinch
99. Dictionary compilation
102. Kitchen utensil
103. Fine lava
104. Unlatches a door, in poesy
105. Actress Taylor
106. Use a straw
107. Kyushu volcano
108. Betelgeuse's constellation
110. Scruffs
111. Prepare to braise
112. Napoleonic marshal
113. More reasonable
115. "Rosshalde" author
116. "Cara ___," 1954 song
117. Wood sorrel
119. Like a switch-hitter
122. Signet
124. Vandyke's relative
127. Tether
128. Dennis's Mame
130. Collusive behavior
132. Cat, in Catania
133. Admittedly
134. Simon's sporty slob
135. Newspaper section, for short
136. "There's no music in ___ ...": Ruskin
137. Pressure units
138. Clayey rock
139. Eleven's numerals

DOWN

1. Conks
2. He loves: Lat.
3. Acquittal
4. Site for lots of bucks
5. Kissel and Opel
6. Yellowhammer St.
7. Leaned
8. Travail
9. Zither of yore
10. Mule "on the Erie Canal"
11. Conductor's aide
12. Arranges in rows
13. Chromosome parts
14. Impertinent one
15. Discriminator against older people
16. Deli favorites
17. "___ to the land of the dead": Auden
18. French lending institutions
19. African fox
23. Shoe-box ltrs.
26. Sent for
31. Elevating posts
33. Colleague of Paul, John and George
35. Brooch
37. Of a pelvic bone: Comb. form
39. Pawn's superior
40. Where Gideon defeated Midian

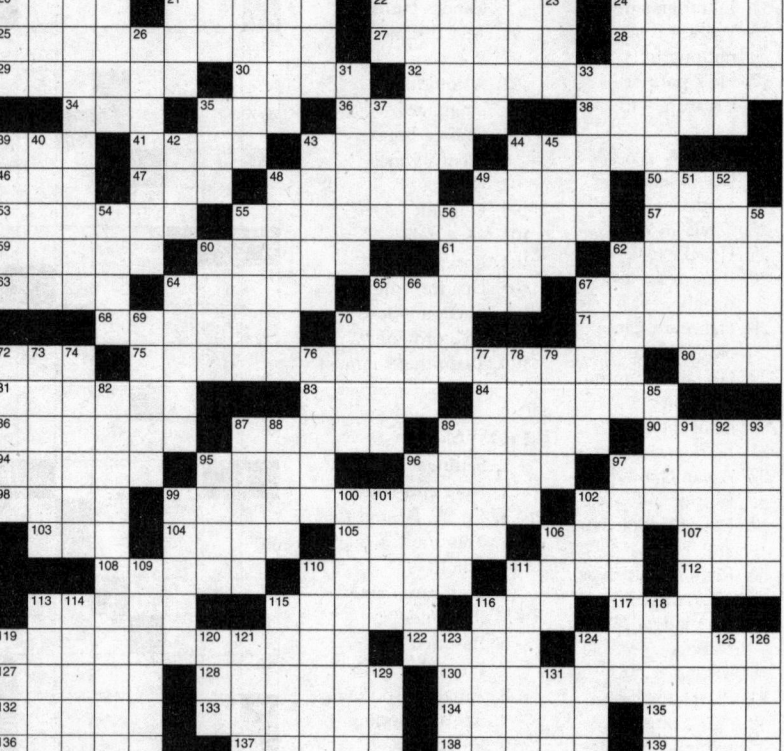

by John Greenman

42. De la Mare poem
43. Observes Yom Kippur
44. Decorated anew
45. Manx tongue
48. Coloring agents
49. "Venerable" theologian
51. Young Durocs
52. More compendious
54. North Sea feeder
55. Awaits
56. Fortification
58. ___ noires (anathemas)
60. Dangerous Hawaiian shark
62. Concurring
64. Throng
65. Debussy opus
66. In the thick of
67. "Need ___ cry?": Burns
69. Indian, e.g.
70. Hawaiian island
72. Strikebreakers
73. "... pretty maids ___ row"
74. The March King's family
76. Muse of bridal songs

77. Cochise was one
78. Down at the heel
79. Uses a dabber
82. Drummers' cousins
85. "Ellie ___," post–Civil War hit
87. Auslander
88. Medics
89. Erases a chalkboard
91. Rationale
92. Soprano Sarah of the Met
93. Crazylegs Hirsch
95. Gourd
96. Bombay royalty members
97. Censure
99. Orléans's river
100. More lawnlike
101. Grosgrains, e.g.
102. Ms. Zadora
106. Andaman, for one
109. Wienie
110. Without gender
111. Mineral in quartz
113. Daub
114. Diminish
115. John Wayne film: 1953
116. Fen
118. City near Babylon's site

119. Kelp, for one
120. ___ chi (Oriental martial art)
121. Litter's smallest
123. Heroic poem
124. A "Pretty Woman" star
125. Fellow, in Madrid
126. Ids' relatives
129. Mag. group
131. The Lone Eagle's monogram

ACROSS

1. Oklahoman
7. Juliet's family name
14. Nail or old plane
18. Uncompromising
19. Complete
20. Ignominy
21. Moundsman who begins a game?
23. River in central India
24. Rara follower
25. Dieppe donkeys
26. Cooked in a French oven
27. Easy gait
28. Garage worker: Abbr.
29. Growl
30. Pretty woman
31. Brass player
32. Seller's patter?
34. Disturb
35. "Tell ___ Sweeney!"
36. Gelid, in Granada
38. Lug of a jug
39. Chorister's big moment
40. A voice vote
41. Botanical interstices
44. Wreckage
47. Yule quaff, for short
49. Newsman Donaldson
50. Touring play?
52. Way from the heart
55. Hank or Phoebe of songdom
57. Paving material
58. Rascals
60. Sandbars
62. Longfellow's bell town
63. Certain utility conduits?
67. Shield border
68. A land was named for him
71. Haydn sobriquet
72. Motorists' org.
74. Halt
75. Thurify
76. Enjoying great popularity?
80. Witch bird
81. Call ___ day
82. Creator of Mrs. Tanqueray
83. Toward the center
85. Actress on "Murphy's Law"
87. Former Austrian Chancellor
89. Fool
91. If not
92. D.C. body
93. She wrote "Delta of Venus"
94. January store event?
98. Liqueur flavoring
100. ___ en scène (stage setting)
101. Rank above viscount
102. "Nightmare" street
105. Cavorted
106. "Look ___ hands!"
107. Capp's ___ the Hyena
108. Star in Serpens
109. Thin as ___
110. Certain undesirable passengers?
113. Galas
114. Joan of Arc triumphed here
115. Terse
116. Biographer Leon
117. Mountain chains
118. Racial; cultural

DOWN

1. Urbane
2. Courtier in "Hamlet"
3. Former Giant's family
4. In the: It.
5. Verdi opera
6. Of sovereignty
7. Mil. officers
8. Ryan's "Love Story" co-star
9. Sea bird
10. Remove stopple
11. Christine of Hollywood
12. "... ___ saw Elba"
13. Son of Odin
14. Miler's footwear?
15. Musical suite
16. Pardon
17. "For ___ me as light and life": Burns
18. Town in E Mexico
20. Lustrous mineral
22. Opera by Handel
27. Long, untapered cigars
29. U.K. stirs
30. Whittled
31. Golfer Sutton
32. Pedro's uncle
33. Vic's radio wife
34. Mielziner and Stafford
36. Overwrought
37. Compunction
39. Basso Cesare
41. Syria's President
42. Wakashan people of Vancouver Island
43. "___ I," 1924 Gershwin song
45. Tactical unit
46. "Arrivederci ___"
48. La-la lead-in
51. Cloak
53. Violent people
54. First Marxist President of Chile
56. Item for Rumpelstiltskin?
59. Hitch
61. Rig trucks
64. Sir, in India
65. Short ride
66. Regretful-sounding garment
69. Part of i.e.
70. Had a yen for
73. Author Rand
77. Piqued
78. Proboscis
79. "Seven Year Itch" actor
82. Spider in the kitchen
84. Part of a shandy
85. Gave a roast for
86. Liven
88. Abet's partner
90. Like Sue of songdom
92. Wine bottle
94. Doughnut: Slang
95. Meteorological line
96. Manipulate
97. Biblical landfall
99. Wrymouths' cousins
100. Twin crystal
102. Nicholas Gage book
103. Sammy Cahn creation
104. Neither fem. nor neut.
106. A spouse, in Savoie
107. Highland miss
108. Bard's stream
110. Morse recourse
111. Bambi's aunt
112. "___ bin ein Berliner"

by Alfio Micci

ACROSS

1. Type of jar
6. Rotisserie part
10. D.A.'s staff members
15. Program problem
18. Metrodome, for one
19. ___ incognita
21. Olympic slalom star: 1984
22. Paul Bunyan's cook
23. Driving hazard
24. Sounding like Niagara
25. Meccawee, e.g.
26. Soprano Souez
27. ___ polloi
28. Like an angry cleric?
32. Hymnist John Mason ___
34. Opel or Citroën
35. Massenet's "___ de Lahore"
36. Winemaking process
37. Like an angry perfumer?
40. Teenager's woe
42. Writer Bernstein
43. Battery part
45. Pacino and Hirt
46. Long tales
48. "... tomorrow ___ this petty pace ..."
50. Over
52. Shed
53. Passover repast
54. Like angry Captain Kangaroo?
59. In any way
60. Beckett's "___ Knife"
62. Some are fine
63. If there should be
65. Woof's kin
68. What the angry clone was?
72. T.L.C. providers
73. Foolish fancies
75. Nixon nix, once
76. Anger, to Cato
78. Spot for a beret
79. Like angry Mr. Burns?
83. Ready at the bar
87. Singer James or Jones
88. Zwei preceder
89. Epicurean activity
91. Blackmore heroine
93. Artist Shahn
94. Florentine flower
96. Eight: Comb. form
97. Stats for Strawberry
98. Like an angry babe?
101. Makes a hook shot
103. Organic compound
105. Chassé, e.g.
106. "Tru" Tony winner
107. What the angry hangwoman was?
112. Skinny follower
115. Hawaiian island chain?
116. Author Segal
117. "An ___ Time of Hesitation": Moody
118. Actress in "Knots Landing"
120. Singer Kiki
121. Half note
122. Subject of a Cantor song
123. Red leader?
124. Uneven
125. Some lilies
126. "Ahem" alternative
127. Estaminets

DOWN

1. Couch potato's favorite show?
2. Woody's son
3. Like Skelton's angry wife?
4. Romberg's "___ Alone"
5. Violinist Milstein
6. Place for affairs?
7. Lima land
8. "Build it up with ___ steel ..."
9. Defame
10. Latin I word
11. Dress accessory
12. Escutcheons
13. Vestige
14. Sevilla matrons
15. Like angry Ma Kettle?
16. Radius neighbor
17. Equipment
20. Valor; virtue
29. Korbut and Petrova
30. Astronaut Evans
31. Scenes; settings
33. Actress Brennan
36. Rhine tributary
37. Sphere starter
38. Emulated Yma Sumac
39. Varnish ingredients
41. "___ Down the Road," song from "The Wiz"
42. Vol. measures
44. U.S. wellness org.
47. Feudal slaves
49. Investigation
50. Angry states for Bumstead's boss?
51. Kind of inspection
55. Digs
56. Farrow's second
57. Parisian's donkey
58. Half of MCCCII
61. End of a Doris Day hit
64. Ethnic hairdos
65. Emulated Irons
66. Cicero, e.g.
67. Like angry Clara Bow?
69. Mule of songdom
70. "And miles to go before ___": Frost
71. Quant look
74. Rather like an ogre
77. Chekhov and Bruckner
80. Completed, in Caen
81. Certain saucers
82. According to
84. Like the angry clockmaker?
85. "Them" creatures
86. Player's org.
90. Famous fabulist
92. Admires
93. Ardent
94. Made available, as time
95. Make a dent
99. Abbr. on an overdrawn account
100. "Holy Mountain" in Greece
102. Peaceful
104. Weird
106. "Haystack at Giverny" painter
107. Actor Ray
108. ___ off (angry as a golfer?)
109. Plane type
110. Electric measures
111. Danish-American journalist-reformer
113. Concerning
114. Play-gun ammo
119. Munson of "G.W.T.W."

by Cathy Millhauser

ACROSS

1. Medicinal plant
5. Recorded proceedings
9. Brazilian coffee
12. Big beetle
18. Kind of food or music
19. Where Qum is
20. French secular clergyman
22. A Roosevelt relative
23. Irate pop singer in Arkansas?
26. Recording process
27. Livy's language
28. Dig up
30. A crowd?
31. Sigma ___ (frat of songdom)
33. Trainer Dundee of boxing
35. City in Argentina
37. At a distance
38. Expense item
40. Poet ___ Manley Hopkins
42. Synthetic fabric
44. Pers. cards
45. Mt. Ida maiden
47. Street shows
49. "___ the Top": Porter
51. Actor Hardwicke
53. Affluent ex-Veep in Virginia?
57. Dash
60. Dash
61. Large sea duck
63. Fence material
67. The Bambino or Iron Horse
69. Mantua money
70. Labor gp.
71. World Series of Golf site
73. Snoopy one
74. Pen point
75. Handles clumsily
77. Grassy plains of Argentina
79. Trespasses
82. Lively horse
84. Its capital is Luanda
86. Stone lined with crystals
87. Singing Jackie in Pennsylvania?
89. Eyed wolfishly
93. Furious
94. Caveat ___
98. Dote on
99. The Greatest
101. Chilly time in Spain
104. Prewedding surprise
106. Nathan Hale's alma mater
107. Burrows' kin
109. Austrian essayist-editor
111. Lasorda's predecessor at L.A.
113. Rep.'s opponent
114. ___ cum laude
116. Dame Edith ___, English poet
118. Manet's "In ___"
120. Eventually
122. Ascetic family of Chief Justice in Carolina?
126. Start anew
127. Large kangaroo
128. "I remember Mama" role
129. Biblical pottage buyer
130. "___ Scared Stupid," 1991 film
131. QB's goals
132. Eddy-MacDonald number
133. Check

DOWN

1. Bat material
2. Trevanian's "The ___ Sanction"
3. Described in brief
4. "Lohengrin" heroine
5. Exposure outdoors
6. Shrinking one
7. George Hamilton acquirement
8. Sharp-cornered
9. Appraise
10. Metal structural unit
11. Opera by Von Weber
12. Summer time in Milwaukee
13. Miami's N.B.A. team
14. Omega's antithesis
15. Attractive 18th-century novelist in Connecticut?
16. Group of nine
17. Will or Ginger
21. Admission
24. School gp.
25. Nocturnal sawyers
29. Sanctified actor in Massachusetts?
31. Fang: Fr.
32. Epitaph starter
34. Period
36. Palindromic time

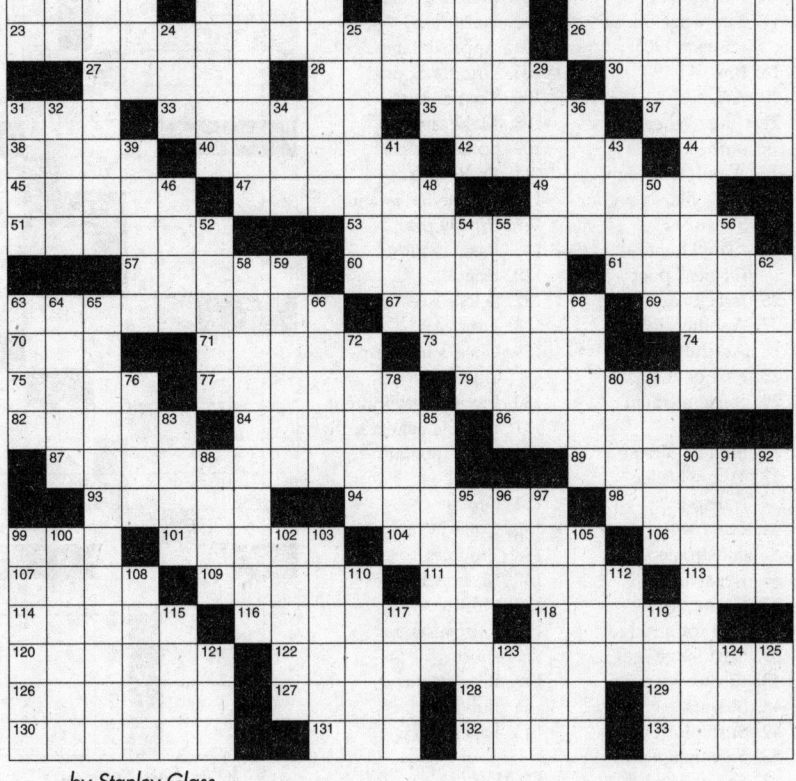

by Stanley Glass

39. Ankles
41. Zeus, to Zeno
43. Modigliani's "The Rose ___"
46. Ref. book
48. Tussle
50. Fulminate
52. Staghorn ___
54. Matisse or Pétain
55. "___ Love," 1982 film
56. Weird
58. Durable columnist in California?
59. Balkan capital
62. Stonewall's boys
63. Drinks gingerly
64. S.A. border river
65. Depressed jazz notable in Massachusetts?
66. Yearns
68. Actor Leon ___: 1881–1951
72. Cowboy's loop
76. Egyptian king
78. Reduces
80. Notion

81. In want
83. Hawk's antithesis
85. Road base
88. Sty sound
90. Driver's exam
91. Author Gardner
92. Judge
95. Northern Connecticut town
96. Pained exclamations
97. Decorative altar structure
99. Esteem
100. Certain horseshoe throw
102. Swell the pot
103. Production measure
105. Vigorous
108. Marsh bird
110. Grassy area
112. Scand. nation
115. Iowa campus site
117. Psyche's beloved
119. Man's septet, to W.S.
121. Suffix with depend

123. New, in Nürnberg
124. Actress ___ Dawn Chong
125. Total

308 HIGHLY PROPER

ACROSS

1. One of the Canary Islands
6. Parrot
11. Kentucky Derby winner: 1955
16. Box
20. Argot
21. "Free Wheeling" auth.
22. A unit of weight
23. The Nile, as a god
24. Storm
25. "The Duino Elegies" poet
26. Israeli coin
27. Another, in Acapulco
28. Part of A.L.U.
29. Aerie resident
30. Dud
31. Sign of pleasure
32. Two-wheeled transport?
34. Carelessly constructed?
36. Regards
37. Germ
38. Seat for a judge
39. Sign language
43. Rocker John
46. Silenus, e.g.
49. Suffix for boy
52. Nev. neighbor
53. Fancy dive?
55. Cornhusker city
57. Packer
58. Means
60. Verve
61. More accurate
62. Fountain of Rome
63. Cut
64. Sincere
66. Part of Muslim prayers
67. Selfish one
69. Threads
70. Summons
72. Dallas-to-San Antonio dir.
75. Sharpen
76. Distinction
78. Kirghizian mountains
80. Certain railroads
81. A cotton fabric
83. Sentence
84. Dash
86. Gloriole
87. Trouble
90. Adlai's running mate: 1956
92. City W of Erfurt
96. A literary Bell
98. Eskimo knives
99. Send abroad
100. Impressions
101. Ballerina Shearer
102. Hair clasp?
104. Approximates
105. Org. for Spock
106. Coat rack
108. Make amends
109. Some carriers
111. Problematic
113. Indonesian islands
114. Prickly pear
115. Pasta request?
120. Brawl?
127. Selene's realm
128. Forgive
129. Cheeks like roses, e.g.
130. Light entertainment
131. Hillside near a loch
132. White poplar
133. Vapid
134. Grave
135. Color of raw silk
136. Troubles
137. Massenet opera
138. Stretch
139. Extremists, for short
140. Rendezvous
141. Publish
142. Lawn tool

DOWN

1. Father: Comb. form
2. Kind of salt or wit
3. Unwilling
4. Broadcaster's problem?
5. Quiz
6. Slough
7. Nearby, poetically
8. Arum lily
9. Out of line
10. Stimulate
11. Mounted
12. Hazard
13. Bouquet
14. Something stated
15. Fill-in
16. James Clavell novel
17. Hand game?
18. Eliot's "cruellest month"
19. Merry
20. Carson predecessor
29. Tree-of-life site
33. Swedish rug
34. Goo
35. Magnate
37. Fillet
39. I.R.S. employee
40. Volcanic crater
41. Otherwise
42. Strainer
43. Oust
44. Unique
45. Clunk
46. "___ Marner"
47. Nomadic Ethiopian
48. Roomy dress style
50. See 26 Across
51. Hector
54. Strapped
56. Painter Joan ___
58. Score for Steffi
59. Workbench adjunct
64. Judah Ben-___
65. Four seasons
68. Exude
69. Title for a Benedictine
71. Spicy dessert?
72. Plan
73. Aloha's cousin
74. Advertising medium?
76. Furze
77. Share
78. Box-elder genus
79. Hunger
82. Film ___
83. Question
84. Chief Justice: 1941–46
85. Tyrolean song
88. Roll up
89. Ice mass
90. Fair
91. English
93. Bullets, e.g.
94. Constellation Lepus
95. Org.
97. Relish
99. Famous last words
103. Exceptional
107. Magnetize
109. Slipper
110. Common connective
112. Meleager's father
113. Certify
114. Knack
115. Winsor's "Forever ___"
116. "Romancero gitano" poet
117. Interdict
118. Abrasive
119. McKinley's birthplace
120. Money of the Mid East
121. Native of Muscat
122. A sturdy chiffon
123. Spaded anew
124. Like Humpty Dumpty
125. Peripheral
126. Piercing
129. Lamebrain
134. Ecological org.

by Barbara Springer

ACROSS

1. Conger catcher
6. Honey of a drink?
10. Helen Mirren film: 1984
13. Actor Tamiroff
17. Shoot from ambush
18. Vince, to Gomer
19. Making iridescent
22. Bracing
23. Arboreal knots
24. Marksmen
25. Grantadvance
28. Oodles
29. Thundering
30. Shem's father, in Lourdes
31. "The Broken Jug" playwright
34. Protruding rock
37. Conditionsituation
42. Degree type
43. Magical conveyance
45. Quay
46. Actor Eisenberg
47. "The Morning Watch" author
48. Perspire
49. Fizzwater
50. Muslim cap
51. Card game
52. Teacher's org.
53. Erode
57. Chum
59. Disentangle, in football.
61. Stumbles
63. W. Hemisphere org.
64. Prefix for form
65. Checks
66. Sagatale
71. "Fickle and restless as ___": Heine
73. Pea petals
74. Scot's veto
75. "The Jolly Toper" artist
79. Lit up
80. U.S.N.A. part
81. Most sordid
84. Porcine parent
85. One less than septi-
86. Cistern
88. Korean boundary river
90. Davis in "The Hill"
92. Spy Penkovsky
93. Mouth: Comb. form
94. Bellow
96. Where to soul search
97. Free (of)
98. Pawpaw
101. ___ fixe
102. Bahamian resort
104. Sweep
105. Contaminate
107. "The Other Side of the Rainbow" author
109. Punchpoke
114. Call into question
117. Odd job
118. Its capital is Lyon
120. Me. storm
121. Toast start
122. Pioneer film producer: 1864–1948
123. Nitti's nemesis
124. Urban rails
125. Forward
126. A sister of Calliope

DOWN

1. Valuation: Abbr.
2. Enoch's cousin
3. Job
4. Peach peels
5. Happen again
6. Lathe spindle
7. Epochal
8. Earth: Comb. form
9. Removed grit
10. Pamper
11. Away from: Prefix
12. Vientiane's locale
13. Chem. compound
14. Cousincousin
15. Opposite of ext.
16. Booker T.'s group
18. Dagger of yore
20. Committeepanel
21. Catania citizens: Abbr.
26. Put to flight
27. Proboscis monkeys
32. Bargains
33. Ancient Athenian freeman
34. Prospect
35. Hoopster
36. Trailing
38. Rorschach, for one
39. Bacchanal cry
40. Adult doodlebugs
41. High ___
44. Zeta follower
47. Viperous
54. Pintquart
55. Fond du ___
56. Some Ghanaians
58. Expertise
60. Born
62. P.O.W. camp of W.W. II
64. Lifetime
67. See red?
68. Dockers' org.
69. Seafood?
70. She was Edna Garrett
71. Earhart
72. Veganova
76. Syrian President
77. Tours river
78. Borg, e.g.
79. Clipped
81. Dull
82. Soft breeze
83. Suffix for simple
87. A neighbor of Norma
89. "Henry ___ Little Secret," 1944 film
91. No rod sparer
95. Joined
96. Wife of Osiris
98. Ballerina Fracci
99. Hearth tools
100. Counties in Fla. and Ga.
103. Walk-ons?
106. They wrote in runes
108. Dresden duck
110. "Nearer, My God, to ___"
111. Cleft
112. Caffeine source
113. Stew
114. Crier's ntwk.
115. Weed killer
116. A semisolid
119. Amour-propre

by Jim Page

ACROSS

1. Give ___ whirl (try)
4. Sahara sections
8. Wrong
13. Unbends
18. Buttonwood
20. Desiccate
21. More unctuous
23. Ron Nessen was one
25. Bug
26. Mentor of Luke Skywalker
27. Wizened
28. Setting for "Hogan's Heroes"
30. Scott Turow book
31. Parts of sonnets
34. Head swellers
35. Sydney-to-Lord Howe Island dir.
36. Puckerel
39. Avine activity
41. It has 32 men
45. Saw-toothed ridge
47. Bar slug
49. Actors Costner and Kline
50. Matthew, in Madrid
51. Clio and Edgar
53. Got the lead out
56. Europe's longest river
60. North Sea feeder
61. Any delicious drink
62. Draft initials
65. Coronet
67. Emulates Dennis Conner
70. Emulate Brian Boitano
71. Responsibility
73. They get cooked with vegetables
76. Run producer
77. Verso's opposite
79. Life-preserver stuffing
80. Coil or curl
82. Wino's ailment
83. Bing Crosby's birthplace
85. Jacob's-sword
87. Man
89. Shish-kebab holder
90. Lines of cliffs
92. Who's station
96. Nero's teacher
98. Tolerated
100. Caboose neighbor, perhaps
101. Phrase on many dietary foods
103. Like
105. "Kenilworth" heroine
106. Thematic letter herein
107. Send packing
110. "We yield our . . . ___ thy soft mercy": Shak.
112. Townshend ___: 1767
114. Ran-tans
116. Kinski role: 1979
117. Gimlet ingredient
121. U.S.A.F. Academy cadet
123. Flare, sometimes
126. Attain acclaim
127. Paid for a hand
128. Scone movers
129. A and B, e.g.
130. Nobelist in Literature: 1923
131. Erotic
132. Printemps follower

DOWN

1. Culp-Cosby series
2. Abecedarian
3. Eagled a par-three hole
4. There are two in mathematics
5. Antarctic arm of the Pacific
6. Addresses
7. Arcane matters
8. Parrot
9. Netman Wilander
10. Ticked off
11. Kind of whale
12. Cruel creditors
13. Gather, as oysters or logs
14. Step on it
15. Countertenor
16. Bad place to lie
17. Goddess of the moon
19. Botanist Gray and namesakes
22. Rent again
24. Site of rods and cones
29. Glaspell's "Norma ___"
32. Implant deeply
33. Like the top of Fuji
36. Distinctive doctrine
37. Woody's frequent co-star
38. Bushes' Millie, e.g.
40. Polynesian apparel
42. Steven's modifier
43. Some form-sheet data
44. Couch potato's meals, often
46. Gun a motor
48. Halloween option
52. Helps with the dishes
54. "___ Home," McCartney song
55. Sordor
57. Lille lily
58. Rubberneck
59. A Met score
62. Out of ___ (grumpy)
63. Jack Nasty
64. Horatio Alger book, e.g.
66. Jelly used as a garnish
68. Gets a circuit ahead in a race
69. Vaudeville performance
72. Family of "The Minister's Wooing" author
74. Rails
75. Monterrey Mrs.
78. Signs
81. Elbow grease
84. Calculus calculation
86. Damage
88. Predicament
90. Last of a familiar hebdomad
91. Part of a worm's body
93. Nipper's co.
94. Rick's pianist
95. Taste
97. Sabot's sound
99. Strips, in a way
100. Clarinet's large cousin
101. "You can ___ horse . . ."
102. Prom queen's date
104. Tenant
108. It's to the left of the Rive Droite
109. Seed coat
111. Actress Petrova
113. Narrow pew
114. Dates frequently
115. Don't dele
118. Dictator's phrase
119. Gold medalist Biondi
120. Ultimatum word
122. Croce's "___ Got a Name"
124. Kin of aves.
125. Like some stares

by Peter Gordon

ACROSS

1. Stocking stuffer
6. Orange gem
11. "Cantique de Noél" composer
15. Colors
19. Doll up
20. Byword
21. Beach resort
22. Superior
23. Naos
24. Variable stars
25. "The World of Words" author
27. Those with telephonitis?
30. Cleanses
31. Thrills
32. Mother of Eos
34. "The Old Wives Tale" dramatist
35. Tannenbaum topper
38. Crush
39. Traveling salesmen
41. Trio from Oslo
42. Prefix for center
43. Gray and Moran
44. Puissant
48. Jumpy noblemen?
52. DII doubled
53. O.T. book
54. Sugarplum, e.g.
55. Fetch
56. Medicate
57. Self-image
58. Rustic
61. Elvis Presley hit
62. Confederate gen.
63. Poulettes?
66. Slow pacifist?
69. Linear measure
70. Puts away
71. Vaquero's relative
72. Radio plugs
73. Confines, in a way
74. About
75. Kind of tape
79. Society-page word
80. Mork's planet
81. Part of the holiday check-out snarl?
84. A sheepdog
86. Indian's protector
87. Under the weather
88. Female kangaroo
89. Firedogs
91. Admits
93. Rudolph's high beam
94. Come out
97. Lee in "Funny Face"
99. Range of NE Italy
100. Alert
102. Busy flautists
108. Spousal symbols
110. Swedish seaport
111. Preceder of 63 Across
112. Futile
113. Magpie
114. German river
115. TV's "___ Indiana"
116. Wrench
117. Very light brown
118. Soubrettes
119. Cob and pen

DOWN

1. Humane org.
2. Quarter
3. Dudley Do-Right's love
4. Job O. Henry had
5. "For want of ___ the shoe . . ."
6. Pony
7. Taos buildings
8. Opulent
9. Seaweed substance
10. Coconut, e.g.
11. Snowcapped peak
12. Magi headbands
13. In the arms of Morpheus
14. Peace Nobelist John R. ___: 1946
15. Superlative for Snow White
16. Fraternal club
17. Tannenbaum topper
18. Simpletons
26. Chastise
28. City in SW Idaho
29. Sequence
33. Dangled
35. 'Tis the season to be chary
36. Sif's husband
37. Solothurn's river
39. Wassail
40. Letter from Paul
42. Renaissance sword
43. D.W. Griffith films
45. Año nuevo time
46. Beersheba's locale
47. Gunwale pin
49. Denounce
50. Brooklyn's "field of dreams"
51. Irish islands
52. Two fortnights
56. Biblical seamstress
59. Swerved
60. Cut of beef
61. Blockhead
63. Coin for Père Noël
64. Copland ballet
65. Car of 1957
66. Basin in W China
67. Forage plant
68. Trifle
71. Sleighs, e.g.
73. Tip
74. Forty winks
76. Prank
77. Country Slaughter
78. S-curve
81. Joe Orton play
82. Wide ties or knots
83. "Matter of Fact" columnist
85. Wash
86. Plodding one
90. Peaceful
91. Peacock spots
92. Became friendly with "to"
93. Enoch, to Seth
94. Loaf
95. Lyric poem
96. Adjective for Loren
99. Observances
101. Eck!
103. Muslim scholar
104. Spanish shovel
105. Soprano Petina
106. Opposite of ja
107. Turns right
109. Miami inst.

by John M. Samson

ACROSS

1. Early N.A. money
7. Board
12. Better
17. ___ facto
21. Director May
22. Conspirator against Peter III
23. A Montague
24. Pippin
25. Tundra hairdresser?
27. Wildebeest country?
29. Cat's-paw
30. Lie adjacent to
31. Lacks
33. Gather
34. Farm towers
36. Shorthander
37. Hack of baseball
38. Aspirin compound
41. Keep ___ on
42. Trumpeter from New Orleans
43. Grew tall and thin
47. Witnesses
49. Napoleon won here: 1796
50. Game divided into chukkers
51. "And ___ bed": Pepys
52. Street sign
53. Funny weasel?
57. Pi follower
58. Overturn
59. Turkish royal court
60. ___ E. Lee: Abbr.
61. Draw ___ on (aim at)
63. Indian matting
64. Tea treats
66. Glissade
68. Kind of knot
69. Map line: Abbr.
71. No longer ahead
73. Come to know
75. Breathe hard
77. Actress Arthur
78. "___ Remember," 1960 song
79. English dry-goods dealers
81. Beach find
85. Stallone's nickname
87. Dried grape
88. Immaculate
90. One on the payroll
92. Actor from Prague
94. Ouphs
95. Jean Kerr's "Lunch ___"
96. Blanches
97. Simulacrum
99. Reckless Olympian
100. Birds in the walls?
104. Grudge
105. Buzzing insects
107. Matches
108. Tie down securely
109. Cronyn and Tandy, often
110. In a natty way
112. Fellies
113. Highland lord
115. Hordeolum
116. Regions of shifting sands
117. Kern show
118. McMahon's drawn-out word
119. Brenda or Bart
121. Singer Baker
122. Miler Andersson
123. Crew cut's antithesis
127. Very early bird?
129. Buffalo celebration?
133. Hang around
134. Esposa de su padre
135. Cleo or Frankie
136. A star in Anaheim
137. Functions
138. Caught sight of
139. Enroll
140. Tripods

DOWN

1. Shrine Bowl team
2. ___ sax
3. B.L.T. option
4. Bolus
5. Prefix with corn
6. Chess pieces
7. Hoyden
8. Wake
9. Escutcheon stain
10. ___ Alamos
11. Twilight
12. Silvery
13. "___ Cane," Jacopetti film
14. Big birds
15. Society-page word
16. Handout
17. Manhattan and Roanoke
18. Pod contents
19. There are 100 in D.C.
20. Anomalous
26. Fragrant marsh shrubs
28. Role for Zimbalist Jr.
32. Spooky
34. Buffet features
35. ___ 500
36. Displayed
37. Bowler's problem

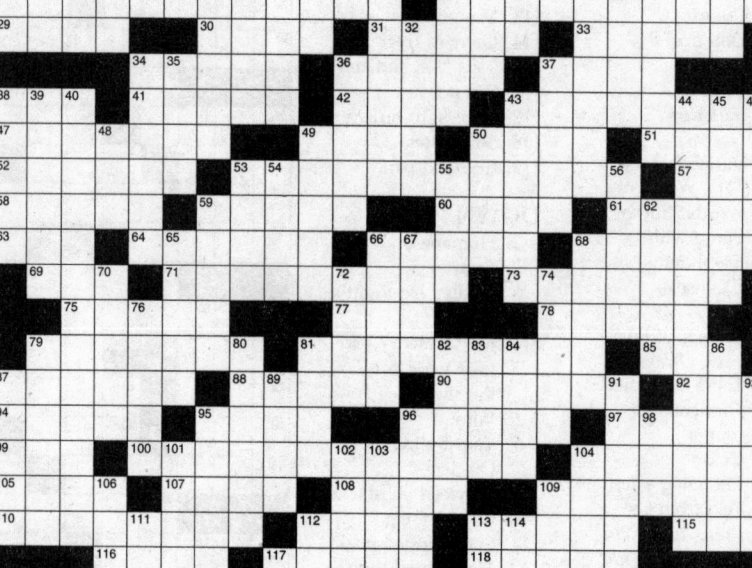

by Norma Steinberg

38. Circa
39. Correspondent of a sort
40. Song-and-dance cat?
43. Serious
44. Pack animals from Santa Monica?
45. Colorless, odorless gas
46. Early TV surname
48. Hold the deed on
49. Smallest amount
50. Nudge
53. Yearn
54. Perpetually
55. Innisfail
56. Jubal ___ of the C.S.A.
59. English Channel port
62. Lures
65. Thirteen witches
66. Ball of yarn
67. Page
68. En ___
70. Backcomb
72. Steinbeck siren
74. Short jackets
76. Foolishly affected

79. A Bond portrayer
80. Chief engineer on the Enterprise
81. Actor Bruce
82. Impart knowledge
83. Four balls
84. Prospectors' objectives
86. Cultured-milk product
87. Enjoys literature
89. San ___ Obispo
91. Washes out suds
93. Disorderly
95. Greets
96. Owl's shipmate
98. Inst. near Harvard
101. Bits of wit
102. Flash
103. Outrageous
104. Super
106. Straggles
109. Insert mark
111. Short wave
112. Like the Roman Forum
113. Sovereignty
114. Actress Marilu
117. Rhonchus

119. B'way hit signs
120. Metal used for trays
121. "___ sae weary . . .": Burns
122. ". . . ___ is in Heaven"
123. Donizetti's "___ Bolena"
124. Lahti resident
125. Surprise from Francis Marion
126. Fronton shouts
127. Actor Gulager
128. Lacuna
130. Golfer Woosnam
131. Quartet in "A Midsummer-Night's Dream"
132. Unit of luminous intensity

ACROSS

1. Beatty film: 1981
5. Trek to Mecca
9. Behave
12. Cordwood measure
17. Frenzied
18. Penthouse?
19. Mrs., in Madrid
20. Tempting dangler
21. Child and Howe, grab, L.B.J. pet
24. Arabian group
25. ___ cantata (sung Mass)
26. A John
27. Like a wet hen
28. "___ Man Answers," Darin hit
31. Dregs
32. Torch
33. P.D.Q.
37. Parsons' homes
39. Swan's victim
40. Haggard novel
42. Mix
43. Performed one's work
44. Spanish blue, look at, young fox
47. Fight seg.
48. Soprano Gluck
49. Brief look
50. Classify
51. Prescribed amount
52. Mauna ___
53. He wrote "A Delicate Balance"
54. Green spaghetti sauce
56. Concert halls
57. Tools, riches, accompany, expand
62. Thespians' org.
63. Rainbow
64. Ethiopian prince
65. Topic, Magi gift, intone, range part, you and me
77. Beatles film: 1965
78. "And ___ with the setting moon": Tennyson
79. Entertainer Della
80. Numero ___
81. Mayan and Mundane
82. A ___ apple
83. Meadows
84. Reclined
85. Tate offering
86. Relative, joy, slip
90. ___ Delgada, E Azores
91. Equal
93. High dudgeon
94. Miller and Blyth
95. Aliens' transport
96. Add value to
98. Touch upon
99. Health clubs
101. Double curve
102. Luau food
103. Squirrel away
104. Puts a stop to
106. Emphasis
109. Center, classic car, put down, headland
114. Brunei's location
115. Washington bill
116. Having roof extensions
117. Flag
118. Canton dwellers
119. Koppel or Knight
120. Stowe book
121. Tangy

DOWN

1. "The ___ Quartet": Paul Scott
2. Big bird
3. U.S. currency
4. Hydroplane
5. Wiesbaden's state
6. Spaces
7. MIV halved
8. Wicked, shameless woman
9. Vanishing table item
10. Antigone's uncle
11. Mountain pool
12. Philippine island
13. Exchanges
14. Sea eagle
15. Dauphin's dad
16. Ands, in Nice
18. Dolts
20. Vie
22. Felt ill
23. Dodge
28. African antelope
29. Uncultivated
30. A kingdom
34. Walked triumphantly
35. Clinquant
36. Trial
38. Marmara, e.g.
39. "Network" director
40. Ray
41. Come up with, as an idea
44. Provençal love song
45. Goal, in Geesthacht
46. Once, once
49. Shine
51. Waterwitch
53. "Just ___ doch-an'-dorris": Lauder
54. Desiccate
55. Emulate Goya
58. Corn porridges
59. Cries of surprise
60. Smelting refuse
61. Except
65. Karloff film: 1940
66. Gentlemen, in München
67. Click beetle
68. Arafat
69. Lorelei's river
70. Ladder part
71. Van Gogh's "Room at ___"
72. ___-do-well
73. Binge
74. Nicety
75. Joins
76. Sub detectors
82. Emperor of Japan
84. McGrew's lady
87. Unnatural; stiff
88. Accustom
89. Matriculated
90. Meat pie
92. Ages
95. Greens dish
97. Volcanic peaks
98. Make up for
99. Thrust
100. Lost color
103. Boswell was one
105. Agitated state
106. Not pres.
107. Intimidate
108. Dernier ___
110. Musical acuity
111. Failed NOW goal
112. Title Drake held
113. Concorde, e.g.

by Betty Jorgensen

ACROSS

1. Dadaist of note
4. Malefic
8. Shoreline peril
13. ___ Sec. of the Navy (F.D.R: 1913–20)
17. Old Ace of Spades
18. Family car
20. Cougar's color
21. Isinglass
22. Four ___ kind
23. Coded order to Adm. Nagumo: 12/2/41
27. Took the tube at Waikiki
29. Diet follower
30. Youngman quip
31. E.T.O. town
32. Riviera acquisition
34. Reveal or pretend
36. Honshu city N of Tokyo
37. "Japanese . . . swooped down on ___": Press: 12/8/41
40. Kind of bread
42. ___ du Diable
43. W.W. I poster man
44. Man with a Plan
50. ___ Island
52. Stack
53. ___ Flow
54. Mindanao's Tasadays, e.g.
57. June 6, 1944
59. Thief
63. Violinist Ughi
64. Thralls and helots
66. Snatch
68. Jawaharlal ___
69. Letter opener
71. Oklahoma and West Virginia
75. Bird or fruit
76. Longed
78. Chimney problem
79. Sedate
81. Fault
82. Kenya's capital
85. Get ready for the O.R.
87. Early penman's chore
89. Umpteen years
91. Requirement
93. Ships, to poets
94. Type of ship not in port: 12/7/41
99. Birchbark
102. Gene letters
103. Row
104. Memorable target: 12/7/41
106. Open-eyed
110. Bonheur and Ponselle
113. "Harper Valley ___"
114. River in Hesse
115. Infirm with age
117. Dweller in a Yemeni port
119. Pen
121. Army partner to Hickam Field
124. "___ on parle . . ."
125. Type of gas
126. Murrow's "___ Now"
127. Hints
128. Strategic port in W.W. II
129. Give it ___ (attempt)
130. Singer-actress Cara
131. Bristle
132. P.O. item

DOWN

1. Inge's "___ Roses"
2. Disproof
3. Site in the news: 12/7/41
4. Suffix for inchoative verbs
5. Kin of savannas
6. Ugandan exile Amin
7. Layers
8. Porticoes for Pericles
9. Visit habitually
10. Baruch's "My ___ Story"
11. Opposites
12. One of the Redgraves
13. "A miss is as good as ___"
14. Audit a course
15. Ancient name for a N European area
16. "Winner ___," 1975 film
19. TV network
24. Cain's "___ Pierce"
25. Ending for pant or scant
26. Plath work
28. Warred
33. Branch of mathematics
35. Ogre
38. Musicians Kipnis and Buketoff
39. Dance-drama of Japan
41. Apiece
45. Doohickey fancier
46. Scattered: Fr.
47. Mystery writer Foley
48. Joy ride
49. Noted Czech novelist
51. ___ alt. (druggist's "every other day")
54. Dey or Brownell Anthony
55. N.Y. city on the Mohawk
56. Newts
58. Derisive calls
60. End of a 7:58 A.M. alert: 12/7/41
61. General Rommel
62. Penitent's activity
65. End
67. Smidgens
70. Ice pinnacle
72. Actress Patterson
73. Old prospector
74. Address for a king
77. Active one
80. Otto, nove, ___
83. Stole
84. Lowdown
86. Examiner
88. Team jacket
90. Alarming person
92. Hades
94. Romanian city and county
95. Class comprising ants, flies, etc.
96. Pawl engager
97. ___-Magnon
98. Observations
100. Sandlot game
101. At a previous time
105. Shady business
107. Reboant
108. Put on the pan again
109. Finial
111. Salk contemporary
112. "Yesterday, December 7, 1941, ___ . . ."; F.D.R.
116. Italian town near Ancona
118. A.E.C. successor
120. Mount in Tasmania
122. Rocker Kiki ___
123. Snooker stick

by Ralph G. Beaman

ACROSS

1. Wellaway!
5. Oral-vaccine man
10. Mid pts.
14. Cartouche
18. Exuviate
19. Gross, in Granada
20. Restored bldg.
22. Middle East prince
23. Foolscap figure?
25. Mediators, occasionally?
27. Finnish poems
28. "Pippin" director
30. Gun org.
31. Greets intrusively
34. "___ diem"
35. Snow-sport conveyor
39. Large-eyed lemur
40. Glisten
41. Business deg.
42. Roman 502
43. Parched
44. Cad in charge?
48. Ending for differ or insist
49. May honorees
50. Samlet; skegger
51. Burden
52. Huff
53. Naval C.I.A.
54. Musical entrances?
58. Catchall term
59. Wine-and-nutmeg drink
61. Herbs, in Yorkshire
62. Noted U.S. surgeon: 1864–1943
63. Long successor on "Cheers"
64. Spelunking sites
65. Decrepit, in Dijon
67. Becomes wan
69. Finishes last
70. W.W. II tanks
73. Actress Raines
74. Nuptial cobblers?
77. Savanna
78. Skim over
79. Glitzy fabric
80. Moroccan coastal area
81. Wing: Comb. form
82. Poodle size
83. Container business?
87. Staffer
88. Baxter role in 1950
89. City in Peru
90. Waistcoats
91. Banks or Pyle
92. Seeds again
94. Bumps a Durant
95. What foes called

supporters of Mary Stuart
97. This, in Tours
98. Luck, in Livorno
99. Gratifies
100. Dermatologist, sometimes?
104. Minor augury?
109. Genuine
110. Maharashtra city
111. Object of Petrarch's affection
112. Variable star
113. Plant juices
114. Candid
115. City SSE of Dallas
116. Male only

DOWN

1. Elec. unit
2. Mauna ___
3. Eisenhut, e.g.
4. Controversial compounds
5. Pointer's best point
6. Butter in the sky
7. Sacks
8. Suffix for baby or old
9. "O short-liv'd pride! ___?" Shak.
10. Make crunchy
11. Succinct
12. Korea's Syngman ___
13. Micmac's cousin
14. Conductive substance
15. Scottish uncle
16. Address for Raleigh
17. Horace's "___ Poetica"
21. Tiered sleeping spots
24. Dancer Tamblyn
26. Due-process process
29. Mountain ashes, to Virgil
31. Cottonwoods
32. Cigar or crown
33. Illegal stratum?
34. Colette novel
35. Use finger paints
36. Equivalent cans in London?
37. Gable-top feature
38. Former quarterback Y.A. ___
40. Suit material
44. Flèche
45. Dred Scott decision Justice
46. Lumpy masses
47. Old cries of triumph

52. Red Cross supply
54. Bando and Mineo
55. Lake in SE Africa
56. Rapper in a courtroom
57. Dolly Varden, e.g.
60. Collect bit by bit
62. Nav. officers
64. Translating device
65. ___-Chu school of philosophy
66. High nest
67. What nudniks do
68. Room recess
69. Precarious perch
70. Lounge furniture
71. "He shall not ___ if he have his own": Shak.
72. Hindu garments
74. Asphalt, e.g.
75. Punjabi potentates
76. Trumpeter Al and family
81. Certain plastic tubes
83. Yearned
84. Exceeded limits
85. Lear's faithful companion
86. Actress Parsons
91. Fleuret's kin
93. Anagram for chase
94. Blackmore outlaw
95. Angelo ___, memorable educator
96. Rand's shrugger
98. Plug up
99. Daze
100. "___ a girl!"
101. La predecessor
102. Walker or Wightman
103. Dove sound
105. Golfer Baker-Finch
106. Pithy remark
107. Braun or Marie Saint
108. Henpeck

by Judith C. Dalton

316 SOUND OFF

ACROSS

1. Hog feed
5. Botswana boss
10. Honchos
16. Spread out
21. Claudia ___ Johnson
22. Carlos Saavedra ___, 1936 Nobelist for Peace
23. Attentive, in Lanark
24. ___ chose (a trifle)
25. Missing ring
27. Convertible
28. Poets Sexton and Marx
29. Persevered
30. Dickens clerk
32. Lower a spar
33. Wrinkles, to botanists
34. "... black as the ___ of night": Read
36. Philly's transit system
38. Rounders
41. Truncated trunk covering
45. Good times
48. Emulate Henry
49. Gas plant's family
50. Suffix with rend or vend
51. Sec.-largest planet
54. Out-and-out
56. ___ mind (remember)
58. Mother of Apollo
59. Calcutta cigarette
60. A Plummer from N.Y.C.
62. Auditions
65. Ai-ling and Mei-ling
67. Certain bottom lines
68. Showy plant
71. Politico Landon
72. Porcelain ware
73. Inspiration for W. C. Bryant
75. Prohibited
77. Vienna. to Hans
78. Kokoon
79. Thespian Thomas
81. No big theory connector
84. Galled
86. Master, in Mexico
87. Fetor
89. Cod cousin
90. Type of screw hook
92. Ploverlike bird of Asia
94. ___ vivant
95. Waterfront inn
96. Staff symbol
99. Skate blade
100. Draggletail
103. Be united
105. Ampersands
106. Aleutian island
108. Summit
111. Early TV sensation
112. Cato's 105 Across
113. Close, poetically
114. Page instrn.
115. Greeks' Greece
117. Still
118. Buzz off
122. Hawk aggressively
125. Senior member
126. ACTION is one
129. What some subscribers do
130. Gide's "___ Die"
132. Snorri Sturluson work
135. James Wright's predecessor
137. Constellation Grus
138. Ericaceous shrub
140. Muffled thud
142. "Landlord of New York"
143. Descry
144. Reunion in Dallas, e.g.
145. Force
146. Pothers
147. Carol starter
148. Chute material
149. Solomonic seasoning?

DOWN

1. Jet-speed unit
2. Fraternal baseball trio
3. Dwarf
4. Quintain
5. Beauty-shop comparative
6. Service person at Lackland base
7. Maid in Japan
8. Scruff
9. Measure
10. Linc. is one
11. "... ___ still a moment": Poe
12. Functioning continuously
13. Kitchen extension
14. Yell out
15. No. 9 on a menology
16. Austere
17. Dearth
18. Rush; charge
19. Cut ___ (transact)
20. Sycophants' oft-used words
26. Slight advantage
31. Bradley campus site
35. Puncheon
37. Pound, in Bayreuth
39. Collier's entry
40. Actress Kurtz
42. It precedes automne
43. From the ___ (long time)
44. ___ catechumens
45. Locale of Rainbow Bridge
46. Quince or pear
47. Dismiss pong's partner
51. Don't give a ___
52. Silvery white
53. Epithelium
55. Photographer Adams
57. Mardi Gras V.I.P.
59. Half a blunder
61. Disposed
63. Fla. cape
64. Fishing net
66. "___ vincit amor"
69. Haphazardly, with "miss"
70. He played in "Waiting for Godot"
72. Faithful
74. Headstall's kin
75. U.N.'s U ___
76. Acey-deucy
77. Particle
79. "Oklahoma!" star in 1955
80. Aggregate
82. Mountie's command
83. Mooch
85. Nouveau ___
88. Make mad
91. It's provided by 93 Down
93. O.R. personnel
94. Book-jacket item
95. Soul chaser: Abbr.
97. First name in "sleuthery"
98. Trilbies
100. Suppressed sob
101. Ill-kempt
102. Epic poetry
104. Fescennine
107. Sesame
109. Old times, old style
110. Lamb of pork fame
113. "Jeopardy" offerings
114. Forfend
116. Luanda native
118. Heretofore
119. Curule-chair occupants
120. Certain minstrel
121. Works clay
122. Predatory dolphins
123. Former Russian measure
124. Maternal kin
127. Lashes
128. Double this for a perfume
131. Lot
133. Lobster boat
134. A co-inventor of cordite
136. Cunctatious
138. "Bleak House" lass
139. Mischievous Olympian
141. Lifesaver of myth

by June A. Boggs

ACROSS

1. Marries in haste
7. TV's Sharkey et al.
11. Period of power
14. Bistro
18. Discovered
19. Concern
20. Ex-coach Parseghian
21. Eye cheesecake
22. Texas trial?
24. Peruvian post?
26. Petulant
27. Half of CDXIV
29. Ravens' havens
30. Sillographers' creations
33. Kingdom east of Babylonia
34. Finished parasailing
36. Escapes notice
37. Glass in Colorado?
40. Up-to-date chap
43. Presses into grains
44. Meadowlands events
45. Travel plan
47. Rolling stones lack it
48. Domestic
49. Terra ___
50. Skelton's script-writing wife
51. Siouan
52. Bahamian baths?
55. Put one's feet down
56. Tommyrot
58. Certain buoys
59. Edicts
60. Lurch
61. Evian or Menton
62. Surface lusters
65. Fair-haired
67. Leslie King became one
68. Escamillo, e.g.
71. August, in Arles
72. Philippines beast?
76. Actress McClanahan
77. No-nukes group
78. Lechwe's cousin
79. City in S France
80. Jujube
81. Seat of fortitude?
83. Vouchers
85. Trances
86. U.S. draft agcy.
87. Nigerian objectives?
89. This is paid to heroes
90. Hot spot
91. Like the grapes of Aesop
92. Day, Duke and Hart
93. Y. A. Tittle was one
96. Strange
97. Fowl dish
98. Song of Norway?
101. Italian jet set?
106. Marble piece
107. A sign of summer
108. Punkies
109. Ocean current off Ecuador
110. Coop group
111. Objective
112. RR stops
113. Squealed

DOWN

1. Simple addition
2. ___ Salonga, "Miss Saigon" actress
3. Propel a randan
4. Has the chair
5. Stands the gaff
6. Eastern Church oraria
7. Pollock's kin
8. Working rule
9. Words of the wise
10. Woodland dweller or deity
11. He painted Helena Rubinstein
12. ___ Ben Canaan, of "Exodus"
13. Devil's-bones
14. Heavenly streaker
15. Turkish chiefs
16. Rove on the wing
17. Fish dish
19. Crooked or ironic
23. Gives the go-ahead
25. Pernod flavoring
28. Lacking reverence
30. Peale appeal
31. Former S.F. mayor
32. Arizona aristocrats?
34. Bryant, but not Gumbel
35. Actresses Olin and Nyman
37. Up
38. Two-cents plain item, once
39. Envelope wd.
40. Indian plays?
41. Third and fourth words of a soliloquy
42. Couples, but not Fred
44. Cup, in Caen
46. Part of the eye
48. Encolure
49. U.S.A.'s best customer
52. Uncool collegian
53. Still on the shelf
54. Above: Lat.
57. U.S. Skater David ___
59. Palpate
62. Wooden legs
63. Great Lakes acronym
64. Varro and Vulgar
65. Foundation
66. Advances
67. Polish or ploy
69. Power failure
70. Pee Wee and Jimmy of baseball
72. Bismuth or bullion
73. Set straight
74. One-billionth: Comb. form
75. Proverbial kingdom loser
80. Like some alleles
82. Cheongsam features
83. Au ___ (with it)
84. Bedrock
85. Flower's petals, collectively
88. ___ on (happenings)
89. Coal car, e.g.
90. Pommels
92. "___ Boot," 1981 film
93. Golly's cousin
94. Key
95. Baritone Opie
96. Birnam, in "Macbeth"
97. These: Fr.
99. P. N. Page's "In ___ Virginia"
100. Broadway's Cariou
102. West Pt. grads.
103. Coll. basketball tourney
104. N.Y.-to-Bos. dir.
105. Turf

by Charles M. Deber

ACROSS

1. Afflicted with ennui
6. W. Hoffman play: 1985
10. Dispatch
15. Con game
19. Hub of old Athens
20. Chess castle
21. Hawaiian porch
22. Poet Pound
23. Joseph's outerwear
26. Eshkol's successor
27. Weighed by lifting
28. N.Y.-N.J. river
29. Correctly reasoned
31. Rules to follow
33. San ___, Italian resort
35. Allergy symptom
36. Like a crazy hombre
40. Commit a gaffe at bridge
44. Battery terminal
46. Olympics host country in 1988: Abbr.
49. Coup d'___
50. Eaglet's birthplace
51. Cherish
53. Stay away from my door!
58. Units of work
59. Small planets
60. Elec. measures
61. Oil, watercolor, etc.
62. Fish with a net
63. Gucci of fashion
64. "Nightline" newsman
65. Ex-ember
67. Note left by a linksman
72. Peer Gynt's mother
73. Virginal
75. Qatar ruler
76. Applied oneself
78. ___ Julius Caesar
79. "I've Got ___ in Kalamazoo"
80. Storm or rainwear
84. End of an O'Neill title
85. Ferde Grofé opus
88. Nice
90. Outlander
91. Jason's vessel
92. Three times a day, in RX's
93. Arboretum specimens
95. Petty tyrant
97. Compass abbrs.
98. "The Rome of Hungary"
100. Wild guess
102. Toper
104. Indigenous
107. Poplars
111. Tenants' contracts
116. Lorelei Lee's creator
117. What to do after the soup course
120. Cambers
121. "Swan Lake" role
122. Capital of the Maldives
123. Another of the same
124. Part of A.D.
125. Now alternative
126. Scraps that Spot gets into
127. Lipizzan, e.g.

DOWN

1. One of the musical B's
2. Fairy-tale heavy
3. What the irate raise
4. Middle of Q.E.D.
5. Passé
6. Escort's offering
7. Go sky-high
8. Hebrides island
9. Read on the run
10. Skier's milieu
11. A daughter of Picasso
12. Rock producer Brian
13. Essex's title
14. Mess
15. Big rigs, for short
16. Plaid, for one
17. Song for Marilyn Mims
18. Crumbly soil
24. Incense emanation
25. Go headlong
30. Earth goddess
32. Tar's unit of distance
34. "___ Old Smoky"
36. Mother of Helen of Troy
37. Pawnees' neighbors
38. Bachelor's boast
39. Paravane
41. Have to have
42. Bobbles the ball
43. Actress Scala
45. Diamonds in Don Juan's deck
47. Bacchanalia
48. Thrift-shop transaction
52. Transude
54. Cobras' cousins

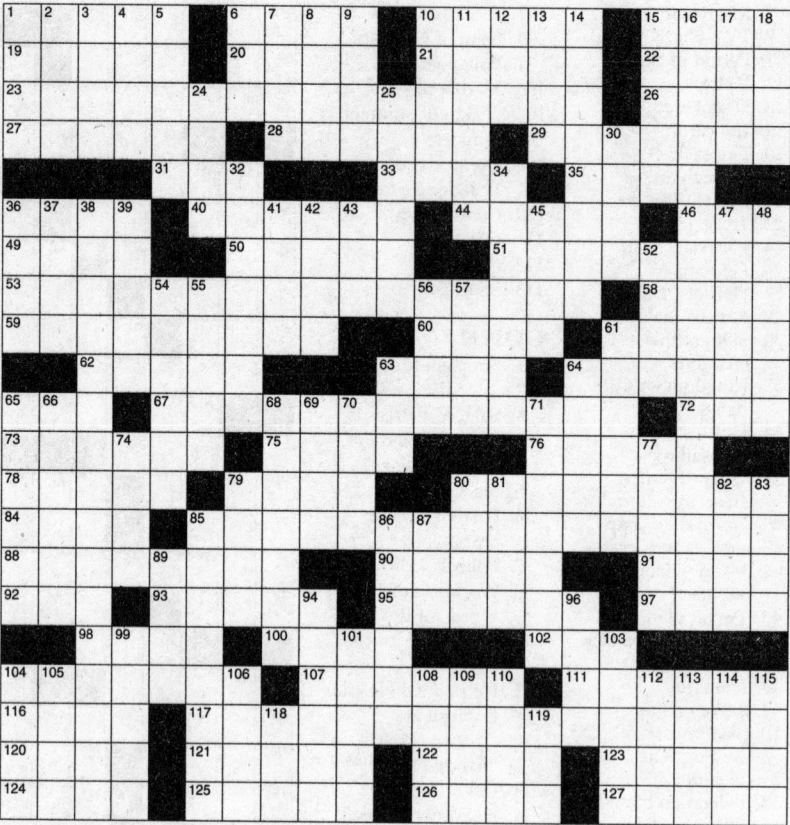

by Maura B. Jocobson

55. "Oh! ___ danced . . ."
56. Asian border river
57. Cato's 2550
61. Three-card games
63. Longest Swiss river
64. Well-recognized
65. Receive readily
66. "___ compare thee to a summer's day?": Shak.
68. Denies the truth of
69. Financial Fed
70. Decorate a lily
71. Large lizards
74. Capital of Elam
77. Nile dam
79. "Comus" composer
80. Tizzy
81. Terminer's partner
82. Slight advantage
83. Vintage cars
85. Fort
86. Section of Fez
87. Guido's high note
89. Goblet feature
94. Horse's home
96. Theda's colleague
99. Plaster of paris
101. Do tailoring
103. Works at the bar
104. Exile island
105. High time
106. Give over
108. Exec's reminder
109. Second caliph
110. Table staple
112. Mine access
113. Developer's interest
114. Borgia in-law
115. Not barefoot
118. "6 Rms ___ Vu," 1972 play
119. Aye

ACROSS

1. Fine horse
5. Freshwater fish
10. Trammel material
14. Soupçon
18. Agouti's cousin
19. ___ bell (seemed familiar)
20. Russian collective
22. Baltic island
23. Guiness-Davis film: 1959
25. "The Grass Harp" writer
27. Diminutive suffixes
28. Greek poet who rode a dolphin
30. The mind: Comb. form
31. Accountant's listing
34. Never ___ moment
35. Menlo Park family
39. Tryon novel, with "The"
40. Redford, e.g.
41. Dunderhead
42. Pompey's head
43. Agnes, in Acapulco
44. Garner-McQueen film: 1963
48. Chinese pagoda
49. News windups
50. Lineup on a fine report card
51. Foe of S. Grant
52. Argot
53. Erode
54. Book parts
56. Kind of consciousness or book
57. City NW of Waco
58. Stem cutters
60. Ripples
62. Chair worker
63. Goes off course
64. Hock and sack
65. Williwaw
67. Rome's Spanish ___
69. ___ of Good Hope
70. "Show Me ___ Go Home"
73. Santa's sounds
74. Kind of help
76. Straggle
78. Plump roasting fowl
79. Hematite and galena
80. Ardor
81. Amonasro's daughter
82. Japanese admiral et al.
83. Hyson, e.g.
84. Whimsy
88. Archibald of N.B.A. fame
89. Type of vb.
90. Miss Hogg of Tex.
91. Like some fruit
92. Dostoyevsky novel, with "The"
93. Made jottings
95. ___ means (certainly)
96. Family of an actor in the "Godfather" films
98. Witticism
99. Site of a 1431–43 council
100. Ky. college
101. Talents
105. Albany or Austin, e.g.
110. Major Hoople's "drat"
111. Framework
112. ___ Baleares, off España
113. Jazz singer Simone
114. Lacoste of tennis fame
115. Suburb of Paris
116. Leaning
117. Apprehend clearly

DOWN

1. Fitting
2. Stadium sound
3. Stich specialty
4. Lacking foundation
5. Pitcher Saberhagen and namesakes
6. Fads
7. A son of Seth
8. Vizier's superior
9. Sunday performer in Mexico
10. Belafonte hit
11. Cedric ___ (Little Lord Fauntleroy)
12. Floor
13. Haw's partner
14. Repeated musical passages
15. Auto of yore
16. Topic of an Emerson essay
17. Cohort of Larry and Curly
21. Constable and Turner paintings
24. Policeman, at times
26. Hubbub
29. Mystical mark
31. Bêtes ___
32. Of a Sicilian mount
33. Michael Redgrave film: 1946
34. Seaweeds
35. Disburdens
36. Walt Whitman poem
37. Shade
38. Part of a turbine
40. Noggins
44. Acuminate
45. They may be split
46. Takes effect
47. Greek resistance force of W.W. II
52. ___-banc (British motor coach)
54. Goddess of hope
55. Emulated Harvey Birch
56. Algonquians
59. Cucumbers
61. Open a soda bottle
62. Monastic symbol
64. "___ was one-and-twenty": Housman
65. Clupeid fishes
66. Amerinds of N.M.
67. "A ___ the Dark," 1964 film
68. See 9 Down
69. Farm mach.
70. True's partner
71. Ultra
72. Beginnings
74. Tightly sealed
75. Long series of woes
77. Screen part
82. Black pigment
84. Where Congress meets, with "the"
85. Long series of wanderings
86. Russian river
87. Coal region of central Europe
92. Arctic sight
94. Nylon constituent
95. Max, Buddy and Bugs
96. Part of a rose
97. "There's no music in ___ . . .": Ruskin
99. Orders
100. A Crosby-Hope destination
101. Antic
102. Ripen
103. Disallow
104. Mai ___ (rum drink)
106. Hissed reproof
107. Part of pewter
108. Up: Comb. form
109. Nomologist's forte

by Mary M. Murdoch

ACROSS

1. Balm of Gilead
7. Berlin-to-Dresden dir.
10. ". . . ___ and hungry look": Shak.
15. Billiard shot
20. Popular uprising
21. Foxhole
22. Actress Thomas
23. Sharpness
25. Scrub
26. TV letters
27. Ponerology topics
28. Pine-tar product
29. Iranian sweet
32. Match king Kreuger
34. Home of N.Y.'s Blackbirds
35. ___ buco, Italian dish
36. Simon ___, St. John the Divine carver
37. Flash of light
39. Coal bed
40. Cassette
43. Gasthaus
44. Washington aspic
46. New York pasta
51. Lady Penelope Devereux
52. Succès d'estime
53. Monad
55. Family of Reagan's first Sec. of Treasury
59. He lived 912 years
60. ___ Tamid (synagogue lamp)
61. His Monday is our Sunday
63. Upon
65. Modernist
66. Pochette
68. Redacts
69. ___ ha-Shanah
70. Power proj. of 1933
71. Chilean grouse
75. Mulct
76. Crack
77. First American in orbit
78. Boundary
79. Actor Vidal
80. Some Princetonians
81. Foot form
82. Portion of a potion
83. Panamanian breakfast food
87. Hill inhabitant
88. Sock exchange
89. Fit for farming
90. Kin of bravo
91. "The Facts of Life" Charlotte
92. Bear, in Brest
93. Like Maine woods
94. ___ Dhabi, Eastern land
96. Lip
100. Wrong
102. Gaelic
103. Countrified character
105. Shocked
108. Illinois refresher
112. California seafood
116. Laconian clan
117. A Barrymore in "E.T."
118. Riyadh resident
119. Below, in Bonn
120. Peace-loving
122. Hero of Hindu epics
126. Constanta coin
127. Gazelle gait
128. New Mexican breads
132. Of a trunk in a trunk
134. Drug-culture leader in the 60's
136. King in I Kings
137. Anne Brontë's "The ___ of Wildfell Hall"
138. Record holder
139. Rousseau classic
140. Minor minor
141. Father of Spanish drama
142. Kirstie of "Cheers"
143. Khedive
144. Ethyl chaser
145. Ball-park offering

DOWN

1. Beak, in Bologna
2. Beijing baby sitters
3. Comedian Jay and family
4. Uzbek corn mix
5. "___ cara," Bellini aria
6. ___ Lazarus, "Miss Peach" cartoonist
7. Freshet
8. Husky's home ground
9. Whistler creation
10. Antarctic ice shelf
11. Pahoehoe, e.g.
12. "___ bragh"
13. Tennis term
14. Most prying
15. Massachusetts chew
16. The maples
17. Muffler menace
18. Frittata
19. Lackey
24. Musical notational sign
30. Please Nemesis
31. Suburb of Pittsburgh
33. Rose bowl
38. Concupiscence
39. Hart
41. Hockey's ___ Ross Trophy
42. Equine extremities
44. Sulawesi seaport
45. Hebrew letter
46. Some Brit. lords
47. Beatitudes verb
48. Whale: Comb. form
49. Court follower
50. Penitent's activity
54. Electees
56. Ayn Rand novel
57. Alternate locale for 128 Across
58. Afternoon fare on TV
61. Grenoble girlfriend
62. Okhotsk or Andaman
63. Plath work
64. Horse-drawn Indian vehicle
67. Golfer Woosnam
68. Lay or leather attachment
71. Level
72. Lass who got an A
73. Chanson topic
74. Preys for jays
75. Berg detachment
76. Kansas or Massachusetts cabbage
77. Fierce look
79. "___ a Rose": Friml
80. Ripken of the Orioles
82. New Jersey sinker
83. Inspiring intense fear
84. Punjabi princess
85. Featherweight boxer Attell
86. Tea V.I.P.
88. African antelope
89. I.R.S. collection time
94. Neighbor of Scorpius
95. Gautama
97. Sort of key
98. Actor Erwin
99. An Arab rep.
101. Two-syllable foot
102. Being, in France
104. Spadille, sometimes
106. ___ time (never)
107. One at Roanoke, e.g.
109. Like a quodlibet
110. Preclude
111. U.S. lexicographer-educator: 1869–1946
112. Casa units
113. Leaf area
114. Daphne turned into this tree
115. Involve necessarily
120. He's Hunter on TV
121. What aristarchs do
123. Encore
124. Shelly ___, jazz drummer
125. "There was ___ danced . . .": Shak.
127. Husband
129. Helmet border
130. Slumgullion
131. Start of Caesar's boast
133. Hill, to an Arab
135. Ratite bird

by Calista Luminati

ACROSS

1. Lyric poem
4. Bad days on Wall St.
7. Applied nutmeg
13. Reel
18. Strong dislike
20. Spanish loss in 1588
21. Tawed leather
22. Husband
23. Kite or eagle
24. *Ash*
25. *Customer group reveres*
27. Presided
29. Alley yowler
30. Followed a scent
31. Side issue
32. Stack role
33. Novelist Kingsley ___
36. Spanish currency
38. Louis XIV, e.g.
40. Gannet
42. Artist Shahn
43. Variety of gypsum
48. Young congers
49. S African fox
51. "Faith ___!" (*words by Faber*)
52. *Part of D.A.R.*
53. English poet laureate: 1790
54. Fleur de ___
56. Violinist Bull
57. Make lace
58. Actor Frobe
59. Capital of Sicily
61. Tourist attraction
63. Noted Russian-born artist-designer
64. Wear away
65. Nobelist in Physics: 1910
67. Thrash
71. Oblong eatery
73. Vehicle for Ben Hur
75. Slots spot
76. Ruby or river
79. Res followers
80. Luau instr.
81. Limit; restrict: Abbr.
82. *Stretch*
83. *Trainer*
86. Perry's creator
88. Create
89. Its capital is Jakarta
90. Assist
91. "Goodnight" girl
92. Cariou from Canada
93. Dishing out
96. Marshes
97. Bow or knot, in Lisboa
100. Pres. after J.A.G.
102. Popeye's tattoo
104. Motorists' gp.
107. Struck with fear
109. *Some boxing preliminaries*
113. *Lepidopterist's thought while chasing a butterfly?*
114. Maroon
116. Stone
117. Data for a computer
118. Like clothes after a diet
119. Extreme selfishness
120. "___ thou these great buildings?" Mark 13:2
121. "Gunsmoke" actor
122. ___ Moines
123. Singer Davis

DOWN

1. Convex molding
2. Jeans material
3. Gaelic
4. Grime
5. *Unusual occurrences*
6. Lip curl
7. Crusader foes
8. Babbles
9. Hinder
10. Broadway musical hit
11. Tokyo, once
12. "Pride and Prejudice" character
13. Leeward island
14. Ordinary looking
15. *Exhausted*
16. Siouan Indians
17. Alan and Cheryl
18. C.P.A.
19. Cambodian coin
26. Colza oil source
28. Medicinal-plants adept
31. *British P.M.: 1902–5*
33. Warned
34. Red planet
35. Officeholders
37. N.M. Indian
39. Avenaceous
40. *Butchery*
41. Manifest
42. The Bears of Waco
44. In conflict with
45. Asian holiday
46. Epoch
47. Q-U connection
48. Advantage
50. Shade tree
53. Partial paralysis
55. Nebraska neighbor
59. Contrition
60. Take heed
61. Bestowed liberally
62. Tries hard
66. Strong illumination
68. Tree exudation
69. *Deep*
70. Kind
72. A chemical compound
74. Half a bray
76. Half of MCCII
77. Eternity
78. Objective
80. Mineral found in dried lake basins
82. Bruce or Laura of acting fame
84. Sad
85. *Iroquoian Indian*
87. Cattlemen
88. Casino cube
94. Irregular strophe in a chanson de geste
95. Fireplaces
96. *Cargo*
97. Network
98. "A cottage in ___": Godley
99. *Poodle or Doberman*
101. Author Turin
103. Hooted, in a way
104. Pineapple
105. Tall story
106. On the Java
108. Hershfield's Homeless Hector, e.g.
109. Lucerne landmark
110. Heroic poetry
111. Get-up-and-go
112. Red-coated cheese
115. Hide ___ hair

by Ernst Theimer

ACROSS

1. African republic or lake
5. Attempt
9. Caravel or coaster
13. Nephrite
17. Son, in Sonora
18. Greenhorns
20. Blue shade
21. Inky, poetically
22. Thyroid cartilage projection
24. Doctor Mirabilis
26. Athenian statesman
27. Fierce anger
29. Treeless plain
30. Kind of walk
31. ___ Taylor, memorable musicologist
32. Curdle
33. Saar ___, German territory
36. Many: Comb. form
37. Collected
41. Nuncupative
42. "Dream Children . . ." author
45. In the manner of
46. Widely prevalent
47. Baltic island
48. Seine land masses
49. Gyre
50. WNW's reciprocal
51. A bit at a time
55. Hustlers after rustlers
56. Ten-sided figures
59. "A Passage to India" director
60. They're often wild
61. Catherine de Médicis, e.g.
62. Organization for high-I.Q. folk
63. City of NW Turkey
64. Meager
66. Gallic girlfriend
67. Circular, towerlike fort
70. Implied
71. Chancy social engagement
73. ___ Gatos, Calif.
74. Actress Sommer
75. Scheme
77. Subject of Plato's Symposium
78. Steadfast
79. Highlands uncle
80. Tatterdemalions
84. An O'Neill
85. Spanish inns, English style
88. Kind of wrench
89. Province of SE China
90. Metropolitan thrush
91. Sub's "ears"
92. Mashhad money
94. "___ for tennis?"
97. Central Asian range
98. Pacific island group
102. Pretended disdain for the unattainable
104. Misleading clue
106. Sported
107. Needlework loop
108. Gannet
109. First-act finale in "La Boheme"
110. Home of Vance A.F.B.
111. Without
112. World's longest river
113. Emulates Dorcas

DOWN

1. Fellow
2. Coati's coat
3. "Momo" author: 1978
4. Residence
5. Pursue stealthily
6. Melville work
7. Some Dadaist works
8. N.B.A. stringbean
9. Cotterways
10. Companion of mighty
11. Frazil
12. Troubles
13. Patroness of France since 1922
14. Initial quartet
15. Kind of prize or post
16. Composer of "The Princess on the Pea"
19. "Black Beauty" author
20. One of a Dumas trio
23. Analyze verse
25. Dissipate
28. Plexus
31. Breed of hog
32. Milky
33. Used a gimlet
34. Originate
35. Yegg
36. ___-nest (hoax)
37. Effrontery
38. Scaramouch
39. Beethoven's "Für ___"
40. Jutlanders
42. Head over heels?
43. "Die Lorelei" poet
44. Climbing vine
49. Drench
52. Lacquer ingredient
53. Kingsley's "___ White"
54. Alleviated
55. Procacious
57. John Denver album
58. Essential part
60. Coercion
62. Its people were decorated for bravery: 1942
63. Long loaf of bread
64. Use a teapot
65. Majorca's capital
67. "Lower Manhattan" painter
68. Half sister of Liza
69. Ottoman dynasty founder
71. Quagmires
72. Put off
75. Old Testament book
76. Narrative poem by Byron
78. Tie fabrics
81. ___-tung, former Chinese leader
82. Bone below a humerus
83. Knacks
86. Doted on
87. Bell sound
89. "Age of Aquarius" musical
91. Komatiks
92. Indy 500 winner: 1986
93. One of the Horae
94. May Sarton's "___ Are Now"
95. High time
96. Cosmonaut Gagarin
97. Neat as ___
98. DXVII x III
99. Savage Island
100. Once more
101. York and Friday Abbr.
103. Celestial Altar
105. Ages and ages

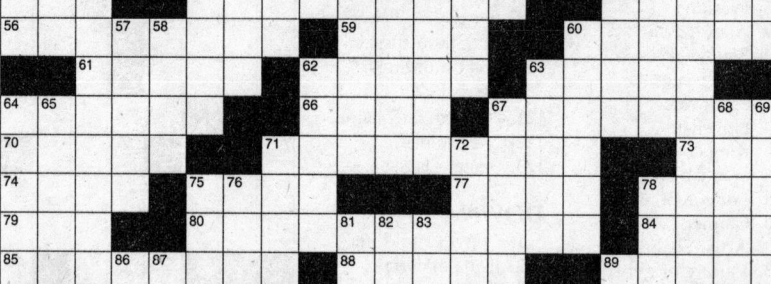

by Gloria Evans

ACROSS

1. Chamfers
7. Lifts for skiers
12. Tach reading
15. "The Old Devils" author
19. Jolson song hit: 1920
20. Red dye
21. Baseball stat
22. ". . . for ___ of woman born": Shak.
23. Last Hawaiian queen
25. Rhine feeder
26. Chesterfield, e.g.
27. Long
28. Impaired gradually
29. Bay of Fundy attractions
31. Auspices
32. Alma-___, capital of Kazakhstan
33. Certain cocktails
35. Jot
36. NE N.J. city
37. La Scala's home
40. Medici protégé: 15th century
44. Brit. lexicon
45. Most venerable
48. Implement for catching a crab?
49. Bermuda ___
51. Broadway Joe
52. De Mille specialties
54. Gull-like predator
55. The Father of Microbiology
59. Boxer Griffith
62. Ky. fort
66. City in Provence
67. Cosmonaut Gagarin
68. Katmandu is its capital
69. Zola heroine
70. Haunt
71. Tennis term
73. Sora
74. Expiate
76. Gravesend goodbye
79. Little Iodine's creator
81. Erstwhile
82. Type of type
83. Small, round window
86. Seaport in Yemen
88. Nurse Maass
89. Lassos
93. White piano keys
97. "Artie" author
98. Of the number six
99. Conquistador's goal
100. Everglades lake
104. Croats' neighbors
106. Wickiup's cousin: Var.
108. Recorded proceedings
109. Co-Nobelist in Medicine: 1977
112. Tidbit for Hansel
113. Sacred image
114. Stone marten
116. Plenteous
117. Soil: Comb. form
118. Norman city
119. Mouths
120. Irish writer-teacher
124. Gould railroad
125. A.E.C. successor
126. Painter of waterlilies
127. "Dolce far ___"
128. German state
129. Comic-strip word
130. Bagnold and Markey
131. Scheduled

DOWN

1. Prophet rebuked by an ass
2. Dispossession
3. Odin's realm
4. Sculptor Nadelman
5. Singer Rawls
6. C. P. and Phoebe
7. Cancel, as a contract
8. Spanish dance
9. Botanist Gray
10. Japanese money of account
11. Stew
12. Computer product
13. Roman bigwig
14. Trumpeter Wynton ___
15. Photographer Adams
16. Cantonese chicken dish
17. Unbeliever
18. Monterey Bay city
24. "Hitchy ___," ragtime hit
30. Clock numeral
34. Slants
38. U.S.N. biggie
39. A 1963 Oscar winner
41. An anagram for nail
42. Don Marquis's cockroach
43. Like a certain bucket
46. Bed or home follower
47. "And ___ I plight thee . . ."
50. ___ uno
52. Flock member
53. Trifle
56. Neighbors of radii
57. Muse for Marceau
58. Hemingway's "The ___"
60. Secular
61. She, in Sedan
62. Knot in wood
63. Intl. alliance
64. Formation of words like "buzz" or "hiss"
65. Site of Kubla Khan's garden
72. Lanford Wilson's "Serenading ___"
75. Febrero preceder
77. Personal quirk
78. Imam's deity
79. As a result of this
80. Legal org.
84. Pedestal part
85. Aficionados
87. Japanese P.M.: 1982–87
90. To, to Sandy
91. Presumptuous
92. Sensualist
93. Marks
94. Indians of the Dakotas
95. Cornwell's pen name
96. Reversal
101. "East of Eden" protagonist
102. Won
103. George and T. S.
105. Under the influence
107. Intramolecular
110. Not working
111. Disaccustoms
115. Salinger girl
117. Ancient city near Argolis
121. Many, many moons
122. Violinist Kavafian
123. Soybean product

by Nancy Nicholson Joline

ACROSS

1. Start of a Stepquote
5. U.K. air arm
8. Agcy. dealing with nutrition, etc.
11. Clayey soil
15. Plant of the lily family
17. Styptic
19. Alpine snowfield
20. Anaglyph
21. The ___ Lewis Trio
22. Composer Rota
23. Jejune
24. Members of an I.R.A. wing
26. A Woody work: 1973
28. Pother
29. TV sales pitch
30. Tear, to Tacitus
31. "Aida" composer
32. By its very nature
36. Singer Reddy
37. Phone's dial letters at "7"
38. Blind cetacean
40. Reverie
41. Littoral flier
43. Actor Byrnes
44. Stepquote: Part III
46. Otiose
47. Townsmen
48. Partly open
52. Certain topsails
54. Grab
56. Hence
60. "The Way We ___"
61. Bagpiper
63. Due follower
64. Hen's pen
65. Whinny
67. Bruited
69. Tails
73. Shining examples
76. Nigerian native
78. Least messy
79. "___ go bragh"
80. Stepquote: Part V
83. Nil, in Nimes
84. Stephen and Phil
87. Latin trio starter
88. Another by 31 Across
92. City-bus route
94. Feral
96. Kind of seal
98. Smog or fog
99. Objective
101. Morman missionary elder
104. ___ fixe
105. Witnessed
106. ___ fatales
109. Fastens anew
110. Ten mills
111. Core of a canine
112. Regan's father
114. Stepquote: Part VII
116. He may be good or bad
119. "Dies ___"
120. Fragrant rootstock
122. Air: Comb. form
123. Jazz session
126. Indo-European
128. Unlike the distant future
131. Moon goddess
133. Drags one's feet
135. Lingerie item
136. Corrida cry
137. Limited
139. Penumbra
140. Gist
141. Part
143. Steels, in Savoie
144. Expiate
145. Weapon, to Ney
146. It's surrounded by glair
147. Bandleader from Barcelona
148. Seas, to Simone
149. Airport stat.
150. Society-page word
151. End of Stepquote

DOWN

1. Old German coin
2. Aaron's feats
3. Gaul's chariot
4. Stepquote: Part II
5. Skedaddled
6. Aka
7. Provided capital
8. Heavens
9. Exercise for a dentist?
10. Additionally
11. Sousa products
12. Juliet's emotion
13. Assail verbally
14. Appeared, as in a fog
16. Affirmative
18. Twilight times
19. Salon offerings
20. Audit maker
21. Invitation letters
25. Fortitude
27. Drench anew
30. Songlike
33. Shore sport
34. Strew hay
35. Sermonizer's desk
39. Ultra high resistances: Abbr.
42. Extreme
45. Stepquote: Part IV
48. Barley beard
49. Army vehicle
50. Oratorio part
51. Backslid
53. Hebrew prophet
55. Suffix with tank
56. Oddball
57. Euros, for short
58. Ibex or markhor
59. Make a choice
62. Uses logic
66. Stags
68. Actress Joanne
70. Saarinen
71. Lateen, e.g.
72. Macerate
74. Regimen
75. Geisha's case
77. "___ new world": Shak.
81. Cassowary's kin
82. Stepquote: Part VI
84. Contention
85. Sludge
86. Handyman
89. Of reproduction
90. Flood or spring
91. Chef's need
92. Fidel's pal
93. Counters game
95. Guam, to U.S.
97. However
100. Extravagantly theatrical play
102. Snickers
103. Flanders river
106. Nutria or marten
107. Venomous-snake genus
108. Arranged in rows
111. Shackles
113. Hyperbola
115. Stepquote: Part VIII
116. Ingests
117. Author of the Stepquote
118. Turn
121. Carry Nation target
123. Fancy cake
124. Noncombustible gases
125. Traipses
127. Passion
129. German President: 1919–25
130. Prom queen
132. Architect Jones
134. Ram's dam
138. U.S.A.F. body
140. Ginnie or Fannie ___
142. Skimp, with "out"

by Lawrence M. Rheingold

ACROSS

1. Beam
6. Kura tributary
10. Piquant
14. Babushka
19. Upper house?
20. Hebrew letter
21. Twinge
22. Certain long bones
23. Irish breakfast? (Seuss)
26. Sesame
27. Ohio college town
28. Phoenician vessel
29. Pretoria's locale
31. Top of the world
33. French school
34. Pisa-to-Leghorn dir.
37. Vinegar: Comb. form
38. Provo plant
40. Diamond, actually
44. Associate
46. Mongoose's prey
47. Don Juan's kiss
48. Ace
50. Mideastern capital
53. Threesomes
55. Large moldings
56. Bring to terms
58. "A Sailor's Admiral" subject
59. Comber's comb
61. Patient helper
62. Mollycoddled
64. Holds
65. Come out
67. Deserts
69. Author Foley
72. Elk
74. Nobelist in Physics: 1912
75. Slouch
77. Abrades
79. Be a majority
83. Whiteness, in Palma
84. Little Red Hen, once
85. Bearded sheep
86. Reveal
88. Slugger Van Slyke
89. Weaken
90. Company lover
91. Warehoused
94. Radiance
96. "Echoi" composer
98. Pro ___
99. Like the oak leaf
101. Classified words
104. Ornamental pink
108. Play it again
110. AMEX overseer
113. Forbears
114. Nike's reveries? (Conford)
117. Frozen dessert
118. Novelist Hostovsky
119. Aye-aye's home
120. Wyeth model
121. Pleasure Island sounds
122. Headway
123. Sediment
124. Artemis gave him stardom

DOWN

1. Roman-fleuve
2. Round up
3. Domain
4. Tsk!
5. British marquee
6. Greek
7. Derby-winning filly: 1915
8. Peace Prize co-Nobelist: 1911
9. Ignominy
10. Talia Shire film: 1986
11. Ernst's eight
12. Brontë's trap? (White)
13. ". . . rosebuds while ___" Herrick
14. Beneath the Laptex's surface
15. Witty Cosby? (Nicholson)
16. Author Sewell
17. Indian prince
18. Intuit
24. Builder
25. Cape
30. Protestant org.
32. Actress Garber
34. Part of a rusty nail
35. Mexican state
36. Pepper missing? (Handford)
37. Dada daddy
39. Frenchman
41. Vereen's born? (Isadora)
42. Douay Bible book
43. Like prying Parker
45. Medical suffix
49. Teaching
50. Tennis great
51. Start of Mass.'s motto
52. Pleistocene Age
53. Asgard resident
54. Inroads
57. Inquisitive Carlin? (Rey)
60. Fox shelter
63. Type of truck
66. Drizzle
67. Actor Julia
68. Shady ones
70. Current unit
71. Penn, to Pennsylvania
73. Outfielder's error? (McClintock)
74. Genetic initials
76. Pakse's land
77. Nos. people
78. "Abou Ben Adhem" poet
80. Orsk's river
81. "The ___ My Fingers," Arnold hit
82. King of ancient Egypt
87. People of SW China
92. An antonym for restores
93. Morse "E"
95. Annelid
96. Jimmy Nelson's canine dummy
97. Gethsemane's locale
100. Showed partisanship
102. Caesuras
103. Seed: Comb. form
104. Judge Priest's creator
105. Livy's love
106. Abel's love
107. Brillant, as a color
109. Mirror, in a way
110. Sun: Comb. form
111. Therefore
112. Greenish blue
115. Ergate or kelep
116. ___ Borch, Dutch artist

by John M. Samson

ACROSS

1. Fellows
5. African republic
9. A machine load floating?
14. Dance for Miranda
19. Declare an oath?
20. Bear malice
21. Buccaneers of ___ Bay
22. Arrogate
23. Kind of bus
24. Part of a Presley autograph
25. Crucible
26. Lollobrigida and Manes
27. Wicked Arabian port?
30. Loyalty Islands port
31. First mate
32. Grounded Australian
33. Weed in a garden, e.g.
35. Bacon slices
39. River to the Rhine
41. Bemoan
44. Colette's "The ___ One"
45. Friable
48. Shingles, e.g.
50. Heaths for Heathcliff
51. "___ Aweigh"
54. Where the Crimson Tide rolls
55. A lump on a battery part?
56. Chou En-___
57. Paper measure
59. Elsa or Sylvester
60. Netherlands city
62. Timeless
65. Novel ending
66. Wee, in Dundee
69. Poetically close to a cob?
72. Dancer Eddie ___ Jr.
73. Slack part of a sail
74. Credos
75. An NCO
77. Kind of down
79. DL × IV
80. San Jose-to-Reno dir.
82. Freud contemporary
87. I.R.S. targets
90. Union or Victoria
92. Relaxed
93. Ouster
94. Seventh sign
95. Entertainer Luft
96. Elegant
98. "Like Niobe, ___ tears": Shak.
99. More suspicious
101. Most abashed
103. An objective of NOW
106. Bks. before publication
107. Sanctions
110. Bacon's place in a B.L.T. with vegetable?
116. Chivy
117. Swindles
118. Benison
119. In any way
120. "Cheyenne," for one
121. ___ de ballet
122. Toward the mouth
123. Scribes
124. Defense on a court
125. Skull protuberance
126. Danson and Knight
127. Assuage completely

DOWN

1. Priest of the East
2. Desirous
3. Cooked
4. Gurth, in "Ivanhoe"
5. Scarabaeid beetle
6. Actor Rhodes of "Daktari"
7. Do repent?
8. Jeans material
9. Aleutian island
10. More cautious
11. Accord
12. Homophone for spade
13. Computer in "2001"
14. Rio's mountain
15. Stage whisper from Elsie?
16. Actor in "The Good Earth"
17. Health food
18. Cathedral area
28. Supervise
29. Suppress
30. Tevye portrayer
34. Some wheys
35. Italia's capital
36. Hit like ___ of bricks
37. Word to a fly
38. Kind of triangle
40. To the left of a visit in an itinerary?
42. Broadway area
43. Antagonism
46. Kind of virus
47. Here, to Pierre

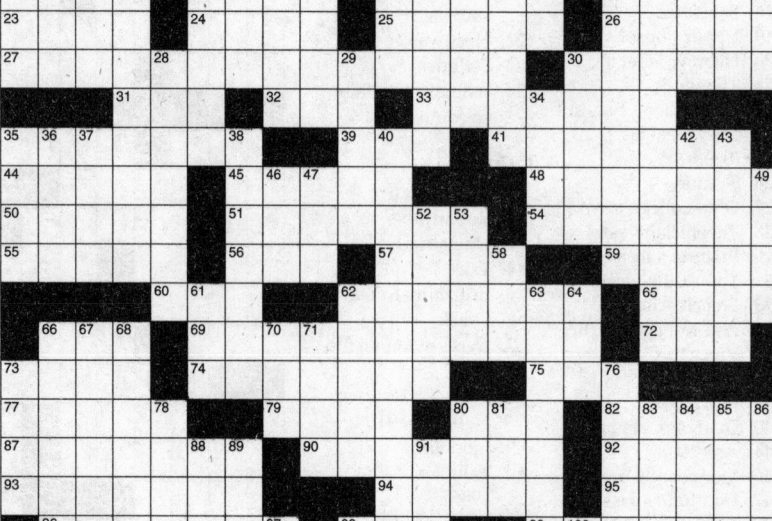

by Robert H. Wolfe

49. "Jalousie" composer: 1927
52. Kin of tombolos
53. Flesh: Comb. form
58. L-P connection
61. Light stroke
62. T. S. Eliot's "Sweeney ___"
63. Storehouse of a sort
64. Liq. methane for shipment
66. Small piece
67. Flaubert's "___ Bovary"
68. Sleeping with flowers?
70. Guernsey or Jersey
71. Objectives
73. Sight follower
76. An adjective for Sears Tower
78. Ebert and Siskel, e.g.
80. Beak
81. Preceder of easter
83. Porch adjuncts
84. Actress Singer
85. Puzzler's favorite Anglo-Saxon
86. Kind of admiral
88. Ayn and Sally
89. Coaster
91. Covered with terra cotta
97. Cleric
98. A beat in a musical direction?
100. Corrects texts
102. Puppeteer Lewis
104. "R.U.R." protagonist
105. Prior to a golfer's warning?
107. Over a toy?
108. Regan's father
109. Kind of show
111. Org.
112. Gun charge
113. Eye layer
114. Ten mills
115. Gaelic
117. B.S. part

ACROSS

1. Top of the line
5. Indian symbol
10. Ophidian
13. Modern frontier
18. Solemn promise
19. Japanese seaport or dog
20. Defrost
22. Rink structures
23. Wound memento
24. Knight's weapon
25. Bathe
26. Some exams
27. Soapmaker's dearth?
29. Sommelier's dearth?
32. Very, in Vichy
33. Marabou
34. Cannel
35. Mitty or Cronkite
38. Weather satellite
39. Light foundation garment
43. Like ___ from the blue
44. Fishmonger's dearth?
46. Surrealist Salvador
47. Misplace
48. Singer Petina
49. Blundered
51. French co.
52. Forage plant
53. Orator's dearth?
57. Inquired
59. Imperturbable
61. Ways
62. Slaver
63. Bowling division
64. Loiter
65. "The ___ Madelon Claudet"
66. Burning
67. Guardian spirits
68. Contaminated
71. Model-airplane wood
72. Miniskirt maker's dearth?
75. Genetic inits.
76. Pizarro's gold
77. Max Sr. and Max Jr.
79. Les Etats ___
80. Feminist Carrie Chapman ___
81. Betsy whose work was saluted
83. Like Savalas
87. Mother-of-pearl
88. Distasteful
90. Utter inadvertently
91. Scraped one's shins
92. Israeli P.M. Eshkol: 1963–69
93. Chris of the courts
94. Cast a ballot
95. Tailor's dearth?
98. Census taker's dearth?
102. Aquarium fish
103. Addict
104. "Mule Train" singer
106. Guns a motor
107. Teheran resident
108. ___ Porsena
109. Computer key
110. Verve
111. Kind of committee
112. Bar drink
113. Vertiginous
114. First name in scat

DOWN

1. The ___ (Springsteen)
2. Every's companion
3. Linger
4. Choke
5. More like Wilt
6. Gives the nod to
7. Fork part
8. Bel Kaufman's "Love, ___"
9. Toscanini, notably
10. Least favorably
11. Its jaws give pause
12. Sandburg's "bucket of ashes"
13. Greek sculptor-architect
14. Let out conditionally
15. Gelling agent
16. Hibernian
17. Tee preceder
21. ". . . despise those ___ them" : Thucydides
28. Guitar feature
30. Unguis
31. Strong point
33. ___ table (dine)
35. Where they plug the leeks
36. Cancel a space flight
37. Dentist's dearth?
38. Change course
39. "The agony of de feet"
40. Railroad engineer's dearth?
41. Architect Gottlieb ___ Saarinen
42. Even-steven
44. Papal cape
45. All set
48. What "veni" means
50. Mild imprecation
53. Egyptian amulet
54. Praying figure
55. Large book size
56. Neighbor of Nev.
58. By and by
60. Spring bloomer
62. Naturalist Fossey et al.
64. Thick
65. This may be posted
66. Duelist Burr
67. TV moderator Moore
69. ___ nous
70. Passé
71. Irish king Brian ___
72. Vexatious
73. Two pints
74. Military group
78. From the beginning
80. Insouciant
82. Italian beachhead: Sept. 1943
84. Main side of a coin
85. Take to the hills
86. Jumped over the candlestick
87. Alliance acronym
89. Of sacred Hindu books
91. Seedy Manhattan area
93. Room for jugs and linens
94. S.A. country
95. Wimp's cousin
96. Greenland base
97. Russian ruler
98. Honey ___, Rose Kennedy's dad
99. Holler
100. Face shape
101. Annapolis inst.
102. Acapulco aunt
105. Cuckoo

by Frances Hansen

ACROSS

1. ___ Drive, near Salerno
7. Pure ___ driven snow
12. Frenzied
17. Lots of sailors?
21. Get back
22. Purplish red
23. Mennonite group
24. Director Kazan
25. Batman?
27. Book that's full of meaning?
29. Loot
30. "And the morne ___ outgrabe": Carroll
31. "My Antonia" character
33. Pays out
34. Lennon's widow
35. ___ a rail
37. Sting operators?
38. Comic Gilliam
41. Lesser of two ___
43. Fin units
44. Tin men?
48. Some guards
50. ___ dive (throw a fight)
52. Hereditary factor
53. Go cruising, in a way
54. Pluto, to Cleo
55. Poetry buff?
57. This may be a little Scottish
58. HIJKLMNO?
59. Correspond
60. Word to a refusenik
61. He wrote "The Chosen"
63. Epic finishes?
64. Playwright Howe
65. Style of pinafore
66. Author of "A Serendipiter's Journey"
67. Word after see and before Sea
68. Canines on the Concorde?
72. Chose chow
73. It has an eye, but it sees not
75. Synthetic fiber
76. Meager
77. Pretense
79. Material for mending a broken heart?
81. Family drs.
84. Ceremonial prayer
85. Baum barker
87. Seafood choice
88. "The Morning Watch" writer
89. Makes emends?
90. "If I ___," Beatles song
91. Roman ruins site in France
93. ___ Public (average person)
94. Touse or towse
95. Rogers's rye?
98. Bush's chief of staff
99. ___ cava (cor. part)
101. Former Met diva
102. Sphere to fear when pooling?
103. He has estranged feeling?
104. Tangles up
106. Maine river
107. Decide against the diner
109. Oregon or Santa Fe: Abbr.
110. Broadway musical: 1982
111. Snips once more
113. It's all in Rhine's mind
114. Pac-Man's home
117. Sharpens
118. Goddess who knew her oats
120. Lone Star sch.
124. Clip joint?
126. Work of a biased composer?
129. S. Grant beat him
130. Pass over
131. This is silly!
132. Taiwan brew
133. Close the eyes, in falconry
134. Stunned
135. Hilaire Germain Edgar ___
136. Hutch items

DOWN

1. Rainbows for Noah?
2. And now, a word from Morris
3. Pedro's 58 Across
4. K.D. of country music
5. Healthy
6. How herds of cattle arrive?
7. Explosive mixture
8. Of the kind mentioned
9. Reliable fund?
10. Loki raised her
11. Testy person?
12. Curtain material
13. Pierre's girlfriends
14. He comes in time
15. Blue ribbon
16. Deceitful sculptor?
17. Leader of 66
18. Buck character
19. Celtics' "33"
20. Simon does it
26. Pinched
28. Certain newspaper page

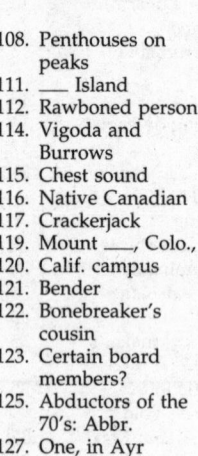

by Joel D. Lafargue

32. Have ___ to the ground
36. Mawkish
37. TV's Denise Huxtable
38. More dilatory
39. Aromatic tea
40. Country club?
41. Mideast bigwig
42. Commemorative stones
44. Passover repast
45. Search party near the Oval Office?
46. Cracked
47. Appeased thirst
49. "___ Tu," 1932 song
51. Pac. counterpart
52. Memorable, melodic Marvin
55. Parson's place
56. Place apart
59. Lord, for one
61. G.I.'s devil-dodger
62. Music to Manolete's ears
64. Woman's one-piece undergarment
65. Kirk's journey?
66. Rich gear?
68. Garb for a Stapleton?
69. Snitch
70. Kingston group
71. Ref. book
72. Lustrous gems
74. Part of Q.E.D.
76. Mount
77. Chop chops
78. Occult
80. Tell about being tardy?
82. He does the write thing
83. Hollywood P.S.?
85. Sees to
86. First name of a star on the bars
88. Par excellence
90. Maid, in France
91. Jargon
92. Ruhr roe
93. Member of a French dozen
95. Collected, as votes
96. Do a double take
97. Canine's neighbor
98. Twaddle
100. Poe maiden
103. Befuddled
105. Helper bringing a drink?
106. Leaked through
108. Penthouses on peaks
111. ___ Island
112. Rawboned person
114. Vigoda and Burrows
115. Chest sound
116. Native Canadian
117. Crackerjack
119. Mount ___, Colo.,
120. Calif. campus
121. Bender
122. Bonebreaker's cousin
123. Certain board members?
125. Abductors of the 70's: Abbr.
127. One, in Ayr
128. Ball of fire?

ACROSS

1. "The labor of ___ . . .": Milton
6. Holds court
10. Gait
14. Gorgons' mother
18. Humorist Myron ___
19. "___ to bury Caesar . . .": Shak.
21. O.T. book
22. On the summit
23. "Halt, salts!"
24. Yclept
25. Loupe
26. Wheys
27. With 4 Down, hand wave
29. Theater critic Barnes
31. With 14 Down, Hollywood's "cattle call" spot
33. Dictators
34. Peppard and pals
35. Actor Delon
36. Disgusts
38. Mortgage, e.g.
40. Cookies
43. "___ homo"
46. Model de la Fressange
47. Horn of a crescent moon
48. Philadelphia eleven
49. Eureka!
50. Ballerina Spessivtseva
51. Do over the bathroom
53. Rent
54. Chaste
56. Mauritian casualty
59. Actress Jones (Mrs. Addams on TV)
62. Dumbarton Oaks, e.g.
63. Get the lead out?
65. Monts ___, French range
66. Bet
67. With 47 Down, theme of this puzzle
70. Brazilian dance
74. Soprano Berger
76. Sacred: Comb. form
77. "There is ___ in love": I John 4:18
78. Prince Philip, e.g.
81. Very, very short time
82. Thrips, e.g.
83. ___ favor (Pablo's please)
84. R. Carson's "Silent ___"
87. Berry and Howard
89. Ref's decision
90. "Say good night, ___": G. Burns
93. Roscoe Coltrane's deputy
94. "___ Only Just Begun," P. Williams song
95. El ___, Tex.
96. Per ___ (yearly)
97. Himalayan sight?
98. Part of E.T.A.
100. Dine in a meadow
102. Goddess of peace
104. Birthmark
106. With 91 Down, glider's cushion
108. Wherewithal
109. With 95 Down, poultry preparer
112. Tony ___, Sinatra role
113. Allegation, in law
115. "All together, musicians!"
117. "Go fly ___!"
118. Spirit
119. Buttinsky
120. Historian Nevins
121. Pomme de ___ (potato)
122. Lear's loyal follower
123. Johnson of "Laugh-In"
124. An NCO
125. Made a boo-boo

DOWN

1. "For ___ and bells . . .": Lowell
2. Popular PBS program
3. "___ Day's Night," Beatles film
4. See 27 Across
5. Lure
6. Chantlike
7. Colombian Indian
8. Back-fence yowlers
9. Silvery fishes
10. One versed in disputation
11. Featherweight Attell
12. Moulin Rouge dance
13. Ford flop
14. See 31 Across
15. ". . . to be secluded ___ . . .": Donne
16. One-third of a 1970 film title
17. Kind of glass or lamp
20. Actress McClurg
28. Brand or Chamberlain
30. Worth
32. LEM's creator
37. Coryphaeus
39. D. W. Griffith product
41. Part of a hammerhead
42. Fast flier
43. ". . . a sparrow in the ___": Yeats
44. Treasure chaser
45. "___ diva," Bellini aria
47. See 67 Across
48. Architect Saarinen
50. Randolph Scott films
52. Cheryl ___ of "Charlie's Angels"
55. Frost's "The Road Not ___"
57. Spanish Main booty
58. Bravura
60. Welles and Bean
61. Browses
64. Homophone for use
67. Speak like a fishwife?
68. Placer material
69. J.F.K.'s favorite chair
71. "Gin a body ___ body": Burns
72. Supports
73. Robot Detoo in "Star Wars"
75. Proboscis
77. Capital of ancient Assyria
78. Schmaltz
79. N. Ireland Protestant
80. Kilmer subject
83. Tourn. won five times by J. Nicklaus
85. Hint at
86. "La Tulipe ___": Balzac
88. Showing clearly
91. See 106 Across
92. Mosque priest
94. Emulate Gorgeous George
95. See 109 Across
97. "Old ___," Disney film
98. Negates
99. Propel a triplane
101. Director of "Two Hundred Motels"
103. "Do I dare to ___ peach?": Eliot
105. Buzzing sound.
106. Long day's journey
107. What a dibble makes
110. To be, to Bernadette
111. Want
114. Autumn in N.Y.
116. Pitch

by Jeanne Wilson

ACROSS

1. Co-author of a 1930 tariff act
6. Helot
10. Minstrel
14. One of Oberon's subjects
19. Singer Ronstadt
20. Cupid
21. Malarial malaise
22. Corbin's "L.A. Law" role
23. Dancer Dolin
24. Knee
25. Barrett or Jaffe
26. Lesions
27. Subjects of this puzzle
31. Sloth, e.g.
32. "How __ the lady?": Shak.
33. Thee, in Tours
34. Panay native
37. Anguine fish
39. Type of jet engine
41. "Treasure Girl" song for Gertrude Lawrence: 1928
46. Secret society, Italian style
48. "Funny sheets"
50. Catapult
51. Classic introduced by Whiteman: 1924
53. Scotch admixture
54. The old sod
55. Sun. homily
56. British customs documents
60. Binaural
63. Bitter
67. Bond rating
68. Cynical song introduced by John Bubbles: 1935
75. Avant-gardist
76. Tin Pan Alley org.
77. "I beg __ pardon now": R. Wilbur
79. Raised-letter printers
85. Function
87. Mother of Hermes
88. Den
89. Song introduced by Ginger Rogers in "Girl Crazy": 1930
95. Song Al Jolson made famous
98. Playwright Ionesco
99. Of the skull
100. Estimated
102. Actress Merkel
103. Mariner's greeting
104. Pisa-to-Verona dir.
105. Monogram of House Speaker Mr. Sam
106. Abba of Israel
108. Rabble
110. Song introduced by Gertrude Lawrence in "Oh, Kay!": 1926
120. "A __ Is a Sometime Thing": 1935
121. Tied
122. Clinton's canal
123. Haute-Savoie spa
124. Ancient Greek dialect
125. Hawk
126. Shade of green
127. Type of musical show
128. Malicious and sly
129. Salver
130. Mimicked
131. Coasters

DOWN

1. Scoria
2. Song in "Let 'Em Eat Cake": 1933
3. Upon
4. Fragrances
5. Chesapeake Bay island and sound
6. Grandiose tale
7. Edits
8. Musical composition
9. Fulfillment
10. Movie vamp
11. Expectant
12. Old Norse poem
13. Paucity
14. Vogue
15. Successively
16. Crucifix inscription
17. Nothing, in Nice
18. Start of a reply to Virginia
28. When it's warm in Chile
29. An equilateral parallelogram
30. Fair
34. Land measures
35. Gauguin's island paradise
36. Serai
38. Young men
40. Zilch
41. To venture, in Versailles
42. Head of the Sanhedrin
43. Painter Grabar

44. Yield
45. Varro and Vulgar
47. "Porgy and Bess," e.g.
48. Sorceress encountered by Odysseus
49. Order from Delbert Mann
52. Bear a lamb
57. Swiss river
58. Freshwater worm
59. Emporium event
61. Zwei preceder
62. Wallet fillers
64. Former N.Y.C. skyline letters
65. Endings for pant and scant
66. U.S. mil. award
69. Little corn grower
70. Soubise, e.g.
71. Chevet
72. Mandarin's residence
73. "__ Alive," Bee Gees hit
74. Man from Marietta
78. Willow: Fr.

79. Charles Laughton's wife
80. Gullets
81. Partiality
82. Department of NW France
83. Marsh growth
84. Inst. at Dallas
86. Apiece
90. Former name of Guyana: Abbr.
91. Extend a subscription
92. Alga causing fishy taste in water
93. Headache remedy
94. Temporary stops in journeys
96. Huxley's "Ape and __"
97. Last word of Mo.'s motto
101. Scenarist Lehman
103. Roman's sacred shield
107. Anchor position
109. Chamfer
110. "Strike Up the Band" song: 1930

111. Where to watch Hawks
112. Bit part
113. "I loved you __": Hamlet
114. Weblike tissue
115. Sole
116. Mind
117. Split
118. Whittier's "__ Muller"
119. Chemical suffixes
120. Minn. neighbor

by Michael A. Rampino

ACROSS

1. "___ may look on a king": Heywood
5. High-school subj.
9. "Murder, ___ Said," 1962 film
12. Like a flapper's hair
18. Type of hit
19. "East of Eden" temptress
20. Loser to H.S.T.
21. "___ in the Sun"
22. Odd magazine?
25. Closed or open position, in golf
26. Mayan or Mundane
27. Suffix for Capri
28. Troy, to Ajax
29. Rameau's "Les ___ galantes"
30. Sheridan play, with "The"
33. Site of Phillips University
34. Town in N India
36. Annapolis freshmen
37. Gang of swans?
40. Org. for the rah-rah people
43. Certain wrench
44. "___ Foolish Things . . . ," 1935 song
45. Chinese warehouse
46. Black, in poesy
47. Distress letters
48. "Honi ___ . . ."
49. After a bit
50. Protracted
51. Former Scandinavian notables?
55. Concerning
56. What a hairline sometimes does
59. Like some beavers
60. Kind of box or joint
61. Wiped out
62. Turkish money
63. Minn. city
64. Wooden stand with a curved top
65. Doctrine
66. They're sometimes grand
67. Counterweight in a lab
68. Photos from Merthyr Tydfil?
72. A Siouan
73. ___ gin fizz
74. River at Bern
75. Wood, the boat builder
78. Saws with the grain
79. Lollapalooza
80. Assuage
82. He recruited Lafayette
84. Part of a TV set
85. Chemical flower?
87. Patten or huarache
88. A.B.A. members
90. To be, in Aix
91. Type of clause
92. Site of a Liza Doolittle triumph
94. Anatomical cavity
96. A verb for you
98. Cole Porter's "___ Clown"
99. Like betting partners' feelings?
101. Balance sheet for Amos?
105. "___ santé!"
106. This won't fill a filly
107. What Mr. America pumps
108. Pan-fry
109. "___ thou now O soul": Whitman
110. Strange need
111. Kind of house
112. Hundred-weights: Abbr.

DOWN

1. Tropical timber tree
2. Niña and her sisters
3. "Worm of the Nile"
4. Article printed daily
5. What Dana sailed before
6. Secular French clergyman?
7. Part of TNT
8. Actions banned on many campuses
9. What to take a reverse in
10. Her lover drowned
11. Where the Pison flowed
12. Kind of relief
13. Action often taken on campus
14. Wishy-washy
15. Pops outlawed?
16. Lo! to Lucretius
17. Rick ___, talk-show host
18. Tibetan bearers
23. Antarctic sea
24. Adjust
31. Featherweight Attell
32. Dawson of football fame
33. Have an ___ (look after)
34. He makes vein efforts
35. Afire with ire
37. X's for Xanthippe
38. "Sweet ___! run softly . . .": Spenser
39. Revolver of a sort
41. Satisfied
42. Cats, goats or rabbits
44. A-one
46. May and Stritch
48. Tore
49. Smooth and connected, in music
51. Tenants
52. Summer refreshments
53. Boxing ploys
54. ___-tail (cirrus cloud)
56. Heads of certain colleges
57. Capricious
58. Egyptian manipulator?
60. Fen footing
62. Actress Ulric
63. Fabric texture
65. Like some vault locks
66. Skin
68. Agent
69. Punjabi princesses
70. Bogus
71. Perm term
75. Rover
76. Metrical feet
77. Quitclaim
80. Showed interest
81. Zeppelin, e.g.
82. "___ Kapital"
83. Ref. book
85. Paravanes
86. Mean
87. ". . . after they've ___ Paree"
89. ___-puissance (omnipotence): Fr.
92. ". . . more deadly than ___ dog's tooth": Shak.
93. Capital of Fiji
94. Espy
95. Dies ___
96. Like ___ of bricks
97. Declaim violently
100. Call at Wimbledon
102. Homophone for air
103. G.I.'s award
104. Nomologist's forte

by Arthur W. Palmer

ACROSS

1. Hamelin's problem
5. Mars, to Sophocles
9. "___ the Sheriff," 1974 tune
14. Galatea, originally
20. Remains in a tray
22. Security trouble
23. Beat the goalie
24. Infuse with oxygen
25. "Where Babies Come From"
27. Tangled stuff
29. Musical suite
30. Princess perturber
32. Actress ___ Dawn Chong
33. York symbol
34. Injure severely
36. ___ Stevens (TV's Peter Gunn)
38. Assent asea
39. CBer's licensed cousin
42. Kin of Micmacs
46. Fern grouping
50. Tax-deferred acct.
51. It multiplies by dividing
53. Bridge requirement
54. Took command
55. Garden spot
56. Perpetrate
57. "___ Lazy River"
58. Final checks for Karpov
61. Refrigerant
62. Character actor Benny
63. Sign on a staff
64. Earl ___ Hines, jazz pianist
65. Work on pumps
66. "___ live and breathe!"
67. Property talk
70. Egyp.-Syr. alliance: 1958–61
71. Shrove Tuesday follower
73. B.A. part
74. Not at all
75. Badger
77. Chevy's "Foul Play" co-star
79. Taxi riders
80. Fashionable
81. String beans
82. Path for Pluto
83. Cupola
84. Tag-team victories
87. Ziegfeld
88. Creative graduate course
91. "Gloria in Excelsis ___"
92. Skirted the basket
94. Trio of trios
95. Castor's slayer
96. Don ___ de la Vega (Zorro)
98. Grate glower
99. They pull in pushers
100. Examinee's T or F
101. Upolu native
102. Release
103. Toy-pistol ammo
104. Make tracks
106. Ascribe
107. Meditative discipline
108. Customary itinerary
113. Road ending
114. Prior to, to Prior
115. Czech. neighbor
116. A democrat is one
117. Bat Masterson's weapon
119. Italian bread?
120. Personification of reckless ambition
121. Anvil location
124. Decorative design
129. Aid an Italian town
134. Small role in "The Road to Morocco"
136. Kind of engine
137. Runs amok
138. Frankenstein's flunky
139. One of us
140. Unwavering
141. One year's record
142. Roric
143. Use the VCR

DOWN

1. Speak hoarsely
2. Hammett canine
3. Heyerdahl
4. Spanish muralist
5. Star in Aquila
6. Hudson contemporary
7. Dodge City lawman
8. Terrier type
9. Doctrine
10. Egyptian amulet
11. Malarkey
12. Former President of Nicaragua
13. Start for Ballesteros
14. Siberian sled dog
15. Sideboard display
16. Johnson of "Laugh-In"
17. Make doilies
18. All-purpose trk.
19. Profit chaser
21. Zip over the surface
26. "___ Mater," ancient hymn
28. Male mergansers
31. Served perfectly
35. Stained
37. Hosp. personnel
39. Dreadful place to hole up
40. Parts of irises
41. Way
42. Of religious rites
43. "...a man or ___?"
44. Hairdresser's union
45. Convoy constituent
47. French ruling family of yore
48. Strong brown paper
49. Gripper for the Gipper
52. Coal case
53. Sounds of hesitation
58. Cuban blade
59. Comte de la Fère
60. Spring phenomenon
61. Iron: Comb. form
63. Consecrated oil
64. "Little Shop of Horrors" storekeeper
65. Bookworm
67. Mooched
68. Gives power to
69. More or Mann
72. Anderson's "High ___"
76. Nile reptile
78. Light-amplification device
79. Nice piece of change
80. Monk or monkish
81. Less stocky
82. ___ about
83. "___ your fathers thus...?": Neh. 13:18
85. Undo
86. Squatter in 1889
87. Stand stock-still
89. Unsuitable
90. Feline sound
93. Sat in session
96. Weir
97. Limbs of the Devil
99. Sartre novel
101. Radio transmission
103. Gallant
104. Hit sign
105. Strobile
108. Embossed
109. "Den I wish ___ Dixie"
110. Saloonkeeper's nemesis
111. Sweat and tears, e.g.
112. Table linen
118. Imprint permanently
119. Actress Hartman
122. It turns litmus red
123. Fad
125. Lacking slack
126. Educator Willard
127. Use a harvester
128. What the "poor dog" had
129. Personals
130. Watch the baby
131. Visit
132. Madrid Mrs.
133. Icel. or Ire.
135. Heap of hay

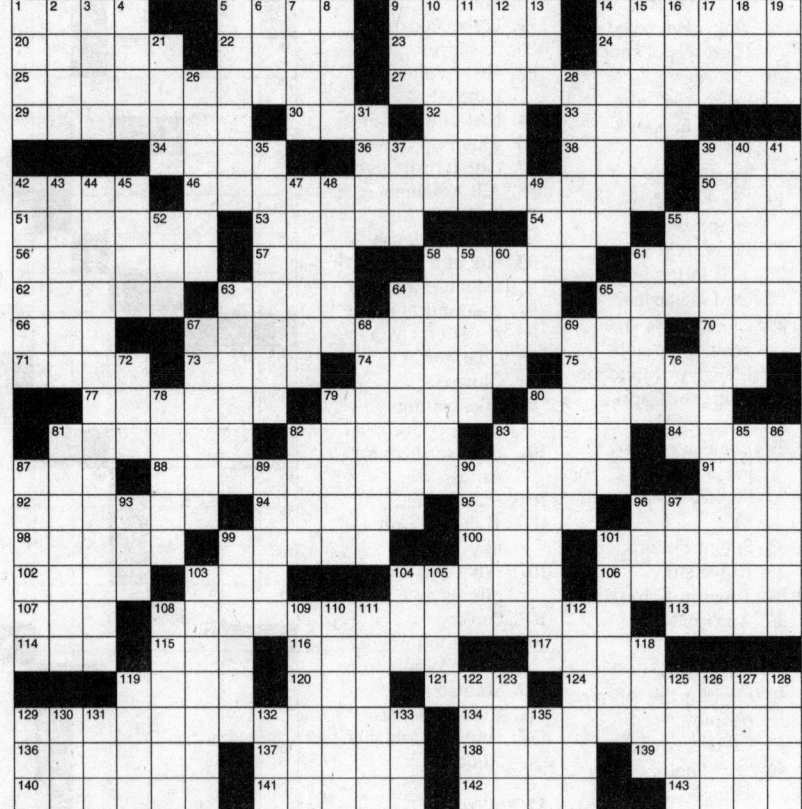

by Caroline G. Fitzgerald

ACROSS

1. Mecca trek
5. "Ars gratia ___"
10. Farmer's field: Abbr.
15. Kin of cock-and-bull stories
19. Actress McClurg
20. Jazz clarinetist Jimmie ___
21. Plain
22. Hornswoggle
23. Chauvinism in the fold?
25. Goat on a bender?
27. Occur
28. Gogol's "___ Bulba"
30. Appearance
31. Bother
34. Lab tube
35. Heat, at times
36. Culpabilities
37. English composer and family
38. Mediterranean flower
42. Provence city
43. Wild hogs' quartets?
45. Barker of the movies
46. Related
47. Profess
49. Lived
50. Year in the reign of Louis XII
51. Trick ending
52. Formal 1 Down parties?
56. A Koblenz river
57. Where boards are formed
60. Helm position
61. Rayon maker's solvent
63. "La Tulipe ___": Dumas
64. Acclaim
65. Xanthippe, e.g.
66. Flippers
68. Anonymous Richards
69. Clobber
71. Finish
72. Stable fables?
74. British medical org.
76. Irish river
77. Thunderstruck
79. Kind of resort
80. Minn. neighbor
81. Snooker stick
82. Cousin of a Cotswold?
86. Siepi, Hines et al.
87. Cop making a collar
90. Subleased
91. Out-of-the-way
92. Pouter's look
93. Song of praise
94. Extended a subscription
95. Apathetic
98. Ganef's job
99. Judges' seats
100. Nothing but bovines?
102. Lagomorph exes?
107. ___ many words
108. TV dragon
109. Earthen pot
110. Winter wind in Hawaii
111. Like Paul Pry
112. Deeds of paladins
113. A Simpson
114. Gurge

DOWN

1. Layer
2. Flap
3. Sine ___ (indefinitely)
4. Like a diadem
5. Monkeyshines
6. Drive out of bed
7. Suit for Belli
8. "Holiday ___," 1942 film
9. It has a tercet
10. Hepburn or Hepburn
11. Crow
12. Classic cars
13. "Ten thousand saw ___ a glance": Wordsworth
14. Hazard on Mont Blanc
15. Former U.A.W. head
16. Mull Island neighbor
17. Sound made by Big Ben
18. Kind of terrier
24. Off ramps
26. Result of a shaver's flub
29. Takeoff specialist
31. Mocha stone
32. Dithers
33. Colt on the loose?
34. Kind of car
35. Contrite one
37. "Life Is Just ___ of Cherries"
38. Fr. titles
39. Barnyard crone?
40. Number of Little Foys
41. Pearl Buck's "The ___": 1936
44. Little hooter
47. Like London in 1666
48. Field rodents
50. Bates ___ ("Psycho" locale)
53. It's sometimes saved
54. Mr. Oop
55. Slightest
56. Blackbird
58. Chunk, in Chelsea
59. Uris's "___ 18"
61. Lenten symbol
62. Coffer
64. Subject to planation
66. Siouan Indian
67. ___-propre (self-esteem)
69. Bias
70. Virtuous
72. Squint
73. Outlander
75. Schussed
77. "___ History": Toynbee
78. Word heard on a roller coaster
80. Praenomen sharer
83. Panegyrics
84. Homophone for seize
85. Kaffee
86. Put on the sidelines
88. Take on
89. Kind of bank
91. Tenant
93. Lapwing
94. Poker ploy
95. Castor, e.g.
96. Exclamation of dismay
97. Writer Macdonald
98. Salutation to a señor
99. French statesman: 1872–1950
101. Key, in Cannes
103. P.G.A. tourer
104. Angler's need
105. Type of table
106. Right to decide

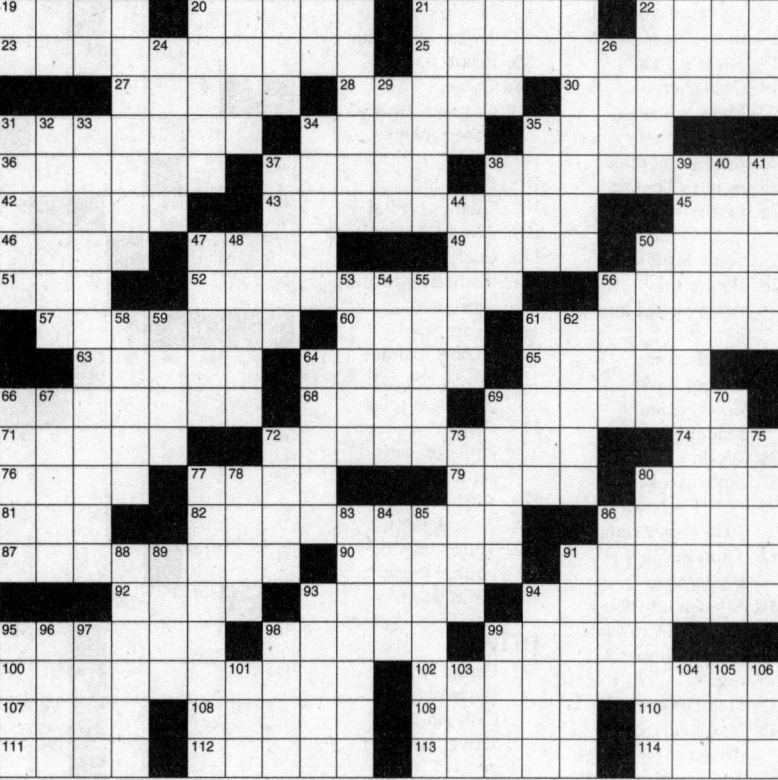

by Virginia Yates

ACROSS

1. ___ in a lifetime
5. Palm of the hand
9. "...as a wild bull in ___": Isa. 51:20
13. Street's boss
18. Okla. city
20. Make worse
22. Light-footed
23. Belgian moppets?
25. Actress Thomas
26. Leroy Anderson's "___ of the Ball"
27. Some legal writs
28. Where the Ambrosian Library is
29. Malefactor
31. Sole of a plow
33. Cosmetician Madeleine ___
34. Worker on a hill
35. Stolen sockeye?
39. "___ De-Lovely," 1936 Porter song
42. Thornburgh's predecessor
44. Kilauea effusion
45. Hoover Dam's lake
46. Hugh Johnson's org.
47. Highlands hillside
48. Like many U.K. drinks
51. Trans-central cord
54. One of the Aleutians
55. Baseball's Paul or Lloyd
56. Oriental restaurant cartel?
58. Pear variety
59. Have the miseries
60. "___ the Rear" (old song)
61. Bangladesh capital's former spelling
65. Undersized pickpocket?
70. He was TV sleuth Jones
71. Dahl or Francis
73. Make a selection
74. Fuzzy surfaces
76. Roughage fanatics?
79. Bowler's woe
81. Ridges between ice walls
85. "___ or five attend him": "Twelfth Night"
86. Simple wind instrument
88. Coiffeur's creation
89. Univ. degrees
90. Desdemona's handkerchief, e.g.
92. Shamrock land
93. London trolleys
94. Tic-toe connector
95. Beauty salon?
99. Creek
100. City in S France
102. Desert juniper
103. Tragi
105. Propounds
107. Guam's capital
109. Almost, to the Bard
110. Coalesce
111. Gorbachev in A.M. action?
117. "Gare Saint-Lazare" painter
118. Where concert musicians relax
119. Hindustani emperor: 16th century
120. Kitchen attraction
121. A York river
122. They sometimes bounce mgrs.
123. Ratio words

DOWN

1. Outlet for N.Y. horse players
2. Only, in Bonn
3. Driver's main course?
4. Gaul's chariot
5. De ___ of 92 Across
6. G.I.'s supervisors
7. Some coll. linemen
8. A Dadaist
9. Ducks
10. Ad ___ (to a sickening degree)
11. Chanson follower
12. Hardy protagonist
13. Material wealth
14. "Encore!"
15. What beefy waiters get?
16. Southwest stewpot
17. ___ tetra (aquarium favorite)
19. Slanting
21. Belligerent sea groups
24. Oil: Comb. form
29. Cobra's relative
30. Like argon
31. Laminated rock
32. Tool for Archimedes
33. Some propositions in logic
36. Make a fist
37. W.W. II India-Burma road
38. Marian, for one
40. ___ et quarante (Monte Carlo game)
41. Assyrian monarch
43. Thalassic expanse
48. ___ Jima
49. Timberlane of fiction
50. Prune
52. Dishes out
53. Jewish holiday eve
57. Antediluvian
58. Alberta park
59. Qty.
61. Touches gingerly
62. Spanish weight unit
63. Gambling spot for littlenecks?
64. Recent, to a geologist
66. Marathoner Allison ___
67. ___ facto
68. Kind of engine
69. Distress
72. Flees to a J.P.
75. Org. dating from 1897
77. Ambience
78. Fast-food magnate
79. Hindu outergarment
80. Spectrum producer
81. "___ Nell," Gershwin musical
82. Leftovers from a TV roast?
83. Come clean
84. Ponselle and Raisa
87. Incontrovertible
91. Catchwords
93. Wright or Brewer
95. Córdoba coin
96. Thought, to Pascal
97. Fortifies anew
98. Windmill impeller
101. "___ Eat Cake," 1933 musical
104. Harold ___, English political scientist: 1893–1950
105. Cougar
106. ___ about (circa)
107. Jason's ship
108. Spiritual mentor
112. Indonesia's ___ Islands
113. ___ de guerre
114. Diamond cutter's device
115. Basketball Hall-of-Famer Holman
116. Twelve doz.

by Bert Rosenfield

ACROSS

1. Ex-head of Japan
8. Town of the Big Red
14. San Diego wives, perhaps
20. "There is three ___ in this matter": W.S.
21. Gazed idly
22. Weaver bird, formerly
23. St. Louis runs
25. Maltreat
26. " 'Fraud!' ___ the maddened thousands"
27. Pop-ups, usually
28. Lou Piniella
29. Houston: No hits, no runs, no errors
33. Bull chaser
34. Neat as ___
35. Winning pennant: 1979
42. Imputes
47. Broke up or in
49. Belgian Congo, today
50. ". . . sin to prefer life ___": Juvenal
51. In order
52. Flourisher
54. St. Louis base of yore
56. Generation
57. Oakland players
58. "___ Grows in Brooklyn"
59. Miss Thompson
61. Power source
62. Diminutive
64. Painter Claude ___, né Gelée
66. Crinkly fabric
72. ". . . in the twinkling ___ eye": 1 Cor. 15:52
74. Kind of measure
76. Small bay
77. Coach's area in Kansas City
82. Enchantress
83. Chicago recruiter
85. Devoid of native minerals
86. Racing sled
87. Backslide
88. Source of igneous rock
89. More obtuse
91. Base security
92. Calif. pitching arms, slangily
94. Countertenor
95. Top pitcher
96. Squeeze-play sign in the Bronx
104. Four balls to a Torontonian
109. Silk, in Savoie
110. Kiel, e.g.
111. Tip of baseball
112. Feller and Garcia, for years
117. Raw material
118. Foiled by a Fisk throw
119. Eddy role
120. For this reason
121. Nevertheless
122. Individuals

DOWN

1. Kind of moth
2. Sharif et al.
3. Spar
4. It's quarry
5. Optic membrane: Comb. form
6. Haunt
7. Simile words
8. Deny
9. Canine, e.g.
10. Raise aloft
11. Joe Palooka's bride
12. This, in Tours
13. Ins and outs of tennis
14. Import
15. Dull
16. Home plate?
17. Debauchee
18. Hostess Maxwell
19. Spore
24. A Mo. patron?
28. ___ riot act
30. Tycoon, for one
31. Gluck works
32. Digger
33. Vent or view leader
36. Boston or ground follower
37. Old Testament book
38. ___ accompli
39. In play, as a ball
40. Tract
41. Pathogen
42. Facing Orel
43. Kind, in Calais
44. Odd job
45. Aftermath
46. Writer of suspense tales
47. Ramp alternative at a stadium
48. Detroit's batting-practice backstop
53. Employees
55. Wreath evergreen
57. Unisex gown of old Greece
60. Drysdale or Mattingly
61. Taradiddle
63. British hoods
65. Gimlet's larger cousin
67. Stocking fabric
68. Early Peruvian
69. Hill
70. "The Cat in the Hat" man
71. Feminine endings
73. Capp's Fearless fellow
75. Parish priest
77. City NW of Napoli
78. "Is it a hit ___ error?"
79. Peteman
80. Egyptian dancing girl
81. True, in Ayr
82. Minx
84. Confuse
86. Highly volatile fuel: Abbr.
90. Chicago-to-Detroit dir.
91. Get some shuteye
93. Pickpocket's prize
94. ". . . devotion is ___ love": Coleridge
97. "And this shall be ___ unto you": Luke 2:12
98. Netman Yannick's family
99. Exist
100. Family of a 1944 Nobelist in Chemistry
101. ___ a customer
102. San Rafael's county
103. Someone ___ (another's)
104. Banter
105. Poker payment
106. Manager of the ___
107. Help with the dishes
108. ___ breve (2/2 time)
112. Trainer's aid, often
113. Pt. of U.S.N.
114. Fitting
115. Devilkin
116. Tot's "little piggy"

by Caroline G. Fitzgerald

ACROSS

1. Stone paving block
5. Book of the Bible
9. Part of Montana's shoe
14. Sea dogs
18. Astronaut's milieu
20. White heron
21. Poet Garcia ___ of Spain
22. Primitive: Comb. form
23. Lait topper
24. The Summit in Houston
25. E.T., e.g.
26. Feeling contrite
27. Commotion
29. Franklin D. Roosevelt Museum site
32. Menlo Park name
33. Darling or Hiller
34. Actor O'Brien: 1915–85
35. Cynic
37. Modified, with "down"
40. Grocery item
41. New wine
42. Pluck
44. Jennifer O'Neill film: 1971
50. Bright
51. Gary Grimes in 44 Across
53. Jogs
54. Adjective for 69 Down
55. Introduction
57. Steeple adornment
58. Your, of yore
59. Aim high
60. Synthetic fabric
61. Tree of the rose family
62. N.Y.C. dept.
63. Not any, in law
65. Toronto's prov.
66. Part of N.B.
67. Sky enigma
68. Agency
70. Gives joy
73. Film or play that is the key to this puzzle
77. Teetotal
80. "___ of Endearment"
81. Hopped-up drink
82. Holier ___ thou
85. Two-cupped garment
86. "___ It Up," Little Richard hit
88. Spooks' den
89. Completed hang gliding
90. Make shipshape again
92. In a weird way
95. Southwestern stewpots
97. Hamlet's exclamation
98. Annoy
99. "___ . . . in infamy": F.D.R.
100. Dirk
101. Moth's glossa
103. He wrote "The Name of the Rose"
104. December messages?
108. Word with pin or fold
109. Jane or Zane
110. Zimbalist's teacher
111. Events at ovals
113. Finds a second renter
115. Idols
118. Allowed
120. Bind
121. T. Williams play
126. Tip givers at the Big A
129. Heavenly butter
130. "___ Male War Bride," 1949 film
131. Sky: Comb. form
133. Lustrous fiber
134. Recumbent
135. Outward
136. Dustin Hoffman title role: 1974
137. Swiftly
138. Mediocre
139. Real author of Baron Munchausen's tales
140. ___ fixe
141. Unique thing

DOWN

1. Schismatic group
2. Raison d'___
3. Shakespearean play
4. Pattern
5. A Cabinet dept.
6. Cheshire borough
7. "The ___," 1976 Polanski film
8. Status reached by Streep
9. Quahog
10. Actress Montez
11. Innisfail
12. Dice throw
13. Citrus fruits
14. Bull: Comb. form
15. Adjust precisely
16. Frog
17. Saw, in Siena
19. Superman portrayer
20. Emulate Horner
22. Pushes
28. Ancient Assyrian king
30. Talking bird
31. German reservoir dam
33. Cancel
35. Tops
36. Forage plant
38. Charms
39. Some ancient Greeks
40. Day after day
41. Saint-___, French port
43. Plant part
45. Benin native
46. Kyoodle
47. The Gorgons and Graces
48. German city on the Lippe
49. "Night Music" playwright
51. David Lean's milieu
52. Kid
56. Actor in "The Ghost Goes West"
58. Todd and Ritter of films
59. Isomeric
61. Certain Muslim
64. Capsize
68. French Republic personification
69. One of the seals
71. Menu item
72. Grief symbol
74. Ethereal
75. Rescue
76. Expert witness in a sanity trial
77. At right angles to a ship's length
78. City in S Netherlands
79. Wrapping material
83. A. Miller play
84. One's sibling's daughters
87. Game in "The Sting"
89. Taffrail's locale
91. Home of Aeneas
93. Part of T.G.I.F.
94. Attorneys' jargon
96. Suffer
98. Hopi village
100. More fitting
102. Kokoon
105. Undo
106. Shekels
107. Spurs
109. Third Reich secret police
112. Frightened
114. Ashley or Hobson
115. Mule's cousin
116. Goodbye, in Granada
117. Gland: Comb. form
119. Silly
121. Lamebrains
122. Service org.
123. Lines on maps: Abbr.
124. P.D.Q.
125. Vendition
126. Frisbee, e.g.
127. Sushi ingredient
128. Haruspex
132. Bangkok-to-Hanoi dir.

by Jacques Liwer

ACROSS

1. It verges on Virgo
4. Skewed
8. Architectural recesses
13. Decamped
17. Portoferraio's island
19. Wife of King Latinus
20. Patch up a road
21. Vehicle for winter Olympics
22. She weds poet—gets lots of mail
25. "God's Little ___"
26. Southern constellation
27. Childish, in Chartres
28. Like Brown's walls
29. More reasonable
32. Joust standards
33. Elopes
34. The Red Cross needs it
35. Heart part
36. "___ Crazy"
37. "___ the ramparts . . ."
38. She weds novelist—OPEC applauds
43. Ubiquitous abbr.
46. Japanese foot covering
48. Casino cash-collector
49. City in Uruguay
50. Spanish river
51. Gin
53. Atlas aid
56. Wild guess
57. Raise ___ (create a commotion)
58. A Morrow medium
60. Señorita's snack
62. Parts of soft palates
64. Corolla petal
66. She weds boxing champ—plays in fast lane
70. Dental deg.
71. Alters a line
73. Stairway post
74. Huge star in Cygnus
76. Flightless birds
77. Consumer
79. Trite
82. Bits of marginalia
85. Observe carefully
86. Scurvy fighters
88. State founder
90. Oratorio part
91. Echidna's morsel
92. She weds ex-Surgeon General—elopes in roadster
96. T-bill payout
97. Netman Camporese
99. Sandy tracts in England
100. Like street talk
102. Irritate
104. Jams; pickles
107. Angler's casting plug
108. ___ lazuli (shade of blue)
109. Upright and grand
110. Aphorism
111. Arabian port
112. She weds former N.Y. mayor—turns down lights
117. The horror of Gomorrah
118. Auguries
119. Bows out
120. Tug's tow
121. Broadhorns
122. Rib
123. Apple or pear
124. When the French fry?

DOWN

1. Noted ecdysiast
2. "Spoon River" poet's monogram
3. Kabuki costume adornment
4. One cause of trysts
5. Bonnie bairn
6. Six-time N.L. home run leader
7. Cold wind from the Andes
8. Places for matériel
9. Kind of dollars
10. She knows roses
11. Wilson and Hines
12. Jrs.' elders
13. Taste in general
14. She elopes with explorer—smooth running assured
15. Swamp stalker
16. G. Cooper role
18. Everything, in Emden
19. These go to a higher court
23. Desert, in Diamante
24. Unc's mate
28. Relative of 15 Down
29. Dry cleaners' problems
30. N.Y. city
31. She weds actor—develops odd typing technique
32. Yeats and Keats
35. Conn. town
36. Small sphere
39. Troy, to Horner
40. Pallid
41. Singer John
42. Dirigible description: Abbr.
44. Group of three
45. Pine fruit
47. George's collaborator
50. Shield for Jeanne d'Arc
52. Dutch treat
54. FitzGerald's rhyme for "thou"
55. Scheherazade's stock in trade
59. Narrow-minded
61. Tara native
63. French oenophiles' delights
64. Tarkington's "In the ___"
65. Dud
67. Scipio, to Hannibal
68. Visorless cap
69. Gland: Comb. form
72. Suffix for Canton
75. Letter from Greece
78. Novelist Haggard's title
80. "___ moi le déluge"
81. Coins in Tirana
83. Trace
84. Bacchus attendant
87. Khartoum residents
89. Absentees at airports
92. Say Hey Willie
93. Boot camp's cousin
94. Ragtime dance
95. Kind of line
98. Monks, in Metz
101. Critic James and family
102. Wash. cape
103. Lowest point
104. Froth
105. "Adriana Lecouvreur" composer
106. Belasco portrayer: 1940
107. Runyon's $100
110. Brief gander
112. Little bit
113. Outside: Comb. form
114. Top gun
115. Pithy saying
116. Ram's dam

by Victoria Black and Alex F. Black

ACROSS

1. Andalusian port
6. Imarets
10. Disney's inventive mouse
14. Senegal's capital
19. U.S. rocket stage
20. What a swain presses
21. Niagara Falls sound
22. Evergreen shrub
23. Marriage, to Cicero
27. Flavorful
28. Lovelace's colleagues
29. Toils
30. Choler
31. Whirled
32. Satirist Freberg
33. "Marry'd in haste, ___": Congreve
42. Ivanhoe, e.g.
43. Opercula
44. Shower gift
45. Stole
46. Victorian expletive
47. She wrote "My Life": 1975
49. Tie material
50. Trifles
51. "Husband and wife ___": O. W. Holmes
58. Large wts.
59. Finished parasailing
60. Wrong
61. Fries quickly
62. Inverness uncles
63. Guidry or Darling
64. Other
65. Barrel parts
68. Rise on a wave
70. Chapeau ___ (a cocked hat)
71. Audit maker
74. What man and wife shouldn't have, according to Farquhar
78. Director Flaherty's "Man of ___"
79. Nothing
80. Cockle
81. Algerian port
82. "We'll ___ a cup o' kindness yet": Burns
83. Type of goat
85. Something real
87. End of a Stein line
88. "___ is born married": John Ray
93. Mr., in Munich
94. Watercourse
95. Lover of Tithonus
96. Stalactite locale
99. Islamic spirit
101. River of N Ecuador
106. Marriage, to Menander
109. Father of English empiricism
110. Frangipani, e.g.
111. Undiluted
112. Big cousin of a dik-dik
113. End of an O. Henry tale
114. Counting-out word
115. Record, as a wedding
116. Force units

DOWN

1. Margays and civets
2. Muslim title
3. Profound
4. Tout's dope
5. Kinshasa resident
6. Publisher
7. Streisand film: 1987
8. Pen point
9. Checked
10. Like honeymooners
11. Debatable
12. Dull-witted ones
13. Grads, not long ago
14. Orate
15. Certain Christian doctrinists
16. Ukrainian capital
17. Part of a French play
18. Thornbacks
24. Actor Calhoun
25. Husband and wife, e.g.
26. Bone: Comb. form
31. "Dum ___ Spero," S.C. motto
32. Incline
33. Gilly or democrat
34. Profs' concoctions
35. Fashion
36. Romola's creator
37. Shelters, in Savoie
38. Difficult journeys
39. Wolfpack member
40. Stir up
41. Bridge positions
42. The Shakers, e.g.
47. Annoy
48. Site of first Olympics
50. Swing around
52. Petruchio, e.g.
53. Valentine for moviegoers
54. "___ My Souvenirs," 1927 song

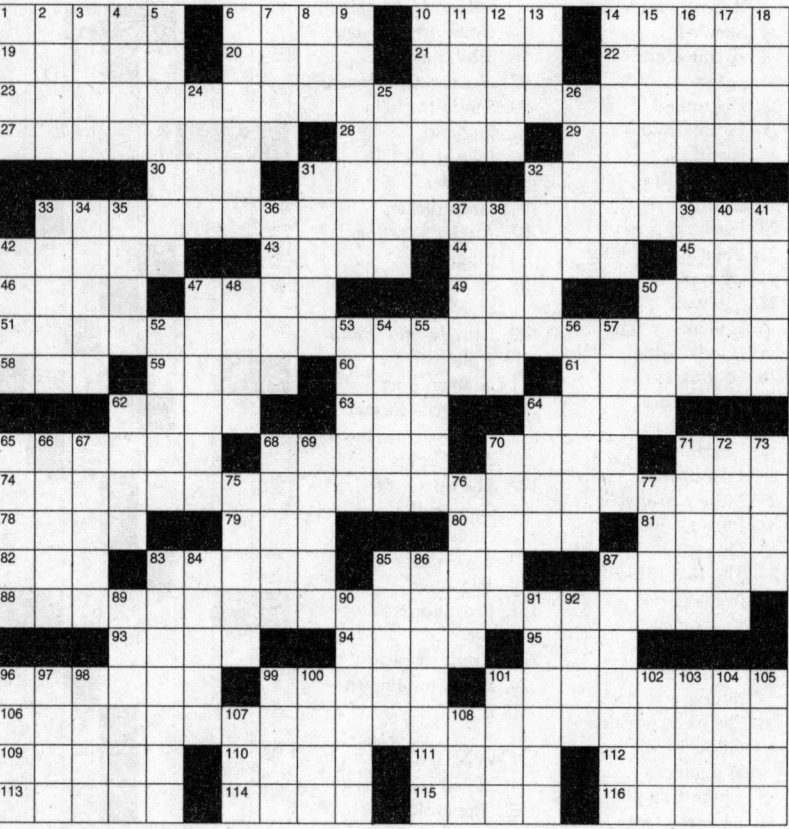

by Michael J. Parris

55. "Cielito ___," Spanish song
56. Oblique
57. Renaissance poet
62. Tied
64. Actian and Augustan
65. Groom's wear in yesteryear
66. Pentateuch
67. On the alert
68. Liners
69. Biblical spy
70. ___ retreat (flee)
71. Color: Comb. form
72. A.F.B. in N.H.
73. "Judith" composer
75. Walking ___ (happy)
76. Bedtime for a señora
77. Matador's foe
83. Frozen dessert
84. Horn-shaped structure
85. Montmartre money
86. Like S.T.C.'s Mariner
87. Used a cupel
89. Certain elongated snails
90. Cantankerous
91. Nullify
92. Sullen
96. Briton or Breton
97. Take ___ (say "I do")
98. Last of a Caesarean trio
99. Nephrite
100. Privy to
101. Kin of P.D.Q.
102. Depend (on)
103. Actor Dixon
104. Spanish movies
105. Auto pioneer
107. Dactyl or hallux
108. Poseidon's domain

ACROSS

1. Horned vipers
5. Alpine pinnacle
10. Title for Macbeth
15. Troon, e.g.
18. Use a bubble pipe
19. Madrid art museum
20. Student of Fauré
21. Cantina cash
23. Subject of this puzzle
25. "Can-Can" tune
27. Some playing marbles
28. Blackout while young F.A.S. sang
30. Woolly Andean
31. Had effect
32. Stops working
33. Pride of one in a pride
34. Bits of land
37. Ship to remember
38. Sevens and elevens
42. Chief buyers of performers' albums
43. "Anything Goes" tune
45. Neck warmer
46. Muslim chiefs
47. "___ Do It": 1928
48. State
49. Stuffy chap
50. Schisgal play
51. "Gay Divorce" tune
55. Light too bright for sight
56. Zetetic
58. Pouty looks
59. Kind of bullet
60. A prelate and a playwright
61. Seals, as pipe joints
62. Lake Volta is here
63. Triangular sail
65. Stupefy
66. Tricked
69. Where two become one
70. "The New Yorkers" tune
73. Violinist Kavafian
74. Move wearily
75. Unit of loudness
76. Roof segment
77. Shepard's "Fool for Love" won one: 1984
78. Lap pooch
79. "Red, Hot and Blue!" tune
83. Napoleonic general or red hog
84. Regular dates
86. Major Hoople's cries
87. Lighter fluid
88. Earsplitters
89. A.L. M.V.P.: 1960–61
90. Bender
91. Tar
94. Expand
95. Fragrant
99. Musical featuring "I Hate Men," "So in Love," etc.
101. "Born to Dance" tune
103. Dividing word
104. Cauthen or Pincay
105. Taffeta sound
106. "Fish Magic" artist
107. Long time
108. Motivates
109. Rorschachs, e.g.
110. Vocal impertinence

DOWN

1. Basics
2. Token taker
3. Chopin or Gomulka
4. Adds instruments to make a lusher sound
5. Victor's take
6. Missed a pop-up
7. "Peanuts" plaint
8. He wrote "The College Widow"
9. Pirate
10. Its rhyme scheme is ABaAabAB
11. Aureoles or glorioles
12. English Channel feeder
13. Ida. neighbor
14. Kind of shoe
15. Typewriter bar
16. Indiana birthplace of 23 Across
17. A ___ Able
22. She bear, in Barcelona
24. Dramatic designs
26. Barracks decoration
29. Médoc product
32. Gounod opera
33. Companionable, in Cheshire
34. Natives of Sic.
35. Musician's transition
36. Musical featuring "My Heart Belongs to Daddy"
37. Racing sailboat
38. Actress Patterson et al.
39. "Mexican Hayride" tune
40. River at Tours
41. Lyricist Carol Bayer ___
43. Petemen
44. Pluto, to Plato
47. Fabric for an amice
49. Sycamore
51. Gulf of Guinea feeder
52. Tickle
53. "___ This Earth," 1988 film
54. Because of
55. Cornucopia item
57. Shape manually
59. Pin inserted into a gunwale
61. Flood controller
62. Windfall
63. Finns' neighbors
64. Dole out
65. What some gentlemen prefer
67. Occipital protuberance
68. Dorothy, to Em
70. Is schneidered
71. Hautboys, e.g.
72. E. Indian timber trees
75. Brandy-based drinks
77. Shows verbal superiority
79. Language student's problem
80. Coryphaei
81. Grendel, in "Beowulf"
82. Most peacockish
83. Cynosure in Florence
85. Appends
87. Kiosks
89. Carpenter's ___ box
90. Possible cause of "seen us" trouble
91. Perform Christies
92. "___ kleine Nachtmusik": Mozart
93. Regarding
94. Dry spot except in a rainy season
95. William Hoffman play: 1985
96. Altman's "Welcome ___"
97. U.S. composer: 1874–1954
98. Fair marks
100. Little fox
102. Veneration

by Louis Sabin

ACROSS

1. French landscapist
6. Start of most of a passage by 66 Down
12. Lang syne
16. Kind of boat or train
21. Andean animal
22. Author Fallaci
23. Not fooled by
24. TV role for Sharon Gless
25. Stand-in for Standish
26. Bay west of Myanmar
27. Word on a coin
28. Four Holy Roman emperors
29. Yellowish brown pigment
31. "___ Evil," 1971 film
32. Entrance to 128 Across
34. Reflexive pronoun
36. Income from a tenant
38. Que. neighbor
39. Ethiopian prince
40. Alpine frock
43. Tomcat
44. Second passage: Part VI
46. Prefix with sphere
50. Aussie's warning cry
51. "On ___ Boat to China"
53. G. & S. character
57. Way out
58. O'Neill trees
59. Hexapods
61. Blue shoe material
62. ___-Lenape Indians
63. First U.N. Secretary General
64. Pakistani language
65. Squiggle or spiral
67. Boast
68. Humdrum
70. Humiliate
71. Hero of a 1922 play
72. River at Leeds
73. Maroons
74. ___ fide
75. Enzyme suffix
76. Turmoil
78. Inc., in Britain
79. Second passage: Part IV
81. Feverish
82. Rest
85. Court call
86. Josip Broz
87. Some kayakers
91. Exactly divisible by two
92. Singer Loretta ___
94. Pythias's pal
95. Blind spot
96. Crosby or cherry
97. Café au ___
98. St. Pierre and Miquelon
99. Child-advocacy org.
100. Tiff
101. Les ___-Unis
103. Chitchat
105. Krupp's milieu
106. A U.S. Open champ: 1968
107. Strait of Dover port
109. Radials on a Rolls
110. Web-footed beast
111. Half a tetrad
112. Second passage: Part II
114. Home of Johnny Reb
115. D.C. suburb
117. Hoppy drink
120. ___ Allen belt
121. Voltaire's forte
123. Wife of Henry II
128. Locale featured in this puzzle
131. Of a former Venetian ruler
134. Name in "The Raven"
135. Verve
136. Others, to Ovid
137. Used a pantograph
139. Admiral Andrea ___
140. Rude awakener
141. Musical epilogue
142. Regatta site
143. Sidled
144. Hemmed and ___
145. Earl of Avon
146. End of first passage
147. Movie units

DOWN

1. Skirmish
2. Partner of Stan
3. Writer Dotson ___
4. Straws in the wind
5. Like beachcombers or surfers
6. Criminal coterie
7. Provokes
8. The Mets or the Muses
9. With enthusiasm
10. Fatuous
11. First passage continued
12. Like wet cement
13. Record of one year's events
14. Counterfoil
15. Hoyden
16. Bats' hangouts
17. "Our Gang" author
18. Actress in "The Maltese Falcon"
19. String-quartet member
20. Ayes
30. Young friend of 66 Down
33. ___ 500
35. Gambols
37. Mesh; web
41. Iditarod terminus
42. ___ Plaines, Ill.
44. Second passage: Part V
45. End of second passage
46. Lends a hand
47. Apply muscle power
48. Lesser
49. Start of second passage
52. Event
54. Part of N.M.S.Q.T.
55. Revere
56. Less passé
59. Man of Ahvaz
60. Mr. in Madras
64. Wolf-pack member
66. Pen name of Charles Dodgson
69. Aardvark's dinner
70. In a preoccupied way
75. Some choir members
77. Mecca for cowboy poets
79. Second passage: Part III
80. Marksman, at times
82. Old fiddle
83. Señora Perôn
84. Disciplinary
87. Sensitive one
88. A sibling of Cottontail
89. City near Boys Town
90. Filled
93. Bark
94. Get rid of
99. Propels a shot
102. Like some mirrors
104. Rustic
105. Tpk. or hwy.
108. Dueling trophy
110. Mint family member
113. Intertwine
116. Indigent one
117. Covered with water
118. Liza's sister
119. Furnish funds for
121. Slyly sarcastic
122. Composer Ned
124. Battery terminal
125. Norway, to the Norse
126. Bay window
127. Uses books
129. Engraver Gustave
130. Land owned absolutely
132. Scopes's supporter
133. Bottom of the barrel
138. FD&C Blue No. 2

by Timothy S. Lewis

ACROSS

1. A golf stroke
5. Aspirin target
9. Chest sound
13. Colorful fish
17. Pianist Gilels
18. Hitler's mistress
19. Particulars
21. ___ citato
22. Nick's spouse
23. Lofty sanctum
24. Jury
25. Pour forth
26. Tennyson title
28. Popular hymn, with "The"
30. Korea Bay feeder
31. Amphora
33. Liking, in Lyons
34. Ball game for 20
37. Do a double take
39. Freshwater turtle
44. Summons to court
45. Changed one's status
47. Indian of N.M.
48. Tolkien horse
49. ___ drop of a hat
50. Start of a tot's chant
51. Alternate movie shots
52. Problem in some concert halls
53. Life stories, briefly
54. Flock of quail
56. Seria or comique preceder
57. More uncertain
59. Stop, in Montréal
60. Rejects disdainfully
61. Wright wings
62. Focal point
63. Baker's aide
64. Mortarboard feature
67. City in Puerto Rico
68. Ariel's boss
72. Crockett's last stand
73. Heat and Jazz
74. Capital of 78 Across
75. Algerian port
76. City on the Adda
77. Sheltered at sea
78. Department of N France
79. Except
80. Getting ___ years
81. Suffer
84. Fonda or Rabbit
85. Uncalled for
87. Imprimeur's need
88. "When the Frost ___ the Punkin": Riley
89. Old verb ending
90. NASCAR event
91. A glove leather
94. Ill-tempered
99. De Mille epic of 1932, with "The"
105. U. of New Mexico athlete
106. City on the Po
107. Movement
108. Comment from Garfield
109. Bond's alma mater
110. Beethoven's "Für ___"
111. Source of a fragrant oil
112. Soprano Berger
113. ". . . ___ forgive those . . ."
114. Necklace unit
115. Level a Soho flat
116. Curious

DOWN

1. "Chariots of Fire" star
2. Parisian's "Help!"
3. Alpine snowfield
4. Become limp
5. Spinning
6. Choke's locale
7. Starling's N.Z. cousin
8. Sap
9. Comeback
10. "Thereby hangs ___"
11. Furnish
12. Crisis
13. Skater Protopopov
14. Quince
15. Etcher's need
16. Kind of bun
18. ___ Allah, Iranian religious leader
20. Calumniated
27. Mast chains
29. A Eur. country
32. "___ du lieber!"
34. Tamarack
35. Hi from Ho
36. Occurred to a person suddenly
38. Old letters
39. Yeti's homeland
40. With opposing aims
41. Meadowlands horse
42. Entomb
43. "___ a Stranger": Thompson
44. Between hic and hoc
45. Rail supports
46. Used the tub
49. "___ of Divorcement," 1932 Cukor film
54. Gators' kin
55. Old English money
56. Uncloses, in poesy
58. Role for Liz
59. "Judith" composer
60. Tea tidbit
62. Passageway
63. Position for a gymnast
64. Kite's weapon
65. Romberg's "One ___"
66. Berlin's "___ Salome"
67. Antae
68. Fares
69. Poet's inspiration
70. Fictional talking bird
71. Lulu
73. Photographer's need
74. One waiting in ambush
77. Record material
78. Forebear
82. Had a hankering
83. Hook: Comb. form
84. Memorable chanteuse
86. "___ Girls"
90. Mrs. Gorbachev
92. Laurie of songdom
93. Peas' spots
94. "Iacta ___ est"
95. Barflies
96. Medieval weapon
97. Tops
98. Maumee Bay feeder
100. Mezzo-soprano Petina
101. Feds
102. Deli purchase
103. Long, long periods
104. Intersection

by Alfio Micci

342 DITTO

ACROSS

1. Type of beer
5. Vainglory
9. At the stern
12. Rival of U.S.C.
16. Isle of Hawaii
17. Long narrative
19. Deadness symbol
21. Robards and Bateman
22. Part of a markka
23. Diarist's activity
24. Patriotic song words
27. ___ shrike of Madagascar
28. Monogram of T. Wolfe's eminent editor
29. Trifle
30. Kind of panel or year
31. Where Warden Lawes worked
32. Pipe elbow
33. Zero
36. One of Carmen's people
37. Was left on base
38. Vilipend
40. Multi-star 1963 movie
46. Spotted cat
48. River in N Chile
49. Mazuma
50. Use finger paints
51. Dowitcher
53. Sacred: Comb. form
55. Welkin
56. Tenon's mate
59. Tucker's partner
60. Strauss's "___ Italien"
62. Black tea
64. Phrase from a W.W. I song
68. Zoological suffix
69. Equality
70. Intention
71. Like certain seals
72. Side of a triangle
73. Actor Bruce et al.
75. Hampshire or Yorkshire
76. Curved inward
79. Medium is one
80. Broad sash
82. Varsity member's prize
86. "When . . . marching ___!"
90. Retail sign
91. Formal order
92. Type of jet engine
93. Alphonse, to Gaston
94. ___ up (riled)
95. Composer of "The Seasons"
97. Scandinavian goddess of the future
99. An Afg. neighbor
102. One of the Hoggs of Tex.
103. An Asian capital
104. Doubled phrase in a novel ending
108. Fit for use
110. Fanfare
111. Lagging
112. Visit by a medic or clergyman
113. "The Wreck of the Mary ___"
114. ___ a time (singly)
115. For shame!
116. Swedish rug
117. Fr. holy women
118. Preadult person

DOWN

1. Electric wall receptacle
2. ___ about (date-setting phrase)
3. Contemptible one, to Cato
4. Mount ___, N.Y.C. exurb
5. Ta-ta
6. Designer Cassini
7. Labyrinth king
8. She wasn't hopeless
9. "Doe, ___ . . ."
10. Loving
11. Add up
12. Biased in choice
13. Summoning, as sheep, in Ayr
14. D.C. panda
15. Water plant
16. Thin layer or plate
18. Force out of place
20. Critiques
21. Corbett, Jeffries or Braddock
25. Unpaid sitter
26. Words before tongs
31. "In Spain they say '___'"
34. Wight is one, Wong isn't
35. Thai language
37. Banned pesticide
39. Boor, in Brest
40. G. M. Cohan's ancestors
41. Hawaiian fish
42. Vocally
43. Do a farrier's job
44. Magic Johnson's team
45. Sylvan nymphs
47. Baker or Bryant
52. Chick's sound
54. "Rosmersholm" playwright
56. Do-re-mi
57. Province or city in NW Spain
58. Wood for railroad ties
59. City in Perm Oblast, U.S.S.R.
61. Goulash
62. A European capital
63. Small hooters
65. Neighbors of ulnae
66. Belgian painter: 1860–1949
67. "___, the gang's . . ."
74. Given new quarters
75. Domain of Anna's boss
77. Sinatra-Minnelli show stopper
78. Of the heart
79. Gained a lap
81. Car's front shield
83. Papeete native
84. Neon is one
85. Impede progress
87. Schnapps
88. Opens hightops
89. "___ hooray!"
95. Bull and Nile, as gods
96. Win by ___ (narrowly outrace)
97. Gravestone, perhaps
98. Certain keynote
100. Monastery head
101. Sharp N.H. city?
103. Boniface
104. In a bad way
105. Interlaken's river
106. Lines on an A.A.A. map
107. ". . . I ___ wed"
109. Mandrel, e.g.

by Ralph G. Beaman

ACROSS

1. Muammar el-___ of Libya
8. Sheer; utter
13. Hula hoops, once
18. Idealists
20. Like a diorama
22. Actress Veronica from Philadelphia
23. Gunslinger's forte
24. Week, in Mexico
25. Love, in Roma
26. Powerful explosive
27. Fabulous finale
29. Mikhail of ballet
31. Colorless: Comb. form
32. George's lyricist
34. European wooden shoes
35. Egyptian king
39. Conjunction
40. W. Webster's gp.
43. Pyrite and pitchblende
44. Actress Beulah: 1892–1981
46. Where Jeanne d'Arc triumphed: 1429
49. Mid East ladies' rooms
50. Common code
52. Author Feodor
55. Film director Akira
57. Corresponded
59. Cereal fruit
60. Low digit
61. Touched down
62. Host of the 1992 summer Olympics
63. Cousin of Tony and Oscar
66. Philosopher Friedrich
71. Catch
72. They're bitten and banged
74. Anglo-Saxon money of account
75. Co-star of "Rocky III"
77. Type of minnow
78. Texas footballer
80. Deng ___, Chinese leader
85. Zbigniew of Carter's Administration
87. Squash variety
89. Myanmar group
90. "...fears that I may ___ be": Keats
91. Sergeant's "___ were!"
93. ___'acte (intermission)
94. Librarian's admonition
95. Recipe amt.
97. Philosophical writer Charles Louis de Secondat
101. Dormant
104. Ltd., in the U.S.A.
105. Tennyson poem
106. Philosopher-theologian Soren
110. "Se ___ español"
112. Wilde was one
115. As a friend: Fr.
116. English cloth measure, once used for tax purposes
118. Chief artery
120. Shore bird
121. Assented
122. Example
123. Awaits action
124. Namesakes of Actress Cannon
125. Poet Omar

DOWN

1. Egyptian village
2. ___ impasse
3. Biblical verb
4. Agr. is one at D.C.
5. Medics' assistants
6. King of Egypt: 1936–52
7. Graft, in a way
8. Wall and Fleet: Abbr.
9. "And ___ played on"
10. "Aeneid" starter
11. Nurtures
12. Nairobi native
13. Intone
14. Harold of "Ghost-busters"
15. In a frenzy
16. Zilch
17. Alt.
19. Namibia, once: Abbr.
21. German submarine film: 1981
28. Fancy wheels
30. Atrocities
31. Rodeo rope
33. Continue, as a subscription
35. Accepted
36. Language of Pakistan
37. Eye drop
38. Canyon mouth
40. Chinese cinnamon
41. Pressman's activity
42. A ___ apple
45. Rock stars, to some
47. ___ a conclusion (prejudges)
48. French spa
50. Leader before Hua
51. Author Wister
53. Of the ear
54. Eve's third
56. Make conventional
58. Wooden ship without an upper deck
63. Hardens
64. Passover staple
65. "And ___ to go...": Frost
67. Perfect test scores
68. Actor Estrada
69. Shire of "Godfather III"
70. Arabian prince
73. Kind of bug
76. Film by 55 Across
77. Common lab tests
79. Synthetic material
80. Delete
81. False: Comb. form
82. Fire: Comb. form
83. Hoopster Archibald
84. Teacher, in India
86. Small bunch of flowers
88. Seashell often used as a horn
92. Little bit
96. Rang
98. Enclose a waterway
99. N.A. Indian language
100. Amounts
101. Carrying a weapon
102. Playlets
103. Li'l Abner's mother
106. Retain
107. "Picnic" playwright
108. Generate profits
109. Tabula ___
111. "___ Blue?": 1929 song
112. Vinous
113. Peruvian native
114. Rain cats and dogs
117. Begley and Bradley
119. Minstrel's song

by Randolph Ross

ACROSS

1. Muddle of nowhere?
5. Waist cincher
9. "... comes in like ___"
14. Fairway clump
19. "___ Named Sue"
20. Brawl
21. Wordsworth work
23. Plant used for making pipes
24. Complication
25. New Guinea, to Indonesians
26. Combat flight
27. Uncovered wagons
28. Start of Burma Shave Ad # I
31. Frat letter
33. Far East feast
34. Lizard called a fringefoot
35. Skater Brinker
36. TV alien
37. Part II of Ad # I
40. Assign (to)
42. ___ the Irish
45. Some awnings
46. Violinist Bull
47. Part of D.C.
48. Swindle
50. Heaviest U.S. President
54. High-gloss paint
57. "___ to Be You," 1924 song
59. Tractor-trailer
60. Have nixed emotions?
61. Start of Burma Shave Ad # II
67. John McGraw's wunderkind
68. More orderly
69. Without
70. Gdansk coins
71. Diagnostic aid
73. Sesame
74. Infant
75. ___ T'ung, last Chinese emperor
77. Long ago
78. Part II of Ad # II
81. Essence
85. "___ Irish Rose"
87. Irk
88. Actor McKellen
89. ___ precedent
90. Alphonse's companion
93. Shirt or coat preceder
94. White herons
97. Fled
98. Part III of Ad # II
103. A long time
104. Outstanding
105. Wirepuller
106. Keenness
107. Louis and Bill
109. It lessens
111. Legal claim
112. "___ Oncle," Tati film
113. Architect of Boston's John Hancock Bldg.
115. Viscous
117. Literary collection
121. Part III of Ad # I
125. Bishopric
126. "When I was ___...": Gilbert
127. Toronto's prov.
128. Harrison or Reed
129. Composer Delibes
130. Part IV of Ad # I
135. José's friend
137. Saloonkeeper's nemesis
139. Jibe
140. Innisfail
141. Inspected the joint
142. Petcock
143. Certain horses
144. French violinist: 18th century
145. Admittance
146. "___ Billie Joe"
147. Doctrines
148. Beatty film: 1981

DOWN

1. The Duke of ___, "Rigoletto" role
2. Units of resistance
3. Belt having 12 signs
4. Head set?
5. Peaceful
6. An anonym
7. Stitch line
8. Coop group
9. Smooth ___
10. Seek
11. Concerning
12. Available
13. Chess master Ivo ___
14. Boil down
15. Oldster's nest egg
16. Artistic quality
17. Group of eight
18. Flavor
20. A plum brandy
22. Astounding
29. From Santiago, e.g.
30. One of a class of amides
32. Moiety
38. Mote
39. Winner over T.E.D.
41. Actress Schneider
42. In a supple way
43. Groom's pal
44. Hosiery style
47. Playful tunes
49. Gentles
51. Smell ___ (suspect)
52. Anger
53. Kinski film
54. Gooey stuff
55. Kin of TNT
56. Perfume
58. Rules out
62. Turner's tool
63. "King of Hollywood"
64. Côte d'___, Riviera area
65. Anything extravagant
66. Styne products
72. Nobelist in Literature: 1923
74. What Jack did
75. Cheer
76. Strength
78. Prong
79. With head held higher
80. Style of film lighting
82. "Able was ___ saw Elba"
83. Lead off
84. Strong-scented Old World herb
86. Singing Tower sponsor
90. Verdon of "Damn Yankees"
91. Hey, sailor!
92. ___ curve, in math
93. Sexton or Nemerov
94. Shade of blue
95. Ruth and Gehrig, e.g.
96. Lower parts of duets
99. Kin of "The Emperor Jones" actor
100. His domain is lover's lane
101. Enclave
102. Pueblo dweller
108. Solti's title
109. "Baked in ___"
110. Do a scene over
114. It lingers on
116. Taken care of
117. A "Hellzapoppin" star and family
118. Cape Cod's ___ Bridge
119. Loosened
120. Dental compounds
121. Harness strap
122. Macho guy
123. Be alive
124. Ovum-to-be
126. Middle name of 20th U.S. President
131. Actor Andrews of TV
132. Delhi wear
133. Writers Betti and Moretti
134. Binge
136. Eur. tongue
138. Initials on army mail

by A. J. Santora

ACROSS

1. Wampum item
5. Hammerlock or half nelson
9. London cleaning woman
13. Degrade
18. Singer James
19. Caravansary
20. Let up
21. Insurgent
22. Why is the gardener so happy?
26. Catalogued
27. Entreaty
28. Quarterback Y. A.
29. "The ___ Green," E. Williams play
30. Ran in the laundry
31. Pull up stakes
32. Helmut's ice
33. Mister, in Malaysia
34. Writer Vidal
35. Movie mogul
39. How does that change the gardener's plans?
45. Portrayer of western villains
46. See 40 Down
47. Make tracks
48. Pahlevi's namesakes
49. Lilting melodies
50. Whitman or Wilbur
51. Aim
52. "___ Boat," Belafonte hit
53. Fish eggs
54. "Mens sana in corpore ___"
55. A sister of John Boy
56. Rubik of the cube craze
57. What kind of gift has he bought her?
64. Linguist Chomsky
65. Archibald of the N.B.A.
66. Psyche's lover
67. Day, in Durango
68. Woman warden
71. Actor Robert or Alan
72. In ___ (having trouble)
73. Treaty between nations
74. ___ con pollo (Spanish dish)
75. West of Hollywood
76. Small barracuda
77. Korea's Syngman
78. Do they plan a large family?

84. Winglike parts
85. Carries the day
86. ___ accompli
87. "Ich bin ___ Berliner": J.F.K.
88. Knife handle
89. Swindles
90. Fishing boats
93. Accomplice
96. Where to find Wailuku
97. Lop-eared dog
98. What do you see in their future?
102. Fashion designer Simpson
103. Author Ludwig
104. "Invisible Man" Claude
105. Singer Paul from Ottawa
106. Feasted one's eyes
107. One of a seagoing trio
108. Hunky trailer
109. Masher's grimace

DOWN

1. Big-A action
2. Moral precept
3. "___ clock scholar"
4. Does some woolgathering
5. Start of a toast
6. Toward the mouth
7. China's Zhou En-___
8. Showcases
9. Granted, as territory
10. Sounds of merriment
11. "___ live and breathe!"
12. Patch up a painting
13. Mountain ridge
14. Deliver one to the jaw
15. First shepherd
16. Withered
17. English cathedral town
19. NOW fights this bias
23. Toxic substance in a snake's fluid
24. Former queen of Italy
25. Cacomistle
30. Exploded
31. Bates's wayside stopover
33. ___ knowledge (Eden landmark)

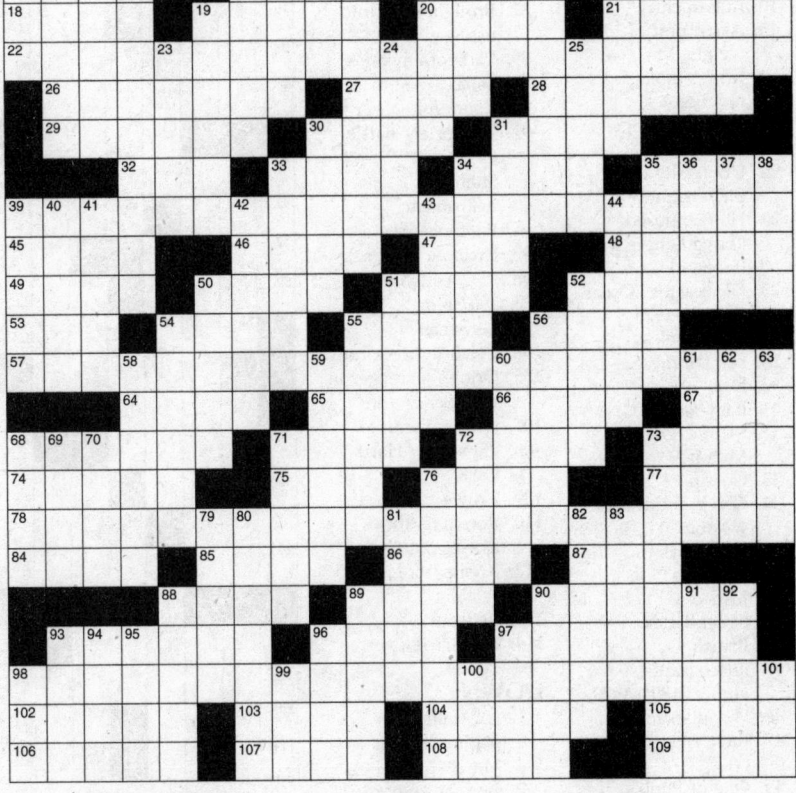

by Frances Hansen

34. Vast South American region
35. Key of Beethoven's Fifth
36. Marquis de Venosta's mistress
37. "Pictures ___ Exhibition"
38. Ponselle or Bonheur
39. "Do I ___ Waltz?"
40. With 46 Across, an "Untouchable"
41. First of the Cavalier poets
42. Unnamed person
43. Option
44. Praying figures
50. Other name of Lalitpur, Nepal
51. Garbo
52. Closet item
54. Grab some shut-eye
55. I.R.S. quarry
56. Printers' errors
58. Garb in regal garments
59. Falk-Arkin film, with "The"

60. Send back a manuscript
61. Gem State
62. "___ Easy," Sinatra favorite
63. Winner at Saratoga: 1777
68. Baby's first word, often
69. Russian inland sea
70. "___ Little Tenderness"
71. Catkin
72. Orbit point
73. Victoria of filmdom
76. Man of La Mancha, e.g.
79. Edgar or Emmy
80. Tennis score
81. Run ___ of (hit a snag)
82. French auto-racing locale
83. Tael
88. Put an edge on
89. "Cheers" waitress
90. Like a hedgehog
91. N.H. city
92. Quench one's thirst

93. Musical finale
94. "Hear ye!"
95. Golfer Irwin
96. "___ Leben," Wagner's autobiography
97. The pokey
98. Drinking spree
99. "Brother Rat" inst.
100. ___ Paulo, Brazil
101. Men's org. founded in 1889

ACROSS

1. Short haircuts
5. Perfume ingredient
10. Indian chief
15. Asian unit of weight
19. In ___ (going nowhere)
20. Ezra or Irving
21. Ham it up
22. University or playwright
23. He composed "Love Letters in the Sand"
25. "Best actor" Oscar winner: 1976
27. Nevertheless
28. Les femmes
30. Rota
31. Easy gait
32. Melancholy, to Milton
33. Gossip
34. Greek goddess of wisdom
37. "___ Keys to Baldpate"
38. Joshed
42. Greek letter
43. British lexicographer-author: 1894–1979
46. Wood sorrel
47. Ravens' strident cries
49. One of Pooh's friends
50. Stretches the budget
51. Gator's relative
52. Smell ___ (suspect)
53. U.S. poet who wrote "The Bridge"
57. Morley's "Kitty ___"
58. Bishop, e.g.
60. Had expectations
61. Rhythmical beat
62. Male duck
63. College in Lewiston, Me.
64. A man of morals
65. Gleam
66. Abbot's right-hand man
67. Deighton's "___ in Berlin"
69. It's used on a cue tip
70. Boston Celtics star
72. Goddess of discord
74. Elias or Gordie
75. Despina, in "Cosi fan tutte"
77. ___ rule (generally)
78. Attract
79. Quest of Indiana Jones
80. He painted "Old Battersea Bridge"
86. Actress Munson
87. Brought back into use
89. Parts of a horse's collar
90. Room for action
92. Author of "Battle Cry"
93. Shankar's instrument
94. Footnote abbr.
95. Excel on the track
98. "___ Laughing," 1967 film
99. Lengthen
103. Celebrity-roast host
105. Orioles' manager in 1970 Series win
107. Actress Sommer
108. He wrote "Hard Cash"
109. Crows, e.g.
110. Rock's partner
111. Device on a loom
112. Kirstie from Wichita
113. Velocity
114. Ko-Ko's dagger

DOWN

1. ___ California, peninsula in Mexico
2. German composer: 1895–1982
3. Loni's husband
4. Addison's writing partner
5. Gone con?
6. Neckpiece
7. Pawn
8. Tolkien creature
9. Modesty, in Madrid
10. Change the flower bed
11. Native ruler in Africa
12. Tittles
13. Ingested
14. If red, these may mislead
15. "Valse ___"
16. "___ She Sweet?": 1927 song
17. Behold, to Brutus
18. Oven used to anneal glass
24. Bombinate
26. One's strong point
29. Lewd look
32. Magazine for military stores
33. Miami's county
34. Chest for valuables
35. Twyla, the choreographer
36. Director of "The Big Sleep"
37. Censure
38. Used a tandem
39. N.B.A. player with the Sacramento Kings
40. What an élève attends
41. Cyprinoid fish
44. Steamed up
45. Coty or Cassin
48. Barren
51. Part of N.A.A.C.P.
53. Cod's kin
54. Bergère, e.g.
55. Revolving part on a machine
56. Imitation
57. Blend
59. Not curly, as hair
61. Hang fire
63. Finishing nails
64. Of hearing
65. Snipe's habitat
66. Performed diligently
67. Signs used in printing
68. Climbing plant
69. Carbonize
71. More despicable
73. Controlling influence
75. Type of spaghetti sauce
76. Cyclones play here
80. Large drinking bowl
81. Singer Houston
82. H. Broun's "Pieces of ___"
83. Turkish inns
84. Jostled
85. Marie Antoinette, for one
88. Changed, as leaves
91. Awards for mystery writers
93. Insinuating
94. "___ Seeing You"
95. River in central Europe
96. Ubangi feeder
97. The gate
98. Butcher shop: Fr.,
99. Coloratura Mills
100. Sight from Warwick Castle
101. Psychic affinity
102. Film director Kenton
104. Electrical unit
106. A founder of Dadaism

by Jeanette K. Brill

ACROSS

1. Kin of kerplunk
6. Couple
10. Swashbuckler
15. Raiment
16. Drab shade
17. Tied in red tape in Mongolian center?
19. Tardy for shuttle in Orioles' home?
21. Neither oui nor non
23. Ale, in Aachen
24. Publish
25. "If ___ a Rich Man"
26. Actor Mineo
27. Rim
28. Bungled bus transfer in Ontario metropolis?
31. Central points
32. Shake a drink
34. Uno y uno
35. Lollapaloozas
36. W.W. II bomber
37. Ant. for ant.
38. A ratite
40. World-weary
41. Salamanders
42. Bright lights
43. Opposite of eso
44. Tar
45. Feral feline
47. ___ March to the Sea
50. Door hinge
54. Way off base
55. Papal name
56. Nanjing nursemaid
57. ___ Finklea, a k a Cyd Charisse
58. Evert's ex
59. Charges
60. Field yield
61. Cycle
62. Sow sound
63. Crooned
64. French president: 1954–59
65. Looseness
66. Preppy, e.g.
67. Independence
69. Ointment
70. Vichy resources
72. Needle feature
73. Kind of pie or board
74. Did lawn work
76. Sci-fi awards
78. ___ majesté
79. Juliette Low's gp.
82. Van Pelt and Ricardo
83. VCR button
84. Mo. in hiver
85. Juan Carlos's realm
87. Biblical well
88. Boarded wrong train in Pyrenees capital?
91. Bath residue
92. Fresh ___ daisy
93. Narc's prey
94. Composer Copland
95. Photographer Morath
96. Cramps a cowboy's style
98. Lost tour group in South Pacific site?
101. Marooned on monorail in Sunshine State mecca?
102. Cockney crony
103. Tibetan guide
104. Ketch tippers
105. Goad
106. Steel splint, in armor

DOWN

1. With decorum
2. Fogged in, in Pacific Northwest gateway?
3. British measures
4. Onassis nickname
5. Entice
6. Factories
7. ___ surface missiles
8. Campus climber
9. Electrical unit
10. Runs, in a way
11. Tierney title role: 1944
12. Stake
13. Inits. for Judith Anderson, e.g.
14. Dines at a restaurant
15. Convent head
16. Causing fear and anxiety
17. Type of mobility
18. Footprints
20. Corrosive
22. Director Kazan
25. Arrow poison
29. Cajoles
30. Missed connections in this puzzle
31. Overshot exit ramp in Dallas's sister city?
33. Well-to-do
36. Nice seasoning
39. Debatable
40. Hackmen
41. Hudson contemporary
42. Late for the 7:58 in Gotham?
44. Cinch
45. Lt. Col. North, to friends
46. Duplicate
47. Mistimed excursion in S California locale?
48. Delbert Mann's 1955 Oscar winner
49. Old name of Xiamen
51. I.R.S. procedure
52. List of candidates
53. Divided, in heraldry
54. "Thanks ___!"
55. Confined
59. Counterfeit, in Paris
60. Cather's "Death ___ for the Archbishop"
61. Analyzes a sentence
63. King of the Meccans: 1953–64
64. South Dakota, the ___ State
65. Dregs
68. Israeli hot spot
69. Herringbone
71. Loser to D.D.E.
73. Without a doubt
74. Shore-dinner item
75. Cousteau's fld.
76. Capital of the Treasure State
77. D.O.D. div.
79. Some fancy dives
80. Mired in customs in Far East banking hub?
81. Light role on TV
82. Page
83. White water
84. Chipped
86. Awards
88. TV's "Trials of ___ O'Neill"
89. Milk: Comb. form
90. "___ of robins . . .": Kilmer
93. Dingle
97. ___ franc of W. Afr.
98. Mike's complement
99. Eg. and Syr., once
100. Contemporary of T.S.E.

by Jane S. Flowerree

348 CROSS-EXAMINATION

ACROSS

1. Drab; not stylish
6. Mirador
11. Fa-la connector
14. "From the Terrace" author
19. Suffered
20. Kowalski portrayer: 1947
21. Small case
22. Hemidemi-semiquavers
23. Kalmar-Ruby question
25. What "is" is
26. Pinch
27. Kind of guard
28. Banquet platform
29. A Capulet's question
32. Eyes and ears
34. Straggle
36. Testified
37. Dreamer
39. Question from Bugs
42. Tied the knot
43. Construe
44. Fry in butter
45. Part of a shandy
46. Russian C.I.A.
48. Site of Vance A.F.B.
49. Less populated
51. Agrippa's apparel
53. Part of M-G-M's motto
57. Capek play
58. Beatles movie: 1965
59. Ed Koch's former question
61. Wimbledon winner: 1987
63. Papa Bear of football
65. Cavatina
66. Arenaceous plant
67. Singer John
69. "Raving, ___, money-mad": B. R. Newton
71. Laves lightly
72. Wilde was one
74. Knock-knock question
78. Business abbr.
79. River in the Carolinas
82. Bony
84. Campus costumes
88. High praise
91. Shakespearean tinker
92. Meistersinger Hans
94. Hone
95. Veronese question
97. Surfeit
98. Past
99. ___ prosequi
100. Gouda's competitor
101. Kind of plate
104. Deneb or Mizar
105. "Sail ___ Union . . .": Longfellow
107. "Israfel" poet's monogram
108. Wasted time
109. Chanson de ___
110. Eliz II, for one
112. Part of a Gallic question
115. Glistened
117. Six bells on the midwatch
119. Sarah ___, Met soprano
120. In shipshape fashion
121. Jack Yellen's question
124. Juncture
125. Spline
128. Jacob's first wife and namesakes
129. Close by
130. Half-baked question?
134. A first name in fragrance
135. June heroes
136. Rock having roelike grains
137. Official language of India
138. Dutch genre painter
139. ___ Lanka
140. Like a bugbear
141. "___ by land . . ."

DOWN

1. Cockcrow
2. Eight, in Oaxaca
3. Routine question
4. Left in the lurch
5. A mi. = 1,760 ___
6. Fragrant root
7. Beams
8. Tavern
9. Tokyo, once
10. Depressed state
11. Printer's directive
12. Yours and mine
13. Drive of a kind
14. Ready for use
15. Question for Bossy
16. Relaxed
17. Used an auger
18. Questioned
20. Wild goose
21. Appraiser
24. Harem rooms
30. ___ nibs
31. It has seven vertebrae
33. Needlefish
34. So
35. Have status
37. Savage
38. Yearbook
39. Road to conflict
40. Furrow maker
41. "Absinthe" painter
44. Unhealthy looking
47. Carefree rover's activity
49. Hush!
50. Anjou or Comice
52. Physicians' org.
54. Juan's uncles
55. Anent
56. Some NCO's
59. Meteorological areas
60. Letters at Calvary
62. Mrs. B.'s question
64. O. Henry prod.
65. Itchy
68. Name in TV ratings
70. Capri, to Capriotes
73. Hyson and gunpowder
75. Endings for draft and employ
76. City pests
77. Classical geometer
79. Impignorate
80. A nymph pursued by Pan
81. Environmental subj.
83. Scat!
85. Question for Bennett Cerf
86. Void
87. Squirreled away
89. It has 21 dots
90. Senior
91. They wear fatuous smiles
93. Prefix for thesis
96. River in South Africa
101. Ten
102. Foofaraws
103. Pivot
104. Mukluk material
106. Colorful marine fish
109. Columbia, in a song
110. Most bashful
111. Embellished
113. Corrects
114. Zorro's mark
115. Mealtime prayer
116. Exec's car
117. Judicial writ
118. City in the Ruhr valley
120. Snappish
122. Rifle part
123. Ravine that is often dry
124. Cookery direction
126. "The Breeze ___," 1940 song
127. Letters for day six
131. Ad ___ committee
132. C.S.A. state
133. Cry of amused surprise

by Valerie Meunier

ACROSS

1. Papier-___
6. German grandma
9. Lhasa ___
13. U.S. Open golf champ: 1959
19. Profit
20. "Up to ___," Al Smith's autobiography
21. Becloud
22. Joint: Comb. form
23. Class Casanova
26. Grills
27. Yegg's diamonds
28. "...but the end is not ___": Matt. 24: 6
29. Alma mater of the 39th Pres.
30. U.S. dancer-choreographer: 1931–89
31. "The Jazz Singer" was one: 1927
34. Appropriate
35. Grip
38. Noted theater in Paris
39. Boy with the Best Physique
41. Ex-coach Parseghian
44. ___ nova
45. Oscars' kin
46. Joyce's ___ Livia Plurabelle
47. Angular border design
48. The law, to Mr. Bumble
49. Vast amount
50. Send to Coventry
51. Crossworder's Latin verb
52. Class Actress
56. Ecclesiastical vestment
57. Asseverate
61. Convenes
62. Sea-urchin features
63. Emitted
64. Cumberland, e.g.
65. Democritus or Dalton
66. Alarms
67. Site of ancient Olympics
69. Pedants
70. Ailurophiles' rewards
71. Teacher's Pet
75. Place for avions
76. Hybrid animal
77. Capital of the Maldives
78. Lincoln or Maxwell
81. Ligatures
82. Arabian sultanate
83. Allen or Lawrence
85. Snicker
87. "___ It," 1940 song
88. Class Clown
90. Extract forcibly
91. Bar where Hemingway hung out
93. Inlets
94. "Pathétique" or "Appassionata"
95. Type of phobia
97. Squeals
98. Actuary's concern
100. Upsilon follower
101. ___ Bueller, Broderick role
103. Big Woman on Campus
107. Used
108. Okla. Indian
109. Actress Alicia
110. Waste producer
111. Forsyth's "The ___ File"
112. Young salmon
113. Pili or macadamia
114. Weasel's kin

DOWN

1. Ontario neighbor
2. Guacamole items
3. Negligent
4. L.B.J. beagle
5. Guido note
6. Formerly
7. Doubtful
8. Wheat beard
9. Maltreaters
10. David Hare play
11. Iranian archeological site
12. Table scrap
13. Hack
14. "But he's an ___ knave": Shak.
15. Zeno, e.g.
16. Class Musician
17. A Gardner
18. Promising
24. Aneurin Bevan, familiarly
25. Ask
32. Aegean island
33. Concert follower
34. Non compos ___
35. Tristan da ___ Islands
36. Genus of flax
37. Dash
39. "Fear of Flying" author
40. Lively party
42. Most authentic
43. Certifies
45. Far from fresh
47. Shrine site in Portugal
49. Entangles
52. "...o'er ___ and hills": Wordsworth
53. Actor Bruce or Havers
54. Shelley's "Paradise of exiles"
55. Savory jelly
56. Famed English potter
57. Autocrats
58. Out of court
59. Class Athlete
60. Bird and Holmes
62. Fence straddler
65. Confuse
68. Suzanne from San Bruno
71. Karloff role
72. Norwegian kings
73. Comedian Jay
74. Crockett or Jones
76. "I never saw a ___": Dickinson
78. Most shoddy
79. Dilettante
80. Shopkeeper
83. Move like a snake
84. Pester
85. Jefferson's bill
86. North follower
88. Oregon and Santa Fe
89. Cicero, e.g.
92. Wall hanging
94. Bishopric
95. Hair style
96. Turned right
97. Pro ___
98. Japanese aborigine
99. Punkie
102. Kind of chest or dog
103. Bull
104. Kurosawa film: 1985
105. The ___, of rock fame
106. Dicer or skimmer

by Nancy Nicholson Joline

350 CAREER CHANGES

ACROSS

1. Sew loosely
6. Gyrate
10. Iced
15. Choir member
19. Russian cooperative
20. Amonasro's daughter
21. Lured
22. Cross
23. Supply new weapons
24. Lowest high tide
25. Bitter
26. Designate
27. Candlemaker becomes mystery writer
30. Duck down
31. Sigma
32. Montague heir
33. Attention getter
34. Unit of land measure
35. Church tribunals
36. Nicholas II, e.g.
37. Give the once-over
41. Depreciate
44. Policeman becomes landscape painter
46. Courted danger
47. Honored
48. Actress Balin
49. Secular
50. Auto-racing name of fame
51. Stews
52. Literary monogram
53. "___ vincit amor"
54. Dutch commune
55. Poet Marianne ___
56. Help!
57. Haggard novel
58. Gymnast becomes singer
61. Doorkeeper becomes Broadway composer
66. Tote
67. Essay
68. Friendship
69. Author Rölvaag
70. Slacken
73. Nitrous oxide; e.g.
74. Heath
75. Mountain mint
77. Actor Baldwin
78. Calendar abbr.
79. Iranian river
80. Well-mannered
81. Arrow maker becomes aerospace scientist
84. Upholstery material
85. Not gregarious
86. Marmalade ingredient
87. Sop
88. Louis ___ of the N.B.A.
89. Foot: Comb. form
90. City south of Florence
91. Crone
94. Gitche Gumee craft
97. Palace official becomes basketball star
100. At the summit
101. Appellation
102. Pernicious
103. Fate
104. Otherwise
105. Opponents
106. Kind of china
107. "___ Talking": Rivers-Meryman
108. ___-do-well
109. Voltaire was one
110. Discordia, to Demosthenes
111. Marsh plants

DOWN

1. Vt. granite center
2. Locations
3. Remains
4. Time period
5. Ranch worker becomes pollster
6. Sleep inducer
7. Flinders
8. Site of Hells Canyon
9. Calif. wine valley
10. Cordial welcome
11. French general, in-law of Napoleon
12. To the point, in law
13. Coconut fiber
14. Terminate
15. Pilgrim becomes golfer
16. Burden
17. Weighty volume
18. River to the Baltic
28. Eminent
29. Contemporaries of Hudsons
30. Formerly, once
34. Handle, to Hadrian
35. Strafe
36. Unsteady
37. Travelers' rests
38. Israeli statesman
39. Twice LXXVI
40. Mexican Indian
41. Condiment bottle
42. Indo-Aryan language
43. Site of the Krupp works
44. They come along for "deride"
45. Ocean pollutant
47. Face of a building
51. Pro
52. More spacious
53. Cry of amused surprise
55. Phiz
56. Disfigured
57. Le Carré character
59. Barrelmaker becomes rock musician
60. Now, now!
62. Greek letter
63. "___ With Love," Poitier film
64. Cream
65. Rent again
70. Indian prince
71. Greek underground in W.W. II
72. Exec's reminder
73. Kittiwake
74. Cultural
75. Sideshow pitchman becomes game-show host
76. Winglike structures
78. At a distance
79. Decisive experiment
80. Twain biographer
82. Beget
83. Latticework
84. Increases threefold
87. Islands off the Fla. coast
89. Florentine palace
90. Relish
91. Western local-color writer
92. Directed toward
93. Growls
94. City on the Orne
95. Tamarisk
96. Proboscis
97. Oenologist's interest
98. Cupbearer of the gods
99. Kent's girlfriend
101. Tiny amount

by Judith Perry

ACROSS

1. Breezy idiom
6. Ali Baba, e.g.
13. Strong dislike
19. Former federation in SE Asia
21. Steve Martin romp: 1987
22. College town east of L.A.
23. Start of message
26. Cherish
27. Plaines preceder
28. "Fiddler" matchmaker and namesakes
29. Einstein's birthplace
30. Down East
32. Summer in Noisy-le-Sec
33. ___ Islands, Blackbeard's base
37. Divided into areas
38. Baseball stat
39. B'way signs
43. "Hallelujah, I'm ___," Jolson film
44. Connection
45. Do some ushering
46. Whitman or Disney
47. More of message
53. Relative of et al.
54. Telephoned
55. Matriculate
56. E.T., e.g.
57. Quailed
59. Black eye
61. Same difference
62. He went over the wall
64. Character actress Parsons
66. Part of HEW
69. Actor Ed and family
71. Fritz, Carl or Rob
74. Mountain range in Russia
75. Smoke detector
76. Viking landfall
77. Sighs of satisfaction
79. More of message
84. ". . . Baked in ___"
85. World's longest river
86. Spooky-sounding lake
87. Columnist Barrett
88. Minister to
89. Ship-plank curve
90. Specified, as a date
92. Glyn or Wylie
94. Panay people
95. The original "golden boy"?

96. Claire of "Claudia"
97. Chief French naval base
100. Hot-pie ingredient
101. Reduced to a mean
106. End of message
110. Emulate Circe
111. Mother-of-pearl source
112. Silverware city in N.Y.
113. Moped about listlessly
114. Colorful spectral type
115. TV-tube element

DOWN

1. Struck hard, old style
2. Memorable Cowardly Lion
3. Winglike parts
4. Zilch, in Zaragoza
5. Plaster of paris mineral
6. "Comus" composer
7. ___ Reagan Jr.
8. Borden weapon
9. Villain, informally
10. Mean
11. Have ___ for news
12. A neighbor of Wyo.
13. Zest for food
14. Not a soul
15. "___ a Man," Ciardi book
16. Speck
17. Les Etats-___
18. Botanical pouch
20. Bastard wing
24. Estuary
25. Confrontation feature
30. Bop pioneer Thelonious
31. Singer Paul
33. Bunyan's Blue Ox
34. Touches on
35. Rabbit coop
36. Fifi's friend
37. Pizazz
38. Snappy comeback
39. Puffed up
40. "The Shadow" medium
41. Ancient, to poets
42. Songwriter Jule
44. Sri ___
45. Accent
48. Extreme
49. Western spread
50. Wahine's neckwear
51. Kind of tube or man

52. Somewhat like the Sears Tower
58. At ease
59. Oil-yielding tropical plant
60. Flit-fetcher of yesteryear
61. On the qui vive
63. In a wan way
65. Wipe out
66. Attacks with vigor
67. Skip the wedding march
68. Dined at home
70. Nandu's look-alike
72. Secretary of War: 1829–31
73. Nose: Pref.
75. Silly
76. Hitler's "___ Kampf"
78. Wound souvenir
80. ". . . leave no tern ___": Nash
81. St. Petersburg's river
82. God of war
83. Belligerent Greek god

90. Balm of ___
91. Commendable principles
92. January, in Trujillo
93. Voice box
94. Clover type
95. Possibly
96. "___ Got Five Dollars," 1931 song
97. Pueblo Indian
98. Vision: Comb. form
99. ___ the air (unsettled)
101. State firmly
102. Busy as ___
103. "___ Out of My Head," 1964 song
104. Taro root
105. Cannon of cinema
106. Fashion's whimsical line
107. Fun and games for 82 Down
108. Balderdash!
109. Bambi's aunt

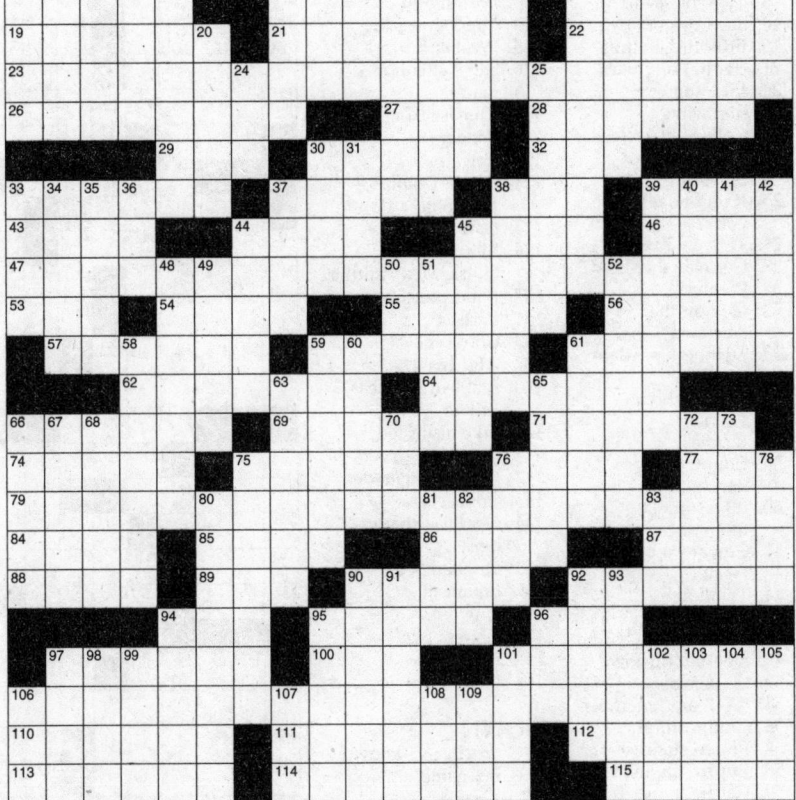

by Frances Hansen

ACROSS

1. Strident
6. Type of seaman
10. Seed oysters
15. Ethically neutral
21. Capital of Guam
22. Like some highways
23. College at Oxford
24. A source of potassium
25. Kafka novel, with "The"
26. This, in Taxco
27. German shepherd?
29. Pointer?
32. City on the Alabama
33. Steinbeck's Adam
34. Tee neighbor
35. Carriage
36. Razzias
38. Country singer Bandy
40. Like some toothpaste
42. Cowboy's buddy
43. Heaters
44. Twaddle
47. "Jagged Edge" actress
49. Siberian huskies?
53. ___ Canals
54. "A-Team" member
56. Composition
57. Potato state
58. Improvise, in jazz
59. Cardigan or Pembroke of Wales
61. Amanda Plummer role
63. Lammed out
64. Lures game
65. ___ dictus (otherwise called)
66. Court order
67. Verdure
70. Some are G.P.'s
71. Challenge a juror
73. The Scourge of God
75. An amino acid, for short
77. Boxers?
85. Salmon follower
86. Present; current
87. ___ foudre (French thunderbolt)
88. Pronto
91. Spend the summer
95. Admiral Maximilian von ___
97. Grain thresher
98. Another boxer?
100. ___ Cassin, Nobelist for Peace: 1968
101. Poker hand, also called kilter
102. Perfume ingredient
103. Placid
104. Fabled deliverer
106. Blanc's opposite
107. Bustle
109. De Maupassant
110. Boston bull
113. Firedog residue
115. West end
116. Salt's attention getter
117. Chinese isinglass
118. Bender
120. Low
121. "___ a Dolphin," 1957 film
123. Dale starter
124. Monogram of "Little Men" author
127. Pond protozoan
131. Laissez ___
133. Chow chow?
137. Afghans?
140. Emblem of Great Britain
141. Like neglected carpets or dryers
142. Black nightshades
143. Copacetic
144. Goatlike Roman deity
145. Single-celled organism
146. Unwrote
147. Actress Eve
148. Poker stake
149. Drum wire

DOWN

1. "...he ___ known my name"
2. Accede
3. Fulminates
4. Shapes up, in a way
5. Fifty percent
6. Antarctic penguin
7. Beat
8. Trajan's tongue
9. Impetuous ardor
10. Type of story
11. Chair
12. Televised
13. Famed Uri family
14. Garment size
15. Start of a child's song
16. Certain cat or dog
17. What towser has
18. Like Caesar's steak, perhaps
19. A Spanish liqueur
20. Dearth
28. Famed pantyhose peddler
30. Reddish brown
31. Ear part
37. Weapons
39. Holy Roman emperor: 962–73
41. Terriers?
42. Chemist's small container
43. Chewed on
44. ___ 91, source of 1 Down
45. Invited
46. Basketball defense
47. Pen
48. Old Roman cuirass
49. Actress Granville
50. Aswan's site
51. Notion, in Nimes
52. E.T.'s vehicle
53. Nape drape
55. Large marble
60. Surgical dressing
62. Seize
63. Graylag's cousin
64. Pug?
67. Frozen
68. Summer time in N.Y.C.
69. V.M.I. group
72. They start as elvers
74. Provoked
76. As ___ (generally)
78. Ship deserter
79. More gloomy
80. Having a flimsy texture
81. Not windward
82. Sprinkle
83. Repugnant
84. Nice ___ (prude)
88. Annapolis frosh
89. Eastern U.S. capital
90. Hussy
92. Ferruginous
93. Speak or fetch, e.g.
94. "Puppy Love" composer: 1959
96. Greek vowel
99. Hostelry
101. Voiced speech sound
104. Manhattan district
105. ___ kind (poker holding)
106. Canceled by NASA
108. Stunt person, e.g.
111. Like some wild animals
112. Outfits for baby
114. Rowdy
118. Stay until the end
119. Hawthorne character
121. Fonda was this in "Easy Rider"
122. Echo was one
123. Miao, e.g.
125. City in Nigeria
126. "...and ___ to steer her by": Masefield
127. Peak
128. Heath
129. Philanthropist Cornell
130. Secondary matters
132. Empress Ivanovna
134. Communications word
135. Shade trees
136. Irish President: 1938–45
138. A hallucinogen, for short
139. Methuselah, to Enoch

by June A. Boggs

ACROSS

1. Next of skin?
5. Low life forms
12. Forgetful
19. Deed, in Dijon
20. Actors Edward and William
21. Make unfriendly
22. Colleen McCullough's music makers?
24. Family of Grant's first Veep
25. Fluffy fare
26. Shut up
28. Tinge
29. Fashion designer Simpson
31. Danza latina
32. Potent hallucinogen
33. Pants style
36. N.L. team
38. Three-pointed tooth
43. Entertain
44. Humbug
45. Beat it, Ringo!
46. Rock producer Brian ___
47. Soccer great
48. Candia
50. Abbot's aide
52. Folded, filled tortilla
53. R.E.O. middle
54. This bunch
55. Synthetic fabric
56. Of 60 Across
57. Lifeboats
59. Sofa
60. Back burner?
61. What this country singer needs?
66. Purpose
67. Clergyman
68. Handel handled this well
70. ___ deux (dance for two)
73. Burglar
74. Seasoning
75. Vandalize
76. Tract
77. Excitement
78. Poe's "___ in Paradise"
79. Satiate
80. Critic Reed
81. Chesterton's "___ Survey"
82. Dobbin gets hitched to it
83. Horse or car
84. Kind of clause
87. Where Bush whacked Dukakis
89. Wore
90. Singer Sumac
91. At the tip of one's lung?
93. A Jackson Secretary of War
95. Walk like Festus
97. Mythical beasts
100. Quartet members
103. Rooter for hockey's Oilers
105. Barn-dance song?
108. Proximity
109. End the reign of rain
110. Be next door to
111. In any case
112. Notched, as a leaf
113. Harmony, for short

DOWN

1. Boater or bowler
2. Reverberate
3. News bit
4. Practice
5. See eye to eye
6. One of the "M" boys of baseball
7. Pluto, e.g.
8. Sponsorship
9. Crosby was one
10. First ___ (above all else)
11. Krupp city
12. Lotion ingredient
13. Clement
14. Seaman's clock
15. Makes law
16. What Stan Getz has?
17. Suburban people?
18. "___ Magnifique," 1953 hit song
21. How to play polkas?
23. Call-in song
27. Darkness hrs.
30. Why the musical was R-rated?
32. Aggregate
33. Clothed in a fanon
34. Ms. Bloomer
35. Pouring out the whines
37. An hors d'oeuvre
39. Smooth out
40. Bad dog
41. Orejon, e.g.
42. Spot for a slot
48. Scold
49. Shorten a sail
50. Sidewalk brick
51. Pitcher Nolan
52. Jay Silverheels role
54. That bunch
55. Costa ___, San Jose native
56. Parlor set
58. Dutch cheese
59. Scenery of a sort
60. Like a smoothie
62. Manicure
63. Rictus
64. Actor Assante
65. Theater district
69. Acrylic fiber
70. Shave
71. Hawkish god
72. Erotic music maker?
73. Touched
74. Energy source
77. Tallahassee is its cap.
78. More complex
79. Laydowns, in bridge
81. In the style of
82. Glisten
83. Fake
85. Current unit
86. Big bird of myth
88. Stayed to the end of
92. Pear choices
94. Fiesta Bowl site
95. Singer Cantrell
96. "___ a Song Go..."
97. All-purpose trks.
98. Tweed twitter
99. Bandy words
101. Girl in a Kenny Rogers hit
102. Amaze
104. Kind of virus
106. Sinatra's coda?
107. Blah, blah, blah

by A. J. Santora

354 ACADEME

ACROSS

1. Panier handle
5. Pen
8. Small containers for liquids
14. Rose fruits
18. Hit musical
19. Aunt, in Avila
20. Actor Oscar
22. Chinese nurse
23. Part of a typing exercise
26. ___ dixit
27. Gompers or Goldwyn
28. Berliner's 44 Down
29. Brood of pheasants
30. Tatter's output
31. Rhode Island's founder
34. Cava or contracta preceder
35. Fanfare
36. Alarm
38. Scrams
40. Carols
41. Innocent
42. Soil aggregate
43. Misfortune
44. Darling
46. Parrots
47. Norma or Charlotte
48. Troubles
50. Peace pipe
54. Lips
55. Converter
57. Epiphany trio
58. Eschews
60. Actress Pola
61. Postponed
63. Turkic or Mongolic language
65. Bill
67. Glance
68. ___ d'hotel
69. Architectural rib
70. Gentle as ___
72. Firth in Scotland
73. Tel ___
74. Small hand drum
76. Pout
77. Thesmothete
79. Pilaster
80. MOMA display
81. Small talk
85. Companion of file
86. Curve
87. High degree
88. Desdemona's detractor
89. Old Italian coin
92. ". . . ___ promise, serv'd no private end": Pope
94. Scatter
95. Smart, swift equines
96. "___ Three Lives": Philbrick
98. Half of a test name
100. Place
101. Privy to
102. Latin I word
103. Grows
106. Lifted an anchor
107. Broadway's Juliet: 1934
111. Dismounted
112. Military ornament
113. Operate
114. North Sea feeder
115. Affirmative votes
116. Separate seed
117. Color of a fez
118. Side dish

DOWN

1. Deeds
2. Capital of Okinawa
3. Glasses
4. Gentlemen just below knights
5. Allay
6. Obsession
7. Tibetan ox
8. Transplant expert
9. Aussie marsupials
10. "Coal-ition" initials
11. "Golden Treasury" item
12. Spritelike
13. Czech car
14. "___! happy land!"
15. Pierce
16. Inventor of first digital calculation
17. Nautical ropes
21. Chop
24. Ubangi feeder
25. Part of a basilica
32. Certain girders
33. Dangerous mosquito
34. Longfellow subject
35. Chemical compound
36. Resort
37. "Kindness"
39. Coast, in a way
42. Mount ___, Colo. peak
44. Surface for a Sabre
45. Devonshire seaport
49. Nimble
51. Like lager
52. Historic Hungarian city
53. Ocean flux
54. Havoc
56. Bond
58. Rose contemplator
59. Sliced or diced vegetables
62. River in Switzerland
63. Lackaday!
64. Of immediate interest
65. Woolen cap
66. ___ Longa
71. Paris subway
72. Jazzy Jelly Roll
75. Pique
76. Any sudden aid
78. NM town
81. False topazes
82. A Madison Ave. method
83. Ripen
84. Draw
89. Glide
90. Troupial
91. Baltic republic
92. Wallace work
93. Scholar's collar
94. Fly high
96. Clumsy
97. Hindu's brass water vessel
99. Palm leaf
101. Harry's successor
102. Olympian once imprisoned in a jar
104. Italian isle
105. Ruck
108. Pub request
109. Stray
110. Snooker stick

by Barbara Lunder Gillis

ACROSS

1. Ares, in Rome
5. Ruth St. ___
10. Org.
15. Synthetic estrogen, for short
18. Parisian possessive
19. Wash out
20. Prefix for dactyl
21. Forwarded
22. Julian's father
24. Alan's father
26. Skylit courts
27. "L'Elisir d'amore" heroine
29. Dispossess
30. Editor's notation
31. Actor Keach
32. Schlep
33. Like some castles
36. Paul, in Pisa
37. Comes ashore
40. Laborers of yore
41. Margaret's father
43. Adlai's opponent
45. Part of C. in C.
46. Julia ___ Howe
47. Contrary: Abbr.
48. Chamber music piece
49. Benz product
50. Natalie's father
54. Sign
55. Wind flowers
57. Pontificate
58. Molts
59. Slogged
60. Night lights
61. Seed: Pref.
62. Acknowledged
63. Softly, to Solti
64. Saddle adjuncts
67. Gabby of westerns
68. Charlie's father
70. Tibetan gazelle
71. Western Indians
72. Comic Olsen
73. Blackbirds' habitat
74. Cut
75. N.H.L. goal
76. Carrie's father
81. Aspect
82. More like pelite
84. Glittery fabrics
85. Expunges
86. Pinza or Plishka
87. Criterion
88. Lord Rutherford's concern
89. Cranston of "The Shadow"
92. Chutzpah
93. Composer Frederic and Nicolas
97. Peter's father
99. Jane's father
102. Nitti's nemesis
103. Awaken rudely
104. Late 50's auto
105. Old Irish alphabet
106. Jap. Big Board
107. Displaces
108. Drives
109. Benefit

DOWN

1. Goya subject
2. "Thanks ___!"
3. Rhine tributary
4. Ominous
5. Judged
6. Surrealist Max
7. Negative prefix
8. Altar vow
9. Sam Houston was one
10. Pastel hue
11. Hardhearted
12. A grandson of Ham
13. Pitchblende, e.g.
14. Moorish capital
15. Marginal mark
16. Windups
17. ASAP in the OR
21. Frugal one
23. Concrete spreaders
25. Coeus or Crius
28. Gless's co-star
31. N.Y.C. restaurateur
32. Fiesta Bowl site
33. Mohammed's birthplace
34. Estogrul's son
35. Jamie's father
36. Urban oases
37. Twofold
38. Michael's father
39. Berlin's were blue
41. Loathed
42. Haley book
44. Billion years
46. Petered out
48. "___ is human"
50. Swellings
51. ___ home (out)
52. Sigurd's horse
53. "Lili" star
54. Spine
56. Gnu features
58. Operatives
60. Yes follower
61. Bullock
62. "The Profane Art" author
63. To grow dim, in Dijon
64. Flings
65. Alt's asset
66. Gluts
67. Attila, e.g.
68. Methods
69. Wedge: Pref.
74. Salon services
76. Large antelope
77. Unsettle
78. Shows off
79. Hunter and Richardson
80. Suppress
81. Potable's potency
83. "___ will is the wind's will": Longfellow
85. Antiknock fluids
87. Frangible
88. Like a country gentleman
89. Fast time
90. Citrus coolers
91. Store gds.
92. Cohort
94. Actress Swenson
95. Minot's loc.
96. Ditto
98. Tête holder
100. Maestro de Waart
101. Campus org.

by Nancy Ross

ACROSS

1. Fragrance
6. Jasper Johns medium
10. Ramble
14. "___ and Lovers": Lawrence
18. Bicycle parts
19. Dispassionate people
22. Lamb who wrote about a pig
23. Field of study
24. GOOD-TIME FELLOW'S SPREE, with "out": 1915
26. April 16, 1989, to 20 Down
28. Amonasro's daughter
29. Money-exchange allowances
30. Heart vessel
32. Drifts
33. Rose Bowl pts.
34. Camel's backbreaker?
35. Writer Bontemps
36. Pie edgings
37. UFO passenger
38. Renowned Canadian physician
39. Emulated Van Winkle
40. Kind of disk
43. HE KEEPS A FILLING STATION: 1914
45. Religious deg.
48. Terminates
49. Loves too fondly
51. God of love
52. Van Gogh's brother
53. Penal and Napoleonic
54. Juan and Eva
55. Wife of Osiris
56. Max, Buddy and Bugs
57. North Sea feeder
58. London's "White ___"
59. "Oro y ___," Mont.'s motto
61. Ancient Greek instrument
62. Syr. neighbor
63. LIFE OF RILEY: 1917
66. Il Duce's daughter and son-in-law
67. Whinnies
69. Jazz pianist Fatha
70. Butler or Morse
71. Sports palaces
72. DIVERSION: 1914
74. Forced emigrants: Abbr.
77. Old Athenian tunic
78. Poe's "___ in Paradise"
80. Aquatic flier
81. Bind with a ship's ropes
82. Great Lakes acronym
83. Beget
84. Del Rio film: 1928
87. Rock cavity's crystalline lining
88. Hot box
89. Zola novel
90. Comb: Comb. form
91. Gala in Galicia
92. Footlike part
93. Stage illumination
96. Gift for a third anniversary
97. Deserves
98. What a mantis does?
99. "Now the hungry lion ___": Shak.
100. Loudness
102. Old World lizard
103. Fencing defense
104. Links org.
107. Bagnold's "___ Blandish"
108. Staggering
110. Moon of Uranus
111. Prohibitionists
112. MISERY: 1918
114. HUSSEIN IN GOTHAM, with "A": 1957
117. Royal Indian
118. Scottish group
119. Catnap
120. Some are close
121. ___ St. Lawrence, G.B.S.'s home
122. Olden times
123. German river
124. Church council

DOWN

1. Garden pest
2. Hampton ___
3. Gumbo
4. Ott or Brooks
5. Nepalese, e.g.
6. Legendary Gaelic hero
7. Murrow's "See ___"
8. Clark Kent's girl
9. Mr., in Milano
10. Straight: Pref.
11. Olive genus
12. Department in E. France
13. "Once Upon a ___," 1959 musical
14. Most logical
15. Praying figure
16. Wimps' cousins
17. Puts into words
18. Ailurophobe's cry
20. SUBJECT OF THIS PUZZLE
21. Pelted
25. Plumed bird
27. What Mauna Loa can do
31. Undercooked
34. Laths
35. Pallid
36. TV ads honors
37. "___ moi le déluge"
38. Preminger or Bismarck
39. Groove
40. Nopal and saguaro
41. Shawms' successors
42. THIS DAY AND AGE: 1936
44. Hatching post
45. KLONDIKE EVENT: 1925
46. Poor boys
47. Capt's deck chief
49. Patron saint of France
50. Assns.
52. French philosopher: 1828–93
54. Ottoman title
55. Stagehands' union
56. Hitler's mistress
58. Dickens villain
60. Lascivious look
61. "___ of Athens"
63. Formal content of a culture
64. Paroxysm
65. Dutch artist Poortvliet
66. French Revolution song
68. Corroded
70. Pool person
71. Give thrust to
73. Like ___ of bricks
75. Phony gem
76. Supernumerary's weapon
77. Karate stroke
78. Shades
79. Vocal
81. Guitar's fingerboard ridges
83. One of Lyon's rivers
85. Court gp.
86. Hodgepodge
87. Anne Frank's book
89. Average state
91. Like the legendary Fosdick
93. Rural deities
94. ___ dixit
95. Cretans or Spartans
96. Scicolone on screen
97. Writ of execution
99. Two-time Oscar winner
100. May 8, 1945
101. Base for the Black Bears
103. Kind of ring
104. Home of the Cougars
105. Spun
106. Questions
107. Poet Teasdale
108. At a distance
109. Film maker Clair
110. Excited
111. Actress Cannon
113. U.N. arm
115. Captain on the ark, to Philippe
116. "___ Do I Love You?", 1927 song

by Arnold Moss

ACROSS

1. Disks for a deejay
5. Schwarzenegger and Stallone, e.g.
10. Track segment
15. Chem. room
18. Uninspired
19. Mexican horse-drawn cabs.
21. Bluster from de Bergerac
23. ___ Ghazi, Khan, Punjabi town
24. Frank Lloyd's fiscal views?
26. Elaine of Astolat's son
28. Hindu habiliments
29. Serve up
30. Larcenous rodent
31. Porcine
32. Actress Skipworth, et al.
35. Stop ___ dime
36. Jack's dance step?
41. Tuition
42. Norwegian river
44. Tartan wearers
45. Gainer or pike
46. A social sci.
47. Paucity
50. Utah ski center
52. ___ one's laurels (is content)
54. Gary's pocket money?
58. Floral scent
60. Breathing space?
63. Custer's last Major
64. Kinkajou
65. Actor Erwin
66. Addressed to Robert's family?
72. Attention
73. Mont ___, Alpine pass tunnel
76. Solothurn's river
77. Epicene
80. Violet perfume base
81. Horace's haymakers?
85. Related by marriage
87. Air trainee's aim
88. Cuisinier's creation
92. Ampersands
93. "___ corny as Kansas . . ."
95. Bando and Mineo
97. Body of poetry
98. Habitat
99. Helmut's dismissal?
104. Prefix with pay or plan
105. Hen and pen
107. Mardi Gras V.I.P.
108. Item widened in disdain
110. ___ mike (automatic pilot)
111. Home of Hercules' lion
113. Favoring (with "to")
114. Animus directed at Sam?
118. Actor O'Shea
120. Fraudulent
121. Wine cask
122. Glacial gravel ridges
123. Tina's ex
124. Red celestial body
125. Polk's predecessor
126. Nidus

DOWN

1. G.P.O. category
2. Woman of fashion
3. Vulturine S.A. hawk
4. Celery unit
5. Lord ___ of W.W. II
6. Capricious
7. Annina in "La Traviata"
8. Part of the U.K.
9. Slangy denials
10. Kindled
11. Word from Charlie Brown
12. Gray or blond preceder
13. Arctic menaces
14. Chinese linguine dish
15. Joseph's acres?
16. Fruit drink
17. Erstwhile Turkish honorific
20. Biblical comforter
22. Ayes' opposites
25. Type of hygiene
27. Tate display
30. About 36 pounds, in Pinsk
32. Post–W.W. II org. member
33. Re the new arrival
34. D.C. bigwig
37. Debris
38. Hoffman product
39. Aware of
40. Reflect
43. Roguish
46. Por ___ (therefore, in Toluca)
48. However, in short form
49. Kind of shell or sole
51. Demons of Arabic myth

by Bert Rosenfield

53. Draw on
55. Modernist
56. Language of Isr.
57. One or another
59. Actor Calhoun
60. Fungal spore sacs
61. Repetition
62. Agnes's workout?
67. Excoriate
68. Epithet
69. Elizabethan letters
70. "___ spiro spero," S.C. motto
71. Piece of cake
74. First baseman and s.s.
75. Cinque follower
78. L-P filler
79. Contribution of a sort
81. Branch of a plant
82. Middling
83. Name of two Danish kings
84. People
86. Exactitude
89. Judge definitively
90. Mob goons
91. Düsseldorf donkey
92. Doughboys' gp.
94. Litterbug
96. Sound
99. Union general at Gettysburg
100. Golf's Champagne Tony
101. Put forth effort
102. Pie fancier
103. E.T.O. amphibian
106. Seed covering
109. Shakespeare's testy Athenian
111. TV science program
112. Mine entrance
113. Eddy gently
114. Twelfth-century starter
115. Satisfactory, to NASA
116. Chickadee's cousin
117. Napoleonic marshal
119. Meal leftover

358 INTERLOPERS

ACROSS

1. Propagates
5. Wood sorrels
9. Master beginner
13. Coincide
18. Nerd
19. ___ snuff (O.K.)
20. ___ Vista, city S. of San Diego
21. He wrote "Advise and Consent": 1959
22. "___ Want for Christmas . . ."
23. Cauda
24. Two-walled fortification
25. Stupid
26. Excitement over a national park?
30. Tours summers
31. Donatello specialty
32. British noble family
33. Wheat bristle
35. Check
37. ___ dieu (kneeling bench)
38. Charwoman's utensil
42. Member of the fold
46. Watergate evidence
50. Kind of therapy
51. Unusual bloke
52. Kálmán operetta
53. One of a nautical trio
55. "The Haj" author
56. "Hasta luego!"
58. Sugar daddy?
63. Tusked cetaceans
65. A, German
66. Wires
67. Endangered geese
68. Eng. start-up
69. Chestnut's kin
71. Blind ___
74. Malarial malady
75. Data and his ilk
79. Pei's winning work?
83. Of gold
84. Pro ___ (shared equally)
85. Emulate Julia Child
86. College sports org.
88. Hindu god
89. Creamy shade
91. Attar for 12 Down?
95. Wax-covered cheese
96. Like a trillium's leaves
98. ___-poly
99. Author Buscaglia
101. Resort of a sort
102. Man in a lodge
104. Cochise, for one
109. Beige
112. Under-the-counter ne'er-do-wells?
117. Gasconades
119. Extricate
120. Hip
121. Cinders of comics
122. Idaho senator: 1907–40
123. Like Redford
124. Rise high
125. Write Waugh
126. Hair-raising
127. Australian lake
128. With competence
129. "___ Fence Me In"

DOWN

1. Hangs in there
2. Little hooter
3. Author Cather
4. Avocet's kin
5. Lasts longer than
6. Ledger scanners, for short
7. Have ___ (tackle)
8. Without others
9. Sit at ___ of (be a disciple)
10. "Age of Anxiety" poet
11. Poles, Serbs, etc.
12. Welles role
13. Say more
14. Horticulturist's habitat?
15. Litter's smallest
16. Old tongue
17. Some are private
20. Attribute to
27. Away
28. Pianist Peter
29. Author Santha Rama ___
34. Inst. at Ogden, Utah
36. Darwin's ship
37. Esposito of the N.H.L.
38. Brighton sight
39. Jeopardy
40. Ammonia derivative
41. Items to count
42. Credit union's offer
43. "___ partridge in a . . ."
44. She wrote "My Life": 1975
45. Forest denizen's sweet?
47. Rubbish
48. Pierre's seraph
49. Gilt, e.g.
54. Moved in a curved course
57. Trim
59. Condescend
60. Uncover
61. Kind of tube or circle
62. Pelvic bones
64. Caper
69. Place to get pesetas
70. Necessitate
71. Hillside dugouts
72. Drudge
73. Hatchbacks, e.g.
74. NASA nods
76. Crocus or gladiolus
77. Aprile Millo, for one
78. Horn-swaggler's forte
80. Windbag
81. Hobgoblin's word
82. ___ 500 (event for Al Unser)
87. Depending on luck
90. Kennel sound
92. Author Caldwell
93. Grew swiftly
94. Arm bone
97. Pt. of Newfoundland
100. Saturn's spouse
102. Macho
103. John Lithgow, e.g.
105. Winning
106. Viola's kin
107. Reddy or Moody
108. Solar-lunar time differential
109. Refluxes
110. "Lizard of the Nile," for short
111. ___ avis
113. Grease job
114. Sub ___ (secretly)
115. Pommel
116. Useful Latin Abbr.
118. Retiring

by Virginia L. Yates

ACROSS

1. Neither fem. nor neut.
5. Thin-skinned area
9. Spring
13. Reporter's exclusive
18. Juárez water
19. Neophyte
20. Moon valley
21. Veil material
22. Actor Sean
23. Fail to include
24. Infix
25. Summer snake
26. Nobleman views oceanic wastes
30. Flowering shrub
32. August sign
33. County component
34. Vane reading
35. Auricles
36. Source of a syrup
39. It's W. of the Urals
41. Excavator overlooked secondary weather phenomenon
49. Ed or Leon
50. With full force
51. Greek Cupid
52. Biblical idol
54. Carmine
55. Old English bards
56. More dreadful
58. Foulard
59. NASA sites
60. Earthquake
62. Gourmand's joy
65. Virtuous relatives ran after insects
71. Gridiron gear
72. Selling places
73. Type of sch.
74. Prefix for form
75. "Aqui se ___ español"
77. Child's wear
79. "Major Barbara" auth.
82. Jeer
84. Funnyman Foxx
85. "___ by land . . ."
86. Donkey's cry
87. Ecclesiastical group dined on chicken
92. Earth: Pref.
93. Assuages
94. In two
95. Uraeus symbol
98. Early pulpit
101. Squids squirt it
102. Rubs out
103. Sedate singer remained vile
109. Careless hurrying
110. Clean a fluke
111. Yemeni, e.g.
112. English
115. Ethyl oxide
116. Slender candle
117. Ceremonial act
118. Galway's locale
119. Fabric joints
120. While preceder
121. Have to have
122. Mulligan

DOWN

1. Atlas page
2. A cause of grayness
3. Red from rays
4. Tenerife, Fuerte-ventura, etc.
5. Milkmaid's perch
6. Choir rendition
7. Rainbow
8. Distinction
9. Bar dance
10. Exile island
11. On the ball
12. Actor Armendariz: 1912–63
13. Tin
14. Chaws
15. Of yore
16. City on the Allegheny
17. Inherently
20. Do a lawn job
27. Hind
28. Terry or Glasgow
29. Washstand item
30. Truman's birthplace
31. Wicker's "___ to Die"
36. Sensitive plant
37. P.D.Q. kin
38. Penultimate Greek letters
40. Eve's genesis
42. Thane of Cawdor
43. Docs
44. Cork folks
45. Bellini opera
46. Carbohydrate ending
47. Glossy fabric
48. Sully
53. Tour segments
55. Stuff to the gills
57. Recite quickly
59. W.W. II craft
60. Sicilian street
61. Superlative suffix
63. Mideast gulf
64. Edinburgh beret
65. Engine sound

by Richard Silvestri

66. Three-time Olympic skating champion
67. Suspect's out
68. Brownish hue
69. Silent screen star Nita
70. One thing after another
76. Cartoon bark
77. Literary collections
78. He rose over Ty
79. Lube-job area
80. Wilkes' other half
81. Methods: Abbr.
83. Future finch
85. Honshu city
86. Gets around
88. Spectacular falls
89. Mausoleum
90. Tenant
91. ___ avis
95. Incinerator residue
96. One of 50
97. Turkish title
99. Sew with loose stitches
100. "Sesame Street" grouch
101. Ait
102. Declined
104. Piece of news
105. Undermines
106. Tall tale
107. ___-Lackawanna RR
108. Prom partner
113. Infuriation
114. Just on the market

ACROSS

1. Town SW of Padua
5. Scrub
10. Moroccan capital
15. Hangars
20. Square columns
21. Creator of Truthful James
22. ___ Levant, French island
23. Divided country
24. WHAT HE WAS DOING
28. Three: Prefix
29. San ___, W. R. Hearst's castle
30. Sopranos Calve and Eames
31. Items thrown by Eris
32. Carry on
34. "___ we forget . . ."
35. Crisp topping
36. Bar Mitzvah, e.g. Ceremony
37. Kind of market
39. Lament
40. An act of suppression
44. WHAT HE SAW
49. Shamus
50. Stag's mate
51. Railroad stations
54. Home on a tor
55. Evans' mate
57. Bridle part
58. H. Clay, to A. Jackson
59. City on the Po
60. Dispatch boat
61. Desist
62. Mère's man
63. U.S. voters since 1920
64. Haze-smoke mixture
65. Pastors' homes
66. ___ shrew
67. Wagnerian earth goddess
68. Basso Italo ___
69. Filly's father
70. WHAT HE ASKED
79. Fixes the squeaks
80. Nine: Pref.
81. Dark-suit nemesis
82. Me, to Miss Piggy
83. "Oft in the ___ Night": T. Moore
86. Plied with potions
87. With 76 Down, Dino's big hit
89. Part of h.c.l.
90. Entire
91. Small nightclub
92. Emblem on a Greek flag
93. Street show
94. Nose-bag contents
95. Liquidated Russian: 1953
96. Prepare oysters
97. Apt. managers
98. Kind of virus
99. Forbid
100. WHAT SHE REPLIED
103. Ancestry
105. Unsubstantial
106. Bloch symphony
110. Seraglio rooms
111. Opium source
113. Great: Pref.
115. European tree
116. In disgrace
119. Bridal path
120. Cleanse the throat
122. Bonaparte's Marshal
123. WHAT HE SIGHED
127. Lustrous fiber
128. A.L. home run leader: 1944
129. Landed estate
130. Units of force
131. Ancient chariot
132. "Sing ___ songs for me": C. Rossetti
133. Oscar, e.g.
134. Germ

DOWN

1. Snare
2. Try hard
3. Chinese truth
4. They're often smoked
5. Impossible fancy
6. Bowling alleys
7. Rye disease
8. Abbr. on an envelope
9. O.T. book
10. Equatorial Guinea's Mbini, formerly
11. Grads
12. Procreated, biblical style
13. Sticky substances: Abbr.
14. Famed mummy
15. Doubting Thomas
16. Emulated Bugs Bunny
17. Of an epoch
18. Streeter's "___ Mable"
19. He directed "The Odd Couple"
20. Kind of turf
25. Easter blossoms
26. Pile up the leaves again
27. "Hotel" author
33. Cover with a rounded roof
35. Bobwhite
36. Kind of rocket
38. Bohemian
39. Calif. county
41. Notions
42. Racket
43. Hereditary factors
45. Kenyan rebel
46. To be, in the past
47. Member of largest Indian group in U.S.
48. French Prime Minister: 1847–48
51. Chauncey from N.Y.: 1834–1928
52. January, in Avila
53. Hidden
56. Half a fly
57. Continue a subscription
59. Commotions
60. One of a Latin I trio
61. Jeweler's weight unit
63. In a distorted way
64. Charger
65. Bearings
67. Caesar's early post
69. Vaudeville acts
71. Lazes
72. Pope: 795–816
73. Put in place (second spelling)
74. Kind of brace or bend
75. "Seward's Folly?"
76. See 87 Across
77. Also-ran
78. Buzzards' cousins
83. Side arm
84. Macbeth's title
85. Tiny amounts
86. June bug
87. For real
88. Pawn
89. Pranks
91. Inclinations
92. Circumspect
93. Mystical poem
95. Potassium supplier
96. Heists
97. An East African
99. Covered with morning moisture
101. Region of N. Europe
102. Ten o'clock scholar, e.g.
104. A sheep dog
107. Liquid used in perfumery
108. Worked on a ship
109. Chasm
111. Ancient people of Great Britain
112. Tessie ___, music-hall star
113. ___ Carta
114. Mistake
116. Discharge
117. Japanese female divers
118. Mobsters' exits
119. Concerning
120. Bite like beavers
121. Finishes
124. Longing
125. One of the Hoggs
126. By the ___

by Betty Jorgensen

ACROSS

1. Costume
6. Gown for Calpurnia
11. Harris or Silvers
15. Buddhist mound
20. Tex. shrine
21. Bane of grain
22. Site of St. Columba's abbey
23. Cicero's bread
24. Proper pistol handling
27. The skull reminded Hamlet that he ___
29. City RR's
30. Titillates
31. Requires
33. Main arteries
34. Loci
35. Composition theme
36. Compatriot
37. Gypsy husband
40. "Bali ___"
41. Eagle's nest
42. Soft cheese
43. Actor Torn
46. Beth preceder
48. Baghdad ruler more cantankerous
52. Three ___ match
53. Find another chair for
55. Months after Shebats
56. U.S.S.R. news agency
57. Rampart
58. Artist's stand
59. Modish
60. Right, in law
62. Poser
63. Manner
64. "Card game simple," says king of Siam
67. Angry
68. Gumshoe
69. Comedian Sahl
70. Heavy weights
71. Cease
72. Rock salt
75. Thong
76. Carpentry tools
78. Justified, as margins
80. Blue Jays or Cardinals
81. Shine
82. Fleur-de-___
85. Babbitt's creator
86. Bug the landlord
90. French seaport
92. Site of a knight's fights
93. Lifeless, old style
94. Electric catfish
95. Swift brute
96. Dairyman's anathema
97. Spades or clubs
98. Consecrate
100. Detroit headache
101. Macerate
102. Must be signed in ink
106. Within: Comb. form
107. Commercials
108. Cellini's skill
109. Common solecisms
110. Greek vowel
112. Lair
113. Periods of note
114. Spile
115. Kind of type
117. Trim anew
120. Stone pillar
121. Turn inside out
122. Mispickel or cinnabar
125. Stare at a certain seascape
127. Scales for singer Reese
130. "The Loved One" author
131. Bertolucci film
132. Emulate Zayak
133. Ribs of leaves
134. Weavers' reeds
135. Literary contest
136. Cut wood
137. Indulge in cabotinage

DOWN

1. Security
2. Jewish month
3. Browns
4. Japanese apricot
5. Dead Sea product
6. Giant redwood
7. Faith
8. Curved moldings
9. Acreage
10. An A.B.A. member
11. Certain tollgate employees
12. Lariat eye
13. Agnes, in Avila
14. Boston's Cardinal
15. Wire winder
16. Linger
17. Military force
18. Type size
19. Inquires
25. Collision
26. Preceders of febreros
28. Elis

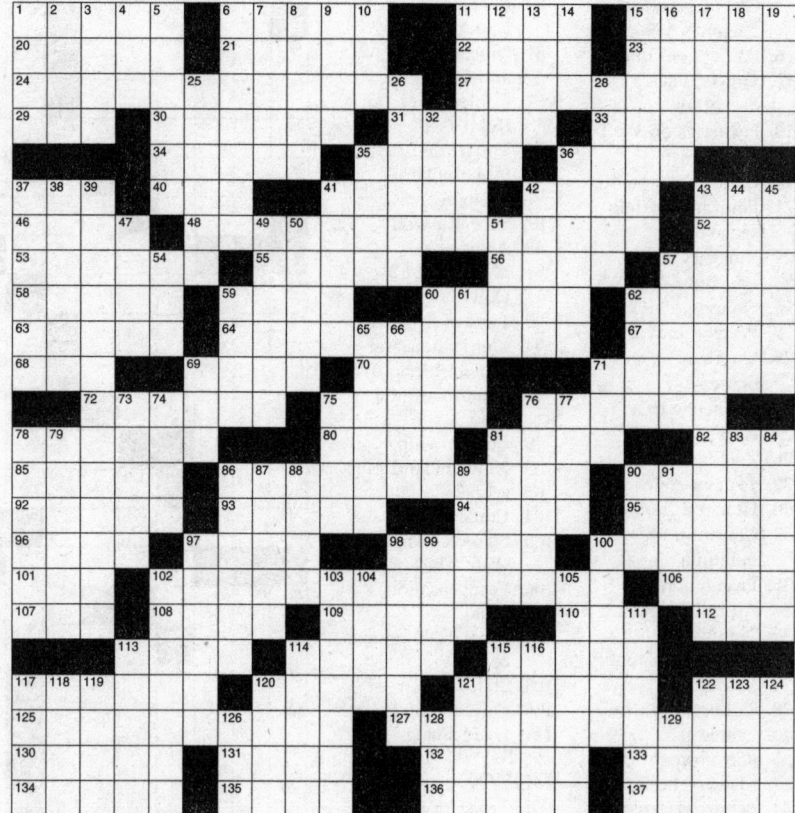

by Ernst Theimer

32. Eastern potentate
35. Annealing over
36. Grain beard
37. Most attenuated
38. ___ of quinine
39. Licorice eaters' dentures
41. Speedily
42. Egghead
43. Worker indicating single lane, e.g.
44. Estuaries
45. Portable platform in a warehouse
47. Sense
49. Pakistani city
50. Dostoyevsky's "The ___"
51. Type of collar
54. Rarebit ingredient
57. More unpleasant
59. Coagulate
60. Electrical generator
61. Grate
62. Carriage
65. Bear witness
66. Rails
69. Kind of way
71. Grackle
73. Philippine idol
74. Minus
75. Sadr or Salm
76. Satisfy
77. C. P. Snow's title
78. Site of famed rock temples in India
79. Hidden
81. Grind
83. She signs "Liebestod"
84. Runner on a plant
86. Frequents
87. Priest's scarf
88. Meat entrée
89. Small birds
90. Seeded player's delight
91. Watercourse
97. Celestial being
98. Relied (on)
99. Mineral: Comb. form
100. Go to bed
102. Outcasts
103. Cathedral church of Rome
104. Small bottle
105. Extended a subscription
111. Lively
113. Melancholy poem
114. Office worker
115. Relative acquired
116. Egg-shaped
117. Tiers
118. Same, in Savoie
119. Guide for Holmes
120. Self-satisfied
121. Actress Chase
122. Paducah's river
123. Budget item
124. Gaelic
126. Biographer Winslow
128. Double curve
129. Muffin

ACROSS

1. Girl in Maude Nugent's 1896 song
6. Poe's "gold bug"
12. Enticed via deception
19. Hysterias on Wall Street
20. Civil
21. Point in a certain space orbit
22. Vinegary
23. Raucous fan
24. "Johnny ___," Wyman movie
25. Unprized possession
27. Challenge to a surfer
28. Zenith's antithesis
29. Type of code
30. Homer's "homer"?
32. Cousin of an ophidiid
33. Prohibition
34. Ad infinitum
35. Thimblerig
37. A star of "Naughty Marietta"
38. Signoret film: 1967
40. Fannie ___ (Government issue)
41. Malevolence
44. Better prepared
47. College-credit unit
48. Knocked for a loop
52. Crimson Tide's archrival
53. Intuitive good judgment
56. Wrigley Field flora
57. Adorned
58. Gaelic
59. Colberteen, e.g.
60. Dawson or Deighton
61. Perambulates
62. Roe v. ___ (historic case)
63. Hawkeye's unit
64. Jerry's Anne
66. Within: Prefix
67. "The Way We ___"
68. Dignity
69. New Zealand statesman: 1878–1943
70. "Ich bin ___ Berliner"
71. Their job causes lots of interest
73. Swallow
74. Evil spirits
76. Geological periods
77. Bears witness
78. Chose
80. Bill's possible future
81. "Spandau . . ." author
82. Composer of "Le Roi d'Ys"
85. Rouget de ___ ("Marseillaise" composer)
87. Slice of bacon
88. Acquiesce
91. Mistress of 82 Down
92. Type of flycatcher
94. Metric thousand
95. Brownish photo
97. Hundredth of a peso
99. Certain whip
103. New England prep school
104. Come forth
105. Sheridan work, with "The"
106. Compensation
107. Blunt
108. What 2,000 pounds comes to
109. States
110. Out of bounds
111. Disseminate

DOWN

1. Protector of Joshua's spies: Var.
2. Silver center in N.Y.
3. Easy target
4. Less friendly
5. Ending for an inchoative verb
6. Celestial bodies
7. Lou Gehrig portrayer
8. Greeting on Maui
9. T.H. Benton's "Self-Portrait With ___"
10. Egyptian sun disk
11. Victoria's consort, to friends
12. Illegal blow
13. ". . . Mahagonny" is one
14. Propelled a gondola
15. Director-author Kazan
16. Immersed
17. Verily
18. Almost
19. Potential queen
26. Four-time Wimbledon winner
31. ___ Palmas
34. Correct
35. ___ célèbre
36. "The eyes are not ___": Eliot
37. Poetic twilight
39. Buenos ___
40. First telegrapher
42. Caesar's "myself"
43. Origin of a drive
44. Pollen source
45. Largest land mass
46. A source of mother-of-pearl
47. Swarms
49. Enlarges
50. Himalayan challenge
51. "The ___," Hardy's poetic drama
53. Actor Lafcadio ___
54. Informal garb
55. Facilitates
62. Evasive speech
63. A colleague of Danton
64. Casino game
65. Enthusiast
67. Habit
68. Travesty
69. Mentioned
71. Truncate
72. Fulfill a Hippocratic promise
75. Bovine comment
77. Airport area
79. Gambling cube
81. Striking
82. The house, to Pedro
83. Catkins
84. First baseball commissioner
86. Emulate S.C. in 1860
87. Home of the storied Mouse Tower
89. Producer of inertia
90. Machine for cleaning cotton
92. He prepares the way
93. Blessed ___
94. "Elephant Boy" co-director
95. Be frugal
96. N.A.A.C.P., e.g.
98. Guzzle
100. Part of N.A.
101. Rip along or rip
102. Plato's "Symposium" topic

by Stanley Glass

ACROSS

1. Short-legged horses
5. ___ Ababa
10. Drop heavily
14. Broadway's Jane
18. "___ the Great," E. Dumm cartoon
19. Early or late Crawford
20. Vibrant
21. Piece of Marilyn Mims
22. WHERE'S THE STATION?
24. WHERE'S THE SECOND?
26. He caused earthquakes
27. Unpleasant sound
29. Capricious indulgences
30. Month, in Milano
31. Pub drink
32. Skin or slick preceder
33. Cozened
36. Sheppard-Turpin guns
37. Elongated, as a spheroid
41. Month before Nisan
42. WHERE'S THE FINDING?
46. Like "cats" in the 40's
47. Rock group
48. Letters
49. Harness
50. Heraldic design
51. Kelep
52. WHERE'S THE ARIAN?
56. Scenic view
57. Swear anew
60. Viracocha worshiper
61. Iraqi neighbors
62. Kind of dropper
63. Ancient Greek city-state
64. Five of trumps
65. Grading systems
67. Amenhotep IV's god
68. Earlier bid
71. Construe
72. WHERE'S THE TILL?
74. Part of TNT
75. Stratum; level
76. Former Chinese leader
78. The life of Riley
79. A Sinatra
80. And the rest: Abbr.
81. WHERE'S THE SHOPPING?
85. Presage
86. Belittle
88. Designer Oscar de la ___
89. Usurp
90. It's between the U.S. and Eur.
91. Bourrée or forlana
92. Quality; nature
94. "I did but ___ little honey . . .": I Sam. 14:43
97. Twofold
98. Injured a joint
102. WHERE'S THE WAVE?
104. WHERE DO WE GET LACE?
106. Couple
107. Parts of pumps
108. Strand
109. Space on the face of a bird
110. Commits a bull
111. Kin of a hydria
112. One of the Dryads
113. Assyrian war god

DOWN

1. Quibble
2. Potpourri
3. Petitions
4. Intrigants
5. Footless ones
6. "An Essay upon Projects" author: 1697
7. Cockcrow
8. City in Peru
9. He practices pettifoggery
10. Flat double fold in cloth
11. Heeltap
12. Ab ___ (from the start)
13. Of necessity
14. Fishing fly
15. Battle of ___: July 3, 1940
16. Playwright Sir Arthur ___ Pinero
17. The Four ___, singing group
20. Reddening
23. Litigated
25. "Cats" libretto author
28. Paris's ___ Neuf
31. Roman burial stone
33. Senegal's capital
34. City NW of Trieste
35. WHERE'S THE PITCH?
36. Pack tightly
37. Dawber or Shriver
38. WHERE'S GREENWICH?
39. Beats, to Puccini
40. Flèche weapons
42. Ammonia derivatives
43. Sharp projections
44. Alcohol heaters
45. Falstaffian
50. Skin exfoliation
53. Runs amok
54. Table bay is one
55. Currants, e.g.
56. Javanese carriage
58. Four-time Wimbledon winner
59. Perpetually
61. Farm machine
63. Half a Samoan island's name: Var.
64. Cues in group singing
65. Commended for gallantry
66. Colligate
68. End of Mont.'s motto
69. Pelagic raptors
70. Cheerful
72. Bank abbr.
73. "Festina ___" ("Make haste slowly")
76. Of a lower social order
77. Triton
79. Mexican baker's product
81. Anon
82. Ancient Germanic people
83. Triclinium meal
84. Put a fence around
87. Teachers, at times
89. Swaddle
91. Reno roller
92. Rollick
93. "___ ed Euridice"
94. VCR insertion
95. In the distance
96. Rustle
97. Clay used as a pigment
98. Kin of a parvis
99. Ancient temple
100. Raw-silk shade
101. Sambar
103. Quo modo
105. Clock, in Köln

by Jack L. Steinhardt

ACROSS

1. Former Turkish official
6. European flatfish
9. Append
12. Sandal part
17. Anew
18. Bruce of N.F.L. fame
20. Oahu souvenirs
22. Sacramento's ARCO, e.g.
23. Plantation owner's enemies?
27. German measles
28. Ancient weight
29. ___ the finish
30. Spicy sausage
33. Grown-up grig
34. Katmandu native
36. Frowning elater?
40. Palpebras on the eyes
41. Goad
42. Ljubljana native
47. Arabian commander
48. Warm oneself pleasantly
51. Peruvian plant
53. Yearned
54. Lepidopteran structure?
60. Roman fountain
61. Newspaper sec.
62. Egg: Comb. form
63. Mandela's gp.
65. Soak flax
66. Hyde Park locusts?
74. At the age of: Lat. Abbr.
75. RR stop
76. Half of CCCII
77. Vishnu incarnation
78. Exaggerated comedy
81. Egyptian demagogue?
88. Small handbill
89. Botanist Gray
90. Ghazels
91. Latin I verb
92. Catherine or Josephine
95. Kettledrum
99. One's own: Comb. form
100. Future moth for Lot's wife
105. Site of Cromwell's first victory
109. Operate
110. Cuts short
111. Delicate
112. Japanese admiral and family
114. Lift ___ (make a slight effort)
116. Untrustworthy Puccini heroine?
123. Have ___ for news
124. Ego
125. Fencing cry
126. Historic Pueblo Indian village
127. Worthless item
128. Polka follower
129. Kind of storehouse: Abbr.
130. Gas used in TV tubes

DOWN

1. Larrigan's kin
2. Past
3. Posed
4. Struck
5. Eskimo jacket
6. Reynolds or Gibson
7. Lotion ingredient
8. Corrida ticket
9. Cakes' companion
10. Judge
11. Holy, to Dante
12. Bando of baseball
13. Follow
14. "At the Sign of the ___ Pédauque": A. France
15. Christie and Held
16. Glue
19. One of a pair of genes
21. Tendons
24. Insensible
25. Like corduroy
26. Jacket feature
30. Connacht county
31. A seventh-century Irish bishop who became a saint
32. Certain bank offerings: Abbr.
35. Vote to accept
36. Quahog
37. Sumerian god of wisdom
38. Rorschach item
39. French cashier's stamp
43. Man, to Brutus
44. First month, in Lima
45. At no time
46. Redacts
48. The Wrights: Abbr.
49. Pituitary hormones
50. New growths
52. Omani, e.g.
55. "___ gratia artis"
56. Peak
57. A pome caused her to leave home
58. About
59. Habituated
64. A Munster county
66. Blunder
67. Kingdom
68. Anchor position
69. S.A. rodent
70. Vestment
71. Tad's marble
72. TV role for Alvin Childress
73. Greek letter
79. Wax: Comb. form
80. Build
82. Copernicus's field: Abbr.
83. Scottish rope
84. Actress Montez
85. Co-Nobelist for Peace: 1978
86. Ludwig and Jannings
87. Core
93. Master, in India
94. Position
96. To look, to Miguel
97. Broad-faced banks
98. Star in Orion's belt
99. Neighbor of Syr.
101. Overacted
102. Miscellaneous assortment
103. Heed
104. Southern constellation
105. Family of a Portuguese navigator
106. Cheerful
107. Zeal
108. Former name of Lake Malawi
113. W.W. II battle site
115. Polish river
117. European gull
118. Newt
119. Bar need
120. Ending with penta or deca
121. Med. group
122. Thrash

by Joy L. Wouk

ACROSS

1. Caesar's partner
5. Skelton's script-writing spouse
9. End of a G. Eliot title
14. Soldat's hat
18. Di's ex
19. Dry
20. Emcee's opening word
22. Members of the peerage
24. French actress with chutzpah?
27. Jane Wyatt role in "Star Trek IV"
28. Record before showtime
29. Thwacks
30. ___ Gay; W.W. II bomber
32. Potter in "M*A*S*H"
33. Is human?
34. Sinuous
36. Maurois or Malraux
37. "Get lost!"
38. ___ standstill
40. Singles
41. Little charmer
42. Shaven
43. Espionage agent
45. Prying tool
47. "Crimes and Misdemeanors" director
48. Street weapon
49. Buddy
50. ___ seaman
51. Base runner's ploy
52. Of G.B.S.
55. Lovable evolutionist?
59. "But of course!"
61. Anagram for artisan
62. Roofing of a sort
64. Camus essay
65. Commit perjury
66. He wrote "John Brown's Body"
67. What 66 Across was
68. Integrity
70. Ghost of Christmas ___
71. Fearsome beasts
73. Strongman in a bar
76. Actress Lamarr
79. Internal obstruction
81. Tidy, in Ayr
82. Scandinavian kings
85. Governor of Guam
86. Palaver
88. Miss Kitty's business
90. Tartness
92. Turkey Day pie
95. Presidential Twinkle-Toes?
97. Matrons, in Madrid
98. A piece of resistance
100. Artificial: Abbr.
101. "___ the season . . ."
102. Caddis or crewel
103. Ballerina's rail
104. Pluto, to Plato
106. Opposite of ant.
107. One way to be in love
109. Bulwer-Lytton novel
110. Author of "The Counterfeiters"
111. Clairvoyance, for short
113. Functions
114. Corneous; callous
115. Artist's purchase
117. Dumbo's wings
120. Novel by Kathleen Coyle
121. Polite blokes
122. "En ___!"
123. Schleps
126. Kimbrough and Post
128. Muscular magazine editor?
131. Calif. county
132. Lacking a key
133. Mother Hubbard's quest
134. Neb. Indian
135. Asseverates
136. Fusty
137. Brings to court
138. Diminish

DOWN

1. Letters on a U.S.S.R. player's jersey
2. Chicago's airport
3. Prepare fare for an affair
4. Obsolescent receptacle?
5. O.K. Corral shootout participant
6. Helps with the dishes
7. "Winter of Artifice" writer
8. Author ___ Virginia Woolf
9. Speckles
10. Tall and thin
11. Parabases
12. Pinero's title
13. Tarkington opus
14. ___ Sutra
15. Pitcher's stat.
16. Leader in Mexican outerwear?
17. Like some sports
21. Sondheim's "___ the Clowns"
22. Bundle of cotton
23. Arty party
25. Vane point
26. Roadside stop
31. Miner's delight
35. Adored
36. "___ Lang Syne"
37. God riding a bull called Nandi
39. Red Deer's locale
41. Assure victory
42. Stock item
43. Master, in Madras
44. Kind of geometry
46. Joy Adamson's pet
47. Got off
48. Close
49. Pts. of a jigsaw puzzle
50. Change
51. Thin board
52. Area for a taffrail
53. Baba and Pasha
54. Gorbachev's refusal
56. Travis or Quaid
57. Expiate
58. Indian monkey
60. Not sotto voce
63. Hang out with
67. Sprightly dance
69. Clarinetist Jimmy of jazz
70. Madrid museum
72. "___ Goat-Boy": Barth
74. Apache chief
75. Prufrock's creator
76. Easter entrées
77. Mrs. Kovacs
78. Actor from Asti?
80. "Beau Geste" locale
81. Kind
83. Number for Hawaii
84. Toklas's companion
86. Ex-quarterback Bradshaw
87. T. Mann's "___ and His Dog"
89. ___ majesty
90. "Ma, He's Making Eyes ___," 1921 song
91. Jan.-to-Jan. periods
93. Embers
94. Lionel output
96. "___ cockhorse . . ."
99. Parisian airport
103. German cannon's name
104. Indian religion
105. Duly and truly, e.g.
106. Nickname Piaf had
107. Slip-ons
108. Sci-fi master
109. Nol of Cambodia
110. Mouthwash
112. Montenegrin, e.g.
114. "For ___ jolly . . ."
115. Sight from Buzzards Bay
116. Setting
118. Lariat
119. Attach, as a button
121. Places for workouts
122. Actress Rowlands
124. Yes votes
125. Koko's weapon
127. Moo
129. Salt pillar's husband
130. Singer Rawls

by Norma Steinberg

ACROSS

1. U. of New Mexico team
6. Baby-care item
10. Chevets
15. Kind of case or flight
19. "What's in ___?": Juliet
20. Pitcher Hershiser
21. Numbers game
22. Frogner Park locale
23. Actress Shire
24. Maginot, for one
25. Barrie title from "Julius Caesar"
27. Porter-Spewack title from "The Taming of the Shrew"
29. Major chaser
30. Copiers
31. Part of Q.E.D.
32. Enl. men
33. Roosevelt and Teasdale
35. W. Texas city
36. "O ___ Ben Jonson!"
38. New Haven, City of ___
39. "___ of the Mind," Shepard play
40. Does a diaskeuast's job
43. McGinniss title from "Macbeth"
48. Latin American dances
51. O'Neill play
53. Vagus, e.g.
54. Belgian resort town
55. Spanish liqueur
58. Gardener's tool
59. Bring up
60. Tossed off, as an exam
61. "___ Shelter," Rolling Stones hit
63. Paderewski
65. Capital of Turkey
67. Memorable Israeli political leader
68. Forsyth title, with "The," from "Julius Caesar"
72. Douglas Hyde's republic
73. George Eliot's weaver
75. Join a cause
76. Type size
78. Netman Nastase
79. Bryce Canyon locale
83. More comfortable
85. "Remember ___ wife": Luke 17:32
86. "___ 'em!"
87. Actress Jones of "L.A. Law"
89. Lewis or Weems
90. Ekberg and Loos
92. Maugham title from "Twelfth Night"
96. Pack fruit with the best on top
98. Clement
99. This may be floppy
101. Burbot
102. These are sometimes round
105. "___ la vista"
106. Distress
107. Sheet of ice asea
111. Moderate
112. Ten: Comb. form
113. Christie title from "Twelfth Night"
116. Kingsley title from "Twelfth Night"
118. Lombok neighbor
119. Miller's salesman
120. Like the White Rabbit
121. ___-Powell, Boy Scouts founder
122. Kind of rug
123. Tradition
124. Lean-to
125. Gather
126. Bath-towel word
127. Hordeola

DOWN

1. Potato pancake
2. Broadcasting
3. Model-airplane material
4. Lunts' comedy title from "Twelfth Night"
5. Place to caulk
6. "The Two Towers" author
7. Former president of Costa Rica
8. Mardi Gras follower
9. One of the Monty Python troupe
10. Municipal-council member
11. Writer of inferior verse
12. Census figs.
13. To be, in Brest
14. Kind of story
15. Some head coverings
16. Met bass-baritone
17. Calumnies
18. Fiber from a jute
26. Ulnae's neighbors
28. Way out
34. TV extra-terrestrial
35. Oldest street in L.A.
37. M.D.'s org.
39. Part of T.A.E.
41. Muralist Rivera
42. Ade's "Fables in ___"
44. "All the Things You ___," 1939 song
45. Betrayer; traitor
46. Lehár specialty
47. Nothing, in Nicaragua
48. Weaken
49. Plantae's counterpart
50. Edward Lear specialty
52. Undo
57. Lay doggo, in London
58. Teatime goody
60. Leacha title from "Henry VIII"
62. Palindromic word
64. "Eroica" key
66. Formerly named
69. ___ up (got smart): Slang
70. In reserve
71. Hwy.
73. Abbr. for a potpourri
74. Dogpatch denizens, e.g.
77. Ar chaser
80. Conduce
81. What an ampersand means
82. Annoying situations
84. In a risqué manner
88. Omissions
91. Sine qua ___
93. Issued
94. Tendon
95. Erhard's therapy
97. De Larrocha and Markova
100. Algiers native quarter
102. Singer Lou from Chicago
103. West Indian fetish
104. Sew loosely
105. Ibsen's Gabler
106. Freud contemporary
108. Air Force Chief of Staff: 1961–65
109. Indian or orange
110. Anglo-Saxon laborers
112. Tot
114. Bern's river
115. ___ fours
117. Arab's outer garment

by Nancy Nicholson Joline

ACROSS

1. Prohibits
5. Hector's hometown
9. Contained
13. Tearful comedienne Pitts
17. One of the Waughs
18. Seductively beautiful woman
19. Bakery worker
20. Kin of 18 Across
21. "I'm alive," ___
23. "Eat your cookie," ___
25. Do a slow burn
26. Hinder
28. Texas border city
29. Horner's capture
30. Imitated Marceau
31. Oop's abode
32. Tote laboriously
35. Powerful beam
36. William Carlos Williams verse epic
40. Locomotive, e.g.
41. "Storm approaching!" ___
43. Aujourd' ___ (today, in Tours)
44. Chews the fat
45. Tennis units
46. Ben Hur's drag strip
47. Verlaine's birthplace
48. Ditty
49. "You mongrel," ___
53. First Viscount Templewood
54. In a seemly way
56. Like a road full of furrows
57. Elopement need, maybe
58. Lincoln bills
59. Linton Heathcliff's wife
60. Eunuch's milieu
61. Teed off
63. Henry Christophe's land
64. Mason's activity
67. Burlington's Bean
68. "Have a candy bar," ___
70. MacDowell's "___ Wild Rose"
71. Like Shangri-la's horizon
72. Usher's offering
73. Novello of "The Lodger"
74. Telegram's period
75. "The Sultan of Sulu" playwright
76. "I work in a lab," ___
80. Reagan's second Attorney General
81. Cardinal and scarlet tanager
83. Plea to a departing one
84. Squiffed
85. Butterfly's sashes
86. Lathered
87. Restrain
88. A Ladd from Huron
91. Brazilian novelist Jorge
92. Field game devised by Indians
96. "Fire's going out!"
98. "I'm dying,"
100. Behind which Polonius hid
101. Nut for soft drinks
102. Church pledge
103. Tatum's dad
104. See 42 Down
105. Confederate
106. Mignon trailer
107. Fashion's Oscar ___ Renta

DOWN

1. Kin of tchus and pfuis
2. Turkish standard
3. Last mount Moses climbed
4. Krantz bestseller
5. Pole near a tepee
6. German industrial valley
7. Galena or bauxite
8. Aleichem's language
9. Underground water tank
10. Yearned
11. Villain's grimace
12. Mom's title
13. Buttons' replacer
14. La Scala harp
15. Gets the picture
16. Ruin
18. Caused to be arraigned
20. Assuaged, as one's conscience
22. "Oklahoma!" aunt
24. Not so untidy
27. That old ratite bird
30. East China Sea island
31. Gave a hoot
32. Discard as useless
33. Going to Jerusalem prop
34. "I teach," ___
35. "___ people go . . ." Exodus 5:1
36. Vought's comical Dink
37. "I let him in," ___
38. Bizarre
39. "My Day in Court" author
41. Loaf ends
42. With 104 Across, foul play
45. Emulate Fawn and Ollie
47. Exemplar
49. Number of "swans-a-swimming"
50. Wedding-gown aisle-sweeper
51. All together, in music
52. Moral precept
53. Made tracks
55. Pirouette
57. Rod of tennis
59. Untouchables, for one
60. Salome danced for him
61. Kind of bear
62. Molder
63. Gets wind of
64. Quay for the Robert E. Lee
65. Hangman's loop
66. Stared slack-jawed
68. Pays attention
69. Poker pot
72. Piercing
74. Coastal region
76. Female oracles
77. Like some vaudeville shows
78. Toward the mouth
79. Clever comeback
80. ___ Castle (Havana fort)
82. Of the north wind
84. "Filthy" money
86. Fragrance
87. Secrete
88. Fellow
89. Super-sandwich
90. Spain's longest river
91. Mil. truant
92. Man from Riga
93. Terrier type
94. Dr. Dolittle's Sophie, e.g.
95. Felix Unger's daughter
97. Trappist cheese
99. Whop

by Frances Hansen

ACROSS

1. State in E. India
7. Shaped like an oak leaf
12. Teddy, for example
18. Roll
19. Occasional TV fare
21. Small cavity
22. Regard
23. Type of cheese
24. Bigoted
25. Mr. Bumble's declaration in "Oliver Twist"
28. Chokes; stifles
29. Muscle protein
30. Custard dessert
31. One's companion
34. Former Ringling star
35. Burgeon
36. Relieve
38. Seat of Wayne Co., Utah
39. Begley and Lopat
40. Dweller in Hades
41. "Messe de Requiem" composer
42. Call-call answer
44. Kind of shooter
45. Business abbr.
46. Tree of C. America
47. According to Kipling, "The ___"
57. Hound's strong point
58. "But never ___ my love": Shak.
59. Amatory
61. Merry, to a Basque
62. Avian brood
63. Like a ghost
65. Granular snow
66. Lozenge
68. Repudiate
69. Shankar's instrument
70. Statement preceding 47 Across
74. Never, in Nürnberg
75. ___ polloi
76. Colorless
77. Kronborg Castle features
80. Syncope
82. Message medium
85. Monogram of a suffragette
88. Prop, e.g.
89. Orale
90. Actresses Bonet and Eilbacher
91. Fox hunter's goad
92. Year in the reign of Antoninus Pius
93. Anguish
94. Recoils
95. Has-been's place
96. Statement made by Alice
101. Screenwriter Lehman
103. Course participant
104. Offensive
106. Give a rendition of a poem
107. Suave British actor: 1906–72
108. Listen
109. Pertaining to a cenotaph
110. Makes sound again
111. First name of 107 Across

DOWN

1. Pay dirt
2. "Cyrano de Bergerac" playwright
3. Mexico's ___ of Tehuantepec
4. Escarpments
5. Closes a falcon's eyes
6. "Aeneid" starter
7. Lection
8. Forward a letter
9. Billy___, pop singer
10. Confessor's earful
11. Grub
12. Patten, e.g.
13. Retinue
14. Architect Saarinen
15. Impressive entries
16. U.N. arm
17. Just out
19. Flavorsome
20. Informal footwear
26. Muted trumpet sound
27. Lenard's "Winnie ___ Pooh"
28. Scheduled
32. Costello or Gossett
33. Hood's exit
35. Pahlavi was one
36. Told all to the fuzz
37. Dark purple
40. MacDonald branch, e.g.
41. Decree
42. Give a leg up to a yegg
43. Canada, once
44. Regretful
46. College of N.C.
47. Brilliance
48. This makes Rover no rover
49. Great Barrier Reef sight
50. Kind of orange
51. Dogfall, in wrestling
52. Curve of a ship's plank
53. Motilal or Jawaharlal
54. E.C. Bentley's sleuth
55. Vinegary: Comb. form
56. Type of engagement
57. Drain
60. Celtic Neptune
62. What this is
63. SST's, e.g.
64. Ashcan target
67. Heron's kin
68. Burlesque act
69. Tunisian port
71. A hit song of 1922
72. Do some piloting
73. Dazzles a disciple
77. Brit. raincoat
78. Shipment from Saudi Arabia
79. Loan
80. Hunger, to Henri
81. History
82. Watches
83. Glacial deposits
84. "Krapp's ___ Tape": Beckett
85. Family name of Princess Diana
86. Like sumo competitors
87. Sandy's remark
89. More like Arbuckle
90. Hampton of jazz
91. Japanese religion
93. ___ fagioli (Neapolitan dish)
94. Producer Sir Alexander
95. Emulate Katarina Witt
97. Do a plasterer's job
98. Nope's opposite
99. Scene of many a strike
100. Berlin's "He's ___ Picker"
101. Forage plant
102. Macerate
105. E.T.O. leader

by Dorothea E. Shipp

EXTERMINATE THE PESTS! 369

ACROSS

1. Plant of the nightshade family
7. Mexican fare
12. Instrumental silencer
16. ___ doble (corrida march)
20. Head garland
21. Cheerful
22. Son of Judah: Gen. 38:4
23. Tabriz location
24. Garden State borough
27. Factor in football
28. Pheasant brood
29. U.S. film critic-author
30. What Mollie Bloom said finally
31. Hero
33. Square-root signs
37. Postpone
39. TV's "I Married ___": 1987
40. Coeur d'___, Idaho
41. Norman town
44. Guanaco's descendant
46. Petty prince
50. Patrick Dennis's aunt
51. Thomson-Stein opera: 1947
54. Distrustful
55. Defective vision
57. Sambar, e.g.
58. Achilles' tissues
60. Seasoning for Bardot
61. Give orders
63. Oppenheim sleuth
65. Yesteryear
66. One of the Jackson Five
67. Black cuckoo
68. Yearn
70. Flowed to and fro
73. Panamanian province
75. ___ homo (religious picture)
77. Felis pardalis
80. Kind of physics
83. "Vaya con ___"
84. Snit
85. Sum of interest to Bohr
87. A son of Bilhah
88. Strauss's "Die ___ ohne Schatten"
89. High, in the French Alps
90. Know by cognition
91. Natives of Benin City
93. Type of print
95. Diet periods
97. Emulate Charles Carroll
99. Mrs. Sprat's fare
101. Steeplechase, e.g.
102. Diary abbr.
105. Honshu city
108. Rhythmic sequence
110. Auden's "The ___ of Anxiety"
111. Garage employee
114. Home of Irish kings
116. Spite
117. Fiber from a jute
119. Isherwood's treatise on philosophy: 1970
122. Prof's concoction
123. Photographer Adams et al.
125. Calif. resort
126. "Picnic" playwright
127. Struck a Philistine
128. Composer Janáček
130. Covered with frost
132. Twisted
134. French painter-lithographer
138. An S.S.R., once
140. Chadian town
141. Qualified
142. Augur
143. Dicey predicament
149. Baron Munchausen, e.g.
150. Turkish regiment
151. Oppositionists
152. Bowl-game locales
153. Optical device
154. A Yugoslav, once
155. Last word of Genesis
156. Mercutio's nemesis

DOWN

1. Make picots
2. "A Chorus Line" show-stopper
3. Staff
4. Nabokov opus
5. Bridge holding
6. The end
7. Number of Trevi coins
8. Ethereal
9. Checked the joint
10. Singular reflexive
11. Hordeolum
12. Cable-car V.I.P.
13. Coll.'s big sister
14. Like Kate in Act V
15. Anos openers
16. Featherlike
17. Hardscrabble
18. Nigerian singer
19. Unique fellow
25. Natives of Cardiff
26. Emulated Yorick
31. Rental document
32. Hurdles for would-be Ph.D's
33. Open shelter
34. Protein acid
35. U.S. election routine
36. Bungling
38. Having long, rounded grooves
42. Wineglass leftovers
43. City on the Oka
45. He played Gershwin
47. Historic 1974 event
48. Alpine crests
49. Tower used in air races
51. Films' M. Hulot
52. Cicero was one
53. Birler's footing
56. Titan who fathered Prometheus
59. Where Cain settled
62. Methuselah's father
64. Saps
66. Musical chord
69. S.A. country
71. Let out
72. New World rodent
74. Book appendixes
76. Desist
78. Jewish month
79. Like Marquand's Apley
81. "All ___ and Heaven Too"
82. Tall story
86. Sword-shaped, as a leaf
88. Ale vessel
92. Pouch-shaped
93. Persona non ___
94. Yevtushenko's "Babi ___"
96. ". . . ___ in the inn"
98. Vasco da ___
100. Pullulated
103. Sweet or split chaser
104. Enthralled
106. Muslim judge: Var.
107. ___ Islands, off Ireland
109. Perfume resin
111. Roman helmet
112. Cookout item
113. Moral precept
115. Pier of Hollywood: 1932-71
118. A star of "Dr. Strangelove"
120. Swerving
121. Dogma
124. John Philip's namesakes
127. In after-workout condition
129. Monument marker
131. Rhodes of Polo Grounds fame
133. Expect confidently
134. Like Bunyan's tales
135. N.Y. stage award
136. ___ Bator, Mongolia
137. Tower
139. Corvette or packet
143. Port on Huon Gulf
144. J.F.K. visitor
145. Collar part
146. Nancy Walker character
147. "Black gold"
148. Singer Cole

by Kenneth Haxton

ACROSS

1. Castle feature
5. Violin's predecessor
10. Girasols
15. Paraphernalia
19. "Othello" villain
20. Poetry muse
21. A Heep of literature
22. River at Rennes
23. Tallyho for dancer, pitcher, saxophonist, and actor
27. Conserve
28. Concealed obstacles
29. Ammonia derivative
30. Like Hume's tomes
32. Letter opener
33. Tahiti togs
35. Bower
39. White poplar
41. Handles roughly
42. The old grind for two actresses and two authors
50. Hemsley sitcom
51. Houston, to Warwick
52. Footpace
53. Type of vaccine
54. TV network's concern
56. Hooch or all-night flight
59. Clown in "Pagliacci"
60. Saturn attachment
62. Dispatch boat
63. Kitt from S.C.
64. Faulty cobbling for jockey, philosopher, runner, and TV actor
70. Humphrey's widow
71. Poet Lizette Woodworth ___
72. Centers; hubs
73. Structure on a predella
74. Lined with mother-of-pearl
75. Following the sun
80. Saul's uncle and grandfather
81. Tony Peña's glove
82. Abbreviated attribute
84. Arrow poison
85. Culinary blunder for actor, TV narrator, comedian, and essayist
91. Belgian river
92. This features Achilles wrath
93. Yoga position
94. Resembling
98. Cry of woe
99. Takes advantage of
102. Sky: Comb. form
103. Numbers game
105. Rats
110. Outdoor chore for author, singer, showman, and President
115. Stake
116. Acronym for an ex-treaty
117. Shade of green
118. Con
119. Inlets
120. Stand-in for Standish
121. Goren partner Helen ___
122. Use a scythe

DOWN

1. Wolverine st.
2. Locale of Diamond Head
3. Turkish titles
4. Pyramid, e.g.
5. Catherine de Medici was one
6. Subject to planation
7. Censor
8. Numerical suffixes
9. Advise
10. Increased faster
11. Vintner's gear
12. Broadcast
13. Billiard opening action
14. Andress film: 1965
15. Thingamajig
16. Sprite-ly
17. In conformity with
18. Harrison and Reed
24. G.I.'s devil-dodger
25. Brad and spad
26. Ankle: Comb. form
31. Gagne ___ (French breadwinner)
33. Hekzebiah Hawkins's daughter
34. Terrifies
35. From a distance
36. Hero in a Sanskrit epic
37. A Maverick of TV
38. Hawks fly here
40. PB&J alternative
41. Tie-breaking contest, e.g.
43. Loose overcoat
44. Bach's output
45. Common Latin phrase
46. Hebrew instruments
47. So much, to Verdi
48. One of Job's friends
49. Trondheim toast
55. Identifier
56. Croupier, e.g.
57. Enlarging gradually
58. Feasted
59. Goes from gate to runway
61. Effervescing device
63. Surpasses
64. Ade medium
65. Czech coin
66. Bizarre
67. Clear a tape
68. Right-hand page
69. Hawkeye
74. More refined
76. Madre's sisters
77. Quechuan
78. Element #10
79. Actress Rowlands
81. L. L'Amour's "The Haunted ___"
82. In the capacity of
83. Indic language
86. Parachute material
87. Explosive force
88. Make jubilant
89. Nightclubs
90. Thrash
94. Honeyed word
95. He may come from Qum
96. The Street Singer's theme
97. Rameau's "Les ___ galantes"
98. Winged ant
100. Franklin invented one
101. Support for Soyer
104. A Nobel Institute site
106. Ski lift
107. Clair de ___ (porcelain)
108. Spanish demonstrative
109. Corvette, for one
111. Hockey star Tikkanen
112. Electrical unit
113. Paper ball
114. Tease

by Norman S. Wizer

ACROSS

1. Strains the brain
6. Segovia's companion
12. Gerald Ford, by birth
18. Peer
19. Amusements
21. Notable Watergate figure
22. Eritrea's urethane riches
24. Believe; trust
25. Blue
26. Lucy lover
27. Produced milk
29. He wrote "The Sultan of Sulu"
30. Sinatra film: 1954
34. Auguries
37. Menace with reata
41. ___ Bator, Mongolia
43. Pile
44. Douse
45. Ending for scant or pant
46. Crandall and Webb
47. Pfc. superior
48. Arab garments
49. P.D.Q. realtive
51. Some radio buffs
53. Arias
54. Act like Mrs. Mitty
55. Country lass
57. Orange-red chalcedony
58. Beginning
60. More like Poe's midnight
62. Owing
64. New England eleven, familiarly
65. Owe a pony and a gun
68. Elide
70. Grammer of "Cheers"
71. Forsakes
75. Dealt
77. Word with miss or beer
78. Italian card game
79. Tatami
80. Dame Myra
81. S-shaped curves
83. A Bolger co-star in 1939
84. Skin
85. Lodge member
86. ___ Reekie (Edinburgh)
87. Author of "One Human Minute"
88. Core
91. Verb ending
92. Trim a photo
93. Act I—"On a secret mission"
95. Grassy plant
97. Explosive
99. ___ de deux
100. "... and take it for ___ worse": Cowley
102. Organic compound
104. Kimono sash
107. Webster or Clay
109. They span hybrid gestation
114. Italia's second largest city
115. Of ancient writing
116. Barton, e.g.
117. Took off
118. Jim Varney role
119. Silly ones

DOWN

1. Lee's men
2. Shade of blue
3. Coagulant
4. Winding of jazz fame
5. Luge lover
6. Tawdry
7. Application
8. Ending for a niña's name
9. "___ the season..."
10. Gris-gris
11. Stood for a second term
12. Movie whale
13. Dean and Downey
14. Revoke a legacy
15. Mexico's tourist expense
16. A tickbird
17. Finisher in "Wayne's World"
19. A gal. has eight
20. This could be a challenge to find
23. He went to town
28. W. Harrison's successor
29. Stout choices
31. Bathsheba's first mate
32. Profound
33. "___ Boot"
35. Capital of Campania
36. Gymnastics move
37. Article of food
38. Imprison
39. P.R. man's concern
40. N.J. township
42. ___-ran
50. Put this up or chase flies
51. Box for oolong
52. Cook up
53. Point of view
55. Corresponded
56. Aachen article
57. Mock
59. "Once ___ time..."
61. Stomach churners
62. "Casablanca" heroine et al.
63. Cylindrical seat
66. Protected, at sea
67. Soft food for invalids
68. Blackmailer's words
69. Place to hobnob all night in disguise
72. Muscat-eer?
73. Stupor: Comb. form
74. Painter of "The Feast of St. Nicholas"
75. Kojak and a Huxtable
76. Sullen
78. Soft and crumbling, as bricks
82. Hand warmer
83. A tribe of Israel
84. Favorites
86. Paint solvent
87. Auction unit
89. Flavor
90. Fish preparation
93. George Washington ___
94. Prepare another draft
96. Reach
98. He outranks the sarge
101. Walked on
103. G.E. subsidiary
104. Grimm character
105. A First Lady of the 50's
106. "Uh-huh"
107. An arm of the U.S. exec. branch
108. A Hope-Crosby location
110. Directional ending
111. Actress Charlotte
112. U.F.O. crew
113. Required

by Randolph Ross

ACROSS

1. Fiery felony
6. ___ law (Germanic code)
11. Type of herring
16. Residue
19. Stiller's wife
20. Bandleader Louis
21. Enforcement powers
22. Watering hole?
23. Ait
24. "The Shield of Achilles" poet
25. Decathlete Johnson
26. Darn
27. Wrestling holds
29. Fernando's fast food
31. Is under new management
33. Yoko
34. Elec. units
37. Fill this puzzle
39. Quail
40. Syndicated columns?
44. Bury
45. Smith and Capp
46. Bucolic
47. Eschew
49. Tex. battle site
52. Memorable stutterer
53. "___ thee late a rosy wreath": Jonson
54. Halfway-like
57. Out of the race
59. Dublin or nothin'?
62. Cool quaff
63. Kind of frost
64. Aesopian finale
65. "My Fair Lady" lyricist
66. Wilbur works
68. Muslim wise man
69. Greek letters
70. Nod off
72. Scolded
73. Pseudologist
74. Stalemate
77. Hiked through campgrounds?
79. Librarians' clientele
81. Article
82. Physicist Bohr
83. Soviet sea
84. Merchandise
85. Group of badgers
86. Brilliance
88. Ens' followers
89. What Salk conquered
93. Beer foam?
98. Carry out
100. Wildebeest
101. Vend
102. Symbol of strength
104. He dyes for a living
105. Cartoon tiger
107. Dickens's Madame ___
110. Bern's river
111. Pepper pot ingredient
113. Capitol Hill body
116. Building projection
117. Racket
118. Kovacs
119. Depside is one
120. Arabian gazelle
121. Silly pair
122. Stormed
123. Facients
124. Après-ski drink

DOWN

1. ___ acids
2. Take umbrage
3. Jaundiced
4. Mine finds
5. Brussels-based org.
6. Bursts of energy
7. Indonesian island group
8. Palpebra
9. "___ a man who wasn't there"
10. Rummy game
11. Promenade
12. Green or jacket
13. What a pause does
14. Fit to ___
15. Advice to an inept gardener?
16. Agreement
17. Londoner's pantry
18. Mooring rope
28. Scots' negatives
30. Anthracite
32. Barrette
35. O. Henry
36. Swung around
38. Craft
41. "___ Camera"
42. Moths' meeting?
43. A.M.A. members
48. Muddied
49. Third king of Judah
50. Statistician's Abbr.
51. "I long for ___ . . .": Wordsworth
52. Discovery sounds
53. Mosque priest
54. Cathedral
55. Jewel thief's loot
56. German article
58. ___ Française (French national theater)
59. One-liners, e.g.
60. Jejune
61. Sixty minutes, in Siena
64. Dillon of "Gunsmoke"
67. Sounds from tack-sitters
68. Brinker of fiction
69. Spin a log
70. Agr. is one
71. Fall call
72. D.S. Freeman book
73. Abominate
75. Wrath
76. Ar's chaser
78. Attaching ropes
79. Churlish children
80. Porter's "DuBarry ___ Lady"
83. TV sitcom
86. Ferber or Millay
87. Gave reluctantly, with "up"
88. Make eyes at
89. Dressage maneuver
90. Soup ingredient
91. Ascertains
92. Here, in Haiti
94. Made a pact
95. Church officials
96. Vile
97. Lost muscle tone
99. ___ incognita
103. Singer Smith
106. Mediocre
108. Soho pad
109. Baltic island
112. Nesselrode, e.g.
114. Actress Christensen
115. Sun. discourse

by Jeanne Wilson

ACROSS

1 Long narrative poem
7 Outlaw Kelly
10 Uses a ring, maybe
17 Camp Pendleton group
19 Summer treats
21 Brand of sports drink
22 Long time that just flies by?
24 An Easter egg hunt may have one
25 Long bones
26 Nickname of a boxer who converted to Islam?
28 Board member: Abbr.
29 3 for 2 and 4: Abbr.
30 A camera may be set on this
31 Matter to the jury
32 Mao's grp.
33 Wing, say
36 Supermarket checkout action
39 It gets in the groove
42 Bee product?
47 Befalls
50 Enjoys a hammock
51 Slip into
52 Whom bouncers might bounce
53 Law firm aide, for short
54 Not just approximately
55 Conventioneers' place
57 Duo that might review films based on arcade games?
62 In a workable manner
67 Most fibrous
68 Like some siblings
69 Water color
70 Ticks off
71 What King Arthur's men would like to have seen more of along the way?
73 Offensive basketball position
75 Where a haircut may end
76 Claim of a sort
77 ___ for the long haul
81 Don't chug
82 Stage after pupation
84 Monte ___
86 "Therefore, I have proven the existence of jalapeños!"?
90 With 40-Down, a 1975 horror novel
91 Some crockery
92 Director's second try
96 1940's spy grp.
97 Sound made with outstretched neck
99 Rings of islands
101 O.A.S. member: Abbr.
102 Sitarist Shankar
104 Grizzlies who give great interviews?
108 Movie with a posse
110 Photographer's setting
112 Possible response to "My boss is leaving and I hate his replacement"?
114 Fitting into a joint
115 Phrase usually before a colon
116 1972 U.S. Open champion
117 Stew
118 Cartoonist Avery
119 Got behind, with "for"

DOWN

1 Printer's unit
2 Pope of 1963–78
3 Rubber gaskets
4 Printer's unit
5 Speed-skating gold medalist Karin
6 Common Market letters
7 Angina treatment, for short
8 O.A.S. member: Abbr.
9 "Citizen Ruth" actress, 1996
10 Senators' wear
11 "Trainspotting" star Bremner
12 Short-finned ___
13 Uncommon delivery
14 It's used with some frequency
15 Singer-Brickell
16 Where scenes are seen
18 Title with a number, perhaps
20 Heroine of TV's "Alias," for short
21 Cut back
23 Kook
27 Brunch buffet items
30 Father-and-daughter fighters
32 Small brain size
34 Places for fish
35 Forest sticker
36 Part of a heartbeat
37 Cool ___
38 Stubborn one
39 Where God sent Jonah
40 See 90-Across
41 Officer with a half-inch stripe: Abbr.
43 Stepped
44 Substantiate
45 Outhouse issue
46 Simple bunk
47 Part of "The Alphabet Song"
48 Italian-born explorer of the New World
49 Blintz relative
54 Destructive stuff
55 Grass and such
56 Disbeliever's cry
58 Sub
59 Hockey stat
60 Mag. staff
61 Grabs some chow?
63 Put a stop to
64 King Louis XII's birthplace
65 "Network" director, 1976
66 Kind of question
69 Sault ___ Marie
71 Letter before resh
72 Each
74 Trader ___
77 Test results, sometimes
78 United Feature Synd. partner
79 Warm assent
80 Joan Collins's villain on "Batman"
82 U.N. agcy.
83 With, in Wiesbaden
84 Non-dean's list grades
85 Reading and the like: Abbr.
87 Chanted sounds
88 Device with a scroll wheel
89 Con junction
93 Surpass in gluttony
94 Ominous-sounding phrase
95 Put down roots?
97 Reims's department
98 Universal donor blood type, for short
99 Skintight material
100 Tomfool finish
102 Hindu avatar
103 Fat as ___
104 Classroom handout
105 E.P.A. pollution
106 Batter's ploy
107 The Auld Sod
108 "In that range"
109 About
111 Plane heading?
113 Onetime Mideast union: Abbr.

by Trip Payne

ACROSS

1. Obstinate person
4. Plagiarizes
9. Nessus, for one
14. Red alga
18. Lecture
20. Pillage; plunder
21. Black Sea port
22. Eldest of the Pleiades
23. Rapid rise
25. Dormant future shoots
27. Wives of Fatima's descendants
28. Automatic pistols
30. Formal avenue
31. Eucharistic dish
32. Kipling's "Soldiers ___"
33. Swiss river
35. Bodies of writing
37. Greek sea goddess
41. Prokofiev's lupine trapper
42. Okla. Siouans
43. Slyly sarcastic
44. F.D.R. measure
45. Actress Alicia
46. Most ceraceous
48. Naval assents
49. Bottom line
50. Actress Talmadge
53. Emulate Doré
55. Poet Hart ___
57. Flower parts
58. Stomach acidity
60. Curling teams
61. Great supply
66. Star-packed teams
68. Town in Ethiopia or Kenya
69. Type of estate
70. ___ fixe
71. Turkish city
72. Put out a candle
74. Conifers
79. Animal and plant lives of regions
80. Scapegoat
82. Species of Mexican yuccas
84. Soup or jacket preceder
85. A.P. rival
86. Uncle Milty
87. Greek goddess of victory
88. Terrier breed
90. Amour-propre
92. British general in the Seven Years War

95. ". . . ___ perfumed sea": Poe
96. Member of a Jewish sect
97. Competitor
98. Crownlet
101. "L'Heure Espagnole" composer
102. Ester of acid from cork
105. ___ Highway System
108. Origination of first life on earth
110. Causes (oneself) to go
111. Item on an alley
112. Blower on the proboscis
113. Rheo or thermo follower
114. Pushkin refusal
115. Laurel and Musial
116. Aquarium denizen
117. Compass dir.

DOWN

1. Sordini
2. Scold severely
3. Sousa march
4. June beetle
5. ___ Church, N.Z. sect
6. Eye part
7. Sis sibling
8. Systems that turn motors in time with generators
9. Streets, in Sonora
10. Growing out
11. Cole and Turner
12. Brownish gray
13. Sprinted
14. Mystery writer Eric
15. Part of Europe, once
16. Assistant
17. Make an incised mark
19. Defense discipline
24. Liquid measure
26. French pastry
29. Voltaire tragedy
32. Private student
33. Sand, to Chopin
34. Plant lice
35. Comic Jay
36. Poisonous
37. Haphazardly
38. Irrational
39. Boles
40. Furniture designer
41. Moccasin

43. Vanzetti's co-defendant
46. German woods
47. Early Mohammedan converts at Medina
51. Disdain
52. Disease with muscular spasms
54. Type of root
55. Condiment holder
56. Stair part
59. Roi's mate
61. Recording equipment
62. Largest S.A. country, to inhabitants
63. Lie snugly
64. King of England and Denmark
65. Brownie
67. Colonialist Cecil
68. Miss.'s ex-Governor
73. Last stage
74. Prodded
75. Pompey's way
76. Outer layers of cells of an embryo

77. Hair-raising
78. Antonio or Francisco
80. "To ___ not . . .": Hamlet
81. Crab-eating mongoose
83. Hissing
86. Indistinct
88. Group of 13 witches
89. Portuguese town
91. Arden, for one
92. Prowls after prey
93. Miss. delta town
94. Spanish painter Lo Spagnoletto
96. Fastener for a cloche
98. Lhasa native
99. Like a squid's discharge
100. Fits to ___
101. Punjabi potentate
102. Easily split rock
103. Pedro's aunts
104. Ferrara family name
106. Kin of aves.

107. Vietnam offensive
109. Caviar

by Kenneth Haxton

ACROSS

1. "___ Ike" button
6. A son of Jacob
10. Make sense
15. Flutters the sheets
16. Luster
17. Publication makeup
19. Ceremonies
20. Precocious Ivy Leaguer!
23. Alt.
24. Connery and Penn
26. New Orleans hoopla word
27. Buttons, for one
28. Writer Earl ___ Biggers
29. Borrowed
31. Alias
32. Bête ___
34. Stopped at a motel
36. Beat pounder
37. What a Mexican whistles
39. Cries of joy
40. Concorde bows to big birds!
43. Switches
44. Roh ___ Woo of the ROK
45. God, to Verdi
46. Certain gales
49. U.S. Open tennis champ: 1966
52. "Le ___ d'or"
54. Command at sea
55. ___ Mahal
58. Arduous
60. Thigh armor
62. Rollo's men
64. "Bus Stop" playwright
65. Egotist ties his knot!
68. Goddess of victory
69. Devil
71. Ivanhoe's love
72. Intensifying agent
74. Dolce ___ niente
75. Twin City suburb
77. Refrain start
79. Moved quickly
80. Karate ploy
82. Some Bx. trains
84. "Blame It on ___," 1984 film
85. Like deciduous trees
87. Snowman elected!
93. Globetrotters' home
94. Fall on Broadway
96. Crossette
97. Judicial attire
98. Kind of city
99. Pants maker of song
100. Actress Franklin
103. Budget concern
104. Nigerian city
105. "___ bleu!"
107. Cheryl Tiegs, e.g.
108. ___ time (never)
109. Vehicle made of ballpoints!
113. Inlet in SE Conn.
115. Yalta figure
116. Special collars
117. Steps for pairs
118. ___ the hills
119. Type of dancer
120. Aromatic compound

DOWN

1. Hospital person
2. Paris art palace lifted!
3. "Sliver" author Levin
4. Five-time Horse of the Year
5. Heart
6. ___ apso
7. Moray, e.g.
8. Kind of sign
9. Director Bergman
10. Valuable Nigerian tree
11. U.S. publisher
12. Great Lake being emptied!
13. U.S.A. draft program
14. Flag-waver
15. Wild pink catchfly
16. Like some Gospels
18. Insignificant ones
19. Excavate again
21. Fall tool
22. Keats feats
25. "___ would sink a navy...": Shak.
30. "Emerald Point ___," TV series
33. Endings for ball and harp
35. Understandings
38. Cato's "Go!"
39. Sharpen
41. In Hades
42. Pacify
43. Inured
47. Comedy title starter
48. Rained hard, in Yorkshire
49. French painter Delaunay
50. Blake's burns bright
51. Polished, in a way
53. One of five, for short
55. Threefold
56. Invited
57. Scoff
58. Dust-up
59. Ancient Thracians
61. Turkish inn
63. Gigantic citrus produced!
66. Variety of neck
67. Partner of hopes
70. Western capital auctioned!
73. Nosy one
76. Consider
78. They transfer property
80. Mazuma
81. Sports site
83. Put up with
85. Actress Carole
86. Composer Lecuona
88. Wane
89. Cuban province
90. One fostering a felon
91. Chang's game
92. Renaissance sword
93. Tore
94. Arrow part
95. Foo yong, for one
99. Checks over
101. Native of Muscat
102. Inventor Howe
106. Where Brunei is
110. Sidekick
111. Greek letter
112. Harding beat him
114. Rock star Adam ___

by Bert H. Kruse

ACROSS

1. Resell tickets
6. Exposition
10. Jersey
15. W.W. II gen.
18. "Luck and Pluck" author
19. Suffix with major or kitchen
20. Splinter
21. Darling or Silver
22. ASK FOR IT
26. Hot tub
27. Rate of speed
28. QB Warren
29. Lawn item
30. A HA'PENNY WILL DO
35. Least cordial
38. Sahara area
39. Fla. county
40. Lenya of "The Threepenny Opera"
41. Former V.I.P. at the Met
43. Like some stadiums
44. Suffix with Finn or Lett
47. Do this, then reap
48. CAN SPRING BE FAR BEHIND?
51. Boy preceder
52. Workshops
55. Kalpa, to a Hindu
56. Eisenhower aide, in 1953
58. Excise, to a doctor
59. Use a Frisbee
61. Bluebloods
62. Peculate
64. LET HIM GO
67. Roman goddess of chastity
68. Came to rest
70. Israeli statesman
71. Blackish butterfly
73. Wakes
75. Penn., e.g.
76. Pets
79. Encolure
80. WEAR IT
84. Actress Joanne
85. Andress film: 1965
86. Actor from London
87. Xmas centerpiece
88. Certain fighter
90. Horn blower Al
91. Day, to Don Quixote
92. Entreated
93. YOU'LL BE A MAN, MY SON
101. Boredom
102. Greenish-blue color
103. Produce interest
104. In favor of
107. TRY TRY AGAIN
113. Dauphin's père
114. Straying
115. Courteous bloke
116. Undo
117. Bos. or N.Y.
118. Sitologists' subjects
119. Olden days
120. Categories

DOWN

1. Asserts
2. Sound on cobblestones
3. Orinoco contents
4. Was in charge
5. Set forth
6. Command to a canine
7. Bewildered
8. Suffix with Adam or Eden
9. Appear again
10. Argot
11. Skeet feat
12. Campus climber
13. Essex contemporary
14. Surpassed
15. Tempted
16. Producer-director Stanley ___
17. Ingress
20. Massé or carom
23. Mile on the water
24. World's most common name
25. Sadness
30. "O ___ we trust...": Tennyson
31. Outlet
32. Blue Moon of baseball
33. Domesticates
34. Start of a Yule hymn
35. Ingrid in "Casablanca"
36. Codger
37. 'TWERE WELL 'TWERE DONE QUICKLY
41. Whipping rod
42. Conforming
43. English poet
44. THIS MUST BE BELGIUM
45. Dutch genre painter
46. Medieval merchant guild
48. Like a homunculus
49. Stuffed pepper
50. Winds
51. Bhutanese, e.g.
53. Unit of distance
54. Keys
57. Movie role of 86 Across
59. Onward
60. Burns's Allen
62. Duplicate events
63. Pentateuch
65. Nobel novelist: 1946
66. List of runners
69. Check
72. Natives of San Juan: Abbr.
74. Goldbrick
77. Fulmar's kin
78. Impleaded
81. Duck, in Dresden
82. Study of causation
83. "___ Sorge," Sudermann novel
86. Headed a committee
88. Frisks
89. Whippersnapper
91. Couple
92. El Misti's locale
93. Oenologists' concerns
94. Sitting pretty
95. Not qualified
96. ___ bono?
97. Certain collars
98. ___-être (perhaps): Fr.
99. Amt. paid to an atty.
100. Dispatch
104. Anjou or Comice
105. Lie on the oars
106. Genethliacons
108. ___ Lanka
109. Three, in Torino
110. Sun ___-sen of China
111. Modernist
112. ___-Magnon

by Charles M. Deber

ACROSS

1 Hearty response?
8 Flutist Jean-Pierre
14 Wife of Priam
20 Japanese art form
21 Beethoven's Symphony No. 3
22 Emulates Hyperides
23 Cartoon Comrade of Boris
24 Fail to hit in the clutch
26 Chain letters?
27 On the level
29 Popular ice cream
30 Rodgers and Hammerstein's "___ It Kinda Fun?"
31 Bocelli, of the Italian opera
34 Is apparently
36 Show stoppers?
37 Wagner soprano
39 In love
43 Engine sound
46 Kid's game
48 Any of the Dolomites
50 Gertrude who swam the English Channel
51 Center of Athens, with "the"
53 High-priced designer wear
58 Like some crystal balls
60 Time on end
61 Mrs. Herbert Hoover
62 So far
63 Worked
64 Sites of some minibars
66 Scold severely
68 Lemon ___
69 Midwest city famous for furniture manufacturing
72 Rat-___
76 Euclid's element?: Abbr.
77 Suffer an embarrassing defeat, slangily
78 Washington locale
80 "___ Teen-age Werewolf" (1957 flick)
84 Where Dr. J first operated professionally
86 Understanding
87 Abated
88 Noted 20th-century mathematician, philosopher and pacifist
92 Happen
93 Fleet
94 Summer coolers, for short
95 Psi category
97 Miller, for one
98 Fishers, at times
100 Hair attachment
104 Defendants, in old law
106 Put an ___
108 1990's sitcom star
113 84-Across, e.g.: Abbr.
116 Aloe ___
118 Naive
119 Thrilla in Manila participant
120 Longtime Indy 50 competitor, say
123 1992 Disney hit
125 It may help when changing your mind
126 Current event?
127 Cacti used for hallucinogens
128 Agrees
129 Honors, in a way
130 Part of a heartbeat

DOWN

1 Swimming sites
2 Qum native
3 Magnate
4 Turkish title
5 Was successfully disguised (as)
6 New England college whose mascot is the Lord Jeff
7 Crown
8 Does more garden work, maybe
9 ___ Fuente cigars
10 Choice bit
11 Singer Zadora
12 Teen spots?
13 Actresses Cheryl and Diane
14 Bouncers
15 Coastal flier
16 Jars
17 Western tribe
18 European capital
19 ___ prof.
25 Bakery selections
28 Architect Jones
32 Debate stopper
33 Aleutian island
35 Hot time?
38 Mideast carrier
40 Four's inferior
41 If not
42 It may go out on a limb
43 Agreements
44 Northern residence
45 Reason for engine trouble, perhaps
47 Put in
49 Learn
52 Summer refreshment
54 Turndown in Munich
55 ___ plume
56 Arctic wear
57 Part of a seasonal song
59 Beat, but barely
64 Sorority letter
65 Fills up
67 "The Thin Man" role
70 Horse color
71 Long
72 Biting
73 Gus Van Sant film "___ For"
74 Divert
75 Part of a Christmas decoration
76 Arboretum
79 Botanist Gray
80 Support beam
81 As it ___
82 French weapon
83 It may leave a bad taste
85 Cunning
87 2002 British Open champion
89 First animal?
90 Insignia on some fighters
91 Three-time U.S. Open champion
96 One with many imitators
99 British rifle
101 Country singer Randy
102 Source
103 Preliminaries
105 Lamb products
107 Stability
109 Clears the field
110 Couldn't not
111 Architect Saarinen
112 Salon activity
113 Welcomes
114 Evening in Rome
115 Collar support
117 Woody's son
121 Classic car
122 Suffix with concert
124 Part of a URL

by Alan Arbesfeld

A CHRISTMAS CONCERT

ACROSS

1. Mother: Comb. form
6. Kind of tide
10. Pasturage
13. Seasonal ringers
19. Earthy oxide
20. Actor Jack
21. Pixie
22. Interstice
23. Mi re do re mi fa sol
26. Dec. 25 adjective
27. Shipworm
28. Paves anew
29. Bothers
30. River to the Baltic
31. "___ furtiva lagrima . . .": Donizetti aria
33. XXVII divided IX
34. Erector ___
35. Alter follower
36. La la si la do ti ti ti la si
43. With 50 Down, sol fa mi re do re mi do
47. Burdensome
48. Lessen
49. Squirrel's cache
50. Religious reformer of Bohemia
51. Hallowed woman: Fr.
52. Argentine river
53. Water wheel
54. The least bit
55. City in Morocco
56. ___ favorite
57. Student group
58. Maltreat
61. Scottish firth
62. Sniggles
63. Sol la sol mi sol la sol mi
66. Identical
70. Dodecanese island
71. Nestle
72. Heart chambers
73. Fervid
77. Arafat's org.
79. Byron's twilight
80. Manhandles
81. Marie Antoinette, e.g.
82. Former agcy. concerned with planes
83. Team of oxen
85. Sing like a bird
86. Mount of a Magus
87. Rock ___
89. With 118 Across, do re mi re do re mi re do sol sol sol sol

90. Do do sol do re sol
92. Rhea, to the Romans
93. Min. part
94. Coal size
95. Colonial bird
96. Like the Sahara
100. Twisted paper sweets-holders
105. Worlds, to René
107. Herbal beverage
109. Futile
110. Mi fa mi ri mi fa fi sol
112. Airborne team member
113. Pet name
114. One-time Korean president
115. Native of Mashhad
116. Passover feasts
117. East, in Essen
118. See 89 Across
119. Loudness units

DOWN

1. Saying
2. Yearned
3. "And ___ were shepherds . . .": J. S. Bach
4. Direct attention (to)
5. Crocus or gladiolus
6. Aye
7. Extreme
8. "In the ___ snow is glist'nin' "
9. Feelings
10. More suspicious
11. House additions
12. Labor org.
13. OSHA concern
14. Olympic hawk
15. Aerie
16. Carry
17. Having wings
18. Maglie and Bando
24. Rowdies
25. Dispenses with
29. Intrinsically
32. Ark maker in the Douay Bible
34. Bearcat maker
35. Lab heaters
36. Join freight cars
37. News organ?
38. Sweet treat
39. In the sack
40. Cleaning cloths
41. Other, to Pedro
42. Trotsky or Uris
43. New Year's Eve activity
44. Élève's milieu
45. Atoll material

46. ___ Kringle
50. See 43 Across
54. Danish-born reformer
55. Repel, with "off"
56. Feed-bag morsel
59. "Address to the ___ Guid": Burns
60. Actor Erwin
61. "___ entered in those wise men three"
63. Toper
64. Goals
65. Setting in "Brigadoon"
66. Lead players
67. Island off Venezuela
68. One-thousandth: Comb. form
69. Atelier stand
70. Emulated shepherds in a crèche
72. Accumulate
73. Ancient strong box
74. Interpret

75. Fast-stop site
76. Chemical endings
77. Sudden terror
78. Alan, Cheryl or Diane
82. Bistros
83. Channel north of the Isle of Wight
84. Beggars or lawyers
85. Elk
88. Repair a brick wall, in a way
89. Conquered
91. Organic compounds
95. Pale
96. Houston baseballer
97. Nobelist in Physics: 1930
98. Foolish
99. Arnaz and others
100. Food dish
101. Western Indian
102. Bark
103. Central point
104. Danish weights
105. Conductance units
106. Reverberate

108. Egyptian goddess of fertility
110. Abbott's first baseman
111. Col.'s command

by Walter Covell

ACROSS

1. Historic Syrian city
7. Prague, to a Czech
12. Ballet's "Le ___ des Cygnes"
15. Penn pronoun
19. Curie's discovery
20. Ceremonial acts
21. Bodkin
22. Blessed
23. Busy Athenian's breakfast?
25. Dissimulation
27. Lake near a temple of Diana
28. Holiday greeting by Zorba?
30. Go lickety-split
32. Union unit
33. Grossly stupid
34. Mirror
37. Slumgullion
38. Actor Adler
41. Chaney
42. Squash
45. Son of an unc.
46. Fragrant evergreen
50. Budding classicist's statement about future plans?
56. Caucho yielder
57. Remainder
58. Lined up
59. Small constellation
60. Bourse
61. Resolution time for José
62. Guitar ridge
63. Vatican name
64. Wearing garments
65. "___ than none"?
70. Sinatra's cohorts
73. Tom's friend in "Typee"
74. Fork unit
75. Silk makers
79. Challenging
80. Li'l Abner's son
81. Was checkmated
82. Unfamiliar
84. Pig ___ poke
85. Song of the Aegean sailor?
88. Bit role
90. Auspices
91. Coptic Church title
92. Agcy. with an eagle
93. Accounts officer on a ship
95. Appearance
98. Induce
100. Mutiny inciter
102. Concerning
104. Son in "Desire Under the Elms"
106. Concurring words by Theocritus?
110. Spiked shield boss
114. Approached directly
115. Lettered composer?
117. Pow!
118. Ending for boff or pay
119. Expected
120. Conductor Fritz
121. ___-majesté
122. Male aoudad
123. Sumerian moon god
124. Safeguard

DOWN

1. "Man of ___," Flaherty film
2. Baikal or Peipus
3. Round cheese
4. Larks' cousins
5. Baby seal
6. City in Nebraska
7. O.T. book
8. Most abundant
9. "And jeers ___": F.P.A.
10. Bray
11. "While memory holds ___ . . .": Shak.
12. Caribou herdsman
13. Wrong
14. Close tightly
15. "___ slaves who fear to speak": Lowell
16. Masters, as skills
17. "___ Dream," Wagnerian aria
18. Witness
24. "Wheels"
26. Pianist Rosalyn
29. A Pequod owner in "Moby-Dick"
31. Spanish, to Spanish
34. Spherical object
35. Lee J. Cobb role
36. Apply chrism, old style
37. "Tartan" producer Lesser
39. Elevate
40. ". . . ay, there's ___": Shak.
43. Catchall sentence ender
44. Author of "Hop-Frog"
45. L.A.-to-Reno dir.
47. Twofold
48. Ms. Nazimova
49. "The Third Man" director
51. M-1 rifle
52. Premature
53. Mars: Comb. form
54. TV-antenna device
55. Effortlessness
60. Tumblebug
62. Czars' jeweler
63. Calico pony
66. Egyptian god of artisans
67. Runagates
68. Kind of story
69. O'Hara's "From the ___"
70. "Blondie" cartoonist Young
71. Singer Cantrell
72. Saroyan's "My Name Is ___"
76. Turkey's President: 1938–50
77. Algae extracts
78. Kin of vibrissae
81. Blake's "The Book of ___"
82. Sad sound
83. Clumsy craft
85. Areas off fairways
86. Tyre monarch
87. A parent of a dzo
89. Embodiment
94. Eloquent speaker
95. Author Alcott
96. Surpass in firepower
97. Ottoman Empire founder
99. Jackal-headed god
100. Poilu's term for his foe
101. "Star Wars" director
103. One of a cap'n's aides
104. Region N of Afr.
105. Eric of movies
106. Small sailboat
107. Tissue layer
108. Costa loser
109. Dog buried in Hyde Park
111. Carte before the course
112. Fox or Rabbit
113. Story-time heavy
116. Stag attendees

by Louis Baron

ACROSS

1. Schickele's Bach
4. Diva Lucine
9. Exactly vertical
14. Boxing refs' calls
18. Stead
19. Koran chapters
20. Kind of show
21. A lagomorph
22. Napoleon slept here: 1814
23. Pamphlet
24. Swelling in plant cells
25. Egyptian sun disk
26. Targets for Walter?
29. Lightweight champ Carlos: 1960's
31. Kremlin connection
32. B'way sign
33. High dwelling
35. Org. for Snead
38. Kind of basil
39. Sigma preceder
41. Antenna for singer Eddie?
44. Parts of dols.
46. Suppositions
48. Tito's real name
49. Loretta of "M*A*S*H"
50. "Casablanca" lady
53. Poison for Nero?
56. Luigi's "Enough!"
57. Attendance check
59. Suckling's output
60. Old French coin
61. Writer St. Johns
62. Muffin
64. Penultimate Greek letter
65. Swindles
69. Ball holder
70. Zhivago's portrayer
73. Medieval land tenure
75. O'Neill play: 1917
76. Will disclosures
78. Subvert
80. Type of buoy
81. "Oklahoma!" aunt
83. Jailbird
84. Went
86. What 1988 was
88. Phil the Fiddler's creator
91. What Michael uses to handle people?
93. Approximately
94. Aaron or Raymond
95. Dies ___
96. "___ Got Sixpence"
97. Actress Jillian
99. Fruit for Buster?

103. San Francisco's 49___
105. "___ World Turns"
109. Susan of "L.A. Law"
110. Hawley-___ Tariff Act
111. Denise of "The Garry Moore Show"
113. Wetlands
115. Kind of acid
117. Observers of a W.Va. legislator?
119. Schoenberg's "Moses and ___"
121. Shaw's phonetic spelling of "fish"
124. Fanon
125. Peak
126. "You're the pants on a ___ usher": Porter
127. Spring harbinger
128. Carter and Gwyn
129. Play re Sadie Thompson
130. Memorable jogger James
131. Southfork family name
132. "Why, thou ___ God . . .": Shak.
133. Stat for Saberhagen

DOWN

1. "___ Talk," 1959 film
2. Pre-election event
3. Summons for Dan?
4. Actor in "The Addams Family"
5. Group of crows
6. Berlin's "He's ___ Picker"
7. Speeds away
8. Brooke or Mary
9. G.R.F. was one
10. Terhune dog
11. British actress Mary
12. Learn by heart
13. Grin and ___
14. Bangkok native
15. Comedian Mickey's dupes?
16. Product of 51 Down
17. Member of Cong.
18. Nobelist Walesa and namesakes
27. PA sch.
28. Scand. nation
30. Asian festival
33. Sore
34. Hard wood
36. Spunk
37. Charleses' dog

40. British actress Wendy
42. Conventual superior
43. Jacob's brother's namesakes
45. Namibia, once: Abbr.
47. Ninth mo.
50. Steamed
51. Deposits
52. Wintry phenomenon
54. Korbut and others
55. Propitiatory bribe
56. Shepherdess of rhyme
58. One of the Dioscuri
60. Mr., in Milano
63. Adjust unsatisfactorily
65. Hindu queen
66. Houston player
67. Siphonaptera members
68. Iron: Comb. form
71. Grown-up pullet
72. Burden, to the Bard
74. ___ City, Calif.
77. Acidulous
79. Throw

82. Biggest part for Sue?
84. Dempsey challenger: 1923
85. Half of MCII
87. Jehoshaphat's predecessor
88. First four subheads
89. Attract
90. Fur for Redd?
91. ___ Bay, Yellow Sea inlet
92. Caused a rubber check
98. Drug cop
100. Theol. degree
101. Political exile
102. English cathedral town
104. Composer of "The Wiz"
106. Movie thriller in 1977
107. Lysander's love
108. City on the Ruhr
112. Maine town
114. Nuclear trial, for short
116. Chalcedony

117. Ex-Met director
118. Ridge
119. Sandy's only word
120. Jarry's "Ubu ___"
122. Kimono sash
123. Can

by Jim Bernhard

ACROSS

1. Part of the pinna
5. A savory jelly
10. Russian range
15. Reveal secrets
19. Mangle
20. Greek river
21. Generally valid
22. Mezzanine section
23. Unprepared
25. Sedate
27. Spates
28. Like lager
30. "Golden" songs
31. Film comic Roscoe
32. Aegean island
33. Sotto ___
34. Wielded
36. Indian police station
37. Left
41. Comminute
42. Susceptible
44. Dockers' org.
45. Troubles
46. Psychic
47. New Look man
48. Old Irish alphabet
49. Gelid
50. Obdurate
54. Thai coins
55. Broadcast
58. Billingsgate
59. Stitch
60. Pax, to Praxiteles
61. Catkin
62. Line on a letter
63. "Ay, ___ inch a king": Shak.
64. The Indian, for one
65. Idleness
68. Malayan palm
69. In flagrante delicto
71. "...to shining ___"
72. Cause for a lawsuit
73. Cannes evening
75. ___ fixe
76. Puchero, e.g.
77. Pindar product
78. Fatuitous
82. Parts of some hammers
83. Extremely old-fashioned
85. Rags-to-riches author
86. Electric catfish
87. Balanchine ballet
88. Hand measures
89. Monsieur's egg
90. First textbook
93. Kind of acid
94. Applauds
98. Excitable
100. Munificent
102. One of the Near Islands
103. Ariz.'s Mo or Stu
104. Small streets
105. Spanish demonstrative
106. Brit. decorations
107. Ill-natured
108. Arabian princes
109. Castle

DOWN

1. Swipe
2. Flat plinth
3. Adonis' killer
4. Boards a Pullman
5. Made amends
6. Injections
7. Darlings
8. Canaan follower
9. Of the founder of Thebes
10. Reveal
11. Haley book
12. Xiamen, formerly
13. Mae West role
14. Tall glass for beer
15. Cutlers' products
16. New Jersey city
17. "___ on Film"
18. Spots for bulbs
24. Gave a party for
26. Spanish hero
29. Jillian and Rutherford
32. Unkind kind of degree
33. "In ___ veritas"
34. Nick the golfer
35. Pusillanimous
36. Yonder
37. Insinuating
38. Parsimonious
39. Buck up
40. Super Bowl team: 1980
41. Trot or lope
42. Josh
43. What i.e. stands for
46. Like Rudolph's nose
48. Parched one's paradise
51. Dubbed
52. Voodoo fetish
53. Moslem law
54. Pressure: Comb. form
56. Upright
57. Actress Ralston
59. Both, in Bonn
61. Caustic
62. Heroic horse
63. Molder
64. Mirador
65. More bizarre
66. Adolescents
67. Veers away
68. Alphabet half
70. Low cards in pinochle
73. Flavorful
74. Algerian port
76. Mariner
78. German philosopher: 1770–1831
79. How the Niagara flows
80. Actor Rachins
81. Despicable
82. Comic Poundstone
84. Metrical foot
86. Pupils' delight
88. Whiff
89. Relative of sienna
90. Star in Ursa Major
91. Deteriorates
92. "Tell ___ the Marines!"
93. Jewish month
94. Hindu fire god
95. "Wishing will make ___"
96. "Take ___ your leader"
97. Neighbor of Wyo.
99. "___ mein holder Abendstern," Wagner aria
101. "___ no orator...": Shak.

by Warren W. Reich

ACROSS

1. Ale ingredient
5. Rostand or Rimbaud
10. As red as ___
15. Dingle
19. N.T. omission
20. Incite
21. Choleric
22. Footnote abbr.
23. Australia
27. Various
28. Earthen pots
29. Sartre novel
30. Burden
31. Athanasian or Nicene
32. Argot
33. "Journey into Fear" author
36. Musical upbeats
37. Point ___, Calif. cape
41. Hard to find
42. Tail-dragging nursery group
45. "___ Heldenleben": Strauss
46. Experts
48. Haggard queen
49. Dr. Seuss's "Hop on ___"
50. Literary initials
51. "___ Clear Day . . ."
52. Innsbruck thrills: 1976
59. Exist
60. Dessert wines
62. Speedily
63. American wildcat
65. Arty party
66. Yawning
67. Positioned for push-ups
68. Photog's copies
70. Coeur d' ___, Idaho
71. Scrutinies
74. Like some dicts.
75. Bugliosi best seller
78. Haw's opposite
79. Baby of opera
80. Itinerary info
81. DX ÷ V
82. Thesmothete
84. Corolla petal
85. Chapeaux for writer Jean
91. Hawk
92. Ouster; dislodgement
94. Maki or vari
95. Scholastic propositions
97. Rock attachment
98. Checks cagily
99. Jetty
100. Mister, in Monza
103. Yellowish green
104. Increase Mather was one
108. English actress's family treasures
111. Aweather's opposite
112. An eye opener
113. Tubby
114. At the peak
115. Winter Palace resident
116. Agate and pica
117. Eminent
118. Hanging ends

DOWN

1. "The night ___ thousand eyes"
2. Work
3. Crocks
4. High follower
5. Disquiet
6. Looks too long
7. "Gadzooks!" relative
8. This comes short or long
9. Support
10. Random
11. Like E.M.K.'s "A"
12. Diner come-on
13. Biblical suffix
14. Like "Grease" characters
15. Weaken
16. Bedouin robes
17. Business
18. Icelandic saga
24. Lake in Ireland
25. Coleridge's "gentle thing"
26. Jerry-built
31. Angler's basket
32. Light fabric
33. Woolf's "___ of One's Own"
34. Unexpected gain
35. Rye coating
36. Gardener's bane
37. What to "give me"
38. Reitman film: 1986
39. Book, in Brescia
40. Start
43. Turkish empire founder
44. Modern frontier
47. Civil War battle
53. Came into being
54. Pub offering
55. Reaches
56. Czech
57. "Casablanca" costar
58. Examines minutely
61. Lug of a jug
64. U.S.N.A. graduate
66. At the ready
67. A larceny size
68. Homing device
69. Verdi princess
70. ". . . it is ___ of life": Proverbs 13:12
71. Workman, e.g.
72. Sierra ___
73. Transmits
76. Knight's shaft
77. Neutral colors
83. Cause an axle to break
85. U.F. student
86. Beg
87. Events for Phil Mahre
88. Broom for Twiggy?
89. "Each and All" poet
90. Up in arms, e.g.
93. Old French coin
96. Make sound
98. Task
99. Aplomb
100. Beat it!
101. What Pandora let loose
102. Mother of the Titans
103. Trap leader
104. Assemble
105. Jot
106. Portmanteau word
107. Three of these make a tbs.
109. Journalist-reformer Nellie
110. TV option

by Tom Mixon

ACROSS

1. Expressed by word of mouth
6. Muddle
10. Spring water, e.g.
18. Writer Calvino
19. "... I obeyed as ___": Gibbon
20. Beach baskers
23. Substitute
25. Horror film
26. Beat the incumbent
27. Boorish one
29. "Play ___ It Lays," 1972 film
30. Actress Talbot
31. Width for Big Foot?
32. Happy syllable
34. "Tristram Shandy" author and family
36. Galena and prill
37. Grenoble's river
39. Torrid
40. Gilbertian princess
43. Has-___ (faded star)
46. "In vino ___"
49. Asps
53. Sharp-witted
55. A case for Cicero
56. Board a Concorde
58. Extravagantly ornate
60. Einstein's "The World ___ See It"
61. Express ways?
63. Summer quaff
64. Russian river
66. Civil War side
68. Map-in-a-map
69. Theme of this puzzle
73. "... from ___ dream of peace": Hunt
76. Swerves
77. Ancient Irish king
78. Jackie's second
81. "We are ___": Queen Victoria
84. Eureka!
86. QB Bradshaw was one
88. Neptune's scepter
89. Propose
91. One in a pool
92. Like some railways
93. Menu listings
95. The yoke is on them
96. Philosopher Lao-___
97. Cheerful, in Cherbourg
98. "Over the Rainbow" composer
100. Colorful fish
104. Gregorian plain songs, old style
108. Gender
109. Nabokov novel
112. Hearty's partner
113. Well, in Metz
114. Barbarian
116. French schools
118. "And the crack in the tea cup ___ ...": Auden
121. A Dionne, e.g.
123. Signs of middle age
124. Ruin
125. Mall unit
126. Sauce ___ (interest stimulator)
127. Sorbonne summers
128. Chemical compound

DOWN

1. Woven cotton fabric
2. In harmony
3. Rear
4. Ye ___ tea shoppe
5. Ex-pitcher Eddie and family
6. Chinese chairman
7. Some members of the Eng. gentry
8. Spirits
9. Beak
10. Kind of blonde
11. Antiquated
12. Bring together
13. Pumice, etc.
14. Links norms
15. Lizard of the western U.S.
16. Mammal of Afr. or Ind.
17. Odin led them
21. Neural network
22. Titles in Mex.
24. Form of address for an abbot: Abbr.
28. Theme definition
33. "... after the people ___": Proust
35. Subject of a Stein line
37. Division word
38. Time period
41. Force
42. Fabric decorations
43. ___ au rhum
44. Plant form
45. River at Chartres
47. Call ___ day
48. Interwoven series
50. Zesty feelings
51. Also ___ (losers)
52. Snicker chaser
54. Gear
57. Superlative suffix
59. Subject of a Keats ode
61. Dix and Bragg: Abbr.
62. Melville's captain
65. Destroy cells by certain antibodies
67. Result
69. A Gettysburg general
70. Approved, for short
71. They attack snacks
72. Inst. at Hanover, N.H.
73. Colonizer
74. British actress Diana ___
75. Diet follower
78. Author Haley
79. Tale by Chateaubriand
80. Ferrum
82. Les États-___
83. Patron of musicians
85. Bern's stream
87. College or collar
89. Boyfriend
90. Economics org.
94. Dangerous downpour
97. Web-footed sea bird
99. Cover story
100. Sounds of surprise
101. N.Y. Shakespeare Festival producer
102. ___ in the dark
103. Artist Matisse
105. Lafcadio ___, U.S. journalist-author
106. Tight topper
107. Perilous performance
109. Ration
110. Farm-machine name
111. Late bloomer
113. ___ Khan, Mongol conqueror
115. Secrete
117. Goes for
119. "Omoo" to "Typee": Abbr.
120. Suffix with Siam
122. "___ Knife," Beckett book

by Jeanne Wilson

384 STRUCTURAL WORKS

ACROSS

1. Anthropologist Margaret
5. Comprehension
10. Old cries of contempt
14. Bust's opposite
18. Peak
19. QE2, e.g.
20. Sweet smelling
21. Taj Mahal site
22. Wilder novel
26. Turned's partner
27. Thrown skyward
28. What QB's wish to gain
29. North Sea feeder
30. G-men
32. Narwhal
33. Kaiser rel.
35. Glossy silk fabric
39. W. H. Hudson novel
45. Like knobs
46. Bog
48. Knead, formerly
49. Malayan boat
50. Vicki Baum novel
52. Writer Hammett
54. Riga native
55. Hautboy
56. Aquatic mammals
59. In the least
60. He wrote "The Hairy Ape"
62. Eats with others
64. "L.A. Law" actress
65. Walpole novel
70. Wheel projection
73. Church parts
74. Painter Andre: 1880–1954
78. Adjust oneself
80. Hammer targets
81. "Die Frau ___ Schatten": R. Strauss
84. ___ time (pronto)
85. Sartre, e.g.
87. Tuchman work, with "The"
89. Tumult
90. Orleans-to-Paris dir.
91. Garment with short flaps
93. Tocsin
94. Remarque novel, with "The"
97. Goes back in thought
99. Suffragist's monogram
100. Rowan, e.g.
101. Ratio words
102. Snoop
105. Miss Hogg
107. Cloud type
109. Hudson port
114. Hawthorne novel, with "The"
118. As to
119. French ballot boxes
120. Street show
121. Garbo film: 1927
122. Tardy
123. Bar denizens
124. Large numbers
125. Deneb, e.g.

DOWN

1. N.T. starter
2. Second hearing
3. Iowa college town
4. Five-time Presidential candidate
5. Moved smoothly
6. Disencumber
7. Aberdeen ___ cattle
8. Ooze
9. Pertaining to obtaining
10. Typewriter part
11. Leghorn
12. As recently as
13. Learners
14. ___-relief
15. Monster
16. Utah city
17. Legendary Giant
20. Actor Davis et al.
23. Pleat again
24. Poets' temples
25. Doctrines
31. Disband troops
34. Small singing bird
35. Certain American
36. A 1961 Oscar winner
37. Radio's "___ With Judy"
38. Having prophetic power
39. Victory, in Aberdeen
40. Applelike fruit
41. Yukon neighbor
42. Mountain nymph
43. ___ prosequi
44. Quip
47. A Siouan
51. Composer of "The Planets"
53. Dispatch
56. Bank items
57. Piccadilly Circus figure
58. Business abbr.
61. Shoemakers' needs
62. Head
63. Done
66. Renter
67. Not so chubby
68. A New Hebrides island
69. Ripken, for one
70. Film maker Frank
71. Deborah of "Dynasty"
72. Rabat's country, to Marie
75. Sadat
76. Dull
77. Standards
79. Gists
81. Straight: Pref.
82. Garden tool
83. Sudanese people
86. Notorious
87. Wall painters' associates
88. Table, in Napoli
91. Radium discoverers
92. Hebrew measures
95. Theater award
96. Induces scratching
98. Stories in a maison
101. Grenoble's river
102. Singer Collins
103. Author Jaffe
104. Mongolian felt tent
106. Hair style
108. Of grapes
110. Some containers: Abbr.
111. "Thanks ___"
112. St. Petersburg's river
113. North Sea feeder
115. Bishopric
116. Explosive
117. Recent

by Joy L. Wouk

ACROSS

1. Contained
5. Summon
9. Flick's footstep
13. Pal of Porthos
18. Heathen
19. Melville novel
20. Creator of "Little Iodine"
22. Rumba relative
24. Director-dramatist
28. Cato's "to be"
29. Osprey's relative
30. Azimuth
31. Bernard ___ Haar, Dutch poet
32. "Call Me Madam" prototype
33. Also
34. Home-school orgs.
35. Francis, for one
36. Epicedia, e.g.
38. Rival of 87 Across
40. Teredo
41. Berlin products
43. Collar
46. "Stout-hearted ___"
47. Stomata
48. Actor-hero Murphy
49. Pop
50. Author-clergyman
56. Granny Smith, e.g.
57. "___-Bitsy Spider"
58. New Zealand beetle grubs
59. Turns rancid
60. Huff
61. Fable, e.g.
63. Mindanao municipality
64. Pilaster
65. Mark Antony's bodyguard
67. Decline
69. Certain berths
72. Expert
73. Australian-American singers
80. Essay
81. Oise cathedral town
82. Lothian slope
83. Market town of Normandy
84. Sculptor Nadelman
86. Metal containers
87. Radames's beloved
89. Faucet
90. Loath
92. East Coast fish delicacy
94. West Coast naturalist
96. Former N.Y.C. mayor
98. Presidentertainer
102. Rehan and Huxtable
103. On the ball
104. Adores, with "upon"
105. W.W. II scene of action
106. King, in Castilla
107. Fuses
108. Gods for Galba
109. Tenuous
113. Actress Louise
114. Stens and Brens
115. Author Bagnold
116. Diminutive suffix
117. Calcined
120. Society-page word
123. Actress O'Connor
124. OPEC member
125. Actor Pickens
126. Bridge champrima donna
131. Macadamized
132. Stendhal hero
133. A son of Adam
134. Cookie pan
135. Transmission parts
136. Auction
137. Affirmatives
138. Cry said with a sigh

DOWN

1. Horse-drawn vehicle
2. Goads
3. Halt
4. Genetic initials
5. Snakes often charmed
6. Last words
7. Body of knowledge
8. Birler's need
9. Silent-film star of "Forever Amber"
10. Picador
11. N.L. home-run champ: 1942
12. Scheme
13. Sigh, in Stuttgart
14. Motifs
15. Cods' relatives
16. Baron of "Der Rosenkavalier"
17. Jigger
18. Buonarroti masterpiece
21. Undivided
23. Hawaiian beverage
25. Where rhodopsin abounds
26. French operatic baritone: 1848–1923
27. Author of "Hatter's Castle"
34. Factory-adjusted
35. Vicious eel
37. Musicologist Taylor
39. Nobelist von Behring: 1901
40. Some babies
41. Nobel Peace Prize winner: 1984
42. Japanese veggies
43. Kind of ball game
44. Journalist St. Johns
45. Bistros
47. Exclusive rights
48. Hitchcock's "To Catch ___"
49. Seedy blueberries
50. Jacket part
51. "Rienzi" or "Jenufa"
52. Author Sinclair
53. Where to see "The Last Supper"
54. Go beyond
55. Rapidly
62. Not at home
63. Panel divider
66. Lampoons
68. Afore
70. Kid
71. Difficulties
72. Describing some cheeses
74. Salad green
75. Tangle; snare
76. Where the Lomani flows
77. Essential oil
78. Vicuña's relative
79. A companion to Doc
84. Dodge
85. SAC commander: 1948–61
88. Let up
90. Slightly open
91. TV's Barnaby Jones
92. Scram!
93. Judges' suites: Abbr.
94. Apportions
95. Shoshoneans
97. "Psychic Warfare..." author
99. Prussian cavalrymen
100. Mailer or Lear
101. Civet, e.g.
107. A Bette
108. Greek wreath component
109. Scythe shafts
110. "David and Lisa" star
111. Omits
112. Absolve
113. Word with cotta or firma
115. Muse or Dryad
117. Statute
118. Pile
119. Lagomorph
121. Inquiring interjections
122. Selves
124. Journey, for Juvenal
125. Comedian Mort
127. Ames and Begley
128. Pay dirt
129. Uraeus
130. Youth org.

by Mary Virginia Orna

ACROSS

1. Spartan slaves
7. Health resort
10. R.N. specialty
13. Assagai
18. Kazoo's cousin
20. Conflict partly logomachical
22. Beside oneself
23. A 1939 song by 64 Down
25. Seed covering
26. Light amplifier
27. Con men
29. Use a swizzle stick
30. Nuisance
34. Press for payment
35. "Dinner ___," 1933 film
37. Afore
38. Professional standard
40. God of revelry
43. Made serious
45. A 1942 song by 64 Down
50. Twist out of shape
51. Metalworker
52. Will, the historian
53. Bring up a subject
56. Murrow's "___ Now"
59. Verse form
61. Vier preceder
62. ___ tai (rum drink)
65. Cure
67. Has to have
68. Be on the payroll
69. Opposite of dep.
70. Single-seeded fruit
71. Benefit
73. Poor grade
74. Hindu good spirit
76. Take a sip
78. ___ million
79. Sigmoid shape
80. Indigo
81. Theoretically
83. Habit
85. Prophetic
87. Lots and lots
89. Pianist's perch
92. Birthplace of Goliath
93. A 1972 song by 64 Down
97. Reproduce in kind
100. Shade of blue
101. Electrical rectifier
102. Once named
103. "Tender ___," 1983 film
107. Keydets' sch.
109. Avian crop
110. Bosnian
112. Metric weights
113. Do a double take
115. Runs in neutral
117. A 1929 song by 64 Down
124. Trombone section
125. Rustic
126. Stone Age tools
127. Belief
128. QB's measures
129. Modernist
130. Middle East waterway

DOWN

1. Glutton
2. Italian author
3. Youth
4. Symbol of royalty
5. Work the land
6. Sam or J. C.
7. Incision aftermath
8. Lap dog, for short
9. Schooner contents
10. Strong string
11. Milk: Pref.
12. "___ Wife," Kelly play
13. Mind the baby
14. Chief exec.
15. A 1933 song by 64 Down
16. Get-up
17. Brought up
19. In itself
21. Euphemistic expletive
24. Man of La Mancha
28. A 1946 song by 64 Down
30. Seat at St. Patrick's
31. Ordinal endings
32. Leveling wedge
33. Monkeys or trees
35. Houston athlete
36. Conveyance for skiers
39. Et follower
41. In the thick of
42. Shylock's practice
44. Wear away
46. A 1935 song by 64 Down
47. Literature Nobelist: 1929
48. Like llamas
49. Packed in the hold
54. Largest asteroid
55. Fatha of jazz
57. Clarifying words
58. Sawbuck
60. Robin of ballad fame
62. "Call Me ___," musical with songs by 64 Down
63. Coliseum
64. Subject of this puzzle, born May 11, 1888
66. Disconnect
72. Endured
75. Knot-tying location
77. Fencing piece
78. "Believe It ___"
82. Allays
84. Kind of boom
86. News bit
88. Scottish skiing surface
90. Olfactory datum
91. Mother of the Gemini
94. Donated
95. Cell dweller
96. Morning coat?
97. Declare firmly
98. Ride
99. Overly sentimental
104. Wrote a puzzle definition
105. Tittles
106. Superlative suffixes
108. Venous fluid for Venus
111. Venerable one
113. Gravure prefix
114. TV part
116. Fixed
118. Singer Whitcomb
119. Compass point
120. Disencumbered
121. "___ a Lovely Day Today," 1950 song by 64 Down
122. "When I Leave ___ World Behind," 1915 song by 64 Down
123. Half a Gabor

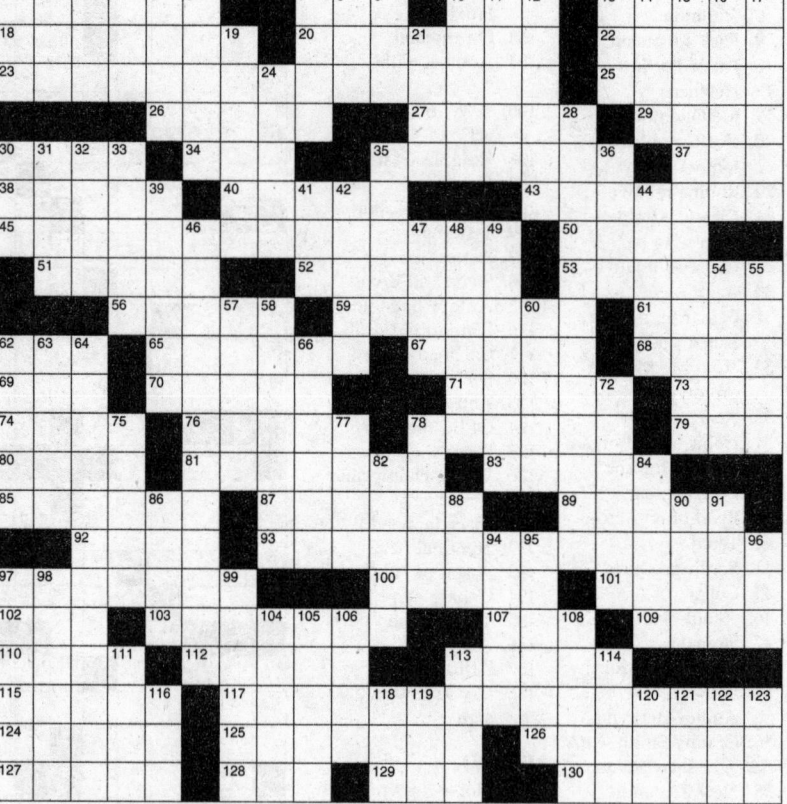

by Richard Silvestri

ACROSS

1. Baker's aide
5. Flak sound
8. Laughing matter
12. Sell hot tickets
17. Meadow mouse
18. "If ___ a Hammer"
20. Colorful fish
21. Small drum
22. Actor Baldwin
23. Novelist de la Roche
24. Apiary sight
25. Rainier realm
26. Happy cloud
27. Signora on a camel?
30. Problems in the boot?
32. Count the pennies
33. Corrida contender
34. Mrs. Henry Wallace
35. Same old routine
36. Gael's land
40. Turn into
43. Sharp taste
45. Oriental nanny
47. Stephen Foster's "Old Uncle"
48. Antarctic cape
49. Ever so simple?
52. Short smoke
53. Matelot's milieu
54. Splinter group
56. Rita's Khan
57. Sizable
59. Licorice-tasting cordials
62. "Sail ___ Ship of State!"
63. Off a pedestal
65. Working woman's choice?
68. Bisector's results
69. Mouth piece
70. Fragrant plants
73. Actress LuPone
74. Rosary bead
75. News clipping
76. Fam. member
77. Ostrich look-alike
78. Italian obi?
84. Grant license to
86. Paver's pitch
87. Grigs
88. Anna of "Nana"
89. Edits TV goofs
90. Singles
92. High, in music
93. ___ for tat
94. Parlor piece
95. Go ___ (deteriorate)
98. How to keep the dottore away?
102. Second line of a nursery rhyme?
106. Familiar campus figure
108. Derivation
109. Zwei chaser
110. Breton brainstorm
111. Run in neutral
112. Shade of green
113. Algae extract
114. Parking lights
115. Give the elbow
116. Slyly disparaging
117. European blackbird
118. Grasshopper's critic
119. Whilom

DOWN

1. First czar of Russia
2. Muligrubs
3. "Uncle Vanya" role
4. Any sense organ
5. Part of a target-practice command
6. Copper: Pref.
7. Ocarina's kin
8. Andrew and Lyndon
9. Grand-scale
10. Goalie's successes
11. Union of the personal soul with God
12. 70 mph wind
13. Hors d'oeuvre item
14. Rhyme scheme
15. Math points
16. Malayan outrigger
19. A Dickens family
25. Rum cocktail
28. Chou ___
29. Dowdy one
31. Hotel amenity?
37. Not to be believed
38. King's tenure
39. Brink
40. The Crimson Tide, for short
41. Earl of Avon
42. Lampooned likeness
44. Brobdingnagian
46. Greeting from Michael Caine?
49. Impersonate
50. Hip follower?
51. Hilo howdy
55. Raison d'___
58. Very much
60. Table staple
61. Cannon salute
62. Comics cave man
63. Spume
64. Alas!
66. Outward images
67. Goddess of discord
68. Biblical villain

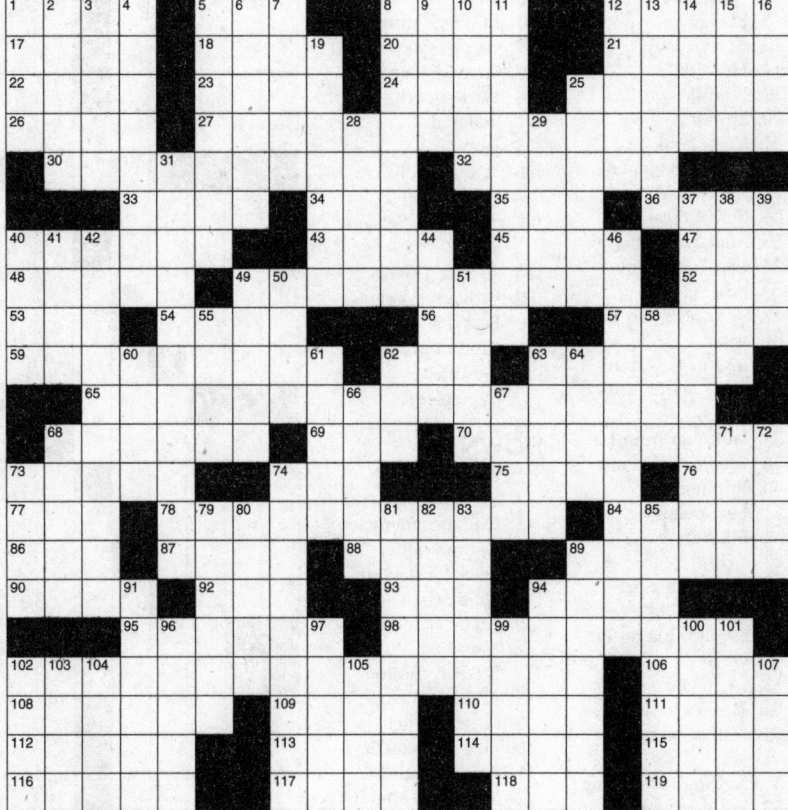

by Maura B. Jacobson

71. Cut a photo
72. Shoats' moms
73. Falstaff's henchman
74. Netherlands city
79. Think it through
80. "Oklahoma!" aunt
81. Cry of encouragement to Mary Lou
82. Fisherman's net
83. Digestive aid
85. Kind of cinch
89. Least timorous
91. Contrived
94. Sacred
96. Voice a view
97. Requiem
99. Daises
100. Fervor
101. Egg innards
102. Ward healers
103. Press
104. Sir, in Africa
105. Treasured
107. Iambic measures

ACROSS

1. "Rug" area?
6. Pledge
10. Catch flies
14. Fla. city
19. Eremite
20. Surfeit
21. Cook book
22. More developed
23. Very, to Verdi
24. O.K. Corral man
25. Mad as ___ hen
26. Old Testament book
27. Start of a four-line verse
31. Jose or Giovanni
32. Story start
33. Miscue
34. Hoffman from L.A.
38. Brahman, for one
40. Implore
41. Leb. neighbor
44. Pilasters
45. Arias
46. Speaker's place
47. Concerning
48. Second line of the verse
53. ___ day's wonder
54. Tropics topic
55. Half an aromatic oil
56. Netting for snaring
57. Fr. holy woman
58. Bearing
59. Manilow's "___ It Through the Rain"
60. Surgical tool
61. Skerry
62. Coin receivers
63. Nap
64. Computer component
67. Avignon's river
68. G & S executioner
69. Thrash
72. Inclined, as a ship
73. Lotto's kin
74. Whale
75. Marquand sleuth
76. Third line of the verse
80. "Ich ___," Prince of Wales' motto
81. Suffix with canon
82. Sow sound
83. Fanon
84. Admiral Benbow, e.g.
85. Hitch
86. Walk daintily
88. Knots
89. Top of the crop
91. Kan. senator
92. Pisan Mr.
93. Last line of the verse
101. Praying figure
102. Campaigns
103. German one
104. Wickerwork material
105. Patois
106. "Down with!" in Dieppe
107. "The Four Seasons" star
108. Actress Taylor
109. Is overly fond
110. Past due
111. Kind of processor
112. English hymnologist

DOWN

1. Blind part
2. Blackjack, in Soho
3. Faulkner character
4. Regan's father
5. Place for devout petitions
6. Arctic or Indian
7. "Sustineo ___" U.S.A.F. motto
8. African antelope
9. Mesmer's field
10. Like hen's teeth
11. Actor Mandel
12. Iowa State site
13. Assemblage
14. Stubborn
15. Mussolini's son-in-law
16. Like an adage
17. Their, in Tours
18. Radius's locale
28. Took the cake
29. Bankbook Abbr.
30. Worthless writing
34. Cockcrows
35. Without a scratch
36. "Platoon" director
37. Use the VCR
38. He wrote "Little Johnny Jones"
39. Landed
40. "Public Good" publisher: 1730
42. Inscribed pillar
43. Criticize harshly
45. Nectarous
46. Pairs
47. Unisonally
49. Yours of yore
50. Kyoto garments
51. Make merry
52. Tajo of the Met
58. Kind of millionaire
59. Novelist Karmel
60. Compare
61. Korean port
62. Paisley
63. Asher Lev's creator
64. Islamic prophet
65. Lard constituent
66. Free from illusion
67. Put a new label on
68. City on the Ashuelot
69. "Marching as ___": Baring-Gould
70. Under any circumstances
71. "The Loom of Years" poet
73. Like Congress
74. Smart
75. Pianist Hess
77. Shore from Tenn.
78. Far from musical
79. A moist Cheddar
85. Bouts
86. Chocolate ___
87. Under the weather
88. Captain's boat
90. Scope
91. Mr. Chips portrayer
92. Sam of golf
93. Beethoven's "Archduke," for one
94. Isla de Pinos site
95. Cylindrical structure
96. Chinese preceder
97. Prophet's words
98. Lollobrigida
99. Cad
100. An Algonquian
101. Antediluvian

by Alfio Micci

ACROSS

1. File's partner
5. Kimonos
10. Water bottle
16. Shady spot
21. Bacchanalian cry
22. This can be grand
23. Deli-menu item
24. Varnish source
25. + 4
28. Ala. city
29. Couple
30. Plantation group
31. ¿Como ___ usted?
32. Jewish month
33. Spuds
35. Outlets for admen
36. Pair of pistols
38. Bounder
40. Wax-coated cheese
43. ___ capita
44. Give ___ on the back (praise)
48. Aunt, to Maria
51. Gorcey or Durocher
52. − 2
56. With regard to
58. Del. industrialist
60. ___ da capo
61. Flat straw hat
62. Soup scoop
64. Most confident
66. RR systems
67. Intact
68. + 998
70. Synthetic
73. Not frequent: Abbr.
74. Colorful shawl
75. Sound
77. Plant shoot
79. Tree toad
80. Yin kin
83. Fire residue
85. Crotchety one
87. Pungency
91. "... ___! the lark ...": Shak.
93. Grain sorghum
94. Peacock-feather spots
99. Look for prey
101. Imitate, in a way
103. − 3
107. Radiant
109. Tse-tung
110. Hunting dog
112. French wine region
113. ___ account (reprimand)
114. Fountain offering
116. Kerry county seat
118. ___ and terminer
119. − 1
122. Low island
124. Summertime in N.Y.C.
125. Ridicule
126. Gold: Pref.
127. Music halls
128. Broadcast
130. Boggs of baseball
132. Sly and nasty
135. Cold-weather wear
139. Indian term of respect
142. Eject, as in volcanic action: Var.
146. Fashionable
148. Diacritical mark
149. Novelist Karmer
150. + 58
153. Con man's targets
154. Prima ballerina
155. Sao ___, Brazil
156. Main man
157. "___ porridge hot..."
158. Snakebird
159. European lindens
160. The Ohre, to Hans

DOWN

1. Contradict
2. Pastoral pipe in Palencia
3. Keep bases empty
4. German commander, W.W. II
5. Wand
6. Makes a choice
7. "I'll ___ for Christmas"
8. "Maid of Athens ___ part...": Byron
9. ___ Koh, Afghan range
10. Religious mission
11. Air: Pref.
12. Bumpkin
13. Arabs' apparel
14. Nonwoven fabric
15. Intertwines
16. Groundwork
17. + 6
18. Artful
19. Madame Bovary
20. Nurture
26. Perfume ingredient
27. Gets one's bearings
34. Litigated
37. Sprang up
39. The March King
41. Eureka!
42. Involves in difficulties
43. Pliable
45. Course of action
46. Without principles
47. Nobelist Mother
48. Controversies
49. Dumbfounded
50. Fervency
52. Its capital is Lille
53. Actually existing: Lat.
54. Granite State flower
55. Town on the Adriatic
57. Kazan
59. "Canoe row a boat?" is one
63. Catch sight of
65. − 8
69. Jacob's substituted bride
71. Virginia follower
72. Tourist attraction
76. Some pineapples
78. High point
81. Cards raise this
82. Solecist's failing
84. Pulpits
86. Instr.
87. Typewriter device
88. Wild sheep of Asia
89. Hung loosely
90. + 28
92. South African enclosure
95. Reverberate
96. Oldest of the Bridges
97. Crescent-shaped figures
98. French composer: 1890–1962
100. Like George Apley
102. Chieftain, also called Rolf the Ganger
104. Coup d'___
105. M.P.H.
106. Found
108. Single-celled organism
111. Colorless, flammable liquid
115. Mass of ivy
117. Tombstone man
120. Made an estimate
121. One who cuddles
123. He wrote "The Hour Glass"
128. One and a half: Comb. form
129. Bend out of shape
131. Humiliate
133. Clumsy
134. The Furies of myth
136. Studio floodlight
137. Like very much
138. Sir, in Zaragoza
139. Meathead
140. Pea-plant petals
141. Israeli dance
143. "Pocket" bread
144. Calpurnia, to Caesar
145. Revise and correct
147. Statesman Cordell ___
151. Violinist Bull
152. Orion's beloved

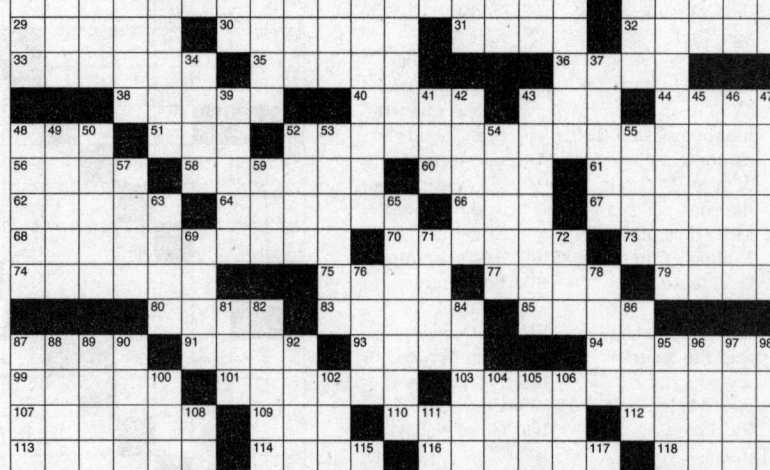

by June A. Boggs

ACROSS

1. Make picots
4. Feigns
9. Over, in Ulm
13. Wire nail
17. Biblical verb
18. Sun: Pref.
19. Scruff
20. Flattens flats
22. "You're all litterbugs," said the janitor ___
24. "I'm on TV," said the chef ___
26. Muezzin's place
27. Kipling poem
29. "___ these truths..."
30. "I'm petrified," said the quarrier ___
31. Sky Whale
32. Rid Rover of insects
33. G. Burns role
34. Asp's cousin
35. Skier Jean Claude
36. "Forever" girl
39. "I'm in a rut," said the ditchdigger ___
41. Peace, in Pamplona
44. Calf meat
45. Yum-Yum, e.g.
46. Wagers
47. Game fish
48. The whole shebang
49. "Blast it!" said the dynamiter ___
53. Pound unit
54. "Alice" illustrator
56. Mrs. Will Durant
57. Ill-prepared
58. Rank-smelling
59. Topknot
60. Roman coins
62. Sky blue
64. Flat, in Italy
65. Kennedy compound, e.g.
67. Distort, in a way
68. "We need water," said the gardener ___
70. Slip
72. Exaction
73. See 85 Across
74. Dry, cold wind
75. TV ad award
76. Marmee's youngest
77. "No juice," said the electrician ___
81. Dallied
82. Like a Morse message
83. Nine: Pref.
84. "The ___ Sanction"
85. With 73 Across, an earth belt
87. With full force
88. "I'm all ears," said the corn farmer ___
92. "Viva ___," 1952 film
93. Savoy dance
94. Bassanio's friend
95. "It's permanent press," said the saleswoman ___
97. "Excuse my gear," said the truck driver ___
100. Salk's conquest
101. Bookbinding leather
102. Ex-Dodger
103. It, in Mexico
104. N.J. governor, once
105. Chevot
106. Grani or Bayard
107. "I ___," said the prophet, predictably

DOWN

1. Namely
2. "... ___ clock scholar"
3. "___ Wore Red," 1960 film
4. Scutum in the sky
5. "The Young Bugler" author
6. Math form
7. Wire measure
8. Hairy legume
9. Rude
10. Thai money
11. Finials
12. Dau, or bro
13. "Tight shorts," said the boxer ___
14. "I itch," said the barber ___
15. "...who lived in ___"
16. Singer Reese
17. G.I. awards
21. A Chaplin
23. Earlier
25. Harps (on)
28. Of the ear
31. Tenet
32. Simple song
34. Whalebone whale's food
35. Bell sound
36. Oahu drink
37. Dissolve
38. "I'm packing it in!" said the cotton picker ___
39. On a disk
40. Red as ___
41. "They escaped," said the pig man ___
42. A Johnson
43. Kind of suit
45. Half of MMXXIV
47. City in Crete
49. Stage direction
50. Singer Vaughan
51. A Castle
52. Cap projection
53. "Oklahoma!" hero
55. Perfumery ingredient
59. Quoter
60. Teed off
61. U.S.C. rival
62. Recorded proceedings
63. Kind of lens
64. Yearned
65. Col. Tibbet's mother
66. HOMES part
68. Knocked 'em dead
69. "Little Eyolf" dramatist
71. Wand
73. This gives you a sign
75. ___ goose (ruin)
77. Share
78. Boucher's teacher
79. Hindu land grant
80. Hidden marksmen
81. "Mittinata" composer
82. Braincases
84. Charged
85. Old card game
86. Polish city
87. Book of maps
88. Reichstag leader before Ebert
89. Fireplace, in Yorkshire
90. DeGaulle's birthplace
91. Spinner or weirdo
92. A code in the head?
93. Spill over
96. Altar above
98. Not gross
99. "___!" said the hansom driver rightly

by Frances Hansen

391

ACROSS

1. Pro votes
5. Shinbone
10. Bucks' mates
14. "Big" creation theory
18. It's nothing to Graf
19. Japanese port
20. Sea birds
22. Ending for buck or smack
23. Stare-downs
25. Crazy talk
27. Ava's was barefoot
28. Honks
30. Red crystal mineral
31. Division word
32. Pickle fluid
33. Charter
34. Plants with two seed leaves, for short
37. Thin pancakes
38. Certain surveyors?
42. Make amends
43. Wreck winders
45. Knock
46. Props for TV weathermen
47. Train, to José
48. Seasons in Pau
49. Middling
50. It's below a sop.
51. Greens, cooked
55. Right-hand page
56. Stains, old style
58. Strive
59. Former actor Ralph
60. Natalie and Nat King
61. Actress Spacek
62. Hindi master
63. Upper house building
65. "___ Grows in Brooklyn"
66. Listeners
69. Citrus workers' brawls
70. "Gyp sheet"
72. Caddy's contents
73. "... an old man in ___ month": Eliot
74. Kind of opera
75. Clumsy one's cry
76. Rat followers
77. O.T. book
78. Separate rockers
82. Electron tube
83. More comely
85. Kind of fever
86. Brought about, deviously
87. Go after game
88. Compendious
89. Dear followers, sometimes
90. City facing Lake Huron
93. Musical paces
94. Head-shaped, to botanists
98. Original box
100. Extra troughs
102. Jai ___
103. Macho fellows
104. City on the Mosel
105. Legendary Greek hero
106. Acuff and Rogers
107. Waistcoat
108. Units of loudness
109. French father

DOWN

1. Anchovy sauce
2. Stringed toy
3. Flush
4. Cuttings
5. Idols of sorts
6. "___ nice to have a man around..."
7. ___ Ullah, Persian religious leader
8. Wrath
9. Haydn's homeland
10. Frenzied
11. What spellbinders do
12. Partner of odds
13. Part of a min.
14. Ameliorate
15. Collegio offerings
16. Mime-dancer Parenti
17. Tenn.'s Albert
21. Contracts
24. "Festina ___"
26. Ambiences
29. Sow sound
32. Mixture
33. Gave a knife new life
34. Ladies in León
35. Writer Calvino
36. Egyptian courage
37. Southern bros.
38. London docker
39. Pot base
40. Subject of 24 Down
41. Track of the pack
43. Hillsides, to Burns
44. One of several early U.S. satellites
47. Kipling's "Soldier's ___"
49. Murrow's "___ Now"
51. Groups of devotees
52. Small antelope of Somalia
53. A Caucasian
54. Early Japanese immigrant
55. Concealed again
57. Like fertile land
59. ___ a wet hen
61. "It Seems Like Old Times" composer
62. Additions: Abbr.
63. Sell tickets illegally
64. Presbyter
65. "Who touches ___ ...": Whittier
66. Greek marketplace
67. Author of "The Cloister and the Hearth"
68. Glutted
70. Poet who was Flaubert's mistress
71. Cacophony
74. Source of Popeye's strength
76. Small landing field
78. Acrobatic feat
79. Name of 14 popes
80. Part of a lamp
81. Hockey statistics
82. A boldface type
84. Proposition
86. Windshield mechanisms
88. Parisian pates
89. Hindu garment: Var.
90. Churchill's "___ Country"
91. Inflatable beach mattress
92. Say the rosary
93. Milky
94. Enoch's father
95. Adjutant
96. Skier's convenience
97. To live, to Livy
99. Accelerate
101. Favoring

by Judith C. Dalton

ACROSS

1. Contort
2. Short and sharp
3. "Wonderland" character
4. Scottish river noted for salmon fishing
5. Jackson's first Secy. of War
6. Shoot from cover
7. The Hawks fly here
8. Autumnal hue
9. Arresting expression for this crossword
11. Happy
12. Aerie newcomer
13. Austrian state
16. "Vilia" composer
17. Guidonian note
18. Word on Japanese freighter hulls
19. Friend in a fray
20. Former head of 80 Up
21. Jostled
24. Mil. educational institution
25. Pod population
27. Gilmet's cousin
29. Colleen
31. Traumatize
32. Bandleader of "Heartaches" fame
34. Asian nation
35. Chemical suffix
36. Poe's "To ___ Paradise"
37. Overseas addresses for G.I.'s
39. Some exercises
42. Forget-me-___
43. Jewish group in Iberia
45. Series, in Sevilla
46. Where to give a rap
47. Petulant
49. Leave high and dry
51. Every corner or con man has one
54. Group of Muslim scholars: Var.
56. Watt power!
58. Ancient Peruvian
59. Russian pianist ___ Gabrilowitsch
61. Item used in Carver experiments
63. Medium
64. Emblem of Wales
66. Took apart
68. He tried to blow up Parliament: 1605
70. "Oysters ___ Season"
71. An echo's performance
73. ___ of Kutch, salt marsh in India
74. Some coll. buildings
75. Fuss
77. Mine entrance
79. Sandarac, e.g.
81. Singing King
82. Straight
83. Snooper
84. Like a runt
85. Ton preceder
88. "... fury like a woman ___": Congreve
90. Two wives of Henry VIII
91. Tennis divisions
92. Stead
93. But, to Cato
94. Vicuña's habitat
95. Library listings
96. Kin of paraments
97. Seine terrains
98. "The flowers that bloom ___, tra la": Gilbert
100. Kanga's kin
101. Jambalaya base
102. Philippine island
103. Italy's "City of a Hundred Towers"
104. Prefix with chord or meter
108. Popular bag
112. Be clement
117. Cheerful conclusion?

UP

10. Reduced estimate
11. Jove, to Juvenal
13. Proofreader's direction
14. Unbend
15. Tibetan trailblazer?
16. Occupation
17. Sailor's saint
19. A foe of Sparta
20. Norse gods
21. Dik-dik's big cousin
22. X out
23. Like many an attic
25. Flexible
26. Ancient kingdom in SW Asia
28. Eur. country
30. Actress Suzanne ___
33. Lake ___, N.H. vacation spot
38. Colossal collisions
40. Famed Italian architect ___: 16th century
41. Pitcher's plate
43. Area in Manhattan
44. A Stooge
47. French legislative body
48. Cries out sharply
50. Gunpowder component
52. Doctorow's "___ Lake"
53. Late Art Deco illustrator
55. Trenet's "La ___"
57. NASA space probe
60. Last movement of Beethoven's Ninth, e.g.
62. Biblical weeds
65. "I'll learn him or ___": Twain
67. Works for two
69. Danish island
72. Hair dyes
74. Capital of Bangladesh, old style
75. Woody's wonderboy
76. "___ Irae"
78. A hit tune of 1967
80. Actor's org.
81. Ranch worker
83. Fully, to an attorney
84. Barracks wall décor
85. Emulating Hillary or a solver of this puzzle
86. Ancient native of S Mexico
87. Loch without a key?
89. Shah ___ ed-Din: 19th century
90. Naval forces
91. One way to cook eggs
94. Tropical American bird
99. British gun
104. Exams for would-be Ph.D.'s
105. Mulligrubs
106. To have a hole-in-one or two?
107. Convince
108. French working girl
109. Got one's goat
110. Made a perfect serve
111. Egyptian god of pleasure
112. Angler's lure
113. Go-between for illicit affairs
114. Poker pots
115. Cheers
116. Hurricane center
117. Snobbish
118. Segments
119. Malevolent
120. Cubs or Mets
121. Hanging ends

by John Russell

ACROSS

1. Catamount
5. Color also called meadowlark
10. Inspiration for Blake
15. Zodiacal sign
18. Retired
19. Lip: Comb. form
20. Coeur d'___, Idaho
21. Inlet
22. Where Daniel was cast
24. Authorized
26. Twin of sorts
27. Ryan's daughter
29. Type of orange
30. Chew
33. Watchful guardian
34. A.U.S. or U.S.N.
35. Neglect
36. Shanks
37. Spotted racers
41. Quick, straight drink
42. Certain black-nosed rabbits
44. Wattlebird
45. Moisture of morning
46. A Margaret Mead subject
49. Soot or porn
50. Painter of American Indians
51. Site of 1952 Olympics
53. Brown feline from Africa
57. Actress Prentiss
58. Certain papers
60. Etchers' purchases
61. Vandal, e.g.
62. Slip-ups
64. Partita
65. Divisions of hockey games
66. "...draw thy breath ___": Hamlet
67. Whiner
68. Shoe part
69. ___ and end-all (whole)
70. Disasters
72. Alewife's kin
75. Yeast for Vassar
76. Franklin's mother
77. Ingredients of gimlets
79. Cohan's "___ Popular Man"
80. Airport info.
81. Conspirator
85. Hot, old style
87. Guitarists' arpeggios
89. Family in "Look Homeward, Angel"
90. Algonquian Indian spirit
91. Shake ___ (hie)
92. Old Spanish coin
93. Spotted cats
94. Emulate Lorelei
96. City at the foot of Mt. Etna
97. Avid
98. Grayish wildcat
100. Not absolved
105. Give ___ on the back
106. Turkish decree
107. Limerick starter
108. Otherwise
109. Insane
110. Diarist of the 17th century
111. Wader in the Everglades
112. Assess

DOWN

1. Expand, in a way
2. Honshu port
3. Alcott's "Little ___"
4. "...___ in the house?"
5. Allot
6. An Oscar winner in 1986
7. Reed
8. Dog with two Tins on his tail
9. Panacea
10. Caused by touch
11. Intestinal obstruction
12. Microbe
13. Tolkien tree
14. ___ the wheel (devise unnecessarily)
15. Find
16. Knievel
17. Dict. published in England
21. Source of a perfume ingredient
23. Eyes the girls
25. One Eve had three
28. Pearl Mosque site
30. Err
31. Choreographer de Mille
32. Ounces
33. Peace Nobelist: 1987
34. Singer Cassidy
36. E. Indian herb roots
37. Certain moldings

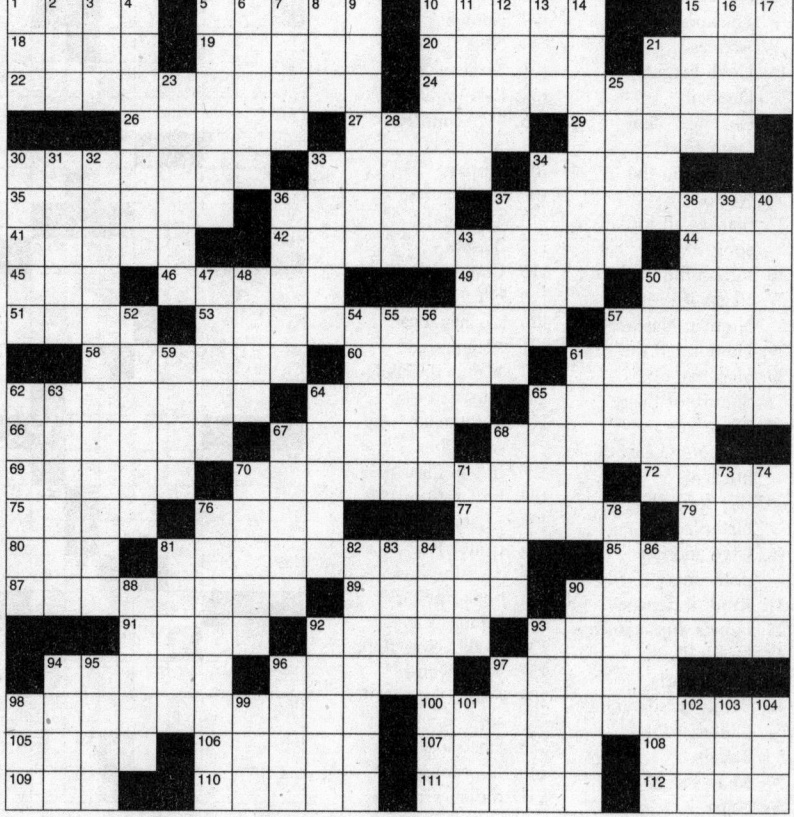

by Jack R. Harnes

38. Garfield lovers' emotion
39. Greeted
40. Sub detectors
43. Digression
47. "Green Pastures" role
48. Degs. for industrialists
50. Herbs liked by felines
52. Horseweed
54. ___ Ste. Marie
55. Less cordial
56. Peterman's purchase
57. Nice recreation area
59. Labor
61. An Attorney General under Reagan
62. Tippler
63. ___ time (singly)
64. Actress Dey
65. Wilbur product
67. A son of Priam
68. Dilutes
70. Sort
71. End of Mont.'s motto
73. Friendship
74. Secures by fitting into a groove
76. Incidental excursion
78. Frightened
81. Cigar tree, e.g.
82. Violent struggles
83. Physics Nobelist: 1944
84. Medial sounds
86. More irate
88. Guido's lowest note
90. Lodestone
92. Warbucks
93. Ville V.I.P.
94. Paper-mulberry bark
95. Mild oath
96. Snooze
97. Always
98. Fill too tightly
99. Ouse tributary
101. Modern lang.
102. Huge SE Asian fish
103. N.Y. time in winter
104. Duant

394 INDIAN FILE

ACROSS

1. Plaster of paris
6. Thickness
9. Arrives
14. Heidi heights
18. Dresser
19. Gazetteer item
20. High crest
21. Not ___ in the world
22. Start of an Indians song
26. Indian film: 1975
27. Vegas lead-in
28. Netman Nastase
29. He minded the stoa
30. Hero tag-on
31. Suburb of Liège
32. Small kite
35. C. Moore beast of burden
38. Big Bertha's birthplace
40. Give another polishing
41. Kind of dancer
42. How's that again?
43. "Vissi d'___," Puccini aria
47. Banky of silents
51. Guitarist Paul
53. Tavern
54. More viscid
56. Gaga
60. With an ___ the ground
62. Famed chef
63. A Beery
64. ___ Vanilli (lip-sync group)
65. ___ vera (skin conditioner)
66. Red dyes
67. Fusses
69. Sea barrier
70. A Seoul G.I.
71. "___ Love You So," Humperdinck hit
72. ___ hit (single)
74. Put up
77. Brandy-based cocktail
81. Sally ___ cake
82. Ebenezer's word
83. Drug buster
85. Mart part
86. "___ Born"
89. This goes with something
90. Aka
92. Rubber tube
93. Squiffed
94. Less deceitful
95. Acts for
97. Sea snail
98. Weed
99. Kerouac's "Big ___"
101. Tameins' kin
102. Lake Indian
103. "My country, ___ . . ."
104. Surpass
106. Reddish hog
110. Captured
113. Biased
116. Conference city
117. Hot tub
120. ___ hepatica
121. Asian range
123. Memorable Belgian musician
125. Montpelier is its cap.
126. Indian film: 1969
133. Indian film: 1976
134. ___ barrel (in trouble)
135. "___ the Rose," book by Stark Young
136. Snake River flopper
137. More weird
138. Fringe benefit of a sort
139. Head lock?
140. ___ Moines
141. Indian princess

DOWN

1. Battleship part
2. Palindrome part
3. Vend
4. Cruise
5. Attire
6. Warm up an oven
7. Riga man
8. What a bore evokes
9. Ned of radio news
10. Hunter in the skies
11. Milano's subway
12. Kitchen tag-on
13. Far from altruistic
14. Throb
15. Insect stage
16. Do not rush in dressing
17. Seventh sons
18. Pot or double follower
19. Cold
21. ". . . lovely as ___": Kilmer
23. Sesame
24. Seep through
25. Long time
33. Indian comforter
34. Way out
36. Indian film: 1970
37. Haw preceder
38. Kind of market
39. Indian film: 1957
42. Venom
44. Get up
45. Rend
46. Mistypes
48. Abner's companion
49. Nonwinners at the track
50. Hun of Norse myth
52. "The ___," Indian film: 1956
53. Indian film: 1950
54. "___ Sleep," Odets play
55. Coarse fabric
56. Division word
57. "High" time
58. Lose color
59. Sommer from Berlin
61. "Thanks ___!"
66. Makeup
68. Mackerel's kin
73. Slyly sarcastic
75. Simplicity
76. Hill's partner
78. Continue
79. Once, once
80. Dakota Indians
84. Tears
86. ". . . ___ forgive those . . ."
87. Use a blender
88. Grant of "Being a Woman"
89. The libido
91. U.S.A.F., e.g.
94. Ichorous
96. Team
100. Western Indian
103. Bony fish
105. "Flintstones" child
107. Brown study
108. Supervise
109. Go at top speed
111. Word in the Kan. motto
112. Madeline from Boston
113. Buffet features
114. Hot spot
115. Waggish
116. Some do get the hang of it
117. Razor's edger
118. Pet ___
119. Tailor
121. Sentient
122. These give ade
124. Red ___ (night flight)
127. Sneak around
128. "Dial ___ Murder"
129. ___ tea
130. Mansard extension
131. Where Braves visit Mets
132. Little Big ___

by A. J. Santora

ACROSS

1. Lille's department
5. Cause distaste
10. English estate feature
14. Arnaz, Sr. or Jr.
18. Thine, in 1 Across
19. Miss ___, J. R.'s mother
20. Sans assistance
22. Bow out gracefully
23. Baker's largess
25. Madison Ave. worker's largess
27. Hurdle, in a way
28. Shankar's instrument
30. The "Soviet Riviera"
31. Once again
32. Vladimir Ilyich Ulyanov
33. Blanch
34. What a choir requires
36. Alberta tourist center
37. Fondled
41. Gator's cousin
42. Assembly worker's largess
45. Medieval French poem
46. "Portnoy's Complaint" author
47. Yalie
48. Pacino and Hirt
49. Zilch
50. Org. founded in Bogotá: 1948
51. Roofer's largess
57. Temple or Rice II
58. Divided proportionately
60. Mrs. Ethan Frome
61. Silverweed
63. Sacked
64. Victoria ___
65. He played to the balcony
66. Bees do it
67. Ah Sin's creator
68. Set one's goal toward
71. Lt. Cable's love
72. Reaper's largess
75. Singer Sumac
76. Pilaster
77. "A Chorus Line" finale
78. Welsh-rabbit brew
79. Gist of the matter
80. Slave Turner
81. Washerwoman's largess
87. Beards grown by some farmers
88. Gladstone's political rival
90. Rich cake
91. Ankles
93. Part of a Racine product
94. Conclusion
95. Roast, in Reims
96. "... 'tis no sin for ___ labor ...": Shak.
99. Purim celebrates his destruction
100. Set free
104. Garment worker's largess
106. Corn farmer's largess
108. Memorable basso Pinza
109. Largest book size
110. Of a Great lake
111. Owlish comment
112. Silas Marner's apparatus
113. Beethoven's birthplace
114. Certain orgs.
115. ___ of Court, British bar group

DOWN

1. Part of N.R.A.
2. Kiowa's cousin
3. Columnist Barrett
4. Expedition
5. Stimulate the memory
6. Jostle rudely
7. Nag
8. German article
9. Diminishes
10. Lap dog's opposite number
11. Northern highway
12. Lot's refuge city
13. He may be tight
14. Throws down the gauntlet
15. Quiz
16. Kind of car at the bar
17. "___ boy!"
21. Steep slope
24. ___ consequence (trivial)
26. Heraldry bands
29. Dope
32. "___ Lazuli," Yeats poem
33. Bel ___ (mild cheese)
34. Bellowing

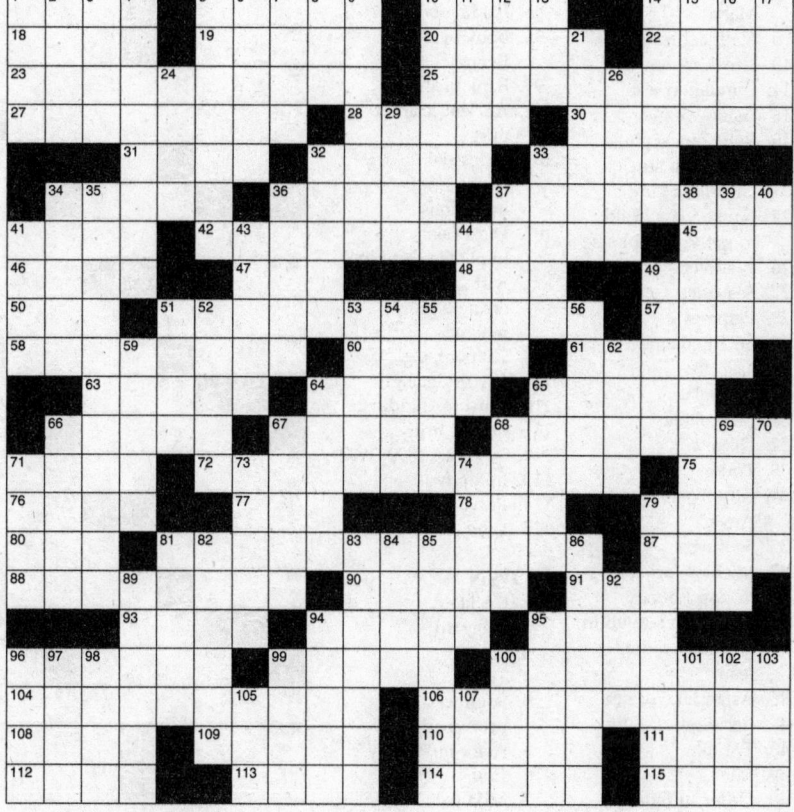

by Frances Hansen

35. Electrician's largess
36. Did a cotton-pickin' job
37. Naos
38. Nurseryman's largess
39. Betimes
40. "Vaya con ___," 1953 hit
41. Riding whip
43. Fished for congers
44. Certain Hindu ascetics
49. Like hospital areas
51. Young salmon
52. Shopping-list notations
53. ___ Ike of comics
54. Hat materials
55. Complete: Comb. form
56. Plant aperture
59. Lariat
62. Wall St. acronym
64. Confronted
65. Rubbed the wrong way
66. Biblical mount
67. Vietnamese capital
68. "A flea and a fly in ___"
69. Man from Muscat
70. Pied Piper's entourage
71. Touch down
73. Mont. county
74. Observes Lent
79. Popular Mexican music
81. Ipso ___
82. Excused from duty
83. Secretary of State: 1929–33
84. Eugene O'Neill's daughter
85. Adornments for some surreys
86. Runners
89. Kidnapper's demand
92. Crown of Osiris
94. Oliver's wicked tutor
95. Continued in a musical-chairs game
96. The third man
97. Author de la Roche
98. Exchange premium
99. Heavenly headgear
100. Baseball stats
101. Presently
102. Black, poetically
103. N.Y. times
105. Alcoholic Roy
107. Kid ___, jazz trombonist

ACROSS

1. Site of the Taj Mahal
5. Nautical term
10. Greek letters
14. Dandelion, e.g.
18. Asian weight
19. Religious sayings
20. Modify to suit
21. Gudrun's king
22. Nurse joins Weld to get Porter phrase
26. Well versed
27. Sea duck
28. Palpates
29. Small change?
30. "___ the ramparts . . ."
31. ___ colada
32. Distant
33. Torsk
34. City SW of Buenos Aires
35. Sediment
37. Michael Jackson hit
40. Young Rooney backs N.M. town in quest for radio team
46. Asian lake or sea
47. Resident of: Suffix
48. Trouble
49. Idle
50. Order to Fido at historic site has a certain pop style
58. Footlike part
59. Fast fliers
60. Rib or pan
61. Soothes
62. Deg. for a cellist, e.g.
63. Spring mo.
64. Cpls.' bosses
65. Certain pipe
67. City in Bolivia
69. Fit to ___
70. Actor Majors
73. Tote bag on back of singer stirs up a form of business
77. Celebes ox
78. Title for Eliz. II
79. Panay native
80. Some ratites
81. Movie great gets behind bandleader in producing "Explorers"
89. Mouths
90. Gainsay
91. Iroquoian group
92. Hide ___ hair
93. Cousin of a twp.
94. Broadway musical since 1982
95. Folding bed
96. Book by Peter Evans
99. Bank deals
101. Ancient Roman port
103. Industrial Revolution inventions
105. Dickensian hypocrite combines with actress to create typing method
108. Guipure, e.g.
109. Glyceride, e.g.
110. Must for Pindar
111. On the briny
112. ___ War: 1899–1902
113. In a jiffy
114. Pravda founder
115. Kind

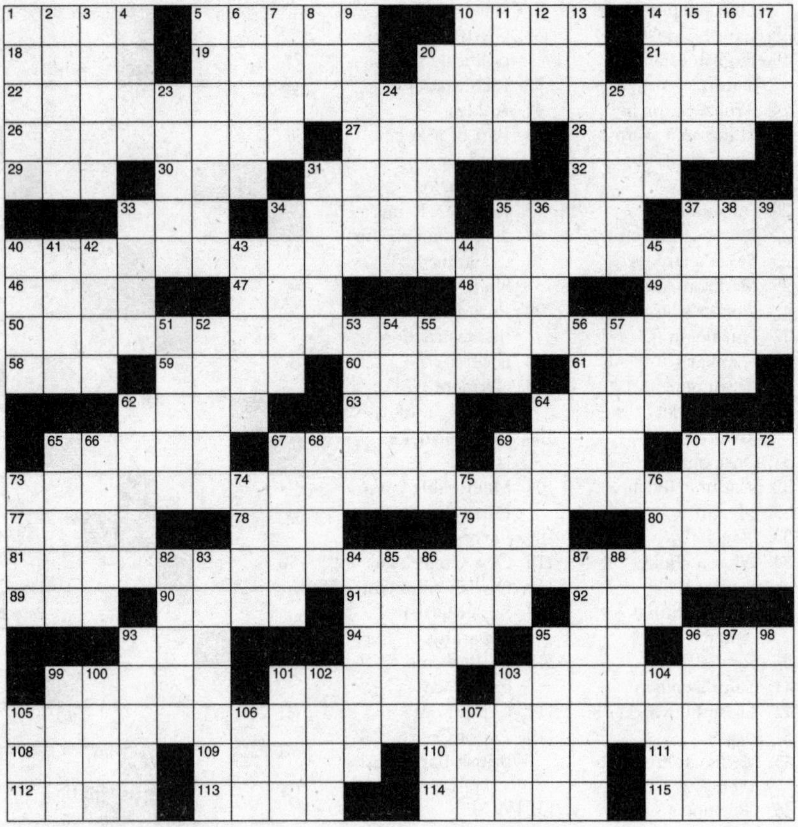

DOWN

1. Cockloft
2. Haggard
3. Shoals
4. Too
5. Southwestern promenade
6. Actor in "Fanny": 1961
7. Mild oath
8. Own, to Robert Burns
9. White wine
10. Rim
11. Wild goat of Nepal
12. Quick to learn
13. How goose-steppers march
14. Tout's subject
15. And others: Abbr.
16. Building additions
17. Cutting tool
20. ___ abet (be an accomplice)
23. Talk foolishly
24. Sheer fabric
25. Under, poetically
31. Hard puzzle
33. Serene
34. Racing sailboats
35. Shot, as of liquor
36. Concept: Comb. form
37. Atlanta baseball player
38. Wood trimmers
39. Colorist
40. Northern nomad
41. Escutcheon border
42. Simon ___ (elimination game)
43. Gloves for Gehrig and Berra
44. Beards of grain
45. At ___ for words
51. Ottoman Empire founder
52. Specialty of some sharks
53. Herb resembling spinach
54. Source of coconut oil
55. Actress Black
56. French painter Fernand ___
57. Subsequently
62. Twofold
64. This may be posted
65. Goof
66. Mary's TV friend
67. Fresh
68. Cadets' inst.
69. Certificates, in Durango
70. Gentle soul
71. Month after Av
72. Besides
73. A certain J.F.K. departure
74. Gab; yak
75. Robertson and Evans
76. Newcomer in January
82. Minneapolis suburb
83. British character actor and family
84. Any delicious drink
85. Scupper
86. A. J. Cronin's "The ___"
87. "___ wood" (superstitious statement)
88. Barbarians
93. "Star Wars" villain
95. Prickly pears
96. Unequal: Comb. form
97. Allude (to)
98. ". . . one of them ___ and grows old": Shak.
99. River in China
100. Head of a tale
101. Aware of
102. "Nana" star: 1934
103. Ill-tempered
104. Actresses Claire and Balin
105. Att.'s degree
106. G.I.'s hangout
107. Prefix with eminent

by Dorothy Smitonick

ACROSS

1. Radio's "Our ___ Sunday"
4. Honored with entertainment
9. Hamper
14. Douglas Fairbanks Sr. role
19. A land in S.A.
20. Love feast
21. Houston gridder
22. Wild blue yonder
23. Gloaming
24. Type of sermon
27. Groom's milieu
29. Beat, in a way
30. Give forth
31. Baudelaire's "Les Fleurs du ___"
32. "B.C." character
33. Prepare
35. Corkers
37. Vehicle in a Monroe film
38. Cupidinous
40. Elmer Gantry's wife
41. "Family Ties" role
42. Span member
43. Compeer
45. Stem joint
47. Stem
49. Bond foe
53. "...Lord is ___ indeed": Luke 24:34
54. "Trust ___," 1934 song
55. Sign-language developer
56. Anadama or panettone
59. Roman attachment
63. Trifle
64. ___ were (seemingly)
65. Forward
66. Display pretentiously
67. Time piece
68. Roman magistrate
70. Drop-lid desks
72. Eureka!
73. "The Queen of the ___": Rice
75. Having color
77. Wood sorrels
78. Thrash
79. Harvard president: 1869–1909
80. He's often robbed
81. Scotch ingredient
82. Common contraction
83. Storied pachyderm
85. Frank Sinatra
88. Kind of box
90. He "loves mambo"
92. Confound it!
93. "..., tekel, upharsin"
94. State tree of Tex.
96. ___ Grande, city in Ariz.
99. Ebro and Segura
101. Muslim general
102. Part of a trident
103. Chorus syllables
105. TV's "Just the Ten ___"
107. Cur. unit
108. Put the kibosh on
109. Invent extender
111. Marijuana
113. Insincere show of sorrow
117. Grape, in Concordia
118. Shoptalk
119. "___ Work...": G. Will book
120. "...___ that kills": Housman
121. Side of a triangle
122. "Home, Sweet Home" lyricist
123. Earl of Avon's family
124. Minuscular
125. Possessive pron.

DOWN

1. Company for Carson
2. Singer Franklin
3. Leslie-Burke song: 1935
4. Safe preceder
5. Type of moth
6. Oribi's hue
7. Majestic
8. Notorious marquis
9. Etna has one
10. Holey
11. Kin of a dalmatic
12. Nothing more than
13. Emergency treatment
14. Spice
15. Polo Grounds hero
16. Equilateral parallelogram
17. Co-Nobelist for Peace: 1907
18. Choice words
25. "___ Can Whistle," Sondheim musical
26. Chintzy ones
28. Grill item
34. Surpass
36. Caucho-producing tree
39. "___ Spiro, Spero" (S.C. motto)
42. Table for Tacitus
44. "...I am ___": Romeo
46. Mars and Venus, e.g.
48. Staggers
49. General's ___ camp
50. Written, e.g.
51. And not
52. Become publicly known
53. Sweeping
57. Thing, to Tiberius
58. Sepulcher
60. Independence Day
61. Remove husks
62. Worktable, in Etaples
66. "Old Dog Tray" composer
68. Vexillum, e.g.
69. Her mate is ruff
71. Marshy
74. High-minded
76. Gutta
78. Enunciation
80. Robed scythe carrier
84. Slugged
86. Of milk
87. Galley essential
88. Irish euphemism
89. Similitude
90. Kisser
91. Luanda resident
93. Rash
95. Became distant
97. "...the mountains of ___": Gen. 8:4
98. Brackish
100. More sophisticated
104. One more time
106. Layered coifs
108. Canvassers' concern
110. "Willard" creatures
112. Ethereal
114. Temporary beginner
115. Gazetteer letters
116. Financier's Fannie ___

by June A. Boggs

398 50 K's

ACROSS

1. Newsstand
6. Large brown bear
12. Flair
17. Klingon foe
21. Painter-writer Kokoschka
22. Anxiety, in Aix
23. King of Hollywood
24. Yemeni seaport
25. Destiny
26. N.Z. songbird
28. Composer Luigi ___
29. Russian river
30. Blackguards
32. Peon's mite
33. Fanatic
35. Yellow-fever mosquito
36. Sale sign
37. Cold-climate craft
39. Org. founded in 1915
42. Junket
43. Patch of land
44. Tarbell, e.g.
48. "Merry Mount" composer: 1934
50. Laughing jackasses
52. Philip Johnson's org.
53. Singer Baker
54. French physician-novelist: 1894–1961
56. Originator of Jellicle Cats
57. Richmond V.I.P. set
58. Recoil
59. Delirious
60. Primary locations
61. Actor Sam: 1891–1984
63. Calligraphers' needs
64. Catkin
65. Stick with these!
66. Whalebone
67. Compass pt.
68. "Either/Or" questioner
70. Hearth shelves
71. Massive mammals, for short
73. Standing start
74. Documentary film hero
75. Legendary victims of the Romans
77. De Mille epic with "The": 1927
81. ___ Cruces
84. Conjured up
85. Actress Hope or Jessica
86. Palindromic French quisling
87. Gasp
88. More pleasant
89. Signs on
90. Hairy herb
91. Luncheon follower
92. Post station in India
93. "Lili" film composer
94. Coronation gown
95. Buckwheat cereal
96. All-purpose trk.
97. Zorba's creator
99. Devilish
100. Betty Boop quality
102. Solar disk
103. Integument
105. Admiralty abbr.
106. Tarsus
107. Pastoral poem
108. Mr. Spock's father in "Star Trek"
109. Shrub of the rose family
112. "And giving ___ . . ."
113. Deep-seated
114. "Keystone" character
117. Part of 39 Across
118. Indian tobacco mixture
122. Skewer
124. Hindu discipline
125. Play the part
126. Aria for two
127. Mr. Kovacs
128. Jedi's furry friend
129. Advantages
130. Teeter
131. Bumpkin

DOWN

1. "The Mikado" executioner
2. Baroness Blixen, a.k.a.___ Dinesen
3. Gumbo basic
4. Danson role in "Cheers"
5. Eruption site: 1883
6. Beethoven trio, Op. 121a
7. Hardy one
8. Salaam preliminaries
9. Blue flag
10. Qty.
11. Memento
12. Russian beer
13. Bilbao boy
14. Nabokov title
15. Daunt: awe
16. Coconino County cutie
17. A Hawaiian
18. Iconoclast's target
19. "Splitsville," once
20. Clove hitch, e.g.
27. First president of Mali
31. Broadway gas
34. Listeners
36. Forth
37. Russian islands
38. Circus performers: Abbr.
39. Jeans' alternative
40. Screenwriters Garson and Michael
41. Sen. Bradley was one
43. Grosse ___, Mich.
44. Pondered
45. Gossip's delight
46. Noted French engineer
47. Poe-tic birds
49. N.Y.S.E. abbr.
50. Klemperer role
51. "Let independence ___ boast": Hopkinson
54. Carved gemstones
55. Baseball's Crab or Hoot
59. Bestowed abundantly
60. Founder of famed Academy
61. ___ Starker, famed cellist
62. Palo singer?
65. Yardstick
66. Bracelet, e.g.
68. Pittsburgh slugger, turned announcer
69. Tam-tams
70. Direct
72. Raise or increase sharply
74. Abounding with snow
75. Takeoff
76. Emulate Odom
77. Namesakes of 2 Down
78. Lifeless
79. Gold coin in Edam
80. Small racing vehicles
82. Key work
83. Places
85. Digestive enzyme
87. ___ de soie (cloth for dresses)
89. Filbert
90. Actor-folk singer from Vienna
93. City in Ill.
94. Noisy grasshoppers
95. "Cuckoo's Nest" builder
97. Cattle, in poesy
98. Handel's "___ the Priest"
99. Regimen
101. Ancient temple site
103. Female saint: Lat.
104. City on the Vistula
107. F.D.R. and D.D.E., e.g.
108. Swivets
109. Celestial terrier?
110. Till
111. Shakespearean baddie
112. End of vigil
113. Arrow poison
114. Quirk
115. Steinbeck protagonist
116. Strip off
119. N.Y.C. subway
120. Worn-out horse
121. Cloud, to Baudelaire
123. In favor of

by Sandy Graf

ACROSS

1. Bushel's partner, in song
5. Dippy or dotty
9. Rec. measures
13. Packed away
19. Opposite of aweather
20. Turgenev's birthplace
21. Ham___ (emote)
22. Balzac
23. Kin of rhoncus in the bronchus
24. Yemeni capital
25. Hawaii's bird
26. Ulster town
27. S P A C E R
30. Avian midwives?
31. Auction chaser
32. Bro or sis
33. Murray and West
34. African antelope
35. S N I V E L
41. Street in a horror film
44. Eatery order
45. Long. sidekick
46. Famed muralist
47. Hindu Kush's locale
48. Pilasters
51. U.S. motor capital
52. "Vaya con___," 1953 song
54. Unsightly
55. Ululate
56. ___ cordiale
60. Readies an oven
62. D E V I L
64. Haw., once
65. Prefix for adroit
66. Sordino
67. Double DI
68. Hammett canine
70. Numbers' person
73. Lion's pad
75. S T R E S S E D
78. Comes in again
82. Vacuum tube
83. Breakout at high school
84. Leed's river
85. Deal-consummating word
87. Abbr. in a to-let ad
88. Pipe
89. Place to place tokens
90. Skater Babilonia and namesakes
92. Small whale
93. Arm of the Med.
94. L.B.J. beagle
95. S P O R T S

101. Mountain in Thessaly
104. Product of a Spanish pine
105. Philippine volcano
106. A Greek goddess of vengeance
107. Flock of turkeys
109. L E V E R
113. Greek
114. "Mary Magdalene" painter
115. Mopsus or Melampus
116. Greet
117. Metal balls used in pétanque
118. Egyptian solar deity
119. Radiator sound
120. Blast or carp precursor
121. Make jagged
122. Twerp's cousin
123. Being, in Barcelona
124. Haricot, for one

DOWN

1. Unit equivalent to 3.26 light years
2. Beetle type
3. Relish-tray item
4. Bewail, Irish style
5. A 1982 Oscar winner
6. Land fit for cultivation
7. Actress Rowlands
8. Opposite of apterous
9. Aural insensitivity
10. Audio systems
11. Castigated
12. Little sea pike
13. Kind of fir or cypress
14. Role for Todd or Silverheels
15. "___ of Old Smoky"
16. C A R E S
17. Composer Satie
18. Reps.' rivals
28. Fanon
29. Hit, old style
36. D. Arnaz's costar
37. Building wing
38. Badger's African cousin
39. Stumble
40. To use, to Nero
42. Rhythmic cadence
43. The Say Hey Kid
47. Menuhin's teacher
48. Polite interruption
49. Smoked salmon

50. D E N I M
51. Device for collecting plankton
53. Vessel with a long, sharp prow
56. Habituates
57. Thread: Comb. form
58. Bis
59. Fiat
61. Kind of master or hunter
63. Skip
68. State of lawlessness
69. Mil. banners
71. ___ colada
72. Copycat
74. A contemporary of Loti
76. Did the human thing
77. Top kick
78. Madcap
79. Haste, in Hanover
80. Calais entrée
81. Scoria from a volcano
86. Separate
88. Infatue

91. "Well-boiled icicles" man
92. Uppity one
93. Calumniate
95. Least furnished
96. Coil about
97. Hardest to find
98. Swimming, in heraldry
99. Gold look-alike
100. Star of "Bombshell"
102. Fence straddler
103. Aeschylus's "___ Against Thebes"
107. Physics Nobelist: 1944
108. Steinbeck character
109. Herring measure in Hereford
110. S. African fox
111. Check
112. "___ Funny That Way"

by Bernard Meren

ACROSS

1. Festoon
5. City in Egypt
10. Expression
14. "___ a horse with wings!": Shak.
18. Islamic judge
19. Be obtrusively conspicuous
20. Sacher or Linzer
21. Director Clair
22. Yonder
23. Chinese pleasure craft?
25. Old strongbox
26. Feed feasters
28. Eurasian region of Middle Ages
29. Good-for-nothing
31. Appeals
33. Remove TV broadcast
34. Surfeit
35. Adieu, in Bath
37. Some buoys
39. Lacrimator
42. Tires
45. Dummy
47. Psalm verse ender
49. "Twelfth Night" heroine
50. Hind
51. ___ Rapids, city in Minn.
53. Lesions
55. One-eyed god
56. Countertenor
58. Suitcase marker
60. Round
62. "___ Merrilies," Keats poem
63. Boa
65. Brief piece of writing
67. Cause: Fr.
69. Entanglement
70. Valor
71. "___ Get Started With You," 1936 song
72. Denmark's ___ Islands
73. Type of maid
74. Finder of the Holy Grail
77. Birthplace of Hippocrates
78. Quarrel
80. During
82. Soccer great
83. Actress Sommer
85. Daughter of David
87. He was Hutch on TV
88. Kid
89. Property claims
91. French pioneer in treating the mentally ill
93. British actor Roger ___
95. Giant jets
96. Clayware
98. Knob on a pipe organ
100. Check for Checkers
102. Canadian lake
103. Ovid's "you love"
105. 1965 U.S. Open winner
108. Stuck
111. Capital of Laconia
113. Exultant
115. River mouth
116. Don Giovanni, as a seaman?
119. Cry on a roller coaster
120. Bureau attachment
121. Was mistaken
122. N.Y. city
123. ___-majesty
124. Gainsay
125. Fume
126. Front cover of a book
127. Monoski, e.g.

DOWN

1. Hilum
2. Disk for sealing letters
3. Apothegm
4. Long-necked vessels?
5. Avers
6. Erwin of early TV
7. Penury
8. Indo-European
9. Set in order
10. President of France: 1954–59
11. Four in refrigerators
12. Fret
13. A-Q combo, in bridge
14. Handel specialty
15. Transport protectors?
16. Ever
17. Authentic
20. High order of angels
24. Nobelist in Literature: 1957
27. Site of Gray herd
30. Pole, e.g.
32. Shipboard psychiatry?
36. Wheezer's menace
38. Great Lakes vessel?
39. Slumber on a two-master?
40. Strange
41. Ratted
42. Land of Qum
43. Aïda or Radamés
44. Phrase for a disorderly sailer?
46. Japanese galley utensils?
48. Pt. of E.T.A.
52. Mother-of-pearl
54. Fur seal
57. Tom Joad, e.g.
58. Boil down
59. First name of a memorable loner
61. Horologe face
64. Alphabet: Abbr.
66. Hollywooders going steady
68. Photo
72. Book leaf
75. Landed
76. American Socialist: 1855–1926
77. Large seaweed
79. Friend, in Angers
81. Affaire d'honneur
84. Plea
86. Recorded anew
90. Fortune-teller
92. Miller protagonist
94. Italian gulf
95. Boat covers?
97. Polishing machine
99. Kind of car or maid
101. Bando of baseball
104. Orarion
106. ___ Levy, Cohan's first wife
107. "Tears" poet
108. Start of a kindergarten chant
109. "Divine Comedy" illustrator
110. Bell the cat
111. Ferret out
112. With, to Pierre
114. Quitclaim
117. Uno e due
118. Graze

by Arthur S. Verdesca

ACROSS

1. Washington city
7. Dart
12. Saint of Avila
18. Embodiment
19. Food mixture in a small mold
22. Conceive
23. Richard Strauss's flower pendant?
25. Washing utensil
26. Tatum or Ryan
27. Bakery worker
28. Verdi's philanderer?
30. Modified leaf
32. Used purchase
33. Sharklike fish
37. Cicatrix
39. Oater
44. Obeisance
45. One of the Dakotas
47. Sound from 46 Down
48. TV backdrop
49. "___ Old Cowhand"
50. Wagner's advice to Elsie the cow?
52. Service trucks
53. Sri Lankan seaport
56. Desert region
57. Scot's "own"
58. Henry James's forte
59. Pharynx tissues
61. Chubby rodents
63. Querulous
64. Area enframed by an arch
66. Muslim sacred book
68. Evaluate
71. Gone up
73. Billhooks
77. Midler or Davis
78. Thai language
79. Palmer's org.
81. Ocular pest
82. Olympic hawk
83. Wagnerian yuppie?
86. Harness part
87. Victory, in Berlin
88. Bitter vetch
89. Dialect
90. Locust
92. Attired
94. Played for a fool
95. Sire
97. Lagoon shapers
99. "___ is an island": Donne
100. Meyerbeer's bottom line?
104. River in Central Africa
105. Betel palm
110. Go back
111. Wagner's short-order cook?
115. Fielding novel
116. Fish sauce
117. Panay seaport
118. The woad plant
119. Indian antelope
120. Journalist James

DOWN

1. Poi source
2. Eden's earldom
3. Pomander
4. Great Barrier Island
5. Postman's pickup
6. Prince Valiant's son
7. Disconnected, as notes
8. Spicy stew of game
9. Gen. Bradley
10. Rect. figure
11. Pacific porgy
12. W Austrian native
13. Roman officials
14. M. Clair
15. Shrine Bowl team
16. Printer's direction
17. Baltic island
20. French painter: 1881–1955
21. Goddess of discord
24. Prevaricator
29. King Arthur's nephew
31. Her mate is ruff
32. South African coin
33. Porcelain
34. Proceeded toward a target, with "in"
35. Icon
36. Puccini's advice to his dallying heroine?
37. Treats a fever?
38. African river
40. Puccini's vacation activity in India?
41. Singer John
42. "Tears" poet
43. ___ Parker (busybody)
46. Ram's ma'am
47. Sharpens, with "up"
50. Rich source
51. Highlands Celt
54. Shiner
55. Receptacles for coal
58. A virus, for short
60. Worthless trifles
62. Drooping
63. Kong's first love
65. Opera trailer
67. Lollapalooza
68. Humble
69. Canary's relative
70. Do a conn job
72. Lyric poem
74. Put on
75. Fine cloth fiber
76. Fat: Comb. form
78. "___ the Flies," Golding novel
80. Japanese mountain
83. Entire; complete
84. Snake sound
85. Give courage
90. Turkish chief
91. Coterie
93. "Quality Street" playwright
94. Extreme
96. Cassowary's cousin
98. Rescind
99. Silent-screen star
100. Lobster pot
101. Blood: Comb. form
102. Arden and Queler
103. Lucy van ___, in "Peanuts"
104. Señorita's fingernails
106. Letters from Greece
107. Exude
108. A Gypsy language
109. Presently
112. Mos. and mos.
113. Call ___ day
114. Rifle range at Saint-Cyr

by Arthur S. Verdesca

ACROSS

1. Wilkes-___, Pa.
6. Jar of antiquity
13. Commotions
18. Sci-fi character
19. Headgear for a peer
20. Woodworking tool
21. Lady Mary Wortley Montagu's Rx?
24. Cartoonist Fisher
25. Israeli seaport
26. ___ off (angry)
27. Pacific islands
29. Diva Galli-Curci
31. Hotel ___ Invalides, Paris
32. Chit
34. S. Africa's ___ Paul Kruger
35. Consumer advocate
36. John Milton's Rx?
42. Let's assume
43. Brace
44. Opposite of sml.
45. Barnyard butter
46. Fade in the stretch
48. Change: Comb. form
51. Samples
54. John Fletcher's Rx?
58. Literary monogram
59. Former A. L. team
62. Like dark clouds
63. Midnight fluid
64. Cry of triumph
65. Sunny side of a mountain
66. Kind of jet
67. Trip segment
68. General at Gettysburg
70. River in E England
72. Gob
73. Attention getters
75. Cricket sides
77. Super-being
78. France of France
80. Me. city
81. Author of "Ulalume"
82. Tennyson's Rx?
84. Groups of three
86. Emulated Edwin Booth
87. Guidonian note
88. Pitch detector
89. Personal quirk
91. Kind of tax
93. Dance, in France
96. Sir Henry Wotton's Rx?
102. Carp
104. Honey, in prescriptions
105. Conquistador's booty
106. Rec. of brain waves
107. Picture
109. Calif. observatory
113. Abbr. in grammar
115. Director Flaherty's "Man of ___"
116. Nabokov lady
117. Byron's Rx?
121. Expunge
122. Jill or John of films
123. Part of a stage
124. Shoemakers' forms
125. States
126. Tower name

DOWN

1. Florida neighbors
2. City near San Francisco
3. Lip
4. Fix
5. Represent on the stage
6. Cause of eruptions
7. Stooge in charge
8. Imitates Polonius
9. Foursquare
10. Cousin of vague or flot
11. Bacon's Rx for becoming "a full man"?
12. F.A.A. airport serv.
13. French flatfoot
14. Spike the punch
15. Aleutian island
16. Carbolic acid
17. Kind of partner
21. Biggers' sleuth
22. Attach
23. Noon or midnight, e.g.
28. One of the "Little Women"
30. Rembrandt's birthplace
31. Base or hospital areas
33. Famed folk singer
37. Truck-stop sign
38. Indonesian island
39. Gaelic
40. Winery container
41. Correct
43. Musician's transition
47. Teraphim
49. Tony's relative
50. Pertaining to the open seas
52. Early 1900's school of painters
53. Poet-novelist May

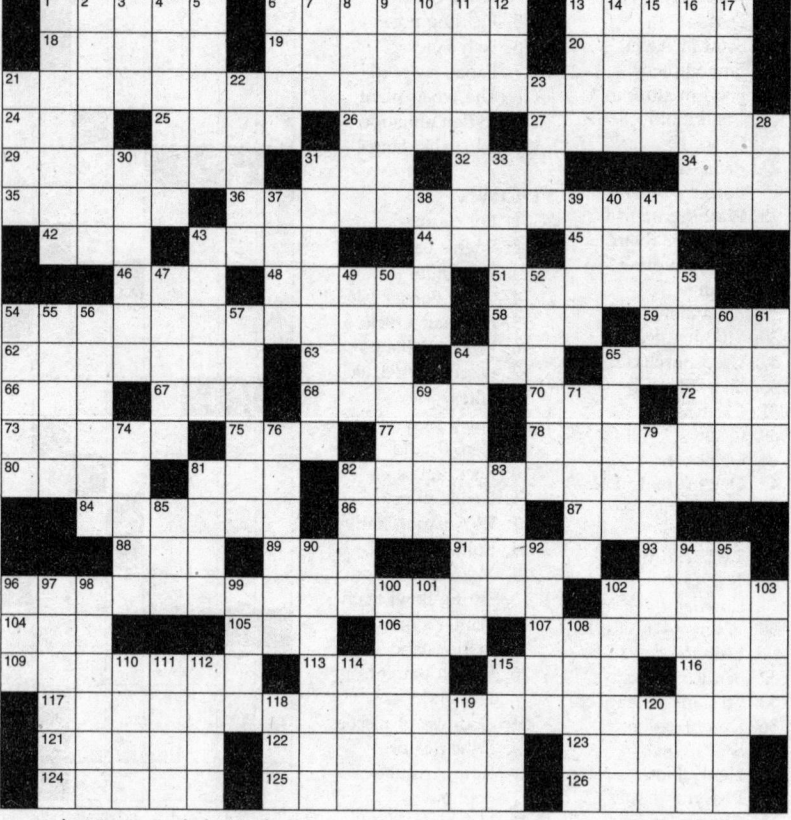

by Nancy Nicholson Joline

54. Frat-party garb
55. D-day beach
56. Geometry verb
57. Perkins of the theater
60. Naturalist Edwin Way ___
61. Broadcast
64. Wonderland croquet ball
65. Menotti role
69. "___ Explain," Billie Holiday song
71. ___ up (paid)
74. "Sons and Lovers" hero
76. Sage of Greek myth
79. Work-break item
81. Bois de Boulogne, e.g.
82. Grand National or Iditarod
83. Gram or logic preceder
85. Screenwriter ___ Diamond
90. Chemical compounds
92. Film director Kurosawa
94. Odom or Post
95. Basswoods
96. Elec. unit
97. Stool pigeon
98. Site of cave temples in India
99. Israeli dance
100. Settle snugly
101. City in W Algeria
102. Cocktail accompaniment
103. Limericks man
108. They lived in Chichén Itzá
110. Harem rooms
111. A sloop has one
112. Inspires reverence in
114. Warlike Olympian
115. Tots
118. Pedro's aunt
119. Tolkien creature
120. ___ Filippo Lippi

ACROSS

1. Medicinal bark
7. While on the contrary
13. Finial
16. Music-industry acronym
19. Circus swing
20. Spanish city
21. Crumbly soil
22. Oil source
23. Hemingway title
25. Harden by heat
26. Harvest
27. Arrow poison
28. Eagles' nests
29. Of a religious festival
32. Basketball player
33. Pay attention
34. Settle by intervention
35. It comes in reams
36. South Pacific island group
37. Goneril's father
38. Level
40. Water from steam, e.g.
45. ___ de foie gras
46. Musical instruments
49. Diversion
50. Unexceptional
52. Former Raider QB
53. Liquid vessels
54. Small flasks
55. Thieves
56. Tolstoy et al.
57. Closely related
58. Greeted
60. Sicilian volcano
61. Sailor
62. Hurdy-gurdies
63. Brewer's yeast
66. Streetside pillars
70. Dried orchid tubers
72. Parsonage
73. Unfortunate event
75. Tenon's target
77. Suffers longing
78. Roil anew
79. Worker along the Thames
80. Flower parts
81. Dexterous
82. Spurious wing of a bird
83. Indulgent, in a way
85. Receives with approval
87. River islets
88. Couples
89. Roasting stick
91. Feel indignant
93. Elaborate meal
94. Grossly stupid
98. Restaurant order for two
100. Threaten
101. Bristlelike parts
102. French king
103. "Cavalleria" temptress
104. Cameraman
107. Early Christian pulpit
108. Carpentry need
109. Radiator adjunct
110. Resident of Haifa
111. Former Boston ace
112. City in Nev.
113. Landed properties
114. Discipline

DOWN

1. Radio interference
2. East Indian garment
3. Algerian cavalry soldier
4. Pyrexia
5. Demolish
6. Clown fish's home
7. Capital residents
8. Lifted with effort
9. Projecting rims
10. Shower
11. Lover on the run
12. Scheduled
13. Fortify
14. Budgerigar
15. Of the small intestines
16. Key work
17. Establish
18. Abele or aspen
24. Empties
30. Groovy
31. Fit to be surgically treated
34. Bad guy
36. Harnessed oxen
37. Weighted
39. Primitive family symbols
40. Qualified
41. Caucasian inhabitant
42. Part of N.A.A.C.P.
43. Ross and Rigg
44. Incensed
45. Solve grammatically
47. Close by
48. Ladies of Spain: Abbr.
51. Compass dir.
52. Brown ermines
54. Loud outcry
55. Range of view
57. Salmon or frog, e.g.
59. Household gods
61. Rove; ramble
64. Munitions depot
65. Untidy
67. Chew
68. Dravidian language
69. Former U.K. coin
70. Blaze and Brenda
71. Delineate
72. Marceau forte
73. Yugoslav town
74. Noun-forming suffix
76. Yacht race
77. Trails
79. Muscovite's land
80. Advantageous
82. Sideways
84. Complete failure
86. Precook
87. Gandhi's namesakes
89. Beats it
90. Irrational fear
92. Confine at the zoo
93. Doe or ewe
94. Weinberger et al.
95. Put back on the burner
96. Engraved pillars
97. European songbird
99. Armbones
100. Dissolve
105. Bryant or Loos
106. Hasty; reckless

by Donald V. Lee II

QUOTATION MUTATIONS

ACROSS

1. Singer Franklin
7. Burghoff role
12. Swedish explorer Hedin
16. Arrow-poison tree
20. Lewd one
21. Act, in a way
22. Wing: Comb. form
23. Part of TV
24. Herb's promise for kids?
27. Kemo ___
28. Acts dreamily
29. At ___ (free)
30. Takes forty winks
32. Chew the ___ (ponder)
33. Deficiency: Comb. form
34. NASA cart
35. Dill of the Bible
36. Honors
38. Jim Lawrence's advice to teetotalers?
44. Stadium surface
45. Diseases of rye
46. Orient expresser
47. Buffalo Bill
49. Upgraded trail
52. Tyke protector
54. Encapsulate
57. Sticky stuff
58. Shield border
59. More demure
63. Tops
65. Fake goldleaf
67. Agitate
68. Bonkers
69. Covered
70. Heap of stones
72. Part of the U.K.
74. All-purpose trk.
75. Fillings after drillings
77. Make a collar
79. Grandpa on "The Waltons"
81. More osseous
82. Start of Julius's phrase for a carpenter?
85. Cradle tenders
88. ___-do-well
89. Colima cover-up
90. Frightful
92. Thai's neighbor
94. Anil, e.g.
96. Challenger
97. Legal claim
98. Radiate
99. Prefix with chord or meter
101. Cabot Cove's Jessica
103. Cows, to Cowper
104. Ask repeatedly
105. Apex
106. Hoopster Manute ___
107. Bacon products
110. Kind of bear
112. Brain passage
113. "The jig ___!"
115. Smell ___ (be suspicious)
116. Marina sights
121. Burbot
123. Harry's phrase for a goalie's crease?
128. Certain summaries
131. Kind of surgeon
132. Libation station potation
133. Smeltery pile
134. He wrote "The Brave Bulls"
135. Partner of Old Lace
137. Mouth, to a zoologist
140. Actress Massey
141. Feedbag filler
143. René's words for a lurker?
146. Soft cheese
147. Mixers' frozen assets
148. Tushington and Moreno
149. "Bridget Loves ___"
150. Koko's weapon
151. New Zealand parrots
152. About
153. Old lemons

DOWN

1. Thin silk for hoods
2. Change a shade
3. Parrot's activity
4. "... men have found a ___ love": Chesterton
5. TV's Ramsey et al.
6. Ham saver
7. Dub over
8. Arabian commander
9. Tintinnabular sound
10. To ___ (exactly)
11. Race a motor
12. Astringent
13. Last-word power
14. Notched, as a leaf
15. Horace's good news for a student?
16. Old musical syllables
17. France's wish for Marcel à la Neville?
18. Photo collection
19. Uses a gin
22. Gloat
25. Everest stat.
26. One with eagle eyes
31. A memorable Erwin
34. Actress in "Signore e Signori"
35. Hailing call
37. Fielder's boot
39. Most of the U.K.
40. Topple
41. Corn bread
42. Forte of a good hosp.
43. Kind of stick
48. Bush rival in 1988
50. Touched down
51. Galley mark
53. Gilead's lack
55. More contrite
56. Kilmer opus
59. Hunk
60. "Ecce ___," Titian painting
61. George's retail-failure admission?
62. Isole ___ (isles off Sicily)
64. Desert relief
66. Cartouche
69. T.R.'s advice to a strong mason?
70. Elm fruits
71. Thin pancake
73. Tackle
76. Opposite of hawed
78. Two, once
80. Species of wheat
83. Grant
84. Papal vestment
86. Flavoring for a Cannes cordial
87. Some NCO's
91. Sediment
92. Places
93. ___ above (better)
95. Author-lecturer Mills
97. Site of knights' fights
100. A certain fool
102. Flood
103. A tippy canoe?
104. Pod denizens
108. Author Bellow
109. Cometic path
111. Hoopla
114. Imposters
117. Wraths
118. Juliet or Cordelia
119. Shipbuilding peg
120. Tropical, herbaceous plants
122. U.S. flight org.
124. Moran and Gray
125. Lobo group
126. Most domestic
127. Minn.'s St. ___ College
128. Messy ones
129. Pine
130. Progeny
136. Exile isle
137. Leg part
138. Mal de ___
139. Algerian port
140. Angered
142. Bishopric
144. Between, in Bologna
145. Eng. title

by Robert H. Wolfe

ACROSS

1. ___ Gan, Israeli city
6. Thrills for Domingo
10. In shape
13. Extreme sluggishness
19. Tony musical winner: 1980
20. Actor Mischa
21. Stir
22. One-celled organism
23. Dentist's office?
26. Underlying structure
27. Thai measure
28. Up to now
29. A Carter on TV
30. Swell
31. Garb
34. Poet who wrote "Opportunity"
35. A.L. Batting Champion: 1955
38. Mussolini's kin
39. Reason for marital breakup?
41. TV network
44. Rich dessert
45. Teeny-___
46. Lake in NW Italy
47. Become agitated
48. Upward curve of a ship's plank
49. Identical
50. Author Nin
51. ___ dixit
52. Jogger's complaint?
56. Lo-cal
57. Modernized
60. Baptism and confirmation
61. Kind of jury or larceny
62. Separated
63. Showed concern
64. Crude borax
65. Breakfast food in Dixie
66. Hall's musical partner
67. Type of periodical
68. Canary's trill
69. Tidal bores?
73. Everybody, in Bonn
74. Choice words
75. Crooner or cherry
76. Teachers' degs.
79. A.E.S. and H.S.T.
80. Yvette's sky
81. Rhône feeder
83. Commandment verb
85. Writer LeShan
86. "Equus"?
88. ___ counter
89. Actors Charlie and Martin
92. Cartoonist Gross
93. Ellington's "Mood ___"
94. Appraises
96. Nursery trio
97. Turkish title
99. Half a dance
100. "___ Fideles"
102. Square in an arena?
106. Learned
107. Craggy hill
108. ___ and anon
109. Speedily
110. Gore or gusset
111. Siamang
112. Melchior, by birth
113. "Ores" man

DOWN

1. What an ophthalmologist does
2. The Wright way?
3. Armed services
4. Pac.'s sister
5. Mai ___ (rum drink)
6. A wise herb?
7. Unseat
8. Rent
9. Qum native
10. Ribbed silk fabric
11. Pedestal object
12. Smart set
13. U.S.A.F. group
14. Muscat native
15. This is sometimes round
16. Clemens beauty?
17. R.I.P. notice
18. Risque
24. Bill and Louis
25. TV in England
32. Bank depositor's div.
33. Kind of deer
34. Dutch genre painter
35. Gold weights
36. Tall story?
37. Rover's restraint
39. Kind of truck
40. Rich
42. Inhuman
43. In a gentle way
45. Conjurer's rod
47. Chaplin's early films
49. Prune a tree, in Scotland
50. Verify
52. Crib toys
53. Salt Lake City team
54. Kitchen utensil
55. "Irresistibelle"
57. Marathoner's challenge
58. Released conditionally
59. Dentists?
61. Four noggins
63. Seasonal songs
64. Chinese secret society
66. Some are holy
67. Word on a biblical wall
69. Where cash might be stashed
70. "The ___" (Ore.'s motto)
71. Eng. foes' fast craft
72. Having tendrils
76. David Copperfield, e.g.
77. Refined grace
78. More potent
81. Type of bandage
82. Asserted without proof
83. Indonesian coin
84. Secreted
87. Displaced person
88. ___ Carlo Menotti
90. Nobelist in Literature: 1946
91. Nitrite, e.g.
94. Sitarist Shankar
95. S. Yemen seaport
96. L-Q connection
97. TV show starring Sherman Hemsley
98. Star of "American Gigolo"
101. N.Y. summer time
102. Greek letter
103. Actress Le Gallienne
104. Highlands headgear
105. Inst. in Troy, N.Y.

by Jeanette K. Brill

ACROSS

1. Trial run
5. Italian cats
10. Least risky
16. Cast
17. Kin of auloi
18. Zenger, for one
20. Rainer's 1937 Oscar film
22. McLaglen's 1935 Oscar film, with "The"
24. George's lyricist
25. Squander
26. Pyle and Banks
28. Birthplace of Henry IV of France
29. Zing
30. Motherless calf
31. Less polished
32. George ___, baseball Hall of Famer
33. Marine mollusk
35. Carpenters' pins
36. Ranee's garb
37. Mature
38. Aplenty
39. Most uncommon
40. Scott role in a 1970 Oscar film
42. Some modern apts.
43. Humor
44. Medieval helmet
45. Babbled
46. "Platoon," e.g.
47. ___-do-well
48. Safari member
49. Tatum O'Neal's 1973 Oscar film
53. "Jamaica ___"
54. Actress Binnie
55. Crystalline amino acid
56. League of hoops
57. First name of three wives of Henry VIII
59. High points
60. Like Tithonus
61. Betimes
62. Soap plants
63. "Fatal Attraction" Oscar winner
64. Challenges anew
67. Some are racers
68. Knife expert
69. Oscar film: 1968
70. Casino employee
71. Tossed dish
72. More villainous
73. Gives access
74. Most stocky
77. Pyrrhuloxia or jacana
78. Subject of Amendment XVII
79. Pomanders
80. Former name of a Carib. island group
81. Bambi's aunt
82. "Moses" waterway
83. ___ distance (endure)
84. Mary Martin role: 1954
85. Appear afresh
87. George Burns's 1975 Oscar film, with "The"
91. Yukon vehicles
92. Teed off
93. Chooser's call
94. Magazine filler
95. Hosni's predecessor
96. Act

DOWN

1. Lemmon-MacLaine Oscar film
2. Work unit
3. Michigan region
4. Loren's 1961 Oscar film
5. Enters
6. Ebb
7. Sped
8. Asian holiday
9. His writing led to "Cabaret"
10. Slender rod
11. Palmer, et al.
12. Marching-band musician
13. Adam's grandson
14. Riv. boat
15. Modifying agent
16. "A Letter to ___ Wives"
19. Most genuine
20. Track info
21. Philistine deity
23. "I see but one ___ be clear": Stendahl
27. A sorry lot
30. Boot camp, e.g.
31. Less genial
32. Abdul-Jabbar of the Lakers
34. Metric unit
35. Edmond of "The Count of Monte Cristo"
36. Biting drama
38. Vandyke's kin
39. Prowls after prey
40. Lose one's grip
41. "Rocky" setting
42. Narrow opening
43. Clones
45. Serious risks
46. "Duck Soup" group
48. Specialized shoeworker
49. Kitchen tool
50. H. Fonda's 1981 Oscar film
51. Way overweight
52. Consumer spokesman
54. Incumbent
55. Parol
58. Panted
59. Charlotte ___, V.I.
60. Asian range
62. I. Bergman's 1956 Oscar film
63. Picks out
64. Thief
65. Stritch and May
66. Arliss's 1929 Oscar film
67. Bristlelike organs
68. Lurched
70. Most crowded
71. Japanese fare
73. Cratchit's book
74. Mack Sennett girl
75. Convinces otherwise
76. Cambridge cans
78. Suit material
79. ___ Rica
82. W. Beatty film
83. Eat, in a way
86. Brando film, with "The": 1950
88. Samovar
89. "All About ___"
90. Nectar collector

by Louis Sabin

ACROSS

1. Sticky stuff
6. Melville protagonist
10. Troy suffered one
15. Succeeded: Colloq.
16. Betel-nut producer
17. Ruined
19. Give oneself airs
21. Election results
23. Shoshone
24. Dozed
25. Shingle man
27. Venetian bigwig
28. Tropical tree
30. Inventor Howe
32. Perch
33. Rose's love
34. Divinity with a load on
36. Curtain on stage
38. Caboodle's pal
39. Wave lift
40. Dugong
42. African republic
44. Griffith Gaunt's creator
45. A Waugh
47. P.I. trees
48. Proverbially cheap item
49. Toy
54. Prisoners
58. Latin love
59. Bard's before
60. Veloz's dancing partner
62. Anger
63. Sayer's "The ___ Tailors"
64. Experimented
66. Actor John and family
67. Custard
68. Antarctic cape
69. Masticate
71. French born
72. Catch
73. Cook one's ___ (dash another's hopes)
75. Try to overcome insomnia
79. Foot part
80. El Paso's Vikki
81. Plant affliction
82. Emulate Kermit
84. Claims
87. Kind of firecracker
91. Fern part
92. Little, in Lothian
93. "Giant" ranch
95. Passover feast
96. Highlands girl
97. Hangs onto
99. Short smokes
101. Crème ___ crème
102. Up and ___ (Slang)
103. Knightly weapons
105. Subway item
107. Author Yutang
108. Apportion
110. ___ around (cutting capers)
113. Moe, e.g.
114. Charged particle
115. Testify
116. Bearded, botanically
117. Kind of house
118. Undermine

DOWN

1. Kneecap
2. Commotion
3. French cathedral city
4. Kind of fight
5. Kennedy and Barrymore
6. French artist
7. Name in a will
8. Thespian
9. Shaw's "___ and the Man"
10. Most dependable
11. Lifeless
12. Certain N.Y. time
13. Flesh-revealing photo
14. Attired
15. Undergo change
16. Gazing fixedly
18. Motor
19. Immature monarchs, e.g.
20. Homeric products
22. Beginning
26. Thwart
29. Ghastly
31. Indian tongue: Var.
35. Only
37. Villain
39. Pituitary location
41. Dry foe
43. "Taras Bulba" author
44. Incursions
46. Hold dear
48. Certain two-wheeled carriages
49. ___ arms
50. Kind of acid
51. Known, in Nice
52. Musical chord
53. Pay attention
54. Actress Leigh
55. Italian metropolis
56. Heaven: Pref.
57. Dispatches
61. Sally ___ (tea cake)
64. Eighteen-wheeler
65. Aristocratic
67. Aped a butterfly
69. Cell-producing gland
70. Student at times
74. Lollapalooza, to a flapper
76. Encourages
77. H.R.E. part
78. Regrets
80. Lauren Bacall vehicle
82. Cargo units
83. ___ stone (famous tablet)
84. Vocal approval
85. Dines at home
86. It was a Bearcat
88. Barbershop sweetheart
89. Fix brakes
90. German urge
91. Lie
92. Using a squab
94. Grate
97. W.W. II field marshal
98. Net
100. More reasonable
104. Whirl
106. Squash or melon
109. Cart or ball ending
111. Kind of luck
112. ___ and reel

by Bert H. Kruse

408 CELEBRITEASE

ACROSS

1. City in Calif.
5. Rebuffs
10. Make merry
15. Chancel item
20. Noted research physician
21. Membranes
22. Writer Jong
23. Worsted
24. Shaking like ___
25. Guam's capital
26. Plump roasting fowl
27. Book by J. B. Cabell: 1937
28. Items in Liz's closet?
31. Made a bridge play
33. Ar chaser
34. Cousin of a wrymouth
35. "It ___ laugh": Pinero
36. Bouquet beauty
37. "___ for All Seasons"
39. Together: Mus. dir.
40. Tip
41. Party for Elke?
46. Ruffian
47. The Great Compromiser
51. Seething
52. S.E.C. member
53. Townsend ___: 1934
55. Clement people
58. Shea performer
59. Cassandra, e.g.
63. Medical suffix
65. Cavity in a cactus
66. Vow
68. Teresa has it?
70. Long looker
71. Straight or sharp follower
73. Some cats and dogs
75. Queen Elizabeth's Aussie vessel
76. Julius of songdom
79. Robin Hood's quaff
80. Accumulate
82. Herds of whales
84. Discontented one
86. Most spooky
90. Specify
92. Walter got set for a race?
96. Writer Wiesel
97. Milk curdler
98. Dot on a map
99. Highwayman
101. Nabokov book
102. "...lovely ___"
104. Towel designation
106. ___ generis
107. Western
109. Intertwine
110. Temperate
112. The ex-Mrs. Bono's hairdressers?
116. Queen of mystery
119. Ownership document
120. Always
121. Vocations
123. Private eye Peter
124. Jeanne or Cécile: Abbr.
125. Andress film
128. Strips a ship
129. Lorne's favorite side dish?
134. Concerning
135. Ryan or Tatum
137. Qum resident
138. Wrathful
139. Problem for Fido
140. Present occasion
141. Hebrew month
142. QE2, e.g.
143. Beeweed or starwort
144. Gallant mount
145. Tales or exploits
146. Aglets

DOWN

1. Song sounds
2. Minds
3. Clock face
4. Lowdown
5. Flower parts
6. Within the law
7. "When I was ___ ...'"
8. Sheet of stamps
9. Ocean front
10. Emulate a diseur
11. One of the dryads
12. Bigwigs
13. He wrote "The Name of the Rose"
14. Japan's Feast of ___
15. Guarantee
16. Jack's favorite dessert?
17. Voyages
18. Jibe
19. Tall grass
20. Cloy
29. Foster
30. Seize power
32. Actress Charlotte
36. Chinese principle
37. "___ Blue?"
38. Blanc and Ferrer
39. Flooded
40. Christmas tree
41. Greek island
42. Voodoo
43. "Be prepared:" e.g.
44. Mata ___
45. Designer Cassini
46. Entire scope
48. Arrowsmith's first wife
49. City on the Rhône
50. River of Flanders
54. ___ credit
56. ___ de deux
57. Dudley Moore film
60. Pitcher
61. Trial's partner
62. One feared by xenophobes
64. Beehive's relative
67. Celeste in her nest?
69. Salted, as a noix
72. Sampler
74. Coleridge's "gentle thing"
77. Aug. 31 follower
78. How pongids behave
81. Wife of Tyndareus
82. Embden and Toulouse
83. Moffo and Moses
85. Lollygagged
87. Happify
88. Partisan
89. Shreds
90. Minute amount
91. Summer in St. Tropez
93. Snooped
94. Guided trip
95. Of the ear
100. Jughead
103. Famed Concord family: 19th century
105. Film segment
108. Spring mo.
111. Tax org.
113. Illusionist Doug
114. Keeps
115. Hot spot
117. Bandleader Lanin
118. Allow
119. Fought one-on-one
121. Suppers, in Sevilla
122. Catkin
123. Table prayer
124. Governing body of France
125. Ade medium
126. Despises
127. German reservoir
128. Lady of Spain
129. Actor Wilder
130. Fourth of HOMES
131. Pinza was one
132. Residue
133. Diva delivery
136. Negative word

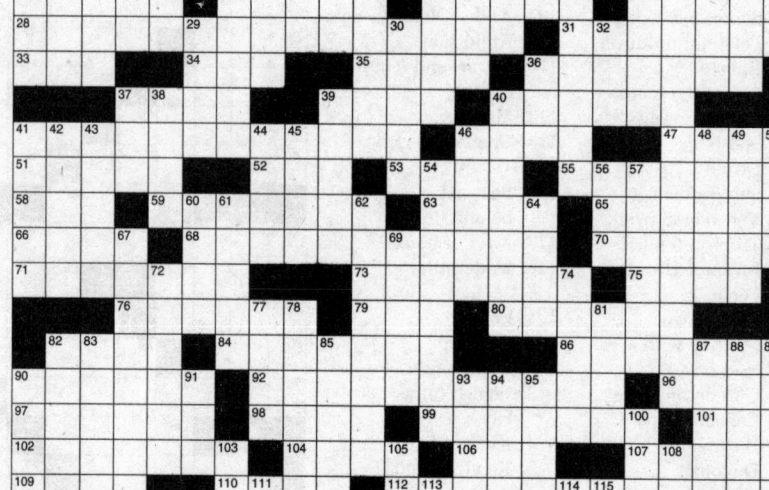

by Shirley Soloway

ACROSS

1. Concavity
5. Extemporize
10. Submerge
15. Declines
19. Blunderbore, e.g.
20. Tropical vine
21. Fluke larva
22. Ice field
23. Take a back seat
26. Driver's shout
27. Saki and Sand
28. Release
29. Potted
31. Interstices
32. Ah Sin creator
33. Dynamo parts
34. Half a score
35. Amiens's river
36. Unfruitful
37. Fenway foursome
40. Belaboring
42. Corn serving
45. Indonesian island
46. Pots' companions
47. "Topaz" author
48. European capital
49. Doak Walker's coll.
50. Flinch
51. Insipid
53. Plods
54. Most convenient
56. Disparage
57. Ticket type
58. Act as gofer
62. Sofa
64. Carry on
65. Went over again
68. Throbs
69. Awn
71. Emulated Pan
72. Swedish coin
73. Molted
74. Skirt length
75. Limerick poet
76. Manger
77. Sizzling
78. Be successful
82. Viking alphabet
83. "Boys Town" actor
85. Peace Nobelist: 1987
86. Light bed
87. Expel
89. Cupids
90. Beat
94. Fissured
95. Derogatory
96. Aurora ___
97. River in Xanadu
98. Borge will do this for laughs
101. Kind of market
102. Cave being
103. Strained
104. Unicorn fish
105. Asian festivals
106. "Solstice" author
107. Chipped in
108. Roman clan

DOWN

1. Dad
2. Girl watcher
3. It may be whooping
4. Convention orator
5. President of Mexico: 1946–52
6. Cubes
7. Neighbor of Burma
8. Bavarian river
9. Nightstand sight
10. Scriptural
11. Pussyfoot
12. Taro part
13. "___ Liza Jane"
14. Bands stand for them
15. Lacking vigor
16. Boast
17. Shipworm
18. Pips
24. Holiday happenings
25. Nobelist in Physics: 1938
30. Mountain lake
32. Kind of chestnut
33. Flavorful
35. Private rooms
36. Incinerate
37. Blowout
38. Soprano Gluck
39. Proclaim widely
40. Medieval guild
41. Protect
43. Filamentous plant
44. Rubicund
46. Rifle
48. Spreads
50. Dinner drinks
51. Mixture
52. Alfred of acting
53. P.G.A. winner 1949
55. Old hat
56. Rating symbol
57. Brown shade
59. Characteristic
60. Gazelles
61. Asian nation
62. Cummerbund
63. Repeat
66. Buffalo's county
67. Society entrants
69. Alfred of testing
70. Impatient
71. Excuses
74. Sonata movement
76. Jitterbug
78. Source
79. Mark and Dorothy
80. Wear away
81. Cardinal's cap
82. Logger's sport
84. Neb. tribe
86. Crooked
87. Rough sketch
88. Lunar trench
89. Tarsus
90. Aplomb
91. Dress design
92. Connection
93. Fussy couple?
95. Bagpipe player
96. Propensity
99. "Watchful" name
100. One with a clutch

by Judith Perry

410

DROPOUTS

ACROSS

1. Rigel, e.g.
5. Trade
9. Bath, for one
12. Herald's cloak
18. Fine fabric
19. Kennedy relative
20. Auto
21. Lariats
22. Fabian's opinion of Cesario: Shak.
25. "By their ___ ye shall know them"
26. Third
27. Peter's ___ (old tax)
28. Saturate
29. Church niche
30. "When I was ___ . . ."
31. Twangy
33. Flings
36. Author St. Johns
37. Above all
41. Poilu's weapon
42. Sultry
44. Kind of soup
47. Invent facts
48. Sward
49. Wings, to Ovid
50. "I've ___ had!"
51. Horne from Brooklyn
52. Bigger pic
53. "___, said . . . Chaucer": Spenser
57. Folk-tale creatures
59. Auditors' concerns
61. Tempers
62. Painting style
63. It can be scanned
64. Po metropolis
65. Lorelei
67. Islamic Messiah
69. Rel. of a bracket
70. Hampered
73. Prepare to deplane
75. Loud confrontation
77. Mme., in Madrid
78. Estuaries
79. Kind of sax
81. Mother of Jabal and Jubal
82. Folding bed
83. Literary monogram
84. Decrees
86. Tommyrot
87. Yield
88. Early ascetics
90. Squash variety
92. Weighty works
93. Smudges
95. Rounded moldings
96. Overcrowd
98. Part of AFL-CIO

100. Shapes
102. Walked aimlessly
106. Stage
107. How the deathfires danced for the Ancient Mariner
109. James Webb's "___ of Honor"
110. Baby raccoon
111. Some tides
112. Fad
113. Spare
114. Vane dir.
115. Yawn
116. Foil

DOWN

1. Lath
2. Subdued
3. Acidity, to an M.D.
4. Iterate
5. Author Hite
6. Undulating
7. Azimuth
8. Populated
9. Kind of sheet
10. Tuileries, e.g.
11. Tennyson's wrecked seaman
12. Piscatorial sport
13. Service begun May 15, 1918
14. Geegaw
15. One of the Cook Islands
16. Seed, in tennis
17. Sociologist's deg.
19. Seraglio sections
23. Apices
24. Prosperity
30. Ta-ta, in Tours
32. Section of "Le Tartuffe"
33. Joshua's fellow spy
34. Coliseum
35. Fisherman's quarry
36. Far East nurses
38. Start of Stephano's song in "The Tempest"
39. Luxury craft
40. Barm
42. Type of arch
43. Pressure product
45. Actor Buddy
46. N.B.A. team
51. Jogger's cousin
53. As far as
54. Nerve: Pref.
55. Black of "Nashville"
56. Gershwin's "Of Thee ___"
58. Author Lofts
60. Dangerous mosquito

64. Resort lake in the West
65. Caterpillar hairs
66. On edge
67. Guillemot
68. Indigo sources
69. Attention getters
70. Gaseous element
71. Wear away
72. Trysts
74. Fast-food specialty
76. A Polynesian tongue
80. Endure
84. Free
85. Cloy
86. ___ around (cavorting)
87. Liken
89. In decline
91. Search carefully
92. Shadow
94. Spike
96. Kind of paper
97. Norma and Charlotte
98. ___ majesté
99. Belt
101. Shea stats.
102. Hazard for Strange

103. Cinch
104. Fringe
105. Endure, in Edinburgh
106. Singer Tillis
108. Pedagogue's org.

by Judson G. Trent

ACROSS

1. Actor Will
5. Old Dutch coins
10. Mechanical repetition
14. Proportion
19. Gallimaufry
20. Confused
21. Always
22. Etchers' needs
23. Size of type?
26. Tippy craft
27. Sailor's dread
28. Stowe book
29. Ride in a roadster
31. Theater award
32. Objectives
33. The Little ___ (nursery-tale character)
37. French clerics' titles
40. "A House ___ Home": P. Adler
42. O'Hare tenant
43. Heraldic fur
44. Tiff?
47. Most M.I.T. grads
48. Kin of a dalmatic
49. Immature egg
50. "___ some other name!": Juliet
51. Morse symbol
52. Poivre's partner
53. Superficial prettiness?
58. Roll up
59. Sterne's "___ Shandy"
61. Indian princess
62. Layman in a monastery
64. Inc.-tax pros
65. Small vessel for oil
66. Afflictions
67. Galahad's mother
69. Ind. town
70. Freshwater fish
74. Rhythmical cadence
75. Spread before a strut?
78. High priest
79. ___ up (confine)
80. Shad delicacy
81. "___ Triste": Sibelius
82. Scottish bonnet
83. Casca's time for action
85. Short laugh?
89. Mention for military honors
90. Lands a fish
92. Turns down
93. Football grip
94. Passionate
95. Decorates a cake
96. Indifferent
98. Some rabbits
100. Court celebrity
101. European buntings
105. Belief
108. Pintail duck?
111. Break a commandment
112. Testa's cousin
113. Dissonance
114. Smidgen
115. Carbonizes
116. Foundation
117. Unrefined
118. De ___ (unwanted)

DOWN

1. Objective
2. German river
3. "___ Kleine Nachtmusik": Mozart
4. Chanticleer
5. Author Runyon
6. Eared seal
7. Man, for one
8. Gumshoe
9. Pilchard
10. Gives power back to
11. "Metamorphoses" poet
12. Half a score
13. Work units
14. More risque
15. Hold ___ to (compare favorably with)
16. "___ Men," 1987 film
17. Altar words
18. Simple sugar
24. Greek letters
25. Mail
30. School V.I.P.
32. Mine ceiling
34. Berra of baseball?
35. Surrounded
36. Snuggle
37. Command from Bligh
38. Farm machine
39. Weight allowance?
40. Moslem faith
41. Zenith
42. Bide ___ (stay awhile)
44. Trans-Atlantic
45. AZ city
46. Skilled
49. "Barefoot boy, with cheek ___": Whittier
54. Flynn or Fauntleroy
55. Actress Prentiss
56. Living ___ (cohabiting illegally)
57. From bad ___
58. Scram
60. Polish's partner
63. Henri's kindness
65. Czech dramatists Karel and Josef
67. Mark Twain's burial place
68. Schubert songs
69. Part of speech: Abbr.
70. Traverses
71. Baby-powder base
72. Like a pterodactyl
73. Eras
76. Port of entry in N. Spain
77. Ties
84. Santa, e.g.
85. Locus
86. Letter by Paul
87. Nape
88. Letting go
89. ___ a day (retires)
91. High-hats
93. Auden's "___ Stranger!"
96. Ankh, for one
97. Sioux
99. Strikebreaker
100. Sacred bull of Egypt
101. Taft's state
102. "Omnia vincit ___"
103. Defense org.
104. Kind of bean
105. U.S. agency: 1933–43
106. S. Korean president: 1988
107. Stowe girl
109. Altar in the sky
110. Hide ___ hair

by T. W. Underhill

ACROSS

1. ___ House, Washington D.C.
6. Onto
11. ___ veau (sweetbread)
16. Items in stacks
21. Small stream, in England
22. Split
23. Outward
24. Praying female figure
25. Set ___ (prepare to snare)
26. Union general
27. Diplomat Silas
28. Devilfish
29. Closet pest?
31. Superman?
33. Having droopy auricles
34. Facial bone
36. Subject of some roasts
37. Hardy heroine
38. Singer Callas
39. Arrow's little cousin
40. Vexed or rubbed
44. Bribed
45. Stuffs
46. Morning hrs.
47. Valhalla gods
50. What an arsonist sometimes does?
53. Stigma
54. Sing Sing warden-author
55. Rake
56. Bill's partner
57. Donizetti heroine
58. Russian sea
59. ". . . ___ away the sin . . .": John 1:29
61. Posture at bat
64. R.I.P. notice
65. Surveying instrument
67. Quaker in a grove
69. Menhaden
71. Whale constellation
72. Trick alternative
73. Boy singer of the 30's
74. Barge
77. Ritual meal
78. Famed former miler
82. Music halls
83. Strut
85. Nova ___
87. An armadillo
88. "Hamiltons"
89. Gibbon
90. Prado offering
91. Certain gaits
92. Conductor Jeffrey ___
93. Rossini's Figaro when depressed?
98. Kayo blows
99. Some RR's
100. Painters, e.g.
101. Crazy as ___
102. Author of "Tristram Shandy"
103. Summers, in Arles
104. Fold
105. Partner of aid
107. "To every thing there is ___ . . .": Eccl. 3:1
111. Made with pickets
112. Led
117. Mystery novel?
119. Moonshiner?
122. Fanon
123. Conjecture
124. Rejoice
125. Rhone tributary
126. Passé
127. Bone: Pref.
128. Type of angler
129. J'___ (I was, in Paris)
130. Curves
131. Vance of whodunits
132. Crystalline crust
133. Purposes

DOWN

1. Melee
2. Graph starter?
3. Anchor position
4. "___ war": F.D.R.
5. Parrots, e.g.,
6. Hordes
7. Handles
8. Of grandparents
9. Advise, in Yorkshire
10. Sap
11. Memorable sportswriter
12. Summer refresher
13. Brenda or Bart
14. Of Denmark: Comb. form
15. Toothless
16. Alley frequenters
17. Some exams
18. ___-arms (mounted soldier)
19. ___ nous
20. Bet
30. Talking horse of TV
32. Inserts on skirts
35. Domesday Book money
38. "Cape Martin" painter
39. Pythias's friend
40. Assyrian city
41. ___ pin drop
42. Egyptian dam
43. Fox hunt?
44. Thin porridge
45. Ashcan School painter
46. Whodunit factor
47. Theme
48. Union unit
50. Display of daring
51. Pairs
52. A Mendelssohn opus in E flat major
53. An Ivy League jewel?
59. Rollers in the 1790's
60. Oliver or Thomas
61. Ship's poles
62. Triter
63. Actress Verdugo
66. Rent
68. Bishopric
70. Gods, to Galba
72. Lachrymose
73. Beaten, in Brest
74. Soprano Lehmann
75. Beau ___
76. Polite blokes
77. Clupeid fishes
78. Element used in metallurgy
79. Acuminate
80. Ever, in poesy
81. Ballet ___
84. Blackthorns
86. English explorer
91. Games for would-be-millionaires
93. Engine
94. Establishment not requiring union membership
95. Advertising hoopla
96. Not aweather
97. The common plantain
100. Sows again
102. A Belgradian
104. Piece of fourth-class mail
105. Confuses
106. Swarthy, in Savoie
107. Home
108. Koran chapters
109. Les ___ Unis
110. Formal mall
111. Loren's married name
113. Jai-alai basket
114. Twitch
115. Weird
116. Garb
118. Disdainful interjection
120. Hedge that bars cattle
121. Finnish city or river

by Jack R. Harnes

ACROSS

1. An October birthstone
5. Valjean of "Les Misérables"
9. ___ button
14. Tailored
18. Enthusiastic review
19. Old card game
21. Statistic for Tyson
22. Noyes play
23. Take heart
25. The lady vanishes
27. "Downstairs" folk
28. Worsted-cloth strainer
30. Aspirations
31. Irish lake
32. Disguise
33. Lemon
34. Contemptibly small
37. Speaks childishly
38. Devilfishes
42. Cartoonist Peter and family
43. Night out
45. Easter treat
47. Explorer Ericson
48. Entertainer Eartha
49. Cribs
50. Moore of the movies
51. Cardiologist's chart: Abbr.
52. All gone
56. Plumbers' tubes
57. No place to skate
59. Winged
60. Inflicts
61. Sometimes it hurts
62. Dogs sans pedigree
63. Lake dwellers
64. Bronco busters
66. Eastern inn
67. "Agon" and "Serenade"
69. In harmony
70. Timeless
72. Luau instr.
74. Gaelic
75. Fang, in France
76. Actor Richard
77. Devil's walking-stick, e.g.
78. Year in Claudius I's reign
79. Abandoned bride
83. Roll along
84. Adams, Harding, Hayes or Taylor
86. Needed an eraser
87. Bureaus
88. People of NE India
89. Battery terminal
90. King Balak's land
91. South African township
94. Concert hall
95. Describing picnics
99. No room
101. Skip breakfast
103. Sandwich source
104. Hotel de___ (town hall, in Tours)
105. It was nothing to Nero
106. Hindu hero
107. Extremities
108. Disburdened
109. "___ of the Mind," Shepard play
110. Neuter, as a pet

DOWN

1. Globes
2. Peel
3. Affirm
4. Cut grass
5. He's on the spot
6. Emulate Duse
7. Moslem names
8. Town in Iceland
9. Something to keep
10. Cliff dwelling
11. Cole and Turner
12. German pronoun
13. Cheeses named for an English village
14. ". . . ___ little failed much": R.L.S.
15. Shankar specialty
16. Bibliographer's "same"
17. Place in space
20. Try again
24. Marx and Malden
26. Saudi Arabian town
29. Coleridge's "sacred river"
32. Please: Ger.
34. Maldives capital
35. Upright
36. Little left
37. Cabinetmaker's machine
38. Barrel spigot
39. Counting-out word
40. Green leaves
41. Hebrew letter
43. English letter
44. R.I.P. notices
46. Peach or Piggy
48. Emulates Mme. Defarge
50. Chemical compound
52. Make used to
53. Composer Gabriel: 1845–1924
54. Mongolian range
55. Montand's morning
56. Laborer, for short
58. Goddess who is no hawk
60. Stout's Nero
62. Center of activity
63. Former Defense Secretary
64. Asian weight
65. Roman patios
66. Affected ones
67. Run, as dye
68. Trapshooting variety
70. Veins' contents
71. Concur
73. Sniggles
75. "___ zeffiretto" ("The Marriage of Figaro" duet)
77. Strike three
79. Something plighted
80. Freshened
81. Gap, in Grenoble
82. "The Silver Bears" author
83. Landing place
85. Mother of Achilles
87. Chain gang
89. Astaire's sister
90. CCCLI tripled
91. Nigerian singer
92. Poet Wilfred
93. Barbarous
94. Watteau works
95. Sprinter or skier: Abbr.
96. Speak sharply
97. Projecting molding
98. Anthem's beginning
100. By way of
102. Aunt, in Acapulco

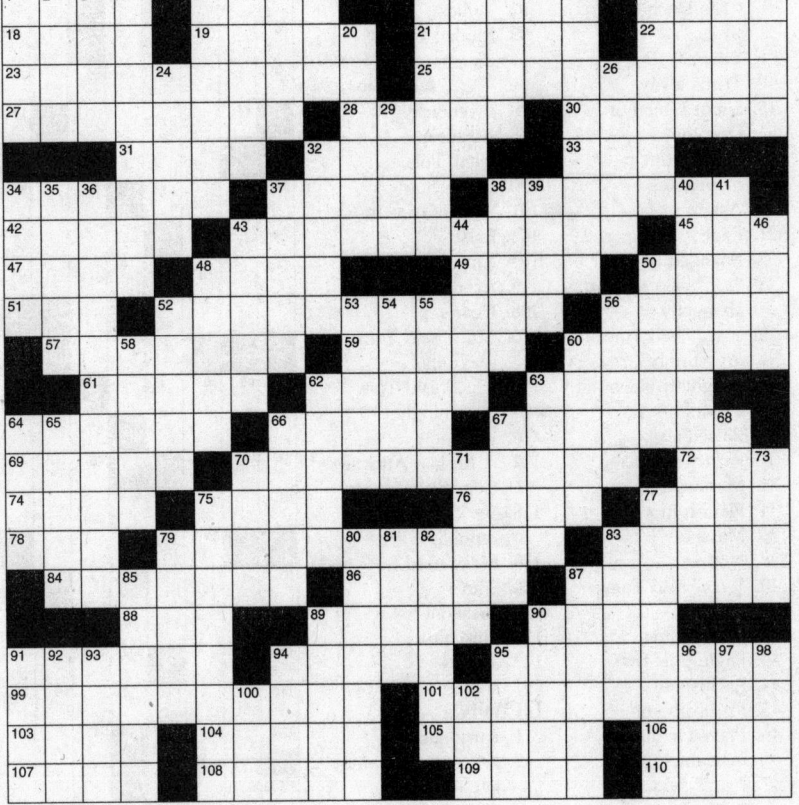

by Nancy Scandrett Ross

ACROSS

1. John Webster's "The Duchess of ___"
6. Ethereal ring
10. Trims away
15. Silent Lillian or Dorothy
19. First victim's namesakes
20. Askew
21. Rage
22. Engaged in
23. "___?" asked Tom abstractly
25. "___," said Tom divertingly
27. Spaghetti wheat
28. Credulous
30. Raised strip
31. Falsify
32. Measures
34. Flatter, in a way
36. Massive
38. Notice
40. "___," said Tom initially
42. Signal flares
43. Eagle plus two
44. Exclusively
45. Precise point
46. Played a shrill instrument
47. "___," said Tom haltingly
50. "___," said Tom unsparingly
54. Wolf's kin
55. Barley beard
57. Underdone
58. ___ Friday
59. Tycoon Turner
60. Tire print
62. The revenuers
63. Wall Street figure
64. Levin or Lansky
67. "___," said Tom grandly
69. Avifauna
70. Pink-slipped
71. Word, in Nice
72. Priest, to Pedro
73. "___ pig's eye!"
74. Doughboys' successors
75. Smell ___
77. Creek
78. "That's a ___ on me!" said Tom freshly
82. "___," said Tom dramatically
86. "___," said Tom rhetorically
89. Gulf of Aqaba port
90. Dutch airline inits.
91. Roald or Arlene
92. Pallid
93. Mother Goose dieters
95. "___," said Tom ravenously
98. Adduce
99. Silent Pola
100. Early show
101. Sources of ruin
103. Exist
104. Kin of strep
106. Acerbic
108. Hearts
110. "___," said Tom playfully
113. "___," said Tom disarmingly
116. Brief note
117. A Reagan Attorney General
118. De Valera's republic
119. Make used to
120. Glut
121. Vermont town
122. Hire out
123. Trifled

DOWN

1. Fairy queen
2. "At once, ___, and yet a rose full-blown": Herrick
3. "___," said Tom gracefully
4. Coquettish
5. Progeny
6. Cloche, e.g.
7. King of comedy
8. Lake Erie city near Cleveland
9. Most favorable situations
10. Omega's predecessor
11. Magnetic one
12. ___ Alverio (Rita Moreno)
13. Run to seed
14. Complacent
15. Prepare fish
16. "___," said Tom automatically
17. Alley coup
18. Sweethearts
24. Encroached
26. Blunt refusal
29. "___," said Tom flatly
33. Sans others
35. Disney film: 1982
37. Employer
38. Grand in scope

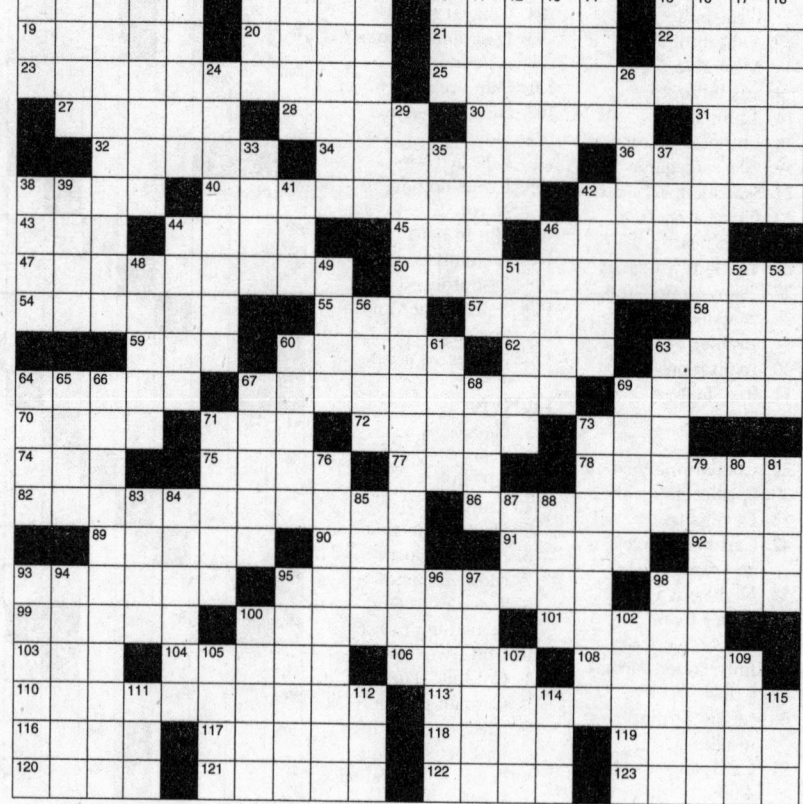

by Mel Taub

39. Me. city
41. Mont. neighbor
42. Bench penalties
44. Weasel's kin
46. Iron: Pref.
48. Famous
49. Special cop
51. Citizen Tom
52. Algerian neighbor
53. Pipe elbows
56. Bewail
60. Powerful person
61. Actress Conn
63. Donnybrook
64. Wise trio
65. Stairwell sign
66. "___," said Tom privately
67. Maugham's ___ Nesbit
68. Aba wearer
69. Ryan or Tatum
71. Snack-bar drinks
73. Red-handed
76. "___," said Tom dolefully
79. "___," said Tom sagely
80. All in order

81. Irish river
83. Winglike
84. Somewhat tardy
85. Romans' 156
87. Pledge of unity
88. Apparel
93. Symbols of sluggishness
94. Xerxes's realm
95. City near Vesuvius
96. McGuffey work
97. ___ olde England
98. Melville's "Benito ___"
100. Russell, Ball and Lansbury
102. Kind of game for Nolan Ryan
105. Like a pussycat
107. Asunder
109. Kind of bet
111. Minuscule
112. Waco nickname
114. Peevish fit
115. He's often raised

ACROSS

1. New Zealand native
6. J. F Cooper subject
11. Off the mark
16. Out of breath
17. Namibia's game preserve
19. Grow together
21. ___ million
22. Polluted waters at Port Said?
24. Draw forth
25. Bedouin's workout?
26. Start of a Hardy title
27. Lump of earth
28. Town near Steubenville, Ohio
29. Boot bottom
30. Corn or verse preceder
31. TV's Donahue
32. Bu. or pk.
34. To, to Burns
36. East Indian sailor
38. Yamamai's kin
39. N.L., M.V.P.: 1952
42. Pou ___ (vantage point)
45. Donne's geographical error?
49. Fairy-tale sign-off
51. Certain lodge members
52. Apt. house, e.g.
53. Lasso
54. Methuselah's claim to fame
56. Kindergartner
57. Coal scuttle
58. Alfonse's polite ami
59. Valentino?
65. He played Ashley
66. Violinist Bull
67. Moscow square
68. Toastmasters, for short
69. Sierra Nevada resort
70. Beersheba's region
72. Be philanthropic
74. ___ Yisrael (Palestine)
75. Title for an aged Islamic rancher?
79. Rembrandt's last name
80. Bentsen, for one
82. Function
83. Numbers each leaf or page
85. TV's Headroom
86. Swift Atl. plane
87. Decant
89. Cube root of eight

90. Opposite of wax
93. Cover story
97. He wrote "The Gremlins"
98. Noted Indian diplomat
99. Mideast mecca for star-gazers?
103. Trudges
105. Persian Gulf diet observers?
106. Orbital high point
107. Voted in
108. Tribute
109. Ind. hoopsters
110. Tire imprint
111. Natives of Ecbatana, e.g.
112. Some collars

DOWN

1. Philippine island
2. Artery disorder
3. Of a verse form
4. Coty or Clair
5. G. & S. princess
6. Fuel for a lorry
7. "___ to Be You," 1924 song
8. Leopold's codefendant
9. Bone: Comb. form
10. "___ in the Hat": Seuss
11. Needle-shaped
12. DCL doubled
13. "Not for these ___/ The song . . .": Wordsworth
14. Feeling, in Ferrara
15. Writer Germaine de ___
16. Sad
18. Wonderstruck
19. City on the Garonne
20. Ultimatum word
23. Tool for Bunyan
25. Common Muslim name
27. "Death on the Nile" author
31. Ill. coal city
32. Jackie's second
33. Impish
35. Noah's landfall
37. Where Arabian knights park their steeds?
38. Nanny has three
39. Saharan sights
40. Plus
41. Widmark's first film role
42. Radio annoyance

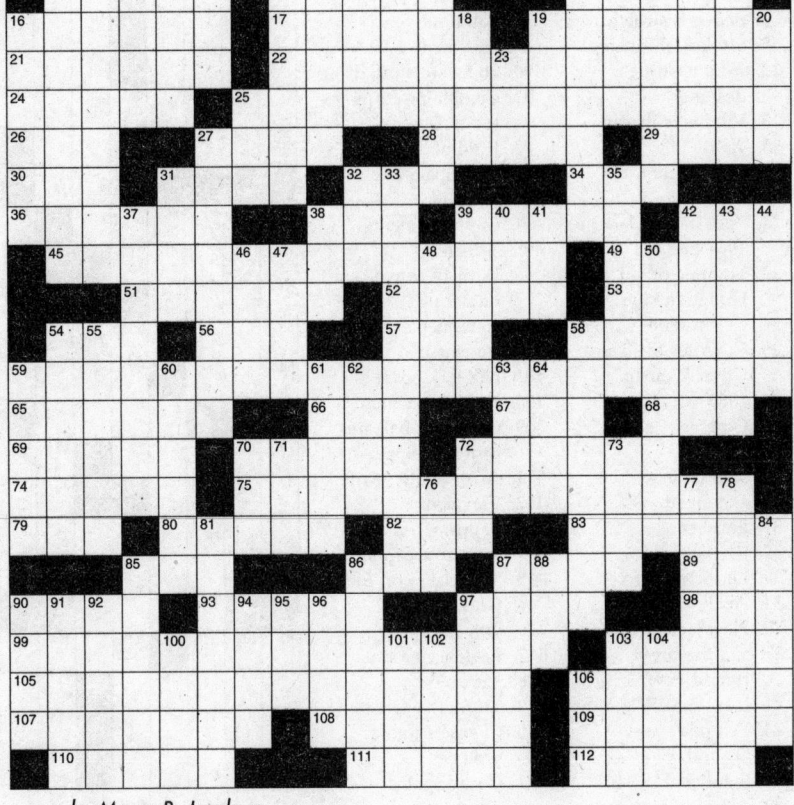

by Maura B. Jacobson

43. Grand ___ (Western range)
44. Chimp's cousin
46. Presently
47. Aardvark's diet
48. Peek
50. "Call me ___" (drowning Arab's cry?)
54. Tired, in poesy
55. A land of plenty
56. Terrible: Slang
59. Do tailoring
60. Granada gala
61. Navajo's home
62. Sch. before jr. high
63. Gator's kin
64. Comedian Jay
70. Nope
71. Estonian river
72. A.E.S. defeater
73. Son of Odin
76. D-day craft
77. Four-fifths of the atmosphere
78. Matronly ladies
81. Grand ___ Ruler (B.P.O.E. bigwig)
84. Winos

85. Threat
86. "Cheers," e.g.
87. Brief respites
88. Electrical unit
90. Finnegan's ___": Joyce
91. No longer a minor
92. More trendy
94. De ___ ("Green Pastures" role)
95. Balin or Claire
96. Alcott girl
97. Requiem
100. Mideast bread
101. Alas!
102. Scan the print
103. Tiff
104. Like crazy hombre
106. Rue Morgue murderer

ACROSS

1. Suffix with gab or song
5. Beaver's structure
8. Strokes of fortune
13. "Status stripe" designer
18. Vilnius is its cap.
19. At all
21. Composition for eight
22. "___ in the Dark," 1964 film
23. Tommie of Gil Hodges's Mets
24. Celebration
25. Cowriter of "The Other Woman": 1983
26. Gibe
27. Start of a statesman's statement
31. Early car
32. Rivulets
33. Lettuce type
34. Anchovy sauce
36. Haw's companion
37. ___ the press (brand new)
41. City in SW Ga.
44. Felt one's way around
48. Statement: Part II
50. More difficult to find
51. Strauss's "___ Italien"
52. Mutt and Jeff, e.g.
53. Land map
54. African ruler
55. C.P.A.
57. Wrinkle
58. Bretons or Britons
59. Statement: Part III
61. Shadow
62. "Diary of ___ Housewife"
64. Heavy-weight
65. "Abbey ___," Beatles album
66. Ephthalite
67. ___ about (approximately)
68. Double this for a Chilean river
71. Something to break
72. Tree house
73. Statement: Part IV
75. Healing: Comb. form
78. Rousseau hero
80. Skin
81. Differently
82. Juan's 2 Down
83. Burt Reynolds's ex
84. ___ Jose
85. Solid rain
86. Statement: Part V
90. Some are stuffed
91. Combining form for 10 Down
92. Kind of band
93. Participate in a langlauf
94. Circle segments
95. Adherent
96. With 15 Down, quoter of statesman's statement
101. N.Y.P.D. order
103. End of statement
109. Capital of Baleares province, Spain
111. Arrowsmith's wife
112. Carry on
113. Baptism, e.g.
114. Ancient weapon
115. "Luncheon on the Grass" artist
116. Tokyo tipple
117. Legless creature
118. Let up
119. Tripura or Orissa
120. Charlie's comic brother
121. Go up against

DOWN

1. Walking shoes
2. Shell crew
3. Mosshorn, e.g.
4. Soothing word
5. Vilified
6. Disinclined
7. Distribute
8. Regains consciousness
9. Maple genus
10. Nihala or Nunki
11. Actress Copley
12. Awkward try
13. Furniture feature
14. Springsteen's "Born in the ___"
15. See 96 Across
16. Shape of a hogan
17. "Leave ___ Beaver"
20. Extend onself
28. "Half Magic" author
29. Horn emanations
30. Toddlers' perches
35. Emulated Jessica
38. Out ___ (no longer available)
39. Thrash or thresh
40. Oliver Stone product
42. Med. student's subject
43. Top-level business gps.
44. Super
45. Stallone role
46. Mythical hunter
47. Where Machu Picchu is
48. Spiked the punch
49. Language of Picasso
55. Niels Bohr's subject
56. Place of worship
57. Reason
58. Rob Reiner's dad
60. Server
61. "___ of Riley," former TV sitcom
63. Humorist Sahl
67. Hero of the 1936 Olympics
68. Cotton packer
69. Atlas feature
70. He wrote "Night Music"
71. Braggart
72. Curtain fabric
74. Lunchmeat emporium
75. Little bit
76. Bonn expletives
77. "You Turned ___ on Me," 1936 song
79. Marquand's sleuth
80. Hopper and Turner
84. Hide the loot
85. Glow
87. Doomed area in a Chekhov play
88. ___ Bud, a Dickens heroine
89. Flatter, in a way
90. Evaded
93. Elegant
97. Fabulous fiddle
98. Potboiler's product
99. "___ Africa," 1985 Oscar winner
100. Penurious
101. Cathedral section
102. Haydn's nickname
104. Attorneys' degs.
105. Accomplishment
106. O'Neill's daughter
107. Worry
108. Author of "The Valachi Papers"
110. West of Hollywood

by Shirley Soloway

ACROSS

1. Rudimentary
6. Sacred choral piece
11. Scrooge's invectives
15. Scalawags
21. January, in Juárez
22. Massenet's forte
23. Petroleum cartel inits.
24. Shoulder-to-elbow bones
25. SILVER
28. Rubbed with rubber
29. Sinker
30. Inn's descendant
31. Robert Burns's one
33. Leaking radiator's sound
34. Self-important person
36. Nipa palm
38. Escorted anew
40. Convert into cipher
42. Ferrigno and Rawls
44. Two-toed sloth
46. Put down
47. Vega or Rigel
48. Preceders of xi's
51. KRYPTON
56. Discernment
58. ___ of iniquity
59. Brewer's need
60. Bireme gear
62. Depend (on)
63. Collapsed, with "in"
66. Oriental units of weight
68. Ring up
70. Greek goddesses of the seasons
71. Petri-dish contents
72. Ciro ___, 17th-century Italian painter
73. Bagel-like roll
74. Mortise's partner
75. Hero of "Giants in the Earth"
76. Classify
77. Intones
79. Woe
80. Undefiled
82. Pointillist's prop
83. Printing machine operators
86. Simone's school
87. Undeveloped state
88. Bloody Mary's daughter
89. Apt anagram of aye
90. Swizzles
91. La ___, Milano's opera house
92. Concede
94. Raison d' ___
95. Holmes's creator
96. Where Hercules slew the Hydra
97. Service club
98. Moral nature
99. Mil. truant
100. Dish list
101. Ear: Comb. form
102. Cariou or Deighton
103. Maligns
105. NEON
113. Celestial sphere
114. One of Manhattan's rivers
116. To's companion
117. Getz or Kenton
118. Positive
119. Ef, e.g.
121. ___ cum laude
124. Painting and poetry, e.g.
126. Oomph
127. Dutch or French follower
128. Catch in the act
130. University in Oxford, Ohio
132. Civil War general
134. Like a solarium
136. IRON
141. Mustard-family vegetable
142. Cannel
143. Cove
144. Take flight to unite
145. One of the Furies
146. Brontë's Jane
147. Idyllic spots
148. Actress Spacek

DOWN

1. ___ canto
2. Upward: Comb. form
3. Sentences
4. Mars: Comb. form
5. Doone of fiction
6. Super Bowl M.V.P.: 1990
7. Aperture: Abbr.
8. Rain cats and dogs
9. Boo-boo
10. Sapor
11. Kind of algebra
12. Eliot's cruelest mo.
13. "___ Rebel," 1962 tune
14. Bergman's "___ from a Marriage"
15. TV spy film of 1980
16. Computer-display pointers
17. "...the way of a man with ___": Proverbs
18. MERCURY
19. Fraternity V.I.P.
20. Caesar or Luckman
26. "___ in New York," 1935 song
27. Greece, to Greeks
32. Full
34. Hirt and Jolson
35. Trifle
37. Roast or roaster
39. Henna, e.g.
41. Preserves
43. Passover feast
45. End of a Poe title
49. Prussian cavalryman
50. Eye problem
52. Rubicund
53. COPPER
54. Disks for a dee-jay
55. Adz and awl
57. Perfume additives
61. Word with body and way
63. "Li'l Abner" cartoonist
64. Ripening device
65. PLATINUM
66. Coat with an alloy of tin and lead
67. Funnyman Johnson
68. Covered with evergreens
69. IODINE
70. Knock over a joint
72. Discomfits
73. Iraqi port
74. Doctor
76. Squirrel away
78. "¿___ Usted español?"
79. Beams
81. Herb of the lily family
83. Blueprint
84. A first name in architecture
85. Dundee denials
87. Oysters' hues
90. Seed planter
91. E.M.K. is one
93. Muddies the waters
94. Lab burners
95. Pedestal part
96. Diminish
97. Sand's "Elle et ___"
98. "Frae morn to ___..."
100. Headcheese, e.g.
101. Social disintegration
102. Archway element
104. Maker of verses
106. Conditions
107. Grouse
108. Thespian Hagen
109. Woodchucks
110. Black gums
111. Bismuth, e.g.
112. Corded fabric
115. Hypnotic state
120. Borne by the wind
122. Singer Osmond
123. Better
125. Strongboxes
127. Double
129. Keep afloat
131. Inactive
133. When Yazdegerd III died
134. Mme., in Madrid
135. However, for short
137. Deface
138. Four-star off.
139. Periods of prosperity
140. Turhan ___, 40's film actor

by John Greenman

418   LAW-SCHOOL DROPOUT

ACROSS

1. Norwegian saint
5. Utter
10. World toter
15. Put away
19. Painter of "Aurora"
20. Trunk
21. ___ Vista, Mexican War battle site
22. Put an edge on
23. What are contracts?
25. If you pass the bar, what will it mean?
27. Birthplace of Columbus
28. Marner of Lapham
30. Pined
31. ___ Aires
33. Skid-row denizens
34. Cans, in Canterbury
35. Heraldic design
36. Presently
37. Kind of spoon
41. Dips
42. Which former female arbiter do you most admire?
45. Wine: Comb. form
46. Individualist
47. Mr. Flintstone
48. Bible book
49. Couple
50. Cahn-Styne product
51. Name at least one historic trial
55. Choreographer-director from Chicago
56. Cancels
58. Arab nobleman
59. Yosemite National Park river
60. A poplar
61. Takes off the cream
62. Pace
63. Tooth problem
65. Ill will
66. Out of the ordinary
69. Singer of "Stop the Music" fame
70. What is a talesman?
73. Refrain word
74. Arikaras
75. Kind of plane or dynamics
76. Grandmother of Timothy
77. Banking game
78. Lodge
79. What's equity?
83. Uses a kitchen appliance
84. Umpire's command
86. Kind of deck
87. Bits for Benji
88. Drenched
89. Horse follower
90. Be a witness
92. Where filets are often ruined
95. I.Q. tester
96. Spanish ice-skating figures
97. Define statutes
99. Name a prominent former court figure
104. Florence's river
105. Silly
106. Lustrous
107. Weaving need
108. Kind of drop
109. Lebanese tree
110. River and lake in Scotland
111. Crosses out

DOWN

1. Scepter's adjunct
2. Irish Neptune
3. Black bird
4. Nervous Nellie
5. Exec's brain, on occasion
6. Roads scholars
7. Silkworm
8. Apocryphal bk.
9. "The Barber of Seville" composer
10. Tasty mollusk
11. Helicons
12. "___ is more": Browning
13. Hill maker
14. Liner schedules
15. Chinese province
16. Go oystering
17. Erstwhile
18. Cull
24. Heredity determiners
26. Present
29. Party to
31. Prep cap
32. What exactly is a brief?
33. Emerson's middle name
34. Henry VIII was one
37. Sometimes it's ugly
38. Quitclaim is a deed, name some others
39. Rent
40. Over
41. Bank transaction
42. Originate
43. Soak flax or lumber
44. "The Golden Bowl" author
47. Heaters
49. African villages
51. Dutch genre painter
52. Dervish
53. Peaceful harmony
54. Convened anew
55. Our largest bone
57. "___ Irish Rose"
59. Biblical wall words
61. Game trail
62. Spring bloom
63. Brazilian Indian
64. Knockout of a place
65. Perk up a straightedge
67. Halt
68. Asian nation
70. Arrangement
71. Marry modestly
72. Costello or Groza
75. Puzzle variety
77. Damaged-goods rendition
79. Famed fabulist
80. "Faerie Queene" poet
81. Away
82. Cyrano's creator
83. Chopper part
85. Who starts the most suits?
89. City near Assisi
90. "Body all ___": O. Hammerstein
91. Dull sounds
92. Scholastic test, for short
93. Israeli port
94. Fish or pear
95. Finishing nail
96. Schenk or Harbach
98. One, in Paris
100. Cruise port, for short
101. Boston or Chicago team
102. Weeder
103. Bad ___, German spa

by Bert H. Kruse

ACROSS

1. Served perfectly
5. River in E. France
10. Part of a Latin paradigm
14. Competent
18. Rich fabric
19. Muster
20. Major Joppolo's post
21. Wampum item
22. Disco queen Summer?
24. Nicaraguan music makers?
26. Pledge
27. "Ici on ___ français"
29. Sham
30. Enameled metalware
31. Like Modigliani's "Reclining Nude"?
33. You're on one now!
36. Stair part
38. Old name of the Bulgarian port called Varna
42. "___-porridge hot . . ."
43. Obtuse
44. Fortunetelling card
46. City in E. Brazil
47. Violinist Kavafina
48. Int. group established in 1948
49. Song from "A Chorus Line"
50. Supercilious person
51. Orch. section
52. J.P.'s office?
58. Jewish month
59. Strict disciplinarian
61. Author of "The Making of a Surgeon"
62. Akin on the father's side
64. Upbeat, in music
65. Like some seals
66. Oneness
67. Least moist
69. Latin American dance music
70. Warehouse
73. Singer Stevens
74. Like a confirmed bachelor?
77. Nice article
78. Eager
79. Menuhin's title
80. Erwin or Symington
81. Diarist Anaïs ___
82. Fortify
83. Type of type
85. Rowdydow
87. Name in 1921 headlines
89. "X" math?
91. Play a higher card
92. German city on Belgium's border
93. Memo from rock singer Slick?
96. West Point mascot
97. Mite, e.g.
100. He doesn't like company
101. Clique
104. Gen. Jaruzelski and Lech Walesa?
106. Sock in the mouth?
109. Give forth
110. Baritone role in "I Pagliacci"
111. Sappho's Muse
112. Part of a pitchfork
113. Star in reverse?
114. Old Icelandic poetry
115. Sorrow
116. Kin of etc.

DOWN

1. Eisenhut, e.g.
2. Cavil
3. Arabian prince
4. Reduces in rank
5. Chancel seat
6. Win by ___ (inch ahead)
7. Writer Sarah ___ Jewett
8. ___ compos mentis
9. Goes by
10. Gustaf ___, former Swedish king
11. Painter of "Olympia"
12. Formicary denizen
13. Underwater projectile
14. Head of a convent
15. Brummell or Bridges
16. Cry from a crow's-nest
17. Edible corm of the taro
20. Stinging to the taste
23. Tosca's emotion
25. Valuable possession
28. Cries of triumph
32. Are they to the manor born?
33. Involuntary muscular contraction
34. Five: Comb. form
35. Like minoxidil?
36. Paine or Mather product
37. Reckless
39. Weekend libation?
40. One of Tirpitz's vessels
41. Buffalo man in a rink
43. Shelters for sheep
44. Not live
45. Shortly
50. "À votre ___!"
52. Sound of escaping steam
53. Components of monograms
54. Totally
55. Vikings
56. Faint light
57. Aunt, in Arles
60. Cornered
63. Encircle
65. This bore may cause excitement
66. Improper
67. Ibsen's forte
68. Competitor
69. Pique
70. Stage direction
71. In readiness
72. Companion of a mortise
75. Writer Singer
76. Archipelago unit
83. Dugouts
84. Arrange in degrees
85. Cornea irritant
86. Turned inside out
87. Dried tubers of orchids
88. Needle-shaped
90. Wading birds
91. Portuguese money of account
92. Glasgow or London
94. Impala's big cousin
95. Water wheel
96. Words to live by
97. Unoriginal person
98. Robin Cook novel
99. Finished parasailing
101. Pea or egg follower
102. "___ Really Me?": 1963 song
103. Suburb of Pittsburgh
105. School of whales
107. Relative of plata
108. Anguineous fish

by Jeanette K. Brill

420 TITLE SEARCH

ACROSS

1. Encourages a felon
6. Constantine slept here
11. Portrait sculpture
15. Printer's dot
16. Musical direction
17. "King ___ Road," 1965 song
19. Castro's predecessor
20. See 67 Across
23. Toothed: Comb. form
24. Maternally related
26. Yorkshire city
27. Month for lovers
28. C times XXXV
29. Zwei follower
30. Vesicle
31. Prefix for puncture
32. Ray
33. See 67 Across
38. Con
39. Suffix used by physicists
40. The 23rd Hebrew letter
41. "Fawlty Towers" star
42. Hypocritical talk
44. Melody
46. Spinning devices
47. Backward, nautically
50. Duroc's home
53. Tibetan monk
55. City on the Loire
58. Scrooge word
59. Wind of S. France
62. Ego
64. Former Spanish enclave in Morocco
65. Kind of sch.
67. Heart of the matter
69. Dispatch
70. Star's car
71. Greet
72. Dolt
74. Sign of triumph
75. Scaly crust
77. Buddies
79. Carrie or Louis
80. Playground time
82. Jazz dance
84. Ursula Andress film
86. Isinglass
87. Gun aimed at a bomber
89. Capp and Capone
91. Daisy ___ Scraggs
92. Mezzo Stevens
96. See 67 Across
101. Perfume measure
102. Bridle part
103. Wine experts' comb. form
104. Earthquake site: June 21, 1990
105. Grimace
106. Super serve
107. Base Gehrig covered
109. Some Renoir paintings
111. Thrice minus twice
112. See 67 Across
116. More drippy, as paste
118. A sister of Eunomia
119. Pupils' locales
120. Jubilant
121. Pipe part
122. Ethyl acetate, e.g.
123. Gulls

DOWN

1. Self-service restaurant
2. See 67 Across
3. Certain railways
4. Parisian head
5. Top-notch performer
6. Nonbeliever
7. Map abbr.
8. Sitter's feature
9. One of the Waughs
10. Least batty
11. Movie Messala
12. Sky sightings: Abbr.
13. P.O. item
14. See 67 Across
15. Outlaws
16. Paravane
18. Puts up
19. Pump, in Peru
21. Meadowlands team
22. Obloquy
25. Calla, e.g.
30. Kind of servant
33. Language of Helsinki
34. Motorists' org.
35. Like a street after sleet
36. Worker's rights org.
37. Part of Asia Minor
43. Branch
45. How madcaps act
46. Corolla part
47. Actor Walter and family
48. Of a Frankish people
49. See 67 Across
50. Narrow furrow
51. Joan Sutherland specialties
52. Gab
54. Ballerina Park
56. Writer of suspense tales
57. Teams
60. Olivia of the Met
61. Guided
63. Harbor sights
66. Human
68. Large cask
73. Ten: Comb. form
76. Centers of attention
78. Plumed hat
81. See 67 Across
83. Trading place: Abbr.
85. Big name in New Haven
86. Affected
87. Facing the pitcher
88. Pretentious
90. Brandy-based cocktail
91. Hoover Dam's lake
93. Satires' cousins
94. Tipsy
95. Eastern V.I.P.
97. Legal wrong
98. Nielsen or Uggams
99. Comes onstage
100. Bind tightly
107. Exquisite
108. Gossip tidbit
110. Sea in the W. Pacific
113. Permit
114. Fruit center
115. Expert ending
117. Carpet feature

by Nancy Scandrett Ross

ACROSS

1. Rawboned person
6. Created
10. Textile city in N. France
16. But
19. Put to the test
20. "When I was ___...": W.S. Gilbert
21. Banana kin
23. Randan implement
24. Song for market tip that bombed?
26. Song for late Oct. 1929?
27. Southwest Indian
28. Tied
29. Pew accessory
31. Polanski film
32. Correspond
34. Influenced
35. Author of "The Fountainhead"
36. Debussy opus
38. Pincers
39. "I begin to smell ___": Cervantes
41. Located
42. Bach's "___ of Fugue"
44. Song for a broker's day?
49. Type of volcanic crater
50. Unbend
53. Value
54. Nobelist Wiesel
55. Gospel
58. ___ of Good Feeling: 1817–24
59. Kingly
60. Insincere language
61. Barley beard
62. Singer John
64. Arabian Sea gulf
65. Puts a new cover on a book
67. Sirius or Vega
68. Dr. Seuss's Thidwick
69. Cannonballed
70. Tokyo, formerly
71. "I Promessi ___," Manzoni novel
73. Swabbed
74. Hopeful plunger's song?
79. Brings forth
83. "___ Chan," T.N. Page story
84. Free electron
85. R.b.i. is one
89. Actress Irene from Greece
90. Bus station
92. Largest of the Galapagos
95. What esse means
96. Habituate
97. Film on bronze
99. Harold of Tin Pan Alley
100. Down Under lumberman
101. Wood shaper
102. Hit man or hero
104. Largest natural lake in Wales
105. Dürer's "Paumgartner ___"
106. Topple a tower
108. Palestine plant
109. Takeover song?
113. Slow mover
115. Refrain in old songs
116. Anti votes
117. Too
119. Cartouches
120. Dance
122. Bill
125. Pace
126. Attend Choate
128. Mercury's winged sandals
130. Clouseau's servant
131. Item stored in a buttery
132. Insider's song?
135. Bullish investor's song?
137. Kennel adjunct
138. Artificial
139. Actress Thompson
140. Longest modern note
141. Nationwide mil. instruction
142. Give the ___ (fire)
143. Very, in Lyon
144. More eccentric

DOWN

1. Barker's come-on
2. Desire fiercely
3. Did some ranch work
4. Eden's earldom
5. Set
6. Business tycoon
7. Outlander
8. Stunned
9. A biographer of Henry James
10. Everything
11. Snack-bar drink
12. Actress Stevens: 1934–70
13. French summers
14. Former D.C. team
15. Kinsman
16. Song for bluechip stocks?
17. Cafe patron
18. Dilo and dita
21. Henry Morgan was one
22. Antelope of E. Africa
25. Gumbos
30. Beethoven's "Für ___"
33. Carpenter's heavy beam
37. Wilbur concern
38. Balzac's "Le ___ Goriot"
39. Secret
40. Cambodia's monetary unit
41. Agitated states
42. Nile delta city
43. Ishmael's mother
44. Small herring
45. Hives
46. River in W. Africa
47. Manatee
48. Humerus neighbor
49. Aromatic resin
51. Rebelled
52. Faded
56. "___ d'arte," Puccini aria
57. Defective new auto
60. Ghanaian money
61. Consort of Pericles
63. Truncate
65. N.F.L. "zebras"
66. Danish weights
72. Placer material
73. Polynesian's supernatural force
74. Relative of a gore
75. Emulated Pearl White
76. Fast
77. Wintry
78. Weak-eyed worm hunter
79. Hoplite's weapon
80. Ling-Ling, for one
81. King of Siam's song for Wall St.?
82. What Aristophanes called "Area'chick"
85. Poles for some clowns
86. Silverheels role
87. Right-angled to a keel
88. "___ Promise": Maurois
90. Bender
91. Acuminate
93. "The Sheik of ___," 1921 song
94. Tree trunk
98. "Drake" poet
100. Summon, in a way
103. Dionysus specialty
104. Sac or city once sacked by Tatars
107. O.K. Corral figure
110. Emulated Red Jacket
111. Some of the Iroquoians
112. Without face value, as stocks
114. Dejection
115. Banish
117. Port city on Hokkaido
118. Soft palate
119. Confused struggle
120. Philippine Island
121. Occupation
122. Subdued
123. "The stag ___...": Scott
124. Shipworm
126. Catcher Tony
127. Harangue
129. Register
130. Wag
133. Badger
134. Avant-gardist
136. Oil-yielding tropical tree

by Edward Marchese

ACROSS

1. Castile
5. Ontario tribesmen
10. N.Y.C. river
16. Piece of cake
17. Novelist Troyat
18. Birdman
20. CUPID
22. Hurdle
24. Farrell's knee bend
25. Peter and a Wolfe
26. "The Perfect Fool" composer
28. Prime-time time
29. Small "small"
30. Canary's cousin
31. Label anew
33. Athenian vowel
34. Asunder
36. Spruce
38. TV bee
39. Poor surfer
41. Voice
43. "Santa Claus Is Watching You" singer
45. Indeed
46. Rats!
48. They were: Lat.
49. Tower of Bombay
50. Alluded
54. Old age, of old
55. VIXEN
58. European capital
59. Oder tributary
61. In holiday spirits
62. Behold, to Brutus
63. Western lizard
64. DANCER
66. Jacky
67. Mild oath
69. Catcher Tony
70. Shelved
72. Convex moldings
73. Transient things
75. Marble
76. Abstruse
78. Ferric
79. Dr. Salk
81. John, in Cardiff
82. William Conrad role
84. Zingers
86. Ham
90. Swiss sledder
91. Bastes
92. Hang behind
94. Likely
95. "Artie" author
96. Tape over
98. Soft-palate projection
100. Divinity deg.
101. Letter opener
103. White poplar
105. Useful
106. A sister of Europa
107. Nov. 11 honoree
109. DASHER
112. Conspicuous
113. Propose
114. Mold
115. Where Virgil wrote the "Georgics"
116. Rating symbols
117. Focal points

DOWN

1. Suchlike
2. Third of thrice
3. French explorer in Colonial America
4. Modern medium
5. Dijon darlings
6. Resound
7. One of Eve's grandsons
8. White-tailed bird
9. Deep breath
10. COMET
11. Parsees' sacred writings
12. Cowboy's rope
13. Pomeranian's place
14. Lord Wimsey's alma mater
15. DONNER (popular variant of Donder)
16. Islamic leader
19. Charter car
20. Panel strip
21. "Sunny" composer
23. Psyched up
27. Praying gure
30. Brenda of comics
32. Belgian port
35. Copland ballet
37. Missionaries of Charity founder
38. Remedy
40. Ponti cal cape
42. Lake in a cirque
44. RUDOLPH
45. Biography
47. Wobbling
49. Kind of cross
50. Roulette bet
51. Bar, to a barrister
52. BLITZEN
53. An aunt of Princess Beatrice
55. Swiss canton (former spelling)
56. Mites
57. Adapted to the desert
60. Mme., in Madrid
61. Male cat

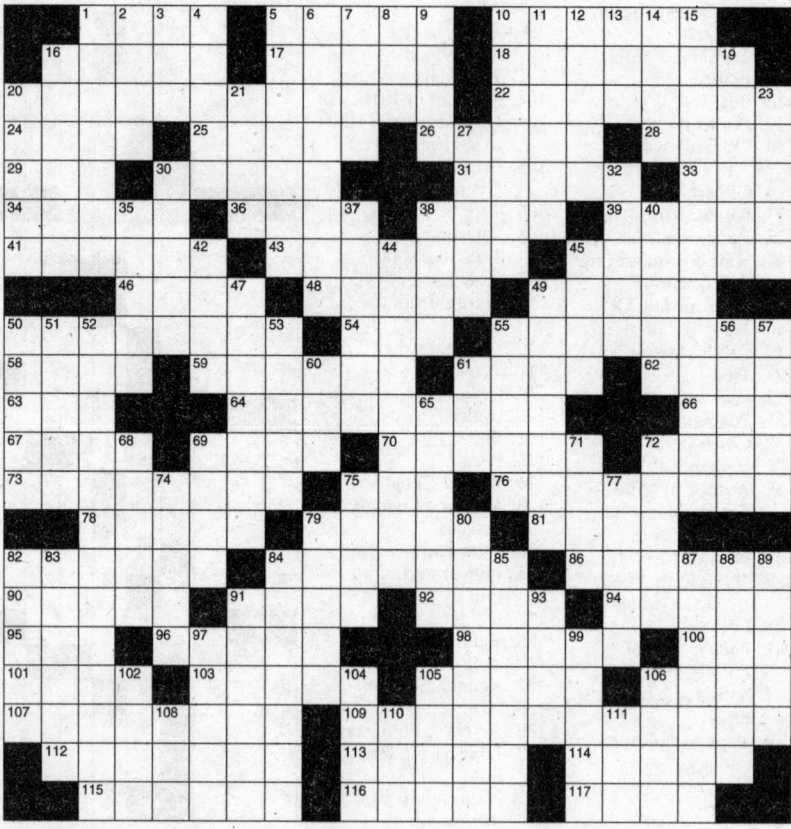

by John M. Samson

65. Garment for Geraint
68. City in the Ruhr region
69. Keystone State's eponym
71. "Paci c" bird
72. Substance
74. "Santa Claus" star
75. Epigrams
77. Super Bowl XVIII site
79. Pink Panther, e.g.
80. PRANCER
82. Caliber
83. I.R.S. inquiries
84. Bristles
85. Deliverers
87. Even choices
88. Plenary
89. Forti cation
91. E. Texas river
93. Abyss
97. Badgerlike mammal
99. Trammel of a sort
102. Reception room
104. Heroic verse
105. City in SE Turkey
106. Husband of Jezebel
108. Torn or Taylor
110. Sternward
111. Philosopher ___ Hsi

ACROSS

1. West Coast nine
7. Juniper
12. He cameth before the refrigerator
18. Apply chrism
19. Intimidate
22. Comb. form for 12
23. Mozart's bride in 1782
25. Frittata, e.g.
26. A deadly sin
27. Unsubstantial
28. Mental inventions
30. Mansard borders
32. Diarized
34. Comes earlier than
38. Arithmetical sign
39. Incongruity
44. Outlying
45. Mecca for turiste
47. Dessert choice
48. Thought: Comb. form
49. Calcar
50. Italian town or gulf
52. Roman historian
53. Boxlike sleigh
54. Absquatulated
57. Alpha, beta and gamma
58. Man's slipper
59. Esculents
61. Bolt-head sides
62. Niblick sockets
63. Invocational figure
64. Rambler mfr.
65. Standoffish
67. Mathematically validated
70. Dike, Eunomia and Irene
72. Balloon cabin
75. Salieri, to Mozart
76. Kin of "By Jove!"
77. Rostrum
78. Lurch
80. Uniform
81. Pine cone
84. Grown-up chigger
85. Set of three
86. Sounds at a shower
87. Gula and cyma
89. Reserves
91. Stipulations in a contract
93. ___ the Impaler (15th-century Romanian prince)
94. Butter makers
96. Of a Mesolithic cultural stage
98. Conductor Walter
99. Rouen rooms
102. Harsh; bleak
103. Offensive odor
108. Radio's "___ the Magician"
109. Mozart opera: 1791
113. Tin and lead alloy
114. Racine tragedy: 1691
115. Home of Abraham
116. Velarium, e.g.
117. Teams of horses
118. Emulated Red Jacket

DOWN

1. S. American rodent
2. Shortly
3. Vietnamese monetary unit
4. Upheave
5. Importune
6. Dep.
7. Most comfortable
8. Tinker's target
9. ". . . ___-feather'd sleep": Milton
10. "We ___ the World"
11. Mortar-mixing tool
12. Mozart opera: 1781
13. Dermal blemish
14. Whence the Pison flowed
15. Deliquesce
16. Tops
17. Actor Pendleton
20. Certain fabrics
21. Where Perry triumphed
24. Wheel hub
29. Millet
31. Bolted
32. Film featuring Mozart's Piano Concerto No. 21
33. Nudnik or buttinsky
34. Buttress
35. "George White's Scandals," e.g.
36. Correct
37. Mozart opera: 1787
38. Through, for each
40. "Amadeus" director
41. Stop on ___
42. Demolish
43. Vacillates
46. Punty or mandrel
47. Short segment
51. Nautical chain
54. Spanish custard
55. Actor Cariou
56. Williams and Ralston
58. Crucifix
60. Chanteur Jacques ___
61. Plane curve
62. Nene cry
66. Chilean stream
67. Disturbed
68. Moon or Spoon
69. Unconcealed
71. U.S. satellite
73. French area, rich in coal
74. Permute
77. Apoidea member
79. Slighter
81. Mozart's birthplace: Jan. 27, 1756
82. Possessive adjective
83. Conducted
88. Sopherim
89. Phoebus
90. Suggest; volunteer
92. Whitman died here: 1892
93. Call on
95. Scottish philosopher: 1711–76
97. Wife of Tyndareus
98. Bobby Orr was one
99. Use maxilla and mandible
100. A "Shampoo" star
101. Oppositionist
102. Jamboree
104. Its chief town is Portoferraio
105. Illegality
106. Western Indian
107. Lacerate
108. Acct., often
110. Querying sounds
111. Use a ray gun
112. Between pi and sigma

by Jack L. Steinhardt

424 COMBINING FORMS

ACROSS

1. Spoil
6. Step on
11. Gator's relative
15. Unfurnished
19. One of the 400
20. Nomad
21. Amonasro's daughter
22. Alt.
23. Kind of accompaniment
25. Engender
27. Distant actor?
28. Around an attorney?
29. Comprehend
30. Collector from John Q.
32. Bell sound
33. Pinnacles
37. Decree by Hussein, e.g.
40. Santa's bane?
42. Total
43. Harness parts
44. A cause of mental and physical disturbances
45. Sea anemone or hydra
47. Shortened form, for short
48. One-tenth of a musician-comic?
50. Silica gem
54. Von Richthofen's title
56. Refuges of sorts
57. Concocted
58. Duffer's curving drive
59. In the center of
61. Hawaiian goose
62. King and Newton
63. Position Jackie Robinson usually played
65. Ling-Ling, e.g.
67. Head nun
68. Emerges
69. Diet
70. Championships
72. Octad in a gallon
73. Narrow opening
74. Corn or oat follower
76. Tennessee ___ Ford
79. Wise brush?
80. Very small country singer?
82. Mardi Gras, e.g.
83. Burdened
86. Talks back
87. Some small dogs, for short
88. Part of a barn
91. An amphibian
92. Phoenix's source of rebirth
93. Screenwriter Lehman
94. Mexican president: 1851–53
96. J. Wilbrand's discovery: 1863
97. Sault ___ Marie
98. Bad Christie character?
101. Deficiency of a designer?
109. European annual herbs
110. Earned 10%, perhaps
111. Lotion ingredient
112. Weight
113. Williams of "Happy Days"
114. Entirety
115. Units on space vehicles
116. J.F.K. sights
117. "Brigadoon" composer
118. Pledged

DOWN

1. A social grace
2. "Norma ___," Glaspell novel
3. Eur. country
4. Good reply to a dope pusher
5. Locks
6. Treasure follower
7. Columnist Barrett
8. Course for a horse
9. Kind of ton
10. Soviet committees
11. Cockney family in comics
12. Laughter, in Lyon
13. Balm or spice
14. Building burned by British: 1814
15. Initiated
16. Home of many Tlingits
17. Stated again
18. Leveled
24. Norma and Charlotte
26. Friendship
31. Supplied troops again
33. Jezebel's husband
34. Acronym for a sunscreen ingredient
35. Activity at a joyful reunion
36. Dry comic?
37. Like krypton
38. "Jailhouse ___," Presley hit
39. Coalition in 1941
40. Hammett figure
41. Slow flow
44. Rehan and Neilson
46. More than one actress?
49. A Darling dog
51. Harmless reptile of N.A.
52. Bullets, in poker
53. An end to motion
55. Yarborough's top cards
58. Marten
60. A.D.A. member
61. Dallas-to-Tulsa dir.
62. Thai temple
63. Enervates
64. Term for a worm
65. Bread, in Brest
66. Anagram for Sinatra
69. "In Like ___," 1967 Coburn film
70. Darnels
71. Escapees from a mythical box
73. Cousin of a hootamaganzy
74. Grill or grid
75. Sybarite's delight
77. Parts of La France
78. Port side when sailing south
81. Arcadian
84. Piers
85. Famines
87. Arranges beforehand
88. Man is one
89. Troupial
90. "___ is humble . . .": Cowper
93. Followers of zetas
95. Pochards
96. Probes
97. Type of stealer
99. Slapstick staples
100. Bridle hand
102. Comic Jay ___
103. ___ dixit
104. Accrete
105. Brumal blanket
106. "Tell ___ the Marines!"
107. ___ Islands (Attu et al.)
108. Slothful

by Robert H. Wolfe

ACROSS

1. Agreed
6. Jam
10. Imprecates
15. Enforce
21. Papal cape
22. Loathsome one
23. Walking ___ (gleeful)
24. Planetarium
25. "Roar of the Bull" author?
27. "The Office Machine" author?
29. Purfles
30. Mortgage
31. "Mercure" composer
32. Choose
33. Comprehend
34. Dull surface
35. Holy Roman emperors
36. Bonnet item
37. Russian lake
40. Memorable stutterer
41. Hershfield's "___ the Agent"
42. Scads of money
43. Healer's org.
46. Sport of a sort
48. "Cooler in July" author?
51. Astronaut Shepard
52. Street shows
53. Composer-singer: 1936–73
55. Crooked
56. Impression
57. Jetson's dog
58. Thesaurus man
59. Helps a hood
60. Near the hip
61. Roman despot
62. Baldwin-Wallace locale
63. Reproductive cell
64. Kind of sale
65. Actress Joanne
66. "Too Hot to Handle" author?
68. More unruffled
69. Keaton or Baker
71. Fragrant loop
72. Nosed
73. Attentive
75. "Living with Elsa" author?
80. Dummy's pair
83. Dismays
84. Hyenas' homes
85. Day centers
86. Inhale
87. ___ a pig (obese)
88. Guillemot
89. Mythical hold-up man
90. Billiards immortal
91. Fire fodder
92. Pay to play
93. Like Harvard Yard's walls
94. King or Lombard
95. Site of the first Olympics
96. "The Onion Row" author?
98. Greyhound's small look-alike
99. Retreat
100. Tear
101. To be, in Paris
102. Irish assembly
103. Alpine road
104. ___ glance (instantly)
105. Roman shade
107. Painter of jockeys
108. Bustle
111. V.P. under G.R.F.
112. ___ nous
113. Straighten
114. Melville book
118. "The Apple of My Eye" author?
121. "Beaches" author?
123. Explosive containing TNT
124. Climbing plant
125. Commedia dell' ___
126. Daunted
127. Dub again
128. Disclosed
129. Act
130. Lock

DOWN

1. Banter
2. Dies ___
3. Creator of the "Oz" books
4. Pipe elbows
5. Society gal
6. Better mannered
7. Shoelace tags
8. Witch
9. London's ___ Gardens
10. Gift
11. Not this one
12. Cuomo or Lanza
13. City NW of Marseille
14. Mrs., in Mexico
15. Vie
16. Emulates Demosthenes
17. Silkworm
18. Electric units
19. Native Canadian
20. Explorer of Australia
26. Gladdens
28. Unowned
31. Amen
34. San ___, Calif.
37. Ropelike piece
38. Hit man
39. "A Beer is a Beer" author?
41. "It's ___ day for the Irish"
42. Ex ___ (one-sided)
43. "Vatican Days" author?
44. Cope
45. Stag's weapon
47. Of aircraft
49. African republic
50. Jugs
51. Actress Renée of silents
53. Dante illustrator
54. Time, e.g.
58. Nonconformist
59. Shower time
60. S.A. Indian
62. Honorarium
63. Litigants
64. Rudiments
66. Lots
67. Trumpet sound
68. Teams of horses
70. Perfect types
73. Emulated the nursery wolf
74. Shoulder, in Sedan
75. Magna ___
76. Personnel director
77. Unimpaired
78. Dover delicacy
79. Backpack
81. Box elders, e.g.
82. Darling
84. Dueler's move
86. Hamlet
88. Makeup item
89. Reluctant
90. Salutes
93. Served in a hospital
94. ___ Kai-shek
96. Adjective for a morel
97. Principal mass of a tooth
98. Bet
100. Redeem
102. Set apart
105. Press, TV, etc.
106. Sadat
107. Plow inventor
108. Not in harmony
109. Title Christie held
110. Arabian gulf
114. To dare, in Durango
115. Confusing network
116. People
117. Track concerns
119. J.F.K. listing
120. Belli's deg.
121. Wander idly
122. Newt

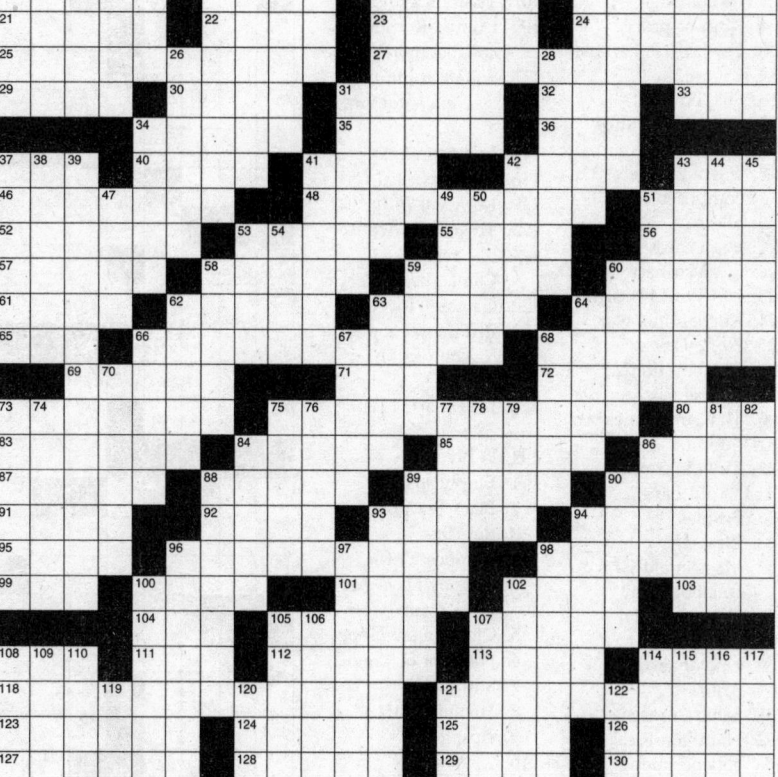

by Bert H. Kruse

ACROSS

1. Germany's Otto ___ Bismarck
4. Kind of prof.
8. Lewis's Timberlane
12. Excuse
16. Shaped
17. "___ Kick Out of You"
18. "Gypsy Love" composer
20. File
21. High cards
22. ___ Marmara
23. Old World lizard
24. Kitchen follower
25. Stone-Day collaboration?
29. Coarse silk
30. That, in Cannes
31. Inhibit
32. Tiny, in Scotland
33. "Auld Lang ___"
36. Besides
38. Elsa, e.g.
42. MacDonald-Graves collaboration?
46. Volcano crater
49. Asian weight
50. One of seven: Abbr.
51. Saharan ridges
52. Hamilton-Rice collaboration?
58. Sophia or Isabel
59. Actress Alicia
60. Wilder's "___ Town"
61. Keddah, e.g.
65. Warren-Kingsley collaboration?
72. North Sea feeder
73. Long time
74. "High ___": M. Anderson
75. One Muppet of two
76. Saint-Exupéry-Borodin collaboration? (with "The")
82. Russian mountains
87. Mouths
88. Arabian V.I.P.
89. Pokey dwellers
90. Wouk-Tolstoy collaboration? (with "The")
96. "___, Lover!," 1954 song
97. Henri's soul
98. ". . . Cupid ___ longer an archer": Shak.
99. Bearish period
102. Vedic god's thing
105. "___, That Kiss," 1931 song
107. Tristram's love
109. Conrad-Koestler collaboration?
115. Square column
116. ___ and sometimes Y
117. In a tumult
118. Use a musical fork
119. Rock star Billy ___
120. Town in Provence
121. ___ Sap, Cambodian lake
122. Galatea's lover
123. Prunes trees
124. ___ off (irate)
125. Hem
126. H.H.S. arm

DOWN

1. Empty space
2. Black Sea port
3. Retreats
4. Composer of "Happy Days Are Here Again"
5. Close an envelope
6. Follower of Zeno
7. Stiff fabric
8. Hammer part
9. Auspices
10. ___-al-Arab
11. Euphemism for "hell"
12. So-called, in Provence
13. Plaster holder
14. Tasso's patron
15. Mimic
16. Brewers' needs
17. Rainfall-chart lines
19. Basket fiber
26. Trouble, in Ayr
27. Orwell's school
28. Not in a whisper
34. Orderly
35. Hungarian city
37. Harem rooms
39. "___ Heidenleben": R. Strauss
40. Petition
41. Draft org.
42. Rivers in England and Ontario
43. Collect, as grain
44. World banking org.
45. King of Thebes
46. Corday's victim
47. Anoint, old style
48. Spry
53. ___-di-dah
54. H.S. subj.
55. Flavor
56. Rapa ___ (Easter Island)
57. Sea eagle
61. Threefold
62. Beatles' Starr
63. Suffix with form or reform
64. Equals
66. Moray
67. Japanese carp
68. Under one's control
69. Swab
70. Bungled
71. ___ Willie Winkle
77. Musical syllable
78. Pasternak girl
79. Body of African warriors
80. She wrote "Seven Women"
81. Having a skull
82. Hole maker
83. Trygve of the U.N.
84. Explosive letters
85. Nimitz and Byrd
86. "___ thee late a rosy wreath": Jonson
91. Group of eight
92. Fine
93. In a violent rage
94. Infant under one month
95. Price
99. Loafer
100. Persephone's love
101. Chromosome parts
103. Verona's river
104. Rhône feeder
106. A king of Judea
108. Ready for action
109. Multiseasonal pelter
110. Inner: Comb. form
111. Upon
112. Regretted
113. Trill or troll
114. Shoe part

by Joy L. Wouk

ACROSS

1. Ghana's capital
6. Reformer Jacob
10. Ancient fertility gods
15. Increases
19. Extensive
20. Atlanta arena
21. Burros
22. Station, in Paris
23. Ship's stern sail support
25. Display site
27. Eyelid problem
28. Sulky
29. Ending for hip or tip
30. Abrades
31. Gulf of Lions feeder
33. Afrikaner
34. Redness symbol
36. World-weary
39. Knave of Hearts' loot
41. Salt, in St. Lô
42. Pitcher
46. Enfold
47. "De ___," Seneca essay
50. Rod
51. Narrow channel
53. Dockers' org.
54. He calls K's
55. Did a preliminary survey
58. Douceur
59. Plummeted
61. Real, in Rouen
62. Vincent Lopez's theme song
63. Muslim Messiah
65. Monasteries
67. Anglo-Indian "first-rate"
69. Emulated Izaak Walton
70. Uncouth
71. The person summoned
72. Painter Andrea del ___
73. Deli hero
75. Grinder
76. Nimbi
79. Commedia dell' ___
80. Virginia of the lost colony
81. S. American wildcat
82. Its cap. is Bismarck
83. ___ alai
84. Sophomores at a Columbus col., e.g.
89. Call ___ day
90. Fourth book of the N.T.
91. British unskilled laborer
92. Dally
93. Queen's title: Abbr.
94. Seine
95. Car starters: Abbr.
97. Gosh!
98. Authority
100. Bore
102. Junior's col.-entrance exam
104. Lion's pride
105. Metal plate
108. Cousin of B.M.I.
111. Fairies
112. Picket
113. G.I.'s necessity
117. O. Henry product
120. Item on a Binet-Simon test
122. Japanese seaport
123. Pluck
124. Tabor
125. Metric measure
126. Weeps convulsively
127. Male and female
128. Simple sugars
129. Kin of blush

DOWN

1. Certain missiles, for short
2. Bk. reviewer
3. Snug
4. Demolition men
5. Humorist George
6. Kind of nose or candle
7. Turkish inn
8. Sec.
9. Pose
10. Stitches loosely
11. Eighth son of Jacob
12. Hebrew lyre
13. Actor Ayres
14. Pisa-to-Leghorn dir.
15. Related parrilinearly
16. June honorees
17. Minute amount
18. Stitches
24. Cpl. or sgt.
26. Petulance
29. ___ voce
32. Legatee
33. Popular diet item
34. He hit 358 home runs
35. Peace Nobelist Wiesel
36. Poker play
37. More unconvincing
38. Use
40. Hindu fire god
41. Stone pillar
43. Kind of tax
44. Slur over
45. Speedy
48. Amend
49. Lots of lots
51. Feed the furnace
52. Esteem
56. Western Hemisphere acronym
57. Printer's device
60. Shirt size
64. Nobelist in Chemistry: 1922
66. ___ d'être
67. Amassed
68. Western lizard
69. Units of capacitance
71. Trite
72. Twilled fabric
73. Mecca pilgrim
74. Borneo ape
75. Delicate purple
76. Scottish river
77. Gourmand
78. Ray
80. Comforter
81. Roe
85. Adventure tale
86. Ardors
87. Actress Martha
88. Widgeon
96. Car accessories
98. "She Didn't ___," 1931 song
99. Murky
101. Yellow dye
103. Bost. is one
104. Actress Dressler
106. Astringents
107. Kind of shirt
108. Inquiries
109. Begone!
110. Baseball's Georgia Peach
111. Entertainer Redd
112. O-T connectors
114. Bearing
115. "Utopia" author
116. Ace
118. College degrees
119. Dactyl, e.g.
120. Altar words
121. Concorde

by Peggy Devlin

ACROSS

1. Wrongly
6. Runs in neutral
11. A light: Slang
15. Collegian's pad
19. Saltarello, e.g.
20. Nantes's river
21. René's laughter
22. Fencing tool
23. CONSTITU-TIONALS?
26. Enclosed trucks
27. Hitchcock movie: 1964
28. Some amplifiers
29. Wraps up
31. Prima ballerina
32. Heredity factors
33. O.T. book
34. Summits, in Siena
36. Heretofore
38. Dike
42. Silly person
45. Watch over
47. Ranks of nobility
50. MORNING SHOWER-SHAVE RITUAL?
55. Morocco, to Marcel
56. Rim
57. Spanish river
58. Pintail ducks
59. Tex. shrine
60. Bridge expert Culbertson
61. Test photos
64. Backward
66. Plant also called avens
68. Abel Janszoon ___
69. Univ. in Dallas
70. J.F.K. Abbr.
72. Asian wild ass
76. Rama I's domain
78. "Iliad," for one
80. Ancient Greek geographer
81. Singer Tillis
84. Lasso
86. Slatterns
88. Dupe
89. Japanese sash
90. Limpid
91. BOGART TWIN FEATURE?
94. Lowered in social position
96. North Korean river
97. Ar chaser
98. Driving hazard
99. Insect's lower lip
105. Muscovite
107. Summit
110. City NE of Rome
111. Humorous
115. Stored away
118. Tropical bird
120. Zoroastrian sacred writings
121. Whip
122. HIRED GUN?
125. Commedia dell'___
126. Khayyám
127. Like some walls
128. Former county in Scotland
129. Kern's "Very ___, Eddie"
130. Rink feature
131. Mother-of-pearl
132. Bean and Shepard

DOWN

1. ___ a dozen
2. ___-arms (soldier)
3. Prefix for mission
4. Picturesque
5. Old-age infirmity
6. Chinese river
7. Condemn
8. Editor's concern
9. Utensil on a pencil
10. Moon goddess
11. Late governor of Conn.
12. West role
13. Vexed
14. Legal term for "middle"
15. Ardent
16. Oct.'s gem
17. Tear apart
18. Army meal
24. Poured
25. Church architect
30. COMPLETE NOBLEMAN?
35. Biblical patriarch
37. Welfare of the community
39. Short-tailed rodent
40. Author Ludwig
41. Glimpse
42. Skilled
43. Native-born Israeli
44. Aegean island
46. Dantès's creator
48. "To ___ and a bone...": Kipling
49. Men's house slippers
51. Impends ominously
52. Tarnish
53. Slacken
54. Suffix with journal
55. Loose robe
62. HONORABLY WON SWEET-HEART?
63. Escargots
65. Duplicate, for short
67. Actress in "Winterset"
71. A singing Boone
73. Measure
74. Muslim Satan
75. Functions
77. Murray and Marsh
79. Peculiar
81. Seed containers
82. Genesis man
83. Nursery-rhyme trio
85. Asian weight
87. Critic's disapproval
92. Chariot-of-fire prophet
93. Rumanian region now shared with the Ukraine
95. Restrained
100. Garb
101. "Lulu" composer
102. "___ the water shall float" (old English saying)
103. Quebec bay
104. Causing excessive pupil contraction
106. Perfumery compound
108. French wine region
109. Water swelling
112. Port city for Pompey
113. Harsh
114. Merits
115. Metal dross
116. Arum plant
117. Concerning
119. Not ever, to Blake
123. Droop
124. E.T.O. head

by Edward Marchese

ACROSS

1. Nautical term
6. Sleight of hand
11. May or Charles
15. Pulverize
19. Cruel master
21. Mennonite
22. Arabian gulf
23. Carroll heroine
24. The indestructible Miss Bailey
27. Some art models
28. Terminate
29. Lunatic of old
30. Amorite king
31. Tun
32. Large European tree
33. Lab burners, once
34. Card-game leftovers
37. Burrowing rodent
42. More underhanded
43. Party of a sort
44. Monopolize
46. Wading bird
47. The lovable Mr. Holden
50. U.N. org.
51. Eastern Church monasteries
52. Scup
53. Swiss river
54. Brouhaha
55. QE1 or QE2
56. Like certain beaches
57. Fast
59. Fragment
60. Der ___ (Adenauer)
61. Russian communities
62. Rhodes of Africa
63. Famous evolutionist
64. Gentleman farmer's degree
65. Mork in tatters
68. Flavoring substance
69. Bury
71. Capital of Seine-Maritime
72. Set straight
73. N.Y.'s geographic center
74. The irrepressible Midler
76. High priest
79. Dahl or Francis
80. ___-et-un (gambling game)
81. Desiccated
82. Foie ___ (table delicacy)
83. Gardening tool
84. Indian princess
85. Do a framer's job
87. Icy
88. So
89. Ballad
90. Broadcast
91. Fox or jackal
92. Poetic contraction
93. The adorable Miss Pickford
96. Ancient Greek colony
97. Herb for McClanahan
98. Bonnie one
99. Common mosquito
100. Spread out
101. Sheathe
103. Nodded
104. "The pig was ___"
105. ___ de Calais
106. "Life is an ___ itself . . .": O. W. Holmes, Jr.
107. Quaid or Rodman
110. Cousin of kvass
113. Icy pinnacle
116. Miss Heming as a partner in crime
119. Period
120. Cordon ___ (top chef)
121. Edict in Odessa
122. One who sidesteps
123. Social attribute
124. Hall, in Hamburg
125. A concern of Whittier
126. Stood up

DOWN

1. Mont Blanc, e.g.
2. "I've ___ to London . . ."
3. Mild expletive
4. Airport Abbr.
5. Pinochle play
6. Expert
7. Verily
8. Encircled
9. St. John or St. Thomas
10. Bonos' baby
11. Members of a medieval sect
12. Juan's goodbye
13. Colonial Quaker
14. Siamese twin
15. Popeye's nemesis
16. Divest
17. The Red Baron, e.g.
18. Permissive word
20. Ocelli
23. Crown of flowers
25. Eastern potentate
26. Tendon
31. Curriculum ___
33. Poetic tribute
34. Bizarre
35. Tomlin shooting the rapids
36. Seek
37. Subject of Tennyson's "In Memoriam"
38. Serves
39. Hardy friend at Pikes Peak
40. Pebbly rubble
41. Speed
42. Gurth, in "Ivanhoe"
43. Thrash
45. Bridge whiz
47. Euphorbia
48. Poor
49. Poor man's mink
54. Circe, e.g.
56. Ess
57. Violin precursor
58. Small seeds of grapes
59. Debra of Hollywood
61. Bea Arthur role
62. Dracula, for one
63. Sere
65. Lorelei's river
66. Bee sound
67. Blusher
68. Satellite's path
70. Lacks
72. Sweet Rosie
73. Eurydice's beloved
74. Jag
75. Designator
77. Singer Kazan
78. "Ding-Dong! The Witch ___"
79. Actress Mary
80. Windmill parts
82. Columbus's hometown
84. Awaken
85. Frosty
86. Ages
87. Manxman, e.g.
89. Croats and Czechs
90. Postscript
91. Kind of audience
93. Etiolate
94. Quantity alongside a barn
95. Spooky
100. Rational
102. Excess of solar over lunar year
103. Nine: Comb. form
104. Diarize
106. ___ weed, rangeland plant
107. Mild expletive
108. Leisure
109. Hindu god
110. Actor ___ Ray
111. Residue
112. Raison d'___
113. Ready for action
114. Govt. agency
115. Fabled big bird
116. Network initials
117. Monogram of a musical Duke
118. Means of propulsion

by Irene Smullyan

430 KITCHENWARE

ACROSS

1. Composer Bartók
5. Rcd. player
10. Extremely
16. ___-de-sac
19. Likeness
20. Hawkeye's friend
21. Heft
22. Jackie's second
23. PLATES
27. Moistens the bird
28. Mystic character
29. Total
30. Ollie's sidekick
31. Porker's pad
32. Health club
34. Cash
37. Short and very staccato: Mus.
39. Manipulators
41. Mouthward
43. Fight segments
46. CUPS
52. Attention getter
53. Family car
54. Jr.-to-be
55. Glacial ridges
56. Scuttlebutt
58. Nita of "A Sainted Devil"
60. Oil cartel
62. Dispatched
63. Expunged
65. Olive and castor
67. Guidonian note
68. BOWLS
77. Be human
78. Change for a five
79. Seek help from
80. Airplane runner
84. Kind of work or spirit
86. U.S. export
89. Actor Lloyd: 1902–85
90. Writer Tyler
91. Malaria Fever
93. Wolfish looks
95. Wimp's cousin
96. POTS
101. Titania's spouse
102. Composer Rota: 1911–79
103. Polonius hid behind one
104. Carries on
106. Harvest goddess
109. A North Caucasic language
110. Cry of triumph
113. Mind
115. Kind of cat
117. Biblical preposition
119. Of a poetic foot

121. PANS
126. Business Abbr.
127. Starry
128. Ms. Dinsmore
129. Road for Caesar
130. Fair grade
131. Live
132. Movie units
133. Action word

DOWN

1. Supports on ships
2. Prominence
3. Crummy
4. French novelist Claude
5. Blossoms
6. CB buff
7. Fragrant river?
8. Old Testament book
9. U. of Maine locale
10. "The ___ Dogs": Burns
11. Broody
12. Clears (of)
13. Arctic abodes
14. Foolish fancy
15. List ender
16. Asian language
17. Word with Major or Minor
18. Mortgage
24. "Demian" author
25. Fitted piece
26. Portuguese money
33. Harold of songdom
35. Work units
36. Bumpkin
38. Kind of artist
39. Greatest
40. Fountain order
42. Ladle's kin
44. Cannon of films
45. Noted muralist
46. Told all
47. Ruark novel: 1962
48. Musical subjects
49. Intrepidity
50. "Mood ___," 1931 song
51. Pincerlike claw
57. Legal thing
59. Half a fragrant oil
61. Incline
64. Music for two
66. Unsaturated alcohol
69. Large
70. Birthplace of Henry VIII's first wife
71. Indian or orange
72. Sue for payment
73. Jungle sights
74. Cove
75. Impolite look

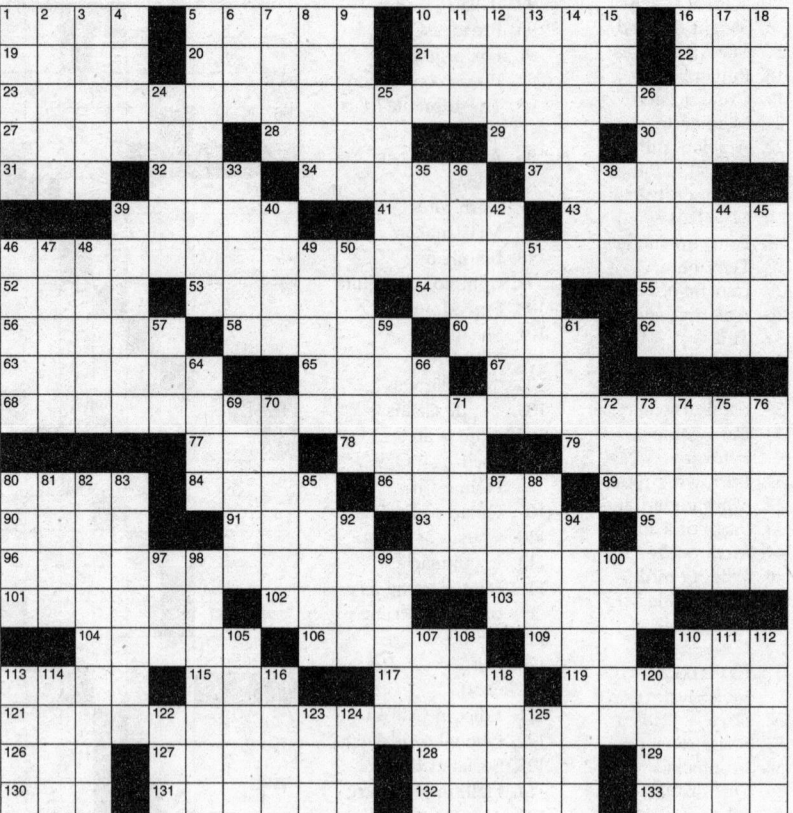

by Alfio Micci

76. Metal eye at the end of a lariat
80. Me. river
81. Bellpull
82. Logician's conclusion
83. Pays expenses
85. Bernstein's field
87. Bergman role
88. Jawaharlal ___ of India
92. Slave of yore
94. Herrings' kin
97. Long, long time
98. Display delight about
99. "Julius Caesar" setting
100. Water nymph
105. Conventicle participants
107. Pierce
108. Trite
110. Ebb
111. Scout, at times
112. Harsh
113. Auditory
114. Plant shoot
116. Lovely woman

118. Seine feeder
120. Twelfth-cen. date
122. Bern's stream
123. Downcast
124. Toby contents
125. Homophone for 124 Down

ACROSS

1. Not up
5. Mich. city
10. Shadow
14. Play players
18. TV's Anderson
19. Bread
20. Yes ___ (ultimatum words)
21. Palo ___
22. Start of a verse
24. Resins
25. Certain wader
26. Conceal, in a way
27. Verse, Part II
30. High peaks
31. Chimney lining
32. ___-Magnon
33. Plow part
36. Fasten anew
38. Intoned
42. Hang fire
43. Urge
45. "Burnt Norton" poet
47. Widow of 37 Down
48. Siamese measure
49. Chanteuse Horne
50. Indian otter
51. Amaze
52. Verse: Part III
59. End of a Pope title
60. Poi makings
61. Salt tree
62. Ones, to Burns
63. Squelched
64. Bad reviews
66. Queue
69. Gone up
70. Humor
74. Verse: Part IV
79. Bible book
80. Drops dropping
81. Pro ___ (proportionately)
82. Stat. for a slugger
83. Masefield heroine
84. Frenzied
87. Type of type, for short
88. End of a loaf
89. French forest
91. Mournful tunes
93. Deputized group
94. Adipose
95. Fr. companies
96. Semaphores on a RR
98. Verse: Part V
104. Dash water about
108. Shoshonean
109. Archibald of the N.B.A.
110. End of verse
112. Article
113. Bismarck's st.
114. Producer Hayward
115. Viaud's pen name
116. Ancient Asian
117. Ballerina's leap
118. Redacts
119. Tore

DOWN

1. Lily plant
2. Beethoven's birthplace
3. Ref. books
4. Steadfast one
5. Concentrate
6. Actor Jack
7. ___ de France
8. Carry or Cat
9. "Don't rock ___"
10. Resin used in perfumes
11. One of a Kipling trio
12. Edge along
13. Sullivan song, with "The"
14. Paper type
15. Russian range
16. Recipe direction
17. Related
19. L-Q connection
23. Heraldic wreath
28. Uplifting fellow?
29. Smell ___ (be suspicious)
31. Eastern inn
33. Mast appendage
34. Erica
35. Cordial flavoring
36. Mystical mark
37. One of the Fab Four
38. Half of CCVI
39. Thoroughly wreck
40. Accustom
41. "The Flea" poet
43. Hook's opposite
44. "___ Bad Boy"
46. Youths
51. Prepares a sting
53. Carter country
54. Sonata part
55. Put away
56. Titus, the conspirator
57. U. of Maine site
58. Actress Elissa ___
63. Inked
64. Michelangelo work
65. Record of a single year
66. African boss
67. "___ of the Jungle," early TV show
68. "I Let ___ Go Out ..."
69. Journalist Jacob
71. Penates' partners
72. Derides
73. Roman magistrate
75. Scene of a G.W. coup
76. Noted loser
77. Essays
78. Easter finery
84. ___ B'rith
85. Puerto ___
86. Dec. visitor
88. Lodging places
90. Start of a Wolfe title
92. Equipped
93. Map out
96. Makes yarn
97. Elated
98. Caprice
99. Table d'___
100. Parroted
101. General Hampton
102. Coup d'___
103. Astronaut Slayton
104. Ella's forte
105. De ___ (too much)
106. Chap, in Córdoba
107. Wallace of silents
111. Yalie

by Mary M. Murdoch

ACROSS

1. Up to now
6. Smeltery leavings
11. Sound seeking silence
14. Supplement
17. "Cheers" barkeeper
18. Slanting type
19. Absence of the skull
21. Lacking a key
22. Mexican's moola
23. Former N.Y. Senator
24. Start of an impetuous person's prayer, with 101 Across
27. Small whale
28. Quality of having limits
32. Jumbo cymbal
36. Red Queen's advice to Alice
41. Sign for Churchill
42. Writer James and family
44. "Can do" serviceman
45. Clump of ivy
46. Pious talk
47. Boston suburb
49. German river
50. ___ capita
51. Word after omni or mini
52. Taunt to an early motorist
54. Relative of a prom
55. Central American
58. Units of syllabic length
59. Jewish month
61. Armenia's capital
62. Ordinary
65. Impetuous guest's question
69. French head
70. "Twelfth Night" lass
72. Sty sound
73. Mexican O.K.'s
75. Little weak coffee
76. Chess pc.
77. Actress Sally
81. Wino
82. Word before rata
83. Merry sounds
85. Symbolic show-biz city
86. In a while
88. Hush-hush agcy.
89. Pina ___ (rum drink)
91. Sp. misses
92. Neighbor of Arg.

93. Impetuous motorist's sounds
96. Wires: Abbr.
97. Status honored in May
99. Private eye
101. Rest of 24 Across
110. Number-2 golf club
113. Brought under control
114. Relating to gulls
115. Shipment of fliers
116. Mall units
117. Worn away
118. Chang's twin
119. Opp. of NNW
120. Ruhr city
121. Famous golf cup

DOWN

1. Japanese P.M.: 1964–72
2. Swan genus
3. "Ae ___ Kiss," Burns poem
4. Word jugglings: Abbr.
5. Kind of pitcher
6. Particle, in Scotland
7. Memory or Drury
8. Syrian city, to the French
9. Tall veldt grazer
10. Nova ___
11. ___ leave it
12. Like a sachet
13. Lost-article checker
14. Black cuckoo
15. Cacophony
16. Hammarskjöld
17. Prefix for adroit
18. Freshwater fish
20. Solar disk
25. Passages
26. Foot part
29. Shifty
30. Cambodian coin
31. Prepare the table
32. Kind of plank
33. Type of arch
34. Eft
35. Impetuous person's advice
37. Asian partridge
38. Welty product
39. One of the tides
40. Dakota Indian
43. N.Y.C. artists' area
46. Brusque person's command
48. Home for a Viking
50. Study hard
51. Grill's partner
53. Cheer

by Will Weng

54. Peddle
55. Eases
56. One of the Turners
57. Singleton
59. Mine access
60. Juan or Carlos
62. Plant
63. Swedish poet Hansson
64. Stays to the end
66. Minor prohibition
67. Sonora is one
68. Cavatina
71. NYC line
74. Followers: Suffix
76. Polish city
77. Ruler who fled: Jan. 16, 1979
78. Notable French artist-designer
79. Coin of Iran
80. Impertinence
82. Type of device on which a door swings
83. Dearie
84. A resin
86. ___, esse, fui . . .
87. Spanish treasure

88. Certain barriers
89. Some seines
90. Opposed
93. Pétain and Matisse
94. Husky-voiced
95. Bowler
98. Greet
100. Cautious
102. Uncles, in Toledo
103. Concerning
104. One of the ages
105. Boxing units: Abbr.
106. Walked on
107. Pheasant group
108. Special person
109. Mat. day
110. Former mlle.
111. Writer Fleming
112. Get Beat poetry

ACROSS

1. Hawthorne's birthplace
6. Russian river
10. Artist Chagall
14. Comedian Mort
18. Miniver Cheevy's love
19. Glorifies
22. Aka Lamb
23. Medicinal plant
24. USUAL VACATION?
26. DOUBLES
28. Brando role in "I Remember Mama"
29. Qaddafi's gulf
30. Actress Hughes
32. Soupçons
33. Evita Peron, e.g.: Abbr.
34. A ___ minute
35. Match
36. Hardy's partner
37. Marcus Aurelius's M.D.
38. Brownish gray
39. Mexican's estate
40. Handled by food pros
43. AVENUE GOING EAST AND WEST
45. Angle or color preceder
48. Greek GQ man
49. Having ups and downs
51. Opie's Bee
52. British gun
53. Loblollies
54. Square
55. French wrinkles
56. "Borstal Boy" author
57. Degenerates
58. Actress Witherspoon
59. Haut monde
61. Quibbles
62. Tough wood
63. TOOL FOR A PAIR
66. Backpackers
67. Exit
69. French composer Erik
70. Map key
71. Least furnished
72. DISCIPLE OF ANANIAS
74. As written: Mus.
77. Position properly
78. Wilbur and Kunitz
80. Train for many N.Y. commuters
81. Tel ___

82. Narrowly defeated, with "out"
83. Some are wild
84. Brief joy rides
86. "To a rag and ___ . . .": Kipling
87. "Twice-___ Tales"
88. ___ spumante
89. Home, for one
90. Carpenter's tool
91. Sappho creation
92. BIKINI, E.G.
95. Miss America, e.g.
96. Yawns
97. A tropical ray
98. Centennial choice for U.S. President
99. Dragonfly
101. Some Russian planes
102. Actress from Greece
103. Gibraltar, e.g.: Abbr.
106. Money in Santander
107. TV's Sawyer
109. European thrush
110. Erin, to a Gael
111. TRIKES' COUSINS
113. FLETCHER-SHAKESPEARE PLAY, WITH "THE"
116. A carny
117. Kin of etc.
118. Saunter
119. Bristly
120. Damascenes: Abbr.
121. Anderson or Fonteyn
122. Actress Armstrong
123. Mohawk months

DOWN

1. Cloaca
2. Author Turin
3. U.N.'s Trygve and kin
4. Opponent of Luther
5. Trident and Titan
6. Rembrandt's birthplace
7. Film day-player
8. Okinawan city
9. Jungfrau, e.g.
10. "Miracle team" of 1969
11. Provençal love song
12. Inlet
13. Rhythm maker
14. Tuaregs' region
15. Marble or Walker
16. Hailey best-seller
17. Bargain price
18. Pennines or Carpathians: Abbr.

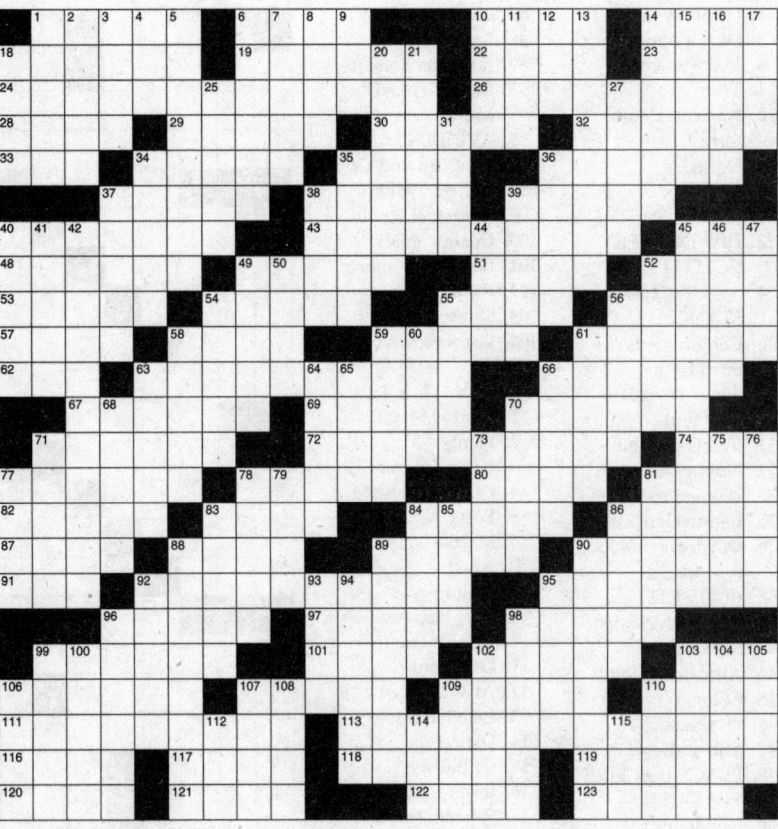

by Arnold Moss

20. Tropical armadillo
21. Cloying
25. Enticed
27. Emit violently
31. Summers, in Soissons
34. 61-'61 man
35. Obscene
36. Mortgages
37. Tunney and Kelly
38. KIND OF TRUCK
39. Jujube or loquat
40. Director of "It Happened One Night"
41. Goodbye, in Granada
42. CRITICS' SEATS
44. Baby soother
45. CONGRESSIONAL REQUIREMENT FOR AMENDMENTS
46. Former Spanish coins
47. Caravansaries
49. Dawns, poetically
50. Toward the mouth
52. Reno "natural"

54. Keep going effortlessly
55. Flycatcher
56. He makes good scents
58. Stallone feature
59. Estoy, ___, esta
60. Secular
61. Burns's prop
63. Drift
64. Bass-baritone Simon ___
65. Crazy
66. Will personae
68. Classic von Stroheim film
70. Radiation term
71. Offspring
73. Honorary degree
75. Prongs
76. Ward off
77. Aware of
78. Spreads
79. Auricular
81. Borders on
83. Willow twig
84. Clefts
85. ___-cake (child's game)

86. Top ratings
88. Challenged a ruling
89. Tangy
90. Support of kings
92. "La Plume de Ma ___"
93. Bovary or Lazarus
94. New Orleans eleven
95. Author of "The Makropoulos Secret"
96. Attic natives
98. Filberts
99. Loser to Truman
100. Tribe of Israel
102. Plays tug of war
103. Simple one
104. Lock
105. Actor Auberjonois
106. Series of book copies: Abbr.
107. Mite
108. Key
109. A double-reed
110. "___ Perpetua," motto of Idaho
112. Greek long e
114. Sphere
115. Modernist

ACROSS

1. Delhi dress
5. Fem.'s opposite
9. Make amends
14. Trim
18. Ancient: Comb. form
19. Ogee, e.g.
20. Yclept
21. Swear
22. HAVING VERY COLD FEET
24. ___ CIRCUMSTANCES
26. Certain reeds
27. Send back
29. Some Yugoslavs
30. Play parts
31. Venus's island
32. Nubby yarn
33. Women-to-be
35. Lightweight silk
36. Daydreamer's food
37. A votre ___
38. ELVIS HIT
40. W.C.'s chickadee
43. Sale proviso
44. African republic
45. Colors
46. Here again
47. Mil. address
48. PLACE FOR FIVE-YEAR-OLDS
52. Divide into segments
53. Answers
55. Abodes
56. Switches
57. "Was-saw" connector
58. Temptress
59. Singer Te Kanawa is one
60. Ransacked
62. Cowboys' nightspots?
63. Bêtes noires
66. Loos or Baker
67. YANKEE SKIPPER, ONCE
69. Chemical ending
70. Inhabitants: Suffix
71. Obi, e.g.
72. Flags
73. Buzzy body
74. Doze
75. THE BIG HOUSE
79. "Santa ___," Italian song
80. Britches
81. Pineapples, in Peru
82. Agrippina, to Nero
83. Heart parts
85. Eye nerve
86. Tackle tidbit
87. Sense
88. Brewing
89. NYC components
93. RIGHT-HAND MEN
95. ACCIDENTAL
97. Maynard and Olin
98. Actress Taylor
99. Mother of Aeolus
100. Goalies' goals
101. Helper, for short
102. Reads meter
103. Shane portrayer
104. Logger's travois

DOWN

1. Actress Mia ___
2. Plenty
3. Begins anew
4. OCTOPUS ARM
5. Posts
6. Martial ___
7. ___-fi
8. Rialto pony, e.g.
9. Thimbleweed
10. Airport lineup
11. Leave out
12. Avant-gardist
13. Enlightens
14. Dialect
15. Of birds
16. Income, in France
17. Saharan tracts
18. Mil. rank
23. Computer units
25. Pianist Rubinstein
28. Biblical land
31. Date element, often
32. De Mille-Copland ballet
33. Quebec peninsula
34. STEPPED UP
35. Full nelsons, e.g.
36. Hall of Fame boxer
37. European coal basin
38. Elissa of old films
39. German pronoun
40. UPKEEP
41. Bank no.
42. Barely gets by
44. Laid booby traps
46. Jacket copy
48. '50s war zone
49. "Watch"-ed river?
50. Moscow's main street
51. Whomp up ___ of pottage
52. Sandbank
54. Skins
56. Emerson, Mencken, et al.
58. Raw fish dish
59. Hot and humid
60. Wet weather
61. Dividing word
62. Groundwork
63. Wild hogs
64. Walking ___ (ecstatic)
65. Bristle
67. Whines
68. Writer Asimov
71. Thesmothetes
73. Of the throat
75. Father: Comb. form
76. Is against
77. LaToya's brother
78. Monogram ingredient
79. TARDY STATE
80. "Remembrance of Things Past" author
82. Hamlisch, to pals
83. French girlfriends
84. Has a premiere
85. Frequently
86. Foretold
87. Writer-actress Chase
88. Karenina or Christie
89. Combo
90. Contribute
91. Weeded
92. Neb. and Mo., e.g.
94. Agcy. succeeded by the N.R.C.
96. Gun org.

by Charles M. Deber

ACROSS

1. Ornamental stud
6. Betel palm
11. Designates
15. Painter Benjamin
19. More cunning
20. Ancient Greek populace
21. Willow
22. First Chinese dynasty
23. A work by barnyard collaborators?
26. Agenda component
27. Pay dirt
28. City in S. France
29. Giraffe's kin
30. Suffragist Lucy
31. King Mark's castle
34. Female swan
35. Steno's need
37. Strut
38. Apian darners?
40. Clairvoyant
41. Window glass
44. ___ Paulo, Brazil
45. Manor or tutor ending
46. Nicaraguan rebel
48. Keeps in office
53. In a frenzied state
57. Leftist clupeids?
60. Exclamation of relief
61. Greediness
63. A main street in Roma
64. Kipling's ___ Khan
65. Portable lodge of a certain shape
66. Famed conductor
68. ___ show (spectacle)
69. Wheel spokes
70. Flower stalk
72. Pyromaniac
75. ___ code
76. Lagomorph from Llangollen?
79. Congou and hyson
80. Glass gardens
82. "Two ___ People," 1938 tune
83. ". . . ___ of little faith?": Matt. 8:26
84. Some hosts, for short
87. Grouts
88. Poem by Byron
92. Equine political demand?
95. Howard and Russell
97. Long-legged shorebirds
99. Joplin work
100. Callas's style of singing
102. A king of Crete
103. Routine duty
105. ___ Nostra
106. Twitching
107. N.L. batting champ: 1966
108. Canine dental visit?
112. Stigma
113. Entreat
114. Stale
115. "Ici on ___ français"
116. Spanish painter
117. Editor's notation
118. Intuit
119. Ledger item

DOWN

1. Some neckwear
2. Nimbi
3. Freedom
4. Mouse-spotters' cry
5. Refrain syllable
6. Confound
7. Shays or Tyler
8. Cassowaries' cousins
9. Mountain pass
10. Slanting
11. Oberon's spouse
12. On a pinnacle
13. Vitus ___, Danish navigator
14. Affirmation
15. Plastered pachyderm?
16. Bars, legally
17. Home of St. Catherine
18. Emulated Petruchio
24. Former Hungarian prime minister
25. Twists
30. Bargain
32. Tea, in Tours
33. Rhine feeder
36. Some of Tony's kin
38. Withered
39. Norse Fates
41. Wilbur or Merrill
42. Singer Gibb
43. Utmost
46. Dernier ___
47. Toxophilites
49. Kind of trip
50. Marilyn's "Bus Stop" role
51. Opera's Stratas
52. Bonbons
53. Ark's landfall
54. Victor of Hollywood
55. Kitchen item
56. Marsupial motel?
58. Deteriorate
59. Author Levin
62. Parts of dols.
64. Hit letters
66. Joad and Kettle
67. Williams athlete
70. A whale
71. Hold tightly
72. Incite
73. Saws with the grain
74. Hampshire's home
76. Snatch forcibly
77. Indonesian island
78. Actress Arthur
81. A Dr. Kildare portrayer
85. Diadem for Di
86. Turf
88. Fond du ___, Wis.
89. Alias
90. Tenants
91. A, e.g.
92. Integrity, English style
93. Accompany
94. Rids the body of
95. Mediocre
96. Concavity of a joint
97. Accumulate
98. Dulls ender
100. Kipling poem
101. A Lauder
104. Vast
105. Soldo or solidus
108. Bohemian martyr
109. Due follower
110. He checks the bks.
111. Is down with

by Nancy Nicholson Joline

ACROSS

1. Lively frolic
5. More untidy
13. Bobby of nursery rhyme
20. Khayyám
21. L.A. suburb
22. Tax
23. Betty Botta
26. Climb aboard
27. Commotions
28. Pianist Dame Myra
29. Wreath, in Wahiawa
30. Crabtree of "Topsy"
32. Peer Gynt's mother
33. Lincoln bill
34. Attitudinize
35. Mollusk merchant
40. Lanchester from Lewisham
41. Harrison from Huyton
42. Tune for two
43. Achaean Aurora
44. Certain knit goods
46. "___ at the pane...": Browning
49. Elicits
54. Charge
55. Symbol of remembrance
58. Eliot's "Coker"
59. Whoopee!
60. Breeze
61. Bannister's distance
62. Horned viper
63. Obtuse
64. Peter Piper
70. Laughing stock
71. ___ Alamos
72. Toulouse-Lautrec's birthplace
73. Roguish
74. Uncouth one
75. Borodin's "Prince ___"
77. "The ___ Storm": P. White novel
79. Neal-Douglas Oscar vehicle
82. Wrong places to change horses
85. Commedia dell' ___
86. Labor leader George
88. Wave, in Huelva
89. ___ bene
91. Queen before Sophia
93. In the altogether
94. Sister Suzie
99. Invent a new word
101. Having a part of
102. Droop
103. Matisse or Bergson
104. Hostel
105. Escort
106. Burnsian "do not"
108. Pear-shaped
111. Caesar
115. She wrote "Gigi"
116. Catherine II was his widow
117. Pericles's philosophy prof
118. Concord
119. Bertrand and Lillian
120. Son of Ares and Aphrodite

DOWN

1. Defrauds
2. Neglect
3. Embossed, as a fabric
4. Recommendation
5. He needs no mike
6. Peppery
7. Some are martial
8. Garbo and Nissen
9. Showy
10. Become effete, in a way
11. Old French coins
12. Soak timber
13. Stuff into a hold
14. Like Richard III at the end of Act V
15. Priestly robes
16. Scourge in 1918
17. Rip or Renée
18. S-shaped lines
19. Spooky
24. The two
25. Theopholus or Theogenes
31. Tracts
33. "A ___ and a fly in a flue"
34. Aquino coin
35. The ego
36. Writer Wiesel
37. Kind of speech
38. Ball part
39. Gallery
45. Psychoanalyst Erikson
47. Guillaume's girlfriends
48. Lobster's feeler
50. N. Norwegian
51. Puck or Feste
52. Heyerdahl
53. Manner or method
56. Mont. motto metal
57. Compensate
60. First-rate
62. Bower
63. Firmament
64. Arkin-Moreno film: 1969
65. Barely made out
66. Ice field
67. Birthplace of 117 Across
68. Suffix with sheep or wolf
69. Kadiddle-hopper
70. Predicament
75. "___ soon shake your windows...": Dylan
76. Ramps
77. Superlative endings
78. Tithe portion
79. Short cannon, once
80. Wavy, in heraldry
81. Beautician, often
83. Early
84. "September ___," Chabas painting
87. Invigorate
90. Point-guard specialties
92. Absence of bad germs
94. Individual
95. "...our help ___ past"
96. Medieval merchant guilds
97. Neglect
98. Snick-a-___
99. Lake herring
100. Gibson garnish
105. Morsel
106. "___ et droit"
107. Seed covering
109. Mythological wine maker
110. Paid athletes
112. Farm layer
113. A metallic elem.
114. Part of R.S.V.P.

by Caroline G. Fitzgerald

ACROSS

1. Amex-listing info
6. Libran symbol
11. Space
15. Sch. groups
19. Tile picture
20. In the wrong
22. About
23. ___ avis
24. He's an unwelcome caller
26. He's unfriendly
28. On the briny
29. Canines, e.g.
30. Pasadena flowers
32. Sanctuaries
33. Kin of aves.
34. Peyton or Park
35. Porn
36. Vernal harbingers
37. Fellowship
38. Cacophonous
39. Lot's hometown
40. Sifts
43. He's in the museum
45. Chew the fat
48. Dear
49. Burger shape
51. Sci. dealing with currents
52. ___ dieu (kneeling bench)
53. Shoe ties
54. Lords it over
55. Long hikes
57. Be miserly
58. Germanic exclamations
59. Lunkhead
60. Dense or mawkish
61. Jousting weapons
62. Danson or Knight
63. He got a tax break
66. Used a tumbrel
67. Withstand
69. D sharp
70. Dirt
71. Bible poems
72. She's a go-getter
74. Airport timetable info
77. Hits hard
78. Squamous
80. Is indebted
81. Zola's "The ___ Shop"
82. Locales
83. Spin
84. Showy flower
86. Idaho city
87. Cover person
88. Chum, sometimes
89. Perky rhythms
90. Wooden shoes
91. Erhard's gp.
92. He's belligerent
95. Paces
96. Penned
97. It has skits and songs
98. Lark
99. Dialects of regions
101. "Easy ___," of radio fame
102. Blackthorn fruits
103. "___ Love You," 1934 song
106. American wildcat
107. Ellington's "___ Doll"
109. Separate
110. Germ
111. He's determined
113. She's hanging around
116. "___ Smile Be Your Umbrella . . ."
117. Took off
118. ___ de corps
119. "___ the Chief!"
120. Brides in Barcelona
121. Hoop hangings
122. Mill runs
123. Cries of surprise

DOWN

1. Dumbwaiter
2. Keys' cousins
3. Festive
4. ___ et ubique
5. Carlyle's native land
6. Choose
7. Minos's realm
8. Foot part
9. Eng. ___
10. Hugeness
11. Paella ingredient
12. Responsibility
13. Bruins legend
14. Orderly
15. Heat, for short
16. Easy basket
17. City on the Rhône
18. Finds words
19. Yuppie degrees
21. Complaining bird?
25. Is inclined
27. He has nerves of steel
31. Charon's river
34. Uses a lever
35. Kinds
36. Peignoirs
37. Uses a telescope
38. Archibald of N.B.A. fame
39. Smooth
40. Chair-back piece
41. Harness strap
42. He's a sweetie
44. Micawber's boss
45. She gives you a second chance
46. Ventilated
47. Charpoys
49. Cocoon residents
50. Hardy villain
52. Loren's spouse
54. Bellows
55. Of sound
56. Like some dirt roads
57. Severe
59. Containers for oil
60. Taint
61. Sticks it out
63. Runs in neutral
64. Union activist Chavez
65. "I am monarch ___ I survey": Cowper
66. Wendell or Jeff of films
68. Of birth
70. Frocks
71. Helen's kidnapper
73. Part of a yard
75. Discrimination
76. In ___ (untidy)
77. Knight's aide
78. Effulgence
79. "___ Boy," Wouk story
81. Gillis of TV
83. Desires
84. Devout
85. Actress Sommer
86. Exposes
88. San Francisco, once
89. Trysters' hideaway
90. Elastic
92. Flag
93. Churlish child
94. Instructions for cooking
95. Infant fern
96. Author Cather and namesakes
98. Viewpoints
99. More frosted
100. Welly's "___ Wedding"
102. Like some ends
103. Positive-thinking man
104. Religious blocs
105. Thought: Pref.
106. Night birds
107. Transmitted
108. Creative pursuits
109. Info at depots
110. Ferry's berth
112. Infinitesimal
114. Mimic
115. Jazzman Winding

by Norma Steinberg

438 Eponyms

ACROSS

1. Writer Jong
6. Writer Ayn
10. Blonde shade
13. NATO's defunct cousin
18. Scanning device
19. Hershfield hero
20. Sandpiper
21. Southwestern Amerind
22. Feminist who helped women make great strides
25. Ford's successor
26. Famed observatory
27. Field marshal who had something up his sleeve
29. Ibsen character
30. Heavyweight champion: 1934–35
32. Melville work
33. Notables
38. "___ quam videre" (N.C. motto)
40. Impertinent
44. Relative of D.S.O.
45. Rhythmical cadence
46. Craftier
47. Rational
48. Red-ink item
50. Operatic toast of two continents
52. "Judith" composer
53. Lamb who had a Mary
54. Heraldic wreath
55. A memorable Nelson
56. Trollope's "Ayala's ___"
57. Dandie ___ (terriers)
59. Uncle ___ of early TV
60. Rot-resistant woods
61. Rubber trees
62. Loves too fondly
63. Gush
64. Human beings, e.g.
67. City on the Loire
68. Lunch-counter features
72. Baal and Baphomet
73. "La Plume de ma ___"
74. Cartel formed in 1960
75. Karate blow
76. Abound
77. His signature led all the rest
79. Mata follower
80. Relative of bye-bye
81. Eaglewood
82. Thine, in Aix
83. Chemical ending
84. Croat, e.g.
85. Kin of a strada
86. Painted a sign over
90. A.A. Fair's real first name
92. London domicile
94. Bird of prey
95. She saw a ray of hope in the dark
99. Gave in
103. Rescuer
104. Staunch defender, contender and bitter-ender
108. Winkles out
109. "___ bin ein Berliner": J.F.K.
110. Auricular
111. More abstemious
112. British informers
113. Upsilon preceder
114. Pant
115. Ala. city

DOWN

1. Paleozoic, e.g.
2. Freeway exit
3. Inkling
4. Memorable diva
5. Melodious
6. Indian chief
7. NE is one
8. Nothing
9. ___ volente
10. Mail
11. Soothsayer
12. Wrangle
13. Etymon of spaghetti
14. First fast-food fancier
15. Recorded proceedings
16. Now partner
17. Above, poetically
21. "I Am ___": Van Druten
23. TV sitcom
24. Comedian Olsen
28. ". . . ___ any other name . . ."
30. Ball star
31. Italian city
33. Punted
34. Mezzo role in "Don Carlos"
35. Varnish ingredient
36. Tips off
37. Mushroom features
38. Opts
39. Smooth and lustrous
41. Sweater size
42. Kind of circle
43. Shucks
46. Shows approval
49. He made his mark by not making his mark
50. Canonical hours
51. Ethiopian province
56. Hardy villain
58. Early car pioneer
59. Estuaries
60. "___ of troubles": Erasmus
62. Sierra Nevada pass
63. Money in coin
64. Bollards
65. Perfect
66. Gabriele D'Annunzio, e.g.
67. Western lake resort
68. Bobbin
69. ". . . ___ of yon gray head"
70. Actor Greene
71. Looked unseen
73. Early invader of Mexico
74. Double quartet
77. Turnkeys
78. Ancient Japanese capital
87. Cal. or Georgia
88. "She ___ on it so light": Shak.
89. Last
91. Wild scenes
92. Light, triangular shawl
93. Sign of early August
95. Goya subject
96. Maintain
97. Military group
98. Costa ___
99. Sale condition
100. Letters on a Russian plane or athlete
101. Vile anagram
102. Per ___
103. E.M.K. is one
105. Nautical record
106. Alma-___, Soviet city
107. Hunter's org.

by Kay Sullivan

ACROSS

1. Airport feature
5. Prosaic
9. Residue of grapes
13. "Evita" role
16. Squinch, e.g.
17. State in NE Brazil
18. Nymph of the hills
20. McQueen film, with "The"
21. Colette character
22. Agitated movement by a singer
24. Nursery-rhyme pet
25. Family of a U.S. inventor
27. Balsam-yielding tree
28. Some bridges
30. Ouse feeder
31. "___ Millions," O'Neill play
34. Caspian feeder
35. Cities in R.I. and the Isle of Wight
39. Holds up
41. Comic Ole
44. Eye docs
45. Arose
47. Exequy
48. G.I.'s devil-dodger
49. Certain Wall Street options
51. Increase stitches
53. Expels
56. Article of merchandise
57. Critical
59. Lady of Spain
60. Possessions
62. Rorem or Sparks
63. College officials
65. Robert of "Quincy, M.E."
67. Aqueous resting place
69. Detail
70. Bellini's Druidic priestess
72. Armbone
73. Guido di Pietro, or Fra ___
76. Golfer's 19th hole
77. Where Dresden china is made
81. Yoko Lennon, née ___
82. Dissolute
84. A lady's maid to Cleopatra
86. Words on a Wonderland cake
87. Fish dish
89. Marine hazards
90. Burton of "Roots"
92. Dregs
93. Amount of assessment
95. Extol
97. Polish river
99. Old-timer
100. Ridge on a mountain
101. Blowhard's output
103. First steps
105. Because
107. Disdainful look
109. Bruce of films
110. Thesmothetes
113. "___ company . . ."
115. Yehudi Menuhin's teacher
118. Fail to use
119. Coveted award for a playwright
123. Acidity
124. Houston school
125. Champ after Braddock
126. What to spend in Shiraz
127. Arp's art cult: 1916
128. Wapiti
129. School book
130. Refuse to grant
131. Light British carbine

DOWN

1. Fashion
2. Song for Sutherland
3. Transport for a pitcher
4. U.K. prince
5. Thuringian article
6. Scold vehemently
7. "___ With a View"
8. Chanteuse's specialty
9. Jan. and Aug.
10. Metric measure
11. Funny Foxx
12. Students at the U.S.M.A.
13. Great dog for an actor
14. Abode
15. Points of decline
17. Historic commune near Naples
19. Unit of force
20. Sunday statute
23. Creator of "Melencolia"
26. Greek cupid
29. De ___ (superfluous)
32. Founder of British India
33. Crowded quarters for a thespian
35. Like some stock certificates
36. Bring out
37. Transmitter for an entrepreneur
38. Kind of jerk
40. Backyard gossip
42. Slipped or tripped
43. Destitution
46. No-nos for a pianist-songwriter
50. Popular cartoonist
52. Org. founded in 1949
54. Paintings by a hot pianist
55. Inscribed stone slab
58. Input data
61. Banks of baseball
64. Pertaining to tissue
66. Celestial body
68. ___ metabolism
71. Arthur's coat
73. Close, to Keats
74. Damage to a screen star
75. Sky: Sp.
78. Feline in music
79. Kuwait ruler
80. Hangouts
81. ". . . ___ perfumed sea": Poe
83. ___ T'ung, Chinese emperor: 1908–12
85. Gardner and namesakes
88. Glut
91. Primers, e.g.
94. Fast period
96. Scarsdale, etc.
98. He reconstructed St. Paul's
101. English feudal tribute
102. Change text
104. Steps
106. Covering for a chimney
108. Miss O'Grady
110. Tender
111. The screen's Jannings
112. Turn around
114. Medical procedure
116. System of rules
117. Algerian port
120. Fort in N.J.
121. Superlative suffix
122. One of the Khans

by Bernice Gordon

ACROSS

1. Young salmon
5. Medieval estate
9. She loved Narcissus
13. British service-woman of W.W.I
17. Woodwind
18. Up and about
20. Porch
21. Earth goddess
22. Vulgar group avoided argument
26. "Die Fledermaus" maid
27. African timber tree
28. Annoy
29. Retiree's nest egg
31. Reconnoiters
32. Plants used for raising nap
33. Active chemical substance
37. Choreographer Tommy
38. H.H.H.'s state
39. Four couples expect big argument
46. French violinist: 18th century
47. Behold: Lat.
48. Precipitation in Dundee
49. Baseball stats.
50. Commanded
51. Solitary
53. Rabbit fur
55. Lighter and tender
56. Easter lead-in
57. ___ Nevada
59. Platitude
60. Intelligent men find fault with falsehoods
65. "Popo" author: 1980
66. Archer's goal
67. Mama or Peggy
68. Bury
69. Bog
70. Vents
71. Sir, in Madrid
74. S. state
75. Curve
76. Mantle
78. Take aliment
79. Silly people bilk fat relative
86. Rex or Donna
87. Broadway muggers?
88. Kitchen appliance
89. Orbs
93. Daffy Duck, e.g.
95. Cagers' gp.
96. Emulate Gulliver
97. Comportment
99. More experienced
103. Assistant held up sober young man
106. Orison finis
107. Leases
108. Moor plant
109. Portent
110. Dry run
111. Tokyo drink
112. To live, to Livy
113. Proceed

DOWN

1. Negri of silents
2. Retired
3. English poet laureate: 1715–18
4. Car stopper
5. Partner of wide
6. Fabulist: Var.
7. Okla. Indians
8. Preachy
9. Cultural characteristics
10. Betty of songdom
11. In what way
12. Allowing for contingencies
13. They cross warps
14. Mountain ridge
15. "... makes Jack ___ boy"
16. Aqua and motor endings
19. Detour traffic
20. Sea duck
23. Chapeau for Corot
24. Went for the pitch
25. Revolutionary diplomat
30. Actress Alicia
32. Rhea or Cronus
33. Kind of estate
34. "___ kleine Nachtmusik"
35. Ripened
36. Score
38. Lunatic
40. Tennis coup
41. ___ de corps
42. Tumults
43. Calculators of sorts
44. A tenth part
45. Sinuous letters
51. French artist
52. Load
53. She was an O'Hara
54. Prado offering
55. Consecrate
56. Pries
57. Infrequent
58. Imperfect merchandise: Abbr.
59. Person exercising power
60. Twist
61. Pat needs this to maintain composure
62. Bristles
63. Gawked
64. Most frigid
69. Tiercel and cob
70. Copy
71. Assembly
72. Head of a tale
73. ___-do-well
76. Mariner's aid
77. Nonattender
78. Veto
80. Goofed
81. Antennae
82. Rings
83. Allayed
84. Time without end
85. Wealthy man
89. Hessen or Hamburg
90. Coach
91. A brother of Zeus
92. Happening
93. Philippine island
94. Byways
97. Moist and chilly
98. Outfits
100. British title
101. Whence the Pison flowed
102. Tear
104. Where cows browse
105. Scottish river

by Norman S. Wizer

ACROSS

1. Parisian gangster
7. Cleanse thoroughly
12. Of an armbone
17. The Censor
21. Ameche-Verdon film: 1985
22. Department of France: 1815–1975
23. Daughter of Tantalus
24. Words of understanding
25. Fast player with lots of clout
27. Outfielder, at times
29. "___ Not Unusual"
30. Shock
31. Lessen
33. ___ double take
34. Half of XIV
35. Ancient Celtic priest
37. Bivalve mollusk
41. Hammarskjold
44. Desires
46. Cast amorous glances
48. Vowel changes in verb forms
50. Battologize
52. One way for runners to score
55. Hanoi holiday
56. Garb
57. Pick up the tab
58. Valley
59. Get one's goat
60. Don
61. Religious composition
62. Germ cell
64. Mistake
65. A son of Seth
66. Criterion for Kelly
68. Carnegie ___ U.
69. Ump's relative
70. This can be acute
72. War god
73. "Lili ___"
74. Small land masses
76. Wept
78. Concerning this
79. Irritates
81. Contented sounds
82. Musical ennead
83. "___ Sleepy People"
86. Portion of bacon
87. Yogi Berra was one
90. In the distance
91. John or Sean
92. Stadium pentagon
94. Dispatch boat
95. Daily rat race.
96. Lettuce variety
97. Player in an old song
98. Gripper of sorts
99. Art of horsemanship
100. Laders' org.
101. Strike-calling umpire
104. Flower part
105. Swivel wheels
107. Water wheel
108. Looks over hastily
110. Crandall or Ennis
111. Come back in
113. More rational
115. Numero ___
116. Ship-shaped clock
117. Position properly
119. Will topic
122. Wood sorrel
125. What a pinch hitter will do
129. At the end, for 25 Across
132. Declare positively
133. Baseball's Pee Wee
134. Standards
135. Nicotinic acid
136. Opposite of raves
137. T.N. Page's "___ Chan"
138. Dutch jurist Huig de ___: 1583–1645
139. Mystery awards

DOWN

1. Start of "Hamlet"
2. Larboard
3. Galatea's lover
4. ___ a plea
5. Jack or Tim
6. Sap
7. Dutch boat
8. Bulb's cousin
9. Mountain nymph
10. "Born in the ___"
11. Instructed again
12. Still bright
13. Gay tune
14. "Drake" poet
15. Broadcasting syst.
16. Unlike some scrawls
17. Homopterous insect
18. Rowan
19. Peg for Peete
20. Above, poetically
26. French critic-historian: 19th century
28. Outcry, in Rouen
32. Spleen
36. Turn
38. Wire
39. Where to see Rickey Henderson
40. Hunter beloved by Eos
41. Layette item
42. Bring into harmony
43. Hit or walk
44. Caution
45. Raid
47. Fogies
49. "Tristram Shandy" author
51. Branco and Mayo
53. Penury
54. Egypt–Syr. once
57. Bridge charges
59. Norse chieftain
61. Certain NCO's
62. Unfailing
63. Entreated
64. Montmartre chapeau
67. Rear
68. ___ nostrum (the Mediterranean)
70. Standish's stand-in
71. ___-do-well
73. "The evil that ___ . . .": Shak.
75. Title in colonial India
76. Scoter
77. Songwriter Harold
78. Ski jumper ___ Bulau
79. Lebanon language
80. Situated at the foundation
81. Styx ferryman
82. Water nymphs
84. Falsify
85. Severe trial
88. Roman helmets
89. Eye layer
90. American cartoonist
92. "___ porridge hot . . ."
93. Author Stanislaw ___
95. Needlefishes
97. Small agricultural enterprise
98. Gymnast's activity
99. Chorus reject
101. Star in Cygnus
102. Emphatic negative
103. Kind of bunt
104. Watercourse
106. Domingo, et al.
109. Most adorable
112. Olympic athlete Johnson
114. Kind of rocket
118. Opposite of a win
120. Foolish person
121. Geraint's wife
122. Grampus
123. French leather
124. Sothern and Harding
125. Breach
126. Eggs, to Ovid
127. Derek vehicle
128. Earl Grey, for one
130. Correlative
131. Kind of rule

by Jeanette K. Brill

ACROSS

1. Ibsen heroine
5. Part of NASA gets the gait
9. "___ c'est moi"
14. Bal. sheet worker
17. Jai ___
18. Gomorrah neighbor
19. Mason's concern
20. Attention-getting word
21. Pits turn into little arbiters
22. March along
23. Conjecture becomes embezzlement
25. Change a bulb
27. Certain taxes
29. ___ l'oeil
30. Tati's ta-ta
31. Russian area goes south
33. Stormy ___ (sea birds)
34. Nathan, to David
35. Tusked swine
37. Stupid guys become little cutups
39. N.Y.C. observes it
40. Soak flax
41. "To ___, to Greece, and into Noah's ark": Cowper
43. Bill-of-exchange signer
46. Intoxicating
48. Foxhole kin becomes illuminated
51. Batik expert
52. Restaurateur goes to a Jordanian peak
53. Entomb
54. Author goes to college
56. Time to irrigate
60. Bilbao visitor
62. Actress Claire
64. Silvertip
65. Kind of sauce
66. "Robust ___ alone is eternal": Gautier
67. Santa becomes less egotistical
70. Prefix with Raphaelite
72. Guido's high note
74. Depend (on)
75. Ade's "___ Horne"
76. Crab, lobster or shrimp
79. "Clair de lune" composer
81. "Streamers" playwright
83. Casked-wine process
84. Suffix from a trig function
85. Actress Raines
89. Bet becomes emporium gelt
91. Arabian prince
94. "... a sea of ___": Shak.
96. Safecracker
97. Forest humus
98. Blotter ltrs.
100. River duck
101. Eliel's son
103. Monogram of Garfield's successor
106. Pliant
108. Doughnut-shaped rolls
110. Computer buffs
112. Prepare a diamond
113. Oily resins
115. Fiendish
117. Cocktail becomes a coxswain
119. Lithe animal
121. "Wishing will make ___"
122. Attain justly
123. Pinguid
124. Whistle-blowing times
125. Baltic native
126. Concordes come to N.Y., N.J., etc.
127. Baseball Hall of Famer
128. WWI admiral
129. Mmes., in Mexico

DOWN

1. Petrarch's beloved, et al.
2. Wimbledon champ: 1959
3. Reptile becomes drowsy
4. Usher's beat
5. Bassanio's beloved
6. Hoopla
7. Col. Pickering portrayer
8. Charlatan of old
9. Dazed, miler becomes obsessed
10. Robt. ___
11. Twitches
12. Elephant boy turns into Arabian dad
13. Jousted
14. Foolish fancy
15. Colonized
16. Pardon
18. Social pos.
20. Suffix for comment
24. "... wherefore ___ Romeo?"
26. Reddish browns
28. Clocked
32. Leaflike plant part
33. ___ diem
36. Fish gets a cheer
38. Sault ___ Marie
42. Abruzzi town
44. Fastidious: Slang
45. Willy Loman's quest
47. Work units
48. Rock singer ___ Ford
49. Hardened
50. Football's Greasy, et al.
52. Mongol throng
55. Wind dir.
57. German navy V.I.P.: 1928–43
58. Mall becomes a warren
59. Power of the movies
61. Far from loquacious
63. Writer gets a connection
64. Looked good on
68. Philadelphia hockey player
69. Anderson's "High ___"
71. High-strung
73. Role in 20's Broadway hit
77. Emerged, as an article
78. Enthralled
80. Like movies, once
82. Swiss river port
86. ___ Alamos
87. Sleepy one becomes a woodsman
88. Perpendicular to the keel
90. Son of Odin
91. Punishes by fine
92. Bandicoot
93. Utensils on pencils
94. Tic-___-toe
95. Roman army units
99. Vagrants' area changes into children's line
102. Ancient ascetic
104. Awn
105. Ties
107. Like a quilt
109. Bar legally
111. Ballooners, e.g.
113. Odd number becomes the opposite
114. ___-majesté
116. ___ Antiqua
118. Philippine tree
120. Low digit

by Jim Page

ACROSS

1. With, to Rene
5. Gains
9. Maui bye
14. Brawl
19. ___ avis
20. Gershwin's "___ Rhythm"
21. Arabian desert
22. "___ Lady": Cather
23. Actress visits doctor about piercing weapon
27. Dead Sea Scroll guardians
28. Prince's "Purple ___"
29. Musical three-note intervals
30. Exploits
31. Monza moola
32. River near Eboli
33. Watchdog for 89 Across
36. Actor Jeremy
38. Ibsen products
43. Ex-senator with former pitcher on time
50. Highway for Hadrian
51. Steve Martin's "___ Jerk"
52. Dice throw
53. Comic Johnson
54. Baby boys, in Barcelona
56. An Alcott
59. Pony-express haul
60. Queue
61. Gazelles
63. Role for McArdle
65. Proverb ending
67. Typing method of actress with director
75. Hue holiday
76. Hymn of praise
77. "To ___" Burns poem
78. Kind of race
82. Bad day for Julius
85. Israeli port
87. Loren's mate
88. Oppenheimer subject
89. Environmental sci.
90. Past one's prime
92. Gang follower
93. Justice joins wife slayer, gets bruised
100. ___ Nevada
101. Twenty
102. Where kine dine
103. Ham ___ (overact)
106. Medical suffix
107. Brings down the house, in Kew
112. Expectorant mixture
116. Nothing, in Nice
117. Latent
119. Life time of comic hero with pop singer
122. Simon's later name
123. Thrill
124. Copycat
125. Virginia ___
126. Connery and Penn
127. Hogan's cousin
128. Actor from Philadelphia
129. Kind of cast or vision

DOWN

1. Like Natural Bridge
2. "___ Triste": Sibelius
3. Clear the boards
4. Was solicitous
5. Taunt
6. Vain one's traits
7. Pull
8. Kind of night
9. Fireplace accessory
10. ". . . ___ hungry look": Julius Caesar
11. Ninth-cent. Gallic language
12. Wounds
13. Venerate
14. Command
15. Sailor's saint
16. Mutton cut
17. Italian family
18. Biblical verb endings
24. Geese genus
25. Nigerian money
26. Uncontrolled
34. Coal mine
35. Turkish title
37. Bristle
39. "We've ___ and a debt . . .": J. R. Lowell
40. Dame ___ Hess
41. Oppositionist
42. Prune, in Ayr
43. Ultimate
44. Wombs
45. Ulyanov
46. Multiply
47. Stallone-type role
48. Uris protagonist
49. Vestige
55. Bluish gray
57. Can. province
58. Breaks
59. Mythical sorceress
60. A Colonel of W.W. II
62. Andress film
64. One ___ million
66. Alias
68. City near N.Y.'s Thruway
69. Laced boot
70. Matriculate
71. John Brown's bane
72. ___ Arenas, Chile
73. Daisylike flower
74. Creepy
78. Bowl calls
79. Ornamental case
80. Mezzanine part
81. ___ patriae
83. Med. person
84. Wawaskeeshes
86. Jewish month
89. Click beetle
91. Actress Sandra ___
94. People buyers?
95. Needle-shaped
96. Candidate
97. Sere
98. Item thrown in some games
99. Ballet railing
104. Like failed goals
105. "Positive Thinking" exponent
108. Spiritless
109. Hindu garment
110. TV's Georgia ___
111. Engraved pillar
112. Recipe amts.
113. Three-sided blade
114. Comic Rudner
115. Solway Firth tributary
117. He's a hue man
118. Scarebabe
120. Baize feature
121. Cockney desire

by Robert H. Wolfe

ARTIFICIAL INTELLIGENCE

ACROSS

1. Twerp
5. Mother of Pollux
9. Ponselle or Luxemburg
13. Redemption
19. Domingo specialty
20. Use a goose
21. Livy's way
22. Beethoven's third
23. Sensible cipher
26. Creeds
27. Vex
28. Potsdam pot
29. Brainy comber?
31. Falls behind
33. Fish with bobbing bait
35. Betel
36. Williwaw
39. Wilkes-___, PA
41. Changes actors
46. Some are proper
47. Clever bevel?
50. Honolulu movie sleuth
51. Inter ___
52. Shell, to Pierre
53. Freezes
54. Fabulous racer
55. Seemingly inviting
57. Scottish architect
58. Become known
60. Atchinson is here
61. Spaceship adjunct
62. Thrive
63. Underworld god
65. Polished gem?
69. Pts. of dollars
70. Comestables
72. "Bei ___ Bist Du Schoen"
73. Forked pole
75. Flowed forth
76. Ankle cover
77. Falstaff's favorite tavern
80. Etna output
81. Use a distaff
82. Cotton pods
83. Luigi's yesterday
84. "___ o'clock scholar"
85. Bright bankroll?
87. Major and Minor
88. Sheet material
90. Oxlike antelope
91. Stepped on it
93. Medicine container
95. Yang's opposite
96. Proclivity
97. Prudent pastures?
102. Cherished
104. Loutish
109. "___ Fideles"
110. Profound painting?
113. Companion of ambrosia
114. Hibernia
115. Colliery entrance
116. New Rochelle college
117. Aromatic compounds
118. Censures
119. Rel. of the Amex
120. Auspice

DOWN

1. Use a tocsin
2. Dies ___
3. Arcarologist's subject
4. No longer due
5. Hereditary
6. NOW members' aim
7. Birdbrains
8. Part of A.D.
9. Kind of rifle or cartridge
10. Way to play ponies in N.Y.
11. Gets the point
12. Tapestry type
13. Ring noncombatant
14. Hussein's language
15. Monte Carlo roulette bet
16. In ___ (originally positioned)
17. Adolph or Phil
18. Alda TV vehicle
24. Bulging jars
25. Make current
30. Little women
32. Stages of the Pleistocene Epoch
34. Like some locks
36. Cobbler's concern
37. Fast money?
38. Tenn.'s ___ Mountains
39. Neighbor of Yugo.
40. Bivouac
42. Yearns
43. Piercing pecorino?
44. Tell's apple, e.g.
45. Looks the villain
46. Catch a culprit
48. "Or ___ thou guide Arcturus . . .": Job 38:32
49. Lapidary's interest
52. Eventuated
56. Père's frère
57. All ears
58. Court failures
59. Sheds
62. Stupefy
63. Wattle
64. Perform in a think tank
66. Cricket official
67. Mirthfully
68. French school
71. Mont ___ (highest of the Alps)
74. Aviary sound
76. Bad Ems is one
77. Uniting force
78. W. Rumanian city
79. Cease functioning
81. Besmirch
82. British hood
85. Deli devices
86. Race horses yet to win
87. Author Sinclair
89. Incarnation
92. Instigate
94. Shunned one
96. Famed Civil War photographer
97. Dwindle
98. Nine days after nones
99. Product of a schism
100. Ferrara family
101. Antitoxins
103. Galway Bay Islands
105. Money changer's fee
106. Breathing space
107. ___ qua non
108. Pizzazz
111. Tuck's partner
112. It's for poets

by Warren W. Reich

ACROSS

1. Brief effort
5. Cassandra's gloomy prediction
9. Protrude, as the chin
12. Isaac Wise, e.g.
17. Attended
18. Utah ski resort
19. Allie's TV friend
20. Mrs. Irving Berlin
21. They can take a yoke
22. Ancien régime queen
24. Wall Street acronym
25. States firmly
26. NO CLOWNING, SIR!: 1988
29. U.S.A. LAST!: 1946
31. Early fig-leaf wearer
32. Face-stubble time
33. He dealt in pelts
34. Flower's Saturday-night special?
37. Most indolent
39. Operatic Eugene
43. Valor; virtue
44. D.A. WARM? LIAR!: 1937
46. Zilch
47. Low place
48. "You ___ mouthful!"
50. Whitewalls
52. Cole or Turner
53. Tolkien tree-giants
55. PACK BUNS, ED!: 1985
59. Keen
61. Loathed
63. Staring open-mouthed
64. Joined in a common cause
65. One quart, roughly
66. Cantankerous
67. MacLeod of "The Love Boat"
68. Kitchen gadget
70. "Common Sense" author
71. Marie von Trapp's title
74. Old Testament book
75. ONLY US, HANS!: 1983
77. Pitfall
78. The works
79. Gibbs of "227"
81. Large antelope
83. March 15, in Milano
84. Coral ridge

86. BLOBS OF RED!: 1976
90. O'Grady of song
92. Lord Mountbatten's wife
94. Previous
95. Stoppered the wine bottle
96. Coup ___
98. "___ We Got Fun?": 1921 song
99. Mason's burden
100. SEND LEE!: 1956
103. DUNCE SLAIN? YES!: 1989
109. Leaf angles
110. Compassionate
112. Play for time
113. Actor Julia from San Juan
114. "Giant" actor Sal ___
115. Plato topic
116. Jewish month
117. Pound or Stone
118. Forever, in poesy
119. Spider's parlor
120. Import tax
121. "Ich ___," Prince of Wales's motto

DOWN

1. Clumsy craft
2. Hirsch sitcom
3. Final word
4. Arnold or Tony
5. Weedy grass
6. Actor Vidov
7. Auricular
8. Flaherty film
9. Traffic tie-ups
10. Salt Lake City player
11. "Hello, sucker!" Guinan
12. Logic
13. Santa Anna's deposer
14. Tricolore hue
15. Spin a log
16. Part of M.I.T.
19. Abdul-Jabbar
23. Stowe's ice-crosser
27. Campus climbers
28. "The Art of Love" poet
30. Filched
33. In ___ (quickly)
34. Went white
35. Papas from Greece
36. SWELL ESTATE!: 1977
37. Put on cargo

38. Part of a daily dozen?
40. RUINS GIN? EEK!: 1980
41. Fuming
42. Well-known
44. Rheostat part
45. Ararat docker
49. Fall bloomer
51. Round of cheers
54. Fish catcher
56. "Mack the Knife" singer
57. Ecstasy's partner
58. Diamond corners
60. "Make my day" Eastwood
62. Iron or shovel preceder
64. Duelist Burr
66. Honkers' home
67. Festive affairs
68. Travelers' Midwest mecca
69. Propelled a gondola
70. Young hen
71. Plantation hand
72. Thompson or Hawkins

73. Looked through keyholes
75. Angels love these letters
76. Made dull
80. Taper off
82. Talk inanely
85. A crab on the roof?
87. Hoaxes
88. Ken ___ of "thirtysomething"
89. Cortices
91. Systematic
93. Wrestling hold
95. A bit nippy
97. Lopsided
100. Doe or Roe
101. Ramp sign
102. "___ kleine Nachtmusik"
103. Brahmin
104. Korean border river
105. Trollop
106. Hakenkreuzler
107. Smoke meat
108. Dash
111. Dander

by Frances Hansen

446 SKOAL!

ACROSS

1. A fruit for a spirit
6. Feel one's way
11. Clay or Webster
15. Sharpen a razor
20. Strong drink, for short
21. Glaswegian's great-grandchild
22. Man in the van of a clan
23. Italian philosopher 1866–1952
24. Certain turkeys
26. Deltas
28. Quarrel
29. Cerveza ingredient
30. Containers larger than six-packs
31. Without profit
32. "___ the Single Girl"
34. Necessity for a screwdriver
35. Cold ___
36. Vintner's vessel
39. NFL eleven
40. Elder (girl): Fr.
41. Wort ingredient
42. Utters, in Br'er Fox jargon
45. Heighten
47. Howe won here: 9/11/77
49. Monogram of Garfield's successor
50. Cover for the iris
51. Banshee sounds
52. ___ 'acte
53. Lewd material, for short
54. Common noun endings
55. Computer channels
56. Likeness
58. Singer Page
59. Burden
60. Deserve
61. British coins, for short
62. Bon ___ (cheap): Fr.
63. Hooper or Nielsen: Abbr.
64. Maugham book
68. ___ Vineyard
69. Harding's Secretary of Commerce
71. He summons: Lat.
72. Asiatic peninsula
73. ___ in bond
75. Plays a child's game
77. Beatty or Rorem
80. Lucy ___, the bride of Lammermoor
81. Complain
82. S.A. sorrels
83. Commercial Abbr.
84. Food and drink
85. Barbara's Oscar-winning role
86. Author of "Taras Bulba"
88. The Vaisyas, for one
89. Actress in "Tea and Sympathy"
90. Distinctive air
91. Hungarian wine
92. Hector, Hercules, et al.
93. Scotland's longest river
94. West Indies island chain
97. Beguiles
98. Simple sugar
99. Jigger
100. Wined and ___
101. Melkarth
102. French soul
103. Ursid
104. Four-time Wimbledon winner
105. Saki and family
107. Consents
110. Rickey ingredients
111. Sacred bird
112. Rudiments
116. Expire, à la Tennyson
118. Famed essayist and caricaturist
121. Fix the clocks again
122. Concerning
123. Costar in "The Seven Year Itch"
124. Forearm bones
125. Give an ___ (look after)
126. Brewer's need
127. Old Spanish sherry
128. Union general

DOWN

1. London taverns
2. Fabulist: Var.
3. ___ vitae
4. Gowdy and namesakes
5. N.T. book
6. Coburn's Pulitzer Prize play, with "The"
7. Summer TV fare
8. Mountain nymph
9. Seed holder
10. Draft or train endings
11. ___-jack, the Canada jay
12. "I ___ dream": M.L. King Jr.
13. Model ___ de la Fressange
14. Schnapps country: Abbr.
15. Stamp out
16. Kegs carrier
17. Newspaper section, for short
18. "Der Rosenkavalier" baron
19. Annoyance
22. Swapped
25. Home of Juárez
27. German firearm
30. Directs a ship's navigation
33. White-tailed birds
34. Lab items
35. Subject to 23 Across
36. Airplane's course
37. Rub with oil
38. "Coming ___": Burns
40. Saharan
41. Valuable vases
42. Kingston Trio hit: 1962
43. Singer Kitt
44. Kooks
46. Jillian and Sheridan
47. Poisons
48. Emulate Penelope
51. Ingredient of a barman's cubes
53. Cocktail ___
55. ___ Alaska
56. Newton or Hayes
57. ___ adagio (very slowly)
58. Coins of Belgrade
60. Prowl after prey
62. Drakes or harts
64. Wine is one
65. Kind of squash
66. Sharp; biting; cold
67. Affliction on skid row
68. Taj ___
70. Playful mammal
72. Genuine one
73. "___ the Future," 1985 movie
74. Family of a music-hall star
75. A treasurer of Nehemiah
76. Apparel at an "Animal House" orgy
78. Respect
79. Goddess, in Grenoble
81. Insert mark
83. Word on a Japanese freighter
85. Prevailing mania
86. Hopeless one
87. Approved
88. Rostropovich's instrument
90. Horrified
91. Prongs
92. Undertaker's purchase
95. Hard
96. Amuse
97. Jack or Josephus
99. Takes care of
101. Champagne feature
103. Assail
104. Nizer subject
105. Highball ingredient
106. Fla. cape
107. Israeli port
108. "Cabaret" costar
109. Kind of wine
110. Hyena created by Capp
113. ___ fide
114. Everett of TV and films
115. Widgeon
117. Stage freight?
118. Tequila country: Abbr.
119. Disciple's emotion
120. Strange, in Soho

by James E. Hinish, Jr.

ACROSS

1. ___ Alto
5. A step up
10. Fog's companion
14. Wetland
19. LXXVII × II
20. ___ nous
21. Dividing word
22. Air a view
23. Gatherers of honey for Georges?
25. A flier or fryer for Frédéric?
27. More glittering
28. "___ de Lune"
30. Soaks
31. An old story from Paul?
34. Fakes
36. Ampersands
37. Slanting
41. Charlie and clan
42. Drudge
44. Jr. high, e.g.
46. Town SE of Brussels
48. Resound
49. German state
50. Bull (transliteration from the Greek)
53. Jason's ship
54. Chi. airport code
55. A growler for Giacomo?
58. Actor Shackelford
59. Ready
61. Suffixes with attend and appear
62. Boring tools
64. Viking Ericson
65. Certain pitches
67. Fabricator
68. Pulpits
70. Safe place
71. Actress June from N.Y.C.
74. Residue
75. Footwear for Franz Peter?
79. Bk. notation
80. Type type, for short
82. Certain fishermen
83. Lament
84. Skin opening
85. Eatery
87. Mineo or Maglie
88. Custom
89. Polonius hid behind this
90. Extras
92. Bambi, for one
94. Municipal maps
95. A lure by Ludwig?
100. Protozoans
104. Loathed
105. Aquarium accessories
109. A watercolor by Wolfgang?
111. A few things for Franz to do?
113. Miscued
114. Certain entrance fee
115. Lincoln's late cousin
116. Start of Idaho's motto
117. Approaches
118. Spurry or henbit
119. ___ Carte, opera company
120. Enlist again: G.I. slang

DOWN

1. Chem. pollutants
2. Came to rest
3. Judy's girl
4. Projection
5. Gums
6. Ilka Chase's "___ We Cry"
7. Cubic meter
8. Before, to the Bard
9. Take back
10. Minor Prophet and namesakes
11. "___ Own Write," Lennon book
12. Attack
13. Apex
14. Every 30 days or so
15. Chevet
16. "Cherry-___" Herrick poem
17. Green bean
18. Coop group
24. Clips
26. Adherents
29. Inc. in the U.K.
32. New Zealand native
33. Uncouth person
34. Bake eggs
35. Applause for George?
38. Eggs: Lat.
39. A cove for Cole?
40. "The ___ Sanction," 1975 film
41. Field yield
42. Tempo
43. Example of 5 Down
44. Part of SST
45. Irritable
47. Stewart and Serling
49. Exterior boundary
50. Fire starters
51. Bronowski's "The ___ of Man"
52. Shore-dinner tidbit
55. What socks come in
56. More innocent
57. Oil, in Orléans
60. Favorite
63. Cheerful
65. Dolphins' former coach
66. Tag
68. Foray
69. Port for Pompey
71. Attention getter
72. Other women, to El Cid
73. Ayes' opposites
76. "Steppenwolf" author
77. Type of testimony
78. Sun. speech
81. Headed
84. One who babbles
86. Portrayer of many O'Neill protagonists
88. Teased
89. Cryptonym's cousin
91. Cardinal's quarters
92. Kind of line to sign
93. Woodward role in 1957
94. To a degree
96. Man in the van of a clan
97. "... Poker Flat" author
98. Impertinent
99. Cutting edge
100. Sitcom starring Sherman Hemsley
101. The man for all seasons
102. Biblical scribe
103. Humorist Arthur (Bugs) ___
106. Locale of Beauvais
107. Q-V connection
108. Octagonal sign
110. Observed
112. Wedding words

by Charles M. Deber

ACROSS

1. ... "THE PALLID PROF" by J. B. Poquelin?
7. Men, e.g.
13. Seasoning herbs
19. An ointment
20. Of the moon
21. Ancient marketplaces
22. ... "RIGHT? RIGHT!" by A. Loos?
23. Slender and sharp
24. Expand
25. Paradigm
26. ... "GRAND IMAGES" by H. Gardner?
28. "The law is a ___": Dickens
29. Occupied
31. Convert into cash
32. Got a hole-in-one
33. Newspaper-publishing family
36. Part of Scotland
40. Year or frog preceder
43. Islet
45. Pronoun for the Andrea Doria
46. Medicinal root
48. ... "O'ER THE LENT HERB" by P. Osborn?
53. Nicholas II & Ivan IV
54. World-weary
55. Lotion ingredient
56. Jockey's garb
58. Milieu for Levine
59. Effort
61. Blockheads, in Brest
63. Pasture
64. Cries of disgust
65. ... "AVE, SALVADOR" by M. Stewart & J. Herman?
68. ... "SAGAN'S TARS" by A. Miller?
71. Identical
72. ___ de plume
73. Hollow out
75. Cather's "One of ___"
76. Uncle in 36 Across
77. Organizational regulation
79. Generator's power output
81. Observant one
84. Bamboo lover of China
86. ... "MOLDING MOLD" by E. Williams?
90. Harmonize
92. Norse poem
93. Mythical piper
94. Parts of joules
95. "More matter with ___ art": Shak.
96. Did some sowing
99. Fixations
101. Steal
103. F's forerunners
105. Job of TV's Teddy Z.
108. ... "HOSTESS TO THE IMPECUNIOUS" by J. Gay?
114. Jockey, at times
116. Dwell
117. Frame braces
118. Plant also called germander
119. Ballerina McKerrow
120. Reference works
121. French ordnance
122. Book of prayers
123. Blush
124. Least forthright

DOWN

1. System of tenets
2. Spreads
3. Sleep, food, etc.
4. Carry on
5. Imperfective, as a verb
6. Maiden-name preceder
7. ___-de-mer (trepang)
8. Former Congolese prime minister
9. City on the Wabash
10. He lived 905 years
11. Upsets
12. Tantrums in public
13. Misfortune, in Hibernia
14. Spry
15. Guadalcanal, Malaita, et al.
16. New Persia
17. Lasting into the wee hours
18. Homophone for seize
20. Col. entrance exams
26. TV sound signal
27. Insecticide in disrepute
30. Niggardly
32. Asch's "The ___"
33. Pleasurable
34. A Lauder
35. Bat wood
37. Dorset town
38. Matches
39. Family of a memorable cartoonist
40. Lugworm
41. Signed up, as a G.I.
42. Humiliations
44. "The ___ Dogs," Burns poem
47. French connections
49. Actual
50. Israeli airline
51. Stir until foamy
52. Grade sch.
57. Land a haymaker
60. Like a skeleton
62. Relished
64. Public uproars in England
65. Hooked at the tip
66. Numskull
67. Oriental nurse
69. Scraggy
70. Intoned
71. Calyx segment
74. Byrd book
77. Interdict
78. Mineral resembling feldspar
80. Skinny follower
82. Brain specialist's rec.
83. T.L.C. givers
85. Trash-cans-on-Thames
87. Collegian's prerogative
88. Tricky drawback
89. Actress Markey
91. Living near the ground, as insects
97. Part of a journey
98. Human incarnation of a deity
100. Breakfast food
102. Hopper of Hollywood
103. Shakespearean forest
104. Food fish
105. Southwestern porridge
106. Chromosome constituents
107. Lovers' date
108. Trombone, to a jazzman
109. Half: Prefix
110. Those niñas
111. Rarely, old style
112. Toward the mouth
113. Raise a question
115. Gudrun's victim
118. Airgun ammo

by Walter Covell

ACROSS

1. Gaiters
6. Zounds!
10. Duct
14. "___ Thirteen": Faulkner
19. Stash
20. Fifth-largest desert
21. A wife of Esau
22. "Kitchen" of Manhattan
23. "___ Grows in Brooklyn"
24. The color purple
26. Islamic devil
27. "___ on the Drina": Andric
29. Isak Dinesen book
31. Uncanny
32. Kobo and Burrows
33. Tessera
34. Leaf beets
37. Rich man in Luke 16, Vulgate version
39. Mountain ashes
43. Remedy
44. Frost book
48. Fermi or Caruso
51. Pluck
52. Was off base
53. Dactyl, e.g.
54. Demeter's dad
55. Hebrew letter
56. Employed busily
57. "The Seaman's Friend" author
58. Monarchy
60. Aerie components
61. Swimmer Weatherford
62. E. M. Forster novel
66. MX and Sickle
69. Herrick's creation
70. Dark period in a Koestler book
74. Give a hang
75. Many a "Brother Rat" character
76. In academia a 4.00, e.g.
78. Muslim messiahs
79. Levin or Wolfert
80. Criterion
81. Fulminate
82. Shell-game decoys
83. Graham Greene novel
86. Orange-neck goose
87. Soprano Resnik
88. Throws off
90. Books, to Zola
92. ___ Ifni, Morocco
94. Fed
95. Al-Qahirah, to Flaubert
97. Isaak Babel book
101. James Joyce book
105. Result of a wedge shot
106. Place to write letters
108. "Land of cotton"
109. Running: Comb. form
110. Cape of Chile
111. Large kangaroo
112. Moliére's "L' ___ des maris"
113. Tip
114. Of French rock music in the 60's
115. ___ Mawr
116. Passover feast

DOWN

1. Vamoose
2. It's often beaten
3. End of an E. Caldwell title
4. Deighton book
5. Be angry
6. Islands off Sicily
7. Overcharged
8. Author Prevost
9. Cube with 21 spots
10. Most ambiguous
11. Emulates Robert Giroux
12. Minute: Comb. form
13. A purloining
14. A rainbow followed this
15. New Testament book
16. She outwrestled Thor
17. Bankrupt Federal org.
18. She, to Soldati
25. Poet Service
28. Org. that audits
30. Springless mattress
32. Get around
34. Tab
35. Novelist Barbusse
36. Role in "Green Pastures"
38. It's worn on an obi
40. Fragrance
41. Kern's "___ But Me"
42. Kind of preview
45. Light: Comb. form
46. Inventive
47. City SE of San Jose
49. Pointed ends
50. ___ Peak, N.M.
51. Romany realm
56. Small part of an oz.
57. Thomas Mann novella
59. Bensalem is one
60. Gumshoe
61. Alice's cat
63. The Salt Palace, e.g.
64. Shoo!, in Dogpatch
65. Benedictine titles
66. Less amicable
67. "Daybreak" director
68. Fort in N.C.
71. Fainéant
72. Eeyore's creator
73. Squiggles
75. Homeland of 25 Down
76. Street urchin
77. Painter Mondrian
80. Container for coffee
81. Group anew
84. Supple
85. Estate
89. Scamper
90. "___ Liza Jane," 1916 song
91. Fleurs-de-lis
93. Antsy
94. Celebrity
96. Minor judge in Judges
97. Chances
98. Tittle-tattle
99. Bacchic shout
100. ___ Islands, off New Guinea
101. Gloomy
102. O.T. book
103. Ruffle
104. Melampus or Mopsus
107. "Charlotte's ___"

by John M. Samson

450 SVITTLES

ACROSS

1. Supergiant in Scorpio
8. Put two and two together
15. Agreement
19. Arrowhead, e.g.
20. Bleach
21. Gate City of the West
23. Cassava grains
24. Dinner course, dressed up?
27. News nugget
28. "Get ___ the Church . . ."
30. Gaelic
31. Brazilian dance
32. Putting salt in one's coffee, e.g.
35. Lincoln's "Cap'n ___"
38. Tipples
40. Cowpoke's poker
41. Switch positions
44. Work
45. Make ___ in (progress)
47. Have the flu
48. ___ Lanka
49. Energy
50. Debussy's sea
51. Grilled fare gets splintered?
55. Like good news
57. Cliques
58. Apprizes
59. Free
60. Marathon winner: 1972 Olympics
61. A Borgia in-law
62. Donees
64. Ictus syllable
65. Jaeger
66. Bad Soden is one
69. Dame Myra ___
71. Hammett dog
73. Restaurants?
76. Yearn
77. Question
79. Ethyl's end
80. Spore clusters
81. Ears catch note of derision?
88. Capone nemesis
91. Calculator key
92. Featherweight champ: 1942–48
93. Burden
94. Lanyards
96. Put away
98. Pitcher Saberhagen
99. Bestow a right upon
101. Fined
104. Shutter parts
106. Washer's swasher
107. Reply to "Why?"
108. Inebriated vege-taters?
110. Chance
111. Macadam stickum
112. Lennon's "___ Do You Sleep?"
113. Kind of sided
114. German river and Hungarian city
115. Game of chance
116. Result of 8 Across
117. Cosmic times
119. Uke ridge
121. It opens sesame
122. Crude vessels?
124. Heart chambers
126. Medley
128. Arena for the Hawks
129. Sonora sandwich
133. Easter quarry fragment?
138. Unaffected
141. Flock of geese
142. Skier's turn
143. Put into law
144. Tolkien tree creatures
145. Squeeze out
146. Diapers, in Dover

DOWN

1. Oppositionist
2. Undiluted
3. Drink without moderation
4. Out on ___
5. One Grande
6. List extender
7. Grill counterfeits?
8. Kind of sphere?
9. God, in Genoa
10. Johnny's bandleader
11. Grand Exalted Ruler, e.g.
12. Go together
13. Intersection maneuver
14. Darius's subjects
15. Campaigner, for short
16. Nice souls in Iowa?
17. Chihuahua houses
18. Sadie of "Rain"
20. This, in Spain
22. Hair colors
25. Warmish
26. Achilles' killer
29. Aurora, in Greece
33. Attu canoe
34. Marine area
35. Diaskeuasts
36. Numismatic tails
37. Immovability
39. Decelerates
41. Finished
42. Ramses' river
43. Shake center, colored blue?
45. Kauai hi
46. Adriatic gulf
51. Act pts.
52. Gas: Comb. form
53. South African province
54. Choler
56. Madison Avenue come on
61. Heart track, initially
63. Candlestick Park info
65. Dirks of yore
66. Sarcastic remarks from the deli?
67. Cuzco country
68. Broadway play: 1985
69. Chest fastener
70. "___ homo"
72. Cigarette end
74. "Holiday ___" Crosby film
75. "Ad astra per ___"
78. Important ore of boron
82. Realm of Boreas
83. "Hell is ___": T. S. Eliot
84. Filbert
85. Kind of pudding
86. Narcotics
87. Reno raisers
89. Fabric for a filly?
90. "Make ___ Happy," 1960 song
95. Blackthorns
97. Principal's cousin
98. Kind of relief
99. One kind of maniac
100. Forage plant
102. Isaac's firstborn
103. Corium
104. Evens out
105. Fall tool
106. Desire, in this puzzle
108. Butter trees
109. Not ventro
115. Relations
118. Traffic stopper
120. Fax predecessor
122. Siberian city
123. Adhered
125. Colliery access
127. Whip lash
128. Huge hideosity
130. Esthetic course for freshmen
131. Calvados capital
132. Auto maker
134. Infantry gps.
135. Weber's "___ Freischutz"
136. Rhea's relative
137. Chisel
139. Literary oddments
140. Spigot

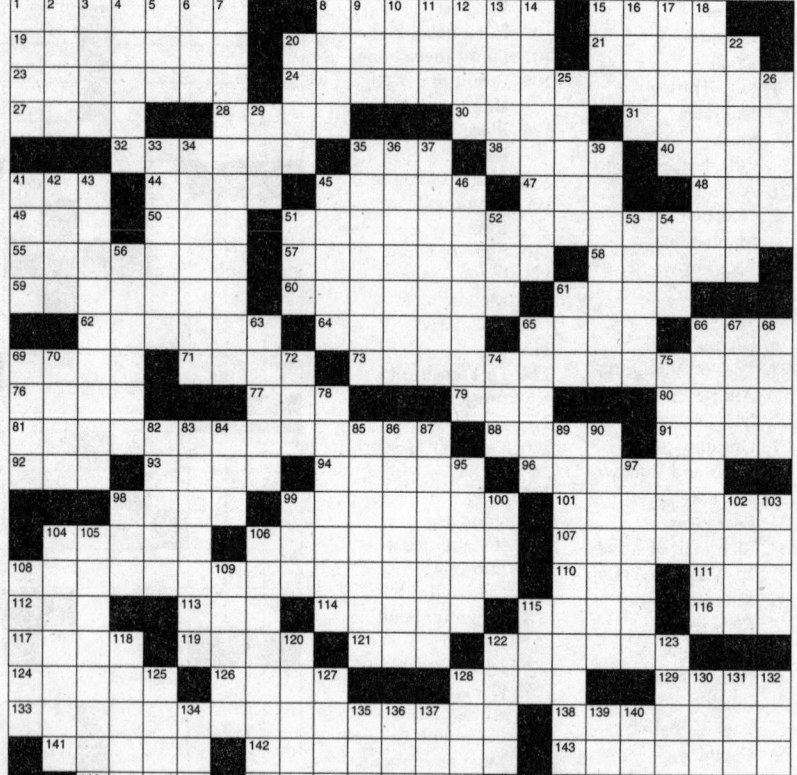

by Phyllis Fehringer

ACROSS

1. Van
5. Mary Janes
10. Calyx part
15. Lamb of pork fame
19. Being: Fr.
20. A manager of the Cards in 1990
21. Wing of a sort
22. Flows
23. Verdi product, full of froth?
25. Foolish, tree-climbing bird?
27. Subjugates
28. Alan, Cheryl and Diane
30. Glide nonchalantly
31. City in S. France
32. Latin teacher's command
33. Violinist Bull
34. Barbiturate
37. ___ Domingo
38. Sweeps under the rug
43. Kin of Tonys
44. Indecent planter?
46. Crooked
47. Impart
48. A concern of ecologists
49. Frost
50. River duck
51. Shaver
52. Obdurate bricklayers?
56. British shindig
57. Mouthpiece of a sort
59. Root used as a cleanser in Mexico
60. Egg box
61. Goes in with
62. Marsh bird
63. Groom
64. Bowling term
66. Caused by
67. Obstructs
70. Fleet St. product
71. Vague Donatello?
74. Skeet feat
75. Radiation dosages
76. G-men
77. Some votes
78. ___ qua non
79. Sèvres summer
80. Rash maitre d'?
84. Ky. college town
85. Justification
87. Avifauna
88. Half a decade
89. Bel Kaufman's "Love, ___": 1979
90. White wine, in 90 Down
91. Rex ___, film critic
92. He's got the goods
95. Move crabwise
96. Kin of floribundas
100. Emaciated hunting dog?
102. A short, thickset haddock?
104. Lotion ingredient
105. Finnish bath
106. Rich cake
107. Destiny, to Domenico
108. Tear
109. Co-Nobelist for Peace: 1978
110. Hairnet
111. Merganser

DOWN

1. ___-majesty
2. School 007 attended
3. Turkish river
4. Got off a 747
5. Hay; stubble
6. "High ___" 1959 song
7. Cuprite and limonite
8. Stray
9. Waxy substance
10. "___ Iwo Jima," 1949 film
11. Give the slip to
12. Places
13. Cover girl Carol ___
14. Postpones
15. Classroom item
16. A Prot.
17. "Child of the Sun"
18. Pale
24. Mythical beasts
26. Word on a Czech's check
29. Bohemian
32. Kind of line
34. Display in a toy shop
35. West Indian fetish
36. Unsubstantial ship?
37. Capital of Valais, Switzerland
38. Beldam
39. Suffixes used in medical terms
40. Moist cámise?
41. Sky: Comb. form
42. Airport tower
44. "Swinging ___," Haggard hit
45. Burn ___ in one's pocket

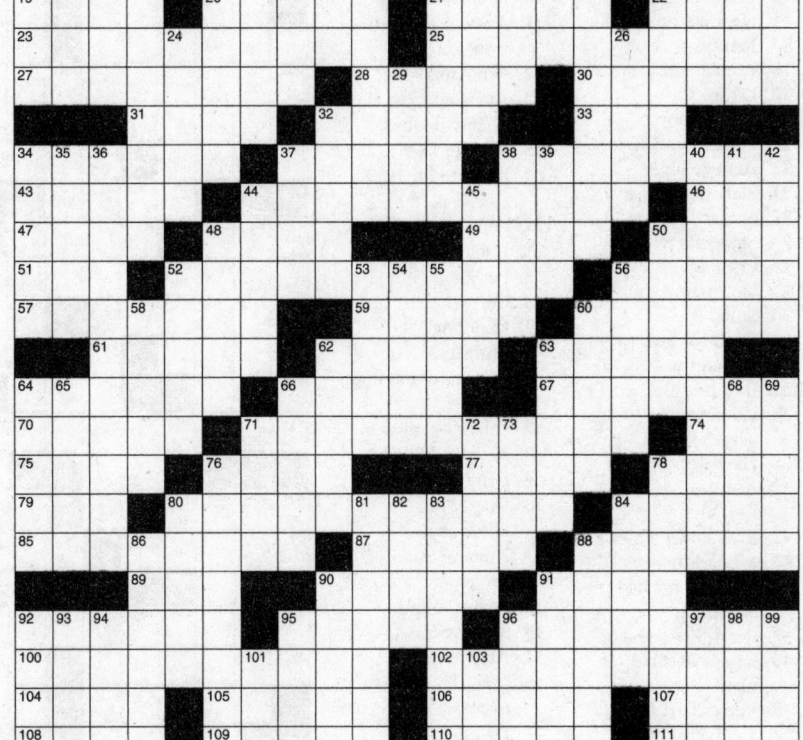

by Harold B. Counts

48. British guns
50. Basse ___, city in Guadeloupe
52. Filthy places
53. Having hair like Elsa
54. Friendship
55. City NNW of Gdansk
56. Rail for Susan Jaffe
58. Tender places
60. Tendrils
62. Like bubble baths
63. Supply food commercially
64. Throw about
65. Statue in the Duomo at Florence
66. Fuddy follower
68. Ringworm
69. Lieu
71. Gist
72. Loosen
73. European deer
76. Salad ingredient
78. Bon-voyage bashes
80. Despises
81. Bushy-tailed hoarder
82. Asian lake
83. Dresses
84. Dr. Spooner's "___ wenches"
86. Changed colors again
88. Wan
90. Where Duccio painted
91. Right-hand page
92. Ski lift
93. Cameo, for one
94. Soon
95. Ornament
96. Charger in Mexico City
97. Thailand, once
98. Varese's Palazzo d'___
99. Betoken
101. Chinese pagoda
103. Fashion

452 PROMISES, PROMISES

ACROSS

1. Dines late
5. Munch
10. Tribulations
14. Nedda's husband
15. Finery
18. Fainéant
20. Errors at Wimbledon
21. Pericles and Cicero
22. Actress Piper
24. Start of a verse
27. Singer Laine et al.
28. Stengel's wife
29. Composer ___ Hoffmann: Inits.
30. Suitable
31. Deadeye and Rackstraw
32. Bull fiddle
33. "Lakmé," e.g.
36. City NW of Leipzig
38. Harrow's rival
40. Institute in Brooklyn
41. Ross and Palmer
42. Mil. address
45. Endings for lobby and palm
47. Pearl Mosque site
48. Japanese salad plant
49. Verse: Part II
57. ___ Bell (Emily Brontë)
58. Shabby
59. The least bit
60. Popular apéritif
61. Greenish blue
62. Prospero's servant
64. Cautious
66. Greek Juno
67. Bowler or boater
68. Neighbor of Md.
69. Secular
70. Jeans fabric
71. Verse: Part III
78. "But is it ___?"
79. Composer Khachaturian
80. Bridge bid
81. Draft org.
82. Nettles
85. Streetcars
86. Command to Gabriel
88. Peep show
89. Euripides tragedy
90. Twofold
92. Curly coiffure
96. Syr. neighbor
97. Australian isl.
98. Louis challenger
99. J. F. Cooper subject
100. End of verse
107. Strict
108. Part of G.P.A.
109. Some women's fashions
110. Less well done
111. Ancient chipped stones
112. Tam-tams
113. Ayers and Hoad
114. Loamy deposit
115. Pulitzer Prize playwright: 1953

DOWN

1. Limoges item
2. Let go
3. Cores
4. Middling
5. Throngs
6. Cousins of hammerheads
7. Guam's capital
8. Marshal Dillon
9. Drop heavily
10. One of the Flintstones
11. Anita or Alan of songdom
12. Jewish month
13. Soap operas
14. Arum lily
16. "De ___," Seneca essay
17. Postulate
19. Like breeze-kissed water
20. Reality
23. Adlai's running mate: 1956
25. Camper's shelter
26. Dep.
32. Greenish-yellow pear
33. E. Power Biggs' instrument
34. Henry's last Catherine
35. State of France
36. Lamarr of films
37. At the summit
39. Involuntary contractions
40. Kind of bull
41. Causing jolts
42. "... the rat that ___ malt"
43. Knight's weapon
44. Flattened at the poles
46. Metaphor's cousin
50. Trouble
51. Comprehend
52. Plants resembling spinach
53. Remote
54. Indehiscent fruits
55. Night's brightest star
56. Birds of passage
62. Mine entrances
63. Domicile: Abbr.
64. Soothes
65. Towel word
66. The bottom line, to Blass
69. Vicuña's cousin
70. Salesman's car, frequently
72. Appraise
73. Ontario Indian
74. Guardian's concern
75. "Dies ___"
76. Role in "King Lear"
77. Weary
82. Southern dish
83. Bacon portion
84. Advent
85. Seed coats
87. Banshee's activity
89. Actress Clarke of old films
90. Kneaded mixtures
91. Save
93. Projecting rim
94. American Beauties
95. Mel and Ed of baseball
97. Shea areas
98. Jalopy
99. Post used in air races
101. Parched
102. Teen detective of fiction
103. ___ Levi (Yves Montand)
104. Market
105. Chamber-music piece
106. O. Henry title word

by Nancy Scandrett Ross

ACROSS

1. A 1977 movie
5. "Batman," e.g.
9. "But war's ___ . . .": Cowper
14. Pollution problem
18. Chums
19. Shirley Temple's first
20. Thin layer
22. Famed hill near Dublin
23. Fusses
24. Custer's last major
25. "The guests ___ . . .": Coleridge
26. Time periods
27. With 65 Across, source of 40 and 87 Across
29. ___ B'rith
30. Rolling stock
32. Nap, in Nayarit
33. Sell or tell
35. Science that's on the rocks
36. Ticked off
38. ___ de plume (pen names)
39. Writer Calderon
40. Start of a quotation
49. Inductance unit
50. White bubbles
51. Covenant
52. Greek peak
53. College studies
54. Blame bearer in a song
55. Occur as a consequence
57. Understood
58. Also
59. Facility
60. Singer Laine
61. Schism
63. Imagoes
65. See 27 Across
68. Set back
71. Family of Portnoy's creator
73. City south of Moscow
74. Graf ___
76. Caviar
77. Mold
79. Expert
81. Salutation of a sort
82. Meerschaum
83. All atwitter
84. Dock support
85. A-F links
86. First: Comb. form
87. End of quotation
92. Wallet stuffers
93. She may wear a chador
94. Munster's pet
95. Divulges
99. Order from Hunter
101. Kind of license
105. He wrote "I Marry You"
106. Dish for a king?
107. Author of the quotation
109. Indigo
110. Obscure
112. Belém, Brazil
113. Dagger of yore
114. Canonical hour
115. Tso-lin of Manchuria and family
116. Balm
117. To be, to Bernadette
118. ___ bien!
119. Beginning
120. Canapés
121. Be zetetic

DOWN

1. Girasols
2. Spokes
3. Complete copy
4. Tax men
5. Token, sometimes
6. "Happy Days Are Here Again" composer
7. Landed estate
8. Call at a barn dance
9. Country-rock group
10. Parsley, e.g.
11. What one swallow doesn't make
12. La Bohème
13. Chem. ending
14. Bargain
15. Cuomo or Lanza
16. Chimp's cousin
17. Like long-winded orators
21. Essay
28. Pitiless
31. Simba's sound
34. Seaver and Sneva
35. Attendants on Aphrodite
37. "___ Dream": Wagner
39. Uncle of Joseph
40. "They went ___ way"
41. King of Judea
42. Celebrity's following
43. "Dog Day Afternoon" director
44. ___ Downs
45. Column style
46. Recondite matters
47. Calais-to-Rouen dir.
48. Sunbather's goal
54. Hawkeye's unit
55. Barkin of films
56. Patricia of films
57. "Fish Magic" painter
59. Major chaser
60. Parrot's mandible covering
62. G.H.W.B., e.g.
64. Steady Eddie of pitching fame
66. Home of the slave
67. Coward's "To Step ___"
69. Frosh teasers
70. Murrow's "___ Now"
72. Callahan-Roberts song
75. Basketball defense
77. Short noncom?
78. Cry of discovery
80. Start of a W.S. title
81. Opossum shrimp
82. Shams
84. Ottawa chief
85. Poison
86. "Is life ___?": Gilbert
88. "Mum's the ___": Cervantes
89. Settle
90. Inflatable life jacket
91. Seems
95. "___ Sleep," Odets play
96. Under full legal age
97. "Common Sense" author
98. Van Gogh slept here
99. Open, tartlike pastries
100. Islands off Sicily
102. Anne Sedgwick novel: 1911
103. Rhone feeder
104. Nerve
106. Radar action
108. Lozenge
111. Greek letter

by Jeanne Wilson

ACROSS

1. Cinch belt's cousin
5. Economist Smith
9. Sahara filling station
14. Shoot the breeze
17. C.I.O. partner
20. Canyon phenomenon
21. The Venerable ___
22. Gorge with a stream
23. Macrogametes
24. Kind of brother
25. Advice to Clouseau
28. Physiotherapist
30. Busy place, 4:00 P.M., London
31. Mexican standoff
32. Surroundings
34. Patriotic women's org.
35. Depletion
37. Witness
38. Indian foot soldier
40. Shelley subject
43. Stone pillar
45. Am. equivalent of a concierge
49. Diamond point
50. Locust
53. Collars
55. Moderate
56. Data fed to a computer
58. Eliminate malfunctions
59. Masonic doorkeeper
61. Operated
62. Immature, in a way
64. African plant
66. Conversation à deux
69. Harangue
71. Kyd work
74. Mingle
75. Allot
76. Embdem and quink
79. Age, as cheese
82. Interstices
85. Mun. official
86. Justification for existence
89. Australian bird
90. "Swanee" lyricist
94. Harness part
95. Provide new weapons
97. Aspersion
98. Vatican governing body
100. Wrists
102. Detroit action
104. Enamel work
108. Place
110. Uncover
112. Roman household god
113. Flies heavenward
115. One-tenth
118. Casino game
119. They call K's
121. Boite de ___ (nightclub)
122. Levantine garment
123. Glacé
124. Muddle with drink
126. Insinuating
128. Some N.Y.C. trains
129. Reared
130. Apologue
133. Negotiate
136. One needing an att.
137. Kin of a morganatic marriage
141. Originally called
143. Tells or sells
147. Beyond the megalopolis
148. Ambassador's stand-in
151. Taste
152. Suffix with verb
153. To love, in Paris
154. Robert (père) or Allan (fils)
155. Fustian
156. Nov. 1 group
157. Painter ___ Borch
158. Nervous
159. Sow chow
160. Purposes

DOWN

1. Conventicle group
2. Feel compassion
3. Strawberry's patch, once
4. Canapé
5. Antonym for adore
6. Profound
7. Wood-trimming tool
8. Dissolve
9. Tender
10. Part of a shandy
11. Pinnacle
12. At hand
13. Spots
14. Montague's son
15. ___-garde
16. Exceeds
17. Nonwindy side
18. Goatlike creature
19. Hugo's "Toute la ___"
26. Biggers hero
27. Give a leg up
29. Cancel
33. Give power to
36. A king of Judah
38. Long, slender cigar
39. Camaraderie
40. Unhinged
41. Top of a suit
42. ___ au rhum
44. Café au ___
46. Superior
47. French state
48. French director Clair
49. Puppeteer Baird
51. Dead end
52. Borodin's prince
54. Bristle
57. Chinese pagoda
60. Burgundy and Bordeaux, sometimes
63. Arrival at J.F.K.
65. Bacon bringers
67. Unit of elec. current
68. Tante, in Spain
70. Poetic contraction
72. First word of "Home, Sweet Home"
73. Sherry or Dubonnet, often
75. Singer Davis
77. Please the cordon bleu
78. "To ___ with Love"
80. Printemps follower
81. New Deal org.
83. Tried to equal or surpass
84. Big ___, Calif.
87. Peruvian plant
88. Slip or trip
91. ___ generis (unique)
92. "___ longa . . ."
93. Mayo and Yaqui
96. La Méditerranée, e.g.
97. Urbanity; tact
99. Shortly
101. Pocket bread
103. Bldg. material
104. Wodehouse's Drones ___
105. Brocaded fabric
106. Repugnance
107. Hibernia
109. Word feminizer
111. Was first
114. "A ___ time saves nine"
116. Belgian pilgrimage town, to a Parisian
117. Annapolis grad.
120. Up to now
122. Third letter
125. Type of hound
127. Fantasized
129. Kind of particle or ray
131. World-weary
132. Grease pencil
134. Wroth
135. Peg for Peete
136. Skim off grease
137. Kind of hall
138. Stage direction
139. Has dinner
140. Sports org.
142. Dutch cheese town
143. Mail rtes.
144. Persia, today
145. ___-Lease Act: 1941
146. Concordes
149. Thing, in law
150. Carte preceder

by Joan P. Leemhorst

ACROSS

1. Commodity
5. Tender or hooker
9. "Sesame Street" grouch
14. Turkish chiefs
18. Arabian gulf
19. "___ la Douce"
20. Keyless
22. Cooked
23. Agalite
24. Grin broadly
25. Franchi or Mendes
26. Glissaded
27. What the passenger told the cabbie
28. Devoured
29. A.M.A. members
31. Fragrance
33. On a yacht, briefly
34. Kind of eclipse
36. Forerunner
41. Norwegian kings
43. Antique auto
44. Curtis and Bennett
46. Of the ribs
48. Too bad!
52. Beloit or Berea
54. Hebrew letter
56. Person Cinderella said was cruel
57. Can. province
58. Letter
60. Journalist Stewart
62. Volume of sayings
63. Ghislanzoni's great libretto
66. Cassowary
67. Kansas motto word
70. David, to Goliath
72. How the gradualist said he proceeds
74. Comedienne Kelly et al.
76. Shankar's ax
77. N.Y.C. subway line
79. Mtg.
80. ___ de France
81. Strasberg or Hayward
83. ___ Mauler (Dempsey)
86. ___ de veau
87. Undo
90. What perils test
94. Outside: Comb. form
96. Comedian Russell
98. Chalkboard
100. Fuss
101. Unisonally
103. What the politician was told to do
104. Scrutinizes
106. Commence
109. Queen Sophia's predecessor
111. Fledgling's abode
113. D-H connection
114. Possess
119. Parnassian number
121. Depict
123. Evangelist Roberts
125. Alt.
126. Indigo
127. Date
128. Wan
129. Ceramic piece
130. Reduce a sail
131. Judgment
132. Vegas machine
133. Takes a chair

DOWN

1. Escalator warning
2. Actress ___ Isaacs Menken
3. Depend
4. Construct a cipher
5. Child's cover-up
6. Cuprite and limnite
7. Loving
8. Domesticated
9. Alliance for Progress grp.
10. Hesse novel
11. Marine body
12. Rich Norman cheese
13. Barometer
14. Commercials
15. ___ Heights, in the Mideast
16. Singer Baker
17. Passover feast
21. Mean-spirited
30. Cheap cigar
32. What arroz is
35. Davis Cup team
36. Cinquefoil feature
37. New: Comb. form
38. Mountain pass
39. Part of Armstrong's statement
40. Surpass
42. Lowest female voices
45. "Erie Canal" mule
47. Keen
49. Abhor
50. Years, to Yves
51. Belle, Bart, and Brenda
53. Vaults
55. Slightest
59. Okla. oil center
61. The end, in Epernay
63. Aim high
64. Type of type
65. Hate
68. Penn. is one
69. Durations
71. "Where ___," 1969 Kanin film
73. Queues
75. Sleep, to Segovia
78. Feared fly
82. Cowardly
84. Loser to D.D.E.
85. What Levin called his heroines
88. In medias ___
89. Sixteenth Hebrew letter
91. Fond du ___, Wis.
92. N.Y. zone, at times
93. Distress call
95. Item for a shell
97. Punishment for sin
99. Actual
102. What the painters said they needed
105. Herons
106. Sub detector
107. Cord
108. Lennox or Potts
110. Extra charge
112. Halts
115. Grand ___, Evangeline's home
116. ___ Alto
117. LXIX × VIII
118. Ridge
120. Pixie
122. Beat for a P.O. man
124. Rent

by Charles M. Deber

ACROSS

1. Dade City's county
6. Long time
10. Plaudit
15. Fence's take
19. Certain voices
20. ___-ha-Shanah
21. Pine product
22. Strauss's "Die Frau ___ Schatten"
23. Landing places
24. Berlin product
25. Out of the way
26. Pedestal section
27. "Officious ___"
31. Actor Danson
32. Blind a falcon
33. Brachium's locale
34. Noon has two
35. Last exit
37. Abner's adjective
39. Solecist's contraction
41. Caboodle's mate
44. N.Y. Phil. output
45. "Armageddon ___!"
51. Pollen distributor
53. Tokyo, once
54. Febrero predecessor
55. Record the pace
56. The McCoy
58. An Arnaz
59. Contrite ones
61. Cytology inits.
62. Muezzin's God
64. Knish emporium
66. White-flag time
68. "Humus ___"
74. One of the Dryads
75. Equal, in Metz
76. Gunwale pin
79. Yard for Johann
82. Uncharged particle
84. Nautical raptors
88. Cameo's stone
89. Family name in baseball
91. Au revoir's kin
92. Bright signs
94. Aberdeen's river
95. "Universe ___"
100. Air: Comb. form
101. Snoopy's pair
102. Bartlett or Seckel
103. Churchill's letter
104. Islam's second city
107. Eureka!
108. Copy
110. ___ Comeau, Quebec town
114. Sideburn's neighbor
115. "Acrostic ___"
121. Exchange premium
123. Baited device
124. Trident part
125. Puff up
126. Leningrad's river
127. Just ___ in the bucket
128. Concert halls
129. Be gaga about
130. Migration
131. Not yet dry
132. Lather
133. Covers with frost

DOWN

1. Actress from Greece
2. Mrs. Roosevelt
3. Cubic meter
4. Dramatic tenor Franco ___
5. Tasmania's top peak
6. Pianist Schnabel
7. Dom DeLuise et al.
8. Theow's cousin
9. Dresser's "___ to the City"
10. Kindergarten pests
11. Hebrew R
12. Book by poet Ciardi
13. Word in a Caesar report
14. Upright
15. Earth layer
16. "Ament ___!"
17. Chilean landscape
18. Crystal-lined stone
28. Blabbed
29. Incan sun god
30. Kind of pro
36. Dog-show crasher
38. Aloof
40. "The Fourposter" as a 1966 musical
41. Lottolike game
42. Trav. papers, e.g.
43. Matador
45. Marine mammals
46. "The Sultan of Sulu" playwright
47. Eyeball section
48. Tribunal
49. K-O hookup
50. Where cows browse
51. Lingerie item
52. Reclusive fish
57. Off-schedule
59. Make parallel
60. Bambi's tail
63. Cape or Trader
65. Make do with
67. Say the same
69. Joyous hymn
70. Atelier
71. Incentive
72. Farrell or Jackson
73. Wayne film: 1953
77. Cleaning substance
78. Somerset river
79. Gen. Arnold
80. Violinist Bull
81. "Manon Lescaut ___"
83. Dakota Indians
85. Taught new software
86. Japanese drama
87. Whine tearfully
90. ___ nad Labem, Czech city
93. Reno-to-Las Vegas dir.
96. Bus or potent preceder
97. Snake: Comb. form
98. Sloped sheds
99. Soprano Renata
104. Intended
105. Gung-ho
106. Shilong's state
107. Skilled one
109. Entreaties
111. Forster's "___ With a View"
112. "___ do all . . .": Macbeth
113. Creator of the Moffats
116. Cancel
117. Patola, e.g.
118. Psyche's love
119. Singer Sayao
120. Construction piece
122. Acorn that made it

by Louis Baron

ACROSS

1. Kind of plan
9. Cloisonné
15. "¿Quién ___?"
19. Potential vitamin A
20. Lassie's family
22. Quahog
23. Unisex Shakespearean play?
25. Aleutian island
26. Nautical direction
27. Vic's radio wife
28. Zeus, to Cronus
29. Rooms at the top
31. Transformed
33. Snack
35. Swiss river
36. Souls
40. Eliot poem on the rewards of dieting?
44. Waters the garden
45. Truth, in Confucianism
46. Site of the patella
47. Pablo's uncle
48. Country song from a Gershwin musical?
54. Kind of price
56. Actress Rehan
57. "___ right with the world"
58. Diva Stevens
60. Theater part
61. Pillages
64. Olympic event
66. At full speed
69. Woolf work on the joy of housework?
72. Kepi part
73. "L' ___ c'est moi"
74. Norman and Walloon, e.g.
78. Traverse
80. Land in Eur.
82. Bank claim
83. Scandinavian coin
84. N.B.A. men
87. Fitzgerald's tale for tots?
92. Parseghian
93. Fervor
95. City in Neb.
96. "Ars gratia ___"
97. Updike work on cooking wild game?
101. ___ Pointe, Mich.
102. Blessing
103. City on the Oka
104. Guides
108. Unbranded calf, to cowboys
110. Alma-___, Kazakhstan city

112. Chip in a chip
113. Cartoonist Soglow
117. Alan or Robert
118. Freed-Brown film musical re commuters?
122. Match
123. Air: Comb. form
124. Went over again
125. Exam for a teen
126. Long-running show
127. "Hamlet" setting

DOWN

1. Recorded proceedings
2. Knightwear
3. Famed artist/designer
4. Rake
5. Porter's "___ De-Lovely"
6. Stops
7. Former Indochinese kingdom
8. "Pagliacci" wife
9. Writer Umberto
10. Emulates Xanthippe
11. "Tennis, ___?"
12. Common bait
13. Tokyo before 1868
14. Rowan and Martin's show
15. Beetle or gem
16. Change
17. Glutton's activity
18. Cassowaries' kin
21. Conductor ___ Pekka Salonen
24. Like some tape
30. Estimates
31. Tabula ___
32. Relative of etc.
34. Tokyo drinks
36. Onward
37. ___ guerre
38. Russian log huts
39. Debussy's "La ___"
41. Straddler
42. One expanse
43. Grand Canal man
45. Cookbook Abbr.
49. Ohio/Mississippi city
50. Archeological site in India
51. Part of aka
52. Grain disease
53. Vienna, to Strauss
55. Franz or Kevin
59. Not so hard
62. "Common Sense" author
63. Dictionary Abbr.

64. Singer/actress Lenya
65. Italian exclamation
67. Flaherty South Seas film: 1926
68. Pointed instrument
70. Engage
71. Correct text
72. The life of a hobo
75. Mud hens
76. ___-Rivières, Quebec
77. Sixth follower
78. Cicatrix
79. Bowl-shaped antennas
81. Absolute
82. Trip tripper, for short
85. Lorelei's bailiwick
86. Prepared
88. Bagel topper
89. Hector's protector
90. Lincoln and Maxwell
91. ___-Magnon
94. Worshipful
98. Oscar winner of 1951
99. Three sea miles

100. Last syllable of a word
101. Hails
105. Japanese land unit
106. ___ nous
107. Lucy's TV pal
108. Northern nomad
109. Horned viper
111. Collections of sayings
113. Algerian port
114. Tex-Mex treat
115. Opera-house feature
116. Marcel's wave
119. Abner's father
120. Social followers
121. Cycle starter

by Nancy Nicholson Joline

458 NOTA BENE: SCALE BACK

ACROSS

1. Dress trimming
6. Receded
11. Chest wood
16. Rambouillets
21. Pompeiian cover-up
22. Veiling
23. Genetic enzyme
24. Señor's mark
25. DO
28. Lazzarone
29. Durango dough
30. Swiss unit for watches
31. Org.
32. Young pilchard
34. Exist
35. Caught a bug
36. Debauchee
37. Spit curl
38. TI
43. Type of brandy
46. "Friends" role
47. Cavort
48. Foot, to Fabius
51. Uzbek, for one
52. Goalie's place
54. Muscovite
56. Singer Vaughan
58. LA
63. Josip Broz
64. Cast lead-in
65. Lake near Novgorod
66. Sniffs out
67. ___ State (Oklahoma)
69. Standoff
71. Galatea's love
72. Sky Harbor, e.g.
73. SOL
77. Tries very hard
81. Get around
82. Handel's forte
87. Asked for earnestly
88. "A linen stock ___ leg...": Shak.
90. Singer Lopez
91. Whilom
92. Roster
93. FA
96. Equalizes
98. Write a ticket
99. "Play ___ It Lays," 1972 film
100. Jeans material
101. Say "I do"
102. Grimace
104. A Yemeni capital
106. Sheep-ish?
107. MI
113. Menu
115. Dover domestic
116. Convex moldings
117. Light touch
120. Song from "South Pacific"
122. Insincerity
123. Extended family
124. Monterrey Ms.
125. Liqueur flavoring
126. RE
130. No way!
131. Classical ennead
132. Ben or Paul
133. English poet
134. Sheath, for one
135. Inscribed pillar
136. Gators' kin
137. Highway hazard

DOWN

1. Mexican dance
2. Wedding worker
3. Was selective
4. Hoagie
5. "Dulce et decorum ___..."
6. Savoie star
7. Fries' partner
8. Fair-haired chaps
9. Sand's "___ et lui"
10. "Agnus ___"
11. Coal-tar distillates
12. Attains a goal
13. Dragonfly
14. ___ rule (generally)
15. The Gray
16. Saddle features
17. Out of sight
18. Poet Havelock
19. "Lest we lose our ___": Browning
20. Goriot, par exemple
26. Somersaults
27. Spanish measures
33. Molecule member
35. ___ acid
38. Actress Sanford
39. Cathedral fixture
40. A Coward
41. The lower world
42. Mr. Chomsky
43. Assigns parts
44. To this point
45. Summer capital of the Raj
48. Carnera of boxing
49. Gourmand
50. Two-reel movie
52. French blueblood
53. Dizzy
54. Beethoven's "___ Solemnis"
55. Medic chaser
57. Surmounting
59. Depicted
60. Wearies
61. Bare
62. Water silk
67. Relating to life
68. Thereabouts
70. Chalet feature
71. Unanimously
72. "___ plan, a canal..."
74. Uneven
75. Playwright Garcia ___
76. Where Hamal twinkles
77. Guard, to a con
78. Treasure follower
79. Appraised
80. Netman Lendl
83. Make good
84. Actress Dunne
85. Of an element important in electricity
86. Frustrate, alternatively
88. Willow
89. Turner or Cole
90. Mighty one
93. Like some pockets
94. Chianti or Soave
95. He lost to Dwight
97. Comedic brothers
103. Draft status
104. ___ chance (may succeed)
105. "As the ___ a bird...": Blake
106. Beef cut
107. Stressful times
108. Lay blame
109. Colorful Coco
110. Pass up
111. Ootheca
112. Signs of spring
113. Rattan worker
114. Extant
117. Threefold
118. Expiate
119. Like many windows
120. Troupe
121. Beliefs
123. Author Heyerdahl
124. Street sign
127. Passé
128. Inst. in Henderson, Tenn.
129. Sales pitches

by William Lutwiniak

ACROSS

1. "___ cold and starve a fever"
6. Perfume bottle
10. Kitchen utensil
15. C.S.A. troops
19. More mature
20. Con
21. Rub with rubber
22. Brainchild
23. PRECISE changes in letter sequence
27. Roosevelt or Teasdale
28. Churchillian sign
29. Zola novel
30. Rods' counterparts
31. Refusals
33. Murphy of movies
35. Flying saucer
37. Pig's digs
38. Kermit's kin
41. Two, of yore
42. Listing
44. ALTERED altered thrice
51. In the thick of
52. Windy City airport
53. Pindar's products
54. Prejudice
55. Hither's partner
56. Auspices
57. Norse deities
59. The King
60. Director Flaherty's "Man of ___"
61. Tuckered out
62. Actor Everett ___: 1909–65
63. PARSING into variations
69. Originates
70. "___ Irish Rose"
71. A grandson of Jacob
72. Fla. exports
73. Bridges
74. Barr. or sol.
75. ___ vous plaît
78. Hymn sign-off
79. Journalist Jacob
80. Basketry twig
82. Yea or nay
83. DIVERSE rearrangements
88. Unconscious states
89. Singer James et al.
90. Bouquet
91. Letters in danger
94. West role
95. Holding
96. Raw silk's hue
98. "Romola" writer
100. Island off SW Alaska
101. Galena, e.g.
102. Biography
106. RELAPSE into three other forms
112. "___ Misbehavin' "
113. Kind of bore or wave
114. Sapient
115. Mystery writer Hammond ___
116. Pastures
117. Rimes
118. "Zounds!"
119. Discombobulated

DOWN

1. Popinjays
2. Lamb's pen name
3. W. German river
4. Off one's rocker
5. Pendulum's path
6. Bud vessels
7. As to
8. Chowed down
9. Driver's permit: Abbr.
10. Spruce up a room
11. Cara or Castle
12. Havanan's house
13. Psychic power's inits.
14. Defendants: Law
15. Carty of baseball
16. Anthony and Clarissa
17. Rakish cap
18. Procacious
24. Anne Baxter role
25. Kind of ink
26. School for Simone
32. Explorer Johnson
33. Jug
34. Valley
35. Verbalize
36. Douglas and Oregon
38. Fracas
39. San ___, Italy
40. Tyr's father
41. Refrain syllables
42. Saying more
43. Scandal sheet
45. Ella and Josh
46. Tangible object
47. Red dye
48. Low couch or sofa
49. "Knots" author
50. Curves
56. N.Y. Indians
57. Mont Blanc's range
58. Original Olympics site
59. Crazy Legs Hirsch
60. "___ and Old Lace"
61. "Pleasure's ___ . . .": Byron
62. "No Exit" author
63. Caesar, e.g.
64. Time preceder
65. Marksman, e.g.
66. White water
67. Degrade
68. He wrote "Marius the Epicurean"
73. Twine fiber
74. Affectations
75. Middling
76. Inventory listing
77. Mother of Pollux
79. Ancient people of Gaul
80. Bone: Comb. form
81. Pew or perch
82. Noxious
84. Electrical units
85. Flame keepers of old Rome
86. "___ to You," Dexter-Paris tune of 1946
87. River near Nice
91. Flower element
92. Hardy, to Laurel
93. City S of Florence
95. "And every woe ___ can claim": Byron
96. Slipped up
97. Bee chaser
99. Fillies' fodder
100. "M*A*S*H" TV star
101. Thessalian peak
103. Fleming and Carmichael
104. Be on the lam
105. Pronoun for the Andrea Doria
107. Numerical ending
108. Brazil's ___ Branco
109. Ovine female
110. Equip a ship
111. Actress Zadora

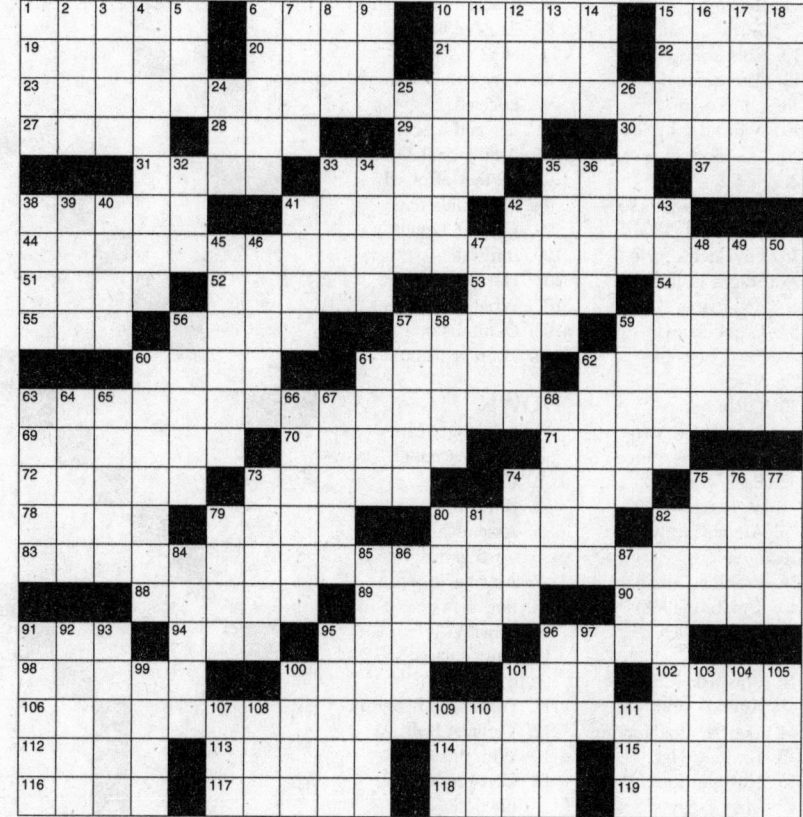

by John Greenman

ACROSS

1. Reeking
5. Surly
10. Cote sound
13. Abominated
18. ___ Nostra
19. A hundred paise
20. ___ food
21. Sadat
22. Charlemagne (800)–Francis II (1806)
25. Lovelace's forte
26. Stages in lives of organisms
27. Legal claims
28. Parts of books
29. Viscid
30. Eucharist containers: Var.
31. Faint appearance
32. Early French monarchs
35. Ate elegantly
36. Loyalties
39. Wahines' dances
40. T'ai Tsu (1368)–Chuan glich-ti (1644)
42. Wawaskeesh
43. Agenda unit
44. Generic dog's name
45. Grafted: Her.
46. Norman town
47. Miss Piggy's pronoun
48. Paleolithic period
52. Brazilian state
53. Lamb or Bacon
55. Staggers
56. Neutralize
57. Chirp
58. Runs away
59. "___ d'Arthur": Tennyson
60. Animal tracks
62. Eat away
63. Agitates
66. Gripes
67. February 29
69. Gumshoe
70. Arrow poison
71. Tale
72. Tenor Shicoff
73. Whine
74. Eliot's "The Hollow ___"
75. When dinosaurs roamed the earth
79. Firth of Clyde island
80. Supposes
82. Fatuous
83. Plundered
84. "The Pumpkin ___," 1964 film
85. Coquette
86. Tracks relentlessly
87. ___ Zee Bridge, N.Y.
89. City on the Meuse
90. Located
94. ___ and a holler
95. A.H. 1 or A.D. 622
97. Mother-of-pearl
98. Pangolin's feast
99. Like a Cheviot
100. Innisfail
101. Hardwoods
102. What, in Weimar
103. Delirious one
104. Poop or orlop

DOWN

1. Folksinger Phil
2. Terhune novel
3. Cuba, e.g.
4. Reverie
5. Assemblages
6. Card game
7. Asian evergreen
8. Bog
9. Sensitivity
10. Numismatist's concern
11. Possessive pronoun
12. Violinist Bull
13. With pleasure
14. Consecrate by unction
15. Today, in a way
16. Tranquillity
17. Prohibitionists
20. Fast on one's feet
23. Mob actions
24. Kind of doubles
28. Shade of gray
30. Grape variety
31. "Beau ___," Wren work
32. Edge of cask
33. Auburn and Marmon
34. Ice Age
35. Biblical verb
36. Adder's armament
37. "___ Rhee," Civil War song
38. Kin of 46 Down
40. Center
41. Patricia and Tom of films
44. What time does
46. A votre ___! (Cheers!)
48. Court hearings
49. Ship's lowest deck
50. Indigent
51. Size of Bigfoot or Yeti?
52. Full of froth
54. Left Nod
56. Staghorn
58. Lehár or Schubert
59. Radio and TV
60. Be miserly
61. Anguished one
62. Saarinen's namesakes
63. Jacques's title in song
64. Anatomical tissues
65. Rise on a wave
67. Device used in microsurgery
68. Concerning
71. Red Sea republic
73. Foretold
75. Changes genetically
76. Houston eleven
77. Architect Jones
78. Like
79. Debate
81. Flavor, in Ferrara
83. Bustle; confusion
85. Edicts
86. Chemical compound
87. Lake ___, source of the Blue Nile
88. Cries of discovery
89. Irkutsk river
90. Hood's blade
91. Flag
92. ___ Blair (George Orwell)
93. Moist and chilly
95. Deviate from course
96. Pride of ex-Sen. Norris

by Michael J. Parris

ACROSS

1. Olympics site: 1960
5. Coolidge from Nashville
9. Casca thrust
13. Boast
17. Son of Shem
18. ___ de Caldas, Braz.
19. Taurus neighbor
21. Kind of trumpet
22. Golfer Miller's dance is held in shaver's place?
24. Bolshoi's "Sleeping Beauty" looks fishy?
26. Irish river
27. Ibsen's "___ Gabler"
29. More jittery
30. Kind of bike
31. Rare object, sometimes
33. Customer
35. Group of eight
37. Threadlike
39. Shrine Bowl teams
43. Timid
47. Coe or Cram
48. Prof's protection
49. Nerve cell
50. Taken ___ (surprised)
52. Age; time: It.
54. CCC divided by C
55. Livestock
56. Sun-rooms
58. Sometimes they're shady
61. Oxford's emporium is hip?
63. Stocks, bonds, etc.
64. Flesh: Comb. form
65. Bull thrower
67. Simple sugars
68. Gets off the Yankee Clipper
71. Goober's cover causes misery for comics kids?
76. Lady ___ Lamb
77. A 1984 running mate
78. Hatred: It.
79. Eggs, to Ovid
80. Town in Norway
81. Journalize
82. Henley action
84. Galileo et al.
87. Slew
89. Miniature ornamental structure
91. Cubic meter
92. TV actress Garber
93. They sing so low
94. "Peyton Place" star
96. Yuletides
98. Alum
102. Harum-___
104. Actress Gallagher
106. Aisle-seat finder
109. Collection of Turners comes down on Ann and May?
111. Awed by leading man's pickup?
113. "___ boy!"
114. Chopin work
115. Flat sign
116. "The mind is like ___": Wilbur
117. Dawson's ex
118. Humdinger
119. Prune: Scot.
120. Dozes off

DOWN

1. Midianite king
2. Baltic island
3. Singer Nixon
4. Lock up
5. Composer Francesco Antonio ___
6. I, in Bonn
7. "___ to Handle," 1938 film
8. Ski resort
9. Quartz variety
10. Sticky sweet
11. Lend a hand
12. Excite
13. Anchor hoister
14. Mature
15. ___-Neisse Line
16. Simple card game
18. Before: Prefix
20. Koko's weapon
23. Manolete's concern
25. Hugo's "L'___ terrible"
28. Borrowed-money outlay causes imminent shortages?
32. Tranquilize
34. Texas city
36. Shackles are put on chain gangs?
38. Actress Chase
40. Litigant's activity
41. Wedges for wheels
42. Six, in Seville
43. Some: Sp.
44. Call at a deli counter
45. Dr. ___, "Buck Rogers" scientist
46. Don Pasquale's nephew
47. Sudan's ___ Mountians
48. Contemptible person's implements nurture fungi?
51. False gods
53. Hat material
57. Of a songbird suborder?
59. Prevaricates
60. Kind of current
62. Viscount's superior
63. R.A.F. promoter
66. Some Spanish murals
68. Cargo lifter
69. Clean the slate
70. A Ford aide
72. Tusked whale
73. Cut from a film
74. Scourge of serge
75. Theater section
76. Friday et al.
77. Trepidation
83. Get off one's high horse?
85. Large tank forces
86. Draws closer
88. ___ cassis (a liqueur)
90. Beyond doubt
92. Madrilène flavoring
93. "Homestead" artist
95. "Stuffed Shirts" author
97. Malt-drying ovens
99. Aired "The Honeymooners"
100. It's west of Curaçao
101. Open a bottle
102. P.M. of Japan: 1964–72
103. Jar or box: Abbr.
105. Danish weights
107. Fast jet
108. NASA space capsules
109. Terhune canine
110. Calembour
112. Wassail drink

by Jim Page

ACROSS

1. Over again
5. Mil. weapon
9. Art-school subj.
13. Balin or Claire
16. "Kenilworth" heroine
19. City in Alaska
20. ___ gras
21. Tie down
22. British mothers
24. Ka ___, Hawaiian cape
25. Rossini opera, with "The"
28. Making braids
30. Young oyster
31. Folkways
32. Like some fires
34. Plus factor
36. More tender
37. Owns
38. Roof ornament
39. Director Peter
40. Needle holders
41. Schubert instrumental work, with "The"
47. Id relative
48. Berlin public square
49. Lamentable
50. Hindu god of love
51. Mussorgsky vocal composition
54. Silkworm
55. Kind of jury
56. Fathers of dauphins
57. Bavarian river
58. Medics, at times
60. Annapolis's river
63. Tennis stroke
64. Cousin of a smash
67. Excessively
68. Duelist's sword
69. Directional warning
72. Word history
77. Saint-Saëns zoological fantasy
82. "Two heads ___ than one": Heywood
83. Contralto Anderson
84. Dramatist James
85. Curmudgeon's word
86. Summer in Phila.
88. Black Hawk was one
89. Visionary plan
91. Fast-talking comedian
96. Piedmontese city
98. Portico
99. Light tans
100. Kind of coal or pump
102. Sibelius tone poem, with "The"
108. Brit. money
109. Philosopher who served as a sculptor
111. Certain tides
112. Rod "The ___" Stewart
113. Rimsky-Korsakov's "Flight of ___"
115. Aquarium fish
116. Puccini heroine
117. Luzon peak
118. Palindromic sheep
119. Patron saint of France
120. Genesis verb
121. Nonconformist
125. Lovely lasses
126. Diamond shape
127. Erstwhile campus cutup
128. Stravinsky opera
133. Vital statistic
134. ___ de veau
135. Indefinite time
136. Epitaph starter
137. School Wellington attended
138. Legal matter
139. Punty
140. Author S. S. Van ___
141. Autocrat
142. Sunder

DOWN

1. Kelep
2. Classic Japanese drama
3. Exhaust smoke, e.g.
4. Loser, proverbially
5. "___ Die," Gide work
6. Emulate Peter Funk
7. Kind of bass
8. Learn by heart
9. Phil the Fiddler's creator
10. Piles
11. "Unaccustomed ___ am . . ."
12. "For want of a nail ___ was lost"
13. Quacks
14. Invalid
15. Mozart's middle name
16. Others, to Ovid
17. Director Delbert
18. Peterman
23. Famed basso
26. Dye vessel
27. Brother of Eris
29. Trifle
33. Hazy purple
34. Intimidates
35. Lily of the West
36. Some photocopies, for short
40. Puckish
41. Weight allowance
42. Lasso
43. John Ford 1952 film, with "The"
44. Family name in "A Rage to Live"
45. Asian ruler
46. Makes edging
48. Indigent
49. Worldwide
52. Home of ouzo
53. Stubbornly willful
55. Corsican Pasquale
59. River in a Burns poem
60. Coterie
61. Biblical Hebrew measure
62. Change direction
63. Embankment
65. Get off the A
66. Moral standard
69. Kind of training
70. Basketball tourn.
71. ___ Kippur
73. Verily
74. Gerald Ford, by birth
75. Kind of plum, for short
76. Theoretic primordial source of all elements
78. Liszt and Prévost, e.g.
79. Foster
80. "Bake me a cake . . . ___ you can"
81. Bishopric
87. Predilection
89. Buddhist shrine
90. Doves' sounds
91. Buttinsky
92. Pituitary hormone: Abbr.
93. Corner overhead
94. Type of engine
95. Cut back underbrush again
97. ___ Pea, small comic character
98. White dwarfs
101. What a Scot wears under a kilt
103. "It Happened ___," early Colbert film
104. Fixations
105. Leave one's native land
106. Relative of a mesa
107. Mine entrance
109. Buck
110. Incited a criminal
114. Sub
115. Actress Garr
116. Scant
119. Dumb
120. Actor Gazzara
121. Munich's river
122. Hauling charge: Abbr.
123. Cuprite and tinstone
124. A daughter of Phoebe
125. Eponym of an Eastern state
126. Kind of table
129. Polloi leader
130. Refrain syllable
131. Nol of Cambodia
132. Result

by Kay Sullivan

ACROSS

1. Tick, e.g.
7. Succinct
12. Til
18. Pertaining to the nostrils
19. Nonterrestrial
20. Wild asses
22. Anna Mary Robertson
24. A 1914 Oriole who took wing
26. Lubricate
27. Caught sight of
28. Certain trucks
29. Buck's mate
30. ___-ha-Shanah
32. Brave who really could hammer
34. Connors or Wallace
35. Epithet of Athena
36. Lesions
37. Young tag-on
38. Subdued
39. Scorch
40. Angered
41. Even
42. Woodpeckers
43. Having paddles
45. Jet-engine housing
46. Type of pinafore
47. Open grating
50. Jester
53. Husband of Jezebel
57. Jack or Julie
58. Heddle's place
59. Naso of Rome
60. Mythical beast
61. Obloquy
62. Long Island troubadour
64. Manuel de ___, Spanish composer
65. No score
66. Garb for Lakmé
67. Canning equipment
68. Fine brushes
69. Düsseldorf donkey
70. Plans on reheating
72. Stop
73. One-eyed god
75. That ship
76. Doctrine
78. N.M.U. member
81. Island off Ireland
83. Iron-containing pigment
84. Daunting
88. Crazy Legs Hirsch
89. Dross
90. Errand boy: Slang
91. "Sting like ___": Ali
92. Claim on a property
93. Actor in "Hold Back the Dawn"
95. Grain for Vassar
96. Kind of dye
97. 1957 Nobelist in Literature
98. Shadows, to Jeanne
100. Bishopric
101. Bacharach's partner
103. U.S. novelist-poet
106. Conceal
107. Soul
108. Quiescent
109. Broke up a shutout
110. Part of a potpourri
111. Carolina river

DOWN

1. Certain cats and goats
2. Covered cart
3. Caspian's neighbor
4. ___ Tin Tin
5. State adjoining Ill.
6. Administrative division of Greece
7. Interfered
8. Carried away, as property
9. Perron parts
10. Down at the heels
11. Naval off.
12. Grew serious, with "up"
13. Captivate
14. Antipolio pioneer
15. Ripens
16. Matelot's milieu
17. Scholarly
21. O'Neill's Yank, e.g.
23. On land
25. Listens to
28. Glut
31. Netman from D.C.
33. Stage device
34. F. ___, Oscar winner in 1984
36. Mud eel
38. Country singer Bandy
41. Former Yankee pitcher
42. Tie
44. Medicinal plant
45. Game in "The Color of Money"
46. Follow surreptitiously
47. Take panes with one's work
48. Judges' garb
49. Habituate
50. Mulligrubs
51. Spots for slots
52. Type of grape
54. Handel's birthplace
55. "Deutschland über ___"
56. A sixth-day creation
58. Cambio in Calabria
62. Storage building
63. Hunky-dory; copacetic
64. Sow and hoe
66. Gyre
68. More discerning
71. River or Indian
74. Two watch-laps
76. Postponement
77. Breakfast fare
78. Hebrew word in the Psalms
79. Doolitle and namesakes
80. Small interstices
81. Referred (to)
82. Deserters
83. Dutch painter: 1638–1709
85. Disconcerted
86. Let go
87. Relaxing of international tensions
89. Heavy silk fabric in the Middle Ages
90. Significant first words
93. Show indecision
94. ABC's Arledge
97. Dear, in Italy
99. Shot or dragon preceder
102. Caesar's 700
103. Reverse of par
104. Olympic brat
105. Uno, due, ___

by Jeanette K. Brill

ACROSS

1. Wrinkled
7. Terse diner sign
11. Gen. ___ Arnold
14. Kind of plan
18. Former U.K. judicial writ
19. ___ cog (err)
21. Team's best pitcher
22. Boesky or Lendl
23. Memo to a gabby vintner
25. Use a death ray
26. Miles of films
27. Far out
28. Combiner with dyne or doxy
29. Arcane
31. Monogram of the 21st V.P.
32. Covert's cousin
34. Pollster's unit
36. Took the bait
37. Saison chaude
38. Sol of ours
39. A-U vowel connection
40. Nine-to-fiver
41. Rue ___ Paix
43. Memo to a sluggish walnut processor
50. Shebat, ___, Nisan
51. Opp. of WSW
53. Cinnabar, for one
54. One on the watch
56. Institute in Brooklyn
58. Kin of strathspeys
60. Cohan song: 1907
64. Effulge
66. Sartre novel
69. Word in Kan.'s motto
70. Kant's concern
71. Memo to a careless Bonn teller
74. ___ Downing Street
75. Small pikeperch
77. New Zealand's discoverer
78. Fatuous
80. Lacking a breastbone
82. "___ Kick Out of You"
84. Nary a soul
85. Came down in buckets
87. Durango demonstrative
88. Land-based newt
89. ___-Cynwyd, near Philadelphia
92. Memo to a waiting taxidermist
97. Riza Khan Pahlevi, e.g.
100. Bouquet
102. Alternative to hup
103. Like sushi
105. Guido's note
106. ___ Gulf, Aegean Sea inlet
107. Evince affection
110. ___-bel-Abbès, onetime Foreign Legion home
111. Afghan coin
112. Kind of shoe
114. Arabian kettledrum
116. Wynonna Judd's mom
118. Dark time, in ads
119. Israeli burp gun
120. Memo from a bored stripteaser
122. Acronym for an aircraft's ascent
123. Where Trevino got his start
124. AFB in Fla.
125. Auricles
126. "It ___ ancient Mariner"
127. Boundless: Abbr.
128. Garth, in "Ivanhoe"
129. Is written

DOWN

1. Supposed to be such
2. Keen
3. Memo to a lazy galena miner
4. Petri-dish filler
5. Siamese coins
6. Ike and Monty's bailiwick
7. Gravel ridge in a glacier
8. Found a perch
9. Antler subdivisions
10. Meadowsweet
11. Noisette
12. "___ of Identity," S. Holmes adventure
13. Squash, for one
14. Memo to a hasty seamstress
15. Warded off
16. ___ Trench
17. Thespian or thesmothete
20. Kind of pile
24. Where Alberich struck gold
30. TV network logo
33. L.B.J.'s birth month
35. Sourdough's sack
42. Prefix with tank or trust
44. Part of a golf club
45. A "Real McCoy"
46. Fresh crews
47. Bandleader-songwriter Jones
48. American news execs' org.
49. Name of cities in Ill., Kan., Ohio and Pa.
52. Whatnot
55. Former Brooklyn pitcher
56. Cue in group singing
57. Sitar solos
58. Out of the labor mkt.
59. Finland, to Sibelius
61. Memo to a U.S.M.A. recruit
62. "When the sheep ___ the fauld . . ."
63. John ___ Garner
65. Coated with tin-lead alloy
67. Metalworking tools: Var.
68. Conductor Ansermet
72. Yorkshire town
73. U.S. architects' org.
76. Memo to a dilatory chess player
79. Reactions to solar-plexus punches
81. "Yo te ___" (Avila avowal)
83. Kind of cross
86. Updike's "The Same ___"
89. African dog
90. Houseplants used medicinally
91. Lynn from Ky.
93. Disquiet
94. Put a play on again
95. Furbelow
96. Cabbage Patch dolls, e.g.
98. Homecoming V.I.P.'s
99. Some chemical compounds
101. Soft-drink tycoon Candler
104. Improvise
107. Defraud
108. A moon of Uranus
109. Houston and Coleridge: Abbr.
110. Rhone River augmenter
113. Dancing dress
115. "Oh, to ___ England . . .": Browning
117. Author Bontemps
121. Unfortunates of W.W. II

by Bert Rosenfield

ACROSS

1. Salami purveyor
5. Provoked
10. Ledge
15. Poznán natives
16. Sound-shield screens
17. Parents
19. Paar's light?
21. Supplication
23. Diminutive suffix
24. "There runs __ by Merrow Down": Kipling
25. Begrudges
27. Educational org.
28. Sked. abbr.
29. Fashionable
30. Rubens' medium
31. Kind of flint
32. Tumult
34. Wreaths
36. African fox
37. Cheat
38. Speech sound
40. Well-groomed
42. Chinese city on the Wei
43. Hold for Ozzie?
45. Himalayan ointments
46. Optical network
49. Bergonzi, for one
51. Short song
52. Pertaining to the fibula
53. Harry's spouse
56. Kind of electricity
58. Soprano Frances: 1883–1952
59. Cozy
60. Type of suit
61. Color of Faye's dress?
63. __ Lanka
64. Hector's protector
66. Talented
67. Fitted together
69. Orson or lima
70. In a somnolent way
72. Intimidate
73. Metropolis on the Missouri
75. Platform
76. Bristles
78. The Finnish language
81. Boggs of baseball
82. Contemporary persons
84. Hope's feline?
86. Twigs for grafting
88. Foal's dad
89. Descry
91. Michelangelo masterpiece
92. Fence picket
93. Wallace's transmitting device?
94. Obtuse
96. TV network north of the U.S.A.
97. Afflict
98. Aggregates
100. Young pheasant
101. Lorain's lake
102. Hairlike
104. Einstein's frock coat?
107. City ESE of Napoli
108. Snow leopard
109. Electrical unit of capacitance
110. Excavations
111. French heads
112. Out of

DOWN

1. Precept
2. Actress Sommer
3. Pope who was lionized?
4. Imam's faith
5. Slights
6. Pool game
7. Retired
8. Rocky crag
9. Feudal thrall
10. Mentally infirm
11. Execrates
12. Strays
13. Majors or Marvin
14. Olibanum for Sinatra?
15. Colonial Dutch landowner
17. Emend
18. Mug for Gertrude?
19. Actress Seberg's slacks?
20. Inland sea
22. Yin's partner
26. Pries into
29. Feeling, e.g.
31. Sullies
33. Condiments
35. Pertaining to rocks rich in silica
36. Handy one
37. Food: Pref.
39. Great quantity
41. Musical embellishment for 93 Down?
42. Italian evening
44. Celebrated or celebrity
46. Buys back

47. Writer Hobson
48. Illinois city
50. Auto race
52. Planet for a canine?
53. Bored
54. British nobles
55. Dulcet Tell?
57. Dye's partner
58. Hirt and Pacino
62. Take care
65. Mexican shawl
66. __-de-camp
68. Smear
69. Salten book
71. Tablets
72. Yield, as land
74. Skirt spreaders
76. Famed French historian: 1842–1906
77. Hide securely
79. Parfait ingredient
80. __ seat (enviable position)
82. A steam locomotive
83. Certain evergreen trees
85. Be silent, to Solti
86. Short gaiter
87. Dens

88. Workers' job actions
90. Lock of a type
93. Soprano in "One Night of Love"
95. Rod
98. A partner of there
99. Announcement of a kind
100. Liquid measure
101. Zaragoza's river
103. Cato's 151
105. Regret
106. Household spirit

by Wilson McBeath

ACROSS

1. Kind of check
5. Wave modifier
10. Cosmetician Max
16. Erwin of early TV
19. Ziti topping
20. Idolize
21. Rub with a rasp
22. Eschew
23. EL
25. GEE
27. Assist at a wedding: Slang
28. Eyes amorously
29. Divests of honors
31. "Lady" of song
32. Menial
34. Change timers
36. Contracts a cold
37. Not impetuous
39. Feel contrite
41. Raison d'___
43. Spotted piece
44. Expended effort
46. BEE
49. Midwinter malady
52. Autumns, in Avila
53. Kirk and Hartman
54. Yokum or Doubleday
55. Stats for Mike Greenwell
56. Authority
57. Piquant quaff
58. Sixty-thousandths of a min.
59. Bogus
60. Building wing
61. EX
64. These go from alpha to omega
65. Luge or pung
67. ___-do-well
68. Side petals
69. Supernatural spirits
70. Wars of the ___
72. Diagonal weave
74. Major appliance
75. With calm assurance
77. Soy or Roy
78. Cuban cat
79. Norman town
83. Most reasonable
84. ESS
88. Maneuverable, as a sailboat
89. Puccini's forte
90. Heart's-ease
91. Houston gridder
92. Fleet
94. Cheerleaders' calls
95. Kolo or merengue
96. Incense
97. Placid
98. Guido's note
99. VEE
101. Bedroom
102. Pages
104. "...'E won't split on ___": Kipling
105. Sheep tender
106. Cooked beans, Mexican style
108. Egyptian dancing girl
110. Oleoresin
112. Roll top, e.g.
115. To no ___ (fruitlessly)
116. Graduates
118. Skating feats
120. Imitate
121. TEE
124. ZEE
127. Juillet-aout periods
128. Kitchen utensil
129. "___ You Glad You're You?"
130. Kind of jury
131. Actor Neill
132. Fondle
133. Circus areas
134. Comedian Mort

DOWN

1. Pay hike
2. KAY
3. Gelid
4. Laughton role: 1932
5. Last part
6. Most indolent
7. Use a divining rod
8. Constellation near Norma
9. Certain pewters
10. Oberon's subjects
11. Simmering
12. Jockeys' goads
13. N.M. art colony
14. Eccentric
15. Early Olds
16. JAY
17. Port on the Po
18. Not hardened
19. East Coast porgy
22. Felled, as a dragon
24. Concurs
26. Admitted
30. Infield coverage
33. Light gases
35. Come-on
37. Models
38. N. African bigwig
40. Evidence
42. Monarchs of yore
43. Blockhead
44. Forfeits
45. To any extent
46. More expansive
47. Matter-of-fact
48. Rotund
50. Tilts
51. Manipulates
53. Fla. exports
55. Textile fibers
57. Set of beliefs
58. "Night Court" actor
59. Eyetooth
62. Start
63. "Common Sense" man
64. Italian port
66. Laundromat items
69. Bowl at Jacksonville
71. Thessalian peak
72. More laconic
73. Undulatory
74. Less frequent
75. Kind of bull
76. EN
77. Swindler's scheme
78. Greek physician
80. EM
81. "Jezebel" popularizer
82. Money follower
83. Type of subject
84. Inclinations
85. Region of ancient Asia Minor
86. Carp pettily
87. Anxiety
90. Walked the floor
93. Pistol-packing
95. Run-down nightspot
96. Western resort
97. Strident
99. Lowers
100. Babbles
101. Unites firmly
103. Actors Estrada and Rhodes
105. Voodooist's activity
106. Wheezes
107. Patti LuPone role
108. Bring into agreement
109. Henry and Clare
111. Burdened
113. Turn rancid
114. Superman's alter ego
116. State
117. Moslem woman's garb
119. Placebos
122. "___ Horne," Ade book
123. Antipollution org.
125. "___ tu," Verdi aria
126. ___ Filippias, Greek town

by John Greenman

ACROSS

1. Italian violin
6. Engrossed
10. Biblical book
14. Swiss canton
19. Balzac's "___ Birotteau"
20. Take on
21. Bomb
22. Soap plant
23. SALINAS VALLEY
25. UKRAINE
27. Estranges
28. O'Casey's staff of life
29. Wilde's forte
30. What yeggs crack
34. Tubing joint
35. Potok novel, with "The"
39. XIII × IV
40. Olympics awards
45. Hard beds
47. Harpsichordist Landowska
49. Anticipated
50. Recoiled
51. Second after tau
53. Bloch's Bates
55. Dante's "La ___ Nuova"
56. Hollow out
57. Scraps for Fido
58. Baylor of basketball
59. Edmonton skater
60. Lofty verse
62. Thug
63. Utopia or Pianosa
64. Bungle
66. GUYANA
70. Uh-huh
71. Affidavit taker
73. Advance
74. Plunder
76. Try to find water
77. Columbia's team
78. Penrod's dog
79. Tot
82. "Jake's Thing" novelist
83. Kids' rocker
84. Big brown bird
85. Patchwork
86. Lesotho coins
88. Day's march
90. Niobe was one
92. Epistle
93. Ellington monogram
94. Bow ceremoniously
95. Cambridge coll.
97. The Hardy Boys, e.g.
99. Hebrew "T"
100. Mistle thrush
105. Flattery
111. GOPHER PRAIRIE
113. DEVONSHIRE
114. Mother's mother, e.g.
115. Turgenev's birthplace
116. Poet Sexton
117. Novelist Shaw
118. Dylan Thomas's homeland
119. Sweet pear
120. Corp V.I.P.'s
121. Big Brother, to Orwell

DOWN

1. Zoological suffix
2. Kind of ticket
3. Holly found in Dixie
4. British or U.S. poet
5. ALBANY
6. Scarlett's Butler
7. Man Friday
8. Fourth Estate
9. Decimal unit
10. P.M.
11. Erich Segal book
12. Corrida charger
13. Hammett hero
14. Incoherent one
15. Chinese border river
16. Matchless
17. Place of exile: 1814
18. Graphite
24. Swoon
26. Chinook
31. According to
32. DUBLIN
33. Phantom
35. Product-banning org.
36. Tee-hee
37. LONDON
38. Visit dreamland
41. Auld Clootie
42. YOKNAPA-TAWPHA COUNTY
43. Iron Age period
44. Turfs
46. Lost weekend
47. Kenosha loc.
48. Rival of Sparta
49. Team supporter
52. Trout or marble
54. Least
57. Grand Ole ___
59. Bones
61. Grim Grimm character
63. Anent
64. Ultimate goal
65. Bunkmate
67. Springe
68. Sea cow
69. Caulking material
72. Desirable quality
75. Driver's one-eighty
77. C.S.A. hero
78. Aberdeen's river
80. Swiss artist
81. French I verb
83. Austere
85. ROME
87. Waterloos
89. Author's assn.
91. Fla. city
96. Palpitate
97. Kilmer title
98. A Lyon river
99. Melodies
100. Merganser
101. Village in John 2:1
102. Coin of Teheran
103. Duck, to Doblin
104. First name in architecture
106. Fleming novel
107. Wrongful act
108. Amana's state
109. "Step" followers
110. Oahu avian
112. R. N.'s forte
113. Sir Launcelot du ___

by John M. Samson

ACROSS

1. Holdups at sea?
6. Young salmon
10. Messy mass
14. Push-button predecessors
19. Make trouble
20. Sun-tan lotion ingredient
21. N.Y. college
22. Fisher in a whirl?
23. Soprano Mitchell
24. Brass instrument
25. Took a powder
26. Take off
27. Unemployed renter?
29. Lassie or Elsie?
31. Serpentine dagger
32. Little Red Book author
34. Delta collection
35. Flopsy and Mopsy
39. Resort near Lake Louise
41. Honey-loving deer at the rear?
46. Roman officials
47. Man of the people: Var.
49. Steve who took a dive
50. Haymaker
51. Bug
52. Leonine lingo
54. Manner of expression
55. My gosh, it's molding!
56. Amber, formerly
57. World lifter
59. Cinder chaser
60. Wimbledon forecaster?
62. Subject of sommeliers' argument?
64. All-purpose vehicle
65. Writer Levin
66. What some lords have?
73. Berlin's Christmas-eve dream?
80. ___ dixit
81. Emulate an ecdysiast
82. Unusual peep show?
83. Obscure
84. Happen again
86. Official stamp
87. Currier's colleague
88. Sordid
89. Copied painstakingly
91. David in the valley of Elah
93. "O ___ when we cry . . ." U.S. Navy Hymn
94. Twitch of a rabbit's nose?
96. Newscaster Leslie
97. Most serene
98. Sheepskin morocco
100. Elev.
101. HBO, e.g.
102. Computer bug's danger?
107. The good doctor?
113. African nation
114. Italian seaport
115. Operatic prince
116. Medic who monkeys around?
117. Upright
118. Cake decorator
119. Nearly gone goose
120. Saucy charmer
121. Necessary evils
122. Supplements, with "out"
123. Turns right
124. Choose

DOWN

1. W. African country
2. Made a hole-in-one
3. Versatile plane, for short
4. Styne song
5. More animated
6. Jargon
7. Grads
8. Toga
9. Venus de Milo's concern?
10. Mugger's forte?
11. Poet Ridge
12. "___ so near . . .": Job 41:16
13. Thoughtless remark?
14. Censors
15. Thought
16. Jewish month
17. "No evil deed ___ on"
18. Clairvoyant
28. Scraps of a sort
30. Blister
33. Actress Alicia
35. Odilon ___, French painter
36. Era of commercials?
37. "Carmen" composer
38. TV censor's signal
39. Prove false
40. U.S. playwright who's on his toes?
42. Visitor's quarters
43. Romantic interlude
44. Tot's favorite, after "choklit"
45. Dr. spelled out?
47. Spoon's elope-mate
48. Molls and dolls
51. Feels contrite
53. Ostriches, e.g.
56. Rosters
58. Rock debris
61. Jamaican export
63. Suffix with nectar
66. Circumference
67. The works, to Cato
68. Wild writer?
69. Two-spot
70. Mined matter
71. Iranian coins
72. What a bad will might do?
73. Part of Orville's machine?
74. German river
75. Cockney employer?
76. Girder
77. Angry look
78. Soil component
79. Lovers' meeting
85. Radial make-overs
88. Ravel preventer
90. Designing man
92. Shrew
93. "Greater love ___ no man . . ."
95. Hack
97. Nuclei of experts
99. N.Y. destination in a song
101. Hag
102. Coin opening
103. ___ colada
104. Wild goat
105. Unit of force
106. What Kilmer couldn't make
108. Pulitzer Prize author
109. Huge Russian lake
110. Gold cloth
111. "Beowulf" is one
112. Budget item

by Dale O. Burgener

ACROSS

1. Splendor
5. City on the Ganges
10. Bundle of wheat
15. Luzon river
19. Culture medium
20. Like ___ (quickly)
21. Ham's affirmative
22. Tie
23. "___ want for Christmas . . ."
24. IHS: Isa. 59:20
26. Lode
27. Comet seen on Dec. 24
29. "The Glass Key" actor
30. Liberate
32. English horn
33. Memorable warship
35. Combed cotton
36. Farrier
39. Winold ___, painter of Indians
41. Trunk
42. Pablo Picasso's daughter
44. Short salutation
45. Waipahu's island
47. D-I links
50. Book by poet Ciardi
51. IHS: John 10:11
55. Papal name
56. Pre-Christmas activity
58. One + one to Burns
59. Attributes
61. London borough
63. Père Noel's affirmative
64. Caine role
65. Porter's "Kiss ___"
68. Bests in brainpower
71. Be imminent
72. Carroll's girl
73. New Guinea port
74. Mother of Samuel
76. Sheets, etc.
78. N.C. State's conference
79. Biblical verse
83. Yule ___
84. IHS: Luke 23:35
89. Verdi opus
90. Whoa!
92. ___ meridiem
93. S. A. armadillo
94. Warmhearted
96. Wintry floater
98. Share evenly
100. Certain Yemeni
101. "___ Along," Merrill musical
103. Perplexed

105. Start of Mont.'s motto
106. Adjective for "Metamorphoses"
108. "___ Rhythm"
109. Helter-skelter
114. Rudolf of opera
115. IHS: I Tim. 6:15
118. Biologist Metchnikoff
119. "Picnic" playwright
120. Cat Nation tribe
121. Slur over
122. Present
123. Hardy's "Pure Woman"
124. Delta preceder
125. Permanent place?
126. Concerning

DOWN

1. "I Kid You Not" author
2. Eye amorously
3. Algerian neighbor
4. IHS: Isa. 9:6
5. ___ Noster
6. Notable netman
7. Unit of heat
8. Trondheim loc.
9. Studios for Seurat
10. Nobel's compatriots
11. Wasted no time
12. "Spoon River" poet's monogram
13. Box-elder genus
14. Attack area for Graf
15. Unfavorable
16. IHS: John 6:35
17. Elevate
18. Bearded
25. Rich pastry
28. College room
31. Roman household deity
34. Desiccated
36. Hot tubs
37. Hodgepodge
38. Potpourri
40. ___ Camel, W.W. I plane
41. Article in common use
43. Lithe
44. Dream, to Dante
46. Kin of oho
48. Enter or arrive
49. Drenched the lawn
52. Naval C.I.A.
53. Case for pins
54. Plays
57. Open to all
60. IHS: Rev. 1:8
62. Ravines

by John M. Samson

63. See red?
65. They hum in Dec.
66. "Adam Bede" novelist
67. IHS: Rev. 17:14
69. Tortilla con carne
70. Flavor
71. Map within a map
75. Bobbsey twin
77. Hurry up!
78. Do something
80. French novelist
81. Adam's birthplace
82. Hindu garment
85. Directional letters
86. "Ye are the ___ the earth": Matt. 5:13
87. Apostolic letters
88. Thurmond of N.B.A. fame
91. Telethon call-ins
95. James ___ Jones
97. French friend
99. Peak of S. Colo.
101. Apochrypha book
102. Of the birds
104. Eliot's cruelest month
105. Comedian Ole

107. Ibsen's Helmer
108. Same: Lat.
110. Taro root
111. Ally of Sparta
112. Ski tow
113. Mother of Artemis
116. Flange
117. Suffix with pay or play

ACROSS

1. Riata
6. Respond to stimuli
11. Set the oven at 350 degrees
15. Franks' accompaniment
20. Fill with joy
21. Shout loudly
22. Actor in "Support Your Local Sheriff"
23. "Creatures that by a ___ nature teach": Shak.
24. Physicist born on March 14, 1879
26. Kentucky Derby winner: 1980
28. Fishing net
29. "___ a Kick Out of You"
30. Norwegian monetary unit
32. Chirp
33. Watched
34. Bustle
35. List of candidates
36. Seven-day cycle
37. Depth charge
38. Recording in writing
40. Deep-seated
44. Opined
49. Cayuga, Seneca, etc.
53. "Ben ___," 1959 film
54. Apportions
55. Actor in "Scarface": 1932
57. More profound
58. Wife of Zeus
59. For the most part
60. ___ Major
61. ___ on (trampled)
62. Gene Anthony Ray's role in "Fame"
63. A 1492 vessel
64. Outpatient facility
65. Bear
67. Bell-shaped flower
68. Archdiocese
69. Egghead
70. Interlace
72. Sharp-crested ridge
73. Condense
76. Architects' org.
77. Clothing
80. Moslem faith
81. Folding
84. Nurtured
85. Cut with an ax
88. Barrel part
89. Actress in "The Big Chill"
90. "Forever ___," Winsor novel
92. "Sliver" author
93. "___ you do?"
94. "Moonstruck" star
95. Got on one's feet
96. Carpenter's activity
97. Medicinal plant
98. Coquettes
100. "Thanks ___!"
101. ". . . there is ___ and a great man . . .": II Samuel
102. Wedding response
103. U.S. women's singles champion: 1979 and 1981
105. Interwove
107. River in southern Alberta
109. ___ to (adheres)
111. First ___
112. Emit smoke
113. Raid
115. D.C. group
117. West German river
121. Journalist-author Alexander
123. Brazilian seaport
124. Mascara recipient
125. Musical vamp
126. "Crisis" publisher: 1776–83
128. Pool V.I.P.
132. Label again
133. Singer James
134. Meantime
135. Newmar or Andrews
136. Test choice
137. Part of Y.W.C.A.
138. Prado display
139. Absquatulates

DOWN

1. Tenant's document
2. Bowling lane
3. Italic language
4. Spirited horse
5. "___ the ramparts . . ."
6. Checked
7. Catcher Howard
8. Hgt.
9. "Producer's Showcase" producer
10. Instant
11. Sired
12. Couer d'___, Idaho
13. Welles role
14. Flightless bird
15. Milwaukee team
16. Calif.'s motto
17. "I cannot tell ___"
18. Nutcracker's suite
19. Where to find a drip?
21. Depart!
25. Gaea's brood
27. O, e.g.
31. Prevailed uncontrollably
35. Is frugal
36. Nictitated
37. French president: 1954–59
39. Function
41. March movie
42. Sixth-largest continent
43. Sturdy wagon
44. Highway exits
45. May or Stritch
46. Carmel V.I.P.
47. Caffeine-rich nut
48. Flowing off gradually
50. Keep
51. "Brigadoon" lyricist
52. Footless animal
56. Black bird
58. Hayes or Traubel
60. Clothed
62. Enticed
64. Robbery or arson
65. Short plant stalk
66. "A Tramp Abroad" writer
67. More subdued
69. Hired assassin
71. Siestas
74. Leaf
75. A Queen
78. Costello's partner
79. Angered
80. Beloved of Tristram
82. Artery
83. A gun inventor
86. Show
87. Alar
89. Stylish
91. King Guzzle's kingdom
92. Actor Teeter
93. Hit musical of the 60's
94. "American Bandstand" host
95. Smooth
96. Made haste
98. ___ the breeze
99. Monetary unit of Ecuador
101. Correctly
103. Of adolescents
104. Activity for Sam Snead?
106. Two-wheeled carriage
108. Albee products
110. Outer coat enclosing the eyeball
113. Makes a pretense of
114. N.Y. city
116. Watering place
117. Wicked
118. Start of a Dickens title
119. Ade book: 1896
120. Annual Pasadena display
121. Queens stadium
122. "The ___ Baltimore," Wilson play
123. Leatherwings
126. Type of bus ticket: Abbr.
127. Thimblerig object
129. Division word
130. Marshal of France: 1804
131. Famed racecar driver's monogram

by Bette Sue Cohen

ACROSS

1. Title of courtesy, once
5. S.A. wood sorrel
8. French floor
13. Sudden tug
17. On the Indian
18. ___ de jambe (ballet movement)
20. Kind of renewal
21. "Big" or "Z," e.g.
22. "Death's Duel" author
24. Paint splashes
25. "___ we all?"
26. Conquistador Juan de ___
27. Sec. of State: 1977
29. English writer Arthur ___
30. Alley button
31. Haul into court once again
32. Franklin's father was born here
33. Voice of Tweetie Pie
35. Saloon where 50 Down bent an elbow
38. "A ___ the Misbegotten" (Robards vehicle)
43. Idi ___
45. Suffix with musket
46. "The Hungarian Rome"
48. "___ is sinking to-day": Ufford
49. Sloth, for one
50. "Return of the ___"
51. Meadow
52. Immerses
53. Scottish pudding
55. Whence comes take-home
58. Fran of "Kukla . . ."
59. ___ damnée (willing tool)
60. Made a path
61. Biblical shepherd
62. Prop finish
63. Tic
66. Monday-morning quarterbacking, e.g.
69. That is: Lat.
71. Charged particle
72. A eucalypt
74. Unbend
75. Extinct bird
76. ___ of paris
78. "Henry the Fifth, thy ___ invocate": Shak.
80. Aegean island
84. Calico ponies
85. Chinese dynasty
86. ___ Porsena
88. Gelderland city
89. Innuits, e.g.
91. Fancy
93. 650, to Cato
94. Expressions of disgust
95. Washington Square Players' vehicle by 8 Down
96. Tony role for Dewhurst: 1974
99. Invitation reqs.
102. Mother-of-pearl
103. Grown dearer in price
106. More underhanded
110. "___ Napoli": T. A. Daly
111. "Lest we lose our ___": Browning
112. Island off Venezuela
113. Amazon tributary
114. Super-model Campbell
116. Changed a menu selection
118. Powhatan, to John Rolfe
119. Customary drink
120. Some I.D.'s
121. Blood fluids
122. One Beatle
123. Rose element
124. J. F. K. visitor
125. Calls for silence

DOWN

1. Bowes, e.g.
2. Together
3. Working up old material again
4. Veronese neighbor
5. Gaucho's gold
6. Transported
7. Vehicle for Garbo
8. This E.G.O. arrived Oct. 16, 1888
9. Santa Fe or Oregon: Abbr.
10. Fermi focus
11. "The Thief" actor
12. Marks with scars
13. Time past
14. Hails
15. Numbered cloud
16. Etta ___
19. Tooth: Comb. form
21. Vehicle for Lunt: 1928
23. Venison
28. Handle a problem handily
34. The old bean
36. "Tears" poet
37. Forecaster
39. Town in Liberia or Italy
40. Bone hollows
41. Tear-jerkers
42. It curdles milk
43. Panatela residue
44. "Cara ___," 1954 song
47. Manta, e.g.
50. He and Hickey took the stage together
54. Chat idly
56. Alder tree: Scot.
57. Israeli city
58. Circa: Abbr.
61. Vehicle for Cohan: 1933
63. Fragment
64. Buff pumps
65. Mother of the Fates, to Plato
66. Roscoe: Abbr.
67. Monogram for Jesus
68. Rod
70. Pop
73. Hague's "___ Fables"
75. Danny's girl
77. Blend batter
78. F-J link
79. Pilgrimage to Mecca
81. Extends liability coverage
82. Poetic piece
83. French possessive
87. Dean and Edward
90. Card game
92. "And mine ___ one": Shak.
94. Adjective for Snow White
97. Cupcake toppers
98. Alum
100. "___ porridge hot . . ."
101. Weevil feature
104. German Republic's first president
105. Nothingness states
106. Upstart
107. Hyena, of the comics
108. Snow-blind?
109. Epochal
115. Lost lamb's call?
117. Q-U connection

by Jim Page

ACROSS

1. Vista
6. Ready
10. Actor McKellen
13. Hillbilly's chaw
18. Northern N.D. town
19. Case
21. Largest Garden State city
22. Dan and Fred are somewhat amicable
24. Word-of-mouth bettor
25. Company V.I.P.
26. Masculine
27. Cutting tools
28. Russian peninsula
29. Conceive
31. Suffix with press or fail
32. Simon's "Plaza ___"
33. Shoe size
34. With William, singer Dinah props burning logs
39. Literary monogram
42. Eat
44. Gametes
45. Dock worker
46. Arabic letter
47. Periods
48. Drugstore cowboys
51. Wire measure
52. Blackboard
54. Stephen T. takes Harry to Plato, for one
58. To ___ (precisely)
59. Indian weight
62. Kind of virus
63. Declaim
64. Part of H.H.H.
66. Brigadier general's insignia
68. Vital fluid
70. One of the brass
71. Fastened
72. Presently
73. S.A. Indian
74. Foxy
75. Aleutian island
76. Former Giant great Mel joins Charles and George for emperor's favor
82. Public disorders
84. Bricklayer's burden
85. Wise legislators
86. Baseball Hall-of-Famer Rixey
90. Charged particle
91. Specific otary
93. Asian holiday
94. Moods
96. Opposite of ques.
97. William Allen needs Ted to make a Looking-Glass character
101. Poets' guides
102. Open a cage
104. Doze
105. Inform
107. Older
109. Eager
111. Three, in Berlin
112. Solmization syllables
113. Decorated anew
114. Why Morley, Glenn and Claude prefer snakes to lye
118. Emulates Cicero
119. Put up
120. Ham it up
121. Bushy legumes
122. Blue
123. Tinted
124. Thick

DOWN

1. Cagliari is its capital
2. Kind of horse race
3. Alienate
4. O.T. book
5. Montcalm and Wolfe, e.g.
6. Plunders
7. As to
8. Last Greek consonant
9. Nice hot time
10. West ___ (American archipelago)
11. Philippine timber tree
12. Napoleon's marshal's family
13. Currant pickers
14. Expect
15. Ned and Lou make harbor
16. Algonquian Indian
17. A soup base
20. M. Gide
21. Cold characteristic?
23. Operated
30. Simpletons
31. S.A. arrow poison
32. Go edgewise
35. Sacred
36. Finished
37. Marzipan base
38. Dim
40. Kind of pass
41. In a pleasant manner
43. Winding wind
49. Mire, in Ayr
50. Malayan skirts
53. The Elbe, to a Czech
55. "Vissi d'___," Puccini aria
56. ___ Paulo, Brazil
57. Kind of wine
59. Sun parlors
60. Maternal kinship
61. What James and evangelist Billy rarely were wont to do
65. Single
67. Closed
68. Swag
69. ___ Alamos
70. Graduation costume
72. Ermine in summer
77. "___ Wedding Journey": Howells
78. Egg cell after meiosis
79. Designer Cassini
80. "How use ___ breed a habit . . .": Shak.
81. Aye-aye, for one
83. Surgeon: Slang
87. Stance
88. Gifts
89. Taxpayer
92. Stock holdings
95. Officiated at Shea
98. Stabbed
99. Central points
100. Paved, in a way
103. E. Indian tree
106. Foot: Pref.
107. Welfare hotels
108. Architect Saarinen
109. Nile serpents
110. Spanish linear measure
111. Peace symbol
115. Roulette bet
116. Fingerlings
117. Soul, in Savoie

by Ernst T. Theimer

ACROSS

1. Scoundrel
4. Angels' headgear
9. ___ as the eye can see
14. Fixed or frozen follower
19. Fabulist George
20. Two-line verse
21. Beach
22. Weather, to a poet
23. Israeli airport
24. Tailor trousers
25. Pauline's problem
26. Exhausts
27. Silkworm
28. Routines
29. Frauds
30. Inclination
31. Get lost, after four
35. They may justify means
36. Total: Abbr.
37. Appraise
38. Bought time?
40. In particular
43. L.B.J. beagle
45. Diamond and Lagerlöf
48. W. S. Porter
49. Mata ___
50. Devour, after five
53. Penn and Tell, for short
54. Famed marbles
56. Map
58. Selves
59. Max and Buddy
60. Parboils
62. Newman and Revere
63. Bullfrog's sound
66. Right to the jaw, after four
68. "Dames ___," 1968 musical
69. Double features
70. "Mikrokosmos" composer
71. Stadium sounds
73. That, in Toulouse
74. Closefisted
75. Slightest
76. French vineyard
79. Broiled entree, after three
83. Land contract
85. Frightens
87. Eroded, as a river
88. America's Uncle
89. Warehouse function
90. From now on
94. West African country

96. "Tin ___," 1987 film
97. Osiris's wife
100. Specialization, after eleven
105. Christie's Miss ___
107. Novelist Sinclair
108. On one's toes
109. Afore
110. An Astaire
111. Shoe plate
112. Actress Verdugo
113. Operated
114. Frenzied
115. Lasagna or linguine
116. Flax fabric
117. 1 or 66, e.g.
118. Chest: Pref.
119. Skills, in Sevilla
120. Untidy
121. Word of assent

DOWN

1. Writer Carr
2. Cherish
3. Commemorates
4. Disappointments, after four
5. "... and pulled out ___"
6. Numbers game
7. Black Sea port
8. Sun. talk
9. Humane org.
10. Shaves a sheep
11. Style
12. Beard of grain
13. R.C., e.g.
14. Play parts
15. Deli specialties, after seven
16. Sea songstress
17. Correct a text
18. Exams
29. Hitler's architect
30. Freud contemporary
32. Arabian sultanate
33. Frome or Allen
34. Lioness or Lanchester
39. Yalie
40. At present
41. German physicist
42. Baseball's Sparky
44. Parachute strings, after four
46. Breed of cattle
47. Fur piece
49. Certain U.S. resident
50. Baby powder
51. Lasted
52. Mount in Tasmania
55. Dig
57. Wagtail's cousin
59. Dessert, after four

60. Caterpillar's hair
61. Greek portico
62. Leave, after seven
63. Half of DCC
64. American ostriches
65. Tin Man's plea in Oz film
67. Type of school
72. Prof. rank
75. Dud
76. Thanksgiving fruit
77. ___ U.S. Pat. Off.
78. Employ
80. Coal container
81. Bonnie's beau
82. Half: Pref.
84. City in Ohio
86. Length times width, e.g.
89. Melts
91. Like a small egg
92. Most mature
93. Will's contents
95. Net minder
97. Mohammed descendants
98. Former Egyptian president
99. Dunne or Castle

101. Tiny amounts
102. Queues
103. Speechify
104. M. Descartes
106. Walesa
111. Nos. man
112. Shade tree

by Charles M. Deber

ACROSS

1. Highly seasoned fowl dish
6. Bamboo outrigger
13. "___ on Film"
17. Prohibits
21. Pleiades hunter
22. Containing a radioactive element
23. Whine
24. Irish island
25. "They must be crocuses"
27. Ballet bend
28. Sitarist Shankar
29. Quarter of four
30. Eras
31. Bone depressions
33. Spurred, with "on"
34. Nursery king
36. Revealing
37. American Revolution general
38. "...tomorrow is another day"
44. Tearful
45. River in Venezuela
46. Rumor
47. Wind sound
48. Ear: Pref.
51. Faction
52. Partake
53. Britain's emblem
55. Ancient Greek physician
57. "...but we must cultivate our garden"
60. Sudden burst of activity
63. J. Wilbrand's discovery
64. Think
65. Extinct people of Brazil
66. Dry table wine
68. Jai-alai ball
70. Actor Novello
71. Free-swimming aquatic life
73. Recluse
76. Entwiners
79. U.S. painter: 1871–1951
81. Mother-of-pearl
82. Gaucho's rope
83. Practice
86. Adriatic port
88. Controlled the water flow
92. "___ a Californian...": Frost
93. Comedian's foil
95. Coney
97. Hail!
98. In the thick of
100. Puppy cry
101. "Mine never shall be parted, bliss ___": Milton
104. "...yes I said, yes I will Yes"
106. Church officer
107. Squealers
109. ___ Sadat
111. Injury
112. Fed. benefit legislation: 1935
113. Ugandan exile
115. Into pieces
118. "West Side Story" girl
119. Helmet-shaped plant part
121. "I been there before"
124. Showed clemency
126. Certifying officer
127. Imitate an owl
128. "Tiny Alice" playwright
129. Richardson novel
130. R.I.P. notice
132. "___ Misérables"
135. ___ Horizonte, Brazilian city
136. Attorney's concern
137. "...now it's already Tennessee"
142. Former labor leader
143. Russian river
144. ___ often (repeatedly, to a fault)
145. Tots' hero
146. Zeus's wife
147. Trust with "on"
148. Car fuels: Brit.
149. Water mammal

DOWN

1. Where Dryden lived
2. ___ for one's money
3. Citrus fruit
4. Unruly throng
5. Helle's stepmother
6. Government concern
7. Comic Johnson
8. Soviet news agency
9. Geom. figure
10. We, in Roma
11. Explosive laughs
12. Ore. port
13. Attach
14. "The ___ Archipelago": Solzhenitsyn
15. Nobelist Wiesel
16. Shoe width
17. Gondolas
18. "Good night, Grace"
19. Prowl after prey
20. Sarcastic
26. Polynesian drum
32. Popular plastic
33. "___ bragh!"
34. Waxed, old style
35. Be in debt
36. Ky. college
37. Gazelle of Tibet
38. Braggart
39. Sedative
40. Pest
41. L.B.J.'s V.P
42. Madison Ave. come-on
43. Lamp-shade support
44. Growing in elevated areas
47. Calif. city
49. Domingo or Kraus
50. Humdingers
52. Plaice's place
54. Dancer Michio ___
56. At the vertex
58. Mezzo-soprano Jones
59. Philanthropic person
61. Less bland
62. Verse rhythm for Keats
67. Marco Polo was one
69. Sediment
72. Harmful fly
74. Within: Prefix
75. Actress in "Winterset"
77. French quisling
78. Lack of muscular coordination
80. Nineveh was its capital
83. Hoarfrosts
84. Ludwig and Jannings
85. "...people don't do such things"
87. "___ and the Rock": Wolfe
89. Biographer of Michelangelo, et al.
90. "___ fear to kindle your dislike": Shak.
91. Molelike mammal
94. Choose
96. Capek play
99. Kerry city
102. Weakly
103. French wave
105. Ray or beam
108. Pan-fry
110. "Chances ___," Mathis hit
114. Kind of sch.
116. Shore-dinner morsel
117. Nation of Minsk
118. Muscle: Pref.
120. Small interstice
121. Plain
122. Afr. horned mammals
123. Ecclesiastical court
124. State of Malaysia
125. West Point freshman
126. Twangy
129. Peel
130. Actor Kruger
131. Life sci.
132. Alfred ___ of stage fame
133. Patron of Tasso
134. Lead-role player
136. Mongrel
138. Universal-time initials
139. That woman
140. Service gp.
141. Ship's channel

by Edward Marchese

ACROSS

1. He played Mr. Chips
6. Joyous celebration
10. Barb of a feather
15. "Driving ——— Daisy," Uhry play
19. A symbol of purity
21. Elbe feeder
22. Major Joppolo's post
23. Region
24. Lively, to Solti
25. ENDURE YOURSELF!
28. Still burning
29. Loti contemporary
31. Hermes' mother
32. Mahoganylike wood
33. Sister of a padre, e.g.
34. ———-de-boeuf (a window)
35. Biblical sage: Prov. 30:1
37. Sleep, food, etc.
39. Divided
41. PORTRAY YOURSELF!
45. Painter George ——— Tour
47. One of the Joneses
48. Zinke player
53. Hunter's hideaway
56. Fellies
58. Felt eager
59. "Do not go gentle ——— . . .": Thomas
60. Most magnificent
63. SNUB YOURSELF!
66. Govt. man
67. Special kind of plane
69. What Bassanio pressed
70. Somber
71. ——— publica
72. Improper
74. ——— out (makes last)
76. Bellini's Norma, e.g.
79. Type of steam locomotive
81. PROMOTE YOURSELF!
85. One amok
88. Bone: Comb. form
89. Charles of the silents
90. Heath
94. Bath-to-London dir.
95. Wk. day
97. Boat cover
99. Greek letters
101. Muscat resident
102. UNDERSTAND YOURSELF!
107. Turncoat
109. ——— Nagy, Hungarian hero
110. Choreographer Ailey
111. Scene of Perry's victory
113. Loamy deposit
114. Pertaining to Gaius Julius
116. Certain Jayhawker
119. Polanski movie: 1980
120. OPPOSE YOURSELF!
128. Cowboy's cow catcher
131. Victor at Gettysburg
132. Reeking
133. Heraldic band
134. Flock member
135. SHAPE is part of it
138. ——— Beach, Fla. resort
140. Kafka heroine
142. Bani-———, ex-president of Iran
143. WELCOME YOURSELF!
147. Issued
149. Cartoonist Peter
150. Jubal's invention: Gen. 4:21
151. Biblical trader
152. Pribilof Islands, e.g.
153. Yellow-fever conqueror
154. "To a Steam Roller" poet
155. Actor Auberjonois
156. Monoskis

DOWN

1. One of the Websters
2. De Havilland or Hussey
3. To wit
4. Eureka!
5. Bye-bye
6. Hollow, as a pipe
7. "Iacta alea ———"
8. Work or play preceder
9. Verdi opera
10. Trujillo of the Dominican Republic
11. Nabokov novel
12. Gin poles
13. Biblical preposition
14. Manhattan section
15. Stomach
16. Incensed
17. Sans ——— (type style)
18. Leader before Mubarak
19. Lively dance
20. Disney character
26. Of a 24-hour period
27. "Mon ———," Tati film
30. He, in Napoli
36. Having secret meaning
38. British radio navigational aid
40. Livy's tongue
42. Swathe
43. Chilean mountains
44. "The Plague" author
45. Habit
46. Last stage of strategy, in chess
49. Exclamations
50. Within: Prefix
51. Bayard or Bucephalus
52. Statue with limitations
53. Edible fiber
54. Bedeck
55. Nightmares
57. Stallion
58. Toscanini
60. Kókon
61. Fret
62. Summer Olympic site: 1964
64. Copter cousin
65. City NE of Venice
68. Composer Janácek
73. Make happy
75. He wrote "Where the Money Was"
77. Photographer Morath
78. Nile end
80. A martial art
82. Eyepieces
83. Erect
84. TV's "Quantum ———"
85. Ward healer
86. Soul
87. Pic ———, Andorran mountain
91. Writers Levin and Wolfert
92. "——— Cradle": Vonnegut
93. Burrows of Broadway
96. Sexologist Havelock ———
98. Ajaccio and Algeciras
100. Heliacal
103. Rebecca, Benjamin and Adam
104. ——— Marie Saint of films
105. Because
106. ——— du Sahel, town in Mali
108. Buck book
112. Concluding part
115. Time periods
117. Sin
118. Small anchors
121. Gulch
122. River at Frankfurt
123. Tray
124. Push and shove
125. Sounded off
126. Rot-resistant woods
127. Cousin of wimpish
128. "Villa" composer
129. Informed
130. Catcher in the Rhine?
131. Cuban jazz artist Santamaria
136. Molecule part
137. Matador charger
139. Department in N France
141. City north of Des Moines
144. Israeli airport
145. Otology subject
146. Diva Merriman
148. Suffix for manor or baron

by Jacques Liwer

ACROSS

1. Con game
5. Mighty mite in a computer
9. Withheld
13. Kitchen ender
17. Ancient Greek flask
18. Mozart portrayer in "Amadeus"
20. Structural bar
22. Center
23. Fleet V.I.P.'s
25. Movie star of the 30's
27. In a pleasant manner
28. Dated
30. Ideate
31. Dress material
32. Residue
33. Spare
34. Ess follower
35. Veranda
37. Dispatch
40. Approached
42. Fade-out
44. Kind of seal
46. Not so much
47. Honshu city
48. Fay of old flicks
49. Kirghiz range
50. Scamp
51. Reconnaissance groups
55. "___ of robins . . .": Kilmer
56. Cunégonde's creator
58. Suit material
59. Survives
60. Satiric twist
61. Henry IV's birthplace
62. States of pique
63. Student's action or electives
65. Folk-rock singer Jim
67. Certain barren area
70. Please, in Bonn
71. Fairy-tale title
73. "___ tu," Verdi aria
74. Composer Siegmeister
75. Hawthorne's "The Marble ___"
76. Cambodian neighbor
77. Godunov, e.g.
78. Itch
79. Christina Crawford book
83. Sanguine
84. Bypasses
86. Mignon lead-in
87. ___ capita

88. Table scraps
89. Group once ruled by J.E.H.
90. Descent
94. Beautiful woman
96. Full follower
98. Arlington, Va. structure
99. Alan Bates movie: 1966
101. Taking the lead
103. Fancy
104. Spanish commune
105. A hydrocarbon
106. Word with shoppe
107. Saucy
108. Modernists
109. Jane of fiction
110. "Camino ___," Williams play

DOWN

1. Syrup source
2. More lucid
3. "A grief without ___ . . .": Coleridge
4. Reconciles
5. Byron's "___ Harold's Pilgrimage"
6. Burly antecedent
7. "Now ___ me down . . ."
8. P.O. item
9. Affinity
10. London statue
11. Reduce
12. Actor Reed
13. Prickly: Comb. form
14. "And there's little ___ . . .": Kingsley
15. Tough trip
16. Rocket attachment
19. Chabrier favorite
21. Dormant state
24. Like lions or zebras
26. Elm's offering
29. Kin of P.D.Q.
33. Horne and Nyman
35. Nimble
36. Drenched
37. Delhi garb
38. Daredevil's trait
39. Famine's antithesis
40. Remote telecast
41. Very loud
42. Condemn
43. Small centipede
45. Morse-code signals
46. Actress Ullman
47. Scorching
49. Singer Baker
51. Rhone feeder

52. In ___ (having difficulty)
53. Attain
54. More loyal
55. Leaf-stem angles
57. Stale
59. Makes beloved
62. Patten's cousin
63. Mind
64. Mushroom caps
65. Finn and Sawyer, e.g.
66. Actor Santoni
67. Hell kite
68. Squirrel's nest
69. Lieutenant, to a private
71. Emulates Petruchio
72. Freeman's "R. ___"
75. Arm
77. Escamillo, for one
79. ___ Castle, historic Cuban fort
80. Sheds
81. Sweet syrup used in the East
82. First to come
83. Fashion's Oscar de la ___

85. Almond confection
87. Turpentine component
90. "Villa" composer
91. Spry
92. Town ENE of Lucknow, India
93. U.S. conductor-composer
94. Seek's companion
95. Lulu
96. Funeral sight
97. Palindromic name
98. Like heaven's gates
99. Monetary unit of 76 Across
100. Layer
102. Creator of Arthur Gordon Pym

by Alfio Micci

ACROSS

1. Jack preceder
5. Grimalkins
9. Italian coin of yore
14. Young pest
18. Bombay bigwig
19. Kauai greeting
21. Polynesian garment
22. Miff
23. His business is looking up
25. Unresolved
27. Actor Alan from Allestree
28. Tones down
30. Becloud
31. Chrysler cars of 1928–61
34. Grape variety
35. Assumes
39. Weapon for D'Artagnan
40. Luster
41. In a pacific way
42. Graduate-school hurdles
43. Sort of friend
45. By way of
46. One-stripe G.I.'s
47. Low blow
48. Had regrets
49. Guns an engine
50. Yes, to Nanette
51. Regardless of
55. Palmists' interests
56. Naval unit
58. Inclined
59. Hindu scripture
60. Soviet range
61. Ceramists' needs
62. "When the ___ breaks . . ."
63. Harasses
65. "Whom shall ___ . . .": Isa. 6:8
66. British sneaker
69. Befuddled
70. Elated
72. Be human
73. S. Korean soldiers
74. Actress-writer Chase
75. Time past
76. So long, in England
77. Half of MIV
78. The world over
82. Any rich man
83. Ornamental shrub
85. Laconian serf
86. Break one's word
87. More irascible
88. Noted name in polio research
89. River into Monterey Bay
90. Big A offshoot
91. Keglers' milieu
92. Macho type
93. Dreamily romantic
97. Like 93 Across
102. Domingo specialty
103. ___ nous
104. Part of a TV transmission
105. Parched
106. Obey a cheerleader
107. In a stupor
108. Combo
109. Gush forth

DOWN

1. Browning's "___ Lippo Lippi"
2. ___ Cruces, N.M.
3. Carpenter with six legs
4. Precooks
5. Stage name for Mr. Iskowitz
6. Fugard's "A Lesson From ___"
7. Collins and Mix
8. Haggard romance
9. Cool Italian dessert
10. French dynast
11. "The Angry Hills" author
12. Hideaway
13. Surpassed in audacity
14. City on the Weser
15. Inlet
16. "The Greatest"
17. ___ Borch, Dutch painter
20. More chichi
24. "Cybele" author
26. Backpacker
29. Once more
31. "A ruddy ___ manly blood": Emerson
32. Scolding
33. Phrase from "America the Beautiful"
34. Van Dine's Vance
35. Ha-ha
36. What Jimmy Stewart was in during 1937
37. Twist of fiction
38. Former name of Lake Malawi
40. Bathhouse of a sort
41. Air-show feature
43. Frustrates
44. Seed coverings
47. Victoria and Reichenbach
49. Saturn features
51. Lasso
52. "La Valse" composer
53. Apt anagram for notes
54. Veda adherent
55. Summa cum ___
57. Persea and poon
59. A thousand kilograms
61. Caricaturist Berger
62. Scottish offspring
63. "Viva Maria!" actress: 1965
64. Arc de Triomphe locale
65. Printer's roller
66. Weevil feature
67. Philosopher José ___ y Gasset
68. Cleans the slate
70. Not so fresh
71. English stargazer: 1868–1939
74. Beholden
76. Lilliputian hallmark
78. Condos
79. Expressed gratitude
80. Wife of Hercules
81. Phoenician name of Dido
82. Hold up
84. Like some modern music
86. Martinet
88. ___ Coeur (Paris landmark)
89. European finch
91. Figure-skating jump
92. "If I ___ Million," 1932 movie
93. Hawthorn
94. Vein yield
95. Wildcatter's quest
96. Genetic initials
98. Keeve
99. Opposite of nope
100. Afore
101. Kind of line

by Warren W. Reich

HOW TO ACHIEVE HAPPINESS

ACROSS

1. Start of a Stepquote
6. Noted conductor-composer
12. Singer Anita ___
17. Anno ___
18. Emend
19. Skipped over
21. Rife
22. Paradigms or paragons
23. Solve a "weighty" problem
24. Mellow
25. Kind of duck or sisal
27. Woodworkers' machines
29. On this side: Prefix
30. Seat in a bay window
32. Stepquote: Part III
34. Map abbr.
35. Like some bloomers
36. Zola and Berliner
38. One in a roll book
40. Kind of box
41. Chub
42. Insipid
44. Elman's teacher
45. Clandestine
46. Eagerly expecting
48. ___ Rabbit
49. Beau Brummell, e.g.
50. "___ Memorandum," Stepquote source
54. Subject of a long Frost poem
58. Plath work
59. Third person: It.
60. Light-amplification device
61. Old French coin
62. "___ Macabre"
63. Stepquote author
65. Independently
67. From ___ Z
68. Caesar's "I seize"
70. ___ Domingo
71. Inflections
72. Most abundant Atlantic Coast fish
74. Hurdles in Hollywood
76. Vendition condition
77. Joan or Marian
78. Hot spot for hops
79. "McGraw's boy"
82. Heart
83. Part of a lamp
85. Jelly ingredient
89. Courses for horses
90. Puccini opera: 1926
92. La ___, town in Spain ("The sunny spot")
94. Einstein's fourth dimension
95. Amazon estuary
96. Stepquote: part V
98. Red-ink entry
99. March 15 in Milano
100. Venus ___
102. In olden days
104. Hwy.
105. Jury panel
107. Screed
109. More reticulate
111. Crown protector
112. Scab, as after a burn
113. Regard highly
114. Purpose of a hansa
115. These make flights
116. End of Stepquote

DOWN

1. Grand; imposing
2. Elec. unit
3. Practical
4. Sicilian resort
5. Stepquote: Part II
6. Archbishop
7. Edit
8. Anne Baxter role: 1950
9. Perfume container
10. Nantucket native
11. Future fledgling
12. Left Bank headgear
13. Alternative to lagers
14. Baby sea otter
15. School
16. Diseur
17. First European to reach India by sea
20. Home of a sidewinder
21. Tore
26. Saroyan hero
28. "Some ___ meat. . . .": Burns
31. Certain ointments
33. Stepquote: Part IV
35. Existed
37. Recipe verb
39. Swarm, in Sedan
40. Presides
43. Losses of last letters
45. Preserve
47. Airs via video
48. Honeysuckle, e.g.
49. Ignominy
50. Choleric
51. Sheer fabric
52. Dickens villain
53. He's faithful to Homo sapiens
54. Dispatch
55. Intended
56. One of Sheridan's "Rivals"
57. McAuliffe's reply in 1944
58. Costa loser
60. Singer Cristy ___
64. Aromatic Himalayan plant
66. Ufficio ___, Italian mail center
69. Collier's access
73. Caucasian, to a Polynesian
74. Author Davidson ("Loose Change")
75. Signal after tattoo
77. Increase Mather was one
79. Reason
80. Plain
81. Arranged in thin plates
82. Radioactive minerals
83. Chorines: Slang
84. Give it ___ (attempt)
86. Divine messenger
87. "To a newspaperman a human being is ___ . . .": Fred Allen
88. Teacher, at times
90. Scot's cap
91. Hindu's "tree of the gods"
93. U.S. folk singer
95. A Shakespeare contemporary
97. Stepquote: Part VI
100. Stowe book
101. Relative of "Jaws": 1977
103. Caesura
106. "___ Stranger Here Myself," ultimate source of Stepquote
108. Hawaiian tuna
110. ___ Aviv

by Eugene T. Maleska

ACROSS

1. Diner staple
5. Gibe
10. Broadcasts
14. Secrete
19. Caravansary
20. Comicality
21. Warhol style
22. Where St. Paul was shipwrecked
23. In company
24. Papas or Bordoni
25. Water wheel
26. Actress Burstyn
27. Like a poor pickpocket?
30. Dogs, when riled
32. Mason's burden
33. Baum dog
34. Leo's pride
35. Cut
36. "Auld Lang ___"
37. Depend
38. Typeface
40. Fleet or Easy
42. Comfort
45. Thames boats
46. Short queries
47. ___ Islands, near the Shetlands
51. Lancelot's hair-raiser?
54. Houston pro
56. Took long steps
57. Gillette razor
58. Out of bed
60. Act up a storm
62. Asian weight
63. Drink lead-in
65. Culloden Moor wear
66. Securities expert
67. Some records, briefly
68. Nancy three-some
69. Inventor Howe
71. Prickle
73. Post or Balbo
75. Grain coats
76. Elected
77. Throng
78. Except for
81. Ream unit
82. Fraser of tennis
83. Rainbow
86. Tommie of baseball fame
87. Loser at Little Bighorn
89. Monkey's uncle?
91. Leyte neighbor
93. Wampum item
94. Hebrew measures

95. Command at West Point
96. Completed
97. Relay finisher
99. Welles of "Touch of Evil"
101. Gentle renters?
104. Critic
105. Nero's 1105
106. Fix loosened laces
108. Most exceptional
109. Do over
111. Vague and Zorina
112. First space travelers
113. Indonesian island
116. Choice words
117. Label designation
118. Suit or chute fabric
119. Navy noncom
122. Mischievous
124. Would-be Duses?
128. ___ acids
129. Halley novel
131. Bar-mitzvah reading matter
132. Any rich man
133. Boxlike sleighs
134. Swiftly
135. Boot out
136. A.L. batting king: 1954
137. Ringlet
138. D-day craft
139. School furniture
140. Shade of blue

DOWN

1. Greeting
2. Cuckoopint, e.g.
3. Emulated Kathleen Barne
4. Utilitarian style of design
5. Evasive
6. Article of virtu
7. Indication
8. Former Senator from Hawaii
9. Author of "Lee's Lieutenants"
10. Fine china
11. Trireme tool
12. Architectural curve?
13. Tourists, at times
14. Merganser
15. Starting five of Chamberlain, Bol, Ewing, et al?
16. Kegler's venue
17. Unyielding
18. Merchant guild
19. Cummerbund
21. Unity
28. Galsworthy novel

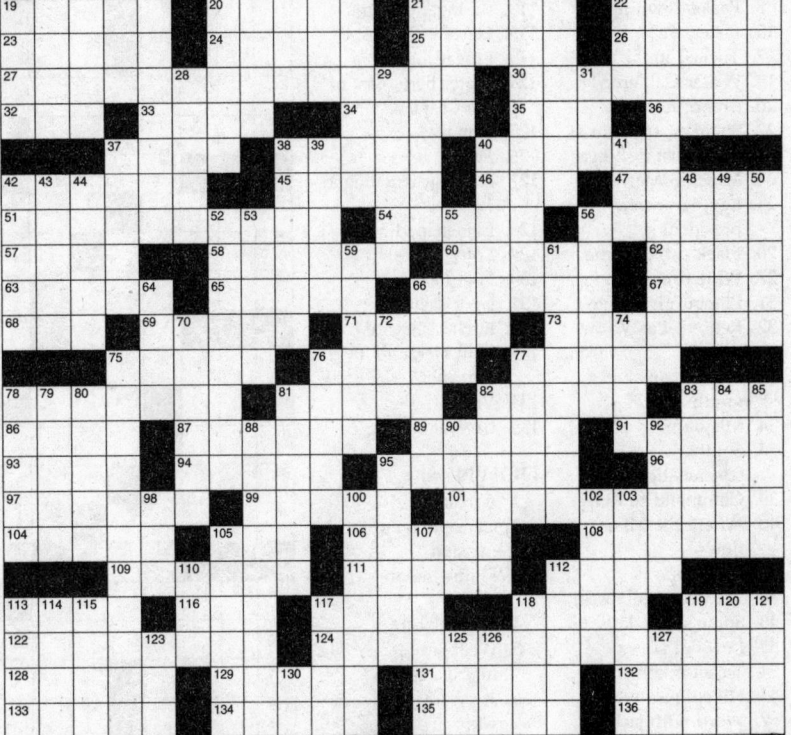

by Louis Sabin

29. Long-stemmed palm
31. Run up a tab
37. Hindu tunes
38. Spring months
39. Talk-show invitee
40. Peale appeal
41. Triton
42. Brinker's blade
43. Surmounting
44. Turkish coins
48. Barbecue choice
49. "___ Psyche": Keats
50. Conger chaser
52. Post-spat activity
53. Nobelist after Wiesel
55. Zola's "La ___"
56. African wildcat
59. ___ Lederer (Ann Landers)
61. Elevenses cart
64. Actress Garr
66. Athens of America
70. Calvary soldier
72. Tool for Mrs. Wiggs
74. Vexes
75. Raised unreliable fish?
76. The mating game

77. Actress Berger
78. De Brunhoff elephant
79. Rocket stage
80. Jump away in sudden fear
81. Antithesis of surfeit
82. Italy's third largest city
83. Song by Tosti
84. Shoe strips
85. Peak
88. Places to pawn Stephen King's books?
90. A Muslim month
92. Venerate
95. Allergic response
98. Bauxite or galena
100. Kitty Hawk name
102. Bore
103. "Ah, woe!"
105. Dillon or Earp
107. Picked up the tab
110. Miss Piggy's pronoun
112. Powers
113. Modify to suit
114. Maholi or maki

115. Sheeplike
117. "Cheaters"
118. Nibble
119. Kind of servant
120. Shakespeare contemporary
121. Pelion's support
123. Setback
125. Noah's bird
126. Flag
127. Flagstad or Gluck
130. Make doilies

480 FIRST-NAME GAME

ACROSS

1. Sailor, e.g.
4. Flirt with
8. Packs down lightly
13. Lister, e.g.
17. Tucked in
19. Writer Calderon
20. Brand new
22. Shankar, the sitarist
23. Dramatist de Vega
24. Mine, in Marne
25. Egypt's second president
26. Black cat, to some
27. Wine dregs
31. Pittsburgh athlete
32. Reno-to-Las Vegas dir.
33. English royal family
34. Misplace
35. Southern constellation
39. Command to Fido
40. Where the Miami flows
43. Shipshape
46. ___ over (collapses)
48. Some salad days
52. Low-cut shoes
54. Ticket-booth sign
55. Hiked, in a way
57. Word with jack or stick
58. Housebreaks
60. One of the Near Islands
62. Penny dreadful or shilling shocker
64. A marzo date
65. Clear
66. Certain tides
68. Greek letter
69. This, to Caesar
70. Fishes
77. Choler
78. Brazil's ___ Branco
79. Africa's largest city
80. ___ de la Cité
81. Year Claudius I died
82. Bon vivant
85. Atop
86. Western squatter
90. Annealing oven
92. Most crafty
94. A.L. member
96. Narrow groove
97. R. Wilbur's "Walking to ___"
99. Cartoonist Dean
100. ___ Blair (George Orwell)
102. ___-froid (calmness)
103. Supporting
105. Guys
107. Tear apart
109. Fun and games
113. Basinger of films
115. Fence in
119. Linear measures
124. Water body east of the Caspian
125. Cringe
126. Space
127. A Phillies' manager: 1987
128. Egg-shaped fruit
129. Lofty
130. Poet Lazarus
131. Lyricist Evans
132. Eucharistic rite
133. John Herzfeld TV film: 1987
134. Views
135. Lawyer's thing

DOWN

1. Arrests
2. Cancel a bombing mission
3. Plains Indian shelter
4. Most abject
5. Weapons manufacturers
6. A portmanteau word
7. They are often split
8. Heredity factors
9. Med.-sch. subject
10. Rumple
11. Attention getter
12. Cryptesthetic people
13. Validates a will
14. Debussy opus
15. Open
16. Paul McCartney band
18. Darkroom activity
21. Victorian expletive
28. U.N. agency
29. Ski wood
30. Clubs, e.g.
36. Juno, to Cato
37. Check
38. Furthermore
40. Elect
41. "Ben-___"
42. Cohan's "___ Popular Man"
44. Tabriz native
45. Auto court
47. Cleave
49. Diplomat Root
50. Rock bottom
51. Off-color
53. Scornful looks
56. Keep in custody
59. Runways

by Peter Swift

61. Take a powder
63. Scoops
67. Impertinent lass
70. Parts of wads
71. Mirador
72. River Quay
73. Dough
74. Flock
75. Boo-boo
76. Author's "jackpot"
83. Teases
84. Kind of caterpillar
87. Singing syllable
88. German article
89. Scandal sheet
91. Herpetologist's subject
93. Celebes, e.g.
95. Boring
98. Betsey ___ (Dickens character)
101. British movie theaters
104. End
106. Title Pinero had
108. TV adjunct
109. Sacred song
110. Trajan's courtyards
111. Furrows
112. Misjudged
114. Traditional customs
116. Edmonton hockey player
117. Slyly sarcastic
118. Kin of 21 Down
120. Actress Witherspoon
121. Enthusiastic
122. Fermented drink
123. Seward Peninsula city

ACROSS

1 White-collar position
7 Big guy
11 "Did you ___?!"
15 Moo goo gai pan pan
18 Sonata movements
19 Not the most reliable set of wheels
20 –
22 Little-known
24 It surrounds the Isle of Man
25 "New Look" pioneer
26 Eastern way
27 Half-German/half-Indian film hero
29 Cymbal in a drum kit
30 –
34 3-D figures
35 "I hope to see London once ___ I die": "Henry IV, Part 2"
36 Cognizance
37 Carnegie's cronies
39 Comment made after jumping in a pool, maybe
42 State strongly
44 Faultfinders
47 Throaty sound
49 Eye sockets
52 Certain ID check
53 Cross shape
54 Obstructor of congress?
57 –
59 ___ Sunday, the fourth Sunday in Lent
60 Farm pitcher
61 "The Time Machine" race
62 Agatha and Dahlia, in P. G. Wodehouse books
63 What this puzzle's circled spaces represent
69 Subject of a Michelangelo sculpture
72 Westminster area
73 LL Bean competitor
77 Made fun of, in a way
78 Ring duo
81 –
82 Hairstyling need
83 2000 Elton John/Tim Rice musical
84 Fluoroscope inventor
86 Traditional Christmas Eve meal in Germany
87 Drink served in a tall glass
89 Hoof handlers
92 Rtes.
93 –
97 Startled cry
98 Reuters competitor
100 Refresher
102 Casino fixture
108 Hunter slain by Artemis
109 Gillette brand
110 "What ___ care?"
111 Five or ten, say
112 Unsuccessful, as a mission
114 –
118 Bear in mind
119 Appropriate
120 Blubberless marine mammals
121 Leftmost digital watch no.
122 Recycle bin fillers
123 Tap sites
124 Boon to Scottish tourism

by Patrick Berry

DOWN

1 Fuddy-duddy
2 1998 De Niro thriller
3 Under a false name, briefly
4 –
5 G
6 Sleeping sickness carriers
7 Sports ___
8 Cereal grass
9 Schindler's business partner in "Schindler's List"
10 Sonatas, e.g.
11 Like some mushrooms
12 Florida's ___ Beach
13 "Hostel" director ___ Roth
14 1950 film that retells the same events four times
15 –
16 Mountain nymph
17 "Beauty is truth, truth beauty" writer
19 Potsherds
21 Passed (away)
23 "What nonsense!"
28 Intersected
31 Grp. involved in "the Troubles"
32 Flavor lender
33 Ludicrous
34 M.I.T.'s ___ School of Management
38 Ending with defer or refer
39 "Goldberg Variations" composer
40 Daughter of Uranus
41 Count
43 Super-duper
45 Big ___
46 Appeals to
48 Out of sorts
50 –
51 The place of one's fodder?
52 Does a run
55 Snakes with vestigial limbs
56 Escort's offering
58 Lettuce type
59 Country
62 "Son of ___!"
64 It serves many courses: Abbr.
65 Juicer
66 Former Hong Kong leader Tung ___ Hwa
67 Lacking sense
68 One of the Bobbsey Twins
69 Star followers
70 Group that includes the U.A.E.
71 Picks
74 Girder with flanges
75 It may come with a gift
76 –
78 Render unavailable
79 First of all
80 Molière comedy, with "The"
81 Became an item
83 –
85 Brother of Ham and Japheth
88 Honored alumni, usually
90 –
91 Rest cure destination
94 Bugs that live in trees
95 Actress Merkel
96 Ancient Turkish dynasty founder
99 Mini-maps
100 Whistle wearer
101 Garden spot
103 Shabby treatment
104 Soirees
105 Pillbox quantities
106 ___ ware (Japanese porcelain)
107 Clipped
109 Hot room, colloquially
113 Gilbert & Sullivan princess
115 Carry with effort
116 Collection agcy.?
117 Took in

ACROSS

1. ___ dixit
5. Actor Gulager
8. Turnery gear
13. Reflexive pronoun
15. Precarious spot
19. Ghastly
20. Norman Mailer book, with "The"
22. Small sandpipers
23. Bitter disagreement
24. Socagers, e.g.
26. Year in Alexius I Commenus's reign
27. Ancient wall word
28. Rhinoceros beetle
30. Mascara neighbor
31. Menilite is one
32. A son of Gad
33. Burt Lancaster role: 1960
37. Slightly tapering
39. City in Tuscany
40. Lunar plain
41. Long-beaked fish
42. Like many needs of the needy
43. Mother superior
45. Pisa divider
46. More pious
48. Opposite of saludos
49. Rapid movements in music
53. "...blue ribbons ___"
54. Book by President Carter
56. Diamond man
57. Sticks, e.g.
58. Ditty
59. Indian of N.M.
60. "Star Wars" role
61. Ordinal suffix
62. Actor who produced a director
67. Town west of 91 Down
68. Servant
70. Writer Gardner's namesakes
71. Rigorous
73. Sky bear
74. Sour ale
76. Folkways
77. German admiral
78. Uniform
79. Kind of battery
80. Gospel author
82. Benjamin Britten opera
84. Its symbol is a lion
87. Remunerates
88. Fraction
90. Nimble
91. Theda contemporary
92. Photog. abbr.
93. Slopes
96. Priest saying Mass, e.g.
99. Cato the Elder was one
101. Setting for a Christie classic
103. "Roxana" author
104. English poet-novelist: 1886–1967
105. Slant a certain way
106. Small springs
107. Inst. at Nashville
108. Arnold ___, memorable actor-puzzler

DOWN

1. Ship that brought Miss Liberty to the U.S.
2. Tijuana tender
3. Toil
4. Outflowing branch of a lake
5. Fidel's compadre
6. Scourge of serge
7. One-horned fish
8. Track circuits
9. Ibsen character
10. O'Neill play: 1920
11. Swingers of the 40's
12. Store fodder
13. Always, in Aachen
14. Throne of Israel contender: I Kgs. 16
15. Babiche
16. Doesn't heed
17. Circumspect
18. A suburb of Pittsburgh
20. Hoarfrost
21. Pope's crown
25. Explosive initials
29. Opening maneuver
31. Chimp's cousin
33. Gimlet ingredient
34. ___ van Delft, Dutch painter
35. Midget, in Marseille
36. Baseball's Mike or Tom
38. Stalker in a salt marsh
39. Agitated fits
42. Song popularized by Debby Boone
43. Idolize
44. Sevilla savants
45. Capp and Hirt
46. "Launching the Boat" painter
47. Explorer of N.M.: 16th century
48. Grieg dancer
50. Gaunt
51. Edmonton athlete on ice
52. Whacked
54. Bush's alma mater
55. Glyceride, e.g.
60. Life guard, at times
62. More sapient
63. Literary scraps
64. Superman portrayer
65. One who prods
66. Like street talk
69. Environs
71. Pump part
72. Notable periods
75. Belles-___
76. Impetus
77. Victim of 95 Down
79. Parthenope, for one
80. Emulates Jehu
81. G.I.'s, at times
82. Czech capital, to Czechs
83. Prowl after prey
84. Norman Bates's place
85. Kind of oven
86. Father of Remus
89. St. John follower
91. Gauguin's birthplace
93. Shoe widths for Bigfoot?
94. Military station
95. Hit signs
97. Montreal player
98. Accts.
100. Truncate
102. Chit

by Daniel Girardi

ACROSS

1. One of the Dioscuri
7. Bird of the night
12. Helen of Troy's mother
16. "___ Suspicion," 1943 film
21. Seek ambitiously
22. Nose: Comb. form
23. Concern on Wall St.
24. Ancient city of Egypt
25. CHOREOG-RAPHER
27. ASTRONOMER
29. "___ Cardboard Lover," 1942 film
30. Corrigenda
31. Sacred song
33. Malediction
34. Novelist Murdoch
35. Certain fighter
36. "Mondo ___," 1963 documentary
37. Gelada or pongo
40. Actress in "The Wedding Night"
41. Actress Patricia and actor Tom
42. Capitol Hill list
46. Used a treadle
48. Rich cake
49. Equipped with weapons
50. Defendants, in law
51. Hat adornments
52. CINEMA-TOGRAPHER
54. Mother of Eris
55. Added spirits
56. Carouse
57. Strip
58. Sherlock portrayer, often
59. Actor in "A Summer Place"
60. Capital of Lombardy
61. Coagulated part of milk
62. The March King and family
63. Tennis division
64. FARMER
67. "___ is . . . a refuge from home life": Shaw
68. Hole-___(ace)
70. Congrio, e.g.
71. Eminent
72. Made zzz's
73. LOCKSMITH
78. Scottish cap
81. Piscator
82. Jejune
83. Posts
84. Deli order
85. Rhea's role in "Cheers"
86. Go with the gale
87. Parsonage
88. Compare
89. Fourth-largest Great Lake
90. POULTRYMAN
93. "___ to my remains . . .": Dryden
94. Prepare flax
95. Texas longhorn
97. Author of "The Dynasts"
98. Girl in a calypso song
99. Ramate
101. Dance in a single file
102. Actor in "The Guardsman"
103. Wager
104. Gunfighter at the O.K. Corral
105. Standard
106. Flex
107. A Houston athlete
109. Uses a discus
110. Comedienne Anne and kin
112. Like a March hare
115. LIFEGUARD
117. REPORTER
120. Turned white
121. Puerto ___
122. Red dye
123. Intransitive verb
124. Segal's "Oliver's ___"
125. Stagehand
126. Takes five
127. Unit of electric current

DOWN

1. Singer Johnny
2. He wrote "Off the Court"
3. Boom
4. Sesame
5. Architectural fillet
6. Alters the text
7. Destine
8. "___ Up, Doc?": 1972 film
9. Director Wertmuller
10. Ref. book
11. Protection for a loafer
12. Famous racing site
13. Nice school
14. Condemn
15. Actress Harding
16. Brought into harmony
17. Fruitless
18. Blame
19. Wickedness
20. Arc. dweller
26. Was human
28. Squama
32. Capital of the Beaver State
35. Christie's "___ at End House"

by Bette Sue Cohen

36. Deloul, for one
37. Fameuse and pippin
38. Hairy covering
39. TEACHER
40. Komatik, e.g.
41. Roman Catholic devotion
42. Wept
43. MODEL
44. Rooftop sight
45. Money in Iran
47. Hemsley TV vehicle
48. Actress Feldshuh
49. Ward off
52. Canasta play
53. Magnum ___
54. ___ couture
56. Hot under the collar
58. Spoils
60. He may do some stripping
61. Zygote
62. Clogs or pumps
64. "She ___ Yellow Ribbon," 1949 film
65. College in Ore.
66. Carrot, briefly
67. Place for a bracelet
69. ___ prosequi

72. Trapper
73. More loyal
74. Screen
75. Blake of "Gunsmoke"
76. Dog in "Annie"
77. Señor's response
79. Meeting outline
80. When Grundy was born
81. Vinegary
82. Yearned
84. Heyerdahl's "Kon-___"
86. Precipitous
87. Actress-dancer Champion
88. Native of Riga
91. He commits grave crimes
92. Moll's companion
93. Large handkerchief or scarf
95. Kind of cat
96. Pulse
98. Saki
100. Lower
101. Drive-in waitress or waiter
102. Memorizes
105. Name in fashion

106. Suit
107. Premed subj.
108. Town WSW of Caen
109. BARBER
110. Muddle
111. Check
112. Spouse
113. Ripening agent
114. Streeter's "___ Mable"
115. Wife of Saturn
116. Work unit
118. Garden implement
119. Young seal

ACROSS

1. Ashen
5. Transparent fabrics
11. New Testament book
15. Cher's former partner
19. Old Irish war cry
21. Fold-up furniture
23. Easy existence
24. Shunned, in a big way
25. Franciscan Abbr.
26. "Ah! je ___ seule," Massenet aria
27. Composer Ned
29. Becomes sunny
30. Enforcement, figuratively
32. Expressions of inquiry
34. Commotion
36. "Do as I say, not ___"
37. "___ sow,..."
38. M.I.T., R.P.I. et al.
40. Lamb product
42. Nantes negative
43. ___ Lingus, Irish airline
45. "Holy" city?
47. Irish terriers, e.g.
50. Actor Hayakawa
53. Noted
55. Huarache, e.g.
59. Press on
60. Attacks flies
61. Fast plane
63. Fast's companion
64. "___ Blu, Dipinto di Blu"
65. Pismire
67. J.C. Oates book
69. Ireland, poetically
71. Silk from Assam
73. "We're off ___ the Wizard"
75. Coward's "To Step ___"
77. Vols' home
78. Popular Irish ballad
80. Like Croesus
82. Tree in an O'Neill title
84. Donate, in Dundee
85. ___ France, famed liner
86. Pastoral paths: Abbr.
88. Monoskis
90. Islands off the Irish coast
92. Lincolns' unpopular kin
94. Loire valley attraction
96. Ocellus
97. Prunelle flavoring
99. Engross
100. Ade's "___ Horne"
101. Word before mo
104. Synge or O'Casey work
106. Probe deeply
108. Late, in Lyon
112. Game-show group
115. Ex-astronaut on the Hill
117. Twice CCLI
118. Type of power
119. Start
121. "Ragged Dick" author
123. Son of Lamech
125. Latin I verb
126. "My Wild ___"
128. Vehicle for Molly Malone
131. Five-liners named for an Irish port
132. Wee hoarders of legend
133. Observed
134. Sch. groups
135. Bakers' needs
136. "...thrive as best ___" Shak.

DOWN

1. Jai-alai ball
2. Originates
3. River of Ireland
4. Cork-to-Kilkenny dir.
5. Health food also called bean curd
6. ___ potatoes (certain home fries)
7. Meat-and-vegetables combo
8. Former Indian P.M. Shastri
9. Historic Hungarian city
10. Fight ___ (avoid)
11. Tarkington's "The Magnificent ___"
12. First Family at Albany, once
13. Hear a case
14. Anti-child-abuse org.
15. Computer units
16. Acquire
17. ___-well (idler)
18. Heavily favored
20. "Gee whiz!"
22. Spaniard's greeting
28. ___ la Paix, Paris thoroughfare
31. Rib
33. Having tiny openings, as leaves
35. Modern music form
38. St. Patrick's land, for short
39. Move like a snake
41. "Certainly!"
44. Faulkner female
46. First word in Mass. motto
48. O'Flaherty product
49. Laugh in derision
50. Indefinitely, in legal lingo
51. The ___ Isle
52. Slates
54. A West African language
56. Heavy Irish tweed
57. Silly
58. Most suitable for Sprat
60. Bar seat
62. High and low phenomena
66. Norw. news service
68. Actor Gavin of "The Love Boat"
70. ___ canto
72. Llamas' locale
74. Out of ___ (disjointed)
76. Sliced off sharply
79. Scream
81. Followers of: Suffix
83. County in NW Ireland
87. Disgraceful
89. James Joyce collection of short stories
91. Right-hand page
93. The old ___ (Ireland)
95. "Not with ___...": T.S. Eliot
96. Dutch commune
98. Energy unit
101. Loot
102. "Annie ___," 1838 song
103. Prompt
105. Where to find McCarthy, McKinley and McGrath
107. N.Y.U.'s hue
109. Tocsin
110. Helen Hunt Jackson novel
111. Ready for Morpheus
113. Big Bertha's birthplace
114. Oven for annealing glass
116. In recent days
118. Riza Pahlevi, once
120. Scenery changer
122. S. Korean president: 1948–60
124. Basics
127. Fall mo.
129. Environmental watchdog agcy.
130. Wheel spoke: Fr.

by Charles E. Gersch

ACROSS

1. Stag or buck
5. Bracelet add-on
10. Trite
15. Lighter or tender
19. Prolific auth.
20. Bast fiber
21. Alleviates
22. Approximately
23. Jack London classic, with "The"
25. "___ Western Front"
27. Squeeze the tube
28. Like Times Square
30. Medicinal seeds
31. Wear away
33. Encouraged, as a team
36. Mubarak's predecessor
39. Mar
41. Lengthen
45. Scottish magpies
46. Facing a glacier
47. Wood sorrels
48. Brother
49. Killer whales
50. Author ___ Congwen
51. Kennel adjunct
52. R.B.I., for one
53. Electrical unit
54. Author of the European Recovery Plan
59. Grant
60. Divides into three parts
62. Carols
63. Worshiper
65. Approaches
66. Italian poet
67. In wild confusion
68. Designer Cardin
70. Eton boy's mother
71. "... closer than ___": Proverbs
74. Berlin's "He's ___ Picker"
75. A. Conan Doyle work
78. Epoch
79. Autry or Kelly
80. The Greatest
81. Tax shelters, for short
82. Ski lift
83. Aim
84. Allen or MacMurray
85. Seraglio
87. Kissed by Henri
88. Certain
91. ___ chance! (good luck!)
92. Stair part

93. Records
95. Be behind
98. Dethroned Titan
101. Parts
103. Process of bone formation
107. Drug effect, sometimes
110. ___ Journal (financial daily)
112. Envelope wd.
113. ___ prosequi (court entry)
114. Hogan's cousin
115. Gaelic
116. Catch flies
117. Hydroxyl compounds
118. Jannings and Ludwig
119. Hammett's "The ___ Curse"

DOWN

1. Herb or weapon
2. Strong as ___
3. Attic
4. Pleads with
5. Set of beliefs
6. Hemmed and ___
7. "___ Blue?"
8. Brooklet
9. Docs
10. Further adventure
11. Stocking color
12. "___ was saying . . ."
13. Mr. Iacocca
14. Los ___ Unidos
15. Cramming, with "up"
16. Scraps
17. "Norma ___," Glaspell novel
18. Low digits
24. Harms
26. "___, you noblest English!": Shak.
29. Alternative to that
32. Fragrant compounds
34. Happens again
35. Zesty feelings
36. Variant
37. Drying structure
38. Evelyn Waugh novel: 1928
40. Ping follower
42. "___ Over"
43. Kind of union
44. Trencherman
46. Movie takes
47. Fanon
50. Arcane
52. Dart
54. Equipment

55. Growing out
56. Island or rabbit
57. Paris subway
58. Herd of stud horses
61. Suit fabric
64. He created "the sack"
66. Biblical king
67. Abreast the middle of a ship's side
68. Called, in a way
69. One of the Forsytes
70. Frays
71. Arabic demon
72. Delete
73. Scarcer
76. Poker Flat creator
77. Field of granular snow
82. Like some suits
84. By ___ starts (intermittently)
85. Ululate
86. Alaskan island
87. Actress Ekland
89. Seventh-___ stretch
90. Substantive
91. Daniel and Pat
94. Amusing

96. Spur wheel
97. Burros
98. First son of Eliz.
99. Biblical loyalist
100. Prefix with chord or meter
102. Noah's eldest
104. Antitoxins
105. Birthplace of Frederick II
106. "Nana" star: 1934
108. A ___ (yours, in Toulon)
109. U.N. arm
111. Spire ornament

by Thomas W. Underhill

ACROSS

1. Turkish title of respect
5. Israeli seaport
9. Watch part
13. Moist
17. Gravy container
18. Archibald ___ (Cary Grant)
20. "___ Grows in Brooklyn"
21. Jannings or Ludwig
22. Ex-President and his supporters?
24. Actress Sally's home construction?
26. Crowd feedback
27. Abzug or Spewack
29. Aegean island
30. Major follower
31. Benedict or Matthew
32. Dernier ___ (last word)
33. Profundity
36. Omni, for one
37. Future benedict
40. View amorously
41. Boston Celtic fan's favorite pastime?
45. Actress Gardner
47. Times of note
48. Therefore
49. English river
50. Former silver coin of Spain
51. Juan Carlos, e.g.
52. Tennis player Margaret's recreation area?
56. Ridge or rib
57. Cowboy hats
60. Share equally
61. Former First Family of Egypt
62. Capacious
63. Clearance sale, in Caen
64. Kitchen gadget
65. Walk cautiously
67. Layer
68. City or game
71. E.T., e.g.
72. Actor-dancer as composer?
74. S.E.C. member
75. Earlier Thailand
76. Scrutinize carefully
78. Stake of a sort
79. Daminozide
80. Tanning agent
81. Café pianist on tour?
85. Church part
86. Contemporary
88. TV backdrops
89. Lost color
90. Inst. at Troy, N.Y.
91. Resources
93. Chard
95. Attack
98. ___ Tshombe, Congolese statesman
99. Unsportsmanlike loser
103. First Chief Justice afoot?
105. Dinah's vacation?
107. "Judith" composer
108. Rose-colored dye
109. Expressing purpose
110. Mech.-eng. degree
111. What arroz is
112. Campus org.
113. One way to go
114. Relating to aircraft

DOWN

1. Israel's Eban
2. Increase in value
3. Hinged fastener
4. Decathlon participants
5. Alaskan native
6. Desist
7. Furor
8. Shield, in Savoie
9. Yet
10. "Don't ___ on me"
11. Lamprey
12. ___ Hat, Alta.
13. Confine
14. "Porgi ___," Mozart aria
15. Type of skirt
16. Entreaty
19. Lod deli tongue
20. Drifting about
23. Plaster backing
25. Scrawny animal
28. Danish composer: 1860–1939
31. Zeal
33. Activists
34. Wading bird
35. Golfer's musical instrument?
36. Watchful guardian
37. Santa Lucia, e.g.
38. Comedian's favorite diet food?
39. President of U.N. General Assembly: 1948–49
41. Look well on
42. Literary device
43. Sculpt
44. Screen
46. Welladay!
50. Copland composition
53. Spine
54. Cantab's rival
55. "M*A*S*H"-er and kin
56. Songstress Vikki
58. Freud's "___ und Tabu"
59. Anon
61. Perfumed bag
63. Hinder growth
64. Singer Page
65. Pravda source
66. Troy
67. Deneb is one
68. "Peanuts" character
69. Drudge
70. Like cups and pitchers
73. Egyptian cottons
76. More strident
77. Swindle
79. Execration
81. A dark brown
82. Back payment?
83. Sights on the Seine
84. Examine again
87. A participant in a bill-of-exchange transaction
89. Sense
91. Love-in-___ (garden plant)
92. Kind of boom
93. "___ Godunov," Pushkin play
94. Upright
95. Slightly open
96. Patola
97. Adjust for sound and sight
99. A flatfish
100. Bed of roses
101. Affirm
102. Item sent to a D.J.
104. Chinese statesman Wellington ___
106. Cut down

by Jeanette K. Brill

ACROSS

1. Noted naval historian
6. Rib
11. Elbow
16. Iowa church society
21. Plowed land, in Pamplona
22. Frighten
23. Wretched abode
24. Kind of soprano
25. Start of a verse
29. Guy's gal
30. A code in the head?
31. Bacchanalian bash
32. City on the Thames
33. Nuclear device
35. Essential
36. ___ avis
37. Wee one
38. Caesar's cohort
39. Suborder comprising the swifts
41. Manufacturers' org.
44. More of verse
52. Had a bite
53. Cat-___-tails
54. Fanons
55. ___-les-Moulineaux, Paris suburb
56. ___ kebab (barbecue treat)
59. Beverage choice
60. Forsyte tale, e.g.
62. "Exodus" hero
63. Dilute
64. More of verse
69. One of a facial pair
70. Wine tub
71. Served perfectly
72. Walking ___ (elated)
73. Of age: Lat. Abbr.
74. Appearance
76. Humdinger
77. Inst. at Columbus
78. Hits a fly
81. Singer Vikki
82. Result
83. Padded footstool
87. More of verse
92. Catskills resort
93. New Deal inits.
94. Supporter
95. Umberto the writer
96. Cowboy's cow catcher
97. Month, in Metz
98. Butterfly's title
100. Cordage fiber
102. ___ Remo, Italy
103. More of verse
109. Bishopric
110. "Zut ___!"
111. Viaud's pen name
112. Golfer's gadget
113. To-do
114. Snap
116. Arbor feature
120. Argot
123. Mont or Mel
124. Algonquian
125. A lady-in-waiting to Cleo
127. End of verse
132. Pale shade of blue
133. Burst forth, as a volcano
134. Duck
135. Doc
136. Gogol's "___ Bulba"
137. Oater group
138. Hinder
139. Common verbal contraction

DOWN

1. An upstairs girl
2. Passion
3. Non-Hawaiian, in Hawaii
4. Fawn upon
5. Catch in the act
6. Lorre in "The Maltese Falcon"
7. Longer in the tooth
8. Actress Thompson
9. Three, to Luigi
10. Home of the brave
11. Hindu god, called The Destroyer
12. Hailey book: 1965
13. Pigskin-shaped
14. Indian writer Mehta
15. Yalie
16. Casbah country
17. Actress Loy
18. Soviet inland sea
19. Pleasant
20. ___-deucey
26. Drumroll
27. Gold or copper
28. Tints delicately
34. Arch
35. Viva follower
36. Snow White's sister
38. Role for Arnold
39. Actress Gardner
40. Prolonged parley
41. N.H. city
42. Neighbor of Perugia
43. N.J.'s governor: 1954–62
44. "The king ___ his countinghouse"
45. Of a race: Comb. form
46. Whitelaw and Ogden
47. Up to
48. All even
49. Theater section
50. "To ___ bone . . .": Kipling
51. Dante's "New Life"
57. Make comfortable
58. Joan of Arc's "crime"
60. Laurel or Musial
61. Browning's "___ Vogler"
65. Morse-code word
66. Withstood
67. Bartender's need
68. Of the mail service
74. Dueler in the sun
75. Group helping D.P.'s
76. "___ Make Believe," 1927 song
77. Inhabitant: Suffix
78. Pundits
79. "Here ___ a-wassailing," Yuletide air's start
80. Reach one's goal
81. Museum honcho
82. Building wing
83. "___ Mio"
84. Tuscan marble center
85. Lab analysis
86. Bright lights
88. ". . . enter ___ of friends": Cowper
89. Winglike
90. "___ la giubba," Leoncavallo aria
91. Arthritis med.
99. Smith and Pacino
100. "Tell ___ the marines!"
101. Regard highly
104. G.I.'s K ___
105. "Take Me ___," 1959 Broadway hit
106. Serrated
107. Slippery customer
108. Parcel postmen do it
113. Designer Rykiel
114. Falls into a chair heavily
115. ___ couture
116. Swap
117. Allude (to)
118. Muslim decree
119. Black buck
120. Painter Mondrian
121. "___ baby!"
122. Russian ruler
123. Eng. units of heat
124. Causerie
126. Religious group
128. Fall mo.
129. Gold, in Genova
130. "___ Got Five Dollars," 1931 song
131. Singer Sumac from Peru

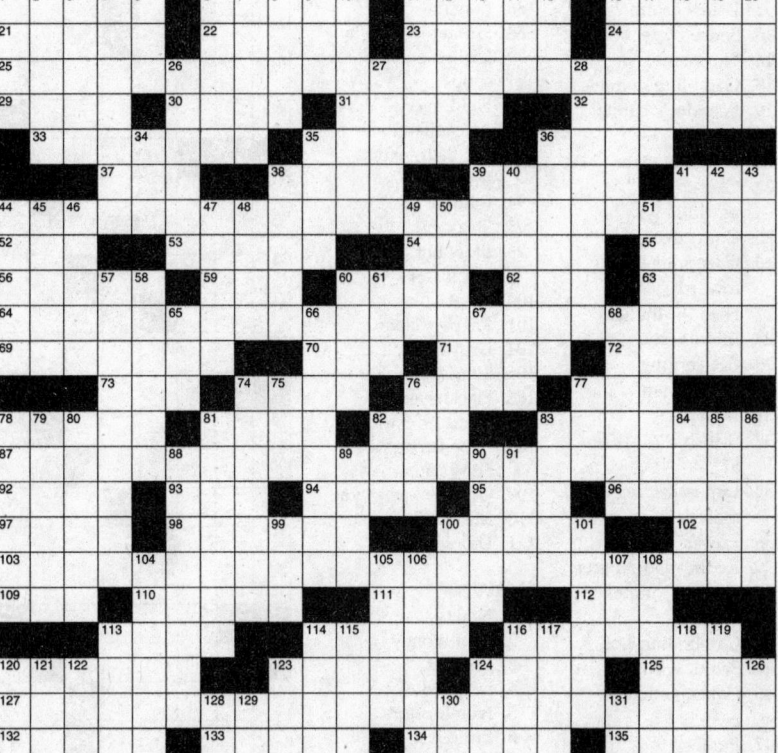

by Frances Hansen

ACROSS

1. Israel's Abba
5. Police group
10. Sense by feeling
14. Norman town
18. Gambling game
19. Ecuador's capital
20. Cupid
21. Brazilian state
22. Carpenter's patriotic lyric?
25. Court decree
26. Gaze intently toward
27. Feed on the lea
28. Illinois city
29. Concerning
30. "Superman"
31. Permit
32. British P.M.: 1945–52
35. Lint-collecting material
36. Frost's "In the ___"
39. Redheaded Arlene
40. Barber's dinner course?
43. Cambodian Lon
44. Scold, with "down"
46. Cakes' unlikely partner
47. Parched
48. Gudrun's husband
49. Dos Passos trilogy
50. Gardener's direction?
55. "Borstal Boy" playwright
56. Coloring substances
58. Domain
59. Negative verbal contraction
60. She was a lady, in song
61. "Bei ___ Bist Du Schoen," 1937 hit
62. ___ four (tea cake)
63. Condemned
65. Nicholas Gage bestseller
67. Polarized
70. Pixyish
71. How a new lumberjack fells a tree?
73. Tic-tac-toe row
74. Northern wind of southern France
75. "___ baby!"
76. Past
77. Took in a movie
79. "Yech!"
80. Leather-worker's dictum?
85. Take out, editorially
86. Bargain
88. Hunter in the sky
89. Dished out the soup
91. Field mice
92. Alb adjunct
93. ___ Sadr, exiled Iranian
94. John or Bo
95. Steak cut
96. Blow hot ___ (vacillate)
100. Pivotal
101. Reapers' span?
104. Droves
105. Sitarist Shankar
106. Hackneyed
107. "L'___, c'est moi"
108. "The Banana Boat Song," familiarly
109. Oil-cartel acronym
110. Male and female
111. Dawson's ex

DOWN

1. Newts
2. Thai money
3. Precinct
4. Stripped
5. Non-hipsters
6. Entirely
7. Out, in the Transvaal
8. Had a bite
9. Los Angeles nine
10. Long parley
11. Astonish
12. Like a certain ranger
13. Grand ___, Evangeline's home
14. Tailor, facetiously
15. Mason's discouraging advice?
16. Property claim
17. Tidbit for Dobbin
21. "Home, Sweet Home," e.g.
23. Coty or Descartes
24. Polite Italian word
28. Get ___ on (find a clue)
30. Stitch again
31. Kate's TV friend
32. Total
33. Anklebones
34. Ditchdigger's knightly period?
35. River deposits
36. Billiard shot
37. Pitcher Ryan
38. Flash
41. Untouchables, e.g.
42. Comedian Mort
45. Where the Riksdag meets
48. Eagle's home
51. Writer Bagnold
52. Bristling with weapons
53. Marie Antoinette, notably
54. "Mack the Knife" singer
55. Grable, White and Boop
57. Ike's wife
59. Jack Benny's exclamation
62. Southwestern lagniappe
63. Clean programs
64. Few: Comb. form
65. Sing the praises of
66. Matilda or Ananias
67. Twist's wicked tutor
68. Prospero, e.g.
69. Loved, not wisely, but too well
71. Rand's shrugger
72. Western resort
75. "A year, a month, ___...": Marlowe
78. "Hooked"
80. Luther, Larry and Polly
81. Wandering
82. Vital space-shuttle part
83. Ducats
84. Takes a gander
87. El ___, fabulous treasure city
90. Gibb or Gump
92. Among the quick
93. Tack up
94. "___ deer, a female..."
95. Wrap with ropes, at sea
97. "___ be in England...": R. Browning
98. Limerick man
99. N.Y. times
100. Wilson's deg.
101. Sibling of Sis
102. Galena or bauxite
103. Dilemma

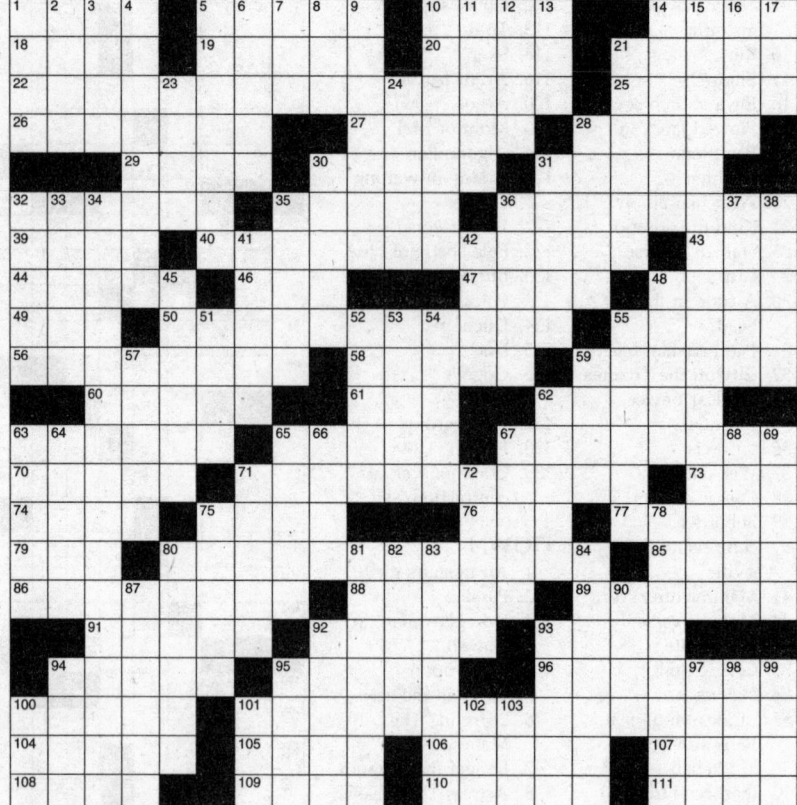

by Frances Hansen

ACROSS

1. Bear hug
6. Small shrimp
12. Signified
19. Marx's "___ Speaks!"
20. Hinders, in a way
21. Patrick Duffy, e.g.
22. N.I.H. toast to Perot?
24. Being produced
25. Harmony
26. Wired to Europe
27. Grand backers
30. Excite anew
33. Causing horripilation
37. Old campaigner
38. Claim
40. Tebaldi role
41. Quell
43. Univ. degs.
44. Yoko ___
45. Winter melon
47. Lauder, for one
48. U. of Chicago legend
50. Champ's dramatic account?
55. Soissons soul
56. Biotite
57. Bungo or Rob Roy
58. Pitcher catcher
59. Tough problem
61. Inventor Nikola ___
63. Hag
66. Jacks, e.g.
68. W.W. I craft gambling with turbulence?
72. Surreptitiousness
75. One cubic meter
76. Autocrats
79. Venezuelan writer
80. Psyche parts
83. "As You Like It" lass
85. Harper and Spike
87. "___ Heldenleben": Strauss
88. Congressional register?
92. Iowa city near Oskaloosa
93. Dian Fossey subject
95. Soprano role in "The Barber of Seville"
96. Patriotic org.
98. Conger
99. Make corporate changes
101. Glassmaker's oven
103. Icon feature
104. Big-bang letters
105. Indian "guitar"
106. Nematodes
109. Playwright Sean
111. Hardships
113. Corroborate
115. Certain footwear
118. Boxing, to Pincay?
123. Prepares for another challenge
124. More sanguine
125. Dale or Dwight
126. Darnels
127. Cheetahlike
128. First time out

DOWN

1. Thorax: Abbr.
2. Citizen of Vientiane
3. Discretion follower?
4. Shiny fishing lure
5. Elvis's gift from Ezra?
6. Basted
7. Arabian V.I.P.'s
8. Strip of stripes
9. Balm of Gilead
10. Eating leftover
11. Four pks.
12. Shady magnate's into apples?
13. Organic compound
14. "Ironweed" star
15. Caters to
16. Navy's C.I.A.
17. River to the Yangtze
18. Part of the U.K.
21. "Serpico" author
23. Gamboge or dammar
26. Thigh armor
27. Burst of energy
28. Yellow-tailed thornbill
29. View from the Vosges Mountains
31. Jambalaya base
32. Epps or Moreno
34. Cover a book again
35. Certain nuclide
36. Ingredients of perfumes
39. Ex-Philly Larry ___
42. '70s Highflying stk.?
46. ___ standstill
49. One of the Magi
51. Ruler division
52. Japanese seaweed
53. Advertising signs
54. Thrusting swords
57. Suffragette Carrie Chapman ___
60. Reduced, as goods
62. Syringa
64. Opp. of day
65. Do a bouncer's job
67. Bread for Wimsey?
69. Mann-Kramer sucker bet?
70. Part of a familiar palindrome
71. Gwyn or Quickly
72. Asparagus shoots
73. Capital of Taiwan
74. Screenwriter Lehman
77. Leases again
78. Moon goddess
81. Hades
82. Pix from movies
84. Bergman role in "Casablanca"
86. Like a pretzel
89. Bark in "Annie"
90. Draft status
91. Cowardly Lion portrayer
92. Obtained
94. Monks' adviser
97. Distant
100. Rebels
102. RNA sugar
103. Like some arguments
107. Angers
108. Hawk's home
110. Suffix with talk or form
112. Clarified butter in India
114. Calhoun of films
115. Opposite of sml.
116. Eastern Church chalice cover
117. Jeff Davis's govt.
118. Future grads.
119. Kind of fly
120. Collar
121. Wildebeest
122. Concorde, e.g.

by Jim Page

ACROSS

1. Opposing teams
6. Vexed
11. Rockies crest
16. Space renter
17. Of ships
18. Misogynist's attitude
20. Ocean-loving snake?
22. Phantasm
24. Fall back
25. Form of currency
26. Meet the need
28. Squat, broad-mouthed jaw
29. In the center
31. Dutch export
33. Tattered
34. Silkworm
35. Showed nerve
37. Hazard
39. Make leather
40. Expresses joy
41. Dinner course
43. D.C. ballplayer, once
45. Fanatic
46. Bad breaks
48. Deck
49. Like Hume's tomes
50. Framed ursine goatees?
55. Stiffens
59. Indonesian islands
60. CMXXXVI ÷ IX
61. Rope
63. Balanced
64. "The __ Sanction"
65. Reeking
67. Conference site: 1945
68. Put to the torch
69. Suffix with Boswell or Burns
71. Antarctic penguin
73. Through
74. Raccoon's cousin
76. Doubly stylish
78. Pass for a sports-loving beast?
81. Be unresolved
82. Darn it!
83. Roof section
84. Icy dessert
87. Poorly structured
90. Lost turgor
94. Suit fabric
95. Shopper's tote
96. Take to task
98. Show fear
99. __'acte
100. Lahore garb
102. Alpine communication
104. Initiate
105. Role for Arnold Moss
106. Appointment
107. Pardon
109. Sesame
110. Judge
112. Wilbur's fleabag?
116. Jacket part
117. Acedia
118. Not as removed
119. Chemical compound
120. Cleric-poet
121. Launderette machine

DOWN

1. Like Australia or Hispaniola
2. Electees
3. Crows' cousins
4. Stage
5. Roil
6. Animate
7. Zodiacal animal
8. One of Frank's exes
9. Siberian tribesman
10. Londoner's lift
11. Give homework
12. Comeback
13. Devon river
14. Stock-market simians?
15. Portuguese resort
16. Unanimously
19. Fine-wooled sheep
20. Dashing fellow
21. Ohio city
23. Prepare turkey
27. Culture base
30. Mock
32. Spot or mark, in Madrid
36. Fleur-__
38. Prides' dens
40. Turns right
42. Fraternal fellow
44. Short-tempered
45. Fictional castle
47. Withdrew
49. Having teeth
50. True
51. Bellowing
52. Nary a soul
53. Bad dog
54. Satanic
55. Shire of "Rocky"
56. Philippine palm
57. Splice
58. __ jury
62. Critic's blessing
65. Dim
66. Certain couturier's creations

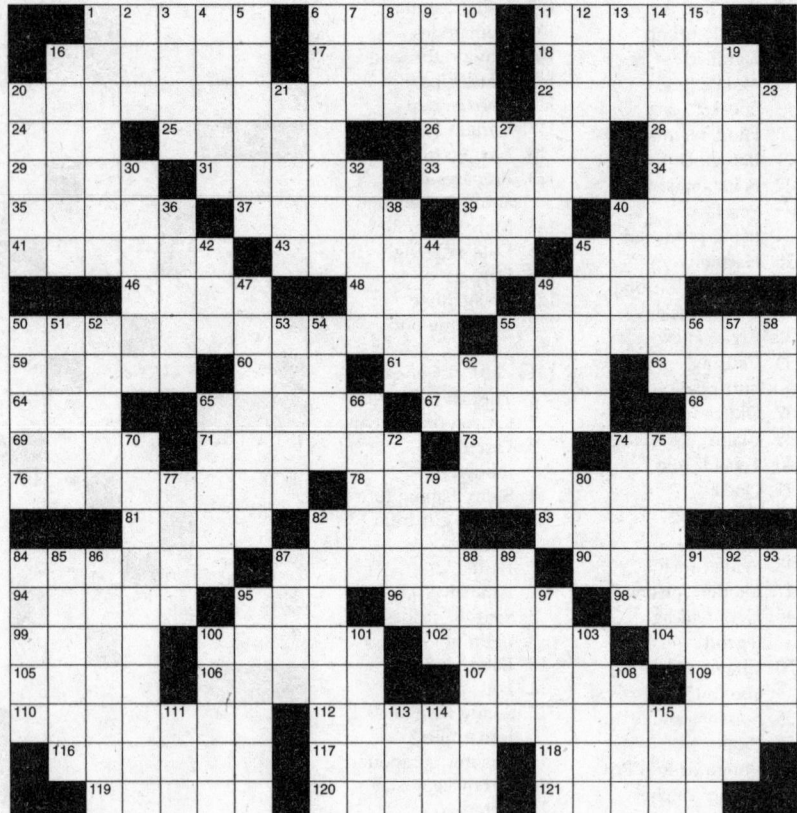

by Louis Sabin

70. Herpetological fruit?
72. S.A.T.'s
74. Municipal
75. Large American cat
77. Sow
79. Actor Keach
80. Marble
82. Codified
84. Commemorative slab
85. Baseball group
86. Altar-lights site
87. William's joint ruler
88. All-out
89. Church official
91. Tizzy
92. More spooky
93. Waggish
95. Shoemaking specialist
97. Require
100. Allen or Lawrence
101. Race: Comb. form
103. Measure of capacity
108. Bangkok native
111. Eastern observance
113. Boniface's domain
114. Emulate Slaney
115. Mine find

ACROSS

1. Errand boy
6. Yankee backstop, once
11. Jewish month
15. Mirror reflection
20. Emulate Cicero
21. Starry hunter
22. Fly alone
23. Jaybirdlike
24. Where Mr. Jones lived?
27. Where Mr. Jones got engaged?
29. ___-de-France
30. Grievously
31. Hate
33. Mailer or Lear
34. Omit
35. Muslim ruler
36. Whirlpool
37. Typesetter's concern: Abbr.
40. Jane, to Peter
41. Late bloomer
42. Italian eight
43. Small hat
46. Fat
48. Where Mr. Jones's fiancée lived?
52. One of a Latin trio
53. Interstice
55. Motet anagram
56. One, in Köln
57. Companion of Aeneas
58. Carved pillar
59. Actress Garr
60. Designates
62. Michigan city
63. French painter
64. Where the Joneses were married?
67. Actress Jackson
68. Kind of wrestling
69. Neighbor of Ont.
70. Abundant
71. Lowly
72. "And ___ is to the living . . .": M.M. Dodge
75. Athenian lawgiver
76. Northern nation
78. New ___, Conn.
80. Hair style
81. "Thief" star
82. PAT preceders
85. Help
86. Where the Joneses had cocktails?
89. An Allen
91. Climbs, in a way
92. Cline classic
93. Appends

94. Lermontov's "___ of Our Time"
95. Laugh riot
96. Item in a chest
97. More timid
99. City SE of San Francisco
100. Sea eagle
101. Where Mrs. Jones threw her bridal bouquet?
105. ___ out (supplemented)
106. ___ Moines
107. Finn's neighbor
108. Broadcast
109. Prill or pyrite
111. Many ft.
112. Ring event
113. Begot
114. Brazilian dance
116. Peace in Israel
119. Gay ___
120. Impede
121. Underworld god
124. Where the Joneses go for Christmas?
126. Where the Joneses live?
129. Wear away
130. Penny ___
131. "Bubbles" author
132. Plunder
133. Golf great
134. Gist
135. Kilmer poem
136. Wing

DOWN

1. Asian desert
2. Spoken
3. Confront
4. Ordinal suffix
5. Della and Pee Wee
6. Rude
7. Was human
8. Ransack and rob
9. Poly's partner
10. Actress Alicia
11. "To make up a year / And ___": Emerson
12. Sorrow, in Sonora
13. Winglike
14. Cartoonist Chast
15. "Is there beauty ___?": Dostoyevsky
16. Wills of baseball
17. Actor Tamiroff
18. Japanese wooden clog
19. Actress Barbara
25. Kubrick film: 1962
26. Gong

28. Heel-___
32. Toot
35. Tennis great
36. Certain collars
37. Whey
38. Bad-tempered one
39. Where the Joneses spend their weekends?
41. Actor in "The Addams Family"
42. Bay window
43. Where the Joneses honeymooned?
44. TV role for Kate Jackson
45. Of the mail
47. Relief
49. Everlasting, poetically
50. Navigational system
51. Greek commune
54. Court call
57. Coeur d'___, Idaho
59. Workers' joyful letters
60. "There is ___ like an old . . ."
61. Solar disk

62. Skipped town
65. Visit
66. Imagist Doolittle
67. F.B.I. agents
69. Marjoram, e.g.
73. ___ Bernard
74. Colleen
75. Egyptian port
76. Actress Dee
77. Means' partner
78. Converted the chips
79. On land
81. Cryptographer
83. Mended
84. Headbands
86. Defeat decisively
87. Discontinue
88. Scottish hobo
89. Pinna
90. Quaker pronoun
92. Appropriate
96. Mental shock
97. Easy or Grub
98. Pay attention
99. "So Big" author
101. Inundated
102. Protection for locks
103. Ireland, to a Gael
104. Navigator's need

110. Singer Kitt
112. City SW of Algiers
113. Annual visitor
114. Elbe tributary
115. Plentiful
116. Females
117. Shofar, e.g.
118. Tub plant
119. Yearn
120. Legatee
121. Actor in "Family Plot"
122. As to
123. River of Charon
125. Camote
127. F.D.R.'s successor
128. Staff

by Bette Sue Cohen

ACROSS

1. Add new insulation
6. P.O.W. camp
12. Genii
18. Entrance court
19. Myself, in Melun
20. Cather lass
21. Drug-related
23. A woman's cloak of yore
24. Fervent; strong
25. Skipjack
27. In any way
28. Conked out
29. Very, in music
32. Scale-song phrase
34. Tall Asiatic tree
35. Stick in one's ___
37. Exactly
39. Marker
41. "___ the season . . ."
42. Inventor of an early telescope
46. Roman magistrates
48. Reading room
51. Pinna
52. Refer (to)
53. Females, casually
54. Execrates
56. Deride
57. What to call a Spade
58. Solar deity
59. Fax relative
61. Fan
65. Baker or Bryant
67. "___ take arms . . .": Hamlet
69. Fouls up
71. ___-ground missile
72. Pines
74. Average
76. Father of "robots"
78. Some sighs
79. Cheeses
81. Calmed
83. Octo
84. Hard to get
86. Peruvian gold
87. Measure of film sharpness
89. Break
90. About the science of viniculture
92. Letters on a chasuble
93. Founded (on)
95. French I verb
96. Payment due
99. Land between Aram and Edom
101. "Network" director: 1976
103. Metrical feet
106. Canaveral grp.
108. Scrutinized
110. Branchlike
112. Cohort
114. Former
116. Schliemann and Carter
119. Two-___ (tandems)
120. Christmas-berries: Var.
121. Relative of dill and carrot
122. Conductor Ansermet
123. Gen. with G. Washington
124. Sandy tracts, in England

DOWN

1. Speedy
2. Of a people
3. Viennese park
4. Terriers
5. Denounce
6. ___ Canals
7. Iceberg feature
8. Infections caused by protozoans
9. Smooth: Comb. form
10. Church Society since 1714
11. In an icy manner
12. Genetic letters
13. Site of a fire god's smithy
14. Boxer Jake La___
15. Playlet
16. Worker with black alloy on metal
17. ___ à manger (dining rooms)
19. Postgrad degrees in public works
20. Alternately responsive, as verses
22. Third king of Judah
26. Assam export
30. Skiers' maneuvers
31. Assamese native
33. More embarrassed
36. Achieve
38. ___ all, folks!
40. Dixie tree
43. Child: Comb. form
44. A ___ (from boyhood, to Pliny)
45. First, in Berlin
47. "Vive ___!"
48. Evaluate
49. Title Macbeth held
50. Blood condition: Comb. form
55. This, to Pedro
56. Artifice
58. Polish manually
60. Old chest for valuables
62. Retinue
63. Moral code
64. Spill-wiper on TV
66. C.E.O.'s aide
68. George ___ Welles
70. Class with common attributes: Comb. form
73. Holy
75. Ancient Ethiopian capital
77. Part of N.E.A.
80. Means to ends
82. In a stupid way
83. O. Henry's Jimmy
84. Tall beer glass
85. Operation by an obstetrician
88. Bit
90. Abnormal swellings
91. Domesday Book money
92. Kibitz, in a way
94. Estonian river
97. ___ the belfry
98. African fly
100. She twice played Elizabeth I
102. "The Devil knows how ___": Coleridge
104. Palais social events
105. Nigerian native
107. Upbeats, in music
109. Roman day
111. U.S.C. rival
113. Victorian oath
115. Tough actor
117. Very long time
118. Quarter of four

by Ralph G. Beaman

ACROSS

1. Who or which
5. November exhortation
9. June honoree
12. Record spinner
18. TV host Philbin
20. Burr role
22. Bring about
23. Sweaterman?
25. Posts for harbor houses
26. Banished Olympian
27. Soviet range
28. Like foo yong
29. Seine sights
30. English walled city
32. "The Morning Watch" writer
33. Surfeits
35. Arcade in ancient Athens
36. Pistil packin' papa?
39. Platters for 12 Across
42. Within: Comb. form
43. They take panes
44. Otherwise
45. "___ Heldenleben": Strauss
46. Trifle
47. Algerian seaport
48. Sheltered at sea
50. Places
51. Minnow man?
56. At the apex
57. The Dark Cont.
60. Cav. units
61. Aix-les-Bains attraction
62. Paternally related
64. Eddy in "Rose Marie"
66. Actress Van Doren
67. Oath taker
68. One of the Huxleys
69. Limnite and hematite
70. Tiny margin
71. ___ Moines
72. Celebrity
73. Man of war?
78. River in Corsica
79. Charged atoms
80. Antonym of c.c.
81. Greek underground: W.W. II
84. Sitcom alien
85. Showy lily
87. Apportioned
89. Mimic
91. Less than lg.
92. Highwayman?
95. Tether
97. "___ Sleep," Odets play
99. Pitchers' handles
100. Poacher's pitfall
101. H.S. subject
102. Pisa's river
103. Hellkite
105. Stem: Suffix
106. Winter melon
108. Porky patriot?
111. Two thousand pounds
112. Toothless
113. Factory
114. Dissimilar
115. Former chess champ
116. Monoski
117. City in S France

DOWN

1. Sticky sweet
2. Pagans
3. Consents concerning
4. Sesame
5. Wakefield's clergyman
6. Nuncupative
7. Rocky peaks
8. Terminate
9. N.Z. or Aussie W.W.I solder
10. Saws
11. Impugn
12. Underworld god
13. Dub
14. Quaestor's cousin
15. Superman's outfitter?
16. Bible book
17. Aye
19. One of the Carolinas
21. Bouts
24. Manumit
31. Clean energetically
32. Sellers' notices
33. Food from orchids
34. Cries of surprise
36. Bates and Badel
37. Zola heroine
38. Profound
40. Carnation variety
41. Hidden gunmen
43. Complain
47. Like Grendel
48. Shaking
49. Elegance
50. ___ Lang, Superboy's friend
52. Some penultimate words
53. Timothy and family
54. J. Baker and M. Hess
55. Deviating, as a storm-swept ship
57. Mixture
58. Leaflet, to a botanist
59. Motorman?
63. Actor Richard
65. Advice to Nanette
66. "And day's at the ___": Browning
67. Tasty
70. Polygamous group
74. Bad-news ball
75. Midday
76. Port near Cadiz
77. Jumped
82. Sanction
83. Resin ingredient
85. African whip
86. Many, many eras
87. Leave high and dry
88. Wynn and Sullivan
90. Is contrite
93. Yucatán's capital
94. Annul
95. Leftover dish
96. Ready for use
98. Raccoon's relative
100. Repelled a mugger
101. Author of "The High and the Mighty"
102. French violinist: 18th century
103. Jezebel's god
104. City near Padua
106. Alouette's neck
107. Chemical suffix
109. Superiors of sgts.
110. Diminutive suffix

by Victoria Black and Alex F. Black

PLEASE THINK TWICE!

ACROSS

1. Playwright Racine
5. Jazz form
10. Thank-you-___ (road bump)
14. Bellow
18. Farm unit
19. Meyerbeer product
20. "Kiss Me, Kate" co-writer Spewack
21. Sailor's saint
22. National League nine
24. S.A. capital
26. Some Swiss paintings
27. Galsworthy novel
29. Some yuks
30. Speaks tipsily
31. Eyelashes
32. Domino
33. Counterfeit
34. Frenchman's girlfriend
35. Like Smetana's Marie
39. British service-women in W.W. II
40. Great Lake
43. Yamamai's kin
44. Wave, in Pau
45. Flat fish
46. Piques at their peaks
47. Ancient Greek contest
48. Remick or Marvin
49. Super Bowl team: 1988
53. Shun
54. Acted as a figurehead
56. Blore and Porter
57. Hesitated
58. April 1 Abderites
59. Spain's Louvre
60. Army honchos
61. Most perspicacious
63. Oar fulcrum
64. Like the Sabbath
67. Turns rapidly, in Ayr
68. Rodgers and Hammerstein classic
71. Capital of medieval Armenia
72. Stuff to smelt
73. Mickey to avoid
74. Teen bane
75. Budge
76. Galba's "Go!"
77. Helen's abductor
81. Conductor Zubin ___
82. Forgives
84. Dispute, in Durango
85. Punchless punches
86. Snake eyes
87. Prophets
88. Rose oil
90. Sings à la Crosby
93. Apt anagram for notes
94. Cather's "___ Lady"
95. Locks
97. Memorable humorous poet
102. Pine
103. Valuable wood
104. Vienna's river, to Strauss
105. Learning
106. Campfire collection
107. Specks
108. Mothball
109. John L.'s widow

DOWN

1. Elbow
2. Old French coin
3. Rainbow
4. Jewelry item
5. Gaffe
6. Dueling pieces
7. Honey bunch
8. Neb.'s ex-Governor
9. Hobby
10. Tragedy by Euripides
11. Came to earth
12. Dalmatic's relative
13. Wild ducks
14. Scold
15. Actor Vidov
16. Oriental maid
17. Howard and Cey
20. Faith
23. Grads
25. Cardinal points
28. Omnium-gatherum
30. World's longest river
31. Deloul, e.g.
32. Kind of nest
33. More reasonable
35. Divulges
36. Edward or Norman
37. Undermine
38. Had a meal
39. Gobble
40. Prods
41. Root and branch
42. Midwest whitefish
45. Sparling
47. Nautical cry
49. Noted German sculptor: c.1440–1533

by Bert H. Kruse

50. Fish-eating bird
51. Papal garment
52. Bill attachment
53. Take out
55. Christmases
57. El Greco's birthplace
59. Rec. player
60. Dark-colored goose
61. Unexcitable
62. ___-surface missiles
63. Awards named for Ms. Perry
65. Distinct parts
66. Money in Ankara
68. Developers' interests
69. Grandiose tales
70. Cluck of disapproval
73. Used artifice
75. Anagram for dyes et al.
77. Known, in Nantes
78. Without interference
79. Mortgage
80. Forays
81. Asian ornamental pine
83. Like a goner
87. Watergate figure
88. "___ needs a good memory": Quintillian
89. Brimless hat
90. Tobacco in the cheek
91. Carty of baseball
92. Subject of a Keats tragedy
93. Glaswegian, e.g.
94. ___ time (never)
96. Nigerian native
98. Last word in denials
99. Bill's partner
100. Biblical craft
101. Early Olds

ACROSS

1. Arethusas, e.g.
7. Calif. white oak
11. Complete defeats
15. Carp-family member
19. Gone up
20. In ___ (bogged down)
21. Rung
22. Insect stage
23. With no sweat
25. Puccini heroine
26. Informed on
27. Glance askance
28. Anglo-Saxon dialect
30. Alabama commodity
31. Irregularly notched
32. Sets free
33. Plumbism
35. Uttered
36. Variegated chalcedony
37. Dobbin's fare
38. Foster's "De ___ Races"
42. Zambezi feeder
43. Kind of table
47. Arabian gazelles
48. Fen
49. Overwhelm
50. Plant angle
51. Suppose
52. Inborn
54. Prats
55. Unlikely
56. Sapience
57. Uses an exit
58. Paravane
59. Fling about
60. Overalls fabric
61. One of the Seven Wonders
63. Emulates Hirt
66. Expenses
68. Tomcat
70. Hirsute
71. Fabulist
72. Heisman, e.g.
74. Tantrums
76. Algonquian spirit
77. Huge land mass
78. Crowd response
79. Cringes with fear
80. Michelangelo, to Lorenzo
81. Greffier or chartulary
83. Opposite of 12 Down
84. Intersection
85. Cartel acronym
86. Gauntlets
87. Glyph
88. Maypop
92. S. European liquor
93. "G.W.T.W." locale
97. Age
98. Ruined photographs
100. Waiter's notes
101. Type of bean or horse
102. Devil's delight
103. Absolute
105. Tatting output
106. Actress-singer Carter
107. Bogus
108. Midday
109. January, in Ibiza
110. You are, in Mexico
111. Jack or Robert
112. Intuits

DOWN

1. Sibyl
2. Tree
3. Urticaria
4. French river or department
5. Dad's refuge
6. Daughters' mates
7. Declaimed violently
8. Stocks
9. Oner
10. Linguistics expert
11. Beaked
12. Alfresco
13. Shoe part
14. Cervantes or Velázquez
15. Melancholy
16. Nicolo of Cremona
17. Swiss district
18. Seasonal beverage
24. Abrading action
29. Chicago embrace?
34. Condescend
35. Runner or rhizome
36. Al ___, Cairo newspaper
38. Orange food
39. Neighborhoods
40. Of minute proportions
41. Indian tea
42. Largest of the Tremiti Islands
43. Raggedy Ann or Andy
44. Kidnapper, e.g.
45. Aspire
46. Type of gold or paradise
48. Roman Catholic title
49. Shapes
52. Numismatic unit
53. Amends
54. Fires; axes
56. Is indebted
58. Reactionary
60. Weak-minded, in Dixie
62. Gig implements
64. Siberian forest
65. Classified
67. Marksman
69. Like some lenses
70. Owls
71. Former monetary units of Riga
72. Poi base
73. Abie's beloved
74. Box chaser
75. Makeup applicator
76. Type of code
78. Assemble anew
80. Legal clauses
82. ___ gratia
83. Profitable holes
84. Awry
86. Nimbus
87. January birthstone
88. Streisand hit
89. Relating to bees
90. Bracket for candles
91. Peggy Lee hit
92. Puckers
93. Conch-shell blowing demigod
94. Male dreamboat
95. Aptly named novelist
96. Kingdom of Burgundy, once
99. Naut. detection apparatus
104. Part of a chord

by Donald V. Lee II

ACROSS

1. ". . . a tall ship and
   ___ steer her by":
   Masefield
5. Actor Hoffman
11. Little Iodine's
    creator
16. "___ moss-trooping
    Scot was he": Scott
19. U.S. columnist
20. Like some beds
21. Standoffish
22. Chinese dynasty
24. Very meager pay
26. Texas
28. Drain
29. Lowest points
30. Groups of three
32. Small change
33. On hand
35. Baseball pitch
36. Dennis and Duncan
37. Fatigue symptom
39. Turner of TNT
40. Fishing net
41. Binds
42. Daylight dimmers
44. Ratifies
45. Defaults
47. Half a score
50. Manned a shell
51. Military bigwig
54. Soft cheese
55. Residue
56. Hershiser et al.
57. Valhalla V.I.P.
58. Flunky
59. Effortlessness
60. French composer
61. Timber wolves
63. Nagged
65. Sell out
67. Rome's river
68. Mount ___, Jordan
69. Bard's "before"
70. Share top billing
73. Parish-Perkins tune:
    1934
77. Ukr., once
78. Sol.
79. Ft. soldiers
80. Mosquito
81. Became cheerful
83. Thusly: Colloq.
85. Tamar's half-
    brother
86. Swap
88. Fox terrier of films
92. Myrna's kinfolk
93. "___ a man with
    seven wives"
94. "A Rage to Live"
    author
95. Wan
96. A biol. sci.

97. Figurative signs of
    joy
100. Of ___
     (undistinguished)
101. Together: Comb.
     form
102. City: Ger.
103. Nitrous ___
     (laughing gas)
104. Melodic
105. Quotidian
107. Black tea
108. Fine, mod style
110. Natives: Suffix
111. Be calculating
113. Movable pointer
115. Some Italian
     singers
117. Bolivian city
118. Sword
119. ___ Sark, a Channel
     Islands ruler
120. Glasgow veto
123. A discarded title
     for "G.W.T.W."
125. "When ___ sang
     together . . .": Job
     38:7
128. Verb ending
129. Al ___ (chewy)
130. Author Welty
131. Activates anew
132. Sounds seeking
     silence
133. ___ down (scold)
134. Double dagger
135. Being, to Brutus

DOWN

1. Edison's middle
   name
2. Blue gems
3. Preschooler
4. Vent one's view
5. Scottish port
6. Relax
7. Fashionable
8. Shoelace ends
9. Cyprinoid fish
10. Young bird
11. A binary
    compound
12. Solo
13. Coloring agent
14. Former Brooklyn
    pitcher
15. "A pair ___ cross'd
    lovers . . .": Shak.
16. Accompany
17. G.I. publication
18. Poker pot
19. Spectral types
23. Scottish headland
25. Ovens
27. Isolated rocks
31. Washer cycle

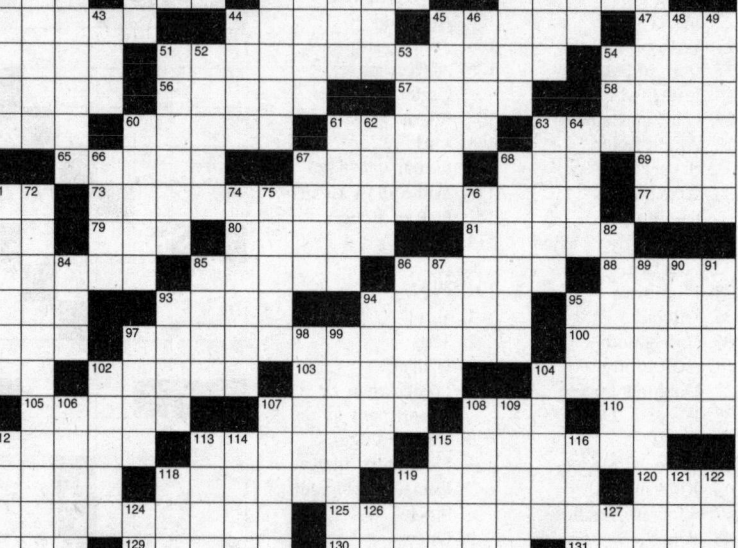

by John Greenman

34. Promise-breaker
35. Feel effects of a
    head blow
36. Dormer part
37. Habitat
38. Bow or Barton
40. Fuse ores
41. ___ Carlo Menotti
43. Dentist's deg.
44. State firmly
45. Brimmed headgear
46. Doric column edge
48. Sea ducks
49. Indigent person
51. Misrepresent as
    genuine
52. Goddess of peace
53. Prize eponym
54. Prevent
60. "___ Use Raising a
    Shout": Auden
61. Bed sheets, etc.
62. Nigerian V.I.P.'s
63. French nobleman
64. New Guinea
    people
66. "___ Born"
67. Commotion
68. Alaskan Indians
70. Maria of opera

71. Like some omelets
72. TV roles for Glaser
    and Soul
74. Plaint
75. Slowly, to Solti
76. Trumpet
82. Fervor
84. Part of i.e.
85. In the thick of
86. Bara of silents
87. Comedienne
    Martha
89. Meteors
90. Clipped
91. Poker payments
93. "Je dis," in English
94. Basketry twig
95. Swiss river
97. Take by surprise
98. Lariat loop
99. Urged
102. Carly or Paul
104. City SE of
     Cleveland
106. High hideaways
107. Ballet movements
108. Honshu seaport
109. Verdi works
111. Loudness unit
112. Irritable

113. Chili con ___
114. Whipper-snappers
115. Greek isle
116. Flaming
118. Remorseful one
119. "___ Dinah," 1958
     hit tune
121. Phoenician love
     goddess
122. Ar successor
124. Bizarre
126. Hawaiian syndicate
127. Vane dirs.

ACROSS

1. Ms. Picasso
7. Start of a famous speech of defiance
12. Dead Sea ___
18. Ethically neutral
19. Clarsach player
21. Capital of Taiwan
22. Effect
23. Herod ___ I
24. Mesh
25. Female goat
26. Mister, in Munich
28. Small snake
29. Gist
31. A drug, for short
32. Speech: Part II
36. River at Zaragoza
39. African antelope
40. Rio ___ Plata, S.A. estuary
41. Hebrew prophet
45. Struggles clumsily
48. Trellises
51. Quoits players
52. Arab garb
55. Large mackerels
56. Speech: Part III
61. Knock
62. Bantu language
63. Le jour de ___ (New Year's Day): Fr.
64. Eating place
68. Forbid
73. Panhandle
74. Pointer
78. Also not
79. Bargain word
83. ___ de guerre
84. In a foolish way
88. Speech: Part IV
93. Chaplains, to G.I.'s
95. N.J. river
96. W.W. II German cipher machine
99. Warning
100. Coiner?
101. Formicidae
103. Attu native
104. Actress Pitts
105. Crucifix
106. Trickle
108. "___ la Douce," 1963 movie
109. End of the speech
115. Activity during a riot
118. "Uhuru" author
119. Recesses
123. Skill, in Sedan
124. Remove by dissolving
125. Victors in Gaul
126. Wapiti's cousin
127. Contents of an onomasticon
128. One who attempts

DOWN

1. Salaried
2. Ordinance item, for short
3. Easy gait
4. Mouths
5. Papier ___
6. Kind of ego
7. Joker
8. Printers' mistakes
9. Silly
10. Tore
11. Psychic's claim
12. Bargain
13. Bel ___ (singing style)
14. Fix
15. Gemstone
16. Gangster Diamond
17. Schumann product
19. Conceal
20. Sri Lanka group
27. Student's new chance
30. Pass
32. Building promoters
33. Parts of a cent.
34. "___ Geordie," 1956 movie
35. ___ square (honest)
36. Salamander
37. Moral flaw
38. ___-ha-Shanah
42. Blackbird
43. Buccal
44. Mil. draft org.
46. Spanish baby girls
47. Hang loosely
49. Passage
50. "The Merry Widow" composer
52. Actress Alicia
53. Word of disdain
54. Witch bird
57. "Beauty ___ the eye . . ."
58. Had chits out
59. Eng. prof's degree
60. Skid-row denizen
64. Youngster's 2 Down
65. G.O.P. member
66. Lists of things to be done
67. Get one's goat
69. The Bee Gees, e.g.
70. Entity
71. Mountain pass
72. Rugby play
75. Motionless
76. "___ fan tutte," Mozart opera
77. Wife of King Latinus
80. Rotten
81. Newsy note
82. Jolson and Pacino
85. Paris-to-Senlis dir.
86. Sight from Taormina
87. Land in ancient Palestine
89. In a tumult
90. Mark or Mamie
91. Certain beards
92. I come in: Sp.
93. La___, Bolivia
94. Ga. neighbor
97. It's the word
98. ___ loss (puzzled)
100. Fish or war follower
102. Infield hit
105. Car-wash step
107. Israeli leader
110. Seine tributary
111. A Sudanese people
112. First author of the "Oz" books
113. Commedia dell'___
114. Clothing, informally
115. Roman household deity
116. Lyric poem
117. ___ Peak, Ariz.
120. Trifle
121. Moss Hart's "Act ___"
122. Ukr., once

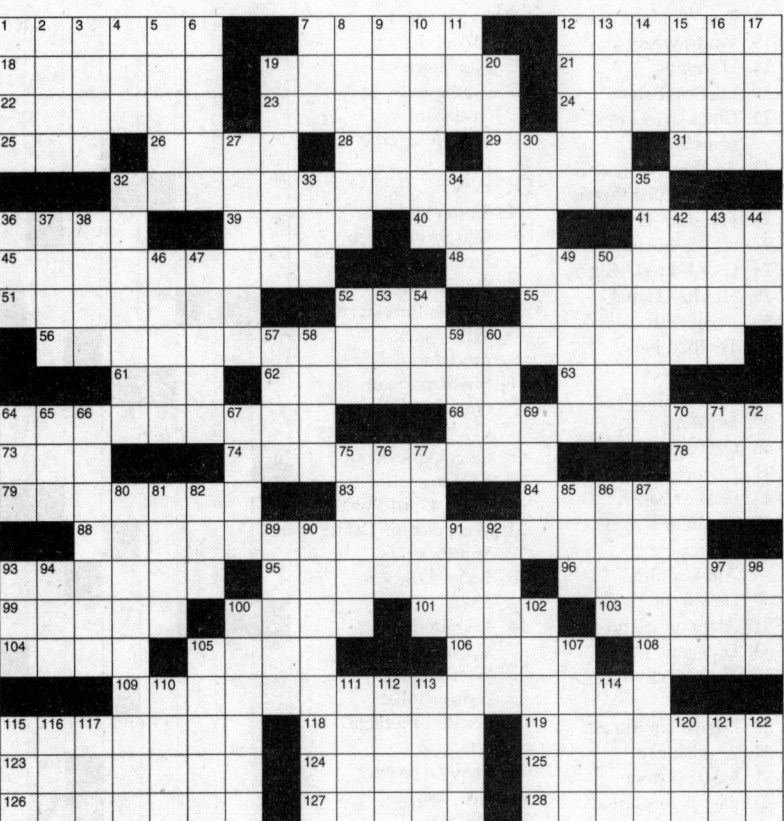

by Jacques Liwer

ACROSS

1. Tiny Tim's problem
9. Water wheel
14. Hornbills
19. Like sandstone
20. Cheddar colorer, sometimes
22. To shine, in Sedan
23. Cross Word Puzzle
26. Filmdom terrier
27. ___-de-boeuf
28. Like J. Fred Muggs
29. Hindu's camel
30. Early Olds
31. Toothed bars
33. Suppresses
35. Encircled
39. Stratum
40. Cabbage
41. Perfumes
43. Slice of bacon
45. Again and again
49. "Welcome ___," Altman film
50. DeSoto or Hudson
51. Aleutian island
53. Divagate
54. This covers the world
57. French condiment
59. Scottish cap
61. Flagged down
63. Fannie or Ginnie follower
64. Essay
66. Club clubber
68. Cross Word Puzzle
73. To find, to a fra
74. Crusty entrees
75. Had a hero
76. Dance in 3/4 time
77. P.I.
78. Rating number
79. Poem's chapter
81. Foreshadow
82. G.I.'s need
85. Lisper's hurdle
87. Carbon particles
89. Anchorage
91. In the thick of
93. Honors
97. W.W. II hero Murphy
99. "___ and Sane Fourth" Masson
101. Grommet
102. Like zebras
105. Writer of ridicule
107. Prior, to Prior
108. Yak
109. Man in the van
111. Noah's eldest
113. Lagomorph
114. Cross Word Puzzle
118. Key
119. Lampooned
120. Escorted
121. Noblemen
122. Young bulls, in Yorkshire
123. Woven together

DOWN

1. Smiley's creator
2. Middle of a Stein line
3. Sheepskins
4. Actress Purviance
5. Wit or pick preceder
6. Mediterranean entrant
7. Craftier
8. Ongoing shows
9. Engine encl.
10. Cross Word Puzzle
11. Weapons for Lafitte
12. Sundries
13. Longfellow's bell town
14. Ma's doting
15. Oscar winner: 1985
16. Welsh onion
17. Dane's dollar
18. Fourth canonical hours
21. In some respect
24. Claudia ___ Johnson
25. Within: Comb. form
32. Author McFadden
34. A U.N. arm
36. Wooden clog
37. Genesis man
38. Deg. for a legal eagle
40. Lincoln Ctr. attraction
42. Spring break
44. Gammon
46. El Greco became one
47. Orator Edward
48. Kelly or Beatty
50. Indicator of pitch
52. No sirrees
54. Spirit, to the Sun King
55. April 15
56. Student, hopefully
58. Raison d'___
60. Elem. number
62. One, in Ayr
64. Spaniard's yearly income
65. Act listless
66. French cheese district
67. H. C. Andersen's birthplace
69. Sir Edmund P. Hillary, e.g.
70. "___ been had!"
71. Makes a choice
72. ___ gratias
76. Canaille
77. Hundred-___ shot
79. Apograph
80. To ___ (precisely)
83. Damsels
84. Curie title
86. Jazzman Kenton
88. Suffix with verb or herb
90. Wagoner's command
92. "Who ___ call Himself a man": Cummings
93. Glowed anew
94. Cinema's Little
95. Earthy; worldly
96. Headed the committee
98. Mark for removal
100. Garibaldi, e.g.
102. Cash substitute
103. The ones here
104. Winchester, for one
105. Face card?
106. Dovetail wedge
110. Dice throw
112. Colleague of suffragette Stanton
113. Hindu spring festival
115. Some coll. linemen
116. Hearths: Abbr.
117. Like sushi

by Nancy W. Atkinson

ACROSS

1. Milady
6. Epps of "Higher Learning"
10. Epic
14. Avow
19. Berries
20. Divergence
22. Roo's mom
23. Wells sequel to "Jude the Obscure"?
25. Garret
26. Genet play, with "The"
27. Bribed
28. "Storm" novelist
29. Maple fruit
32. Pianist Peterson
33. Trilled like a grasshopper
34. Old French coin
35. City on the Songka River
37. Drawing rooms
39. E. E. Smith cousin of "I Am a Camera"?
42. Manhandle
45. Bustle
46. S. C. river
47. Throw out
49. Holm or key
51. Fissure
53. Doggone!
54. Sprightly
55. Rose's enemy
56. Sacred
58. Hollandaise, e.g.
59. Zealous
60. Ende book that's hard to put down?
65. Robots
66. Fronton basket
67. Vidi, in English
68. Diva Marilyn
69. Rivera of stage fame
70. Beau Brummel
72. Lille's department
76. Slovene or Slovak
77. John Ridd's Lorna
78. Cable company
80. Resort of SW France
81. Idle hours
83. Tolkien book about the World Trade Center?
86. Bedouins
88. N.Y. city
89. Danube tributary
90. Singular
93. Walking on the Rue Royale
95. Of the number six
96. Nocturnal mammals
97. Novelist Jong
98. "Now I ___ down . . ."
100. Brick building
101. Pohl book about Fishburne?
106. Befuddle
107. Intrudes
108. Actress Shire
109. King salmons
110. Wilbur or Nemerov
111. Eleonora of "Cenere"
112. Sticky stuff

DOWN

1. Inner frame
2. Alas, to Arndt
3. Cutting tool
4. Aesopian characters
5. Mosque turrets
6. "Amores" poet
7. Bulk
8. "Exodus" hero
9. Part of a cell
10. Roman burial stone
11. Marksmen
12. Prod
13. "___ Veronica," Wells book
14. Activity in which camels may be executed
15. Adams book about the Nautilus?
16. Program in
17. Nimble
18. Rushed
21. Ballerina Alonso
24. ___ Dolorosa
28. Whoop
29. Up to now
30. Tolerate
31. City SW of Buenos Aires
32. Assault
33. Clepsydra, e.g.
35. Shakespearean drama
36. Stage org.
38. Gone up
40. Scoops for soups
41. Chilean poet
43. End of a Poe title
44. "Historia naturalis" author
48. "I conquered," to Caesar
50. S. C. summer time
52. Lem novel about Mike Tyson?
54. Danza's "Taxi" role
55. "Thou ___ lady": Kingsley
57. Wave on la mer
58. Sonnet unit
59. Postulate
60. King in "Peer Gynt"
61. Dike, Eunomia and Irene
62. Parroted
63. Hold back
64. Judge, in Judges
65. Some A. L. batters
69. Marine collective
70. Fussed over
71. Meat packers' union
73. "Werther," for one
74. Less manifold
75. Long unused
77. "La Dame aux camélias" playwright
78. Discharged
79. El Capitan locale
82. Evening gatherings
84. Cry to the hounds
85. Winter apple
87. Wrap of Juarez
90. Country, to Nietzsche
91. Rice field
92. Lyric poem
94. Embroidery loop
95. ___ Darya, Asian river
97. Author Wortman
98. Vientiane locale
99. "Comus" composer
101. Marceau character
102. Nashville col.
103. U.N. agency
104. Veto
105. Author Talese

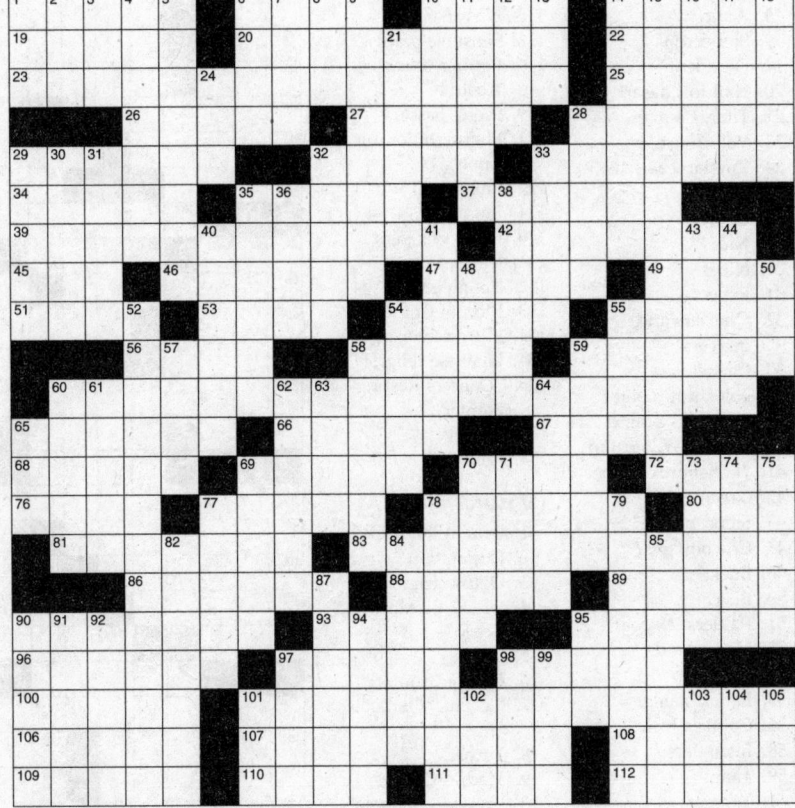

by John M. Samson

ACROSS

1. Early seafarer
4. Antic
9. Stonecrop
14. Decadent
20. Hail to Caesar!
21. Titania's man
23. Valor; virtue
24. Russian czar: 1645–76
25. Boozer
26. Nice
29. Nicer
31. Expect
32. Quarters and quavers
33. Capacious
34. Solos times eight
36. Shylock's pound
38. "G.W.T.W." group
41. "Lohengrin" role
42. Green cup
43. Stood up
44. Cowboy gear
46. Buck
50. Bias
51. Raiders' ex-coach
52. Netherlands township
55. Letter opener
56. Comic's forte
58. Interstices
59. Tangy
61. Tangier
63. Drag
64. Disconnects
66. To take off, at de Gaulle
67. Dash
68. Clears the slate
69. Libertine
70. Avoid bogey
73. Flat
77. Flatter
80. Forage plant
81. Take cover
82. OPEC members
85. Driving areas
86. He's unique, so to speak
87. Early astronaut
90. Hawks fly here
91. Better
96. Best
98. Diatonic spans
99. Flowering
100. Galba's successor
101. Court hindrance
102. Decreased?
103. Actress Burstyn
104. Churchman
106. More auspicious
107. Parts of carts
108. African pastureland
110. Southern Johnnies
114. Meese and Muskie
115. Nirvana
116. Sensitive plant
118. Former coin of Austria
119. Secret passers
121. Filling station for camels
122. Rainy
124. Rainier
130. Plumber's joint
131. Kind of price
132. Rough-edged
133. Rice, in China
134. W.C.'s chickadee
135. Japanese religion
136. "Dancers Resting" painter
137. Surfeits
138. Junk mail

DOWN

1. Pain in the neck
2. Declaration
3. Oxford lengths
4. Le ___ de Monte Cristo
5. Busy as ___
6. Five of trumps
7. "___ tu," "Ballo" aria
8. Turner
9. Madras dresses
10. Horace's "he was"
11. Phrontistery
12. All-purpose trk.
13. Most contemptible
14. Aristotelian element
15. Escape
16. Actor Parker
17. Outside: Comb. form
18. Shooting match for Jacques
19. W. Erhard's therapy
22. Stair post
27. Merit
28. Bridge site
30. Drat!
35. Scorch
36. Money for Monet
37. Opposite of brevis
38. Tenor Bergonzi
39. Javelin
40. Balance-sheet entry
43. Faye and Cooper
44. Less arcane
45. Holey roller
47. Harem room
48. Eye part
49. Recent
50. Struck
51. Disencumber
52. Young Athenian
53. Caller, in a way
54. Is comparable to
56. Pentateuch
57. Savings for sr. citizens
58. John Jacob
60. Of an armbone: Comb. form
61. Grappa's cousin
62. "Desire hath ___": Burton
65. Roberta or Bernadette
70. Simon acquaintance
71. In ___ (so to speak)
72. Oppose
74. Anyone that
75. Clinked
76. Brainstorms
77. Greek theater
78. Napa trailer
79. Over
82. Pine martens' kin
83. Poet who invented the dithyramb
84. Look ___ (respect)
87. TV hookups
88. Italian dynasty
89. Rhine tributary
91. French river
92. Pungent
93. Discontinues
94. Roof pointer
95. Annie and Monty
97. Reine's mate
100. Michigan car maker
103. Were
104. Hanger hangouts
105. Santa ___ Islands
107. Shake ___ (hurry)
108. Border stamp
109. Gives off
111. Dermal affliction
112. Folk song
113. Manners
115. Five in a row!
116. Karpov coups
117. Expert
118. Levees
119. Tibia's locale
120. Half a quarter gallon
121. Pelion supporter
123. Relative of a wheeze
124. What, in Weimar
125. Etna ejecta
126. Vail verb
127. Vein's glory
128. Strong ale
129. "___ Vidderne," long Ibsen poem

by Phyllis Fehringer

ANSWERS

1

```
OHARA  JAWAT  OATH   MEET
SOLED  ADASH  SCAR   ARNO
ALLAH  NIXIE  CELEBRANT
GEODE  EEE  PEARL  ISSUE
EDWARDTUDORAROYALHEIR
     PEI    FIR   LUNK
MEETSTOMCANTYAPOORLAD
ODS    TAO   CHE    KILO
BYCHANCETHEYSWAPROLES
SEETO   SEA   ALOU   ICE
    STENT  ENG  GLINT
DIS  ANNA   DOE   LUIGI
EDWARDWITHTOMSSUPPORT
ELAN   HAH   MEL    BOA
REGAINSRULEBYLOCATING
    NATE   OPE   ONA
THEGREATSEALOFENGLAND
EAGRE  MATSU  XIV  OLLIE
STEAMPIPE  PAINE  RIATA
LISP  ONEA  ELDER  ASTER
ANTE  MASK  REEDS  SHERE
```

2

```
PEPSI  FETID  CUSP   ORBS
OLEIN  ENVOI  ASWE   POLO
MARSHAMOANS  LEER   EBAN
ELL  ALMS  IMELDACAROMS
     ELSIE   AIMS  REBATE
GAMETE  MANSE   DINE
AGAVE  COT  SUSANTANGOS
NOTE  ANTA  SUM   MOORE
GREERGROANS  BARD  TALC
ASSAIL  ITEM  TERMITE
     YVONNECAROLED
PAPEETE  STLO  AGLEAM
DOLE  ASKS  SANDYSINNED
ISLAM  TAJ  RARE   SNEE
SHARONTONES  LAD  BUSTS
     VEIN  STUDY  KARNAK
DEWITT  ASAP  CANEA
JULIEWANDERS  ARTS  RAE
ICED  ONEA  LESLEYHALTS
VANE  RIAL  ETTAS  EVERT
ELAN  KALE  TSARS  EADIE
```

3

```
ATTAR  CRAVAT  ALACARTE
MERLE  SALAMI  VAGARIES
BROADWAYFLOP  OCARINAS
ORINDA  SALE   NEST
YESSES   ABIE   EAMES
     RACKETANDBALLGAME
ARPS  THERE  GUIDE  ARAM
RIOTS  ISA  MECCAS  VIII
USUALS  ETTE  ESP  PEALS
BELGIANYOUTHS   TAO
ANTENNA  BAA   ELLESSE
GAS   TAXIDERMYNEED
SCAMS  CPA  ALEX  SPARTA
LONE  REARMS  CUT  SCRIM
AREA  ANIMA  CORKY  TANS
KINDOFTRAINORBOAT
ENTER   CLOP   BURIAL
     ISLE   RIAL  BRENDA
OLDJOKES  AMERICANICON
VOCALIST  MARINO  ENURE
ANISETTE  INSETS  DERNS
```

4

```
ELPASO  TIEDUP  SETTEE
SORBIC  SERPENT  ADORES
TWICETOLDTALES  VIRILE
EEN  VARY  CPA   SATAN
     TRAVELEDTHROUGHTIME
ABE  YAR  ITSME   ODOR
OBESE   RAT  HUM  CRAWL
RASHAD  ASTEP  ARIADNE
ILK  NODS  SLAM    OAT
EDIT  TAKESTOTASK  OVER
NEMO  TICTACTOE    RIDE
TRON  TENTIMESTEN  ASAP
YEW  GONE   SPAR   AMO
LASTCAR  GNOME  YEAGER
ELIHU  ONS  TAO  ATEST
FAME  POOCH  TVS    SLO
TIPTOETHRUTHETULIPS
LIMES  OSE   AGES   PER
GEEGAW  TOTELLTHETRUTH
ARSENE  AGONIES  PIERCE
PETRIE  TENSED  SCATHE
```

5

```
SOFTG  RESTER  BRET  ABAFT
ONEAL  ESKIMO  YOYO  NOBLY
PULLUPSTAKES  AARP  GROAN
STEELIE  IRISHMEN  OZONE
     AGR   ATTA   OTRO
TRADEINS  PLAYITSTRAIGHT
RELOAD  FED  EROICA   ROI
APLUS  CARESS  MPH  SCENE
PLEBE  ATIP  PRIES  POUTER
PEAL  QUOD  PEENS  BETRAYS
ETRE  ULNA  LEEK   BLEST
DESC  OKAYBUDDYDRAW  AFAR
HOTEL  AMBI  AARE   IRMA
SECEDED  ALEUT  MINE  NEON
PLACED  PRISM  PANE  ICERS
ROCKS  SEM  PLESSY  TABOO
IRA  FTROOP  OAK  HELIUM
GOODBYEMRCHIPS  SEAMLESS
VAIN   AIDE   ULT
SAYOK  OPENSEAS  FACTORY
ADORE  PAPA  ARTOFTHEDEAL
CIGAR  ACID  TEEPEE  CELLO
SNAKY  DECA  EDWARD  HAYES
```

6

```
GEMINIS  ULEE  WEBS   DSM
RIOTACT  PATCHEDUP  RAE
ESREVERPSYCHOLOGY  AIS
ENEMY  IRA  HINT  SCOWLS
TEA  OVAL  DDE  YAPPER
RUBTHEYAWGNORW  MAUDS
     LYONS  RNA  WHELM
AWFUL  PEA  POWER   OHS
THREEFACESTSEW  TALBOT
TIE  ROBUST  HONI  SEINE
ENDE  EASEL  ORING  SLAW
NEEDS  SATE  WINGIT  ILA
DRRUTH  CARRIAGENRUTER
SSI  OINKS  YEN   ISYET
CORDE   MAS   MAINE
KUKLA  OUTINTFELFIELD
ONHIGH  SIN  RATS   AOL
WITNEY  EMIL  ANE  SWINE
TAR  BENDOVERSDRAWKCAB
OTO  INATRANCE  EMIRATE
WEN  NATO  CZAR  DIMPLED
```

7

```
MARSHA   SAHARA   CABANAS
ACETOL   ICEMEN   ELEMENT
JONATHANSWIFT     LAVERNE
SPORTING      OID      BENDER
      TERN   NOELCOWARD
ADJUST   DOMED   GAMA   LOS
LEAPT   TITAN   FLAGPOLE
TIMS   TRAIN   EGAD   EAUDE
AGE   FRANCISBACON   RIIS
RNS   AIMEE   ABLE   OUTSET
   HILTS   ITS   SIBYL
STINKO   PUMA   CLOSE   AAA
HILL   NORMANMAILER   MIG
OATER   TEAM   ANDES   PORN
PROTESTS   SCADS   ROUTE
SAN   FLEA   EMORY   TOPROW
   GEORGESAND   LOOS
IMPART   ENS   PARTICLE
MAOISTS   JEFFREYARCHER
PLOTTER   ONLOAN   HOLIER
SALSODA   YEARNS   STEAKS
```

8

```
ALLAH   ROC   ITAL   RASPS
MULTI   USO   LUNA   BOCCIE
AMAL5SSEL   IRKS   IDEATE
SEMANAS   OSAKA   GOTMAD
STANDEE   NICE   FATLY
   TONTINE   YEARO4LORD
TAPIRS   CAVS   USTEN   VIR
ERICS   MODEM   DCI   SPODE
ANT   SINE   OBOIST   RIGA
RETAKEN   MOORS   IBIDEM
   GOLDSMI3XAMINED
RATINE   HENNY   GENESIS
AWOL   STRAIT   ADOS   ORA
KAREN   RIG   RELIT   CROON
ESS   OPINE   YALE   GLENNS
SHIF2RKERS   SOMALIS
   ERIES   CHEW   DINETTE
CAVERN   SHULA   ENTREES
ARABIC   DOOM   BOST1VENT
POLLEE   DROP   LAT   RENEE
TWEED   EELS   ERE   ASSTS
```

9

```
COLD   ASAP   LAID   ABCS
OTERI   SMOTE   ERNO   DEAN
BRAINMUFFIN   SOSO   HERA
ASFLAT   ACHESMURDERER
   TART   LEAR   AROSE
LACEYCOMEHOME   ADMEN
ODOR   NOLAN   SNIP   TAR
GASSED   BLUEGRACESTATE
OPT   TEASES   OATES   APOD
STASHED   ETTU   STEMS
   WOMANWITHAPASTE
INGAS   OHTO   WHEREOF
PERM   RADII   ELINOR   DLI
STAINEDUPCOMIC   REGIME
ASI   IDOS   BIZET   ONAN
   NOSIR   BAITATHOUSAND
ALYCE   APES   IMPS
BAKEINTHEUSSR   GREASE
ONNA   AINT   THETHINMANE
ICON   TOOL   LIARS   DENIM
LETS   ONME   ONLY   REDO
```

10

```
BOSS   JUNC   PODS   SHAWN
RAWLS   SITAR   APOEM   COREA
ATEAT   ELATE   CARTA   ANTIS
THEBESTTHINGTHATCAN   ERS
SST   EFT   OER   TOAST   RDA
   HAPPENINLIFEISWHENYOU
AREO   DEED   SPAY   ESO
SHARP   SALA   REPOS   TSPS
TORTES   TERP   LATIN   AROO
   STARTWORKATEIGHTOCLOCK
TEA   SPONDEE   THEBAR
IVY   URSA   AND   RARA   ELA
PIERRE   SUCCESS   MUS
SOMEBODYSAYSITSTIMEFOR
ELEE   SOLES   TATA   PREVIN
   ANKA   BASSI   GABS   SIEVE
   ORB   INTO   COLA   GREW
COFFEEBREAKANDYOUDONT
UMA   ALIEN   REA   SEW   HEE
REC   WANTTOGOSTEPHENKING
ELIZA   DARLA   TITLE   EARED
RELAY   SIEGE   AVOID   RETRO
STEPS   NEAL   RENE   LYON
```

11

```
ARES   DELEGATE   FORUM
CORE   OLEANDER   ARENAS
CURE   MIGRAINEIMAGINER
ELAPSE   INTO   LILA   GEE
DENSE   COE   SIGIL   LORDS
EAT   ROUND   GRAY   GLOBE
DURABLE   PALED   ELEVEN
   ARIA   HOLLOW   RDA   EDT
MONDAYDYNAMO   MUIR
ELTON   REINS   BASTE   LAG
SEER   MINOT   SLOTH   WADE
HOR   DIVAN   SHARI   TITAN
   AXES   ANEMICCINEMA
EAR   TEL   ASIDES   ANON
RIOTER   TINTS   BRISTLE
ARMOR   LONE   ABATE   TAM
SCANT   EXURB   LIT   SLAVE
EON   RANI   ELLS   STALER
SOCRATICACROSTIC   VERS
   LEADON   CANBERRA   ANNO
   STEMS   TREETOAD   STEN
```

12

```
TOPMOST   POLKAS   TBAR
ATTACHE   MOVEABLE   AERO
GOAHEADBAKEBYDAY   BARA
   ELL   USER   SUPERSTAR
PATROL   THREW   LULU   TYS
AGE   TOOT   AIM   PATCH
WHATSTHEBATTER   SHEEN
NASH   TROT   TOOTH   SPEW
   ACTOFGOD   WOO   DARLA
MOBIUS   LENO   BARRELS
ETO   BABYYESBABYNO   SIP
ROBBERY   ELSA   NOOSES
LOBES   TAP   SANDHILL
ELYA   REVEL   DEMI   ARMS
   EDUCE   ARUBEWITHAVIEW
   EXACT   UNI   NEED   DIE
OVA   REED   AGLET   ADHERE
HARDLINER   SAGO   TRA
ASEA   PUTABANONTHEBOON
REST   TREMBLES   RESIDUE
ASTA   ERASES   INSTORE
```

13

```
IPECAC   EDITS     DOESIN
LILACS   METEOR   POSTURE
SKIRTTHEISSUE     ILLEGAL
 ESAI  ARGOT  POLLO   ATL
   FIBRIN  CHOKES   PREY
ACHE  LET  NAM   ASHARP
THO  TOMATOSOUP   OMELET
TINCANS  ONE  LITUP   UVA
USERID  GMS  PESOS   AMIR
  YIPE  NEEDY   DEEPFAT
 KNEE  SPINDRIED  LEAN
MAURICE   SEATS    JIMI
OPTS  HESSE  MET   EDERLE
LUC  MINUS  TIM  TEENIER
ETHNIC  BROADSWORD   ENS
 ERIKAS  USS  EDE   OSTE
AREA  CREDIT   GLADYS
LER  NOCTI  EJECT   AMFM
LEISURE   BABETHEBLUEOX
AVOIDED  SLUDGE   MINUTE
NESTEA   ADIOS   WEDDED
```

14

```
TELSTAR  EDGAR   ANAGRAM
INAHOLE  KORDA   SEQUELA
LIKENEW  GEORGEKAUFMAN
EDEL  XII  WILD    AFORE
    FRANKLINPADAMS
PTA  ANDEAN  NARC   HURT
REMENDS  USSR   EQUATOR
ONEDGE  ATTHEAL  UNRIPE
BORNFREE  SOBIG  ECOLES
REAO  ALF  EUROPE   LESS
   FRISBEE   TENONED
CODE  SEALUP  SQR   GRIP
HAIRDO  TORII  UNWOODED
ISABEL  DNUORNI  OISEAU
LINEMAN   SNEE  COSSACK
ISAR  TORO  NOSALT   SHE
   ROBERTBENCHLEY
AMAZE   AGHA   IOC   AFRO
DOROTHYPARKER   KOOKIER
ANGORAS  NUKES  ITSONME
HOOTOWL  SMELT  ATAVISM
```

15

```
SIDEBAR  BABAS   BATMAN
IRONAGE  ARDORS  ATONCE
BEATLES  MOUNTRUSHMORE
 RENT  OILED  LIE    POD
LOCUST  EULA   ESSEN
ERAS  NAN  TACIT   ASCAP
SILT  LITTLEWOMEN   ALSO
SOLSTICE  ADS  PRO   TOSS
ELI  ARENAS  LSD   IVES
RENAMES  LEGATO  SURETE
 GIP  TOPRATING   KIR
SABRAS  BOSTON  ORACLES
CRIB  HAS  NACHOS    ELO
HERA  ARC  ARE  LOVELAND
WADS  DOUBLESGAME   AVID
ASSES  URALS  RUE   RENE
  UPSET  ODES   LOGSON
ARP  REA  IONIA   PONE
SEINFELDSTARS  SEASONS
PAPIER  STINGY  SWISHED
SPENDS  CASTE  TERESAS
```

16

```
CAR  ADELA  RASP  ADAGIO
ADO  GENUS  ENTO  REMORA
TAMTAMOSHANTER  SPIGOT
SMARTEST  MELEES   ANON
 AHA  RAGED   THROB
CANCANOPENER  FOOTRACE
ALEE  STUBS  SALOME  NOL
STARS  OLE  LOG   DRAMA
TOT  CHOPCHOPSUEY  ANAT
  COALS  ERROR  ESTATE
DETERGE  MOE   VALISES
EVONNE  ALINE  MARIO
FEMS  NONONONSENSE  LAM
INTER  UNO  CDI   RAISE
ELO  ESTOPS  MOIST  FLIT
SYMMETRY  CHOWCHOWLINE
 TANGO  DRESS    REO
CHIT  WIRERS  BARNACLE
SOUSED  BYEBYEELECTION
ELMIRA  LENI  STONE  ALI
ATBEST  ERSE  SHUTS  OLD
```

17

```
CAPLET  SAFETY  PLANETS
ASLOPE  ACADIA  IGNORED
SKATINGSHRINK  LEGATES
TIN  GNU  ATESTS   SHED
SNEER  PARDO   UNITS
 MARPLE  RADNER   SCAT
LENDMEYOURSHEARS  HALO
ATEASE  UNE  ARF  CANDY
CHIS  FADING  NIA  OREOS
TIGHTER  OARS   STORK
ICE  ORIENTALSHRUG   SUB
 HOSES  APAL  ETIENNE
IDEAL  STL  EMOTER  TADA
DAVIS  OOH  OVI   USERID
EMER  CINCINNATISHREDS
SPRY  ARIOSO   KUCHEN
 SANKA  TASSO   PERCH
ASHY  SNAPON  NOH   ELA
PICASSO  SANTASSHELVES
TROPISM  INCODE  TRAUMA
ASPERSE  AGENDA  ODDEST
```

18

```
SLIM  BIC  ATELESS   BLAH
KONA  UMA  CAMILLA   EASE
IFIHADANICKELFOR   RUNE
PAGERS  ORRERY  WAVERED
STORE  WEEUNS  SENATORS
   DOH  ETO  TRAIT
BOZ  COSM  ONCE   CLAMPS
TEHACHAPI   ORB    ILK
BANTUS  ISM  EVERYTIMEI
AROOM  DECEIVE   AEOLIA
  PUTADOLLARINTHE
GAELIC  NEEDING   OFOLD
BANKIDHAVE   ENT  ALTMAN
UNA  ADE   GRANDMAMA
SGTMAJ  DYCK  SOWN   YRS
  USUAL  SAN   OAK
SORBONNE  LIONEL  ISAAC
CLEANED  LESTER  DELRIO
ALAR  1/20WHATIHAVENOW
LIMA  SOOTIER  CEL  DELE
DESK  TROTSKY  AXE  SLID
```

19

```
C R A G   · T A M P · R Y A N · E C L A T
Z O L A · S U S I E · I A M B · N A O M I
E L L S · C R I S T · G R E A T B R A I N
C L A S H O F T H E T A N S · B E A T T Y
H E Y Y O U · · I R A · · W O R T H Y
· · C R E A T I V E W R I N G · ·
R C A · K E R N · I S O L D E · S K E W
A L L · E D G I N G · N O S E · S H I V A
P U L P Y · · M O A T E D · · E A R N E D
· B A A · O P I A T E · V A L S I G N S
· B R I D E S H E A D R E V I S E D ·
W O R K P E R M · R A I N E S · K A L
O D E S S A · W H Y N O T · R S V P S
M O V I E · D O H A · S T R O D E · I G O
B R E T · M O R I T Z · A W E D · D A Y
· B I N G T H E B U L L E T ·
A L G O R E · S E P · P A C K E T
C L E A V E · C E N T E R S O F G R A V Y
P E T L A R C E N Y · F I L A R · U T E P
A U G E R · O L D S · U S U R Y · M I N E
S T O N Y · E L S E · P E G S · B E T A
```

20

```
C H A I R · L A M B · C A R B · P A O L O
C A L L A · A L A R · A R E A · R E D U B
S H O O F L Y P I E · M I N U T E R I C E
· A U N T I E · D A B A · M I T O S I S
· · A S T R O · D E R A T · T E S T E E
A U K · H E R D · L O B O · A N T
C H I P P E D B E E F · B E A N S A L A D
T O W E R · E N T R E A T S · E T U D E
S H I N O L A · S A Y S · O P T S · R E L
· M O O N S E T · E S T E E · T I L E
H O M E F R I E S · C O R N B R E A D
E V A N · A M A T I · T R E S T L E
M U D · C L A M · S H O E · E S O B E S O
A L A M O · T I T T E R E D · O L D E R
L E M O N S O L E · C O D D L E D E G G S
· T V A · E A S T · S A I D · Y O O
B U S I E R · S L O O P · Y E S N O
E N C O R E S · B R E T · S E E S A W
S P O N G E C A K E · S H E L L S T E A K
T E P E E · O V E R · T A C O · T E R R A
S N E R D · W A Y S · S T O W · S O O T Y
```

21

```
H A S E K · R I F L E · L I B E R A L
E L O P E R · T A N D E M · E L E V A T E
R E T I R E M E N T A G E · C O H E R E S
· · C R E O L E · E R S T · I R E N E
A S W E · F R E E Z I N G P O I N T ·
S O A N D S O · E N D E A R E D · P O E
T U T E E · C H A R · A T H E N A
E N T · G U N C A L I B E R · T I E R E D
R D S · A T O L L S · O L E G · M U F T I
· I L S A S · S N E E R · E R E W E
· A N E · H O U R S I N A D A Y · E C O
S N A G S · A R E A R · H U R S T
A T B A T · P E A T · A S M A R A · S I L
C H U T E S · S P E E D L I M I T · C L E
H E L E N A · S O O T · E B O L A
A R B · T H E S E A T S · A B S O R B S
· R O L L O F T H E D I C E · N E E T
P A L E R · I N F O · E R R A N D
O C U L I S T · U N L U C K Y N U M B E R
L I N E A T E · S E I K O S · S T A R R Y
A D D E N D S · E S T E R · S N O R E
```

22

```
T E A B A G · A R C H I E · O P E N E D
A R G Y L E · B A A I N G · E V I L E Y E
O M E L E T P R I N C E O F D E N M A R K
S A R A · E A S E · T A I N T · T E E
· W H A T D I D J U I C E S A Y ·
M A O · E S S E N · A P S E · A C I D
E T H E L S · P S S T · H O R M O N E
D A H L I A S · B A C T · M A K E S F O R
A L O U · I H A M W H A T I H A M · F I N
L E W D · L E V O · A R I D · Y O D E L S
· W E T · L E V I · T E D S · P O E
S C A R E D · R I N D · U L E E · G A E L
O A F · H O U S E K I P P E R S · O N L Y
U N F R E E Z E · I L E S · A P H O N I C
S A L I E R I · L E A P · I O D A T E
A L E C · L A S T · S T R A W · N E E
· E G G S I S T E N T I A L L Y ·
S T L · O W E T O · E A R N · U V E A
T H E Y N E V E R S A U S A G E A M E S S
A R G O N N E · D A R R I N · I N M A T E
B U S M A N · A P P O S E · S T Y L E T
```

23

```
C H E F S · H A S A T · R A F · T O G A
O A S I S · E C O L E · O L L A · A J A X
W H A T T I M E W I L L Y O U B E H O M E
L A I T · N A T S · L U S T · A R I S E
· E R A T O · A S A · · S L I T
W H E R E W I L L Y O U B E T O N I G H T
I O N · H E N · E E N · U L A N · R A O
T H O S E · P T A · L O I R E · S O L O
H O W W A S Y O U R D A Y A T S C H O O L
· A R R O W S · I V S · · H A V E
R A N S O M S · R N A · U N L A D E D
E D G E · · M U G · A R C A R O
W H O A R E Y O U G O I N G O U T W I T H
H A R T · N E R D S · H E E · E S T E E
E S E · V L A D · H A M · T O R · T A C
W H E N W I L L Y O U D O H O M E W O R K
· E A R S · A A A · O R A R E
G R E C O · K A H N · A R C H · I S L A
W H Y D O N T Y O U G E T A H A I R C U T
D I A L · S U L U · T R I C E · A D A G E
S A N E · B E T · I N T E R · M O R S E
```

24

```
A S T E R · R A F T S · S A R A · A M I D
S L A V E · E C L A T · A R E S · N U D E
F O R E S T G R U M P · F I A T · G T O S
I T S · A R O S E · B A S S I N E T
T H I S T L E S · S A R I S · E L E E
· W H A T S M Y W H I N E · W A R D S
A L G A E · E O E · G R A F · M I O
C A R P A T B A G G E R S · T E A B A L L
T W I · U R I A H · E C O · C L O Y E D
S N A C K B A R · A D A M S · L O I S
· L E A V E I T T O B E E F E R ·
S W I T · O R B I T · G A I N S A Y S
S H I F T S · S E E · I R A T E · N E O
M A N T L E S · G R I P E S O F W R A T H
E N D · E X E S · · E S E · R A T I O
W A Y O F · T H E P R O F U S S E R
· S A B U · A R N I E · S T O N E A G E
· M E L O D I C A · S P U R N · L E G
E M M Y · L A V A · F E R R I S P U L E R
G L E E · E T E S · T R I E D · U K A S E
G I R D · G E R E · D E E R E · B E N E T
```

25

```
IRONIC  ARTSALE  EDAMES
NEVADA  BEATSIT  SAVANT
RAISETHESTAKES   APACHE
EDNA  LISTENS   CUP  HAN
DYE CID   DISCO   EYING
  MAKEAGRANDENTRANCE
SMILE  HOOT  INCA   PEEL
CLINE  FOOT   TAX    PSS
RINGBELLFORSERVICE
AMI   ROD   EERIE  ORDER
VENDOR   WASPS   ENSURE
EDGES  SNARE  LON    GEE
  CHIPOFFTHEOLDBLOCK
CRO   TAN   URGE  ROUTS
SLED  CRAG  DEMO  PARTS
  TAKETHEMONEYANDRUN
ARIDE  METER   ION   OCT
MIN  RYE   SIDEARM  MARY
ENDURE  GETDOWNTOCASES
NELSON  STEEPEN  TUXEDO
STEERS  TEASERS  EDISON
```

26

```
PRESUME    CABALA   METHOD
RACEGOER   BANANAS  IGUANA
IDONOTLIKEMYDADSBROTHER
MILD   OKD   MEAL      ASE
POISONEDKINGWEDMYMOTHER
      CANE  MILA   ARHAT
TOT  ASS    DEL   SEANCE
ILETTHEMTHINKTHATIAMMAD
TIME   ABOU  TOAST   EURO
OOPSISTABBEDOPHELIASDAD
     TRI  ABBE   EST   IDO
APO KLU  TABITHA  ELO NOS
DRX  ELS    SHAG      ILK
NOBODYHELPSMEINMYPLIGHT
AMOI    ERICH  TELE  RAIN
NOWLAERTESANDIWILLFIGHT
IRISES   DOE   PIE    SOS
  SKEIN     OWNS  DELI
SWORDSARESWITCHEDINAJAM
WAS     RAMP   UAR    DOGE
ATHEATRICALENDINGHAMIAM
SHELVE  DECIDES  SAILINTO
HERMAN  SEESAW   TSETSES
```

27

```
RICHIE  SCRAPS   CREASE
EROICA  TAIPEI  SAURIAN
VENDERBENDERS   ASSERTS
ELSE  PUNTER  SAUTE  LII
LAIRD  STA  AISLE   VEAL
ENS  OCTOBERVEST   PASTE
DDT  CHER  LEAST  PAUSED
   TAD   LAYS   POLL
SHADOW  VINETUNES  TREK
COLOR  GILDS  NITE  LAVA
ARID  BASIS  MIXER  IBAR
RANG  EMIT  METER  SNIDE
FLEE  VATHEADED  SWEDEN
   REEL   SLID   LIE
GRAVEL  ACTIN  AONE  TBS
LEVAR  VILECABINET  EAT
OVEN  GAMER  LLD  STARR
SER  SAMSA  ENAMOR  ARNO
SNARLUP  REVERENCEBOOK
EGGNOGS  ELEVEN  MALONE
DEEDEE   DYNAST   PREMED
```

28

```
HASHED   MEDICI   OBLATE
OSMOSE   OLOROSO  LEADIN
WHITECHRISTMAS   ELNINO
TET    RISE    MALI   DEGS
ONEPIECE   PEACOCKBLUE
    ARA   FAX   BOYO
  THESCARLETPIMPERNEL
SRO   ERSE   CARL    DOVE
HOOCH  UTIL  LILAC   CIT
HOTHOUSE  ELLE  BOA  TDS
  THECHARACTERSINCLUE
BBS  KOD  ETDS  ADJOURNS
LEO  HENIE  TONI   WINCE
DEMS  CORA  CTNS    EEE
GREENAROUNDTHEGILLS
   COMO    EOS    DEA
  PLUMPUDDING  BREADBIN
HEAR   TARN   PIES   ILE
ATTICA  MUSTARDPLASTER
RETTON  SMEARED  INTEND
PREYON   STIMPY   POSSES
```

29

```
FRAS  TRESS   LOLA   HIST
RENT  RURAL  IDIOT  INTO
OTTO  UNITE  FOURBAGGER
GROUNDSKEEPER  TINHORN
SONTAG    SPA   STARDATE
  STELA   ILS   ALDEN
WHO  TRIPLEPLAY   ADDUP
HUBBY  APER  AILS  NOISE
ASIA  CRAG  ENROLL  URSA
THELMA  LACED  ROOSTERS
  LONG  LORES  BOAS
SNAPPERS  WIRED  SLIPON
IOLA  DIEPPE  WIDE  DUKE
BAIRD  NATO  RUNE  BERRA
SHAKO  MAKEUPGAME   EAR
  FROME   ELF   ONEAL
SCREWING   AFL   TSETSE
MELAMED  RELIEFPITCHER
OPENINGDAY  ADORE  HEIR
DIRK  SENSE  NICER  ERNE
SAKS   TAPS   SNIPS  REED
```

30

```
CITRIC   FOSS   LAMPPOST
ONEIDA   IBET   CAFETERIA
KIEVINCLINE   ACCRABATS
ETS    TOM   SPARE   BLOT
  HOPIN  BUSIEST  ALENE
BEIJINGBEAUTY    ARTY
LAROSA  YELPS  FROM  MOB
OTT    MET    LAM   TONE
WASONTO   SEPIA  AVENUE
  ROOST   PRAGUENOSES
  TAIPEIPERSONALITY
MINSKSTOLES    TRACE
BERGEN  TILDE  TWEEDLE
ALEE  OWE   BRO    EEN
ADD  STIR  COCOA  HASPED
   AUST  CAIROPROCTORS
POSSE  HOODLUM   OLEAN
INNS   BLESS   OLD   ERA
SEOULFOOD  KABULSTONES
ANOMALIES   IDOS  TIPTOE
NOTEPADS    NEXT  ODESSA
```

31

```
DIM   SEAL    STDS    IRONY
EVES  CALEB   CREW    NOVAE
BANK  ASIDO   HOPE    ABETS
ANTIQUETAXCOLLECTOR
CHINUPS   OSOLE   OUTAGE
LOOSE   BUFFALOTAXBILLS
EEN  STYLE   SPEC    CLOT
     STR  MEMO    MCI
JAMESES   TAXFREEATLAST
AMAT  EKE  RILED   READER
KITS  LATAXDODGER   TOGA
ENSURE  ANEAR  ELI   OBEY
SOUPYSALESTAX   SAWYERS
     ESL   ELOI   GIA
MBAS  TEAT   UNPEN   HIC
GIMMETAXSHELTER   GUARE
STEELE   PEELE   EDITION
   MANYHAPPYTAXRETURNS
MAORI  ANTI   URKEL   RIME
ALIEN  ASIT   SCENE   NEAR
PARDO  SECS   SSTS    RNS
```

32

```
LAVAS   BEEFED    ATTILA
ORACLE  ANNEXES   TRITON
SOLTIFAREDWELLAMIDOWN
ECLIPTIC   ECLAT   LINES
SKINS   RACERS    VOILE
   GOB   ROY   SENS   SLEW
DOMINOSOLEFATRELATIVE
AKIN  WELLDONE   REV   KEN
TAX   NEY   OCTO   AMEND
UPENDED   ESTH    FUSTY
MIDORITIRESOFANLASOLO
   SYNOD   ACRE   FORTRAN
MACHO   SEEA   LAO   DYE
ALI  FMS  PELLICLE   TIER
LATIFAHSOLDONADMIRERS
LIEN   RAHS   WED   SNO
   FAVRE   CASSES   GLOAM
STAID  IBSEN   MOLELIKE
LAREDOFANSTIMINGSOLID
AXILLA   TOASTEE   STPETE
BIDDER   BRYANS    AEDES
```

33

```
TAVI   PEPA   HORN   ASKEW
IRA(QR)OUTED  AR(AB)IC CHERI
MACARTHUR   NAINA  HOPIN
BRANDT   IAN  NARRO(WX)ING
RANG   OAXACAN   FLOOR
ETTE  BO(YZ)NTHEHOOD  A(CD)C
   BELA   HICS   STRAP
HESIOD   FLYFISH  ONEONE
ORING   AFOOT   KIDMAN
LI(GH)TS  MARKSMEN   ATF
TESH  SPIRE  ELEGY  IBET
   ELI  REDIRECT  ELI(IJ)AH
PAYFOR   TIN(KL)E   AMORE
AVOIDS   ALSATIA   URSULA
LO(UV)RE   PLIE   CANS
WE(ST) CHI(MN)EYSWEEP  CCCP
   PE(OP)LE  PICASSO  OAHU
BALLPEENS   PIS   IRONER
ALIAS  GETUP  HOUS(EF)LIES
MARCO  MEESE  MAKESENSE
ADREM   SMEE   EKED   REED
```

34

```
RUSTLE  CHANCY    DRAPES
ENTAIL  HONORE    PROMISE
STARVE  ISTRESSROMANCE
IRIS  MORTISE   TYNE   CAD
DORIDEARACE   BRIE   PEPE
EDS  ANTS   ALAN   BORER
   ARTS   TRYSUNGLASSES
SMOCKS   WHOOPED   ERE
NORTE  REVUES  JAG  AFT
IPAINTMODERN   GOVERNOR
VETO  RITA   DIVE   AGRI
EDENTATE   NEVERINSTOCK
LSD  RUT  SOLEIL   THREE
   AIM  ICELESS   TREADS
DANCEARMINARM   DOOR
ELAND  APOD  BRAN   RBI
RISE  AVON  IDOLENGTHEN
IMA  ALIS  ARANEID   HORN
DELVEINTOVERSE   FRINGE
ENLARGE   RENTED   RENDER
STYRON   CRESTS   OCEANS
```

35

```
REVAMP   SHEBA   SPINACH
IMADEIT   OILER   HONALEE
MORALMAJORITY   ONATEAR
   MIAMI   TOTALECLIPSE
ALVAN  ILL  TONI   ELOPES
BLINDALLEY   RSVP   NOSY
OAKTAG   TVS   RENTA
INK  LAB  EASTERISLAND
LOISLANE  SNOW  UNE  SEA
   HERDER   DREG   AHAB
SHAKESPEAREANSONNET
WHEW   SALA   KAPLAN
EEL  RAW  DADS  REDNOSED
BALANCEDDIET   LEI   ABU
   RATER   EON   SLALOM
LISI   PURE   WEATHERMAP
INNEED  IONA  TWA  AMITY
SCOTLANDYARD   ADANO
PARTITA   AMERICANDREAM
ESTATES   LENIN   STEELER
DESSERT   SLAPS   ERRORS
```

36

```
DUFF  DROSS   TEASE   SALT
EVEL  RELIT   ALLOY   OLIO
BEAUTYPAGE   GALLEFFORT
TARTARE   HELENA   HETERO
   TROLL   PEND   COTE
FINEST   AHEAD   MALINGER
ATARI  SVEN  SCALED   ILO
KATY  SOAR   AILS   PSAT
ELI  SERGEATARMS   LACTO
ROOMMATE   LAGOS   GATHER
   NAILS   ABRAM   LATEN
SNARLS   BLURT   DISHRAGS
HALLE  PYGMYELOPES   URE
ECHO  CUTE   ASIS   CZAR
ERE  CORERS  SKID  CREST
TEMPLARS   PATEN   SHERPA
   RATS   SOLO   GLUED
ASSERT   SCULPT   ABREAST
TENFARMERS   PENNWINNER
OTOE  EERIE  ELIZA  ZONE
MAWR  EXAMS  RELAY  ANDY
```

37

```
BUMPS   MINUTE   SERFS
OPORTO ONAROLL  TAURUS
ITCOULDBEVERSE  ARMADA
LOAM  SEIZE  IAMBWOMAN
  IDEAL  ARENA  IRENE
ITSSONNETSLASTLEGS
RACED   HATS  OLE  JET
ABARDSEYEVIEW ENCLOSE
QUM  PLENA  OAT  REUSE
  PLAIN GOGOL  SEALED
ASSONANCEWILLHAPPEN
GLOATS  EASEL  YATES
ADULT  FDR  LOONY  LPS
PALMOIL AHAIKUDROPOUT
ESS  RES  ALAI  SACRA
  ITSTHESAMEODESTORY
BASSI  CESAR  TOGAE
IDYLLCHAT  BEIGE  NASH
ERRATA RHYMEDOESNTPAY
REINER  SEMITES  TIESUP
  MADRE  RASSLE  ADELE
```

38

```
REBEC SPAD  BAIT  GLOP
EBOLA AHSO  INTO DRONE
CROWMAGNON  DICK RISEN
SOREAT  ONOR  THESADSAC
  SCRAM  REBA  DEMILLE
MSG HELP  SEALY  WARE
UTEHOSTEL FLOAT  OAST
LONI  TONIC  IOWABUNDLE
LOOPS SHEAF SIMON  EYE
  PAPA  GRIT NICKERED
OTOEBEINENGLAND
CAPSULAR BENE  OENO
HER RETAP  SEMIS TRANS
ERIENOISES TEMPI LITE
FOOD  NIPAT APACHEFOG
  RING LEGUP RHEO SPA
ACETONE LASE  ONCEA
SOSIOUXME HARM ACTIVA
TYSON  TIPS HOPIPASSED
OPENS OREO ETTA KEANE
RUSS  LEWD NOUN EASTS
```

39

```
BIP  EFTS  ITMAY  ATSEA
ESAU NOAH DROVE CHINS
COUNTERMEASURES TECHS
OLLIE TMEN EARTH AKA
MASTERMIND BLT EATEN
ETES AYES ELIS WRENCH
SEN STE FLUS FREER
  CHARTERMEMBER MDSE
MAGOO SIZE EDINA
CLAMOR PINTA LATERAL
COOPTED OZARK MASQUER
GLUEDON YEMEN STUDIO
TRURO IRAS SEISM
ETTE GANGSTERMOVIE
SHIRR OPES SIN OSS
CRAMER SELA TOTE SNEE
AMEBA PSI WATERMETER
SAM GAHAN ARON OCALA
THROE BETTERMOUSETRAP
WEIRD ERIES ALTO SINE
ADAYS TETRA CEOS ODS
```

40

```
SQUATS NONAMES FOSTER
GUNGHO IKEBANA REMOVE
TITHED CLASSIFIEDADAM
STOA ASEA CODERS LANE
  SICKO VANS ANALYST
JUSTSAYNOAM ASONE
ANT UNSEWN ESP TSAR
CLASPS NEWYORKJETSAM
KIRK WASSAIL EON WVA
TROTTED DNA YANKEES
AHUNDREDGRANDAM
HEWLETT OIL MESSAGE
ELI ATO OLEMISS ROLE
FIGHTINGMADAM RATTED
ASIE OST HACKER INA
BASSO FRYINGPANAM
MINIMUM TRUE NOISE
ALES MUSEUM PEWS RSVP
HOWCANTHATBEAM TOATEE
ASTUTE OOHLALA ESTATE
LESSER DRSEUSS REEBOK
```

41

```
BABA  SALUKI  JAPE  PALE
OMAR TIEPIN ARAL EVAN
POSTCEREALS INTERDICT
RESIN NORMANMAILER
SPLAT APT LEEZA SCARY
THELETTERMEN GSA
OISE ROSIES OLDALBUMS
PCS JANETS AVIATE RET
LOVETO ENEMY RASTA
DELIVERANADDRESS KIRI
ERASER NIL AMINOR
AMYL STICKTOITIVENESS
FILED URALS SOMERS
ENO ESTATE CARPAL RFD
NEWISSUES CHAPEL SELA
MCS THECOLLECTOR
SLIME SUAVE SRS RAISE
TERENCESTAMP WILTS
UPANDATIT ITSCANCELED
NETS MANY SATIRE NERO
TREE PEGS ESPRIT ESSO
```

42

```
SHEA SCAD OLDS REPACK
AUSTRALIA WIRE ETALII
LATTEFORDINNER PENPAL
BENSON EGGCARTOON
MACABRE MUM EARNS
AROSE DATASET STA SCI
MIRE BUTENE TELSTAR
MORALFIBBER EPEE COCO
ASA AIMEE OMAR DYLAN
ILOILO EDGER ALLOY
SPRINGFIELDRIFLE
PANED AERIE TITANS
LBARS MULE LUCRE BOO
ANKA HILL TEETHERBALL
SEESRED AGORAE ASIS
MRS OAR SOANDSO SWEDE
ADDIS ATE DEALSIN
SUPPERBOWL STEELY
ETHANE PAINTEDDESSERT
ENACTS ONEA LIONTAMER
DETEST REST LENA DUTY
```

43

```
PROPMAN   ALABAMAN   TROGGS
LARAINE   COLLAPSE   HARARE
IHAVEADREAMTHATONEDAYON
ARNESS  ETNAS  AISLE   LEWD
NAG     SLY        HEAP  STE
THEREDHILLSOFGEORGIATHE
    ELSIE  TUREEN    LED
  SONSOFFORMERSLAVESAND
IOWE   TSP  MOAS  LES  GOOK
CONGAME  TWO  LOGON  GENRE
KNEEPAD     END  TOTAL   PAY
  DDAY   THESONSOF   SEGA
EAU   ROSIE   TIP   SYNERGY
CSPOT  TEPID  CYD  HENREID
KITH  TAG  MARC  EGO   AIRS
  FORMERSLAVEOWNERSWILL
OIL    TRIALS     STAIN
BEABLETOSITDOWNTOGETHER
RAN   OPAL        OAF    ONE
ERIC  ADDUP  ICALL  NUANCE
ATTHETABLEOFBROTHERHOOD
THRASH   ANATHEMA   ERASURE
HYATTS   TATTERED   COLORED
```

44

```
WIGWAGS   NATASHA   HOGAN
AMIABLE   AGATHAS   EVITA
SPAREINTHETRUNK   MAVEN
TENT  MEWS   TIED   ALERT
ENTS  MCI  FOU  SPAN  URE
SDS  MEATFROMHOGS   APES
   BAR   SRA   INSPECT
ENMASSE   OTHER   HITHER
MEANT  VOW  OLES  ARSENE
BULK   INNUMERABLE   GHI
RTES  CAT  PEN  DOT  THAN
ARI  NONAMERICAN   IONS
CANTER  PONE  UTE  PESCI
ELDEST   ODDER   SMARTEN
   INTENSE   LIB   ERS
REVS  GOODTOLOOKAT   SST
AMI  PERM  HBO  NIL  RATE
VIDEO   ALIS   BEST   AREA
AGUAS   PLACEFORSINNERS
GRAVE   SINKSIN   IMOGENE
EELER   TAKESTO   NEMESES
```

45

```
POTOMAC   LADD   CHARMAN
UTERINE   AMOI   MOODIEST
BOARDINGPASS   ENRAVISH
SEMI    SEATASSIGNMENT
   SAVEIT   YET   EES
JAG   BIDS   CARRYONBAG
UPRISE  TAX  TROI  NOLTE
NIECE    DIS   YER   TARA
CABINPRESSURE   SIDEBAR
ONE   THAD   CATO   GEOS
    READYFORTAKEOFF
LIES   SOSO   INRI   QUA
HEADSET   BUSINESSCLASS
ANNI   DUG   ELI   IOTAS
LOANS  PAPA  EXO  MENAGE
FLIGHTPLAN   PHEN   RET
   AWE   UNA   BEASTS
  HOLDINGPATTERN   ABBA
SALIENCE   BAGGAGECLAIM
ALLERGEN   ERIE   ACTUATE
CLAUSES   LIFT   RUSTLES
```

46

```
LOOT   STASI   LEIA   SWOOPS
TENNISMATCHPARTS   KALKAN
HOUSEHOLDANIMALS   ORELSE
ENS  PROCURES  LOMAN  ATE
   POET  SENTBY  CALS  HER
COULD  WKS  EROTIC   NODI
BOBFOSSE    AREA   BEAMON
OLOF  WESTSIDESTORYGANG
ZEE  BOA  THORS   SEDERS
   DANMARINO    EWE   FOG
ARIOSO  WASIN  MARS  ALMA
NEWJERSEYBASKETBALLTEAM
EZIO   ESSE   IRANI  OATERS
WAN  RAN   DINOSAURS
   FOSSAE  GETTO  ESS  GAP
GIVESPERMISSIONTO   ARCS
ANITAS   RASP   ENMITIES
STOA  BIGTOP  AWN  ENIDS
MEL  SLAV  STRATI   JETE
ARE  AEREO  ICESKATE  SRO
INNATE  SHEASTADIUMGROUP
NECKED   ASSUMESOWNERSHIP
STEADS   TOPS   DEMIT  ATOZ
```

47

```
SHEILA   SPAREME   ADAPT
WALLIS   AURORAS   ADAGES
IMEETSANTAMOREANDMORE
GEMSTONE   ADA   DIONNE
   ERA   MANET   OMN
GOCART  TACOS  FRA  NAME
AZAN   FAZE   SUET   ITAL
MANYSTORESENTHRONEHIM
EWE  WANT  SOARS  ALONE
 ASSENT   IMPUTE   KISSER
  CASSINI   NURTURE
WATERY   CARESS   ALONSO
AVANT   PERES   AHAB   URI
SOMEONEMUSTBEJOKINGOR
TIER  ARAT  ALAE   RANK
EDDY  STN  LOMAX  PHAROS
   STU   HEMAN   MAE
  REPAIR   AGA   SIGNPOST
THEYVEBEGUNTOCLONEHIM
SELLER   TAMIAMI   DEPONE
KEYED   ORESTES   ARISEN
```

48

```
PASCAL   ENDUPAT   OPPOSE
APOLLO   COINAGE   WHORLS
REPAST   HURRYUPANDWAIT
   POISON   ATEIN    TEE
AMA  ROO  IVO  DAMPNESS
RANKANDFILE     SOREST
ARKINS   ROLLUPS   ROW
BILL  BANS  NIPANDTUCK
SEEDINESS   SPLATS   TOA
   AMOS  SHIEST  SWEAT
BEFRUITFULANDMULTIPLY
LURES   MESONS    NEIN
ORA   CANAPE   THEGREASE
TOUCHANDGO   ARID   BLUR
   OAR  SENTFOR  SEAMAN
  CHARON   RANTANDRAVE
THETIMES  AAR  CII   YES
ARR    SWARM    THEFTS
COMEOUTANDPLAY   FIESTA
IMAGES   STOLEUP   LOCKER
TENORS   HERESTO   ENTICE
```

49

```
FARER   COALGAS   GRILLS
ADORED  ISRAELI   RUNOUT
MEDICO  THETRILLISGONE
ELICIT  ANET   IDEAMAN
DEN  TOSSPOT  ATLI  SRO
  SEE  THETORNBIRDS
APTER  AID  UNI  ORATE
SOHO  ERR  THEIR  NEARS
SIE  TICKHEADED  BETA
ANT  ADHERES  BADSEED
ICI  PEERED  PELURE  MED
LINGERS  DELIRIA  EMU
SAKI  TINSKINNED  NIP
NERTS  OVATE  ESS  WANT
ARTIE  MES  BMI  LINGO
  HANGBYATHREAD  AND
SAS  TESS  HOTNESS  APB
TRACTOR  LENA  ISOBAR
YOUHAVEMYTANKS  ROMANA
ESTATE  MERCIES  SEABED
SEEDER  VASTEST  DRYLY
```

50

```
SPUD  MADAM  PROW  HARPO
HARI  ORONO  RACY  ALEAN
EISENHOWERSEYES  YEAST
PLATEAUS  RUMBAS  EXGOV
  XIS  EONIAN  SEA
VANBURENSWREN  WHINER
ARIES  OSSA  STRIA  SLO
POPE  MANE  PIZZERIA
IMP  NIXONSNICKS  ETATS
DAYGAMES  NEMESES  NYET
  OBI  ROUEN  AGA
AMMO  CEREBRA  ABBESSES
ROOST  WILSONSWILL  ELL
MONEYMEN  TATE  MAIO
ORR  LORDS  SCAR  ORTHO
REOPEN  COOLIDGESCOUP
  ERR  MARNER  ORA
LASES  MARCIA  PEEKABOO
EGRET  BUCHANANSCANNON
ARONI  EREI  EMEAT  DAZE
HAWSE  SARD  ROUTS  SIEG
```

51

```
HAL  SEWN  HADNT  CITED
IDA  PROA  MARIAH  ASHER
REDBARON  OPIATE  NOELS
ELDER  DAMUP  NUN  ALG
DESERTS  TRITER  SPARKY
  FORT  ANNA  AONE  EAU
EASTWOOD  EMILIO  EARL
ALEE  DCUP  SELLS  BETTE
RECAP  KREBS  EYEDROP
NAUSEA  ELLIE  ABACUS
SSR  CHARLESSCHULZ  MEN
  HIATAL  BATHO  SIMPLE
  TRIBECA  WHANG  LAKER
FLYNN  TURNA  WOOF  KIND
LOBO  MARKER  ROUTINES
ELL  APPL  AMCS  DRAM
AAAUGH  YIPPEE  GYROCAR
  NNE  AHS  UNDER  INONE
ARKIN  LAYUPS  LILFOLKS
RHETT  DIEPPE  LEIF  ALI
MOTES  ARTSY  EFTS  SEN
```

52

```
SAMIAM  IHAVEIT  ALCOA
EMILIA  SALIERI  SHEARS
CALLMYCHILDREN  HEARTH
  LIANA  RIA  HEAVEHO
CLINTTRAPS  CROSSPEROT
HOBO  TRIO  HEPTA
AWAITS  INN  ONE  IGLOO
PERSEUS  CRACKOFRIBS
  CRUMB  YUL  EPAULET
SHOPS  REMAPS  EYE  MIRA
COLA  CLAWBREAKER  ITOR
OMIT  RID  BESTED  JOHNS
REVENUE  AAS  EDUCE
CLINEDRIVES  POTTAGE
HYATT  LIB  MIR  LEANON
  TULSA  ASHE  GOOD
CLAYPERSON  CLOGCABINS
ALSORAN  AHA  ARGON
GAYNOR  CRAVINGLUNATIC
EMENDS  ROLONDA  SURETY
YATES  ICINESS  ESDRAS
```

53

```
SSR  SAHARA  APER  ADS
UTEP  OLEMISS  LULU  REO
RADICALRIGHT  PRESSMAN
FIREUP  ADIEUS  GESTALT
ANODE  FLED  CHE  IONIA
CIV  TADS  ROADRACING
ENE  RIMS  ROOTS  INK
  GREECE  DULUTH  BRUNEI
  RMS  SERINS  COOPERS
EMCEE  UPLAND  LSU  SOL
LAH  DERAIL  RAFAEL  TSE
IRA  IAN  RIOTED  ESSES
AIRMASS  SOMBER  BTU
SOMALI  LAURIE  TATERS
  IRE  INTEN  GENE  ENS
RIFLERANGE  MRED  NAW
ATRIA  LET  NEIN  LATKA
GRANDMA  ONTIME  FAIRER
TIPSIEST  RECOVERYROOM
ADP  NIKE  ACHIEVE  ELIE
GEE  GRAD  HERDED  LLD
```

54

```
BOMBS  IPSA  ♠SODA  LOU♦
EMORY  MOAB  BERYL  ERNS
LADEN  PUMA  YALIE  BEIT
THEACEOF♠S  SONAR  STU
SALK  ITE  HOMING  ACTED
  FARED  LUCS  STEEDS
SARAZEN  BRISK  ETONS
AVAST  THRIVE  ALANS
TENT  EAVES  DOM  ERIE
INK  PALAVER  ♦JIMBRADY
AGE  ABODES  AMUSES  GEE
TESSTRUE♥  GLIDERS  TAL
ESTO  AIR  FLING  LIME
  CEDES  LEVEES  AIMAT
FILES  VINES  MARTENS
SCRAMS  PEND  ROLFE
WHOLE  SANTAS  ITO  ROSE
EEN  RINSE  NIGHT♠ACTS
ERTE  NOSEE  INGE  CLEAT
TIOS  ♠WORK  DOER  ALATE
♥ENS  SENSE  ENDS  RYNES
```

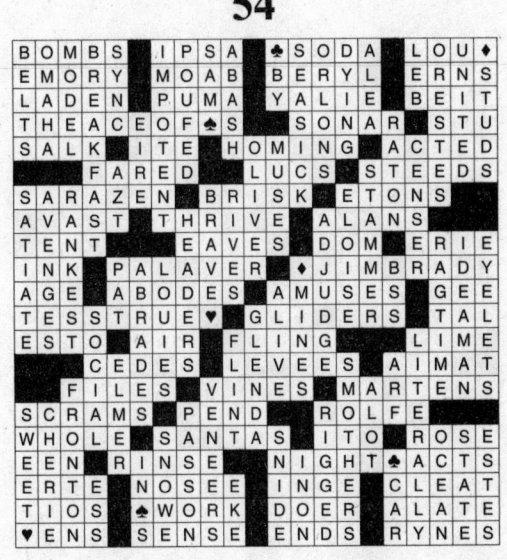

55

```
DIVIDE·ALPINE·MANGLES
EVILER·MARNER·ASCRIBE
MOVERRHYMESWITHHOOVER
IRANI·OSAGE·CURE··SENT
···EDOM··SORB··RENTS··
RIA·ELAM·TMAN··HEROD
ANNO·AGASP·OUTAGE·EMI
ISGROVERHENCEAGROOVER
SILAS·ALTO··LINE··ISNT
EDITS·ATEAM···LABEL
RECOILS·PLAYA·TELSTAR
·REATA···DODGE··ITALO
ATOI·DORA·IYAR··HOPES
DOLOVERSBECOMELOUVERS
ERE·INSOLE·SATUP·ERTE
NIOBE··NELL···AGED·SSS
··IRAQI··YAPS··ONUS··
DAIS··LUSH··TRESS·GLADE
ILLHAVETOTHINKITOOVER
CALORIE·CREASE·SUPERS
KEEPING··HARMED·ETERNE
```

56

```
ASHAMED··COBALT·TARRED
CHARADE··ANOMIE·ORANGE
MONODIC··LOUIEANDERSON
EDDS·TOLL··TENTOONE
··LET··ROSS··SIG··OSOLE
ERE·REUNITES·MOC··TNUT
LEAVESMINUTIAEOUT·ORO
ANOINT··DOES··DRAWMEN
TAUNT·POKY·RTS··TREAD
EMIT·MAMA··TRANSIENT
DEJA·OVERSEAIOUS·TOMA
·AGGREGATE··RUNS··SPAS
ABEAT·ACE··GETS··MOONS
FLOSSIE··HERO··DELETE
ABA·HENRIROUSSEAUOILS
CERF·RIO··SIDEWAYS·AES
ENDUP·GAM··ANAT··EAU
·TRAMROAD··ABCD··ISIT
SEQUOIAEXPERT·RUMMAGE
INURED·RIALTO·OCTAGON
STEAMS··SELLER·WESTERN
```

57

```
DERIDES·ERECTS·MATZOS
OVERAGE·REMORA·AIRING
GETALOADOFTHIS·STYLET
INUSE·SID··EVERS··TLC
TEN·GOFIGURE·WEARIES
·REAGAN·BARETTA·LYONS
··URI··SLUGS·INSTANTS
HANGINTHERE··REDTAG
IRE·PERE··RERAN··AIDA
NIX·PROMS·MAD··SHINED
TOTHE·TAKEAHIKE·ENDED
ASTORS··OLE·GILDA·ODE
TOOL·AMWAY···NERD·OER
··DERAIL··MARKMYWORDS
BESTLAID··MANES··OAR
OMAHA·DESALTS·BUYSUP
POTENCE·CUTITOUT·NRA
·TIL·ANEAR··CPO·LATIN
FIRING·CLEANUPYOURACT
AVENUE··HEEDER·ESCAPEE
BESETS··ORNATE·DUELERS
```

58

```
CARGO·MUSIAL·PAT··ISLE
ROUEN·ORANGE·ERR··SHIV
INTHE·WILLIE·ABE··TUBE
TEHRAN·MAINST·INKSTER
··ILIE··ANG··OUTDO·OLE
STAG·LEMME··ARTE·UVULA
ARG·BELA···CAPER·FETED
LINER·EYESORES·MASSEY
CLOVE·DOGWOOD··TEXT
HOMERS·ROE··NOMAD·INDO
OBER··LEA····ALI··TAOS
WENG·ATLAS·POX·CAUCUS
·LAME··BEGONIA·GREBE
SHEARS·FREEDOMS·HELLO
TILDE·ELUDE··USDA·LEU
RESET·LAZY··TIMER·JESS
ARI·HEINZ··ART··TATE
YANKEES·INDIAN·GIJOES
CROW·RID··EMPLOY·TURBO
ACRO·IOU··WILIER·UNCAP
THEN·ENE··STEALS·SEANS
```

59

```
AGHAS·FRED··SAID··DEFER
LEANT·LONI··PATE··AQABA
INTERRUPTS·INSC·BURBS
BETWEENYOUANDME·SIFTS
IRE·ALG··SLOWED·APRIL
SAD·MAA·SITU··EAT·ODE
·NEXTTONOTHING··AMES
TUBER··RAG··ANTESUP
UTES·CHIP·ABIE··ORES
BOYS·AUK·SARK·CABARET
APO·AFTERTHOUGHTS·FDA
SINGLET·AYES·LEO·DEUX
ADOS··PIED·MARM··ECCE
·QUONDAM···WAD··FATED
BOUT··BESIDEONESELF
APE·TAR·ANON·PGA·SSS
ZESTS·REBIND·OAT·TAW
ANTAE·INBLACKANDWHITE
ATILT·ESAI·UNASSAILED
ROOKS·RULE·TORO·RELEE
SENSE·EELS··STER·EDENS
```

60

```
SPACED··STIES··VASSAR
TENUTA··SPIRAL·AIRLINE
ASEPARATEPACE·LEMONDE
GEM·TEAL··HEALS··GIRL
STINK·NILES·PRO··BASES
·ACONFEDERACYOFDUNES·
··LEIA··DEVO··AMISS··
METERS··SOL··RENT··HES
PANELS··RATIOS·ALCOVE
ACC·THETURNOFTHECREW
THONG·AAA··LEI··SUNNI
RIDEANDPREJUDICE·SIN
ONETWO·IRONON·ACTING
LED·KNOB··WES··STRING
··RECUR··IDAS··EEEE··
THERETURNOFTHENAIVE
SEERS·RIO··NEROS·KNISH
HALE··SANTO··ARAB·CPA
AREARUG·THERUNWAYJURY
MUNDANE·ENCASE·BEANIE
SPASMS··ROOTS··ATBATS
```

61

```
OSCARS  OHMS   ACHES  LOM
SHOWUP  TORI   CHANT  AVA
LAMEBRAINED    QANDA  KEN
ORE  LYNNWOOD  TUNNELER ERN
EDIE  ISR    WILED   NODE
EWOK  FLEET  ITSY    GOFOR
DANWELLS     ERESTU  SERGEI
ARI LOO    EATER  TAMENESS
MET AWN  NEVERFEAR   VIM
HONE  SIDED  ERG   PATS
WORSEN        GRIEFS
COHN  LUC   TBSPS   NEIL
EDO  LIBRARIES   HAD   IDA
NEWSWEEK   ELATE  AMU  FUN
TSETSE    TIGERS  REPRESENT
ISERE  SPEE  SPINS   INGS
LATE  GLAND  EVE   MATA
IFI  CROSSWAY  GLASSEYE  ERR
TIT  PIVOT  WOUNDEDKNEE
ELI  OPERE  PINK   NIECES
RES  SENDS  ANKA   SAGEST
```

62

```
ATLAST     TISHA    LEAFAGE
CHASTE  OSTEAL     ALPACAS
MOTHEROFPEARL      BARRELS
ERE  PERM    MAYI    LIE
    FOSTERPARENT   CRASS
CABANAS  AONE   TORO   FLA
ABODE   NIL    PEARTREES
SNYE  GIBSONGIRLS    EWES
HESITANCE   ARNEL   SAPPY
IRONIES     EMITS   OTRO
NSF  CLOSERELATIVE   IUM
   SAKS   CAROL   SAVANNA
SPURS  BOSON   COLLECTED
IRMA  LITTLEFOXES    READ
DUMBBELLS    UNO    MORSE
ENE ANKA  BANC   AMASSER
SERBS  ONEOFTHEGUYS
    ETS  DUAL   VEST   EFT
MARRIED  BROTHERSINLAW
ABALONE  IDAHOS    EMILIO
REPENTS  ESTEE    DETERS
```

63

```
HAHAS    ICIEST    BARMAN
APITCH   HEATERS   ORIOLE
JETHRO   ALMANAC   AMPULE
   PEEPAT   ODA    ACRID
STARWIREDPARENTSMONEY
WORM   GYROCAR   ICER
ANAIS   OUSE    STANDPAT
MADCONSUMERREPORTSSPY
ILE  OOH   ALE    YAP
   ATSEA  CANOE   BOCCIE
JETTHEATLANTICMONTHLY
EXITED   OUTDO   HUGER
EEG   NCO    NIT    BIT
PREMIEREINTERVIEWTIME
STRESSED   ETTA    OILON
   ROMA   ISRAELI   ELFS
GEORGEDETAILSHOMELIFE
MARIO   CAL    ACACIA
ATTEND  CLAVELL   CONRAD
TOESIN  LIMINAL   SLEDGE
SNATCH  CINEMA    ESSEN
```

64

```
ABCS   GATHER   ODD   BESTS
HARE   AREOLA   SOW   USAGE
ALITTLESOFTSHOE     SCRIP
BIBLEBELT      EARLYSHIFT
    OCALA   BAR   STATE
CHAOS   GUSTS    LORRES
HAUS  FREUDIANSLIP    AXE
ETTE  IOLA   ANTE    PICA
SHO  CLAIMJUMPER    ALLEN
SAMEHERE  ELATE   MARLS
USERS   MUNRO   NGAIO
SIFTS   TODAY   TUESDAYS
ASFAT  MOVIESHORTS   DEL
HULS  GALE   URSA   ATNO
IZE  YELLOWJACKET   NITA
BURGOO  NOVAK    PAEAN
RURAL   NSA    EASEL
BOXINGRING    SALARYCAP
AMONG  CLASSACTIONSUIT
ROUGE  HTS  STAMEN   ETNA
MOTOR  YSL  SERENE   SSTS
```

65

```
LABELS    FOILS    MANAGED
ARAMIS    SUNSET   IMPROVE
PALEST    THELORDSPRAYER
SMARTS  ORCA  AUEL    BARN
   AGE  ELMAN   PERES
WOMENSWEARDAILY      EATS
AWS  TENN  ANS    REDONE
FLAPPER   WAR    CORONER
TESTERS   SHEPHERDSPIES
TSAR  BAER  ALOE    TORE
    MRSOLEARYSCOW
COME  AMOI  THEE    HEMA
APOSTLESCREED     CHERUBS
REDTAPE   USA    LATERAL
PREACH  PTS   ROAR   PSU
AMBO  WHISTLERSMOTHER
   SCOOT   OASIS   PRY
SPAS  ROTA  THEO   SEISMO
AROOMOFONESOWN     INPLAY
CONFINE   INURES   TULANE
SWEATER   CAPED    SPEWER
```

66

```
ASTIR   MASSE  LOTUS   EMBAR
MYRNA   AMAHL  ARENT   FOLIO
IRISHSYMBOL    KINDOFTHUMB
SILT  HOARD   ENCORE   ARAB
SALINA  NADER   GENES   ITTY
   GORE   ITEM    NESTOR
SALADINGREDIENT     EDSELS
PRET  DOTS  DAU   SARI  DAH
ATTEND  BETA   RAMON   UTICA
NOT  OASES  SLANGFORMONEY
GOSIGNAL  III  CRANE   LASS
   SOAP   SANTE    YARE
APSO  NINTH  GAS   IMMATURE
VILLAGECOMMON   ONSET   BON
ONEAL  NOWAY   KILN   RAGOUT
ITE  ACTS  ELS   NEED  EASE
ROTATE  PLACEFORAPUTTER
   CENSER   RAGE    BEGS
MARC  TAMAR  MOREL   SHAMES
OMAR  ELITES  INLET   HOLA
LIMEOROLIVE    COLOROFENVY
DEBTS  MINER   PRAYS   RADII
SLOES  EAGLE   ASIDE   IDEST
```

67

```
SHAPED   PIMPLES   MAITAI
CENTRE   OCARINA   AUBURN
OXTAIL   WERELIVINGINAN
TIE CELEB   GEM   EDAM
INCA TELEGRAM   PARES
AGEWHENLEMONADEISMADE
 DEEDS RACY  ADD   LAY
REIN    BYE    SLAVE
TANG OAK RATA  SECEDES
WITHARTIFICIAL   VEX
ADS ALFREDENEUMAN  BEE
 PRO INGREDIENTSAND
REGIONS DEBS  STS  TKOS
OCEAN  HAS      GOES
ORO ROI OLAV  CHARD
FURNITUREPOLISHISMADE
 GOBEL ASSENTED  SLOB
LESE DAR  TAXIS  APB
WITHREALLEMONS NESSIE
HOTOIL PAROLEE GASKET
ONEWAY OPENERS SMEARS
```

68

```
BRACE HASH  ALVA  MELON
ROLLS ELSA  DOER  ALOFT
ABOUTFAITH JUNIORMYTH
 BEEHIVE  USEDUP
 SEVEN  CIDER  SLAPON
AFB TEA BONG  ALTEREGO
NORBERT ALDENTE  MELD
SLUR HANOI YEAS  AWES
ALTA DISGRACE PAINED
ROADHOGS NOTA  LODE
AWL ACHE ITO SHOW WBA
 FIST SASH SUMATRAN
POMPOM GRUESOME AERO
SOUP ROBO MECCA  CARD
TORA ALGEBRA NECKTIE
INTIMATE NEIN WOO HOS
RAHRAH ANTRE  ARSON
 ROSCOE  WAIKIKI
DEADLYTHIN PLAINTHONG
ENDUE LEST EXIT OINKS
WOOZY OSEE PITH PLAYA
```

69

```
DANCERS ACT SKEE  PUB
ATEALOT PERSONAL POPE
MEATLOAFPLATTERS OILS
NATS DYER COHEN APSIS
 MOES SWEETKISS STONE
 YUP HOSES  SHANKS
ARDENT ZEN  CAMERA
BAR SALON POLICESTING
STICH IND HOSTEL ROM
 FRAPPE DANTE LASSOS
ETUDES VINAS RECOUP
FLEXED FACTS MADCAP
OIR ARISTO TIS UPPER
BOSTONCREME ETHOS LEE
JUNTAS ANT JEKYLL
SCORES THORN  SON
UHURA FREEBREAD FIBS
MOREL LETAT SPED TOCK
MINT HEARTASSOCIATION
ICES SETASIDE COMESTO
TEY TRAS NIE ARIDEST
```

70

```
DERMAL THECARS  REGAL
ARTURO RESOLED VOLARE
PRESSCLIPPINGS AXILLA
 COHORT FIR ALY OED
MILAN LEOI CABLE SONE
ICET IAM GLOBETROTTER
CODERS EGIS  LEICA
ANGLERS OVALS RETREAD
HOE CALLLETTERS ADALE
REDEYED SYNE PLUGIN
ISLA LEASH RABBI SLAY
MAITAI STUB TERNATE
ANNEX STATEPOLICE SSW
STERILE RULER CURACAO
INAWE IPSO ROCOCO
TELEGRAPHKEY MAL CURE
AXIS ARIAN SAID RETAR
MPG LID VOS  STAKES
TIEDIN PATRIOTMISSILE
ARRIVE ANTOINE WIENER
MESSY SASSIER INSANE
```

71

```
INFO TREY BASAL PITHS
LOIN HAMM ADELA ATOOT
ERLE EPIC BURLS SANTO
DAIS FILADELFIAPHLYER
ESP RODE ORTS GRASSLE
 PEERS PIUS  RNAS
 HINDU SANT MAAM EFG
FANTOMPHIGHTERS STIEB
EVERS EENS OLE  YALTA
REP EIRE SRO PORTIAS
RAHS FOTOPHINISH SPRS
UGLIEST DUE NYSE TAE
LOADS NIL BOAC NOHIT
EAGLE FYSICALPHITNESS
 TSE BEET ABIT GRIPE
 BRAT OLEO  SNATH
STAREAT MILL ATOP OAS
PHRENCHFILOSOFER RUBY
RELEE ELLEN VIVA IRAN
IREST REARM ERIN OTTO
GENES SENSE NEET SHED
```

72

```
OFFHAND  DEFOG  SELES
REAIRING DENOVO EXULT
BRITISHRAINCOAT DAMME
 RASE EDDO TLC UMBER
SHA TIGERSTEESHOT ERN
TAMPA UNITED  ACTER
ALOU REP SAD  TONJON
ROUT FUR FELICE CAGE
KEN KOS CARLIGHT ACER
STEEN GOBI EEE ASKED
MYTHREESONSROLE
RUMPS OER BRET GODWE
OPAL BLACKEYE ART UVA
ETNA REVERE USE INOR
GOINTO ERA ANY CDLI
 CERTS FRESCO REEVE
TRU AHAUNTEDHOUSE RES
HIRED UNE VIER ISAK
AGILE CHAYEFSKYSATIRE
NOSIR EATERY SEALANTS
ERTES SPORT SLEDDED
```

73

```
ROOSTS  FINKS  CACHET
ANXIOUS INANE  AIRHOLE
MEETMEINSTPERIOD LOUIS
SAY  MAKE  SANK  OUSTS
MESAS  HERES  SID  TIE
EXES  IDEST  EMBOSS
HELPEXCLAMATIONPOINT
AVOID  YEWS  DRAPER
DIVA  BLTS  SKEET  DIAS
OLE  OULU  TEAR  BROWNE
NOBODYAPOSTROPHESFOOL
ENURES  DAHL  LOTT  JFK
SEGA  AGERS  DEBS  HIFI
TAPIRS  SAAB  SUMER
QUOVADISQUESTIONMARK
BUMRAP  SAUNA  TRIP
RIP  AAH  ACHED  APSES
AXIOM  MAAS  OWEN  LIP
SORRYCOMMAWRONGNUMBER
STEERER  BRISK  SOMEONE
YESMAN  ISLES  GALWAY
```

74

```
HASTO  SPAR  GAZA  BASTE
ALTER  PELE  REED  ISOUR
ROAST  CATS  ACEOFCLUBS
PUTTERAROUND  EYELET
EGO  REE  MEECE
SUNDAYDRIVER  BALLPARK
UNO  SEABED  GARNI  VIE
MINCE  PREYSON  POSTAGE
STEAL  PET  BAAL  TALON
VIA  CRISPUS  LORE
WEARINGOFTHEGREEN
SEHR  ENNEADS  SAN
ARENA  SEES  TIA  STATE
DOESNOT  STUDENT  ESSEX
ADZ  CLOSE  NEARTO  SAT
TEESHIRT  MISSINGLINKS
TOVES  AOK  ROD
SAFARI  INTOTHEWOODS
IRONMAIDEN  OLIO  CIVET
MAIZE  DELL  PENN  ADELA
IMEAN  IFFY  SOAK  LONER
```

75

```
ROTATE  SEWARD  ART  MOE
UNISEX  TRIVIA  LEOTARD
BULLETSESSION  OPPOSED
ESE  PEAT  EATS  TACITLY
FIEND  LUTE  PALE
WAITED  SUPERMANET  RBI
ERSE  SMUG  IBAR  SPAN
SCHMO  OLAF  SLAG  DCLIV
PUNKROCKET  BERATE
EDB  ISAY  SHIRE  REINER
LEARNED  STUDS  PEPPERS
ECLAIR  SPEND  SOAS  TSE
VOLVOS  MARKETTIME
AREIN  MARS  DARN  ADMAN
TUTS  TICS  RATS  EASE
EMO  JUNKETFOOD  CHALKY
FRAN  ALIT  LAURA
OFFICES  AMIN  SEND  MTA
TRIPODS  RACKETANDRUIN
RAREBIT  ALKENE  ELATED
AYE  INS  LEADEN  REMEDY
```

76

```
SEETHE  BREWED  MISDEALS
ALTHEA  AEROSOL  INTENTON
WINIFREDWINKLE  CREATURE
SEAN  LILAC  LATHER  OBIE
LOGOS  MTOSSA  NAM
ELIZABETHBOOP  PENUMBRAE
RANOVER  IRR  LOME  ENG
RYNES  PATOIS  SMU  TBAR
ALAS  STEVENCANYON  AHOLE
TOT  RUINERS  CYRUS  ZEROS
AWESOME  KRAUS  TANGS
WOODROWWOODPECKER
HADIT  INEED  RECTORS
ELOPE  OCTAL  TAILORS  PEI
ACTED  CHARLESBROWN  DELE
LOTS  CAP  SNEAKS  MINOR
EVE  KNUR  DTS  STENTOR
REDGUARDS  JOSEPHPALOOKA
AER  TENURE  RAINS
ENOL  REREAD  SORTA  GEAR
PANORAMA  BARNABASGOOGLE
OPERATIC  SINUSES  ENVIED
SERENELY  CATERS  ROSSES
```

77

```
TOTEM  TONYAS  LOAND
ECOLES  SWEEPEA  MURRAY
THEYDOPENDANTS  APIECE
ROSSINI  REAP  NINERS
CINCINNATIBANGLE
HEW  CEASES  ROTE
OSHEA  LAI  OBESE  SEAL
SAINTNECKLACE  SEEPAGE
PUTTIES  SLEEPY  MORAN
ESTATES  CARA  ASTRID
RAW  THELOONYPIN  INS
ADAGIO  RUTH  SANDMAN
DATED  POIROT  SMUGGLE
INCLINE  CALAMITYCHAIN
OOHS  INGES  SOO  HAITI
ALTE  STANCE  DAD
BIRDSANDTHEBEADS
MINEOS  TREE  RIPOSTE
ELTORO  LOCKETORLUMPIT
OBRIEN  ESTEVEZ  ENRAGE
WOOLS  SALEMS  KITES
```

78

```
ACDC  AMATI  MALICE  HAG
RAIL  DELON  ALSTON  ERR
MRDEEDSGOESTOTOWN  RIO
ANITA  RALES  BOPEEP
BANANA  ATMOS  DEBACLE
SERUM  ILIAC  FELLTO
CASPER  CLARKGABLE  MAI
AVE  LEVEE  AMAS  BERN
MEND  GARYCOOPER  GESTE
PRIORESS  OUTER  CORTEZ
COUNT  CHITS  SLOTH
CHALET  BLADE  SHEPHERD
HONED  JEANARTHUR  AGEE
ANDY  BOAC  IONIC  RAW
TKO  FRANKCAPRA  CAJOLE
LAREDO  ALLOT  ROOMY
ANDREWS  INDUS  HAREMS
BELIES  DOYEN  KABOB
AGA  ITSAWONDERFULLIFE
TEC  NETMAN  EMITS  ORAL
EVE  GREENS  RUSSE  WAXY
```

79

```
GADGET  CUSPS   BOBTWAY
AMARNA  ARIANA  AVERAGE
TIMOTHYHUTTON   LINESUP
   SWOON   TRINI   APES
BOSSIER   TEETH   HYDE
ELLEN  EDWARDALBEE  TIM
REESE   ERIN    ERASURE
RIP  BARE  SHA  DESALES
ACTOFLYING  ALPES  RANA
   BATES  ARTOO  VANES
   FEN  SIGNATURE  ENT
SLURS   VOGUE   KANGA
TALL  SUEDE  REPROACHES
OBLIGES  SSW  TILT  IDO
NEONATE   ARTE   ATTIC
ELF  MIDDYBLOUSE  CROCK
LIEN   SAULT   DOCENTS
TEEN   LORNE   MINUS
ABALONE  DYNAMITESTICK
TAKENIN  SADDER  NELLIE
INSTEPS  NASTY   DRESSY
```

80

```
SNAPBEAN  SHAD  HADAFIT
LENAOLIN  LUXE  OPALINE
OBDURATE  ARISTOPHANES
BRALESS  ONTOPOF  LISZT
   FOOT   OLDSMOKEY
PAT  NIMBLE  TYRES  ABE
SHED  CLAIROL  OSLO  REX
SORE  SIDESLIP  POPEYE
TYPEA   ABOVE   TEAOR
   IMPALA  AVERAGE ISNT
BBC  TRUEST  LESAGE  ODS
LETA   CLOTHES   EDGEIN
AFUSS   UNDER   KNAVE
MORAYS  SNOWPEAS  TBAR
ERE  NEAR  SOILAGE  OLIO
DES  CANIT  NASALS  ENS
   MYDIGNITY   LEWD
OMITS  BENEATH  OSTEOID
DANIELORTEGA  PROTRUDE
EXALTED  ESEL  ENFEEBLE
AINTHAY  DELL  DEFEATED
```

81

```
MEALPLAN  SHASTA  SEEST
ANNERICE  TECTUM  ELMER
READONESFORTUNE  REEVE
IMHOME  TIM  PAX  OGRES
MIENS  TOBACCO  ITAINT
BEI  PAR  CHARS  FONTAL
ASMARAN  SHOWSUPINTIME
   RAW  LISPS  DEMI
SAMSNEAD   CAT   NONCE
SELFPERCEPTION   MALI
EXCUSES  MEARA  SPEEDER
REEL   LARGERTHANLIFE
BREST  PIN  SHELTERS
   HTEN  ALLEY  LET
JETPROPULSION  MARSHES
AGREED  SITES  CIS  EVA
MOANED  MINERAL  DALEY
ATBAY  GTO  SUN  PETERS
IRENE  RIGHTONTHEMONEY
CIRCA  AREYOU  BALINESE
APTER  DESPOT  EYETESTS
```

82

```
SEEMS  TRY  LOFT  TSETSE
TACIT  WEE  INOR  SHALES
YSHNIKOVSBECUE  RERENT
ETOILE  MODELSHIP  TSE
   VENTRAL  USES  TAR
METES  RUNT  PEATIEST
ICER  SIN  ORGS  RENNIE
ERA  MLVI  NYU  ATREST
NUMSGAINS  MIDIS  PLOPS
   YMCA  TOOTIN  STANCE
ATTN  KLEYSRACUDA  VEST
SHOCKS  ALPERT  OBOE
PEKOE  STIRS  ASTENDERS
   SPIRES  EOS  HART  RAH
ACETIN  SYNE  IRS  CITE
LASHEDAT   CORD   MACES
SLR   SEGA   ONESTOP
OHO  ABRASIONS  OPIATE
RELATE  THOLDISOMETERS
TREMOR  HELL  DOW  DORIS
AESOPS  ASEA  EYE  SLOPE
```

83

```
OSHA  CASA  CARD  HELP
CHESS  ALUM  OMNIA  AQUA
THEHOUSENOWLEANS  PUNY
   PANT  BEALS  EYELIDS
MARIMBA  OBIE  PRONE
ORATION  WATCHYOURSTEP
PODS  SES  TAR  OSHEA
EMO  NOTHINGSLEVEL  ELS
RANSOM  AMIR  EXAM  ERES
ALIS  KILO  SIGNORE
RBIS  LOTSOFROT  LOOS
ROOMERS  MOOD  SERF
EMUS  IANS  ERTE  HAMLIN
HAN  ANTATTRACTION  ESO
ENDER  IER  SNO  LAST
MOSTLYOFWATER  STROKER
   HOOPS  IRMA  TOOTSIE
SYRINGE  SPEED  AUTH
LAIC  INDUSTRIALTHATIS
ALDA  SEIZE  GAOL  SIENA
PEEL  RAYS  ELKS  RENT
```

84

```
FRACAS  CHARISMA  FRAS
LOCALE  DECAMPED  COUNT
ENTRANCERAMPAGE  PUNTA
ANI  SNO  DEAN  WALTER
SYN  KENTS  SLOUGH  LODE
GNAT  EMCEE  NEE  IHAD
AMOUNT  NIAS  CHET  NITA
LAUDS  BDRM  NOON  REMET
BYTE  MEEK  POOLAREA
AHA  LIAR  RASPY  HIGHS
NEGROS  FAUVISM  ONEOUT
MEOWS  OILER  EONS  ORE
   CLAMORED  ASHE  OVEN
TALKY  ITER  MUSS  CREST
ACAB  GLAD  VIDA  CHARTS
KABA  LEG  SELIG  HELD
EDEN  ERECTS  SERAC  ALA
FELDON  HATS  IRK  MAX
IMEAN  CRITICALMASSAGE
VIRGO  RELEGATE  DIGGER
EASE  OPERETTA  ENTERS
```

85

```
PAST  NEON    FOOL    HAGS
AGEE  EATUP   OSLO  DALAI
WHENIPRONOUNCETHEWORD
SANDMAN   USDA  SUCKERS
   EELS  SNEER    BEE
LARA   PICAS  DERIDING
SILENCEIDESTROYIT  CUL
ENID  AXEL   OURS  MITA
EEN  LITERATURE  DIETS
PRETTILY  ECONO  HENRYS
    RACE  SCROD  POCO
INDIGO  MOTET  PUBORDER
SOAPS  POLISHBORN   OVO
LITE  ROLE   OLIO  CEOS
ASE  WISLAWASZYMBORSKA
MESSAGES  ESTOP   RATE
   ADS   DELOS  FDIC
AGENDUM  APOP  RANKLES
NOBELPRIZEWINNINGPOET
ATALE  EDER  NONET  OLGA
TONY   DADS  BEDE  TASS
```

86

```
NEVER  ABAFT  PLAT  MAT
AVILA  REWORK  NINAFOCH
BASIE  ALOSER  INSTANCE
 NAH  BALDMOUNTAINDEW
NEBULA  IONS     NIPA
OSIRIS  CYCLONE  SLEETS
ACLOCKWORKORANGECRUSH
MELO  FILS    DORM
   TWOTO  LABS  SASHAYS
GILBERTGRAPENEHI  ALEA
ADMEN  NOMINAL   PILLS
RENE  FREDANDGINGERALE
POORBOY  ERGS  CERIC
   EGAN   GIBE  RUSS
THEMAGNIFICENTSEVENUP
ROSERY  LOCULUS  TEAZLE
ARCA    TETE   SEMITE
IMOGENECOCACOLA   SPR
LORRAINE  ARTHUR  HOPIS
ENTERSON  PURINA  ADELA
RES  LIST  GOODY  LADYS
```

87

```
SADISM  ECLAT  SHIP  CAB
AGATHA  ARESO  EASE  ANA
LIFTOPERATOR  ANAPESTS
ALF  PLANTMANAGER  ATIE
DEY  PER  EEK  NUS  GRIGS
   WESTER   GAL  WALNUT
MFA  HASABALL   AMIGA
WELLDAYS  IAGO  KNEED
IRITIS  TARRAGON  WRIT
FIG  SYR  NET  AIDA  RAM
EDH  COURTREPORTER  ERA
YET  JUNE  NAY  SAD  CPI
NATO  GLANDULA  TEUTON
 TECHS  FEEL  JOHNSONS
STAKE  CLERICAL  ERS
SHEREE  HAD  OXIDES
TANGY  POM  ONE  VIS  CAN
EDDA  MAKEUPARTIST  RIO
REASSURE  STOCKANALYST
ERN  ALOU  MIMEO  ETOILE
OST  YELP  ACIDS  YENNED
```

88

```
CADGE  SAHL   BOTHA  CHUMP
ADORE  OBOE  TABOOS  LANAI
MA NOV ERBOARD  WHENLI FEB EGINS
PLAYOUT  SAGE  RID  RAMONA
YENS  THEE  ALMOST  IVANA
   STEAL  SVEN   HELEN
EDDIE  D AUG HTER  METER JAN ET
PR OCT OR  SHEA  LE MAY S  EGGO
EMOTED  RNA  OTOE   PALER
TIRESOME  KNISH  QUAVERY
ENES  ORDER  TATAS  SPED
RED  MAR DIGRAS  MINT JUL EP  NRA
DILL  YEMEN  TEPID  BEAR
WORRIES  MOXIE  SAUTERNE
ONION  C APR IS  PXS  PRAVDA
NUNN  RITE  HAHA  ONERS
TSK  PLACE  DRAGON  PUSSY
   PROMO  TEAL  UNSET
STEER  THEYRE  SEP ALS  LIMA
SWEDEN  TIE  IDOL  ITHACAN
HANDMA DEC ARPET  CA JUN COOKING
OBELI  CREEPY  ANTE  SELES
ESTEE  ATSEA   STAR  TRYST
```

89

```
SUCCEED  SHEATHS  ADLIB
ISRAELI  LUMPIER  MAINE
FEELLIKEAMILLIONBUCKS
TUT  SENT  NEER  ALBEIT
SPECK  DEFEND  STE  NEB
  HITE  ONT  LOUD  SSE
WHENIMSIXTYFOUR  JETT
TAO  SPEEDY  EUREKA
ELM  KOREA  DALI  INCUR
ALE  IFS  MIMOSA  TERRA
BARS  FORTYNINERS  TICK
ACUTE  NEARED  MER  CHI
GENES  AMAD  CLARA  KIN
 ASHARP   GOODEN  ENG
BRED  ONEARMEDBANDITS
REV  BUDD  IAN  SERT
ENE  ERS  CONTRA  YACHT
AERIAL  DOTH  ALEE  ROI
TWENTYFIVEORSIXTOFOUR
HASTE  OVERLAP  ECLIPSE
ELTON  BASSETS  CHEESES
```

90

```
RAISE  ILSA  ACURA  AFAR
OMNIA  NEED  LANES  HUME
POURSOVERASCRIPT  ALBS
ERS  EBERT  POT  ROI  LII
DEE  DIRE  EAVE  INDUCED
   JUSTDESSERTS  INONE
STRIP  SAM  SRA   BATS
WEIL  STATUS  ULSTER
ANGLICAN  DIT  TONS
NAH  BRIDALPATH  ORDERS
ENTREE  LOGIC  KISMET
ETTORE  WASASHOEIN  ECO
 OLIN  IST  MONORAIL
BLASTS  BENING   ALTE
SCAB  REA  AGE  ASSES
CARAT  URBANGORILLA
OVERRAN  SSTS  ANIL  DAG
TIA  ETC  TIE  SPATE  ONE
TART  BAZAARHAPPENINGS
IRMA  ATEIN  ALEE  DANES
ESSE  TEENS  MART  ENERO
```

91

```
SCAPE   STRUNGUP  SINGLE
ADMAN   TEARINTO  PAIRED
BRILLIANTBLUESMANKING
ROTE  GIST  ESSEX    FIE
EMERALD  ASS    SHAFFER
    MIO  BIT  KAI  ALLENS
AUTOMOBILEJOCKEYFOYT
BSA  ISLA  LURKER
DOVES  INCASE  SESSILE
USER  INCA  TSP  PADOVA
CHRISTIANSCHOLARLEWIS
TONNES    TEA  RELY  ABCS
 WASTAGE  SULKED  PLATE
  ATEASE  REEL  LET
 WARPEDCOMEDIANFIELDS
POLEAX  HEE  TNT  FEN
ROTATES    GOT  ROSTERS
ADE    TRASH  OVER  ISEE
YARDAGEATTAINERTITTLE
TREATY  MAINMENU  BLEED
ODDMEN  STRAPSIN  NESTS
```

92

```
PLACID   SCUSI   ULULATE
AURORA   WAVER  PEMOLINE
SNOOKYOOKUMS  BABYFACE
SAUL   SPOIL   GENRE  RAL
ATSIX  INNAMORATA  SASE
DIEOF  NEG  ERATO  CHEER
OCS  IBID  ANDYS  SHODDY
    OLEO  ARTE  CIAO
SOTHERN  DEARHEART  VOW
PHRASE  OVAL  ARF  STILE
UBER  TUBES  GRIEF  ANDA
NONET  TON  CAPE  RINGER
KYD  SWEETLOVE  LANGTRY
    MAYS  AMER  UNDO
ASPIRE  TAMIL  BCCI  DAR
LEAKS  LILAC  ARE  CHIVE
INRE  SUGARSUGAR  TUPAC
GIS  LUCRE  PAINE  BORA
HONEYPIE  LITTLEDARLIN
TRIPLETS  ETHEL  APIECE
 SPHERES  GEESE  MESSES
```

93

```
LORCA   BATHER   SCOUR
AVERSE  ARRIVE  SHERPAS
MEMOIR  CRANED  TABASCO
BROWNRICE  DRAKEHUNTER
DATS   CHAS   ITS   AMA
ACE  AUBURNTUFTS  EDGER
 TRUISMS  ARNIE  VARESE
  NRA  GROWN  SITE
BELIEF  CRETE  SPRAWLS
BLOOD  FEED  DELLA  QUIT
LION  LADE  SAIL  UNDO
SASS  IRATE  ATIT  SEALS
 SEMINAR  MAVEN  THERES
  ILED  RIVER  ERN
PECTIN  FILER  ARRESTS
ALOHA  LIBERTYBARD  REP
CAN   SER   SOON   LAVA
KINGSTEMPLE  DUKERIDER
UNOILED  HOLDEN  NATURE
PETROLS  AGEOLD  ASHCAN
 SEDGE   RECESS   HEELS
```

94

```
LOGE   MUSTS   SEWS  ELLA
TYROL  ABOIL  ALEC  FOIL
OCALA  NOLTE  BALI  FLEA
RENDS  DAVIDGOLDFIELD
NEGOTIATE  FIT  SINN
   DINT  DURAN  UDALL
DIRECTER  OLDGOLDSIDES
IDEO  ODEUM  SESAME  IST
KOLN  ATIP  SERI  ONES
ELI  BHUTANI  ETCH
 CATONAHOTGOLDROOF
  BUNS  OLEOOIL  AGA
NAGS  CEST  NANO  GROG
ERA  OHAIRS  DORIS  OGRE
HIYOGOLDAWAY  ANTELOPE
IDEAL  EDENS  DYAD
 KEYS  ELO  POWERBOAT
GOLDANDOLDLACE  HEINE
NOVA  LOAF  YENTL  ALLIN
ANEW  TOFF  NODAL  RLESS
PENN  APTS  EGADS  TYRE
```

95

```
AGRA   SWAMI  GONER  SCAT
SLOB   SEWER  ALAMO  THRU
HOPEDREAMS  LIVIA  REIN
CRETE  DIP  OVALS  ELSE
AIR  BLYTHESPIRIT  ASTI
NASSAU  SILT  ERA  IMEAN
  PRIG  SARTRE  ASIA
TIDY  GAP  NOR  TWANGER
RBI  DISSEDHILLARY  RCA
AERIE  RYN  SPOOKY  DALI
IRENE  ACDC  SOLE  CUMIN
PICK  ONHOLD  PIT  OOMPH
SAT  ALGORERHYTHMS  ASA
ENLARGE  FYI  AAA  FRET
 YWCA  ONSITE  TUTU
ESTES  TVA  NIPS  VERBAL
TWOA  THEBIGTIPPER  IRA
HOYT  ERROL  SEE  SASSY
NOAH  SEIKO  SOCKSESSES
ISLE  TACOS  ADIEU  KENO
CHER  STEVE  GEESE  STEN
```

96

```
COULD   DACHA  OPERA  TBSP
OSTEO   ETHAN  PAPAL  HEIRS
ICIER   TBIRD  EROSE  AGGIE
LACKEDHANDSONEXPERIENCE
SRA  NERTS   BEVY   ESTEEM
    COS  ISERE  BON  STDS
TRADEIN  STOL  FLOE
WASUNDERCAPITALIZED  PAM
APIECE  HALS  ALENE  ALAMO
STALE  CORY  SPEND  DROPIN
    IAN  STEPS  COINAGE
RUBBEDPEOPLETHEWRONGWAY
ENRAGES  RIATA  HAM
SCOURS  FALLS  SAAB  TISCH
ELIDE  MATEO  AMIR  NICOLO
TEL  TALKEDMYSELFOUTOFIT
 LIED  OILS  UNSNAPS
EMIL  LID  TRUST  ETC
SONATA  SEAT  ELSIE  BAH
QUITWHENPUSHCAMETOSHOVE
UNTIE  LOATH  ARECA  SINAI
EDINA  ALCOA  PARTY  ELGIN
 SOAK  NOEND  ABYSS  STOLE
```

97

```
HOHUM FANJETS RUBITIN
AROSE STEAMUP INARAGE
WILMA THERITEOFSPRING
HODAD OED SCALED LIL
ALI SPINES ITER STE
WENTAT STREAMERS EPIC
GULLET INTERS CLINT
SPANIEL ACTON DOINGS
PETEFOUNTAIN ALONE
ORBS SOW NEWGATE OTC
USA MAITAI SHAPES CAR
TEY LIVORNO ENA BENE
ELLEN FLORALSPRAYS
METRES CADRE MARINAS
AXONS CHACHI FANONS
RPMS POOLTABLE TWEETS
LOW RAUL TIERRA LAW
ONO BASSOS AMI ADELA
WELLINTENTIONED RAVEL
ENFORCE MANNING IRENE
STEALER ENTENTE DENTS
```

98

```
SCATHE MARSALA SMEW
ARNHEM CAROUSAL APISH
WATERMOCCAPRIDE MISSY
SWIT ARCHIE DEFENSES
OLGA ILED LBS OBOLS
FEU ASIT MOO BRAZO
FRANKCOVETOUSNESSATRA
EARN HUDSON HUT
MAPLE THINMAN GURGLE
MINT CANTO ETALIA
ENGULF UNGLUES LEVINS
KEENER AUTRE INGE
ORRERY RIMSHOT COOKS
NAG DONATE FALL
GLUTTONYDBADTHESAILOR
LEONA ROI REEK URE
VALSE DAB GOLD GRIN
FIRESALE ARMIES AKEE
ARISE ENVYGAPORESLING
DETER ATOMIZES TRENTE
SOYS HEXANES HINGED
```

99

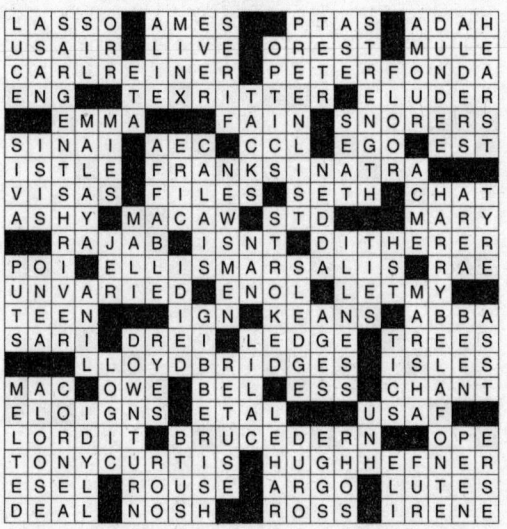

```
PRADO BRAVADO GRAHAM
TREMOR RECITED LATINO
SOFARIHAVENTMADEITFIT
UPSTAGED NEO RETAIL
DIX SWISS ACT
SAILON FLEET AWL DARK
PINE SOAR ALOU AMON
IMPOSITIVEITCANBEDONE
RAU OTOE MACS GARDE
OTTOMAN SPACEK GEISEL
CELESTE ONAGERS
SHEEHY WISEST UNITING
MARLO ENTS ASIA NEA
AHNOWIVEGOTITTHISISIT
LAST CATO TROY SEGO
LSTS ENS STEAM SLATER
API SEAMY ATO
DEBRIS CAT OPERETTA
MERRYCHRISTMASEVERYONE
REDOAK COOLANT INGRID
SPAWNS ANNETTE EASEL
```

100

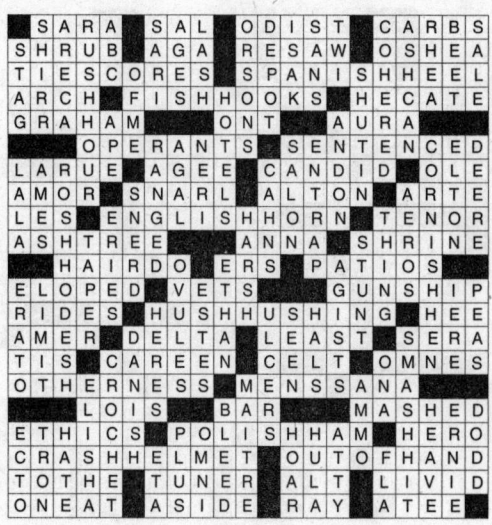

```
SARA SAL ODIST CARBS
SHRUB AGA RESAW OSHEA
TIESCORES SPANISHHEEL
ARCH FISHHOOKS HECATE
GRAHAM ONT AURA
OPERANTS SENTENCED
LARUE AGEE CANDID OLE
AMOR SNARL ALTON ARTE
LES ENGLISHHORN TENOR
ASHTREE ANNA SHRINE
HAIRDO ERS PATIOS
ELOPED VETS GUNSHIP
RIDES HUSHHUSHING HEE
AMER DELTA LEAST SERA
TIS CAREEN CELT OMNES
OTHERNESS MENSSANA
LOIS BAR MASHED
ETHICS POLISHHAM HERO
CRASHHELMET OUTOFHAND
TOTHE TUNER ALT LIVID
ONEAT ASIDE RAY ATEE
```

101

```
LASSO AMES PTAS ADAH
USAIR LIVE OREST MULE
CARLREINER PETERFONDA
ENG TEXRITTER ELUDER
EMMA FAIN SNORERS
SINAI AEC CCL EGO EST
ISTLE FRANKSINATRA
VISAS FILES SETH CHAT
ASHY MACAW STD MARY
RAJAB ISNT DITHERER
POI ELLISMARSALIS RAE
UNVARIED ENOL LETMY
TEEN IGN KEANS ABBA
SARI DREI LEDGE TREES
LLOYDBRIDGES ISLES
MAC OWE BEL ESS CHANT
ELOIGNS ETAL USAF
LORDIT BRUCEDERN OPE
TONYCURTIS HUGHHEFNER
ESEL ROUSE ARGO LUTES
DEAL NOSH ROSS IRENE
```

102

```
PDQ CBS BELLA GAZEBO
EAU RENO ALIAS RAILON
PTA UTAHJOINSTHEUNION
SEDAN GRAB SHOE NANA
RECK IMAGE ENNUI
MICHELOBBEER ESPARTO
SAC YAY SOLOISTS OIL
ICY CLIP ALTA UTNE
MRC THESEAGULL MRMOTO
MALAR ORMANDY PEI
SEENIT ELF SLACKS
GOO OBELISK AKRON
CARUSO DOROTHYDIX ADA
AMOS TWIN EDAM CAR
LIT TSINGTAO RAN KKK
FACTOID OLYMPICGAMES
INEED CRIED OVER
SEWS ROES SELF ANJOU
CROSSOFGOLDSPEECH ABS
ANNUAL ADIEU REPO CIE
RETELL SAVES DAS KTS
```

103

```
S A M B A   A C H   F L I P   C A D S
A L E R T   I Q U I T   R I S E   O L E O
L O W I N   N U R S E   A L S O   M I E N
T H E G O D F A T H E R   A U N T M A R Y
S A D A   R A T   E V I N C E   E A S E S
      N A O M I   L E N I S   E R N
D A D D Y L O N G L E G S   S L E D G E S
U R I   E L U T E   E V I L S   E L I
C O M P A S S   M O M M I E D E A R E S T
T O S A Y   W E E   E E N   E R A S
      T E A R Y   L E T   P A S H A
A C H E   D O E   E S E   U T I L E
F O U R D A U G H T E R S   S A T A N I C
A N E   R I N G O   R E E D S   R O O
R E Y N A R D   K I S S I N C O U S I N S
      O W S   S E T T O   S O R T E
E R A T O   L E S I O N   I N E   A R A M
M O N O N C L E   S O N O F D R A C U L A
B L I P   H A I L   P E K O E   C O B B S
A L T E   A N N E   S T A R R   T W E E T
R O A N   N O G O   S Y M   E S S E S
```

104

```
S T R A Y E D   E D N A   C H I P P E W A
O R A T O R Y   T R E E   R E T A I L O R
P I C T U R E S H O W S   E X A C T I O N
S P E A R   S H I N T O   N I L E
      C E E   A C E   P I A N O S T O O L
A N T H I L L   M T G   E A R L E
T A R   T S E T S E   W E E   S T R A D S
T I E S   T R U M P E T   W A T T L E S
E L E C   M A I M E D   D O T E S
M E T A   S E P T E T   J O K E R   P C S
P R O M P T   P O T S H O T   E S C R O W
T S P   A R M E R   H A S T E N   H O N E
      A V O I D   L O S T I N   E T T E
W A S H I N G   I M P A L E D   F E A T
A S K I N G   D A N   T E R E S A   S C I
S T I N G   L E G   D I N E T T E
P O S T S E A S O N   B O P   C A V
      T O M E   O H I O A N   T O O R A
C O M P O S E R   P U Z Z L E S O L V E R
A L I E N I S T   A G E E   S O L V E N T
R E A G E N T S   R O T S   S W E E N E Y
```

105

```
S H A   R O M E   D R A W A   C E N T
H Y S   T E L E X   C A R O L   R E L E E
O P S   B E A L E   I N G L E   E L I E S
T H E ⊙ O F F I C E   ◯ O F F R I E N D S
P E R T N E S S   R E S T E   I N S O L E
U N T I E D   S U R P A S S   M E T R E S
T E E N S   B A Z A A R   M E R E
D D E   W A S I N   O S S A   A L F
      D A Y   T R U T H S   A L L O R
R U B I K S ◫ S   E N I A C   L E A V E
M E N A C E   R E W I D E N   S O N N E T
A M I L E   S O N I C   B E R M U D A △
L I F E R   C O N C H S   O E D
I T Y   U T A H   C A R T E   F U M
      A D A M   I T A L I C   H O P E R
S U T R A S   A T T I R E D   T O U S L E
A R O I D S   T R A L A   I S A B R O A D
L A Y S O N T H E -   B A C K T O □ O N E
U N I T E   R E A M S   S U I T E   N I A
D I N O S   A N T A S   A L T O S   E E L
S A G S   P A Y N E   P E S O   R S T
```

106

```
S W I S S   A V E R   A L P S   S A L T S
C O O P T   T A T E   F E A R   T R O O P
H O N E Y B U N C H   F A C I L I T A T E
      A L I B I   A L O F T   A L I N E D
D A R K E N   L O N E R   S P E E
O L E S   G O L F G A D G E T S   S P O T
D A D   B E D I M S   S A R A   S T O L E
E M A I L   E N E   L U R I A   D E N
C O N D U C T   S C A L P I N G   D I E
      D E E R S   F O R G O T   T A L E N T
A B A B A   L I N E U P S   A C I D S
P R E L I M   A R I S E S   S K I M P
O A R   R E D M E A T S   P E O P L E D
R B I   D R O I D   B C E   U S A I R
T I N T S   O N O R   C A L A I S   N E O
S A G A   I M A G E M A K E R S   I T I S
      L A S S   S E R U M   L A S S O S
R E C O I L   A M I G O   E V I C T
I S I N D E B T E D   M A N I P U L A T E
E S T E E   E T T E   E R T E   T E N A M
N E E D S   D Y E S   D R E W   E S T O P
```

107

```
  A D M I R A L   L A S T R A D A   H U S H
A R E A C O D E   E S P O U S E D   S I N C E
J U S T I C E O F T H E P E A C E   A R M O R
A L I   P R I M   D E S I   C R E A T E
R E G O   E T A G E S   R I C H A R D I I
    N A I V E   H A H A   A R I   S E A N
M A S T E R O F C E R E M O N I E S
P O T T S   M A O   C R O S S   F E T A L
A R E S   D E A R T H   A N T   P O L I C E D
R O D   C O N N O T E D   G E N U F L E C T S
E N H A N C E   E X I T   N U T S   S O S O
    I S N T   A S R E G A R D S   T U T U
A F T S   O A T H   D I C E   B A R O N E T
M E T E O R I T E S   T I M E L I F E   T S E
S T E N T O R   B U S   T A L E O F   S E T S
    A R T O F   S A C H S   I S O   T E X A S
      E L E C T R I C A L E N G I N E E R
S P C A   A V A   E M I R   A N T I C
W O R L D W A R S   M A N T R A   T U B S
E N A T E S   T A P S   L I E D   T A O
L I V E N   P H Y S I C A L T H E R A P I S T
L E A R Y   O I L S T O N E   E N S L A V E S
S S T S   I M I T A T E S   E S T A T E S
```

108

```
G A B S   S A R A H   B O L D   A E S O P
A L L T H E W A G E   E N C A M P M E N T
E V A P O R A T O R   W E D H O T M A M A
L A B E L E R S   S A N   L O N E L Y
      T E N D   T I M I D   N E T
  S W E D E   D R O O L   F A L S T A F F
N E H R U   F R A N K   P A R I S   T E E
E T E   P O L E S   E G O I S T   P A L L
S T E M   N I G H T F A L L   H A N O I
S O L O I S T S   H I L L S   L A R Y N X
    I D L E S   L O L L S   R E N E W
M I N U I T   C A R L O   B A D D R E A M
U N C L E   A P P E N D I N G   S I R E
F L O E   C A P P E D   O K I E S   G E O
F E M   T O M E S   W I Z E N   P S H A W
S T E P O N I T   J O K E R   B E A T S
      O P T   Y E M E N   D E A N
  K I S S E S   A L B   G U A R D D O G
W A T T I N H E L L   S E A A N E M O N E
I N B A D T A S T E   W A Y N E D A N C E
S T E L E   M E A D   C R E E D   N E E R
```

109

```
ELIZ   MEDEA  MESAS  MBA
DOGS  PALEST  STUNT  EER
KALACHRISTOUGENNA    LAG
OTO  ODS  IANS   BELIEVE
CHOOKSUNGTAN  SEALSKIN
HESSE  PANEL  ELAL  LAST
      SCRIP   SLAM   SAL
SAM  ADA  CLUEIN    ISIS
CRENNA  BUONNATALE  KER
RARES  AYERS   BIGTIME
IMRE  GLEDELIGJUL   AMIS
PAYROLL   INOUT   CRATE
TIC  JOYEUXNOEL  SOAKED
CHOO   REIGNS   MAN  ASA
     RDS  GILS    NOONS
ERIE  PIKE  SPEER  ICAME
MISTRESS   FELIZNAVIDAD
CATSEYE   BRAT  ILE  DLI
ELM  NOLLAIGSHONADHUIT
ETA  ATLAS  EMERGE  ECCE
SOS  LEEDS  SARAS   WEED
```

110

```
MODS  ALGA  ASTI   MESMER
OMIT  LAOS  FURL   EXPIRE
SAVEDBYTHEBAIL   NEEDLE
SNEER  ITER   ASPS  LIED
     RUNNINGPALEMAIL
DIK  MOT   EASES   SEARS
AGIN  ROOSTER   CARPAL
UNSEAT  SHALESHOCK  RYE
BISTRO  SAP  TONI   PIED
STATING  MER  RETIRES
ENES  ALEDORADO   ECOS
DREAMOF  COP   PETUNIA
ACTS  TUFU  MSU  RINSES
BOA  LITTLENAIL  APIARY
EMILIE   TINNERS   AIRE
DALES  TRACT   OED  LAT
     GIVEEMHAILHARRY
LODE  INGE  SEEM   EATME
AMINES  GETWHALEWISHES
PADDLE  ARNO  SIRE  IRMA
PRISMS  ESTE  TOSS  ROOS
```

111

```
MEATS  ASTO  BEBE   RECAP
YALIE  LAIC  RARE   EVADE
SCONE  DUSTDEVIL    NINER
THEGREENHORNET   SETTEE
      EDNA  PUT  THEWASPS
BLONDES   FOR   ODE
RAZE   LADYBUGLADYBUG
ABOIL  BESS  ALLEN   EIRE
MENLO  ACT  PYROS   MANGE
LESOTHO   LILI   TENDER
      MOSQUITOCOAST
GRAVEN  SEAR   CLEARER
RABID  MAUDS  MTA  LURES
IGOT  SADAT  QUES  SLATE
DAYOFTHELOCUST    ETRE
OAR   RIT   BARROOM
ATTICBEE   EUX   SETI
CROCUS  LORDOFTHEFLIES
MARIS  OLIVETREE   LILLE
ESTEE  NISI  IERS  ELLEN
SHERD  TEEN  CENT  STEED
```

112

```
AESOP   CARED   STANCH
LAPPET  SOLUTE  INSTORE
EGLISE  TRENDS  CAPERED
FLINTSTONES  TIEGS   MAG
ENE  TORE   WITS    BASE
JETS  LIMABEANS  SCALES
AYE  HALS  ENNEA   TONS
REDTAPE  MAID   DIRECTS
ARS  GOLDENRULE   HIP
EBBED  BARE  ROOKED  ONO
JAIL  ALLS   TUES   GOGO
ELL  STALER  DIGS  ALLEN
CEL  MOBILEHOME   TRE
TRITONS  DORE   QUIETED
NOTA  MOIRA  AURA   OFA
MIGUEL  ORANGEMAN   SETH
INST   HEAL  LISI   OTS
RAG  WHIST  READINGROOM
APACHES  OSIRIS  TATTOO
GETTERS  RECANT  ONIONS
ETERNE   STATE   GEESE
```

113

```
SOS   SFC   NARC   SPACE
RIPUP  ELAL  UHOH  MARIA
EMILE  NOME  ROLE  INERT
GOATS  SOUNDSOFSILENCE
INTATTERS  NET  SMELTER
SEEN  HOI  RAD   AMASS
      SHAFTED  OLEG  SPA
REJOINS  SAVESONESSKIN
ALOFT  MOP  IDLE  TOAST
FLESHIER  LEGO  SHEATHE
      WETLY  ITE  STEEP
ADMIRAL  HENS  BARROOMS
POINT   TATA  CAT  APEAK
SONGOFSOLOMON   EAGERLY
ERG   AUTO   UNSOBER
BURRO  BAT  IFI   ALEE
ARRANGE  SAX  ASSESSORS
SHOWSOFSTRENGTH   ATLAS
POULE  ICON  OLEO  RAISE
ENTER  RARE  MERC  ARTES
NEEDS  EMMY  TSK   SAD
```

114

```
AL*   BIG*  ATILT  *DAY
PENA  CALEB  SARAH  BALE
ADEN  AKITA  STARE  ETON
ITSNOTEASYBEING*   LENT
ROSERED   WIN   ERITREA
      OER  LAIDTO  SONS
AMFM  BONS  SAMSON   MR*
PEA  CONIC  TEEM   WAIT
ORIG  ANGLO  SHA   GEESE
WOMANIN*  NAY  NEBRASKA
      BORE   SAD   LAIR
SOYLENT*  IAN  PUTTING*
WHEEL   BAN  ELIDE  NILE
AILS  STAB  YIPES  GNUS
MOP  FORGET  *IES  POET
      FIFA  THESIS  ARF
*BERETS   ENT   BROTHEL
CALI  THE.**GRASSOFHOME
ABLE  AMISH  ELLIS  ELMO
RAIN  CANEA  ETUDE  *MAN
DRED  ONEAT  TOME   SSE
```

* = GREEN

115

```
TAROTS  ELK   PHI  USHERS
APOGEE  NEUTRON   NOEXIT
REELER  MAROONS   DUMPTY
ASSEMBLESTOGETHER  LAX
        SIS  TRY  IRIDO
FRISE  THESEA  FESSEDUP
LONERS  MURMUR  THRESH
OLDANTIQUES  LESE  AVID
OLIN  ONUS  STEAM  TIAS
REV  ANKA  ABURST  GEO
SRI  NEWINNOVATION  LAD
DRY  ONEIDA  ARAP  EVE
ROUE  MOTHS  ITIS  ANON
ALAN  EDER  BISECTINTWO
RELOAN  SUPINE  STYLET
ASPIRANT  ESTERS  SAYRE
    ERATO  ARM  OAR
ARR  BASICFUNDAMENTALS
RESTIR  DIETERS  SOIREE
IDOISM  ENCHANT  TALENT
DONUTS  SGT  LOS  SHEATH
```

116

```
JADED  FEES  BBC  STACTE
AMISS  REWRAP  AIR  SALARY
CORPORALENTRANCE  EPOPEE
ALGA  UZI  RORQUAL  ETTES
NEER  GENERALMUSTARD  ANT
ASSTS  SERAPE  EPODE  LIAO
    OTB  OBI  IRAN  ONIN
SEL  ROTC  EEC  MDS  BUGLE
PSI  ALOAD  SABU  FRODO
ITE  PUTRID  RAPTURES  VAS
NOUN  SERGEANTPUNISHMENT
ONTO  BEETLEHEADS  ARTE
FIELDMARSHALSTRIKE  ONAN
FAN  RIGATONI  SENIOR  ORT
AGARS  RIAL  GEESE  REO
CANNY  CON  NIN  SRIS  SSR
ATTU  SWAP  OOM  NEW
RAPS  LINED  UNLASH  TARAS
ARE  COLONELLEAGUER  TEMA
MAPLE  DEFEATS  NUN  TSPS
EXPEND  MAJORSCOURAGEOUS
LIESTO  ECA  AEROPE  EARLE
SARTOR  NEY  SIPS  MUTED
```

117

```
LOCALS  EWER  ORAN  ODE
AMULET  NINO  KALE  HEN
BERATE  ANIMALFARM  ICC
INDIANAMODERATION  ORO
ASSN  LEU  OTHE  SOAPED
    STEALTH  ORC  CREE
AMI  HABS  EDAM  ONFEED
REL  ERA  LAURA  LEAST
MALCOLM  OVERCROWD  TOD
ALIAS  AGUES  OARS  TYPE
NINA  SKEIN  ARRAY  AWET
DEON  HANS  ERRED  SCORE
SRI  DALAILAMA  OTTOMAN
SHARI  AVRIL  PEA  ATT
SPOKEN  NINE  RILL  NEE
SLOE  EPA  SMELLED
WISDOM  ASIS  IDO  ELEE
ITT  MASSACHUSETTSBELL
PHI  SETTLEABLE  ELATED
EEN  VEAL  REAM  NATIVE
SRO  ERSE  DRYS  OPENER
```

118

```
NOSALE  ELM  MARL  DAVID
ARAWAK  SOY  ALAI  ARISE
DANANG  ABRAHAMLINCOLN
ANTRA  QUOTHA  PISTOLES
    ADIEU  LOTS  EEE
SECS  MICKEYMOUSE  STLO
PAL  KORAN  ARP  SOWED
IRAKI  TRACE  EWE  OBIES
ELUANTS  COLONELKLINK
LESTER  SKEET  LINAGE
    SARA  VAT  LAIR
SOCIAL  ANAIS  SCAMPI
BOZOTHECLOWN  CHEROOT
BEBOP  SRO  RASTA  LISLE
IRENE  NEA  URIEL  HAM
OGRE  GROUCHOMARX  HERS
    EOE  REAR  NOMAD
ASSEMBLE  TRACKS  ITALO
CHARLIECHAPLIN  PLAYER
COLLY  NUIT  LAO  AERATE
TOKEN  TAPE  YOW  PRINTS
```

119

```
LAMB  TESTS  ONCE  VOLGA
ELIE  OLEIC  FAUX  OSIER
MAKEYOURCOATREPELLENT
OPERETTA  TREK  EXTORTS
NASTASE  GLEN  SRTA
ASI  IRAN  OTO  BABE
WEEXTERMINATEALLHOMES
RARE  APED  WAVY  ABOLT
ETAS  SMOG  GERE  SICKLE
NAT  OAR  PULL  DATA
STOCKUPTOSAVELIMITONE
ONNO  VERE  ISM  HAE
DAMMED  MAUD  REMS  BOHR
ASAIL  WARD  AIDA  ALUI
WHYCLEANYOURSELFTRYME
NESS  SIT  PTER  EWE
ETTA  EBEN  PREFACE
SPONSOR  UXOR  REVEALER
WEDISPENSEWITHCONCERN
ASONE  SEER  AYEAR  ETES
BORAX  SORT  LEANS  DAST
```

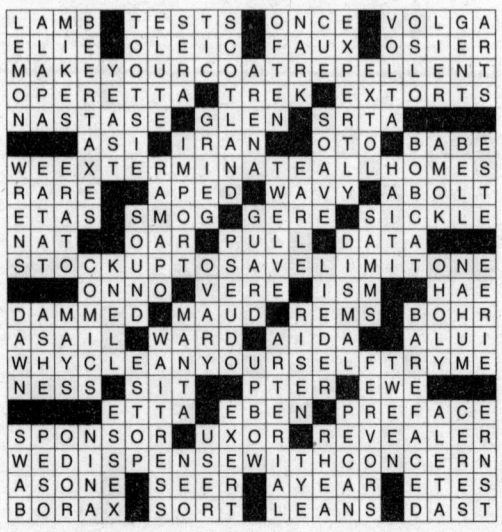

120

```
ADEPT  ACDC  GLOM  SMITE
LEROI  NOAH  RAPA  MILOS
FLAPDOODLE  ELAN  ASSET
    PEW  AEC  BALDERDASH
JUBILEE  KNEW  RATE
ILLNESS  SUA  SAUSAGES
GLASS  POPPYCOCK  LOCI
SAT  SPOKES  ASHES  BOD
AGHA  OUSE  BRIO  HUMBLE
WEEVILS  DRIEST  OBELIA
    RANEES  ALE  TERETE
ENSIGN  EMIGRE  MIRADOR
AUKLET  NOSE  TWIN  LYCO
SRI  ASTRO  THONGS  GTO
ESTA  MOONSHINE  AFOAM
DEERSKIN  PEC  NOTAONE
    AWOL  ARAM  TRICKED
APPLESAUCE  APT  ARA
CAUSA  XRAY  TARADIDDLE
EGRET  EDGE  IBEX  SENAT
DELAY  SUES  CAKE  TSARS
```

121

```
SALIERI · ARAPAHO · ENFORCE
EVANDER · CASHBAR · SALVERS
TOMDICKANDHARRY · STOOGES
INSITU · LEI · LIL · REAP · GTE
· COSAS · USA · ETONS · GIAN
CIGARETTESONAMATCH · RENE
ABET · MOD · CXI · CHEAPO
RENO · BONSAI · RBI · OUTRE
PATROLS · MACBETHWITCHES
EMS · PITS · ALOUD · OON · HEFT
· EEG · TOSSES · LUNG · ISEE
FRENCHHENS · MUSKETEERS
OARS · TILE · PUMICE · NAR
ABIE · EEL · LENAS · SCUT · CIA
MACMURRAYSSONS · READING
STABS · ODE · MAPLES · IVAN
· LEAPER · TEA · SIC · VINE
SAME · CLUBSANDWICHSLICES
KRIS · HASAT · DEI · HEELS
ERS · EINE · ERG · NEE · GAINES
WISEMEN · AREACODENUMBERS
EVASIVE · BEAMING · REALIST
DELETED · SOMEDAY · ASSENTS
```

122

```
EBBED · SNORE · THAT · APR
MORAY · EELED · IONIA · DRE
BOOTEDTHECOMPUTER · DIP
ELMS · ATRA · ETRE · CHICO
DEI · BOUNCEDHISCHECKS ·
SADNESS · ALEE · LITTLE
NEAT · ATLI · OUI · SYS
THREWHISBACKOUT ·
CCI · ASHE · ERTE · MISDO
RANOFFSOMEMEMOS · BATIK
OCCULT · AMC · VERONA
CHUTE · DROVEHISCARAWAY
SERGE · RAPE · ZOOS · EHS
· ORDEREDFOODTOGO ·
DAS · RIA · AIDA · ORAL
ELISHA · SELL · FETTLED
MADEABANANASPLIT · RAE
OMENS · GIGI · EAST · KISS
TEC · TURNEDOUTTHELIGHT
EDA · AREAS · BRAHE · OTHER
DAR · NEST · EULER · BETSY
```

123

```
OVERT · SODAS · GERONIMO
HOPEH · UPDATE · REENACTS
OLIVEASUDDEN · ALDEREGO
· ENTERS · LOADSTAR ·
ALPACAS · GIRL · AROWS
FOOLER · BOREAL · DIMWITS
LAPS · ISOBARS · MILE · LAT
AFL · EASY · CUR · DELTA
MEA · CHER · SMUDGE · NOUN
ERR · LINDENEAR · ELBOWED
· OPAL · SNEERER · LOST
REPENTS · OAKYDOKEY · HAS
EXIT · STILTS · WORD · EDA
VINED · ANA · ABEL · WAY
ELI · EPIC · ARSENAL · DIGS
LEOPARD · ARISTA · LARSEN
· SNARE · SIGN · CALYPSO
· ROSEBUSH · BIONIC ·
PECANESE · ITHADTOBEYEW
CREDENCE · NOBLES · ILONA
SEMESTER · GNOME · SLOES
```

124

```
RIBBED · FLA · OME · ASSAM
ALLURE · REMODEL · STALER
FLANGE · ETAMINE · SULTRY
· STOPINTHENAMEOFLOVE
AIT · ESC · GIG · LIFE ·
BLUEINTHEFACE · ELY · TRA
BOLES · SILOS · ROM · AHAB
ANALOG · SIP · PIGINAPOKE
SASS · ALMS · PIED · ESPRIT
· CLI · HALO · EDITIONS
MUCHADOABOUTNOTHING ·
NARRATOR · APSO · CHE ·
ELAINE · EATS · RUSE · ARCH
WINBYANOSE · HUN · ROMERO
ECUS · ISH · MELEE · LYMAN
RES · ITO · ADAYINTHELIFE
· ONER · MEN · TAO · STY
READBETWEENTHELINES ·
EXTERN · ADMIRER · SERIAL
NANTES · FLEXILE · TRIODE
· MOODY · TYR · ODD · SONNET
```

125

```
MUSE · CZAR · ARCED · SCOTT
ONAN · HIDE · SHALE · CARRE
DIVAGATES · TONIC · ANION
EVAMARIE · LIMN · OMNIBUS
SAGELY · CANBERRA · SITE
· CELL · ROOM · STOOP ·
· OVERLAPS · EURASIAN
MAME · IMRI · EWE · SILENCE
IMITATE · CANARD · SILVER
DECIMALS · SETTOS · SEE
INROMEDOASTHEROMANSDO
· OLE · SUTURE · PREDATES
REBATE · REMASH · BRETONS
PRETELL · NET · OPEC · ERGO
MISERIES · DESPOTIC ·
· SCALP · VETS · HOSS
SPAS · IDOLATER · AERATE
CLIMATE · ADIN · MIGRATES
REMIT · NATAL · MILLINERS
INERT · EMOTE · OGLE · GENE
MARKS · DOSES · ASST · ENOS
```

126

```
FTD · CAB · HENCE · RAGA
LIEF · DODO · ALOOF · IDOLS
INBROADDAYLIGHT · BOOAT
PATERNAL · ELTON · PANFRY
ASSURES · BNAI · PILAF
· DIS · TETHS · BIGDITCH
BASIN · PULLSTRINGS · HAE
ANKA · EURO · ABOY · NELL
BYANARROWMARGIN · MODEL
EATSCROW · OBOES · SASEBO
· ELMOS · PAD · EATME
EASIER · THULE · ETHIOPIA
DROPS · THEPLOTTHICKENS
GINS · LEER · AHAB · INAT
EST · CARSALESMEN · ANDSO
REHEARSE · ARIEL · LDG ·
· INDUE · UNES · MALARIA
MENAGE · LOREN · SADIRONS
ADIME · GIVESAWIDEBERTH
PACER · SMELT · ALAN · AYRE
· MELS · TORSO · DOT · SOS
```

127

```
STEAMS  SEAR  DAMON    PAGO
MAUMAU ULCERATIVE    AIRED
ORGANS MARGARETATHREEOD
OSE  OPTOMETRIST  HOTDOGS
TUN LEO    ENTS    WHAM
 SEVENTUSIV      KLUTE
  TETS NOVASCOTIA  RETTO
PAWNEE QUINTILIAN BRRRR
ELOI EURE ETERNE ARIOT
SLICE JOES  IVES ELECTS
TALER ETD HAZES  OFFS
OYL NICE MOREL  MUTI  BCD
  GENT LORAN PIT VOILE
SPARSE BOVA ERSE ENLAI
TENET SOWETO DORR  FLIT
ARNEB INITIATIVE SHIMMY
BUENO ZENOOFELEA  PARA
  BORGE   LENDNINEON
OLGA  PUCK    ING   NIB
POLITIC ORANGEPEKOE ECO
ELEVENZINGNORGAY FRISKY
DOYEN  ACCENTUATE FORKED
ERNS  REEDY  BLED SNAILS
```

128

```
SSE  WEEMS  STEW   BOORS
IMA  HETUP  PILE ARMLET
BARBARASEVILLE  MINIMA
 SHUT  SECANT  MINIVAN
OHARE  DINAHSCARD  ENG
BURGLAR MEL  ORB  LAYS
EPT SLIME   TRA  REPO
  ALLAN DRENCH  BUCO
REPASSED SRA MOO   TRU
ADORNED  CHAIRED  BERET
BILLET  SHRINER REVUES
ASLOW  CHAINED CEDILLA
TOY MIA VEE  CATALYST
SNUB PALTER  UHLAN
 RUSH ARR  NEVIN  MDS
RENO PLO BAH  ENEMIES
DET ROSATRALEE   BALSA
INHABIT  ACORNS  OAKS
STARES IFIHEDDAHAMMER
CANINE TONI  ETHER  ERA
SLEET  TEST  DOLED  NTH
```

129

```
 SCATS   PAD    BEDBUGS
SWATHE  AILES ALIENATE
LABOUROFLOVE  SIDEDOOR
AHOLD PROSAIC  COP  LMN
VIOL  KEATS ZAXIS  THAI
ELS TERMS  PUTIT  CHOSE
DIESIRAE  FARSI  CHOU
  ORBS  BLEEP  PEARSON
LALAS  ELIS  YARNS  EPA
SALINE BANE  JEST  ARID
CRUDER ONT  MAS  RAMONA
ROMS  VOLK COMO  EDUCES
ASI BIHAC  ASAP  FOLKS
MANIACS  HONES  SORE
 IDLE  DECOY  DELETING
EQUAL TOQUE  SENDS  SIL
MUMS MOGUL  AGNES  YOGI
OAF AID EIDETIC  OATEN
TROPICAL SERJEANTYORK
ETIOLATE TRIOS  URANIA
 SLOSHED  NEE   TOSEA
```

130

```
SCAMS  AORTAS   GRATED
KABUL SPOONED INCOMER
IRATE PETRATINGACRIME
PINTER RAT AGIO   SLIP
POD PIRATES  CLUB  ILE
ECO SONTOSONPHONECALL
RANT SER  CARE  CRANE
 OUT SIRES   LAGO
SEVERANCEPAYS  DATE
TRADITIONAL  PEDESTAL
ISM  NESS SAAB    UVA
REPULSED  AUSCULTATED
 NETS COMMITTEDJURY
PIMA ROTAS    ISA
PITON ALIT  LEA  RAPS
SEVENCENTSOLUTION TRI
LAO YENS LOCARNO  LAS
ANTE  DODD  AIM ERRANT
BUMTOBUMTRAFFIC MINCE
STANDEE SATEENS ASTER
SNAILS  GARRET  NEARS
```

131

```
SMUDGED  UNCROSS  DUCAL
TAPIOCA  POLONIA  OSAGE
ELBAROUNDTHEBEND GENES
ALOT SERE  TELE  OLDEST
LEWIS  SOMME  ACEAE
 GELT SPA KNUCKLGLEFT
AIRSEA SOMBRERO EARLE
PRETEXT BOO  ENTHUSES
LIA TEASPOONS OVEREAT
USSR SLOE  MEEK   SAI
SHEET CURVEERANG DELES
 TUT SLOB  TARS   RSVP
ALSORAN ELABORATE HAI
PETUNIAS ULE  BALLADE
ENACT  FOOTLESS DIAPER
RIGHTOSTONE  BAL  TAKE
 ALANS  SEGOS  SEDAN
FELONY TESH ETTA  ERMA
AXING CORNERTHEMARKOOM
NEPAL OBVIATE  MOLIERE
SCONE DEEPSEA  SKEETER
```

132

```
 THI  OAS PSALMS  HOLED
FRAMABLE OHIOAN  UNITE
LIBELLEE DIRTYOLDOMEN
OBITPARTS NESSUS  PRI
RET    TOTED  TURBINE
ACACIA  ELICIT  ELDER
SATURDAYNIGHTOLIVE
 PROLOG  RODIN   WETS
SAC RIKERS LIANA  DRE
HEROANDOLEANDER VIGIL
ADAPTS   NBA   MENIAL
PINTO HOMEONTHEORANGE
ELK PEABO  TOREUP  GER
DESK PLEBE  EERIER
 OMISSIONIMPOSSIBLE
IDAHO  ELNINO  HEALER
CABLETV  COLAS    OON
HHS REMARK  OWINGNUTS
OLEODUROCHER FLARESAT
RINSE  SORELY UTTERERS
SATAN ATEASE LYE  ODD
```

133

```
UPCOMING·BASE·HERB·MACH
NARRATOR·ODES·ILIE·OTOE
SLAUGHTERHOUSEFIVE·DAMA
EON·EMEER·REGIS·PEALED
AMESS·ECO·SANG·BILLETS
TARPIT·EIGHTCOUSINS·ORE
·ATUB·LIE·ENDING·FUT
CUTRATE·GEOS·ODD·ACTE
ONETRUETHING·ESCROW
LANA·SOO·RATED·RESOLD
ELL·NOWWEARESIX·NOTICER
MOI·ONASIDE·INPEACE·ICY
ANTITAX·NINESTORIES·TAN
NETMEN·AGNES·SIL·SIRE
·LARDED·THREESISTERS
CESS·AER·BAIO·UNCASES
SOI·STEELE·LBS·PSAT
ERN·FOURQUARTETS·TRIAGE
ADDEDUP·PROS·APO·SCRAG
WEIMAR·EVICT·DIANA·AYE
ALAI·SEVENAGAINSTTHEBES
LINT·OVER·TUNE·MOTORIST
LASS·NARY·STAT·SPYBOATS
```

134

```
ELBE·EBBED·DEBT·HELD
DEED·SEEME·ELESS·ELEE
STRESSTEST·SPEECHLESS
·STREETS·EBSEN·HELVE
·EXE·NEER·HEME·
EGGED·DETER·DEMENTHE
GERT·THELETTERMEN·REN
REES·EELS·DEPS·SENT
ESE·TREESHREWS·PENCE
TENSPEED·TEENS·ELDER
·BLESS·SEXES·SMEES
STEEL·WHEES·EVENNESS
THREE·THEDRESSER·TET
REEK·THEE·ESNE·ETTE
EMT·MEETTHEPRESS·KETT
WESTERNS·ELLEN·PERES
·HEMS·ERLE·MME·
THESE·EMBED·KEEPERS
PREFERENCE·GENTLEMENS
REFT·SEDER·EXERT·EEEE
EFTS·NEET·EPEES·SLEW
```

135

```
ANDANTE·BOSUNS·TRUEING
COASTAL·PUSHPIN·HONALEE
HERSHEYKISSESLIFESAVERS
ESAU·SENSOR·POW·WENDS
·MAS·ROE·MBA·GILA·ESO
SWEETTARTSPAYDAYZERO·
LIB·ORTS·ANOLD·SEURAT
OTE·NOT·SAT·EDAM·TORE
THREEMUSKETEERSMILKDUDS
HILL·TIRING·ANEMONES
STEEP·CLEO·AGE·SSA·DNA
·MRGOODBARSNICKERS·
NBC·AND·ERB·ADAY·TULIP
ALISTAIR·TOURER·LANE
BUTTERFINGERSMARSMOUNDS
ESTA·YOUR·USS·HEB·DEA
SHARPS·DECCA·TELE·ABC
·TOOTSIEROLLSBABYRUTH
VCR·LYRE·TYR·OHO·ASA
IRINA·ENE·ROSINS·IANS
SUGARDADDYDOTSREESESCUP
TSELIOT·NEEDIER·LORETTA
ATLASES·ARNESS·FORREST
```

136

```
ARUBA·AMOI·OLGA·AGA
SOLES·APERS·KUOYU·HES
SUNDAYGOTOMEETING·EES
NEAT·SETE·SLEPT·NANA
·ICESHOW·BLUEMONDAY
DAGMAR·ERI·ASTRIDE
OGLED·MITT·SERE·MBA
TUESDAYSCHILD·ROTTERS
SEE·ITO·ARIE·ORNOT
·LEHUA·INNING·ASTI
OHIO·ONWEDNESDAY·CAHN
ROTO·SONTAG·AMPLE·
AMASS·ASOF·ESE·BOP
TELECOM·THURSDAYSGAME
ERY·AMOR·TUTU·TALON
·PREDATE·MRS·TEUTON
GIRLFRIDAY·PATTERN·
OLEO·SIRES·IBIS·TMEN
FOB·SATURDAYNIGHTLIVE
EVE·ENEMY·DIANE·BELIE
REL·LESS·ENTS·STEER
```

137

```
ADMAN·MADAME·ODD#ED
CEASE·MEDICARE·LEANTO
¢ERSOF@TENTION·DENIAL
ERIE·ITS·ELSAS·DENSE
DENTINE·SAD·HESSE·
·RARITY·GAPED·ISM
GLOBAL·TEN%ERS·SHERPA
YEMEN·MER·ALIAS·AVOIR
MANN·TIMING·ALT·NANNY
•PIECES·LEES·MESS·SSS
·REFLEX·CASTLE·
CO★·EDIE·TSAR·SILVER$
ORSON·RAT·UNTROD·ICED
UG&AN·ERROR·LON·BAHIA
PASTAS·NON+SES·FELONY
ENT·TASTE·ISABEL·
·ROGER·RNS·RALLIES
SLIME·CAUSE·GAS·ALVA
TYPIST·GR&¢RALSTATION
&RETTI·EARLOBES·SHAKE
SASSES·LAYMEN·SEDER
```

138

```
SPRAWL·GHANA·GOTAJOB
PRECIS·ALANON·EPICURE
HOWARDSTERNLY·REMODEL
ERASE·MENDS·WAR·PILL
RAGED·INNY·JODYS·TSE
ETE·BLOC·WARD·INCHES
SARALEE·LIENS·ADEAL
·MACY·OSSIE·OVARIAL
·MARKS·SECS·SUIT·GTO
SLANGY·HERR·ROTC·AHSO
HORDES·ELEANOR·INSTEP
IOTA·HOLY·VIBE·OUTLAY
PSI·FAIL·LESE·HURRY
SENSORS·PINER·ESSA
·SHAPE·UNLIT·ALEYARD
SCHELL·STAY·WARY·PER
TOO·YEATS·RITT·PRIVY
ERRS·GOO·GUSTO·LUCIE
ESTELLE·BARNEYFRANKLY
RELAXES·EMAILS·ANGLEE
STYLIST·DANNY·POSERS
```

139

```
TEM   CHAKA   NOBLE   SMITS
ITO   AILED   IDEAL   TANEY
THUMBVANDYKEANDMORGAN
UNROBES   VOLTA   INCASE
SONJA   BELL   ODIE
   AGA   NOTA   CARSEATS
SEAVERMARTINANDTRUMAN
OLDE   MAGEE   ANTIS   ERA
LEM   ULNAS   LITHE   LENIN
UNI   SEEN   AAA   TIX
MIXBUTTONANDBELAFONTE
ARS   ALD   LUBE   ORA
ONLAY   DATES   SAGAS   TIT
ACE   PUTIN   SPIES   RUNE
SAWYERCAVETTANDCHAPIN
ADEQUATE   RAKE   OAF
LUNT   WIDE   MTGES
STELAE   ABACI   ALBERTA
ARNOLDCLARKANDHOUDINI
MEOUT   RIGEL   AESIR   PAN
PESTO   TASSE   PRONG   EST
```

140

```
BAS   GLOAT   CERES   ILES
ACCT   ROACH   ALONE   GAGE
THROWINTHETROWEL   URGE
HEARINGS   WEDGE   FLAGON
EDMOND   SADIE   ASONE
NOS   CALIF   ALABAMAN
MATTS   HALLOFFRAME   ORA
ECHO   COCA   ATIE   CUED
ARE   BATHTUBGRIN   BUTTE
NEGLIGEE   RAREE   GUSHER
RATEL   DATES   CALEB
AMAZES   ARNIE   AUTOCRAT
NOYES   BROOKREVIEW   AMI
GINS   FOOL   SIRS   TSAR
SRI   DRILLPICKLE   TASTE
TENORITE   AFLEA   AWN
ERASE   SPEAR   METAGE
ESTATE   OTTER   SOPRANOS
LAIN   THREELITTLEPRIGS
ALEG   TALES   OILER   ALOE
LESE   EGYPT   NOOSE   ELS
```

141

```
CRANE   GESTE   GRASPS
SLALOM   ECLAT   REDPOLL
NUTBROWNHALE   ODDITIES
ABRAM   ATIVE   SWEET   DAU
RCA   RIDE   SOLED   VEND
EACH   UPANDATHEM   AORTA
DREI   NINA   BOOR   WILSON
DAWNS   GNP   TALC
GATELEG   DUE   SHUN   AMOS
ERASED   HAIRPLANE   NARC
TITOS   FEND   RAZE   MINOR
USAF   ILIKEHIKE   RACINE
PERM   RARE   ADE   CASHCOW
ABIT   ERE   GOTTA
SABRAS   FAST   ERNE   STOA
TEACH   HAMPERSAND   HORT
ORTH   BACON   ITSO   RIB
MIT   PATTY   BLEST   THROE
PALMETTO   JELLIEDHEELS
LEATHER   ADELE   CORNET
SPEEDY   WESER   LUSTS
```

142

```
FARM   AHALT   ROWEL   PAST
OBOE   COCOA   EDILE   ELLE
GOLDIEHAWN   PENICILLIN
GOLFSHOT   NEALE   UBOATS
LOIS   PERIL   COST
PAGING   TURIN   MANEATER
LIRE   HARRYSTRUMAN   ARU
AMESS   HOG   ESE   LVI
TEE   UNITEDNATIONS   KIN
HERRIOT   EOLIC   OILING
GOTO   ANNIE   SWAN
SLATES   ARTES   TEARGAS
AIR   DETROITTIGERS   BLT
HES   RIA   NIL   HAOLE
ITO   STUARTLITTLE   BOER
BONFIRES   RACES   AWAKEN
INAS   DEVIL   STAT
HARLAN   ROMAN   TWISTOFF
ATOMICBOMB   EISENHOWER
LOPE   EASEL   STAAT   INLA
SPED   SHADE   SARTO   RSTU
```

143

```
CLINE   SAFE   SPAT   AWE
AIDED   CRAMP   MORSE   LEA
STEVELAMSMALEVETS   GAR
TRAINER   TENOR   SOTHERN
SELL   ALS   TAPIRS   AERIE
ADEPT   MANORS   LIES
SCRAM   TRAPATOYOTAPART
THEDAY   YUL   SOURS
RICHTER   SAMBA   MBE   ISR
IDEE   GAP   NEARS   NANCE
NEDRAGESINANISEGARDEN
GREED   TREND   WAR   LINT
SSS   ACT   TRYST   ROSEATE
SNARE   AEF   WINNER
DRAWALEVELAWARD   READS
RAGA   SPIROS   KEENE
AMANA   ALNICO   EVA   DRAM
GLISTEN   EROSE   OVERAGE
NIN   LENOSETAGATESONEL
ENS   ARENT   SKATE   ALONE
TET   SODA   ADES   ULNAE
```

144

```
SLOP   HERE   VESTAL   ARF
HYDE   ALERT   ELTORO   LEO
ARIA   CLEAR   REAGAN   TAR
HENRYKISSINGER   BECALM
TENSE   SUE   DISARMS
SCARNE   BED   DECOR
NINETYPERCENTOF   MOPED
INTEL   EXIT   OILY   ELUDE
PEI   STAG   MUTE   DIGIN
SNARL   SAGA   MONETS
THEPOLITICIANSGIVETHE
RACINE   WANT   ARLES
ANODE   CITE   STUD   ODO
MOLES   DISH   SEAM   ASPEN
PIERS   OTHERTENPERCENT
MESSY   AID   LEANTO
INFANTE   FIR   SLANT
BOUNTY   ABADREPUTATION
ELM   IMAMAN   ELENI   EDGE
ATE   AIRING   DINGO   ROLE
MED   LEASES   EDEN   SLED
```

145

```
PIA    PRESTO    ASOF   SALUKI
INN    RESTON    MAUI   INTRUST
THECOMPUTERISINCREDIBLY
TAMARIND    ADS   LOEW   LAP
SLIWA    SAGS   BARN   GUANO
FASTACCURATEANDSTUPID
AGHAST    LAD    ASS
OPTS   EARP   JET   SALTAWAY
LEOCHERNE   ANOTHER   ALETA
LORRE   MANISUNBELIEVABLY
INTUIT   CDROM   OWLET
EYEBROW   ENERO   LOGROLL
WHARF   RANTO   NAUSEA
SLOWINACCURATEAND   INCAS
HURON   CHALETS   BRILLIANT
OVERTAKE   TEO   LUXE   CRTS
KID   TWA   RESIST
THEMARRIAGEOFTHETWOIS
SHORE   EENY   TPKS   OBOES
HEN   PUNT   SUE   SAILINTO
AFORCEBEYONDCALCULATION
HORMONE   PLIE   LEADEN   ANY
GENOAN   EATS   PETITE   NSA
```

146

```
GAELIC    ANITRA    GOCOLD
AREOLA   GRUNION   URANIA
FARCES   EIDOLON   TATTER
FLYINTHEOINTMENT   CODE
ELOISE   ROACH
APR   ERNO   PLAIT   HEGEL
ROEBLING   FIANCE   AREGO
ATTAINS   TEENIE   DOINGS
BEATIT   ALIAS   HOTNESS
LEIS   HAULIN   ELEGIT
ENLIVENS   XTC   TRICHOID
HEATEN   HUDSON   ERNE
BEATTIE   UTERO   THRICE
ARCHER   PROSIT   THEYEAR
MILER   TAMIKO   PRETENSE
SCUBA   UNITY   FOAM   TES
ENATE   LASCAR
ARIL   BULLINACHINASHOP
REDFIN   LUNETTE   GITANO
PEERCE   EXCITOR   ESALEN
SLAYER   DEALER   RAGTAG
```

147

```
CIDER   SHAG   DAZE   ATWIST
ANAME   HOMO   SILEX   FIANCE
FLYINTHEOINTMENT   RESTON
TARTAR   UNEASE   OVERSHOT
ABA   LIVINGON   CRASS   ETH
NOTE   BAITANDSWITCH   PLUS
REAL   LIST   LEV   CHIP
ROSE   ADONIS   DOIN
BBC   CATCHASCATCHCAN   EPA
ALASKA   HORTON   RAINCOAT
RUSHER   ORRIN   ITEMS   OFNO
BETAS   SPEAR   GROWS   LODEN
AMOR   COSBY   FROND   FERULE
RANDOLPH   JOANIE   LASTER
ANE   BYHOOKORBYCROOK   YDS
STEM   PLANKS   AWED
CLAY   DNA   PAIR   DADA
LAOS   BITETHEBULLET   DEPP
ALT   ALVIN   DOLLEDUP   CRI
NOWADAYS   MEGALO   BOLLIX
ARISER   KEEPEROFTHEPEACE
TITTLE   ELLER   UMAS   ENROL
ECHOED   TIDE   TEXT   STETS
```

148

```
SODAS    APASS    CLARETS
EVENED   RADIAN   EATENUP
NESTER   ANUPHILLBATTLE
TRI   MACRAE   ANO   DORIC
UGLI   WAAC   REVS   REPS
POUNDEDTHEPAVEMENT
WARS   EPI   EMILE   FRI
TROIS   INTHELONGRUN
HITTHEBRICKS   ENEMIES
INTHEMAIN   SAMS   SORT
DESPOT   RETOOL
BATS   EROO   NOURISHED
ANIMALS   NOTUPTOSPEED
HADAGOODTIME   TERRE
STY   INURE   PTS   ASEA
JOINEDTHEHUMANRACE
TOJO   DADE   EDIT   SCAN
IREST   MEN   ALDERS   USA
GOTHEEXTRAMILE   ATOMIC
ENTENTE   SNIDER   PATENT
ROASTED   TOADS   NONOS
```

149

```
BEACHES    PUEBLO    TOPOFF
ARCHAIC   ATTAIN   ARTURO
STRINGOFPEARLS   PLATES
SEE   GETA   RAE   ROSSES
ARTCOLLECTION   TSE
SHIRR   THAIS   COSTA
MEDUSAS   ABE   HOOT   INON
ARES   PAIROFJEANS   EDNA
CON   SETTER   ANTS   SPIER
KIT   TRUE   FIR   WINDY
CITE   PRICELIST   INGA
DAFOE   SAD   PUSS   BYE
FLYUP   MALL   MOUNTS   ISM
CLIP   DAYAFTERDAY   SLAM
SYNE   ETES   ADD   SEVILLE
GEARS   FRIES   INSET
ADM   DOUBLEPARKERS
SEADOG   EON   IDEA   CEO
TARARA   CONNCETINGRODS
ANKLET   KNEELS   TEENAGE
RESIDE   SYLVIA   SEDATES
```

150

```
SAVANT    SAWDUST    CARD
CLOVER   PREENER   SOFAR
OPTIMAL   UTILITY   ALFIE
THEDOCOFNIGHT   OFF   ALS
SAD   EPI   CHI   CURE   IRS
IFS   GELT   ROTOR   ROE
ADELE   ABLE   GEMS   TSAR
DIXIE   LAM   DOTE   BROODS
REPEL   BROCADES   RIFF
ITE   SMU   ADULT   ACUTER
FED   MEMBERATLODGE   HUH
TRIBAL   ANTIC   ASP   EGO
TILT   FRESHMAN   ACHED
SPILLS   FORT   ETC   DRONE
POOL   ELLS   SATE   DATES
ERN   PANEL   RITA   GYM
APT   ABCD   BAN   CRO   MBA
ROO   YEA   HOCKTHEHERALD
GIMME   SPANISH   POWERED
USAGE   ESTONIA   MENIAL
NESS   DISSENT   ESTATE
```

151

ABACULUS · ATTAR · ARABIA
WELLNIGH · BOONE · RADIOS
ELVISTHEPELVIS · CROONS
AVEC · ALE · BAER
ETHELREDTHEUNREADY
HAT · IDE · ORANGE · SLOE
ALOES · GNAW · OLD · OTT
WILTTHESTILT · OLATHE
SETOSE · ERA · SOMUCHAS
ENE · IMA · IPSOFACTO
RICHARDTHELIONHEARTED
ELECTORAL · OAR · HAR
PARISIAN · TIS · NICETY
ASSISI · MACKTHEKNIFE
ARK · PTA · AIRE · ESSAY
DEED · AUGURS · UNO · STE
EDWARDTHECONFESSOR
WADE · NAG · COED
SLEDGE · JOHNTHEBAPTIST
GELLER · ONSET · STRAINER
TOYERS · BETTY · TUSKEGEE

152

FLA · ISM · CASTS · SKIMPS
RETASTE · ODIUM · SPINOUT
ANOTHER · BONGO · WORLDLY
COMMONCAWS · OREO · YELL
ARIOT · HRE · BOTHERS · REE
SEC · BAABAASHOP · WANTS
SPENT · DIMES · PATH
EARNEST · GATOR · DENTIST
BLOATS · SONES · FINESSED
BLAKE · COODEGRACE · SAS
URE · LOAF · LESE · PTS
ADS · PURRFORMER · CHOIR
LECTURES · CEASE · HAIRDO
ADHERES · STANS · DELAYED
ACED · SCADS · ARIEL
CACHE · MOOVIESTAR · BIB
ICH · STOLLEN · ERG · AGORA
CUTE · ILED · NEIGHSAYER
ETERNAL · INFER · LATRINE
RESTERS · NOONE · ELAPSES
ORTEGA · GREED · SOB · HST

153

GUM · CSPAN · ACERB · GAMUT
ALE · HAUTE · POLAR · IRANI
SUNDAYNIGHTLIVE · LENIN
LOINS · TAO · USED · ANITA
TAROT · TERMS · BRACES
ATAD · CAGE · UNA · MOIST
REHEARSE · PBS · MARV · USS
ASS · JOHNBOY · FINDE · EWE
DOCTOROW · UNSER · SEE
AMOK · HAILE · REAR · ODER
PLATEAU · MEDIT · TSTRAPS
OPUS · TRAM · NEHRU · HAYS
KIN · ITSME · EVEARDEN
END · NADER · SERFDOM · WAS
DEY · SCAN · FDR · FAREWELL
FLUKY · SEA · HIYA · ILIE
CAROLS · TRYTO · IDLED
UTICA · AZOV · ANT · GREEN
SADAT · SUPERBOWLMONDAY
PLATO · ALINE · RISEN · UTO
SLYER · PUTTY · STUNS · PEN

154

CASE · ADAMS · PAAR · POKE
HULA · MODEL · SINCE · OBIT
IRAS · PIANO · PETRI · LOSE
PAVEMENTDEFICIENCIES
MERGES · AGES · VAT
ALLEGES · TIO · CEDILLA
LEONA · NAILTECHNICIAN
CANT · NOOSES · WHIT · ONT
ODE · RIVET · PEEL · KINK
VERTICALINSERTIONS
ENSILE · EEL · SEISMO
PERSONALTIMECENTER
CUSS · CHAT · VITAL · RLS
POS · HAIR · ORATOR · CATO
ENERGYDOCUMENT · BATON
INROADS · NED · REASONS
ARR · SWIG · SMELLS
AIRBORNEPARTICULATES
TERI · GUISE · EARED · BOLL
BRAN · ENDED · ALONE · ARLO
SONG · NEER · PESTS · STAT

155

ETNA · DADA · BORES · AYE
LOAFS · ELAN · ENACT · LORE
BUTTERFLYTRACTOR · DURA
OCT · LEIS · FETES · OPERAS
WHIFFLE · PAGE · DENOTE
SELL · DEERINGOVER · LAD
RYES · YAMS · OBI · IND
DOTTER · ATON · LUFFS
PST · CHARLESSHEEP · BOAT
ATH · IRIS · UCLA · ELIXIR
TOENAIL · SCRUM · PLIABLE
TOKILL · AHEM · PELT · ALA
EGAN · LIONREPORTER · GEM
DEREK · DICE · MASTER
ASA · ONT · ACAD · SAPS
ATT · PALKANGAROO · PLUS
THERUB · EENS · DENSEST
LEGATO · BLAND · IDEO · APE
ASON · MYLITTLEBIRDADEE
WEAK · BEAME · EMIT · EMEND
STS · SABER · RUDY · ADDS

156

MARCIA · LIL · WACS · SPIN
ANOINT · EDER · OMAN · PONE
DIDNT[BAT]ANEYE · MINA · ALTE
ALICE · TOADS · [BAT]TERFRIED
MENORAH · LEIF · YALE · CRI
ICE · INDUS · SELENE
[BAT]TLEMENTS · ENATE · USSR
IRIDS · IOTA · MERMAN
SINS · DANSE · [BAT]ONROUGE
TAN · CINE · RATA · SCREAM
ALEMAN · STIPEND · HASSAM
STINGS · EARN · ETAL · ERI
SAB[BAT]ICAL · ESTHS · ROIL
SYSTEM · DOOR · SAUNA
SCAM · ELENA · MOUNT[BAT]TEN
PALATE · DACHE · STR
ATE · VAST · PROP · THICKET
TAKEASTA[BAT] · OLLIE · CHORE
ILSA · TINA · [BAT]MANRETURNS
APES · OLGA · SECO · DETEST
LAIT · NEON · SEN · TREATS

157

S	T	E	P	S		F	E	A	R		O	H	N	O		F	A	T	A	S
A	R	G	O	N		L	A	R	A		Z	E	A	L		I	D	O	N	T
S	E	A	N	O	C	A	S	E	Y		A	N	N	E	B	R	O	N	T	E
S	Y	N	D	R	O	M	E		B	U	R	R	O		A	T	R	E	S	T

STEPS FEAR OHNO FATAS / ARGON LARA ZEAL IDONT / SEANOCASEY ANNEBRONTE / SYNDROME BURRO ATREST / ETRE MURKY WIRE / SOIREE VERGE SHREDDER / UNSER JOHNERSKINE ITE / LEAD BAIT AIRS ACHE / FAA VACLAVHAVEL BIKED / AMCHITKA AILED GADFLY / AUNTS RUNGS SURER / BOSLEY HENGE OPENDATE / ARIAS GUNTERGRASS NRA / RIMS FARE AVIS SCAM / BOO WALTWHITMAN DEICE / INVOICES ONEAL BEASTS / BLIN ANNAL WOIM / ATTILA BLESS THERIGHT / LEOTOLSTOY EDWARDLEAR / INNEW TUNE TOIL RETRO / STORY USED SANE ESSEN

158

RACE MARI ARARAT BEAD / LEGAL EDITS BODICE OTTO / ILONA GOOUT SUDANRATHER / PANAMAANDPAKETTLE ITISI / TID ILIE MINEO ALLOTS / LIZA MIS LINT STREEP / EVEREST GONE SCOOT SIGN / BESET HUNGARYCOOPER ALI / HAS NOEL ERATO ABZUG / DANA TRIMS DOILY AVIATE / ELON AUTO COMP AMENDER / COR ARGENTINATURNER ONI / REMOVES ANON PINE ARIA / EVADED BAKER OWNER MANN / TENOR SALEM BRAG SEE / ARD BOHEMIAFARROW ERASE / LAYS DERAT ARID RELINES / ROYALS STES SIC CATS / BOONES STAUB POSH ATS / AMONG BOLIVIANEWTONJOHN / SENEGALGORE CUPEL COLOR / IGET PEEPER KNUTE ANITA / NAYS TWEEDS SPOT AGAS

159

UPSET ABIT STOCK DOES / POWER BOSH HANOI ENDO / OPERA HARECOMESTHESUN / NEE DOOR RAVEL ERICA / THEIR MANED CHAPTER / ASSAIL LIVID SLURRED / SCORN BADEN CHANDU / TALK MYDINGOLING DIRT / ORE SALES ZEN WEWON / MICRON STORE RANOUT / KUWAIT THINK MUSCLE / CASALS DRAPE BELIEF / UTILE OID GREEN FAR / PECK OWLBEAROUND GOBI / THRACE BENNY CELLO / ENHANCE CADET PALLET / SLEEVES NOSIR PESTO / ATALE SOLER GOAT WBA / GORILLAMYDREAMS OTHER / AREO CRUEL CREE FAINT / LORN DITSY TEND FUMES

160

CUBS ERROR PAPA CODEX / OGEE MAURO IMAS OLIVE / SHELLINGOUTCASH HIVED / ISRAELI TOADS BEVIN / WAIN RETRO FIRES / MASADA MUTED FINERIES / ODORS NOBODYELSES OLA / LOUD TORO PITT PNIN / ARN LAWOFFICERS BESOT / REDROBIN INLET DESOTO / IAMBS MODUS SEAOF / MANRAY LORIN STARSHIP / ORGAN MIDDAYMEALS ONE / TELE WALE ALIT SUET / ICI GENTLEWOMEN TERRE / FAKERIES CHUMS FEASTS / EXERT ZLOTY HILL / TAPED LOOMS EXISTED / BACON PINGPONGRACKETS / AROSE BLEU LEROT ITEM / TOWER AIDE DOONE NESS

161

ASH ALTERS TAPS HASH / TKO MEANIT ELENI ISLE / HUSKYVOICE LATIN TEAR / OLEO DEVILSADVOCATE / SLAV DISSECT LEIGH / AERO AHAS TRISTE / CHECKOUTTIMES REENTRY / LETSUP MANE IDES GEAR / ORT SMELT DEI SPADE / GOES BENCHPRESS HOLES / HAYS ASI SEES / LABOR SETTINGSUN TOTS / ADIOS IRA SANER MOI / NEAT BEEF PESO OFFING / CALIPER FLASHBULLETIN / ELINOR RYAN ALAN / GOTTA TITTERS DIRE / SMASHHITRECORD EDEN / KANT ALTAR DAILYBREAD / ILKA SELMA OILIER ACE / PEAR SEAL STEINS LTD

162

RIVET PISA ATT KALE / GENEVA UGHS ROUE IMAM / ABREAK FEASTOFFLOWERS / PEOPLEOFTHESOUTHWIND / ELMS OSO STEM SIN / SSE ENSUE USHER / GREATMOUNTAINPLACE / STEN ONCOURSE AURA / MOONEYED ALERTED PLUM / AUTOSALE ALIS / GREATRIVER SNOWCAPPED / ELAN NOTREADY / AMES CASINOS GERTRUDE / NAPA OUTHUNTS IOLA / TRIBEOFSUPERIORMEN / EXCEL SNEER ITS / ETA ODER ENC ASIA / TOWNOFTHELARGECANOES / SKYTINTEDWATER ALIBIS / LOEW ERNE NINA NOTANY / OSSO ATM DOOM SEARS

163

```
VAMP  ABANDON  AMASSED
OLEOS LUCIANO  ROMANCE
TAROT IRONIES  DRACULA
ETCHES GRASP PETS BAR
REY ATHENS IRANI ESTE
 ADAIR LEON CUL
CALLINS DECO PINATAS
ORATED SUAVE DEADPANS
MISERS ORNE TOP OSCAR
BAH ISOBAR ERS NESTS
 BANANA ASIDES
FACES DEN SERENE SEA
AGARS IRE CLAY BIGMAC
RESTORES BRITS AROUSE
RETIRES TOES FRONTED
 ETA CROW BORNE
PAWS CLOAK BEEPED HAM
OLE STYX SOULS DUBOSE
KINGPIN CASSIUS KIOWA
ENCLAVE ULSTERS ETHAN
REHIRES MEASLES SANS
```

164

```
HECTOR GALAHAD FAMED
EROICA EXAMINE VACATE
MARGERYMETALEPRECHAUN
STEELIES JAN ARTEMIS
 OTT SPORT NBA
TOASTY BARRY ODE APIS
OCHO AARE INON VINO
WHOSAIDHISNAMEWASESAU
IER NCOS AMAIN PRAWN
TRAITOR TABARD MOANED
 NONEBUT SEATING
ASPENS ATREST RAGEDAT
MAORI CROIX TIME ORE
ALOTOFHERAPLOMBISGONE
DALI LESS ABEE ERIN
ODEA ORT COZEN HALSEY
 SRI MONEY TIT
AGOUTIS ILE WISHBONE
SINCESHESAWESAUSEESAW
ARMLET SEDATED ENDIVE
PLEAD PRAYERS SASSES
```

165

```
DOLCE STEW ASAP ACED
AREAS OVOID EARL MAMA
DRISTANANDISOLDE IRAN
ASAHARA TRALA AENEID
 BANGTHETUMSSLOWLY
LOST TAO SITES
AXIOMS GLACE EDITORS
PERPETUALMOTRIN EUBIE
PYE NOV ALOUS LEDA
 ENTIRE BJANDTHEBAYER
 RAMAPO DOESIN
FAMILYSUCRETS ASLEEP
ALEX SCORE REB LEA
RELIC THEAGEOFANACINS
RELEASE MONTE EOCENE
 SCRAP TEC ILEA
BUFFERINSUCCOTASH
ARIOSO KAROL BOOTIES
LION ONALEVEOFABSENCE
SENT GERM EASEL EXTRA
ALAS ETAS TUNA STOUT
```

166

```
 GAMED HARASS SEETHE
ERNANI DOVELET CACHES
NETWORKINGGIRL ARREST
ICE ENCE BAUER UBI
DODGECITYSLICKERS ITA
 RITT SOU ELEA GAT
TAPINS AGUES DOCENT
AGAPE REPENT RACY
DOPE OBOL JESS EASE
ARE BLEAKHOUSEPARTY
 ARCADES ONS COPTERS
 MYLEFTFOOTLOOSE IER
COST YSER ANNE EDNA
SOOT TABARD BLEST
HANSON DAYAN FRERES
ETS TOME STA ELAN
ALT COOLEYHIGHSOCIETY
 IRA NEURO AUTO CAV
UNUSED GODFATHERGOOSE
SECADA EDERLES EARLES
ORKNEY DELAYS DOTER
```

167

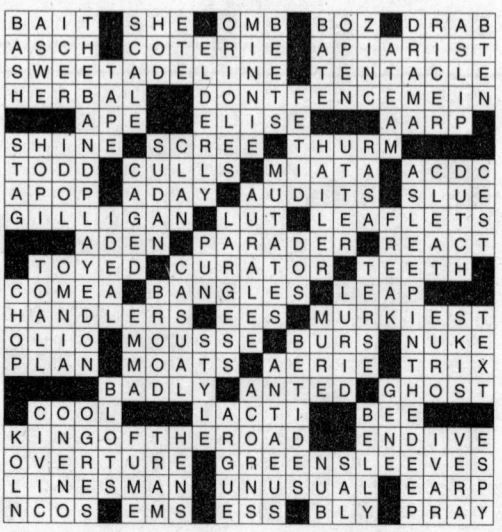

```
BAIT SHE OMB BOZ DRAB
ASCH COTERIE APIARIST
SWEETADELINE TENTACLE
HERBAL DONTFENCEMEIN
 APE ELISE AARP
SHINE SCREE THURM
TODD CULLS MIATA ACDC
APOP ADAY AUDITS SLUE
GILLIGAN LUT LEAFLETS
 ADEN PARADER REACT
 TOYED CURATOR TEETH
COMEA BANGLES LEAP
HANDLERS EES MURKIEST
OLIO MOUSSE BURS NUKE
PLAN MOATS AERIE TRIX
 BADLY ANTED GHOST
COOL LACTI BEE
KINGOFTHEROAD ENDIVE
OVERTURE GREENSLEEVES
LINESMAN UNUSUAL EARP
NCOS EMS ESS BLY PRAY
```

168

```
TIBIAL TRIMMER FASTER
ENESCO RESCALE INHALE
ACHIER AFRIENDINDEXED
SLO DEVIL IRON SAGA
DULL NINES ONAN BIT
ADDON NEXTPROFIT GLEE
LETMESEE ALA TARTNESS
ESHARP PLATA NERO
 EXTERNALCITY TOMLIN
RAM SWOON ENTAL TEASE
ALAS SATAN GALAS STLO
SANTA DICES CINES EEN
PIXELS THENAKEDAPEX
 EPPS EDENS MAMBOS
SUBPOENA NED BASTILLE
APES CAMEOROLEX ERODE
LGE PENT RIDER SOLD
ARTE BARR ELLIS MAC
MARXISTCOLLEGE VENETO
IDEATE ELAINES EGERIA
SEEMED SLYNESS DOESNT
```

169

```
MORBID  PRAY  ASS   SNIP
OTOOLE  REFERENCE   IONA
WHOLLSTOPTHERAIN  TBAR
SOFTWORDS   MAP  ACTONE
     ITO  AHOT  IMPEDED
WHATNOWMYLOVE  GERRY
EELED  EAGLE  COL  SIGH
BAAL  ASTRAY  FATS  KEA
STRETCHED  BURR  RENEW
    TITO  ELIJAH  EROSE
SOLAR  PUBLICITY  FEWER
CREPE  ABASES   THEM
RATED  ROSE  APHORIZES
ITS  SOAK  CALLME  TAMP
MEGA  HUT  CARLA  RESEE
OLEIN  HOWCANIBESURE
ACCEDED  ANKA   SEC
BARREL  TLC  SEALERIES
OCAT  DOYOUWANTTODANCE
MAZE  SUPERSTAR  VENICE
BOYD  RES  WAGE  EDITED
```

170

```
LAMAR  SPAN  TATAS  TAPER
ALINE  OLEO  AREIN  OLIVES
DINER  FORT  CLARA  RESENT
  IWENTTOABOOKSTOREANDI
WAS  AES  LUM  CHE  NEER
ASKEDTHEWOMANBEHIND  DRS
SHIPS  OMITS  AUX  OTIC
ACRE  CEOS  CHRIS  STALAG
BATEAU  THECOUNTER  CREME
INS  IRAE  MAIM  TISH  ROT
ADAS  SERF  HAUNT  COCO
WHERETHESELFHELPSECTION
HELM  ORDER  UMPS  EROS
IAM  GREG  TROT  ERIC  MOW
GREBE  WASSHESAID  LAREDO
STRAND  RITES  MISE  ITOR
DIES  LOY  BRETT  SCHUL
NAG  IFITOLDYOUTHATWOULD
AMER  ALA  ELL  RIO  SSS
DEFEATTHEWHOLEPURPOSE
INFEST  IDIOM  SOLI  SOLON
ADESTE  TETRA  ORNE  IRANI
SNEAD  INSAN  FEAR  ETHEL
```

171

```
SCAM  LADD  CANS  ALIBI
PACA  ISEE  RIATA  FATAL
ONTHEBALL  ORCAS  OBESE
IWILL  BTU  WELLGROOMED
LEVELHEADED  LOATH
AREEL  INSIDEOF  ETON
EAT  SLING  REDD  MINI
STOAS  IGLOOS  APPEASE
PARCHESI  IAN  ASOR  REC
STORM  ASK  AGGREGATE
STRAIGHTSHOOTER
BONAPARTE  REA  LIMES
APE  UNTO  DEM  ADAPTIVE
REGATTA  RHEIMS  TAXIS
BRER  SINO  PIPER  PEA
SAVE  PASSWORD  NONCE
AVOWS  DOWNTOEARTH
APOWERHOUSE  IER  ALCOA
LABAN  IBSEN  FAULTLESS
FLOYD  PETES  ELSE  ANAT
AMESS  RAKE  DETS  STYE
```

172

```
ETAL  SEEM  JOSTLE  STOW
MUTE  ULNA  OBERON  PAVO
BROWNRICE  HOWARDBAKER
ERN  AMOY  NNE  SCOOTERS
RECRUIT  ROD  SHAWS  SIT
STEERS  EUROPE  TRUCE
QUEENSMERCY  LOOPED
ECRU  DASH  ATAMANS
SHEIK  SUPPLY  LEHR  WAD
COATI  TEARY  TUTTI  ARE
APPENDS  COMER  EIDOLON
PIE  GRIME  PROMO  ENNUI
END  SADA  THAYER  REUSE
UTTERLY  BRIM  ETES
MOSSES  CAPITALCITY
ATEAM  HONORE  COERCE
CHE  PAYER  AND  GRADUAL
RESOLDER  ASS  GROS  FRY
ALFREDSMITH  REEDTUFTS
ELIE  LEANTO  INTO  ALOE
SOTS  ESSENE  MEAT  RENE
```

173

```
HOTBED  BALM  VACATER
ETHANE  STRIAE  ACADEME
STENOS  THELITTLEFOXES
SOS  LAROSA  DIREST  ANO
EMU  ALAN  KRONOR  AANDW
SANS  THEYOUNGLIONS
NATO  DEUS  LED  OSIS
LARA  ATHOME  DENOTE
MOSTEVER  EWER  YEMEN
AHOUSEDIVIDED  ERE  ERA
TIRE  RIGOR  MIATA  OCAT
IOI  WYE  WIDEISTHEGATE
NASTY  MENE  TEATIMES
ENEROS  ORANGS  LAVE
ESSO  INN  ORIG  SERF
INTOTHEVALLEY  SUIT
BALSA  TOULON  EBAN  NNE
ELI  PLAYBY  USABLE  NAP
ABSALOMABSALOM  IRVINE
TESSERA  LEVELS  EVINCE
SEEPSIN  EEGS  SEDGES
```

174

```
PASTA  LESSONED  ETCETERA
DRAYS  INITIATE  SAARINEN
QTIPS  LAZYSUSANSARANDON
BENOTE  EXES  HELD  ROSA
ARTS  MRED  EMILS  IDO
CIV  AMEX  KEATS  CAROLS
HOE  TYPHOIDMARYPICKFORD
REVS  AULD  EYE  VIA
DIORS  MUSTANGSALLYFIELD
IANS  RESTE  ARISE  VILLAS
EMITTENT  DIVEST  ROSLYN
MAC  HESS  SAE  BUNK  RKO
CABALA  OZARKS  AMNESIAC
TAHITI  AROAR  PALME  ETNA
AMAZINGGRACEKELLY  GRASS
REM  OUI  CRAY  GOSH
PRETTYPENNYMARSHALL  ASH
ALICES  BERRY  OLOF  YMA
MUS  THANG  MOAB  TWIN
AHAM  SURA  REBA  EPHODS
CALAMITYJANEFONDA  LARGO
TSARINAS  BEETROOT  INTEL
STRAIGHT  SANSKRIT  ETHNO
```

175

```
INVEST  LISTEE   BEWARE
LEANTO  ENTERS   SERAPES
OTTERNONSENSE    CARRELS
    REEK  PEST  MARSH
 OBOE ABIDE SERB  ORCA
GNUSPAPER DELRIO   LAOS
EER  BINET NICENE  BUS
MAROON EDITED  RETABLE
SLOBBER  FAMER  SOVIET
 OSIRIS  FLYROD  NOTES
 PFC  STOP   STOA  CTS
TOQUE ENRAGE  COSTAR
INURED GOMER  MONDALE
STEELER MADAMS STONED
HOE SEASON TIARA  SAG
RONA RIATAS LIONDRIVE
INST SLUE PLINY  ROTE
 TRAWL  MEAT  AMOS
MARIANA JACKALLANTERN
ABILITY ORIENT TEETER
CANADA  EXERTS ERRATA
```

176

```
CRAB SAGAS ARRAS  AGRA
LIMA CLASH TEASE  BRAS
ACOLLECTIONOFPACKRATS
PERSONAE RELIT  EATEN
 ADEN  STILT  MATHERS
SOMME  SLAG   MECCA
AMASSOFHIGHCHURCHMEN
SIR ALINE HATER   REF
STEM KING GALE ALCOVE
 AGENT  ALIT   AEDES
ASTRINGOFBASSFIDDLERS
CHOIR   ROSE   ABODE
RETOOK WARS BEER  BALE
OBE  ELENA SERAI  SOL
AMINEOFKLEPTOMANIACS
 MENAT  RITE   OMNIA
ELAPSED ABATE  CARP
TOBAT  ARETE TASMANIA
ANASSEMBLYOFMECHANICS
GELS LABEL ULNAE  ELEE
ERLE LEASE LINOS  LEDA
```

177

```
REAM KIWI  ARCO  UNFIT
ENZO IRAQ BARRS  TULSA
YOURPLAYSORMINE  TREAT
SCREEDS BARBECUESAWS
 HELGA NEMO   PRES
 GRACES DECKS  SLIP
THEEYESAGE RHEAS  IRE
HURLS TWA FLAIR  TUNAS
ELIS BRET EATER  ANENT
MAKEGOODEWESOF STUDIO
 ODS   ELS   SEI
ORALLY PARFORTHECORES
VOTED MINEO AUER  PAVE
ELLIE ELGAR MLI  MAGEE
REO NIGEL FALLSALARM
TOOL LASES IDEALS
 SANK  TARA   UTHER
THEPEASCORPS  SMEARED
RINSE ROBERTTHEBRUISE
ADDED STOWE WAGE  TEEM
MESSY  YENS  OMAR  ESTO
```

178

```
CAREW  SHIVS ANATHEMA
INIGO  ALICIA IAMWOMAN
SONGOFMYSELF LIBERIUS
 PLATES  LEVELLER
HAMLETS  PAWED  EDICT
OCEANS LARIAT BRIDOON
SCAN OROGENY ERSE  GEE
TENTO ADAY ELI  RAISA
EDD USCG NIXONS  STIR
LEM THEEGOIST GIBSONS
 YODA  SUPPORT  LONE
BESTOWS MIAFARROW RVS
ELHI MOPPET  EAST  GAT
ABACI LIS DENG  OVOLO
SOD DAIS FRUSTUM  ASIN
TWOFOLD SEENTO ACCUSE
SWELL YEMEN  ASHAMED
 RATIONAL  GARSON
SCRUTINY LETATCESTMOI
OSOLEMIO ECHOES ELENA
CABARETS STYLE  NYLON
```

179

```
TAINT REPRO HEMPS STEPS
ABNER ALAMO AVAIL EAMON
MISSINGLYNX BENNY AMBLE
ALPS ELON MART   MARIA
LEA BEARESSENTIALS RACK
END EDNA LATE STAT ACES
SEE AYS BABAR  TRANCE
SON FOWLLANGUAGE  AFT
 ASH LOSE ERN  STABLE
SECT AFAR ECHOES TILES
NAHS VAN HIDERS COLLECT
OTO GEL BADGNUS ORE EKE
RECALLS OWLETS BUG EWER
ENOLA ESSAYS PITA BEDS
RULING ICI EPEE  NOR
SPA CRASHINGBOAR  DOW
THEIST OLEOS MAE  ADO
ALEE ETES BORK SALT FUR
PUMA GORILLATACTICS FRA
IGORS MEET ARGO  ALAN
COOKE TYPES HARERAISING
ASSET WOLDS ADAGE DENTE
LIENS OBESE GETAT SAGES
```

180

```
BASKETS  BIGGAME  LUCAS
OCTAVIA  INORDER  OZONE
THEYALLCONTAINA  SIMON
HYPO LEON AYN  SOL  PUN
 HERNIATE  STROMATA
RUBBERNECK  RENUMBER
AMOUR OHAIR XES   ODIN
TBONES EROTICA USESUP
ORS EDAM ETUDES   ODE
NOTECARD PSAS  SHATNER
 MELISSA  NEATENS
JUBILEE CURD GARDENED
UTA  GRILLE VASE  ELI
SARDIS SEVENAM DAYGLO
HOER TER KOREA  CURED
MARIANAO  TIMBERLINE
THEFIRST  FRIENDLY
RAT GAT INE GOUP  LALA
ARENA EUROPEANCAPITAL
STRUT INATROT  TSARINA
HESSE TAKEONE  SONATAS
```

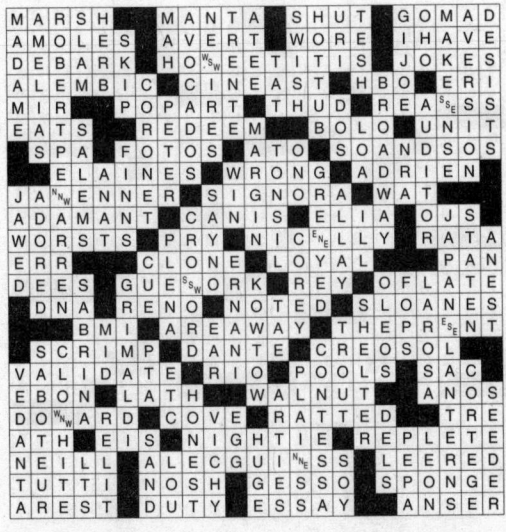
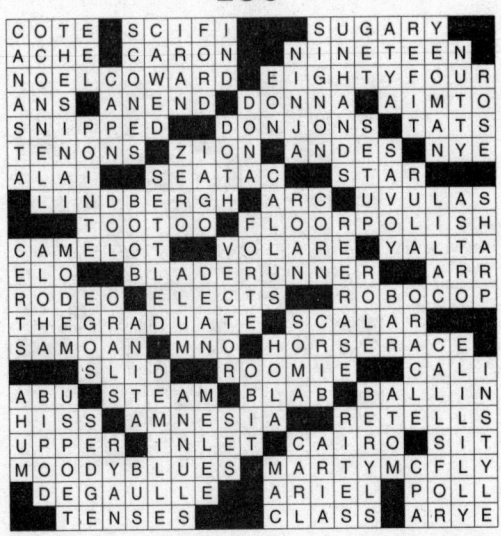

181

```
ARAFAT   CHICAGO      BRAG
PAULVI   IHATEYOU     IRENE
INDIANAGOVERNOR       DUANE
ATEN  ERR  EMF    TSONGAS
ONCD  EARL    ALOT    EASE
HEINIE    SCREWEDIN
BIS   SLANGFORMONEY   SEN
AVOWAL    EARLY    DELUXE
SYNODIC   LATIMES   SACCO
ELGRECOS  NINEVEH   ICON
ESS  ICET    GAGA    DER
GATT  TOWARDS   NARCOSIS
OGRES  ASSENTS   SPOUSAL
SUEDES    NEAPS   INTOTO
HES   TYPEOFPROTEST   REB
SCHROEDER     TEATRO
SPCA  IRKS    ASPS   ASAP
TRAUMAS    TBA   STE  CLAP
PARSE   CITYINAUSTRALIA
ADEER   HOOKEDUP   CORONA
TOYS    EUTERPE     HESTER
```

182

```
DANCED   CRUDES    UPSTAGE
EMILIE   HEGIRA    ROTATED
SILENTBUTLERS      CRASHES
IDEA  AIM   ITES   HORSE
NICK   REED   LISTENED
MUMSTHEWORD    JONES   IRE
EPEES   RPM    TAU    CAIN
NEDS     MURMURINGPINES
INI   PBA   LEON   SOLID
ADA   ROT   UAR    ATONERS
LETMEWHISPERINYOUREAR
DEALERS    LAS   EMP   QUO
TIROS   ALGA   TYS   UNO
SHUTMYBIGMOUTH      AITS
HOPE    LIP   IOS   ARRET
ESS   BALLS   DUMBWAITERS
ATTORNEY   SONE   ACRE
ALIGN   ATMS   ARC   RAGA
SMIDGEN   QUIETAMERICAN
EARTHLY   UNNEAR   SHAMED
DESOTOS   ATONCE   SOLELY
```

183

```
TUBBS   AQUA   GSPOT   CAMP
APART   LUNE   UHURU   ARIA
RIDER   DIDO   MOPINGPONG
FLEURDELIMOS      IMPUTE
ASA   ASI   RIB    ANT   SIB
CHICKENALAMOKING      LENO
METHYL   RIN   PILAF   EDGY
ELHI   ESME   KILL   OWN
PASTA   SMUTS   REALES
PROMISED   TAME   AKIHITO
RUMOR   WATERDROP   MOLTO
ANANIAS   HAME   RIPARIAN
MENDES   HADON   ALARM
ART   ATIT   ICES   OLID
FOWL   REESE   SNL   SANITY
OPIE   OSCARMODELARENTA
REN   ONE    TCU   EGG   GOD
ENDURO   MOPSILOVEYOU
ITSNOMOUSE   AGUE   LOINS
GOOD   ELISE   LESE   ENNIO
NERO   RERAN   SSTS   SAINT
```

184

```
ROACH   EVAN   BUD    SITES
ARNIE   DIRE   AHAB   PSHAW
METALLICMIXTURE    ALATE
AGO   PET    LATHES   CANOE
DANA   SHOP   XES   TIEMEUP
ANITAS   NEWER   AID   ISTS
SOOTHEFEARS    BLANC
IONESCO   DILL   EGGS
SCARY   VIENNESE   ROUTE
CAME   PEZ   GETA   CODDLED
UNE   DIRECTORWOODY   LEG
BANJOES   LUNA   VUE   CELA
ADDON   HERSCHEL   SATYR
ASIN   NOON   TARDIER
NEVER   BOWLINGLANE
RIFF   AWN   PARKA   LOOSER
ENROLLS   AIR   EYRE   STAN
AFIRE   MAPLES   ATT   ORE
PENCE   APPORTIONSHARES
EAGER   NEAT   ECHO   EXIST
DRESS   RLS   PEON   YEATS
```

185

```
MARSH   MANTA   SHUT   GOMAD
AMOLES  AVERT   WORE   IHAVE
DEBARK  HOWSWEETITIS   JOKES
ALEMBIC  CINEAST   HBO  ERI
MIR   POPART   THUD   REASSESS
EATS   REDEEM   BOLO   UNIT
SPA   FOTOS   ATO   SOANDSOS
ELAINES   WRONG   ADRIEN
JANWENNER   SIGNORA   WAT
ADAMANT   CANIS   ELIA   OJS
WORSTS   PRY   NICENELLY   RATA
ERR   CLONE   LOYAL   PAN
DEES   GUESSWORK   REY   OFLATE
DNA   RENO   NOTED   SLOANES
BMI   AREAWAY   THEPRESENT
SCRIMP   DANTE   CREOSOL
VALIDATE   RIO   POOLS   SAC
EBON   LATH   WALNUT   ANOS
DOWNWARD   COVE   RATTED   TRE
ATH   EIS   NIGHTIE   REPLETE
NEILL   ALECGUINNESS   LEERED
TUTTI   NOSH   GESSO   SPONGE
AREST   DUTY   ESSAY   ANSER
```

186

```
COTE   SCIFI      SUGARY
ACHE   CARON      NINETEEN
NOELCOWARD   EIGHTYFOUR
ANS   ANEND   DONNA   AIMTO
SNIPPED   DONJONS   TATS
TENONS   ZION   ANDES   NYE
ALAI   SEATAC   STAR
LINDBERGH   ARC   UVULAS
TOOTOO   FLOORPOLISH
CAMELOT   VOLARE   YALTA
ELO   BLADERUNNER   ARR
RODEO   ELECTS   ROBOCOP
THEGRADUATE   SCALAR
SAMOAN   MNO   HORSERACE
SLID   ROOMIE   CALI
ABU   STEAM   BLAB   BALLIN
HISS   AMNESIA   RETELLS
UPPER   INLET   CAIRO   SIT
MOODYBLUES   MARTYMCFLY
DEGAULLE   ARIEL   POLL
TENSES   CLASS   ARYE
```

187

```
DIVAS  MCS   SLAB  ALMOST
AGENT  OOH   TORE  DEAVER
BORNONTHEFOURTHOFJULY
STY  NITA  IGNITE  TOLES
     SET  NOBIGDEAL  RENT
DEFLATE  CREE  LAB   SES
ALLEGIANCE     PATTIS
SLADE  SEAS  TOTHEFLAG
HAT  SIAM  SODA  ROOFED
   TASTER  PENA  CAINE
THESTARSPANGLEDBANNER
SARAI    RUSS    BAILEE
PLEDGE  KALE  TORN  MOI
FROMSEATO  TALI  SAENS
   GASLIT  SHININGSEA
FIN  SEL  THEO  GLUESON
ENOS  SEPARATES   IFS
THREW  RERIGS  LOAF  ODE
IAMTHEYANKEEDOODLEBOY
SLATED  RIEN  AMP  EXILE
HELOTS  LESS  DOS  STEED
```

188

```
CHIC  MOMMA  APR  PLATED
AONE  IDEAL  ROO  JETHRO
PRELUDETOAKISS  SATEEN
ASSENTTO  MOSSY   ACIS
     STES  AERIE  BOSCO
FACTOR  ANDAN  FORTKNOX
ALAE  MUSTANGSALLY  TOR
LAMS  SOI  TIDY   GIZA
SIP  JOHNCOUGAR   TANEY
END  ELEE  PROLE  SHREDS
     ASTER  SEGAL  CAIRN
DEVITO  APRES  FLAN  TSE
AMITY  TOASKYLARK   ATA
RODE  CARO  OAR   ILES
ETA  SEVENSAMURAI  MOVE
RECHARGE  TROVE  NAPPED
     CANTS  PADRE  OTRA
STOL  ASTOR  KNEECAPS
CARVER  CHEROKEENATION
UPDATE  TAL  WINOS  EDNA
MESHED  HWY  STONE  DEEP
```

189

```
MESH  EPOS   PELF   WEARE
ILAY  PARA  DALAI  ACMES
RILE  ICES  IHAVE  RHEAS
THENETHASFALLENUPONME
HUMANOID  ALA   DNA
   UMS  DROVER   ITHACA
  THEREISMAGICINTHEWEB
TRINE  AID  RKO  SMALL
HUND  PACT  FAUSTA  PYLE
ORDINAL  RAID  HINT
MOUSEOFVIRTUEANSWERME
   ALAE  CIEL  TEALEAF
MESA  ALLMAN  ODOR  CART
ECOLE  FAO  ADA   PITTS
NOMANHATHACCESSBYDAY
UNESCO  ERRATA  MAG
   AMA  MNO  MISMATCH
IPUTMYSELFINTOTHYFILE
AESOP  BRAUN  HOTE  IBIS
MAINE  AGILE  USER  RIPS
BRAID  DOCS  DENS  EASE
```

190

```
AZAN  ABYSS  LARK   GASH
SONY  QUOTE  AREEL  ALECTO
TONE  URGER  HEBREWLETTER
AGE  DAGAMA  TAURUSDOZERS
RES  ORES  PRISSY  WET  DEE
TOA  RIS  HEE   BABOOS
EGG  BASTA  BODE  FLAMENS
   RISE  INCUBUS  AIRED
BATTERINGARIES  CZAR  MGM
APTITUDETESTS  DEANS  IRR
CHARLIE  ISTS  PET   NEC
CIR  ENA  MAS  SEA  CPA  NEL
ACI   LER  NEWT  HELLENE
TAU  LOTUS  NORTHTOALASKA
ELS  IVAR  SCAPECAPRICORN
   OBELI  HOMERUN   ATTY
SLURRED  ASSN  PAEAN  APR
ACETAL   TDS  XTC  GTE
NRA  BAY  MEDUSA  FATE  EON
CANCERSPIDER  REALES  MNO
OPERAGLASSES  WILTS  VIII
RESUME  THEDA  INSET  INTR
ARTE    ELSE  NEEDS  MIES
```

191

Starred letters
stand for:
R — Red
O — Orange
Y — Yellow
G — Green
B — Blue
I — Indigo
V — Violet

```
Y'SEA   I'GIRLS   ANKARA
OPTIMA  SONNETS  LOLLED
CARNAC  NONSTOP  G'BEANS
AGEE  LEAF  URAL   LEM
LEE  ORK  ISPY  EKESOUT
ASPS  CEE  CYS  USES  DAN
  ASK  SKID  MLLE  CERT
GEWGAWS  EEN  OTELLO
ONA  DOS  GREGORY  IBSEN
ORR  IRS  YODA  STRIVE
DAMASK  R'O'Y'G'B'I'V  HEALER
AGENTO  ARES  ARR  INV
SENTI  FLIRTER  PIA  CUE
   SCREEN  RNA  ENTRAPS
COPY  HARD  EONS  KID
ARA  VOLT  SEL  CDI  SPAT
TANNEST  IOTA  RIN  ASH
   FIR  YARD  DENG  PIPE
ANIONS  RAINBOW  V'SAREB'
CASBAH  SQUEEZE  SIRENS
ETHELR'  IMAGED   SIRS
```

192

```
PUMA  PROP  BANG  DEJECT
ETON  ILKA  AMIE  OCULAR
SAVINGSANDLOAM  NUMINA
THETOP  PINTO  ADAPTED
   AMERICAONLIME  SERE
BAR  ONI   IMARET
LIED  GLIDE  ARS   THAT
ODIUM  HERECOMESTHESUM
BANDONTHERUM   ENGINE
   MILAN  SAMS  LOUDER
WAAF  CYRIL  NATAL  MESS
ILLUSE  SCAM  NOTUM
TOILES  HOTCROSSBUMS
THELITTLEREDHEM  SAXON
ANON  ROT  TSADI   TONI
   FEDORA  SHE   RAP
SCAB  OMISTRESSMIME
TONESUP  IONIA  SMELLY
ANNALS  ASCRAZYASALOOM
ROOMIE  CAKY  ENDE  EPIC
TRYSTS  HOSS  DOOR  DENA
```

193

```
CHA  STAIR  SPASMS   CTS
RON  PALME  CANTATA  OWE
INDIANAPOLISJONES    MEL
SORBS    ISO  SOW  PEOPLE
PROM  FAS  ETTU  PAVLOVS
NAM  KASHMIRI  DISEASE
ERE  ITS  OLYMPIAIRVING
SID  MIATA  ELAND  ITON
SAAB  GUITAR  ALOES  IOU
     OVULE  BOON    LOON
   SWEETATLANTABROWN
    MOLD  HELM  QUEEN
PAD  ASNER  DEJURE  SCAN
ERAS  TONED  EARNS  ALI
RICHMONDWOOLF  ITO  NFC
ORIOLES  PROFITED  NAH
SCARLET  MARY  NOR  MIRO
TUCKIN  PAM  AHA  SOBOL
AOK  NASHVILLEWILLIAMS
MME  ERODING  RADIO  LEO
POR  TOSSES  DYING  SON
```

194

```
SCORED  PRATT  CAKED  SODA
MALDIVE  AIMEE  ABATE  EMIT
ALLIGATORPEAR PANAMACANAL
LANG  ARDEN  TAINT  AVERSE
      CEO  DAINTY  ARID
ARF  CHANS  CANA  CREDENCE
REACHED  CORRAL  GAMS  DAHL
MARRED  HALLEYSCOMET  TAI
ADMIT  BODES  HALED  SHIRT
DEEP  PEPE  TAIL  STOOGE
ARR  KALEIDOSCOPE  TANNER
    SCAMP  NOONE  CEREAL
ABALONE  TENGALLONHAT  VAC
BOMBER  CAME  BEAK  ZENO
ARABS  MALTA  SLEPT  VOLGA
SAN  ROMANNUMERAL  DENVER
EGAD  EVES  INIGO  CONKERS
DECEASED  DOLL  NAOMI  TSE
      BIER  RUBIES  SHE
UNMADE  RAVES  ALBEES  TARP
REARADMIRAL TRIALANDERROR
ALACK  EASEL  EAVES  AROUSE
STES  DEERS  DEARY  YENTAS
```

195

```
   LAMBS  CABLETS  RFD
ASARULE  SPREADON  ORES
GAMBLERSCARDGAME  MAST
ELI  LAKER  SOO  BALANCE
NANA  RILES  GOGODANCER
TRANS  NEWEL  NAY  EXINE
SYSTEM  SYNAPSE  GRISTS
    IDOL  AMI  TATI
STATECAPITALS  AGEISTS
CIGAR  TEN  SETTLES  HOT
ALEX  WIRER  RAILS  MIRE
MEN  SAMURAI  ICI  AERIE
PRATTLE  TVSUNSETSTRIP
     RELS  ELL  DOST
SHOOTS  STRANGS  VELLUM
TERMS  GAR  MAAMS  TEENA
ELABORATES  SLAPS  DAMN
BITONAL  SAE  ARRAN  NOG
ECON  FIFTYSIXTIMESTWO
RARE  TOILETRY  NOTIONS
   LYS  STEERER  GASPS
```

196

```
ASS  MOCKERS  MANO  RAP
LAIR  FELLOVER  CLOP  NERO
ERGO  ELDORADO  GASTRITIS
CANTATA  TEND  DEBT  CAFES
    ALAN  ASA  YEAR  AGILE
STAVE  GNP  LIE  MISSAL
TELEX  ECU  DEF  GALA  ETC
EMILIA  ADDITION  SKISHOP
APSE  SHANANA  DIG  EMIGRE
KITSCHY  AVER  OTIS  ORION
    SAYA  PYRO  REZA  GLENN
SOFAR  EDU  OPP  KAL  ELWAY
TROLL  NEED  ROTC  OMNI
AGOGO  ACHE  OTHO  MAEWEST
CARTAE  ITS  CARRIER  HAAR
KNEADED  NICEGUYS  UNTRUE
SHE  ROTO  CHE  KLM  OUNCE
TRYONE  EST  SEA  ROSES
OMEGA  TAIL  BOO  RATS
BASEL  DRNO  MONO  OHHENRY
ELIHUROOT  PIMENTOS  HAHA
STAT  MISO  ALPACINO  TIER
EAR  STEW  SCHLEPS  LAD
```

197

```
DEMI  PANDAS  MACH  HASH
EROS  IGUANA  ELLE  OLIO
FAREWELLMYVOLLEY  WING
   PROPEL  ROAM  CAVES
THEMATINGOFTHESHREW
WHO  ENS  ARRET  NEED
RESIN  SPIRO  CZAR  BLY
AMINSTREET  MOAT  SLOE
PEST  EEL  GLOM  CHINA
   OWLS  FAREOFFLYING
 ANAMERICANGYRATED
 PRIVATEELVIS  ONEL
RAINY  BLUE  DNA  DASH
OLEG  SCUD  AUNTIEEMMA
BEL  LEOS  BETSY  URIEL
  YUMA  OREOS  MAR  NAT
 LOOKINGFORMRBAGODOR
MARGE  CRAM  UTOPIA
ETTU  THEMOSQUITOASCOT
THOR  IOTA  DULLES  CINE
SENT  ORAN  SETTLE  ODAY
```

198

```
SEATTLE  CADETS  JAFFA
ANGORAS  UNIQUE  FAROES
KONRADADENAUER  ARMORS
ELON  LIE  ELASTIC  EDGE
   MAME  ASSET  DEADAIR
SKEDADDLE  DOODADS  DET
HONOR  ISNT  RYES  POD
ESSENCE  ERASED  CHAISE
    SEA  ICAN  ZOROASTER
GAT  LADADOG  ALLTIME
ISR  OLIO  ERI  SMUT  VIC
STILLER  DADAISM  EST
MINIDRESS  KELP  BED
ORIELS  LASSOS  TOREROS
  DNA  RARE  NASA  OVERT
BRA  CRAWDAD  CANADADRY
REDHEAD  HELEN  TEST
ILIE  COPPOLA  ENO  TINE
LIAISE  FOREVERANDADAY
LENDER  CUSTER  PASTEUR
OSSIE  STEERS  ALCESTE
```

199

H	O	F	F	A		E	T	H	I	C	S		C	A	D	S		M	A	T	T	E
E	L	L	E	N		A	R	A	B	L	E		E	R	I	E		E	L	I	A	S
A	L	A	S	K	A	T	O	J	O	I	N	U	N	I	O	N		N	I	T	R	O
R	A	G	T	A	G		P	J	S		E	S	T	E	R		S	W	E	A	T	S
				G	A	I	A		S	C	A	R	S			S	W	A	N	N		
F	I	R	E	S	I	N	C	H	I	C	A	G	O		S	E	A	L		I	S	H
O	T	A	R	I	E	S		N	O	S	E		T	H	A	N	K		C	H	I	
C	A	W	E	D		T	A	U	R		P	O	E	M		O	N	S	E	T		
A	L	L	I	E	D	A	R	M	I	E	S	L	A	N	D		S	N	A	I	L	
L	O	S		E	L	I	O	T		E	A	V	E	S		E	M	E	N	D	S	
			S	L	A	M	S		D	R	Y	E	R		F	L	O		K	O	O	
K	E	N		H	U	N	S		P	O	R	E	S		S	O	L	O		S	N	L
I	D	I			E	I	S		B	R	I	A	R		G	O	R	E	N			
M	I	X	E	R	S		S	A	I	N	T		S	O	N	A	R		R	S	T	
	T	O	R	M	E		T	W	O	G	E	R	M	A	N	Y	S	U	N	I	T	E
C	O	N	G	A		S	A	D	R		O	I	L	Y			R	O	G	E	R	
O	R	R		N	A	T	T	Y		S	P	A	R			P	E	A	N	U	T	S
T	S	E		S	L	U	E		S	T	O	C	K	S	C	O	L	L	A	P	S	E
			S	O	M	A	S		L	O	A	T	H		T	O	E	D				
L	E	I	L	A	S		C	O	P	R	A		A	R	C		E	P	O	C	H	S
A	L	G	E	R		P	R	O	H	I	B	I	T	I	O	N	R	E	P	E	A	L
S	O	N	I	C		T	O	N	I		L	O	U	D	O	N		N	A	D	I	A
T	I	S	C	H		A	P	S	E		E	U	G	E	N	E		A	L	E	R	T

200

	S	W	U	M		A	B	A	T	E	R		C	R	A	C	K	
	S	W	I	P	E		M	E	R	I	D	A		O	H	I	O	A	N
S	W	E	D	I	S	H	P	R	I	S	O	N		R	E	N	A	M	E	D
T	A	L	E		H	A	L	A	S		O	R	N	E		T	I	G	E
A	N	T			M	I	T	E	I	N	V	E	E			K	A	N
B	E	E	P		W	I	F	E		M	A	E	N	A	D		C	A	T	T
S	E	R	E	N	I	T	Y		S	P	O	R	T		A	M	A	Z	E	S
			T	I	N	E		C	L	A	M		S	C	E	N	E	
F	U	M	I	N	G		G	R	E	C	I	A	N	U	R	N		P	A	T
I	R	A	T	E		S	H	E	E	T		L	A	G	O	S		I	M	A
L	A	K	E		F	E	A	S	T		A	P	I	A	N		S	L	I	P
I	L	E		G	I	A	N	T		A	L	I	A	R		T	H	O	L	E
A	S	H		A	B	R	A	S	S	B	A	N	D		W	A	I	T	E	D
			O	O	Z	E	S		A	R	T	E			L	O	L	L	
F	O	L	D	E	R		D	A	N	A	E		C	I	R	C	L	E	T	S
A	B	Y	E		S	O	A	P	E	D		S	A	N	D		S	N	O	W
L	O	W		D	R	P	R	E	S	U	M	E				C	P	A
S	I	A	M		P	E	T	E		T	R	I	A	L		E	R	I	N
E	S	T	A	T	E	S		N	A	M	E	F	O	R	A	T	R	U	C	K
	T	E	T	O	N	S		D	R	I	V	E	N		C	R	A	S	S
	R	H	O	D	A		S	A	V	E	R	S		E	A	S	T	

201

R	E	L	A	Y		C	O	M	P			L	E	V		S	P	A	T
A	L	A	M	O		A	W	O	L	S		S	A	P	P		A	A	R	E
D	I	V	I	D	E	D	L	O	Y	A	L	T	I	E	S		P	R	O	M
I	S	E		A	T	E			F	A	R	C	E			T	O	T	U	P
A	I	R	S		O	N	E		S	E	P	I	A			I	R	E	S	T
N	O	N	O		C	L	E	F	T	P	A	L	A	T	E		D	E	S
S	N	E	R	T		E	L	R	O	Y		D	I	R	A	C			
			T	E	N	D	E	R		L	A	S	E		C	O	U	P
	S	C	E	N	A		C	U	P	I	D		S	C	A	M	P	I
B	A	H	R	A	I	N		P	A	N	A	M	A	S		A	R	P	E	L
E	M	O		B	R	O	K	E	N	P	R	O	M	I	S	E		A	N	E
A	P	P	A	L		V	E	T	O	E	R	S		R	E	S	E	N	D	S
N	A	P	P	E	D		L	E	N	N	Y			M	A	R	Y	S
S	N	E	E		A	P	P	S			C	H	O	I	R	S		
			D	R	A	M	A		R	E	H	A	B		S	A	W	E	D
L	E	S		S	P	L	I	T	L	E	V	E	L	S		T	H	A	R
I	M	A	C	S		N	A	I	V	E		E	T	S		Z	E	R	O
E	C	L	A	T		B	A	R	R	E			A	N	Y		E	L	S
D	E	A	N		S	E	P	A	R	A	T	E	D	C	O	U	P	L	E	S
T	E	D	S		A	L	E	S		L	O	Y	A	L		N	O	I	S	E
O	S	S	O		L	A	T			M	E	D	E		G	L	E	S	S

202

C	O	B	S		A	D	D	I	S		P	L	O	P		C	O	W	L
A	L	E	C		P	E	A	C	H		A	L	I	V	E		A	R	I	A
R	I	G	H	T	O	F	W	A	Y		B	E	F	O	R	E	H	A	N	D
P	O	S	E	I	D	O	N		S	P	L	A	T		F	L	I	N	G	S
			M	E	S	E		S	T	O	U	T		O	I	L			
D	U	P	E	D		S	T	E	N	S			P	R	O	L	A	T	E
A	D	A	R		A	F	T	E	R	T	H	E	F	A	C	T		H	E	P
K	I	S	S		M	A	I	L			T	A	M	E		S	E	M	E
A	N	T		I	N	V	A	R	I	A	N	T		S	C	A	P	E
R	E	P	L	E	D	G	E		I	N	C	A			S	A	U	D	I	S
			E	A	V	E	S		P	O	L	I	S		P	E	D	R	O
C	U	R	V	E	S		A	T	E	N		P	R	E	O	F	F	E	R
I	N	F	E	R		I	N	S	T	I	L	L	E	D			T	R	I
T	I	E	R		D	E	N	G			E	A	S	E		T	I	N	A
E	T	C		L	E	F	T	O	F	C	E	N	T	E	R		O	M	E	N
D	E	T	R	A	C	T		R	E	N	T	A			W	R	E	S	T
			A	T	L		D	A	N	C	E		S	O	R	T			
T	A	S	T	E	A		B	I	N	A	L		S	P	R	A	I	N	E	D
A	F	T	E	R	S	H	O	C	K		O	U	T	O	F	P	L	A	C	E
P	A	I	R		S	O	L	E	S		S	H	O	R	E		L	O	R	E
E	R	R	S		E	W	E	R			E	R	A	T	O		A	S	U	R

203

A	L	F	A		T	M	A	N		A	B	A	T	E		P	I	E	C	E
T	O	R	N		H	A	R	A		L	O	V	E	D		E	D	G	A	R
P	R	U	N	E	W	H	I	P		P	O	A	C	H	E	D	E	G	G	S
A	R	I		C	A	R	E	S	S		R	I	A		G	A	N	N	E	T
R	E	T	R	A	C	E	S		N	A	I	L		P	O	N	T	O	
			P	E	R	K	S		S	O	N	S		B	A	I	T		O	I	L
T	R	U	S	T	S		D	O	U	G	H	N	U	T	S		A	D	D	A
S	I	N	C	E		L	E	Y	T	E		I	N	S	T	A	L	L	E	R
A	C	C	U	S	T	O	M	S		L	A	N	K	Y		R	E	E	S	E
R	O	H	E		A	L	I		F	R	T			A	T	E	S	T	S
				P	O	T	A	T	O	C	H	I	P	S					
D	A	K	O	T	A		C	O	O		S	L	T		S	L	I	T	
E	R	N	I	E		A	M	E	N	D		B	L	O	O	D	L	I	N	E
L	I	O	N	T	A	M	E	R		C	A	R	E	T		R	O	G	E	T
T	A	C	K		C	R	A	B	S	A	L	A	D		C	Y	P	H	E	R
A	S	K		G	H	A	T		I	K	O	N		F	A	C	E	T	
		W	A	R	I	S		B	L	E	U		C	O	L	E	S	L	A	W
P	O	U	R	I	N		P	R	E		D	A	R	R	Y	L		U	R	I
S	T	R	I	N	G	B	E	A	N	S		D	U	M	P	L	I	N	G	S
A	R	S	O	N		A	L	I	C	E		I	D	E	S		S	C	U	P
T	A	T	T	Y		T	E	N	E	T		N	E	R	O		T	H	E	Y

204

B	A	N	G		M	E	R	E		F	R	E	E		P	A	W	L
A	D	E	L	A		C	E	D	A	R		R	I	G	A		E	C	H	O
T	O	H	A	V	E	A	N	D	H	A	V	E	N	O	T		T	R	I	P
A	P	R	I	O	R	I		A	S	S	E	S	S		S	P	R	I	T	E
	T	U	R	N	I	N	G			E	R	N	E	S		A	I	D	E	S
				K	E	Y	L	A	R	G	O		T	U	R	F			
P	I	N	T	O		M	O	U	S	S	E		S	A	B	R	I	N	A
A	L	O	H	A		U	R	G	E			F	O	R	E		E	A	S	T
L	E	V	E	R	E	T		S	A	H	A	R	A		R	E	D	O	W	A
			A	S	T	I			A	L	T	E	R		O	F	M	A	N
H	O	F	F	M	A	N		A	S	S	E	T		H	A	L	O	I	N	G
E	V	O	R	A			Y	A	C	H	T			E	M	I	R	
L	O	S	I	N	G		G	R	E	E	C	E		B	I	T	E	T	H	E
D	I	S	C		O	G	E	E		A	L	A	I		H	S	I	E	N
	D	E	A	D	E	N	D		D	I	N	I	N	G		S	T	E	W	S
			N	A	R	A		C	O	N	T	E	S	S	A	
I	R	A	Q	I		W	A	R	N	S		A	L	L	P	A	S	S
M	E	D	U	S	A		M	I	N	U	E	T		E	E	L	B	A	C	K
O	B	I	E		T	H	E	M	A	L	T	E	S	E	F	A	L	C	O	N
L	E	N	E		K	A	N	E		T	U	L	I	P		T	E	R	R	E
A	L	A	N		A	L	D	A		S	I	L	T				R	E	N	E

205

```
SPRAY BRAT  MAHAL  GAMBA
PROBE LURE  TIMORE ODEON
QOMUPPANCE  ICEBAG SMART
RAPT ETO STEREOTAIPING
    SEDAN  ODORS  TRET
SOS VAN  SCRUB  RIAL AIS
PRESENT PEIPINGHOT LUNT
AMOUNT GEL CANINE  ESTE
DOUR  ARILS TANS  CATON
ELL TYRESOME IRE LADINO
DUB RATES  ERROL RAVINE
 REAMED CANON  CADENT
RONDEL MOREL AUGER APB
FATTEN MAU SLOWBERN TRA
APHID CARL  OLLAS  DIET
KIER CHILDS DEN  SMOOTH
INRE HANOIANCES STATUTE
RES BASE GOONS TRI SYD
 PART AMATI LIANA
 CAENDIDCAMERA AFT MILE
SADAT SUCCOR HAIFALUTIN
ANISE ERRORS ARNE ASSAI
PETER DEANE  BEEN  BEARD
```

206

```
SPOT HOOD CABAL  SADIST
OAFS YALE ADALE  TRENTE
ATME PRAM SHRIFT ERASER
PHI THEVOICEOFTHETURTLE
ESCAPED CARNE ENS  MEAT
DOESIN TRADES ARGO EPEE
FAT SPHERED  ANOINT
AGNUS LETUS FANON IRENE
OLDTO EGIS GUM TESTATOR
ROMEO ARE MERINO ELIHUS
TRE NASA LITTLEFOXES
AYNS REPEAL INCARE ERST
 ARISEMYLOVE LISA  OOH
INAPIE SHEREE PLO SCORE
PALOALTO RUR KEEL TAMER
AGIRL OFTEN SERVE IRADE
 STOWED CONCISE OTT
OVEN RIRE FENNEL ALLTHE
FIRE ISA BILGE FRESHET
FORWHOMTHEBELLTOLLS ERY
ELATED HOARSE AHOY ATOM
RETORE EMITS FIAT SOSO
STANDS DELES TOTO  OPEN
```

207

```
SPATS EGAD VENT  THESE
CACHE GOBI ADAH  HELLS
ATREE AUBERGINE  EBLIS
THEBRIDGE OUTOFAFRICA
 EERIE ABES  TILE
CHARDS DIVES  ROWANS
HEAL NORTHOFBOSTON
ENRICO GRIT ERRED  TOE
CRONUS YOD PLIED  DANA
KINGSHIP TWIGS  DEREK
 APASSAGETOINDIA
ICBMS LYRIC  NOONTIME
CARE CADET GPA MAHDIS
IRA CANON RAIL SHILLS
ENGLANDMADEME  NENE
REGINA EMITS  LIVRES
 SIDI GMAN CAIRE
ODESSATALES DUBLINERS
DIVOT CROSSWORD DIXIE
DROME HORN EURO ECOLE
STEER YEYE BRYN  SEDER
```

208

```
HAVE ALVA  CODA  HASTY
EVEL NAILS OMEN  ONERA
MARLOTHOMASMANN NEWEL
ELAINE LANTERN BOVINE
NOM SABA TUT  PARENT
NICETY BOBHOPELANGE
 LATERALS  LATER
TREK ROMA SATE  YAMS
HOSEA NUMB AFIRE  BAER
ROD LBJ EARL NOCTURNE
ITA BEAARTHURASHE YIP
LOVESONG MOTE EOS MOO
LUIS FIRMA EDAM STARS
TSPS SEAN REAM  ERSE
 ICIER MERRIEST
LEEGRANTWOOD INSTIL
ENDMAN RMS TEDS  NEE
TARGUM OPENSEA LEMMAS
AGAIN GRACIEALLENFUNT
LUGED HACK DRIES  ALTO
LEERS ALES PATS  SLOP
```

209

```
TRALA  AMMO  PSST  CAP
RESOD OLEIN RECIT IMI
AUFWIEDERSEHENHERMANN
MNO ELIXIR ASTO EMOTE
PERFUME DUNNE  ONAIR
 AHA BANANA LUCIAN
INCENSE SHALOMSHIMON
ALAIN ALI RASE  ORO
COVERALLS ASSIN RONAN
EVA INS REMOTE  IYO
SELF TATASIRALEC HOPI
 OWE HENNER LEA RUT
HAVEA TELEX EVILDOERS
AMA GOIT SET DRYLY
SOLONGMARLON RESIDES
 REVERE AURORA COO
 CERES INTRO AIRSICK
SHARI PAST MOOGOO SYN
HASTALAVISTAFRANCISCO
ARC NINON SNELL KNELT
YEA ESSE EDDY  YALES
```

210

```
LASHINGS IRATE SPOUTS
ESTONIAN SEPAL PAWNEE
ASITWASINTHEBEGINNING
TREAT COLA SCAR SOSO
 RANKLES  TRET
WIELD YET HOAR AERATE
ERDA TARES TWOS EAVES
PANGLESS ADORNED TIES
TEASELS POESY RADIATE
 ELATING RETINTED
ASSERT INERTIA EGGERS
RETREADS  ARTICLE
TREADLE MODES HESSIAN
HEES ENTAMES TESTCASE
UNLET ERIE SHIES AGES
REEDED OMNI UPS ANOAS
 DROP CAMPERS
CAPO ERIS EMIL OTATE
ONEMUSTCONSIDERTHEEND
CARESS ALEUT ROOMRATE
ASTRAY LOOPY STRASSEN
```

211

```
ARETHA  RADAR  SVEN  UPAS
LECHER  EMOTE  PTERO  TELE
ACHICKENINEVERYTOT  SABE
MOONS  LARGE  REPOSES  CUD
OLIG  LEM  ANET  ESTEEMS
DONTGIVEUPTHENIP  TURF
ERGOTS  POLO  CODY  ROAD
BIB  ENCYST  GOO  ORLE
SHIER  AONE  ORMOLU  ROIL
LOCO  CLAD  SCREE  ENG  UTE
AMALGAMS  ARREST  GEER
BONIER  ICOMEISAW  MAMMAS
NEER  SERAPE  ALARMING
LAO  DYE  DARER  LIEN  EMIT
OCTA  ANGELA  KINE  PRESS
CUSP  BOL  ESSAYS  SHE
ITER  ISUP  ARAT  YACHTS
LING  THEPUCKSTOPSHERE
SYLLABI  ORAL  ALE  ORES
LEA  ARSENIC  STOMA  ILONA
OATS  ISLINKTHEREFOREIAM
BRIE  CUBES  RITAS  BERNIE
SNEE  KEAS  ANENT  EDSELS
```

212

```
ABETS  ARLES  BUST
BULLET  OTTAVA  OFTHE
BATISTA  THEPENNYOPERA
ODON  ENATE  LEEDS  FEB
MMMD  DREI  CYST  ACU
BEAM  FOURSAINTSINACTS
ANTI  IUM  TAV  CLEESE
CANT  AIR  GYROS
ASTERN  STY  LAMA  BLOIS
BAH  MISTRAL  SELF  IFNI
ELEM  STRIKETHREE  SEND
LIMO  HAIL  DULLARD  VEE
SCURF  PALS  NYE  RECESS
STOMP  SHE  MICA
ACKACK  ALS  MAE  RISE
THELITTLEKITTENS  DRAM
BIT  OENO  IRAN  MOUE
ACE  FIRST  NUDES  ONCE
THELITTLEPIGS  RUNNIER
IRENE  IRISES  ELATED
STEM  ESTER  DUPES
```

213

```
LUAU  BROIL  OCALA  SMOG
AMPS  ROLLO  LOREN  TARA
PEPELEMOKO  DIRTYHARRY
PAL  EVER  STILET  ANISE
EAGER  BEHEST  WIDE
TASS  OPINE  HARICOT
AWNED  EDEL  SAUCY  UNA
SINAI  JESSEJAMES  PRES
PSI  AWOL  SMILED  PRINT
STEAMIEST  OVIS  JOIEDE
GORY  APENA  GAPS
REPINE  SLED  NONMEMBER
INOLD  BOLERO  BABY  EXO
VOLE  COLEPORTER  ELLIS
ALL  BUYER  PAMS  DOLLY
LAYERED  KNEED  OGEE
AXIS  ASSIGN  ABYSS
ENDUE  ARCADE  INOL  TAN
GOLDFINGER  AUNTIEMAME
GLEE  STING  DATES  ARAM
YARD  MELEE  EROSE  ORSO
```

214

```
FARUK  ANAPEST  ALAPA
ARLENE  ROMANCE  NODICE
COMEMEETMYPRETTYPACER
TEADANCE  ION  ITERATE
DEO  CHEST  PHD
BEAVER  SHARE  ITI  BSA
ATRI  SKIN  ASON  RABE
SHESPAWINGATTHEGROUND
SET  ARADA  BORED  OWNED
ELEANOR  PERIL  ROSARY
MUSTAFA  MALTESE
VOLARE  PIUTE  HATSOFF
ICING  AISLE  ELUDE  SRO
SHESEESAHANDSOMERACER
ARNA  SPRY  ATUB  SANE
EST  THY  DIVED  ESPRIT
SRA  VADER  ONO
COMICAL  OKA  INCURRED
ANDWANTSTOHORSEAROUND
BOXING  ORTOLAN  GOALIE
RINSE  PEASANT  ENDED
```

215

```
OMIT  GALBA  STEAD  LEA
PALOS  ARIEL  AISLE  OLD
SCARP  MURAL  TENAM  GEE
ROSEMARYAIDEDECAMP
BOREOUT  SIN  DARNIT
FRANKIEMEMORYLAINE
LASTS  ITON  ERN  TMAN
ALES  MACAW  DIRE  READE
TED  PAGAN  MOROCCO  RAW
EARTHAFIRSTAIDKITT
SCORIA  AMI  REESES
KEVINCANADIANBACON
IDA  TANAGER  ORALS  CCC
MATAS  IDES  ELISE  TARA
PREC  STE  ULAN  EAGER
HOWARDONANEVENKEEL
ACHENE  EAT  ELDERLY
FREDWASHERANDDRYER
TEM  ARPAD  MARES  AORTA
EDA  REUNE  EMILE  ROOKS
RON  DREAD  DUPES  TOOK
```

216

```
ARSON  SALIC  SPRAT  ASH
MEARA  PRIMA  TEETH  SPA
ISLET  AUDEN  RAFER  SEW
NELSONS  TACO  REOPENS
ONO  AMPS  SOLVE  WINCE
TWICESOLDTALES  INTER
ALS  RURAL  SHUN
ALAMO  ATES  ISENT  MID
SCRATCHED  JAMESCHOICE
ADE  HOAR  MORAL  LERNER
PEOMS  HAKIM  BETAS
DROWSE  RATED  LIAR  TIE
PASSEDTENTS  BORROWERS
THE  NIELS  ARAL  WARES
CETE  ECLAT  OES
POLIO  HEADOFTHEGLASS
EXECUTE  GNU  SELL  OAK
STAINER  RAGS  DEFARGE
AAR  TRIPE  HOUSE  LEDGE
DIN  ERNIE  ESTER  ARIEL
ELS  RAGED  DOERS  TODDY
```

217

```
BAS  REPO  MINERS   CABLE
URN  AVON  ATONAL   OCEAN
STEEPEST  RETINA    RUNIC
THEXINTHEGRIDSCENTER
LURID  LENO    OKAYED
ERST  HUGO  FRAMER    IVS
GODOWNSEVENSPACES
SWADDLE    AUGERS   ENTER
RECESS  HBO  ORS   CRISPS
SEEM  TRAUMA       CHIS
PROCEEDSIXTOTHELEFT
THRO      EARNED    TEAS
POSIES  SES  HET   DOTELL
ATHOS   OPENTO    PATELLA
COUNTUPELEVENMORE
TET  REESES   ACIS   TEED
DOTARD     ARCS    SONAR
FOURLETTERSCLOCKWISE
TAWNY  TRAVIS   UNHINGED
SYNCS  TAMEST  REAP   MUG
RESET  APPLES   ERRS  APE
```

218

```
PATES  TRES   TAI   ESPRIT
ATONE  AIRCRAFT    SALARY
CARACASMARACAS     TRACER
ILO  RTE   ENTRY    ANISE
FAIRWAY  MAGI     CAPON
INDOOR  ROMECHROME   EVE
STATE  THUS   OAHU    TOL
MAL   BAER   EBNER   TULA
DURBANTURBAN       WRAP
COLOHEL   OVALS   ALIENS
AMATIVE   CRUSE  PLANETE
BERATE  BOULE    ALIGNED
ALEG   DALLASPALACE
REDE  SULFA  ABLY     SST
ETO  ARIA   UREY    MATTE
TST  BRONXHONKS    BARREN
ORRIS   IRAS    DANTEEN
ROMEO   AFTER  EUR    ARY
ENAMOR  BAHAMASPAJAMAS
NOTICE  CREDENCE   ODETO
TROTHS  SER   DEER   GOREN
```

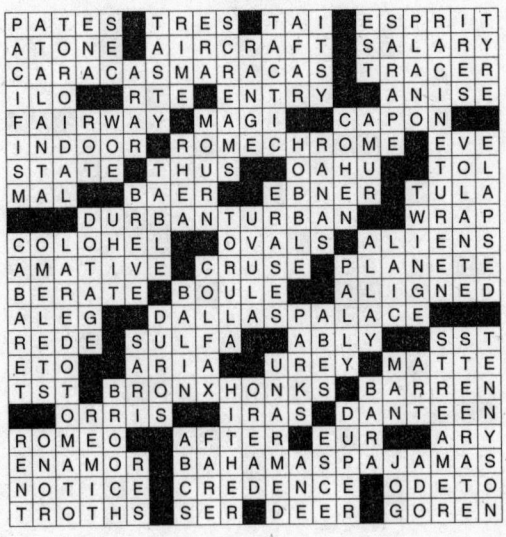

219

```
LIB   GAPER   SPAD    USES
ISLE  ORONO   HAND   ENTRE
STUMBLINGBLOCKS    DRAIN
PLEIADES   BERTH   TEEMED
SETTLES   BENTS    REMAP
TEN   ERNE    CANADIAN
ASHER   FLYINGANT    NRA
HOODS  CAL   ONUS    AGER
ELL   RIDINGCROP    SIGNE
MODERATE  ARLEN   MADRAS
IMAGE   PLAIN    CAMEO
PANICS  HADIN   LAMEDUCK
ANGLE  DATINGGAME    NEA
YIPE  COLT    AMP    SEDER
USA  LOVINGCUP     TASSO
PETSTORE   ALAN     MAR
TEENS   ODIST   TURNESA
AVERSE  FLINT   AIRVENTS
BERET  PRINTINGPRESSES
LANNY  EAVE   NORSE   TULE
ELSE   WYES   GRAYS    EAT
```

220

```
STRAFE   SLEEVE    LEWIS
PRESENT  EARNING   ARANA
LITTLEROCKGARDENPARTY
ABOIL  ENTE   TORAS    SOY
TERN  ESCARP  UREY   MANI
SST  CASE  ELAS    STOWED
TAMEST   KALE    ETHS
SPARRED  HAIL    DARETO
CRUETS  LETNOT   MENORAH
RESTE   OLEG   ODIN    SRO
INT  LISBONFIREDOG   ELL
PSI  SEES   INRE    LAMED
TANGENT  TESTER   PAVANE
PORTAL   PHON   MARINER
MARS   ELEF    TROVES
GONETO  VEER   ELIS    MUM
ALAN  SHEA  YAWPED   SANA
MIL  USURP  TOES    PATRI
BELGRADESCHOOLTEACHER
OREAD  STIPEND   SUNRISE
LEYTE   SNARES    REESTS
```

221

```
DISUSE  BLUFF   ATIC    JUL
ENISLE  RIFLE   THRU    ENE
BUTTERORSOURCREAM     EDA
TRIEDON    NAIVE    MRED
SENDS  LEADS  PSI    SEERS
BIGDEAL    KEYLARGO
SMOKINGORNON    WAITSON
SAUSAGEORBACON     MEL
INTURN  NEY   ARAB   ROODS
TRA  LEB    ELMIRA    AVEC
SEGO  SOUPORSALAD    FILL
OMEN  SESAME   EVE    DIA
NONOS  RAGE   ATA   ENGULF
UKE  REGULARORDECAF
TIMRICE   TABLEORBOOTH
ONEONONE    SEABAGS
SHOWS  SIP   RHODA   SERUM
PAWN  CULTS    NETZERO
ALI  FRIESORONIONRINGS
REN  LUTE   REPEL   DONEES
ERG  OXEN   EXTOL   SPEEDY
```

222

```
MALIC  LASSO   GOOD    SNAP
IMAGO  ADAIR   ESAI    HALO
MADAM  BOONE   NATE    OBIS
INEVER    GOURMETCOOKS
CADETCORPS   PEARCE    BEE
CALORIES       SON
ATHOL  IRONWEED    KOPECK
HOUSEBOY  GETDONE    EQUI
LASCARS     IWO    TRUES
THINS   ANTEATER    OMARS
MLS   SWEETCORN     PIT
STOLE  CHANCERY    OSTIA
LUNAR   AIL      BRETONS
ABET  STLOUIS   LARCENER
GAYEST  ENCLOSER    RESTS
ARI   LAWNDALE
ARM  BETCHA   BASKETCASE
POCKETCHANGE      SCALED
HUGE  CHEZ   ALLEN   ORANG
ITEM  HERE   SLAKE   DENSE
DEEP  YSER   HYPED   ESSES
```

223

```
S P E C   H I R A M   P A O L I   P E A R
O R C A   A D E L A   O R L O N   L E N A
D A H L S D O L L S   W A L T S W A L T Z
S T O I C A L   A M E B A   T E S S I E
      C A T S   D R U R Y   B R A M
M A J O R   S A Y S O   F O U L A R D S
A B U   F R A N C K S F R A N C S   H O T
T E L   S E L A H   A U N T   R O D E
E L E C   A Y R E S A I R S   B A D G E
R E S O U R C E   I N S E T   A M E E R
  J A I M E   C L A I R   T S A R S
A B E T S   A R K I N   D E P L O R E S
P E W I T   G U Y S G U I S E   D O R A
A R E S   A R N E   N O L L E   A G O
I L L   A R I E L S A E R I A L S   D O N
R E S P I R E S   P U N I C   P A S T E
      A D A M   S O B I G   A B I E
A D R I A N   S L U E S   P E A R S O N
J E A N S G E N E S   L A P P S L A P S E
A C M E   E T A P E   E X A L T   T R I P
R O S S   D E P T S   D E L E S   E Y E S
```

224

```
H O T C A K E   S T U D   A N A B A S I S
I C H A B O D   U R G E   R E D O L E N T
S H A V I N G C R E A M   C L A M B A K E
S O W E D   Y A M E N   C A L I B E R S
      M E D   R I D D L E D   S S R
E M B A R R A S S   A O N E   Y A T S E N
L I E N   A L O E S   T O S S   W A H O O
S S W   B L A N D E S T   A T A N E N D
A S I   O L I C   T W O S   L O Y   R I O
L A Z Y   I L I E   P A V E   A M A S
R A D I O   S T O N E W A R E   P L A N E
I D E M   K A Y O   P E R C   C H I N
B A R   F I T   M I E N   H A R E   T N S
A G I L I T Y   M A C K I N A W   A C E
L I N E N   R E Z A   H A M O N   G N A W
D O G M A S   N O G S   L E N I N A K A N
      O N T   F O O T P A D   A I L
L A N C E L O T   E T H E R   C A G E R
R E T A I L E R   T R E A S U R E H U N T
E P I D E M I C   H E R R   P E N A N C E
P E T E R O S E   I O O I   P L E D G E S
```

225

```
S Y L P H   D I V E   C O S T   L A M P
T I A R A   A M I D   A D M A N   I R A E
A P R O N   C A V E   M O O L A   T Y R O
B E D P O S T M A S T E R K E Y C H A I N
      O I L Y   R O L E S   H E N N Y
H I S S   A L S A C E   E D E M A
A T T E S T   C R A F T S   O R A N G E
H E A D L I G H T H O U S E F L Y B A L L
A M Y   A N E   S O I T   A L L   A X I S
    S I G N   A W L   P R A Y   T O N I
L E T I N   E R N S   J I L T   G E S T E
E L A N   U S E D   M E N   T R O D
A I R E   R E T   P A R C   E O N   S C M
S H O W C A S E W O R K H O R S E S H O E
H U S S A R   A L L I E D   T R A M P S
      L I M E S   E N D E A R   R O T H
A L B E E   A S H E N   D U A D
B E A N B A G P I P E D R E A M W O R L D
A N N A   I N A N E   E A R P   A N O I A
S T A T   L U N G E   F R I T   R Y D E R
H O L E   M A S S   T E N S   E X E R T
```

226

```
P O L A R S   B A W L E D   Y A L U   B A R
A M U L E T   A P I E C E   A V E R   I V A R
C O N F L A G R A T I O N   W O E B E G O N E
T O G A   R O A C H   S K E W   A L B I O N
      S L A D E   B L E E D   I N F E R N O
S O D   P E T S   L E E R Y   A L I E N
P R I V E T S   S A L A   E N O S   D E I
I N S E T S   I N D I F F E R E N T   F E R N
R A C E S   S L I D E   A G A N A   A L L O T
A T O P   E L O P E   A V A S T   B R A I S E
L E N   D I V E R S I O N   P L U M B E R
  S E R E N E   E M U   G E E G E E
A D O R I N G   O V E R T O N E S   R O M
L I L A C S   L A V E R   O D A L S   T A R O
O T A T E   S E R I N   A R I S E   T O T A L
O T T O   S T A N D O F F I S H   T O N I N E
F O E   K O K O   L E E T   T H R O N G S
    D O I L Y   I D E A S   P R I M   G E T
A D D E N D A   S N E E R   A L O N E
S E E M E D   T I N T   D R A N K   A L A I
I N C U R I O U S   E N T E R T A I N M E N T
A T O R   N U N S   S E A B E E   N O T A T E
E Y E   G R A Y   T O A S T S   G A S P E R
```

227

```
A B U   G O P   C U B E S   A W A C S
B O N F I R E   A R O S E   P R E L A T E
A T T I R E D   M I S S A   U M P I R E S
S T I L L L I F E   C A L L L E T T E R S
E L L E S   C U T E   Y I E L D   S E E
D E W   A L M O N D   O S S   B I S O N
  R E F E R E E   S I G N S   P O L
    U R I S   R I L E   B O W L E R S
S C A L E D   B E L L L Y R E S   L I E N
H A L L   K A T E   S E A L S   O T T O
E M I L   B O N E   O G L E   O H I O
L E S E   O R A L S   S M E E   K E E P
L R O N   W E L L L I K E D   B A I R D S
S A N G R I A   E R I N   V E N N
    T O E   V A D I M   D E L I G H T
N I C H E   R E L   S P E A R S   O R A
O N E   G O A L S   S A N D   A G N U S
R U S S E L L L O N G   S K I L L L E S S
T R A M M E L   W O R S T   C E L E S T E
H E R O I N E   E R A S E   T W E E T E R
  D E G A S   D E F E R   S D S   Y E T
```

228

```
T O O T S Y   S C A D S   E T U I S   C A R L
O R I O L E   C O V E T   A R R O W   O L E O
P I L L O W   O U I J A   R E I N E   M O T O
H A I L T H O U E V E R B L E S S E D M O R N
A N N   H O U R   C O E D   T E A P O Y
T A G S   S T E M   T E T O N   F A W N
    A W A R D E D   R A M A D A N   D R E W
T A U R I N E   D R A B   H A Y D N   O P A
O W N I N G   E L U D E   A U X   L A C T I C
W A C   C A N E   S T R U M   T O B A C C O
I S L   E R I N Y S   H I T   S A V O R
T H E N L E T U S A L L M O S T M E R R Y B E
  A B A C I   L E E   S N A I L S   A R T
S P A R E T H   A U G H T   O N L Y   R A H
P A P Y R I   T N T   E W E R S   L I N D E N
A L I   T O P A Z   M O N K   P I C A S S O
T O S S   N U D I S T S   S E D A T E S
  P A S T   O M A H A   L E N T   A R A W
O S C A N S   I T I N   F I L S   E V A
G L O R Y T O G O D A N D P E A C E T O M E N
L I N K   O R A N G   I S A A C   O E N O N E
E G A L   R A Z E E   N O R S E   N E U T E R
D O N E   Y E A R N   G N A T S   E D S E L S
```

229

```
MARC  CHARM  ADDS  BSTAR
ALAR  AONIA  URAL  OHARA
JANETFLAIR  GENA  DORAN
ANISEEDS  LOUISWAYWARD
     CASS  SEES    MAE
ALOES  BONITA  HANDFUL
KILN  MERLELAGGARD  ANE
INIT  ERIE  NANA  PYLE
NEV  JANEDITHERS  REED
REMADE  BROWS  STARTS
RAKES  FEARS  TARTU
MOTTES  PEACE  ALIENS
ACAT  LARRYBAGMAN  AHA
DARE  KERR  BOER  TWIG
ALD  JESSICABANDY  HARE
MAYPOLE  SOLACE  MEYER
ENL  TERA  SCAR
AUDREYJOTTER  SEACOAST
SEAMS  ELIA  EDWINSOOTH
OLDIE  TANG  TAINT  TULE
PEATS  ENTE  TIMEO  STOW
```

230

```
LOREN  AMANDA  FACE  BLOB
AMOLE  MAROON  ALAN  BEENE
PABLOPICASSO  COLEPORTER
PRES  SNORE  DATUM  RATTAN
SAUNA  BIPOD  RASH
FTC  ALT  TERZA  BANTAMS
AREHOMES  LEEREMICK  ATA
RICAN  TOAD  TRADES  DREG
OXIDE  JESTER  AGED  LAGER
FILE  MELEE  EASED  PAYOLA
FEB  EDWARDALBEE  CAPOTE
DULLER  LIB  TARIFF
DERAIL  DEANACHESON  OCS
BIMINI  LIBRE  LAPEL  MNOP
IVIED  WINO  SAILED  LITRE
TALL  SHEENA  SNEE  IRENE
ENL  HENRYVIII  SURVEYED
SENORAS  ENACT  PEE  NAY
EDIT  DORAN  RARER
ATRAIN  DARTS  DENIS  MATA
MAOTSETUNG  THOMASEDISON
EMMET  ANTA  EUROPE  ULTRA
NEAR  PEEN  WEARER  ELIOT
```

231

```
LESSON  MILSAP  ALMOST
ATTUNE  AREOLA  MOISTEN
THECLOTHOFMAN  MANCALA
TEARY  CONTENTSOFTABLE
ELMO  RENI  RAYE  EER
SHEL  SAS  GIRD  DEE
LOVEOFLOTS  BAUD  READ
USE  JESU  TRADEOFBOARD
GLAMOR  THREAD  ROONEY
SOLI  NAHUM  STINTED
THOUGHTOFSCHOOL
SATIATE  VITRO  ESAI
REPENT  CHEESE  BATONS
PLENTYOFHORN  WEIR  RNA
MARS  PLIE  DAYOFBREAK
SHY  PREY  CST  LISA
HOO  ODAY  RAID  STAT
NORETURNOFPOINT  SPADE
ANIMATO  WAROFTHEWINDS
PILATES  NTUPLE  RANGES
TENORS  YESSES  ANGORA
```

232

```
BESS  ATPAR  ATAT  BOSOM
ANEW  IRATE  HUME  AGAVE
ACRE  MILITIAMEN  LEVEE
SHEEN  PENINSULA  LEERS
INT1  PAGE2  LINE3  MME
LAME  ELL  STACY  SEA
FADED  REECHO  6ENTAS
ODEA  RIGHT  ROOSTS
PART4  TAKE5  AOK  6WEEK
SPRAGUE  ARMED  SARI
ELO  MABELL  CALLED  TSP
KOOL  FLITS  CRITICS
GAME7  ASU  8EENS  9PINS
STPAUL  TREAD  ANAT
HARPER  ODETTA  ICAME
SHY  NEAPS  IRR  MEME
LOB  DATE  0FEET  #SON
EMAIL  LOTTERIES  SARAH
GENRE  INCIDENTAL  GAME
ALDAS  SCAD  STOLE  ATEN
LYSES  METE  HOPED  SASS
```

233

```
WALRUS  CALORIC  ALEPPO
ITAINT  ATANEND  MIXERS
LOOFLIRPAEHTSEMOCEREH
LISTENIN  IRE  IRISES
STD  FAGOT  NET
ABBESS  MOTHS  BUT  TRAM
NOOR  DILL  MEET  OONA
YAWYMNOMIEMROFTIAWUOY
ASI  IONIC  AERO  MASSE
STETSON  ODOR  SISTER
ERNESTO  ONEACAT
SWANEE  HEXA  LABELED
HILDA  ONUP  STILL  AME
ELURDROWSSORCAKAERBOT
ALLI  ACME  YORE  IOTA
FOAL  ITE  BWANA  CLARET
PLO  MAINE  AHO
BOPEEP  AGT  FLATBOAT
YADOTDIRGEHTPUGNIOGMI
ENDORA  ENLIVEN  COLLIE
TEAPOT  DASTARD  ENDEAR
```

234

```
CLASP  CAST  BRAG  PEAT
LILLE  URTH  PRAGA  LENA
ANAIL  ITER  HUBER  ERNS
NONPLUS  MOURNINGHAYES
ABIE  BLED  LAS
EMERGENTS  ANAS  ELAINE
RECURRENTREIGN  SANDER
USLTA  ARE  CEIL  STEAL
PTAH  RESIST  TAR  DATE
TAT  PIG  DOREN  HOVELS
SEAR  ELEMI  OBEY
ESTATE  REWON  RET  PAT
PULE  ATT  STELES  SOMA
ILIAC  SOPH  EVA  SOLAR
TENDER  THUNDERINGHERD
ARGYLE  SANO  HALETODAY
RIP  RCMP  SLAM
UNHEALTHYHEIR  ELAPIDS
LEOI  AMINE  LANG  JONAH
AMEN  TANGS  ARIA  OCALA
RODS  ENTO  FELL  ROSIN
```

235

```
ADELA  GRAMPUS  DALAI
DOCILE ATTAINS DESIGN
ONHALLOWEENAMEDICSAID
STOREDUP  ANA  ESKIMO
    GET  WAGON  AME
HAMMER RITES ARID OAF
AREA  SONT  ACIS  ELLE
ILLJOINYOUONTHESTREET
TEO PLEAS VILE  IRANI
INN TEAL HEXAD STONED
    KIDD TARES HEAL
SPLICE TOGAS TERN  ADE
KOALA  IDIC LANAI  TIA
IWILLNOTDOTHETRICKING
MENS ORLY ADAY  ALAR
PRE OBIE BRIAR SCYTHE
    BLE SEARS BOA
BEATEN  CAT  CANTICLE
ILLJUSTBETHERETOTREAT
VOLANT ENTERED FLENSE
AWARD  DAYRATE  ESTHS
```

236

```
VON  ASST  CASS  PLEA
MADE IGETA LEHAR RASP
ACES SEAOF AGAMA ETTE
LUSTFORLIFEWITHFATHER
TUSSAH  CET  STIFLE
SMA SYNE TOO  LIONESS
THEEGGANDICLAUDIUS
MAAR TAEL AFR  DUNES
ANGELSTREETSCENE
REINA  ANA  OUR  TRAP
ALLTHEKINGSMENINWHITE
TEES EON  TOR  ERNIE
LITTLEPRINCEIGOR
ALTAI ORA EMIR  CONS
WINDSOFWARANDPEACE
LETMEGO AME ISNO SAG
INDRAS  OOH  ISOLDE
HEARTOFDARKNESSATNOON
ANTA AEIOU ARIOT TUNE
IDOL DIGNE TONLE ACIS
LOPS  TEED  EDGE  PHS
```

237

```
KNOB DAD ADA  EOS MATH
RIFE AGO FISHNET ERIE
AXON PENELOPECRUZLINE
FILE HIHO PITY DOODAD
TEDDANSONSTRUCTION
INIT HEEP REM  KEG
ACACIA AGAR HERSCHEL
RUNTS DEUM CHESS LYRE
EYDIEGORMEFOODS RABIN
APR MEOW LILO MOREEN
OSCARDELARENTACAR
MINION REEK DIAZ  PFC
ACING JODIEFOSTERCARE
NECK SAMSA LUTE EASEL
GIUSEPPE MOTS TASSEL
ONS MEA BRAU  SICS
MEANJOEGREENEHOUSE
STMARK OWED EGAD URAL
TAMMYFAYEBAKKERY LIST
EPEE OUTSOLE SEE ECHO
WEST RKO KAY TDS THAN
```

238

```
HOBSON SPT BREL  RASH
ERRATA ARA LICIT ELLA
LIONET MISSINGTHEBOAT
LOKI  EATING  HENLEYS
ONETRACKMIND  RECTO
NYASA  EDEMA  AROMAS
RAH MORASS RETIREMENT
ELOI RESETS DEN  STE
GAMMA DIG WHISTLESTOP
TIEUPS DORIA  RAGLAN
SLADE UPI  TAIGA
OCTANE SERVE CATNIP
SPRINGFEVER ELF READY
ICE ORA SPELLS  DILL
PIPEDREAMS ASSURE LEE
STEVIE SPOUT STAUB
ENSUE OVERCHARGING
EMERGES STEREO  ATOR
TIMEONHISHANDS DENISE
ONUS TESTE ADA RODNEY
NEST ROSS LYS USAGES
```

239

```
SMACKED GR&MA ASSAILS
MOTHER& RURAL B&ANNAS
UNHINGE INERT AIRGAPS
STOAT R&D ACH  ANGE
UNS BIGSHOT GALACT
EAST SERIF RAS  SOLAR
GR&IOSO ORA NOTES EPA
GO& ALL NOUN  &SO XED
SNOWSUIT SLOWSUP C&LE
NOTICER TIEUP  HELI
ODER TITER REM&S ORAN
PENS TENOR PACKERS
EMIT MISDEAL CHILDREN
NEG &ON SNAG EMS ADO
ASH RIGHT KWA EPERGNE
INTRO SUE &OVER ETAL
RESECT BLUFFER  SCI
GLEE EVI RAT  TIMED
BEANERY SALMI IRATELY
IMPASSE ITEMS POTABLE
OUTL&ER SERVE ICEL&ER
```

240

```
SASH BACHS RAKE  FLOG
HITE ALOOP AMADO RAUL
ADOLESENCE MAYONAISSE
HALLMARK CRAZE ADESTE
BELT DIODE  IRAN
ALPERT WHATA KLONDIKE
TEENY VIOLINCELLO ROM
TART TILT REAL  BRAM
ISM COMMITTMENT VOILE
CHINASEA REAPS DEODAR
SUDAN GENRE DONNE
DESTRY COVEN CONTESSA
ELATE DELITERIOUS CAN
GABY SITE ISNT  PENN
ATL ACCUMMULATE TANTE
SHEATHES IRINA VERTEX
STUD BRANT MALI
GOTHAM PLANK SALESMAN
EMBARASSED ASPHIXIATE
ROAM NOTSO GOADS AZOV
MORE USSR EDDIE NOPE
```

241

```
AMISS  IDLES  GLIM   DORM
DANCE  LOIRE  RIRE   EPEE
INTENTIONALWALKS   VANS
MARNIE MASERS  ENFOLDS
ETOILE GENES   DEUT
   CIME ERENOW   LEVEE
ASS  TEND      EARLDOMS
DAILYDOUBLE  MAROC  LIP
EBRO  SMEES  ALAMO  ELY
PROOFS  ASTERN  GEUM
TASMAN SMU  ETD  ONAGER
   SIAM  EPOPEE  STRABO
PAM  RIATA  DRABS  GULL
OBI  CLEAR  DOUBLEBOGIE
DECLASSE    YALU    ESS
SLEET   LABIUM   MICA
   ACME  TERNI  JACOSE
STASHED  TROGON  AVESTA
LASH  DESIGNATEDHITTER
ARTE  OMAR  IVIED  NAIRN
GOOD  CAGE  NACRE  ALANS
```

242

```
SLAW   RATSON   AFB  PABST
HULA   ENAMOR   SRA  LLANO
ICEDTHECUPCAKES   AARON
FIREHAT      LESSISMORE
TETRIS  WASTEDHISMONEY
      CHRISTO      HAS
WHACKEDTHEWEEDS     WEB
YELLEDAT   GREAT   SANA
LEDA      PLUGGEDHISCDS
ELOPERS  OAT   DIAGNOSE
     SAP  DWEEB   SNO
TRISTRAM   REO   TERRACE
HITTHECEILING      ORAL
ACED  SENNA   CAPITALS
REM  RUBBEDOUTAGENIE
     ASA    LOWBORN
CLIPPEDCOUPONS   SOAVES
HISTORIANS     AIRLIFT
ABLER  KNOCKEDOFFEARLY
IREST  EON  ENDORA  INAN
NESTS  SEE  RETOOL  NATE
```

243

```
BALD   TAHR   ATHOL  TOOTH
ONER   ABOY   SHANA  UMBRA
ANNOYREPEATEDLY   BAJER
REALISTE  MOREY    HEEP
   LEU  BOLES   SERAC
OUSELS  MARAT  FORESTAL
SNERD  TAKETOCOURT   ODA
ADAY  SITE   AINS   AFAR
GET  UNDISGUISED   IDIE
ERITREAN  USNA   ADDERS
   NOBELS  YUK   CAGIER
BOATED   SORE  OMISSIVE
ALBA   WITTYREMARK  SAM
SEAL  BOCA   TEIL   RIPE
SAY  JERKYMOTION  CHOIR
INWARDLY  ETHAN  TRENDY
   ISLED  NAHUM   HOT
PINT   EASEL  ANACONDA
ENDUP  TWILLEDMATERIAL
WROTE  LEVEL  OMRI  INFO
SEWER  CREDO  TOYS  COTE
```

244

```
RASH   AGO   RAGA   SPARTA
ATTY   DELAINES    AIRIER
BRED  INDUSTRIALGIANTS
BIRR  MELTER  AMAID  DIT
LUNAS   AURA  TARN  ESSA
EMEUTE  CMS  PIT  ALTAR
   LATEEN  SOCIALLIONS
SEMINAL  BETT    DUG
AVEC  TEARLE  OBER  PISA
LITRE  ENOLA  VENERATED
ATTARS  SWAMPER  DANITE
DALMATIAN  JERRY  STOOP
ASES  RTES  ENDASA  RUST
   LII   ATTU  ECDYSES
BACKPACKERS    EERIER
ARLES  ACE  NBA  SPAHIS
STEW  MAZO  PUIS  SIENA
TIA  SALON  OBLIGE  DAMN
SCREENDOOROILERS   EDAD
   LUPINO  MANASSAS  ROTE
EPINAL   YEAS   TSE  SNED
```

245

```
LADLE   PTAH   CTS   SKAW
OLEIC   AULA   PHOTO  TUBE
GAMMA   CRIS   LATIN  OLES
ONEBROKENHEARTFORSALE
    TIREE   ANGEL   ESKER
GRACELAND   STERILE
ROPA  ETS  MEAD  NIN  MAE
OLIVER   BELI   GSTRING
IFEELSOBAD  NBA  SEESTO
NEDDA  FARED  ERRORLESS
     IFICANDREAM
VALDAOSTA  ARYAN  HEFTS
ABOUND  SRS  ALLTHATIAM
CAPITAL  HAMS  ETHENE
ASE  OTE  SENS  APA  ALTA
   NEGATED  SURRENDER
SPAHI   AWARE   IRANI
AREYOULONESOMETONIGHT
LODE  NERDS  HOOT  SOROR
EVEN  ISLET  MOLL  ANODE
MESA   EDE   SMEE  MASSE
```

246

```
   CHARTER  THAT  INUSE
   THENERVE  HOLE  NIGER
WRONGTOEVERSPLITTHEM
OUR  LOIS  GOTO  THE  PIU
KEEPER   BONE  BEERCANS
   ISTOBESELDOMLYUSED
AEC   JAL   ROSE   RTS
ISMOREORLESSOK    AAA
GUINNESS  WHONEEDSTHEM
UNREAL  READERS   LEOVI
ADA   SOSO    OSLO   PES
NETTY  SPORTIN  GIJANE
AREIMPORTANT  CARRACER
   MAR  ARENTNECESSARY
CSI   ELIO   LOO    CBS
TOENDSENTENCESWITH
ELEGISTS  LEAR  LOAFER
OLD  EKE  ATAD  IDLE  AYE
ALLTIMEWORSTMISTAKES
RESET  SORE  ANNEALED
STUDS  PLOD  NOTEPAD
```

247

```
ERITREA  ITSLATE  PAGES
VETOERS  NATASHA  AROMA
INCOMETAXRACKET  SIDED
COHN  UNSER  FOSSE  LEI
TIESINTO  TAO   HOMERS
SRS  THENOELPRIZE  ASST
TEL    KNEE    DOALLS
GRIM  CHIT  SAIN  ETAS
ORIN  CHEESEURGERS  MUS
MANHOLES  WIT  DISSECT
ANKARA  SPRITES  SOURCE
HOOTERS  HUN  TEENSIER
ALF  LOOMINGDALES  ICEE
ADES  CELS  ICON  MEAD
IDEALS  OHOH    SEQ
SISI  LEAKFORECAST  RDA
GOATEE  NFL  LOWSPEED
TDS  NEATO  LOPER  ACED
MATTE  FATHEROFTHERIDE
ATEAM  ALTERER  AMMETER
JERRY  RESTSON  SOIREES
```

248

```
SLOP  SCAM  SHAD  URANUS
HERA  ARLO  LADE  CANAPE
OMIT  TOOT  ARAB  ARISEN
ONETOUCHOFVENUS  AMANT
TONIER  ARA  OGPU  ALDA
STEIN    SYCE    APPT
SLAB  EARTHSCIENCE
ETH  SLIP  WIREMAN  IRA
ERIA  ISING  CAM  STATES
SIGN  AENEID  PLUTOCRAT
CHN  CHALIAPIN    TAT
BYJUPITER  PLENUM  OTIS
OCULAR  AID  PRESA  REVE
OLM  LORDSOF  SERA  DEE
NEPTUNESHELL    DSMS
ASIA    SAID    EINER
SDAK  CRAB  ARE  INAPET
TUNED  MERCURYCHLORIDE
ACINUS  DIET  ELUL  INON
MATINS  EDNA  RAGE  NANO
PLANET  SETH  STES  GLEN
```

249

```
ARC  PRIER  MATT  PALER
PAH  RONDE  AURA  PEYOTE
THENEWCOLOSSUS  REEVES
RUPEE  ABATES  INSERT
GOUDA  PODE  OOO    ONE
LIBERTYISLAND  BRIEFED
IDS  EAUDE  OPTIMAL
LCI  MANIA  PRISM
ASTATIC  FREDERICA  BEE
AMOUR  ATTEND  ANON  EMS
ROBLES  ARTIEST  DEBRIS
HOR  MIAS  TANKER  LOTTE
UTE  BARTHOLDI  ASSAYED
SHALL  REINS    PTA
TIELESS  BAEDA  PGA
SPHERES  THEGOLDENDOOR
TOE  ATH  ETAL  NETOP
RUFFED  ORACLE  EGEST
ARRIVE  MOTHEROFEXILES
KEENER  EPEE  OPINE  ELL
EDENS  REDS  SAKES  SKY
```

250

```
LAMP  ANGUS  ISER  DUMB
EMIR  MOIST  SHEAF  ORAL
SOLESATSEA  GOLDENBUOY
SENAT  TARES  ROI
ASPERSE  MUSES  ARIETTA
LORNA  TORTE  LYS  HAS
INIT  THEREINSCAME  ERS
CANS  EIRE  YALE  EDGE
IRT  THEPLANESMAN  TEES
ASSURERS  COPTS  THATS
OKIES  ATHOS  ADAIR
SOFAS  OLEIC  CROUCHED
OFFS  SOREDTHEROWS  UNE
OTOE  ADDA  RELS  ANDI
NIX  TWOONTHEISLE  LTRS
EME  RTN  RISES  ALEUT
RESHOOT  DISCS  CAVERNS
ATO  COSTA  BOGEY
KNIGHTMARE  PLAZASWEET
ENNA  HEMIC  EATER  AREA
YEAR  TEST  EMEND  YARN
```

251

```
TAPING  NAMED  ADMAN  DRAG
OPENER  OBOLI  SAONE  EIRE
PORGYANDBESS  SWONDERFUL
ERSE  NODE  TAUNT  RAFTS
RTE  CUTEST  ALMS  AGRI
SOLED  RONDE  STROLLER
SOLEDAD  DANCE  FETAL  ERE
PLOVER  CONCERTOINF  ATOM
RIVER  HORSE  ERN  BETE
AVER  FARSI  BARGES  MAMIE
YAW  BUTNOTFORME  TRISECT
ALERTS  ROE  CRIMEA
RELEASE  THEMANILOVE  TOL
ASKED  DREADS  OLIVE  NCAA
ICER  ACT  ATONE  HEATH
DADS  OFTHEEISING  PARKER
EPI  FARES  ERICA  CARVERS
RENDERED  PRISE  GASSY
OUST  LEIS  SMERSH  ASH
FORTE  SANER  EDNA  ELLA
IGOTRHYTHM  OHLADYBEGOOD
ELLE  REATA  ORARE  LEANON
FEED  SATIN  TEXAS  YCLEPT
```

252

```
ALAS  PYE  DAMP  HEAPS
SAVES  IONA  OLIO  ASCOT
PRINTJOURNALISM  SPOOR
EVASION  OTTO  TEMP  UBI
CAT  RYE  LIAR  ISO  SAD
TEES  REALCREAM  OFFTHE
CHIRP  ISME  DELI
CANOED  RFD  ASI  TACET
UNARMED  LARCH  TEARGAS
METES  REAMER  DANSEUSE
SMU  DAYBASEBALL  ITT
HOROLOGE  GEMINI  OATES
ANALYZE  FETED  CARFARE
WELLS  ERE  SEX  SCORNS
BIEN  ORCS  IDAHO
WALESA  SNOWSKIER  TRAP
AMO  ICE  CETE  SUR  EMU
RON  GLOW  KAAT  ALCAZAR
SEDGE  ROTARYTELEPHONE
ABEAM  GOAD  SLAT  TENDS
WASPS  IDLE  ERS  MEAT
```

253

```
LABORS  GASTON  JACOBY
IMARET  SORCERY IBERIA
SAIDBENTOMRSBENMYDEAR
 STOOLIE    ASI  EDSELS
    ZEN  TOWIT   BAS
IDAHOS THULE MUN   OOH
SARA  BOAZ  MOLD  ANNO
ANOTHERSTORMYDAYIFEAR
AZO ELIS  SALE  NAILS
CAMBRIC  PATTON SCULLY
   ROOKIES  TRAVAIL
STRAIT SPICED EUSTACE
IRONS  OPAH  ARLO  NON
SAIDMRSBENITISNTRIGHT
ALLY APAR ROHE  LEAR
LAY  DAR CLONE STERNE
   AIR  IRATE  EWA
 MEDIAS  NEW  ALAMEDA
TOWASTEADAYGOFLYAKITE
OTELLO  METEOUT ELEVEN
VENEER  EXERTS  RESENT
```

254

```
MACS  GASPS  HARSH TACT
EBAN  ABEET  ELITE ARLO
SONOFZORRO  ITFOR  STAR
SUCRE  WAIVEROFPREMIUM
   ETUN   SEX    PASSE
UCLA ALPH PCTS MONTES
PELT MAST LOOT  IDI
OLE LETCH OMOO SEACOW
REDTIDE EPISTLES  UVA
SCOUR  TET HELI  ETES
THU OMAHA LENIN  STR
PIER PASO COX  GLAIR
TAC PETULANT PLAINES
ALKALI AGER RERIG GAI
 NIN THAR AVON  ACCT
TAPING ETRE CASK MOTE
ELISE   RAT    STER
ABSENCEOFMALICE ERNIE
CATT ARNIE COURTLIEST
UNIT SLING ONETO CRAT
PYLE HENNA ASSET ASKA
```

255

```
 GROSS  SAFER  ASSISTS
CLOTHE CURIE STARCHES
HOUSECLOSING SENTIENT
ABS STOUTS  TOAD  SETA
MUTT STRIKEBACK  SNAG
BLEEP  INSTEP  AGOD
EARTHMEN OLE FURROWS
RRS OUTGUN ARMADA FEW
 ITSA GIS  SATIN TRA
 DIDOS ELENA NEEDLING
TENOF PRICETAGS FUMES
INCLINER EATME SIXER
EDO NAPES DAM WANE
URN IDIDIT ROMANA FAN
PACKSIN NEW ADELAIDE
 LAHR GRASPS ERNAS
SPUN BEERCHASER CAPT
SASS DUAD ALLDAY GTO
TRIACIDS MOVIETRAILER
STONEAGE OWENS ELVERS
 INSOLES BERGS REEDS
```

256

```
CAAN  POSH  SIENA PRAHA
URDU  OAHU  ONTOP RENAL
BEDMINTON PTERODOCTYL
ASSERTED BREST  ARIES
  RAIN  ALAR  HADAT
CABANA  PUNIC  BATISTE
ADIT CAMPROMISE ENERO
LIKE  GAT  PEAR  GNUS
LEE CHRYSANTHEMOM TRI
AURORAE SORER GABION
 SEINE ASTIR  SERUM
MADRES  IGETA CRAZIES
IDO DORMATOLOGIST NRA
DOZE MARS  TWO  ETAL
AREAS RESTAURUNT NASA
SENSATE IRINA ROLLED
 IVIES ERAS  GINA
 DANAE ENNIS DEMERITS
POMEGRANITE CROMIGNON
POISE SOLOS TIDE EDIE
DRESS ARENT SPED DOLE
```

257

```
LARA  GAGA  ALBERT SSTS
AMEN  ATOM  CARRIE CHOP
CU★D  POLO  QUALMS RARE
ESTATE DEPUTIES  TEMPE
YESNO  ★BOARD   BEEPED
 TOAD ALIE  AREACODE
RIFE BIT ENCORES HOOD
ENO HEAD★T ACAT
WHOSHOTJR PRADO  IBET
RATHER  AMMO DEFERRER
ILIAD BIGDIPPER MAORI
TENNYSON CO★S MINNIE
EDGE MOTEL SATIRIZES
 AGOG APTEST  EST
DOFF RINGO★R FAT A★TE
ENLISTEE VIOL  RYAN
SLURPS NESSIE  PADUA
KESEY DOORBELL ★TLING
TATA LIKESO ABEL YMCA
OVEN LOANER COVE SLAT
PERT DRYDEN SWAT TYPE
```

258

```
LISTS  PARADE  LECTER
ARTOO  USURERS OTOOLE
YOURLUNCHBREAK DANCIN
ENDS HUE RIP ACE ROAD
TIE SUM DIV ETONIAN
TEN THERECEIVER VICAR
ESTEE ROB  TORN OLLIE
 DEPORT EEK PAR URU
VOILE YOURMEMORY SEN
SOFTEN RRR SAND  IDI
ELF RUST NAB DEMO OAF
ATA CLAM TIA OPENLY
GAB THEJACUZZI RINSE
RIO HEE DAM URGENT
ARTUR PRAM RKO ESTES
METRO SOMEONESEAR ALA
LAWSONS ROD SIS RES
AMEN INN AIR BAD ITCH
RACIER INCOMPUTERDATA
CLAUDE EARLAPS CAREY
HOPMAN TEENSY  ASSES
```

259

```
SORTS   MADE   ERECTS
ASTAIRE SABIN  DESERET
CHARGEACCOUNT  ISOLATE
TAL SARAH TAHITI  LITE
IVES DETER HURON  BLIP
VESTS DEMOB SER  ALENE
ESTATE REVISED  GEORGE
    NOLA  ENES   BRIC
CIRCUITRIDER CROOKING
ASYET LID TABLEAU  COE
REDS MANIA CROAT  CHIN
TRE GINGOLD END  SHORT
SERPENTS OUTLETSTORES
  ONEA  PEER   HOUR
CROWER MUSTARD  SNARED
REVES SOB SPARK  GLOVE
AGER STALK PIANO  EMIT
NERD PINING NIOBE  ACE
ENLIVEN CURRENTEVENTS
STAVING ATOMS  TSARIST
  SPEEDY  NEWS   SENNA
```

260

```
SLID  AMBER  PLEA  CZARS
KYLE  PEASE  HALT  ROGET
UNEM🔔ISHED A🔔FORADANO
ANTIBES  WIRE  MANILOW
    LUCY  COCAS   TIA
CHILOE ROLEO  ATTACHED
ROSEY 🔔EOFTHEBALL  ERI
AGA  SEVE   TIRE   SNAG
MA SAVEDBYTHE🔔  PARTI
SNEAKOUT REINS  CANYON
 ALINE ROMEO  HARE🔔
ONDINE CAMEO  BERTRAND
RAJAS 🔔ADONNALILY  MIR
AMAS TAVI  DIRE   ATO
NUN RE🔔IOUSNESS  SANTO
TRIBUNAL NOELS  CATNIP
  IND  ALLEE   LALA
SLANTED TODD  IRELAND
HILAIRE🔔OC LA🔔EEPOQUE
ARETE CONK ELUTE  SUNS
WAXER OWES DEMON  SANK
```

261

```
PORED ATRIA TRACK  QUITE
ETHNO LOONS HUMAN  UNDER
THEJOULEOFTHENILE  AVIAN
RETORTS KORAN  SLEDGE
ARTY ATT ARCO  LOGROLL
  SHARER KETCH  MASHIE
IFAT RULED TRI   EMMA
NERO ELSE NOEL  REDOES
FREUDGREENTOMATOES  NYE
SUMATRA ASHRAM  COMET
ASI SIZE TEE NYSA  ETHER
REAL PER RRS ORB  DEMO
ASNER TECH MET BILE  REB
DEIST HAVANA  NECTARS
WPM THEPERILSOFPAULING
HEYDAY LENA EIRE  ANGE
EDGE USE ISAAC  ITES
ERASER GESSO  MULLER
LOLITAS SAVE SAS  COCA
 GHETTO LEVER  SPRAWLS
GARNI IAMCURIEOUSYELLOW
AZTEC ELECT CRANE  PLENA
BOERS SENSE TYROS  OATEN
```

262

```
SHEBA REALM SCALE  DARNS
EELER ELLIE EOSIN  ESTOP
SALEM CROON NOTES  CHEWY
SLAPSAROUND  SKINCARE
  STRAYS  FAIR  OPENSUP
TVS RAN ESTATE NEE  ENE
HILLOCKS AIDE ARCED  ARP
ELAINE EAVE AWEEK  BRA
CLUNG SPORTSFAN  COSTA
IAGO ALTER AHERD  LANCED
ASH AMIE SHREWD  REREADS
 TALENTS ONE  SADDEST
OBELISK IDLING BAGS  ART
PERLES IDEES RAISE  ELEE
ETHAN SLUSHFUND  STOLA
ROY PALES  ANTE  IMAGES
YOU ARLES GIRT  RESOLUTE
ETS COL ARNESS MAO  ESS
WHERETO AMEN  PAPACY
 STOWAWAY SMALLCHANGE
NAFTA IMINE CARGO  IHEAR
ABOUT NERDS ASSAY  NORMS
NERVE GREAT THEES  GOOSE
```

263

```
SIERRA ASPACE  RIALTO
ANCHOR STATUE  ARMORY
ITSYBITSYWORLD  GRAVEL
LETT ENURE BERLE  TEA
RAH SUMER RNA  MISTS
TMC TAN ASYOULOVEIT
PRISON BEACH  RELEASE
REC NOEL CTR SEG  TEM
AND JUDETHEUNKNOWN
TVA UNA WEDGIE  SHOTS
TOYER MAE XES  ITHOT
ISLED TESTAE PST  ERR
FRIGIDHANDLUKE  SEA
LTS AUT EST ERIN  KAY
ERASERS ATILT  MERITS
FILTHYHARRY ESP  REN
TALES EVA MALES  SNO
LYE PRANK ATOLL  TYPE
TRIPLE STENCHOFAWOMAN
SUNLIT AMORES  GERARD
ENGELS NOMORE  SEENTO
```

264

```
RUSTS  IRKS  PALPI  OHM
ASIAN  NOAH  ATOLL  SOON
IENJOYEDYOURBOOK  ANNA
LUG BALDEAGLE  PACKETS
SPAN HAY LAOS  OASES
  EGOS  NUTTIER   TRA
WHOWROTE FDR  ITFORYOU
HEPTO INDIA  ODETTA
ARE UNCLOG SKIMS  POI
TERESA STEPINS  SPUN
STAVES DARLING  RHETTS
 ITES PODESTA  COLLET
CEN MEROE TWOCAR  ONE
SAUNAS PEARL  THOSE
IMSOGLAD TER  YOULIKED
NIK ALLOWED  SPYS
CLIFT ILLS LES  SLAY
HELLENE TEAMMATES  APO
ERLE ITWHOREADITTOYOU
DUES NOYES AMEN  ALERT
NTH ANEST RANG  BERTH
```

265

```
BASIN . PLASMA . NODICE .
ALONE . ROUGHEN . ERASERS
JACKARMSTRONG . DETECTS
ARI . TANTE . ODOR . SERIES
. MELEE . . STEROL . DEL
NITON . LEWISLAWES . . FAA
GNAWS . OMEN . . DTS . AITS
OGLE . ABBA . PRIOR . HEHS
. HUBERTGREEN . SELLE
SECRETED . ALANS . SPADER
UNHEARD . OLAND . SHARETT
SCANTY . CROCK . CHARTRES
PARTS . BARNEYFRANK . .
ISLE . TATAS . RAKE . ARLO
REED . ABE . MATE . PREEN
EDS . GARYPLAYER . ENACT
. REB . STELAE . ALOST
SIERRA . OSER . PALPI . SUI
ATAVIST . MARGARETCOURT
MEDIATE . ASYLUMS . APRES
. RENNIN . NESTLE . NEEDY
```

266

```
THELEFT . SHIER . GASHED
MAXILLA . TRANCE . OTOOLE
ALANDERSHOWITZ . REMAKE
NOM . ETTE . STOOGE . AXED
. ALCAPONE . . NOVEL
GODLIER . ERG . ELITISMS
APOEM . ASA . RESEDA . OUT
MALCOLMFORBES . MAM . PTA
ELL . SARD . RAT . SLITHER
. YAMAHA . TOSEA . NAIL
SPLIT . MAEWEST . DELAY
HATS . ELAND . BRASIL
WIRETAP . ISE . LAOS . ONE
ANT . ARA . KERMITTHEFROG
ATO . KISMET . ADS . GEESE
CONTESSA . SSR . SCANNER
. ANTON . WCFIELDS . .
BEAK . ONSIDE . LALA . MFA
EXPECT . ABRAHAMLINCOLN
VISUAL . RANTAN . ERUPTED
STEPPE . DROSS . REBATES
```

267

```
IMPEDE . RAMADAN . CRISPS
SIEVED . ACADEMY . HOODOO
HERELIESTHEFAMOUSWATT
. STRETCH . SEI . BREAKS
. TOO . SATAN . ELY
NEARER . MONET . PSI . REAP
OPRY . CARY . MAIS . ELSA
SOMEWHEREABOUTTHISLOT
EXE . HULK . RUTTY . NEILS
EYEBALL . DOOZIE . SHEEDY
. ALCOVES . ENDOWED
BEANIE . OVALLY . BORSTAL
ELMAN . SLIGO . ZORI . RNA
AMONGTHESEPATIENTDEAD
SERA . RATE . CEOS . ONCE
TRES . ALS . DURAN . JESTED
. BIL . TYLER . FIN . .
. WISETO . ONS . MIGRATE
WHOKNOWSWATTLIESAHEAD
BONIER . TIMEOUT . AGASSI
COASTS . STORAGE . WESSEX
```

268

```
PAPAL . AGED . MSGT . CABAL
ABASE . RIVE . OLEO . AROMA
BESTSELLER . BUMPERCROP
ASSESSED . VISES . ETHERS
. ROTS . HILTS . FREE
SECOND . ROSIE . MAILROOM
TROIS . MOTHERLODE . SBA
OGOD . DOGE . ADE . RACER
POP . NOBELPRIZE . DEBASE
STEPONIT . RUNE . DESIRES
. RATELS . ARA . CASTES
RESTATE . STAN . IMPOSTER
ENTERS . REELECTION . ALA
IVORY . SHE . ARAT . STEN
NOW . SMOKINGGUN . DAUNT
SYNCOPES . MORES . HABEAS
. OBOE . SPEED . MAYO
ISSUER . SCALE . GAGSTERS
HAPPYTIMES . NOMISTAKES
AGILE . RUNS . EDEN . AGENT
DATED . ETTE . RENE . RESTS
```

269

```
SADA . BLAH . MAMA . NOISE
WREN . BROMO . OLAF . ANGER
ABET . LABOR . REST . TILER
MOREMONEYSHORTERHOURS
IRELAND . EAST . ROAN
. ODDS . ACRE . ELAN . DUN
STOPA . CHAT . AXIS . KENO
MOVETOTHEREAROFTHEBUS
AVIS . POEMS . SITE . EATME
RAN . SAP . COSI . ARN
THEYAREAPERFECTCOUPLE
. ANT . BEAU . UHS . RIG
SPOCK . PARR . SETTO . PISA
ILLHAVETOPUTYOUONHOLD
MEET . EDEN . NORM . AIRES
IDO . ANOS . FINE . ECOL
. ATOM . COTE . LAMOTTA
TRUSTMETHISDRESSISYOU
AERIE . TOIL . EUBIE . OPEN
PAGAN . ERTE . ALOES . PEAT
EMEND . READ . FENS . HATS
```

270

```
RASCAL . ENTITLES . SEPAL
ASHORE . TAWNIEST . WALLY
BIASED . SPOCKSSUPERIOR
BANS . TIES . ALLEGE
INTACT . CRISS . SALLY
. CHI . REMO . RIBS . ELSE
MASKEDSUPERHERO . AXIAL
ITE . SENSED . OVER . SPANK
SLAWS . EON . BOUNTYBLOKE
HALO . BRET . EKES . EIO
ASSUMED . GAY . ANGRIER
. KID . PARK . MANS . ECRU
PANSNEMESIS . AMA . BRAND
ALAMO . ANTE . ENERGY . HIE
LUNAR . SCIFISUBMARINER
OMAR . FAIR . NCAA . POT
. TRAIL . STALE . SNAFUS
EASIER . KEEL . LINT
FLYNNMELODRAMA . EVINCE
FINED . PATENTLY . SICKLE
STETS . SCORSESE . PASSEL
```

271

```
ADOG  ANC   PABA   TASTE
TINA  KOREA ONEL   SNAIL
AGENTAGENT  EAGLEEAGLE
RINGO ACLU  LEAD   LATE
INDEMNITYINDEMNITY
SEENO ALP   TOSCA
RAF   RARE  ITA  IATRIC
IRAS  VISIONVISION  ONO
STUTTER GPA CLAN   STY
EILERS WHET ENSUES
SETNO WETNURSES NACRE
FONTAL RUPP BIRRED
AAA  HAIG  ESE MUTTONS
FLU  DECKERDECKER OSTE
BILLER ERA SIDE    SAL
ITISA  FIE TOAST
OCCUPANCYOCCUPANCY
ASSN EMIL GOGH  AMICO
SPACESPACE SPEAKSPEAK
TALUS ENOW TUNGO ACNE
ARABS DONE SOS   NEDS
```

The circled letters spell:
SEEING DOUBLE

272

```
WARD  GRASP RMS  ALASKA
AGER  HILLS EAT  RASPED
DIVIDEDLOYALTY  TITLED
ELEVATES CRATER DRIPS
RELENTS CHETS   ORION
LEO  BOITE  MAINSTAY
ASSES MINCEDHAMS  ESE
LIED COLD  EPEE   SRTA
ALP BROKENFIELD RAFER
STALLERS ELOPE MOLARS
ROUSE  GIT   TABAC
CLAVES SERRA CHRISTIE
ALTER SPLITSCREEN IRE
BAER ATEE  ROSS   SOON
AMI CRACKEDICE  FANNY
LANDSEER ARABS  PIN
CEASE ANGUS  SANDALS
SPORT PASSON PINETREE
ARMIES SHATTEREDDREAM
TEEVEE TEN ELEVE  ANNI
ESSENE ONS RIPER  PATS
```

273

```
ALARM  ALBION HOYT   CAB
COMMA  DOUNTO OLEO  RHEE
COUNTDOWNATTIMESSQUARE
OKS AUGER  SADO  SUMMIT
SEETHE RAG SENOR  APPAL
TERRA KEA MYBACK   ALE
ORY CUTUP  MEGAERG
FORTIETH UTAH SAY  ING
AMIS ARI POROSE  COVERT
REN WHELK  TOO  PESETAS
ALGAE ALLBESTFOR  INONE
DESCEND ERA  TIEUP  ANT
STOCKY KEITEL LPS  PSIS
SUR AMY EERO  ESCORTEE
TASSELS  ROGER   GUY
BIT MARIAH SAX    TORIC
OSHEA VENUS NEB  SPRUCE
OTELLO DELI  CAMEI  DEL
SHOULDAULDACQUAINTANCE
TALL DRNO NEUTER CLEAR
STD  SKIT  GREEDY HARPY
```

274

```
RASP  STELA  ASPS   MACE
ISEE  TRIAL  OCHOA  AXON
BILLBOARDS  BROWNBREAD
SALIENCE OVOID  DRILLS
CREE  BRAID   STAN
PECANS CRASS PORTABLE
ASONE SAINTTHOMAS  EIN
SAWS TARN  ASAP   WAND
TUB EAGLESCOUTS  SARTO
OODLES CHILE  CHIMER
LYRIC PAILS   RIVAL
CABALS PELLE  ADORER
ATONE JETAIRPLANE KAY
RIOT TEAR  UGLY   HERA
ENT PATRIOTSDAY  MOTOR
ROSARIES PHAGE PERSON
GALS SEEDY   CANS
ASSETS AIRED CASSETTE
GIANTPANDA LIONTAMERS
ERIC IDOLS ERROR  ARAT
DENY NONE  DANNY  NOME
```

275

```
LASHES DEWAR  OFFCAST
ASHORE DELETE CREATOR
SHERRYPICKERS TADPOLE
SAIS MLS SMITTEN  ELAN
IRK BOARD SPLOTCH  LCD
EPH RUNOUT EST   APSES
THUR  BRONXSHEARS
LOIN BEANIES  EMIGRE
RESTORE TINS  FARO  RET
ECHO ENTICE  MILAN  ETE
CAEN SHOOSTHEFAT  AGAR
TRI SPURN IODINE  COIN
ORK EERO DEMI  OSBORNE
REHEEL VATICAN   ERIS
POLICESHEAF  HANA
MOTIF SOI RIFLED   NSC
AHS FLOUNCE DAILY  SOO
DEUS IMPLODE ILL  WHIM
ENROUTE ELECTRICSHARE
DRIFTER SIMONE  ATONER
OYSTERS  SCANT  TASTES
```

276

```
NICOLAS TESSERA HARPSON
OOHLALA HONORED ULALUME
STEAMED ELAPSED SOFARAS
HARVARDSFIGHTFIGHTFIGHT
TELIC  NEE   TEAS
VANYA NOX ROMA    ESSA
OPPOSE EMETICS   EXURB
WORKOFABRITISHHISTORIAN
OFFWE LASH  OLE  NEGRI
MAW UNDOES ERWIN   HIM
ALAINS EATS ECUS  PATTI
CARRIERPIGEONNAMEDGIJOE
BABEL ELLE WEDS  ASLANT
ERR BALSA WEEDER   BEY
TAILS ETA USSR   AGEES
HADTHECODENAMECROSSWORD
FEDUP ESTRADA   TAIPEI
NAHA CYAN RES    ITSOK
ARKS ALI   ACTAS
BEETHOVENSFIFTHSYMPHONY
ALTOONA COROLLA LARAMIE
CITROEN ANANIAS EROTICA
ICIETLA SYNAPSE STPETER
```

277

```
COBB  PLANT MARIS DROP
ACLU  RANTS ETUDE IONA
THEYSAYTHECHEMICALSIN
TOA PIUS OTIS  LEANS
   CRISP MILAN PALM
ASHORE HARI  DECAMPS
THEBODYARENTWORTHALOT
WARE  EYED HOURS  ERR
OHS MEALS MERRY SHARI
   LORRE SOWS WEASEL
BUTASANYMOTHERCANTELL
ANODES  ONTO IRISH
LINDY AMINO SPITE SOB
MSG  PROSE FUSE  ACRE
YOUITSNOTTHEPARTSTHAT
 NEMESIS ANEW OTOOLE
  PETE RANDR STENO
ALIEN  PASO SATE  LYE
COSTSOMUCHITSTHELABOR
ESAU MELEE APAIR DURN
DEYS BALDS BARBS ASKS
```

278

```
GASMASK BROILER POTBOIL
ASHANTI LARAINE ARIADNE
SHATNER OCANADA PATRICE
TOMHANKSWINSREPEATOSCAR
ORE  SOBS   RYE
NESSIE MYMAN WARADMIRAL
 ACCRA ROMERO  ALONE
HAITIHOLDSFREEELECTIONS
ODD NOXIOUS TDS PLEASES
NAIVE YAWP DRY  ACID
EGOIST SEIJI UPON PESO
SIMPSONVERDICTNOTGUILTY
TOSS HEIR ENSUE SNEERS
 MEDE RAN GALS ARGOT
STYMIED PAM CASELAW IKE
THEOKLAHOMACITYDISASTER
IRATE ELINOR IMARI
RUSTYNAILS YEARN PENPAL
  ANN  NETS   ARE
CALRIPKENBESTSLOUGEHRIG
AROUSAL ALDORAY MOLOKAI
SEATTLE GENNARO PAISANO
HANSOMS SWAGMAN STASSEN
```

279

```
EPEE ARISTA ATM  GOTHS
DEAL CASPAR CHE  RURAL
STRIKEFORCE CAR ICOME
UNTO FLAT COMINGHOME
ONEIS LAY ARETE  PEP
MISS GET LANDS GAMERS
BATMANRETURNS TAKERS
  GAS APIE FETID
 RESOW FLOSS ENEMIES
BELA ALONE ODDBALLS
ABOVE LANE RAFT OLIOS
SUPERFLY BOFFO  LAME
TEAROSE ARLOS SAYSO
 BORED NOLO SOD
BILLET DOUBLETROUBLE
ARNESS BRINY NOT NEUR
SOV TWAIN AND ADAME
SWINGSHIFT CLOG BARB
UNTIL ALT THEBIGSTEAL
MEESE TEE HARLEM ERGO
EDDIE ADD OTTERS DSOS
```

280

```
MARINA THEFED  SHALOM
ALINES ROMANIA COLIMA
CLENCH OWENDELLHOLMES
KOJAK ODIN  SIMPSONS
STATION EDIFY COST
 CENSE SHLOCK AIRE
ASK GULFS MORESTERDAM
SOSO OHM RETURN  LIB
IDOL PURIM APAR  ESE
SAND HERODIAS VOIDED
 ELIUSVANDERBILT
BARNUM ESCAPEES ERNO
ARE GMEN EMILY  MRED
BOB AENEAS SAE  SEMI
ESEARLJONES STPAT TOE
SELF ONTAPE  ICHOR
FRAY ITALS SKIJUMP
BESIEGES INGA  SIDEA
ALEXANDERILTON ROBERT
RECEDE XAVIERA INWAIT
BETSYS JETSET BEAUTY
```

281

```
WASPS PILAF BERG  CROP
AWARE ITISI AREA  LUNE
RECONNOITER INFLUENCE
BEAUS PERT  ONAGER
IMPACTS ATNO TOSIR
BILBAO PRIZEFIGHT CST
SAULS CROCE ALLEYCATS
EMMY FOAM MILES  HERE
NIB ILLMANNERED  ASIT
ISLET OATER TRAPS
SANTEE SPIDERS LEGREE
EDGED AESIR MINES
ROPE INTERSTATES TAB
ARAL EDDAS HUGS  TOGO
PERENNIAL SHANE CHARS
HST ADOLESCENT PARSEC
ODETS AARE DONATES
HOTTEA INTO SALAS
OBSERVANT HIGHFASHION
SOAR OGEE ENDOF TERSE
TERI ROOM DERRY ADATE
```

282

```
BEAMS ATAD OBIT  SHIFT
ASTEP NOTI BAHR  MARIO
SPELLINGBEES TONITENNILLE
HONORARY MOAB PRAISED
WAVY TIBIAL  ARB
VOWELY PUSSINBOOTS AFAR
IDID LANA  MAH  LIMA
PENN HOVEL STELE DDAY
STIGMATA HORDES PLIE
SERVIAN AONE  FIEND
TOP HEADDRESSES OAF
HAHAS TENS LACUNAS
OVEN ENDURE UNTRODDEN
RIP DAUBS ARDEN  LAY
ALOOP USE LIER  TELE
LAHR CANNONBALLS VERSES
ONA ARIANE  CODA
AGITATE IPSA SALIVATE
GOOSEBERRIES LEWISCARROLL
ADAGE ESNE DOIN  TIARA
REYES DUTY ANTE  SLUES
```

283

```
SODAS   TALON    SPED   BRED
ATRIA SONATA   ARNO  LAMA
SHERLOCKSHOME  LEESMAJOR
HOW ARREARS  RAVE  SENATE
    DIANES  ARSON  ARCHED
PAP SOW   ALOT   ALE
AVER LLOYDSBRIDGE   BAD
PETITE  REUPS  EAST  PERE
ANEMO  WAAF  CONDOR  AVOW
CURSE  WCSFIELD  SPARSELY
YES  GILT  GLEE   CADRE
  CARRIE  ALTAR  BETHEL
MELEE  LOOT  KANS   YRS
HELPLESS  DONSKNOT  ATSEA
IDLE  THOMAS  RIBS  LUSTS
DEAN SOLO  LHASA  TIBIAS
EAR  JIMSNEIGHBOR  ALIE
  AMI   PEEP   REF  LLD
ROMANY  SHACK  RACIAL
OPORTO  PINK  REPLETE  DEB
BERTSPARK  STEPHENSSTILL
ERTE  ISEE  ADRIFT  HORSE
DAYS  CHER   GOODS  YOKED
```

284

```
BLOC  FFF   MUMS   PABST
BELA  AOL  BASAL  AERATE
COALMINE  ELENA  NECTAR
   AORTA  LARDS  ARAMIS
GAMMAS  BELG  AHAS  NENE
ABEAT  MASSACRED  TENS
TBAR  EEGS   WEIRDER
SALIENTS  FINN  EMULATE
   BUS  BUNT  UNBEATEN
STEAM  CODE  ENDE  RTES
MARINELAND  ARCADEGAME
OLID  RIND  CARS  MYERS
VENERATE  JARS   WEE
EMIRATE  CULP  LANDCRAB
   PERSONA  GIRT  OILY
PAVE  ACCOMPANY  UNGER
SETA  ALIA  ORBE  UNCAGE
ATONCE  SCONE  SANTO
CANDOR  SONDE  MEMORIAL
CREAKY  OLEIN  ARE  DOTO
ODDLY  RAIN   NOT  ENVY
```

* The starred entries all begin with the postal abbreviation of a state.

285

```
HARPO  ARGONAUTS  SCHWA
SCOUT  CHARACTER  PLEAS
THETHREEMARTINILAUNCH
   TEASES  ALT  IRE
ASTORS  FMS  PUNKROCK
LAHR  HUGELY  NOBEL  FAN
THEE  MRBIG  ALONE  OWE
MARS  FIASCO  PEAS  SMEE
ARUT  RATE  NTEST  CHARD
NAB  AKIN  DOS  FRIERS
  AUTUMN  WOW  SLOVAK
TIRADE  MEL  HAUS  HAD
BRYAN  SHEBA  AYNS  PARI
REAL  POET  NEVSKI  AYES
INC  TAMAR  CRONE  LYON
NTH  SLAVE  ENCODE  MALE
GETREADY  ESO  BLIMEY
  OTT  DOA  TABOOS
BARQUESUPTHEWRONGTREE
BRAUN  STENOPOOL  ORONO
QUEEG  SYCOPHANT  SYKES
```

286

```
STRATAS  SALVES  CRATES
COEXIST  PLEASE  REMOVE
ANGELHAIRPASTA  EITHER
REA  TERRE  REICHEN  ENA
ALLS  STEAMY  VOID  CLIP
BOITE  LADY  BAAS  MILNE
SCABBLED  BILLS  GULAGS
   ABED  PLIE  TALLIN
SUSSEX  TRUISM  CELADON
PLAID  THEE  SASHES  BRO
INTL  MARSH  ETTES  FATS
FAA  DENOTE  DUES  MOCHA
FENCING  OATERS  CARKEY
  ILLUSE  VIVE  TOGS
DECALS  DEERE  BROMATES
ELVIS  AMAN  NCAA  ALEUT
AMER  TAUS  ETHNIC  ETRE
DOR  SHUNTER  AFTRA  REV
ENSILE  DEVILSFOODCAKE
STENOS  IRISES  RWANDAN
TESTEE  INLATE  SSSSSSS
```

287

```
  ORB  AID  DUH  STRAFE
 BLEEP  SOUTANE  THORAX
TRICIA  STERNER  REBATE
RAVENLUNATIC  OBI  ICER
AVENGES  SEWNUP  NEST
PORT  TEMPS  ABSENT
  STREAK  GUT  OHARA
APACHE  TRAPPERS  NERVY
BELAY  MIC  HERR  RECESS
BABS  VINEGAR  SUTRA
ALAS  EAGLERIGHTS  ACID
  CORES  TALLIES  DODO
SHOWUP  TRIO  ASP  ALDEN
AURAS  HEATHERS  CLEESE
PEERS  ARI  REEVES
  YEARNS  EDSEL  SPIT
TOTE  DECEIT  NEPTUNE
AWAY  OSO  WRENAISSANCE
LINEAR  AVAILED  TARTAN
INTONE  TINGLED  ELVES
AGENTS  SAT  ADS  MER
```

288

```
HEAD  TAFTS  DADAS  SIC
ELLIS  ORION  ECOLE  HMM
REESE  PIANO  STRIA  OPA
OEXCLAMATIONPOINT  RAJ
   REMANS  PEERCE  STLO
SEME  ASS  FEARS  SACHER
HARPIST  BERRA   TRY
ASSADS  POR  DII  HIPPO
HYPNO  WASNAPOSTROPHET
  ECLAIR  AGR  OHOS  ETC
FRY  IST  NAE  BIB  RNS
TAI  DREI  DIE  ANSWER
WHOQUESTIONMARK  AFAIR
ADDUP  TEN  IDS  CRINGE
  MAE  TAMES  BRINGON
BAIRDS  TEXAS  SAY  AERO
AUNT  TEARER  AILEEN
SRI  RACHELCOMMARACHEL
TOV  ARTIS  ERUPT  RIATA
ERE  MEANT  ATSEA  SNITS
DAR  ADDIS  USERS  GLEE
```

289

L	A	M	A		S	W	A	M	P		O	M	I	T		S	T	U	B
E	L	A	N		C	A	N	A	L		S	P	I	R	O		W	A	N	E
N	E	I	T	H	E	R	O	N	E		T	E	L	A	W	R	E	N	C	E
D	E	M	E	A	N	E	D		B	L	I	N	D		H	E	A	T	U	P
			S	U	I			S	E	A	N	S		R	E	G	R	E	T	S
C	A	J	U	N	C	O	O	K	I	N	G		F	E	E	L	S			
A	D	A	P	T		I	L	I	A	D		C	R	A	Z	E		M	O	A
R	A	M		L	I	E	N	S		L	I	M	E		J	I	N	X		
I	N	B	A	D	O	D	O	R		A	T	E	E		M	I	N	C	E	
B	O	S	S	I	E	R		A	T	H	A	N	D		E	G	G	E	D	
		E	N	D	U	R	E	D		I	N	D	I	C	T	S				
A	B	O	V	E		M	I	X	E	R	S		S	A	R	A	C	E	N	
L	A	K	E	R		V	I	N	E		M	I	C	R	O	W	A	V	E	
A	J	A	R		A	B	E	L		P	E	E	T	E		D	A	N		
S	A	Y		P	L	A	T	E		E	N	T	E	R		P	R	I	D	E
		B	A	S	K	S		I	N	T	E	R	N	A	L	I	Z	E	S	
M	A	N	I	T	O	U		A	C	T	O	R		T	A	M				
E	L	A	T	E	R		P	R	I	S	M		S	A	T	I	R	I	Z	E
C	O	N	T	R	A	V	E	N	E		B	O	W	L	E	D	O	V	E	R
C	O	D	E		N	O	S	I	R		E	D	A	M	S		C	A	N	A
A	F	A	R		S	L	O	E		D	E	T	A	T		K	N	O	T	

290

S	C	A	T		S	P	O	R	T		G	L	A	D		S	P	O	O	F
R	O	L	Y		P	A	P	A	W		A	E	R	O		C	L	I	V	E
T	W	O	C	H	I	C	A	G	O	T	E	A	M	S		O	A	S	E	S
A	L	T	O	O	N	A		S	T	A	L	K	S		L	U	C	E	N	T
			O	N	O			I	D	I			S	E	R	E				
S	C	E	N	E	F	R	O	M	M	A	C	B	E	T	H		T	A	N	K
P	A	S		F	A	L	S	E		A	M	O	R		O	B	O	E		
C	R	A	G	S		F	I	G		A	S	I	N		B	A	S	E		
C	O	R	R	A	L	F	O	R	C	A	T	T	L	E		C	U	T	I	N
		O	V	A	L	S		H	E	R	E	S		L	A	Y	E	R	S	
	S	U	E	D	E		N	O	T	E	D		C	O	M	A	S			
S	E	M	P	R	E		P	E	O	N	S		W	O	O	E	D			
A	D	I	O	S		C	O	W	S	A	T	T	H	E	T	R	O	U	G	H
S	E	L	F		A	L	E	E		A	I	D		A	G	R	E	E		
S	M	E	W		A	B	E	S		A	T	R	I	A		A	N	A		
Y	A	R	E		C	O	S	T	O	F	B	E	S	T	S	E	L	L	E	R
		I	G	E	T		C	O	S			P	O	E						
C	Y	P	R	U	S		S	P	U	R	T	S		F	I	N	N	I	S	H
A	S	I	D	E		W	A	L	L	M	A	I	N	O	R	S	T	A	T	E
R	E	P	O	S		I	D	E	A		I	N	A	N	E		I	G	O	R
D	R	E	S	S		N	E	A	R		N	E	E	D	S		L	O	P	S

291

A	B	C		D	I	A	Z		S	P	E	A	R		C	U	B	S	
B	A	H	S		I	N	G	E		M	O	A	N	E	D		A	S	I	T
S	L	I	P	P	E	D	O	N	H	I	S	R	O	B	E		N	A	P	A
	Q	U	O	T	E			A	L	I	T		O	R	A	T	I	O	N	
S	L	U	R	P		B	R	O	K	E	T	H	E	R	E	C	O	R	D	S
H	E	I	S	T		T	A	M	E			A	N	K	H	S				
E	A	T		O	B	E	S	E		A	C	T	S				P	A	R	
D	R	O	P	P	E	D	H	I	S	F	R	I	E	N	D	S		U	R	E
			U	S	E		I	R	O	N		A	D	O	R	N	E	D		
S	A	H	L		F	E	L	L	D	O	W	N	O	N	T	H	E	J	O	B
A	M	I	S	S		T	E	A		E	E	C		O	C	A	L	A		
U	P	S	E	T	T	H	E	C	H	I	L	D	R	E	N		A	B	E	T
T	E	S	S	E	R	A		I	O	T	A		E	S	S					
E	R	E		R	A	N	I	N	T	O	H	I	S	B	R	O	T	H	E	R
S	E	D		S	G	L	S		S	T	R	O	M		O	V	A			
		S	E	D	A	N		B	L	E	U		A	B	N	E	R			
S	P	I	L	L	E	D	T	H	E	B	E	A	N	S		L	E	O	N	E
P	I	C	A	S	S	O		A	L	E	A		S	P	I	E	R			
L	A	I	T		K	N	O	C	K	E	D	O	V	E	R	A	B	A	N	K
A	N	N	E		S	I	N	K	I	N		H	I	L	O		E	R	N	O
T	O	G	S		S	T	Y	N	E		M	E	S	S		Y	E	S		

292

A	L	E	C		A	T	O	P		T	A	R	P		A	L	A	S	
S	O	Y	A	S		L	O	R	R	E		O	V	E	R		L	I	S	A
P	R	E	J	A	N	E	S	S	O	R		N	O	V	O	P	U	S	E	S
S	E	D	U	L	O	U	S		B	I	S	O	N		P	A	M	P	A	S
			L	O	O	T		M	I	C	E		D	O	W	N				
S	A	M	S	O	N		O	C	T	A	R	A	T	E	S		A	G	R	A
A	L	A		N	E	A	R	L	Y		B	R	A	C	E		R	E	S	
G	A	L	A		M	I	X			T	R	A	D	E	M	A	R	K		
A	R	M	E		F	E	B	I	T	O	R	I	A	L		C	O	M	A	E
	M	A	R	T	I	N	I		A	R	I	E	S		P	O	L	A	N	D
		Y	A	W	N	S		S	N	I	P	S		T	U	L	I	P		
E	M	O	T	E	D		M	A	G	O	O		C	A	R	E	E	R	S	
G	A	P	E	R		J	U	N	O	N	N	A	I	S	E		R	I	P	S
G	U	I	D	E	P	O	S	T			T	V	S		E	A	R	S		
E	N	S		R	A	K	E	S		D	R	I	E	S	T		N	E	T	
D	A	M	P		I	N	S	E	P	U	R	A	L		E	R	A	S	E	S
		A	T	M	S		A	S	A	P		B	L	E	U					
O	N	A	G	E	R		S	E	T	U	P		D	I	M	A	G	G	I	O
L	I	M	A	R	O	A	T	S		R	E	D	E	C	A	T	I	O	N	S
A	N	O	N		S	C	A	T		P	R	O	L	E		S	E	R	G	E
N	E	S	S		E	T	T	E		Y	E	L	P		T	E	E	S		

293

	J	A	F	F	E		C	A	P	A	P	I	E		C	L	A	R	O
F	I	G	A	R	O		I	N	S	T	A	N	T		F	A	I	S	A	L
E	V	E	R	Y	C	H	R	I	S	T	M	A	S	S	O	I	F	I	N	D
D	E	R	R	I	E	R	E		E	I	N		A	R	R	E	S	T	S	
			N	N	E		B	E	N	N	Y		H	E	N					
D	O	S	A	G	E		Z	E	N	D	A		S	A	M		I	N	A	N
E	N	O	W		M	O	R	T		R	A	R	E		N	A	N	A		
I	A	M	L	O	V	I	N	G	S	W	E	E	T	A	N	D	K	I	N	D
S	I	M		C	I	N	E		A	L	I	E	N		O	S	S	I	E	
T	R	E	S	T	L	E		R	A	C	I	N	E		A	N	T	H	E	R
		C	O	L	O	N	E	L		T	E	N	A	B	L	E				
S	E	R	A	P	E		O	L	I	V	E	R		P	E	E	R	A	G	E
E	N	E	R	O		S	W	A	M	I		O	L	A	V		G	R	R	
W	O	U	L	D	N	T	I	T	B	E	N	I	C	E	M	Y	D	E	A	R
O	L	P	E		E	A	S	E		A	C	H	Y		I	N	D	O		
N	A	S	T		S	T	E		F	O	R	K	S		D	E	X	T	E	R
			S	T	U		T	O	D	A	Y		P	O	T					
P	A	S	T	I	E	R		A	X	E		R	E	L	A	P	S	E	D	
I	F	I	W	E	R	E	T	H	I	S	W	A	Y	A	L	L	Y	E	A	R
M	A	T	I	N	S		W	O	E	S	O	M	E		O	I	L	E	R	S
A	R	E	N	A		A	E	R	A	T	E	S		P	A	E	A	N		

294

C	A	N	A	S	T	A		M	I	S	S	M	E		A	W	H	I	R	L
O	R	A	N	T	E	S		A	T	T	H	A	T		C	O	A	T	E	E
L	E	U	C	I	T	E		S	T	E	E	R	S		R	O	W	E	N	A
L	O	S		C	H	A			R	R	S		A	I	D		M	A	V	
A	L	E	A	K		G	A	V	E	A	H	A	R	D	Y	T	I	M	E	
R	E	A	D	Y	T	H	E	R	I	O	T	A	C	T		W	I	Z	E	N
		A	S	H	A	M	E	D		O	L	A		V	O	T	E	D		
F	E	W		H	O	L	S	T	E	I	N		P	E	A	R	L			
A	N	I	M	I	S	T		H	O	C			P	I	K	E	M	A	N	
S	T	R	I	F	E		S	A	T	U	P		H	O	N		A	R	E	
T	R	E	A	T		P	O	S	E		A	C	E	S		C	H	I	L	E
E	E	R		V	E	X		X	E	R	O	X		C	O	I	L	E	D	
R	E	S	A	L	E	S		P	A	D		P	R	U	D	E	N	T		
		L	E	R	O	I		P	A	V	I	L	I	O	N		R	E	O	
	P	R	O	F	T		R	U	R		A	C	E	T	A	T	E			
T	R	O	U	T		M	A	K	E	A	N	I	G	H	T	Y	O	F	I	T
H	E	A	D	Y	O	V	E	R	H	E	E	L	S		H	E	A	R	A	
E	F	S		H	U	P		A	U	S			H	E	E		C	O	M	
R	A	T	I	O	S		S	I	M	O	N	S		O	P	A	L	I	N	E
O	C	E	L	O	T		I	N	A	P	E	T		A	E	D	I	L	E	S
D	E	R	E	K	S		S	E	N	S	E	D		D	E	S	S	E	R	T

295

```
SORT   VASSALAGE    SAPS
CROOK  IMPERATOR   ATSEA
OCTAL  DIAMETERS   ROOTS
WHATIS TRINE      ATONES
LIT  BEVY  SAINTEXUPERY
  DEBASE   SNEERERS
  INSIST   EROS    BIG
EBAN ENTIAL DRS  OCALA
LAB   SUNNI  SOILBANKS
SHULTZ DEISM  ROUEN
ANTARES STIES  NISSANS
  MIKES  ANTON  SETSUP
MULETEAMS  VENUS   ILE
ASIDE CIA ISIBLE  TALC
DEB  TALL  ASITIS
  SPIREMES   GODEAD
LITTLEPRINCE COOL  PAT
ENURED  CALLA   NESEYE
ATRIA ENLARGERS RUMOR
PRINT ONESEATER SCANS
SONG  SEWERRATS   KNEE
```

296

```
WEIGHT  CUTOFFS  BRETTS
ASTRAY  ONADARE  AERIAL
NABORS  CANDILES SURELY
DIESTOCK GELDS  SPARKES
  SENATORS    IDEST
ACME  RABAT LOT  ACRE
GRADUALISM  APEG  HUM
EEL PROLE CUI WIM  ALI
RATATAT SNORET ODA REL
SMASH ASONE TOYSTOREY
  CRAPE  TVA  IDLER
DRYHUMOR NOTAL  RANGE
IOU SOS HBIKES SHAPELY
NUM TNT ACE THEIT  RUE
ETA  EDGE  FREESILVER
DENT TRI CROCK  OEDS
  RUINS  HOSTELER
SPTRING ALCAN ORIGINAL
TOUSLE ROOASTER MRMOTO
ULSTER MONTANE  BEATTO
BLEEDS STEELED STREAKM
```

297

```
DIAMETER  DREAMT   SCAM
INCASEOF  AIRMAIL  HARE
GRUNTLEDEMPLOYEE  ANNA
ETTE   APSES   SINNED
  LEONORE     ASSAY
CAPE  FOUNDEDRUMOR  KEG
AVIS  TOTS  LOOSEN ANTE
YIP MEN  MITTEN  SPAHN
CLEMENTWEATHER  PLACER
EATAT IWERE   SHACKLE
  SHADILY  ANGUISH
MUDHOLE  SLEEP  HERBS
ONEIDA  EVITABLERESULT
TILES  FEELIN  RED  BOY
OTIS FERRIC ARCA  JUKE
REB RULYBEHAVIOR  APES
  LEAST    SIMPSON
STEAMS  HASTA    NICE
OBIS  ADVERTENTMISTAKE
DANE  TRAITOR  RIDEOVER
ARKS  STREWN   WAITRESS
```

298

```
SALIERI  ATSTAKE  ATOMS
STRINGER SHARPEN  TORAH
CHAMPAGNEPROMISES BOITO
DOLES HONE  SPAIN HANGAR
SOLD PEWITS LDS DOT  ALI
  BLANC TIE  DOR  AMIN
DRYWOOD  MERRYGANDERING
RESORT  VEEPS  EARNEST
ANERA MALI  CLINE  CIANO
WARDHEALERS LENS  NASCAR
  VEIN  ALAN  OPTIMA
SUBTLE DIPLOMACY NESSEN
ACLEAR  ETTU   EASE
CLASPS LAKE  PARTYWHACKS
SAUTE AIDID  TEED  ALAIN
  IRONMEN BLISS AROUSE
FATFINDINGTRIP  IMPULSE
ATRY IST  RAE  TEMPO
CLU MOO TEA STAMPS  GADS
TACKON TORCH ARIA  AESOP
URKEL SENATORIALCURTSEY
AGENT ANATOLE  WETSUITS
LEDTO DOLORES  ASSENTS
```

299

```
ACERBATE  ACED  WBC  OFT
BEREAVES  RAVE  ERASURE
BEATRIXPOTTER  LIBATED
ASTIR   RUSSELLBAKER
  NEST ARC  LIFELINE
  HATHA TOA  IBERIA
AKA  TACHE NSC DYS  IDA
MONTEL  ASH CTR  TVMOM
ADDS LMN ONO ECG  IPSO
JAMESFENIMORECOOPER
KATHERINEANNEPORTER
ISAACBASHEVISSINGER
JUDE RIA ISR VEE  ANTA
ATESO  LOT SHE  STMARK
YEN RUG BET ISITI  TOE
  CANONS  ADE  KEDGE
TROCHAIC  LAR  EPEE
SAMUELBUTLER    LOOSE
JAIALAI  RAYMONDCARVER
ODDSARE  ECHO  IRANGATE
YES RDS SOON  NEWDELHI
```

300

```
GLACE  LAMP  GONG  OFFER
RELAY  OVAL  OLEO  LILLE
AMORE  SARA  GAIT  EXAMS
SUFFRAGISTSOFLONGAGO
SRTA  VAL  OWL   PASTE
  ROOT POI  BLOT  ILEA
PAVEDWOMENSWAYTOPOLLS
OLA  ASSET  HALO  SNUBS
RALLY  LEO  SANDRA  MAT
TILE ICE  URSA   AULD
  NINETEENTHAMENDMENT
  SLED  ATOI  RED  LAWS
ADD  AMELIA  LEN  MEDEA
ROOST  OAKS  DISCO  IRK
NOWWECANDECIDETOSHAPE
ORNE  ONES  UNA   AREA
  SEPIA  MLK  ITO  NAME
NOTONLYROLLSBUTROLES
COUPS  YOYO  EAST  AVERT
ESTEE  SKED  SKEE  FENCE
LEHAR  TESS  SINS  TREYS
```

301

```
STACK  SLUR  LOGE   TITUS
EAMON  AERO  AVES   OMINE
CRIMEANDISHMENT    TINIA
TRECENTO  SAINT  SHTETL
    TITAN  SUNS  SLEY
SATINE  DELA  SAIC  DIT
EMBOG  PLEASEDASCH  ECA
LIEN  GAEA  ELSE  KIWI
ANA  CONTRATALLY  DUCAL
HOMESWIT  TORTE  SABERS
    STAC  STARA  FORE
RATTAN  RAISA  BLOCKEDT
ABHOR  NONCTUALITY  MAW
ZEUS  SEAT  DUTY  CLUE
ELM  CTUREDTIRES  BOYLE
LEB  HARK  ERNA  PAWNED
    EBRO  EMUS  BRONC
OCELOT  ALISP  OUTSHINE
LOXIA  FROSTISONTHEKIN
ELGAR  INGE  RING  EREDE
ONEND  TOED  EXES  ESSES
```

302

```
SHAFT  DODOS  DANA  SPY
AISLE  HENOCH  EPIC  WEE
GLOAT  OMERTA  SPOT  ARA
SAPPHIREDMAN  TUB  SPUR
    ENRAGED  WRIEST
AMBERLINER  LEO  PIETA
GOAD  EDS  RUBYSTANDER
ALBERT  OLEG  SPURTING
LEASE  CUPIDS  ILK  SAO
    SALONIKA  SARA  ONT
AQUAMARINECOMMANDANTS
CUM  TREE  TRAILERS
CAP  HIE  WORLDS  ASOKA
EVIDENCE  ARAL  TWOBIT
PERIDOTARDS  AAR  ROTA
TREND  SEI  GARNETTLER
    GAMUTS  ARBITER
ZANY  ASE  EMERALDERMEN
OVA  POUR  CETANE  MAIZE
NOV  ERAL  HEEDER  OVERA
EWE  WILY  ORLES  RENAL
```

303

```
  LACED  CHAPS  DATER
POLITE  HEAVE  ISOPOD
MACADAMIANUTS  LYRICAL
ICAN  LOGIC  SCALE  KRI
NILS  CURE  BIOTA  MYNA
ONE  HORAE  SAONE  GOMER
TOSSEDANDTURNED  OVALS
  ILETA  USES  FAIR
CASTES  PAIL  COLLECTS
ASPEN  LOONEYTUNES  IOU
LAOS  EERO  ABLE  DALE
ONI  OFFBROADWAY  TONER
TALIPOTS  IDOS  RAZORS
  EVER  SNUG  AMORE
RODIN  RECKLESSABANDON
ACRES  ARRET  ESSES  ERO
NEOS  AGOOD  ANIS  AFAR
GAT  ALGOL  CASAS  VINS
ENTITLE  LUNATICFRINGE
SEALED  ENERO  RAISES
NOISY  DOVER  EXPOS
```

304

```
BAER  CALLA  STAGS  ABABA
OMOO  ALIAS  ARLENE  GALAS
PANDORASBO  LAINIE  EGANS
STEERS  TORS  INEPERIENCE
ROD  PER  TINES  ISLES
PEA  ENID  FILMS  RENTS
INT  RON  TALIA  BERG  AST
EDITED  BOSTONREDSO  NHEB
COOED  MINTS  EDIE  ADORE
ERNE  HADES  LADED  ATLAST
  SOONER  MAMA  BOOTEE
SAS  CROSSEAMINATION  SRS
CLOYED  RUED  PANDER
ALULAE  ADAIR  WACKY  HERE
BISON  PLOT  RICKS  REPEL
SNAP  LEICOGRAPHY  PEELER
ASH  OPES  RENEE  SIP  ASO
  ORION  NAPES  SEAR  NEY
SANER  HESSE  MIA  OCA
AMBIDETROUS  SEAL  GOATEE
LEASH  AUNTIE  PRICEFIING
GATTO  INDEED  OSCAR  ROTO
AREST  TORRS  SHALE  ONES
```

305

```
  SOONER  CAPULET  SPAD
AUSTERE  PLENARY  SHAME
PARTINGSTITCHER  PURNA
AVIS  ANES  ROTI  CANTER
MEC  GNAR  PERI  HORNIST
  TAILSSALK  JAR  ITTO
FRIO  EAR  SOLO  NAY
AREOLAS  DEBRIS  NOG
SAM  SHOWEDROE  AORTA
SNOW  TAR  IMPS  SHOALS
ATRI  MASSGAINS  ORLE
DISNEY  PAPA  AAA  STEW
CENSE  HIDINGYRE  ANI
  ITA  PINERO  INWARDS
HAN  RAAB  ASS  ELSE
CONG  NIN  SITEWHALE
ANISEED  MISE  EARL  ELM
ROMPED  MANO  LENA  ALYA
ARAIL  SACKBEATDRIVERS
FETES  ORLEANS  LACONIC
EDEL  SIERRAS  ETHNIC
```

306

```
MASON  SPIT  ASSTS  BUG
ARENA  TERRA  MAHRE  OLE
SLEET  AROAR  ASIAN  INA
HOI  HOTUNDERTHECOLLAR
  NEALE  AUTO  LEROI
AGING  INCENSED  ACNE
CARL  ANODE  ALS  SAGAS
CREEPSIN  DONE  LOSE
SEDER  HOPPINGMAD  EVER
  NOS  ARTS  INCASEOF
ARF  BESIDEHIMSELF  RNS
CHIMERAS  VETO  IRA
TETE  ALLFIREDUP  ONTAP
ETTA  EINS  FEASTING
DOONE  BEN  FIORE  OCTA
  RBIS  UPINARMS  SINKS
ESTER  STEP  MORSE
ATTHEENDOFHERROPE  DIP
LEI  ERICH  ODEIN  NOONE
DEE  MINIM  SUSIE  INFRA
ODD  SEGOS  PSST  CAFES
```

307

```
ALOE  ACTA  RIO  CHAFER
SOUL  IRAN  ADDE  DELANO
HOTSPRINGSTEEN  TAPING
  LATIN  UNEARTH  THREE
CHI  ANGELO  MORON  AFAR
RENT  GERARD  NYLON  IDS
OREAD  RAREES  YOURE
CEDRIC  RICHMONDALE
  SCOOT  STREAK  EIDER
SPLITRAIL  YANKEE  LIRE
ILO  AKRON  PRIER  NIB
PAWS  LLANOS  INFRINGES
STEED  ANGOLA  GEODE
 ALTOONASSIS  LEERED
  LIVID  EMPTOR  ADORE
ALI  ENERO  SHOWER  YALE
DENS  KRAUS  ALSTON  DEM
MAGNA  SITWELL  ABOAT
INTIME  SPARTANBURGERS
REOPEN  EURO  NELS  ESAU
ERNEST  TDS  DUET  STEM
```

308

```
 PALMA  MACAW  SWAPS  SPAR
PATOIS  ONASH  CARAT  HAPI
ATTACK  RILKE  AGORA  OTRA
ARITH  EAGLET  LEMON  GRIN
RICHARDSHAW  GERALDBUILT
  EYES  BUD  BANC
AMESLAN  ELTON  SATYR  ISH
CALIF  JOHNKNIFE  OMAHA
CASER  AVENUE  ELAN  NICER
TREVI  DICED  HEARTY  RAKA
  EGOIST  DUDS  EVOKES
SSW  HONE  GLORY  ALAI  ELS
CHINTZ  DOOM  SCURRY
HALO  EFFORT  ESTES  GOTHA
ELLIS  ULUS  EXPORT  IDEAS
MOIRA  ROBERTPIN  NEARS
AMA  VALET  ATONE  MAILMAN
  MOOT  ARU  TUNA
ALBERTDENTE  DONALDBROOK
MOON  REMIT  SIMILE  REVUE
BRAE  ABELE  INANE  SEDATE
ECRU  CARES  MANON  TAUTEN
RADS  TRYST  PRINT  EDGER
```

309

```
EELER  MEAD  CAL  AKIM
SNIPE  SARGE  OPALIZING
TONIC  KNARS  SHOOTISTS
 SECUREDLOANS  SCADS
  AROAR  NOE  KLEIST
SCAR  UNITEDSTATES  NTH
CARPET  LEVEE  NED  AGEE
EGEST  SODA  TAJ  SKAT
NEA  ABLATE  PAL  UNPILE
ERRS  OAS  AERI  REINS
  TOUCHINGSTORIES
 AFAWN  ALAE  NAE  HALS
SMILED  NAV  BASEST  SOW
HEXA  VAT  YALU  OSSIE
OLEG  ORI  BLARE  INWARD
RID  CLASPEDHANDS  IDEE
NASSAU  OAR  TAINT
  TORME  KNITTEDSOCKS
CHALLENGE  CHORE  RHONE
NOREASTER  HERES  SELIG
NESS  ELS  SEND  ERATO
```

310

```
ITA  ERGS  AMISS  THAWS
SYCAMORE  PARCH  OILIER
PRESSSECRETARY  NETTLE
YODA  SERE  STALAG  ONEL
  SESTETS  EGOS  ENE
IMP  NESTING  CHESSSET
SIERRA  SNORT  KEVINS
MATEO  AWARDS  ERASED
  VOLGA  YSER  NECTAR
SSS  TIARA  SAILS  SKATE
ONUS  SWISSSTEAKS  SNAG
RECTO  KAPOK  SPIRE  DTS
TACOMA  IRIS  STAFF
SKEWER  SCARPS  FIRST
 SENECA  STOOD  BOXCAR
LESSSALT  SIMILAR  AMY
ESS  DUST  LIVESTO
ACTS  SPREES  TESS  LIME
DOOLIE  DISTRESSSIGNAL
ARRIVE  ANTED  TEACARTS
 TYPES  YEATS  SEXY  ETE
```

311

```
SANTA  BALAS  ADAM  FLAG
PREEN  ADAGE  LIDO  AONE
CELLA  NOVAE  PARTRIDGE
CALLINGBIRDS  DETERGES
  ELATES  THEA  PEELE
STAR  MASH  DRUMMERS
AHA  EPI  ERINS  POTENT
LORDSALEAPING  MIV  NEH
TREAT  BRING  DOSE  EGO
  MOSSBACK  DONT  REL
FRENCHHENS  TURTLEDOVE
ROD  EATS  RANCHERO
ADS  PENS  CIRCA  VIDEO
NEE  ORK  LADIESWAITING
COLLIE  TOTEM  ILL  DOE
  ANDIRONS  OWNS  NOSE
DEBUT  RUTA  CADORE
OPENEYED  PIPERSPIPING
GOLDRINGS  MALMO  THREE
IDLE  PIET  ALLER  EERIE
TEAR  ECRU  MAIDS  SWANS
```

312

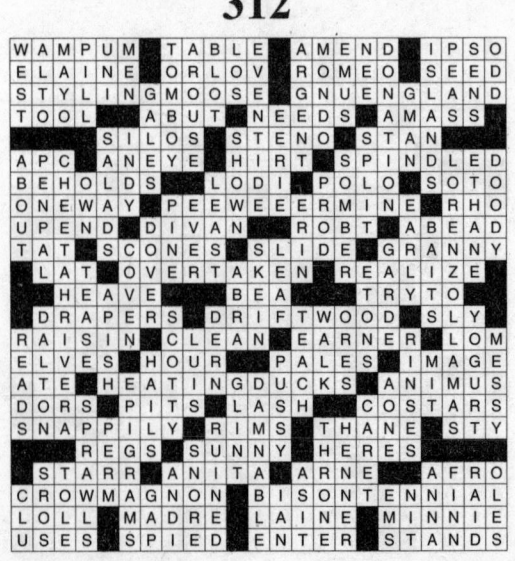

```
WAMPUM  TABLE  AMEND  IPSO
ELAINE  ORLOV  ROMEO  SEED
STYLINGMOOSE  GNUENGLAND
TOOL  ABUT  NEEDS  AMASS
  SILOS  STENO  STAN
APC  ANEYE  HIRT  SPINDLED
BEHOLDS  LODI  POLO  SOTO
ONEWAY  PEEWEEERMINE  RHO
UPEND  DIVAN  ROBT  ABEAD
TAT  SCONES  SLIDE  GRANNY
LAT  OVERTAKEN  REALIZE
 HEAVE  BEA  TRYTO
DRAPERS  DRIFTWOOD  SLY
RAISIN  CLEAN  EARNER  LOM
ELVES  HOUR  PALES  IMAGE
ATE  HEATINGDUCKS  ANIMUS
DORS  PITS  LASH  COSTARS
SNAPPILY  RIMS  THANE  STY
  REGS  SUNNY  HERES
STARR  ANITA  ARNE  AFRO
CROWMAGNON  BISONTENNIAL
LOLL  MADRE  LAINE  MINNIE
USES  SPIED  ENTER  STANDS
```

313

```
REDS   HADJ  ACT    STERE
AMOK  AERIE  SRA  CARROT
JULIASSEIZEHER  OMANIS
   MISSA  ELTON  MAD
IFA  LEES  BURN  PRESTO
MANSES  LEDA  SHE  STIR
PLIED  AZULEYEKIT  RND
ALMA  GLIM  RATE  DOSE
LOA  ALBEE  PESTO  ODEA
AWLSWEALTHATTENDSWELL
   AEA    ARC    RAS
THEMEMYRRHCHANTOVENUS
HELP  AHUSH  REESE  UNO
ERAS  ASIN  LEAS  LAIN
ART  KINGLEEERR  PONTA
PEER  IRE  ANNS  SAUCER
ENRICH  ABUT  SPAS  ESS
   POI  STORE  HALTS
ACCENT  COREREOLAYNESS
BORNEO  ONE  EAVED  IRIS
SWISS  TED  DRED  TART
```

314

```
ARP  EVIL   SHOAL   ASST
LEE  SEDAN  TAWNY  MICA
OFA  CLIMBMOUNTNIITAKA
SURFED  ICIAN  ONELINER
STLO  TAN  LETON  SENDAI
OAHUISLAND  RYE     ILE
FLAGG  GEORGECMARSHALL
RHODE  HEAP  SCAPA
SUBTRIBE  DDAY  HEISTER
UTO  SERFS  GRAB  NEHRU
SIRS  BATTLESHIPS  KIWI
ACHED  SOOT  STAID  SIN
NAIROBI  PREP  SCRIBING
   AEONS  NEED  KEELS
AIRCRAFTCARRIER  CANOE
RNA   OAR  USSARIZONA
ASTARE  ROSAS  PTA  EDER
DECREPIT  ADENI  CORRAL
SCHOFIELDBARRACKS  ICI
TEAR  SEEIT  CLUES  LAE
ATRY  IRENE  SETA  LTR
```

315

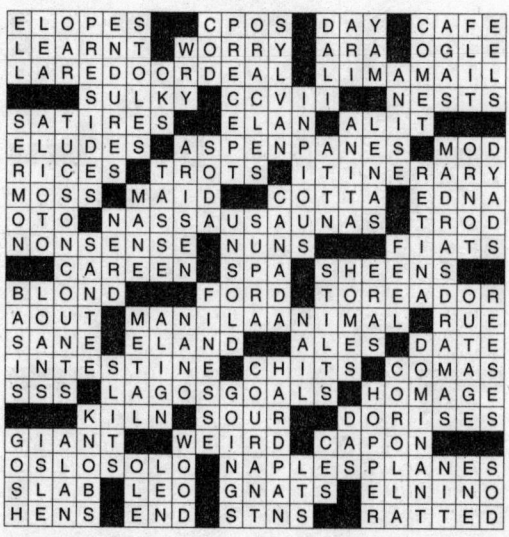

```
ALAS  SABIN  CTRS  MESA
MOLT  CRASO  REHAB  EMIR
PAPEREIGHT  IRECUTTERS
   RUNES  FOSSE  NRA
ACCOSTS  CARPE  SKILIFT
LORIS  SHINE  MBA  DII
ARID  STEERINGHEEL  ENT
MOMS  PARR  LOAD  SNIT
ONI  SINGINGDOORS  ETAL
SANGAREE  YARBS  CRILE
   ALLEY  CAVES  CADUC
PALES  LOSES  SHERMANS
ELLA  BRIDALSHOERS  LEA
SCAN  LAME  IFNI  PTER
TOY  PANBROKERAGE  AIDE
EVE  ICA  VESTS  ERNIE
RERANKS  DENTS  PAPISTS
   CET  SORTE  SATES
ITCHDOCTOR  LITTLEOMEN
TRUE  POONA  LAURA  NOVA
SAPS  OPEN  ENNIS  STAG
```

316

```
MAST  BWANA  CHIEFS  SPLAY
ALTA  LAMAS  TENTIE  PEUDE
COURTOFAPS  RAGTOP  ANNES
HUNGON  HEEP  REEF  RUGAE
STEEDS  SEPTA  WASTRELS
THELEYSOFBROADWAY
UPS  ORATE  RUE  ITION  SAT
TOTAL  BEARIN  LETO  BIRI
AMANDA  READSFOR  SOONGS
HEMS  PHLOX  ALF  LIMOGES
GENTIAN  TABU  WIEN  GNU
MARLO  THEWHOLESHE  IRATE
AMO  ODOR  HAKE  PIGTAIL
COURSER  BON  BOTEL  CLEF
RUNNER  SLATTERN  COHERE
ANDS  ATTU  APOGEE  BERLE
ETS  ANEAR  PTO  ELLAS  YET
ENGELBERTPERDINCK
OVERSELL  DOYEN  AGENCY
RENEW  IFIT  EDDA  ONEILL
CRANE  AZALEA  MOBILEALAA
ASTOR  DETECT  ARENA  DINT
STEWS  ADESTE  NYLON  SAGE
```

317

```
ELOPES  CPOS  DAY  CAFE
LEARNT  WORRY  ARA  OGLE
LAREDOORDEAL  LIMAMAIL
   SULKY  CCVII  NESTS
SATIRES  ELAN  ALIT
ELUDES  ASPENPANES  MOD
RICES  TROTS  ITINERARY
MOSS  MAID  COTTA  EDNA
OTO  NASSAUSAUNAS  TROD
NONSENSE  NUNS  FIATS
   CAREEN  SPA  SHEENS
BLOND  FORD  TOREADOR
AOUT  MANILAANIMAL  RUE
SANE  ELAND  ALES  DATE
INTESTINE  CHITS  COMAS
SSS  LAGOSGOALS  HOMAGE
   KILN  SOUR  DORISES
GIANT  WEIRD  CAPON
OSLOSOLO  NAPLESPLANES
SLAB  LEO  GNATS  ELNINO
HENS  END  STNS  RATTED
```

318

```
BORED  ASIS  SPEED  SCAM
AGORA  ROOK  LANAI  EZRA
CROATOMANICOLORS  MEIR
HEFTED  RAMAPO  LOGICAL
   DOS  RENO  RASH
LOCO  RENEGE  ANODE  KOR
ETAT  AERIE  RREASURE
DONTKHMERANYMOOR  ERGS
ASTEROIDS  AMPS  MEDIA
   TRAWL  ALDO  KOPPEL
ASH  IWENTGAULFINN  ASE
CHASTE  EMIR  GOTAT
CAIUS  AGAL  SOUWESTER
ELMS  GRANDKENYANSWEDE
PLEASANT  ALIEN  ARGO
TID  TREES  SATRAP  NNES
EGER  STAB  SOT
ENDEMIC  ALAMOS  LEASES
LOOS  SERBTHEMAYANDISH
BOWS  ODILE  MALE  DITTO
ANNO  NEVER  ORTS  STEED
```

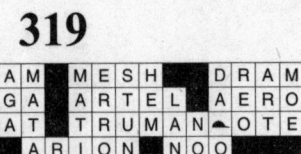

319

```
ARAB  BREAM  MESH   DRAM
PACA  RANGA  ARTEL  AERO
THES EGOAT  TRUMAN OTE
      ETTES  ARION  NOO
NETLOSS ADULL  EDISONS
OTHER  BLOND   ASS   UT
INES  THEGREATES E  TAA
RE S  AAAA   ELEE  CANT
EAT  SPINES  CLASS HICO
SNIPPERS PURLS  CANER
  VEERS  WINES  STORM
STEPS  THE E  THEWAYTO
HOHO  HIRED  SPRAWL  ON
ORES  ELAN   AIDA  ITOS
TEA  RICIOUSNESS  NATE
IRR  IMA  DRIED  IDIOT
NOTATED BYALL  PACINOS
  MOT  BASLE  BEREA
 ABILITIES  STATE ITAL
EGAD  CADRE  ISLAS  NINA
RENE   ISSY  ATILT  KNOW
```

320

```
BALSAM  SSE  ALEAN  CAROM
EMEUTE  PIT  MARLO  ACUMEN
CANCEL  ABC  EVILS  RETENE
CHOCOLATEHERAN  IVAN  LIU
OSSO  VERITY  GLEAM  SEAM
  TAPE  INN  MOUSSEATTLE
MACARONIAGARA  STELLA
PRESTIGE  UNIT  REGANS
SETH  NER ASIAN  ATOP  NEO
  KIT  EMENDS  ROSH  TVA
PHEASANTIAGO  FINE  CHAP
GLENN  METE  OLEG  COEDS
LAST  DOSE  GRANOLAPALMA
ANT  BOUT  ARABLE  OLE
RAE  OURS  PINEY  ABU  SASS
ERRING  ERSE  RURALITY
  AGHAST  LEMONADECATUR
SALMONTEREY  OBE  DREW
ARAB  UNTEN  DOVISH  RAMA
LEU  STOT  TORTILLASVEGAS
AORTAL  LEARY  ASA  TENANT
SLEEVE  EMILE  TOT  ENCINA
ALLEY  RULER  ENE  WIENER
```

321

```
  ODE  DNS  SPICED  SPOOL
AVERSION  ARMADA  ALUTA
CONSERVE  RAPTOR  BA2OD
CLIENT11ERATES  CHAIRED
TOM   TRACED  BYE  NESS
  AMIS  PESETA  ROI
SOLAN  BEN  ALABASTER
ELVERS  ASSE  O4FATHERS
DOERS  PYE  LIS  OLE  TAT
GERT  PALERMO  RUINS
ERTE  ERODE  WAALS  TRIM
  DINER  CHARIOT  RENO
DEE  MIS  UKE  CNF  DIS10D
CONDITI1R  ERLE  DEVISE
INDONESIA  AID  IRENE
  LEN  DOLING  FENS
LACO  CAA  ANCHOR  AAA
ALARMED  LIGHTW8EVENTS
CA90OU  ENISLE  LAPIDATE
INPUT  LOOSER  EGOMANIA
SEEST  ARNESS  DES  MAC
```

322

```
CHAD  STAB  SHIP  JADE
HIJO  TYROS  ALICE  EBON
ADAMSAPPLE  ROGERBACON
PERICLES  WRATH  TUNDRA
  CAKE  DEEMS  TURN
BASIN  MULTI  GARNERED
ORAL  CHARLESLAMB  ALA
RIFE  AERO  ILES  SPIN
ESE  PIECEMEAL  POSSE
DECAGONS  LEAN  DEUCES
  REINE  MENSA  BURSA
SPARSE  AMIE  MARTELLO
TACIT  BLINDDATE  LOS
ELKE  PLOT  EROS  FIRM
EME  RAGAMUFFINS  OONA
PARADORS  ALLEN  HUNAN
  DIVA  SONAR  RIAL
ANYONE  ALTAI  MARIANAS
SOURGRAPES  REDHERRING
WORE  BRIDE  SOLAN  DUET
ENID  SANS  NILE  SEWS
```

323

```
BEVELS  TBARS  RPM  AMIS
AVALON  EOSIN  ERA  NONE
LILIUOKALANI  AAR  SOFA
ACHE  WORE  TIDES  EGIS
ATA  SOURS  IOTA  LODI
MILAN  POLLAIUOLO  OED
OLDEST  OAR  TRIANGLE
NAMATH  EPICS  SKUA
  KEEUWENHOEK  EMILE
KNOX  ARLES  YURI  NEPAL
NANA  DEN  ALL  RAIL
ATONE  TATA  HATLO  ONCE
ROMAN  OEILDEBOEUF
ADEN  CLARA  RIATAS
NATURALS  ADE  SENARY
ORO  OKEECHOBEE  SERBS
TIPI  ACTA  YALOW  OAT
IKON  SABLE  RIFE  AGRO
CAEN  ORA  SEANOFAOLAIN
ERIE  NRC  MONET  NIENTE
SAAR  EEK  ENIDS  SLATED
```

324

```
THES  RAF  FDA  MARL
HOSTA  ALUM  FIRN  CAMEO
RAMSEY  NINO  ARID  PROVOS
SLEEPER  ADO  CML  LACRIMA
VERDI  ESSENTIALLY  HELEN
PRS  SUSU  DREAM  ERNE  EDD
  SHORT  IDLE  CITS
AJAR  RAFFES  SNATCH  ERGO
WERE  SKIRLER  TRE  COOP
NEIGH  NOISED  DRESSCOAT
PARADIGMS  ARO  NEATEST
ERIN  THESUBL  RIEN
FOSTERS  AMO  RIGOLETTO
CROSSTOWN  UNTAME  PRIVY
HAZE  AIM  SEVENTY  IDEE
EYED  FEMMES  RETIES  CENT
  PULP  LEAR  OTHER
EGG  IRAE  ORRIS  AERI  GIG
ARYAN  PREDICTABLE  DIANA
TARRIES  BRA  OLE  STINTED
SHADOW  MEAT  ROLE  ACIERS
ATONE  ARME  YOLK  CUGAT
MERS  ETA  NEE  LOUS
```

325

```
SHAFT ARAS  RACY  SCARF
AERIE RESH  ACHE  ULNAE
GREENEGGSANDHAM  BENNE
ADA TRIREME  TRANSVAAL
      EVEREST  LYCEE
SSW ACET   SEGO  CARBON
COHORT  RAT   BESO
ONESPOT BEIRUT TRINES
TORI RECONCILE HALSEY
CREST NURSE  SPOILT
HAS EMERGE REWARD RAE
WAPITI  DALEN  SLUMP
CHAFES OUTNUMBER AMPO
PULLET URIALS LAYOPEN
ANDY  SAP   MISERY
STOWED GLOW FOSS  TEM
EROSE  FORSALE
CARNATION REPRISE SEC
OMITS DREAMSOFVICTORY
BOMBE EGON TREE HELGA
BRAYS DENT SILT ORION
```

326

```
LADS CHAD AWASH  SAMBA
AVOW HATE TAMPA  USURP
MINI ARON TRIAL  GINAS
ADENOFINIQUITY TADINE
EVE  EMU  EYESORE
RASHERS  AAR  DEPLORE
OTHER CRISP  ROOFING
MOORS ANCHORS ALABAMA
ANODE LAI REAM  FELID
EDE  ETERNAL  ETTE
SMA ANEAROFCORN  FOY
SLAB BELIEFS   SGT
EIDER MMCC NNE  ADLER
EVADERS STATION LOOSE
REMOVAL LIBRA  LORNA
REFINED ALL  LEERIER
REDDEST ERA  MSS
ALLOWS AHEADOFLETTUCE
TEASE SCAMS BOON EVER
OATER CORPS ORAD PENS
PRESS INION TEDS SATE
```

327

```
BEST TOTEM ASP  SPACE
OATH AKITA THAW CAGES
SCAR LANCE WASH ORALS
SHYOFLYE SHORTOFPORT
TRES STORK  COAL
WALTER TIROS CORSELET
ABOLT OUTOFTROUT DALI
LOSE IRRA  ERRED  CIE
ERS SCANTOFCANT ASKED
STOCIAL ROADS DROOL
FRAME DALLY  SINOF
AFIRE GENII  TAINTED
BALSA WANTOFQUANT RNA
ORO BAERS  UNIS  CATT
ROSS BAREOFHAIR NACRE
UNSAVORY BLURT BARKED
LEVI EVERT VOTE
NEEDOFTWEED FEWOFYOU
TETRA USER LAINE REVS
IRANI LARS ENTER ELAN
ADHOC RYE DIZZY ELLA
```

328

```
AMALFI ASTHE MANIC GOBS
REGAIN MUREX AMISH ELIA
COUNTDRACULA DICTIONARY
SWAG RATHS MAREX SPENDS
ONO THINAS BEES
STU EVILS ONES SOLDIERS
LINEMEN TAKEA GENE SAIL
OSIRIS METERREADER SMA
WATER TALLY NYET POTOK
ENES TINA TIER TALESE
RED JETSETTERS ORDERED
NEEDLE ARNEL SPARSE
CHARADE TICKERTAPE GPS
LITANY TOTO EELS AGEE
EDITS FELL ARLES JOHNQ
ADO GINGERBREAD SUNUNU
VENA ALDA EIGHT ALIENEE
ENSNARLS SACO EATIN TRL
NINE RECUTS ESP
ARCADE WHETS CERES UTEP
BARBERSHOP PARTIALSCORE
ELEE ELIDE INANE OOLONG
SEEL DAZED DEGAS PLATES
```

329

```
ANAGE SITS  PACE  CETO
COHEN ICOME OBAD  ATOP
AVAST NAMED LENS  SERA
PARTING CLIVE CENTRAL
DUCES ATEAM ALAIN
REVOLTS LIEN SNAPS
ECCE INES CUSP EAGLES
AHA OLGA RETILE  LET
VESTAL DODO CAROLYN
ESTATE ERASE DORE
STAKE CROSSWORD SAMBA
ERNA HIERO NOFEAR
CONSORT NSEC INSECT
POR SPRING KENS  TKO
GRACIE ENOS WEVE PASO
ANNUM YETI ARRIVAL
GRAZE IRENE NEVUS
THERMAL MEANS CHICKEN
ROME PLEA TUTTI AKITE
ELAN PEST ALLAN TERRE
KENT ARTE  SERG  ERRED
```

330

```
SMOOT SERF  BARD  FAIRY
LINDA AMOR  AGUE  ARNIE
ANTON GENU  RONA  SORES
GEORGEANDIRAGERSHWIN
SIN DOTH   TOI
ATI EELS ION OHSONICE
CAMORRA COMICS ONAGER
RHAPSODYINBLUE SODA
EIRE SER  TRANSIRES
STEREO ACRID  AAA
ITAINTNECESSARILYSO
NEO ASCAP DEATHS
EMBOSSERS USE  MAIA
LAIR EMBRACEABLEYOU
SWANEE EUGENE CRANIAL
ASSESSED UNA AHOY NNE
STR EBAN MOB
SOMEONETOWATCHOVERME
WOMAN EVEN ERIE EVIAN
IONIC SELL NILE REVUE
SNIDE TRAY APED SLEDS
```

331

```
ACAT  MATH  SHE   BOBBED
SMASH ABRA  TED   APLACE
HARPERSBIZARRE    STANCE
ERA   OTE   ILION INDES
RIVALS      ENID  MANDI
PLEBES      CYGNETRING  NCA
ALLEN THESE HONG  EBON
SOS   SOIT  LATER LONG
LAPPSOFMEMORY     ASTO
RECEDES     EAGER MITER
ERASED      LIRAS WINONA
CRISS       TENET PARENTS
TARE  PRINTSOFWALES
OTOE  RAMOS AARE  GAR
RIPS  ONER  SALVE DEANE
SCR   OXIDEDAISY  SANDAL
ATTYS       ETRE  ESCAPE
ASCOT SINUS ARE   BEA
MUTUEL      PROPHETANDLOSS
AVOTRE OAT  IRON  SAUTE
DAREST TEE  PENT  CWTS
```

332

```
RATS  ARES  ISHOT STATUE
ASHES LEAK  SCORE AERATE
STORKSTORY  MATTEDMATTER
PARTITA PEA RAE   ROSE
MAIM  CRAIG AYE   HAM
SACS  BRACKENBRACKET    IRA
AMOEBA CARDS LED  EDEN
COMMIT UPA  MATES FREON
RUBIN CLEF  FATHA RESOLE
ASI   CHATTELCHATTER    UAR
LENT  ARTS  NOHOW HARASS
GOLDIE      FARES MODISH
SCRAGS ORBIT DOME PINS
FLO   SEMINALSEMINAR    DEO
RIMMED MONET IDAS DIEGO
EMBER NARCS ANS   SAMOAN
EMIT  CAP   SCOOT IMPUTE
ZEN   ROUTINEROUTING    STER
ERE   AUS   WAGON CANE
LIRE  ATE   EAR   PATTERN
ASSISTASSISI CAMELCAMEO
DIESEL RIOTS IGOR HUMAN
STEADY ANNAL DEWY TAPE
```

333

```
HADJ  ARTIS AGRIC FIBS
EDIE  NOONE CLEAR ROOK
NOEWETURNS  TOOTENANNY
EXIST TARAS VISAGE
AFFLICT PIPET RACE
GUILTS ARNES MUSKROSE
ARLES BOARSOMES   LEX
TOLD  AVOW  WERE  MDVI
ERY   FOWLBALLS   MOSEL
SAWMILL     ALEE  ACETONE
NOIRE ECLAT SHREW
PADDLES     ROES  SHELLAC
OMEGA PONYTALES   NHS
NORE  AWED  LAST  NDAK
CUE   SHEEPSKIN   BASSI
ARRESTER    RELET REMOTE
MOUE  PAEAN RENEWED
TORPID HEIST BANCS
WHOLLYCOWS  SPLITHARES
INSO  OLLIE CRUSE KONA
NOSY  FEATS HOMER EDDY
```

334

```
ONCE  VOLA  ANET  MASON
TULSA AGGRAVATE   AGILE
BRUSSELSSPROUTS   MARLO
BELLE MISES MILAN
MISDOER SLADE MONO
ANT   POACHEDSALMON    ITS
MEESE LAVA  MEAD  NRA
BRAE  ICELESS DIAMETER
ATKA  WANER NOODLERING
BOSC  AIL   STEPTO
DACCA SHRIMPDIP   EBSEN
ARLENE OPT  NAPS
BRANFLAKES  SPLIT OSAR
SOMEFOUR    OCARINA UPDO
ABS   PROP  ERIN  TRAMS
TAC   PEACHPRESERVE    RIA
ALES  RETEM EARLETS
POSES AGANA ANEAR
UNITE RUSSIANDRESSING
MONET GREENROOM   AKBAR
AROMA OUSE  UMPS  ISTO
```

335

```
YOSHIDA ITHACA MADRES
UMPIRES MOONED ORIOLE
CARDINALPOINTS MISUSE
CRIED OUTS  REDHEAD
ASTRONOUGHTS   PEN
APIN  PIRATEFLAG
ASCRIBES    STAVED ZAIRE
TOHONOR TIDY THRIVER
BROWNBAG AGE THEATEAM
ATREE SADIE FUEL
TEENSY LORRAIN PLISSE
OFAN  CUBIC INLET
ROYALBOX HAG CUBSCOUT
ORELESS LUGE RELAPSE
MAGMA DENSER SAFENESS
ANGELWINGS  ALTO
ACE   YANKEEGOHOME
JAYWALK SOIE CANAL
ONEILL INDIANPITCHERS
STAPLE CAUGHT MOUNTIE
HEREAT EVENSO PERSONS
```

336

```
SETT  ACTS  CLEAT TARS
ETHER EGRET LORCA PALAE
CREME ARENA ALIEN RUING
TEMPEST WARMMANSGEORGIA
ALVA  WENDY EDMOND
SNEERER TONED OLEO
MUST  GRIT  MANOFFORTYTWO
APT   COSTAR TROTS EARED
LEADIN EPI  THINE ASPIRE
ORLON SORB  HRA NUL ONT
BENE  UFO   MEANS PLEASES
AMANFORALLSEASONS
ABSTAIN TERMS ALE THAN
BRA   RIP CIA ALIT REFIT
EERILY OLLAS FIE PESTER
ADATE SKEAN TONGUE ECO
MANSGREETINGS NINE GREY
AUER  MEETS SUBLETS
BAALIM      LICIT LASH
SUDDENLYLASTMAN   TOUTERS
ARIES IWASA URANO RAMIE
PRONE ECTAL LENNY APACE
SOSO  RASPE IDEE  ONER
```

337

```
LEO  ALOP  APSES  FLED
ELBA  AMATA  RETAR  LUGE
EMILYPOSTMASTERS  ACRE
 LEPUS  PUERIL  IVIED
SOBERER  PENNONS  BOLTS
PLASMA  AORTA  GIRL
OER  OLIVEOYLWELLS  ETC
TABI  SLOT  SALTO  EBRO
SNARE  INSET  STAB  CAIN
 RADIO  NACHO  UVULAE
ALA  ANNEBOLEYNALI  LDS
REHEMS  NEWEL  DENEB
EMUS  USER  STALE  STETS
NOTE  LIMES  PENN  ARIA
ANT  MARYTUDORKOOP  INT
 OMAR  DENES  SLANGY
ANNOY  SCRAPES  CHUGGER
LAPIS  PIANOS  GNOME
ADEN  JULIETTELOWBEAME
VICE  OMENS  EXITS  SCOW
ARKS  TEASE  POME  ETE
```

338

```
CADIZ  INNS  AMOS  DAKAR
ADENA  SUIT  ROAR  ERICA
THEFIRSTBONDOFSOCIETY
SAPOROUS  POETS  SLAVES
 IRE  SPUN  STAN
WEMAYREPENTATLEISURE
SAXON  LIDS  BROOM  BOA
EGAD  MEIR  REP  SOUS
COMETOLOOKALIKEATLAST
TNS  ALIT  AMISS  SAUTES
 EMES  RON  ELSE
STAVES  SCEND  BRAS  CPA
POWERTOHANGONEANOTHER
ARAN  NIL  OAST  ORAN
TAK  SCAPE  FACT  AROSE
SHEWHOISBORNHANDSOME
 HERR  RACE  EOS
CAVERN  JINNI  AGUARICO
EVILBUTANECESSARYEVIL
LOCKE  ODOR  NEAT  ELAND
TWIST  EENY  TAPE  DYNES
```

339

```
ASPS  SERAC  THANE  SPA
BLOW  PRADO  RAVEL  PESO
COLEPORTER  ILOVEPARIS
STEELIES  SWOON  VICUNA
 TOLD  FAILS  MANE
ISLETS  MAINE  NATURALS
TEENS  YOURETHETOP  BOA
AGAS  LETS  AVER  PRIG
LUV  NIGHTANDDAY  GLARE
SEEKING  MOUES  TRACER
 INGES  LUTES  GHANA
LATEEN  BESOT  ROPEDIN
ALTAR  LOVEFORSALE  ANI
PLOD  SONE  EAVE  OBIE
POM  ITSDELOVELY  DUROC
STEADIES  EGADS  BUTANE
 DINS  MARIS  TOOT
SEADOG  WIDEN  AROMATIC
KISSMEKATE  EASYTOLOVE
INTO  RIDER  SWISH  KLEE
 EON  STIRS  TESTS  SASS
```

340

```
COROT  MINEIS  PAST  GRAVY
LLAMA  ORIANA  ONTO  ROSIE
ALDEN  BENGAL  UNUM  OTTOS
SIENNA  SEENO  RABBITHOLE
HERSELF  RENTAL  ONT  RAS
 DIRNDL  GIB  HYDOY
HEMI  COOEY  ASLOW  YEOMAN
EXIT  ELMS  INSECTS  SUEDE
LENI  LIE  URDU  CURL  CROW
PROSAIC  ABASE  ABIE  AIRE
STRANDS  BONA  ASE  WELTER
 LTD  YSAIDALIC  ILL
REPOSE  LET  TITO  ESKIMOS
EVEN  LYNN  DAMON  SCOTOMA
BING  LAIT  ILES  PTA  SPAT
ETATS  PALAVER  RUHR  ASHE
CALAIS  TYRES  OTTER  DYAD
 ILCER  CSA  RESTON
ALE  VAN  SATIRE  ELEANOR
WONDERLAND  DOGAL  LENORE
ARDOR  ALII  TRACED  DORIA
SNORE  CODA  HENLEY  EDGED
HAWED  EDEN  EMOUSE  REELS
```

341

```
BAFF  ACHE  RALE  OPAH
EMIL  BRAUN  ITEMS  LOCO
NORA  AERIE  PANEL  EMIT
†INGTHEBAR  OLDRUGGED†
 YALU  VASE  GRE
 LA†E  REACT  TERRAPIN
HALES  †EDTHELINE  TANO
AROD  ATTHE  ABCD  †CUT
ECHO  BIOS  COVEY  OPERA
CHANCIER  ARRET  SPURNS
 ELLS  †ROAD  ICER
TASSEL  PONCE  PROSPERO
ALAMO  FIVES  LAON  ORAN
LODI  ALEE  AISNE  SAVE
ONIN  CARRYONES†  PETER
NEEDLESS  ENCRE  ISON
 ETH  RACE  NAPA
AS†ASABEAR  SIGNOFTHE†
LOBO  TURIN  TREND  MEOW
ETON  ELISE  ORRIS  ERNA
ASWE  BEAD  RASE  NOSY
```

342

```
 BOCK  POMP  AFT  UCLA
LANIA  ILIAD  DOORNAIL
JASONS  PENNI  ENTERING
AMERICA "GODSHED  VANGA
MEP  SOU  SOLAR  SING "
ELL  NIL  ROM  DIED
SLUR  ITSAMADMAD "WORLD
JAGUAR  LOA  GELT  SMEAR
 SNIPE  HIERO  SKY
MORTISE  BIB  AUS  BOHEA
OVERTHERE "SENDTHEWORD
OIDEA  PAR  END  EARLESS
LEG  DERNS  SWINE
ADUNC  SIZE  OBI  LETTER
HOMEAGAINHURRAH "  SALE
 WRIT  ION  AMI  HET
 HAYDN  SKULD  PAK  IMA
HANOI  ITISAFAR "BETTER
OPERABLE  ECLAT  BEHIND
SICKCALL  DEARE  ONEAT
TSK "  RYA  STES  TEEN
```

343

```
QADDAFI  STARK   CRAZE
UTOPIANS THREED  HAMEL
FASTDRAW SEMANA  AMORE
TNT MORAL BARYSHNIKOV
   LEUC  IRA  SABOTS
TUTANKHAMEN  NOR   CIA
ORES   BONDI  ORLEANS
ODAS MORSE DOSTOEVSKI
KUROSAWA WROTE RAISIN
   TOE   ALIT  SPAIN
EMMY NIETZSCHE  SNAG
NAILS  ORAE    MRT
CUTLIP OILER XIAOPING
BRZEZINSKI ACORN SGAU
CEASETO  ASYOU  ENTR
SSH  TSP MONTESQUIEU
   ASLEEP INC  MAUD
KIERKEGAARD HABLA WIT
ENAMI ALNAGE MAINLINE
EGRET YESSED INSTANCE
PENDS  DYANS  KHAYYAM
```

344

```
MAZE  SASH  ALION  DIVOT
ABOY MELEE SONNET ERICA
NODE IRIAN SORTIE CARTS
THISCREAMSLIKEA RHO TET
UMA HANS  ALF PARACHUTE
ASCRIBE LUCKOF  TILTS
OLE DIST RIPOFF  TAFT
ENAMEL ITHAD SEMI  RUE
PITYALLTHEMIGHTYCAESARS
OTT NEATER SANS ZLOTYS
XRAY TIL BABE  HSUAN
YORE THEYPULLTHEIR GIST
ABIES RILE  IAN  SETA
GASTON POLO EGRETS RAN
WHISKERSOUTWITHTWEEZERS
EON OWED SNAKE ACUITY
NYES ABATER LIEN  MON
   IMPEI RESINY OMNIBUS
THEREISNO SEE ALAD ONT
REX LEO OTHERSUBSTITUTE
AMIGO NATION AGREE ERIN
CASED SPIGOT ROANS ANET
ENTRY  ODETO  ISMS  REDS
```

345

```
BEAD  HOLD  CHAR  ABASE
ETTA SERAI EASE  REBEL
THEYVERAISEDHISCELERY
INDEXED PLEA  TITTLE
CORNIS  BLED  MOVE
EIS TUAN GORE  CZAR
HECANMARRYACUTETOMATO
ELAM NESS HIE  RIZAS
AIRS POET GOAL BANANA
ROE SANO ERIN  ERNO
ATWENTYFIVECARROTRING
NOAM NATE EROS  DIA
MATRON ALDA AJAM PACT
ARROZ  MAE SPET  RHEE
MAYBEAFEWRAPSCALLIONS
ALAE WINS FAIT  EIN
   HAFT CONS  SMACKS
COHORT MAUI  SPANIEL
JOYANDEVERLASTINGPEAS
ADELE EMIL RAINS ANKA
GAZED  NINA  DORY  LEER
```

346

```
BOBS  ESTER  RAJAH  TAEL
ARUT STONE EMOTE RICE
JFREDCOOTS PETERFINCH
AFTERALL ELLES ROSTER
   LOPE DREAR  DIRT
ATHENE SEVEN BANTERED
RHO ERICPARTRIDGE OCA
CAWS  ROO  EKES  CROC
ARAT HARTCRANE FOYLE
PRELATE HOPED PULSE
DRAKE BATES  AESOP
SHINE PRIOR FUNERAL
CHALK LARRYBIRD ERIS
HOWE MAID  ASA  DRAW
ARK JAMESWHISTLER ONA
RESTORED HAMES LEEWAY
URIS SITAR  IBID
OUTRUN ENTER ELONGATE
DEANMARTIN EARLWEAVER
ELKE READE TRIBE ROLL
REED ALLEY SPEED SNEE
```

347

```
SPLAT  PAIR   BLADE
ATTIRE OLIVE ULANBAT
BALTIMEMARYL PEUTETRE
BIER PRINT IWERE  SAL
EDGE TONTOCANADA FOCI
SLOSH DOS ONERS STUKA
SYN EMEU JADED NEWTS
NEONS EXO  SALT
OCELOT SHERMANS HASP
ALLWET PIUS AMAH TULA
LLOYD FEES CROP PEDAL
OINK SANG COTY LAXITY
TEEN AUTONOMY CERATE
EAUX  EYE  CHESS
MOWED HUGOS LESE GSA
LUCYS RESET FEV SPAIN
ESEK RALAVELLARA RING
ASA DOPER AARON INGE
FENCESIN AUCKLNEWZEAL
LOFLIDA MATEY SHERPA
GALES  PROD   TASSE
```

348

```
DOWDY  ORIEL  SOL  OHARA
ACHED BRANDO EYUI NOTES
WHOSSORRYNOW VERB TWEAK
NOSE DAIS WHATSINANAME
ORGANS TRAIL DEPOSED
FANTAST WHATSUPDOC WED
INFER SAUTE ALE  KGB
ENID SPARSER TOGA ARTIS
RUR HELP HOWAMIDOING
CASH HALAS AIR SANDWORT
ELTON ROTTING RINSES
WIT WHOSTHERE  INC
PEEDEE OSSEOUS GOWNS
ACCOLADE SLY SACHS WHET
WHOISSILVIA CLOY AGO
NOLLE EDAM FASHION STAR
ONO EAP ODLED  GESTE
SOV PARLEZVOUS GLEAMED
THREEAM REESE TRIMLY
AINTSHESWEET SEAM SLAT
LEAHS NEAR WHATSCOOKING
ESTEE DADS OOLITE HINDI
STEEN  SRI  SCARY  ONEIF
```

349

```
MACHE  OMA  APSO  CASPER
AVIAL  NOW  BLUR  ARTHRO
NORMANCONQUEST  BROILS
ICE  YET  ISNA  AILEY
TALKIE  MEET  CLENCH
ODEON  JERRYBUILT  ARA
BOSSA  TONYS  ANNA  FRET
ASS  MINT  SHUN  AMAT
VIRGINIAHAM  STOLE
DECLARE  SITS  SPINES
EXHALED  GAP  ATOMIST
SCARES  ELIS  DIDACTS
PURRS  MOLLYCODDLE
ORLY  MULE  MALE  CAR
TIES  OMAN  STEVE  TEHEE
SAY  TOMFOLLERY  WREST
HARRYS  RIAS  SONATA
AGORA  RATS  AGE  PHI
FERRIS  CATHERINEWHEEL
RESALE  OTOE  ANA  HASTE
ODESSA  PARR  NUT  OTTER
```

350

```
BASTE  SPIN  GLACE  ALTO
ARTEL  AIDA  LEDON  ROOD
REARM  NEAP  ACRID  NAME
RAYMONDCHANDLER  EIDER
ESS  ROMEO  AHEM  ARE
ROTAS  TSAR  INSPECT
CHEAPEN  JOHNCONSTABLE
RISKED  FETED  INA  LAIC
UNSER  FRETS  RLS  OMNIA
EDE  MOORE  SOS  SHE
TINATURNER  COLEPORTER
LUG  TRY  AMITY  OLE
REMIT  GAS  ERICA  BASIL
ALEC  AUG  ATREK  POLITE
JAMESFLETCHER  TABARET
ASOCIAL  RIND  BRIBE
ORR  PEDI  SIENA  HAG
CANOE  WILTCHAMBERLAIN
ATOP  TITLE  EVIL  KARMA
ELSE  ANTIS  BONE  ENTER
NEER  DEIST  ERIS  REEDS
```

351

```
SLANG  ARABIAN  ANIMUS
MALAYA  ROXANNE  POMONA
IHADPLANNEDTOBEPOETIC
TREASURE  DES  YENTES
ULM  MAINE  ETE
BAHAMA  ZONED  RBI  SROS
ABUM  LINK  SEAT  WALT
BUTIDRANKALITTLETODDY
ETC  RANG  ENROL  ALIEN
SHRANK  SHINER  ALLONE
ESCAPEE  ESTELLE
HEALTH  ASNERS  REINER
ALTAI  ALARM  MARS  AHS
SOEXCUSEMYUNAESTHETIC
APIE  NILE  ERIE  RONA
TEND  SNY  GIVEN  ELINOR
ATI  MIDAS  INA
TOULON  ALE  AVERAGED
HAPPYNEWYEAREVERYBODY
ENTICE  ABALONE  ONEIDA
MOONED  REDSTAR  XENON
```

352

```
HARSH  ABLE  SPATS  AMORAL
AGANA  DUAL  ORIEL  BANANA
TRIAL  ESTA  BERLINCLERIC
HELPFULHINT  SELMA  TRASK
ESS  MIEN  RAIDS  MOE
TUBED  PARD  GATS  PAP
CLOSE  BIGMENINTHEUSSR
SOO  MRT  OPUS  IDAHO  FAKE
CORGI  AGNES  BLEW  TOLES
ALIAS  WRIT  GREENERY  MDS
RECUSE  ATTILA  DOPA
FRAZIERBAERANDPATTERSON
ELLA  ACTUAL  COUPDE
PDQ  ESTIVATE  SPEE  FLAIL
LOUIS  RENE  SKEET  NEROL
EVEN  STORK  NOIR  ADO  GUY
BEANTOWNBALONEY  ASHES
ERN  AHOY  AGAR  SPREE
MOO  BOYON  AIRE  LMA
AMEBA  FAIRE  TASTYRELISH
COZYBLANKETS  LION  LINTY
MORELS  NEATO  FAUN  MONAD
ERASED  ARDEN  ANTE  SNARE
```

353

```
HEIR  AMOEBAE  AMNESIC
ACTE  GARGANS  ALIENATE
THEHORNBIRDS  COLFAXES
OMELET  SILENCED  CAST
ADELE  TANGO  STP
CAPRI  EXPOS  TRICUSPID
AMUSE  CANT  DRUM  ENO
PELE  CRETE  PRIOR  TACO
ELI  THESE  RAYON  SOLAR
DINGHIES  DIVAN  SUN
AGOODFIFECENTGUITAR
USE  VICAR  ORATORIO
PASDE  FELON  CHIVE  MAR
AREA  FEVER  TOONE  PALL
REX  ALLI  SHAY  PINTO
ESCALATOR  POLLS  HADON
YMA  LOBAR  EATON
LIMP  UNICORNS  TENORS
ALBERTAN  SKIPTOMYLUTE
NEARNESS  CLEARUP  ABUT
ATLEAST  SERRATE  SYNC
```

354

```
ANSE  STY  CRUSES  HIPS
CATS  TIA  HOMOLKA  AMAH
THEQUICKBROWNFOX  IPSE
SAMUEL  EIS  NIDE  LACE
WILLIAMS  VENA  ECLAT
SCARE  BEATSIT  NOELS
PURE  PED  ILL  IDOL
APES  RAE  AILS  CALUMET
RIMS  ADAPTER  MAGI
SHUNS  NEGRI  TABLED
ALTAIC  TAB  EYE  MAITRE
LIERNE  ALAMB  MORAY
AVIV  TIMBREL  MOUE
SENATOR  ANTA  ART  CHAT
RANK  ARC  NTH  IAGO
SOLDO  BROKENO  STRAW
ARABS  ILED  STANFORD
SITE  INON  AMO  RAISES
HOVE  KATHARINECORNELL
ALIT  EPAULET  RUN  ELBE
YEAS  THRESH  RED  SLAW
```

355

```
MARS  DENIS  ASSOC  DES
ALUI  ERODE  PTERO  SENT
JOHNLENNON  ROBERTALDA
ATRIUMS  ADINA  DIVEST
STET  STACY  TOTE
MOATED  PAOLO  DEBARKS
ESNES  HARRYTRUMAN  IKE
CMDR  WARD  OPP  TRIO
CAR  NATKINGCOLE  TOKEN
ANEMONES  ORATE  SHEDS
WADED  STARS  SPORO
OWNED  PIANO  STIRRUPS
HAYES  MARTINSHEEN  GOA
UTES  OLE  PIES  SLIT
NET  EDDIEFISHER  PHASE
SHALIER  LAMES  ERASES
BASS  CANON  ATOM
LAMONT  CRUST  CHOPINS
EDDYDUCHIN  HENRYFONDA
BESS  ROUST  EDSEL  OGAM
TSE  BUMPS  ROADS  SAKE
```

356

```
AROMA  OILS  ROAM  SONS
SPOKES  STOICS  ELIA  AREA
CHARLIESNIGHT  CENTENARY
AIDA  AGIOS  AORTA  TRENDS
TDS  STRAW  ARNA  CRUSTS
ALIEN  OSLER  SLEPT
COMPACT  THEDENTIST  THB
ABORTS  DOTES  EROS  THEO
CODES  PERONS  ISIS  BAERS
TEES  FANG  PLATA  TRIGON
ISR  EASYSTREET  CIANOS
NEIGHS  HINES  SAMUEL
STADIA  RECREATION  DPS
CHITON  TOONE  TERN  FRAP
HOMES  SIRE  RAMONA  DRUSE
OVEN  NANA  CTENO  FIESTA
PES  FOOTLIGHTS  LEATHER
EARNS  PRAYS  ROARS
VOLUME  SEPS  PARRY  PGA
SERENA  AREEL  ARIEL  DRYS
ADOGSLIFE  KINGINNEWYORK
RANI  CLAN  SNOOZE  SHAVES
AYOT  YORE  EGER  SYNOD
```

357

```
RECS  HEMEN  IRAIL  LAB
FLAT  ARANAS  GASCONADE
DERA  WRIGHTONTHEMONEY
GALAHAD  SARIS  FEED
PACKRAT  FAT  ALISONS
ONA  TWISTOFLEMMON  FEE
OTRA  CLAN  DIVE  ECON
DEARTH  ALTA  RESTSON
CHANGEOFHART  ATTAR
AIRHOLE  RENO  POTTO
STU  FORTHEBYRDS  EAR
CENIS  AARE  UNMANLY
IRONE  RIGHTSOFMANN
AFFINAL  SOLO  POTAGE
ANDS  IMAS  SALS  EPOS
ECE  SCUTTLEOFKOHL  PRE
FEMALES  REX  NOSTRIL
IRON  NEMEA  PARTIAL
MALICETOWARDNUNN  MILO
COLLUSIVE  TIERCE  OSAR
IKE  MSTAR  TYLER  NEST
```

358

```
SOWS  OCAS  TASK  AGREE
TWIT  UPTO  CHULA  DRURY
ALLI  TAIL  REDAN  DENSE
YELLOWSTONEFEVER  ETES
STATUE  EDENS  AWN
TAB  PRIE  DUSTPAN
LAMB  REDHOTTAPE  CHEMO
ONER  SARI  NINA  URIS
ADIOS  GOLDDIGGERSMINE
NARWHALS  EINE  CABLES
NENES  IGN  BEECH
ASABAT  AGUE  ANDROIDS
BLUERIBBONPRINT  AURIC
RATA  COOK  NCAA  SIVA
IVORY  ROSEBUDOIL  EDAM
SESSILE  ROLY  LEO
SPA  MASON  APACHE
ECRU  BLACKMARKETSHEEP
BRAGS  UNTIE  ONTO  ELLA
BORAH  BLOND  SOAR  ALEC
SCARY  EYRE  ABLY  DONT
```

359

```
MASC  SHIN  LEAP  SCOOP
AGUA  TYRO  RILLE  TULLE
PENN  OMIT  EMBED  ADDER
BARONSEESBARRENSEAS
LAUREL  LEO  TOWN  NNE
ATRIA  MAPLE  EUR
MINERMISSEDMINORMIST
AMES  AMAIN  EROS  BAAL
RED  SCOPS  DIRER  TIE
LABS  SEISM  EATING
CHASTEAUNTSCHASEDANTS
HELMET  MARTS  ELEM
UNI  HABLA  APRON  GBS
GIBE  REDD  ONEIF  BRAY
EIGHTFRIARSATEFRYERS
GEO  EASES  APART
ASP  AMBO  INK  ERASES
STAIDBASSSTAYEDBASE
HASTE  SCALE  ARAB  SPIN
ETHER  TAPER  RITE  EIRE
SEAMS  ERST  NEED  STEW
```

360

```
ESTE  CLEAN  RABAT  SHEDS
ANTAE  HARTE  ILEDU  KOREA
STROLLINGTHROUGHTHEPARK
TRI  SIMEON  EMMAS  APPLES
RAVE  LEST  CRUST  RITE
OPENAIR  MOAN  ELIDING
DREAMWALKING  TEC  DOE
DEPOTS  AERIE  AUTRY  REIN
ENEMY  TURIN  AVISO  CEASE
PERE  WOMEN  SMAZE  MANSES
ERD  ERDA  TAJO  SIRE
WOULDYOULIKETOTAKEAWALK
OILS  ENNE  LINT  MOI
STILLY  DOSED  THATS  COST
WHOLE  BOITE  CROSS  RAREE
OATS  BERIA  SHUCK  SUPERS
RNA  BAN  ILLWALKALONE
DESCENT  AIRY  AMERICA
ODAS  POPPY  MEGA  SORB
FALLEN  AISLE  GARGLE  NEY
IMALWAYSCHASINGRAINBOWS
RAMIE  ETTEN  MANOR  DYNES
ESSED  NOSAD  AWARD  SEED
```

361

```
GETUP  STOLA   PHIL   STUPA
ALAMO  ERGOT   IONA   PANIS
GUNETIQUETTE   KNEWYORICK
ELS  AMUSES  NEEDS  AORTAS
       SPOTS  LEMMA  ALLY
ROM  HAI  AERIE  BRIE  RIP
ALEF  CALIPHORNERIER  ONA
RESEAT  ADARS  TASS  WALL
EASEL  CHIC  DROIT  MODEL
STYLE  LOOEASYANNA  IRATE
TEC  MORT  TONS  DESIST
  HALITE  STRAP  PLANES
EVENED  TEAM  GLOW  LIS
LEWIS  HARASSOWNER  BREST
LISTS  AMORT  RAAD  YAHOO
OLEO  SUIT  BLESS  RECALL
RET  PENCILVAINHERE  ENDO
ADS  ARTE  AINTS  ETA  DEN
   ERAS  STAKE  IONIC
RECLIP  STELE  INVERT  ORE
OGLEAHOMER  DELLAWEIGHER
WAUGH  LUNA  SKATE  VEINS
SLEYS  AGON  SAWED  EMOTE
```

362

```
ROSIE   SCARAB   ROPEDIN
PANICS  POLITE   APOLUNE
ACETIC  HOTTER   BELINDA
WHITEELEPHANT   BREAKER
NADIR  AREA  ILIAD  EEL
BAN  EVER  CHEAT  EDDY
   GAMES  MAE  SPITE
READIER  HOUR  UPENDED
AUBURN  HORSESENSE  IVY
GRACED  ERSE  LACE  LEN
WALKS  WADE  MASH  MEARA
ESO  WERE  FACE  COATES
EIN  LOANSHARKS  INGEST
DAEMONS  ERAS  ATTESTS
  OPTED  ACT  SPEER
LALO  LISLE  BARD  BOW
AMA  PEWEE  KILO  SEPIA
CENTAVO  CATONINETALES
ANDOVER  EMERGE  RIVALS
STIPEND  DEADEN  ONETON
ASSERTS  ERRANT  STREW
```

363

```
COBS  ADDIS  PLOP  COWL
ALEC  PEACH  ALIVE  ARIA
RIGHTOFWAY  BEFOREHAND
POSEIDON  SPLAT  FLINGS
   MESE  STOUT  OIL
DUPED  STENS  PROLATE
ADAR  AFTERTHEFACT  HEP
KISS  MAIL  TAME  SEME
ANT  INVARIANT  SCAPE
REPLEDGE  INCA  SAUDIS
  EAVES  POLIS  PEDRO
CURVES  ATEN  PREOFFER
INFER  INSTILLED  TRI
TIER  DENG  EASE  TINA
ETC  LEFTOFCENTER  OMEN
DETRACT  RENTA  WREST
  ATL  DANCE  SORT
TASTEA  BINAL  SPRAINED
AFTERSHOCK  OUTOFPLACE
PAIR  SOLES  SHORE  LORE
ERRS  EWER  ERATO  ASUR
```

364

```
PASHA  DAB  ADD  STRAP
AGAIN  ELIA  LEIS  ARENA
COTTONBALLWEEVILLAINS
   RUBELLA  MINA  INAT
SALAMI  EEL  NEPALESE
CLICKBEETLEBROWED
LIDS  NEEDLE  SLOVENE
AGA  BASK  OVA  PINED
MONARCHITECTURE  TREVI
  ROTO  OCI  ANC  RET
GRASSHOPPERAMBULATORS
AET  STA  CLI  RAMA
FARCE  SCARABBLEROUSER
FLIER  ASA  ODES  AMO
EMPRESS  TIMBAL  IDIO
  CATERPILLAROFSALT
GRANTHAM  RUN  ABORTS
AIRY  ITOS  AFINGER
MADAMBUTTERFLYBYNIGHT
ANOSE  SELF  SASA  ACOMA
STRAW  DOT  MAG  XENON
```

365

```
COCA  EDNA  FLOSS  KEPI
CHAS  ARID  LADIES  BARONS
CATHERINEDENERVE  AMANDA
PRETAPE  LICKS  ENOLA  COL
ERRS  SLINKY  ANDRE  SHOO
ATA  ONES  CUTIE  SHORN
SPY  LEVER  ALLEN  SHIV
PAL  ABLE  SLIDE  SHAVIAN
CHARLESDARLIN  NATURALLY
SINATRA  THATCH  LETE  LIE
BENET  POET  HONOR  PAST
   DRAGONS  BOUNCER
HEDY  ILEUS  SNOD  OLAFS
ADA  TALK  SALOON  ACIDITY
MINCEMEAT  HERBERTHOOFER
SENORAS  ROAST  IMIT  TIS
YARN  BARRE  HADES  SYN
MADLY  LEILA  GIDE  ESP
USES  HORNY  CANVAS  EARS
LIV  GENTS  GARDE  CARRIES
EMILYS  HELENGURLEYBRAWN
SONOMA  ATONAL  BONE  OTOE
VOWS  STALE  SUES  WANE
```

366

```
LOBOS  TALC  APSES  TEST
ANAME  OREL  LOTTO  OSLO
TALIA  LINE  DEARBRUTUS
KISSMEKATE  ETTE  APERS
ERAT  GIS  SARAS  ODESSA
  RARE  ELMS  ALIE
EMENDS  FATALVISION
SALSAS  ILE  NERVE  SPA
ANIS  SHEARS  REAR  ACED
GIMME  IGNACE  ANKARA
MEIR  DOGSOFWAR  EIRE
MARNER  ENLIST  ELITE
ILIE  UTAH  EASIER  LOTS
SIC  RENEE  TED  ANITAS
CAKESANDALE  DEACON
MILD  DISC  LING
ROBINS  HASTA  AIL  FLOE
ABATE  DECI  SADCYPRESS
WESTWARDHO  BALI  LOMAN
LATE  BADEN  AREA  USAGE
SHED  AMASS  HERS  STYES
```

367

```
BANS   TROY  CALM   ZASU
ALEC  HOURI  ICER  SIREN
HEBREATHED   SHESNAPPED
SMOULDER  DETER  ELPASO
    PLUM  MIMED  CAVE
SCHLEP  LASER  PATERSON
CHEER  HETHUNDERED  HUI
RAPS  SETS   ITER  METZ
AIR  SHEMUTTERED  HOARE
PROPERLY  RUTTY  LADDER
   FIVES  CATHY  HAREM
PEEVED  HAITI  LEVELING
ORSON  HESNICKERED  TOA
LOST  SEAT   IVOR  STOP
ADE  SHERETORTED  MEESE
REDBIRDS  WRITE  LOADED
   OBIS  SOAPY  CURB
CHERYL  AMADO  LACROSSE
HEBELLOWED  SHECROAKED
ARRAS  KOLA  TITHE  RYAN
POOL   ALLY  ETTE   DELA
```

368

```
ORISSA   EROSE   STEPIN
ROSTER  SPECIAL  AREOLE
ESTEEM  PIMENTO  NARROW
  THELAWISAASSAIDIOT
DAMPS  ACTIN   FLAN  ALL
UNUS  SWELL  SPELL  LOA
EDS  SHADE  FAURE  ADSUM
   PEA   INC   EBO
ELEPHANTSAGENTLEMAN
SCENT  TAINT  EROTICAL
ALAI  COVEY  ASHEN  NEVE
PASTILLE  SPURN  SITAR
THEBULLOCKSBUTAFOOL
   NIE   HOI   WAN
MOATS  FAINT  TELEX  SBA
AID  FANON  LISAS  SPUR
CLV  PAIN  KICKS  SHELF
  ACATMAYLOOKATAKING
ERNEST  LEARNER  RANCID
RECITE  SANDERS  ATTEND
STELAR  HEALS  GEORGE
```

369

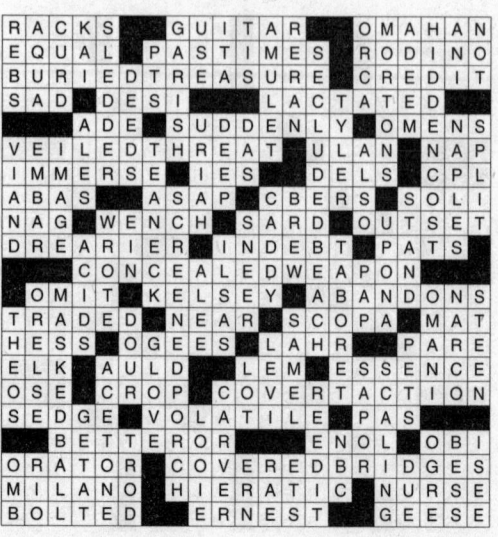

```
TOMATO  TACOS  MUTE  PASO
ANADEM  RIANT  ONAN  IRAN
TENANEWJERSEY  TIME  NIDE
   AGEE  YES  LOVERONDER
RADICALS  DEFER  DORA
ALENE  STLO  LLAMA  SATRAP
MAME  THEEROFUSALL  LEERY
ANOPIA  DEER  TENDONS  SEL
DICTATE  SLANE  AGO  TITO
ANI  PINE  TIDED  DARIEN
ECCE  OCELOT  META  DIOS
   PET  CULARWEIGHT  DAN
FRAU  HAUT  INTUIT  EDOS
GLOSSY  LENTS  SIGN  FAT
RACE  APR  OSAKA  CADENCE
AGE  GREASER  TARA  MALICE
TOSSA  APPTOVEDANTA  EXAM
ANSELS  TAHOE  INGE  SMOTE
   LEOS  RIMED  ENTWINED
TOULAUTREC  RUS  LERE
ABLE  SEER  LISHSITUATION
LIAR  ALAI  ANTIS  STADIA
LENS  SERB  EGYPT  TYBALT
```

370

```
MOAT  REBEC  OPALS  GEAR
IAGO  ERATO  URIAH  ILLE
CHAMPIONHUNTERGETZFOX
HUSBAND  SNAGS  AMINE
   DEEP  SIRS  SARONGS
ARBOR  ABELE  PAWS
FARMERMILLSWILDEOATES
AMEN  AUNT  DAIS  SALK
RATINGS  REDEYE  TONIO
   ALIA  AVISO  EARTHA
SHOEMAKERKANTFIXXSOUL
LAUREN  REESE  FOCI
ALTAR  NACRED  WESTING
NERS  MITT  QUAL  INEE
GREENECOOKEBURNSBACON
   YSER  ILIAD  ASANA
SIMILAR  ALAS  USES
URANO  LOTTO  TATTLES
GARDNERWATERSROSEBUSH
ANTE  SEATO  OLIVE  ANTI
RIAS  ALDEN  SOBEL  REAP
```

371

```
RACKS  GUITAR   OMAHAN
EQUAL  PASTIMES  RODINO
BURIEDTREASURE  CREDIT
SAD  DESI  LACTATED
   ADE  SUDDENLY  OMENS
VEILEDTHREAT  ULAN  NAP
IMMERSE  IES  DELS  CPL
ABAS  ASAP  CBERS  SOLI
NAG  WENCH  SARD  OUTSET
DREARIER  INDEBT  PATS
   CONCEALEDWEAPON
   OMIT  KELSEY  ABANDONS
TRADED  NEAR  SCOPA  MAT
HESS  OGEES  LAHR  PARE
ELK  AULD  LEM  ESSENCE
OSE  CROP  COVERTACTION
SEDGE  VOLATILE  PAS
   BETTEROR  ENOL  OBI
ORATOR  COVEREDBRIDGES
MILANO  HIERATIC  NURSE
BOLTED  ERNEST  GEESE
```

372

```
ARSON  SALIC  SPRAT  ASH
MEARA  PRIMA  TEETH  SPA
ISLET  AUDEN  RAFER  SEW
NELSONS  TACO  REOPENS
ONO  AMPS  SOLVE  WINCE
  TWICESOLDTALES  INTER
   ALS  RURAL  SHUN
ALAMO  ATES  ISENT  MID
SCRATCHED  JAMESCHOICE
ADE  HOAR  MORAL  LERNER
   POEMS  HAKIM  BETAS
DROWSE  RATED  LIAR  TIE
PASSEDTENTS  BORROWERS
THE  NIELS  ARAL  WARES
   CETE  ECLAT  OES
POLIO  HEADOFTHEGLASS
EXECUTE  GNU  SELL  OAK
STAINER  RAGS  DEFARGE
AAR  TRIPE  HOUSE  LEDGE
DIN  ERNIE  ESTER  ARIEL
ELS  RAGED  DOERS  TODDY
```

373

```
EPOPEE   NED    TEETHES
MARINES  ICES   POWERADE
QUICKCENTURY    AGELIMIT
ULNAE  QURANDURAN  PRES
AVG    AUTO   RES   PLA
DISABLE   SCAN   NEEDLE
QUILTBYASSOCIATION
OCCURS  RESTS  DON  SOTS
PARA   TOAT     HOTEL
QBERTANDROEPER  VIABLY
ROPIEST  OLDER  SEABLUE
STEAMS  QUESTBATHROOMS
PIVOT    NAPE     LIEN
INIT  SIP  IMAGO  CRISTO
QEDHOTCHILIPEPPERS
SALEMS   POTS   RESHOOT
OSS   MOO    LEIS   URU
RAVI  QANDABEARS  OATER
APERTURE  QUITYOURSELF
MITERING  INRE  NASTASE
AGONIZE    TEX   ROOTED
```

374

```
μLE   CRIBS  CENτR   AGAR
TALK  HARRY  ANAPA   AMIA
ESCALATION  LATENTBUDS
SHARIFAS  COLTS   ALLEE
PATEN   THREE    AARE
LITERATURES  AMφTRITE
PETER  OTOS  SNIDE   NRA
ANA  WAφEST  AYES    SUM
CONSTANCE  ETCH   CRANE
PηLS    ACOR   RINKS
ABUNDANCE  POWEρUSUS
MURRI  REAL    IDEE
ADANA  SνFF   PINETREES
BιS  BUTT  ISOTES    PEA
UPI  BERLE  NIKE   CAIRN
SELFLOVE  RαBERCROMBY
OERA   HASID   RIVAL
TIARA  RAVEL  SUBERATE
INTERSTATE  ARξGENESIS
βKES  TENπN  NOSER  STAT
NYET  STANS  TETRA   SSE
```

375

```
ILIKE   LEVI    ADDUP
SNORES  SHEEN   FORMAT
RITUALS  YALEGRADATTWO
ELEV  SEANS  MARDI   RED
DERR  ONLOAN  AKA  NOIRE
INNED  COP  AIRE  WHOOPS
GEESEBEATSST   SHUNTS
TAE   DIO    EASTERS
STOLLE  COQ  LIETO   TAJ
TOILSOME  TUILLE  NORSE
INGE  WEDSHIMSELF  NIKE
FIEND  ROWENA  DEEPENER
FAR  EDINA  TRA  DARTED
KNEEING    ELS   RIO
LEAVED   YETITOSENATE
HARLEM  BOMB  EAR  ROBES
INNER  SAM  BONNIE  RENT
EDE  SACRE  MODEL   ATNO
DISPOSABLECAR   NIANTIC
STALIN  ETONS   TANGOS
OLDAS   TAXI    ESTER
```

376

```
SCALP  FAIR   SHIRT   DDE
ALGER  ETTE   SLIVER  RON
YOUDONTSEEWHATYOUWANT
SPA  PACE  MOON     MOWER
YOUHAVENTGOTAPENNY
ICIEST   ERG   DADE   ISH
LOTTE  BING  DOMED  ISH
SOW  WINTERCOMES   ATTA
ATELIERS  EON   STASSEN
RESECT  FLING   ELITES
STEAL  HEHOLLERS  FAUNA
LODGED  PERES   ALPINE
AROUSES   STN  CARESSES
MANE  THESHOEFITS   DRU
SHE  CAINE  TREE   PLANE
HIRT    DIA    PRAYED
YOUCANKEEPYOURHEAD
ENNUI   TEAL  EARN   PRO
ATFIRSTYOUDONTSUCCEED
ROI  ERRANT  GENT  ERASE
SPT  DIETS   YORE  SORTS
```

377

```
PITAPAT  RAMPAL  HECUBA
ORIGAMI  EROICA  ORATES
NATASHA  STRANDRUNNERS
DNA  SERIOUS  EDYS  ISNT
SINGERANDREA    SEEMS
ADS   ISOLDE   SMITTEN
PING  TAG   ALP  EDERLE
AGORA  DONNAKARANDRESS
CLOUDED  EON  LOU  ASYET
TOILED  LIMOS   FLAY
SOLE  GRANDRAPIDS  ATAT
GEOM   EATIT   TACOMA
IWASA  ABA  KEN  EASEDUP
BERTRANDRUSSELL  ARISE
ARMADA  ACS   ESP   BEER
REELERS   HATPIN   REI
ENDTO   FRANDRESCHER
ASSN  VERA  ARTLESS  ALI
VETERANDRIVER  ALADDIN
ERASER  ELNINO  PEYOTES
SAYSOK  ROASTS  SYSTOLE
```

378

```
MATRI   YULE   LEA  SANTAS
OCHER   ELAM   ELF  AREOLA
THEFIRSTNOWELL   FESTAL
TEREDO  RETARS  PESTERS
ODER  UNA   III    SET
EGO  COVENTRYCAROL
DECKTHE  ONEROUS   ABATE
ACORNS  HUSS  STE   NEGRO
NORIA  RAP   FEZ  ODDSON
CLASS  ILLUSE    TAY
EELS  SILENTNIGHT  SAME
KOS   CUDDLE   ATRIA
ARDENT  PLO   EEN  MAULS
REINE  CAA  SPAN  WARBLE
CAMEL  ANDROLL  WASSAIL
ADESTEFIDELES   OPS
SEC  PEA  ANI   ARID
CORNETS  MONDES  TISANE
OTIOSE  WHITECHRISTMAS
DONDER  HON  RHEE  IRANI
SEDERS  OST  SONG  SONES
```

379

```
ALEPPO PRAHA LAC THEE
RADIUM RITES AWL HOLY
AKAPPACOFFEE PRETENSE
NEMI HAVEAHAPPYNUYEAR
TEAR STATE CRASS
GLASS STEW LUTHER
LON PEPO NEPH CEDAR
OMEGATOLEARNGREEK ULE
BALANCE AROW ARA SALE
ENERO FRET PIUS CLAD
ALPHALOAFISBETA
CLAN TOBY TINE ERIAS
HARD ABE LOST STRANGE
INA RHORHORHOYOURBOAT
CAMEO EGIS ABBA NRA
PURSER LOOK CAUSE
BLIGH ABOUT EBEN
YOUTHETAMOUTHFUL UMBO
ACCOSTED SIGMAROMBERG
WHAM OLA USUAL REINER
LESE RAM NANNA ENSURE
```

380

```
PDQ AMARA PLUMB TKOS
LIEU SURAS RAREE HARE
ELBA TRACT EDEMA ATEN
CLAYPIDGEONS ORTIZ
HOTLINE SRO AERIE PGA
SWEET RHO RABBITTEARS
CTS IFS BROZ SWIT
ILSA WOLFESBANE BASTA
ROLLCALL POESY SOU
ADELA GEM PSI RIPSOFF
TEE SHARIF SOCAGE ILE
ESTATES SAP NUN ELLER
CON FARED LEAPYEAR
ALGER KIDDGLOVES ORSO
BURR IRAE IVE ANN
CRABBEAPPLE ERS ASTHE
DEY SMOOT LOR MARSHES
FOLIC BYRDWATCHERS
ARON GHOTI ORALE ACME
ROXY ROBIN NELLS RAIN
FIXX EWING OWEST ERA
```

381

```
LOBE ASPIC URALS BLAB
IRON THETA NOMIC LOGE
FLATFOOTED COOLHEADED
TORRENTS MALTY OLDIES
ATES TENOS VOCE
PLIED THANA SINISTER
GRIND THINSKINNED ILA
AILS SEER DIOR OGAM
ICY HARDNOSED BAHTS
TELEVISE ABUSE BASTE
IRENE AMENT SERIF
EVERY OCEAN OTIOSITY
ARECA REDHANDED SEA
TORT SOIR IDEE STEW
ODE HAREBRAINED PEENS
MEDIEVAL ALGER RAADS
AGON SPANS OEUF
PRIMER AMINO ACCLAIMS
HOTBLOODED BIGHEARTED
ATTU UDALL LANES ESTA
DSOS SURLY EMIRS ROOK
```

382

```
HOPS POETE ABEET DALE
APOC EGGON IRATE IBID
SUTHERLANDSMOTHERLAND
ASSORTED OLLAS NAUSEA
ONUS CREED CANT
AMBLER ARSES ARGUELLO
RARE BOPEEPSSHEEP EIN
ONERS SHE POP GBS
ONA HAMILLSCAMELS ARE
MADEIRAS APACE OCELOT
SALON AGAPE PRONE
REPROS ALENE PERUSALS
ABR HELTERSKELTER GEE
DOE ARR CII SOLON
ALA GENETSBERETS VEND
RIDDANCE LEMUR THESES
ETTE CASES PIER
SIGNOR CHLOR MORALIST
CLAIREBLOOMSHEIRLOOMS
ALEE ALARM OBESE ATOP
TSAR TYPES NOTED DAGS
```

383

```
PAROL MESS AQUAPURA
ITALO ASON SUNBATHERS
QUIDPROQUO HAIRRAISER
UNSEAT SLOB ITAS NITA
EEE TRA STERNES ORES
ISERE HOT IDA
BEEN VERITAS VIPERS
ACUTE DATIVE ENPLANE
BAROQUE ASI FASTLANES
ADE URAL SOUTH INSET
MINDYOURPSANDQS
ADEEP SKEWS BORU ARI
NOTAMUSED AHA STEELER
TRIDENT BROACH STENO
SCENIC ENTREES OXEN
TSE GAI ARLEN
OPAH CHAUNTS SEX ADA
HALE BIEN GOTH ECOLES
OPENSALANE QUINTUPLET
SPARETIRES UNDO STORE
PIQUANTE ETES ESTER
```

384

```
MEAD GRASP PHOS BOOM
ACME LINER OLENT AGRA
THEBRIDGEOFSANLUISREY
TOSSED UPCAST YDS EMS
FEDS UNIE EMP
ALAMODE GREENMANSIONS
NODAL MORASS ELT PROA
GRANDHOTEL DASHIELL
LETT OBOE SEALS ATALL
ONEILL PARTAKES DEY
CASTLEOFOTRANTO
CAM STEEPLES DERAIN
ADAPT NAILS OHNE INNO
PARISIAN PROUDTOWER
RIOT NNE COATEE ALARM
ARCHOFTRIUMPH REVERTS
SBA TREE ISTO
PRY IMA CIRRUS ALBANY
HOUSEOFTHESEVENGABLES
INRE URNES RAREE LOVE
LATE SOTS SLEWS STAR
```

385

```
HELD  CALL  CLOP  ATHOS
PAGAN OMOO  HATLO CHACHA
INGMARBERGMANTONCHEKHOV
ESSE ERNE ARC TER MESTA
TOO PTAS MULE ODES
AMNERIS BORER TUNES NAB
MEN PORES AUDIE SODA
LOUISAMAYALCOTTONMATHER
APPLE ITSY HUHUS SPOILS
PET TALE MATI ANTA
EROS WANE UPPERS ACE
LANACANTRELLAFITZGERALD
TRY SENLIS BRAE STLO
ELIE TINS AIDA TAP
AVERSE SCROD MUIR BEAME
JAMESBUCHANANETTEFABRAY
ADAS SHARP DOTES ETO
REY MELTS LARES SLENDER
TINA ARMS ENID ULE
ASHED NEE UNA IRAN SLIM
CHARLESHGORENATATEBALDI
TARRED SOREL SETH SHEET
GEARS SELL PROS ALAS
```

386

```
HELOTS SPA TLC SPEAR
OCARINA COLDWAR IRATE
GODBLESSAMERICA TESTA
LASER ANTIS STIR
PEST DUN ATEIGHT ERE
ETHIC COMUS SOBERED
WHITECHRISTMAS WARP
SMITH DURANT BROACH
SEEIT RONDEAU DREI
MAI REMEDY NEEDS EARN
ARR AKENE AVAIL DEE
DEVA TASTE ONEINA ESS
ANIL ONPAPER DRESS
MANTIC OCEANS STOOL
GATH THESONGISENDED
INBREED ETAIN DIODE
NEE MERCIES VMI CRAW
SERB KILOS REACT
IDLES PUTTINONTHERITZ
SLIDE PEASANT EOLITHS
TENET YDS NEO REDSEA
```

387

```
ICER ACK JEST SCALP
VOLE IHAD OPAH TABOR
ALEC MAZO HIVE MONACO
NINE FLORENCEOFARABIA
CAPRICORNS SCRIMP
TORO ILO RUT EIRE
BECOME TANG AMAH NED
ADARE ASSISIASPIE CIG
MER SECT ALY LARGE
ANISETTES ONO FALLEN
CARRARAMOTHERHOOD
HALVES LIP AROMATICS
PATTI AVE ITEM BRO
EMU CREMONASASH ALLOW
TAR EELS STEN BLEEPS
ONES ALT TIT SOFA
TOSEED ANAPOLIDAY
PISAPORRIDGECOLD PROF
ORIGIN DREI IDEE IDLE
LODEN AGAR DIMS POKE
SNIDE MERL ANT ERST
```

388

```
SCALP OATH SHAG OCALA
LONER CLOY COMA RIPER
ASSAI EARP AWET NAHUM
THEREWASANIRISHTENOR
DON ONCE ERROR
DUSTIN CASTE PRAY ISR
ANTAE SOLI DAIS ASTO
WHOPUTWHISKEYINHISTEA
NINE HEAT ILANG TOILS
STE MIEN IMADE LANCET
PUNT SLOTS PILE
MODULE RHONE KOKO TAN
ALIST BEANO CETE MOTO
HESAIDITWASTHEONLYWAY
DIEN ICAL OINK ORALE
INN SNAG MINCE GNARLS
CREAM DOLE SIG
THATHECOULDSINGHIGHC
ORANT RUNS EINE OSIER
LINGO ABAS ALDA RENEE
DOTES LATE FOOD NEALE
```

389

```
RANK ROBES CARAFE BOWER
EVOE OPERA REUBEN ANIME
BEHINDTHEFOURBALL SELMA
UNITE SOWERS ESTA IYYAR
TATERS MEDIA CASE
LOUSE EDAM PER APAT
TIA LEO NINEHILLSOFROME
INRE DUPONT ARIA SAILOR
LADLE SUREST ELS ENTIRE
TWOISLANDS ERSATZ OCCAS
SERAPE SANE CION HYLA
YANG EMBER COOT
SALT HARK MILO OCELLI
PROWL PARROT SEVENHCLUB
AGLEAM MAO SETTER RHONE
CALLTO MALT TRALEE OYER
ELEVENGALLONHAT CAY DST
RIDE AUR ODEA STREW
WADE SNIDE PARKAS
SAHIB SPUE TONISH TILDE
ILONA SIXDOLLARQUESTION
MARKS ETOILE PAULO HERO
PEASE DARTER TEILS EGER
```

390

```
TAT SHAMS UBER BRAD
DOTH HELIO NAPE RASES
SWEEPINGLY CHILDISHLY
MINARET BOOTS WEHOLD
STONILY CETUS DEFLEA
GOD KRAIT KILLY
AMBER TRENCHANTLY PAZ
VEAL MAID BETS CERO
ALL EXPLOSIVELY CANTO
TENNIEL ARIEL UNSET
FETID CREST AUREI
AZURE PIANO ENCLAVE
COLOR WITHERINGLY ERR
TOLL ZONE BORA CLIO
AMY POWERLESSLY TOYED
CODED ENNEA LOO
TORRID AMAIN MUSKILY
ZAPATA STOMP ANTONIO
IRONICALLY ENGAGINGLY
POLIO ROAN REESE ELLO
KEAN APSE STEED SEE
```

391

```
AYES  TIBIA  DOES  BANG
LOVE  OTARU  ERNES  EROO
EYECLASHES  MADCHATTER
CONTESSA  TOOTS  RUTILE
INTO  BRINE  HIRE
DICOTS  BLINI  MONARCHS
ATONE  BREAKCRANKS  RAP
MAPS  TREN  ETES  SOSO
ALT  CHARDBOILED  RECTO
SOILURES  ESSAY  MEEKER
COLES  SISSY  SAHIB
SENATE  ATREE  AUDITORS
CLEMS  CHEATINGPAD  TEA
ADRY  SOAP  OOPS  ATAT
LEV  SPLITCHAIRS  DIODE
PRETTIER  LASSA  WORMED
HUNT  TERSE  SIRS
ALPENA  TEMPI  CAPITATE
FIRSTCRATE  SPARECRIBS
ALAI  HEMEN  TRIER  IDAS
ROYS  VEST  SONES  PERE
```

392

```
TWIST  TERSE  DODO  SPEY
EATON  SNIPE  OMNI  RUST
THEGAMEISUP  GLAD  EYAS
STYRIA  LEHAR  ELA  MARU
ALLY  ASNER  ELBOWED
OTS  PEAS  AUGER  LASS
HARM  WEEMS  NEPAL  ENE
ONEIN  APOS  SITUPS  NOT
SEPHARDIM  SERIE  DOOR
SPLEENY  STRAND  ANGLE
ULAMA  STEAM  INCAN
OSSIP  PEANUT  PSYCHIC
LEEK  UNDID  GUYFAWKES
RIN  REPEAT  RANN  DORMS
ADO  STULM  RESIN  COLE
NEAT  PRIER  PUNY  WON
SCORNED  ANNES  SETS
LIEU  SED  ANDES  TITLES
ALBS  ILES  INTHESPRING
ROOS  RICE  PANAY  PAVIA
OCTA  GRAB  SPARE  UPEND
```

393

```
PUMA  ACORN  TIGER  LEO
ABED  LABIO  ALENE  COVE
DENOFLIONS  CERTIFI[CAT]ED
CLONE  TATUM  NAVEL
MASTI[CAT]E  ARGUS  SVCE
IGNORE  CRURA  CHEETAHS
SNORT  HIMALAYANS  IAO
DEW  SAMOA  SMUT  [CAT]LIN
OSLO  ABYSSINIAN  PAULA
EXTRAS  ACIDS  MARRER
BOOBOOS  SUITE  PERIODS
INPAIN  PULER  TOECAP
BEALL  [CAT]ASTROPHES  SHAD
BARM  SARA  LIMES  IMA
ETD  [CAT]ILINARIAN  CALID
RASGADOS  GANTS  MANITO
ALEG  DOBLA  MARGAYS
TEMPT  [CAT]ANIA  EAGER
JAGUARUNDI  UNVINDI[CAT]ED
APAT  IRADE  THERE  ELSE
MAD  PEPYS  EGRET  RATE
```

394

```
GESSO  PLY  COMES  ALPS
BUREAU  AREA  ARETE  ACARE
ONELITTLETWOLITTLETHREE
IWILLFIGHTNOMOREFOREVER
LAS  ILIE  ZENO  INE  ANS
ELANET  DASHER  ESSEN
REWAX  TOE  HUH  ARTE
VILMA  LES  BAR  ICKIER
INFATUATED  EARTO  CAESAR
NOAH  MILLI  ALOE  MADDERS
TODOS  DIKE  ROK  ANDI
ONEBASE  ERECTED  STINGER
LUNN  BAH  NARC  STORE
ASTARIS  ELSE  ALIAS  HOSE
STONED  TRUER  REPRESENTS
WINKLE  HOE  SUR  SARIS
ERIE  TIS  TOP  DUROC
TAKEN  SKEWED  GENEVA
SPA  SAL  ALAI  BREL  VER
TELLTHEMWILLIEBOYISHERE
RETURNOFAMANCALLEDHORSE
OVERA  SORED  EVEL  EERIER
PERK  TRESS  DES  RANEE
```

395

```
NORD  REPEL  MAZE  DESI
ATOI  ELLIE  ALONE  EXIT
TONSOFBUNS  SCADSOFADS
LEAPFROG  SITAR  CRIMEA
ANEW  LENIN  PALE
ALTOS  BANFF  CARESSED
CROC  HEAPSOFJEEPS  LAI
ROTH  ELI  ALS  ZERO
OAS  PILESOFTILES  OWLS
PRORATED  ZEENA  TANSY
FIRED  FALLS  ROMEO
SWARM  HARTE  AIMEDFOR
LIAT  STACKSOFFLAX  YMA
ANTA  ONE  ALE  MEAT
NAT  FLOODSOFSUDS  AWNS
DISRAELI  TORTE  TARSI
ACTE  FINIS  ROTI
AMANTO  HAMAN  RELEASED
BAGSOFRAGS  GOBSOFCOBS
EZIO  FOLIO  ERIAN  HOOT
LOOM  BONN  SYSTS  INNS
```

396

```
AGRA  ABEAM  ETAS  WEED
TAEL  LOGIA  ADAPT  ATLI
TUESDAYANDNIGHTINGALE
INFORMED  EIDER  FEELS
CTS  OER  PINA  FAR
COD  MORON  SILT  BAD
LOSALAMOSANDANDYHARDY
ARAL  ITE  WOE  LAZE
PLYMOUTHROCKNROLLOVER
PES  SSTS  ROAST  EASES
BMUS  APR  SGTS
BRIAR  SUCRE  ATEE  LEE
JOHNNYCASHANDCARRYALL
ANOA  HSM  ATI  EMUS
TEDLEWISANDCLARKGABLE
ORA  DENY  ERIES  NOR
VIL  CATS  COT  ARI
LOANS  OSTIA  MACHINES
LINDAHUNTANDPECKSNIFF
LACE  ESTER  ERATO  ASEA
BOER  SOON  LENIN  SORT
```

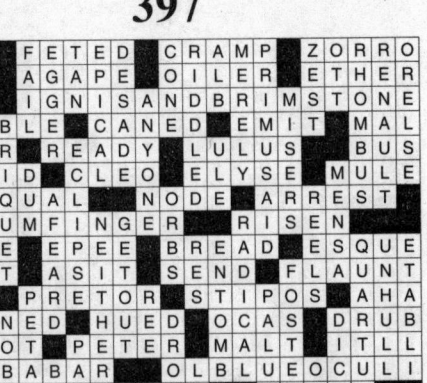

397

```
GAL  FETED  CRAMP  ZORRO
URU  AGAPE  OILER  ETHER
EEN  IGNISANDBRIMSTONE
STABLE CANED  EMIT  MAL
THOR READY  LULUS  BUS
AVID CLEO  ELYSE  MULE
EQUAL  NODE  ARREST
AURUMFINGER  RISEN
INME EPEE  BREAD  ESQUE
DOIT ASIT  SEND  FLAUNT
ERA PRETOR  STIPOS  AHA
DAMNED HUED  OCAS  DRUB
ELIOT PETER MALT  ITLL
BABAR  OLBLUEOCULI
BALLOT  PAPA  DRATS
MENE PECAN  CASA  RIOS
AGA PRONG  TRALA  OFUS
DOL VETO  ORIAL  GANJAH
CROCODILELACRIMAE  UVA
ARGOT MENAT  ANAIR  LEG
PAYNE EDENS  TEENY  YRS
```

398

```
KIOSK  KODIAK  KNACK  KIRK
OSKAR  ALARME  VIDOR  ADEN
KARMA  KIRITEKANAWA  NONO
OKA KNAVES  PESO  ZEALOT
AEDES  ASIS  KAYAK
KKK TOUR  PLAT  MUCKRAKER
HANSON  KOOKABURRAS  AIA
ANITA CELINE  ELIOT  FFV
KICK RAVING  POLLS  JAFFE
INKS AMENT  GLUES  BALEEN
SSE KIERKEGAARD  MANTELS
RHINOS  OUT  NANOOK
SABINES  KINGOFKINGS  LAS
EVOKED LANGE  LAVAL  PANT
NICER HIRES  BORAGE  ETTE
DAK KAPER  KIRTLE  KASHA
UTE KAZANTZAKIS  DEUCED
PERKINESS  ATEN  SKIN  HMS
ANKLE  IDYL  SAREK
SPIREA ANOD  INNATE  KOP
KLAN KINNIKINNICK  SPIKE
YOGA ENACT  DUETTO  ERNIE
EWOK EDGES  SEESAW  YOKEL
```

399

```
PECK  GAGA  TSPS  STOWED
ALEE  OREL  ITUP  HONORE
RALE  SANA  NENE  ANTRIM
STENOSBARSERIT  STORKS
EER REL  MAES  TOPI
CRYLATEARIROHTUA  ELM
BLT LAT  SERT  ASIA
ANTAE DET  DIOS  UGLY
HOWL ENTENTE  PREHEATS
EVILONETLEWD  TERR
MAL MUTE  MII  ASTA  CPA
LAIR  ACCENTEDSEIP
REENTERS  TETRODE  ACNE
AIRE SOLD  RMS  BRIAR
SLOT TAIS  SEI  AEG
HER BIGSPENDERSSENOH
OSSA  CONO  APO  ARA
RAFTER CROWBARRETSIOR
ARGIVE RENI  SEER  HAIL
BOULES ATEN  SISS  ENDO
INDENT NERD  ENTE  STEW
```

400

```
SWAG  ASWAN  CAST  OFOR
CADI  STARE  TORTE  RENE
AFAR  SUNYACHTSEN  ARCA
REGALE TATARY  WASTREL
REFERS NEMO  CLOY
TATAS  NUNS  TEARGAS
IRKS SIMP  SELAH  VIOLA
ROE COON  SORES  ODIN
ALTO DOGTAG  ORBED  MEG
NECKLET SCRIP  RAISON
HITCH ARETE  ICANT
FAEROE METER  GALAHAD
KOS SCRAP  AMIDST  PELE
ELKE TAMAR  SOUL  RIB
LIENS PINEL  REES  SSTS
POTTERY STOP  LEASH
CREE  AMAS  PLAYER
ADHERED SPARTA  ELATED
BOCA LATEENLOVER  WHEE
CRAT ERRED  OLEAN  LESE
DENY REEK  RECTO  SLED
```

401

```
TACOMA  SCOOT  TERESA
AVATAR  TIMBALE  IDEATE
ROSEINLAVALIER  RINSER
ONEAL  ICER  GIGOLETTO
BRACT  RESALE
CHIMAERA  SCAR  WESTERN
HOMAGE TETON  BAA  OLEO
IMAN LOWANDGRIN  UTES
NEGOMBO ERG  AIN  PROSE
ADENOIDS VOLES  WHINEY
LUNETTE  ALKORAN
ASSESS RISEN  SNAGGERS
BETTE LAO  PGA  EYEGNAT
ARES TOWNHOUSER  HAME
SIEG ERS  IDIOM  ACACIA
ENROBED USED  BEGETTER
ATOLLS  NOMAN
THEPROFIT  UELE  ARECA
REVERT FRYINGDUTCHMAN
AMELIA TARTARE  ILOILO
PASTEL SASIN  RESTON
```

402

```
BARRE  AMPHORA  FLAPS
ALIEN  CORONET  LATHE
CHAMPAGNEANDACHICKEN
HAM ACRE  TEED  OCEANIA
AMELITA DES  IOU  OOM
NADER FEASTANDREVELRY
SAY STAY  LGE  RAM
DIE TROPO  TASTES
TOBEDGOSOBER  TSE  NATS
OMINOUS OIL  HAH  ADRET
GAS LEG  MEADE  CAM  TAR
AHEMS ONS  GOD  ANATOLE
SACO POE  RINGINTHENEW
TRIADS  ACTED  ELA
EAR TIC  HEAD  BAL
AWELLCHOSENBOOK  CAVIL
MEL ORO  EEG  IMAGINE
PALOMAR MASC  ARAN  ADA
SODAWATERTHEDAYAFTER
ERASE IRELAND  APRON
LASTS ASSERTS  SEARS
```

403

```
SSSFRS  WHERES  EPI  SCP
TRPEZE  SEVILL  MRL  TRO
TOHVENDHVENOT  BKE  REP
INEE  ERIES  PENTECOSTL
CGER  MIND  MEDITE  PPER
     TONG  LER  FLTTEN
CONDENSTION  PTE  ORGNS
PSTIME  ORDINRY  STBLER
BSINS  CNTEENS  STELERS
LEOS  LLIED  WELCOMED
ETN  SEMN  ROTS  BRM
LMPPOSTS  SLEPS  MNSE
DISSTER  MORTISE  PINES
RESTIR  RIVERMN  STMENS
DROIT  LUL  GRNDFTHERLY
CCEPTS  ITS  PIRS
SPIT  RESENT  FEST  CRSS
CHTEUBRIND  MENCE  SETE
ROI  LOL  CINEMTOGRPHER
MBO  NIL  GRILLE  ISRELI
SIN  ELY  ESTTES  CHSTEN
```

404

```
ARETHA  RADAR  SVEN  UPAS
LECHER  EMOTE  PTERO  TELE
ACHICKENINEVERYTOT  SABE
MOONS  LARGE  REPOSES  CUD
OLIG  LEM  ANET  ESTEEMS
DONTGIVEUPTHENIP  TURF
ERGOTS  POLO  CODY  ROAD
BIB  ENCYST  GOO  ORLE
SHIER  AONE  ORMOLU  ROIL
LOCO  CLAD  SCREE  ENG  UTE
AMALGAMS  ARREST  GEER
BONIER  ICOMEISAW  MAMMAS
NEER  SERAPE  ALARMING
LAO  DYE  DARER  LIEN  EMIT
OCTA  ANGELA  KINE  PRESS
CUSP  BOL  ESSAYS  SHE
ITER  ISUP  ARAT  YACHTS
LING  THEPUCKSTOPSHERE
SYLLABI  ORAL  ALE  ORES
LEA  ARSENIC  STOMA  ILONA
OATS  ISLINKTHEREFOREIAM
BRIE  CUBES  RITAS  BERNIE
SNEE  KEAS  ANENT  EDSELS
```

405

```
RAMAT  SOLI  FIT  TORPOR
EVITA  AUER  ADO  AMOEBA
FILLINGSTATION  FABRIC
RAI  YET  NELL  NIFTY
ATTIRE  SILL  KALINE
CIANOS  STALEMATE  CBS
TORTE  WEENY  ORTA  STEW
SNY  SAME  ANAIS  IPSE
RUNNINGSTITCH  LITE
UPDATED  RITES  PETIT
PARTED  CARED  TINCAL
GRITS  OATES  MONTHLY
ROLL  CURRENTEVENTS
ALLE  ANDOR  BING  MES
DEMS  CIEL  SAONE  SHALT
EDA  HORSEPLAY  GEIGER
SHEENS  MILT  INDIGO
RATES  MICE  AGA  CAN
ADESTE  ENGAGEMENTRING
VERSED  TOR  EVER  APACE
INSERT  APE  DANE  MINER
```

406

```
TEST  GATTI  SAFEST
THROW  OBOES  PRINTER
THEGOODEARTH  INFORMER
IRA  WASTE  ERNIES  PAU
PEP  DOGIE  CRUDER  KELL
SEALEMON  DOWELS  SAREE
RIPEN  GALORE  RAREST
PATTON  CONDOS  CATERTO
ARMET  PRATED  MOVIE
NEER  BEATER  PAPERMOON
INN  BARNES  SERINE  NBA
CATHERINE  APEXES  AGED
EARLY  AMOLES  CLOSE
REDARES  SNAKES  CUTLER
OLIVER  DEALER  SALAD
BASER  LETSIN  BURLIEST
BIRD  SENATE  CASES  NWI
ENA  REDSEA  GOTHE  PAN
REEMERGE  SUNSHINEBOYS
SLEDGES  IRATE  EVENS
INSERT  ANWAR  DEED
```

407

```
PASTE  AHAB  SIEGE
MADEIT  ARECA  UNDONE
PUTONTHESPITZ  RETURNS
UTE  SLEPT  ROOFER  DOGE
PALM  ELIAS  ROOST  ABIE
ATLAS  SCRIM  KIT  SCEND
SEACOW  SENEGAL  READE
ALEC  DAOS  TALK
MACBETHTHING  JAILEMUS
AMOR  ERE  YOLANDA  IRE
NINE  TRIED  LUNDS  FLAN
ANN  GRINDUP  NEE  LAND
TOULOUSE  COUNTMERINOS
INCH  CARR  SMUT
CROAK  ALLEGES  PETARD
FROND  SMA  REATA  SEDER
LASS  KEEPS  STUBS  DELA
ATEM  LANCES  STRAP  LIN
METEOUT  LIPPIZANERING
STOOGE  ANION  DEPONE
AWNED  PENT  ERODE
```

408

```
LODI  SLAPS  REVEL  ALTAR
SABIN  TELAE  ERICA  SERGE
ALEAF  AGANA  CAPON  SMIRE
TAYLORMADESUITS  TRUMPED
ESS  EEL  ISTO  TEAROSE
AMAN  ADUE  CAREEN
SOMMERSHOWER  GOON  CLAY
ABOIL  ALA  PLAN  SPARERS
MET  SEERESS  EMIA  AREOLE
OATH  WRIGHTSTUFF  STARER
SHOOTER  RATTERS  HMAS
LAROSA  ALE  ROLLUP
GAMS  REPINER  EERIEST
DENOTE  PIDGEONTOED  ELIE
RENNET  ISLE  FOOTPAD  ADA
ASATREE  HERS  SUI  OATER
MESH  MILD  CHERCROPPERS
ELLERY  DEED  EVER
CAREERS  GUNN  STE  SHE
DEMASTS  GREENEBEANSALAD
ANENT  ONEAL  IRANI  IRATE
MANGE  NONCE  NISAN  LINER
ASTER  STEED  GESTS  TAGS
```

409

```
POCK  ADLIB  WHELM  EBBS
OGRE  LIANE  REDIA  FLOE
PLAYSECONDFIDDLE   FORE
PENNAMES  LETGO  STEWED
AREOLAS  HARTE  STATORS
    TEN  SOMME  BARREN
BASES  HARPINGUPON  EAR
ALOR  PANS  URIS  OSLO
SMU  WINCE  BLAND  SLOGS
HANDIEST  SLUR  ONEWAY
 DANCEATTENDANCEON
SETTEE  RANT  REHASHED
ACHES  BEARD  PIPED  ORE
SHED  MIDI  LEAR  CRIB
HOT  RINGTHEBELL  RUNES
ROONEY  ARIAS  COT
DRUMOUT  AMORS  PULSATE
RIMATE  SNIDE  BOREALIS
ALPH  TICKLETHEIVORIES
FLEA  TROLL  TENSE  UNIE
TETS  OATES  ANTED  GENS
```

410

```
STAR  SWAP  SPA  TABARD
LACE  OHARE  CAR  RIATAS
AMOSTDEV  COWARD  FRUITS
TERTIARY  PENCE  IMBUE
  APSE  ALAD  NASAL
CASTS  ADELA  CHIEFLY
ARME  HUMID  LENTIL  LIE
LEA  ALAE  BEEN  LENA
ENL  UNCHUNKIST  GNOMES
BALANCES  EASES  OPART
METER  TURIN  SIREN
MAHDI  PAREN  RETARDED
UNBELT  SHINGMATCH  SRA
RIAS  ALTO  ADAH  COT
RLS  UKASES  HOOEY  CEDE
ESSENES  ACORN  TOMES
BLOTS  TORI  CRAM
LABOR  TRIMS  TRAIPSED
PERIOD  ABABINREELANDR
ASENSE  KIT  NEAPS  RAGE
MEAGER  ESE  GAPE  EPEE
```

411

```
GEER  DOITS  ROTE  RATIO
OLIO  ATSEA  EVER  ACIDS
ABNORMALCRAVING  CANOE
LEESHORE  DRED  SPIN
  TONY  AIMS  REDHEN
ABBES  ISNOTA  AIRLINE
VAIR  OYSTERSPAWN  ENGS
ALB  OVULE  OBE  DIT
SEL  FEMALEPIGLET  FURL
TRISTRAM  RANEE  OBLATE
 CPAS  CRUSE  WOES
ELAINE  PAOLI  STONECAT
LILT  AIRPLANEPART  ELI
MEW  ROE  VALSE  TAM
IDES  SUNKENFENCE  CITE
REELSIN  SPURNS  LACES
ARDENT  ICES  COOL
 DOES  ASHE  ORTOLANS
CREDO  CAPTAINHOOKSMAN
COVET  ARIL  NOISE  IOTA
CHARS  BASE  GROSS  TROP
```

412

```
BLAIR  AWARE  RISDE  TOMES
RITHE  RIVEN  ECTAD  ORANT
ATRAP  MEADE  DEANE  MANTA
WHITEMILLER  STRONGCLARK
LOPEARED  VOMER  TOASTEE
  TESS  MARIA  DART
CHAFED  GOTAT  SATES  AMS
AESIR  BYRNESHOLMES  BLOT
LAWES  ROUE  COO  RITA
ARAL  TAKETH  STANCE  OBIT
HANDLEVEL  ASPEN  OLDWIFE
 CETUS  TREAT  BREEN
LIGHTER  SEDER  BANNISTER
ODEA  SASHAY  SCOTIA  TATU
TENS  LAR  ARTE  LOPES
TATE  MOODYBARBOUR  ONERS
ELS  ROPES  ALOON  STERNE
 ETES  PLEAT  ABET
ASEASON  PALED  DIRECTED
BUTLERSTORY  WOODSBREWER
ORALE  HUNCH  EXULT  ISERE
DATED  OSTEO  EELER  ETAIS
ESSES  PHILO  DRUSE  SAKES
```

413

```
OPAL  JEAN  PANIC  TRIM
RAVE  OMBER  REACH  RADA
BREAKHOUSE  ORTHETIGER
SERVANTS  TAMIS  DREAMS
 ERNE  BELIE  DUD
MEASLY  LISPS  SEABATS
ARNOS  AATTHEOPERA  HAM
LEIF  KITT  BINS  DEMI
ECG  INTHEFAMILY  PIPES
THINICE  ALATE  WREAKS
 TRUTH  MUTTS  LOONS
TAMERS  SERAI  BALLETS
ATUNE  ONCEINALIFE  UKE
ERSE  CROC  GERE  TREE
LII  THEBARTERED  WHEEL
ACTRESS  ERRED  CHESTS
 HOS  ANODE  MOAB
SOWETO  ODEUM  ALFRESCO
AWITHAVIEW  ATTIFFANYS
DELI  VILLE  NIHIL  RAMA
ENDS  EASED  ALIE  SPAY
```

414

```
MALFI  HALO  PARES  GISH
ABELS  ALOP  STORM  UPTO
BUTISITART  ITSOURTURN
DURUM  NAIF  RIDGE  LIE
STEPS  IMITATE  BULLY
ESPY  IOWNANRCA  FUSEES
PAR  ONLY  DOT  FIFED
ICANTGOON  ANOPENFRAME
COYOTE  AWN  RARE  GAL
TED  TREAD  IRS  BULL
MEYER  NICEPIANO  ORNIS
AXED  MOT  PADRE  IMA
GIS  ARAT  RIA  NEWONE
ITSALLANACT  BIGTALKER
ELATH  KLM  DAHL  WAN
SPRATS  NEVERMORE  CITE
NEGRI  MATINEE  BANES
ARE  STAPH  TART  CORES
ISAWHAMLET  DROPTHEGUN
LINE  MEESE  EIRE  INURE
SATE  ESSEX  RENT  TOYED
```

415

```
MAORI  PILOT    AMISS
WINDED ETOSHA  ACCRETE
ONEINA THESEWAGECANAL
EDUCE  ARABICEXERCISES
FAR  CLOD   ADENA  SOLE
UNI PHIL  AMT    TAE
LASCAR  ERI  SAUER  STO
OMANISANISLAND  AFTER
 MASONS   CONDO  RIATA
AGE  TOT    HOD  GASTON
AWOLFINSHEIKSCLOTHING
LESLIE  OLE  RED   MCS
TAHOE  NEGEV  DONATE
ERETS  IMAMOLDCOWHAND
RYN  TEXAN  USE  FOLIOS
 MAX    SST  POUR  TWO
WANE  ALIBI   DAHL  RAU
ADENPLANETARIUM  SLOGS
KUWAITWATCHERS  APOGEE
ELECTED  HOMAGE  PACERS
 TREAD    MEDES  ETONS
```

416

```
FEST  DAM  CASTS  GUCCI
LITH  EVER  OCTET  ASHOT
AGEE  FETE  MEARA  TAUNT
THEREAREATERRIBLE  REO
STREAMS  COS    ALEC
    GEE  HOTOFF  PELHAM
GROPED  LOTOFLIESGOING
RARER  AUS  PALS   PLAT
EMIR  ACCT  CRIMP  CELTS
ABOUTTHE  TAIL   AMAD
TON  ROAD  HUN  ONOR  BIO
  CAMP  NEST  WORLDAND
IATRY  EMILE  PELT  ELSE
OCHO  LONI  SAN   SLEET
THEWORSTOFITIS  SHIRTS
ASTERO  ONEMAN   SKI
  ARCS    IST  WINSTON
APB  HALFOFTHEMARETRUE
PALMA  LEORA  RANT  RITE
SPEAR  MANET  SAKE  APOD
EASED  STATE  SYD  DEFY
```

417

```
BASAL  MOTET  BAHS  SCAMPS
ENERO  OPERA  OPEC  HUMERI
LONERANGERSHORSE  ERASED
 DONUT  MOTEL  ANE  SISS
ASS  ATAP  RELED  ENCODE
LOUS  UNAU  LAY  STAR  NUS
SUPERMANSPLANET  INSIGHT
 DEN  HOPS   OARS  RELY
CAVED  TAELS  PHONE  HORAE
AGAR  FERRI  BIALY  TENON
PER  SORT  CHANTS  GRIEF
PRISTINE  EASEL  PRESSMEN
ECOLE  EMBRYO  LIAT  YEA
STIRS  SCALA  GRANT  ETRE
DOYLE  LERNA  LIONS  ETHOS
AWOL  MENU   AURI   LEN
DEFAMES  SIGNILLUMINATOR
ORB  EAST  FRO  STAN  SURE
LETTER  SUMMA  ARTS  PEP
DOOR  NAB  MIAMI  MEADE
SUNLIT  NUMBEREDGOLFCLUB
RADISH  COAL  INLET  ELOPE
ALECTO  EYRE  EDENS  SISSY
```

418

```
OLAF  SHEER  ATLAS  STOW
RENI  TORSO  BUENA  HONE
BRIDGEBIDS  ABSTINENCE
 GENOA  SILAS  LONGED
BUENOS  WINOS  TINS
ENTE  ANON   RUNCIBLE
LADES  ARLINEJUDGE  OEN
ONER  FRED   AMOS  DYAD
AIR  SUITOFARMOR  FOSSE
NEGATES  AMEER  MERCED
 ABELE  SKIMS  TEMPO
CARIES  SPITE  UNUSUAL
ARMEN  STORYTELLER  TRA
REES  AERO  LOIS  FARO
INN  ACTORSGROUP  RICES
BATTERUP  POOP   ORTS
 ASOP  SENSE   ATTEST
PATIOS  BINET  OCHOS
SCULPTURES  ARTHURASHE
ARNO  INANE  NITID  LOOM
TEAR  CEDAR  DOONS  EXES
```

419

```
ACED  SAONE   AMAT  ABLE
LAME  ENROL  ADANO  BEAD
PRIMADONNA  CONTRABAND
 PROMISE  PARLE  PSEUDO
 TOLE    SHIFTLESS
SPHERE  TREAD  ODESSUS
PEASE  CRASS  TAROT  UBA
ANI   OAS    AND   SNOB
STR  HITCHINGPOST  ADAR
MARTINET  NOLEN  AGNATE
 ARSIS  EARED  UNITY
DRIEST  SALSA  ENTREPOT
RISE  SINGLEMINDED  UNE
AVID  SIR   STU   NIN
MAN  AGATE  MELEE  SACCO
ALGEBRA  COVER  AACHEN
 GRACENOTE   MULE
ACARID  LONER  COTERIE
POLESAPART  TOOTHPASTE
EMIT  TONIO  ERATO  TINE
RATS  EDDA  DOLOR  ETAL
```

420

```
 ABETS  ARLES  BUST
 BULLET  OTTAVA  OFTHE
BATISTA  THEPENNYOPERA
ODON  ENATE  LEEDS  FEB
MMMD  DREI  CYST   ACU
BEAM  FOURSAINTSINACTS
ANTI  IUM  TAV   CLEESE
 CANT   AIR  GYROS
ASTERN  STY  LAMA  BLOIS
BAH  MISTRAL  SELF  IFNI
ELEM  STRIKETHREE  SEND
LIMO  HAIL  DULLARD  VEE
SCURF  PALS  NYE  RECESS
 STOMP  SHE    MICA
ACKACK  ALS  MAE  RISE
THELITTLEKITTENS  DRAM
BIT  OENO  IRAN   MOUE
ACE  FIRST  NUDES  ONCE
THELITTLEPIGS  RUNNIER
 IRENE  IRISES  ELATED
 STEM  ESTER  DUPES
```

421

```
SCRAG  MADE   AMIENS    YET
PROVE  ALAD   PLANTAIN  OAR
IAPOLOGIZE    ILLGETBY  UTE
EVEN  KNEELER  TESS    AGREE
LED   RAND   LAMER     PLIERS
      ARAT   SITED  THEART
SUNRISESUNSET   MAAR  THAW
PRICE  ELIE   EVANGEL  ERA
REGAL  CANT   ARISTA  ELTON
ADEN  RECASES  STAR   MOOSE
TORE  EDO   SPOSI    MOPPED
      IFIWEREARICHMAN
SPAWNS   MARSE   ION   STAT
PAPAS  STOP  ISABELA  TOBE
ENURE  PATINA  ROME   PINER
ADZ  TORPEDO  BALA   ALTAR
RAZE  REED  YOUBELONGTOME
   LAGGER  DERRY   NOES
OVERLY  MESAS  STEP   TAB
TEMPO  PREP  TALARIA  CATO
ALE  ONEALONE  IMADREAMER
RUN  MANNERED  SADA  BREVE
UMT   GATETO   TRES  ODDER
```

422

```
SOAP  CREES   HARLEM
CINCH   HENRI   AVIATOR
SAMCOOKESONG   LEAPOVER
PLIE  NEROS  HOLST   NINE
LIL  SERIN  RETAG    ETA
APART  NEAT  MAYA   HODAD
THROAT  STEVENS  VERILY
   DRAT  ERANT  MINAR
REFERRED  ELD  BATTLEAX
OSLO  NEISSE  GALA  ECCE
UTA  TARANTIST     TAR
GOSH  PENA  TABLED  TORI
EPHEMERA  MIB  ESOTERIC
   IRONY  JONAS  EVAN
CANNON  RETORTS  EMOTER
LUGER  SEWS  DRAG  PRONE
ADE  ERASE  UVULA   STD
SIRS  ABELE  UTILE  ASIA
STMARTIN   PARTOFACHURN
SALIENT  OFFER   SHAPE
NAPLES   STARS   HUBS
```

423

```
PADRES   CEDAR    ICEMAN
ANOINT  OVERAWE  DODECA
CONSTANZEWEBER   OMELET
ANGER  AIRY   FIGMENTS
     EAVES  ENTERED
PREDATES  PLUS  ANOMALY
REMOTE  TREVI  PIE  IDEO
OVEN   ORISTANO   LIVY
PUNG  FLED  RAYS   ROMEO
EDIBLES  PANES  HOSELS
   ORANT  AMC  ALOOF
PROVEN  HORAE  GONDOLA
RIVAL  EGAD  BEAK   ROLL
EVEN  STROBILE    MITE
TERN  AHS  OGEES  SPARES
ARTICLE  VLAD  CHURNERS
   AZILIAN  BRUNO
CHAMBRES   GRIM   FETOR
CHANDU  DIEZAUBERFLOTE
PEWTER  ATHALIE  HEBRON
AWNING   SPANS   ORATED
```

424

```
TAINT  TROMP  CROC   BARE
ASTOR  ROVER  AIDA   ELEV
CHAPERONAGE   PROPAGATE
TELESAVALAS   PERIMASON
   SEE   IRS   TINKLE
APEXES  IRADE  SOOT  ADO
HAMES  ANOXIA  POLYP
ABBR  DECIARNAZ   OPAL
BARON  ARKS  MADE  SLICE
   AMIDST  NENE  WAYNES
SECOND  PANDA  ABBESS
ARISES  FARE  TITLES
PINTS  SLIT  MEAL  ERNIE
SAGE  MINIPEARL   GALA
   LADEN  SASSES  PEKES
MOW  NEWT  ASHES  ERNEST
ARISTA   TNT    STE
MISMARPLE  OLIGCASSINI
MODESTIES  REPRESENTED
ALOE  HEFT  ANSON  TOTAL
LEMS  SSTS  LOEWE  SWORE
```

425

```
JIBED  PACK  DAMNS  COERCE
ORALE  OGRE  ONAIR  ORRERY
SAULBELLOW  NORMANMAILER
HEMS  LIEN  SATIE  OPT  SEE
   MATTE  OTHOS   BEE
SEG  ATES  ABIE  POTS  AMA
TREATER  GEORGEADE  ALAN
RAREES  DARIN  AWRY  DENT
ASTRO  ROGET  ABETS  COXAL
NERO  BEREA  SPORE  GARAGE
DRU  ROBERTBURNS  SERENER
   DIANE  LEI   PRIED
HEEDFUL  CHARLESLAMB  EMS
UPSETS  LAIRS  NOONS  DRAW
FATAS  MURRE  ATLAS  HOPPE
FUEL  ANTE  IVIED  CAROLE
ELIS  ESGARDNER  WHIPPET
DEN  RACE  ETRE  DAIL  ESS
   ATA  MANES  DEGAS
ADO  NAR  ENTRE  EVEN  OMOO
JAMESBALDWIN  GEORGESAND
AMATOL  LIANE  ARTE  FAZED
RENAME   BARED  DEED  TRESS
```

426

```
VON   ASST   CASS   PLEA
MADE  IGETA  LEHAR  RASP
ACES  SEAOF  AGAMA  ETTE
LUSTFORLIFEWITHFATHER
TUSSAH   CET   STIFLE
SMA  SYNE  TOO   LIONESS
   THEEGGANDICLAUDIUS
MAAR  TAEL  AFR   DUNES
ANGELSTREETSCENE
REINA   ANA   OUR   TRAP
ALLTHEKINGSMENINWHITE
TEES  EON  TOR   ERNIE
   LITTLEPRINCEIGOR
ALTAI   ORA  EMIR  CONS
WINDSOFWARANDPEACE
LETMEGO  AME  ISNO  SAG
   INDRAS  OOH  ISOLDE
HEARTOFDARKNESSATNOON
ANTA  AEIOU  ARIOT  TUNE
IDOL  DIGNE  TONLE  ACIS
LOPS   TEED   EDGE   PHS
```

427

```
ACCRA  RIIS   BAALS  ADDS
BROAD  OMNI   ASSES  GARE
MIZZENMAST    SHOWWINDOW
STYE   CART   STER   RASPS
RHONE  BOER   BEET
BLASE  TARTS  SEL    EWER
LAP IRA GAT   STRIA  ILA
UMP RECONNOITERED    TIP
FELL   VRAI   NOLA   MAHDI
FRIARIES  PUKKA  FISHED
CRASS   CITEE   SARTO
HOAGIE  MOLAR  AUREOLES
ARTES  DARE   EYRA   NDAK
JAI OSUUNDERGRADS    ITA
JNO NAVVY LAG HSM    NET
IGNS  GEE  SAYSO  EAGRE
PSAT   MANE   PATEN
ASCAP  FAYS   PALE   AMMO
SHORTSTORY  IQQUESTION
KOBE   MOXIE  DRUM   STERE
SOBS   SEXES  OSES   TONER
```

428

```
AMISS  IDLES  GLIM   DORM
DANCE  LOIRE  RIRE   EPEE
INTENTIONALWALKS     VANS
MARNIE  MASERS  ENFOLDS
ETOILE   GENES   DEUT
CIME   ERENOW   LEVEE
ASS  TEND   EARLDOMS
DAILYDOUBLE  MAROC   LIP
EBRO   SMEES  ALAMO  ELY
PROOFS  ASTERN   GEUM
TASMAN SMU ETD   ONAGER
SIAM   EPOPEE   STRABO
PAM RIATA DRABS  GULL
OBI CLEAR DOUBLEBOGIE
DECLASSE   YALU   ESS
SLEET   LABIUM   MICA
ACME   TERNI   JOCOSE
STASHED  TROGON  AVESTA
LASH  DESIGNATEDHITTER
ARTE  OMAR  IVIED  NAIRN
GOOD  CAGE  NACRE  ALANS
```

429

```
ABEAM   MAGIC   CAPE   BRAY
LEGREE  AMISH  ADEN   ALICE
PEARLYEVERLASTING   NUDES
END DEMENT  SIHON   VAT
LIN  ETNAS   WIDOWS
HAMSTER  SLIER  FETE  HOG
AVOCET  SWEETWILLIAM  ILO
LAURAS  PORGY  AARE   STIR
LINER  SURFY  RAPID  PIECE
ALTE MIRS  CECIL  DARWIN
MSA RAGGEDROBIN   ORGEAT
INHUME   ROUEN   ORIENT
ONEIDA  BOUNCINGBET  ELI
ARLENE  VINGT  ARID   GRAS
SPADE  RANEE  REMAT  GELID
THUS  SONG  AIRED  CANINE
OER BLUEEYEDMARY   AEOLIA
RUE LASS  AEDES   SPLAYED
SLEEVE  ERRED   EAT
PAS  ENDIN  DENNIS   ALE
SERAC  CONFEDERATEVIOLET
EPOCH  BLEU  UKASE  EVADER
TACT   SAAL   METER  AROSE
```

430

```
BELA   PHONO  THRICE  CUL
ICON   RADAR  WEIGHT  ARI
BLUEHOMEHOTANDLICENSE
BASTES  RUNE   SUM   STAN
STY  SPA  MONEY   SECCO
USERS   ORAD   ROUNDS
BUTTERLOVINGHICANDEYE
AHEM  SEDAN  SOPH   OSAR
RUMOR  NALDI  OPEC   SENT
ERASED   OILS   ELA
DUSTSUGARGATORANDFISH
ERR   ONES   TURNTO
SKID  TEAM  GRAIN  NOLAN
ANNE  AGUE  OGLES   NERD
COFFEETOSSFLESHANDTEA
OBERON   NINO   ARRAS
RANTS  CERES  UDI    AHA
OBEY  HEP  UNTO   IAMBIC
TINSAUCESAMTAIANDCAKE
INC  ASTRAL  ELSIE  ITER
CEE  RESIDE  REELS  VERB
```

431

```
ABED   FLINT  TAIL   CAST
LONI   MOOLAH  ORNO  ALTO
ONCEONCRETE  LACS   RAIL
ENSHROUD  IBOUGHTABIRD
ALPS   SOOT   CRO
SHARE  RENAIL  CHANTED
PEND  SPUR  TSELIOT   ONO
RAI  LENA  NAIR   STUN
ITSPRICEISOONDIDLEARN
THELOCK   TAROS   ATLEE
ANES   SATON   PANS
BRAID  RISEN  INDULGE
WASNOTHIGHSOTHENIPAID
AMOS  RAIN  RATA   RBI
NAN BERSERK ITAL   HEEL
ARGONNE  DIRGES  POSSE
FAT   CIES   SGLS
WHATIOWEDONA  SPLATTER
HOPI  NATE  GRECIANERNE
ITEM  NDAK  LELAND  LOTI
MEDE  JETE  EDITS   SPED
```

432

```
SOFAR   SLAGS   TST   ADD
MALONE  ITALIC  ACRANIA
ATONAL  DINERO  KEATING
LORDGIVEMEPATIENCE
SEI   FINITENESS
GONG  FASTERFASTER   VEE
AGEES  SEABEE  TOD   CANT
NEWTON  ELBE  PER    BUS
GETAHORSE   HOP   LATINO
MORAE   ADAR   ERIVAN
SOSO  WHENDOWEEAT   TETE
OLIVIA  OINK   SISIS
WATERY  KNT   STRUTHERS
SOT  PRO  HAHA   PEORIA
SOON  CIA  COLADA  SRTAS
URU  HONKHONKHONK  TELS
MOTHERHOOD   TEC
ANDIWANTITRIGHTNOW
MIDIRON  REINED  LARINE
MAILING  STORES  ERODED
ENG  SSE  ESSEN   RYDER
```

433

```
SALEM   LENA    MARC    SAHL
MEDICI  EXALTS  ELIA    ALOE
TWEEKSWITHPAY   TBASEHITS
NELS    SIDRA   TRESA   TRACES
SRA  MILEA  BOUT      LAUREL
     GALEN   TAUPE   FINCA
CATERED  TWAYSTREET  TRI
ADONIS  MOODY    AUNT   STEN
PINES   CORNY   PLIS   BEHAN
ROTS  CORA   ELECT   CAVILS
ASH  THANDEDSAW   HIKERS
   EGRESS   SATIE   LEGEND
BAREST   TFACEDLIAR    STA
ORIENT  POETS  LIRR   AVIV
NOSED  OATS   SPINS   ABONE
TOLD  ASTI   PLATE   ROUTER
ODE  TPIECESUIT   CONTEST
   GAPES   MANTA   HAYES
DARNER   MIGS   PAPAS   STR
PESETA  DIANE   OUZEL   EIRE
TWHEELERS   TNOBLEKINSMEN
GEEK  ETAL   STROLL   SETOSE
SYRS   DAME   BESS   MOONS
```

434

```
SARI   MASC   ATONE   PARE
PALEO  ARCH   NAMED   AVER
FROSTBITIO   EXIOUATING
CATTAILS   REMIT   CROATS
    ACTS   MILOS   RATINE
    GIRLS   HONAN   LOTUS
SANTE  LOVEMEIODER   MAE
ASIS  MALI   HUES   BACK
APO  KINDERGARIO   SLICE
RESPONDS   HOMES   SHUNTS
    IEREI   SIREN   MAORI
RIFLED  BUNKS   BUGABOOS
ANITA  CASEYSIOGEL   ANE
ITES  SASH   SAGS   GNAT
NOD  PENIIOTIARY   LUCIA
    PANTS   PINAS   MATER
AORTAS   OPTIC   BAIT
IMPORT  AFOOT   BOROUGHS
LIEUUIOANTS   INADVERIOT
KENS  RENEE   ARNE   SAVES
ASST  SCANS   LADD   SLED
```

435

```
AGLET   ARECA   TABS   WEST
SLIER   DEMOS   ITEA   HSIA
COCKANDBULLSTORY   ITEM
ORE  ALES   OKAPI   STONE
TINTAGEL   PEN   NOTEPAD
SASHAY     SEWINGBEES
SEER   PANE   SAO   IAL
    CONTRA   REELECTS
AMOK  REDHERRINGS   PHEW
RAPACITY   CORSO   SHERE
ATENT   MEHTA   RAREE
RUNGS  SCAPE   ARSONIST
AREA  WELSHRABBIT   TEAS
TERRARIA   SLEEPY
   OYE  MCS   OATS   LARA
HORSEPOWER   BAKERS
AVOCETS  RAG   BELCANTO
MINOS  CHORE   COSA   TIC
ALOU  HOUNDSTOOTHCHECK
SLUR  URGE   TRITE   PARLE
SERT  STET   SENSE   ASSET
```

436

```
ROMP   SHAGGIER   SHAFTOE
OMAR   TORRANCE   TOLLAGE
BITOBETTERBUTTERBUYER
STEPON  STIRS   HESS   LEI
   LOTTA  ASE   FIVE   POSE
SEASHORESHELLSELLER
ELSA  REX   DUET   EOS
LISLE  ATAP   CALLSFORTH
FEE  ROSEMARY   EAST   OHO
   AIR  MILE   ASP   SLOW
PECKOFPEPPERSPICKER
JOKE  LOS   ALBI   SLY
APE  IGOR   EYEOFTHE   HUD
MIDSTREAMS   ARTE   MEANY
   OLA  NOTA   ENA   NUDE
SOLDIERSSHIRTSSEWER
COIN  INON   SAG   HENRI
INN  BEAU   DINNA   PEGTOP
SIGHINGSCISSORSSEIZER
COLETTE   PETERIII   ZENO
ONENESS   RUSSELLS   EROS
```

437

```
HIGHS  SCALE   ROOM   PTAS
MOSAIC  ERRING  INRE   RARA
BILLCOLLECTOR  CURTREPLY
ASEA  TEETH  ROSES  HOLIES
STS  PLACE  SMUT   ROBINS
   GRANT   NOISY   SODOM
STRAINS   ARTEXHIBIT   GAB
PRIZED  PATTY   ELEC   PRIE
LACES  RULES   TREKS   HOARD
ACHS  DOPE   SOUPY   LANCES
TED  IRAACCOUNT   CARTED
   ENDURE   EFLAT   GOSSIP
PSALMS  SALLYFORTH   ETA
PASTES  SCALY   OWES   DRAM
AREAS  WHIRL   PEONY   BOISE
GIRL  BAIT   LILTS   SABOTS
EST  DONNYBROOK   STRIDES
   WROTE   REVUE   SPREE
IDIOMS  ACES   SLOES   PSI
OCELOT  SATIN   APART   SEED
WILLPOWER   PEARLNECKLACE
LETA  WENT   ESPRIT   HAILTO
SRAS  NETS   TESTS   YIPES
```

438

```
ERICA  RAND   ASH   SEATO
RADAR  ABIE   REE   APACHE
AMELIAJBLOOMER   CARTER
   PALOMAR   LORDRAGLAN
   ASE   BAER   OMOO
PERSONAGES   ESSE   FLIP
OBE  LILT   SLIER   SANE
LOSS  NELLIEMELBA   ANGEL
ELIA  ORLE   RICKY   ANGEL
DINMONTS   MILTY   ALDERS
   ULES   DOTES   SPEW
BIPEDS  TOURS   SPECIALS
IDOLS  TANTE   OPEC   CHOP
TEEM  JOHNHANCOCK   HARI
TATA  ALOES   ATOI   INE
SLAV  ITER   RELETTERED
   ERLE   FLAT   ERN
MARIECURIE   ACCEDED
SAVIOR  NICOLASCHAUVIN
EJECTS  ICH   OTIC   DRIER
NARKS  TAU   GASP   SELMA
```

439

```
RAMP   DRAB   MARC   CHE
ARCH  CEARA  OREAD  BLOB
GIGI  ARNOLDSEDDY   LAMB
EARLES  TOLU  DENTURES
   AIRE   MARCO   TEREK
NEWPORTS  DELAYS  OLSEN
ODS  STOOD  RITE  PADRE
PUTS  ADDON  VENTS  WARE
ACUTE  DAMA  ESTATE  NED
REGENTS  ITO  WATERBED
    ITEM  NORMA  ULNA
ANGELICO   BAR   MEISSEN
ONO  RAKISH  IRAS  EATME
EELS  REEFS  LEVAR  LEES
RATAL  LAUD  NAREW  VET
ARETE  HOTAIR  STARTERS
    SINCE  SNEER  DERN
SENATORS  TWOS  ENESCO
OMIT  WILDESOSCAR  ACOR
RICE  LOUIS  RIALS  DADA
ELK    TEXT   DENY   STEN
```

440

```
PARR  FEOD    ECHO   WAAC
OBOE  ASTIR  STOOP  ERDA
LEWDBROODESCHEWEDFEUD
ADELE  PEARWOOD  NETTLE
   IRA  SCOUTS  TEASELS
REAGENT  TUNE    MINN
EIGHTAWAITGREATDEBATE
ANET  ECCE  SNA    RBIS
LED  LONE  LAPIN  BOATS
   LENT  SIERRA  CLICHE
WISEGUYSCRITICIZELIES
REEVES  TARGET   CASS
INTER  MARSH  AIRS  DON
NCAR  ARC  CAPE    DINE
GEESEFLEECEOBESENIECE
   REED  HAMS  TOASTER
SPHERES  LISPER   NBA
TRAVEL  DEMEANOR  OLDER
AIDEDELAYEDSTAIDBLADE
AMEN  RENTS  SEDGE  OMEN
TEST  SAKE    ESSE   WEND
```

441

```
APACHE  SCOUR  ULNAR  CATO
COCOON  CORSE  NIOBE  ISEE
TRIPLETHREAT  FLYCATCHER
ITS  TRAUMA  ABATE   DOA
     VII  DRUID  SCALLOP
DAG  WANTS  OGLED  ABLAUTS
ITERATE  ONTHEDOUBLE  TET
ATTIRE  TREAT  DALE  RILE
PUTON  MOTET  SPORE  BONER
ENOS  SLIDERULE   MELLON
REF  ANGLE  ARES  MARLENE
   ISLETS  CRIED  HEREOF
ABRADES  COOS  NONET  TWO
RASHER  HOMEGUARD   AFAR
ASTIN  PLATE  AVISO  GRIND
BIBB  DEER  CLEAT  MANEGE
ILA  DIAMONDHEAD  COROLLA
CASTERS  NORIA  SCANS  DEL
REENTER  SANER   UNO
   NEF  ALIGN  ESTATE  OCA
GOTOBATFOR  INTHELONGRUN
AVER  REESE  NORMS  NIACIN
PANS  MARSE  GROOT  EDGARS
```

442

```
LONA    PACE   LETAT   CPA
ALAI  SODOM  ALIBI  AHEM
UMPS  TROOP  PECULATION
REPLANT  TITHES  TROMPE
ADIEU  IBERIA   PETRELS
SON  BOAR  IMPS  EDT  RET
   GAUL  ACCEPTOR  HEADY
LITTRENCH  DYER    HOR
INURN  ETON   DROUGHT
TURISTA  INA  BEAR  SOY
ART  ELFCENTERED   PRE
ELA  RELY  DOC  DECAPOD
DEBUSSY   RABE   AGING
   INE  ELLA  MARTMONEY
AMEER  TROUBLES   YEGG
MOR  AKA  SMEE  EERO  CAA
ELASTIC  BAGELS  USERS
RESEED  ELEMIS  SATANIC
CREWDRIVER  OTTER  ITSO
EARN  OBESE  NOONS  LETT
STS   WANER   SPEE   SRAS
```

443

```
AVEC  GETS   ALOHA   MELEE
RARA  IGOT  NEFUD  ALOST
CLARABOWANDARROWSMITH
ESSENES  RAIN  TRITONES
DEEDS  LIRA  SELE
   EPA  IRONS   DRAMAS
FULBRIGHTANDEARLYWYNN
ITER  THE  TREY   ARTE
NENES  AMOS  MAIL  BRAID
ARIELS  ANNIE   IAL
LINDAHUNTANDPECKINPAW
   TET  PAEAN  AMOUSE
RELAY  IDES  ACRE  PONTI
ATOM  ECOL  OLD   STER
HUGOBLACKANDBLUEBEARD
SIERRA  SCORE   LEA
   ITUP  EMIA   RASES
TEREBENE  RIEN  DORMANT
SPIDERMANANDBOYGEORGE
PETER  ELATE  APER  REEL
SEANS  TEPEE  GERE  TELE
```

444

```
WIMP  LEDA   ROSE   RANSOM
ARIA  IRON  ITER  EROICA
RATIONALNUMBER  FAITHS
NEEDLE  TOPF  SAGEBRUSH
    LAGS  DIB  SIRI
SQUALL  BARRE  RECASTS
NOUNS  ACUTEANGLE  CHAN
ALIA  ECALE  ICES  HARE
BECKONING  ADAM  EMERGE
   KANSAS  LEM  PROSPER
DIS  CULTUREDPEARL  CTS
EDIBLES  MIR  CROTCH
WELLED  SPAT  BOARSHEAD
LAVA  SPIN  BOLLS  IERI
ATEN  SMARTMONEY  URSAE
PERCALE  ELAND  ZIPPED
   VIAL  YIN  BENT
WISEACRES  DEAR  COARSE
ADESTE  PENETRATINGOIL
NECTAR  ERIN  ADIT  IONA
ESTERS  RAPS  NYSE  OMEN
```

445

```
STAB  DOOM    JUT   RABBI
CAME  ALTA    KATE  ELLIN
OXEN  REINE   AMEX  AVERS
WINNINGCOLORS  ASSAULT
      EVE   FIVE  ASTOR
PISTIL  LAZIEST  ONEGIN
ARETE  WARADMIRAL  ZERO
LEA  SAIDA  TIRES  NAT
ENTS  SPENDABUCK  ACUTE
DETESTED  AGAPE  ALLIED
  LITER  CROSS  GAVIN
OPENER  PAINE  BARONESS
HOSEA  SUNNYSHALO  TRAP
ALL  MARLA  ELAND  IDI
REEF  BOLDFORBES  ROSIE
EDWINA  EARLIER  CORKED
  DETAT  AINT  HOD
NEEDLES  SUNDAYSILENCE
AXILS  KIND  STALL  RAUL
MINEO  EROS  ELUL  EZRA
ETERN  WEB  DUTY  DIEN
```

446

```
PEACH  GROPE  WHIG  STROP
USQUE  IEROE  THANE  CROCE
BOURBONREDS  RIVERMOUTHS
SPAT  AGUA  CASES  ATCOST
   SEXAND  VODKA  DUCK
VAT  RAMS  AINEE  MASH  SEZ
ENHANCE  BRANDYWINE  CAA
CORNEA  WAILS  ENTR  PORN
TIONS  BANDS  IMAGE  PATTI
ONUS  RATE  SOVS  MARCHE
RTG  CAKESANDALE  MARTHAS
HOOVER  CITAT  MALAYA
BOTTLED  HOPSCOTCHES  NED
ASHTON  CARP  OCAS  MDSE
CHEER  FANNY  GOGOL  CASTE
KERR  AURA  TOKAY  HEROES
TAY  GRENADINES  DELUDES
OSE  SHOT  DINED  BAAL  AME
   BEAR  LAVER  MUNROS
AGREES  LIMES  IBIS  ABCS
CROSSTHEBAR  MAXBEERBOHM
RESET  ANENT  EWELL  ULNAE
EYETO  MALT  XERES  MEADE
```

447

```
PALO  RISER  MIST  MARSH
CLIV  ENTRE  INTO  OPINE
BIZETSBEES  CHOPINSPAN
STARRIER  CLAIR  STEEPS
   HINDEMITHSMYTH
SHAMS  ANDS  ASLOPE
CHANS  PLOD  SCH  YVOIR
RING  SAAR  TAUROS  ARGO
ORD  PUCCINISPOOCH  TED
PREPARE  ANCES  AUGERS
  LEIF  SLIDERS  LIAR
ROSTRA  HAVEN  ALLYSON
ASH  SCHUBERTSSHOE  PTO
ITAL  EELERS  WEEP  PORE
DINER  SAL  NORM  ARRAS
  ADDONS  DEER  PLATS
   BEETHOVENSBAIT
AMEBAS  HATED  AERATORS
MOZARTSART  LISZTSLIST
ERRED  ANTE  EDSEL  ESTO
NEARS  WEED  DOYLY  REUP
```

448

```
DONWAN  BIPEDS  BASILS
OLEATE  SELENIC  AGORAE
GEEGEE  ACEROSE  DILATE
MODEL  ATHOUSANDCLONES
ASS  INUSE  REDEEM
  ACED  HEARSTS  OSAN
LEAP  AIT  ESSA  SENEGA
ONBORROWEDTHYME  TSARS
BLASE  ALOE  SILKS  MET
  STAB  ANES  LEA  FIES
HELLODALI  ALLMYSUNS
SAME  NOM  CAVE  OURS
EME  BYLAW  LOAD  NOTER
PANDA  THECORNICEGREEN
ATTUNE  RUNE  PAN  ERGS
LESS  PLANTED  TICS
  THIEVE  ABCDE  AGT
THEBEGGARSOPRAH  RATER
RESIDE  TIERODS  BETONY
AMANDA  ATLASES  BALLES
MISSAL  REDDEN  SLIEST
```

449

```
SPATS  EGAD  VENT  THESE
CACHE  GOBI  ADAH  HELLS
ATREE  AUBERGINE  EBLIS
THEBRIDGE  OUTOFAFRICA
  EERIE  ABES  TILE
CHARDS  DIVES  ROWANS
HEAL  NORTHOFBOSTON
ENRICO  GRIT  ERRED  TOE
CRONUS  YOD  PLIED  DANA
KINGSHIP  TWIGS  DEREK
  APASSAGETOINDIA
ICBMS  LYRIC  NOONTIME
CARE  CADET  GPA  MAHDIS
IRA  CANON  RAIL  SHILLS
ENGLANDMADEME  NENE
REGINA  EMITS  LIVRES
  SIDI  GMAN  CAIRE
ODESSATALES  DUBLINERS
DIVOT  CROSSWORD  DIXIE
DROME  HORN  EURO  ECOLE
STEER  YEYE  BRYN  SEDER
```

450

```
ANTARES  ADDEDUP  PACT
NEOLITH  ETIOLATE  OMAHA
TAPIOCA  SMOCKTURTLESOUP
ITEM  METO  ERSE  SAMBA
  BOOBOO  ERI  NIPS  SPUR
ONS  OPUS  ADENT  AIL  SRI
VIM  MER  SLIVERANDONIONS
ELATING  COTERIES  WARNS
RELEASE  SHORTER  ESTE
TAKERS  ARSIS  SKUA  SPA
HESS  ASTA  SEATINGPLACES
ACHE  ASK  ENE  SORI
SCORNONTHECOB  NESS  PLUS
PEP  ONUS  ROPES  STORED
BRET  ENTITLE  AMERCED
SLATS  AGITATOR  BECAUSE
SMASHEDPOTATOES  LOT  TAR
HOW  LOP  EGERS  KENO  SUM
EONS  FRET  ESS  OILERS
ATRIA  STEW  OMNI  TACO
SHARDBOILEDEGGS  NATURAL
SKEIN  TELEMARK  ENACTED
ENTS  EXTRUDE  NAPKINS
```

451

```
LEAD  SHOES  SEPAL  ELIA
ETRE  TORRE  ALULA  RUNS
SOAPYOPERA  NUTTYHATCH
ENSLAVES  LADDS  SASHAY
    ALES  PARSE  OLE
DOWNER  SANTO  COVERSUP
OBIES  DIRTYFARMER  WRY
LEND  SOOT  HOAR  TEAL
LAD  STONYMASONS  BEANO
SHYSTER  AMOLE  CARTON
  JOINS  SNIPE  CURRY
SPARES  DUETO  ARRESTS
TIMES  MUDDYTURTLE  HIT
REMS  FEDS  NOES  SINE
ETE  HEADYWAITER  BEREA
WARRANTY  ORNIS  PENTAD
    ETC  SOAVE  REED
TRADER  SIDLE  TEAROSES
BONYSETTER  STOCKYFISH
ALOE  SAUNA  TORTE  FATO
REND  SADAT  SNOOD  SMEW
```

452

```
   SUPS  CHAMP   WOES
 CANIO  REGALIA  IDLER
FAULTS  ORATORS  LAURIE
ALCOHOLWONTPASSMYLIPS
CLEOS  EDNA    ETA  APT
TARS  BASS  OPERA  HALLE
  ETON  PRATT  BETSYS
APO  ISTS  AGRA  UDO
TOBACCOISPARTOFMYPAST
ELLIS  MEAN  RAP  KIR
TEAL  ARIEL  CHARY  HERA
HAT  DEL  LAIC  DENIM
EXERCISEWILLSHAPEMEUP
  ART  ARAM  SLAM  SSS
GRATES  TRAMS  BLOW
RAREE  MEDEA  DUAL  AFRO
ISR  TAS  CONN  PILOT
THISDIETISTRULYMYLAST
SEVERE  AVERAGE  ALINES
 RARER  EOLITHS  GONGS
 LEWS   LOESS   INGE
```

453

```
ORCA  CAMP  AGAME  SMOG
PALS  AGAR  LAMINA  TARA
ADOS  RENO  AREMET  ERAS
LINESFROM  BNAI  TRAINS
SIESTA  RETAIL  GEOLOGY
  SORE  NOMS  ERMA
THEONELLAMAHESAPRIEST
HENRY  SUDS  PACT  OSSA
ARTS  MAME  ENSUE  KNOWN
TOO  EASE  CLEO  SPLIT
ADULTS  THELAMA  RECESS
  ROTHS  OREL  SPEE  ROE
SHAPE  MAVEN  SIRS  PIPE
GAGA  PILE  BCDE  ARCHI
THETWOLLLLAMAHESABEAST
  ONES  RANI  SPOT
IMPARTS  FREEZE  POETIC
CIARDI  SLAW  OGDENNASH
ANIL  ARCANE  PARA  SNEE
NONE  CHANGS  ODOR  ETRE
TRES  ONSET  DIPS  SEEK
```

454

```
SASH  ADAM  OASIS  RAP  AFL
ECHO  BEDE  FLUME  OVA  LAY
CHERCHEZLAFEMME  MASSEUR
TEASHOP  TIE  MISEENSCENE
DAR  DRAIN  NOTER
 PEON  MAB  STELA  SUPER
BASE  ACACIA  NABS  BATE
INPUT  DEBUG  TILER  RAN
LARVAL  ALOE  TETEATETE
TIRADE  DRAMA  ADMIX
METE  GEESE  RIPEN  SPACES
ALD  RAISONDETRE  EMU
CAESAR  TRACE  REARM  SLUR
 CURIA  CARPI  RECALL
CLOISONNE  SITE  REVEAL
LAR  SOARS  TITHE  MONTE
UMPS  NUIT  CAFTAN  ICED
BESOT  SNIDE  ELS  BRED
 FABLE  TREAT   DEF
MESALLIANCE  NEE  RETAILS
EXURBAN  CHARGEDAFFAIRES
SIP  OSE  AIMER  ALDA  RANT
STS  TER  ANTSY  MAST  ENDS
```

455

```
WARE  BOAT  OSCAR  AGAS
ADEN  IRMA  ATONAL  DONE
TALC  BEAM  SERGIO  SLID
CHYOU  STEP  PPENWO  ATE
  DRS  ODOR  SLG  LUNAR
ANCESTOR  NIT  OLAFS
REO  TONYS  COSTAL  ALAS
COLLEGE  ALEPH  STE  ONT
EPISTLE  ALSOP  ANA
AIDA  EMU  ASTRA  SMITER
STEPB  ALLSTEPFO  OTHER
PATSYS  SITAR  IRT  SESS
ILE  SUSAN  MANASSA
RIS  TEP  ERASE  METTLES
ECTO  NIPSEY  SLATE  ADO
ASONE  SID  INSPECTS
START  ENA  NEST  EFG
OWN  EPLADD  STEP  ORDWI
NINE  RENDER  ORAL  ELEV
ANIL  ESCORT  PALE  TILE
REEF  SENSE  SLOT  SITS
```

456

```
PASCO  AGES  BRAVO  SWAG
ALTOS  ROSH  RESIN  OHNE
PIERS  TUNE  ASIDE  DADO
ACREATUREWITHFINS  TED
SEEL  ARM  ENS  DEMISE
 LIL  AINT  KIT  MUS
 SICKANDTIREDOFITALL
BEE  YEDDO  ENERO  TIME
REAL  DESI  ATONERS  DNA
ALLAH  DELI  TRUCE
 STOPSMOKINGSOMUCH
 ERATO  EGAL   THOLE
HOF  NEUTRON  ERNS  ONYX
ALOU  ADIEU  NEONS  DEE
PERSONIVETOLDTHISTO
 ATM  OES  PEAR  VEE
MEDINA  AHA  APE  BAIE
EAR  ISUSEDINBILLIARDS
AGIO  SNARE  TINE  BLOAT
NEVA  ADROP  ODEA  ADORE
TREK  MOIST  SUDS  RIMES
```

457

```
AMERICAN  ENAMEL  SABE
CAROTENE  CANIDAE  CLAM
TITUSANDROGYNOUS  ATTU
ALEE  SADE  SON  GARRETS
    REMADE  NOSH  AARE
ANIMAS   THEWAISTBAND
HOSES   TAO   KNEE   TIO
EMBRACEABLEEWE  ASKING
ADA  ALLS  RISE  LOGE
DESPOILS  LUGE  AMAIN
   ABROOMOFONESOWN
  VISOR  ETAT  DIALECTS
SPAN   AUST   LIEN   ORE
CAGERS  THELASTRACCOON
ARA  HEAT  ORD  ARTIS
RABBITDELUXE  GROSSE
 BOON  OREL  STEERS
LONGEAR  ATA  ANTE  OTTO
ALDA  SINGININTHETRAIN
PAIR  PNEUMAT  RETRACED
PSAT  GREASE  ELSINORE
```

458

```
RUCHE  EBBED  CEDAR  SHEEP
ASHES  TULLE  RNASE  TILDE
SHORTFOROLIVEDRAB  IDLER
PESO  LIGNE  ASSN  SARDINE
ARE  AILED  ROUE  TRESS
  IMPERSONALPRONOUN
CASSIS  ROSS  ROMP  PES
ASIAN  CAGE  MICA  SARAH
SYMBOLFORALUMINUM  TITO
TELE  ILMEN  NOSES  BOOMER
STALEMATE  ACIS  AIRPORT
   ANGELESORALAMOS
STRIVES  ROVE  ORATORIOS
CRAVED  ONONE  TRINI  ERST
ROTA  USASERVICEACADEMY
EVENS  CITE  ITAS  DENIM
WED  MOUE  SANA  FLEECY
  CONTRACTIONFORIAM
CARTE  CHAR  OVOLI  TAP
BALIHAI  CANT  TRIBE  SRTA
ANISE  SOUNDOFHESITATION
NEVER  MUSES  HOGAN  DONNE
DRESS  STELA  CROCS  SPEED
```

459

```
FEEDA  VIAL  RICER  REBS
OLDER  ANTI  ERASE  IDEA
PIERCESRECIPESPIECERS
SARA  VEE  NANA  CONES
  NOES  EDDIE  UFO  STY
FROGS  TWAIN  ATILT
REDEALTRELATEDTREADLE
AMID  OHARE  ODES  BIAS
YON  EGIS  AESIR  ELVIS
  ARAN  ALLIN  SLOANE
SPARINGRASPINGPARINGS
ARISES  ABIES  AROD
LIMES  SPANS  ATTY  SIL
AMEN  RIIS  OSIER  VOTE
DERIVESDEVISERREVISED
  COMAS  ETTAS  AROMA
SOS  LIL  ASSET  ECRU
ELIOT  ATTU  ORE  LIFE
PLEASERLEAPERSREPEALS
AINT  TIDAL  WISE  INNES
LEAS  HOARS  EGAD  ATSEA
```

460

```
OLID  GRUFF  COO  HATED
COSA  RUPEE  SOUL  ANWAR
HOLYROMANEMPIRE  POESY
STADIUMS  LIENS  SPINES
  ROPY  PIXES  GLINT
CAPETS  DINED  FEALTIES
HULAS  MINGDYNASTY  ELK
ITEM  FIDO  ENTE  STLO
MOI  OLDSTONEAGE  BAHIA
ESSAYIST  REELS  CANCEL
  TWEET  FLEES  MORTE
SPOORS  ERODE  FERMENTS
KICKS  LEAPYEARDAY  TEC
INEE  YARN  NEIL  PULE
MEN  MESOZOICERA  ARRAN
PRESUMES  INANE  PREYED
  EATER  FLIRT  DOGS
TAPPAN  LIEGE  SITUATED
AHOOT  YEAROFTHEHEGIRA
NACRE  ANTS  OVINE  ERIN
ASHES  WAS  RAVER  DECK
```

461

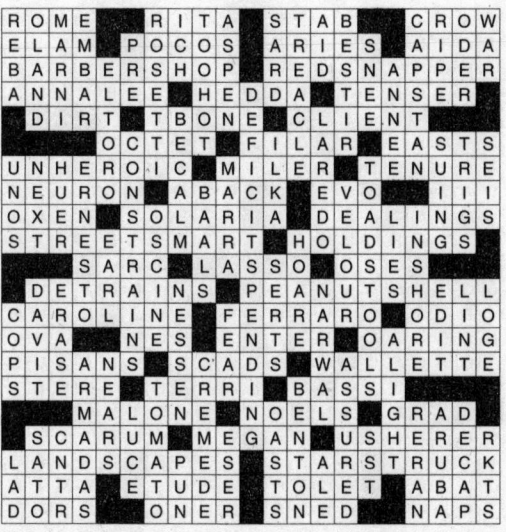

```
ROME  RITA  STAB  CROW
ELAM  POCOS  ARIES  AIDA
BARBERSHOP  REDSNAPPER
ANNALEE  HEDDA  TENSER
 DIRT  TBONE  CLIENT
  OCTET  FILAR  EASTS
UNHEROIC  MILER  TENURE
NEURON  ABACK  EVO  III
OXEN  SOLARIA  DEALINGS
STREETSMART  HOLDINGS
  SARC  LASSO  OSES
 DETRAINS  PEANUTSHELL
CAROLINE  FERRARO  ODIO
OVA  NES  ENTER  OARING
PISANS  SCADS  WALLETTE
STERE  TERRI  BASSI
 MALONE  NOELS  GRAD
SCARUM  MEGAN  USHERER
LANDSCAPES  STARSTRUCK
ATTA  ETUDE  TOLET  ABAT
DORS  ONER  SNED  NAPS
```

462

```
ANEW  ICBM  ANAT  INA  AMY
NOME  FOIE  LASH  MUMS  LAE
THIEVINGMAGPIE  PLAITING
 SPAT  MORES  SMOLDERING
ASSET  SORER  HAS  EPI
WEIR  ETUIS  TROUTQUINTET
EGO  PLATZ  GRIEVOUS  KAMA
SONGOFTHEFLEA  ERI  PETIT
  ROIS  ROTT  SEDATERS
SEVERN  LOB  ADE  TOO
EPEE  ONEWAY  ETYMOLOGY
THECARNIVALOFTHEANIMALS
 AREBETTER  MARIAN  AGEE
  BAH  EDT  SAC  SCHEME
PATTERER  ASTI  STOA
ECRUS  JET  SWANOFTUONELA
STER  SOCRATES  NEAPS  MOD
THEBUMBLEBEE  TETRA  MIMI
 IBA  EWE  DENIS  BEGAT
ICONOCLAST  PERIS  PEAR
STREAKER  THENIGHTINGALE
AGE  TETE  EONS  HERE  ETON
RES  ROD  DINE  TSAR  REND
```

463

```
ACARID TERSE SESAME
NARINE ALIEN ONAGERS
GRANDMAMOSES BABERUTH
OIL ESPIED SEMIS DOE
ROSH HENRYAARON MIKE
ALEA SORES STER MUTED
SEAR IRED TIED BORERS
OARED POD TIER
GRILLE COMEDIAN AHAB
LONDON LOOM OVID YALE
ABUSE BILLYJOEL FALLA
ZERO SARI JARS SABLES
ESEL PRECOOKS ARREST
ODIN SHE DOGMA
SEAMAN ARAN HEME HARD
ELROY SLAG GOFER ABEE
LIEN WALTERABEL MALT
AZO CAMUS OMBRES SEE
HALDAVID ROBERTNATHAN
SECRETE ANIMA ATREST
SCORED PETAL PEEDEE
```

464

```
RUGATE EATS HAP GAME
ELEGIT SLIPA ACE IVAN
PUTACORKINIT ZAP VERA
ULTRA HETERO ESOTERIC
TAH LAIR SAMPLE BITAT
ETE SUN EIO STENO
DELA GETCRACKING ADAR
ENE ORE ESPIER
PRATT REELS HARRIGAN
RADIATE NAUSEA ASPERA
EGO GETONYOURMARK TEN
SAUGER TASMAN IDIOTIC
ASTERNAL IGETA NOONE
TEEMED ONE EFT
BALA DOYOURSTUFF SHAH
AROMA ONE RAW ELA
SAROS CARESS SIDI PUL
ELEVATOR ATABAL NAOMI
NITE UZI SAMEOLDGRIND
JATO TEE EGLIN PINNAE
ISAN UNL ESNE STATES
```

465

```
DELI IRATE SHELF
POLES GOBOS REARERS
JACKOLANTERN ENTREATY
ETTE AROAD ENVIES NEA
ARR SMART OILS SKIN
NOISE LEIS ASSE STING
SONANT SOIGNEE SIAN
NELSON NARDS RETICLE
TENOR LAY PERONEAL
BESS STATIC ALDA SNUG
LAW ALICEBLUE SRI
ARES ABLE NESTED BEAN
SLEEPILY COW OMAHA
ESTRADE SETAE SUOMIC
WADE MODERNS BOBCAT
SLIPS SIRE ESPY PIETA
PALE MIKE CRASS CBC
AIL TOTALS POULT ERIE
TRICHOID PRINCEALBERT
SALERNO OUNCE FARAD
MINES TETES FROM
```

466

```
RAIN TIDAL FACTOR STU
SAUCE ADORE ABRADE SHUN
CITYRAILWAY 1000DOLLARS
USH OGLES STRIPS EADIE
PEON RESET AILS PATIENT
REPENT ETRE DOMINO
LABORED WASPSCOUSIN FLU
OTONOS LISAS ABNER RBIS
SAYSO CIDER MSECS FALSE
ELL FORMERSPOUSE GAMUTS
SLED NEER ALAE GENIES
ROSES TWILL RANGE
POISED BEAN GATO STLO
SANEST CURVEINAROAD YAR
OPERA PANSY OILER RAPID
RAHS DANCE ANGER SERENE
ELA VICTORYSIGN CHAMBER
LEAVES APAL HERDER
REFRIED ALME ELEMI DESK
AVAIL ALUMNI AXELS APE
LINKSDEVICE ZEDINLONDON
ETES OPENER ARENT PETIT
SAM CARESS RINGS SAHL
```

467

```
AMATI RAPT ACTS BASEL
CESAR HIRE FLOP AMOLE
EASTOFEDEN TARASBULBA
ALIENATES SODABREAD
WIT SAFES ELL
CHOSEN LII MEDALS
PALLETS WANDA FORESAW
SHIED PSI NORMAN VITA
CAVE ORTS ELGIN OILER
EPOPEE GOON ISLAND
ERR GREENMANSIONS YES
NOTARY LOAN MARAUD
DOWSE LIONS DUKE TYKE
AMIS SEESAW EMU QUILT
LISENTE ETAPE MOURNER
LETTER EKE CONGEE
MIT TEENS TAV
SCREECHER ADULATION
MAINSTREET LORNADOONE
ENATE OREL ANNE IRWIN
WALES BOSC CEOS STATE
```

468

```
MASTS PARR GLOB DIALS
ACTUP ALOE IONA EDDIE
LEONA TUBA FLED LEAVE
IDLEROOMER TAILBEARER
KRIS MAO SILT
RABBITS BANFF BEEHIND
EDILES DEMAGOG BRODIE
DAZER RILE ROAR STYLE
OGEE RESIN ATLAS ELLA
NETPROPHET BESTCELLAR
UTE IRA
GOODMANORS WHITENIGHT
IPSE STRIP RAREE BLUR
RECUR SEAL IVES SEAMY
TRACED SLINGER HEARUS
HARETIC STAHL CALMEST
ROAN HGT CATV
SPIDERBYTE WARDHEALER
LIBYA BARI IGOR DRAPE
ONEND ICER NENE GAMIN
TAXES EKES GEES ELECT
```

469

```
POMP  PATNA  SHEAF  ABRA
AGAR  ASHOT  WILCO  DRAW
ALLI  THEREDEEMER  VEIN
REINDEER  LADD  RELEASE
   COR  MAINE   CARDED
SHOER   REISS   TORSO
PALOMA  SIRS  OAHU  EFGH
ASIF  GOODSHEPHERD  LEO
SHOPPING   TWA  TRAITS
  EALING  OUI   ALFIE
MEKATE  OUTWITS  IMPEND
ALICE   LAE  HANNAH
LINENS  ACC   PASSAGES
LOG  THECHOSENONE  AIDA
STOP  ANTE  APAR  TENDER
  FLAKE  SPLIT  ADENI
TAKEME   ATSEA  ORO
OVIDIAN  IGOT  PELLMELL
BING  LORDOFLORDS  ELIE
INGE  ERIES  ELIDE  GIFT
TESS  GAMMA  SALON  ASTO
```

470

```
LASSO  REACT  BAKE  BEANS
ELATE  BELLOW  ELAM  RULEIN
ALBERTEINSTEIN  GENUINERISK
SEINE  IGET   KRONE  TWEET
EYED  TODO  SLATE   WEEK
   CAN  NOTING  INGRAINED
RECKONED  FINGERLAKES  HUR
ALLOTS  RAFT  DEEPER  HERA
MAINLY  CANIS   TROD  LEROY
PINTA  CLINIC  STAND  TULIP
SEE  BRAIN  ENTWINE  ARETE
  ABRIDGE  AIA  RAIMENT
ISLAM  LAPPING  BRED  HEW
STAVE  CLOSE  AMBER  LEVIN
HOWDO  CHER  STOOD  SAWING
ALOE  FLIRTS  ALOT  APRINCE
IDO  TRACYAUSTIN  THREADED
REDDEER  CLINGS  AID
  REEK  FORAY  CONG  SAAR
  SHANA  BELEM  LASH  INTRO
THOMASPAINE  MINNESOTAFATS
RETAG  ETTA  INTERIM  JULIE
FALSE  ASSN  GOYAS  FLEES
```

471

```
MARM  OCA  ETAGE   YANK
ASEA  ROND  URBAN  MOVIE
JOHNDONNE  GLOBS  ARENT
ONATE  VANCE  MEE  RESET
RESUE  ECTON  BLANC
  HARRYHOPES   MOONFOR
AMIN  EER  EGER  SOMEONE
SIN  JEDI  LEA  DIPSIN
HAGGIS  SALARY  ALLISON
  AME  TROD  ABEL  ANE
SPASM  HINDSIGHT  IDEST
ION  YATE  THAW  MOA
PLASTER  GHOSTI  ANDROS
PINTOS   HAN  LARS  EDE
ESKIMOS  IDEA  DCL  FIES
THEROPE  JOSIEHOGAN
  RSVPS  NACRE  RISEN
SLIER  EEN  EDENS  ARUBA
NEGRO  NAOMI  REORDERED
INLAW  USUAL  SSNS  SERA
PAUL  PETAL  SST  TSTS
```

472

```
SCENE  RIPE  IAN   BACCO
ALSEN  INSTANCE  NEWARK
RATHERFRIENDLY  ORALER
DIR  MALE  DIES  CRIMEA
IMAGINE  URE  SUITE
NINEE  SHORESAFIRE  RLS
INGEST  OVA  LADER  WAW
AGES  OGLERS  MIL  SLATE
  EARLYREASONER  ATEE
SER  RNA  RANT  HUBERT
ONESTAR  BLOOD  GENERAL
LASHED  SOON  ONA  SLY
ATTU  OTTOSGOODWILL
RIOTS  HOD  SOLONS  EPPA
ION  ASEAL  TET  HUMORS
ANS  WHITEKNIGHT  MUSES
  UNBAR  NOD  APPRISE
SENIOR  AVID  DREI  TES
REDONE  SAFERFORDRAINS
ORATES  PRESERVE  EMOTE
SOYAS  SAD  DYED  DENSE
```

473

```
CAD  HALOS  ASFAR  ASSET
ADE  EPODE  SHORE  CLIME
LOD  ALTER  PERIL  TIRES
ERI  RUTS  SCAMS  ASCENT
BECO  MESEPARATED  ENDS
  AMT  RATE  STALLED
NOTABLY  HER  SELMAS
OHENRY  HARI  TEARI  NTO
WMS  ELGIN  PLAN  EGOS
  BAERS  SCALDS  PAULS
CROAK  UPPE  RCUT  ATSEA
CHINS  BARTOK  ROARS
CELA  NEAR  LEAST  CRU
LAM  BCHOP  DEED  SCARES
SENILE   SAM  STORAGE
  ANYMORE  TOGO  MEN
ISIS  DIVISIONOFL  ABOR
MARPLE  UPTON  ATIP  ERE
ADELE  CLEAT  ELENA  RAN
MANIC  PASTA  LINEN  RTE
STETH  ARTES  MESSY  YES
```

474

```
SALMI  BATANGA  AGEE  BARS
ORION  URANOUS  PULE  ARAN
HUMBOLDTSGIFT  PLIE  RAVI
ONE  AGES  FOVEAE  EGGED
  COLE  BARING  GREENE
GONEWITHTHEWIND  MOIST
APURE  HEARSAY  MOAN  OTO
SIDE  SHARE  LION  GALEN
CANDIDE  SPASM  TNT  OPINE
OTI  SOAVE  PELOTA  IVOR
NEKTON  EREMITE  ENLACERS
  SLOAN  NACRE  REATA
REHEARSE  TRIESTE  VALVED
IMET  STOOGE  HYRAX  AVE
MIDST  YIP  ORWOE  ULYSSES
ELDER  RATS  ANWAR  HARM
SSA  AMIN  ASUNDER  MARIA
  GALEA  HUCKLEBERRYFINN
SPARED  NOTARY  HOOT
ALBEE  PAMELA  OBIT  LES
BELO  CASE  LIGHTINAUGUST
ABEL  URAL  ONCETOO  SANTA
HERA  RELY  PETROLS  OTTER
```

475

```
DONAT  FETE  RAMUS  MISS
GALAHAD ISER ADANO AREA
ANIMATO STANDFASTHOWARD
LIVE ANET MAIA TOON TIA
OEIL AGUR NEEDS CLEFT
PLAYBALLLUCILLE DELA
    INDIANA  CORNETIST
BLIND RIMS ACHED INTO
GRANDEST CUTGRASSGUNTER
NARC STOL SUIT SAD RES
UNDUE EKES DRUID MIKADO
BLOWYOURHORNELENA
MANIAC OSTEO OGLE ERICA
ENE TUE TARP ETAS ARAB
DIGWELLESORSON APOSTATE
IMRE ALVIN ERIE LOESS
CAESARIAN  TOPEKAN
TESS CROSSRIVERSJOAN
LASSO MEADE OLID ORLE
EWE NATO VERO OLGA SADR
HAILSTONEIRVING EMITTED
ARNO ORGAN ESAU SEALERY
REED MOORE RENE SLEDS
```

476

```
SCAM CHIP KEPT ETTE
OLPE HULCE IRAIL CORE
REARADMIRALS NORMASHEARER
GENIALLY PASSE THINK
ORGANDY ASH LEAN
  TEE LANAI SENDOFF
NEARED DISAPPEARANCE EARED
LESS SETO WRAY ALAI
IMP SEARCHPARTIES ANEST
VOLTAIRE SERGE EXISTS
IRONY PAU SNITS
OPTING CROCE BADLANDS
BITTE THETHREEBEARS ERI
ELIE FAUN LAOS TSAR
YEN MOMMIEDEAREST ROSY
IGNORES FILET PER
ORTS FBI LINEAGE
HOURI HOUSE PENTAGON
KINGOFHEARTS SPEARHEADING
IDEA YESTE TOLAN OLDE
PERT NEOS EYRE REAL
```

477

```
FLAP CATS SCUDO BRAT
RANA ALOHA PAREU RILE
ASTRONOMER UPINTHEAIR
  BATES TAMES DIM
DESOTOS PINOT TAKESON
RAPIER SHEEN SERENELY
ORALS FAIRWEATHER VIA
PFCS FOUL RUED REVS
OUI RAINORSHINE LINES
FLOTILLA ATILT TANTRA
URALS OVENS BOUGH
BESETS ISEND SANDSHOE
ATSEA ONCLOUDNINE ERR
ROKS ILKA YORE TATA
DII UNDERTHESUN DIVES
OLEANDER HELOT RENEGE
TESTIER SABIN SALINAS
OTB LANES HEMAN
MOONSTRUCK STARRYEYED
ARIA ENTRE AUDIO SERE
YELL DAZED BAND SPEW
```

478

```
HAVEE PREVIN BAKER
DOMINI REVISE ELIDED
RAMPANT IDEALS REDUCE
AGE BAHAMA LATHES CIS
CAROL ERACL NLAT LATE
EMILES ATTENDEE MITER
DACE TAME AUER COVERT
ATIP BRER DUDE
INTEROFFICE HIREDMAN
ARIEL CAINO LASER ECU
DANSE OGDENNASH APART
ATO CAPIO SANTO TONES
MENHADEN SCREENTESTS
ASIS MAID OAST
MELOTT CORE HARP AGAR
OVALS TURANDOT SOLANA
TIME PARA CEORN DEBIT
IDI DEMILO OFYORE RTE
VENIRE TIRADE NETTIER
ENAMEL ESCHAR ESTEEM
TRADE STAIRS ATALL
```

479

```
HASH SCOFF SOWS STASH
SERAI HUMOR OPART MALTA
ALONG IRENE NORIA ELLEN
SLIGHTFINGERED GROWLERS
HOD TOTO MANE HEW SYNE
RELY AGATE STREET
SOLACE PUNTS ENS FAROE
KNIGHTMARE ASTRO STRODE
ATRA ARISEN EMOTE TAEL
TOAST KILTS BROKER ESTE
EPS ALIAS THORN AVIATOR
BRANS CHOSE SWARM
BARRING SHEET NEALE ARC
AGEE CUSTER ORANG SAMAR
BEAD EPHAS SNAPTO DONE
ANCHOR ORSON BLANDLORDS
RATER MCV RETIE RAREST
REMAKE VERAS MICE
ALOR ORS SIZE SILK CPO
DEVILISH PLEADINGLADIES
AMINO HOTEL TORAH DIVES
PUNGS APACE EVICT AVILA
TRESS LSTS DESKS YALE
```

480

```
HAT MASH TAMPS PLOW
ABED ERMA UNUSED RAVI
LOPE AMOI NASSER OMEN
TREVINOGRANTSTRASBERG
STEELER SSE STUARTS
LOSE HYDRA SIT
OHIO TRIM KEELS TEENS
PUMPS SRO RAISED SLAP
TRAINS ATTU NOVEL IDI
NET NEAPS ETA HIC
BOLGERMILLANDBRADBURY
IRE RIO CAIRO ILE
LIV SPORT UPON NESTER
LEER SLIEST VET STRIA
SLEEP ABNER ERIC SANG
PRO STAYS RIVE
PASTIME KIM ENCLOSE
STEIGERCAMERONSERLING
ARAL GROVEL ROOM ELIA
LIME AERIAL EMMA REDD
MASS DADDY SEES RES
```

481

```
PRIEST  BOSS  EVER WOK
RONDOS CRATE DELAWARE
UNCELEBRATED  IRISHSEA
DIOR TAO RAMBO  HIHAT
ENGLISHCHANNEL  SOLIDS
    ERE KEN STEELMEN
BRR ASSERT  NOODGES
AHEM ORBITS SCAN  TAU
CELIBACY CHICKEN ROSE
HAYFORK  ELOI  AUNTS
   FAMOUSCROSSINGS
MOSES  SOHO  NAUTICA
APED TAGTEAM HANNIBAL
GEL AIDA EDISON  CARP
ICEDTEA  SHOERS  RDS
   COLUMBUS EEK UPI
CATNAP ONEARMEDBANDIT
ORION ORALB  DOI SOME
ABORTIVE JULIUSCAESAR
CONSIDER USURP  OTTERS
HRS CANS KEGS  NESSIE
```

482

```
   IPSE  CLU   LATHE
 ITSELF THINICE ASHEN
RMIESOFTHENIGHT PEEPS
IMBROGLIO TENANTS MCI
MENE  UANG  ORAN OPAL
ERI LMERGANTRY TERETE
  SIENA MARE   GARS
 UNMET ABBESS  ARNO
HOLIER ADIOS ALLEGROS
ONIT YNOTTHEBEST JIM
MAGS AIR  SIA  SOLO
ETH WALTERUSTON  ANET
RETAINER ERLES SEVERE
 URSA ALEGAR MORES
SPEE  EVEN  SOLAR
STMARK PTERGRIMES MGM
PAYS PART  YARE  POLA
ENL ESCARPS VENERATOR
EDILE THEORIENTXPRESS
DEFOE SASSOON UPTILT
SEEPS  TSU  MOSS
```

483

```
CASTOR OWLET LEDA ABOVE
ASPIRE RHINO ECON TANIS
SHALLWEDANCE MOONSTRUCK
HER ERRATA PSALM CURSE
   IRIS PLANE CANE
APE STEN NEALS CALENDAR
PEDALED TORTE ARMED REI
PLUMES MOVIEMOVIE  HERA
LACED REVEL  PEEL BASIL
EGAN MILAN  CURD SOUSAS
SET WILDHARVEST AHOTEL
 INONE  EEL  NOTED
SNORED THEGLASSKEY TAM
ANGLER ARID MAILS TOGO
CARLA SCUD MANSE LIKEN
ERIE THEEGGANDI BEKIND
RET STEER HARDY MATILDA
BRANCHED CONGA LUNT LAY
 EARP GAUGE BEND
ASTRO HURLS MEARAS MAD
ONTHEBEACH THEFRONTPAGE
PALED RICO EOSIN NEUTER
STORY GRIP RESTS AMPERE
```

484

```
PALE TOILES ACTS BONO
ERINGOBRAGH MURPHYBED
LIFEOFRILEY BOYCOTTED
OSF SUIS ROREM CLEARS
TEETH EHS FUROR ASIDO
ASYE INSTS ESSAY  NON
   AER TOLEDO PETS
SESSUE EMINENT SANDAL
IMPEL SWATS SST LOOSE
NEL ANT THEM HIBERNIA
ERIA TOSEE ASIDE TENN
DANNYBOY RICH ELM GIE
ILEDE LNS SLEDS ARANS
EDSELS CHATEAU EYELET
 SLOE ABSORB DOC
SLO DRAMA DELVE TARD
PANEL GLENN DII SOLAR
OUTSET ALGER NOAH AMO
IRISHROSE WHEELBARROW
LIMERICKS LEPRECHAUNS
SEEN PTAS YEASTS IMAY
```

485

```
MALE CHARM STALE BOAT
ANON RAMIE EASES ORSO
COFTHEWILD QUIETONTHE
EXTRUDE LITUP ANISES
 ERODE CHEEREDON
SADAT SPOIL ELONGATE
PIETS STOSS OCAS FRA
ORCS SHEN RUN STAT
REL GEORGECMARSH CEDE
TRISECTS NOELS ADORER
 NEARS DANTE ARIOT
PIERRE MATER ABROTHER
ARAG THEVEYOFFEAR ERA
GENE ALI IRAS TBAR
END FRED HAREM BAISE
DEFINITE BONNE RISER
 NOTESDOWN TRAIL
CRONUS ROLES OSTOSIS
HUCINATION THEWSTREET
ATTN NOLLE TEPEE ERSE
SHAG DIOLS EMILS DAIN
```

486

```
AGHA ACRE  STEM DAMP
BOAT LEACH ATREE EMIL
BUSHLEAGUE FIELDSTONE
APPLAUSE BELLA ICARIA
 ETTE ARNOLD CRI
DEPTH ARENA  FIANCE
OGLE BIRDWATCHING AVA
ERAS ERGO  AIRE REAL
REY COURTYARD COSTA
STETSONS HALVE SADATS
 ROOMY SOLDE PARER
TIPTOE STRIA LACROSSE
ALIEN TUNESMITH ALA
SIAM SCAN  ANTE ALAR
SUN SHORTCIRCUIT NAVE
 MODERN OLEOS FADED
 RPI ASSETS BEET
ASSAIL MOISE SOREHEAD
JAYWALKING SHORELEAVE
ARNE EOSIN TELIC MSEM
RICE ROTC  WEST AERO
```

487

MAHAN COSTA SHOVE AMANA
ARADA ALARM HOVEL LYRIC
IDOUBTIDDEEMITADISGRACE
DOLL AREA REVEL HENLEY
REACTOR VITAL RARA
TOT COCA APODI NAM
WEREYOUTOCALLAVASEAVASE
ATE ONINE ORALES ISSY
SHISH TEA SAGA ARI THIN
INDEEDIDNOTBEGIVENPAUSE
NOSTRIL VAT ACED ONAIR
AET MIEN ONER OSU
SWATS CARR END OTTOMAN
WEREYOUTOCALLAVASEAVASE
ACRA NRA ALLY ECO LASSO
MOIS MADAMA ISTLE SAN
IMVERYTOLERANTTHESEDAYS
SEE ALORS LOTI TEE
STIR PHOTO TRELLIS
PATOIS BLANC CREE IRAS
ITSNOTSOTOUGHIHAFMYVASE
ETAIN ERUPT EVADE MEDIC
TARAS POSSE DETER ARENT

488

EBAN SQUAD PALP STLO
FARO QUITO AMOR BAHIA
THEFRUITEDPLANE ARRET
STAREAT GRAZE ALTON
INRE REEVE ALLOW
ATTLEE SERGE CLEARING
DAHL SCISSORSALAD NOL
DRESS ALE ARID ATLI
USA WESTWARDHOE BEHAN
PIGMENTS REALM WERENT
EADIE MIR PETIT
DOOMED ELENI FILTERED
ELFIN AXIDENTALLY OXO
BISE ATTA AGO SAWIT
UGH AWLORNOTHING DELE
GOODDEAL ORION LADLED
VOLES AMICE BANI
DEREK FLANK ANDCOLD
POLAR BRIDGEOFSCYTHES
HERDS RAVI TRITE ETAT
DAYO OPEC SEXES DORS

489

CLASP SEABOB BESPOKE
HARPO EMBARS MONTANAN
TOYOURWEALTH ABORNING
ONENESS CABLED
STANDS REAROUSE EERIE
POL DIBS MIMI REPRESS
AMS ONO CASABA SCOT
STAGG WINNERSTALE AME
MICA CANOE EAR POSER
TESLA CRONE OPENERS
PITCHINGJENNIES
STEALTH STERE TSARS
PARRA IDS CELIA LEES
EIN CAPITOLTILL PELLA
APES ROSINA SAR EEL
RESTAFF LEHR HALO TNT
SITAR FILARIAE OCASEY
RIGORS BEAROUT
LACESHOE SPORTOFRINGS
RESTEELS ROSIER EVANS
GRASSES SPEEDY DEBUT

490

SIDES IRATE ARETE
TENANT NAVAL SEXISM
BOASWAINSMATE SPECTER
LAG SCRIP AVAIL KORO
AMID TULIP RAGGY ERIA
DARED PERIL TAN GRINS
ENTREE SENATOR ZEALOT
ILLS TIER DEEP
VANDYKEBEARS TENSESUP
AROES CIV STRAND SANE
LOO FETID YALTA LIT
IANA ADELIE VIA COATI
DRESSIER OXSEATTICKET
PEND DRAT EAVE
SORBET MISMADE WILTED
TWEED BAG SCOLD COWER
ENTR SAREE YODEL TIRO
LEAR TRYST REMIT TIL
ARBITER THIRDRATHOTEL
SLEEVE ENNUI NEARER
ESTER DONNE DRIER

491

GOFER BERRA ADAR IMAGE
ORATE ORION SOLO NAKED
BACHELORFLAT PLAZASUITE
ILE SORELY ABHOR NORMAN
ELIDE AMEER EDDY
PTG SIS ASTER OTTO CAP
LARD THELSHAPEDROOM AMO
AREOLA TOTEM EINE ABAS
STELE TERI NAMES FLINT
MANET GRANDHOTEL GLENDA
ARM MINN RIFE MENIAL
ASLIFE SOLON SWEDEN
CANAAN UPDO CAAN TDS
ASSIST THEBALCONY ETHAN
SHINS CRAZY ADDS AHERO
HOOT TOOL SHIER FRESNO
ERN FROMTHETERRACE EKED
DES LAPP AIRED ORE YDS
BOUT SIRED SAMBA
SHALOM PAREE HAMPER DIS
HOLIDAYINN THEAPARTMENT
ERODE ANTE SILLS HARRY
SNEAD MEAT TREES ANNEX

492

REPAD STALAG DÆMONS
ATRIA MOIMEME ANTONIA
PHARMACOPŒIAL MANTEEL
INTENSE BONITO ATALL
DIED ASSAI ADEER ACLE
CRAW TOAT LABEL TIS
LIPPERSHEY ÆDILES
ATHENÆUM EAR ADVERT
SHES DETESTS SNEER
SAM HORUS STAT ROOTER
ANITA ORTO ERRS AIRTO
YEARNS NORM CAPEK AHS
EDAMS SEDATED VIII
SCARCE ORO ACUTANCE
CÆSURA ŒNOLOGICAL
IHS BASED ETRE DEBT
MOAB LUMET IAMBI NASA
PORED RAMOUS ABETTER
ONETIME ARCHÆOLOGISTS
SEATERS TOLLONS ANISE
ERNEST AWAYNE DENES

493

```
THAT   VOTE  DAD   DEEJAY
REGIS  IRONSIDE  INDUCE
EARLOFCARDIGAN  STILTS
ATE  URALS  EGGY  ILES
CHESTER   AGEE   SATES
LESCHE  ANDERSDAHL  LPS
ENTO  GLASS  ELSE  EIN
 SOU  ORAN  ALEE  LOCI
 REGINALDGUPPY  ATOP
AFR  TRPS  EAUX  AGNATE
MOUNTIE  MAMIE  SWEARER
ALDOUS  ORES  HAIR  DES
LION  HENRYSHRAPNEL
GOLO  IONS  ORIG  EAM
ALF  SEGO  METED  APER
MED  JOHNMCADAM  HOPPLE
 ICANT  EARS  MANTRAP
GEOM  ARNO  BEAST  OME
CASABA  NICOLASCHAUVIN
ONETON  EDENTATE  PLANT
UNLIKE  TAL  SLED  ALES
```

494

```
JEAN  BEBOP   MAAM  ROAR
ACRE  OPERA  BELLA  ELMO
BUCCANEERS  EDIBLEBEAN
 KLEES  TOLET  LAUGHS
 SLURS  CILIA  MASK
 SHAM  AMIE  BARTERED
WAACS  GAMEOFCARDS  ERI
ONDE  SOLE  IRES  AGON
LEE  SMALLHORSES  EVADE
FRONTED  ERICS  CRANED
 FOOLS  PRADO  BRASS
SAGEST  THOLE  RESTFUL
TIRLS  SOONERSTATE  ANI
ORES  FINN  ACNE  STIR
ITE  CITYOFLIGHT  MEHTA
CONDONES  RINA  ADES
 ONES  SEERS  ATTAR
CROONS  STENO  ALOST
HITMUSICAL  ANTIQUECAR
ACHE  EBONY  DONAU  LORE
WOOD  DOTS  STORE  YOKO
```

495

```
RCHIDS  RBLE  RUTS  DACE
ARISEN  ARUT  STEP  IMAG
CNVENIENTLY  TSCA  SANG
LEER  NRTHUMBRIAN  CTTN
ERSE  LSES  LEADPISNING
 SAID  AGATE  ATS
CAMPTWN  SHIRE  DRPLEAF
ARIELS  MARSH  FLD  AXIL
RECKN  CNNATURAL  BTTMS
RARE  WISDM  GES  TTER
TSS  DENIM  PHARS  TTS
 CSTS  GIB  HAIRY  LIAR
TRPHY  CNNIPTINS  MANIT
ASIA  RAR  CWERS  PRTEGE
RECRDER  INDRS  CRSSRAD
 PEC  GLVES  GRVE
PASSINFLWER  RAKI  TARA
EPCH  VEREXPSURES  RDER
PINT  EVIL  UNCNDITINAL
LACE  NELL  FAKE  NNTIDE
ENER  ERES  FRST  SENSES
```

496

```
A*TO  DUSTIN  HATLO  A*K
ALSOP  UNMADE  ALOOF  TSIN
*VATIONWAGES  LONE*STATE
SAP  NADIRS  TRINES  CENTS
PRESENT  SLIDER  SANDYS
ACHE  TED  SEINE  GIRDS
BLINDS  AMENS  FAILS  TEN
OARED  FIVE*GENERAL  BRIE
DREGS  ORELS  ODIN  AIDE
EASE  IBERT  LOBOS  CARPED
RATON  TIBER  HOR  ERE
CO*  *SFELLONALABAMA  SSR
ANS  INF  AEDES  LITUP
LIKESO  AMNON  TRADE  ASTA
LOYS  IMET  OHARA  ASHEN
ANAT  *SINONESEYES  ASORT
SYN  STADT  OXIDE  ARIOSE
 DAILY  BOHEA  AOK  OTES
SCHEME  CURSOR  SOPRANI
ORURO  RAPIER  DAMEOF  NAE
NOTINOUR*S  THEMORNING*S
ESCE  DENTE  EUDORA  RE*TS
 SHS  DRESS  DIESIS  ESSE
```

497

```
PALOMA   WEARE   SCROLL
AMORAL  HARPIST  TAIPEI
IMPACT  AGRIPPA  ENGAGE
DOE  HERR  ASP  MEAT  LSD
 HEREBYTHEWILLOF
EBRO  TORA  DELA  AMOS
FLOUNDERS  ESPALIERS
TOSSERS  ABA  SIERRAS
THENATIONANDWESHALL
 RAP  SWAHILI  LAN
BRASSERIE  INTERDICT
BEG  INDICATOR  NOR
SPECIAL  NOM  INEPTLY
 NOTLEAVESAVEONTHE
PADRES  RARITAN  ENIGMA
ALARM  MINT  ANTS  ALEUT
ZASU  ROOD  DRIP  IRMA
 POINTOFBAYONETS
LOOTING  RUARK  GROTTOS
ADRESSE  ELUTE  LEGIONS
REDDEER  NAMES  ESSAYER
```

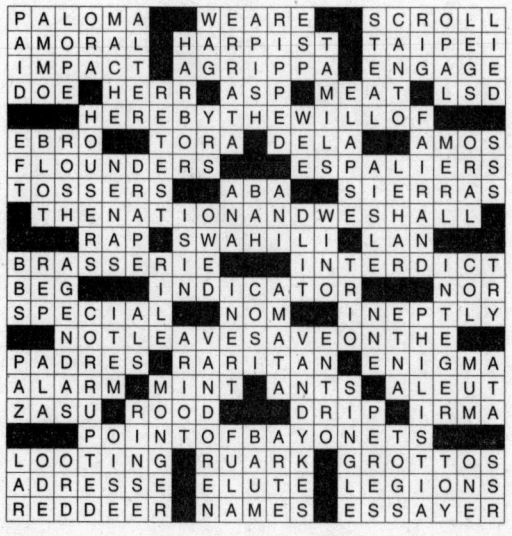

498

```
LAMENESS  NORIA   TOCKS
ERODIBLE  ANATTO  LUIRE
COUNTRYRACEPERFECTBOX
ASTA  OEIL  SIMIAN  OONT
REO  RATCHES  STIFLES
RINGED  LAYER  MOOLA
ESSENCES  RASHER  OFTEN
 TOLA  CAR  ATTU  ROVE
ATLAS  SEL  TAM  HAILED
MAE  ATTEMPT  BOUNCER
EXAMINERFORWORDHEADED
TROVARE  POTPIES  ATE
MINUET  TEC  TEN  CANTO
OMEN  AMMO  ESS  SOOT
BERTH  AMIDST  RESPECTS
 AUDIE  ASAFE  EYELET
STRIPED  IRONIST  ERE
CHIN  LEADER  SHEM  HARE
REFERENCESOFHONOROVER
ISLET  SENTUP  NOTALONE
PEERS  STOTS  ENTWINED
```

499

```
MADAM   OMAR   SAGA    SWEAR
ACINI   VARIATION       KANGA
THEINVISIBLEMAN         ATTIC
      MAIDS   OILED     STEELE
SAMARA        OSCAR   CHIRRED
OBOLE   HANOI   SALONS
FIRSTLENSMAN    ROUGHUP
ADO   SANTEE   EVICT   ISLE
RENT   DRAT   BRISK   APHID
      HOLY     SAUCE   ARDENT
THENEVERENDINGSTORY
DROIDS   CESTA     ISAW
HORNE   CHITA   DUDE   NORD
SLAV   DOONE   ROPERY   PAU
  LEISURE   THETWOTOWERS
      NOMADS   OLEAN   SIRET
SPECIAL   APIED   SENARY
TAPIRS   ERICA   LAYME
ADOBE   BLACKSTARRISING
ADDLE   IMPOSESON   TALIA
TYEES   POET   DUSE   EPOXY
```

500

```
HAM   CAPER   SEDUM   EFFETE
AVE   OBERON   ARETE   ALEXIS
SOT   MEDITERRANEANRESORT
SWEETER   AWAIT   NOTES
LARGE   OCTETS   FLESH   CSA
ELSA   HOLE   AROSE   CHAPS
      DOLLAR   SLANT   FLORES
EDE   DEAR   TIMING   AREOLAE
PIQUANT   MOROCCANSEAPORT
HAUL   SEPARATES   OTER
ELAN   ERASES   ROUE   PAR
BELOWPITCH   OVERPRAISE
ERS   HIDE   SAUDIS   TEES
      ONER   CARPENTER   OMNI
LASVEGASHABITUE   SURPASS
OCTAVES   ABLOOM   OTHO   NET
IRONED   ELLEN   CLERIC
RIPER   AXLES   VELD   REBS
EDS   BLISS   MIMOSA   DUCAT
      SPIES   OASIS   DRIZZLY
WASHINGTONSTATEPEAK   ELL
ASKING   EROSE   STAPLE   MAE
SHINTO   DEGAS   SATES   ADS
```

Big Books from
The New York Times:
The Biggest Name in Crosswords

	50							**51**			

Whether you're a committed "cruciverbalist" or a casual puzzler, St. Martin's Press brings you a continuing line of world-class puzzles from the top names in crosswords.

Every Volume is Power-Packed with 200-Plus Puzzles!

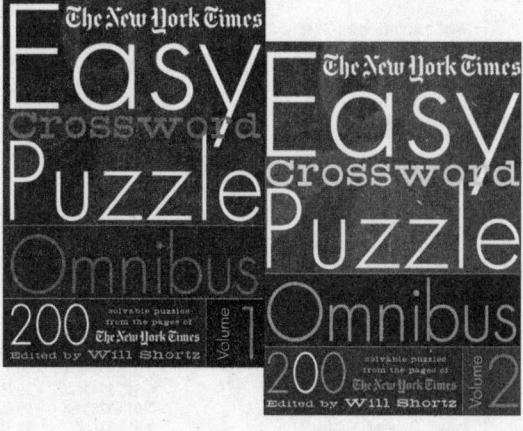

🦅 St. Martin's Griffin

The New York Times

Crossword Puzzles

The #1 name in crosswords

Available at your local bookstore or online at nytimes.com/nytstore

St. Martin's Griffin